MICRO
Office XP

Advanced Course

Mastering and Using

H. Albert Napier
Philip J. Judd
Bruce McLaren
Benjamin Rand
Susan Lehner
Linda Sourek

COURSE TECHNOLOGY
THOMSON LEARNING

Australia • Canada • Mexico • Singapore • Spain • United Kingdom • United States

COURSE TECHNOLOGY

THOMSON LEARNING

Mastering and Using Microsoft® Office XP Advanced Course
by H. Albert Napier, Ph.D. & Philip J. Judd, Bruce McLaren, Linda Sourek, Susan Lehner, Benjamin Rand

Managing Editor:
Melissa Ramondetta

Development Editor:
Robin M. Romer,
Pale Moon Productions

Product Marketing Manager:
Kim Wood

Product Manager:
Robert Gaggin

Associate Product Manager:
Jodi Dreissig

Production Services:
GEX Publishing Services

Copy Editor:
GEX Publishing Services

Cover Design:
Steve Deschene

Compositor:
GEX Publishing Services

COPYRIGHT © 2002 Course Technology, a division of Thomson Learning, Inc. Thomson Learning™ is a trademark used herein under license.

Printed in the United States of America

1 2 3 4 5 6 7 8 9 BM 04 03 02 01

For more information, contact Course Technology, 25 Thomson Place, Boston, Massachusetts 02210.

Or find us on the World Wide Web at: www.course.com

ALL RIGHTS RESERVED. No part of this work covered by the copyright hereon may be reproduced or used in any form or by any means—graphic, electronic, or mechanical, including photocopying, recording, taping, Web distribution, or information storage and retrieval systems—without the written permission of the publisher.

Microsoft and the Office logo are either registered trademarks or trademarks of the Microsoft Corporation in the United States and/or other countries. Course Technology/Thomson Learning is an independent entity from Microsoft Corporation and not affiliated with Microsoft Corporation in any manner. This text may be used in assisting students to prepare for a Microsoft Office User Specialist exam (MOUS). Neither Microsoft Corporation, its designated review company, nor Course Technology/Thomson Learning warrants that use of this publication will ensure passing the relevant MOUS exam.

For permission to use material from this text or product, contact us by
Tel (800) 730-2214
Fax (800) 730-2215
www.thomsonrights.com

Disclaimer
Course Technology reserves the right to revise this publication and make changes from time to time in its content without notice.

ISBN 0-619-05808-0

Mastering and Using

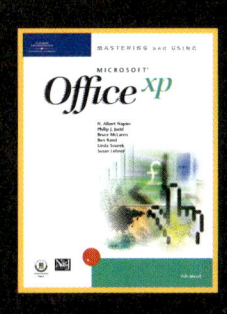

Microsoft® Office XP Advanced Course

The Future Is Now...

Our Napier & Judd series, *Mastering and Using Microsoft Office XP Advanced Course*, is the most comprehensive, instructional tool designed for the user who wants to master and use the application software. This expertly written product provides all the instruction necessary to become certified as a Microsoft Office User Specialist (MOUS) Expert user of Word, Excel, and Access.

Mastering and Using Microsoft Office XP Advanced Course
- Student Text — 0-619-05808-0
- IRK (Instructor's Resource Kit) — 0-619-05810-2
- Review Pack — 0-619-05809-9

The Instructor's Resource Kit (CD-ROM) includes lesson plans, SCANS correlations, scheduling charts, PowerPoint presentations, and much more!

The following companion books, Mastering and Using Microsoft Word 2002, Mastering and Using Microsoft Excel 2002, and Mastering and Using Microsoft Access 2002, will prepare the user for MOUS (Microsoft Office User Specialist) Expert certification. Mastering and Using Microsoft PowerPoint will prepare the user for MOUS Comprehensive certification.

Mastering and Using Microsoft Word 2002 Comprehensive Course
- Student Text — 0-619-05820-X
- IRK (Instructor's Resource Kit) — 0-619-05810-2
- Review Pack — 0-619-05809-9

Mastering and Using Microsoft Excel 2002 Comprehensive Course
- Student Text — 0-619-05832-3
- IRK (Instructor's Resource Kit) — 0-619-05810-2
- Review Pack — 0-619-05809-9

Mastering and Using Microsoft PowerPoint 2002 Comprehensive Course
- Student Text — 0-619-05826-9
- IRK (Instructor's Resource Kit) — 0-619-05810-2
- Review Pack — 0-619-05809-9

Mastering and Using Microsoft Access 2002 Comprehensive Course
- Student Text — 0-619-05814-5
- IRK (Instructor's Resource Kit) — 0-619-05810-2
- Review Pack — 0-619-05809-9

COURSE TECHNOLOGY
THOMSON LEARNING

N&J NAPIER & JUDD Series

For more information about these Course Technology products and others:
Join us On the Internet at www.course.com/masteringandusing

What's New in Office XP

Office XP
- Streamlined, flatter look
- Multiple task panes containing command shortcuts
- Ask A Question Box Help tool
- Smart Tags
- AutoCorrect Options
- Revised Office Clipboard
- Paste Options
- Route documents for review with tracked changes via e-mail
- Speech Recognition
- Improved "crash" recovery features
- New Search task pane
- Digital signatures for documents routed over the Internet

Outlook 2002
- Streamlined setup options
- Expanded virus protection for e-mail attachments
- Calendar color coding
- Calendar sharing over the Internet

Word 2002
- Multiple text selection using the CTRL key
- New task panes to review and apply formatting
- New task panes to apply and create styles
- Select similarly formatted text with shortcut menu
- Revised Mail Merge Wizard
- New table styles
- Revised Track Changes and Compare Documents features
- New drawing tools to create conceptual diagrams
- Native Organization Chart drawing tool
- Revised watermark creation
- New Clear Formatting feature

Excel 2002
- Query data directly from Web pages and XML files
- Import data from a variety of sources, including databases, OLAP data sources, and SQL Server
- Function arguments displayed in ScreenTips as functions entered
- Function Wizard uses natural language query to help find best function available
- Cut-and-paste function examples from Help into a worksheet
- Expanded AutoSum functionality includes commonly used functions such as MIN, MAX, and AVERAGE
- Formula evaluator shows results of nested formulas
- Formula error checking
- Color-coded worksheet tabs
- Smart Tags for paste, fill, insert, and formula checking
- Border drawing to create complex outline borders
- AutoRepublish Excel data to the Web
- Open and save XML files
- Speech playback of cell content
- Graphics can be inserted into headers and footers for printing
- Merge and unmerge cells with a Format toolbar button
- Links Management

PowerPoint 2002
- Collaborative online reviews
- Print presentation with comment pages
- Merge and compare reviewed presentations
- Animation schemes with animation and transitions
- New animation effects
- Motion paths
- Better organization charts
- New diagram types (cycle, pyramid, radial, Venn)
- Task panes for applying slide and presentation formatting
- Outline/Slides tab – Thumbnail of slides in Normal view
- Print preview
- Multiple design templates per presentation
- Visible grids for aligning placeholders, shapes, and pictures
- Adjustable spacing between grids for more control
- Automatic layout for inserted objects
- Embedded fonts (characters within presentation or all font characters)
- Text AutoFit improvements to automatically adjust layout for charts, diagrams, and pictures
- Picture rotation
- Play sounds and animation when a presentation is saved as a Web page
- Password protection when opening a presentation
- Language indicator in status bar

Access 2002
- File format compatibility between Access 2000 and Access 2002
- Create new copy of saved database
- PivotTables and PivotCharts
- XML support
- Extended support for SQL Server databases through Access Projects
- Improved ability to create data access pages
- Relative path support for data access pages
- Multiple Undo/Replace actions

Napier & Judd

In their over 50 years of combined experience, Al Napier and Phil Judd have developed a tested, realistic approach to mastering and using application software. As both academics and corporate trainers, Al and Phil have the unique ability to help students by teaching them the skills necessary to compete in today's complex business world.

H. Albert Napier, Ph.D. is the Director of the Center on the Management of Information Technology and Professor in the Jesse H. Jones Graduate School of Management at Rice University. In addition, Al is a principal of Napier & Judd, Inc., a consulting company and corporate trainer in Houston, Texas, that has trained more than 120,000 people in computer applications.

Philip J. Judd is a former instructor in the Management Department and the Director of the Research and Instructional Computing Service at the University of Houston. Phil now dedicates himself to consulting and corporate training as a principal of Napier & Judd, Inc.

Philip J. Judd

H. Albert Napier, Ph.D.

Preface

At Course Technology, we believe that technology will change the way people teach and learn. Today millions of people are using personal computers in their everyday lives—both as tools at work and for recreational activities. As a result, the personal computer has revolutionized the ways in which people interact with each other. The *Mastering and Using* series combines the following distinguishing features to allow people to do amazing things with their personal computers.

Distinguishing Features

All the textbooks in the *Mastering and Using* series share several key pedagogical features:

Case Project Approach. In their more than twenty years of business and corporate training and teaching experience, Napier & Judd have found that students are more enthusiastic about learning a software application if they can see its real-world relevance. The textbook provides bountiful business-based profiles, exercises, and projects. It also emphasizes the skills most in demand by employers.

Comprehensive and Easy to Use. There is thorough coverage of new features. The narrative is clear and concise. Each unit or chapter thoroughly explains the concepts that underlie the skills and procedures. We explain not just the *how*, but the *why*.

Step-by-Step Instructions and Screen Illustrations. All examples in this text include step-by-step instructions that explain how to complete the specific task. Full-color screen illustrations are used extensively to provide students with a realistic picture of the software application feature.

Extensive Tips and Tricks. The authors have placed informational boxes in the margin of the text. These boxes of information provide students with the following helpful tips:

- *Quick Tip.* Extra information provides shortcuts on how to perform common business-related functions.
- *Caution Tip.* This additional information explains how a mistake occurs and provides tips on how to avoid making similar mistakes in the future.
- *Menu Tip.* Additional explanation on how to use menu commands to perform application tasks.
- *Mouse Tip.* Further instructions on how to use the mouse to perform application tasks.
- *Task Pane Tip.* Additional information on using task pane shortcuts.
- *Internet Tip.* This information incorporates the power of the Internet to help students use the Internet as they progress through the text.
- *Design Tip.* Hints for better presentation designs (found in the PowerPoint chapters).

End-of-Chapter Materials. Each book in the *Mastering and Using* series places a heavy emphasis on providing students with the opportunity to practice and reinforce the skills they are learning through extensive exercises. Each chapter has a summary, commands review, concepts review, skills review, and case projects so that the students can master the material by doing. For more information on each of the end-of-chapter elements see page ix of the How to Use This Book section in this preface.

Appendices. *Mastering and Using* series contains three appendices to further help students prepare to be successful in the classroom or in the workplace. Appendix A teaches students to work with Windows 2000. Appendix B illustrates how to format letters; how to insert a mailing notation; how to format envelopes (referencing the U.S. Postal Service documents); how to format interoffice memorandums; and how to key a formal outline. It also lists popular style guides and describes proofreader's marks. Appendix C describes the new Office XP speech recognition features.

Microsoft Office User Specialist (MOUS) Certification.
What does this logo mean? It means this courseware has been approved by the Microsoft® Office User Specialist Program to be among the finest available for learning Microsoft Office XP, Microsoft Word 2002, Microsoft Excel 2002, Microsoft PowerPoint® 2002, and Microsoft Access 2002. It also means that upon completion of this courseware, you may be prepared to become a Microsoft Office User Specialist.
What is a Microsoft Office User Specialist? A Microsoft Office User Specialist is an individual who has certified his or her skills in one or more of the Microsoft Office desktop applications of Microsoft Word, Microsoft Excel, Microsoft PowerPoint®, Microsoft Outlook® or Microsoft Access, or in Microsoft Project. The Microsoft Office User Specialist Program typically offers certification exams at the "Core" and "Expert" skill levels. The Microsoft Office User Specialist Program is the only Microsoft approved program in the world for certifying proficiency in Microsoft Office desktop applications and Microsoft Project. This certification can be a valuable asset in any job search or career advancement.
More Information: To learn more about becoming a Microsoft Office User Specialist, visit *www.mous.net*. To purchase a Microsoft Office User Specialist certification exam, visit *www.DesktopIQ.com*.

SCANS. In 1992, the U.S. Department of Labor and Education formed the Secretary's Commission on Achieving Necessary Skills, or SCANS, to study the kinds of competencies and skills that workers must have to succeed in today's marketplace. The results of the study were published in a document entitled *What Work Requires of Schools: A SCANS Report for America 2000*. The in-chapter and end-of-chapter exercises in this book are designed to meet the criteria outlined in the SCANS report and thus help prepare students to be successful in today's workplace.

Instructional Support

All books in the *Mastering and Using* series are supplemented with an ***Instructor's Resource Kit.*** This is a CD-ROM that contains lesson plans with teaching materials and preparation suggestions, along with tips for implementing instruction and assessment ideas; a suggested syllabus; and SCANS workplace know how. The CD also contains:

- Career Worksheets
- Evaluation Guidelines
- Hands-on Solutions
- Individual Learning Strategies
- Internet Behavior Contract
- Lesson Plans
- Portfolio Guidelines
- PowerPoint Presentations
- Solution Files
- Student Data Files
- Teacher Training Notes
- Test Questions
- Transparency Graphics Files

ExamView® This textbook is accompanied by ExamView, a powerful testing software package that allows instructors to create and administer printed, computer (LAN-based), and Internet exams. ExamView includes hundreds of questions that correspond to the topics covered in this text, enabling students to generate detailed study guides that include page references for further review. The computer-based and Internet testing components allow students to take exams at their computers, and also save the instructor time by grading each exam automatically.

Student Support

Data Disk. To use this book, students must have the Data Disk. Data Files needed to complete exercises in the text are contained on the Review Pack CD-ROM. These files can be copied to a hard drive or posted to a network drive.

---

*The availability of Microsoft Office User Specialist certification exams varies by application, application version and language. Visit *www.mous.net* for exam availability.
Microsoft, the Microsoft Office User Specialist Logo, PowerPoint and Outlook are either registered trademarks or trademarks of Microsoft Corporation in the United States and/or other countries.

How to Use This Book

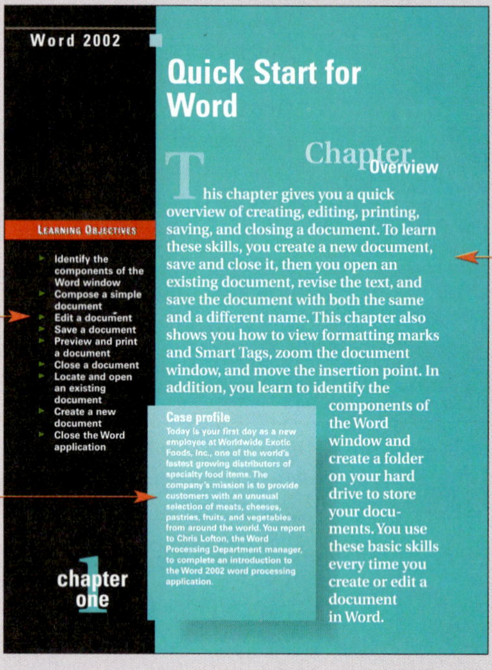

Learning Objectives — A quick reference of the major topics learned in the chapter

Chapter Overview — A concise summary of what will be learned in the chapter

Case profile — Realistic scenarios that show the real-world application of the material being covered

Clear step-by-step directions explain how to complete the specific task

Caution Tip — This additional information explains how a mistake occurs and provides tips on how to avoid making similar mistakes in the future

Task Pane Tip — Additional information about using task pane shortcuts

Quick Tip — Extra information provides shortcuts on how to perform common business-related functions

Internet Tip — Information to help students incorporate the power of the Internet as they progress through the text

Mouse Tip — Further instructions on how to use the mouse to perform application tasks

Design Tip — Hints for better presentation designs (found in only the PowerPoint chapters)

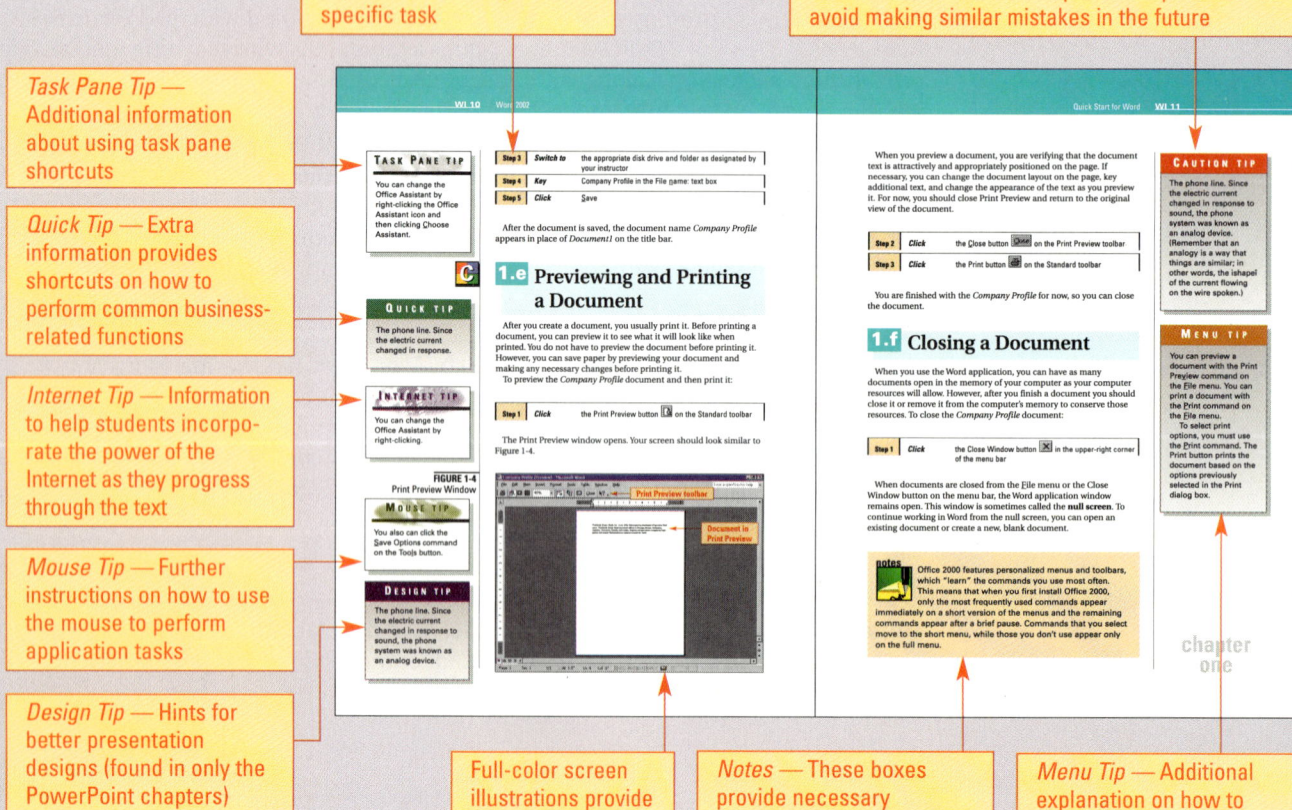

Full-color screen illustrations provide a realistic picture to the student

Notes — These boxes provide necessary information to assist you in completing the activities

Menu Tip — Additional explanation on how to use menu commands to perform application tasks

End-of-Chapter Material

Concepts Review — Multiple choice and true or false questions help assess how well the student has learned the chapter material

Summary — Reviews key topics discussed in the chapter

Commands Review — Provides a quick reference and reinforcement tool on multiple methods for performing actions discussed in the chapter

Skills Review — Hands-on exercises provide the ability to practice the skills just learned in the chapter

Case Projects — Asks the student to synthesize the material learned in the chapter and complete an office assignment

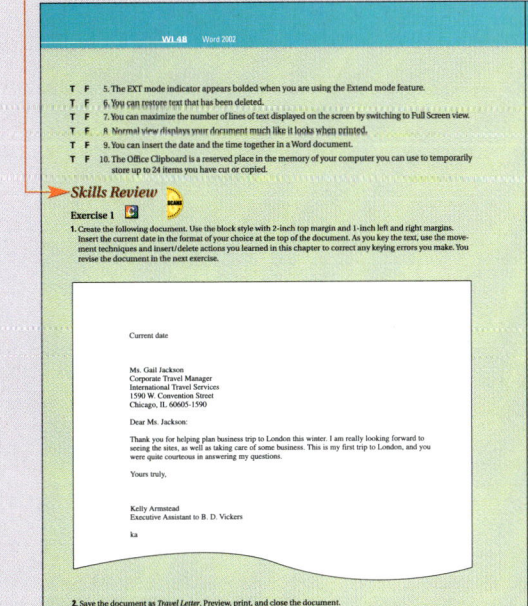

SCANS icon — Indicates that the exercise or project meets SCANS competencies and prepares the student to be successful in today's workplace

MOUS Certification icon — Indicates that the exercise or project meets Microsoft's certification objectives that prepare the student for the MOUS exam

Internet Case Projects — Allow the student to practice using the World Wide Web

Acknowledgments

We would like to thank and express our appreciation to the many fine individuals who have contributed to the completion of this book.

No book is possible without the motivation and support of an editorial staff. Therefore, we wish to acknowledge with great appreciation the project team at Course Technology: Melissa Ramondetta, managing editor; Robert Gaggin, product manager; and Jodi Dreissig, associate product manager. Our appreciation also goes to Robin Romer for managing the developmental editing of this series. In addition, we want to acknowledge the team at GEX for their production work, especially Karla Russell, Kendra Neville, Michelle Olson, and Angel Lesiczka.

We are very appreciative of the personnel at Napier & Judd, Inc., who helped to prepare this book. We acknowledge, with great appreciation, the assistance provided by Ollie Rivers and Nancy Onarheim in preparing and checking the many drafts of the Office unit, the Word unit, the Access Advanced unit, and the appendices of this book and the Instructor's Manual.

We gratefully acknowledge the work of Linda Sourek and Susan Lehner in writing the PowerPoint unit for this series, Benjamin Rand for writing the Outlook unit and the Excel unit for this series, and Bruce McLaren for writing the Access unit for this series.

Contents

Napier & Judd   v

Preface   vi

WORD UNIT — WA 1

14 Customizing Tables   **WA 2**
    a. Using Special Table Features   WA 3
    b. Performing Calculations in a Table   WA 14
    c. Using Table Styles   WA 18
    d. Using Tab Stops in a Table   WA 22
    e. Converting Text to a Table   WA 23
    f. Merging and Splitting Table Cells   WA 25

15 Working with Multipage Documents   **WA 36**
    a. Navigating with the Select Browse Object   WA 37
    b. Verifying Paragraph Formats Using the Reveal Formatting Task Pane   WA 38
    c. Creating Sections with Different Formatting   WA 41
    d. Creating Different Headers and Footers in a Document   WA 43
    e. Using Hyphenation   WA 46

16 Creating Custom Styles and Controlling Pagination   **WA 56**
    a. Creating and Applying Styles   WA 57
    b. Controlling Pagination   WA 66

17 Using the Mail Merge Wizard   **WA 74**
    a. Understanding the Mail Merge Process   WA 75
    b. Defining the Main Document   WA 76
    c. Selecting the Data Source   WA 78
    d. Merging the Main Document and the Data Source   WA 80

18 Using Other Mail Merge Features   **WA 91**
    a. Creating Multiple Envelopes   WA 92
    b. Generating Labels   WA 96
    c. Creating Directories   WA 99
    d. Modifying an Existing Word Table Data Source   WA 101
    e. Querying Data Records   WA 103
    f. Inserting Word Fields   WA 105

19 Sorting Text and Tables — WA 116
- a. Sorting Dates — WA 117
- b. Sorting Lists — WA 119
- c. Sorting Paragraphs — WA 122
- d. Sorting Tables — WA 123

20 Creating and Modifying Document References — WA 133
- a. Inserting Bookmarks — WA 134
- b. Creating and Modifying Footnotes and Endnotes — WA 135
- c. Creating a Cross-Reference — WA 140
- d. Creating and Modifying a Table of Contents — WA 142
- e. Creating and Modifying an Index — WA 146
- f. Using the Document Map — WA 152

21 Working with Drawing Objects and Graphics — WA 161
- a. Creating Drawing Objects — WA 162
- b. Adding Decorative Page Borders — WA 173
- c. Using WordArt Special Text Effects — WA 174
- d. Inserting, Positioning, and Deleting Pictures — WA 176
- e. Inserting and Editing Text Boxes — WA 181
- f. Creating and Editing an Organization Chart — WA 183
- g. Creating an Equation — WA 186

22 Working with Large Documents — WA 195
- a. Creating Master Documents and Subdocuments — WA 196
- b. Creating Multiple Versions of a Document — WA 202
- c. Automatically Format an Entire Document — WA 203
- d. Automatically Summarize a Document — WA 206

23 Using Online Forms — WA 214
- a. Creating and Modifying an Online Form — WA 215
- b. Creating a Document Based on a Form Template — WA 227

24 Integrating Word Documents with the Internet — WA 241
- a. Creating a Web Page — WA 242
- b. Sending E-mail Messages from Word — WA 254
- c. Distributing Documents for Revision — WA 255
- d. Using Digital Signatures — WA 261

25 Using Macros — WA 270
- a. Recording and Running Macros — WA 271
- b. Editing Macros — WA 277
- c. Copying, Renaming, and Deleting Macros — WA 283

26 Managing Files — WA 292
- a. Searching for Specific Files — WA 293
- b. Viewing and Modifying File Properties — WA 299
- c. Protecting Documents — WA 301
- d. Defining the Default File Location for Workgroup Templates — WA 303
- e. Customizing Toolbars and Menus — WA 303

EXCEL UNIT — EA 1

7 Linking Worksheets and Workbooks — EA 2
   a. Grouping Worksheets to Share Data, Formatting, and Formulas — EA 3
   b. Inserting and Formatting a Documentation Worksheet — EA 5
   c. Using Named Ranges — EA 6
   d. Consolidating Data from Multiple Worksheets — EA 9
   e. Creating 3-D References and Links Between Workbooks — EA 12
   f. Working with Multiple Workbooks — EA 15

8 Creating, Sorting, and Filtering Lists — EA 25
   a. Identifying Basic Terms and Guidelines for Creating Lists — EA 26
   b. Entering Data in a List Using Data Validation — EA 27
   c. Using the Data Form — EA 35
   d. Creating Custom Filters — EA 37
   e. Performing Single and Multilevel Sorts — EA 43
   f. Using Grouping and Outlines to Create Subtotals — EA 45

9 Increasing Productivity with Macros, Templates, and Custom Toolbars and Menus — EA 53
   a. Using Macros to Automate Repetitive Tasks — EA 54
   b. Editing a Macro — EA 57
   c. Using Workbooks Containing Macros — EA 61
   d. Creating and Editing Templates — EA 64
   e. Customizing Toolbars and Menus — EA 66

10 Using Problem-Solving Tools — EA 75
   a. Creating Data Tables — EA 76
   b. Using Goal Seek and Solver — EA 80
   c. Creating Scenarios — EA 85
   d. Creating a Trendline — EA 89

11 Using Auditing Tools — EA 98
   a. Using Range Finder to Check and Review Data — EA 99
   b. Identifying Relationships Between Precedent and Dependent Cells — EA 100
   c. Using Error Checking — EA 105
   d. Identifying Invalid Data — EA 107

12 Summarizing Data with Data Analysis, PivotTables, and PivotCharts — EA 114
   a. Using Data Analysis — EA 115
   b. Creating PivotTable Reports — EA 118
   c. Modifying a PivotTable Report — EA 122
   d. Formatting a PivotTable Report — EA 126
   e. Creating PivotChart Reports — EA 128

13	**Working with Charts and the Drawing Tools**	**EA 137**
	a. Creating Special Charts	EA 138
	b. Modifying Charts	EA 141
	c. Using the Drawing Tools	EA 143
	d. Creating and Editing a Conceptual Diagram	EA 151
14	**Importing and Exporting Data from Other Applications**	**EA 163**
	a. Integrating Excel Data with Word and PowerPoint	EA 164
	b. Integrating Excel with Access	EA 172
	c. Importing Data from Text Files	EA 177
15	**Sharing Workbooks with Others**	**EA 186**
	a. Creating and Applying Custom Number and Conditional Formats	EA 187
	b. Using Lookup and Reference Functions	EA 193
	c. Using Workgroup Features	EA 196
16	**Integrating Excel with the Internet or an Intranet**	**EA 213**
	a. Importing Data from the Internet	EA 214
	b. Working with XML	EA 219
	c. Publishing Worksheets and Workbooks to the Web	EA 225
	d. Sending a Workbook via E-mail	EA 230

POWERPOINT UNIT — PA 1

9	**Working with Organization Charts and Diagrams**	**PA 2**
	a. Adding an Organization Chart Slide	PA 3
	b. Formatting an Organization Chart	PA 8
	c. Adding a Diagram Slide	PA 12
	d. Formatting a Diagram	PA 15
10	**Customizing a Slide Show**	**PA 29**
	a. Adding Custom Animation Effects to Slide Objects	PA 30
	b. Adding Sound Effects to Slides	PA 41
	c. Setting Up Presentations to Run Continuously	PA 44
	d. Customizing the End of a Slide Show Presentation	PA 46
11	**Customizing a Presentation**	**PA 55**
	a. Applying a Presentation Design Template from a Different Source	PA 56
	b. Modifying a Presentation Template	PA 61
	c. Customizing Slide Formats and Backgrounds	PA 66
	d. Customizing a Template	PA 70
	e. Creating Folders for Storing Presentations	PA 75
	f. Creating a Custom Show	PA 76
12	**PowerPoint Presentations and the Internet**	**PA 89**
	a. Understanding Hyperlinks	PA 90
	b. Adding Hyperlinks to Slides	PA 90
	c. Previewing a Presentation as a Web Page	PA 100

d. Saving a PowerPoint Presentation as a Web Page	PA 103
e. Editing a Web Page Presentation	PA 105
f. Publishing a Presentation to the Web	PA 107

13 Using Additional Features in PowerPoint — **PA 116**

a. Checking Styles in a Presentation	PA 117
b. Setting Up a Review Cycle	PA 121
c. Reviewing Presentation Comments and Changes	PA 124
d. Using Pack and Go	PA 129
e. Setting Up and Scheduling Online Broadcasts	PA 132

14 Integrating Word and Excel with PowerPoint — **PA 144**

a. Saving a Slide Presentation as a Word Outline	PA 145
b. Opening a Word Outline as a Presentation	PA 149
c. Embedding and Linking in PowerPoint and Word	PA 153
d. Embedding and Linking in PowerPoint and Excel	PA 158

ACCESS UNIT — AA 1

9 Building and Modifying Tables — **AA 2**

a. Defining Data Validation Rules	AA 3
b. Modifying Lookup Field Properties	AA 4
c. Modifying an Input Mask	AA 6
d. Defining Table Relationships	AA 9

10 Working with Advanced Filters and Queries — **AA 20**

a. Creating and Applying Advanced Filters	AA 21
b. Specifying Multiple Query Criteria	AA 23
c. Modifying Query Properties	AA 25
d. Using Aggregate Functions in a Query	AA 26
e. Creating a Parameter Query	AA 29
f. Creating an Action Query	AA 31
g. Creating a Crosstab Query	AA 38

11 Advanced Form Features — **AA 46**

a. Creating a Form in Design View	AA 47
b. Creating a Subform	AA 50
c. Creating a Switchboard Form	AA 55

12 Customizing Reports — **AA 68**

a. Creating a Custom Report in Design View	AA 69
b. Sorting and Grouping Data on a Report	AA 74
c. Adding a Subreport to an Existing Report	AA 83
d. Running a Grouped Report from a Parameter Query	AA 85

13 Using Access Tools — AA 97
- a. Assigning Database Security — AA 98
- b. Compacting and Repairing a Database — AA 105
- c. Using the Database Splitter — AA 106
- d. Using the Linked Table Manager — AA 108
- e. Creating an MDE File — AA 109
- f. Replicating a Database — AA 110
- g. Creating an Access Module — AA 111

14 Integrating Access with the Internet — AA 121
- a. Viewing Web Sites and Sending E-mail Messages from a Database — AA 122
- b. Working with XML Documents — AA 125
- c. Creating and Previewing a Data Access Page — AA 128
- d. Using PivotTable and PivotChart Views — AA 132

APPENDIX — AP 1

A Working with Windows 2000 — AP 1
- a. Reviewing the Windows 2000 Desktop — AP 2
- b. Accessing Your Computer System Resources — AP 4
- c. Using Menu Commands and Toolbar Buttons — AP 6
- d. Using the Start Menu — AP 7
- e. Reviewing Dialog Box Options — AP 7
- f. Using Windows 2000 Shortcuts — AP 8
- g. Understanding the Recycle Bin — AP 10
- h. Shutting Down Windows 2000 — AP 11

B Formatting Tips for Business Documents — AP 12
- a. Formatting Letters — AP 13
- b. Inserting Mailing Notations — AP 15
- c. Formatting Envelopes — AP 15
- d. Formatting Interoffice Memorandums — AP 17
- e. Formatting Formal Outlines — AP 18
- f. Using Style Guides — AP 18
- g. Using Proofreader's Marks — AP 19

C Using Office XP Speech Recognition — AP 21
- a. Training Your Speech Software — AP 22
- b. Using Voice Commands — AP 30
- c. Dictating, Editing, and Formatting by Voice — AP 37
- d. Turning Microsoft Speech Recognition On and Off — AP 45

MOUS Grid — MOUS 1

Index — I 1

Microsoft Word 2002 Advanced

Word 2002

Customizing Tables

Chapter Overview

Tables are generally used to structure data in a document, but they also can be used in other ways to add interest to documents. You can use different techniques to create and work with tables. In this chapter, you use the mouse pointer to draw, copy, and reposition tables. You also use the Tables and Borders toolbar to format tables and table text. Then, you format tables with built-in table styles and create a custom table style. Finally, you convert text to a table and modify a table by merging and splitting cells.

Learning Objectives

- Use special table features
- Perform calculations in a table
- Use table styles
- Use tab stops in a table
- Convert text to a table
- Merge and split table cells

Case profile

After you finish the third quarter sales meeting material for Marisa, you return to the Marketing Department to finalize several documents. First you create a holiday price list cover sheet. Then you revise several documents by creating tables from text, adding calculations to table data, merging, splitting, and copying tables, and reformatting tables with table styles.

chapter fourteen 14

14.a Using Special Table Features

Bill Blake, an account executive in the Marketing Department, asks you to help create the new holiday sales price list. While he compiles the price list, he wants you to create a cover sheet for the document. You decide to do this by drawing tables in which you key the cover sheet text. Figure 14-1 shows the finished cover sheet.

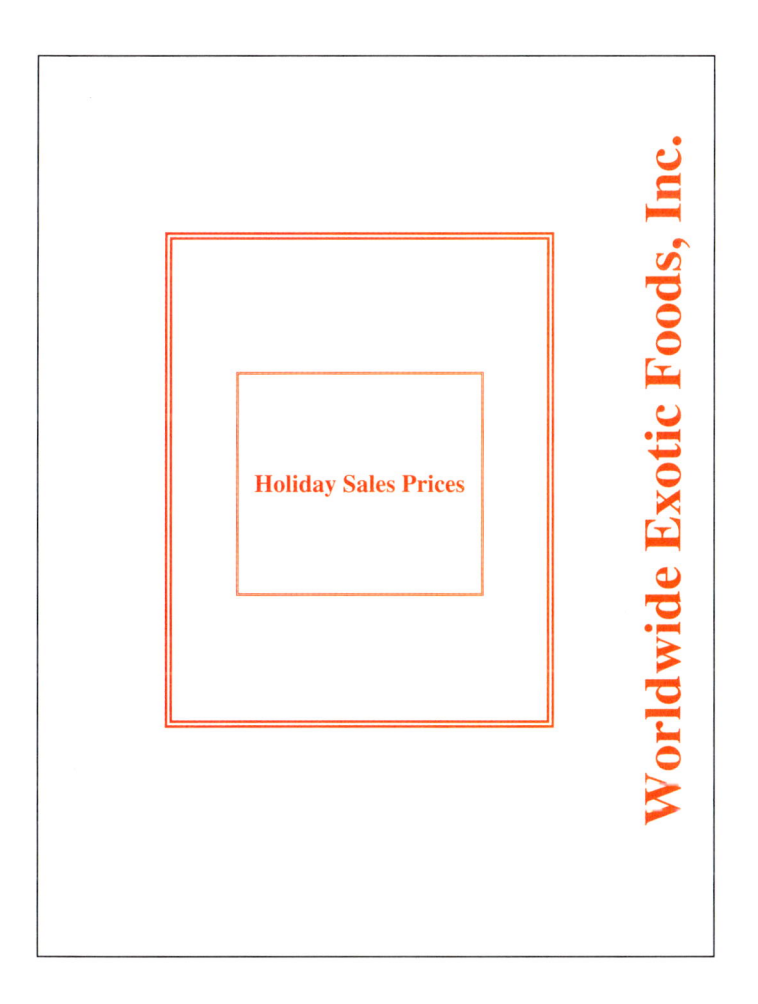

FIGURE 14-1
Completed Holiday Price List Cover Sheet

Word provides several features you can use to be very creative with tables. You can draw complex tables that have cells of different heights or a different number of columns per row, create side-by-side tables, change text direction inside a table cell, and even create a table inside a table cell. You can also reposition, size, and copy a table using the mouse pointer.

Drawing Tables

In addition to creating tables with the Insert command on the Table menu and the Insert Table button on the Standard toolbar, you can draw a table with the mouse pointer. When you use the Insert commands on the Table menu or the Insert Table button on the Standard toolbar, you create a table grid in which the columns and rows are uniformly sized and positioned. Drawing a table with the mouse pointer allows you greater flexibility in determining the size and position of rows and columns. Word provides a separate toolbar, the Tables and Borders toolbar, with tools for drawing, erasing, and formatting a table.

To begin the holiday sales price cover sheet, you create a new, blank document, change the margins, and view the Tables and Borders toolbar:

Step 1	**Create**	a new, blank document
Step 2	**Close**	the New Document task pane, if necessary
Step 3	**Set**	the top, bottom, left and right margins to ½ inch
Step 4	**Click**	the Tables and Borders button on the Standard toolbar

Word switches to Print Layout view, if necessary, the mouse pointer changes to the pencil pointer when positioned in the document, and the Tables and Borders toolbar opens. Unless it has been previously repositioned, the Tables and Borders toolbar appears in its own window near the top of the document. You reposition the Tables and Borders toolbar below the Formatting toolbar to keep it out of the way.

Step 5	**Drag**	the Tables and Borders toolbar up until it docks directly below the Formatting toolbar

When working in Print Layout view, you can hide or display the white space between the top and bottom margin of the page and the top and bottom edge of the page to increase the view of the document text area. You do this with the Hide/Show White Space pointer. To hide the white space at the top of the document:

Step 1	**Verify**	that the document is scrolled to the top and you can see the top edge of the page and the gray area between the page and the Tables and Borders toolbar

> **MENU TIP**
>
> You can view the Tables and Borders toolbar and pencil pointer by clicking the Draw Table command on the Table menu.

Customizing Tables **WA 5**

| Step 2 | *Move* | the mouse pointer to the gray area between the top edge of the page and the Tables and Borders toolbar |
| Step 3 | *Observe* | that the mouse pointer becomes the Hide White Space pointer |

The mouse pointer on your screen should look similar to Figure 14-2.

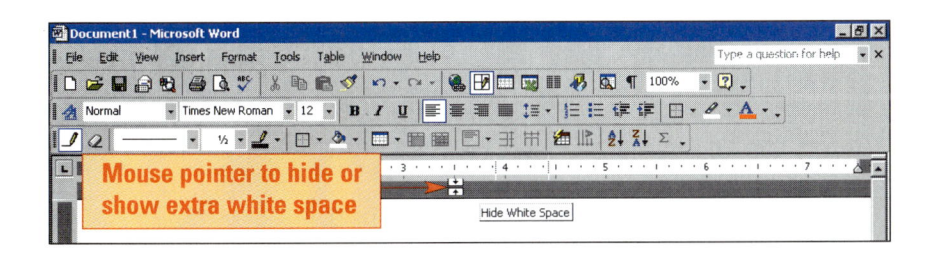

FIGURE 14-2
Hide White Space Pointer

Step 4	*Click*	the gray area between the top edge of the page and the Table and Borders toolbar
Step 5	*Observe*	that the white space between the top margin and the edge of the page is hidden
Step 6	*Scroll*	to the bottom of the page
Step 7	*Observe*	that the white space between the bottom margin and the bottom edge of the page is hidden
Step 8	*Scroll*	back to view the top of the document

Before you draw a table, you can use buttons on the Tables and Borders toolbar to set the table border style, width, and color, or you can turn off the default border. To turn on the Draw Table feature and set the table border options:

Step 1	*Click*	the Draw Table button on the Tables and Borders toolbar to display the pencil pointer, if necessary
Step 2	*Click*	the Line Style button list arrow on the Tables and Borders toolbar
Step 3	*Click*	the thin double-line border option (the eighth option)
Step 4	*Click*	the Line Weight button list arrow on the Tables and Borders toolbar
Step 5	*Click*	the 2¼ pt option
Step 6	*Click*	the Border Color button list arrow on the Tables and Borders toolbar
Step 7	*Click*	the Red square on the color grid (the first color in the third row)

MOUSE TIP

You can use buttons on the Tables and Borders toolbar to add borders and shading to text paragraphs.

chapter fourteen

To draw the table you position the pencil pointer in the document where you want the upper-left corner of the table to begin. Thin guidelines appear on the horizontal and vertical ruler indicating the current position of the pencil pointer. You drag diagonally toward the location of the lower-right corner of the table to create the external table boundaries. Then, you continue to use the pencil pointer to draw the row and column boundaries inside the table. To position the pencil pointer and draw the table:

| Step 1 | *Move* | the pencil pointer 1 inch below the top margin and 1 inch to the right of the left margin |

Your screen should look similar to Figure 14-3.

FIGURE 14-3
Pencil Pointer and Table Drawing Guides

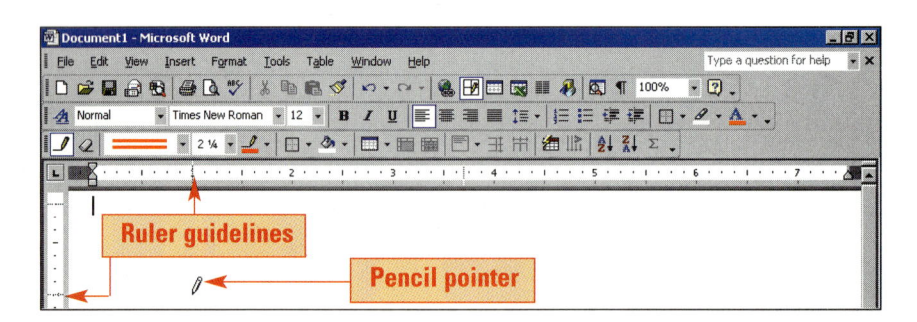

Step 2	*Drag*	diagonally to the right until the guideline on the horizontal ruler is at the 6-inch position and the guideline on the vertical ruler is at the 9-inch position
Step 3	*Release*	the mouse button to create the external table boundaries
Step 4	*Zoom*	the document to Whole Page

You use the pencil pointer to draw row and column boundaries inside the table. To create column and row boundaries with a red, 1-point, single border style:

Step 1	*Click*	the Line Style button list arrow on the Tables and Borders toolbar
Step 2	*Click*	the single line option (the second option)
Step 3	*Click*	the Line Weight button list arrow on the Tables and Borders toolbar
Step 4	*Click*	the 1 pt option
Step 5	*Click*	the Border Color button list arrow on the Tables and Borders toolbar

Step 6	Click	the Red square on the color grid (the first color in the third row)
Step 7	Move	the pencil pointer inside the top boundary of the table approximately 1 inch from the left boundary of the table
Step 8	Drag	down to the bottom boundary until a dashed line column boundary appears
Step 9	Release	the mouse button to create the column boundary
Step 10	Draw	a second column boundary at any position inside the table
Step 11	Draw	a row boundary approximately 1 inch from the top of the table
Step 12	Draw	two additional row boundaries at any position

You now have a 4 × 3 Table (4 rows and 3 columns) with unevenly distributed columns and rows. When you have finished drawing the table, you can turn off the Draw Table feature.

| Step 13 | Click | the Draw Table button on the Tables and Borders toolbar to turn off the pencil pointer |

The mouse pointer changes to an I-beam. You can move the insertion point, select cells, rows, and columns, size the cells, rows, and columns, and key text in the cells just as you can when you create a table using the toolbar or menu commands. A quick way to size rows and columns is with the mouse pointer. To widen the first column and row:

Step 1	Zoom	the document to 75% so that it is easier to see
Step 2	Move	the mouse pointer to the right boundary of the first column (the mouse pointer becomes a sizing pointer with a double-headed black arrow)
Step 3	Drag	the column boundary to the right approximately ½ inch
Step 4	Move	the mouse pointer to the bottom boundary of the first row (the mouse pointer becomes a sizing pointer)
Step 5	Drag	the row boundary up approximately ½ inch

Actually, you don't need the table divided into rows and columns for the cover sheet. If you draw a column or row boundary that you don't need or in the wrong place, it is easy to erase it by turning the mouse pointer into an eraser.

> **MOUSE TIP**
>
> To evenly distribute rows and columns, select the rows or columns (or click in the table for all rows and columns) and then click the Distribute Rows Evenly or Distribute Columns Evenly button on the Tables and Borders toolbar.

MOUSE TIP

You can click the boundary of a cell with the Eraser pointer to remove it.

To erase the row and column boundaries:

Step 1	Zoom	the document to Whole Page
Step 2	Click	the Eraser button on the Tables and Borders toolbar
Step 3	Drag	the eraser pointer over a column boundary to erase it
Step 4	Drag	the eraser pointer over a row boundary to erase it
Step 5	Erase	the remaining column and row boundaries leaving only the external table boundaries
Step 6	Click	the Eraser button on the Tables and Borders toolbar to turn it off

When the pencil and eraser pointers are turned off, the mouse pointer becomes the I-beam when positioned over a table cell. When you place the I-beam in the table, two new objects are added to the table: a move handle that appears above the upper-left corner of the table and a sizing handle that appears below the lower-right corner of the table. You drag the **move handle** to reposition or copy the table and the **sizing handle** to resize the entire table.

You decide to move the table down on the page and make it a little smaller. To reposition and resize the table using the move handle and the sizing handle:

| Step 1 | Move | the mouse pointer to the move handle above the upper-left corner of the table (the mouse pointer becomes a move pointer with four black arrows) |

Your screen should look similar to Figure 14-4.

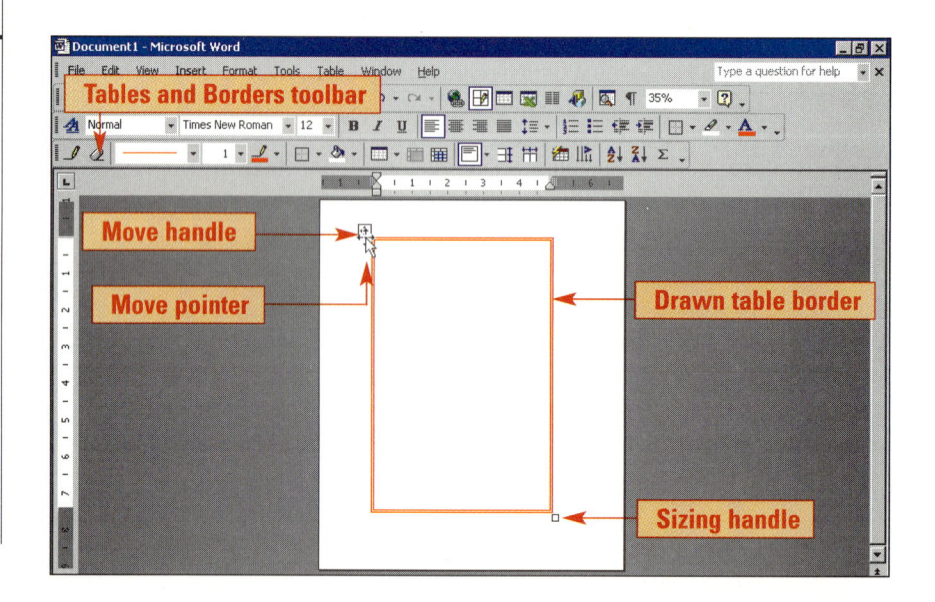

QUICK TIP

You can change the pencil pointer to the eraser pointer by pressing the SHIFT key.

FIGURE 14-4
Table Move Handle and Move Pointer

Step 2	Drag	the move handle down approximately ¼ inch to reposition the table
Step 3	Move	the mouse pointer to the sizing handle below the lower-right corner of the table
Step 4	Drag	the sizing handle up approximately 1 inch

Because this is a cover sheet for the holiday sales price list, you want to add a title to the page. To make the cover page more interesting, you decided to key the title text in a second table placed inside the first table.

Nesting Tables

To help organize text on a page, you can create a table inside another table cell. Creating tables inside other tables is called **nesting**. You can nest tables when you need to organize a subset of data inside a larger table or to create a decorative effect. To draw a nested table:

Step 1	Set	a thin double line, ¾-point, red boundary using buttons on the Tables and Borders toolbar
Step 2	Click	the Draw Table button on the Tables and Borders toolbar, if necessary
Step 3	Move	the pencil pointer inside the table
Step 4	Draw	a smaller table inside the larger one approximately 2½ inches wide and 3 inches long, equidistant from the top, bottom, left, and right boundaries of the larger table
Step 5	Position	and size the smaller table attractively near the center of the larger table
Step 6	Zoom	the document to 75% and scroll to view the smaller table
Step 7	Verify	that the insertion point is inside the smaller table
Step 8	Key	Holiday Sales Prices
Step 9	Format	the text with bold, 22-point, red font

QUICK TIP

You can create a nested table inside a table created with the Table button on the Standard toolbar or the Insert, Table commands on the Table menu. First, create the table. Then move the mouse pointer into a table cell and simply create another table using the toolbar button or menu command methods.

You want the text to be centered vertically and horizontally inside the table. You can vertically and horizontally align text in a cell with a button on the Tables and Borders toolbar. To change the vertical and horizontal alignment of the text in the nested table:

Step 1	Verify	that the insertion point is in the smaller table
Step 2	Click	the Align button list arrow on the Tables and Borders toolbar

QUICK TIP

When you move the mouse pointer over a document in Print Layout view or Web Layout view, the mouse pointer becomes the Click and Type pointer, which consists of the I-beam and an alignment indicator. You can double-click the Click and Type pointer to position the insertion point at a tab stop or horizontal alignment position (left, center, right) anywhere on the page without first creating a blank line with the ENTER key.

| Step 3 | Click | the Align Center button on the grid |
| Step 4 | Deselect | the text |

The text is aligned vertically and horizontally between the nested table boundaries.

Creating Side-by-Side Tables

Side-by-side tables provide greater flexibility in organizing information on a page. For example, in a sales brochure you might have lists of products in multiple side-by-side tables. You could also use side-by-side tables without borders to add a special text effect on a page. You decide to do this for the holiday sales prices cover sheet. To create a new table without borders to the right of the nested tables:

Step 1	Zoom	the document to Whole Page
Step 2	Select	the No Border option from the Line Style list
Step 3	Draw	a long narrow table to the right of the nested tables beginning at the top margin and ending at the bottom margin leaving at least ½ inch between the tables

In addition to the horizontal and vertical alignment of text in a table cell, you can also change the direction of text within a table cell. You add the name of the company, rotated to read from bottom to top in the table.

Rotating Text in Tables

Changing the direction of text in a table cell allows you to add a special effect to the text. It also works well to rotate long column headings over narrow columns of data. When you rotate the text, the text retains its horizontal and vertical formatting. You want the company name to appear vertically against the right boundary of the new table.

To change the text direction:

Step 1	Zoom	the document to 75%
Step 2	Click	the Draw Table button on the Tables and Borders toolbar to turn off the pencil pointer, if necessary
Step 3	Verify	that the insertion point is in the new table
Step 4	Click	the Change Text Direction button on the Tables and Borders toolbar until the directional arrows on the button face are pointing to the right

Customizing Tables **WA 11**

Step 5	Click	the Align Center Right button ⊞ from the Align list on the Tables and Borders toolbar
Step 6	Key	Worldwide Exotic Foods, Inc.
Step 7	Format	the text with bold, 48-point, red font
Step 8	Zoom	the document to Whole Page
Step 9	Move	the mouse pointer to the gray area below the bottom edge of the page to view the Show White Space pointer
Step 10	Click	the gray area below the bottom edge of the page to show the white space
Step 11	Save	the document as *Holiday Sales Prices Cover Sheet* and leave it open

To more accurately position the nested tables on the page, you can use the table positioning features in the Table Properties dialog box. To reposition the table:

Step 1	Right-click	inside the large, outer table
Step 2	Click	Table P*r*operties
Step 3	Click	P*o*sitioning on the *T*able tab of the Table Properties dialog box

Your Table Positioning dialog box should look similar to Figure 14-5.

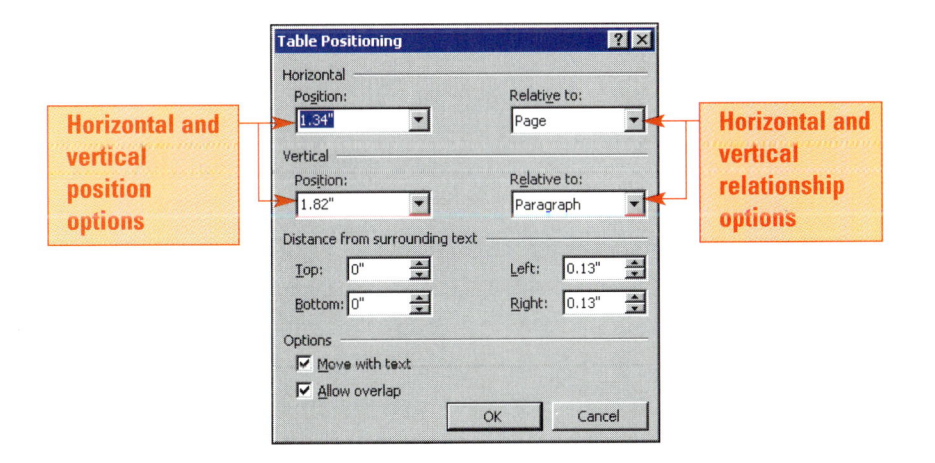

INTERNET TIP

Tables, rather than columns, are used to organize information on a Web page. Many of the options in the Table Properties dialog box are used to create tables on Web pages. Use the dialog box Help button to review all the options in the dialog box.

FIGURE 14-5
Table Positioning Dialog Box

Horizontal and vertical position options

Horizontal and vertical relationship options

The options in the Horizontal and Vertical groups allow you to specify the position of the table in relation to the edges of the page, the margins, a newspaper-style column, or a text paragraph. You can also specify the distance the table boundaries should be from surrounding text. You center the table relative to the left and right margins.

chapter fourteen

Step 4	**Click**	the Horizontal Po<u>s</u>ition: list arrow
Step 5	**Click**	Center, if necessary
Step 6	**Click**	the Horizontal Relati<u>v</u>e to: list arrow
Step 7	**Click**	Margin, if necessary
Step 8	**Click**	the Vertical Po<u>s</u>ition: list arrow
Step 9	**Click**	Center
Step 10	**Click**	the Vertical R<u>e</u>lative to: list arrow
Step 11	**Click**	Margin, if necessary
Step 12	**Click**	OK in each dialog box

The nested tables are centered vertically and horizontally between the margins. Now you want to center the long table containing the company name between the top and bottom margins:

Step 1	**Right-click**	the long table containing the company name
Step 2	**Click**	Table P<u>r</u>operties
Step 3	**Click**	<u>P</u>ositioning
Step 4	**Click**	Center in the Vertical Po<u>s</u>ition: list
Step 5	**Click**	Margin, if necessary, in the Vertical R<u>e</u>lative to: list
Step 6	**Click**	OK in each dialog box
Step 7	**Save**	the document and close it
Step 8	**Hide**	the Tables and Borders toolbar using a shortcut menu

It is very easy to copy a table using drag-and-drop in Print Layout view.

Using Drag-and-Drop to Copy a Table

One way to save time when creating a document that contains multiple similar tables is to create the structure for one table and then quickly copy that table to other locations in the document using drag-and-drop. The marketing manager asks you to finish the *Pastries Projections* document created earlier by another assistant. You need to add a new table based on an existing table and then key different data in the new table. You use the existing table's move handle to select the table and then copy it using drag-and-drop. To open the document and create the new table using drag-and-drop:

Step 1	**Open**	the *Pastries Projections* document located on the Data Disk

Step 2	Switch to	Print Layout view, if necessary
Step 3	Hide	the extra white space above and below the top and bottom margins
Step 4	Move	the mouse pointer to the table to view the move and sizing handles
Step 5	Press & hold	the CTRL key
Step 6	Click & hold	the move handle
Step 7	Drag	the move handle (and selected table) down and drop the copied selection below the "Projected Sales" heading
Step 8	Release	the CTRL key

Your screen should look similar to Figure 14-6.

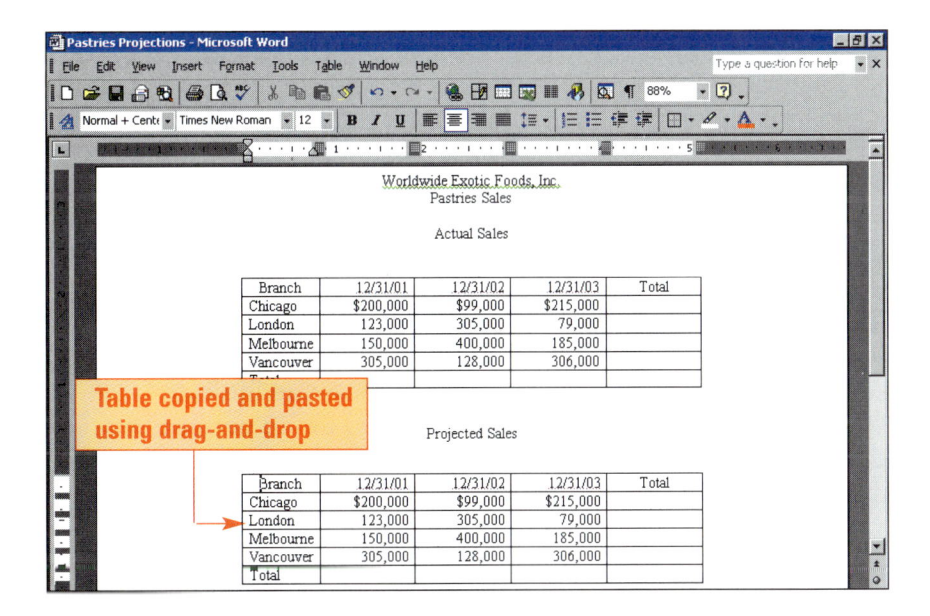

FIGURE 14-6
Table Copied Using Drag-and-Drop

You replace the data in the copied table. To update the data in the Projected Sales table (table 2):

Step 1	Delete	the dates and numerical data in the Projected Sales table (table 2)
Step 2	Key	the following data in the Projected Sales table (table 2):

Branch	12/31/04	12/31/05	12/31/06
Chicago	$210,000	$205,000	$250,000
London	130,000	200,000	389,000
Melbourne	150,000	209,000	302,000
Vancouver	175,000	235,000	408,000

chapter fourteen

| Step 3 | Save | the document as *Pastries Projections Revised* and leave it open |

Now you need to calculate total actual and projected sales by branch and for each year.

14.b Performing Calculations in a Table

Sometimes it is necessary to include numerical totals or other calculated values in a table. One way to add calculated values to a table is to make necessary calculations manually and then key the results in the appropriate cell; however, if you make any changes to the numbers in the calculation, you must then manually recalculate and rekey the results. An alternative is to insert a **formula**, or mathematical expression that performs a computation. For example, you can insert a formula that calculates the total of a series of numbers in a specific row or column. Then if you make any changes to the numbers, you simply update the formula to show the new total.

Inserting a Formula in a Table

The most common calculation for a table is addition. You can also subtract, multiply, divide, and calculate averages, percentages, and minimum or maximum values in a table. Unless you indicate otherwise, Word assumes the calculation you want to perform is addition. Based on the position of the insertion point and the cells containing numbers, Word inserts a formula for addition containing the **Sum function**, a preset addition calculation. For example, if the insertion point is in a column, Word inserts a formula to sum the numbers in the cells *above* the insertion point. If the numbers are in a row, Word inserts a formula to sum the numbers in the cells to the *left* or *right* of the insertion point.

Word inserts the formula as a field code. A **field code** is a placeholder for data or a calculation. To view field codes rather than the results, check the Field Codes command in the View tab in the Options dialog box or the Toggle Field Codes command on a shortcut menu. You can toggle between field codes and field results by pressing the ALT + F9 keys.

To insert the column totals in the Actual Sales table (table 1):

| Step 1 | Move | the insertion point to the last cell in the 12|31|01 column in the Actual Sales table (table 1) |

> **MOUSE TIP**
> You can insert a formula containing the Sum function by clicking the AutoSum button on the Tables and Borders toolbar.

Customizing Tables **WA 15**

Step 2	Click	T<u>a</u>ble
Step 3	Click	F<u>o</u>rmula

The Formula dialog box on your screen should look similar to Figure 14-7.

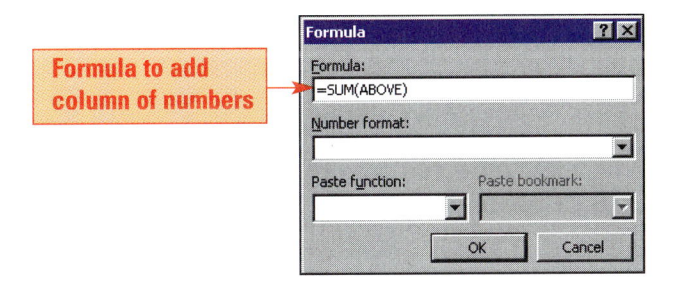

Formula to add column of numbers → =SUM(ABOVE)

FIGURE 14-7
Formula Dialog Box

Step 4	Observe	the =SUM(ABOVE) formula in the <u>F</u>ormula: text box

You can change the format by selecting the appropriate number format, called a numeric picture switch, from the <u>N</u>umber format: list. A **numeric picture switch** consists of a combination of #, or 0 placeholders, a comma, a $, decimal point, percentage indicator, and parentheses. Each of these characters determines how the results of the calculation are formatted. For a complete explanation of numeric picture switch components, see online Help.

You want the results of the calculation to be formatted with a $, a comma, and no decimal places. To apply the desired format, you select a picture number switch that provides the comma and no decimal places and then edit it to add the $. To create a custom format:

Step 1	Click	the <u>N</u>umber format: list arrow
Step 2	Click	the first numeric picture switch (#,##0) in the list, which adds a comma and no decimal places to the format
Step 3	Key	a $ in front of the #,##0 numeric picture switch in the <u>N</u>umber format: text box to add the $ to the format
Step 4	Click	OK

The sum of the numbers in the 12/31/01 column, $778,000, appears in a Word field in the cell. The sum field may be shaded on your screen. You can turn on or off field shading on the View tab of the Options dialog box. Once you create a formula, you can repeat it in other cells by using the <u>R</u>epeat Formula command on the <u>E</u>dit menu or by pressing the CTRL + Y keys.

CAUTION TIP

Be certain to use text or formatted date column or row headings when using the Sum function in a formula to add row or column totals. Word cannot differentiate between the year "2003" in a column or row heading and the number "2003" you want to be included in a calculation. If you include a number, such as the year "2003" as a column or row heading, Word will include that number in its calculation!

chapter fourteen

QUICK TIP

You can key a formula in the Formula text box in the Formula dialog box. A formula must begin with the equal sign (=), it must contain a mathematical operator (+, –, *, or /), and it must include the cell address of the cells to be included in the calculation. A cell address combines the cell's column and row location. In a formula, columns are referenced alphabetically (A, B, C) and rows are referenced numerically (1, 2, 3). For example, A1 is the cell address for the intersection of the first column (column A) and the first row (row 1). To add the contents of cells A1 and B1, key = A1 + B1 in the Formula: text box.

MOUSE TIP

You can edit a formula field by right-clicking the field and clicking Edit Field. You can update a formula field by clicking Update Field on the same shortcut menu.

To calculate the totals for the 12/31/02 and 12/31/03 columns:

Step 1	Press	the TAB key to move the insertion point to the 12/31/02 column
Step 2	Press	the CTRL + Y keys
Step 3	Press	the TAB key
Step 4	Press	the CTRL + Y keys

The totals for the next two columns appear in the cells. Now you can create a formula to calculate the total pastries sales for the Chicago branch office and then repeat that formula for the other branch offices and the grand total. To insert the row totals:

Step 1	Move	the insertion point to the last cell in the Chicago row
Step 2	Open	the Formula dialog box
Step 3	Verify	that the formula in the Formula: text box is =SUM(LEFT)
Step 4	Key	the custom format $#,##0 in the Number format: text box
Step 5	Click	OK
Step 6	Observe	that the total sales for Chicago is $514,000
Step 7	Press	the DOWN ARROW key
Step 8	Press	the CTRL + Y keys to repeat the formula
Step 9	Repeat	Steps 7 and 8 to insert the remaining formulas in the Total column
Step 10	Save	the document and leave it open

When necessary, you can edit a formula to change the function or format.

Editing a Formula

After reviewing the calculations in the Actual Sales table, you decide to remove the $ from the London, Melbourne, and Vancouver totals for consistency in formatting. To edit the formulas to change the formatting:

| Step 1 | Right-click | the cell containing the London total $507,000 |
| Step 2 | Click | Edit Field |

You can insert a new Word field or edit the formula field in this dialog box.

Step 3	Click	the Formula button to display the Formula dialog box
Step 4	Remove	the $ from the numeric picture switch in the Number format: text box
Step 5	Click	OK
Step 6	Edit	the Melbourne and Vancouver totals to remove the $ by moving the insertion point into each cell and pressing the CTRL + Y keys to repeat the formatting change
Step 7	Insert	the similarly formatted year and branch office totals in the Projected Sales table

The document on your screen should look similar to Figure 14-8.

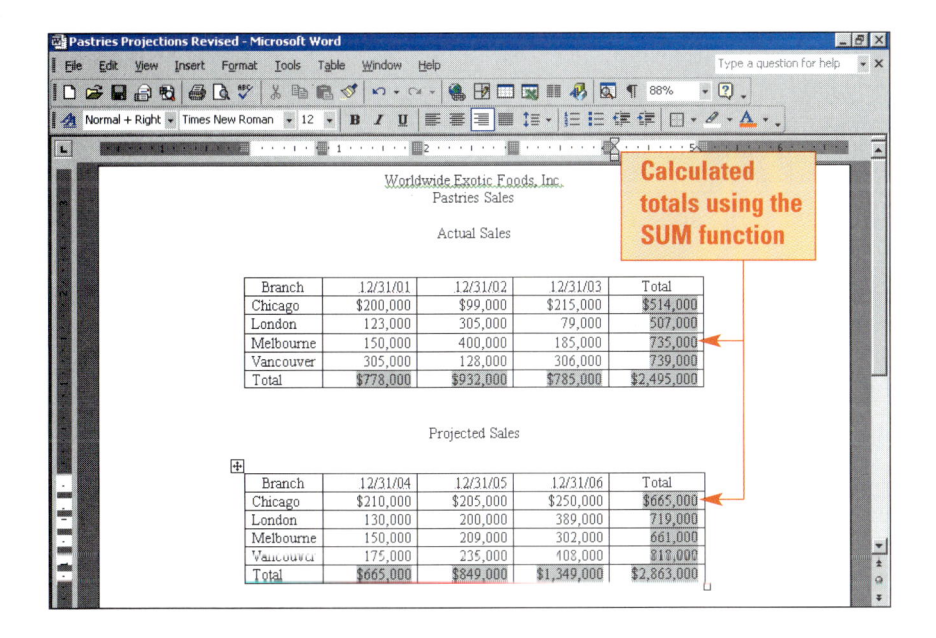

FIGURE 14-8
Tables with Calculated Totals

The marketing director sends you an e-mail asking you to change the Chicago 12/31/05 projected sales amount to $225,000. When you change a numeric value used in a calculation, you must manually update all the formulas that use the changed value. *Unlike formulas created in spreadsheet applications such as Excel, Word formulas do not automatically recalculate when the values used in the calculation are changed.* To change the Chicago 12/31/05 projected sales value and then update the applicable formulas:

Step 1	Change	the Chicago 12/31/05 value to $225,000

Step 2	Observe	that there is no change to either the 12/31/05 column total or the Chicago row total
Step 3	Select	the cell that contains the 12/31/05 column total
Step 4	Press	the F9 key to update the formula
Step 5	Observe	the new 12/31/05 column total, $869,000, in the cell
Step 6	Repeat	Steps 3 through 5 to update the Chicago row total to $685,000 and the grand total to $2,883,000
Step 7	Save	the document and leave it open

After reviewing the *Pastries Projections Revised* document, the marketing director asks you to make the document more attractive. You decide to use paragraph and table styles.

14.c Using Table Styles

A **table style**, also known as a Table AutoFormat, consists of preset row, column, and cell formatting. You can quickly apply a table style to a selected table using the Styles and Formatting task pane. To view and apply a table style to the Actual Sales table:

Step 1	Move	the insertion point to the Actual Sales table (table 1)
Step 2	Click	the Styles and Formatting button on the Formatting toolbar
Step 3	Select	All Styles in the Show: list in the Styles and Formatting task pane
Step 4	Scroll	the Pick formatting to apply list in the Styles and Formatting task pane to view the Table Colorful 2 table style
Step 5	Click	the Table Colorful 2 style in the Pick formatting to apply list in the Styles and Formatting task pane to apply the style to the Actual Sale table (table 1)

The style, which contains a left-aligned positioning, is applied to the table. You like the style, but want the table centered instead of left-aligned. You can modify an applied style everywhere it appears in the current document with the style's shortcut menu. To modify the style:

Step 1	Right-click	the Table Colorful 2 style in the Pick formatting to apply list in the Styles and Formatting task pane
Step 2	Click	Modify

The Modify Style dialog box on your screen should look similar to Figure 14-9.

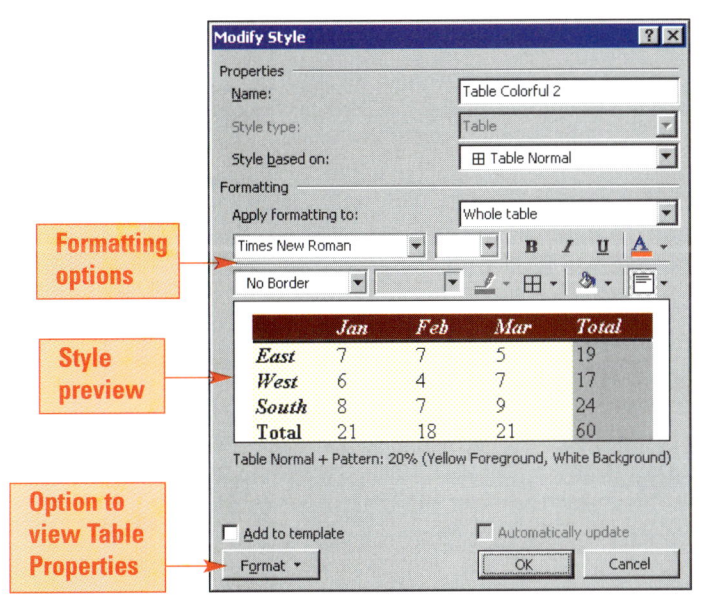

FIGURE 14-9
Modify Style Dialog Box

You can change the font, font size, border style, border width, border color, cell shading, text alignment, and other formatting components for the entire table or selected cells, rows, or columns in this dialog box. You want to change the table alignment property.

Step 3	Click	Format
Step 4	Click	Tabl**e** Properties
Step 5	Click	**C**enter alignment in the **T**able tab in the Table Properties dialog box
Step 6	Click	OK in both dialog boxes
Step 7	Observe	the modified table alignment

You want to format the other table with the same style. To apply the modified Table Colorful 2 style to the Projected Sales table (table 2):

Step 1	Move	the insertion point to the Projected Sales table (table 2)
Step 2	Click	the Table Colorful 2 style in the Pick formatting to apply list in the Styles and Formatting task pane
Step 3	Observe	that the modified Table Colorful 2 style with center alignment is applied

chapter fourteen

Task Pane Tip

You can quickly insert a table based on a table style by clicking a table style in the Styles and Formatting task pane to open the Insert Table dialog box.

Step 4	Select	all the heading text that is not part of either table using the CTRL key
Step 5	Apply	the Heading 4 paragraph style to the selected text using the Styles and Formatting task pane
Step 6	Center	the selected paragraphs using the Formatting toolbar
Step 7	Save	the document and leave it open

You like the basic look of the Table Colorful 2 style, but want to make a few other modifications and then save the modified style so that it can be used in other documents.

Creating a Custom Table Style

When you want to use the same customized table style in various documents, you can create a custom table style. You can create a new table style in the Table AutoFormat dialog box or in the Styles and Formatting task pane. To create a custom style based on the modified Table Colorful 2 style:

Step 1	Click	New Style in the Styles and Formatting task pane to open the New Style dialog box
Step 2	Click	Table in the Style type: list to view the formatting options for a table style

The New Style dialog box on your screen should look similar to Figure 14-10.

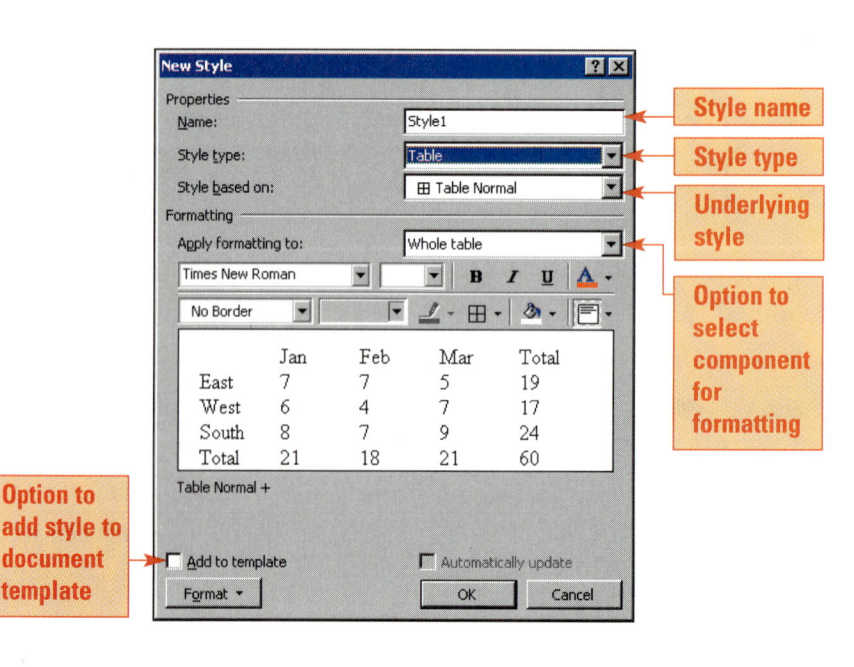

FIGURE 14-10
New Style Dialog Box

Customizing Tables **WA 21**

You give the new table style a name, select the underlying style upon which the new style is based, and make additional formatting changes in this dialog box. This dialog box contains formatting options similar to those on the Tables and Borders toolbar. You want to add a 1½-point double-line outside border and right-align the text in the cells.

Step 3	Key	TABLE MKTG in the Name: text box
Step 4	Select	Table Colorful 2 in the Style based on: list
Step 5	Select	the first narrow double lined border in the Line Style list
Step 6	Select	the 1½ pt size in the Line Weight list
Step 7	Click	Automatic in the Border Color list
Step 8	Click	Outside Borders in the Border list
Step 9	Click	the Align Center Right button on the Align grid

Because you want the new custom TABLE MKTG style available for other documents, you can add it to the Normal template.

Step 10	Click	the Add to template check box to insert a check mark
Step 11	Click	OK
Step 12	Observe	that the custom table style TABLE MKTG is added to the Pick formatting to apply list in the Styles and Formatting task pane

To select both tables and apply the TABLE MKTG custom style:

Step 1	Click	the move handle on the Actual Sales table (table 1)
Step 2	Press & hold	the CTRL key
Step 3	Click	the move handle on the Projected Sales table (table 2)
Step 4	Click	the TABLE MKTG style in the Pick formatting to apply list in the Styles and Formatting task pane (scroll to view this style, if necessary)
Step 5	Deselect	the tables and observe the formatting changes
Step 6	Show	the extra white space above and below the top and bottom margin

chapter fourteen

| Step 7 | **Save** | the document as *Pastries Projections With Custom Style* and close it |

The custom table style is added to the Normal template, which means each new document you create based on the Normal template has access to this custom style. You can delete the custom style from the style list for any specific document without deleting it from the Normal template. To delete the custom table style from the style list for a new, blank document:

Step 1	**Create**	a new, blank document
Step 2	**Observe**	that the TABLE MKTG custom style appears in the Pick formatting to apply list in the Styles and Formatting task pane
Step 3	**Right-click**	the TABLE MKTG style
Step 4	**Click**	Delete
Step 5	**Click**	Yes in the confirmation dialog box
Step 6	**Close**	the Styles and Formatting task pane

When a table contains numbers with differing decimal positions, you can align the numbers with a decimal tab stop.

14.d Using Tab Stops in a Table

You can set tab stops for table cells in the same way you set them for body text, by selecting the tab alignment and clicking the tab stop position on the horizontal ruler. Tab stops can be set for individual cells or a group of selected cells.

The assistant to the marketing director asks you to open a document she created earlier and align the decimal points in a table. To align all the numbers for each column at one time, you first select all the cells containing numbers. When you select cells containing numbers and then insert a tab stop, Word automatically aligns the numbers without inserting a tab character in the cell. To open the document, select the cells, and insert a decimal tab stop:

| Step 1 | **Open** | the *Bonus Rates* document located on the Data Disk |

CAUTION TIP

To delete the custom style from the Normal template, you must use the Organizer feature. To open the Organizer, click the Templates and Add-Ins command on the Tools menu. Then click the Organizer button in the Templates and Add-ins dialog box. Click the Styles tab in the Organizer dialog box. Then in the In Normal: pane, click the style you want to delete, and click the Delete button.

Step 2	Switch to	Normal view, if necessary
Step 3	Observe	that the bonus rate numbers have varying decimal positions
Step 4	Select	all the cells containing the bonus rate numbers
Step 5	Click	the Tab Alignment button to the left of the horizontal ruler until you see the Decimal Tab alignment button
Step 6	Click	the horizontal ruler above the Level 1 column at approximately the 1⅝ inch position to insert the tab stop for the selected cells
Step 7	Observe	that the Level 1, 2, and 3 bonus rate values are now aligned on the decimal point

> **QUICK TIP**
>
> To insert a tab formatting mark in a table cell, press the CTRL + TAB keys.

Your screen should look similar to Figure 14-11.

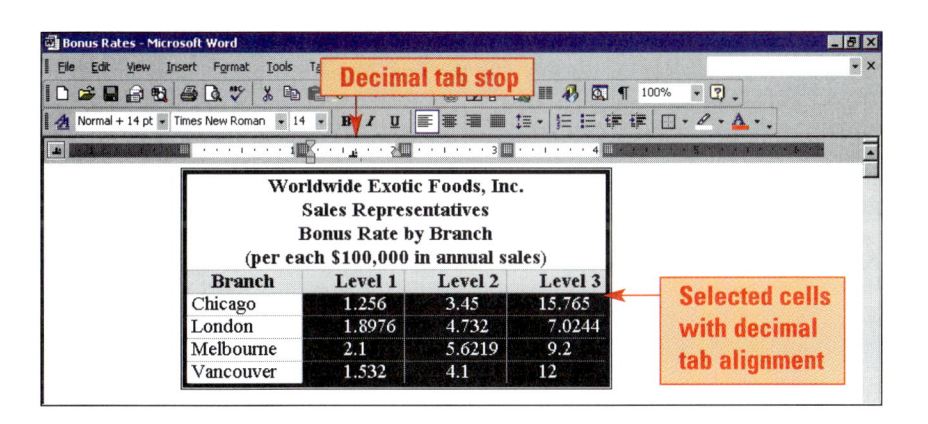

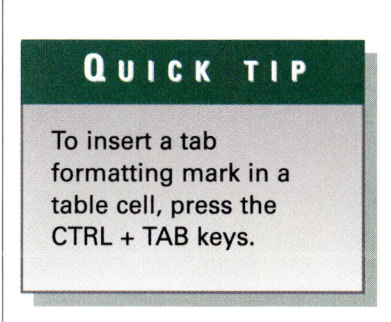

FIGURE 14-11
Table with Selected Cells

Step 8	Deselect	the cells
Step 9	Save	the document as *Bonus Rates With Decimal Alignment* and close it

You can quickly organize body text into a table.

14.e Converting Text to a Table

Selena Jackson, a secretary in the Marketing Department, asks you to format a list of the U.S. marketing representatives by city and state. She already created the list using tab stops and tab characters to separate the information for each sales representative, but she thinks

chapter fourteen

the list is easier to work with in a table. Instead of creating a table and keying the list again, you decide to convert the list to a table.

Data in tables is usually easier to manipulate, format, and calculate than the same data in text columns separated by tabs or other characters. You can convert text columns separated by tab characters, commas, or other characters to a table. You also can reverse the process and convert a table of rows and columns into text columns.

To convert text to a table you first select the text and then point to the Convert command on the Table menu and click the Text to Table command. To begin, you open Selena's old document and select the text to be converted to a table:

> **MENU TIP**
>
> If you create a large table that flows to more than one page, you can repeat the heading row on each subsequent page by moving the insertion point to the heading row and clicking the Heading Rows Repeat command on the Table menu.

Step 1	*Open*	the *Marketing Reps* document located on the Data Disk
Step 2	*View*	the nonprinting formatting marks to see the tab characters
Step 3	*Select*	the columns of text separated by tab formatting marks, beginning with the first Jones row and ending with the Aguilar row
Step 4	*Click*	Table
Step 5	*Point to*	Convert
Step 6	*Click*	Text to Table

The Convert Text to Table dialog box on your screen should look similar to Figure 14-12.

FIGURE 14-12
Convert Text to Table Dialog Box

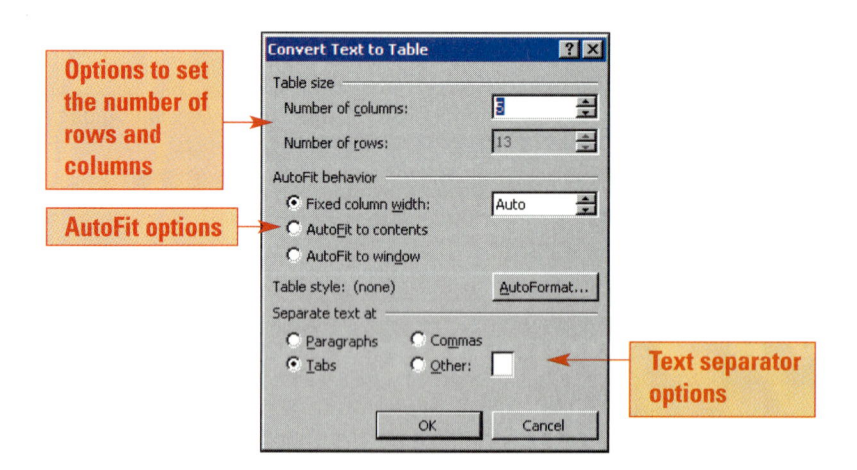

You specify the number of columns and rows as well as the size of the cells using AutoFit options in this dialog box. You also identify the character that separates columns so Word knows when to create a new column in the table. For example, the data in the *Marketing Reps* document is separated by tab formatting marks. Each time Word identifies a tab formatting mark, it places the data to the right of the tab formatting mark in the next column in the table. Word recognizes that the selected text contains five columns of text separated by tab formatting characters and sets those options for you. You can change the AutoFit option to control column width. You also can apply a table style or AutoFormat from this dialog box.

To create a five-column table:

Step 1	Verify	that the Number of columns: text box contains 5 and the Tabs option button is selected
Step 2	Click	OK
Step 3	Deselect	the table
Step 4	Observe	that the tab characters are removed and the selected text is placed in a table with 13 rows and 5 columns

You can edit and format the table as usual. To format the 13 × 5 table:

Step 1	Right-click	the table
Step 2	Point to	AutoFit
Step 3	Click	AutoFit to Contents
Step 4	Center	the table horizontally
Step 5	Save	the document as *Marketing Reps Revised* and close it

You can customize a table to fit specific needs by merging and splitting the table cells.

14.f Merging and Splitting Table Cells

The marketing director asks you to create a worksheet that the marketing representatives fill out by hand when recording client calls. She wants a large column of white space at the left for notations, a large row of white space at the top for the client name and address, and two large cells in the bottom-right corner of the worksheet for the

MENU TIP

You can quickly convert a table to text by first selecting the table and then clicking the Table to Text subcommand under the Convert command on the Table menu.

chapter fourteen

representative's and manager's initials. The rest of the worksheet is to be used to record client calls. She wants two worksheets per page. You decide to use a table to create the worksheet.

To create a new, blank document, and then insert a large table:

Step 1	Create	a new, blank document
Step 2	Key	Worldwide Exotic Foods, Inc. Marketing Representative Worksheet
Step 3	Verify	that the text appears on two lines at the top of the document
Step 4	Insert	two blank lines following the title
Step 5	Center	the title text and format it with bold, 14-point font
Step 6	Create	a 15 × 7 table on the second line below the title

Next you merge and split cells in the table to create the layout the marketing director wants. To merge and split cells:

Step 1	Select	the first two columns
Step 2	Right-click	the selected columns
Step 3	Click	Merge Cells
Step 4	Select	the top three unmerged rows
Step 5	Right-click	the selected rows
Step 6	Click	Merge Cells
Step 7	Select	the last four cells in the lower-right corner of the table
Step 8	Right-click	the selected cells
Step 9	Click	Merge Cells
Step 10	Select	the merged cell in the lower-right corner of the table
Step 11	Right-click	the cell
Step 12	Click	Split Cells to open the Split Cells dialog box
Step 13	Key	2 in the Number of columns: text box, if necessary
Step 14	Key	1 in the Number of rows: text box, if necessary
Step 15	Click	OK

Customizing Tables **WA 27**

Step 16	*Deselect*	the cells
Step 17	*Continue*	to merge and split cells and add appropriate text using Figure 14-13 as your guide

The completed table on your screen should look similar to Figure 14-13.

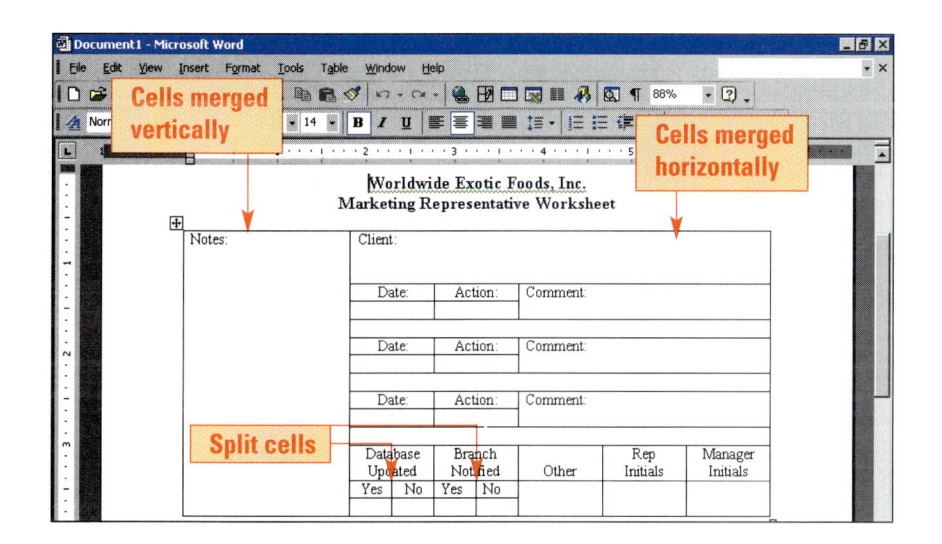

FIGURE 14-13
Completed Table

The director wants two copies of the table on the same page. You can copy the completed table to create the worksheet. To copy the completed table:

Step 1	*Create*	a duplicate second table using drag-and-drop to copy the completed first table
Step 2	*Save*	the document as *Marketing Rep Worksheet* and close it

Tables can effectively present information a wide variety of ways.

chapter fourteen

Summary

- You can draw a complex table with the Draw Table feature and format it with the Tables and Borders toolbar options.
- You can nest tables by drawing a table inside another table cell and you can place tables side by side.
- You can rotate text in a table cell and copy a table using drag-and-drop.
- You can create formulas in tables to add, subtract, multiply, divide, and calculate averages, percentages, and minimum or maximum values in a column or row.
- You can apply table styles (Table AutoFormats) from the Styles and Formatting task pane.
- You can create custom table styles.
- Tab stops can be set for one or more table columns.
- Text separated by commas, paragraph marks, or other characters can be converted to a table and tables can be converted to text separated by commas, paragraph marks, or other characters.
- You can merge and split table cells.

Commands Review

Action	Menu Bar	Shortcut Menu	Toolbar	Task Pane	Keyboard
View the Tables and Borders toolbar	View, Toolbars	Right-click any toolbar, click Tables and Borders			ALT + V, T
Draw a table	Table, Draw Table				ALT + A, W
Change pencil pointer to eraser pointer					SHIFT
Add formula to a table	Table, Formula				ALT + A, O
Repeat formulas	Edit, Repeat Formula				ALT + E, R CTRL + Y
Update a selected formula		Right-click a formula field, click Update Field			F9
Insert a tab formatting mark in a cell					CTRL + TAB
Split a table	Table, Split Table				ALT, A, T
Change text direction		Right-click cell, click Text Direction			

Customizing Tables **WA 29**

Action	Menu Bar	Shortcut Menu	Toolbar	Task Pane	Keyboard
Convert text to a table	Table, Convert, Text to Table				ALT + A, V, X
Convert a table to text	Table, Convert, Table to Text				ALT + A, V, B
Split cells vertically or horizontally	Table, Split Cells	Right-click merged cell, click Split Cells			ALT + A, P
Merge cells	Table, Merge Cells	Right-click selected cells, click Merge Cells			ALT + A, M
Distribute rows and columns evenly		Right-click selected columns or rows, click Distribute Columns Evenly or Distribute Rows Evenly			
Repeat heading row on all pages of table	Table, Heading Rows Repeat				ALT + A, H

Concepts Review

Circle the correct answer.

1. You can draw a table with the Draw Table button on the:
   - [a] Standard toolbar.
   - [b] Formatting toolbar.
   - [c] Tables toolbar.
   - [d] Tables and Borders toolbar.

2. You can hide or show the extra white space above or below the top and bottom margins with the:
   - [a] Show/Hide White Space button.
   - [b] table move handle.
   - [c] table sizing handle.
   - [d] Hide/Show White Space pointer.

3. Vertical and horizontal ruler guidelines help you to:
   - [a] draw a table.
   - [b] resize a table.
   - [c] move a table.
   - [d] copy a table.

4. Creating a table inside a table cell is called:
   - [a] birding.
   - [b] nesting.
   - [c] overlaying.
   - [d] integrating.

5. Word inserts a formula in a:
   - [a] text box.
   - [b] date code.
   - [c] paragraph.
   - [d] field code.

6. Which of the following numeric picture switches will format a Word formula with only a comma and two decimal places?
   - [a] #,##0
   - [b] $#,##0.00
   - [c] #,##0.00
   - [d] $#,##0

7. To update a formula in a table, press the:
   - [a] F8 key.
   - [b] SHIFT + F9 keys.
   - [c] ALT + F9 keys.
   - [d] F9 key.

8. A table style is also called a:
   - [a] TableAutoFormat.
   - [b] TableFormat.
   - [c] TablePosition.
   - [d] TableMode.

chapter fourteen

9. The best way to align the numbers 973.32, 734.871, 34.972 in table columns is to:
   [a] left-align the numbers.
   [b] set a decimal tab stop.
   [c] right-align the numbers.
   [d] center the numbers.

10. Which of the following formatting options is not available on the Tables and Borders toolbar?
    [a] vertical and horizontal text alignment
    [b] text rotation
    [c] line color, style, and width
    [d] bold

Circle **T** if the statement is true or **F** if the statement is false.

T F 1. You cannot create a custom table style.

T F 2. You can convert text to a table but you cannot convert a table to text.

T F 3. Table cells can be merged vertically or horizontally.

T F 4. You can use the eraser pointer to erase row or column boundaries in a drawn table.

T F 5. It is not possible to evenly distribute rows and columns in a drawn table.

T F 6. You set tab stops for table cells in the same manner as body text.

T F 7. You can copy a table using drag-and-drop by pressing the SHIFT key as you drag the sizing handle.

T F 8. The pencil pointer is used to draw tables.

T F 9. You can apply table styles using the Table Formatting task pane.

T F 10. The only kind of formula you can create in a table is to sum numbers in columns or rows.

Skills Review

Exercise 1

1. Open the *Melbourne Deli Sales* document located on the Data Disk.
2. Add a column at the end of the table and a row at the bottom of the table.
3. Add two blank rows at the top of the table and merge the cells in the top row.
4. Key "Melbourne Deli Sales" in the merged top row, and then center and bold the text.
5. Key "Region," "Meat," "Produce," "Pastries," "Beverages," and "Total" in the new row below the title. Key "Total" in the last cell in the Region column.
6. Use a formula to calculate the total sales for each region and for each product.
7. Widen the columns as necessary.
8. Save the document as *Melbourne Deli Sales Revised*, and then preview, print, and close it.

Exercise 2

1. Open the *Melbourne Deli Sales Revised* document you created in Exercise 2. If you have not created the document, do so now.
2. Apply the Table Classic 3 table style using the Styles and Formatting task pane.
3. Change the value of the South region Beverages sales to "107,234.55."
4. Update the Beverages, South, and grand totals all at one time by first selecting them with the CTRL key.
5. Save the document as *Melbourne Deli Sales Recalculated*, and then preview, print, and close it.

Exercise 3

1. Open the *Washington Letter* document located on the Data Disk.
2. Use formulas to calculate the total expenses by Sales District, total expenses by expense item, and the grand total.
3. Edit the formula formatting as necessary to have a comma, and two decimal places. All formulas should have a $ except the totals for Sales Districts 2–5.
4. Modify the Table Professional style to change the table alignment to center.
5. Apply the modified Table Professional style to the expense table.
6. Save the document as *Washington Letter With Calculations*, and then preview, print, and close it.

Exercise 4

1. Create a new, blank document.
2. Display the Tables and Borders toolbar.
3. Draw a 7 × 4 Table with the Draw Table tool on the Tables and Borders toolbar. Use a ½-point thin black line.
4. Select the table and distribute the columns and rows evenly using buttons on the Tables and Borders toolbar.
5. Key the following data:

District	Selling Expenses	Employee Expenses	Overhead
Central	$49,100.60	$12,421.00	$13,921.99
Eastern	41,756.72	5,523.42	8,992.33
Midwest	64,871.86	4,819.89	9,655.76
Mountain	59,256.36	7,085.07	6,332.99
Southern	45,817.32	12,253.57	16,322.86
Western	51,857.52	9,528.88	11,661.30

6. Select the first row, bold and center the text vertically and horizontally, and then right-align the numbers.
7. Insert a row at the bottom of the table and a column at the right of the table.
8. Add the text "Total" to the first cell in the new row and column.
9. Use the AutoSum button on the Tables and Borders toolbar to insert the total for each column.
10. Use the Formula command on the Table menu to sum the Central row. Repeat the formula for the remaining rows.
11. Change the value for Central Selling Expenses to "$59,100.60."
12. Select the three relevant totals using the CTRL key and update the formulas.
13. Insert a row at the top of the table and merge the cells.
14. Key the following title text, centered in 14-point font in the new first row.

    Chicago Branch
    District Expense Report
    Third Quarter

15. Center the table between the left and right margins.
16. Use drag-and-drop to create a copy of the table below the first table. Leave approximately 1 inch between the tables.
17. Save the document as *Chicago Expense Report*, and then preview, print, and close it.

chapter fourteen

Exercise 5

1. Open the *IT Costs Memo* document located on the Data Disk.
2. Display the Tables and Borders toolbar.
3. Draw a 7 × 4 Table with a double, 1½-point black border below the memo body text.
4. Distribute the rows and columns evenly.
5. Merge the cells in the first row.
6. Key the following heading text, centered and bold, in two lines in the first row.

    Information Technology Department
    Adjusted Costs for Second Quarter

7. Key the following data in the remaining rows.

Item	Budgeted	Actual	Difference
Network	$3,455,000	$3,256,000	-$199,000
Communications	490,600	400,000	-90,600
Web Site	1,960,000	1,940,000	-20,000
Systems Design	576,000	650,600	74,600
Programming	96,000	70,000	-26,000

8. Apply bold style to the column and row headings, and then align them at the bottom center.
9. Align the numbers at the bottom left.
10. Set a decimal tab stop at approximately the 2½-inch position to align all the numbers. (*Hint:* The decimal point is implied for whole numbers.)
11. Center the table horizontally.
12. Save the document as *IT Costs Memo Revised*, and then preview, print, and close it.

Exercise 6

1. Create a new, blank document.
2. Set 1-inch top, bottom, left, and right margins.
3. Display the Tables and Border toolbar.
4. Draw a large table with a triple blue border approximately 1 inch from the top, bottom, left, and right margins.
5. Draw a nested table inside the first table with the same border style approximately 1 inch from the top, bottom, left, and right borders of the first table.
6. Change the text direction for the inside table to read from bottom to top and center align the insertion point.
7. Key "Trivia Information About Selected States" in the 18-point blue Comic Sans MS font in the inside table. (*Hint:* If you do not have the Comic Sans MS font, select a font of your choice.)
8. Position the outside table centered horizontally and vertically using the Positioning option in the Table Properties dialog box.
9. Close the Tables and Borders toolbar.
10. Save the document as *State Trivia Cover Sheet*, and then preview, print, and close it.

Exercise 7

1. Open the *Washington Letter With Calculations* document you created in Exercise 3. If you have not completed Exercise 3, do so now.
2. Display the Styles and Formatting task pane.
3. Create a custom table style named "TABLE EXPENSE REPORT" based on the Table Simple 3 table style. (*Hint:* Don't forget to change the Style type to Table, if necessary.)
4. Add the center alignment to the table style for the entire table by changing the Table Properties within the New Style dialog box.
5. Remove the border from the entire table.
6. Change the font for the entire table to Arial 12 point, bottom-right aligned.
7. Change the header row fill to Gray-10% and change the header row font color to black. (*Hint:* Change the Apply formatting to: option to Header row before selecting the fill color.)
8. Change the last row fill to Gray-10%.
9. Apply the new custom TABLE EXPENSE REPORT custom table style to the London Expense Report table.
10. AutoFit the table to contents.
11. Save the document as *Washington Letter With Custom Style*, and then preview and print it.
12. Delete the TABLE EXPENSE REPORT custom table style from the Styles and Formatting task pane and close the task pane.
13. Close the document *without saving changes*.

Exercise 8

1. Create a new, blank document.
2. Create a 15 × 4 Table using the Insert Table button on the Standard toolbar.
3. View the table in Print Layout view and size the table to fill approximately ¾ of the page between the top and bottom margins.
4. Merge all the cells in the first column.
5. Merge all the cells in the top three rows to the right of the merged column.
6. Merge all the cells in the bottom two rows to the right of the merged column.
7. Split the bottom merged cells into 2 columns with 2 rows.
8. Merge the middle column of unmerged cells.
9. Split the middle column into 1 column with 2 rows.
10. Save the document as *Order Form*, and then preview, print, and close it.

chapter fourteen

Exercise 9

1. Open the *Tabbed Branch Data* document located on the Data Disk.
2. Select the tabbed data and convert it to a table.
3. Display the Styles and Formatting task pane and apply the Table Elegant table style modified to add Gray-15% shading to the header row.
4. AutoFit the table to its contents and center it horizontally using the Center button on the Formatting toolbar. (*Hint:* Don't forget to select the entire table before centering it.)
5. Right-align the column headings and numbers.
6. Remove the underline from the column headings.
7. Save the document as *Branch Data Table*, and then preview, print, and close it.
8. Close the Styles and Formatting task pane.

Case Projects

Project 1

A Marketing Department coworker, Liz Benson, wants to know how to prevent a table row from breaking across pages and how to force a table to break across pages at a particular row. Use online Help to research how to control where a table is divided. Write an interoffice memorandum to Liz describing the process. Save, preview, and print the memo.

Project 2

Bill Blake asks you to create an interoffice memo to four London marketing representatives advising them of the profit (sales minus expenses) for the second quarter on the Lush Living basket product. Draw a table to present the data for the four marketing representatives by listing the sales, expenses, and profit for each. Then calculate the total sales, total expenses, and total profit for each representative. Use fictitious data. Format and position the table and table text attractively on the page. Save, preview, and print the memo.

Project 3

One of your coworkers, Mike Stevens, is having trouble with the tables in a document. He asks for your help. He doesn't want the columns in table A to resize as he keys text in the cells. In table B, part of the text is hidden inside a table cell. Use online Help to research these two problems. Then write Mike a memo explaining how he can fix the problems.

Project 4

Bill Blake has created a new Web page for several new products and wants to make certain that two important Internet search tools, Yahoo! and Alta Vista have the URL for the page. He asks you to research how to make Yahoo! and Alta Vista aware of a new URL. Using the Internet, review the Yahoo! (*www.yahoo.com*) and Alta Vista (*www.altavista.com*) Web sites for information on submitting URLs. Write Bill Blake a memo describing the process for both Web sites. Save, preview, and print the memo.

Project 5

A coworker has a large table that she wants to convert to text separated by tab characters and she asks for your help. Use online Help to research how to do this and then create a step-by-step outline of the process. Use the existing table of your choice and convert it to text. Save, preview, and print the documents. With your instructor's permission, use the outline to show two classmates how to convert a table to text.

Project 6

Create a letter and an accompanying envelope to send to the president of Wilson Meat Products, M. L. Wilson, from Bill Blake, account executive, advising Ms. Wilson of the total sales of four Wilson meat products for the third quarter. Draw an attractively formatted and positioned table to itemize the product sales for April, May, and June. Calculate the total sales by product and month. Position and format the table text attractively within the table cells. Use fictitious data. Save, preview, and print the letter.

Project 7

Chris, the Word Processing Department manager, calls to invite you to present a short tutorial on using table styles and creating custom table styles at the next "brown bag" seminar. Use online Help, if necessary, to review how to use table styles, modify table styles, and create custom table styles. Then create an outline of your presentation on table styles. Save, preview, and print the outline. With your instructor's permission, make your presentation to the class.

Project 8

The Marketing Department receptionist is out of preprinted forms and needs to quickly create a temporary worksheet she can use to record client telephone calls. She asks for your help. The information she needs to retain is: date of the call, the client's name, the client's phone number, the marketing representative's name, and a large area in which to note the reason for the call. She wants two worksheets per page. Create a table and merge and split cells as necessary to create a client call worksheet. Then use drag-and-drop to create a second, duplicate worksheet on the same page. Save, preview, and print the document.

chapter fourteen

Word 2002

Working with Multipage Documents

Chapter Overview

When you work with a document created by someone else, it is sometimes useful to browse through the document to get familiar with it and to review the document's formatting. With large, report-style documents, it is also helpful to include a cover sheet as part of the document and to use different headers or footers in the document. In this chapter, you review a document using the Select Browse Object, use the Reveal Formatting task pane to compare paragraph formatting, create section breaks, create different headers and footers, and use hyphenation.

Learning Objectives

- Navigate with the Select Browse Object
- Verify paragraph formats using the Reveal Formatting task pane
- Create sections with different formatting
- Create different headers and footers in a document
- Use hyphenation

Case profile

Now that your work in the Marketing Department is finished, B. J. Chang, the vice president of Human Resources, asks you to assist in the department while his administrative assistant is on vacation. You begin by opening an existing document and checking its formatting. Then you add a cover sheet and alternate headers and footers to the document.

chapter fifteen

15.a Navigating with the Select Browse Object

In addition to navigating through a document by using the Find command, the Go To command, the horizontal and vertical scroll bars, or by moving the insertion point with the mouse and keyboard, you can browse a document by selecting a document component. You use the Select Browse Object feature to select a field, endnote, footnote, comment, section, heading, picture, or table document component.

The default option for the Select Browse Object is to browse by page. To review the Select Browse Object:

| Step 1 | Open | the *Lesson One* document located on the Data Disk |
| Step 2 | Click | the Select Browse Object button ⦿ below the vertical scroll bar |

The Select Browse Object grid opens immediately below the Select Browse Object button. Your grid should look similar to Figure 15-1.

FIGURE 15-1
Select Browse Object Grid

Step 3	Point to	the first icon on the Select Browse Object grid
Step 4	Observe	the text "Browse by Field" in the text area
Step 5	Continue	to review each icon on the grid by pointing to it
Step 6	Point to	the text area of the grid
Step 7	Observe	the text "Cancel"
Step 8	Click	Cancel to close the grid without selecting a browse component

> **MOUSE TIP**
>
> Each icon on the Select Browse Object grid represents a component by which to browse. You can point to each icon and observe the component name in the text area. When you see the component you want to browse by, click its icon.

The paragraph headings in the *Lesson One* document are formatted with the Heading 2 style. You want to find all the instances of the Heading 2 style and replace them with the Heading 3 style. To locate each paragraph heading and reformat it:

| Step 1 | Move | the insertion point to the top of the document, if necessary |

chapter fifteen

QUICK TIP

The Next and Previous buttons below the vertical scroll bar change to reflect the selected browse object, as shown in their ScreenTips, and move the insertion point to the next or previous instance of that object. For example, the Next Page or Previous Page buttons for the default Browse by Page option quickly move the insertion point to the top of the next or previous page. When you select a component other than Page, the Next and Previous buttons change color from black (which signifies Page) to blue. To return the Next and Previous buttons to their default page option, click the Page component in the Select Browse Object grid.

Step 2	Click	the Select Browse Object button
Step 3	Click	the Browse by Heading option on the Select Browse Object grid
Step 4	Observe	that the insertion point moves to the first paragraph heading "Defining the Internet" and the Style button list box on the Formatting toolbar contains "Heading 2"
Step 5	Click	Heading 3 in the Style button list on the Formatting toolbar
Step 6	Observe	the reformatted heading text
Step 7	Observe	that the Next and Previous buttons are blue, indicating they are now the Next Heading and Previous Heading buttons

You can use the Next Heading and Previous Heading buttons below the vertical scroll bar to continue the process.

Step 8	Click	the Next Heading button below the vertical scroll bar
Step 9	Observe	that the insertion point moves to the next paragraph heading "How the Internet Began"
Step 10	Press	the CTRL + Y keys to repeat the Heading 3 style
Step 11	Observe	that the heading is reformatted with the Heading 3 style
Step 12	Follow	Steps 9 through 12 to reformat all the paragraph headings with the Heading 3 style
Step 13	Save	the document as *Lesson One Revised* and leave it open

15.b Verifying Paragraph Formats Using the Reveal Formatting Task Pane

Another quick way to verify and modify paragraph formatting is with the Reveal Formatting task pane. This task pane shows the formatting of selected text and provides options relating to formatting text. To view the Reveal Formatting task pane:

| Step 1 | Move | the insertion point to the beginning of the first body text paragraph, which starts "Millions of computer users" |
| Step 2 | Click | Format |

Working with Multipage Documents

| Step 3 | Click | Re<u>v</u>eal Formatting to open the Reveal Formatting task pane |

You can review the formatting for the selected paragraph, turn on or off the nonprinting formatting marks, and compare the formatting in the selected paragraph to another paragraph. To turn on the formatting marks and compare the currently selected paragraph with another body text paragraph:

Step 1	Click	the Show all formatting marks check box in the Reveal Formatting task pane to insert a check mark
Step 2	Observe	the visible formatting marks in the document
Step 3	Click	the Compare to another selection check box to insert a check mark
Step 4	Move	the insertion point to the beginning of the second body text paragraph, which starts "A network is a"
Step 5	Observe	the Formatting differences list in the Reveal Formatting task pane to see the formatting differences between the two paragraphs

Your screen should look similar to Figure 15-2. The only formatting difference between the two paragraphs is a decimal tab stop setting in the first paragraph. You need to review this tab stop setting and remove it, if necessary.

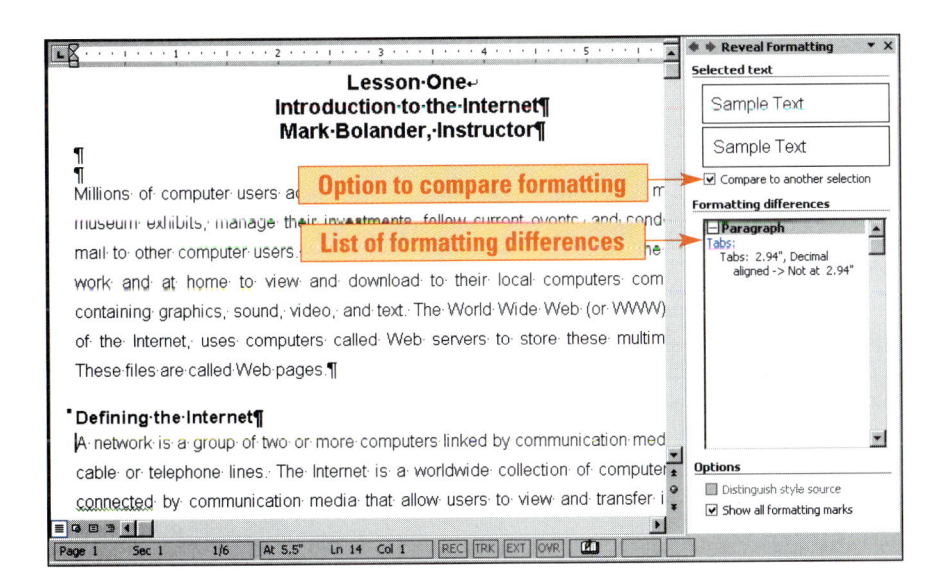

QUICK TIP

You can quickly open the Reveal Formatting task pane and review the formatting for specific text.

MENU TIP

Convert the mouse pointer to the What's This? pointer by clicking the What's <u>T</u>his? command on the <u>H</u>elp menu or by pressing the SHIFT + F1 keys, and then click a paragraph or word. If you click within a word or highlight several words, the Selected text boxes in the Reveal Formatting task pane show that word or phrase.

FIGURE 15-2
Formatting Differences

| Step 6 | Click | the Compare to another selection check box in the Reveal Formatting task pane to remove the check mark |
| Step 7 | Move | the insertion point back to the beginning of the first body paragraph |

chapter fifteen

QUICK TIP

You can check formatting for consistency as you key and format text by turning on the keep track of formatting and the Mark formatting inconsistencies check box as on the Edit tab in the Options dialog box. Formatting inconsistencies are then marked with a wavy blue line to ignore the instance or change the formatting as desired. For more information on checking for formatting consistency, see online Help.

MOUSE TIP

You can clear formatting from selected text by clicking the Style button on the Formatting toolbar and then clicking the Clear Formatting command on the Style button menu.

Step 8	Observe	the Tabs: link in the Formatting of selected text list in the Reveal Formatting task pane indicating a decimal tab stop is set at 2.94 inches
Step 9	Observe	the Decimal tab stop at the 2.94 inch position on the horizontal ruler

This tab stop was set in the document in error and should be removed.

Step 10	Drag	the Decimal tab stop off the ruler to delete it
Step 11	Observe	that the Tabs: link in the Formatting of selected text list in the Reveal Formatting task pane is also removed
Step 12	Click	the Show/Hide button ¶ on the Standard toolbar to turn off the formatting marks
Step 13	Save	the document and leave it open

Clearing Formatting

You can clear the formatting from selected text with the Formats subcommand under the Clear command on the Edit menu or with the Clear Formatting option in the Styles and Formatting task pane. To clear the formatting from the three title paragraphs:

Step 1	Select	the title text at the top of the document
Step 2	Click	the Other Task Panes list arrow on the Reveal Formatting task pane title bar
Step 3	Click	Styles and Formatting to open the Styles and Formatting task pane
Step 4	Click	the Clear Formatting option in the Pick formatting to apply list in the Styles and Formatting task pane
Step 5	Observe	that the text is returned to the default format—Times New Roman, 12 point, left-aligned font
Step 6	Apply	the Heading 1 style to the first two lines of the title text
Step 7	Apply	the Heading 3 style to the remaining line of the title text
Step 8	Center	the title text horizontally
Step 9	Close	the Styles and Formatting task pane
Step 10	Save	the document and leave it open

You are ready to create a cover sheet for the document.

15.c Creating Sections with Different Formatting

When you need to format part of a document with different formatting, such as different margins or page orientation, you can insert a section break. A **section break** stores the section formatting and appears as a double dotted line with the words "Section Break" in the center of the line. Section breaks are inserted automatically when you format a portion of a document with different margins, headers, footers, columns, or page orientation. You also can insert a manual section break and then apply the formatting.

You want to create a cover sheet or title page for the *Lesson One Revised* document that has different margins and vertically centered text. To create a new page for *Lesson One Revised* cover sheet document:

Step 1	*Move*	the insertion point to the left margin of the first body paragraph, which starts "Millions of computer users"
Step 2	*Click*	Insert
Step 3	*Click*	Break

The Break dialog box opens. Table 15-1 describes the four section break types that appear in the Break dialog box.

Type	Description
Next page	creates a page break and begins the new section on the next page
Continuous	begins the new section on the same page
Even page	begins the new section on the next even-numbered page
Odd page	begins the new section on the next odd-numbered page

TABLE 15-1 Section Break Types

You want to start the section on a new page.

Step 4	*Click*	the Next page option button
Step 5	*Click*	OK
Step 6	*Observe*	the double dotted line with the text "Section Break (Next Page)" above the paragraph heading and the section number, Sec 2, on the status bar

chapter fifteen

Your screen should look similar to Figure 15-3.

FIGURE 15-3
Next Page Section Break

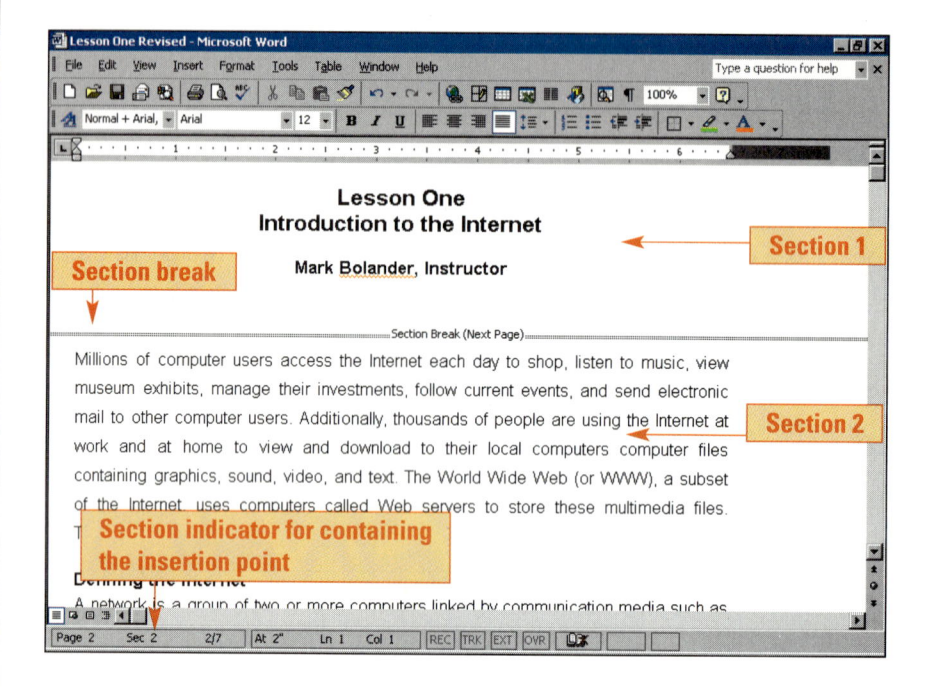

[Screenshot of Microsoft Word window showing "Lesson One Revised" document with "Lesson One / Introduction to the Internet / Mark Bolander, Instructor" as Section 1, a Section Break (Next Page), and body text beginning "Millions of computer users access the Internet each day to shop, listen to music, view museum exhibits, manage their investments, follow current events, and send electronic mail to other computer users. Additionally, thousands of people are using the Internet at work and at home to view and download to their local computers computer files containing graphics, sound, video, and text. The World Wide Web (or WWW), a subset of the Internet, uses computers called Web servers to store these multimedia files." as Section 2. Status bar shows Page 2, Sec 2, 2/7. Callouts: "Section break", "Section 1", "Section 2", "Section indicator for containing the insertion point".]

| Step 7 | **Move** | the insertion point to the top of the document and observe the section number, Sec 1, on the status bar |

You can format each section differently. To change the margins and vertically center the text in Section 1:

Step 1	**Open**	the Margins tab in the Page Setup dialog box
Step 2	**Change**	the top margin to 1 inch
Step 3	**Verify**	that the Apply to: list box contains This section
Step 4	**Switch to**	the Layout tab
Step 5	**Click**	Center in the Vertical alignment: list
Step 6	**Click**	OK
Step 7	**Print Preview**	the document in 1 × 2 Pages

Your screen should look similar to Figure 15-4.

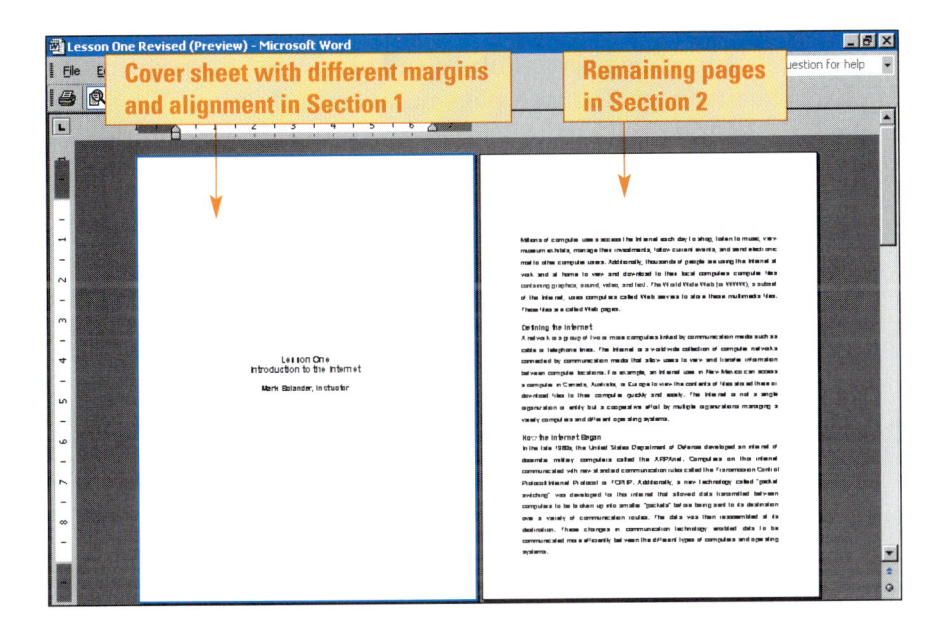

FIGURE 15-4
Document with Cover Sheet

[Screenshot: Lesson One Revised (Preview) - Microsoft Word, showing cover sheet with different margins and alignment in Section 1, and Remaining pages in Section 2]

Step 8	*Close*	Print Preview
Step 9	*Save*	the document and leave it open

To better organize a multipage document, you can add page numbers and informational headers and footers.

15.d Creating Different Headers and Footers in a Document

When you create a header or footer, Word automatically uses the same header or footer throughout the entire document. You can create a different header or footer for the first page of a document or section with the Different first page option in the Layout tab of the Page Setup dialog box. You also can create alternate headers and footers for odd pages (1, 3, 5, etc.) and even pages (2, 4, 6, etc.) with the Different odd and even option in the Layout tab of the Page Setup dialog box.

Because the *Lesson One Revised* document contains many pages, you want to add page numbers to the bottom of the page at the right margin. Additionally, you want to place the instructor's name at the right margin of each evenly numbered page and the text "Lesson One" in a header at the right margin of each odd numbered page. You do not want any header or footer text on the cover sheet.

You begin by inserting page numbers and turning off the page numbering for the first page. To insert page numbers and turn off the page number for the first page in the Page Numbers dialog box:

Step 1	Click	Insert
Step 2	Click	Page N<u>u</u>mbers to open the Page Numbers dialog box
Step 3	Click	Bottom of page (Footer) in the <u>P</u>osition: list if necessary
Step 4	Click	Right in the <u>A</u>lignment: list, if necessary
Step 5	Click	the <u>S</u>how number on first page check box to remove the check mark
Step 6	Click	OK

Next you set up different headers and footers for the odd and even pages. To create alternate headers and footers:

Step 1	Move	the insertion point to the top of the document, if necessary
Step 2	Click	<u>V</u>iew
Step 3	Click	<u>H</u>eader and Footer

Word switches to Print Layout view, if necessary, and displays the First Page Header pane for Section 1. Word creates a different first page header and footer pane because you chose not to view page numbers on the first page in the previous steps. Now you create the odd and even (alternate) header and footer panes.

Step 4	Click	the Page Setup button 📖 on the Header and Footer toolbar to open the Layout tab in the Page Setup dialog box
Step 5	Click	the Different <u>o</u>dd and even check box in the Layout tab to insert a check mark
Step 6	Click	OK

> **QUICK TIP**
>
> When you set alternate headers and footers, Word groups the pages by two (even is left and odd is right), giving you print preview multiple page choices of 2 × 2, 2 × 4, or 2 × 6 Pages.

Working with Multipage Documents   WA 45

The document is set up to show even and odd pages, like you see in a book. To view the Section 2 header pane and add the even page header text:

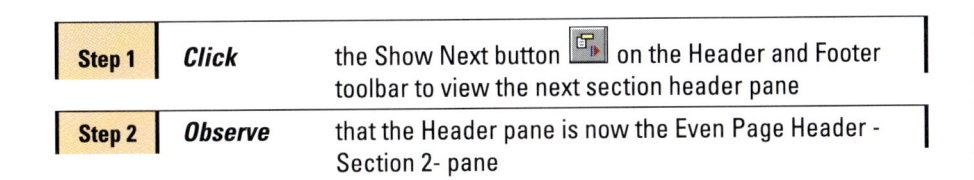

Step 1	Click	the Show Next button on the Header and Footer toolbar to view the next section header pane
Step 2	Observe	that the Header pane is now the Even Page Header - Section 2- pane

Your screen should look similar to Figure 15-5.

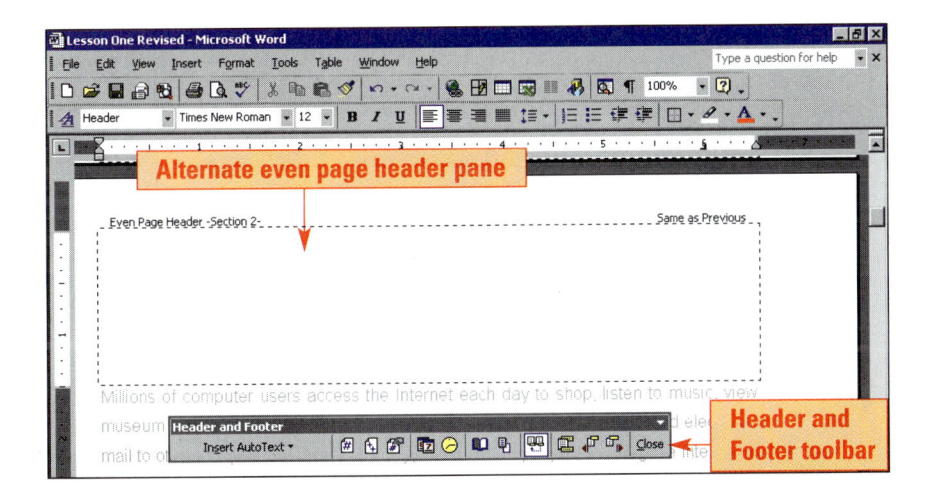

FIGURE 15-5
Even Page Header - Section 2

Step 3	Remove	the Center tab stop and drag the Right Tab tab stop to the right margin in the header pane
Step 4	Press	the TAB key
Step 5	Key	Mark Bolander

You can enter different text for each header in the section. To enter the Odd Page Section 2 header text:

Step 1	Click	the Show Next button on the Header and Footer toolbar to view the Odd Page Header - Section 2 header pane
Step 2	Remove	the Center tab stop and drag the Right Tab tab stop to the right margin in the header pane
Step 3	Press	the TAB key
Step 4	Key	Lesson One
Step 5	Click	the Close button on the Header and Footer toolbar

chapter fifteen

Step 6   *Print Preview* the document in 2 × 4 Pages

The first page stands alone without headers or footers. The remaining pages are grouped into even/odd pairs and contain the alternate headers and page number footers. Your screen should look similar to Figure 15-6.

FIGURE 15-6
Document with Different First Page and Alternate Headers and Footers

> # CAUTION TIP
>
> In a multipage document, it is common to begin numbering pages with the page that follows the cover sheet. You can change the starting page number with an option in the Page Number Format dialog box. If you are using alternate (odd and even) headers and footers, the page following the cover sheet is, by default, an "even" page—page 2. If you change the page number on the page following the cover sheet to page "1," the page becomes an "odd" page. To maintain the odd/even page structure in the document, Word inserts a blank sheet between the cover sheet and the page now numbered "1." The odd/even structure then becomes: cover sheet (odd), blank sheet (even), page 1 (odd), page 2 (even), etc.

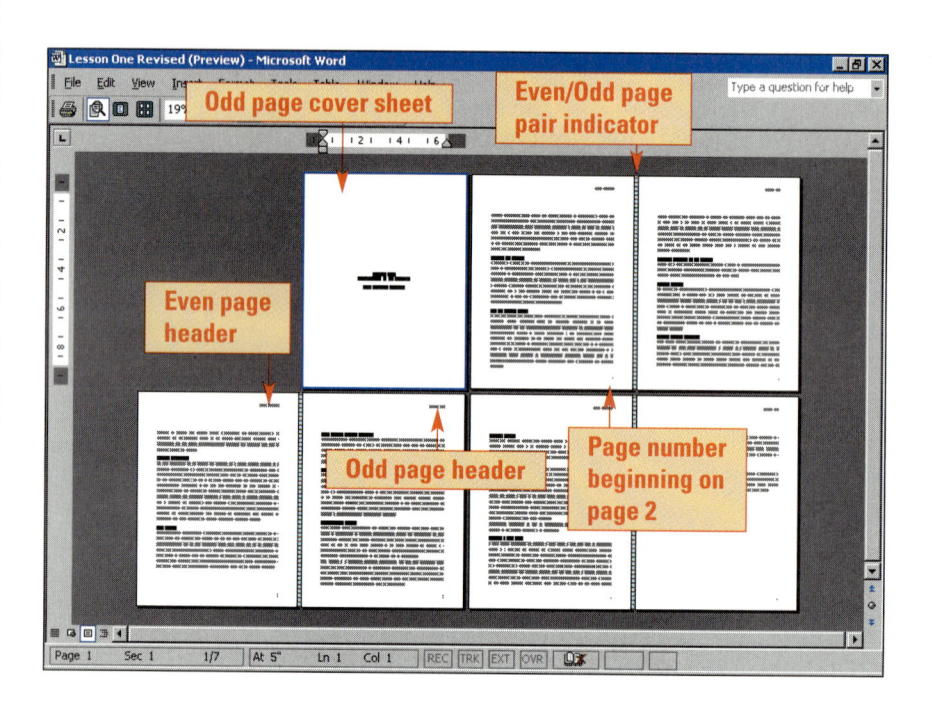

Step 7   *Close*   Print Preview

Step 8   *Save*   the document and close it

Next, you create a payroll stuffer advising all employees about the next month's computer software training classes.

15.e Using Hyphenation

Hyphens are used to join words, such as "drag-and-drop," and to split long words at the right margin. Because word wrap moves a word to the next line if it is too long to fit within the set right margin, left-aligned text may have a very ragged right margin or justified text may have large spaces between words. The end result is less text on a page. **Hyphenation** splits words at the right margin, creating a smoother right margin or smaller spaces between words and more text on the page. The best time to hyphenate a document is after you have keyed,

Working with Multipage Documents   WA 47

edited, and formatted the text. The Hyphenation subcommand under the Language command on the Tools menu provides options to hyphenate text automatically or manually.

You hyphenate the *Training Commitment* document to improve its text wrapping. To open the document and turn on automatic hyphenation:

Step 1	Open	the *Training Commitment* document located on the Data Disk
Step 2	Zoom	the document to Page Width, if necessary, to view the text at the right margin
Step 3	Observe	the ragged right margin
Step 4	Click	Tools
Step 5	Point to	Language
Step 6	Click	Hyphenation

Your Hyphenation dialog box should look similar to Figure 15-7.

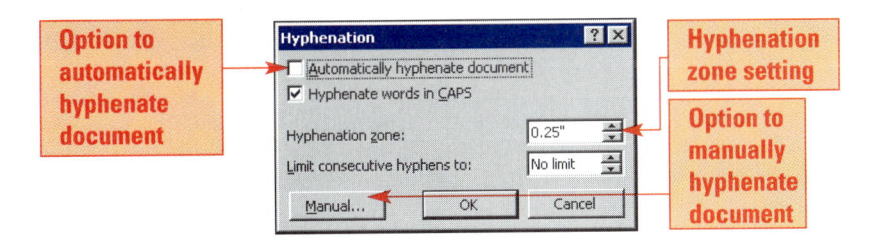

- Option to automatically hyphenate document
- Hyphenation zone setting
- Option to manually hyphenate document

FIGURE 15-7
Hyphenation Dialog Box

QUICK TIP

The en dash, slightly longer than a hyphen, separates words and number ranges such as "5–9." To insert an en dash, press CTRL + the hyphen (-) on the numeric keypad. An em dash (—) indicates a break in a sentence. To insert an em dash, press CTRL + ALT + the hyphen (-) on the numeric keypad. You also can insert an en dash or em dash from the Special Characters tab in the Insert, Symbol dialog box.

The **hyphenation zone** is the distance from the right margin used to determine if words are hyphenated. Words that fall into the hyphenation zone are hyphenated. A large zone increases the right margin raggedness because fewer words require hyphens. A small zone reduces the right margin raggedness, because more words require hyphens. Too many consecutive hyphenated words make a document harder to read, so you can limit the number of consecutively hyphenated words, if desired.

| Step 7 | Click | the Automatically hyphenate document check box to insert a check mark, if necessary |
| Step 8 | Click | OK |

Word automatically hyphenates four words: communication, receive, assigned, and keystrokes. The right margin is less ragged. You use manual hyphenation to control which words are hyphenated. To

QUICK TIP

Most professional documents limit consecutive hyphenation to two or three.

chapter fifteen

QUICK TIP

A nonbreaking space allows words such as 64 MB of RAM or B. D. Vickers or December 31, 2003 to stay on the same line if they would ordinarily be placed on two different lines by word wrap. You keep such words together by inserting nonbreaking spaces between the words. To insert a nonbreaking space, press the CTRL + SHIFT keys as you press the SPACEBAR.

undo the automatic hyphenation and manually hyphenate the *Training Commitment* document using a 0.3 inch hyphenation zone:

Step 1	Click	the Undo button on the Standard toolbar
Step 2	Open	the Hyphenation dialog box
Step 3	Key	.3 in the Hyphenation zone: text box
Step 4	Click	Manual

The Manual Hyphenation dialog box opens with a suggestion for hyphenating the word "com-mu-ni-ca-tion." The flashing insertion point indicates where the word is hyphenated if you click the Yes button to accept the suggestion. You can click another hyphenation position to modify the suggestion and then click the Yes button to accept it. If you don't want to hyphenate that word, click the No button. To manually hyphenate the document:

Step 1	Click	the word at the first (com-) hyphenation position
Step 2	Click	Yes
Step 3	Observe	the next suggested hyphenation "re-ceive"
Step 4	Click	Yes
Step 5	Decline	the next suggested hyphenation "as-signed"
Step 6	Accept	the last suggested hyphenation "key-strokes"
Step 7	Click	OK to confirm the hyphenation is complete
Step 8	Scroll	the document, if necessary, to review the hyphenation
Step 9	Save	the document as *Training Commitment Revised* and close it

Nonbreaking Hyphens

Certain hyphenated words (such as e-mail) should not be split between lines. You can use a **nonbreaking hyphen** to prevent hyphenated words from breaking at the right margin. To insert nonbreaking hyphens in a document:

Step 1	Open	the *Fall Schedule* document located on the Data Disk
Step 2	Observe	that the hyphenated text "left-aligning" breaks at the right margin
Step 3	Select	the hyphen following the word "left"

Working with Multipage Documents   WA 49

Step 4	Press	the CTRL + SHIFT + - (hyphen) keys to insert a non-breaking hyphen
Step 5	Observe	that the hyphenated text "left-aligned" wrapped to the left margin
Step 6	Change	the hyphen in the text "built-in" to a nonbreaking hyphen
Step 7	Save	the document as *Fall Schedule Revised* and leave it open

Optional Hyphens

Sometimes you want to control where a word is hyphenated if it cannot fit at the right margin. **Optional hyphens** join words that can be split if they do not fit at the right margin. An optional hyphen breaks a word or phrase only when it does not fit at the right margin. If the word or phrase appears anywhere else in the line, the optional hyphen does not appear in the document. To insert text and an optional hyphen in the *Fall Schedule Revised* document:

> **QUICK TIP**
> Optional hyphens also are called soft hyphens.

Step 1	Move	the insertion point after the text "using" and the space at the end of the second line in the large paragraph following the heading "*Intermediate Word Processing*"
Step 2	Key	AutoCorrect, using
Step 3	Press	the SPACEBAR
Step 4	Move	the insertion point between the o and the C in AutoCorrect
Step 5	Press	the CTRL + - (hyphen) keys to insert an optional hyphen
Step 6	Observe	that the word AutoCorrect is hyphenated and broken between two lines

To see how the optional hyphen works, you change the margins so that the word "AutoCorrect" does not have to be hyphenated. To view the hyphenated word "AutoCorrect" at the beginning of the line:

Step 1	Change	the right margin to 1½ inch
Step 2	Observe	that the word "AutoCorrect" appears at the beginning of the third line of the paragraph and the hyphen disappears
Step 3	Change	the right margin to 1¼ inch
Step 4	Observe	that the word "AutoCorrect" is again hyphenated
Step 5	Save	the document and close it

To improve readability, you can insert different headers and footers and hyphenate words as necessary.

chapter fifteen

Summary

- The Select Browse Object button provides options for browsing your document by component, such as pictures, comments, or tables.
- You can use the Reveal Formatting task pane to review and compare formatting.
- A section break allows you to change the margins and headers or footers for different pages in a document.
- You can use different header or footer text on the first page or on even or odd numbered pages.
- The Hyphenation tool can hyphenate all possible words automatically or can suggest words for you to hyphenate manually.
- A nonbreaking hyphen is used to prevent hyphenated words from breaking at the right margin and an optional hyphen breaks a word or phrase only when it does not fit at the right margin.

Commands Review

Action	Menu Bar	Shortcut Menu	Toolbar	Task Pane	Keyboard
Navigate through a document by component					
Compare paragraph formatting	Format, Reveal Formatting Help, What's This?			Click the Compare to another selection check box in the Reveal Formatting task pane	ALT + O, V ALT + H, T SHIFT + F1
Insert page or section breaks	Insert, Break				ALT + I, B
Create and modify headers and footers	View, Header and Footer				ALT + V, H
Insert page numbers	Insert, Page Numbers				ALT + I, U
Use Hyphenation tool	Tools, Language, Hyphenation				ALT + T, L, H
Insert nonbreaking hyphen					CTRL + SHIFT + hyphen
Insert optional hyphen					CTRL + hyphen
Insert nonbreaking space					CTRL + SHIFT + SPACEBAR

Concepts Review

Circle the correct answer.

1. Hyphens are used to:
- [a] separate number ranges.
- [b] split long words at the right margin.
- [c] split long words at the left margin.
- [d] add interest to a document.

2. You create alternate Header and Footer panes in the:
- [a] Margins tab in the Page Setup dialog box.
- [b] Header and Footer tab in the Print Setup dialog box.
- [c] Layout tab in the Print dialog box.
- [d] Layout tab in the Page Setup dialog box.

3. The default option for the Select Browse Object button is to Browse by:
- [a] Picture.
- [b] Comment.
- [c] Find.
- [d] Page.

4. You can compare paragraph formatting with an option in the:
- [a] Styles and Formatting task pane.
- [b] Clipboard task pane.
- [c] Reveal Formatting task pane.
- [d] Compare Formatting task pane.

5. When you want to format part of a document with different margins or page orientation, you insert a:
- [a] manual page break.
- [b] header.
- [c] section break.
- [d] hyphen.

6. You can turn off the page number for the first page of a document or section in the:
- [a] Format Page Numbers dialog box.
- [b] Reveal Formatting task pane.
- [c] Break dialog box.
- [d] Page Numbers dialog box.

7. The best time to hyphenate text is:
- [a] at each page break.
- [b] as you key it.
- [c] before you format it.
- [d] after keying, editing, and formatting it.

8. The actions of the Next and Previous buttons below the vertical scroll bar are controlled by the:
- [a] Find and Replace dialog box.
- [b] Hyphenation button.
- [c] CTRL + SHIFT + hyphen (-) keys.
- [d] Select Browse Object button.

Circle **T** if the statement is true or **F** if the statement is false.

T F 1. The hyphenation zone is the area at the right margin in which hyphenation takes place.

T F 2. The Select Browse Object button provides an option to browse a document by comment.

T F 3. You can clear the formatting from selected text with an option in the Reveal Formatting task pane.

T F 4. An optional hyphen is used to join or split words at the right margin as necessary.

T F 5. The Next and Previous buttons below the vertical scroll bar change whenever you select a new browse object from the Select Browse Object grid.

T F 6. A section break allows you to change the margins and headers or footers for different pages in a document.

T F 7. You can view or hide formatting marks with an option in the Styles and Formatting task pane.

T F 8. A nonbreaking hyphen prevents hyphenated words from breaking at the right margin.

chapter fifteen

Skills Review

Exercise 1

1. Open the *British Columbia Report* document located on the Data Disk.
2. Change the font for the entire document except the title to Arial 12 point.
3. Change the top margin to 2 inches, the left margin to 1½ inches, and the right margin to 1 inch.
4. Automatically hyphenate the document using the default hyphenation zone.
5. Go to the top of page 2. Change the top margin to 1 inch and apply it from the position of the insertion point forward in the document.
6. Insert a page number at the bottom center of each page.
7. Save the document as *British Columbia Report Revised*, and then preview, print, and close it.

Exercise 2

1. Open the *British Columbia Report* document located on the Data Disk.
2. Use the Select Browse Object to open the Find and Replace dialog box and then find each occurrence of the text "British Columbia" and replace it with "New York." (*Hint:* Remember to clear any formatting from the dialog box.)
3. Open the Reveal Formatting task pane and compare the paragraph formatting in the document title with that in the first body text paragraph. Note the font difference.
4. Close the Reveal Formatting task pane and change the font for all the body text paragraphs to agree with the font used in the title paragraph. Do not change the font size.
5. Change the left margin to 1 inch.
6. Insert a page number at the bottom center of the page on all pages except the first page.
7. Create alternate headers with your name at the left margin in the odd page header and the date at the right margin in the even page header.
8. Set the Select Browse Object back to its Page default.
9. Save the document as *New York Report*, and then preview, print, and close it.

Exercise 3

1. Open the *Inventory Report* document located on the Data Disk.
2. Change the top margin to 2 inches and the left and right margins to 1 inch.
3. Automatically hyphenate the text using the default hyphenation zone.
4. Go to the top of page 2. Change the top margin to 1 inch and apply it from the position of the insertion point forward.
5. Create a Section 2 header containing centered and bold text "Inventory Report." (*Hint:* Make sure you turn off the Same as Previous button on the Header and Footer toolbar so the header does not appear in Section 1.)
6. Switch to the Section 2 footer and insert a page number at the bottom center of the page. (*Hint:* Make sure you turn off the Same as Previous button on the Header and Footer toolbar so the footer does not appear in Section 1. Don't forget to adjust the center tab stop.)

7. Select the page number and use the Format Page Number button on the Header and Footer toolbar to format the page number in the lowercase Roman numeral style.

8. Save the document as *Inventory Report Revised*, and then preview, print, and close it.

Exercise 4

1. Open the *New York Report* document you created in Exercise 2. If you have not created the document, do so now.

2. View each header and footer pane and delete the header text and footer page number. Then turn off the header and footer options in the Layout tab of the Page Setup dialog box.

3. Zoom the document to Page Width and manually hyphenate it with a 0.4 hyphenation zone. Change the hyphenation of "representatives" to break following the "sen" characters. Accept all other suggested hyphenation.

4. Save the document as *New York Report With Manual Hyphenation*, and then preview, print, and close it.

Exercise 5

1. Open the *Inventory Report* document located on the Data Disk.

2. Display the Styles and Formatting task pane.

3. Use the Select Browse Object and the Next Heading and Previous Heading buttons to locate each paragraph heading and then apply the Heading 2 style.

4. Close the Styles and Formatting task pane.

5. Save the document as *Inventory Report With Heading 2*, and then preview, print, and close it.

Exercise 6

1. Open the *E-Commerce Basics* document located on the Data Disk.

2. Create a cover sheet using a Next Page section break immediately before the first body text paragraph beginning "Commerce, the exchange."

3. Use 1-inch top, bottom, left, and right margins for the cover sheet in Section 1.

4. Center the title text vertically between the top and bottom margins.

5. Insert page numbers at the bottom center on all pages except the cover sheet.

6. Select the page number in the Footer - Section 2 pane and use the Format Page Number button on the Header and Footer toolbar to change the starting number to "1."

7. Use the Select Browse Object button and Next Table button to locate each table. Bold the two-line title text above each table.

8. Set the Select Browse Object button back to its default.

9. Save the document as *E-Commerce Basics Revised*, and then preview, print, and close it.

chapter fifteen

Exercise 7

1. Open the *E-Commerce Basics Revised* document you created in Exercise 6. If you have not created the document, do so now.
2. Use the Reveal Formatting pane to compare the formatting in the first and second body paragraphs.
3. If a formatting error is indicated, correct it.
4. Hyphenate the document manually using a .3 hyphenation zone. Reject the hyphenation of all proper names, Internet, and E- or e-business.
5. Find each instance of e-business(es) in the body text and insert a nonbreaking hyphen. Do not change hyphen in e-business when it appears in a paragraph heading or a table.
6. Save the document as *E-Commerce Basics With Hyphenation*, and then preview, print, and close it.

Exercise 8

1. Open the *Software Training Program* document located on the Data Disk.
2. Select the text beginning "Training Sessions" and ending "...for more details."
3. Open the Page Setup dialog box and change the page orientation to Landscape and the top margin to 2 inches for the selected text. (*Hint:* Don't make the changes for the entire document.)
4. Insert page numbers on all pages at the bottom center of each page.
5. Save the document at *Software Training Program Revised*, and then preview, print, and close it.

Case Projects

Project 1

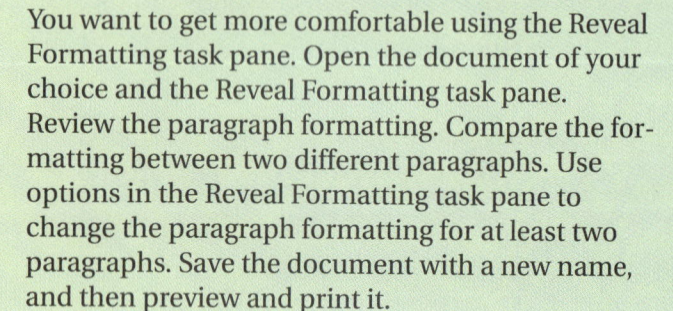

You want to get more comfortable using the Reveal Formatting task pane. Open the document of your choice and the Reveal Formatting task pane. Review the paragraph formatting. Compare the formatting between two different paragraphs. Use options in the Reveal Formatting task pane to change the paragraph formatting for at least two paragraphs. Save the document with a new name, and then preview and print it.

Project 2

Belinda Montez, an assistant secretary in the Human Resources Department, needs help with inserting section breaks in her documents. Using the Ask A Question Box, research the kinds of section breaks you can insert and the type of formatting that can be set for sections. Write Belinda an interoffice memorandum that describes the different kinds of section breaks; give at least five suggestions where a section break could be used. Save, preview, and print the document.

Project 3

B. J. Chang asks you to find several Web pages that provide information for human resources professionals including any online magazines devoted to the human resources field. Connect to the Internet and search for Web pages with information for human resources professionals. Print at least four Web pages. Write B. J. Chang an interoffice memorandum describing what you found on the Web. Save, preview, and print the memorandum.

Project 4

You want to practice hyphenating documents automatically and manually. Using the Ask A Question Box, review how to hyphenate documents including using optional and nonbreaking hyphens. Open a document of your choice and automatically hyphenate the document. Review the document and create nonbreaking and optional hyphens as necessary. Save the document with a new name and print it. Open a document of your choice and manually hyphenate the document. Save the document with a new name and print it.

Create a three-page document that includes a title page and two pages of text. The title page should include the title "Using Word Features," your name, and the current date centered vertically and horizontally on the page. The text pages should describe in your own words how to locate document components using the Select Browse Object, how to create different headers and footers in the same document, and how to use different hyphenation options. Create different first page headers and footers and leave them blank. Insert page numbers centered at the bottom of the page on pages two and three beginning with number 2. Insert your name as a header at the left margin of each even-numbered page and your school's name at the right margin of each odd-numbered page (except the first page). Use hyphenation as necessary. Save, preview, and print the document.

Project 5

B. J. Chang wants to post several open positions on the Web and asks you which Web sites to use. Connect to the Internet, and search for Web sites that allow companies to post job openings. Print at least three pages. Write an interoffice memorandum to B. J. Chang recommending at least two Web sites. Discuss the reasons for your recommendations. Save, preview, and print the memorandum.

Project 6

You are working with Jody and Belinda on the new employee handbook and they have questions about creating the headers and footers for the handbook. Jody asks how to adjust the horizontal and vertical position of headers and footers and Belinda asks how to insert the chapter number and title in footers. Use online Help to look up answers to these questions. Create an interoffice memorandum to both Jody and Belinda listing their questions and your answers. Save, preview, and print the document. With your instructor's permission use the memo as a guide to show a classmate how to adjust the horizontal and vertical position of headers and footers and how to insert a chapter number and title in footers.

Project 7

Jody has two hyphenated documents and now she wants to remove the hyphenation but she doesn't know how to do it quickly. Use online Help to research how to do this. Then write Jody a memo telling her how to remove hyphenation applied both automatically and manually. Save, preview, and print the document.

Project 8

Belinda has opened an old document that contains different alternate and first page headers and footers. She wants to remove all the headers and footers but doesn't know how to do this. Using online Help, research how to delete a header and footer. Then write Belinda a memo that describes how she can remove the header and footer text and turn off the header and footer panes in the document.

chapter fifteen

Word 2002

Creating Custom Styles and Controlling Pagination

Chapter Overview

Styles help shrink the time you need to format documents. In addition to Word's built-in character and paragraph styles, you can create your own custom styles. Also, sometimes you need to control how text flows from page to page. In this chapter, you learn how to create, apply, save, and delete custom styles. You also learn how to control widow and orphan lines as well as line and page breaks.

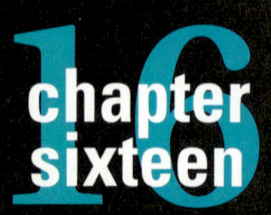

Learning Objectives

- Create and apply styles
- Control pagination

Case profile

B. J. Chang asks you to remain in the Human Resources Department to help his administrative assistant by formatting several documents, including a training schedule. He asks you to use custom styles saved to the Normal template so his assistant can easily format any additional items she adds to the documents or to new training schedules.

chapter sixteen

16.a Creating and Applying Styles

Rather than reformatting text or copying formats from one paragraph or character to another, you can use styles. Using styles allows you to format text easily by applying all the specified formats at one time. You can save styles with the current document or add them to the template, such as the Normal template, on which the document is based. Table 16-1 lists four Word style types.

Style	Description
Character	Determines the appearance of selected text, including font, size, bold, italic, underline, and effects such as all caps
List	Determines the appearance of a bulleted or numbered list, including indentation
Paragraph	Determines the appearance of a paragraph, including text alignment, tab stops, indentation, line spacing, page breaks, borders and shading, numbered and bulleted lists, numbered headings, and the paragraph's position in the page layout
Table	Determines the appearance of a table, including borders, shading, font, font size, column width, row height, and alignment on the page

TABLE 16-1
Word Style Types

You worked with character, paragraph, list, and table styles in earlier chapters. Recall that you can use the Styles and Formatting task pane or the Style button on the Formatting toolbar to apply styles to selected text. You can review styles already applied to text by selecting the text and observing the name of the style in the Style button on the Formatting toolbar or the selected style in the Styles and Formatting task pane. Another way to view the styles applied to selected text is by setting a Style area at the left side of your screen.

Setting a Style Area

When you position the insertion point in a paragraph, the Style button on the Formatting toolbar lists the name of the style used to format the paragraph. If the Styles and Formatting task pane is open, the style applied to the selected text had a dark, selection border in the Pick formatting to apply list. You can quickly see all the paragraph styles applied throughout the document by switching to Normal view, if necessary, and setting a Style area. A **Style area** is a space to the left of the left margin and the selection bar that lists the current paragraph style names for all paragraphs. You set the Style area on the View tab in the Options dialog box.

chapter sixteen

Before you begin to work on the training documents, Chang suggests you set and use the Style area. To create a new, blank document and set a ¾-inch Style area:

Step 1	**Create**	a new, blank document and close the task pane, if necessary
Step 2	**Switch to**	Normal view, if necessary
Step 3	**Click**	Tools
Step 4	**Click**	Options
Step 5	**Click**	the View tab, if necessary
Step 6	**Key**	.75 in the Style area width: text box
Step 7	**Click**	OK

The Style area appears at the left of the screen and contains the name of the style, the default Normal style, applied to the first paragraph. Your screen should look similar to Figure 16-1.

FIGURE 16-1
Style Area

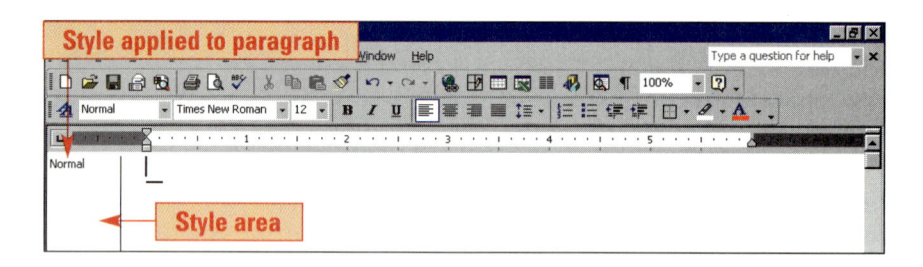

You key and format text to see how the Style area works. To key text and apply a paragraph style:

Step 1	**Key**	Worldwide Exotic Foods, Inc.
Step 2	**Click**	the Style button list arrow [Normal] on the Formatting toolbar

A list of available styles in a blank document based on the Normal template appears. From this list, you can clear the formatting from selected text, apply one of the heading styles, or open the Styles and Formatting task pane with the More command.

Step 3	**Click**	Heading 1

Creating Custom Styles and Controlling Pagination **WA 59**

The Style area now contains the name of the current style, Heading 1. To review the formatting in the Styles and Formatting task pane:

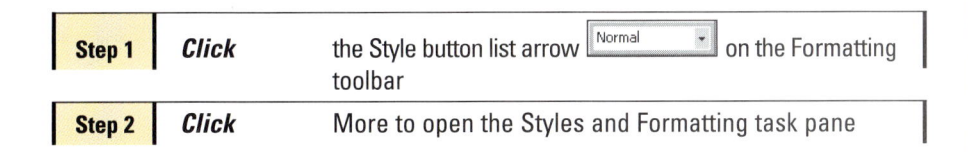

Step 1	Click	the Style button list arrow [Normal] on the Formatting toolbar
Step 2	Click	More to open the Styles and Formatting task pane

The formatting of the selected paragraph appears both in the Formatting of selected text box and, because the default option in the task pane is to display the available formatting, in the Pick formatting to apply list, surrounded by a dark border. Your screen should look similar to Figure 16-2.

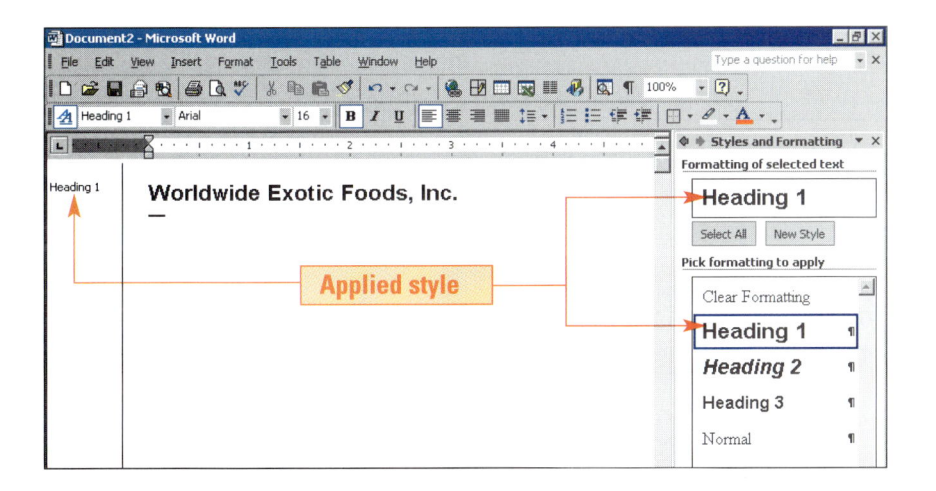

FIGURE 16-2
Formatting in Styles Area and Formatting Task Pane

CAUTION TIP

The list of available styles includes any custom styles added to the Normal template. The list of available styles on your screen may vary from the default list shown in Figure 16-2.

When you modify the formatting, that modification is also shown in the Style button list and the Styles and Formatting task pane.

Step 3	Center	the text
Step 4	Observe	that the formatting notations in the Style button list on the Formatting toolbar and in the Styles and Formatting task pane is "Heading 1 + Center."

You can quickly apply the "Heading 1 + Center" formatting combination that is now available in the document to new text. To key new text and apply the modified style:

Step 1	Press	the ENTER key to create a new paragraph
Step 2	Observe	that the formatting for the new paragraph is the default Normal style

chapter sixteen

Step 3	**Key**	Human Resources Department
Step 4	**Click**	the Heading 1 + Centered modified style from either the Style button list on the Formatting toolbar or the Pick formatting to apply list in the Styles and Formatting task pane
Step 5	**Observe**	that the new text is formatted with the modified Heading 1 style
Step 6	**Close**	the Styles and Formatting task pane

You can size the Style area by dragging its boundary left or right with the mouse pointer. You can quickly remove the Style area by dragging its boundary all the way to the left edge of the screen. To remove the Style area:

Step 1	**Move**	the mouse pointer to the Style area boundary line (it becomes a sizing pointer)
Step 2	**Drag**	the Style area boundary line to the left until it disappears
Step 3	**Close**	the document without saving

Now that you know a variety of ways to work with styles, you are ready to begin formatting the training documents.

Creating a Custom Paragraph Style

When there is no built-in style with the formatting combination you want, you modify an existing style. If you plan to use the modified style in other documents, you can create a custom style and then add the style to the Normal template or another document template. You can base the custom style on another style and specify the style to be applied to the following paragraph. You create custom styles with the New Style button in the Styles and Formatting task pane. You can create a custom style by example by first selecting already formatted text, or you can create a new custom style by selecting all the formatting components.

Chang wants all the training schedule document paragraph headings formatted with a 16-point, bold Arial, Small caps, and a 2¼-inch shadow border. You decide to create a custom style that can be used over and over to do this. You begin by creating and applying the custom style in the *Summer Training Schedule* document. First you format the "Internet Training" paragraph heading, and then you create a custom style by

---

QUICK TIP

You don't have to use a style to be able to reuse formatting in the same document. Formatting combinations you manually apply to text, such as bolding and centering a title using the Formatting toolbar, are also added to the Style button list on the Formatting toolbar and the Pick formatting to apply list in the Styles and Formatting task pane. You can then apply the formatting combination to other text in the same document in the same way you would apply a style.

You can create a custom style by example by selecting formatted text and then clicking the text area of the Style button on the Formatting toolbar. Key a new name for the custom style in the text area and press the ENTER key.

example based on the formatted text. To change the font size and font style, and add a special text effect to the "Internet Training" paragraph heading:

Step 1	Open	the *Summer Training Schedule* document located on the Data Disk
Step 2	Select	the "Internet Training" paragraph
Step 3	Format	the paragraph with Arial, Bold, 12 point, Small caps font using the Font dialog box

The text shows the new font, font style, font size, and Small caps effect. To add a 2¼-point shadow border to the paragraph heading text:

Step 1	Verify	that the "Internet Training" paragraph heading is selected
Step 2	Format	the paragraph text (not the entire paragraph) with a 2¼ pt, Shadow border using the Borders and Shading dialog box
Step 3	Deselect	the text, leaving the insertion point in the paragraph

A 2¼-point shadow border is added to the paragraph. Your screen should look similar to Figure 16-3.

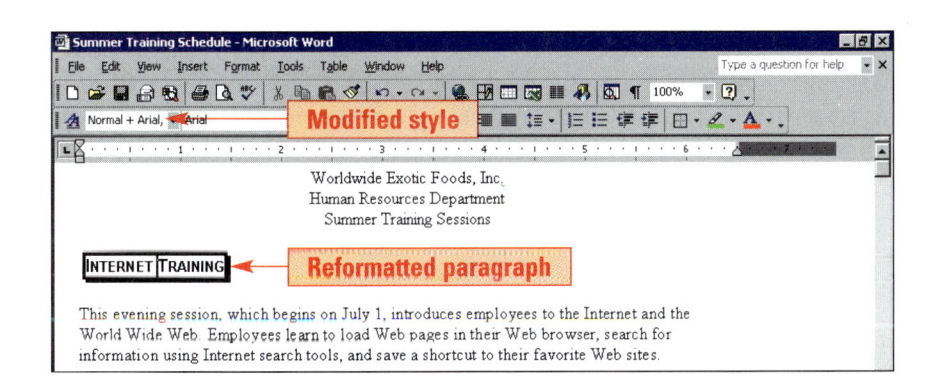

CAUTION TIP

If you apply borders to the paragraph rather than to text, the borders extend from the left to right margins rather than just around the text. If you apply the border to the entire paragraph, you have to indent the paragraph from the right to move the right border closer to the text.

FIGURE 16-3
Formatted Paragraph Heading

Now that the text is formatted, you can create a custom style based on the formatted text. To create a custom style:

Step 1	Verify	that the insertion point is in the "Internet Training" paragraph heading
Step 2	Open	the Styles and Formatting task pane
Step 3	Click	the New Style button in the Styles and Formatting task pane

The New Style dialog box on your screen should look similar to Figure 16-4.

FIGURE 16-4
New Style Dialog Box

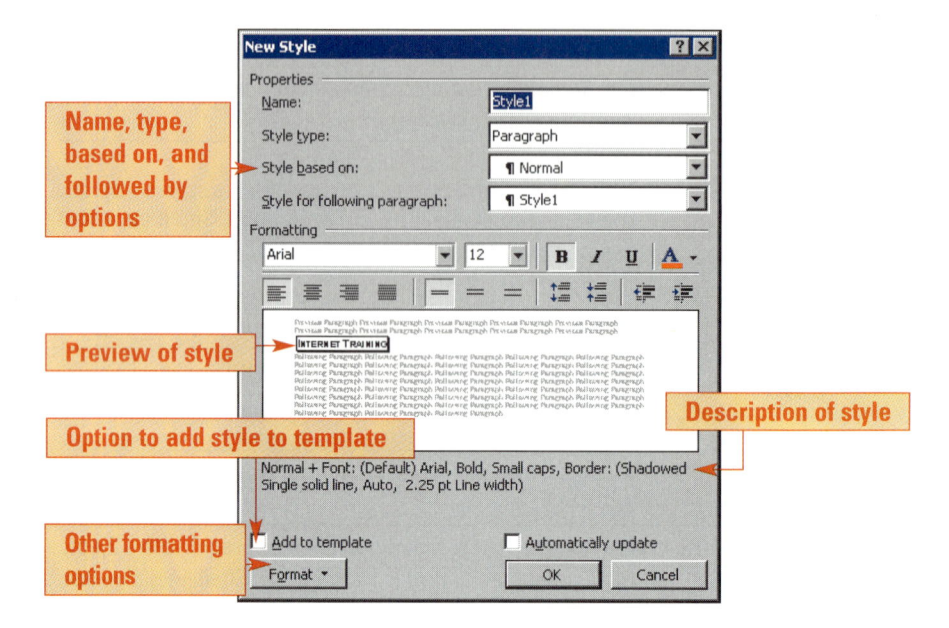

(New Style dialog box with callouts: "Name, type, based on, and followed by options"; "Preview of style"; "Option to add style to template"; "Description of style"; "Other formatting options")

You can name the style, select the style type, select an existing style on which to base the custom style, and specify a style to automatically follow the custom style. The formatting attributes already applied to the paragraph, such as Arial, 12 point, and Bold are already selected on the dialog box toolbar. The formatting is previewed in the preview box and a description of the formatting attributes is included below the preview area. You can click the F*o*rmat button to view a menu containing other formatting commands. If you want the style added to the template attached to the current document, you use the *A*dd to template option.

By keying the custom style names in all uppercase, you can easily identify a custom style from one of Word's built-in styles. To create a paragraph style named COURSE LEVEL, based on the Normal default paragraph style:

Step 1	*Key*	COURSE LEVEL in the *N*ame: text box
Step 2	*Verify*	that Paragraph appears in the Style *t*ype: list box and that Normal appears in the Style *b*ased on: list box
Step 3	*Click*	Normal in the *S*tyle for following paragraph: list
Step 4	*Click*	the *A*dd to template check box to insert a check mark
Step 5	*Click*	OK
Step 6	*Observe*	that the COURSE LEVEL custom style is added to the Pick formatting to apply list in the Styles and Formatting task pane

Creating Custom Styles and Controlling Pagination WA 63

The custom style makes it easy to format other paragraphs the same way quickly. To apply the custom style to the remaining paragraph headings and a modified built-in style to the title lines:

Step 1	Select	the paragraph headings "Word Processing - Level 1" and "Word Processing - Level 2" using the CTRL key
Step 2	Click	COURSE LEVEL in the Pick formatting to apply list in the Styles and Formatting task pane

The COURSE LEVEL paragraph style is applied to the both paragraphs.

Step 3	Apply	the Heading 1 style to the first two lines of the title and center them
Step 4	Apply	the Heading 2 style to the third line of the title and center it
Step 5	Save	the document as *Summer Training Schedule Revised* and leave it open

You can also create a custom style from scratch. To create a custom style for the Dates: paragraphs:

Step 1	Move	the insertion point to a blank line in the document (formatted with the default Normal paragraph style)
Step 2	Open	the New Style dialog box
Step 3	Name	the style DATES
Step 4	Create	a Paragraph type style based on the Normal style followed by the Normal style
Step 5	Change	the font to Arial using the dialog box toolbar
Step 6	Click	the Format button to view the formatting menu
Step 7	Click	Tabs to open the Tabs dialog box
Step 8	Set	Left aligned tab stops at the 1-, 2.5-, and 4-inch positions
Step 9	Click	OK to close the Tabs dialog box
Step 10	Click	the Add to template check box to insert a check mark
Step 11	Click	OK to close the New Style dialog box

chapter sixteen

Once the style is saved, you can apply it to other paragraphs. To apply the DATES custom style:

Step 1	Select	the two Dates: paragraphs using the CTRL key
Step 2	Click	the DATES custom style in the Pick formatting to apply list in the Styles and Formatting task pane
Step 3	Deselect	the text
Step 4	Save	the document and leave it open

After reviewing the *Summer Training Schedule Revised* document, Chang asks you to create special formatting for certain words to draw attention to each training session topic.

Creating a Custom Character Style

You can create custom list and character styles in the same way you create a custom paragraph style. To draw attention to certain key words in the training document, you decide to create and apply a custom character style containing a 14-point bold font. To create and apply the custom character style:

Step 1	Move	the insertion point to the word "Internet" in the sentence following the Internet Training paragraph heading
Step 2	Open	the New Style dialog box
Step 3	Name	the new style TOPIC
Step 4	Click	Character in the Style type: list
Step 5	Change	the font to 14-point bold using the dialog box toolbar
Step 6	Add	the new character style to the template
Step 7	Click	OK
Step 8	Observe	the TOPIC custom character style in the Pick formatting to apply list (the underscored "a" after the style name indicates a character style)
Step 9	Apply	the TOPIC custom character style to each instance of the words "Internet, " "World Wide Web," and "Word" in the body text paragraphs

Because you have added custom styles to the Normal template, you must save the template with the new style. Word automatically saves your changes to the Normal template when you close Word. If you want to save the Normal template before closing Word, you can use the Save All command on the File menu, which saves all open documents and the Normal template. You access the Save All command by pressing the SHIFT key. To save the document and the Normal template:

Step 1	Press & hold	the SHIFT key
Step 2	Click	File
Step 3	Click	Save All
Step 4	Close	the document

When you no longer want a custom style, you can delete it from a specific document or from the template in which it is stored.

Using the Organizer to Delete Styles

You can use the Organizer feature to copy styles from document to document and from template to template or to delete custom styles from a document or template. You open the Organizer dialog box by clicking the Templates and Add-Ins command on the Tools menu and then clicking the Organizer button.

You have finished formatting all the training documents and you now need to delete the custom styles you created and added to the Normal template. To open the Organizer and delete the styles from the Normal template:

Step 1	Close	all open documents, if necessary
Step 2	Click	Tools
Step 3	Click	Templates and Add-Ins to open the Templates and Add-ins dialog box
Step 4	Click	Organizer
Step 5	Click	the Styles tab, if necessary

The Styles tab in the Organizer dialog box on your screen should look similar to Figure 16-5.

QUICK TIP

You can click the Style Gallery button in the Theme dialog box to preview sample documents based on Word templates, the current document with styles from templates, or a list of styles. To open the Theme dialog box, click Theme on the Format menu. When you copy a template in the Style Gallery to your document, styles with the same name override the style formatting currently in the document. Styles with names not in your document are added to the document. Unique styles in your document are not affected.

chapter sixteen

FIGURE 16-5
Organizer Dialog Box

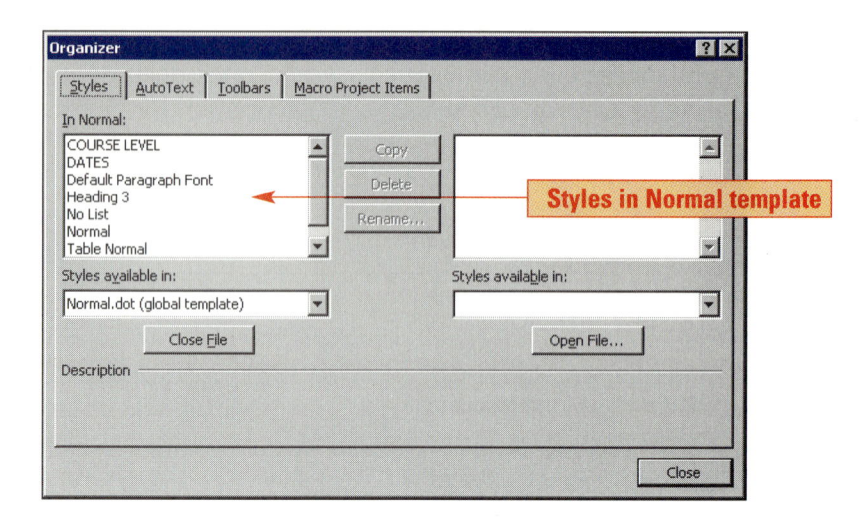

[Screenshot of Organizer dialog box showing Styles tab with list: COURSE LEVEL, DATES, Default Paragraph Font, Heading 3, No List, Normal, Table Normal — labeled "Styles in Normal template"]

You can open two documents or templates and then select and copy styles from one document or template to the other document or template. You can also select and delete styles from either document or template. Because there are no documents open, you only see the styles in the Normal template. To select and delete the custom styles:

Step 1	Select	the COURSE LEVEL, DATES, and TOPIC styles in the In Normal: list using the CTRL key
Step 2	Click	Delete
Step 3	Click	Yes to All in the confirmation dialog box
Step 4	Close	the Organizer dialog box
Step 5	Close	the Styles and Formatting task pane

Next, you improve the appearance of a training document by controlling how text from one page flows to the next.

> **CAUTION TIP**
> You cannot delete Word's built-in styles.

16.b Controlling Pagination

Readers often give more credibility to the content of a document if the document is attractively organized on the page. For this reason, the appearance of the text on each page is very important. Word provides text flow options that allow you to keep single lines from flowing to the top of an additional page, to control page breaks within paragraphs, to control the amount of space between paragraphs and characters, and to create "hard" spaces that keep text on the same line.

Single lines stranded on a page can detract from a paragraph's appearance and message. A **widow** line is the last line of a paragraph that appears by itself at the top of a following page. An **orphan** line is the first line of a paragraph that appears by itself at the bottom of a page. By default the Word option that controls widow and orphan lines is turned on in the Line and Page Breaks tab in the Paragraph dialog box. Keeping lines together on a page prevents Word from placing a page break inside a paragraph. You also can prevent page breaks from occurring between selected paragraphs and force a manual page break to occur before a specific paragraph. You set these options in the Line and Page Breaks tab in the Paragraph dialog box.

The next document Chang wants you to format is the *Lesson Two* training document. He wants you to verify that the Widow/Orphan control is turned on. Then he wants you to use other text flow options to avoid inserting a page break inside a paragraph. To view the Widow/Orphan control option and line break options:

Step 1	Open	the *Lesson Two* document located on the Data Disk
Step 2	Move	the insertion point to the paragraph beginning "Traditional business" at the bottom of page 3
Step 3	Observe	that the automatic page break occurs after the second line in the paragraph
Step 4	Open	the Paragraph dialog box
Step 5	Click	the Line and Page Breaks tab
Step 6	Verify	that the Widow/Orphan control check box contains a check mark
Step 7	Click	the Keep lines together check box to insert a check mark
Step 8	Click	OK
Step 9	Observe	that the automatic page break now occurs above the paragraph
Step 10	Move	the insertion point to the last paragraph beginning "Sellers are" on page 4
Step 11	Open	the Lines and Page Breaks tab in the Paragraph dialog box
Step 12	Click	the Keep lines together check box to insert a check mark
Step 13	Click	OK
Step 14	Continue	to change the paragraph formatting to keep the lines together by forcing a page break above the paragraph for the last paragraphs on pages 6, 7, and 8
Step 15	Save	the document as *Lesson Two With Line Breaks* and close it

Creating and applying custom paragraph and character styles and controlling pagination enhance the appearance of documents.

Summary

▶ There are four types of styles: paragraph, character, list, and table styles.

▶ Styles are saved with the document; they can be added to the template on which the document is based so that the styles are available to all new documents based on that template.

▶ Styles can be viewed in a Style area on the screen to the left of the document text.

▶ You can create custom styles and can modify Word built-in styles using the Styles and Formatting task pane.

▶ You can control how text flows from one page to the next using the text flow options in the Paragraph dialog box.

Commands Review

Action	Menu Bar	Shortcut Menu	Toolbar	Task Pane	Keyboard
Apply a style selected text	Format, Styles and Formatting		Normal	Select text, click style in Pick formatting to apply list in Styles and Formatting to task pane	ALT + O, S CTRL + SHIFT + S CTRL + SHIFT + N (Normal style) ALT + CTRL + 1 (Heading 1 style) ALT + CTRL + 2 (Heading 2 style) ALT + CTRL + 3 (Heading 3 style) CTRL + SHIFT + L (List style)
Display styles in the Style area of the document	Tools, Options, View tab				ALT + T, O
Create custom styles	Format, Styles and formatting		Click the text area of Normal and key style name, then press the ENTER key	Click New Style button in Styles and Formatting task pane	ALT + O, S
View, copy, and delete styles from Word templates or documents	Tools, Templates and Add-Ins				ALT + T, I
Set text flow options	Format, Paragraph, Line and Page Breaks tab				ALT + O, P, P

Concepts Review

Circle the correct answer.

1. **Which of the following is not a type of style?**
   - [a] paragraph
   - [b] table
   - [c] character
   - [d] document

2. **Which of the following is not a basic style in the Style button list?**
   - [a] Heading 1
   - [b] Heading 3
   - [c] Default Character Font
   - [d] Normal

3. **You cannot see which style is applied to a paragraph by:**
   - [a] selecting the paragraph and observing the Style button.
   - [b] clicking the Style Gallery command on the Format menu.
   - [c] setting a Style area down the left side of the screen.
   - [d] moving the insertion point to a paragraph and then opening the Styles and Formatting task pane.

4. **The Style area is a(n):**
   - [a] list in the Styles and Formatting task pane.
   - [b] area to the right of the right margin on the screen in Normal view.
   - [c] formatting option in the New Style dialog box.
   - [d] way to view the styles applied to all paragraphs in your document.

5. **The More command on the Style button list opens the:**
   - [a] Reveal Formatting task pane.
   - [b] New Style dialog box.
   - [c] Styles and Formatting task pane.
   - [d] More Styles dialog box.

6. **A character style:**
   - [a] determines the overall appearance of a paragraph.
   - [b] must be applied to entire words.
   - [c] must be created by example.
   - [d] determines the appearance of selected text.

7. **You can delete styles from the Normal template using the:**
   - [a] Stylizer.
   - [b] Organizer.
   - [c] Identifier.
   - [d] Modifier.

8. **Entering a custom style name in all uppercase characters:**
   - [a] defines the style as a paragraph style.
   - [b] makes the name easier to read.
   - [c] distinguishes the custom style from a built-in style.
   - [d] creates a style by example.

chapter sixteen

Circle **T** if the statement is true or **F** if the statement is false.

T F 1. A widow line is the last line of a paragraph that appears all by itself at the top of the next page.

T F 2. You cannot control when Word inserts a page break inside a paragraph.

T F 3. You can view the Style area in Print Layout view.

T F 4. You can delete built-in Word styles.

T F 5. When you add styles to a template, you must then save the template before you can use the styles.

T F 6. A custom character style is created in the same way as a custom paragraph style.

T F 7. Once you add a style to the Normal template, you cannot delete it.

T F 8. An orphan line is the first line of a paragraph that appears by itself at the bottom of a page.

Skills Review

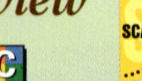

Exercise 1

1. Open the *Legislative Update* document located on the Data Disk.

2. Select the first title line and format it with the Heading 1 style modified for center alignment.

3. Apply the Heading 1 + Centered style to the second title line.

4. Create a custom paragraph style named "MYHEADING" to underline words only and add 12-point spacing after the "SENATE BILL 1004," "AWARD," AND "WORKSHOPS" paragraphs. (*Hint:* Use the Format button in the New Style dialog box to open the Paragraph and Font dialog boxes). The underlying style and the following style should be Normal.

5. Insert a nonbreaking space using the CTRL + SHIFT + SPACEBAR keys before the number "18" in the "SENATE BILL 1004" section.

6. Save the document as *Legislative Update With Custom Styles*, and then preview, print, and close it.

Exercise 2

1. Open the *Word Training* document located on the Data Disk.

2. Apply the Heading 3 style modified for center alignment to the title "WORD TRAINING."

3. Change the title to 16-point font.

4. Create a custom style to underline words only in the topic headings. (The topic headings are in 12-point font.) Name the style "HEADINGS" and base it on the Heading 3 style and follow it with the Normal style.

5. Apply the HEADINGS style to the four paragraph headings.

6. Apply the built-in List Bullet 2 style to all the subtopics at one time using the CTRL key. (The subtopics are in 10-point font.) (*Hint:* Change the Show: option in the Styles and Formatting task pane to All Styles.)

7. Save the document as *Word Training With Styles*, and then preview, print, and close it.

Creating Custom Styles and Controlling Pagination   **WA 71**

Exercise 3

1. Open the *Word Training With Styles* document you created in Exercise 2. If you have not created the document, do so now.
2. Modify the HEADINGS style to change the formatting to Arial, 12 point, bold, Small caps effect, no underline.
3. Modify the List Bullet 2 list style to change the bullet to a different symbol of your choice. (*Hint:* Use the Format button in the Modify Style dialog box to open the Bullets and Numbering dialog box.)
4. Save the document as *Word Training With Modified Styles*, and then preview, print, and close it.

Exercise 4

1. Open the *Preparing For A Speech* document located on the Data Disk.
2. Center the title and make it boldface.
3. Format the "Overcoming Fear" paragraph headings with bold and a double underline. Create a new character style by example using this heading. Name the style "DOUBLE."
4. Apply the DOUBLE custom character style to the remaining paragraph headings using the Pick formatting to apply list in the Styles and Formatting task pane.
5. Save the document as *Preparing For A Speech With Styles*, and then preview, print, and close it.

Exercise 5

1. Open the *Preparing For A Speech With Styles* document you created in Exercise 4. If you have not created the document, do so now.
2. Edit the DOUBLE style so that the paragraph headings are italic instead of bold and have no underline.
3. Reapply the modified DOUBLE style to the paragraph headings, if necessary.
4. Save the document as *Preparing For A Speech With Modified Styles*, and then preview, print, and close it.

Exercise 6

1. Open the *About E-Commerce* document located on the Data Disk.
2. Scroll the document and review the automatic page breaks, several of which break inside a paragraph. Note the widow or orphan lines.
3. Select all the body text below the title.
4. Open the Paragraph dialog box and turn on the widow/orphan protection and the keep lines together protection.
5. Deselect the text and scroll to review the new position of the automatic page breaks.
6. Save the document as *Repaginated About E-Commerce*, and then preview, print, and close it.

chapter sixteen

Exercise 7

1. Open the *Repaginated About E-Commerce* document you created in Exercise 6. If you have not created the document, do so now.
2. Display a ¾-inch Style area and review all the styles applied in the document.
3. Create a custom character style named "MYBODYTEXT" based on the Strong style with an Arial, 11-point font.
4. Apply the MYBODYTEXT character style to all the bold text in the document.
5. Create a new custom paragraph style named "MYNEWHEADING" based on the Heading 3 style and followed by the Normal style and make the font size 14 point.
6. Apply the MYNEWHEADING style to all the paragraph headings at one time using the CTRL key.
7. Review all the style formatting in the Style area and then close the Style area with the mouse pointer.
8. Save the document as *Reformatted About E-Commerce*, and then preview, print, and close it.

Exercise 8

1. Open the *Reformatted About E-Commerce* document you created in Exercise 7. If you have not created the document, do so now.
2. Modify the MYBODYTEXT and MYNEWHEADING styles to add them to the Normal template.
3. Save the Normal template and the document using the Save All command.
4. Close the document.
5. Open the Organizer dialog box and delete the MYBODYTEXT and MYNEWHEADING styles from the Normal template.

Case Projects

Project 1

Viktor Winkler's assistant, Bob Thackery, wants to know how to create custom styles. Use the Ask A Question Box to research creating custom paragraph and character styles. Write Bob an interoffice memorandum explaining how he can create custom styles and then use them in a document. Create a custom style and use it to format text in the memo. Save, preview, and print the memo.

Project 2

The Human resources Department often uses the Contemporary Memo template with custom styles for interoffice memorandums. Create a new template document based on the Contemporary Memo template and create and use custom styles for the boilerplate text. Then create a sample memo using the new template. Save, preview, and print the memo.

Project 3

Viktor Winkler needs a list of e-commerce Web sites that sell products and services to local, state, and federal governments. He asks you to compile such a list. Connect to the Internet, and search the Web for B2G (business-to-government) Web sites. Print at least two Web pages. Create a list of the Web sites you find. Use built-in and custom styles to format the list. Save, preview, and print the list.

Project 4

Lydia Montez, a receptionist in the Human Resources Department, is having trouble using styles. Sometimes her styles change unexpectedly: some paragraphs formatted with the same style look different, and she cannot see all the styles she wants to use in the Style button list. Using the Ask A Question Box, review how to troubleshoot problems you might encounter when using styles. Create a new document with at least four paragraphs describing each of Lydia's style problems and suggest a solution for each one. Use custom styles to format the document. Save and print the document. With your instructor's approval, use the document as a guide to show a classmate how to solve these and other style problems.

Project 5

Bill Martin wants to preview the styles used in several Word templates and then copy the styles into a new document he is creating. Using the Ask A Question Box, research how to view or copy styles from another template into your document using the Organizer. Write Bill an interoffice memorandum explaining how to do this. Use custom styles to format your memorandum. Save, preview, and print the memorandum.

Project 6

B. J. Chang wants to post a list of Web sites offering information about sales and marketing training in the employee lounge. Connect to the Internet, and search for Web sites offering information about sales and marketing training or seminars. Make a list of at least five Web sites. Format the list with custom styles. Save, preview, and print the list.

Project 7

B. J. Chang's administrative assistant is having trouble with text in a large document. She has both widow and orphan lines and wants to remove them. Using online Help, research how to protect against widow and orphan lines. Create an outline that contains the step-by-step process for doing this. Save, preview, and print the outline. With your instructors permission, demonstrate how to protect against widow and orphan lines to several classmates.

Project 8

Bill Martin drops by your desk. He is working on a large document and wants to know if using kerning will help. Connect to the Internet and search for online dictionaries. Then look up "kerning." Open the Character Spacing tab in the Font dialog box, and use the dialog box Help button to review the Kerning for fonts: option. Then write Bill a memo defining "kerning" and how to use it in Word. Format the memo with custom styles. Save, preview, and print the memo.

chapter sixteen

Word 2002

LEARNING OBJECTIVES

- Understand the mail merge process
- Define the main document
- Select the data source
- Merge the main document and the data source

chapter seventeen

Using the Mail Merge Wizard

Chapter Overview

Businesses commonly send the same letter to multiple addressees or create multiple envelopes or labels from a list of delivery addresses. This is done quickly with a process called mail merge. In this chapter, you learn to create multiple letters using the mail merge process by keying the letter in one document, using names and addresses from a second document, and then combining both documents to create individual letters.

Case profile

The Marketing Department sends a letter to potential new customers to arrange a meeting with a sales representative. The letter consists of a standard text combined with names and addresses and other variable information to create a series of personalized form letters. The marketing manager asks you to return to the department to help create these letters.

17.a Understanding the Mail Merge Process

The **mail merge** process is useful when the same text is repeated in many documents. For example, suppose the same letter must be sent to 1,000 customers. You can use the mail merge process to easily prepare 1,000 letters with just two documents! One document contains the letter content and **merge fields**, special codes that are placeholders for a specific data item or variable text such as the customer's name, address, and salutation. The second document contains the variable data that corresponds to the merge fields in the first document; that is, the actual names, addresses, and salutations for each customer. You can then use the Mail Merge Wizard subcommand under the Letters and Mailings command on the Tools menu to combine these two documents to create 1,000 individual letters (often called form letters).

The Mail Merge Wizard is a series of six task panes. In the first task pane, you define the type of mail merge—Letters, E-mail messages, Envelopes, Labels, or Directory—you wish to perform. The contents of the next five task panes vary depending on the type of merge you choose to perform.

The Marketing Department wants to send a marketing letter to three new businesses in Texas. You begin by opening the Mail Merge Wizard and then defining the merge as a Letters merge. To begin:

Step 1	Create	a new, blank document, if necessary
Step 2	Click	Tools
Step 3	Point to	Letters and Mailings
Step 4	Click	Mail Merge Wizard

Word switches to Print Layout view, if necessary, and opens the first Mail Merge task pane. The Step 1 of 6 Mail Merge task pane on your screen should look similar to Figure 17-1.

The default merge type is Letters. You can change the merge type by clicking the appropriate option in the Select document type area in the Step 1 of 6 Mail Merge task pane. When you click an option, a description of that option appears below the list.

chapter seventeen

FIGURE 17-1
Mail Merge Task Pane

[Screenshot of Word with Mail Merge task pane, labeled: Mail Merge types, Description of selected document type, Mail Merge Wizard Step 1 of 6]

MOUSE TIP

When you are familiar with the mail merge process or prefer not to use the wizard, you can display the Mail Merge toolbar and use its features to set up and complete the mail merge process. You can view the Mail Merge toolbar with the Show Mail Merge Toolbar subcommand under the Letters and Mailings command on the Tools menu or with the toolbar shortcut menu.

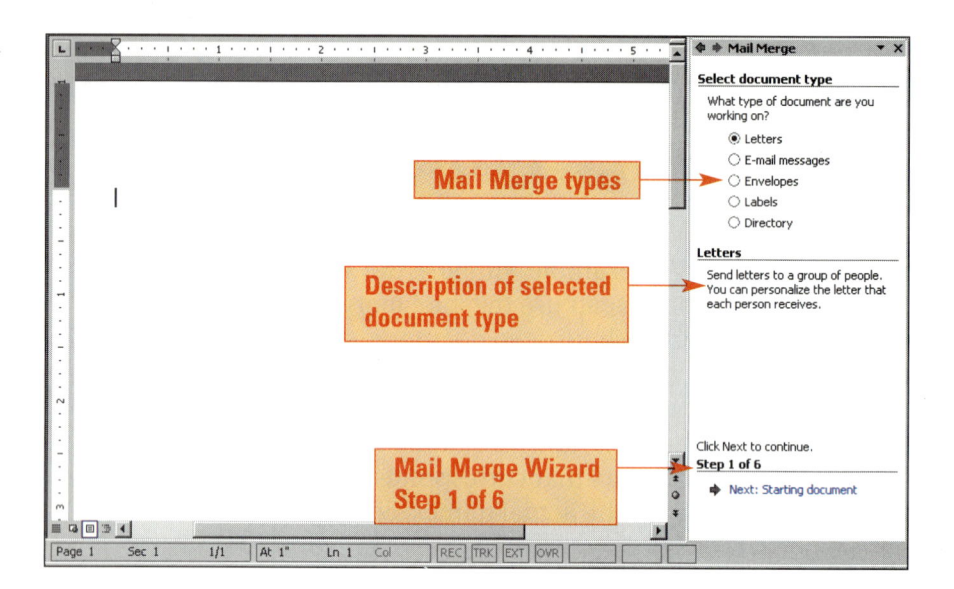

Step 5	**Click**	the E-mail messages option button in the Select document type section of the Mail Merge task pane
Step 6	**Review**	the option description
Step 7	**Click**	each of the remaining document type options and review its description
Step 8	**Click**	the Letters option button in the Select document type section of the Mail Merge task pane

Next you define the main document.

17.b Defining the Main Document

The document that contains the merge field codes and nonvariable text is called the **main document**. You create a main document by keying the nonvariable text and then inserting merge field codes for the variable text. In the next Mail Merge Wizard step, you define the main document, called the starting document by the wizard, by basing it on an existing document. To go to the next wizard step:

| Step 1 | **Click** | the Next: Starting document link at the bottom of the Mail Merge task pane |

The Step 2 of 6 Mail Merge task pane opens. The default option is to use the current open document as the main document. You can also

Using the Mail Merge Wizard **WA 77**

start from a template or from an existing document. You want to base the main document on an existing document, *Marketing Letter*. To define the main document:

Step 1	Click	the Start from existing document option button in the Select starting document section in the Step 2 of 6 Mail Merge task pane
Step 2	Click	the Open button in the Step 2 of 6 Mail Merge task pane
Step 3	Open	the *Marketing Letter* document located on the Data Disk

A new document based on the contents of the *Marketing Letter* document is created.

Step 4	Turn on	the formatting marks, if necessary
Step 5	Zoom	to Page Width, if necessary

Your screen should look similar to Figure 17-2.

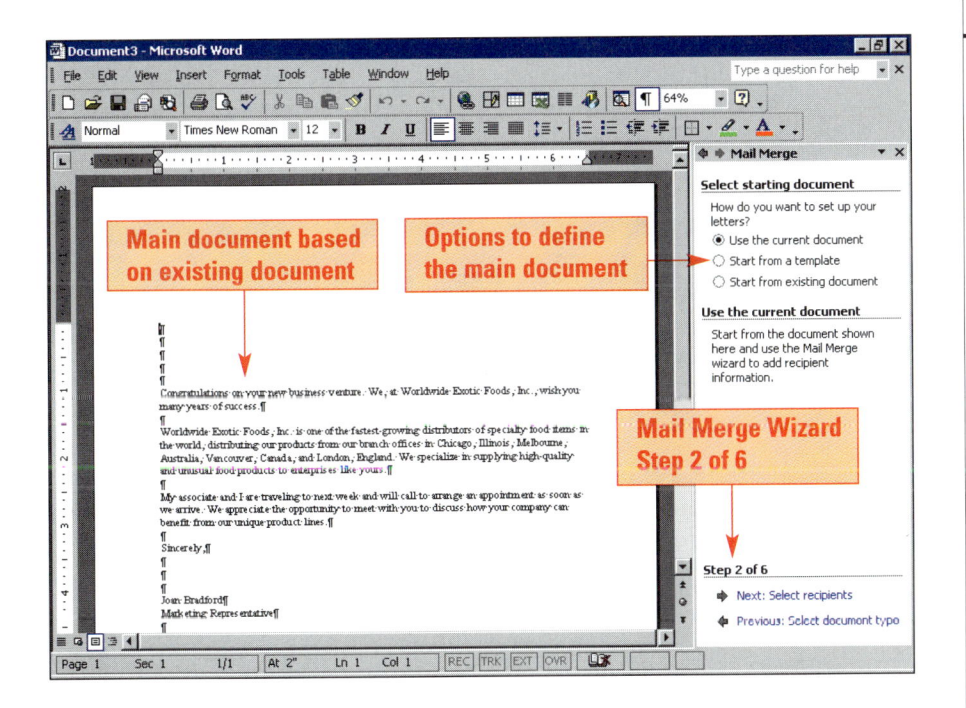

QUICK TIP

When a main document contains the current date, you should insert the date as a date field. This allows you to use the main document multiple times without having to rekey the date.

FIGURE 17-2
Main Document

MOUSE TIP

Word provides a series of mail merge templates you can access by clicking the General Templates link in the New Document task pane and then clicking the Mail Merge tab in the Templates dialog box.

You can continue to the next step, or if necessary, return to the previous step with links at the bottom of the Mail Merge task pane. Now that the main document is defined, you are ready for the next step in the Letter mail merge process—selecting the letter recipients.

chapter
seventeen

17.c Selecting the Data Source

> **QUICK TIP**
>
> During the merge process, you can create and use a simple Office Address List, which is saved as an Access database.

The Letters mail merge process requires that you specify the letter recipients. This information is called the data source for the merge process. A **data source** is a file that contains the variable information to be inserted at each merge field code in the main document. When you merge documents, you can specify an existing data source or you can create a new data source. You can use a variety of existing sources as a data source for a Word mail merge such as a Word table or a list of variable text in a Word document. You also can use an Excel worksheet, an Access table or query, or the Outlook Contacts list.

You are going to open an existing data source, a Word document containing a table with the address information. The table contains a column for each field: title, first name, last name, company, street address, city, state, postal code for the three recipients. To open the Word document data source:

| Step 1 | Click | the Next: Select recipients link at the bottom of the Step 2 of 6 Mail Merge task pane |

The Step 3 of 6 Mail Merge task pane on your screen should look similar to Figure 17-3.

FIGURE 17-3
Step 3 of 6 Mail Merge Task Pane

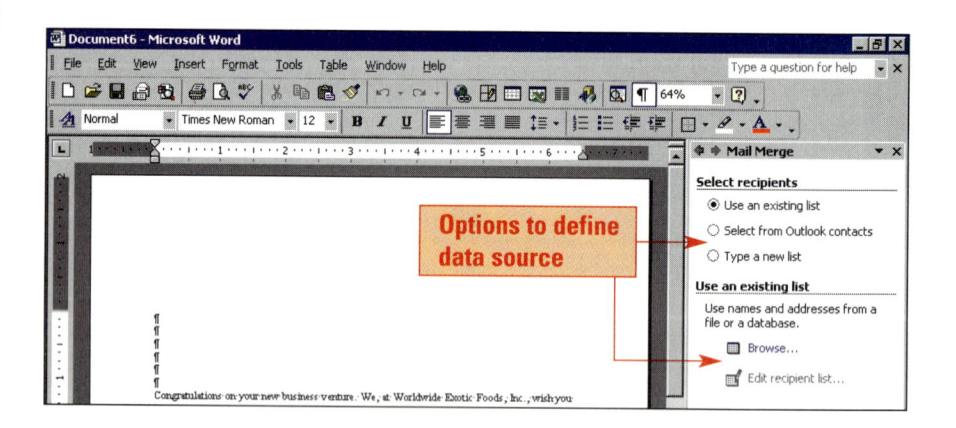

You want to use an existing list of names and addresses as the data source for this merge process.

| Step 2 | Verify | the Use an existing list option is selected in the Select recipients section in the Step 3 of 6 Mail Merge task pane |
| Step 3 | Click | the Browse link in the Step 3 of 6 Mail Merge task pane |

Using the Mail Merge Wizard   WA 79

The Select Data Source dialog box opens. By default, Word stores the Office Address List and other data sources you create in the My Data Sources folder. You need to switch to the Data Disk.

| Step 4 | **Switch to** | the Data Disk |
| Step 5 | **Open** | the *Texas Addresses* document |

The Mail Merge Recipients dialog box on your screen should look similar to Figure 17-4.

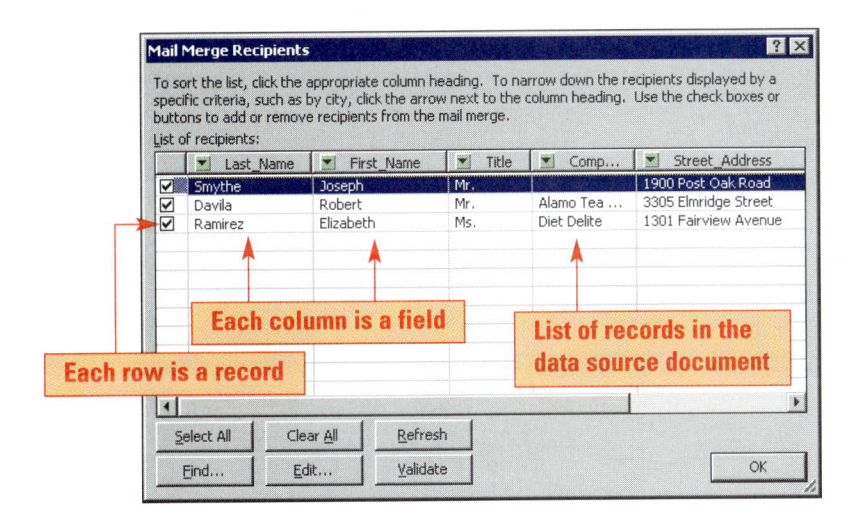

FIGURE 17-4
Mail Merge Recipients Dialog Box

QUICK TIP

Address validation software can be purchased from third-party vendors.

You can sort the list of recipients, select certain recipients by indicating the selection criteria for each column, and select or deselect all the recipients. You can select or deselect individual records by adding or removing the check mark for the record. The Refresh button obtains a fresh copy of the records. The Find button enables you to look for specific records. The Edit button opens a Data Form dialog box that contains the details for the selected record. You can edit the contents of each field in this Data Form. The Validate button is used to connect to address validation software. You use all three records in their current order for this merge.

| Step 6 | **Click** | OK |

You can save the main document and then open it later and use it again for another merge. When you open a main document and start the Mail Merge Wizard, the Step 3 of 6 task pane opens, which allows you to select a different data source or use the attached data source.

| Step 7 | **Save** | the main document as *Texas Main Document* and leave it open |

chapter seventeen

17.d Merging the Main Document and the Data Source

Before you can merge the main document with the addresses in the data source, you need to edit the main document to include the date, inside address, and salutation information. You do this in the next wizard step. To insert the date, the inside address, and the salutation:

| Step 1 | **Insert** | today's date as a field at the top of the document |
| Step 2 | **Click** | the Next: Write your letter link at the bottom of the Step 3 of 6 Mail Merge task pane |

Except for the date, the document and the Step 4 of 6 Mail Merge task pane on your screen should look similar to Figure 17-5.

FIGURE 17-5
Step 4 of 6 Mail Merge Task Pane

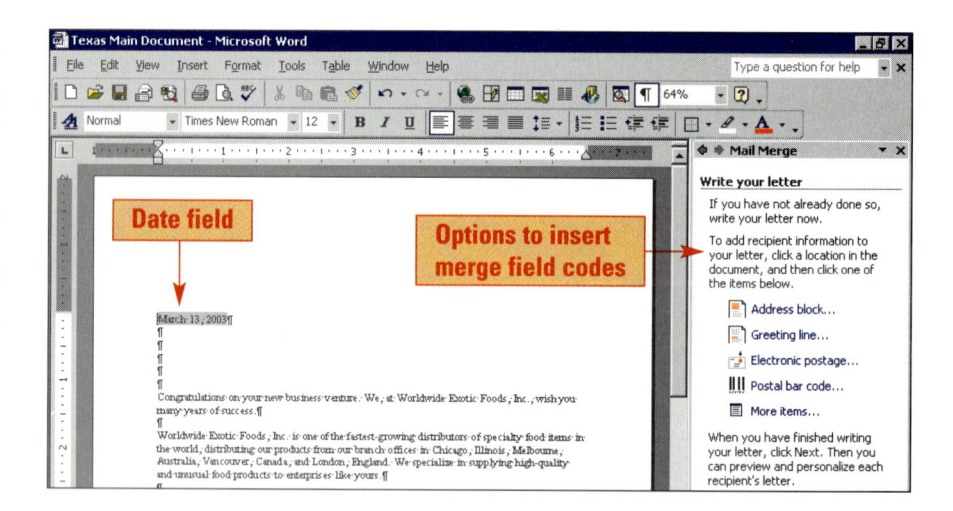

To complete the main document, you need to insert the merge field codes that correspond to the data fields in the data source. You can do this one field at a time with the More items link in the Step 4 of 6 Mail Merge task pane, or you can use the Address block link and the Greeting line link in the task pane to insert all the needed merge fields needed for the inside address and salutation at one time. To insert the inside address:

| Step 1 | **Move** | the insertion point to the first blank line above the paragraph beginning "Congratulations" in the main document |

Using the Mail Merge Wizard   WA 81

| Step 2 | Click | the Address block link in the Step 4 of 6 Mail Merge task pane |

The Insert Address Block dialog box on your screen should look similar to Figure 17-6.

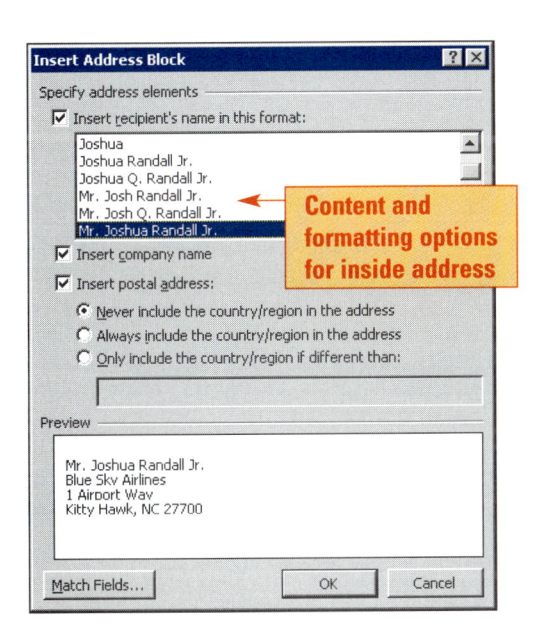

FIGURE 17-6
Insert Address Block Dialog Box

You can select a format for the recipient's name, insert or omit the company name, and insert or omit the postal address in this dialog box. A set of sample names such as "Josh Randall Jr." are listed. You select the appropriate format for Word to use when inserting the recipient's name from this list. Because the *Texas Addresses* document contains a Title, First Name and Last Name field, you use the "Mr. Joshua Randall Jr." format and the company name.

Step 3	Verify	that the Insert recipient's name in this format: check box contains a check mark
Step 4	Click	the "Mr. Joshua Randall Jr." option in the recipient's name list, if necessary
Step 5	Observe	the address preview in the Preview box
Step 6	Verify	that the Insert company name check box contains a check mark
Step 7	Verify	that the Insert postal address: check box contains a check mark

The default option for the address omits the country/region. Because the addresses in the *Texas Addresses* document are all Texas addresses, it is not necessary to add the country name, U.S.A.

chapter seventeen

QUICK TIP

You can format the contents of a merge field by selecting it including the << >> merge field characters. Then format the merge field just as you would any text characters.

You can turn on or off the view the contents of the merge field codes in a document by pressing the ALT + F9 keys.

FIGURE 17-7
Greeting Line Dialog Box

Step 8	Verify	that the Never include the country/region in the address option button is selected
Step 9	Click	OK
Step 10	Observe	the <<<<AddressBlock>>>> merge field in the document

Now you need to insert the salutation. To insert salutation using the Greeting line link in the Mail Merge task pane:

| Step 1 | Press | the ENTER key twice to move the insertion point to the second blank line below the <<<<AddressBlock>>>> |
| Step 2 | Click | the Greeting line link in the Step 4 of 6 Mail Merge task pane |

Your Greeting Line dialog box should look similar to Figure 17-7. You select the form and punctuation of the salutation in this dialog box.

[Greeting Line dialog box image with "Content options for salutation" callout]

Step 3	Verify	that Dear and Mr. Randall and a comma (,) appear in the Greeting line format: text boxes
Step 4	Click	OK
Step 5	Observe	the <<<<GreetingLine>>>> merge field in the document
Step 6	Press	the ENTER key to insert a blank line between the Greeting line and the body text
Step 7	Save	the document

With all the merge fields in the document, you are ready to preview the merge. To preview the merge:

| Step 1 | Click | the Next: Preview your letters link at the bottom of the Step 4 of 6 Mail Merge task pane |

The first letter to Joseph Smythe and the Step 5 of 6 Mail Merge task pane on your screen should look similar to Figure 17-8.

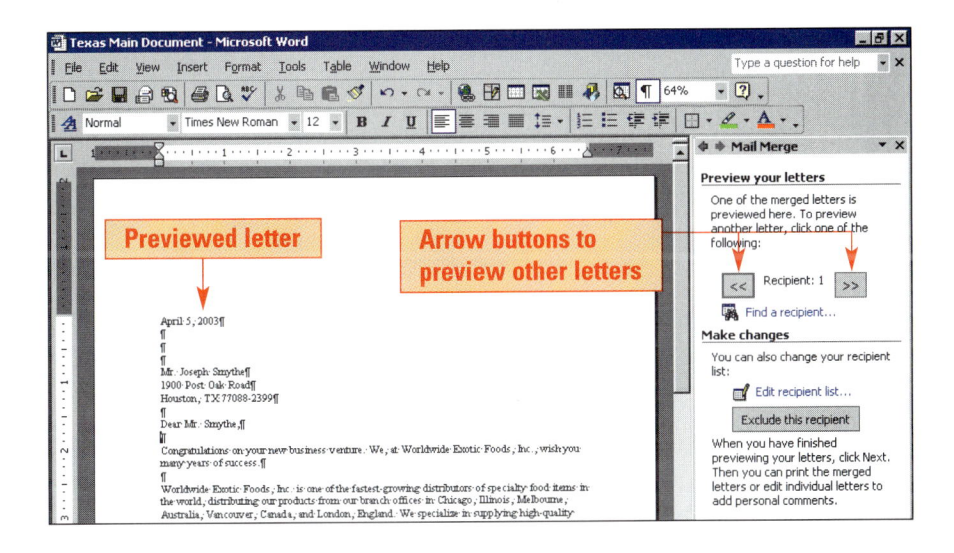

FIGURE 17-8
Preview of First Letter

You can use the arrow buttons in the Step 5 of 6 Mail Merge task pane to preview other letters. You can also edit the data source (list of recipients) and exclude the current recipient from the merge using options in the task pane.

| Step 2 | Click | the right arrow button >> in the Preview your letters section of the Step 5 of 6 Mail Merge task pane to view the second letter |

| Step 3 | Click | the right arrow button >> in the Preview your letters section of the Step 5 of 6 Mail Merge task pane to view the third letter |

If you find any errors as you preview the letters, you can change the main document or edit the data source, if necessary. If you find no errors in the preview, you are ready to complete the merge process. To complete the merge process:

| Step 1 | Click | the Next: Complete the merge link at the bottom of the Step 4 of 6 Mail Merge task pane |

The Step 6 of 6 Mail Merge task pane on your screen should look similar to Figure 17-9. You can send the merged letters directly to the printer or you can create a new document containing the individual letters and then edit each letter, if desired, to personalize it. You want to create a new document containing the individual letters.

CAUTION TIP

If you save a main document after the preview step, the document is saved with the preview data displayed. After closing and reopening the main document, you cannot see the merge field codes. To display the merge field codes instead of the preview data, start the Mail Merge Wizard, back up to the write letter step, and turn off the preview.

chapter seventeen

FIGURE 17-9
Step 6 of 6 Mail Merge Task Pane

[Screenshot of Texas Main Document in Microsoft Word with Mail Merge task pane showing "Complete the merge" step. Callout: "Options to print or save to a new document" pointing to the Merge section.]

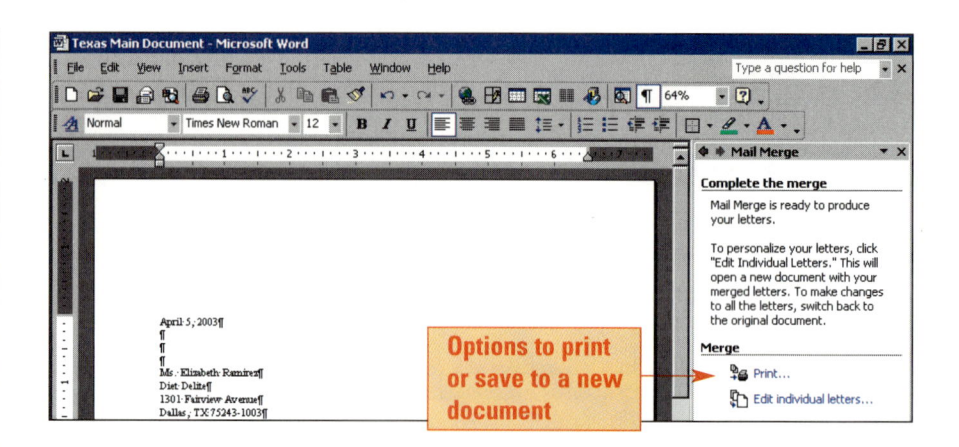

CAUTION TIP

Word may not be able to find the data source for a main document if you moved a saved main document file or its data source from the original save location. To reconnect the main document to its data source, click the Find Data Source button, and then double-click the data source file.

| Step 2 | Click | the Edit individual letters link in the Merge section of the Step 6 of 6 Mail Merge task pane |

The Merge to New Document dialog box on your screen should look similar to Figure 17-10.

FIGURE 17-10
Merge to New Document Dialog Box

[Screenshot of Merge to New Document dialog box with Merge records options: All, Current record, From/To. Callout: "Options to select which records to merge"]

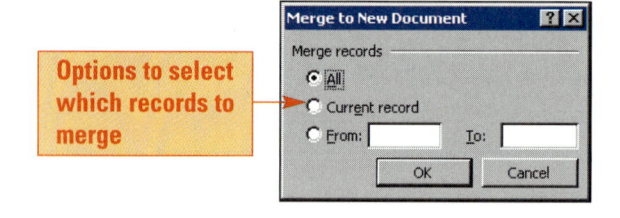

You can merge just the letter for the current record, all the records, or a range of records by specifying the starting and ending record. You want to merge all three records.

| Step 3 | Verify | that the All option button is selected |
| Step 4 | Click | OK |

A new document containing three letters temporarily named *Letters1* is created. The letters are separated by a Next Page section break. You want to save the document.

QUICK TIP

You may want to keep an electronic copy of the merged letters for documentation purposes.

| Step 5 | Save | the *Letters1* document as *Texas Letters* and close it |
| Step 6 | Close | the *Texas Main Document* without saving |

You can easily create multiple letters using the Mail Merge Wizard.

Using the Mail Merge Wizard WA 85

Summary

- A mail merge combines two documents—one containing text and merge field codes called the main document and the other containing variable data called the data source—to create multiple documents.

- A data source can be a Word document containing a table or text, an Excel worksheet, an Access database, or Outlook contacts.

- A main document and a data source can be merged to a new document or directly to a printer.

Commands Review

Action	Menu Bar	Shortcut Menu	Toolbar	Task Pane	Keyboard
Use the Mail Merge Wizard to create multiple letters	Tools, Letters and Mailings, Mail Merge Wizard			Steps 1 through 6, Mail Merge task panes to define the main document and data source and then combine them into multiple documents	ALT + T, E, M
Display the Mail Merge toolbar	Tools, Letters and Mailings, Show Mail Merge Toolbar View, Toolbars Mail Merge	Right-click any toolbar, click Mail Merge			ALT + T, E, T ALT + V, T
View the contents of a merge field code					ALT + F9

Concepts Review

SCANS

Circle the correct answer.

1. The Mail Merge Wizard is a series of:
   [a] three task panes.
   [b] five task panes.
   [c] six dialog boxes.
   [d] six task panes.

2. The merge process does not include:
   [a] inserting a date field.
   [b] defining the main document.
   [c] defining the data source.
   [d] previewing the merge.

3. The default merge type is:
   [a] Letters.
   [b] Fax.
   [c] E-mail messages.
   [d] Envelopes.

4. To complete the merge process, you need:
   [a] a main document only.
   [b] a data source document only.
   [c] a single blank document.
   [d] both a main document and a data source document.

5. A data source cannot be a(n):
   [a] Excel worksheet.
   [b] Access table or query.
   [c] Outlook Contacts list.
   [d] Word main document.

chapter seventeen

6. **The five types of mail merge main documents are:**
   - [a] Letters, Envelopes, Labels, E-mail messages, and Directory.
   - [b] Basic Letters, Envelopes, Labels, and Lists.
   - [c] Form Letters, Envelopes, Mailing Labels, Catalogs, and Lists.
   - [d] Letters, Directory, Envelopes and Labels, E-mail messages, and Lists.

7. **Merge field codes are surrounded by:**
   - [a] [[ ]].
   - [b] {{ }}.
   - [c] < >.
   - [d] << >>.

8. **To create a new document containing the merge letters, you must:**
   - [a] edit the individual letters.
   - [b] print the merge document.
   - [c] save the main document.
   - [d] close the database document.

Circle **T** if the statement is true or **F** if the statement is false.

T F   1. The mail merge process takes data and text from two different documents and creates a combined document.

T F   2. The Mail Merge Wizard task panes provide options for selecting an existing data source or creating a simple Office Address list database.

T F   3. You insert merge field codes into a main document.

T F   4. When you preview a merge, you can view only the first record.

T F   5. The first step in the Mail Merge Wizard task pane is to create a data source.

T F   6. It is a good idea to insert the date as a field in a main document used to create multiple letters.

T F   7. You cannot send merged letters directly to a printer.

T F   8. After you define a data source for a new Letters merge main document, you must then edit the main document to add the date, inside address, and salutation merge fields.

Skills Review

Exercise 1

1. Create a new, blank document, if necessary.
2. Use the Mail Merge Wizard to create a Letters merge using the existing document *Product Preview Letter* located on the Data Disk to create the main document.
3. Use the existing data source *Product Preview Data* located on the Data Disk.
4. Edit the main document to insert a date field.
5. Use the Address block and Greeting line links in the Mail Merge task pane to insert the inside address and salutation. Use the Dear Title LastName format for the salutation.
6. Preview the merge and make any necessary corrections to the main document.
7. Merge all the records to a new document.
8. Save the merged document as *Product Preview Merged Letters*. Do not save the main document.
9. Print the *Product Preview Merged Letters* document. Close all documents.

Exercise 2

1. Create a new, blank document, if necessary.

2. Use the Mail Merge Wizard to create a Letters merge. Base the main document on the *Spring Conference Letter* document located on the Data Disk.

3. Insert today's date as a date field.

4. Use all the records from an existing data source, *Spring Conference Data*, located on the Data Disk.

5. Insert the appropriate inside address merge fields into the main document as indicated below using individual merge fields. (*Hint:* Move the insertion point to the appropriate location in the document, click the More items link in the Mail Merge task pane to open the Insert Merge Field dialog box, click a merge field, click Insert, close the dialog box, and then key the appropriate punctuation such as a space or comma. Repeat the process to insert the next field.)

   <<Title>> <<FirstName>> <<LastName>>
   <<Restaurant>>
   <<Address 1>>
   <<City>>, <<PostalCode>>
   <<Country>>

6. Insert the FirstName field after the "Dear" salutation using the More items link.

7. Preview the merge and then merge to a new document.

8. Save the merged document as *Spring Conference Merged Letters*. Do not save the main document. Close all documents.

Exercise 3

1. Open the *After Holiday Sale Letter* located on the Data Disk.

2. Use the Mail Merge Wizard to create a Letters merge using the current document, the *After Holiday Sale Letter*, as the main document and the *After Holiday Sale Data* document located on the Data Disk as the data source.

3. After inserting the date field and the merge field codes using the Address block and Greeting line links in the Mail Merge task pane, save the main document as *After Holiday Sale Main Document*. Use the Dear Title LastName format for the salutation.

4. Preview the merge and make any necessary corrections.

5. Merge to a new document and save the merged document as *After Holiday Sale Merged Letters*.

6. Print the merged document. Close all documents. Do not resave the main document.

Exercise 4

1. Open the *Confirmation Letter* document located on the Data Disk.

2. Use the Mail Merge Wizard to create a Letters mail merge using the current document, *Confirmation Letter*, as the main document and the *Confirmation Data* document as the data source. Include only the Gonzales record in the merge. (*Hint:* Remove the check mark from the other record in the Mail Merge Recipients dialog box.)

3. Edit the main document to insert the date field and the merge field codes using the Address block and Greeting Line links in the Mail Merge task pane. Use the Dear Title LastName format for the salutation.

4. Save the main document as *Confirmation Letter Main Document*.

chapter seventeen

5. Preview the merge and make any necessary corrections.

6. Merge to a new document and save the merged document as *Confirmation Merged Letter*.

7. Print the merged document. Close all documents.

Exercise 5

1. Open the *Confirmation Letter Main Document* document you created in Exercise 4 and turn on the Mail Merge Wizard. If you have not completed Exercise 4 do so now. (*Hint:* Because this document is already identified as a mail merge main document, the Step 3 of 6 Mail Merge task pane opens.)

2. Use the Select a different list link in the Mail Merge task pane to select the *Texas Addresses* document located on the Data Disk as the data source. Include only the Davila and Ramirez records. (*Hint:* Remove the check mark from the other record in the Mail Merge Recipients dialog box.)

3. Preview the merge and make any necessary corrections.

4. Merge to a new document and save the merged document as *Texas Confirmation Merged Letters*. Do not save the *Confirmation Letter Main Document* document.

5. Print the merged document. Close all documents.

Exercise 6

1. Open the *After Holiday Sale Main Document* you created in Exercise 3. If you have not completed Exercise 3 do so now. Then turn on the Mail Merge Wizard. (*Hint:* Because this document is already identified as a mail merge main document, the Step 3 of 6 Mail Merge task pane opens.)

2. Use the Select a different list link in the Mail Merge task pane to select the *Sales Data* document located on the Data Disk as the data source.

3. Preview the merge and exclude the Matthew Hall letter.

4. Merge to a new document and save the merged document as *Sales Merged Letters*. Do not save the *After Holiday Sale Main Document*.

5. Print the merged document. Close all documents.

Exercise 7

1. Open the *Sales Promotion Letter* document located on the Data Disk.

2. Use the Mail Merge Wizard to create a Letters merge using the current document. Use the *Sales Promotion Data* document as the data source.

3. Edit the main document to insert a date field. Insert the inside address merge field codes using the Address block link in the Mail Merge task pane. Insert the FirstName field in the salutation using the More items link in the Mail Merge task pane. (*Hint:* The data source includes Canadian addresses. Don't forget to include the country in the Address block.)

4. Save the edited main document as *Sales Promotion Main Document*.

5. Preview the merge and make any necessary corrections.

6. Merge to a new document and save the merged document as *Sales Promotion Merged Letters*.

7. Print the merged document. Close all documents.

Exercise 8

1. Open the *Sales Promotion Main Document* you created in Exercise 7. If you have not completed Exercise 7 do so now. Then turn on the Mail Merge Wizard. (*Hint:* Because this document is already identified as a mail merge main document, the Step 3 of 6 Mail Merge task pane opens.)

2. Use the Select a different list link in the Mail Merge task pane to select the *Promotional Data* document located on the Data Disk as the data source.

3. Edit the main document to replace the current salutation using the Greeting line link in the Mail Merge task pane to include the title and last name. Use the Dear Title LastName format for the salutation.

4. Preview the merge and make any necessary corrections.

5. Merge to a new document and save the merged document as *Promotional Merged Letters*. Do not save the main document.

6. Print the merged document. Close all documents.

Case Projects

Project 1

The Worldwide Exotic Foods, Inc. operating departments send overflow work to the Word Processing Department. Dorothy Davis, the marketing assistant, asks you to prepare form letters announcing the opening of the new New Mexico sales territory. The form letters will be sent to a list of prospective distributors in the northern New Mexico and Southern Colorado area. Create a main document with the appropriate text and a data source with at least three records. Use fictitious names and addresses for the records in the data source. Save, preview, and print the main document and data source document. Use the Mail Merge Wizard to merge the documents. Preview the merged data. Merge to a new document. Save, preview, and print the new merged document.

Project 2

Chris Lofton asks you to prepare a list of potential mail merge problems and possible solutions that can be distributed to all the word processing staff. Using the Ask A Question Box, troubleshoot the mail merge process. Then create an unbound report document that lists at least five potential problems and provides a suggested solution for each problem. Save, preview, and print the document.

Project 3

Viktor Winkler, the public affairs officer, drops by the Word Processing Department looking for volunteers to assist with a neighborhood youth group sponsored by Worldwide Exotic Foods, Inc. You offer to send a letter announcing the new summer programs to each family whose children participate in after-school activities with the youth group. Create a main document with the appropriate text and a data source with at least five records. Use fictitious names and addresses for the records in the data source. Save, preview, and print the main document and the data source. Use the Mail Merge Wizard to create the merge. Preview the merged data. Merge to a new document. Save, preview, and print the merged document.

Project 4

The executive assistant to marketing vice president asks you to create a document that explains the procedures for distributing the weekly marketing report to all the branch managers and marketing representatives via e-mail. Using the Ask A Question Box, research how you can distribute the weekly reports to all the managers via e-mail. Create a new document listing the steps needed to merge and distribute the results via e-mail. Save, preview, and print the document.

chapter seventeen

Project 5

Chris Lofton asks you to present a short presentation to a group of junior clerical assistants on how to use the Mail Merge Wizard. Create an outline detailing the topics you plan to cover in your presentation. Save, preview, and print the outline. With your instructor's permission, use the outline as your guide to describe how to use the Mail Merge Wizard to several classmates.

Project 6

The Marketing Department wants to add candy to the product line. Beth Able, a marketing representative, asks you to locate companies who sell handmade or unusual candies. Connect to the Internet and search the Web for companies that sell handmade or unusual candy products. Print at least three Web pages. Write Beth an interoffice memorandum listing the companies you find. Save, preview, and print the memorandum. Attach the Web pages. Create a data source in a Word table that contains the names and addresses of the three companies selling the candy products. Create a main document letter asking for more information about the specialty candy products. Save, preview, and print the main document and the data source document. Use the Mail Merge Wizard to create a mail merge to a new document. Save and print the merged document.

Project 7

The Accounting Department needs to send a letter to all outside sales representatives announcing the new expense reporting form that will be attached to the memo. Create a main document using fictitious information. Create a data source in a Word table. Don't forget to create a header row for the table that defines each column's data. Bold the text in the header row. Key at least three records in the table using fictitious names and addresses. Use the Mail Merge Wizard to merge the main document and the data source to a new document after previewing the merge. Save, preview, and print the main document, the data source document, and the merged document.

Project 8

The Marketing Department asks you to create a form letter inviting new distributors to tour the Worldwide Exotic Foods, Inc. offices next week. Create the main document with appropriate text and create a data source in a Word table with at least five records. Add a header row to the table with appropriate bold column headings. Use fictitious information and data in the main document and data source. Use the Mail Merge Wizard to create the merged letters. Save, preview, and print the main document, the data source, and the merged document.

Using Other Mail Merge Features

Word 2002

Chapter Overview

Organizations often need to create envelopes or labels for large mailings and prepare lists of information, such as addresses or telephone numbers. Also, they must keep their data source documents current by adding and removing records and adding or removing data fields. In this chapter, you learn to create multiple envelopes and labels and special list documents called directories using the mail merge process. You also learn to edit a Word table data source, merge specific data records, and add personalized text to letters during the merge process.

Learning Objectives

- Create multiple envelopes
- Generate labels
- Create directories
- Modify an existing Word table data source
- Query data records
- Insert Word fields

Case profile

The Word Processing Department does a variety of mail merge projects, including the preparation of multiple envelopes and labels, creating documents to be merged with additional keyed text such as personalized form letters, updating various data source documents, and creating different merged lists such as client or employee lists. Chris Lofton asks you to create multiple envelopes and labels from an existing data source, creating personalized form letters by keying additional text during the merge process, updating an existing data source, and creating a client list.

chapter eighteen

18.a Creating Multiple Envelopes

Organizations often send mail, such as form letters, to multiple addressees at one time. Instead of creating each envelope individually, you can create all the envelopes quickly using the mail merge process. You can use the Mail Merge Wizard to merge a new or existing data source with an envelope main document. You also can use the Mail Merge toolbar to create a mail merge main document, such as an envelope main document, and then create or select a data source, and process the merge.

Chris Lofton asks you to create Size 11 envelopes for all the data records in the *Mailing List* data source located on the Data Disk. You create multiple envelopes in the same way that you created multiple letters: by defining a main document, opening a data source, editing the main document to insert merge fields, and merging the two documents.

The buttons on the Mail Merge toolbar allow you to quickly complete the mail merge process. When viewed, the Mail Merge toolbar may appear docked above the ruler with the Standard and Formatting toolbars or it may appear floating in its window in the document area. To view the Mail Merge toolbar:

Step 1	**Create**	a new, blank document, if necessary
Step 2	**Right-click**	any toolbar
Step 3	**Click**	Mail Merge
Step 4	**Dock**	the Mail Merge toolbar below the Formatting toolbar, if necessary

The Mail Merge toolbar contains buttons to create a main document, open a data source, insert the merge fields, preview the merge, and merge the documents to their destination. To create the envelope main document:

| Step 1 | **Click** | the Main document setup button on the Mail Merge toolbar |

The Main Document Type dialog box on your screen should look similar to Figure 18-1.

Using Other Mail Merge Features **WA 93**

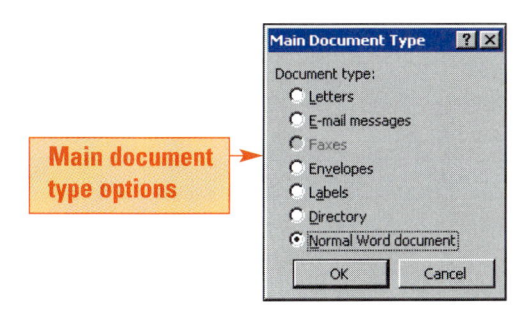

FIGURE 18-1
Main Document Type Dialog Box

Main document type options

Step 2	Click	the En_v_elopes option button
Step 3	Click	OK
Step 4	Click	the _E_nvelope Options tab, if necessary

The Envelope Options dialog box on your screen should look similar to Figure 18-2. You specify the type of envelope to use for the merge process in this dialog box.

Envelope main document options

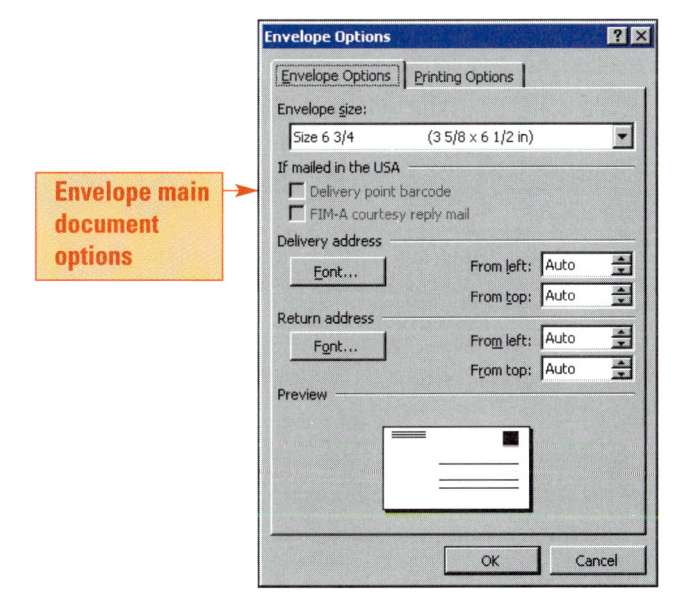

FIGURE 18-2
Envelope Options Dialog Box

Step 5	Click	the Envelope _s_ize: list arrow
Step 6	Click	Size 11 (4 ½ × 10 ⅜ in)
Step 7	Click	OK

Word switches to Print Layout view, if necessary, and displays the new paper size. Your screen should look similar to Figure 18-3.

chapter
eighteen

FIGURE 18-3
Size 11 Envelope

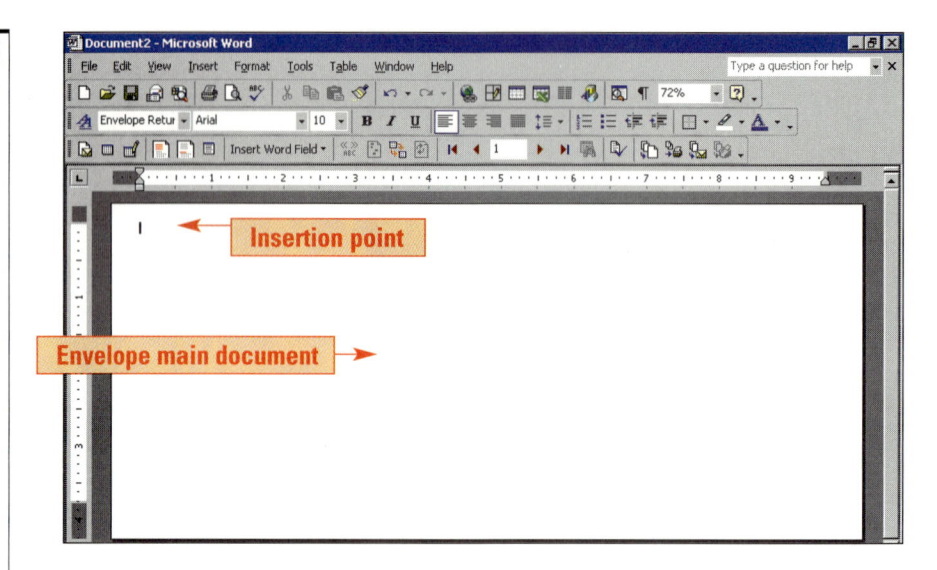

[Screenshot of Microsoft Word document showing a blank envelope with labels "Insertion point" and "Envelope main document"]

The insertion point is in the upper-left corner of the envelope, where you key a return address. Because you are going to merge to preprinted envelopes that already contain a return address, you leave this area blank. To open an existing data source:

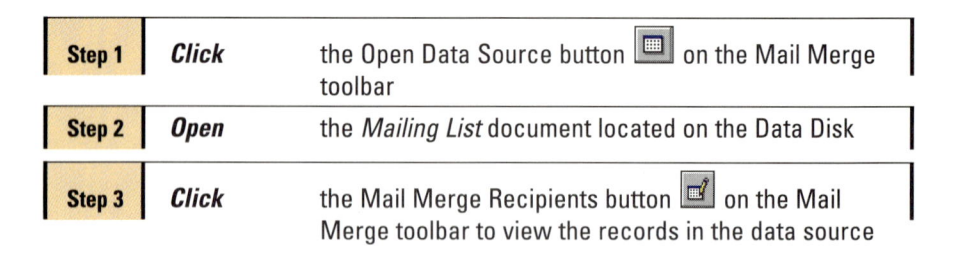

Step 1	**Click**	the Open Data Source button on the Mail Merge toolbar
Step 2	**Open**	the *Mailing List* document located on the Data Disk
Step 3	**Click**	the Mail Merge Recipients button on the Mail Merge toolbar to view the records in the data source

The Mail Merge Recipients dialog box on your screen should look similar to Figure 18-4.

FIGURE 18-4
Mail Merge Recipients Dialog Box

[Screenshot of Mail Merge Recipients dialog box with list of recipients: Washington, Gartner, Lopez, Jefferson, Yang, Delany. Label points to "Data source recipients"]

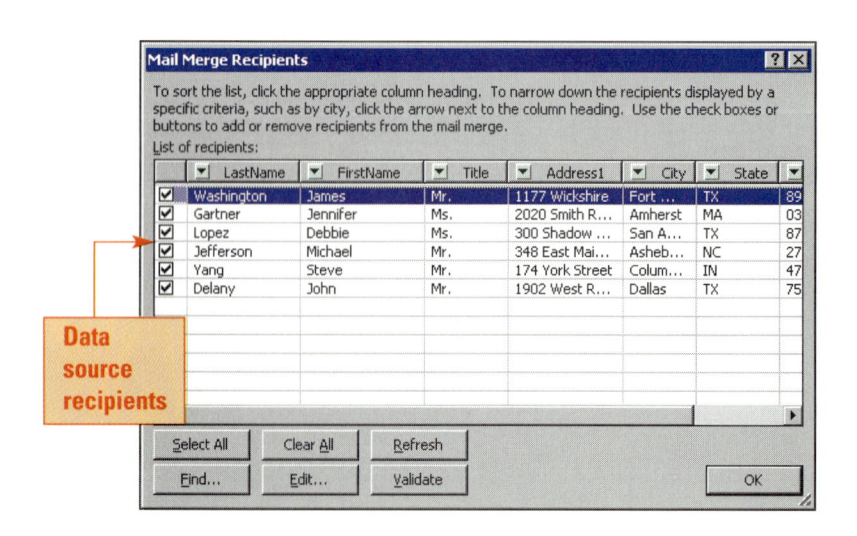

You want to include all the records in the merge process.

Step 4	Click	OK

To insert the Address Block merge field and specify the Address Block options:

Step 1	Click	at approximately the 4½ inch horizontal and 2½ inch vertical position near the center of the envelope to position the insertion point
Step 2	Observe	the hatch mark boundary surrounding the delivery address area of the envelope and the insertion point
Step 3	Click	the Insert Address Block button on the Mail Merge toolbar
Step 4	Insert	the recipient's name in the "Mr. Joshua Randall Jr." format
Step 5	Insert	the company name
Step 6	Insert	the postal address without the country/region
Step 7	Save	the document as *Mailing List Envelope Main Document*

You are ready to preview the merged envelopes. You also do this using buttons on the Mail Merge toolbar. To preview the merged envelopes:

Step 1	Click	the View Merged Data button on the Mail Merge toolbar
Step 2	Observe	the Go to Record button on the Mail Merge toolbar contains "1" indicating you are looking at the envelope for the first record
Step 3	Click	the Next Record button on the Mail Merge toolbar to view the envelope for the second record
Step 4	Click	the Last Record button on the Mail Merge toolbar to view the envelope for the last record
Step 5	Click	the First Record button on the Mail Merge toolbar to view the envelope for the first record
Step 6	Click	the View Merged Data button on the Mail Merge toolbar to turn off the preview

QUICK TIP

By default, Word uses the Envelope Address style for the delivery address.

MOUSE TIP

You can reposition an envelope main document's delivery address area by dragging the hatch mark border, sometimes called a frame or a text box, to a new location on the envelope.

chapter eighteen

INTERNET TIP

If you have compatible e-mail software installed, such as Outlook, or fax software installed you also can merge to e-mail or merge to fax to send multiple copies of the same message to e-mail or fax recipients. For more information on merging to e-mail or fax, see online Help.

You are ready to merge the *Mailing List Envelope Main Document* document with the *Mailing List* data source. To merge to a new document:

Step 1	Click	the Merge to New Document button on the Mail Merge toolbar
Step 2	Verify	that the All option is selected in the Merge to New Document dialog box
Step 3	Click	OK
Step 4	Observe	the new merged envelopes
Step 5	Save	the merged document as *Mailing List Merged Envelopes*
Step 6	Close	all open documents
Step 7	Close	the Mail Merge toolbar

In addition to the envelopes, Chris also wants a sheet of mailing labels with the *Mailing List* data records.

18.b Generating Labels

When you need to print many addresses for envelopes and your printer does not have an automatic envelope feed tray, it is often quicker to print the addresses on sheets of mailing labels. You can use the Mail Merge toolbar to create labels from an existing data source in the same way you created the envelopes. To set up the labels main document:

Step 1	Create	a new, blank document, if necessary
Step 2	Display	the Mail Merge toolbar
Step 3	Click	the Main document setup button on the Mail Merge toolbar
Step 4	Click	the Labels option button
Step 5	Click	OK

Word switches to Print Layout view, if necessary and opens the Label Options dialog box.

| Step 6 | Double-click | 5660 - Address in the Product number: list box (scroll to view this option) in the Label Options dialog box |

To select the data source:

Step 1	Click	the Open Data Source button 🔲 on the Mail Merge toolbar
Step 2	Open	the *Mailing List* document on the Data Disk
Step 3	Observe	that a <<Next Record>> merge field is added to the document for each label position required by the 5660 - Address label format
Step 4	Click	the Mail Merge Recipients button 🔲 on the Mail Merge toolbar to view the records in the data source
Step 5	Click	OK

You must first insert the address merge fields in the upper-left corner of the main document (at the position of the insertion point) and then add the merge fields to each label position. You can do this quickly by inserting the Address Block. To insert the Address Block:

Step 1	Insert	the Address Block at the insertion point with the same options as the envelopes you created previously
Step 2	Click	the Propagate Labels button 🔲 on the Mail Merge toolbar to add the Address Block merge field to all the label positions on the page

Word creates the main document as a large table, with each cell containing a set of merge field codes for a record in the data source. You can change the formatting of label text by selecting all the columns of the table and applying the new format to the merge fields. The data source addresses are formatted with the Times New Roman font. You want to use the Arial font for these labels. To view the table structure and change the font:

Step 1	Show	the table gridlines, if necessary
Step 2	Select	all the columns in the table
Step 3	Change	the font to Arial
Step 4	Deselect	the table columns

Your screen should look similar to Figure 18-5.

chapter
eighteen

FIGURE 18-5
Formatted Merge Fields

Label main document with propagated formatted merge fields

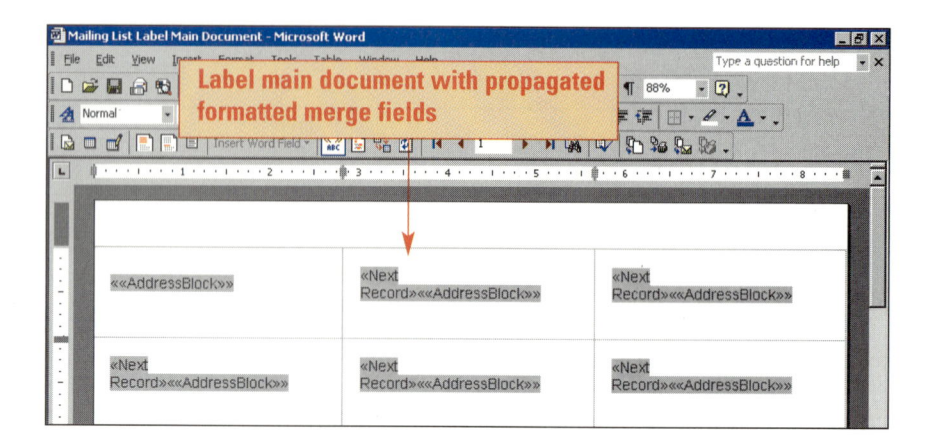

Step 5	Save	the document as *Mailing List Label Main Document*
Step 6	Click	the View Merged Data button on the Mail Merge toolbar to preview the merged labels
Step 7	Click	the View Merged Data button on the Mail Merge toolbar to turn off the preview
Step 8	Click	the Merge to New Document button on the Mail Merge toolbar to create the labels
Step 9	Verify	that All records are selected
Step 10	Click	OK

Word creates a new label document. Your screen should look similar to Figure 18-6.

FIGURE 18-6
Merged Labels

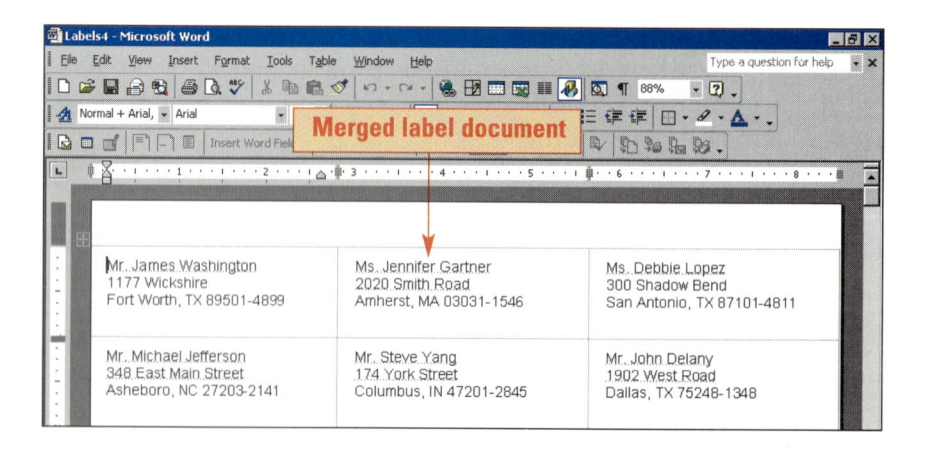

| Step 11 | Save | the document as *Mailing List Merged Labels* |
| Step 12 | Close | all open documents |

Using Other Mail Merge Features **WA 99**

Step 13	Close	the Mail Merge toolbar

Your next assignment is to create a list of distributor names and cities from the *Mailing List* data source.

18.c Creating Directories

In addition to form letters, envelopes, and labels, you can use the Mail Merge Wizard or Mail Merge toolbar to create directories. **Directories** are list merge documents that contain some nonvariable text and variable data, such as telephone lists, client lists, product directories, and so forth.

Chris ask you to create a list of distributors containing the name and city from the data in the *Mailing List* data source. To create a directory merge document:

Step 1	Create	a new, blank document, if necessary
Step 2	Display	the Mail Merge toolbar
Step 3	Create	a Directory main document
Step 4	Open	the *Mailing List* data source

You are now ready to create the main document. When you create a directory or list main document, any text you key in the main document is repeated with each data record that is merged. You key the text you want repeated and insert the merge fields only once for the entire document. To edit the main document:

Step 1	Set	a left-aligned tab stop at 1 inch
Step 2	Key	Name:
Step 3	Press	the TAB key
Step 4	Click	the Insert Merge Fields button on the Mail Merge toolbar to open the Insert Merge Fields dialog box
Step 5	Double-click	the FirstName merge field to insert it in the document
Step 6	Double-click	the LastName merge field to insert it in the document
Step 7	Close	the dialog box
Step 8	Insert	a space between the two merge fields
Step 9	Click	at the end of the <<LastName>> merge field

chapter eighteen

Step 10	Press	the ENTER key
Step 11	Key	City:
Step 12	Press	the TAB key
Step 13	Insert	the City and State merge field codes using the Merge Fields dialog box
Step 14	Insert	a comma (,) and a space between the <<City>> and the <<State>> merge field codes
Step 15	Move	the insertion point to the end of the City: line
Step 16	Press	the ENTER key three times to add blank lines after each record
Step 17	Save	the document as *Distributors List Main Document* and leave it open

The main document on your screen should look similar to Figure 18-7.

FIGURE 18-7
Distributors List Main Document

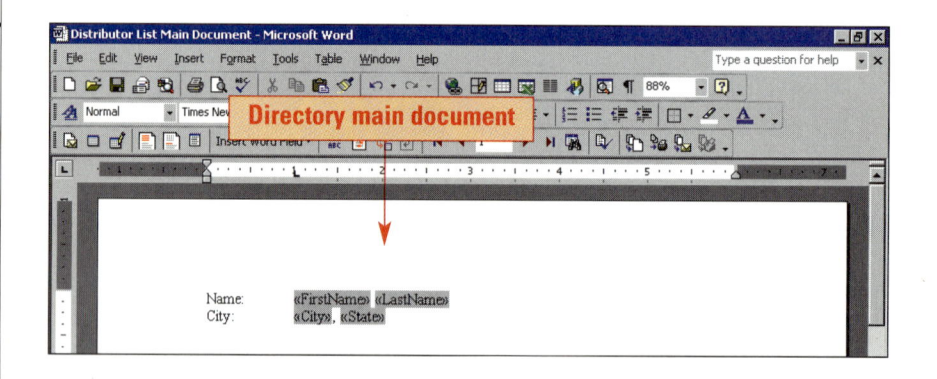

You merge the *Distributors List Main Document* document and the *Mailing List* data source to create a new document. To create the new document:

Step 1	Preview	the merge
Step 2	Turn off	the preview
Step 3	Merge	all the records to a new document
Step 4	Review	the merged directory document
Step 5	Save	the document as *Merged Distributors List*
Step 6	Close	all open documents
Step 7	Close	the Mail Merge toolbar

CAUTION TIP

Only text that repeats for each record should be keyed in the directory main document. If you want to add a text title, table column headings, or headers and footers to a directory document, add it to the merged document.

As you work with a data source in a variety of documents and for a variety or purposes, you find that it often must be updated and revised.

18.d Modifying an Existing Word Table Data Source

Even a well-constructed data source is usually modified over time to add new records, delete records that no longer belong in the data source, and add or remove data fields when the information retained in the data source changes. Chris asks you to update the *Mailing List* document data source by adding and deleting records.

Adding and Deleting Data Records

You can use the Database toolbar to add and delete records from a Word table document data source. To open the data source, display the Database toolbar, insert a new record, and key the data:

Step 1	Open	the *Mailing List* document located on the Data Disk
Step 2	Display	the Database toolbar using the toolbar shortcut menu and dock it below the Formatting toolbar
Step 3	Click	the Add New Record button on the Database toolbar
Step 4	Observe	the new, blank row at the bottom of the table and the insertion point in the first cell
Step 5	Key	the following information in the cells in the blank record, pressing the TAB key to move to the next cell: Ms. Roberta Davis 5465 Braesmont Houston TX 77096-1347
Step 6	Follow	steps 3 through 5 to add a second record with the following data: Mr. David Yanklovic 6925 Spencer Road Kent WA 98032-6925

QUICK TIP

When working with a Word table document data source, you can also add or delete records (rows) and add or delete fields (columns) using the table-editing features instead of the Database toolbar.

Chris tells you that Worldwide Exotic Foods no longer uses one of the distributors on the list. You need to delete that data record from the data source. When you delete a data record in the table format, the insertion point must be in the record. To delete a data record:

| Step 1 | Move | the insertion point to any field in the Steve Yang data record |
| Step 2 | Click | the Delete Record button on the Database toolbar |

Over time, you might find it necessary to add or remove fields from a Word table data source.

Adding Data Fields

You can add more information to an existing data source by adding new data fields. Chris asks you to add the name of the distributor's sales representative to each record in the *Mailing List* document. To add a new field for the sales representatives' names:

| Step 1 | Click | the Manage Fields button on the Database toolbar |

The Manage Fields dialog box on your screen should look similar to Figure 18-8.

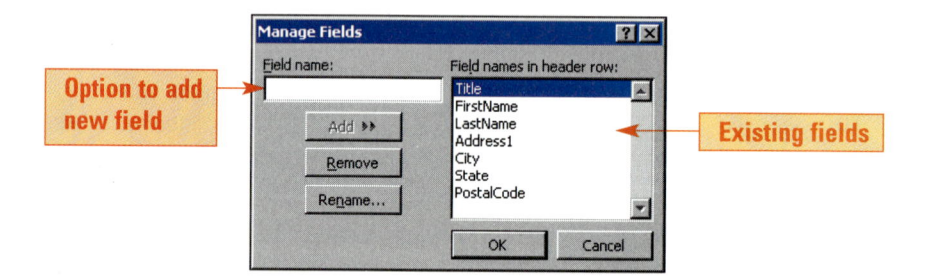

FIGURE 18-8
Manage Fields Dialog Box

Option to add new field

Existing fields

You add a custom field name for the sales representative and then key the data.

Step 2	Key	SalesRep in the Field Name: text box
Step 3	Click	Add
Step 4	Click	OK
Step 5	Observe	the SalesRep column added to the end of the table

Step 6	Key	Malkovich in the SalesRep field in the first record
Step 7	Press	the DOWN ARROW key to move the insertion point to the SalesRep field in the second record
Step 8	Key	Wong
Step 9	Continue	by keying the following sales representatives names in the remaining records, pressing the DOWN ARROW key to move to the next row: *Jackson* *Overstreet* *Ramirez* *Raja* *Nguyen*
Step 10	Save	the data source as *Mailing List Revised* and leave it open

When a data source is large, you might need to locate a specific record or group of records in it so you can review, edit, or delete them.

18.e Querying Data Records

You can select certain records to merge with a main document by setting criteria for fields and field content in the records, which is called a data source **query**. Two ways to query a data source are to sort it or to filter it. You can sort data source records in ascending or descending order by specified field contents. For example, many large mailings should be sorted by ZIP code before being taken to the post office. To do this efficiently, you can sort the data records in ascending order by ZIP code before performing the merge.

You can also filter data records by specifying that only records matching certain criteria be included in the merge process. To filter and merge selected records from the *Mailing List Revised* data source with the *Distributors Letter* main document:

Step 1	Open	the *Distributors Letter* document located on the Data Disk
Step 2	Select	the date field and update it with the F9 key
Step 3	View	the formatting marks, if necessary
Step 4	Move	the insertion point to the fourth blank line below the date
Step 5	Display	the Mail Merge toolbar
Step 6	Open	the *Mailing List Revised* data source you created earlier in this chapter
Step 7	View	the mail merge recipients

You can view the available filter criteria by clicking the arrow next to each column heading. This displays a list of filter options that includes (All) for all records, each unique value in the column, (Blanks) for no value, (Nonblanks) for any value, and (Advanced) for creating a custom criteria. You want to select records for those distributors *not* located in Texas for this merge. This requires a custom filter. When you create a custom filter, you set filter criteria by specifying a data field, a comparison operator, and a comparison value. There are several **comparison operators** such as "equal to," "not equal to," "less than," or "greater than." The **comparison value** is what the field should or should not contain to meet the criteria for selection. For example, to select all the records for distributors not located in Texas the data field criterion is the State field, the comparison operator criterion is "not equal to," and the comparison value criterion is "TX."

To create a custom filter:

| Step 1 | *Click* | the arrow next to the State column heading to view the filter options for the State column |
| Step 2 | *Click* | (Advanced…) |

The Query Options dialog box on your screen should look similar to Figure 18-9.

FIGURE 18-9
Filter Records Tab in the Query Options Dialog Box

Step 3	*Click*	the Field: list arrow
Step 4	*Click*	State (the data field criterion)
Step 5	*Click*	the Comparison: list arrow
Step 6	*Click*	Not equal to (the comparison operator)
Step 7	*Click*	in the Compare to: text box to position the insertion point
Step 8	*Key*	TX (the comparison value)

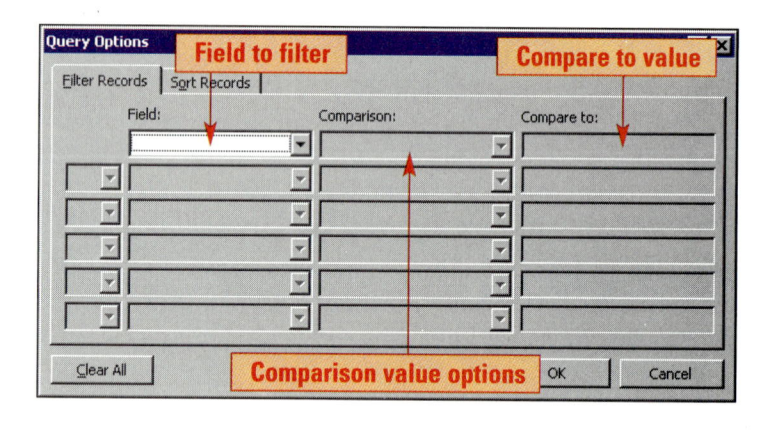

QUICK TIP

The And/Or text box on the left side of the Filter Records tab in the Query Options dialog box enables you to establish more than one set of criteria for record selection. Use "And" if records must meet all criteria; use "Or" if records must only one of the criterion.

Step 9	Click	OK
Step 10	Observe	that the recipients list now contains only three records—the recipients not located in Texas
Step 11	Click	OK

To complete the main document:

Step 1	Insert	the Address Block with the same options as the envelopes and labels you created earlier in this chapter
Step 2	Press	the ENTER key twice
Step 3	Click	the Insert Greeting Line button on the Mail Merge toolbar and insert the salutation using the "Dear Mr. Randall," format
Step 4	Save	the document as *Distributors Letter Main Document*
Step 5	Preview	the merged letters
Step 6	Merge	to a new document
Step 7	Save	the merged document as *Merged Distributors Query* and close it

In addition to the date field code that inserts the current date and the merge field codes that insert variable data from a data source, Word provides many other field codes you can use to control where and how text is inserted in a document.

18.f Inserting Word Fields

Chris wants you to merge the *Mailing List Revised* data source filtered for distributors not located in Texas with a main document and then customize each merged letter during the merge process. You need to add text indicating each distributor's holiday discount as you merge queried records from the *Mailing List Revised* data source. One way to do this is to use the Fill-in Word field. The Fill-in Word field pauses the merge process so you can key variable text at the field location in each merged letter. To begin:

| Step 1 | Verify | that the *Distributors Letter Main Document* document is open |

Step 2	Move	the insertion point to the end of the last sentence in the body paragraph
Step 3	Press	the SPACEBAR
Step 4	Click	the Insert Word Field button [Insert Word Field ▼] on the Mail Merge toolbar
Step 5	Click	Fill-in

The Insert Word Field: Fill-in dialog box on your screen should look similar to Figure 18-10.

FIGURE 18-10
Insert Word Field: Fill-in Dialog Box

Prompt area
Optional default prompt area

QUICK TIP

You can have Word enter default text whenever you do not key specific text at the prompt by entering text in the Default fill-in text: text box. You can enter the same text for each merged data record by clicking Ask once. When you turn on this option, Word prompts you for keyboard entry for the first data record and then uses that input for all remaining data records.

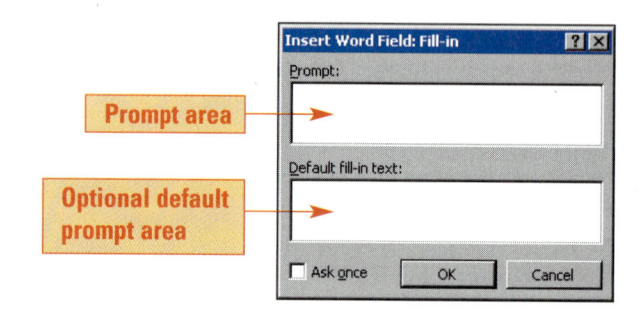

The Fill-in field opens a prompt dialog box and pauses for keyboard input at the position of the field each time a data record is merged. You create the text for the prompt in this dialog box.

To create the prompt text that instructs the user to "Key Discount Text:"

Step 1	Key	Key Discount Text in the Prompt: text box
Step 2	Click	OK
Step 3	Observe	that a sample prompt dialog box opens
Step 4	Verify	that the prompt text is keyed correctly
Step 5	Click	OK
Step 6	Save	the main document as *Fill-in Fields Main Document* and leave it open

Once the fill-in prompt is set up, you can merge the main document and the data source. To begin the merge:

Step 1	Merge	all the filtered records to a new document
Step 2	Observe	that the prompt dialog box appears for the first data record

Using Other Mail Merge Features   WA 107

Step 3	Key	Your holiday discount is 15%. in the prompt dialog box
Step 4	Click	OK
Step 5	Observe	the text "Word is merging record 2. Press ESC to cancel." that appears on the status bar
Step 6	Observe	that the prompt dialog box for the second data record contains the previously keyed text
Step 7	Click	OK to insert the same discount text in the second merged letter
Step 8	Observe	the prompt dialog box for the third letter
Step 9	Key	Your holiday discount is 20%. in the prompt dialog box
Step 10	Click	OK

> **CAUTION TIP**
>
> You cannot see the Fill-in merge field in your document unless you turn on the view of field codes in the View tab in the Options dialog box or press the ALT + F9 keys to toggle the view of field codes.

You have entered the fill-in information for the three records that meet the query criteria. To review the customized form letters:

Step 1	Scroll	to view the customized letters
Step 2	Verify	the fill-in information for each letter
Step 3	Save	the merged document as *Merged Fill-in Fields*
Step 4	Close	all open documents
Step 5	Close	the Mail Merge and Database toolbars

> **MENU TIP**
>
> You can insert field codes with the Field command on the Insert menu.

You can enhance your productivity by using the mail merge process to create multiple envelopes, multiple labels, or lists.

chapter eighteen

Summary

- You can create multiple envelopes and labels with the mail merge process using either the Mail Merge Wizard or the Mail Merge toolbar.
- You can create a list of information such as a client list with a mail merge using a Directory main document.
- Data records can be added and deleted from a Word table data source using the Database toolbar or Word table features.
- Fields can be added or removed from a Word table data source with the Database toolbar or table-editing features.
- Data records can be queried to filter or sort records for a mail merge.
- You can use Word special fields such as the Fill-in field, which pauses for keyboard entry during a mail merge.

Commands Review

Action	Menu Bar	Shortcut Menu	Toolbar	Task Pane	Keyboard
Set up a main document			[icon]		
Open a data source			[icon]		
View the mail merge recipients			[icon]		
Insert the address block merge field			[icon]		
Insert individual merge fields			[icon]		
Preview a mail merge			[icons]		
Merge to a new document, a printer, or e-mail			[icons]		
Propogate labels			[icon]		
Add a new record to a data source			[icon]		
Delete a record from a data source			[icon]		
Add or remove data fields from a data source			[icon]		
To insert a Word field			Insert Word Field		

Concepts Review

Circle the correct answer.

1. **You can add data records to a Word table data source with a button on the:**
   - [a] Formatting toolbar.
   - [b] Database toolbar.
   - [c] Mail Merge toolbar.
   - [d] Forms toolbar.

2. **You can remove a record from a Word table data source by clicking the:**
   - [a] Delete Record button on the Database toolbar.
   - [b] Delete button in the Data Form dialog box.
   - [c] Remove button on the Database toolbar.
   - [d] Delete button on the Mail Merge toolbar.

3. **To select specific records for merging:**
   - [a] insert the Fill-in field in a main document.
   - [b] click the Get Data button in the Mail Merge Helper dialog box.
   - [c] click an arrow filter button in the Mail Merge Recipients dialog box.
   - [d] insert a merge field code.

4. **To create a telephone list, you would use a mail merge main document for a(n):**
   - [a] label.
   - [b] directory.
   - [c] envelope.
   - [d] letter.

5. **You can view the Database toolbar:**
   - [a] automatically by opening a main document.
   - [b] with a shortcut menu.
   - [c] by clicking the Database button on the Formatting toolbar.
   - [d] by clicking the Toolbar button in the Mail Merge Wizard task pane.

6. **To add a new field to a data source, you can click the:**
   - [a] Insert Merge Field button on the Mail Merge toolbar.
   - [b] Insert Word Fields button on the Mail Merge toolbar.
   - [c] Manage Fields button on the Database toolbar.
   - [d] Update Field button on the Database toolbar.

7. **When you filter records, you:**
   - [a] delete them from a data source.
   - [b] sort them for a mail merge.
   - [c] add them to a data source.
   - [d] select them for a mail merge.

8. **By default, Word merges:**
   - [a] only records selected in the Query Options dialog box.
   - [b] all records in the data source.
   - [c] only records from 1 to 50.
   - [d] only records sorted in alphabetical order.

9. **Which of the following is a comparison operator?**
   - [a] below
   - [b] next
   - [c] equal to
   - [d] following

10. **The comparison value is:**
    - [a] the number of merge fields in the main document.
    - [b] the number of records in a data source.
    - [c] what a data field should or should not contain when records are filtered.
    - [d] the number of fields in a data source.

chapter eighteen

Circle **T** if the statement is true or **F** if the statement is false.

T F 1. You cannot add new data records when the data source is in the Word table format.

T F 2. All data records must be included in a mail merge.

T F 3. The Fill-in field prompts you for keyboard input during a merge.

T F 4. Query options can be set to filter or sort a data source.

T F 5. To delete a data record with a button on the Database toolbar, the insertion point must be at the top of the table.

T F 6. You can add and delete fields in a data source.

T F 7. When you create a Directory main document, you should add the document title at the top of the main document before the merge.

T F 8. The Manage Fields dialog box presents options for adding custom fields to a data source.

T F 9. Only text that is repeated should be keyed in a Directory main document.

T F 10. It is not possible to modify a data source after it is created.

Skills Review

Exercise 1

1. Use the Mail Merge toolbar to create a Size 10 envelope for the data records in the *Sales Department List* data source document located on the Data Disk.
2. There is no return address. Use the Address Block to insert the delivery address merge fields.
3. Save the envelope main document as *Sales Department Envelope Main Document*.
4. Preview the merge and then merge all the records to a new document.
5. Save the merged document as *Sales Department Merged Envelopes*, and then preview, print, and close all documents. Close the Mail Merge toolbar.

Exercise 2

1. Use the Mail Merge toolbar to create mailing labels for the data records in the *Sales Department List* data source document located on the Data Disk.
2. Use the Avery label product number 5260 for laser printers.
3. Use the Address Block merge field and remember to propagate the labels.
4. Change the font in the main document to Arial.
5. Save the label main document as *Sales Department Label Main Document*.
6. Preview the merge and then merge all records to a new document.
7. Save the merged label document as *Sales Department Merged Labels*, and then preview, print, and close all documents. Close the Mail Merge toolbar.

notes Exercise 3 requires access to Outlook Contacts folder. If you do not have access to Outlook Contacts folder, you can substitute the *Mailing List* document on the Data Disk as the data source. Your instructor may provide additional instructions for Outlook.

Exercise 3

1. Start Outlook and create a new Contacts folder named "Mailing List." Use the Outlook Bar shortcuts or Windows Explorer to switch to the Data Disk and copy the six contact records (Lopez, Washington, Gartner, Delany, Jefferson, and Yang) to the Clipboard. Switch back to the Outlook Mailing List Contacts folder and paste the records in the folder. Minimize the Outlook window.

2. Create a new, blank Word document, and start the Mail Merge Wizard. Select the Labels document type, select the 5660 - Address label format, and select the recipients from the Outlook contacts. Select the Mailing List Contacts folder as the source of the contact records.

3. Sort the recipients in ascending order by last name in the Mail Merge Recipients dialog box. (*Hint:* Click the Last column header button to sort by last name).

4. Use the Address Block defaults to arrange the labels. (*Hint:* Don't forget to update all the labels with the Address Block merge codes).

5. Preview the labels, and then merge all the labels to a new document.

6. Save the new document as *Merged Contacts*, and print it. Close the merged document, and close the main document without saving.

7. Maximize the Outlook window and delete the Mailing List folder, and then close Outlook.

Exercise 4

1. Open the *Sales Department List* data source document located on the Data Disk.

2. Add the following records to the data source using the Database toolbar.

   Mr. Thomas Carson
   18 South Street
   Dayton, OH 45424-1179

   Mr. Huang Chin
   P. O. Box 1356
   Dayton, OH 45424-1895

   Ms. Lauren Harvell
   347 Smythe Street
   Cleveland, OH 55432-2344

3. Save the data source as *Sales Department List Revised*.

4. Close the *Sales Department List Revised* data source document.

5. Use the Mail Merge toolbar to merge the *Sales Department List Revised* data source with the *Application Letter* main document located on the Data Disk.

6. Update the date field to the current date using the F9 key.

7. Use the Address Block and the Greeting Line merge fields.

8. Save the main document as *Ohio Letter Main Document*.

9. Filter the data source to include only those records for Ohio. (*Hint:* Select OH in the State column filter options list.)

chapter eighteen

10. Preview the merge and then merge all the records to a new document.

11. Save the merged document as *Ohio Merged Letters*, and then preview, print and close all documents.

12. Use a blank document and the Mail Merge toolbar to create Size 10 envelopes for the merged letters. (*Hint:* Refilter the state column for OH.)

13. Save the envelope main document as *Ohio Envelope Main Document*.

14. Preview the merge and then merge all the filtered records to a new document.

15. Save the merged envelopes as *Ohio Merged Envelopes*, and then preview, print, and close all documents. Close the Mail Merge and Database toolbars.

Exercise 5

1. Open the *Spring Conference Data* data source document located on the Data Disk.

2. Add the following record to the data source using Word table-editing tools.
   Mr. Edward Miles
   Bountiful Harvest
   8379 Madison Road
   Edmonton, AB T6G 2R6
   Canada

3. Delete the record for Mr. Mark Jefferson using Word table-editing tools.

4. Save the data source as *Spring Conference Data Revised* and close it.

5. Open the *Spring Conference Letter* document located on the Data Disk.

6. Update the date field with a shortcut menu.

7. Use the Mail Merge toolbar to merge the *Spring Conference Letter* main document with the *Spring Conference Data Revised* data source document.

8. Insert the appropriate individual merge field codes for the inside address and the salutation using the Insert Merge Fields button. Remember to insert the appropriate spacing and punctuation and to insert the country field. Insert the FirstName field in the salutation.

9. Save the main document as *Spring Conference Main Document*.

10. Preview the merge and then merge all records to a new document.

11. Save the merged document as *Spring Conference Merged Letters*, and then preview, print, and close all documents. Close the Mail Merge toolbar.

Exercise 6

1. Create a new, blank document as the basis for a list of chefs invited to the spring conference. Set a left-aligned tab at 1½ inches and key the following text; press the TAB key and then press the ENTER key after you key each line of text.
   Name:
   Restaurant:
   Location:

2. Open the Mail Merge toolbar and define the active document as a Directory main document.

3. Open the *Spring Conference Data* data source document located on the Data Disk.

4. Edit the main document to insert the individual merge field codes manually from the Insert Merge Field dialog box. Use both the first and last names fields for the name. Use the city and country fields for the location. Insert the appropriate spacing and punctuation between the fields.

5. Insert an extra blank line following the Location: line.
6. Save the main document as *Chef Main Document*.
7. Preview the merged records and then merge all the records to a new document.
8. Center the title text "Spring Conference Chef List" in bold, 14-point font three lines above the first record. Change the top margin to 2 inches.
9. Save the merged document as *Spring Conference Chef List*, and then preview, print, and close all documents. Close the Mail Merge toolbar.

Exercise 7

1. Create a new, blank document as the basis for a telephone list for the Human Resources Department in the Melbourne branch office.
2. Set a left-aligned tab at 1 inch and key the following text; press the TAB key and then press the ENTER key after you key each line of text. Double-space after the last line of text.
   Name:
   Company:
   Phone:
3. Use the Mail Merge toolbar to define the active document as a Directory main document.
4. Open the *Melbourne Telephone Data* data source document.
5. Use the Title, FirstName, LastName, Company, and WorkPhone fields for the data source.
6. Edit the main document to insert the individual merge field codes using the Insert Merge Field dialog box. Include the title, first name, and last name for the name. Add the appropriate spacing and punctuation.
7. Save the main document as *Melbourne Telephone Main Document*.
8. Preview the merge document and then merge all records to a new document.
9. Add the title "Melbourne Human Resources Telephone List" three lines above the first record.
10. Save the merged document as *Melbourne Telephone List*, and then preview, print, and close all documents. Close the Mail Merge toolbar.

Exercise 8

1. Open the *Reservation Data* data source document located on the Data Disk.
2. View the Database toolbar. Add the data field "City" to the data source document.
3. Move the "City" column to the left of the "State" column using the Cut and Paste commands.
4. Key the following text for the indicated record in the "City" column.
   Record 1   San Antonio
   Record 2   Bandera
   Record 3   New Braunfels
   Record 4   San Antonio
5. Save the data source as *Reservation Data Revised* and close it. Close the Database toolbar.
6. Open the *Rattlesnake Lodge Letter* document located on the Data Disk.
7. Use the Mail Merge toolbar to merge the *Rattlesnake Lodge Letter* main document with the *Reservation Data Revised* data source document.

chapter eighteen

8. Filter the data source to include only those records where the city is "San Antonio."

9. Edit the main document to update the date field with the F9 key and to insert the merge field codes using the Address Block and the Greeting Line.

10. Insert the Fill-in Word field for the room number in the appropriate location in the second sentence of the second body paragraph.

11. Key "Key Room Number" in the Prompt: text box. Review the sample prompt dialog box and then close it.

12. Press the ALT + F9 keys to view the Fill-in field and add a space after it. Then press ALT + F9 to turn off the view of the Fill-in field.

13. Save the main document as *Rattlesnake Lodge Main Document*.

14. Merge all the filtered records to a new document. Key the following room numbers at each Fill-in prompt.
    1B-109
    2A-115

15. Save the merged document as *Rattlesnake Lodge Merged Letters*. Print the merged document and close all documents.

16. Use a blank document and the Mail Merge toolbar to create Size 10 envelopes for the merged letters. (*Hint:* Don't forget to filter the recipients list.)

17. Save the envelope main document as *Rattlesnake Lodge Envelope Main Document*, and merge the envelopes to a new document.

18. Save the merged envelope document as *Rattlesnake Lodge Merged Envelopes*. Print the envelopes and close all documents without saving. Close the Mail Merge toolbar.

Case Projects

Project 1

During lunch with several executive assistants, you hear the term "switches" used in reference to formatting merged information. You want to know what switches are and how to use them. Using the Ask A Question Box, search for field code help topics. Find and review the topic on formatting merged information. Print the help topic and any referenced topics on switches. Write an interoffice memorandum to Chris Lofton describing how the word processing staff could use switches to format merged information. Save, preview, and print the document.

Project 2

The executive assistant to the vice president of marketing, frequently sends letters to customers announcing new products. He asks you to create several letters and a merged list. Create a data source with at least 10 records containing each customer's title, first name, last name, address, home phone, and work phone numbers. Be sure to have different city data for at least five of the records. Then create a main document form letter announcing a new product. Use fictitious information in your documents. Preview and then merge the form letter main document and the data source to a new document. Save, preview, and print the main document, data source, and the new merged document.

Query the data source to include only records for customers who live in a specific city and merge the queried data source and main document directly to the printer. Create a telephone list main document with each customer's title, last name, home phone number, and work phone number. Preview and then merge the telephone list main document with the complete data source to a new document. Save, preview, and print the telephone list main document and the new merged document.

Using Other Mail Merge Features   WA 115

Project 3

Jody Haversham calls to ask you for tips on creating data source documents. Using the Ask A Question Box, review the requirements for mail merge data sources including which applications you can use to create a data source, tips for planning a new data source, and using documents with data separated by tabs or commas as a data source. Write Jody a memorandum describing how she can find this information in online Help. Save, preview, and print the memo.

Project 4

Chris Lofton wants you to train the word processing staff to use different Word fields to customize merge documents. Use the Ask A Question Box to research how to customize documents using the ASK, FILLIN, IF, and SET fields. Print the appropriate online Help pages. Create an outline of the field help topics to be used as a training tool. Save, preview, and print the outline.

Project 5

Several of the word processing staff are interested in learning more about the different grammatical styles used by authors submitting work to the department. You suggest the department acquire several writers' style manuals. Connect to the Internet and search online bookstores for writers' style manuals. Print at least three Web pages containing a description of a popular style manual. Write an interoffice memorandum to Chris Lofton recommending the department purchase one of the manuals. Save, preview, and print the memorandum. Create a data source with a record for each style manual. Create a catalog main document listing the style manual name, publisher, and cost. Include the repeating text "Style Manual," "Publisher," and "Cost." Preview and then merge the main document with the data source. Add a text title to the merged document. Save, preview, and print the main document, the data source, and the merged document.

Project 6

Roberta Becker, the assistant manager of the Accounting Department, needs to send out a set of collection letters and asks you to prepare mail merge documents for her. Create a standard collection letter to be signed by Roberta containing at least three short paragraphs to be used as a main document. Include the phrase "your past due balance of" in the first body paragraph. Create a data source document with at least five records containing the title, first name, last name, address, city, state, and ZIP code fields. Use fictitious data for the data records. Merge the two documents using a Fill-in field to insert the past due balance. Create Size 10 envelopes for the letters. Save, preview, and print all documents.

Project 7

Chris Lofton asks you to create a Web page for the company intranet that lists the instructions for submitting mail merge work assignments to the Word Processing Department. Consider what information is important for submitting mail merge word processing tasks to a centralized Word Processing Department and then create a set of appropriate instructions others can follow to send their work to the department. Save the document as a Web page. Print the Web page from the browser.

Project 8

James Washington, a new employee in the Word Processing Department, is having trouble with the monthly distributor sales merge letter. The last time the main document and data source documents were used was to prepare letters to the Ohio distributors. Now he wants to merge all the records in the distributors data source, but each time he tries to do it, only the letters for the Ohio distributors are created. He asks for your help in solving the problem. Using the Office Assistant look up the topic "Select data records from a data source." Review the topic and write James a memo describing how he can solve his problem. Save and print the memo.

chapter eighteen

Word 2002

Sorting Text and Tables

Chapter Overview

Information in lists, reports, or tables might be entered in one order, but later prove to be more useful organized in a different order. Rather than having to manually rearrange the data, you can have Word sort it. In this chapter, you learn how to sort dates, lists, paragraphs, and tables.

LEARNING OBJECTIVES

- Sort dates
- Sort lists
- Sort paragraphs
- Sort tables

Case profile

The Sales Department maintains information about its employees, departmental policies and procedures, products, sales data, and distributors in Word report, list, and table documents. Sales Department activities often require that this information be rearranged from its original order. You rearrange a list of employee hire dates, a numbered list of products, report paragraphs, and sales data in a table.

chapter nineteen

Sorting Text and Tables   WA 117

19.a Sorting Dates

The Sort feature enables you to rearrange lists of text, table rows, dates, and document paragraphs quickly. You can sort text alphabetically or numerically, or chronologically. You can arrange as many as three criteria or sort fields at one time in **ascending** order (A–Z, 0–9, earliest to latest) or **descending** order (Z–A, 9–0, latest to earliest).

The Human Resources Department wants a list of sales representatives organized by date of hire rather than in alphabetical order. You sort text in Word documents with the sort commands on the Table menu or with buttons on the Tables and Borders or Database toolbars. To open the document and sort the list by date of hire:

Step 1	Open	the *List Of Dates* document located on the Data Disk
Step 2	Observe	that the dates in the list are formatted with different separator characters
Step 3	Select	the names and dates text
Step 4	Click	Table
Step 5	Click	Sort

QUICK TIP
A date separator is the character used to separate the month, day, and year. When sorting by date, Word recognizes forward slashes (/), hyphens (-), commas (,), or periods (.) as valid date separators. You can sort a list of dates that have different date separators.

Your Sort Text dialog box should look similar to Figure 19-1.

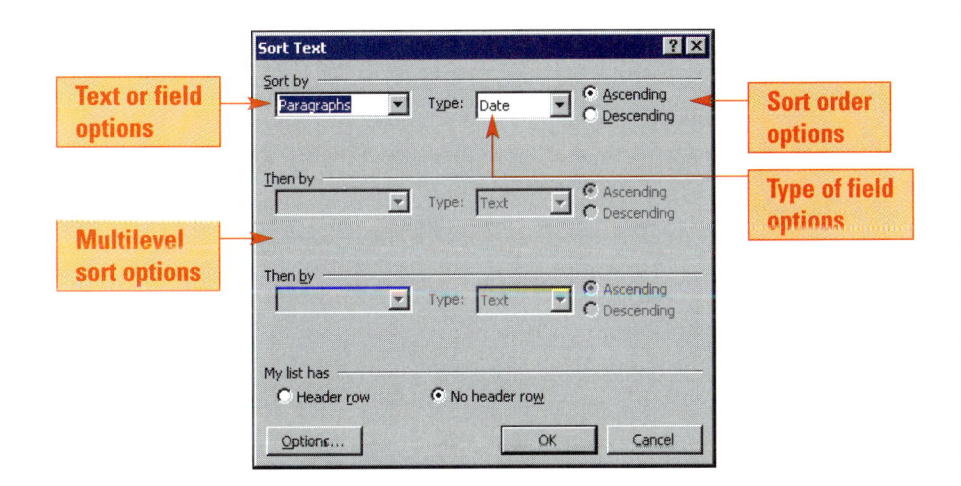

FIGURE 19-1
Sort Text Dialog Box

You use this dialog box to specify the text to sort and the sort order. Before you do that, you must specify the character that separates the columns of text so that Word can identify the individual columns.

chapter nineteen

| Step 6 | Click | Options |

The Sort Options dialog box on your screen should look similar to Figure 19-2. Tab characters separate the columns in the document. You specify the tab character separator in this dialog box.

FIGURE 19-2
Sort Options Dialog Box

CAUTION TIP

It's a good idea to carefully review the options already selected in the Sort Text, Sort Options, and Sort dialog boxes when you open them, as many of the options remained unchanged from the previous selection.

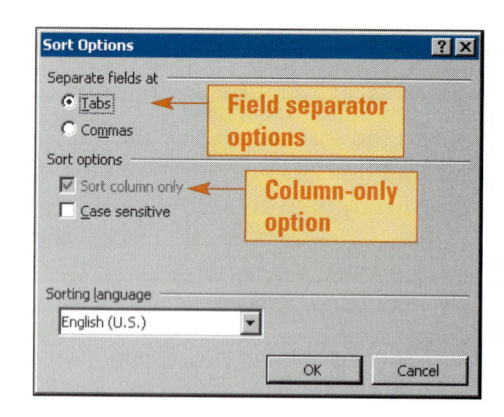

Step 7	Click	the Tabs option button, if necessary
Step 8	Click	OK
Step 9	Click	the Sort by list arrow in the Sort Text dialog box

A list of columns, called **fields**, appears. Each field number in the list corresponds to a column of selected text in the document. There are two fields of selected text: the name text in Field 1 and the data text in Field 2. You select Field 2 and specify the sort order.

Step 10	Click	Field 2
Step 11	Click	the Type: list arrow
Step 12	Click	Date, if necessary
Step 13	Click	the Ascending option button, if necessary
Step 14	Click	OK
Step 15	Observe	that the selected text is rearranged in ascending date order
Step 16	Deselect	the text
Step 17	Save	the document as *Sorted Dates* and close it

In addition to sorting dates, Word also can sort text in lists, body paragraphs, and tables.

19.b Sorting Lists

When you sort Word documents, text that begins with punctuation marks or symbols is listed first, text that begins with numbers is listed next, and text that begins with letters is listed last. Word ignores case unless specified, and then uppercase letters precede lowercase letters; for example, "C" precedes "c". When two items of text begin with the same character, Word looks at subsequent characters to determine which item is listed first.

Sorting a Numbered List

Manny DaVito, a sales representative, created a list of products and wants you to number the list and rearrange it alphabetically in ascending order. The easiest way to number a list is with the Numbering button on the Formatting toolbar. Then, when you sort the numbered list, Word renumbers the list automatically. To create a numbered list and sort it in ascending order:

Step 1	Open	the *List Of Products* document located on the Data Disk
Step 2	Select	the list of products
Step 3	Click	the Numbering button on the Formatting toolbar
Step 4	Click	T<u>a</u>ble
Step 5	Click	<u>S</u>ort
Step 6	Verify	that Paragraphs is selected in the <u>S</u>ort by list
Step 7	Verify	that Text is selected in the T<u>y</u>pe: list
Step 8	Click	the <u>A</u>scending option button, if necessary
Step 9	Click	OK
Step 10	Deselect	the text
Step 11	Observe	that the list of products is rearranged alphabetically in ascending order and renumbered
Step 12	Save	the document as *Sorted Products* and close it

You also can sort columns of text, called fields, separated by tabs, commas, or other characters.

Sorting by a Single Field

The Sales Department receptionist must be able to quickly direct inquiries from distributors and customers to the appropriate sales representative. The sales representatives information is in a Word document that contains a multiple-field list separated by tab characters. To assist the receptionist in directing inquiries, the sales manager requests a list of sales representatives sorted alphabetically by last name. She also wants a list sorted alphabetically by city within state. Finally, she wants a list sorted by ZIP code for Texas representatives. To sort the sales representatives list in ascending order by last name:

Step 1	Open	the *Sales Representatives* document located on the Data Disk
Step 2	Select	the five-column list
Step 3	Open	the Sort Text dialog box
Step 4	Click	the Sort by list arrow

Word identifies each column in the selected text as a field. Field 1 is the first column and contains the last name. Field 5 is the last column and contains the ZIP code.

Step 5	Click	Field 1
Step 6	Click	the Ascending option button, if necessary
Step 7	Click	OK
Step 8	Deselect	the text
Step 9	Observe	that the *Sales Representatives* document list is arranged in ascending alphabetical order by last name
Step 10	Save	the document as *Sales Representatives By Last Name* and leave it open

You can also sort a multiple-field list by more than one field.

Sorting by Multiple Fields

Sometimes you need to sort a document by more than one field. For example, you want to arrange the *Sales Representatives By Last Name* list in ascending alphabetical order by state and then in ascending alphabetical order by city within each state. In this multilevel sort, the state is the most important, or **primary field**, and the city is the next important, or **secondary field**. You could also sort the list by a third field, called the **tertiary field**. The primary field is defined with the Sort by list, the secondary field is defined with the first Then by list, and the tertiary field is defined with the second Then by list in the Sort

Text dialog box. To sort the *Sales Representatives By Last Name* document list by city within state in ascending alphabetical order:

Step 1	Select	the five-column list
Step 2	Open	the Sort Text dialog box
Step 3	Select	Field 4 (the state field) in the Sort by list
Step 4	Select	Text in the Type: list for Field 4, if necessary
Step 5	Click	the Ascending option button for Field 4, if necessary
Step 6	Select	Field 3 (the city field) in the first Then by list
Step 7	Select	Text in the Type: list for Field 3, if necessary
Step 8	Click	the Ascending option button for Field 3, if necessary
Step 9	Click	OK
Step 10	Deselect	the text
Step 11	Observe	that the list is arranged in ascending order by city within state
Step 12	Save	the document as *Sales Representatives By City Within State* and leave it open

You also can sort a portion of a list.

Sorting a Selected Portion of a List

You now want to sort the cities in Texas in ascending order by ZIP code. To select the text to be sorted and then specify the sort criteria:

Step 1	Select	the lines of text beginning with Aaron and ending with Nguyen
Step 2	Open	the Sort Text dialog box
Step 3	Select	Field 5 in the Sort by list
Step 4	Click	the Ascending option button for Field 5, if necessary
Step 5	Click	(none) in the Then by list to turn off the previous sort criteria
Step 6	Click	OK
Step 7	Deselect	the text
Step 8	Observe	that the lines of text for cities in Texas are arranged in ascending order by postal code
Step 9	Save	the document as *Texas Sort* and close it

You can use the Cut and Paste commands to rearrange paragraphs in a document. However, if the paragraphs are adjacent to each other, it may be faster to sort them in a specific order.

19.c Sorting Paragraphs

Word sorts body paragraphs according to the same rules it uses to sort a numbered list, mentioned earlier in this chapter. Based on these rules, numbers are arranged ahead of letters. The easiest way to sort body paragraphs in a specific order is to add a number to the beginning of each paragraph. The number represents the paragraph's order after the sort. For example, if you want a paragraph to be the third paragraph after the sort, key a 3 at the beginning of the paragraph. After the paragraphs are reordered, you can delete the numbers.

The sales manager asks you to reorganize the *Sales Department Expense Guidelines* document. To open the document, number the paragraphs, and rearrange them:

Step 1	Open	the *Sales Department Expense Guidelines* document located on the Data Disk
Step 2	Key	the following numbers as the first character of each body paragraph 6 (paragraph 1) 1 (paragraph 2) 5 (paragraph 3) 2 (paragraph 4) 3 (paragraph 5) 4 (paragraph 6) 7 (paragraph 7)
Step 3	Select	the numbered paragraphs
Step 4	Open	the Sort Text dialog box
Step 5	Select	Paragraphs in the Sort by list, if necessary
Step 6	Click	the Ascending option button, if necessary
Step 7	Click	OK
Step 8	Deselect	the text
Step 9	Observe	the paragraphs in ascending numeric order (scroll to view, if necessary)
Step 10	Delete	the numbers from the paragraphs
Step 11	Save	the document as *Sorted Paragraphs* and close it

You also can sort data organized in tables.

19.d Sorting Tables

Whenever you sort data in a table using the Tables and Borders or Database toolbar, you first must move the insertion point into the column to be sorted. Then you can sort the column using the Sort Ascending or Sort Descending buttons on the toolbars. Marjorie Mason, a sales representative, gives you a document containing deli sales organized in a table by item number assigned to each row and asks you to reorganize the data in ascending alphabetical order by city and then in descending order by product.

To open the document and sort the data in ascending order by city:

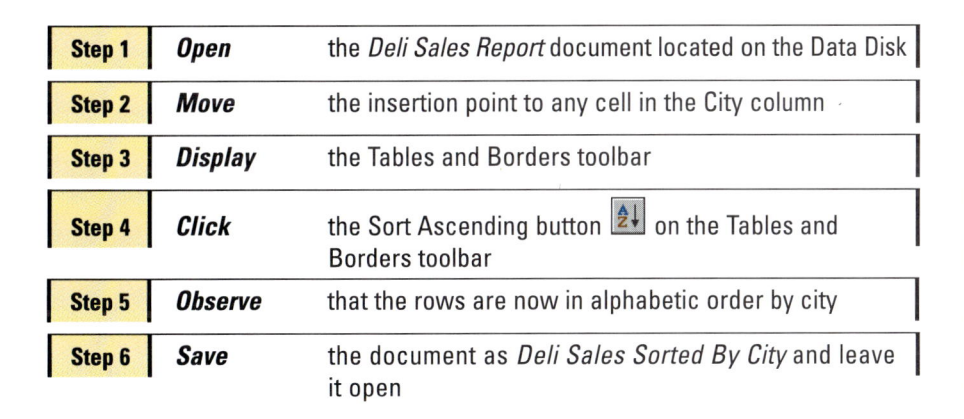

Step 1	Open	the *Deli Sales Report* document located on the Data Disk
Step 2	Move	the insertion point to any cell in the City column
Step 3	Display	the Tables and Borders toolbar
Step 4	Click	the Sort Ascending button on the Tables and Borders toolbar
Step 5	Observe	that the rows are now in alphabetic order by city
Step 6	Save	the document as *Deli Sales Sorted By City* and leave it open

To sort the Bread column in descending order:

Step 1	Move	the insertion point to any cell in the Bread column
Step 2	Click	the Sort Descending button on the Tables and Borders toolbar
Step 3	Observe	that the rows are now rearranged in descending order by the values in the Bread column
Step 4	Save	the document as *Deli Sales Sorted By Bread Value* and leave it open

If you want to sort by more than one table column, you need to use the Sort dialog box. The Sort dialog box opens when working in a table but it contains the same set of options as the Sort Text dialog box you used to sort dates, lists, and paragraphs. To return the table to its original order by using the Sort dialog box:

| Step 1 | Click | T<u>a</u>ble |

QUICK TIP

Word does not include header rows when sorting a table.

chapter nineteen

Step 2	*Click*	Sort
Step 3	*Click*	the Sort by list arrow to display a list of field names (column headings)
Step 4	*Click*	#, if necessary
Step 5	*Click*	the Ascending option button, if necessary
Step 6	*Click*	OK
Step 7	*Observe*	that the table returns to its original order
Step 8	*Close*	the document without saving any changes
Step 9	*Close*	the Tables and Borders toolbar

Sometimes you need to rearrange columns of unrelated data maintained in a table.

Sorting an Individual Table Column

Occasionally, unrelated data is maintained in a table. When you need to rearrange that data, you can sort individual table columns without rearranging the data in the remaining columns; to do that, you first select the individual column and then set the sort options.

The Sales Department receptionist keeps a short reference document that contains the names of new distributors, a list of available discounts, and the names of branch office sales representatives in a table. Each column of the table is not related to the other columns. For easier reference, she would like the discount rates arranged numerically in descending order. To open the *Distributors Reference* document and rearrange the discount column data:

Step 1	*Open*	the *Distributors Reference* document located on the Data Disk
Step 2	*Select*	the Discounts column
Step 3	*Open*	the Sort dialog box
Step 4	*Verify*	that Discounts is selected in the Sort by list and Number is selected in the Type: list
Step 5	*Click*	the Descending option button for the Discounts Number sort
Step 6	*Click*	Options to open the Sort Options dialog box
Step 7	*Click*	the Sort column only check box to insert a check mark, if necessary

Step 8	Click	OK twice to close both dialog boxes
Step 9	Deselect	the column
Step 10	Observe	that the Discounts column is now arranged in descending order and the other two columns are unchanged
Step 11	Save	the document as *Distributors Reference With Rearranged Discounts* and leave it open

The receptionist also would like to have each of the name columns rearranged in ascending alphabetical order.

Sorting Inside a Table Column

You can sort a table column when each cell contains multiple words separated by tabs, spaces, or other characters. The cells in the two name columns contain two words separated by a space. When you identify a separator character inside a column, Word defines multiple fields within the column. For example, the Distributors' Names column contains the first and last names of several distributors separated by a space. The column heading text, "Distributors' Names," is also separated by a space. When you specify a space as the separator character, Word defines two fields in the column: the "Distributors'" field and the "Names" field. You can then use the "Names" field to sort the column in ascending order by last name.

To sort the Distributors' Names column in ascending order by last name:

Step 1	Select	the Distributors' Names column
Step 2	Open	the Sort dialog box
Step 3	Click	the Ascending option button, if necessary
Step 4	Click	Options
Step 5	Click	the Other: option button in the Sort Options dialog box, if necessary
Step 6	Key	a space in the Other: text box
Step 7	Click	the Sort column only check box to insert a check mark, if necessary
Step 8	Click	OK

Now you must tell Word which field in the Distributors' Names column to use.

Step 9	Click	the Using: list arrow for the Sort by group in the Sort dialog box
Step 10	Click	Names (the last name field)
Step 11	Click	OK
Step 12	Observe	that the Distributors' Names column is rearranged in ascending order by last name

The Reps' Names column contains first and last names and column heading text separated by a space. You can rearrange this column just as you did the Distributor's Names column. To rearrange the Reps' Names column in ascending order by last name:

Step 1	Select	the Reps' Names column
Step 2	Open	the Sort dialog box
Step 3	Click	the Ascending option button, if necessary
Step 4	Click	Options
Step 5	Click	the Other: option button in the Sort Options dialog box
Step 6	Key	a space in the Other: text box, if necessary
Step 7	Click	the Sort column only check box to insert a check mark, if necessary
Step 8	Click	OK

Now you must tell Word which field in the Reps' Names column to use.

Step 9	Click	the Using: list arrow for the Sort by group
Step 10	Click	Names (the last name field)
Step 11	Click	OK
Step 12	Observe	that the Reps' Names column is rearranged in ascending order by last name
Step 13	Deselect	the column
Step 14	Save	the document as *Rearranged Distributors Reference* and close it

It's easy to quickly rearrange dates or text in a list, text paragraphs, or data in a table.

QUICK TIP

Records in a Word table document data source can be arranged chronologically, alphabetically, or numerically in ascending or descending order based on the information in the data fields selected for sorting. Other data source records—such as Outlook Contacts, an Excel worksheet, or an Access database table or query—can be sorted using the sort tools available in the source application.

You can also sort data records to be merged with the sort buttons in the Mail Merge Recipients dialog box.

Summary

- You can sort dates separated by a forward slash, a comma, a period, or a hyphen.
- When you sort a numbered list that was created with the numbering feature, the list is automatically renumbered.
- Text can be sorted alphabetically, numerically, or chronologically, using up to three criteria at one time.
- You can sort a selected portion of a list.
- An alternative to using cut-and-paste to rearrange paragraphs in a document is to number the paragraphs, sort them, and then delete the numbers.
- You can sort records in a Word table with menu commands or with buttons on the Database or Tables and Borders toolbar.
- You can sort a single-table column and you can sort multiple words within a single column.

Commands Review

Action	Menu Bar	Shortcut Menu	Toolbar	Task Pane	Keyboard
Sort a numbered list, text in columns, paragraphs, or a table	Table, Sort		↓↑		ALT + A, S

chapter nineteen

Concepts Review

Circle the correct answer.

1. Word can automatically:
   - [a] select sort criteria.
   - [b] format a sorted list.
   - [c] renumber a sorted list.
   - [d] arrange table text.

2. Columns to be sorted are called:
   - [a] rows.
   - [b] a data source.
   - [c] fields.
   - [d] date separators.

3. Which of the following is an incorrect sorting rule?
   - [a] Word first sorts text that begins with punctuation marks or symbols.
   - [b] Word ignores case in a sort.
   - [c] Word looks at subsequent characters when two items of text begin with the same character.
   - [d] Word sorts letters before numbers.

4. To sort body paragraphs in a specific order, you can:
   - [a] cut and paste them.
   - [b] add a number indicating the sort order before the paragraphs and then sort them.
   - [c] select the paragraphs and then sort them alphabetically.
   - [d] insert tab characters in the paragraphs and sort them.

5. Which of the following characters is not a valid date separator?
   - [a] period
   - [b] semicolon
   - [c] forward slash
   - [d] hyphen

6. Data in tables can be sorted with buttons on the:
   - [a] Merge toolbar.
   - [b] Formatting toolbar.
   - [c] Standard toolbar.
   - [d] Tables and Borders toolbar.

7. When sorting table columns that contain multiple words, you must specify the:
   - [a] font.
   - [b] line spacing.
   - [c] separator character.
   - [d] margins.

8. To sort an individual column without disturbing the other columns in the list, you must first:
   - [a] format the column.
   - [b] select the column.
   - [c] specify a separator character.
   - [d] number the rows.

9. In a multilevel sort, you select the:
   - [a] primary, secondary, and tertiary fields.
   - [b] first, intermediate, and last fields.
   - [c] beginning, secondary, and final fields.
   - [d] starting, middle, and ending fields.

10. Information entered in one order might be more useful later when it is:
    - [a] requested by your manager.
    - [b] formatted.
    - [c] organized in a different order.
    - [d] stored on floppy disks.

Circle **T** if the statement is true or **F** if the statement is false.

T F 1. You can only sort numbered lists and text in columns separated by tab characters.

T F 2. When two items of text begin with the same character, Word looks at subsequent characters to determine which item is listed first.

T F 3. Numbers can be added to the beginning of a paragraph to sort paragraphs in a specific order.

T F 4. Ascending order is A–Z and 0–9.

T F 5. Numbers are sorted after letters.

T F 6. A sort can have a maximum of three criteria (fields) at one time.

T F 7. When you sort a table, the header row is also sorted.

T F 8. You can sort a portion of a list.

T F 9. The primary field is the least important sort criterion.

T F 10. A date separator is the character used to separate month, day, and year.

Skills Review

Exercise 1

1. Open the *Anniversary Dates* document located on the Data Disk.

2. Sort the employee name and date list in descending order by anniversary date.

3. Save the document as *Anniversary Dates Revised*, and then preview, print, and close it.

Exercise 2

1. Open the *Chicago Warehouses Audit* document located on the Data Disk.

2. Number the three possible causes paragraphs 3, 1, and 2. (*Hint:* Place the number in front of the text for each bulleted item.)

3. Sort the numbered paragraphs in ascending order using the Sort Text dialog box.

4. Delete the numbers at the beginning of each paragraph.

5. Save the document as *Chicago Warehouses With Sorted List*, and then preview, print page one of the document, and close it.

Exercise 3

1. Open the *Fall Conference Data* data source document located on the Data Disk.

2. Display the Database toolbar.

3. Sort the table by company name in ascending order.

4. Save the document as *Fall Conference Data Sorted*, and then preview, print, and close it.

5. Close the Database toolbar.

chapter nineteen

Exercise 4

1. Open the *Spring Conference Data* data source document located on the Data Disk.

2. Sort the table by the Last field (last name) in the First Last column in ascending order. (*Hint:* Simply move the insertion point into the First Last column; do not select the entire column. Use the Show/Hide button to identify the separator character in the First Last column.)

3. Save the document as *Spring Conference Data Sorted*, and then preview, print, and close it.

Exercise 5

1. Open the *Monthly Sales Report* document located on the Data Disk.

2. Sort the list in ascending order by city within state.

3. Save the document as *Monthly Sales Report Sorted*, and then preview, print, and close it.

Exercise 6

1. Open the *Dividing Words* document located on the Data Disk.

2. Apply the Heading 1 style to the title "Dividing Words" and center it.

3. Number the body paragraphs 3, 7, 2, 1, 6, 5, and 4. (*Hint:* Turn on the view of formatting marks to see the paragraph marks.)

4. Sort the numbered paragraphs in ascending order.

5. Delete the numbers at the beginning of each body paragraph.

6. Space the body paragraphs 1.5 lines and add bullets, using the bullet style of your choice.

7. Save the document as *Dividing Words Sorted*, and then preview, print, and close it.

Exercise 7

1. Open the *Regional Deli Sales* document located on the Data Disk.

2. Convert the text to a four-column table and apply the Table Columns 3 style (AutoFormat) modified to remove the special formatting for the last row. The column separator is a hyphen or dash. AutoFit the table to its contents. (*Hint:* Use options in the Convert Text to Table dialog box to make all of these changes.)

3. Right-align the cells containing numbers and center the table between the left and right margins.

4. Display the Tables and Borders toolbar and sort the table in ascending order by region.

5. Save the document as *Regional Deli Sales Sorted*, and then preview, print, and close it.

6. Close the Tables and Borders toolbar.

Sorting Text and Tables **WA 131**

Exercise 8

1. Create the following document.

> Revised Sales Districts
>
> Texas
> New Mexico
> Minnesota
> New York
> California
> Alaska
> Washington
> Alabama

2. Apply the Heading 2 style to the title and center it.

3. Create a numbered list using the text beginning "Texas" and ending "Alabama."

4. Sort the numbered list an in ascending alphabetical order using the Sort Text dialog box.

5. Save the document as *Sales Districts Sorted*, and then preview, print, and close it.

Exercise 9

1. Open the *Reps Reference Sheet* document located on the Data Disk.

2. Sort the Reps' Names column individually in ascending order by last name.

3. Sort the Bonus Rates column in descending order.

4. Center the contents of the Bonus Rates column.

5. Insert a narrow, blank column between the Reps' Names and Bonus Rates columns.

6. Save the document as *Reps Reference Sheet Sorted*, and then preview, print, and close it.

Case Projects

Project 1

Bob Horseman, a clerical assistant in the Sales Department, created a document with a table that contains several columns of *unrelated* data. He wants to sort just one of the columns—leaving the other column data in its original order—and he asks for your help. Using the Ask A Question Box, review how to sort a single column in a table. Write Bob an interoffice memorandum explaining the process. Save, preview, and print the memorandum.

chapter nineteen

Project 2

The sales manager wants a list of the outside sales representatives and the number of customer calls each representative made during the previous month. Create a list containing three columns of information separated by tab characters. Include at least 15 sales representatives and key the first name in column 1, the last name in column 2, and the number of calls for the previous month in column 3. Use fictitious names and call data. Include at least two duplicate last names. Sort the list in an appropriate way. Key and format an appropriate title. Save, preview, and print the list.

Project 3

The sales manager wants the sales staff to become more familiar with the Web and how to use it to locate information. You are asked to prepare a 30-minute presentation on how to find information on the Web using search engines and directories. Create an outline of your presentation. Include a section describing the differences between directories and search engines. List at least ten search engines and directories in the outline and then sort the list in ascending alphabetical order. Save, preview, and print the outline. With your instructor's permission, use the outline as a guide to give your presentation.

Project 4

Beverly McDonald in the Sales Department wants to send a welcome letter to ten new distributors. Create a main document welcome letter. Create a Word table document data source with ten records. Use fictitious data for the welcome letter and the data source. In order to process the outgoing mail more efficiently, the mail room supervisor requests all multiple mailings be sorted in postal code order. Sort the Word table document data source in ascending order by ZIP code. Then merge the main document and the data source. Save, preview, and print all documents.

Project 5

The Human Resources manager requests a list of birth dates for everyone in the Sales Department. Create a list of at least ten employee names and birthdays using the mm/dd/yy format. Use different date separators in the list. Sort the list in ascending order by birth date. Save, preview, and print the list.

Project 6

David Wilson and Benica Washington, two clerical assistants in the Sales Department, are unfamiliar with sorting text in a Word document. Using the Ask A Question Box, research the rules for sorting text in a Word document. Create an interoffice memorandum to David and Benica describing the sorting rules. Save, preview, and print the memorandum.

Project 7

The Sales Department is sponsoring a softball game between Worldwide Exotic Foods, Inc. employees and several distributors' employees to raise money for a local children's hospital. The sales manager wants to give all participants a custom tee shirt and asks you to locate several companies that can create custom tee shirts. Connect to the Internet, and search the Web for companies that print and sell custom tee shirts. Save at least two Web pages. Write the sales manager an interoffice memorandum listing the companies and sorting their URLs in an appropriate way. Save, preview, and print the memorandum.

Project 8

Sarah Bradley, the Sales Department receptionist, created a list of ten bulleted product items and now needs to rearrange the items. She thinks cutting and pasting each item takes too much time and asks you if there is a quicker way to rearrange them. Write Sarah an interoffice memorandum explaining how to use numbered paragraphs to quickly rearrange items in a bulleted list. Save, preview, and print the memorandum.

Creating and Modifying Document References

Word 2002

Chapter Overview

Document references are a helpful way to insert additional information in your documents. In this chapter, you learn to insert bookmarks, create, revise, and delete footnotes and endnotes, create and use a cross-reference, and create a table of contents and an index. In addition, you use the Document Map to move quickly through a document.

Learning Objectives

- Insert bookmarks
- Create and modify footnotes and endnotes
- Create a cross-reference
- Create and modify a table of contents
- Create and modify an index
- Use the Document Map

Case profile

As secretary of the International Association of Executive Assistants, you spend several hours each week in the association office preparing correspondence, news releases, contributions to the newsletter, and library updates. You find it helpful to use document references, including bookmarks to quickly reference specific topics and footnotes or endnotes to identify the sources of quotations or facts you use in your documents.

chapter twenty 20

20.a Inserting Bookmarks

A **bookmark** is a reference point in a document that you identify by name. Bookmarks are helpful when you need an efficient way to locate text in a large document. A bookmark places hidden brackets around referenced text, which allows Word to quickly locate and select the text. You insert and remove bookmarks with the Boo<u>k</u>mark command on the <u>I</u>nsert menu.

You want to quickly reference individual chapter paragraphs in the *International Chapter News* document drafted earlier. To open the document and insert a bookmark around the Melbourne paragraphs:

Step 1	**Open**	the *International Chapter News* document located on the Data Disk
Step 2	**Select**	the two body paragraphs below the Melbourne paragraph heading
Step 3	**Click**	<u>I</u>nsert
Step 4	**Click**	Bookmark

> **CAUTION TIP**
> Bookmark names must begin with a letter and cannot contain spaces.

The Bookmark dialog box on your screen should look similar to Figure 20-1.

FIGURE 20-1
Bookmark Dialog Box

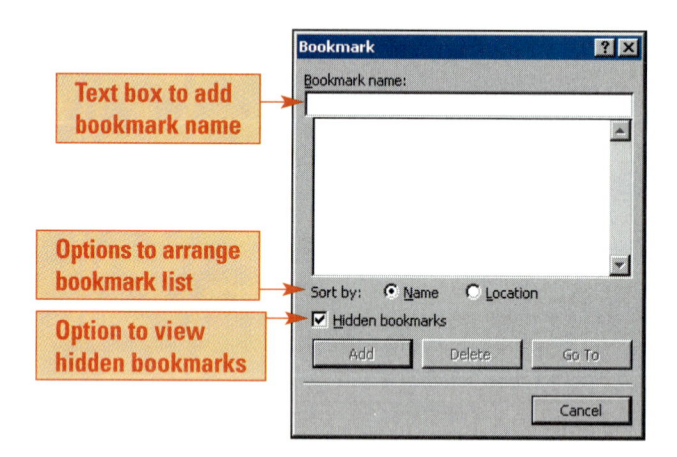

- Text box to add bookmark name
- Options to arrange bookmark list
- Option to view hidden bookmarks

You give the bookmark a name in this dialog box. If the document already contained other bookmarks, you would see them in the list box and could delete them or go to them from this dialog box.

Step 5	**Key**	Melbourne in the <u>B</u>ookmark name: text box
Step 6	**Click**	<u>A</u>dd
Step 7	**Deselect**	the text

You insert other bookmarks the same way. To add a bookmark for the London paragraphs:

| Step 1 | Select | the two London paragraphs |
| Step 2 | Create | a bookmark named "London" |

Now that the bookmarks are in place, you test them. You can go to the text associated with a bookmark with the Go To button in the Bookmark dialog box, or by using the Bookmark option on the Go To tab in the Find and Replace dialog box. To locate the Melbourne text:

Step 1	Double-click	the left side of the status bar (not on a mode indicator) to open the Go To tab in the Find and Replace dialog box
Step 2	Click	Bookmark in the Go to what: list box
Step 3	Select	Melbourne in the Enter bookmark name: list box
Step 4	Click	Go To
Step 5	Close	the Find and Replace dialog box
Step 6	Observe	that the text associated with the Melbourne bookmark is selected
Step 7	Deselect	the text
Step 8	Go To	the text associated with the London bookmark
Step 9	Close	the Find and Replace dialog box
Step 10	Deselect	the text
Step 11	Save	the document as *International Chapter News With Bookmarks* and leave it open

Another way to add references to a document is by using footnotes or endnotes.

20.b Creating and Modifying Footnotes and Endnotes

A **footnote** or **endnote** is supplemental text added to the bottom of a page or end of the document that allows you to identify sources of quotations, facts, and ideas used in the document. You can also use

QUICK TIP

You can turn on or off the view of nonprinting brackets that indicate a bookmark by using the Bookmarks check box on the View tab in the Options dialog box.

To delete a bookmark, open the Bookmark dialog box, select the bookmark, and click the Delete button.

QUICK TIP

In Normal view, Word opens a **note pane**—a separate text area where you key the note text inserts the note reference mark in the note pane, and moves the insertion point to the right of the note reference mark.

By default, Word inserts the footnote text at the bottom of the same page that contains the footnote reference mark. You also can insert the footnote text on the same page immediately below the document text.

---

footnotes or endnotes to insert incidental information that is not part of the document content. Footnotes appear at the bottom of the page that contains the text being noted and endnotes appear at the end of the document text or on a separate page at the end of the document. Each footnote or endnote is numbered consecutively. As you create, edit, add, or delete footnotes or endnotes, Word automatically updates the numbering to keep it sequential.

> **notes**
> This chapter illustrates how to use the Word footnote and endnote features. The formatting rules for footnotes and endnotes vary by the type of source being quoted. You can review the formatting rules for footnotes and endnotes in different style guides. See Appendix B "Formatting Tips for Business Documents" for additional information about style guides.

Inserting Footnotes

Word footnotes consist of a **note reference mark**, a number or symbol placed next to the referenced text and the corresponding note, and the note text. When you create a footnote, Word inserts the appropriately numbered note reference mark at the location of the insertion point. In Print Layout view, Word inserts the note reference mark at the position of the insertion point and at the bottom of the page and then moves the insertion point to the right of the note reference mark at the bottom of the page.

You want to add contact information to the *International Chapter News With Bookmarks* document and you decide to use footnotes. You insert the e-mail address for each association chapter as the contact information. To insert the Melbourne chapter e-mail address:

Step 1	*Move*	the insertion point after the text "Melbourne Chapter" on the second line of the first body paragraph
Step 2	*Switch to*	Print Layout view, if necessary
Step 3	*Click*	Insert
Step 4	*Point to*	Refere<u>n</u>ce
Step 5	*Click*	Foot<u>n</u>ote

Creating and Modifying Document References   **WA 137**

The Footnote and Endnote dialog box on your screen should look similar to Figure 20-2.

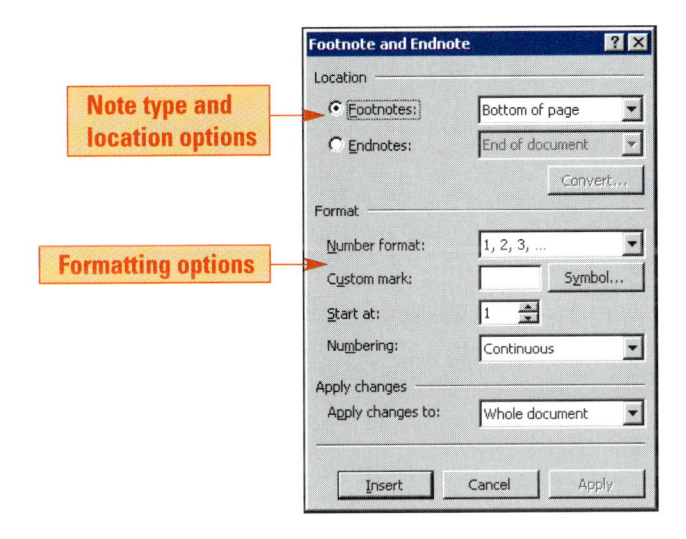

FIGURE 20-2
Footnote and Endnote Dialog Box

- Note type and location options
- Formatting options

You can specify the footnote location, the number format, and the starting number in this dialog box. By default, 1, 2, 3, ... is the automatic numbering format for footnotes. You want to place the footnotes at the bottom of the page using the default numbering format.

Step 6	Verify	that the Footnotes: option button is selected and the Footnotes: list box contains Bottom of page
Step 7	Verify	that the Number format: list box contains 1, 2, 3…
Step 8	Verify	that the Start at: number is 1
Step 9	Verify	that the Numbering: list box contains Continuous
Step 10	Verify	that the Apply changes to: list box contains Whole document
Step 11	Click	Insert
Step 12	Observe	the note separator line, the note reference mark, and the insertion point at the bottom of the page

Your screen should look similar to Figure 20-3.

- Footnote reference mark
- Footnote separator line
- Print Layout view

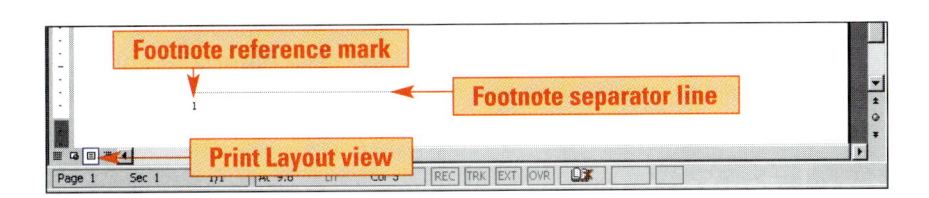

FIGURE 20-3
Note Separator and Note Reference Mark

chapter twenty

Quick Tip

To use a special symbol instead of numbers for the footnotes or endnotes reference marks, click in the Custom mark: text box in the Footnote and Endnote dialog box and then key the symbol you want or click the Symbol button and insert the desired symbol from the Symbol dialog box.

You can use different footnote or endnote numbering schemes in different sections of a document.

Menu Tip

You can open the note pane by clicking the Footnotes command on the View menu.

| Step 13 | Key | Melbourne Chapter e-mail address (melbourne@iaea.net) |

You repeat the same process to insert the footnote for the London chapter. Word automatically uses the next consecutive number. To insert the London e-mail address:

Step 1	Move	the insertion point after the text "London Chapter" on the first line of the third body paragraph
Step 2	Open	the Footnote and Endnote dialog box
Step 3	Click	Insert
Step 4	Key	London Chapter e-mail address (chic@iaea.net)
Step 5	Save	the document as *International Chapter News With Footnotes* and leave it open

You can view footnote text directly in the document in Print Layout view or Print Preview. You can also view the footnote text by moving the mouse pointer, which changes to a notepad-like icon, to the note reference mark to display a ScreenTip with the footnote text. To view the Melbourne Chapter footnote text:

| Step 1 | Move | the mouse pointer to the note reference mark after the text "Melbourne Chapter" |
| Step 2 | Observe | the shape of the mouse pointer and the footnote text in the ScreenTip |

Sometimes you need to edit, add, or delete footnotes.

Revising Footnote Text

After reviewing the London Chapter footnote text, you realize you keyed an incorrect e-mail address. You can edit the footnote in Print Layout view by scrolling to view the note text at the bottom of the page and then making the desired changes. If you are in Normal view, you can open the note pane and edit the text. You edit text in the note pane just as you do in the main document. All the formatting and editing features are available in the note pane.

You need to change the first part of the London e-mail address to "london." To switch to Normal view, open the note pane, and correct the error:

| Step 1 | Switch to | Normal view |

Step 2	Double-click	the note reference mark "2" following the text "London Chapter"
Step 3	Select	the text "chic" in the London Chapter footnote
Step 4	Key	london
Step 5	Close	the note pane
Step 6	Observe	the note text in a ScreenTip
Step 7	Save	the document and leave it open

Inserting Endnotes

To insert endnotes you follow the same process you use to insert footnotes, except you click the Endnote option button in the Footnote and Endnote dialog box. As you create, edit, add, or delete endnotes, Word revises the numbering automatically to keep it sequential. By default, Word uses i, ii, iii, … for endnote numbering.

Because you expect to add more international chapter news to the document, endnotes placed on a separate page at the end of the document are more appropriate. You can quickly convert the current footnotes to endnotes. To convert the footnotes to endnotes:

Step 1	Verify	that the document is in Normal view
Step 2	Open	the note pane
Step 3	Select	both footnotes
Step 4	Right-click	the selected footnotes
Step 5	Click	Convert to Endnote
Step 6	Observe	that the footnotes are now endnotes with the i, ii, iii numbering format

Your screen should look similar to Figure 20-4.

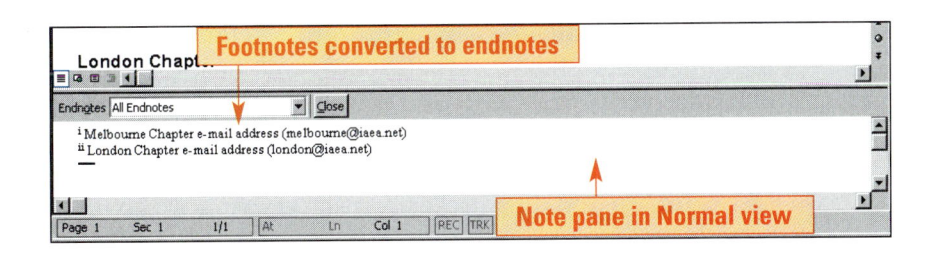

FIGURE 20-4
Footnotes Converted to Endnotes

QUICK TIP

Depending on the style guide you use, you might need to indent the first line from the left margin, or create a hanging indent so that all lines except the first line are indented from the left margin. To do this, switch to Print Layout view, select the footnotes, and use the First Line and Hanging Indent markers on the horizontal ruler to indent the lines as necessary.

MENU TIP

You can convert footnotes to endnotes or vice versa by opening the Footnote and Endnote dialog box, clicking the Convert button, and selecting a conversion option in the Convert Notes dialog box.

QUICK TIP

If you need to quickly find a particular footnote or endnote, you use the Go To tab in the Find and Replace dialog box, which contains options to move the insertion point to a particular footnote or endnote.

You can remove the separator line, if desired, by displaying the note pane, clicking Footnote Separator in the Footnotes list box, selecting the line, and pressing the DELETE key.

Step 7	Close	the note pane
Step 8	Observe	the new note reference marks in the document

Now that the footnotes are endnotes, you need to place them on their own page. To place the endnotes on a separate page at the end of the document:

Step 1	Insert	a manual page break immediately following the last sentence in the document
Step 2	Print Preview	the document in 1 × 2 Pages layout to see the endnotes on a separate page
Step 3	Close	Print Preview
Step 4	Save	the document as *International Chapter News With Endnotes* and close it

You can edit endnote text in the note pane the same way you edit footnote text. You can also edit a footnote or endnote in Print Layout view by scrolling to view it and then moving the insertion point into the note text. Move the insertion point back into the document body when you finish editing the note.

Another tool you can use to quickly locate text in a document is a cross-reference.

20.c Creating a Cross-Reference

When working with large documents that people read online, cross-reference hyperlinks help readers move quickly to related topics. You can create hyperlink cross-references for headings, bookmarks, footnotes, endnotes, tables, equations, figures, or numbered items. You can create a cross-reference to headings formatted with the built-in heading styles. Jody asks you to include a hyperlink cross-reference for the first instance of the text "Web pages" to the paragraph heading Loading Web Pages in the *Using the World Wide Web* document to be distributed to chapter members via e-mail. All the paragraph headings in the document are formatted with the Heading 3 style.

To open the document and then create a cross-reference to the Loading Web Pages paragraph heading:

Step 1	Open	the *Using the World Wide Web* document located on the Data Disk

Step 2	Move	the insertion point to the end of the last sentence in the first body text paragraph ending "…Web pages."
Step 3	Press	the SPACEBAR
Step 4	Key	For more information, see
Step 5	Press	the SPACEBAR

Now you create a cross-reference at this location to the Loading Web Pages paragraph heading. To create the hyperlink cross-reference:

Step 1	Click	Insert
Step 2	Point to	Reference
Step 3	Click	Cross-reference

The Cross-reference dialog box on your screen should look similar to Figure 20-5.

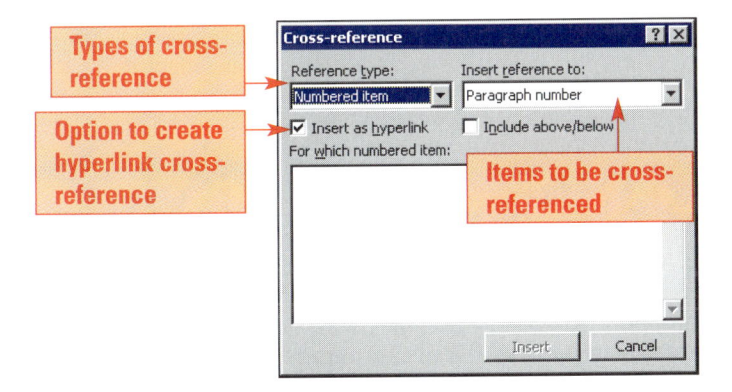

QUICK TIP

If you are not using the built-in heading styles, you can create a hidden bookmark at the appropriate paragraph heading and then create a cross-reference to that bookmark. A **hidden bookmark** creates a reference point that is not visible in the document.

FIGURE 20-5
Cross-reference Dialog Box

You select the reference type and to what the cross-reference refers in this dialog box. For example, if you create a cross-reference to a heading formatted with the built-in heading styles, you select Heading in the Reference type: list and Heading text appears in the Insert reference to: list box. A list of all the formatted headings appears in the For which heading: list box. You then select the heading to which the cross-reference refers.

Step 4	Click	Heading in the Reference type: list
Step 5	Verify	that Heading text appears in the Insert reference to: list box
Step 6	Click	Loading Web Pages in the For which heading: list
Step 7	Click	Insert

QUICK TIP

Word inserts cross-references as fields. When you edit, delete, or move an item referred to in a cross-reference you must update the cross-reference field by selecting the cross-reference, right-clicking it, and clicking Update Field or pressing the F9 key. To update all the cross-references in the document, first select the entire document.

Step 8	*Close*	the dialog box
Step 9	*Observe*	that the text "Loading Web Pages" is added to the sentence as a hyperlink that is not underlined or colored
Step 10	*Key*	a period (.) following the Loading Web Pages link text

You decide to try the link to ensure it works properly. To test the hyperlink cross-reference:

Step 1	*Move*	the I-beam mouse pointer to the hyperlink
Step 2	*Observe*	the ScreenTip advising that you can use the CTRL + Click method to follow the link
Step 3	*Press & hold*	the CTRL key
Step 4	*Observe*	that the mouse pointer becomes a pointing hand, indicating a hyperlink
Step 5	*Click*	the Loading Web Pages hyperlink
Step 6	*Observe*	that the insertion point moves to the Loading Web Pages paragraph heading
Step 7	*Save*	the document as *Loading Web Pages* and close it

20.d Creating and Modifying a Table of Contents

A **table of contents** is a sequential list of the names and page numbers of each chapter's heading and section subheadings. It appears at the front of large reports or books, such as this one. You can list several levels of subsections and their corresponding page numbers in the table of contents, depending on the level of detail you want to maintain.

Identifying Table of Contents Entries with Heading Styles

The Table of Contents feature creates a table of contents automatically based on paragraphs you format with styles. When using Word built-in heading styles, the "Heading 1" style creates a first-level table of contents entry, the "Heading 2" style creates a second-level table of contents entry, and so on through nine heading levels. If you create and format your document headings with custom styles, then you can specify which heading style to use for each level in the table of contents.

Creating and Modifying Document References **WA 143**

Jody asks you to prepare the *Using the World Wide Web* document to be printed and distributed in a binder at the next chapter meeting. She asks you to create a table of contents for the document. You create a table of contents for this document by first identifying the paragraph headings to be included in the table of contents. Generally, you place the table of contents on a separate page at the beginning of the document. To open the document and create a new first page for the table of contents:

Step 1	Open	the *Using the World Wide Web* document located on the Data Disk
Step 2	Insert	a page break above the "Using the World Wide Web" title
Step 3	Move	the insertion point to the new page

Creating a Table of Contents

After you position the insertion point, you then insert a table of contents by clicking the Index and Tables subcommand under the Reference command on the Insert menu. To insert a table of contents:

Step 1	Click	Insert
Step 2	Point to	Reference
Step 3	Click	Index and Tables
Step 4	Click	the Table of Contents tab

The Index and Tables dialog box on your screen should look similar to Figure 20-6.

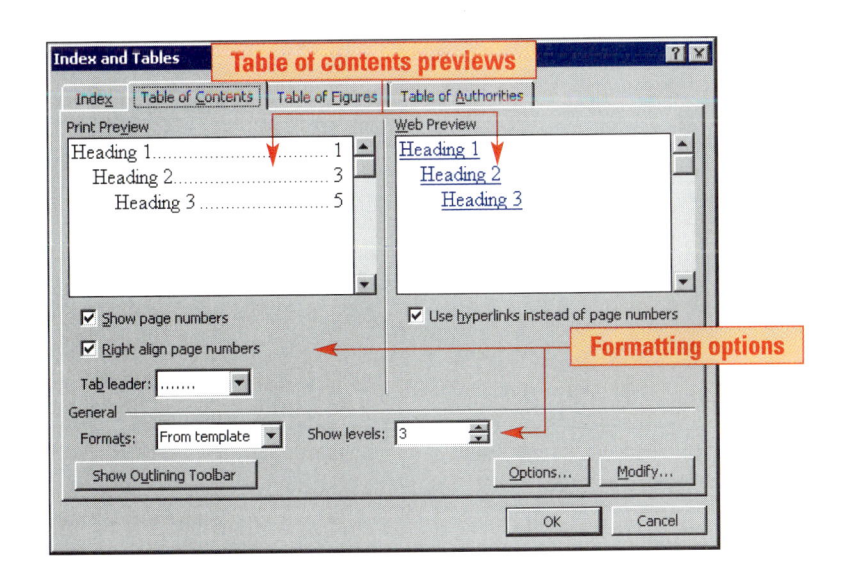

QUICK TIP

If your document contains manually formatted headings instead of styles, you can create a table of contents by first assigning an outline level to each heading in the Paragraph dialog box, or with the Outlining toolbar in Outline view. Then create the table of contents in the desired style with options in the Table of Contents tab in the Index and Tables dialog box.

FIGURE 20-6
Table of Contents Tab in the Index and Tables Dialog Box

chapter twenty

You specify the table of contents format in this dialog box. The Formats: list offers several built-in formats. To see how the various formats look, you can click a format in the Formats: list box and view a sample Table of Contents in the Print Preview or Web Preview box. The Tab leader: list box provides various tab leader options. You decide to use the Classic format with a dotted-line leader and right-aligned numbers.

Step 5	Click	Classic in the Formats: list
Step 6	Click	the Tab leader: list arrow
Step 7	Click	the first dotted-line option
Step 8	Verify	that the Show page numbers and Right align page numbers check boxes contain check marks
Step 9	Click	OK
Step 10	Move	the insertion point to the top of the document
Step 11	Observe	the table of contents
Step 12	Save	the document as *Using the World Wide Web With Classic TOC* and leave it open

You can view specific text in the document by clicking a table of contents entry.

Using a Table of Contents to View Specific Text

The table of contents entries are linked to the referenced paragraph headings in the document. You can use the CTRL + Click method to view the details for any entry on the table of contents. To view a specific paragraph:

Step 1	Move	the I-beam mouse pointer to the Internet Service Providers table of contents entry
Step 2	Observe	the ScreenTip
Step 3	Press & hold	the CTRL key
Step 4	Observe	that the mouse pointer becomes a pointing hand, indicating a hyperlink

| Step 5 | Click | the Internet Service Providers table of contents entry |
| Step 6 | Observe | that the insertion point moves immediately to the Internet Service Providers paragraph heading |

You can add or remove table of contents entries and then update the table.

Modifying a Table of Contents

You can modify the table of contents by modifying the styles used to identify each level of the table or by adding or deleting paragraph headings and then updating the table of contents. You update a table of contents by moving the insertion point to the table and pressing the F9 key.

After reviewing the document, Jody asks you to remove the "Internet Addresses" paragraph heading and then update the table of contents. To remove the heading and update the table of contents:

Step 1	Delete	the "Internet Addresses" paragraph heading near the bottom of page 3
Step 2	Click	in the selection bar to the left of the first table of contents entry "Using the World Wide Web" to select the table of contents
Step 3	Press	the F9 key to update the table of contents
Step 4	Observe	that the table of contents no longer contains the Internet Addresses entry

You can format the table of contents entries by first selecting the entries and then applying the formatting. Because the table of contents is short, you want to double-space it so that it is more attractive on the page. To select and double-space the table of contents:

Step 1	Verify	that the table of contents is still selected
Step 2	Double-space	the table of contents using the Formatting toolbar
Step 3	Deselect	the table of contents

Your screen should look similar to Figure 20-7.

> **QUICK TIP**
>
> You can create a **table of authorities** for legal documents by marking the citations in a legal document and then creating a table of the citations using the Table of Authorities tab in the Index and Tables dialog box. A **table of figures** is a list of the tables, graphs, or pictures in a document. You can use either captions or custom styles to create a table of figures. For more information on creating a table of figures or table of authorities, see online Help.

chapter twenty

FIGURE 20-7
Updated Table of Contents

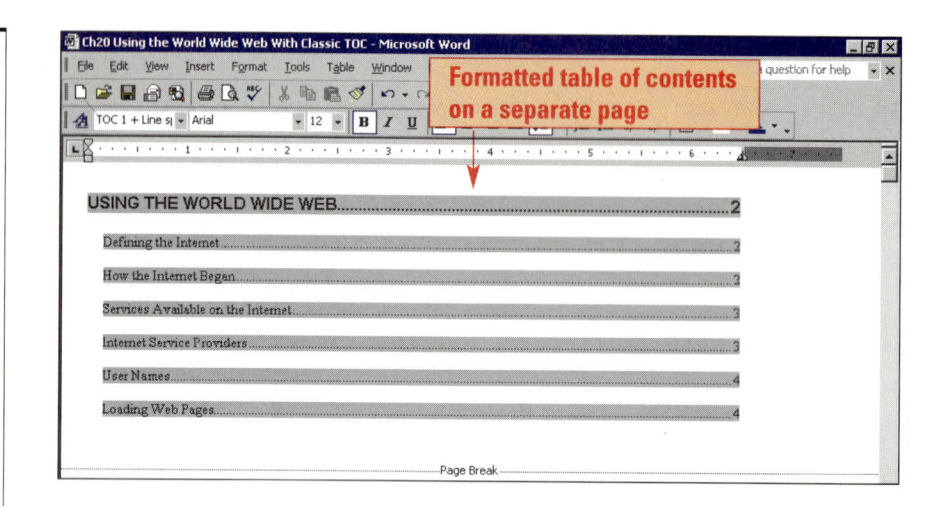

[Screenshot: Ch20 Using the World Wide Web With Classic TOC - Microsoft Word, showing formatted table of contents on a separate page with entries: USING THE WORLD WIDE WEB...2, Defining the Internet...3, How the Internet Began...3, Services Available on the Internet...3, Internet Service Providers...3, User Names...4, Loading Web Pages...4]

Formatted table of contents on a separate page

Step 4 **Save** the document and leave it open

20.e Creating and Modifying an Index

An **index** is an alphabetical list of key words and phrases matched to page numbers. It appears at the back of a long report or book, such as this one. You can create an index entry for a specific word, phrase, or symbol. You can also create a page range index entry for a topic that covers several pages or a cross-reference index entry that refers to another index entry.

Creating an Index

To create an index entry, you first select a word, phrase, or symbol and then mark it as an index entry. Index entries are case-sensitive and text is marked for the index only when the case and spelling match exactly. You can mark a single instance of a word, phrase, or symbol or all instances in the document.

Jody asks you to include the terms "TCP/IP," "Internet Service Provider," "Internet address," and "Uniform Resource Locator" as main index entries in the *Using the World Wide Web With Classic TOC* document. You also can create index subentries that appear under a top-level index heading. You want to include "ISP" as a subentry under Internet Service Provider, "IP address" as a subentry under Internet address, and "URL" as a subentry under Uniform Resource Locator.

> **notes**
>
> For the index activities, use the Find and Replace dialog box to search from the top of the document text (not the table of contents) for the words or phrases to index. Leave the dialog box open until instructed to close it.

To mark the text "TCP/IP" for the index:

Step 1	Move	the insertion point to the top of the document text (page 2 below the table of contents page)
Step 2	Turn on	the view of nonprinting characters
Step 3	Open	the Find and Replace dialog box
Step 4	Find	the first instance of the text "TCP/IP"
Step 5	Click	Insert
Step 6	Point to	Reference
Step 7	Click	Index and Tables
Step 8	Click	the Index tab, if necessary
Step 9	Click	Mark Entry

The Mark Index Entry dialog box on your screen should look similar to Figure 20-8.

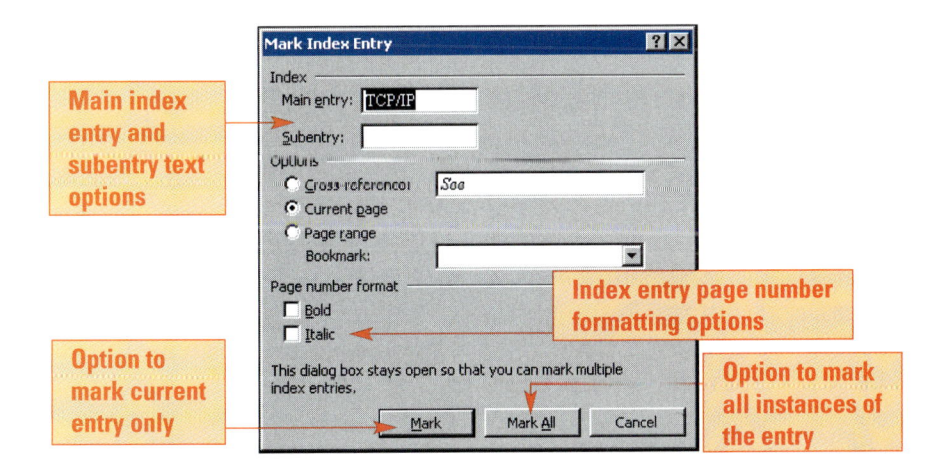

FIGURE 20-8
Mark Index Entry Dialog Box

- Main index entry and subentry text options
- Index entry page number formatting options
- Option to mark current entry only
- Option to mark all instances of the entry

The selected text appears in the Main entry: text box. You can specify the format for the page number of the index entry by inserting a check mark in the Bold or Italic check box. Use the Mark button to mark the selected index entry for the current page only. Use the Mark All button

chapter twenty

QUICK TIP

You can mark an index entry for a range of pages. First, select the text you want referenced in the index and create a bookmark with the selected text. Then open the Mark Index Entry dialog box, click the Page range option button, select the bookmark from the Bookmark: list, and click the OK button.

You also can mark a cross-reference index entry. First, select the text you want to use as the index entry, then open the Mark Index Entry dialog box, click the Cross-reference option button, key the cross-reference text in the Cross-reference text box, and click the OK button.

---

to mark the first occurrence of the index entry in each paragraph. To mark all instances of the word "TCP/IP" for the index:

Step 10	Click	Mark All
Step 11	Leave	the Mark Index Entry dialog box open until instructed to close it

notes You continue to mark the index entries by first locating them with the Find and Replace dialog box and then marking them in the Mark Index Entry dialog box. Rearrange the dialog boxes on your screen as needed and work between the two open dialog boxes.

All instances of the text "TCP/IP" are identified as index entries with the field code { XE "TCP/IP" }. You can see these field codes with the view of formatting marks turned on. You want to add the phrases Internet Service Provider, Internet address, and Uniform Resource Locator to the index. To add the remaining main index entries:

Step 1	Find	the phrase "Internet Service Provider" in the text (not in the table of contents or paragraph heading)
Step 2	Mark	all instances for the index
Step 3	Find	the phrase "Internet address" in the text (not in the table of contents or paragraph headings)
Step 4	Mark	all instances for the index
Step 5	Find	the phrase "Uniform Resource Locator" in the text (not in the table of contents or paragraph headings)
Step 6	Mark	all instances for the index

In addition to the previous phrases, you want to mark the text "ISP," "IP," and "URL" as subentries to Internet Service Provider, Internet address, and Uniform Resource Locator respectively. To do this, you must select the text and create a subentry index entry. To create the ISP subentry to Internet Service Providers:

Step 1	Find	the first instance of the text "ISP"
Step 2	Key	Internet Service Provider in the Main entry: text box
Step 3	Key	ISP in the Subentry: text box
Step 4	Mark	all instances for the index

Creating and Modifying Document References   WA 149

To create the remaining subentries:

Step 1	Find	the phrase "IP address"
Step 2	Create	an index subentry for the text "IP address" for the main entry "Internet address"
Step 3	Mark	all instances for the index
Step 4	Find	the phrase "URL"
Step 5	Create	an index subentry for the text "URL" for the main entry "Uniform Resource Locator"
Step 6	Mark	all instances for the index
Step 7	Close	the Mark Index Entry and Find and Replace dialog boxes

After all the index entries are marked, you then compile the index page.

Compiling an Index

After you have identified the index text, you specify where to place the index in the document, usually starting on a separate page at the end of a document. To insert an index at the end of the document:

Step 1	Move	the insertion point to the end of the document
Step 2	Turn off	the view of formatting marks
Step 3	Insert	a page break
Step 4	Key	Index
Step 5	Format	the word "Index" with the Heading 3 style
Step 6	Insert	two blank lines below the word "Index"
Step 7	Open	the Index tab in the Index and Tables dialog box

You specify the index format in this dialog box. The Formats: list box offers different appearance options. You can see how a format looks by clicking a format in the Formats: list and observing the sample Index in the Print Preview box. By default, all format appearances display the index text in two columns. You can change the number of columns by entering a different number in the Columns: text box.

You create the index in Classic format.

CAUTION TIP

You should compile the index with the formatting marks turned off. Although the hidden text won't print, it can affect pagination onscreen and cause incorrect page entries.

QUICK TIP

The AutoMark button on the Index tab in the Index and Tables dialog box allows you to open a concordance file that identifies specific words to use in an index. For more information about using a concordance file, see online Help.

chapter twenty

Step 8	*Click*	Classic in the Formats: list box, if necessary
Step 9	*Click*	OK

The index entries on your screen should look similar to Figure 20-9.

FIGURE 20-9
Index Entries

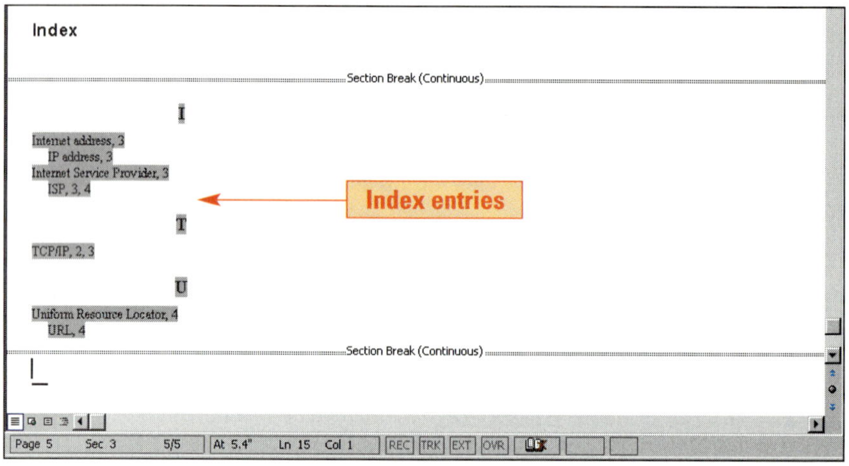
Index
Section Break (Continuous)
I
Internet address, 3
IP address, 3
Internet Service Provider, 3
ISP, 3, 4
Index entries
T
TCP/IP, 2, 3
U
Uniform Resource Locator, 4
URL, 4
Section Break (Continuous)
Page 5 Sec 3 5/5 At 5.4" Ln 15 Col 1 REC TRK EXT OVR

QUICK TIP

In Print Layout view, Word displays the index entries in two columns (the default format).

Step 10	*Save*	the document as *Using the World Wide Web With Classic Index* and leave it open

You can edit or delete an index entry after the index page is created.

Modifying an Index

CAUTION TIP

If you modify index entries in the compiled index pages, your modifications are lost the next time you update the index. Make your editing, formatting, or deleting modifications to the index fields in the document to assure the updated index is correct.

Although compiling an index should be one of the last tasks you perform in your document, you can revise it later if necessary. You can mark additional words or phrases as index entries and then update the index by selecting the index and pressing the F9 key. Because Word inserts index entries into a document as an index field, you edit, format, or delete index entries by modifying the field contents or deleting the field; then you update the index page with the F9 key.

To view the index fields:

Step 1	*Turn on*	the view of formatting marks
Step 2	*Scroll*	the document to see the XE (Index Entry) fields adjacent to the indexed text in the document
Step 3	*Move*	the insertion point to the top of page 2

Jody decides that the TCP/IP index entry doesn't need to be in your index. To delete the TCP/IP index entry:

Step 1	*Select*	the index field { XE "TCP/IP" } (including the brackets) located on page 2
Step 2	*Press*	the DELETE key
Step 3	*Select*	the second index field { XE "TCP/IP" } (including the brackets) located on page 3
Step 4	*Press*	the DELETE key
Step 5	*Turn off*	the view of formatting marks

Now that you've deleted all the TCP/IP entries you need to update the index to remove the listing in the index. To update the index:

Step 1	*Select*	the index entries at the end of the document
Step 2	*Press*	the F9 key to update the index
Step 3	*Observe*	the TCP/IP entries under the "T" heading are removed

To finish the document, you need to update the table of contents to include the Index. To update the table of contents:

Step 1	*Select*	the table of contents
Step 2	*Press*	the F9 key
Step 3	*Click*	the Update entire table option button in the Update Table of Contents dialog box
Step 4	*Click*	OK
Step 5	*Observe*	the new Index entry in the table of contents
Step 6	*Double-space*	the table of contents
Step 7	*Save*	the document and close it

One way to navigate a document you're reading online is to use the Document Map.

chapter twenty

20.f Using the Document Map

MENU TIP

You can view the Document Map by clicking the Document Map command on the View menu.

The **Document Map** feature helps you move the insertion point quickly to different paragraphs in a large document. When you turn on the Document Map your screen splits into two panes: the left pane contains the Document Map with a list of paragraph headings and the right pane contains the document text. When you click a heading in the Document Map, the insertion point moves to that paragraph heading in the document text in the right pane. To be recognized by the Document Map feature, the paragraph headings must be formatted with a built-in heading style (Heading 1 through 9) or an outline-level format using the Paragraph dialog box or the Outline Level button on the Outline toolbar.

Jody asks you to check out the Document Map for the *Loading Web Pages* document you created earlier. To open the document and view the Document Map:

MOUSE TIP

You can choose to view different levels of detail in the Document Map by right-clicking the Document Map to view the shortcut menu and then clicking the Heading level you want to see.

Step 1	Open	the *Loading Web Pages* document you created earlier in this chapter
Step 2	Click	the Document Map button on the Standard toolbar
Step 3	Observe	the Document Map with headings in the left pane and the document text in the right pane

Your screen should look similar to Figure 20-10.

FIGURE 20-10
Loading Web Pages Document Map

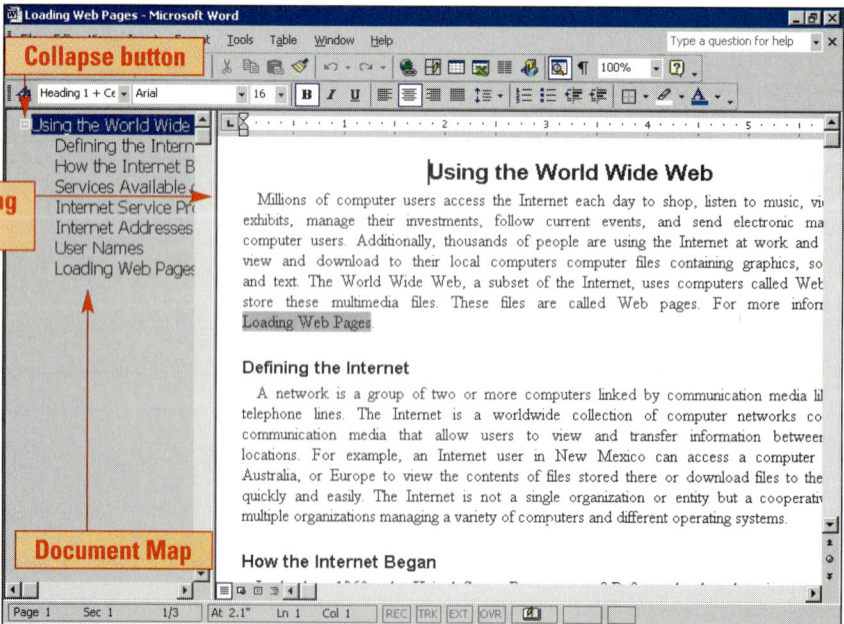

You can expand or collapse the view of paragraph headings in the Document Map. If the Heading 3 paragraph headings do not appear in the Document Map, you can display them. To expand or collapse the view of the paragraph headings in the Document Map:

Step 1	*Right-click*	the Document Map
Step 2	*Observe*	the Expand/Collapse/Show options on the shortcut menu
Step 3	*Click*	Show Heading 1
Step 4	*Observe*	that the Document Map now shows only the title paragraph formatted with the Heading 1 style

To show all the paragraph headings:

| Step 1 | *Right-click* | the Document Map |
| Step 2 | *Click* | All |

You can click any item in the Document Map to move quickly to that location in the document. To move the insertion point to the Internet Service Providers paragraph:

Step 1	*Move*	the mouse pointer to the partially hidden Internet Service Providers heading in the Document Map
Step 2	*Observe*	the ScreenTip containing the complete heading text
Step 3	*Click*	the Internet Service Providers heading in the Document Map
Step 4	*Observe*	that the insertion point moves to the Internet Service Providers paragraph heading in the right pane

To close the Document Map and the document:

| Step 1 | *Click* | the Document Map button on the Standard toolbar |
| Step 2 | *Close* | the document without saving any changes |

The helpfulness of the Document Map becomes even clearer when you work with a very long document.

> **QUICK TIP**
>
> You can also expand or collapse the view of the paragraph headings in the Document Map with the Expand (+) or Collapse (-) buttons in the Document Map.
>
> You can size the Document Map by dragging its right border to the right or left with the mouse pointer.

chapter twenty

Summary

- Bookmarks are an efficient way to mark and then locate specific text in a large document.
- Creating footnotes and endnotes allows you to document sources of quotations, facts, and ideas used in a report.
- Word automatically numbers footnotes and endnotes as you create them and renumbers them sequentially as you add or remove them.
- You can create, view, and edit footnotes or endnotes in the note pane in Normal view or directly in the document in Print Layout view.
- Footnotes can be deleted or converted to endnotes; endnotes can be deleted or converted to footnotes.
- You can insert a hyperlink cross-reference to help online readers move quickly to related topics.
- You can create a table of contents by first formatting paragraph or topic headings with styles or outline level formats and then inserting the table of contents usually on a separate page at the top of the document.
- You can mark text to be included in an index and then compile that index on a separate page, usually at the end of the document.
- The Document Map quickly locates specific paragraph headings in a document.

Commands Review

Action	Menu Bar	Shortcut Menu	Toolbar	Task Pane	Keyboard
Insert a bookmark	Insert, Bookmark				ALT + I, K
Create a footnote	Insert, Reference, Footnote				ALT + I, N, N ALT + CTRL + F
Create an endnote	Insert, Reference, Footnote				ALT + I, N, N ALT + CTRL + D
Move the insertion point to a specific footnote, endnote, bookmark, or comment	Edit, Go To				ALT + E, G CTRL + G F5
View the note pane	View, Footnotes				ALT + V, F
Create a cross-reference	Insert, Reference, Cross-reference				ALT + I, N, R
Insert a table of contents	Insert, Reference, Index and Tables				ALT + I, N, D

Creating and Modifying Document References   **WA 155**

Action	Menu Bar	Shortcut Menu	Toolbar	Task Pane	Keyboard
Mark a table of contents entry					ALT + SHIFT + O
Insert an index	Insert, Reference, Index and Tables				ALT + I, N, D
Mark an index entry					ALT + SHIFT + X
Update a table of contents or an index		Right-click selected table of contents or index, Update Field			F9
Open the Document Map	View, Document Map		🔍		ALT + V, D

Concepts Review

Circle the correct answer.

1. **You create a bookmark with the:**
   - [a] Insert command on the File menu.
   - [b] Bookmark command on the Insert menu.
   - [c] Insert command on the Format menu.
   - [d] Bookmark command on the Edit menu.

2. **A bookmark is:**
   - [a] hidden text that does not affect document text.
   - [b] a quick way to find and select specific text.
   - [c] a method of documenting sources of quotations, facts, and ideas.
   - [d] viewed in the Document Map.

3. **In Normal view, footnotes and endnotes are edited in the:**
   - [a] note pane.
   - [b] Document Map.
   - [c] Bookmark dialog box.
   - [d] comment pane.

4. **Endnotes:**
   - [a] are inserted at the bottom of each page.
   - [b] show the user's initials in the reference mark.
   - [c] can be placed on a separate page at the end of the document.
   - [d] add hidden text to a document.

5. **To create a table of contents, paragraph headings must be formatted with:**
   - [a] bold or underline formatting.
   - [b] heading styles or outline-level paragraph formats.
   - [c] uppercase formatting.
   - [d] bookmarks.

6. **An index is a(n):**
   - [a] list of citations in a legal document.
   - [b] alphabetical list of keywords and phrases and related page numbers.
   - [c] hidden reference point in a document.
   - [d] number or symbol placed next to referenced text.

7. **To quickly open the note pane, you can:**
   - [a] double-click the note reference mark.
   - [b] drag the note reference mark to the bottom of the screen.
   - [c] click the Note View button on the Reviewing toolbar.
   - [d] double-click the NOTE mode indicator on the status bar.

8. **The Document Map allows you to:**
   - [a] display reviewer notes.
   - [b] highlight text.
   - [c] quickly find specific text.
   - [d] browse a document by paragraph headings.

chapter twenty

9. Footnotes and endnotes consist of the note text and a(n):
   [a] bookmark.
   [b] index entry.
   [c] table of contents entry.
   [d] reference mark.

10. Creating a table of contents involves:
    [a] defining where you want to place it in the document.
    [b] identifying the text that will appear in the table.
    [c] inserting the table.
    [d] creating a list of figures.

Circle **T** if the statement is true or **F** if the statement is false.

T F 1. Bookmarks are used to document sources of quotations, facts, and ideas in a report.

T F 2. Footnotes are listed at the end of the document on a separate page.

T F 3. Word automatically numbers footnotes and endnotes inserted in a document.

T F 4. If you decide to use endnotes instead of footnotes after the footnotes are created, you must delete the footnotes and then create the endnotes.

T F 5. You can see the actual footnote at the bottom of each page when viewing the document in Print Layout view.

T F 6. A cross-reference hyperlink can be created for text formatted with a heading style.

T F 7. You insert bookmarks to mark any heading paragraphs you want to include in a table of contents.

T F 8. By default, endnotes appear below the text on the same page as the endnote reference.

T F 9. Once you create an index, you cannot modify it.

T F 10. To quickly find a bookmark, comment, endnote, or footnote, you can use the Go To command on the Edit menu.

Skills Review

Exercise 1

1. Open *E-Commerce Today* document located on the Data Disk.
2. View the Document Map.
3. Collapse all headings to show only the Heading 1 heading.
4. Expand the headings to show the Heading 2 headings.
5. Expand the headings to show the Heading 3 headings.
6. Move the insertion point to the "E-Business Advantages and Disadvantages" paragraph in the text using the Document Map.
7. Move the insertion point to the "E-Commerce History" paragraph in the text using the Document Map.
8. Close the Document Map.
9. Close the document without saving any changes.

Exercise 2

1. Open the *Answering The Telephone* document located on the Data Disk.
2. Move the insertion point to the end of the document.
3. Insert the following footnote at the bottom of the page using the default numbering format. Indent the first line of the note.

   [1]John Spencer and Adrian Pruss, *The Professional Secretary's Handbook: Communication Skills* (New York: Barron's Educational Series, Inc., 1997), 63.

4. Insert a bookmark named "Promise" using the last sentence.
5. Go to the Promise bookmark.
6. Print the selection. (*Hint:* Open the Print dialog box.)
7. Save the document as *Answering The Telephone With Footnote*, and then preview, print, and close it.

Exercise 3

1. Open the *Answering The Telephone With Footnote* document you created in Exercise 2. If you have not created the document, do so now.
2. Convert the footnote to an endnote.
3. Place the endnote on a separate page at the end of the document.
4. Save the document as *Answering The Telephone With Endnote*.
5. Preview, print, and close the document.

Exercise 4

1. Open the *E-Commerce Today* document located on the Data Disk.
2. Move the insertion point to the end of the first body text paragraph.
3. Insert the text "For comparative definitions of E-Business and E-Commerce, see. "
4. Insert a hyperlink cross-reference to the paragraph heading "E-Commerce vs. E-Business."
5. Insert a period after the hyperlink cross-reference.
6. Test the cross-reference.
7. Save the document as *E-Commerce Today With Cross-Reference*, and then preview, print the first page, and close the document.

Exercise 5

1. Open the *E-Commerce Today With Cross-Reference* document you created in Exercise 4. If you have not created the document, do so now.
2. Insert a blank page at the top of the document and create a table of contents using the Distinctive Style and a dashed line leader.
3. Space the table of contents 1.5 lines.
4. Save the document as *E-Commerce Today With Distinctive TOC*, and then preview, print, and close it.

chapter twenty

Exercise 6

1. Open the *E-Commerce Today With Distinctive TOC* document you created in Exercise 5. If you have not created the document, do so now.
2. Delete the paragraph heading "E-Business Value Chains" and the following three paragraphs.
3. Update the table of contents and double-space it.
4. Save the document as *E-Commerce Today With Modified TOC*, and then preview the document, print the table of contents, and close the document.

Exercise 7

1. Open the *Impressions* document located on the Data Disk.
2. Place each paragraph heading and its following paragraph on a separate page. Double-space the document.
3. Display the Outlining toolbar and format the paragraph headings with the LEVEL 1 format.
4. Insert a next page section break at the top of the document to create a new page.
5. Create a table of contents on the new, blank page. Use the Classic format with dotted-line style tab leaders.
6. Insert a next page section break above the table of contents. Change all the margins for the new page to 1 inch.
7. Key the text "IMPRESSIONS" and format it with the Normal style, 24-point Times New Roman font.
8. Center the "IMPRESSIONS" text horizontally and vertically between the margins.
9. View the headers and footers, switch to the footer pane for Section 3, turn off the same as previous footers, insert a centered page number and format it to begin with number 1.
10. Update the table of contents with the new page numbers.
11. Save the document as *Revised Impressions*, and then preview, print, and close it.
12. Close the Outlining toolbar.

Exercise 8

1. Open the *Compensation Procedures* document located on the Data Disk.
2. Double-space the document.
3. Compile an index in the Classic format on a separate page at the end of the document using all instances of the following words. (*Hint:* Remember to match case when searching for and marking words.)

paycheck	commissions
overtime	Personnel Board
holiday	vacation
terminated	retirement

4. Save the document as *Compensation Procedures With Index*.
5. Print the index page.
6. Delete the retirement index item and update the index page.
7. Print the index page and close the document without saving any changes.

Exercise 9

1. Open the *Australia* document located on the Data Disk.
2. Apply the Heading 1 style to the uppercase paragraph headings and the Heading 2 style to the other paragraph headings.
3. Create a table of contents using the Fancy format. Place the table of contents on a separate page before the text.
4. Save the document as *Australia With TOC*.
5. Print the table of contents and close the document.

Case Projects

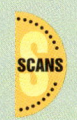

Project 1

The next monthly meeting of the International Association of Executive Assistants includes a 10-minute presentation on troubleshooting footnotes and endnotes. You prepare the outline for the presentation. Using the Ask A Question Box, research troubleshooting topics for footnotes and endnotes. Create an outline itemizing five troubleshooting topics, including possible solutions to the problem. Add a footnote reference to each topic, identifying the online Help page where the topic can be found. Save, preview, and print the outline.

Project 2

You are writing an article about document notations for the next International Association of Executive Assistants newsletter and want to include information about using style guides and documenting an online source. Using the keyword phrases "style guides" and "documenting online sources," search the Web for sites that describe style guides and how to document an online source. Print at least five Web pages. Using your Web sources, create an unbound report document describing several style guides and how to document an online source. Use footnotes or endnotes appropriately formatted for online sources to identify the sources of your information. Save, preview, and print the report.

Project 3

Before the next IAEA chapter meeting, you need to prepare a two- or three-paragraph report concerning a major Internet industry news topic that includes quotes from news sources. Using newspapers, magazines, and the Web, select a current news topic about the Internet and create an unbound report document discussing the topic. Add footnotes or endnotes referencing the source of any quotes, facts, or ideas used in the report including appropriately formatted online sources (refer to Project 2). Add an explanatory comment on any proper name used in the report. Save, preview, and print the report.

Project 4

Jody is having trouble with some of her bookmarks. She isn't getting the results she expects when she edits her bookmarks: an item that refers to a bookmark isn't being updated correctly, and she is getting the error message "Error! Reference source not found" in one document. She asks for your help. Using online Help, troubleshoot these bookmark problems. Then write Jody a memo describing each problem and suggesting a solution. Save, preview, and print the memo.

chapter twenty

Project 5

Although she often creates very large documents, Marisa DaFranco has never used the Document Map. You want to explain to her how easy it is to use. Open the large document of your choice and create and/or format paragraph headings with the Outline level: paragraph formats using the Outlining toolbar. Preview and then save the document with a new name. Use the Document Map to review the document. Write Marisa an interoffice memorandum explaining how to use the Document Map and include the document formatting requirements. Save, preview, and print the memorandum.

Project 6

You know that Word inserts brackets ([ ]) around bookmarked text but have never seen these brackets when working with a document that contains bookmarks. You think viewing the brackets could help identify bookmarked text and want to know how to view them. Use online Help to research how to show the brackets associated with bookmarks. Open a document of your choice, insert a bookmark, and then view the brackets. Turn off the view of the brackets and close the document without saving any changes. Create a Web page, using the theme of your choice, to describe how to create and use bookmarks. Include step-by-step instructions for creating, using, and deleting bookmarks as well as how to view the bookmark brackets. Save, preview, and print the Web page.

Project 7

Mary Whitt is drafting a legal document and wants to include a table of authorities. She asks for your help. Using the Ask A Question Box, research how to create and edit a table of authorities. Write Mary an interoffice memorandum describing the process. Save, preview, and print the memorandum.

Project 8

Following your presentation to the Word Processing Department, participants ask the following questions:

1. Susan Tierney: "How can I create multiple tables of contents in one document?"
2. Mark Acton: "How can I format index entries?"
3. Libbie Daniels: "Can I create a cross-reference for an index entry?"
4. Vera Wilson: "Can I change the font or font color in a Document Map?

Use online Help to find answers to these questions. Create an unbound report document itemizing each question and an appropriate answer. Save, preview, and print the document.

Word 2002

Working with Drawing Objects and Graphics

Chapter Overview

You can add a professional appearance to your documents by the attractive use of drawing objects, decorative page borders, graphics, text boxes, organization charts, and equations. In this chapter, you learn how to apply these finishing touches to your documents.

LEARNING OBJECTIVES

- Create drawing objects
- Add decorative page borders
- Use WordArt special text effects
- Insert, position, and delete pictures
- Insert and edit text boxes
- Create and edit an organization chart
- Create an equation

Case profile

Joyee Martin, the administrative assistant in the travel services office, is out for two weeks on medical leave and you are asked to fill in for her. Joyee drafted several documents and leaves you instructions to use drawing tools, page borders, graphics, text boxes, organization charts, and equations to give the documents an attractive, professional appearance.

chapter twenty one

21.a Creating Drawing Objects

Word has a special toolbar, called the Drawing toolbar, which provides tools for creating and editing drawing objects in a document. **Drawing objects** are graphic items such as shapes, curves, and lines. For example, you can draw lines, arrows, rectangles, squares, ovals, special preset shapes called **AutoShapes**, and three-dimensional shapes by selecting the kind of object you want and then drawing the object with the mouse pointer. You can edit drawing objects to add text and color.

To create a new, blank document and view the Drawing toolbar:

Step 1	*Create*	a new, blank document
Step 2	*Click*	the Drawing button on the Standard toolbar to display the Drawing toolbar

Word switches to Print Layout view, if necessary. To draw a line object:

Step 1	*Click*	the Line button on the Drawing toolbar
Step 2	*Observe*	that the drawing canvas appears
Step 3	*Move*	the cross-hair mouse pointer to approximately the 1-inch horizontal and vertical position within the drawing canvas
Step 4	*Press & hold*	the left mouse button
Step 5	*Drag*	approximately 3 inches to the right
Step 6	*Release*	the mouse button to create the line

The line on your screen should look similar to Figure 21-1.

FIGURE 21-1
Selected Line Object on the Drawing Canvas

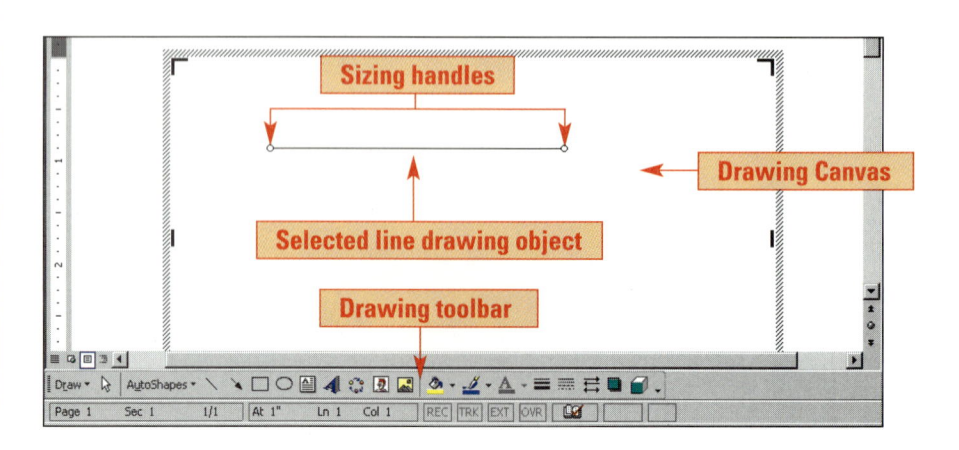

The small clear circles at either end of the line are **sizing handles**, which you drag with the mouse pointer to change the size and shape of a drawing object. When you place the mouse pointer on a sizing handle, it becomes a black, double-headed sizing pointer that you use to drag the sizing handle in the desired direction. If you drag a corner-sizing handle, the object maintains its vertical and horizontal proportion. The sizing handles also indicate an object is selected. You want to deselect the line object.

| Step 7 | *Click* | inside the drawing canvas away from the line object to deselect it |

To follow the same process to draw a line with an arrowhead:

Step 1	*Click*	the Arrow button on the Drawing toolbar
Step 2	*Move*	the cross-hair mouse pointer to approximately ½ inch below the left edge of the line object
Step 3	*Press & hold*	the left mouse button
Step 4	*Drag*	approximately 3 inches to the right
Step 5	*Release*	the mouse button to create the arrow object

To size the arrow to make it shorter:

Step 1	*Move*	the mouse pointer to the right sizing handle (at the arrowhead)
Step 2	*Observe*	that the mouse pointer becomes a black, double-headed sizing pointer
Step 3	*Press & hold*	the left mouse button
Step 4	*Drag*	to the left approximately 1½ inches
Step 5	*Release*	the mouse button
Step 6	*Deselect*	the arrow object leaving the drawing canvas open

To draw a rectangle:

Step 1	*Click*	the Rectangle button on the Drawing toolbar
Step 2	*Move*	the cross-hair mouse pointer to approximately ½ inch below the left edge of the arrow object
Step 3	*Press & hold*	the left mouse button

Step 4	*Drag*	down approximately 1 inch and to the right approximately 2 inches
Step 5	*Release*	the mouse button to create the rectangle object

Your screen should look similar to Figure 21-2.

FIGURE 21-2
Selected Rectangle Object on the Drawing Canvas

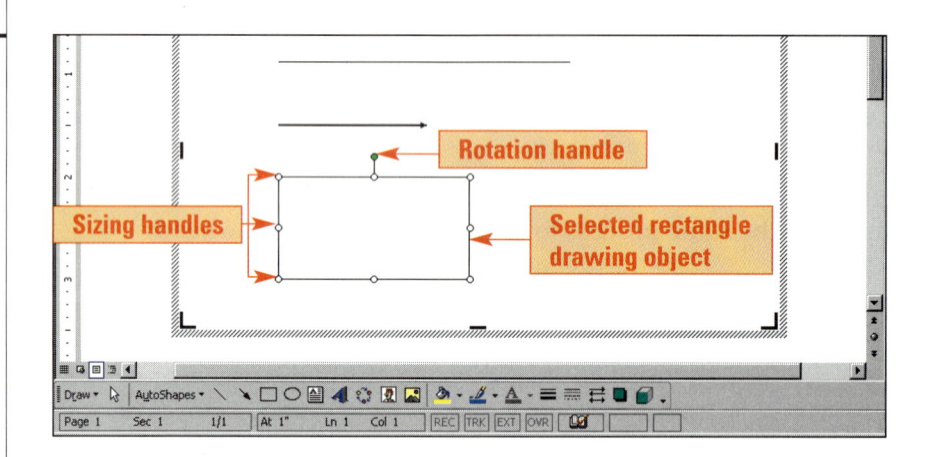

You can also rotate and reposition drawing objects with the mouse pointer. To rotate, size, and reposition the rectangle with the mouse pointer:

Step 1	*Move*	the mouse pointer to the green rotation handle at the top of the rectangle object
Step 2	*Observe*	that the mouse pointer becomes a rotation pointer (a partial circle with a directional arrow)
Step 3	*Press & hold*	the left mouse button
Step 4	*Drag*	the rotation handle 90 degrees to the right (the rectangle object will now be vertical)
Step 5	*Release*	the mouse button

notes
For the remainder of this chapter, you are told to drag an object's sizing or rotation handle or boundary to size, rotate, or reposition it.

To size and reposition the rectangle object:

Step 1	*Move*	the mouse pointer to the upper-middle sizing handle
Step 2	*Drag*	the upper-middle sizing handle down approximately ½ inch

Working with Drawing Objects and Graphics **WA 165**

Step 3	Move	the mouse pointer to the rectangle's right boundary (the mouse pointer becomes a move pointer)
Step 4	Drag	the rectangle to the right until it is approximately ½ inch from the drawing canvas's right boundary
Step 5	Deselect	the rectangle and leave the drawing canvas open

Your screen should look similar to Figure 21-3.

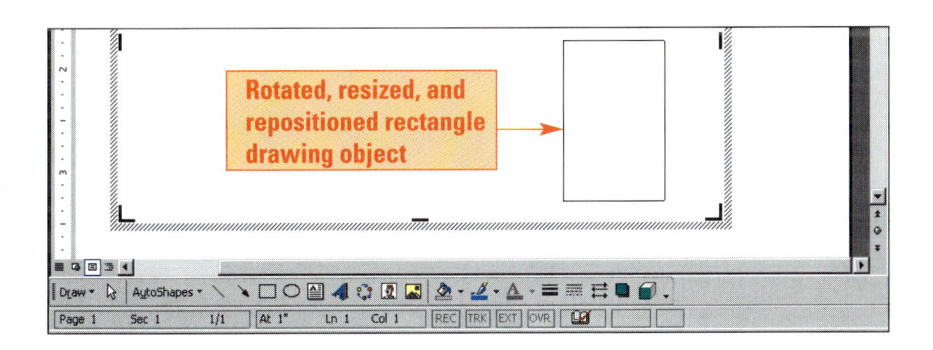

FIGURE 21-3
Rotated, Sized, and Repositioned Rectangle Object

> **QUICK TIP**
>
> You can use the pointer movement keys (UP, DOWN, LEFT, RIGHT ARROW) to move or "nudge" a selected drawing object up, down, left, or right.

You can press and hold the SHIFT key as you drag to draw a line or arrow to keep them straight. To draw a square, you can click the Rectangle button and then press and hold the SHIFT key as you draw the square object. To draw a circle, you can click the Oval button on the Drawing toolbar and then press and hold the SHIFT key as you draw the circle object. To draw a circle object:

Step 1	Click	the Oval button on the Drawing toolbar
Step 2	Move	the cross-hair mouse pointer to approximately ½ inch below the left edge of the arrow object
Step 3	Press & hold	the SHIFT key
Step 4	Drag	diagonally down and to the right approximately 1 inch
Step 5	Release	the mouse button and then the SHIFT key to create the circle object
Step 6	Deselect	the circle object and the drawing canvas by clicking in the document area outside the drawing canvas

> **MENU TIP**
>
> You can move a selected drawing object with the Nudge command on the Draw menu on the Drawing toolbar.

Editing Drawing Objects

You can use buttons on the Drawing toolbar to add text, fill (inside) color, line (border) color, line style, shadow, and three-dimensional effects to drawing objects. You also can edit a drawing object with a shortcut menu and dialog box options.

chapter
twenty-one

Changing Line Style, Line Color, and Fill Colors

To edit a drawing object, you must first select it and then edit it. To edit the line object to make it thicker:

Step 1	*Click*	the line object to select it and activate the drawing canvas partial
Step 2	*Click*	the Line Style button ☰ on the Drawing toolbar
Step 3	*Click*	the 3 pt solid style
Step 4	*Observe*	that the edited line object now has a thicker line style

To edit the arrow object to give it two arrowheads, change the line color, and make it larger:

Step 1	*Click*	the arrow object to select it
Step 2	*Click*	the Arrow Style button ⇄ on the Drawing toolbar
Step 3	*Click*	the Arrow Style 7 style (the seventh style in the list)
Step 4	*Click*	the Line Style button ☰ on the Drawing toolbar
Step 5	*Click*	the 4½ pt solid style
Step 6	*Click*	the Line Color button list arrow ✎ on the Drawing toolbar
Step 7	*Click*	the Blue color on the color grid (second row, sixth color)
Step 8	*Observe*	that the arrow object is now larger, blue, with two arrowheads

You can change a drawing object's fill color by selecting a single color from a color grid. You can fill a drawing object with two shaded colors, a preset color combination, a texture, a pattern, or a picture with options in the Fill Effects dialog box. To edit the circle object to change fill color to a preset color combination:

Step 1	*Click*	the circle object to select it
Step 2	*Click*	the Fill Color button list arrow 🎨 on the Drawing toolbar
Step 3	*Click*	Fill Effects
Step 4	*Click*	the Gradient tab, if necessary

MOUSE TIP

You can resize the drawing canvas with the mouse pointer by placing the mouse pointer on a sizing line in the middle of the top, left, right, and bottom border or a corner bracket and then dragging the boundary. You can move the drawing canvas by placing the mouse pointer on a hatch-mark boundary and dragging it to a new location.

Your Fill Effects dialog box should look similar to Figure 21-4.

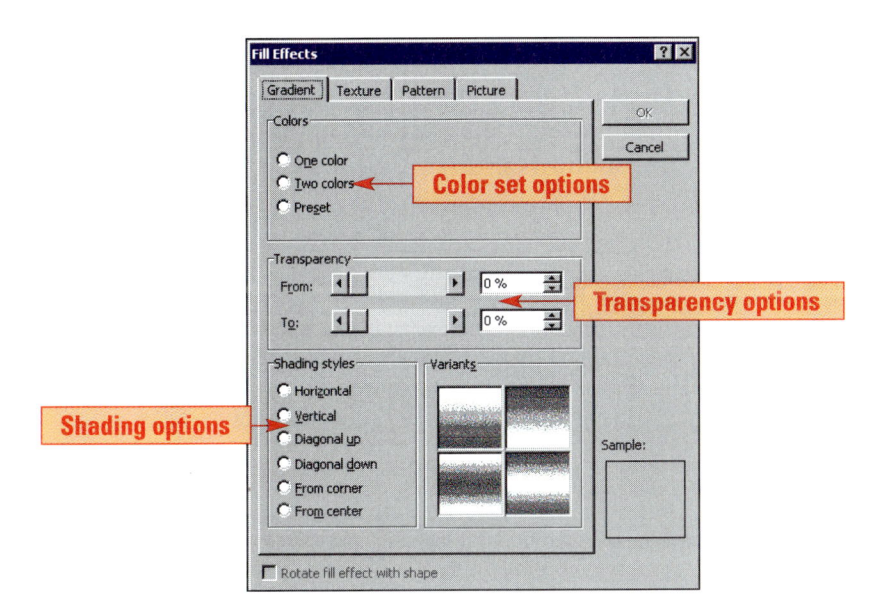

FIGURE 21-4
Gradient Tab in the Fill Effects Dialog Box

Word provides several preset color combinations you can apply or you can manually choose two colors. You can then select the colors shading effects. You apply the Desert preset color combination with the first variant of the From center shading effect.

Step 5	Click	the Preset option button
Step 6	Click	the Preset colors: list arrow
Step 7	Click	Desert
Step 8	Click	the From center option button
Step 9	Observe	the two Variants of the From center shading option
Step 10	Click	the first variant
Step 11	Observe	the Sample: fill
Step 12	Click	OK
Step 13	Observe	the edited circle object

Adding and Modifying a Shadow Style

You can add Shadow effects to a drawing object with a button on the Drawing toolbar. To add a shadow style to the circle object:

Step 1	Verify	that the circle object is still selected
Step 2	Click	the Shadow Style button on the Drawing toolbar

chapter
twenty-one

Step 3	*Click*	the Shadow Style 2 option (first row, second option)
Step 4	*Observe*	the default gray shadow added to the circle

You can modify the shadow style by displaying the Shadow Settings toolbar. To display the Shadow Settings toolbar and change the shadow color:

Step 1	*Verify*	that the circle object is still selected
Step 2	*Click*	Shadow Style button on the Drawing toolbar
Step 3	*Click*	the Shadow Settings to view the Shadow Settings toolbar
Step 4	*Float*	the Shadow Settings toolbar inside the drawing canvas, if necessary

You can turn the shadow on or off, nudge or slightly move the shadow up, down, left, or right, and change the shadow color with buttons on this toolbar. You want to change the shadow color to tan.

Step 5	*Click*	the Shadow Color button list arrow on the Shadow Settings toolbar
Step 6	*Click*	Tan on the color grid (fifth row, second color)
Step 7	*Close*	the Shadow Settings toolbar
Step 8	*Observe*	the new, more complementary shadow color
Step 9	*Deselect*	the circle object and leave the drawing canvas open

Adding and Modifying a 3-D Style

Another way to edit a drawing object is to apply a 3-D style to the object. To fill the rectangle object with the green color and then apply a 3-D style:

Step 1	*Select*	the rectangle drawing object
Step 2	*Click*	the Fill Color button list arrow on the Drawing toolbar
Step 3	*Click*	Green on the color grid (second row, fourth color)
Step 4	*Click*	the 3-D Style button on the Drawing toolbar
Step 5	*Click*	3-D Style 1 on the grid (first row, first option)
Step 6	*Observe*	the three-dimensional rectangle object

You can turn on or off the 3-D effect, tilt the 3-D object, change its shape and direction, change the lighting effect for any side, change the surface composition, and change the color with buttons on the 3-D Settings toolbar. To view the 3-D Settings toolbar and edit the 3-D rectangle object:

Step 1	Click	the 3-D Style button on the Drawing toolbar
Step 2	Click	3-D Settings
Step 3	Float	the 3-D Settings toolbar inside the drawing canvas, if necessary

You want to lighten the color on the front surface of the object.

Step 4	Click	the Lightening button on the 3-D Settings toolbar
Step 5	Click	the button in the center of the grid
Step 6	Observe	that the surface of the 3-D object is brighter
Step 7	Close	the 3-D Settings toolbar

Adding Text to Drawing Objects

You can add text to drawing objects and then format that text using the same formatting tools you use for document body text. To key text in the 3-D rectangle and then format the text:

Step 1	Right-click	the 3-D rectangle object
Step 2	Click	Add Text
Step 3	Key	"Sample text" at the top of the object
Step 4	Select	the text
Step 5	Format	the text with a bold, white color font and center-align it using the Formatting toolbar
Step 6	Deselect	the 3-D rectangle object

Deleting Drawing Objects

When you no longer need a drawing object, you can delete it. You can select and delete individual objects or you can select multiple objects using the SHIFT + Click or CTRL + Click methods and then

> **TASK PANE TIP**
>
> To view a collection of pictures drawn with the AutoShapes tool, click the More AutoShapes command on the AutoShapes button to open the Insert Clip Art task pane.

delete all the objects at one time. You can also use the Select Objects button on the Drawing toolbar to select multiple objects. To select the line object and delete it:

| Step 1 | Click | the line object to select it |
| Step 2 | Press | the DELETE key |

To select the remaining three objects:

Step 1	Click	the Select Objects button on the Drawing toolbar
Step 2	Move	the mouse pointer above and to the left of the arrow object
Step 3	Drag	down and to the right to draw a dashed-line rectangle around the three remaining objects

When you release the mouse button, the three remaining objects are selected.

Step 4	Press	the DELETE key to delete the objects
Step 5	Click	outside the drawing canvas to close it
Step 6	Close	the document without saving

Word also provides a number of preset shapes you can draw.

Drawing, Editing, and Deleting AutoShapes

The AutoShapes tool on the Drawing toolbar contains many different preset shapes you can draw with the mouse pointer. To draw an AutoShape, you first select the shape to draw, move the mouse pointer to the appropriate location in the document, and then drag downward and to the right to draw the shape. When the AutoShape object is the correct size, you release the mouse button.

You can choose to leave the drawing canvas on to help you control the position of AutoShapes in your document or you can turn it off. To turn off the drawing canvas:

| Step 1 | Create | a new, blank document |
| Step 2 | Open | the General tab in the Options dialog box |

Working with Drawing Objects and Graphics   WA 171

Step 3	Click	the Automati<u>c</u>ally create drawing canvas when inserting AutoShapes check box to remove the check mark
Step 4	Click	OK

To create a banner AutoShape in the blank document:

Step 1	Click	the A<u>u</u>toShapes button `AutoShapes ▼` on the Drawing toolbar
Step 2	Point to	<u>S</u>tars and Banners

The AutoShapes menu and Stars and Banners palette on your screen should look similar to Figure 21-5.

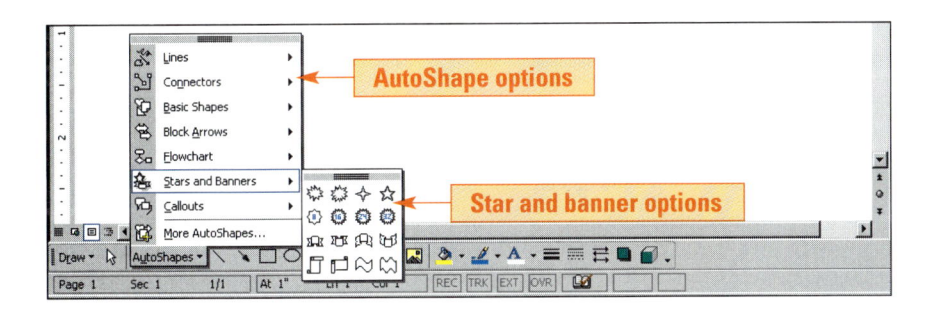

FIGURE 21-5
AutoShapes Stars and Banners Palette

Step 3	Click	the Down Ribbon option on the Stars and Banners grid (second column, third row)
Step 4	Move	the mouse pointer to the approximately ½-inch horizontal and vertical position in the document
Step 5	Drag	down to approximately the 2-inch position and to the right to approximately the 5½-inch position
Step 6	Observe	that when you release the mouse button the selected banner object AutoShape is created

The banner object on your screen should look similar to Figure 21-6.

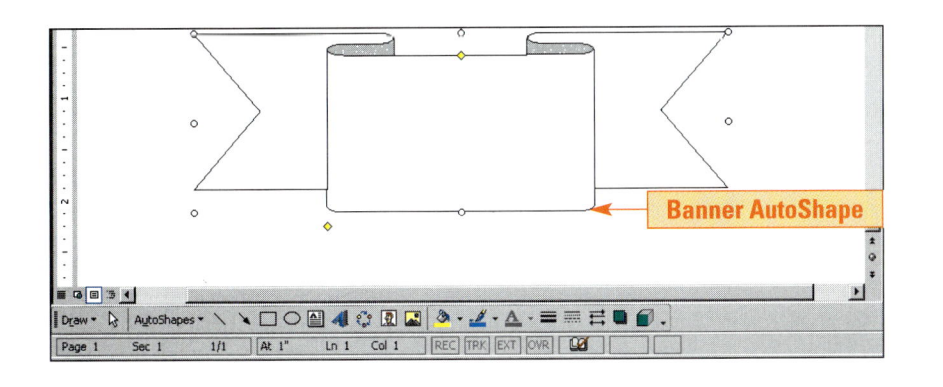

FIGURE 21-6
Down Ribbon AutoShape

chapter
twenty-one

QUICK TIP

You can press the ENTER key when adding text to an AutoShape to move the insertion point down a line.

You can edit an AutoShape to change the line and fill color, the line style, the shadow style, and to add text in the same way you do a drawing object you manually create, such as an arrow or circle. To edit the banner AutoShape drawing object:

Step 1	Select	the banner object, if necessary
Step 2	Change	the line style to 4½ pt
Step 3	Change	the line color to Blue
Step 4	Change	the fill color to Yellow
Step 5	Add	a Light Blue shadow using the Shadow Style 1 style
Step 6	Add	the text "Congratulations!" in the AutoShape approximately three lines from the top
Step 7	Format	the text with an 18-point, blue, bold font and center it horizontally in the banner using the Formatting toolbar

Your formatted banner object should look similar to Figure 21-7.

FIGURE 21-7
Edited Banner AutoShape

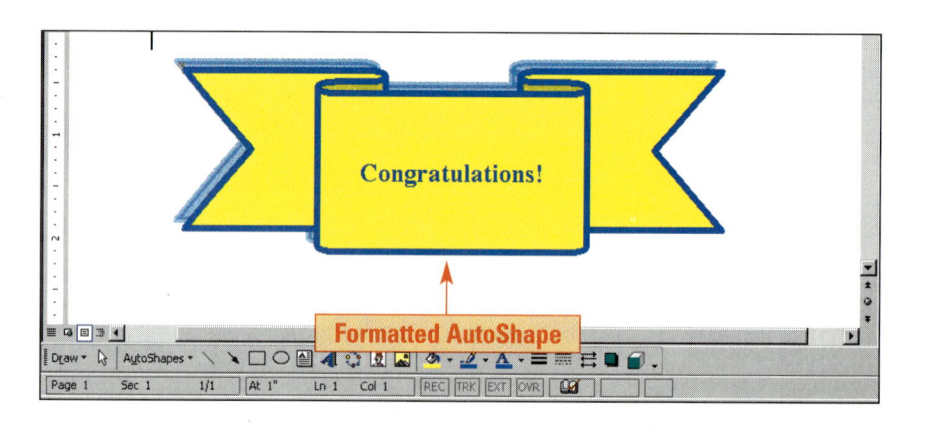

Step 8	Close	the document without saving

The travel services office sponsors a youth soccer team that is holding its annual garage sale next Saturday and Sunday from 10:00 a.m. to 6:00 p.m. at West Side Park. Joyee leaves instructions for you to use drawing objects to modify the garage sale announcement by adding AutoShapes to make the announcement attractive and using drawing objects to create a map to the park. To open and format a document using drawing objects:

Step 1	Open	the *Garage Sale* document located on the Data Disk

Working with Drawing Objects and Graphics   **WA 173**

Step 2	*Draw*	an Explosion 2 AutoShape approximately 2 inches long and 3 inches wide above the "Youth Soccer Club" text (this AutoShape is located on the Stars and Banners grid)
Step 3	*Change*	the AutoShape fill color to Plum
Step 4	*Change*	the AutoShape line style to 3 pt
Step 5	*Change*	the AutoShape line color to Violet
Step 6	*Add*	the text "Don't Miss It!" inside the AutoShape
Step 7	*Format*	the "Don't Miss It!" text with an 18-point, White font and center it approximately vertically and horizontally in the AutoShape
Step 8	*Draw*	lines, arrows, rectangles, and AutoShapes to create the map in Figure 21-8 and use the Plum fill color, White font color, and 9-point font size

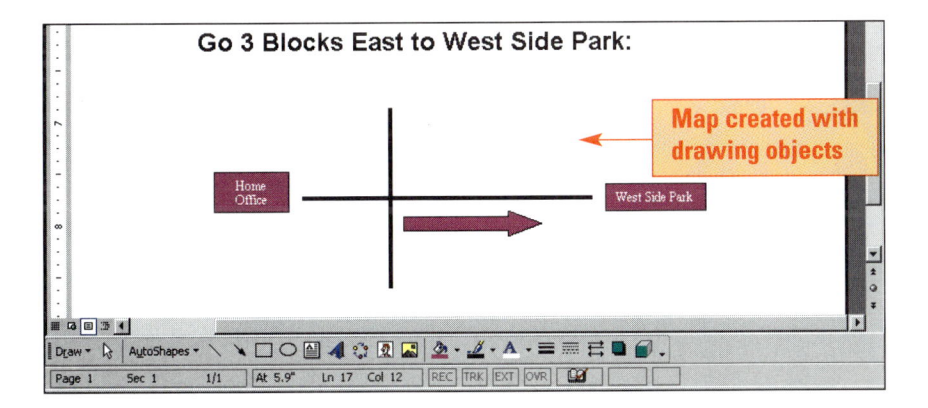

FIGURE 21-8
Garage Sale Map

Step 9	*Save*	the document as *Garage Sale Revised* and leave it open
Step 10	*Open*	the General tab in the Options dialog box and turn on the option to automatically create a drawing canvas

You also can dress up a document with page borders.

21.b Adding Decorative Page Borders

You can add, modify, or remove page borders with options in the Borders and Shading dialog box. You can choose from a preset border or create a custom border by selecting the line style, color, and width.

chapter twenty-one

MENU TIP

You can create special text effects by clicking the Insert menu, pointing to Picture, and then clicking the WordArt command.

CAUTION TIP

Because a WordArt object is a drawing object and not regular text, you cannot use the Spelling & Grammar feature to check the WordArt object text spelling.

Word also provides border art you can use as a page border. To add a page border to the *Garage Sale Revised* document:

Step 1	Open	the Page Border tab in the Borders and Shading dialog box
Step 2	Click	the Box preset option
Step 3	Click	the Art: list arrow
Step 4	Click	a black-and-white art border of your choice
Step 5	Click	Plum in the Color: list
Step 6	Observe	the border preview
Step 7	Verify	that the border is applied to Whole document
Step 8	Click	OK
Step 9	Zoom	the document to Whole Page to view the text, Explosion AutoShape, map, and decorative border and then zoom back to 100% view
Step 10	Save	the document and close it

21.c Using WordArt Special Text Effects

The **WordArt** feature allows you to draw and format a special text object. You can add special effects to WordArt object text by adding shadows and changing the text shape. You edit WordArt objects just like drawing objects to add fill color, change the line style or color, or add 3-D effects. To add a WordArt title to the *Bonaire* document:

Step 1	Open	the *Bonaire* document located on the Data Disk
Step 2	Verify	that the Drawing toolbar is visible
Step 3	Click	the Insert WordArt button on the Drawing toolbar

The WordArt Gallery dialog box on your screen should look similar to Figure 21-9.

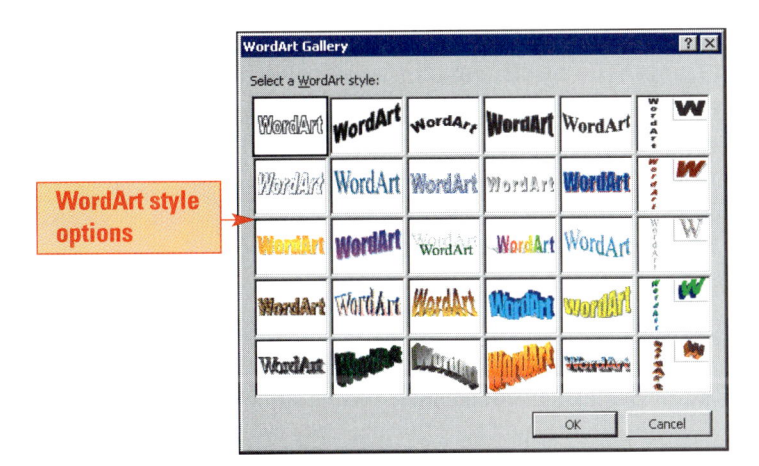

FIGURE 21-9
WordArt Gallery Dialog Box

You select a WordArt style in this dialog box and then key the text in the Edit WordArt Text dialog box that opens. To create the WordArt:

Step 1	Double-click	the fourth WordArt style in the second row
Step 2	Key	BONAIRE in the Edit WordArt Text dialog box
Step 3	Click	48 in the Size: list box
Step 4	Click	OK
Step 5	Click	the BONAIRE WordArt object to select it, if necessary
Step 6	Observe	the black object border and the black square sizing handles

Your screen should look similar to Figure 21-10.

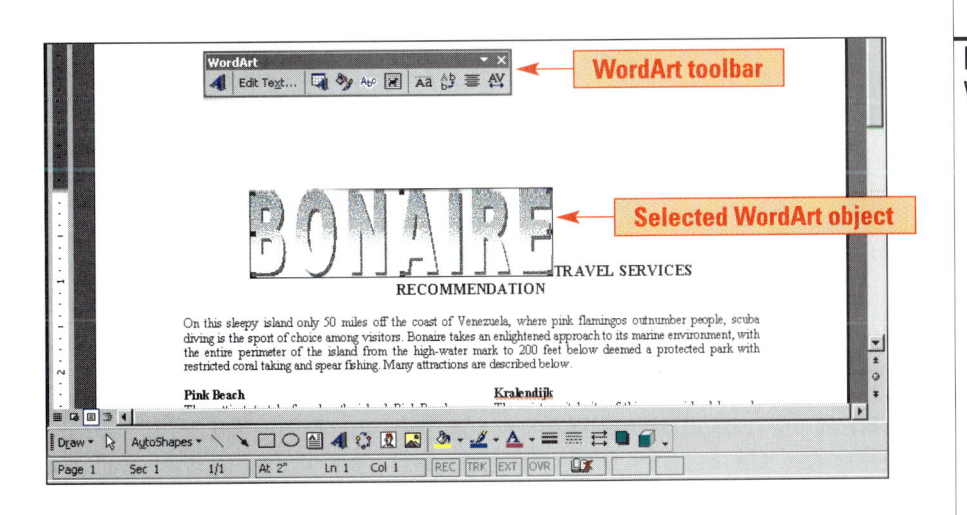

FIGURE 21-10
WordArt Object and Toolbar

chapter
twenty-one

The WordArt drawing object is, by default, placed inline with the text and inserted at the position of the insertion point. You can edit the WordArt object to position the object in front of the text and then drag it where you want it with the mouse pointer. To position the WordArt object in front of the text:

Step 1	Click	the Text Wrapping button on the WordArt toolbar
Step 2	Click	I̲n Front of Text
Step 3	Observe	that there is no border and the sizing handles are clear circles, indicating that you can now move, size, and edit this WordArt object just like any other drawing object
Step 4	Drag	the WordArt drawing object to center it above the "TRAVEL SERVICES RECOMMENDATION" text

To change the shape of the WordArt object:

Step 1	Click	the WordArt Shape button on the WordArt toolbar
Step 2	Click	the Wave 1 shape on the grid (third row, fifth shape)
Step 3	Deselect	the WordArt object
Step 4	Save	the document as *Bonaire Revised* and leave it open

Now you want to add a picture to the Boca Cai text in the second column.

21.d Inserting, Positioning, and Deleting Pictures

Word comes with a set of pictures you can access from the Clip Organizer. You can import pictures into the Clip Organizer from other sources or you can insert pictures in your document from disk files without first importing them into the Clip Organizer. You can also insert a picture from a file located on your hard drive, network drive, or a floppy disk. To insert a picture named *Sunshine* located on the Data Disk at the bottom of the *Bonaire Revised* document:

| Step 1 | Move | the insertion point to the bottom of the document (bottom of the second column) |

Step 2	Press	the ENTER key
Step 3	Click	the Insert Picture button on the Drawing toolbar
Step 4	Switch to	the Data Disk
Step 5	Double-click	the *Sunshine* picture
Step 6	Observe	that the *Sunshine* picture is inserted in the document at the position of the insertion point

Aligning Text and Graphics

Now that the *Sunshine* picture is in the document, you need to move and resize it. You select a picture for editing, sizing, or repositioning by clicking it. When you select a picture object, the Picture toolbar automatically opens. The Picture toolbar has buttons you use to edit the picture. You can size a picture object with the mouse by dragging a sizing handle just like you size drawing objects. To select and size the *Sunshine* picture object:

Step 1	Click	the picture to select it
Step 2	Float	the Picture toolbar over the document, if neccessary
Step 3	Drag	the lower-right corner sizing handle diagonally upward approximately ½ inch

The default layout for picture objects and text is for the picture to be in line with the text. To edit the text wrapping and reposition the picture object:

Step 1	Verify	that the picture object is still selected
Step 2	Click	the Text Wrapping button on the Picture toolbar
Step 3	Click	Square
Step 4	Observe	that the picture object now has clear circle sizing handles and the mouse pointer becomes a move pointer when placed on the object
Step 5	Drag	the picture object to the beginning of the Boca Cai paragraph heading

The text shifts to accommodate the picture object. Because Joyee will be printing the *Bonaire* document on a black-and-white printer, you want to use a black-and-white picture instead of a color picture. You can edit the *Sunshine* picture colors.

QUICK TIP

You can easily rotate selected graphic images and compress them into a smaller file size with buttons on the Picture toolbar. For more information on rotating and compressing graphic images, see online Help

The Text wrapping break option in the Break dialog box allows you to insert a new line break for the text below a picture.

You can delete a picture the same way you delete a drawing object, by selecting the object and pressing the DELETE key.

To change to black-and-white picture colors:

Step 1	Verify	that the picture object is still selected
Step 2	Click	the Color button on the Picture toolbar
Step 3	Click	Black & White
Step 4	Deselect	the picture object

Your screen should look similar to Figure 21-11.

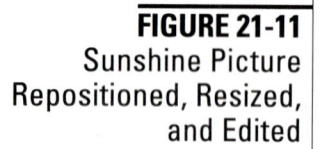

FIGURE 21-11
Sunshine Picture Repositioned, Resized, and Edited

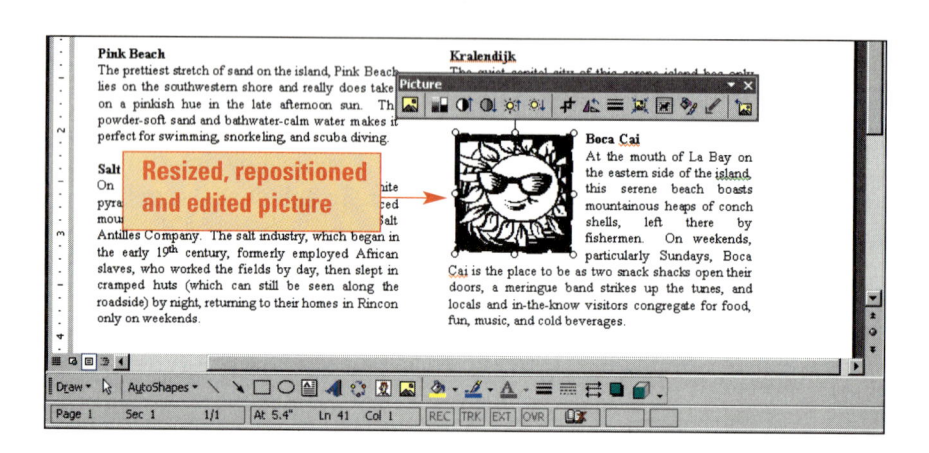

Step 5	Save	the document and leave it open

You also want to draw readers' attention to the first body paragraph in the document. You can do this with the drop cap effect.

Using the Drop Cap Effect

A **drop cap** is an oversized capital first letter used to draw attention to the beginning of a paragraph or line of text. A drop cap can be positioned within the paragraph or to the left of the paragraph in the margin. You want to drop the character "O" in the word "On" at the beginning of the first paragraph. To create a drop cap:

Step 1	Click	in the first body paragraph beginning "On this sleepy island" to select it
Step 2	Click	Format
Step 3	Click	Drop Cap

QUICK TIP

You can add captions automatically to tables and equations as well as graphic figures. The AutoCaption button in the Caption dialog box adds captions to all items of the same type. For example, in a document with multiple tables, you can have Word automatically caption the tables as Table 1, Table 2, and so forth. For more information on using the AutoCaption feature, see online Help.

The Drop Cap dialog box on your screen should look similar to Figure 21-12.

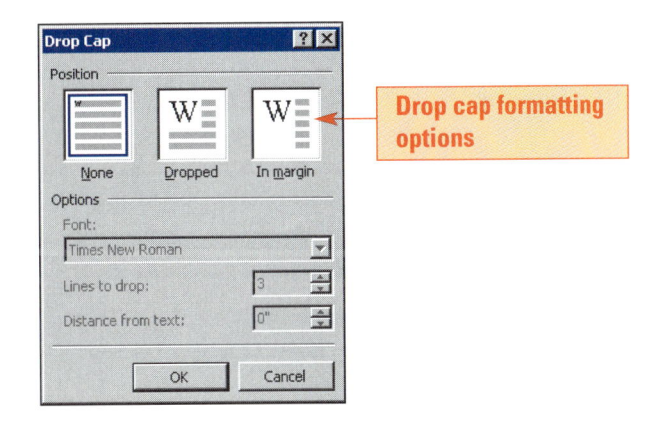

FIGURE 21-12
Drop Cap Dialog Box

(Drop Cap dialog box shown with Drop cap formatting options callout pointing to the Position icons: None, Dropped, In margin)

You select the position of the character, the font, and the number of lines to drop in this dialog box. To drop the character three lines using the default font:

Step 1	**Double-click**	the Dropped icon
Step 2	**Deselect**	the text
Step 3	**Observe**	that the oversized character "O" dropped three lines at the beginning of the first paragraph
Step 4	**Save**	the document and close it

You can position a graphic image behind the text to create a watermark effect.

Creating Watermarks

A **watermark** is a picture or graphic image that appears faintly behind text in a document. You might use a watermark to add the text "DRAFT" or "CONFIDENTIAL" behind text or you can insert a company logo or picture as a watermark. You can create a picture or text watermark with the Printed Watermark subcommand under the Background command on the Format menu. If you select a picture watermark, you open the Insert Picture dialog box to insert the appropriate picture. If you select a text watermark, you key and format the watermark text. Watermark pictures and text are, by default, inserted in the document in Header and Footer view. This enables the picture or text to appear on all pages of a multipage document.

QUICK TIP

You can add a caption above or below a picture by selecting the picture and clicking the Caption subcommand under the Reference command on the Insert menu. By default, Word inserts the caption including a label and number. You can add text to the label or you can create a new label. Also, you can have Word automatically caption all graphic items of the same type. When you insert a caption for a picture formatted with a text wrapping option, the caption is placed in a text box. You can apply the same wrapping option to the text box.

chapter
twenty-one

Inserting a Picture Watermark

The travel services office is hosting a retirement party for a long-time department employee, Richard Klaus. Joyee leaves instructions for you to complete a memo inviting the department staff to the party. You open a partially completed memo and insert a picture watermark in the document. To insert a picture watermark:

Step 1	Open	the *Retirement Party Memo* document located on the Data Disk
Step 2	Click	F*o*rmat
Step 3	Point to	Background
Step 4	Click	Printed *W*atermark

The Printed Watermark dialog box on your screen should look similar to Figure 21-13.

FIGURE 21-13
Printed Watermark Dialog Box

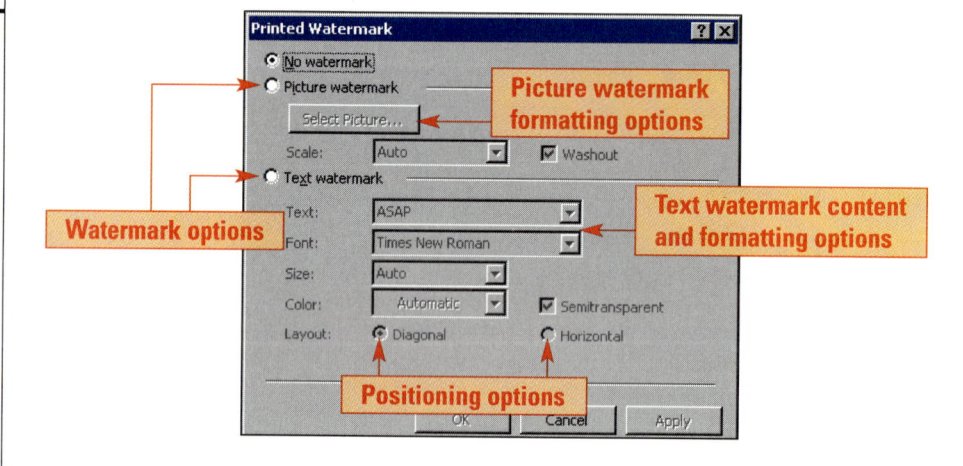

CAUTION TIP

To edit or delete the watermark picture, you must first click *H*eader and Footer on the *V*iew menu to open the Header and Footer view and then click the watermark picture to select it for editing or deletion.

Step 5	Click	the P*i*cture watermark option button, if necessary
Step 6	Click	Select *P*icture
Step 7	Switch to	the Data Disk
Step 8	Double-click	the Retirement picture
Step 9	Verify	that the Sca*l*e: option is Auto and the *W*ashout check box contains a check mark
Step 10	Click	OK
Step 11	Zoom	the document to Whole Page
Step 12	Observe	the watermark picture behind the text
Step 13	Zoom	back to 100%

Working with Drawing Objects and Graphics WA 181

| Step 14 | Save | the document as *Retirement Party Memo With Watermark* and close it |

Inserting a Text Watermark

Joyee left instructions for you to insert the text "DRAFT" as a watermark in the *Service Commitment* document. To open the document and insert the text watermark:

Step 1	Open	the *Service Commitment* document located on the Data Disk
Step 2	Display	the Printed Watermark dialog box
Step 3	Click	the Te*x*t watermark option button
Step 4	Click	DRAFT in the *T*ext: list
Step 5	Click	Arial in the *F*ont: list
Step 6	Click	60 in the *S*ize: list
Step 7	Verify	that the *S*emitransparent check box contains a check mark
Step 8	Verify	that the *D*iagonal layout button is selected
Step 9	Click	OK
Step 10	Zoom	the document to Whole Page to view the "DRAFT" watermark
Step 11	Zoom	the document back to 100%
Step 12	Save	the document as *Service Commitment With Watermark* and close it

You can quickly reposition text or insert new text using a text box.

21.e Inserting and Editing Text Boxes

A **text box** is an invisible container for the text, tables, or charts you want to position in a document. By placing text in a text box, you can treat the text more like a graphic object than regular text. You format a text box in the same way you format an AutoShape. You format the text inside the text box as you do regular body text.

> **QUICK TIP**
>
> You can manually insert a picture watermark on any single page by inserting the picture and using the Text Wrapping button on the Picture toolbar to position the picture behind the text. If you first open the Header and Footer view and then insert the picture in front of the document text, the picture watermark appears on all pages of a multipage document.

> **MENU TIP**
>
> You can click the Te*x*t Box command on the *I*nsert menu to insert a text box.

chapter
twenty-one

> **QUICK TIP**
>
> A **callout** is a text box used to label a picture. Often the callout also includes a leader, or line, to draw the reader's eye from the picture to the label. You can use AutoShapes to create callouts with leaders.

Before she left, Joyee created an announcement for the Office Technology Society. To draw the reader's eye to the OTS membership information, you place that portion of the text in a formatted text box and then position the text box at the right margin. To open the document, select the membership information, and create a text box:

Step 1	**Open**	the *Office Technology Society* document located on the Data Disk
Step 2	**Select**	the OTS MEMBERSHIP paragraph heading, numbered list, and following blank line
Step 3	**Click**	the Text Box button on the Drawing toolbar

A text box is placed around the text. Your screen should look similar to Figure 21-14.

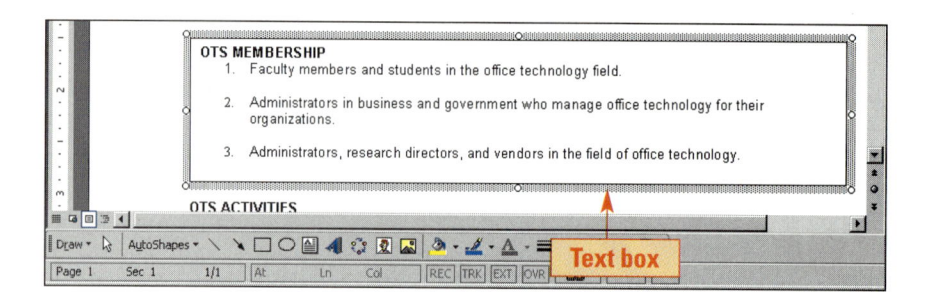

FIGURE 21-14
Membership Information in Selected Text Box

You want to size the text box to be approximately half its current size and reposition it to the right of the OTS PURPOSE paragraphs.

Step 4	**Drag**	the middle-right sizing handle to the left until the text box is approximately half its original size
Step 5	**Drag**	the text box to the right of the OTS PURPOSE paragraphs until they wrap down the left side of the text box
Step 6	**Deselect**	the text box
Step 7	**Save**	the document as *OTS Revised*

By default, a thin single-line border appears around text box text. You can add a customized border to a text box or remove the default border. You also can add fill color to a text box. To add a customized border and fill color:

| Step 1 | **Right-click** | the text box boundary |
| Step 2 | **Click** | Format Text B*o*x |

Step 3	*Click*	the Colors and Lines tab, if necessary

You can add a solid color fill that is semitransparent or completely opaque. To add a semitransparent fill color and a colored border:

Step 1	*Click*	the Color: list arrow in the Fill group
Step 2	*Click*	Light Turquoise (fifth row, fifth color)
Step 3	*Key*	70 in the Transparency: text box
Step 4	*Click*	the Color: list arrow in the Line group
Step 5	*Click*	Red (third row, first color)
Step 6	*Click*	OK
Step 7	*Deselect*	the text box
Step 8	*Observe*	the formatted text box
Step 9	*Save*	the document and close it

> **QUICK TIP**
> You can create an empty text box and then key and format text inside the text box.

An important way to show the relationships among people in an organization is with a chart.

21.f Creating and Editing an Organization Chart

An **organization chart** shows the hierarchical reporting relationships among people in an organization. An organization chart identifies these reporting relationships by placing employees in different levels on the chart, with the top level being the primary reporting relationship. For example, the president of an organization would be shown at the first level on an organization chart, vice presidents at the second level, managers at the third level, and so forth.

> **MENU TIP**
> You format a selected text box by clicking the Text Box command on the Format menu.

Inserting an Organization Chart Object

The travel services office manager needs an employee organization chart. You can create an organization chart with the Diagram button on the Drawing toolbar. To create a new document, key a heading, and insert an organization chart diagram object:

Step 1	*Create*	a new, blank document

Step 2	**Key**	Worldwide Exotic Foods, Inc. Travel Services Office Organization Chart
Step 3	**Format**	the three heading lines with 18-point, bold font and center them
Step 4	**Press**	the ENTER key twice

With the heading text in place, you can create the organization chart object. To create a blank organization chart object:

Step 1	**Click**	the Insert Diagram or Organization Chart button on the Drawing toolbar
Step 2	**Double-click**	the Organization Chart option (first row, first option)

The drawing canvas opens and contains a two-level organization chart. The Organization Chart toolbar also opens. Your screen should look similar to Figure 21-15.

FIGURE 21-15
Drawing Canvas and Organization Chart Object

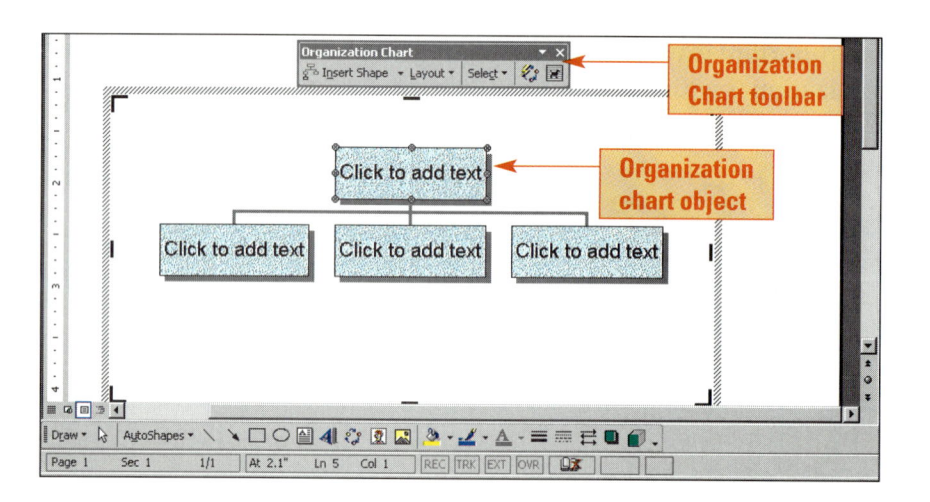

Joyee wants to include the following personnel on the organization chart: L. J. Turner, Office Manager; M. S. Morales, Travel Agent; A. L. Smith, Travel Agent; F. W. Gordon, Travel Agent; and J. J. Martin, Administrative Assistant. The office manager is placed at the first level of the chart, the travel agents are placed at the second level of the chart, and the administrative assistant is placed at its own level below the office manager.

To enter the office manager's name and title in the chart:

Step 1	**Click**	in the top box to position the insertion point

Step 2	Key	L. J. Turner
Step 3	Press	the ENTER key
Step 4	Key	Office Manager

To enter the information for the three travel agents:

Step 1	Click	the first box on the second level to position the insertion point
Step 2	Key	M. S. Morales
Step 3	Press	the ENTER key
Step 4	Key	Travel Agent
Step 5	Continue	by adding and centering A. L. Smith, Travel Agent and F. W. Gordon, Travel Agent in the boxes on the second level

To add the administrative assistant:

Step 1	Click	the Turner box to select it
Step 2	Click	the Insert Shape button list arrow [Insert Shape ▼] on the Organization Chart toolbar
Step 3	Click	Assistant
Step 4	Observe	the new assistant box added to the chart
Step 5	Key	J. J. Martin, A. Assistant, in the new box, and center the text
Step 6	Deselect	the drawing canvas
Step 7	Zoom	the document to Whole Page to view the title text and the organization chart object
Step 8	Zoom	the document back to 100%

Editing an Organization Chart Object

You can edit the organization chart by selecting it and then inserting additional boxes, formatting the text, or changing the color fill of the boxes. To remove the color fill from the boxes:

Step 1	Click	the organization chart object to select it and view the Organization Chart toolbar
Step 2	Click	the Autoformat button on the Organization Chart toolbar

CAUTION TIP

If the Automatic numbered lists option is turned on in the AutoFormat As You Type tab of the AutoCorrect dialog box, Word attempts to create an alphabetical list when you key the initial "A." You can use the AutoCorrect Options button and menu to reverse the AutoCorrect action.

chapter
twenty-one

Step 3	Click	Square Shadows in the Select a Diagram Style: dialog box
Step 4	Click	Apply
Step 5	Deselect	the organization chart object and close the drawing canvas
Step 6	Observe	the reformatted organization chart object
Step 7	Save	the document as *Travel Office Org Chart* and close it
Step 8	Close	the Drawing toolbar

When you need to insert special mathematical symbols or formulas in a document, you can use the Equation 3.0 supplemental application.

21.g Creating an Equation

The Microsoft Equation 3.0 supplementary application allows you to create and edit mathematical and scientific equations. The equations created with Microsoft Equation 3.0 are inserted as objects in your document. The equations inserted by Equation 3.0 do not calculate; however, they do print with the appropriate structure and format for an equation.

You need to insert the formula used to calculate the average age of the corporate travel office employees in an insurance report. To insert the equation:

Step 1	Open	the *Insurance Report* document located on the Data Disk
Step 2	Move	the insertion point to the blank line below the line beginning "The formula for"
Step 3	Click	Insert
Step 4	Click	Object
Step 5	Click	the Create New tab, if necessary
Step 6	Double-click	Microsoft Equation 3.0 in the Object type: list box

The Equation 3.0 application opens. Your screen should look similar to Figure 21-16.

> **QUICK TIP**
>
> When you first launch Microsoft Equation 3.0 (Equation Editor) you may see an Equation Editor tip suggesting that you upgrade Equation Editor to a new, more full-featured version called MathType™ by Design Science. For activities in this section, close this tip window.

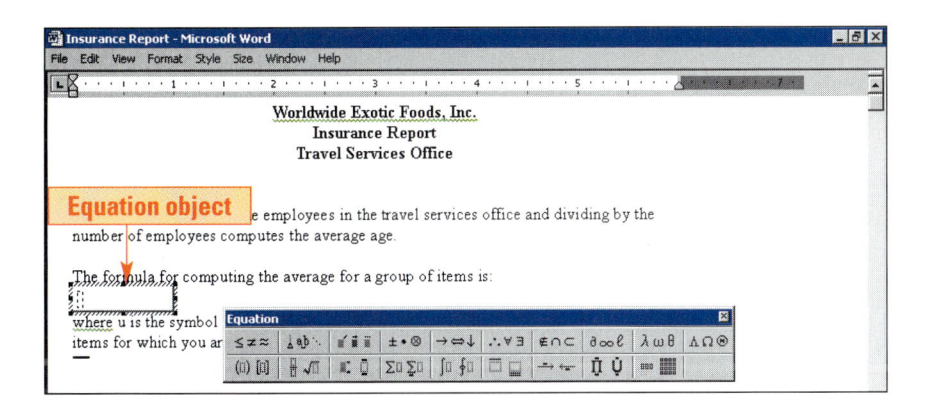

Working with Drawing Objects and Graphics   WA 187

FIGURE 21-16
Microsoft Equation 3.0 Window

You use buttons on the Equation toolbar to insert symbols in the equation object. The first character in the equation is the Greek character μ. To insert the equation:

Step 1	Click	the Greek characters (lowercase) button on the Equation toolbar
Step 2	Click	the μ symbol (fourth row, first symbol)
Step 3	Key	=
Step 4	Click	the Fraction and radical templates button on the Equation toolbar
Step 5	Click	the first template (first row, first column)
Step 6	Click	the Summation templates button on the Equation toolbar
Step 7	Click	the first template (first row, first template)
Step 8	Key	X
Step 9	Click	the Subscript and superscript templates on the Equation toolbar
Step 10	Click	the second template on the first row
Step 11	Key	i
Step 12	Click	the slot at the bottom of the fraction to move the insertion point
Step 13	Key	N

The equation is complete. To close Equation 3.0, return to the document, and position the equation object:

Step 1	Click	anywhere in the document outside the equation object

chapter twenty-one

| Step 2 | **Select** | the equation object and center it using the Formatting toolbar |
| Step 3 | **Deselect** | the equation object |

Your screen should look similar to Figure 21-17.

FIGURE 21-17
Completed Equation

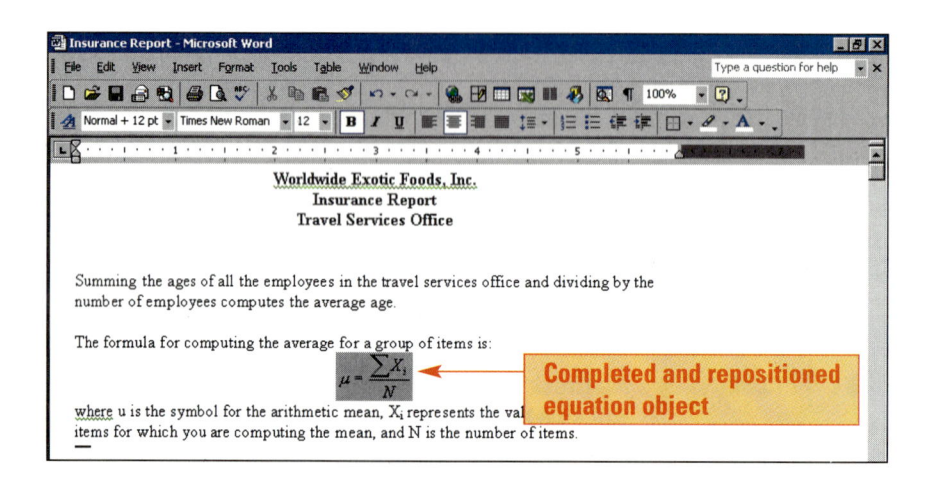

| Step 4 | **Save** | the document as *Insurance Report With Equation* and close it |

The various drawing objects enable you to enhance any document, no matter what its purpose.

Summary

- You can draw lines, circles, squares, arrows, ovals, rectangles, and preset shapes called AutoShapes with the mouse pointer and buttons on the Drawing toolbar.
- You use buttons on the Drawing toolbar to format drawing objects and AutoShapes.
- You can create decorative page borders to add interest to documents.
- You can use WordArt special text effects to add interest to documents.
- Pictures can be inserted, edited, and positioned anywhere in a document.
- The drop cap effect draws the reader's attention to a line or paragraph by enlarging the first character.
- You can add a picture or text watermark to a document so that it prints behind the text on every page of the document.
- You can treat text in a text box more like a graphic object than text.
- You can insert an organization chart object that shows the relationships among people in an organization.
- Microsoft Equation 3.0 is a supplemental application that allows you to construct an equation object.

chapter twenty-one

Commands Review

Action	Menu Bar	Shortcut Menu	Toolbar	Task Pane	Keyboard
View the Drawing toolbar	View, Toolbars	Right-click any toolbar, click Drawing			ALT + V, T
Draw objects and AutoShapes			Various buttons on the Drawing toolbar		
Edit a drawing object		Right-click the object, click Format (object name)	Various buttons on the Drawing toolbar		
Add decorative page borders	Format, Borders and Shading				ALT + O, B
Create WordArt drawing objects	Insert, Picture, WordArt				ALT + I, P, W
Insert a picture from file	Insert, Picture, From File				ALT + I, P, F
Format a picture	Format, Picture	Right-click the picture, click Format Picture	Various buttons on the Picture toolbar		ALT + O, I
Create a drop cap	Format, Drop Cap				ALT + O, D
Create a picture or text watermark	Format, Background, Printed Watermark				ALT + O, K, W
Insert a text box	Insert, Text Box				ALT + I, X
Create an organization chart					
Create an equation	Insert, Object Microsoft Equation 3.0				ALT + I, O
Insert a caption	Insert, Reference, Caption				ALT + I, N, C

Concepts Review

Circle the correct answer.

1. Special preset drawing object shapes are called:
   [a] WordArt.
   [b] Rectangles.
   [c] AutoShapes.
   [d] Text Boxes.

2. WordArt is a:
   [a] text box with formatted text.
   [b] container or box you insert around drawing objects.
   [c] drawing object that contains special text effects.
   [d] large capital letter in the first line of a paragraph.

3. By placing text in a text box, you can:
   [a] change the orientation of text.
   [b] edit the text shape.
   [c] treat text more like a graphic object than text.
   [d] enlarge the first character.

4. A drop cap is a(n):
   [a] oversized capital letter.
   [b] missing character.
   [c] word positioned below the baseline.
   [d] superscript character.

5. A watermark:
   [a] must be inserted on the last page of a document.
   [b] is a picture, text, or drawing object that appears faintly behind text in a document.
   [c] is visible only in Normal view.
   [d] cannot be moved or edited once it is created.

6. Which of the following is not an AutoShapes category?
   [a] Basic Shapes
   [b] Block Arrows
   [c] Hearts and Flowers
   [d] Stars and Banners

Working with Drawing Objects and Graphics   WA 191

7. To draw a straight line, square, or oval, you use a button on the Drawing toolbar and the:
   [a] CTRL key
   [b] ALT key
   [c] SHIFT key
   [d] TAB key

8. An organization chart shows:
   [a] a picture of numerical data.
   [b] the relationships among people in an organization.
   [c] a properly formatted mathematical or scientific equation.
   [d] a grid of rows and columns.

9. Equations inserted with Equation 3.0:
   [a] do not print.
   [b] cannot be edited once inserted.
   [c] do not calculate.
   [d] cannot be repositioned once inserted.

Circle **T** if the statement is true or **F** if the statement is false.

T F   1. Once you insert a picture, you cannot move it to another location in your document.

T F   2. Equations created with the Equation Editor also calculate the results.

T F   3. You can insert a picture but not text as a watermark.

T F   4. The WordArt feature allows you to draw and format objects that contain text effects.

T F   5. Sizing handles indicate a drawing object is selected; the handles can be used to resize the object.

T F   6. Multiple drawing objects must be deleted one at a time.

T F   7. You can add and edit decorative page borders.

T F   8. You can insert pictures from the Clip Organizer or from a file located on your hard drive, network drive, or diskette.

T F   9. In-line pictures are those positioned behind the text.

Skills Review

Exercise 1

1. Open the *Legislative News* document located on the Data Disk.
2. Change the page orientation to landscape.
3. Change the top and bottom margins to 0.75 inch and the left and right margins to 1 inch.
4. Apply a page border around the document. Select an Art option of your choice.
5. Save the document as *Legislative News With Page Border*, and then preview, print, and close it.

Exercise 2

1. Open the *Legislative News With Page Border* document you created in Exercise 1. If you have not created the document, do so now.
2. Remove the page border. (*Hint:* Use the None option in the Page Borders tab of the Borders and Shading dialog box.)
3. Change the page orientation to portrait.
4. Insert the semitransparent text watermark "CONFIDENTIAL" diagonally behind the text in the Veranda, 72-point font.
5. Save the document as *Legislative News With Watermark*, and then preview, print, and close it.

chapter twenty-one

Exercise 3

1. Open the *Service Commitment* document located on the Data Disk.
2. Select all the text and insert a text box. Size the text box horizontally to approximately half its original size by dragging the middle-right sizing handle.
3. Open the Format Text Box dialog box using a shortcut menu. On the Colors and Lines tab, change the text box fill color to light gray with an 85% transparency. On the Layout tab, center the text box horizontally.
4. Size the text box vertically to view all the text, if necessary.
5. Save the document as *Service Commitment With Text Box*, and then preview, print, and close it.

Exercise 4

1. Open the *Civic Association Art Show* document located on the Data Disk.
2. Insert the *ArtShow* picture located on the Data Disk as a watermark.
3. Open the Header and Footer view, select the watermark picture, and size it to approximately half its original size. Use the mouse to move the watermark so it is centered vertically and horizontally behind the text. Then close the Header and Footer view.
4. Save the document as *Civic Association With Watermark*, and then preview, print, and close it.

Exercise 5

1. Open the *Summer Vacation* document located on the Data Disk.
2. Add the title "Summer Vacation" using WordArt. Format the WordArt object as desired.
3. Center the WordArt object at the top of the document. (*Hint:* You may need to insert some hard returns to move the paragraph text down to make room for the WordArt object.)
4. Add drop caps for the first word in each body paragraph.
5. Save the document as *Summer Vacation With WordArt*, and then preview, print, and close it.

Exercise 6

1. Create a new, blank document.
2. Display the Drawing toolbar.
3. Draw a rectangle and fill it with blue. Change the line color to yellow. Change the line style to 2¼ pt.
4. Draw an arrow to the right of the rectangle and change its color to red using the Line Color button. Change the arrowhead style to Arrow Style 7 using the Arrow Style button.
5. Draw an oval below the rectangle and fill it with yellow. Change the oval's line color to red. Change the line style to 6 pt (two narrow and one wide line option). Add the text "Oval" in red, 14-point font in the center of the oval.
6. Using the SHIFT key and the Rectangle button, draw a square below the arrow and fill it with orange. Add the 3-D Style 17 to the square. Change the lighting effect to brighten the top of the 3-D object. Change the 3-D color to gold. (*Hint:* Use the 3-D Color button on the 3-D Settings toolbar.)
7. Using the SHIFT key and the Oval button, draw a circle below the square and fill it with violet. Change the line color to orange. Add a light orange shadow effect to the circle.
8. Save the document as *Drawing Objects*, and then preview, print, and close it.

Exercise 7

1. Open the *Org Chart* document located on the Data Disk.

2. Create an organization chart using the following information. Edwards is level 1; Quinn and Smithers are level 2.

   T. J. Edwards, Manager
   M. S. Quinn, Advertising
   A. L. Smithers, Media
3. Select and delete the empty level 2 box.
4. Insert one subordinate box for Quinn, and add "F. W. Ling, Photo and Art" to the box.
5. Insert two subordinate boxes for Smithers, and add "T. J. Garza, TV and Radio" and "L. V. Cox, Print" in the two boxes.
6. Center the text in each box and change the font color to plum using the Formatting toolbar.
7. Apply the Stripes Autoformat.
8. Add an assistant to T. J. Edwards named "B. Rivera" with the job title "Assistant" and change the font color to Plum.
9. Change the font color of the heading text to Plum.
10. Save the document as *Org Chart Revised*, and then preview, print, and close it.

Exercise 8

1. Open the *Interest Rate* document located on the Data Disk.
2. Between the two paragraphs, insert the following formula that computes the interest owed on a loan for a specific time period. (*Hint:* Format the X in italic using the Other command on the Style menu.)

$$I = P \, x \, \frac{R}{12}$$

3. Center the equation between the left and right margins.
4. Enlarge the equation object approximately ½ inch using the lower-right corner sizing handle.
5. Save the document as *Interest Rate Equation*, and then preview, print, and close it.

Exercise 9

1. Create a new, blank document.
2. Center the title "AutoShapes" in Arial, 14 point, bold font.
3. Display the Drawing toolbar.
4. Using the AutoShapes tool, draw five AutoShapes of your choice anywhere in the document.
5. Use fill and line color as desired.
6. Add text to two of the AutoShapes.
7. Format the text as desired.
8. Save the document as *AutoShape Examples*, and then preview, print, and close it.

Exercise 10

1. Open the *Civic Association With Watermark* document you created in Exercise 4. If you haven't created the document, do so now.
2. Open the Header and Footer view, select the watermark picture, and delete it.
3. Insert the *ArtShow* picture located on the Data Disk at the beginning of the first body text paragraph.
4. Change the text wrapping to Square and size the picture to approximately one-quarter its original size.
5. Reposition the picture near the right margin so that the text wraps down the left side of the picture.
6. Save the document as *Civic Association With Picture*, and then preview, print, and close it.

chapter twenty-one

Case Projects

Project 1
As the temporary administrative assistant in the travel services office, you are responsible for preparing the monthly employee newsletter. While creating this month's newsletter, you experience the following problems working with drawing objects: (1) You cannot rotate a graphic. (2) Colors within drawing objects aren't smooth. (3) The lines in the drawing object are jagged. Use online Help to troubleshoot these problems. Create an outline that describes each problem and a suggested solution. Save, preview, and print the outline.

Project 2
Joyee created a large report that contains several tables, drawing objects, and pictures. She leaves instructions for you to insert captions for the objects and you need to research how to do this. Use online Help to find ways to use captions in a large document. Create a report document that contains a table, picture, and drawing object with captions. Save, preview, and print the document.

Project 3
You want to locate some new graphics (pictures) to use in the employee newsletter and coworkers tell you many Web sites offer free graphics that you can download. Connect to the Internet and search for Web sites that offer free graphics. With your instructor's permission, download at least three new pictures. Create a new, blank document and insert and label each picture you downloaded. Save, preview, and print the document. (*Caution:* Most graphics used on Web pages or offered for sale at Web sites are copyrighted. Be certain you do not download and use any of these copyrighted graphics. If you are unsure whether you can use specific graphics, contact the Webmaster at the site and ask permission before you download the graphics.)

Project 4
Joyee Martin is drafting a five-page report to management on travel services office employee training needs. She wants to dress up the report with page borders and wants you to create a sample report for her review. Create a five-page document that includes a title page. Create fictitious text for the title page, but leave the remaining pages blank. Apply a page border to only the title page. Number all the pages at the center bottom except the first page. Add the text watermark "CONFIDENTIAL" to print on each page, including the title page. Save, preview, and print the document.

Project 5
It's time to create the November travel newsletter. Create the newsletter with the following topics: "Holiday Specials," "New Travel Services Employees," "Trip of the Month," and "Hot Travel Web Sites." Add at least two brief paragraphs of text for each topic. Using the Internet, search for interesting Web sites to include. Insert a paragraph warning readers about downloading a picture or copying Web page text that is copyrighted. Add two Web page references where the readers can find out more about copyright issues on the Web. Use columns, WordArt, drop caps, pic-tures, drawing objects, line and character spacing, and page borders to make the document interesting and attractive. Save, preview, and print the document.

Project 6
Joyee Martin needs help preparing travel services office training materials that include pictures and callouts. You decide to create some examples for her review. Use online Help, if necessary, to research how to create callouts. Create a new, blank document and insert at least three AutoShapes. Add callouts using different callout styles to the AutoShapes. Save, preview, and print the example document. Write Joyee an interoffice memorandum explaining how to create and edit callouts. Save, preview, and print the memo.

Project 7
The shipping manager wants to put the Shipping Department organization chart on the company intranet. Create an organization chart for the Shipping Department using fictitious data. Include three levels in your chart. Save the document as a Web page. Preview, and print the Web page.

Project 8
Jon Swenson, a chartered accountant in the Vancouver branch office, would like to know more about the Microsoft Equation 3.0 application. Open Microsoft Equation 3.0 and use the online Help to locate and review the Equation Editor basics topic. Write Jon an interoffice memorandum describing the application and how to use it. Save, preview, and print the memo.

Working with Large Documents

Word 2002

Chapter Overview

Creating master documents enables you to work efficiently with large documents such as books and reports by separating a large document into smaller subdocuments. This allows multiple people to work on the large document at the same time. Another timesaving feature is the ability to format and summarize the entire document automatically. In this chapter, you learn to create and manage master documents and subdocuments, use AutoFormat to quickly format an entire document, save multiple versions of the same document in one file, and use AutoSummarize to create a synopsis of a document.

Learning Objectives

- Create master documents and subdocuments
- Create multiple versions of a document
- Automatically format an entire document
- Automatically summarize a document

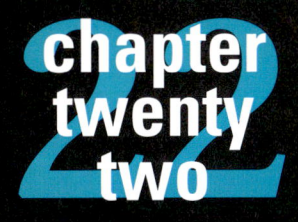

Case profile

You are transferred to the chairman's office to work on several large documents. You work with the chairman's executive assistant to create master and subdocuments. You also use other techniques for working effectively and efficiently with large documents.

chapter twenty two
22

22.a Creating Master Documents and Subdocuments

The Master Document feature allows you to separate a large document into smaller, more manageable subdocuments. The **master document** is a file that organizes and displays a series of smaller, related individual files, called **subdocuments**. Subdocuments are stored in separate files with their own filenames. You can work on all the subdocuments in the master document or you can open and work in an individual subdocument. Subdocuments let work group members access different parts of a larger document at the same time, while the master document keeps track of the subdocuments' overall structure.

Creating Subdocuments

You create a master document and subdocuments from an outline in Outline view using built-in heading styles or outline-level paragraph formats. First identify the outline level where you want the subdocuments created with a built-in heading style or an outline-level paragraph format. If you do not want to change the heading text formatting, use the outline-level paragraph formats. Word creates a subdocument each time that heading style or outline-level paragraph formats occurs in the document.

The executive assistant wants you to open a document about the Internet, and create a master document with subdocuments for each major heading that appears in all uppercase characters. Then, she and several coworkers can work simultaneously on the large document.

Because she does not want you to change the current formatting by applying styles, you apply the outline-level paragraph format Level 1 to the paragraph heading text to create the subdocuments. You can do this from the Paragraph dialog box or from the Outlining toolbar. To open the *Internet Master Document* and format the heading text:

Step 1	Open	the *Internet Master Document* document located on the Data Disk
Step 2	Display	the Outlining toolbar using a shortcut menu and dock it below the Formatting toolbar, if necessary
Step 3	Select	the INTRODUCTION TO THE INTERNET, INTERNET ACCESS, INTERNET CHALLENGES, and LOADING A WEB PAGE paragraph headings using the CTRL key
Step 4	Click	the Outline Level button list arrow [Level 1] on the Outlining toolbar

---

QUICK TIP

You can format the master document as a whole or format each subdocument separately. For example, you can use one template in the master document and a different one in the subdocuments. You also can create a table of contents for the document as a whole in the master document, or you can create a table of contents for each subdocument. And you can print either the master document or individual subdocuments.

Working with Large Documents **WA 197**

Step 5	Click	Level 1
Step 6	Move	the insertion point to the top of the document
Step 7	Save	the document as *Internet Master Document With Subdocuments*
Step 8	Switch to	Outline view
Step 9	Observe	that the Outlining toolbar is expanded to include buttons that create, expand, collapse, combine, split, unlock, and remove subdocuments in the master document

Your screen should look similar to Figure 22-1.

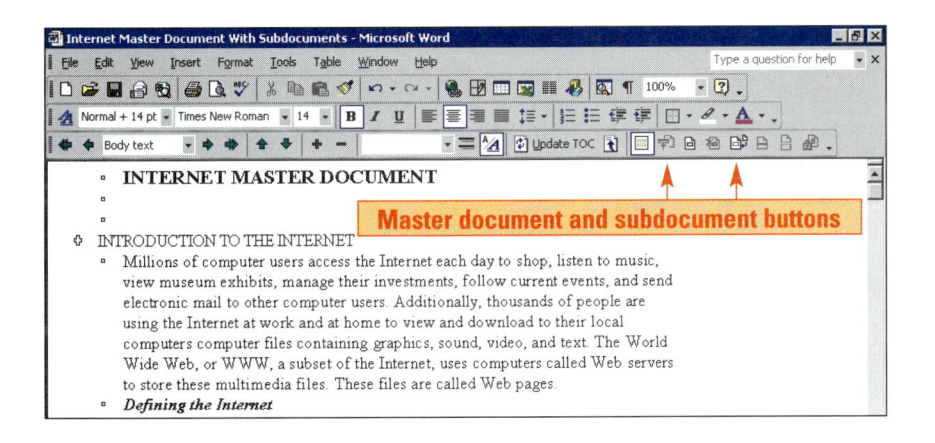

FIGURE 22-1
Document in Outline View

You now create the subdocuments in your master document. To create the subdocuments:

Step 1	Select	the text from "INTRODUCTION TO THE INTERNET" to the end of the document
Step 2	Click	the Create Subdocument button on the Outlining toolbar

Subdocuments are created at each Level 1 heading. Each subdocument is enclosed in a box that contains the text for that subdocument, outline-heading symbols, and a small subdocument icon in the upper-left corner of the subdocument box.

Step 3	Scroll	to view each subdocument and then back to the top of the document

After scrolling to the top of the document, your screen should look similar to Figure 22-2.

CAUTION TIP

Warning! Do not rename or move a subdocument using Windows Explorer, Windows NT File Manager, or MS-DOS. The master document will not be able to locate the subdocument if you do this. To rename a subdocument, display the master document in Outline view, open the subdocument in its own window, and save it with a new name. Then save the master document again.

chapter
twenty-two

FIGURE 22-2
First Subdocument in Master Document

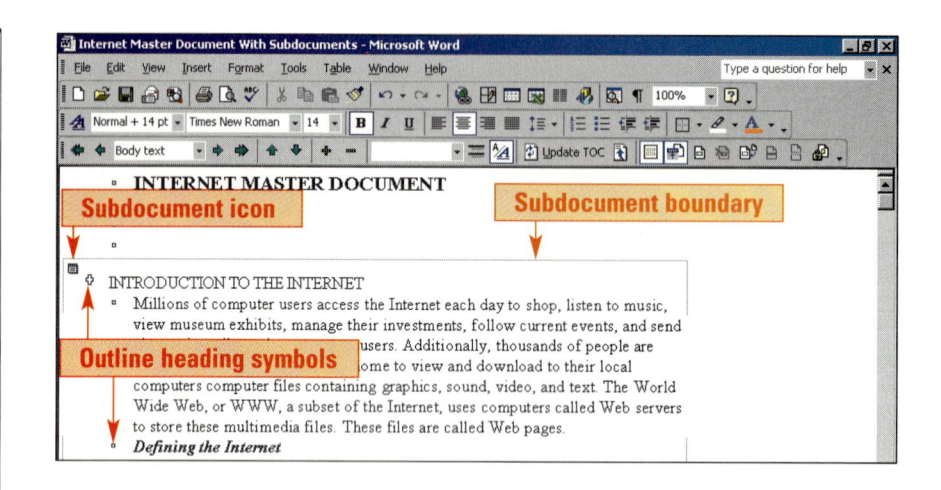

Step 4	*Save*	the document and leave it open

So that you can work with each subdocument independently, Word saves them individually.

Saving Master Documents and Subdocuments

When you save a master document, Word saves each subdocument as a separate file with a filename based on the heading text for that subdocument. The subdocuments are automatically saved in the same location as the master document. When you saved the *Internet Master Document With Subdocuments*, the master document and subdocuments were saved to the same location. To view the saved subdocuments files:

Step 1	*Open*	the Save As dialog box
Step 2	*Switch to*	the disk drive and folder where the *Internet Master Document With Subdocuments* document is stored
Step 3	*Observe*	that the four subdocuments *INTERNET ACCESS*, *INTERNET CHALLENGES*, *INTRODUCTION TO THE INTERNET*, and *LOADING A WEB PAGE* are also saved in the same location
Step 4	*Cancel*	the Save As dialog box
Step 5	*Close*	the document

You can edit subdocuments, split one subdocument into two or more subdocuments, or combine subdocuments into a single document.

Managing Subdocuments

Master documents give you the flexibility to maneuver and organize subdocuments. You can edit a subdocument in Outline view, or you can open a subdocument for viewing or editing in its own window. You can move subdocuments from one position to another within a master document. Finally, a subdocument can be split into two subdocuments and or two or more subdocuments can be combined into a single subdocument.

When you open a master document, each subdocument is represented by a hyperlink. Simply click the hyperlink to display the subdocument in its own window for editing or printing. Or, expand the master document to show all the subdocuments in Outline view and then work on the document as a whole. To open the *Internet Master Document With Subdocuments* and manage the subdocuments:

| Step 1 | *Open* | the *Internet Master Document With Subdocuments* document |
| Step 2 | *Observe* | that the subdocuments are collapsed and each subdocument is represented by a hyperlink |

You can open an individual subdocument by pressing the CTRL key and clicking the hyperlink, or you can expand all the subdocuments and work on them from the master document in Outline view. To open the INTRODUCTION TO THE INTERNET subdocument in its own window:

| Step 1 | *CTRL + Click* | the INTRODUCTION TO THE INTERNET hyperlink |

The subdocument opens as a separate document in its own window. You can edit the subdocument as you would any Word document. After the subdocument is edited, you can save it with the Save command on the File menu or the Save button on the Formatting toolbar. Because the subdocument and the master document are linked, Word automatically saves the changes to both the subdocument and the master document. You close the subdocument just like any other document.

| Step 2 | *Close* | the subdocument |
| Step 3 | *Observe* | that the INTRODUCTION TO THE INTERNET hyperlink in the master document is a different color, indicating that it is a "followed" link that has been used to "jump" to another document |

QUICK TIP

The lock icon below the subdocument icon to the left of each hyperlink indicates the subdocument is locked. By default, all collapsed subdocuments appear locked. A locked subdocument has a read-only file-sharing property, which means that others can open the document and read it but cannot modify it. To determine if the subdocument is actually locked, you must open it or expand all subdocuments. When a subdocument is locked, the lock icon appears when it is expanded or "Read-only" appears on the title bar when it is opened. You can lock and unlock subdocuments with the Lock Document button on the Outlining toolbar.

CAUTION TIP

Whenever you use hyperlinks, Word automatically opens the Web toolbar. You can leave the toolbar open or close it with the shortcut menu. The figures in this chapter do not show the Web toolbar.

chapter twenty-two

QUICK TIP

When you save changes to the master document, Word automatically updates the subdocuments and creates new subdocument files for the newly created subdocuments.

When you save the changes to the master document, Word saves the combined subdocuments with the filename of the first subdocument.

CAUTION TIP

When you combine subdocuments, remove subdocuments, or delete subdocuments and their contents from a master document, the original subdocument files remain on the disk in the directory where they were saved. You can delete these files from the disk by using Windows Explorer or by using the shortcut menu in the Open or Save As dialog box.

If you want to work on the subdocuments from within the master document, you can display the contents of all the subdocuments at one time. To expand the subdocuments:

Step 1	Click	the Expand Subdocuments button on the Outlining toolbar
Step 2	Observe	that the subdocuments replace their hyperlinks

You can move individual topics within a subdocument or reposition an entire subdocument within the master document. You reposition a subdocument by selecting the subdocument and then dragging it to a new position. To reposition the INTERNET ACCESS subdocument after LOADING A WEB PAGE subdocument:

Step 1	Click	the INTERNET ACCESS subdocument icon to select the entire subdocument
Step 2	Position	the mouse pointer on the INTERNET ACCESS subdocument icon
Step 3	Click & hold	the left mouse button to view the move pointer
Step 4	Drag	the INTERNET ACCESS subdocument icon down with the move pointer until a horizontal gray line appears immediately below the LOADING A WEB PAGE subdocument (do not drag to the bottom of the document)
Step 5	Deselect	the subdocument text

You can combine two or more adjacent subdocuments into a single subdocument. When you save the file, Word saves only one file with the name of the first subdocument. The other subdocument files are no longer linked to the master document and you can delete them. To combine the LOADING A WEB PAGE and INTERNET ACCESS subdocuments into a single subdocument:

Step 1	Click	the LOADING A WEB PAGE subdocument icon to select the subdocument
Step 2	SHIFT + Click	the INTERNET ACCESS subdocument icon to select the subdocument
Step 3	Click	the Merge Subdocument button on the Outlining toolbar
Step 4	Deselect	the subdocument text
Step 5	Scroll	the document to view the combined subdocuments

Working with Large Documents   WA 201

You might need to split a large subdocument into more than one subdocument, or you might want to create a subdocument within another subdocument. To split a subdocument, you must place the insertion point at the position where the split will occur. To split the LOADING A WEBPAGE subdocument:

Step 1	Move	the insertion point before the "I" in the INTERNET ACCESS heading in the LOADING A WEB PAGE subdocument
Step 2	Click	the Split Subdocument button on the Outlining toolbar
Step 3	Observe	that the combined subdocument is split into two subdocuments: LOADING A WEB PAGE and INTERNET ACCESS.

You also can create subdocuments within other subdocuments. You want to create a subdocument for the Internet Service Providers text in the INTERNET ACCESS subdocument. To open the subdocument and format the heading:

Step 1	Double-click	the INTERNET ACCESS subdocument icon to open the subdocument for editing
Step 2	Display	the Outlining toolbar with a shortcut menu
Step 3	Apply	the Outline level: LEVEL 1 paragraph format to the Internet Service Providers paragraph heading
Step 4	Save	the document as INTERNET ACCESS to update the copy on the disk (Caution: Word attempts to assign a new name to the document; save it with the original name INTERNET ACCESS and replace the old file) and then close the subdocument

To create the new subdocument:

Step 1	Select	the paragraph heading "Internet Service Providers" and the following paragraph in the INTERNET ACCESS subdocument
Step 2	Click	the Create Subdocument button on the Outlining toolbar
Step 3	Scroll	to view a separate subdocument, Internet Service Providers, within the INTERNET ACCESS subdocument
Step 4	Close	the master document without saving any changes

MOUSE TIP

You can remove a subdocument, making the subdocument text part of the master document, by selecting the subdocument and clicking the Remove Subdocument button on the Outlining toolbar.

You can delete a subdocument and its contents from a master document by selecting the subdocument and pressing the DELETE or BACKSPACE key.

QUICK TIP

You can print all or part of a master document, or you can print individual subdocuments. To print an entire master document, expand the subdocuments and then print the entire document from Normal view. To print an individual subdocument, open the subdocument and click the Print command on the File menu or the Print button on the Formatting toolbar. For more information on working with master documents and subdocuments, see online Help.

chapter
twenty-two

22.b Creating Multiple Versions of a Document

Sometimes you modify a document and then want to keep copies of both the original version and the modified version. Rather than saving each version of the document as separate files, you can save multiple versions of the same document in one file. You want to open the *Unformatted Report* document and let Word automatically format it. Before you format the document, you decide to save the original unformatted document as the original version of the document in a new file. Later, you save the formatted version in the same file. To open the document and save it with a new name:

Step 1	**Open**	the *Unformatted Report* document located on the Data Disk
Step 2	**Save**	the document as *Report Versions*
Step 3	**Click**	File
Step 4	**Click**	Versions

The Versions in Report Versions dialog box on your screen should look similar to Figure 22-3. You can save the current version of the document and view a list of other versions saved in the same file. You can add a comment to identify this version of the document in the Save Versions dialog box.

FIGURE 22-3
Versions in Report Versions Dialog Box

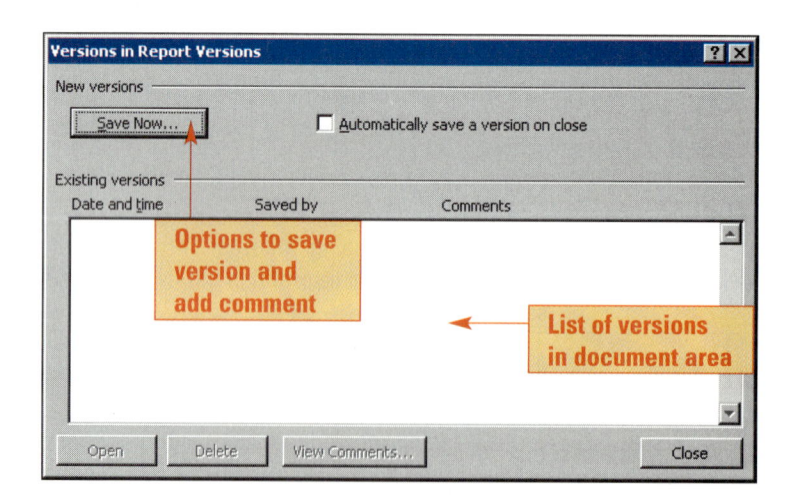

Options to save version and add comment

List of versions in document area

Step 5	**Click**	Save Now to open the Save Version dialog box

The Save Version dialog box on your screen should look similar to Figure 22-4.

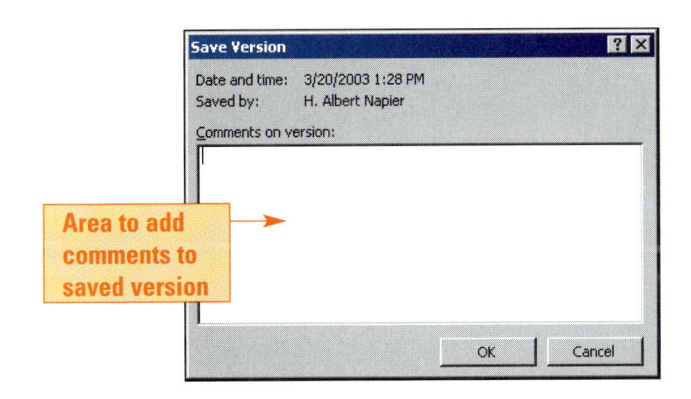

FIGURE 22-4
Save Version Dialog Box

Area to add comments to saved version

Step 6	Key	Unformatted version in the <u>C</u>omments on version: text box
Step 7	Click	OK
Step 8	Observe	that the unformatted version of the document is saved and the Versions mode indicator is added to the end of the status bar to the right of the Spelling and Grammar Status mode indicator

Now you can modify the document and save it as a different version in the same file. When you want to quickly format a document you can have Word make all the formatting decisions for you.

22.c Automatically Format an Entire Document

When you need to format a document quickly, you can use the AutoFormat command on the Format menu to format the entire document based on the built-in styles. Word applies styles based on the position of text in the document. To expedite formatting the *Report Versions* document you decide to use the AutoFormat feature. Then you save the formatted document as the final version in the same file as the original version of the document. To automatically format the document:

Step 1	Move	the insertion point to the top of the document, if necessary
Step 2	Click	F<u>o</u>rmat
Step 3	Click	<u>A</u>utoFormat

chapter
twenty-two

The AutoFormat dialog box on your screen should look similar to Figure 22-5.

FIGURE 22-5
AutoFormat Dialog Box

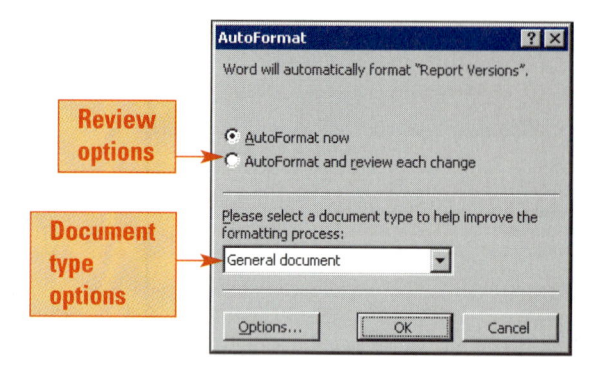

You can let Word format the entire document with or without prompting you to review and accept or reject the changes. You can select a basic document type—general document, letter, or e-mail—to help Word determine the type of formatting to apply. You can view and turn on or off the AutoFormat options in the AutoCorrect dialog box by clicking the Options button.

Step 4	Click	the AutoFormat and review each change option button
Step 5	Verify	that General document appears in the Please select a document type list
Step 6	Click	OK

The second AutoFormat dialog box on your screen should look similar to Figure 22-6. You review, accept, and reject the changes in this dialog box.

FIGURE 22-6
Second AutoFormat Dialog Box

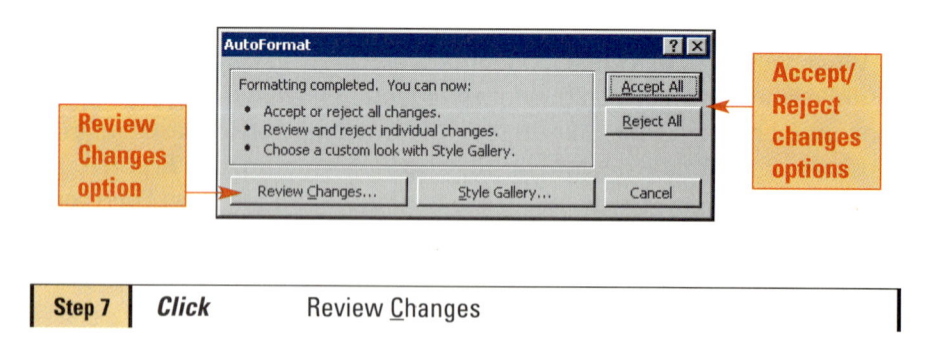

Step 7	Click	Review Changes

Word formats the document using built-in styles. The Review AutoFormat Changes dialog box on your screen should look similar to Figure 22-7.

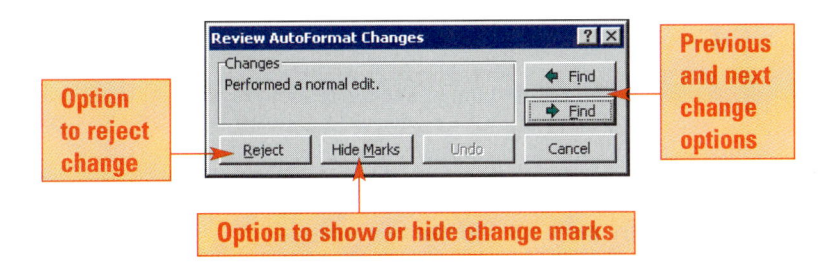

FIGURE 22-7
Review AutoFormat Changes Dialog Box

[Screenshot of Review AutoFormat Changes dialog box with callouts: "Option to reject change" pointing to Reject button; "Previous and next change options" pointing to Find buttons; "Option to show or hide change marks" pointing to Hide Marks button]

Next, you find and accept or reject each of the changes Word made to the document. You move from change to change and accept or reject it using this dialog box. You can show or hide the change marks (a red paragraph mark notation) as desired. You accept a change by moving to the next change. To review the changes:

Step 1	Click	Find to highlight the first change
Step 2	Observe	the referenced highlighted text and the formatting change comment in the dialog box
Step 3	Click	Find to accept the change and move to the next instance
Step 4	Observe	the highlighted paragraph mark and the comment (Applied style Heading 1.) in the dialog box
Step 5	Continue	to review several changes and then cancel the dialog box
Step 6	Click	Accept All to accept all the formatting changes without further review

You save the formatted document as a different version in the same file. To save the document as the final version:

Step 1	Double-click	the Version mode indicator on the status bar
Step 2	Click	Save Now
Step 3	Key	Formatted version in the Comments on version: text box
Step 4	Click	OK to save the formatted version in the same file as the unformatted version

You can look at all the saved versions in a file. To view both versions of the *Report Versions* document:

Step 1	Double-click	the Versions mode indicator on the status bar
Step 2	Observe	the two versions of the document listed in the Versions in Report Versions dialog box

> **QUICK TIP**
>
> To open and edit or print either version, click the Versions command on the File menu or double-click the Versions mode indicator on the status bar.

chapter twenty-two

| Step 3 | *Close* | the dialog box |
| Step 4 | *Save* | the document and leave it open |

To quickly review a large document on your screen, you can have Word automatically summarize the key points.

22.d Automatically Summarize a Document

The AutoSummarize feature provides options to automatically summarize a document by highlighting key text within the document, creating a new document with the summary, inserting an executive-style summary at the top of the document, or hiding the document and displaying only the summary.

To automatically summarize the *Report Versions* document by highlighting key text:

| Step 1 | *Click* | Tools |
| Step 2 | *Click* | AutoSummarize |

The AutoSummarize dialog box on your screen should look similar to Figure 22-8.

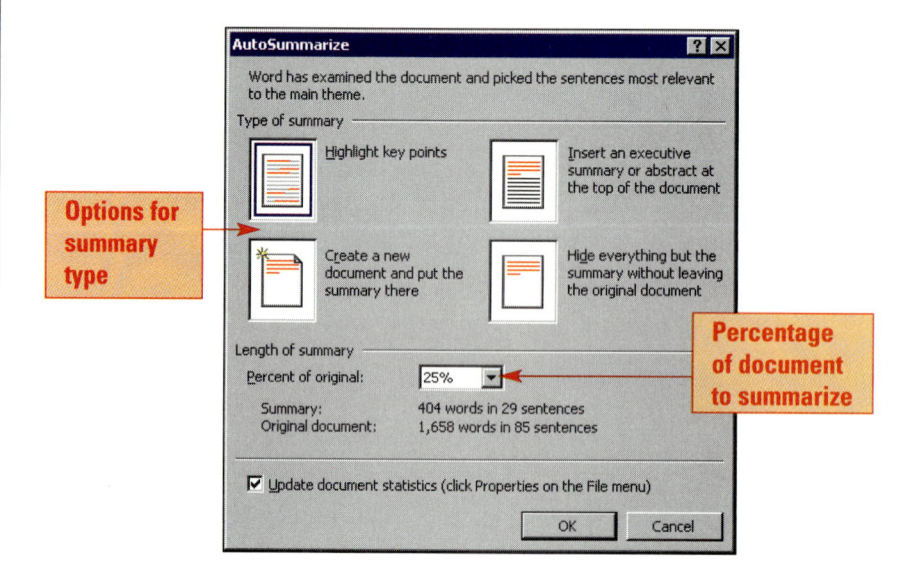

> **QUICK TIP**
>
> To summarize a document, Word analyzes the document and assigns a score to each sentence. Sentences that contain frequently used words get a higher score. The document is summarized to show a percentage of the highest scoring sentences. For best results, make sure the Find All Word Forms tool is installed.

FIGURE 22-8
AutoSummarize Dialog Box

Step 3	Click	the Highlight key points option, if necessary
Step 4	Click	25% in the Percent of original: list, if necessary
Step 5	Click	OK

The key points are highlighted in yellow and the AutoSummarize toolbar appears. You can hide or show only the highlighted summary portion of the document, change the percentage of the document that is summarized, and remove the highlighting using the AutoSummarize toolbar. The Highlight/Show Only Summary button allows you to turn the highlighting off and view just the summarized text. If formatting marks are turned on, the Highlight/Show Only Summary button turns off the highlighting and displays all the text; the text that is not part of the summary has a dotted underline. To view only the summary:

Step 1	Click	the Highlight/Show Only Summary button on the AutoSummarize toolbar
Step 2	Hide	the view of formatting marks, if necessary
Step 3	Observe	that only the 25% of the document that is the summary displays and the rest of the document is hidden
Step 4	Click	the Close button on the AutoSummarize toolbar to turn off the summarization
Step 5	Save	the document and close it

Master and subdocuments, versions, AutoFormat, and AutoSummarize provide techniques for working effectively and efficiently with large documents.

> **MOUSE TIP**
>
> You can include a larger or smaller number of the highest scoring sentences in the summary by clicking the right or left arrows on the Percent of Original button on the AutoSummarize toolbar.

chapter twenty-two

Summary

- The Master Document feature helps you separate a large document into smaller, more manageable subdocuments.
- To create a master document, you can convert an existing document, combine existing documents into a master document, or key original text as an outline in Outline view.
- Word uses the built-in heading styles or paragraph Outline level: formats to identify subdocuments.
- When you save a master document, Word also saves each subdocument as a separate file and automatically assigns a filename to each subdocument.
- You can edit a subdocument in Outline view in the master document or open each subdocument in its own window.
- You can split subdocuments into more than one subdocument or combine multiple subdocuments into one subdocument.
- Master documents and subdocuments can be printed together or individually.
- You can have Word automatically format documents using the built-in styles and then accept or reject each formatting change.
- The AutoSummarize feature summarizes large documents by displaying a percentage of key sentences.

Commands Review

Action	Menu Bar	Shortcut Menu	Toolbar	Task Pane	Keyboard
Display a document in Outline view	View, Outline				ALT + V, O
Select one or multiple subdocuments			Click (or SHIFT + Click) the subdocument icon(s)		
Move a subdocument			Drag the selected subdocument to the new location		
Merge or split subdocuments					
Insert or remove subdocuments					
Create a subdocument					
Expand or collapse subdocuments					CTRL + \
Automatically format a document using built-in styles	Format, AutoFormat				ALT + O, A
Automatically summarize a document	Tools, AutoSummarize				ALT + T, U

Working with Large Documents   WA 209

Concepts Review

Circle the correct answer.

1. **You create and manage master and subdocuments with buttons on the:**
   [a] Formatting toolbar.
   [b] Standard toolbar.
   [c] Outlining toolbar.
   [d] Master Document toolbar.

2. **Which of the following steps is not part of the process for creating a subdocument?**
   [a] Format the paragraph heading text with Word built-in heading styles or paragraph outline-level formats.
   [b] Identify the outline level where the subdocuments occur.
   [c] Select the outline level text to be included in the subdocuments.
   [d] Switch to Normal view and select the text to be included in the subdocuments.

3. **Saving a master document:**
   [a] saves each subdocument with a filename consisting of the master document name and a number.
   [b] saves all subdocuments in a new folder created for subdocuments.
   [c] saves all subdocuments in the same location as the master document.
   [d] does not automatically save each subdocument.

4. **You can let Word automatically format a document with:**
   [a] built-in styles.
   [b] a summary.
   [c] outline-level paragraph formats.
   [d] versions.

5. **Word automatically summarizes a document based on the number of:**
   [a] keywords in each sentence.
   [b] styles applied to paragraph headings.
   [c] subdocuments in the document.
   [d] workgroup members to use the document.

6. **A master document is:**
   [a] a brief summary of a document.
   [b] one of a series of small related files.
   [c] created when you track changes to a document.
   [d] a file that organizes and displays a series of smaller, related files.

7. **When you need to quickly format an entire document, you can use the:**
   [a] AutoText command.
   [b] AutoComplete command.
   [c] AutoFormat command.
   [d] AutoCorrect command.

8. **You can quickly review the key points in a large document by:**
   [a] creating a master document.
   [b] automatically formatting the document.
   [c] automatically summarizing the document.
   [d] expanding the document.

chapter twenty-two

Circle **T** if the statement is true or **F** if the statement is false.

T F   1. You can save multiple versions of a document in a single file.

T F   2. You cannot create new subdocuments within an existing subdocument.

T F   3. Word assigns a score to sentences containing keywords and then highlights a percentage of the most highly scored sentences when you automatically summarize a document.

T F   4. When you combine subdocuments, remove subdocuments, or delete subdocuments, the original subdocument files are automatically removed from the folder in which they were saved.

T F   5. Master documents can be edited only in Normal view.

T F   6. When you automatically format an entire document, you must accept all of the formatting changes.

T F   7. Combined subdocuments are saved with the filename of the first subdocument.

Skills Review

Exercise 1

1. Open the *Unformatted E-Commerce Report* document located on the Data Disk.
2. Automatically format the document without reviewing changes.
3. Save the document as *Formatted E-Commerce Report*, and then preview, print, and close it.

Exercise 2

1. Open the *Formatted E-Commerce Report* document you created in Exercise 1. If you have not created the document, do so now.
2. Use the AutoSummarize feature to insert an executive summary at the top of the document consisting of 15% of the original document.
3. Save the document as *E-Commerce Report With Summary*, and then preview, print, and close it.

Exercise 3

1. Open the *Top Sales* document located on the Data Disk.
2. Display the Outlining toolbar.
3. Select the uppercase headings with the CTRL key and apply the outline Level 1 format to them.
4. View the document in Outline view and verify the outline-level icon at the left of each uppercase heading.
5. Select the entire document and create the subdocuments.
6. Save the master document as *Top Sales Master Document* and close it.
7. Verify that the four subdocuments are saved in the same folder as the master document.
8. Open the *Top Sales Master Document* document and expand the subdocuments.
9. Move the UNITED STATES subdocument to the end of the master document just before the last blank line.
10. Move the AUSTRALIA subdocument to the top of the document above CANADA.
11. Save the master document and subdocuments to update the copies on the disk.
12. Print and close the master document.

Exercise 4

1. Open the *About the New Economy* document located on the Data Disk.
2. Switch to Outline view, select the entire document, and create subdocuments.
3. Save the master document as *New Economy Master Document* and close it.
4. Open the *New Economy Master Document* and expand the subdocuments.
5. Open the Electronic Linking subdocument in its own window.
6. Insert the paragraph heading "Processing Information" formatted with the Heading 1 style above the paragraph that begins "In the new economy, processing information…."
7. Save the subdocument with the same name and close it.
8. Move the insertion point to the "Processing Information" heading inside the Electronic Linking subdocument and split the subdocument into two subdocuments.
9. Save the master document and then preview, print, and close it.

Exercise 5

1. Open the *Top Sales Master Document* document you created in Exercise 3. If you have not created the document, do so now.
2. Expand the subdocuments.
3. Select the subdocuments using the SHIFT + Click method and then remove them.
4. Switch to Normal view and remove any section breaks and blank lines.
5. Save the document as *Top Products*.
6. Save the current version of *Top Products* with the comment "Unformatted version."
7. Select the entire document and create an outline numbered list using the I,II,III style. Use the TAB key to organize the outline: Level 1 are uppercase headings; Level 2 are bold headings; Level 3 are subtopics under each bold heading. (*Hint:* You can use the CTRL key to select several items at once and then indent them at the same time with the TAB key.)
8. Save the outline numbered list as a version in the *Top Products* document with the comment "Numbered list."
9. Use the Versions mode indicator to open the Unformatted version in its own window and then preview, print, and close it. Then preview, print, and close the *Top Products* Numbered list version.
10. Save the document and close it.

Exercise 6

1. Open the *Chicago Warehouses Audit* document located on the Data Disk.
2. Summarize the document 25% and create a new document containing the summary.
3. Save the new document as *Chicago Summary*, and then preview, print, and close it.
4. Close the *Chicago Warehouses Audit* document.

chapter twenty-two

Exercise 7

1. Open the *Word Processing* document located on the Data Disk.
2. Select all the uppercase paragraph headings with the CTRL key and apply the Heading 3 style to them.
3. Switch to Outline view.
4. Select the entire document and create subdocuments.
5. Merge the LETTERS and BUSINESS CORRESPONDENCE subdocuments.
6. Open and print the merged LETTERS subdocument.
7. Delete the STATISTICAL REPORTS subdocument. (*Hint:* Removing a subdocument with the Remove Subdocument button on the Outlining toolbar places the subdocument text in the master document. To completely delete subdocument text, select the subdocument and press the DELETE key.)
8. Save the master document as *Word Processing Master Document* and close it.

Exercise 8

1. Open the *About Master Documents* document located on the Data Disk.
2. Automatically format the document, and review and accept all changes.
3. Save the document as *Formatted About Master Documents*, and then preview, print and close it.

Case Projects

Project 1

Chris Lofton calls to ask for your help. The Word Processing Department has just received the draft (on disk) of a new 15-chapter research report, which must be edited, formatted, and printed within two days. You suggest to Chris that a master document with subdocuments for Chapters 1–5, 6–10, and 11–15 be created so that three word processing specialists can work on the document at one time. Chris asks you to create a procedure memo for the operators describing in detail how they create, edit, save, and print the master document and subdocuments. Create, save, preview, and print the procedure memo.

Project 2

You want to add a Web page to the company intranet that provides links to new Web sites of interest for your coworkers. Using the Internet, review the built-in "Best of the Web" Web site from the button on the Internet Explorer Links bar. (If you are using a different browser, open a comparable Web page.) Review the links. Print at least three Web pages. Create a Word document containing text describing the Web sites and links to the Web sites and save it as a Web page. Save, preview, and print the Web page.

chapter twenty-two

Project 3

While working on the research report, a word processing specialist called you for help solving several problems. Review online Help for solutions to the following problems:

1. The subdocument buttons are unavailable on the Outlining toolbar.
2. Word won't save my master document and the subdocuments in it.
3. I tried to open a master document or subdocument but get a message that the file is in use.

Create an outline itemizing these problems and suggesting solutions. Save, preview, and print the outline. With your instructor's permission, discuss how to solve these three problems with three classmates, using the outline as a guide.

Project 4

Jody Haversham wants to insert an existing Word document into a master document and needs help. Using online Help, research this problem and then write Jody a memo describing how to solve Jody's problem. Save, preview, and print the memo.

Project 5

Joyee Martin wants you to make a short presentation to the next administrative assistants' monthly luncheon on using the AutoSummarize feature. She asks you to cover the basics of the feature and discuss troubleshooting issues. Create an outline of the topics you are going to present at the luncheon. Save, preview, and print the outline. With your instructor's permission, use the outline to describe using and troubleshooting the AutoSummarize feature to a group of classmates.

Project 6

Angelica Hubert, from the Melbourne office, sends you an e-mail. She is trying to automatically format several documents and the results are not what she expected. She asks for your help. Using online Help, research how to use the AutoFormat features, how to turn the features on or off, and how to solve several common problems when using the AutoFormat features. Then draft a document, to be attached to an e-mail message at a later time, that summarizes your research. Save, preview, and print the document.

Project 7

Jeff Bridgestone, in the Purchasing Department, drops by your desk. He read a brief article on saving different document versions in the same file and would like to know more about the feature. Using online Help, research how to save versions of a document. Then write Jeff a memo that describes the process. Save, preview, and print the memo.

Project 8

Joyee Martin needs to put together a list of Web sites that provide current e-commerce news. Using the Internet, search for e-commerce news Web sites. Print at least five home pages. Write Joyee a memo listing the Web sites by name and URL. Include a brief description of the kind of e-commerce news she can find at each site. Save, preview, and print the memo.

chapter twenty-two

Word 2002

Using Online Forms

Chapter Overview

Filling in forms online (also called onscreen) speeds up the order-taking process and helps ensure accuracy because data is keyed once, as the form is completed. Word has the ability to create form templates for documents such as invoices, routing slips, order forms, and schedules. The documents based on these templates are then completed on the screen by filling-in data such as dates and amounts, marking check boxes, or selecting items from list boxes. In this chapter, you learn to create a form template and complete a document based on the form template.

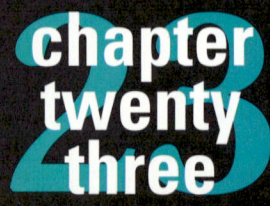

Learning Objectives

- Create and modify an online form
- Create a document based on a form template

Case profile

The Worldwide Exotic Foods Sales Department takes telephone orders and then manually prepares an order form. Later the Accounting Department imports this information into the company's databases. The sales manager believes the process could be more efficient if the sales representatives completed the order form online during the telephone conversation. You assist the sales manager in developing an online order form template.

chapter twenty three

23.a Creating and Modifying an Online Form

A **form** is a document that contains nonvariable informational text (called **boilerplate**) and spaces to enter variable information. Forms, such as Worldwide Exotic Foods' online order form, can include boilerplate text along with fill-in text boxes to key text and numerical data, check boxes to specify yes or no type of information, drop-down lists to select from a standard group, calculations of numerical data, and dates. You create forms as templates with tables for the layout and Word form fields for the variable information.

The Worldwide Exotic Foods sales manager wants you to create an order form that the sales representatives can complete online at the computer as they receive orders from customers. This form will contain the following variables:

1. Buyer's name and address (Sold to)
2. Shipping address (Ship to)
3. Sales representative's name
4. Order date
5. Ship by date
6. Shipping method
7. Item number
8. Item description (Description)
9. Quantity ordered (Qty Ordered)

The first step in creating an online form is to plan the framework and content. A good way to do this is to draw the form on a sheet of paper so that you can visualize how it looks. Also, include any text and form fields to ensure you have room for all the information. It is also helpful to have an end user (such as a Worldwide Exotic Foods sales representative, in this case) review your draft of the form to check for errors or omissions. After you are satisfied with the draft of the form, the next steps are to create a new form template, draw the table structure, enter boilerplate and form fields, and then save the template.

The reviewed and approved form, with variable data organized into four tables, is shown in Figure 23-1.

Creating a Form Template

After you are satisfied with the draft of the form, you begin by creating a new template. You create a form from a template so that each sales representative can open a new document that contains all the boilerplate and blank form fields, and then enter the variable information. After completing the form, the sales representative can save each order separately.

FIGURE 23-1
Completed Order Form

```
                Worldwide Exotic Foods, Inc.
                      Chicago Branch
                 1000 Ellis Street, Suite 1135
                    Chicago, IL 60606-1135
                        (312) 555-7328
                     sales@wwide.xeon.net
                      www.wwidesales.com

                         ORDER FORM
```

| Sold to: | | Ship to: | |

Sales Representative	Order Date	Ship by Date	Shipping Method

Item Number	Description	Qty Ordered

Quick Tip

Forms can be printed on plain paper or on preprinted forms. To print the form on plain paper, simply print the document as you would any Word document. To print only the variable data in the current document on a preprinted form, click the Print data only for forms check box to insert a check mark on the Print tab in the Options dialog box.

To create a new template:

Step 1	**Display**	the New Document task pane
Step 2	**Click**	the General Templates link in the New from template section in the New Document task pane
Step 3	**Click**	the General tab in the Templates dialog box, if necessary
Step 4	**Click**	the Template option button
Step 5	**Double-click**	the Blank Document icon to create the blank template document

Using Online Forms   **WA 217**

Creating the Form Framework

You key and format boilerplate in a template just as you do in a document. You draw the tables to create the form's framework. You can use the Insert, Table command or button to create simple forms, or you can use the Draw Table button on the Tables and Borders toolbar or Forms toolbar to create complex forms. Because this form is complex, you draw the tables that organize the text and fields. You can draw tables to the approximate size and use the mouse pointer (and the ALT key to view actual numbers on the horizontal and vertical rulers) to more accurately size the tables. To begin the form:

Step 1	Set	1-inch top, left, right, and bottom margins
Step 2	Key	the heading text shown in Figure 23-1, with one blank line before and two blank lines after the ORDER FORM text
Step 3	Format	the heading text as 12-point, bold, Times New Roman, center-aligned
Step 4	Move	the insertion point to the end of the document
Step 5	Display	the Tables and Borders toolbar and dock it below the Formatting toolbar
Step 6	Switch to	Print Layout view, if necessary

> **QUICK TIP**
>
> You can open the AutoFormat As You Type tab in the AutoCorrect dialog box and turn off the Internet and network paths with hyperlinks option to avoid creating a hyperlink when you key an e-mail address. Alternatively, right-click the hyperlink, point to Hyperlink, and click the Remove Hyperlink command.

As you follow the steps below, turn on or off the Draw Table feature as necessary. To draw the first two side-by-side tables for the Sold to: and Ship to: boxes on the form:

Step 1	Select	a 2¼ pt single line format
Step 2	Draw	a rectangle approximately 1 inch high and 2.65 inches wide, beginning at the left margin
Step 3	Draw	a same size rectangle approximately starting 0.9 inch to the right of the first rectangle and ending at the right margin
Step 4	Press & hold	the ALT key to view numbers on the horizontal ruler
Step 5	Drag	the left and right table boundaries to resize the tables more precisely
Step 6	Release	the ALT key
Step 7	Key	the 12-point, bold, Times New Roman text in each table, as shown in Figure 23-1

You are drawing the tables to an approximate size; however, your screen should look similar to Figure 23-2.

chapter
twenty-three

FIGURE 23-2
Side-by-Side Tables

CAUTION TIP

When you draw similarly sized side-by-side tables, Word joins the tables by adding a cell without printable borders between the two tables.

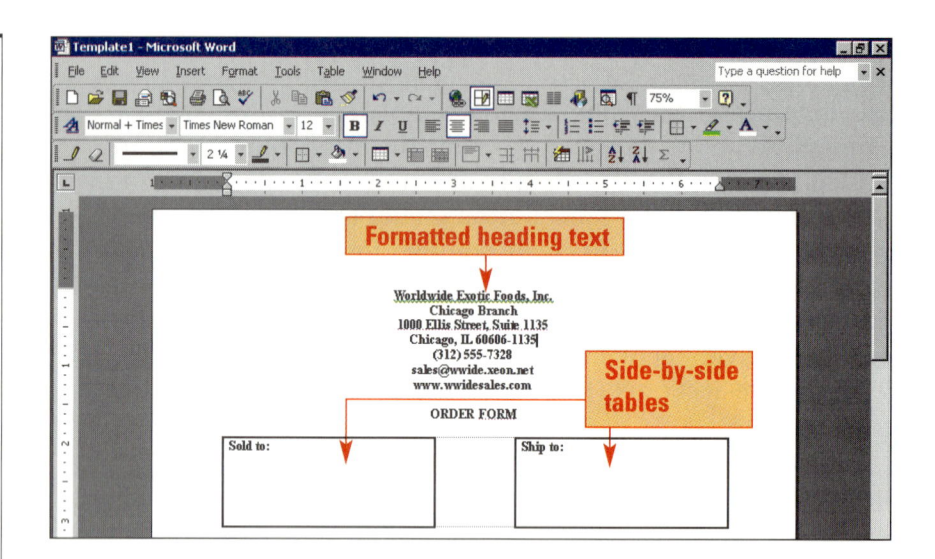

To draw the four-column table below the first two tables:

Step 1	*Change*	the line weight to 1½ pt
Step 2	*Draw*	a rectangle approximately ½ inch high from the left margin to the right margin starting approximately ¼ inch below the first two tables
Step 3	*Size*	the table more precisely by dragging the left and right borders while pressing the ALT key, if necessary
Step 4	*Draw*	a row from the left to the right boundary of the table approximately ½ inch high, using Figure 23-1 as a guide
Step 5	*Draw*	four columns in the new table, as shown in Figure 23-1 (the first and fourth columns are approximately 2 inches wide and the second and third columns are approximately 1.01 inches wide)
Step 6	*Apply*	Gray-20% shading to the first row in the table
Step 7	*Key*	the 12-point, bold, Times New Roman text in the first row of the table, as shown in Figure 23-1
Step 8	*Center*	the text vertically and horizontally

Your screen should look similar to Figure 23-3.

FIGURE 23-3
Third Table

Using Online Forms   WA 219

The fourth table contains three columns where sales representatives enter the variable information about the items ordered. To draw the fourth table below the third table:

Step 1	*Draw*	a rectangle from the left margin to the right margin, starting approximately ¼ inch below the third table and ending approximately ½ inch from the bottom margin
Step 2	*Size*	the left and right and bottom borders with the mouse pointer and the ALT key, if necessary
Step 3	*Draw*	13 rows across the table
Step 4	*Distribute*	the rows evenly
Step 5	*Draw*	a column approximately 1.5 inches from the left border
Step 6	*Draw*	a column approximately 1.2 inches from the right border
Step 7	*Apply*	Gray-20% shading to the first row
Step 8	*Key*	the 12-point, bold, Times New Roman text in the first row, as shown in Figure 23-1
Step 9	*Center*	the text vertically and horizontally

notes
To make templates easy to locate, they are saved by default in the C:\...\Application Data\Microsoft\Templates folder. This chapter assumes you are saving your template in an alternate location. Your instructor may provide different instructions for saving and using your custom templates.

QUICK TIP

You can create a template from any Word document by changing the Save as type: to Document Template in the Save As dialog box.

To save the order form template:

| Step 1 | *Save* | the template as *Order Form Template* in the location specified by your instructor and leave it open |

Creating and Modifying a Form Field

A **form field** (sometimes called a **form control**) is a placeholder for a specific type of variable information in a specific place in a document, such as names and addresses. Text form fields provide space for user to key regular text, numbers, or dates, and perform calculations. Table 23-1 describes the various Text form fields. Check Box form fields enable a user to select an option. Drop-Down form fields provide a list of variables from which a user can select.

chapter
twenty-three

TABLE 23-1
Text Form Field Descriptions

Option	Description
Regular text	text, numbers, symbols, or spaces
Number	numbers only
Date	date only
Current date/Current time	system date/time (you cannot change this field)
Calculation	=(formula) field to calculate numbers

You insert form fields with buttons on the Forms toolbar. To display the Forms toolbar:

Step 1	*Close*	the Tables and Borders toolbar
Step 2	*Display*	the Forms toolbar using a shortcut menu
Step 3	*Review*	the buttons on the Forms toolbar using the SHIFT + F1 Help pointer

This order form requires the following fields:
1. Text form fields for the names, addresses, item numbers, and item description data
2. Number form field for the quantity ordered data
3. Current date form field for the order date
4. Date form field for the ship by date
5. Check Box form fields to indicate the shipping method
6. Drop-Down form field to select the sales representative

You start by entering the text fields at the top of the form. To insert a Regular text form field for the Sold to name:

Step 1	*Move*	the insertion point to the right of the "Sold to:" text in the first table
Step 2	*Set*	a left-aligned tab stop at approximately 0.75 inches
Step 3	*Press*	the CTRL + TAB keys to insert a tab character formatting mark
Step 4	*Click*	the Text Form Field button [abl] on the Forms toolbar
Step 5	*Click*	the Form Field Shading button [a] on the Forms toolbar to turn on the field shading, if necessary
Step 6	*Turn on*	the view of formatting marks, if necessary
Step 7	*Zoom*	the document to 100%, if necessary

The form field is inserted in the table. Your screen should look similar to Figure 23-4.

> **MENU TIP**
>
> You can right-click a form field and then click the Properties command to open the Form Field Options dialog box.

> **MOUSE TIP**
>
> You can double-click a form field to open the Form Field Options dialog box.

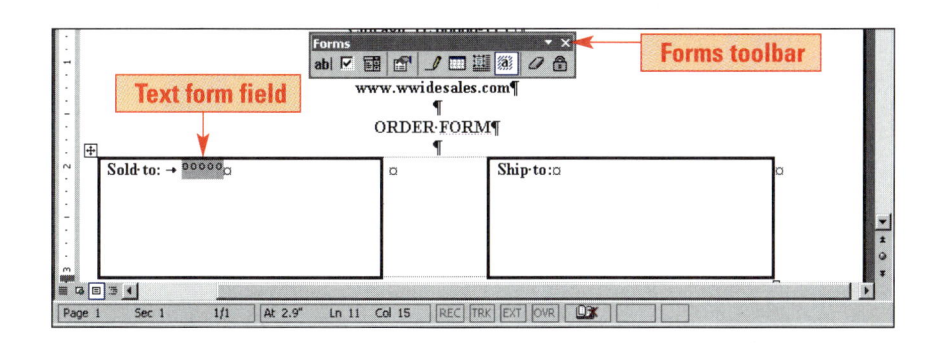

Using Online Forms   **WA 221**

FIGURE 23-4
Inserted Text Form Field

You need to specify the type of Text form field, the length of text the field accepts, and its format. To edit the form field:

| Step 1 | Click | the Form Field Options button on the Forms toolbar |

The Text Form Field Options dialog box on your screen should look similar to Figure 23-5.

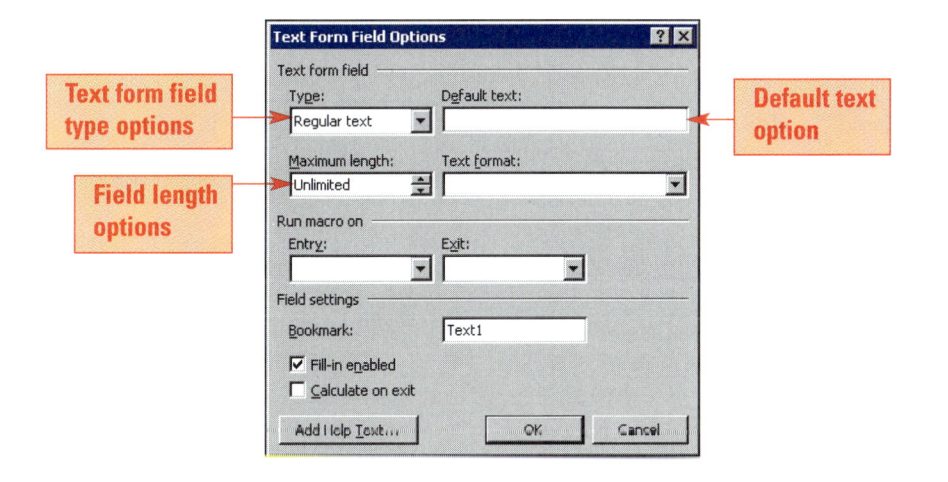

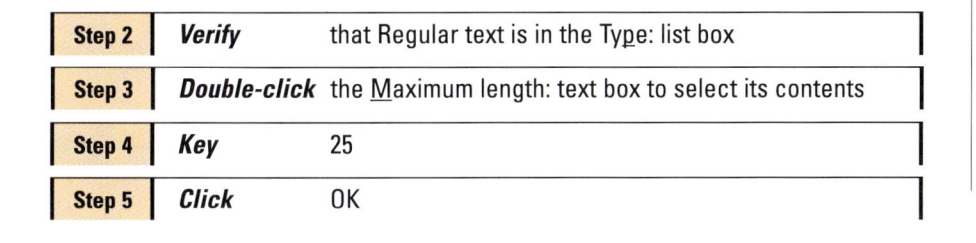

FIGURE 23-5
Text Form Field Options Dialog Box

QUICK TIP

A macro is a short series of programmed instructions. You can run macros automatically when the insertion point enters or exits an individual form field. For more information on running macros in a form, see online Help. Working with macros is discussed in a later chapter.

You select the type of Text form field in the Type: list box. Enter text you want shown by default in the Default text: text box. Specify the maximum number of characters the text form field can contain in the Maximum length: text box. Select a formatting option for the text form field in the Text format: list box. You need a 25-character Regular text form field.

Step 2	Verify	that Regular text is in the Type: list box
Step 3	Double-click	the Maximum length: text box to select its contents
Step 4	Key	25
Step 5	Click	OK

chapter
twenty-three

The form field is edited for 25-character Regular text. The form field is now a dark gray color, indicating it is selected. You need four 25-character Regular text form fields for the Sold to: name and address. You do this by copying the first form field and pasting it in the appropriate location. To insert the next three form fields:

Step 1	*Copy*	the dark gray shaded form field to the Office Clipboard
Step 2	*Press*	the END key to move the insertion point to the right of the shaded form field, if necessary
Step 3	*Press*	the ENTER key
Step 4	*Press*	the CTRL + TAB keys to insert a tab formatting mark
Step 5	*Paste*	the form field from the Office Clipboard at the insertion point
Step 6	*Continue*	by inserting tab character formatting marks and pasting the Text form field until you have four fields in the Sold to: table

You also need four 25-character Regular text form fields for the name and address in the Ship to: table. To insert these fields:

Step 1	*Move*	the insertion point to the right of the "Ship to:" text in the last column of the first table
Step 2	*Set*	a left-aligned tab stop at the 4.6-inch position on the horizontal ruler
Step 3	*Press*	the CTRL + TAB keys
Step 4	*Paste*	the form field from the Office Clipboard at the insertion point
Step 5	*Press*	the ENTER key
Step 6	*Continue*	to insert tab character formatting marks and pasting the text form field until you have four fields in the Ship to: table

You use a Drop-Down form field to create a list of Sales Representative names. To create and format a Drop-Down form field:

Step 1	*Move*	the insertion point to the blank cell below the "Sales Representative" text in the third table
Step 2	*Click*	the Drop-Down Form Field button on the Forms toolbar
Step 3	*Double-click*	the Drop-Down form field

The Drop-Down Form Field Options dialog box on your screen should look similar to Figure 23-6.

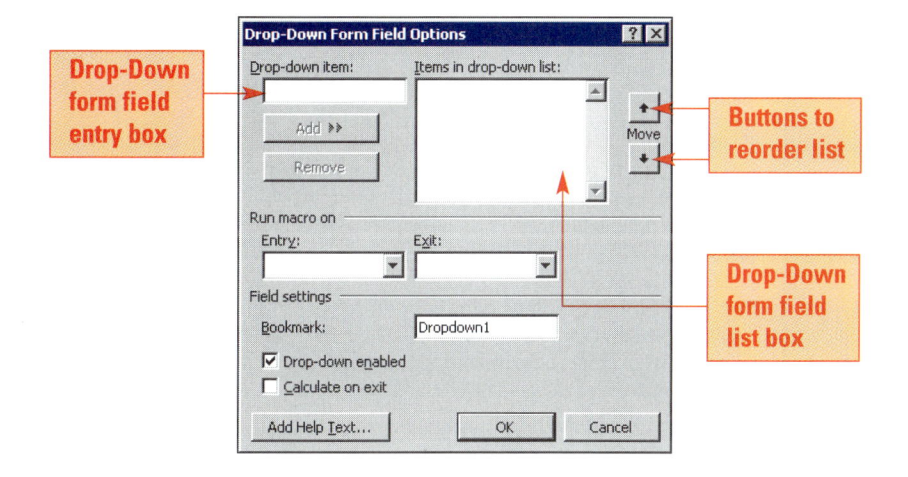

FIGURE 23-6
Drop-Down Form Field Options Dialog Box

You key each item to appear in the drop-down list in the Drop-down item: text box. When you click the Add button or press the ENTER key, the item appears in the Items in drop-down list: list box. Use the Move buttons to reorder items in the list. Click the Remove button to remove selected items from the list. To insert the drop-down list of sales representatives names:

Step 1	Verify	that the insertion point is in the Drop-down item: text box
Step 2	Key	B. Collins
Step 3	Click	Add
Step 4	Key	D. Rendell
Step 5	Click	Add
Step 6	Click	OK

B. Collins, the first item in the list, appears in the cell. Later, when you open a new document based on this form template, the field displays a list box complete with a list arrow.

You use the current system date for the Order Date. The buyer provides the Ship by Date when the order is taken. Word has two Text form fields for dates. The Current date form field is updated automatically with the system date. The Date form field is used when the date data is entered in the form. You format both fields to contain a maximum of eight characters (which includes the date separator /) and to display the month as a two-digit number (suppressing the leading 0 for single-digit months), the day of the month as a two-digit number, and the last two digits of the year.

> **QUICK TIP**
>
> The Date, Current date, and Current time form fields can be formatted using a variety of date/time formats. When formatting a date or time field, Word adds an additional formatting instruction to the field called a **switch**. The general date and time switches consist of "M" for month, "d" for day, and "y" for year. For example, in a date field format switch, an "M" displays the month in a single-digit month as a number such as "8" for August. "MM" displays a two-digit month number with a preceding 0 such as "08." "MMM" displays a three-character month abbreviation such as "Aug" and so forth. For a complete list of date and time field formatting switches, see online Help.

To insert the Current date form field for the Order Date:

Step 1	Move	the insertion point to the blank cell below the "Order Date" text
Step 2	Click	the Text Form Field button **abl** on the Forms toolbar
Step 3	Double-click	the Text form field
Step 4	Click	the Type: list arrow
Step 5	Click	Current date
Step 6	Key	8 in the Maximum length: text box
Step 7	Click	the Date format: list arrow
Step 8	Click	M/d/yy
Step 9	Click	OK

The Current date form field is inserted in the cell and contains the system date. You are now ready to insert a Text form field for the Ship by Date. To insert the Date form field:

Step 1	Move	the insertion point to the blank cell below the "Ship by Date" text
Step 2	Click	the Text Form Field button **abl** on the Forms toolbar
Step 3	Double-click	the Text form field
Step 4	Click	Date in the Type: list
Step 5	Key	8 in the Maximum length: text box
Step 6	Click	M/d/yy in the Date format: list
Step 7	Click	OK

The Date form field is inserted. The sales representative completing the order form will enter data for this field.

Worldwide Exotic Foods, Inc. ships items on a "Rush" basis or on a "Regular" basis. You use a Check Box form field to indicate the shipping method. The Check Box form field is left empty; the user moves to the check box and presses the SPACEBAR to insert an X for the correct shipping method. To insert the Check Box form fields:

| Step 1 | Move | the insertion point to the blank cell below the text "Shipping Method" |

Using Online Forms **WA 225**

Step 2	Key	Rush
Step 3	Press	the SPACEBAR
Step 4	Click	the Check Box Form Field button ☑ on the Forms toolbar
Step 5	Press	the SPACEBAR twice
Step 6	Key	Regular
Step 7	Press	the SPACEBAR
Step 8	Click	the Check Box Form Field button ☑ on the Forms toolbar
Step 9	Center	all the fields vertically and horizontally in their cells using a shortcut menu

> **MOUSE TIP**
>
> You can use the right mouse button to select a cell, row, or column in a table and, at the same time, display a shortcut menu.

You use a 10-character Regular text form field for the Item Number. To insert the Item Number field:

Step 1	Scroll	the document to view the top rows of the last table
Step 2	Move	the insertion point to the first blank cell below the text "Item Number"
Step 3	Insert	a 10-character Regular text form field
Step 4	Align	the cell contents to the bottom left using a shortcut menu

> **QUICK TIP**
>
> You can save the variable data entered in a form instead of the entire form document. This saves disk space and allows the variable data to be imported into an Excel list or Access database. To save the data only when you save a form, click the Save data only for forms check box to insert a check mark on the Save tab in the Options dialog box.

You use a 30-character Regular text form field for the Item Description. To insert the Description field:

Step 1	Press	the TAB key
Step 2	Insert	a 30-character Regular text form field
Step 3	Align	the cell contents to the bottom left using a shortcut menu

You use a 10-character Number text form field for the Quantity Ordered. When you specify a Number text form field, an error message is displayed if the user attempts to enter non-numeric data. To insert the Qty Ordered field:

Step 1	Press	the TAB key
Step 2	Insert	a 10-character Number text field
Step 3	Align	the cell contents to the bottom right using a shortcut menu

chapter
twenty-three

You must insert text form fields for each remaining line of the last table. This allows the sales representative to enter order data in all the rows of the table. Use the copy and paste feature to insert the remaining form fields in the last table. (Copying the contents rather than just the fields also copies the cell alignment formatting.) To copy the form fields:

| Step 1 | Copy | the contents of each cell in row 2 to all the remaining rows in the table |

You can add a help message to a form field that appears on the status bar whenever the insertion point is in the form field. Help for a form field can also be assigned to the F1 key. You want to add a help message to the Ship by Date. To add a help message:

Step 1	Double-click	the Ship by Date field
Step 2	Click	Add Help Text
Step 3	Click	the Status Bar tab, if necessary

The Form Field Help Text dialog box on your screen should look similar to Figure 23-7. You set what type of help message you want and key the help text in this dialog box. You create your own help message text for the status bar.

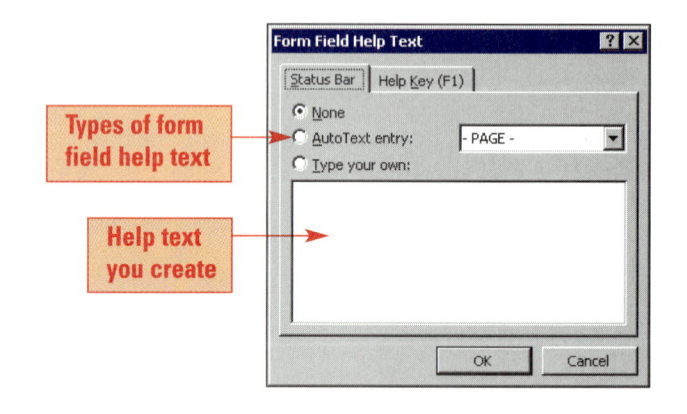

QUICK TIP

Use status bar help messages for short reminders. For more complex instructions, assign the help message to the F1 key.

FIGURE 23-7
Status Bar Tab in the Form Field Help Text Dialog Box

Types of form field help text

Help text you create

MENU TIP

You can protect the template document by clicking the Protect Document command on the Tools menu.

Step 4	Click	the Type your own: option button
Step 5	Key	Remember to ask for the Ship by Date
Step 6	Click	OK in the Form Field Help Text dialog box
Step 7	Click	OK in the Text Form Field Options dialog box
Step 8	Deselect	the form field

After inserting all the form fields, you must protect the template.

Protecting the Form Template

When you **protect** the template, you provide access to only the form fields. Users cannot edit the boilerplate or the form structure of a protected form. They can only enter information in the fields. To protect the template:

Step 1	Click	the Form Field Shading button [a] on the Forms toolbar
Step 2	Click	the Protect Form button [🔒] on the Forms toolbar
Step 3	Close	the Forms toolbar
Step 4	Save	the template and close it

> **QUICK TIP**
>
> To modify a form template, open the template and turn off the protection. Make the desired changes, protect the form, and save it again as a template.

23.b Creating a Document Based on a Form Template

To create a new order form document based on the *Order Form Template* document using the New Document task pane:

Step 1	Display	the New Document task pane
Step 2	Click	the Choose document link in the New from existing document section in the New Document task pane
Step 3	Switch to	the disk drive and folder where your *Order Form Template* is stored
Step 4	Double-click	*Order Form Template*

> **TASK PANE TIP**
>
> If you saved your template in the default location, you can open the Templates dialog box and create a new document based on the template. Another way to create a new document based on the template is with the Choose document link in the New Document task pane. This is an easy way to create a new document from an existing document such as a template that is not stored in the default location.

The first field where you must enter data is selected and contains the insertion point. To move to the next field, press the TAB key. Press the SHIFT + TAB keys to move back to the previous field. You can also click the field where you want to enter data. To enter the variable data:

Step 1	Key	Mary Bowlin in the first field
Step 2	Press	the TAB key to move to the next line in the Sold to: box
Step 3	Key	75 West Highlands Street

chapter
twenty-three

CAUTION TIP

A new document based on the *Order Form Template* opens. Because the document is protected for forms, you can only enter data in each text field, select data from the drop-down list box, or use a check box. The remaining portions of the document cannot be edited unless you turn off the protection with the Unprotect Document command on the Tools menu.

QUICK TIP

When you unprotect the document, you can update selected form fields by pressing the F9 key. You can toggle between a form field and the field results by pressing the SHIFT + F9 keys. You can toggle between all form fields and all field results by pressing the ALT + F9 keys.

Step 4	*Press*	the TAB key to move to the next line in the Sold to: box
Step 5	*Key*	Sydney NSW 20003
Step 6	*Press*	the TAB key to move to the next line in the Sold to: box
Step 7	*Key*	Australia
Step 8	*Press*	the TAB key to move to the first line in the Ship to: box
Step 9	*Key*	Same in the Ship to: box
Step 10	*Click*	the current Sales Representative name to view the drop-down list
Step 11	*Click*	D. Rendell
Step 12	*Press*	the TAB key to move the Ship by: date field
Step 13	*Observe*	the help message on the status bar
Step 14	*Key*	the current date using two digits for month, day, and year
Step 15	*Press*	the TAB key to move to the Rush check box
Step 16	*Press*	the SPACEBAR to insert an X in the Rush check box
Step 17	*Press*	the TAB key twice to move to the first Item Number field
Step 18	*Key*	4568YZ
Step 19	*Press*	the TAB key to move to the first Description field
Step 20	*Key*	Holiday Meat and Cheese Basket
Step 21	*Press*	the TAB key to move to the first Quantity field
Step 22	*Key*	15
Step 23	*Save*	the document as *Completed Order Form*
Step 24	*Print*	the document on plain paper and close it

notes If you saved your template in the default templates folder location, your instructor may provide instructions for removing the *Order Form Template* from that location.

Online form templates can enhance the speed and accuracy of data entry.

Using Online Forms WA 229

Summary

- Online forms can be used to create invoices, routing slips, order forms, and schedule documents; users quickly fill in the variable information on a document based on a form template.
- Form templates can include boilerplate text, fill-in text fields, check boxes, drop-down lists, calculations, and dates.
- Before creating a form, you should design it on paper and then ask an end user to review your design.
- Tables provide a good framework for organizing forms.
- Help messages can be added to fields in a form template and can appear on the status bar or be displayed with the F1 key.
- Form templates must be protected to prevent accidental changes to the text or fields in documents based on the form template.
- Documents based on a form template can be printed on plain paper or on preprinted forms by changing a print option.

Commands Review

Action	Menu Bar	Shortcut Menu	Toolbar	Task Pane	Keyboard
Create a new template	File, New			Click the General Templates link in the New Document task pane	ALT + F, N ALT + T
Insert a tab character in a table					CTRL + TAB
Insert a Text form field			abl		
Insert a Check Box form field			☑		
Insert a Drop-Down form field					
Set form field options		Right-click form field, click Properties	Double-click form field		
Display the Forms toolbar	View, Toolbars, Forms	Right-click toolbar, click Forms			ALT + V, T, DOWN ARROW to Forms, SPACEBAR
Activate form fields and protect a form template	Tools, Protect Document, Forms option		🔒		ALT + T, P, ALT + F

chapter twenty-three

Concepts Review

Circle the correct answer.

1. You protect a form template before you save it so that:
   - [a] an icon for the template appears in the New dialog box.
   - [b] users can easily modify the form template's boilerplate and framework.
   - [c] users cannot accidentally change the nonvariable text or framework of documents based on the template.
   - [d] end users can review the template design.

2. Which of the following is not a Text form field type?
   - [a] Date
   - [b] Number
   - [c] Current date
   - [d] Previous date

3. Nonvariable form text is called:
   - [a] switches.
   - [b] fields.
   - [c] controls.
   - [d] boilerplate.

4. The first step in creating an online form is to:
   - [a] plan and sketch the form.
   - [b] enter the variable data in each field.
   - [c] protect the form.
   - [d] create a new, blank template.

5. The framework for online forms is based on:
   - [a] templates.
   - [b] dialog boxes.
   - [c] drawing objects.
   - [d] tables.

6. A Regular text field can contain:
   - [a] only dates.
   - [b] only the system date.
   - [c] text, numbers, symbols, or spaces.
   - [d] numbers used in calculations.

7. A form field is sometimes called:
   - [a] a switch.
   - [b] boilerplate.
   - [c] an option.
   - [d] a control.

8. Check Box form fields allow the user to:
   - [a] answer yes or no by inserting an X.
   - [b] insert the current date in a field.
   - [c] key variable text in the field.
   - [d] select a variable from a list.

9. The Date field format that includes "MMM" displays the month as:
   - [a] a number without a leading 0 for single-digit months.
   - [b] a number with a leading 0 for single-digit months.
   - [c] the month in two alphabetical characters.
   - [d] the month in three alphabetical characters.

10. You can assign a form field help message to the:
    - [a] F10 key.
    - [b] F1 key.
    - [c] F11 key.
    - [d] F4 key.

Using Online Forms **WA 231**

Circle **T** if the statement is true or **F** if the statement is false.

T F 1. Word provides three kinds of form fields for online forms: Text, Check Box, and Drop-Down.

T F 2. You can never edit a document created from a protected form template.

T F 3. When you protect a form template, users can enter data only in the form fields.

T F 4. Documents based on a form template must always be printed on plain paper.

T F 5. You can save variable data entered into a form without saving a form's boilerplate or framework.

T F 6. Drop-Down form fields allow the user to select from a list of variables.

T F 7. Drawing multiple tables is the best way to structure a complex form.

T F 8. The first step in creating a form is to immediately create a new template and start designing the form on the screen.

T F 9. Filling in forms onscreen slows down the process and increases errors.

T F 10. You use the CTRL key or the CTRL + TAB keys to move from field to field when completing an online form.

Skills Review

Exercise 1

1. Open the *Time Sheet* document located on the Data Disk.
2. Format the first row of the table with Gray-20% shading.
3. Format the entire table with a 2¼-pt outside border and a ¾-pt inside border.
4. Set left-aligned tabs in the tables as necessary to prepare for inserting the form fields.
5. Insert the following form fields.

Variable	*Field Options*
Name:	Regular text, 25 characters
Date:	Current date; 8 characters, M/d/yy format
Dept.:	Drop-Down, with the following departments: Accounting, Legal, Sales
Status:	Check Box Exempt
	Check Box Non-exempt
For week ended:	Date; 8 characters, M/d/yy format
Hours worked:	Number; 2 characters
Supervisor:	Drop-Down; with following names: Roberto Rivas, Elizabeth Washington, Joseph Yang

6. Protect the template.
7. Save the template as *Time Sheet Template* in the location specified by your instructor.
8. Print and close the template document.

chapter twenty-three

9. Create a new document based on the Time Sheet Template template. Use the following data.
Your name
Today's date
Accounting Department
Non-exempt status
For week ended today
40 hours worked
Supervisor, Elizabeth Washington

10. Save the document as *Completed Time Sheet*, and then preview, print, and close it.

Exercise 2

1. Create the form template shown below.

MCBRIDE INSURANCE AGENCY
3414 W. SECOND STREET
CHICAGO, IL 60616-3414

INSURANCE APPLICATION

| Date: | SS #: - - |

| Name: | Date of Birth: |

| Address: | Home Phone: |
| | Gender: Female   Male |

| Employer: |

| Employer Phone: |

| Type of Coverage: | Replacement Value: |

1. Has your driver's license been revoked, suspended or have you been convicted for driving under the influence of alcohol or drugs within the last five years?

   | Yes   No |

2. Do you use your automobile for:

   | Business   Pleasure |

3. Number of drivers in the household:

   | Under 25   Over 25 |

4. How long have you lived at your current address?

   | Years   Months |

_____   _____
Applicant's Signature   Date

Using Online Forms   **WA 233**

2. The three-line heading and the text INSURANCE APPLICATION are 12-point, bold font.

3. Use tables to create a framework for the form, and format the tables with a Gray-10% shading and 2¼-pt outside border.

4. Set left-aligned tabs within the tables as necessary to prepare for inserting the form fields.

5. Insert the following form fields.

Variable	Field Options
Date	Current date; 8 characters, M/d/yy format
SS #	three Number: 3, 2, and 4 characters
Name	Regular text; 25 characters
Date of Birth	Date; 8 characters, M/d/yy format
Address	Regular text, 25 character for each of two lines of text
Home Phone	Regular text, 15 characters
Gender	Check Boxes (Female and Male)
Employer	Regular text, 25 characters
Employer Phone	Regular text, 15 characters
Type of Coverage	Drop-Down, with the following list: Automobile, Homeowners, Renters
Replacement Value	Number, 15 characters, #,##0 format
Yes or No question	Check Boxes
Automobile use	Check Boxes
Number of drivers	Number, 2 characters for each category
Length of time at current address	Number, 2 characters for each category

6. Protect the form.

7. Save the form template as *Insurance Form Template* in the location specified by your instructor.

8. Close the form template.

9. Create a new document based on the *Insurance Form Template* template using the following data.

Variable	Field Options
SS #	123-45-6789
Name	Elvira Jefferson
Date of Birth	03/25/57
Address	7890 Sycamore Avenue
	Chicago, IL 60603-1124
Home Phone	(312) 555-7823
Gender	Female
Employer	Worldwide Exotic Foods, Inc.
Employer Phone	(312) 555-8752
Type of Coverage	Automobile
Replacement Value	Skip
Driver's license	No
Automobile use	Pleasure
Number of drivers	2 over 25
Length of time at current address	Skip

chapter twenty-three

10. Save the document as *Jefferson Form*, and then preview, print, and close it.

11. Create a new document based on the *Insurance Form Template* using the following data.

Field	*Text*
SS #	789-23-3390
Name	Henry Lincoln
Date of Birth	07/10/42
Address	14 East 11th Street
	Chicago, IL 60613-5467
Home Phone	(312) 555-9195
Gender	Male
Employer	Worldwide Exotic Foods, Inc.
Employer Phone	(312) 555-2548
Type of Coverage	Renters
Replacement Value	60,000
Driver's license	Skip
Automobile use	Skip
Number of drivers	Skip
Length of time at current address	5 years and 3 months

12. Save the document as *Lincoln Form*, and then preview, print, and close it.

Exercise 3

1. Open the *Registration Form* document located on the Data Disk.

2. Format the form with tables, borders, and shading of your choice.

3. Set left-aligned tabs in the tables as necessary to prepare for inserting the form fields.

4. Insert the following form fields.

Variable	*Field Options*
Date	Current date; 8 characters, M/d/yy format
Name	Regular text; 25 characters
Address	Regular text, 25 characters for each of two lines
Telephone Number	Regular text, 15 characters
Number of Dependent Children	Number, 2 characters
Registration Fee	Check Boxes for each category
Youth Group	Drop-Down, with the following list:
	West Side Youth, Central City Youth, East Side Youth

5. Add appropriate help message to display on the status bar for each registration fee form field.

6. Protect the template form.

7. Save the template form as *Registration Form Template* in the location specified by your instructor.

8. Print and close the template form.

9. Create a new document based on the *Registration Form Template* using the following data.

Field	*Text*
Name	Millicent Ho
Address	1174 Rosebud Lane
	Chicago, IL 60623-2589
Telephone Number	(312) 555-4963
Number of Dependent Children	3
Registration Fee	Family
Youth Group	West Side Youth

10. Save the document as *Ho Form*, and then preview, print, and close it.

Exercise 4

1. Create the form template shown below.

WORLDWIDE EXOTIC FOODS, INC.
SALES DEPARTMENT
EXPENSE REPORT

NAME:
DATE:

DATE	DESCRIPTION	EXPENSE

2. Set a 1.5-inch top margin, and use the default left, right, and bottom margins. Key all text in 12-point Times New Roman, except the title. Format the title text as 12-point, bold Arial and center it.

3. The Date column should be 0.75-inches wide. The Description column should be 3.75-inches wide. The Expense column should be 1-inch wide.

4. Center the Date column and set a decimal tab for the Expense column.

5. Format the table with Gray-10% shading, a ¾-pt inside border, a 2¼-pt outside border, and a 2¼-pt bottom border for row 1.

6. Center the table between the left and right margins.

chapter twenty-three

7. Insert the following form fields.

Variable	Field Options
Name	Regular text, unlimited characters
Date	Date, 8 characters, M/d/yy format
Date (in table)	Date, 8 characters, M/d/yy format
Description	Regular text, unlimited characters
Expense	Number, unlimited characters, first cell $#,##0.00;($#,##0.00) format, other cells #,##0.00 format

8. Remove the form field shading and protect the form.
9. Save the form template as *Expense Report Form* in the location specified by your instructor.
10. Print and close the template document.

Exercise 5

1. Create a new document based on the *Expense Report Form* template you created in Exercise 4. If you have not created the template, do so now.
2. Enter the following data.

Field	Text
Name	Clifford McDaniels
Date	current date in M/d/yy format
Date	6/27/01
Description	Airline tickets
Expense	350.75
Date	6/30/01
Description	Hotel accommodations
Expense	750.25
Date	6/30/01
Description	Rental car
Expense	220.12

3. Unprotect the form.
4. Enter the text "Total" in the Description column in the cell below "Rental car."
5. Delete the form field in the cell below the last expense. (*Hint:* Display formatting marks.)
6. Enter a formula to calculate the total expenses. Format the formula with the $#,##0.00;($#,##0.00) format.
7. Save the document as *McDaniels Expense Form*, and then preview, print, and close it.

Using Online Forms   WA 237

Exercise 6

1. Create the form template shown below.

REGISTRATION FORM

Date
Name
Department
Address
Phone Number
Course Name
Course Date

---

2. Set a 1.5-inch top margin, and use the default left, right, and bottom margins.

3. Add a 3-pt box border around the form text.

4. Key text in 12-point Arial. Bold and center the text REGISTRATION FORM.

5. Set a left-aligned tab at 1.50 inches.

6. Insert the following form fields.

Variable	*Field Options*
Date	Current date, 8 characters, M/d/yy format
Name	Regular text, unlimited characters
Department	Regular text, unlimited characters
Address	Regular text, unlimited characters for each of two lines of text
Phone Number	Regular text, 15 characters
Course Name	Drop-Down, with the following courses: Beginning Microsoft Word Intermediate Microsoft Word Advanced Microsoft Word Beginning Microsoft Excel Intermediate Microsoft Excel Advanced Microsoft Excel Beginning Microsoft PowerPoint Intermediate Microsoft PowerPoint
Course Date	Date text, 8 characters, M/d/yy format

chapter twenty-three

7. Remove the form field shading and protect the form.

8. Save the form template as *Training Form Template* in the location specified by your instructor.

9. Print and close the template document.

Exercise 7

1. Create a new document based on the *Training Form Template* you created in Exercise 6. If you have not created the template, do so now.

2. Enter the following data.

Field	Text
Name	Janet Holiday
Department	Accounting
Address	3850 West Union Drive
	Chicago, IL 60605-1135
Phone Number	(312) 555-8900
Course Name	Advanced Microsoft Word
Course Date	8/5/03

3. Save the document as *Holiday Registration*, and then preview, print, and close it.

Exercise 8

1. Create the form template below.

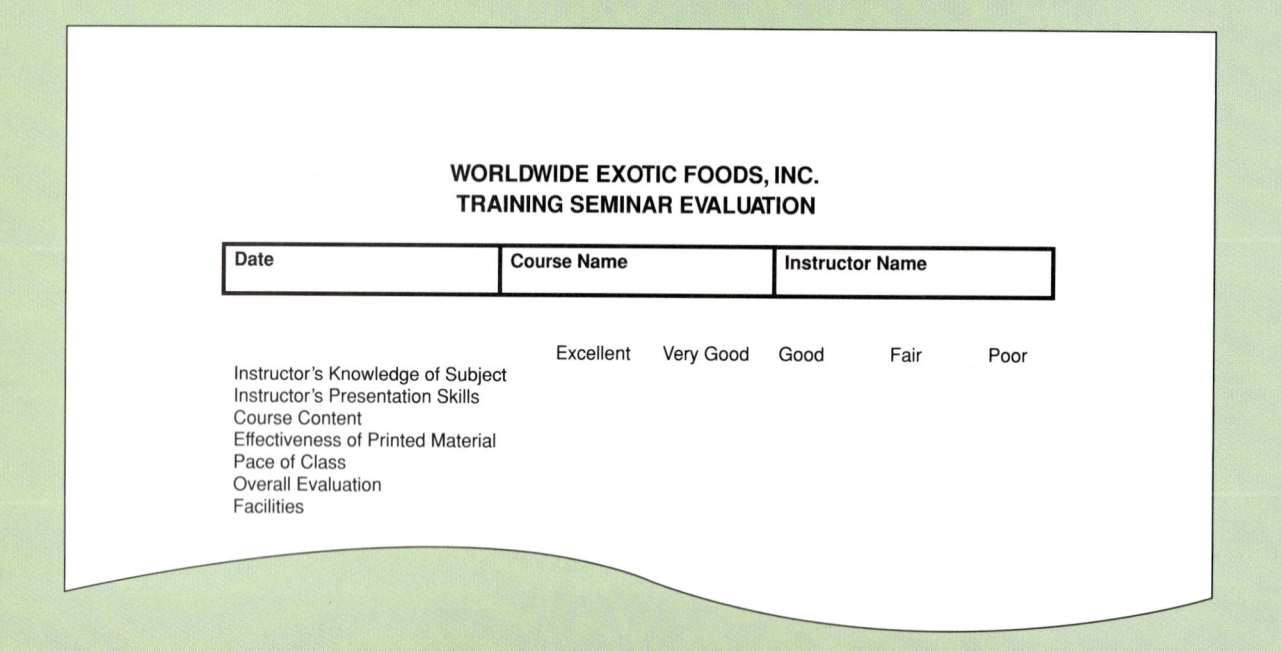

WORLDWIDE EXOTIC FOODS, INC.
TRAINING SEMINAR EVALUATION

Date	Course Name	Instructor Name

Excellent   Very Good   Good   Fair   Poor

Instructor's Knowledge of Subject
Instructor's Presentation Skills
Course Content
Effectiveness of Printed Material
Pace of Class
Overall Evaluation
Facilities

2. The title text is 12-point, bold Arial and centered. The remainder of the text is 10-point Times New Roman.

3. Use tables to create the framework for the form.

4. Insert the following form fields.

Variable	Field Options
Date	Current date, 8 character size, M/d/yy format
Course Name	Drop-Down, with the following courses: Beginning Microsoft Word Intermediate Microsoft Word Advanced Microsoft Word Beginning Microsoft Excel Intermediate Microsoft Excel Advanced Microsoft Excel Beginning Microsoft PowerPoint Intermediate Microsoft PowerPoint
Instructor Name	Drop-Down with the following names: Janice Benevides Tamicka Johnson Brenda Wang David Oliver Frances D'Aversa
Excellent, Very Good, Good, Fair, Poor	Check boxes for each of the following: Instructor's Knowledge of Subject Instructor's Presentation Skills Course Content Effectiveness of Printed Material Pace of Class Overall Evaluation Facilities

5. Remove the form field shading and protect the form.

6. Save the form template as *Training Evaluation Template* in the location specified by your instructor.

7. Print and close the template document.

Case Projects

Project 1

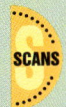

Beverly Williams, the manager of the Office Services Department, needs help creating the online forms used in the department. She asks you to solve the following problems:

1. No arrow displays on drop-down lists in documents created from a form template.
2. Sometimes {FORMTEXT}, {FORMCHECKBOX}, or {FORMDROPDOWN} appear instead of form fields.

Use the Ask A Question Box to research solutions to these problems. Write Beverly an interoffice memorandum describing each problem and suggesting a solution. Save, preview, and print the memo.

Project 2

The sales manager asks you to create an online form that the Shipping Department can use to record items shipped. The information needed on the form is: customer billing name, address, and telephone number; shipping address; order date and ship date; and description and quantity of items shipped. Sketch the layout of the form. With your instructor's permission, have a classmate review the form. Then draw and size the tables to create the layout. Insert the appropriate field codes. Protect, save, and print the template form. The orders will be printed on preprinted forms. Create three orders using the order form template. Use fictitious data for each form. Save, preview, and print the data for each order form.

chapter twenty-three

Project 3

The Accounting Department wants to create invoice forms that contain calculations. The accounting manager asks you how to do this. Using the Help tools, review how to use the Calculation text form field. Write the manager, Bill Wilson, an interoffice memorandum explaining how to use the Calculation text form field in an Invoice online form template. Save, preview, and print the memo.

Project 4

Chris Lofton, the manager of the Word Processing Department, is concerned about the workflow in the department. To avoid delays and enhance scheduling, you are asked to design an online form employees can complete when they send their work to the department. Sketch a draft of an appropriate online form. With your instructor's approval, ask a classmate to review the form. Create a form template based on the reviewed draft. Save, preview, and print the template document. Create an interoffice memorandum to all Word Processing Department users with instructions on how to complete the form. Attach a sample of the form to the memorandum. Save, preview, and print the memorandum.

Project 5

The sales manager wants to see several examples of Web pages that use online forms to gather data. Connect to the Internet and search for Web sites using online forms. Save at least five Web pages. Write the sales manager an interoffice memorandum describing the Web sites that use online forms and the kind of information gathered by the forms. Save, preview, and print the memo.

Project 6

You just read an article in a monthly newsletter discussing various templates available from the Microsoft Office Web site and you want to check out any business form templates that are available. Connect to the Internet and search for the Microsoft Office Template Gallery Web site. Follow the links to preview several different business form templates. Then write a memo to Chris Lofton identifying three templates that might be useful and how to download them. Save, preview, and print the memo. With your instructor's permission, download the templates to the location specified by your instructor.

Project 7

The Accounting Department creates several invoices each day using an online form template. Because the invoice data is used in other applications, the accounting manager wants to save only the variable data for each invoice and asks you if this can be done. Using the Ask A Question Box, locate the online forms topics and review the "Save the data from a form in Word for use in a database" topic. Write the accounting manager an interoffice memorandum describing the process. Save, preview, and print the memorandum.

Project 8

Kelly Armstead in the Purchasing Department needs an online Purchase Order form. Draft the form, review the form with a classmate, and then create the form as a template. Save, preview, and print the template document. Using fictitious data, create a purchase order document using the template. Save, preview, and print the document.

Word 2002

Integrating Word Documents with the Internet

Chapter Overview

Businesses of every kind use Web sites to advertise and sell their products and services to the millions of potential customers who browse the Web each day. In addition, companies have intranets where they post Web pages that only their employees can access. In this chapter, you learn how to create your own Web page, how to create and send e-mail messages directly from Word, how to route documents for revision through internal e-mail, and how to digitally sign a Word document.

Learning Objectives

- Create a Web page
- Send e-mail messages from Word
- Distribute documents for revision
- Use digital signatures

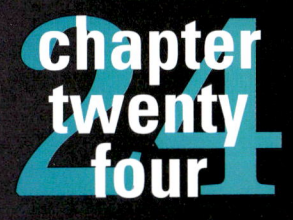

Case profile

The Worldwide Exotic Foods, Inc. Web site development committee wants to create a corporate Web site with a home page and individual branch office pages. You are assigned to assist Nat Wong, the committee chair, in creating the Web site using Word 2002. You create a home page for Worldwide Exotic Foods to promote the company's specialty food products and branch offices, and provide support to employees integrating Word with the Internet.

chapter twenty four

notes It is assumed that you are using the Microsoft Internet Explorer Web browser for the activities in this chapter. If you are using a different Web browser, your instructor may provide additional instructions.

24.a Creating a Web Page

To create a Web page in Word, you can use one of the Web templates on the Web Pages tab in the Templates dialog box. The templates contain preset formatting and sample text you replace with your own text. You also can create a blank, unformatted Web page from a template with the Web Page icon on the General tab in the Templates dialog box. Use this template when you want to create a Web page by selecting your own formatting and text options.

Then you can use the familiar Word tools, such as tables, styles, alignment, or font formatting, to create attractive and professional-looking Web pages.

The Worldwide Exotic Foods home page should contain information about the company's business purpose, and a list of the branch office locations followed by the company's contact information. You begin the home page by creating a new, blank Web page. Then you add a title, apply a theme, insert text, bullets, and a horizontal divider line. To create a new, blank Web page:

| Step 1 | *Display* | the New Document task pane |
| Step 2 | *Click* | the Blank Web Page link in the new section in the New Document task pane |

A blank Web page appears in Web Layout view. Nat wants you to use the company name as the title for the home page. The title of a Web page appears on the title bar of the Web browser used to view it. To add a Web page title to a blank Web page in the document's properties:

Step 1	*Click*	File
Step 2	*Click*	Properties
Step 3	*Click*	the Summary tab, if necessary
Step 4	*Key*	Worldwide Exotic Foods, Inc. in the Title: text box
Step 5	*Key*	your name in the Author: text box, if necessary
Step 6	*Click*	OK

INTERNET TIP

Web pages are encoded using the Hypertext Markup Language (HTML). As you key text or insert graphics, Word translates your actions into HTML code called **tags**. You can view the HTML tags for a Web page created in Word by opening the page in Word and clicking the HTML Source command on the View menu.

QUICK TIP

Word 2002 contains many advanced features for creating Web pages, such as Web frames, cascading style sheets, forms, image insertion and compression, and dynamic Web scripts. For more information on using these and other features to create Web pages, see online Help.

The Word title bar shows the blank document temporary name, not the new title. The new title appears in the title bar only when the page is loaded in a Web browser, such as Internet Explorer. It is a good idea to preview the Web page in a browser as you create or modify it so you can verify the quality and accuracy of your work before you complete the page. You want to verify that the new title "Worldwide Exotic Foods, Inc." appears in the browser title bar. To preview the Web page:

Step 1	Click	File
Step 2	Click	We_b Page Preview
Step 3	Maximize	the Internet Explorer Web browser window, if necessary
Step 4	Observe	the new title in the Web browser title bar
Step 5	Close	the Web browser

Now you want to add a theme to the page. A Web page **theme** contains formatting elements such as color-coordinated graphics and fonts. It is faster to format a Web page by applying a theme instead of formatting each element individually. You use the Theme command on the Format menu to select and apply a theme.

To preview different themes:

| Step 1 | Click | F_ormat |
| Step 2 | Click | T_heme |

> **notes**
> It is assumed that all the themes are installed. See your instructor, if necessary, to install missing themes. Or, substitute a different theme of your choice.

The Theme dialog box opens. You can select a theme from the Choose a T_heme: list box and then preview the background, headings, bullet, horizontal divider line, and text formats associated with the theme. Some of the themes' colors, graphics, and background images can be modified with options in this dialog box. You can set a default theme from the Theme dialog box. When you select a theme, Word sets the Bullets button on the Formatting toolbar with the theme bullet color and style, adds the theme horizontal divider line button to the Borders grid on the Formatting toolbar, and modifies the Normal and heading styles to match the theme.

The Theme dialog box on your screen should look similar to Figure 24-1.

MOUSE TIP

In Web Layout view, the New Blank Document button on the Standard toolbar becomes the New Web Page button and is used to create a new, blank Web page.

QUICK TIP

You also can add or modify a Web page's title when you save a Word document as a Web page by clicking the C_hange Title button in the Save As dialog box and keying the new or revised title.

The Word Web page themes are consistent with the themes in Microsoft FrontPage, providing for a common look between Web pages created in both applications.

FIGURE 24-1
Theme Dialog Box

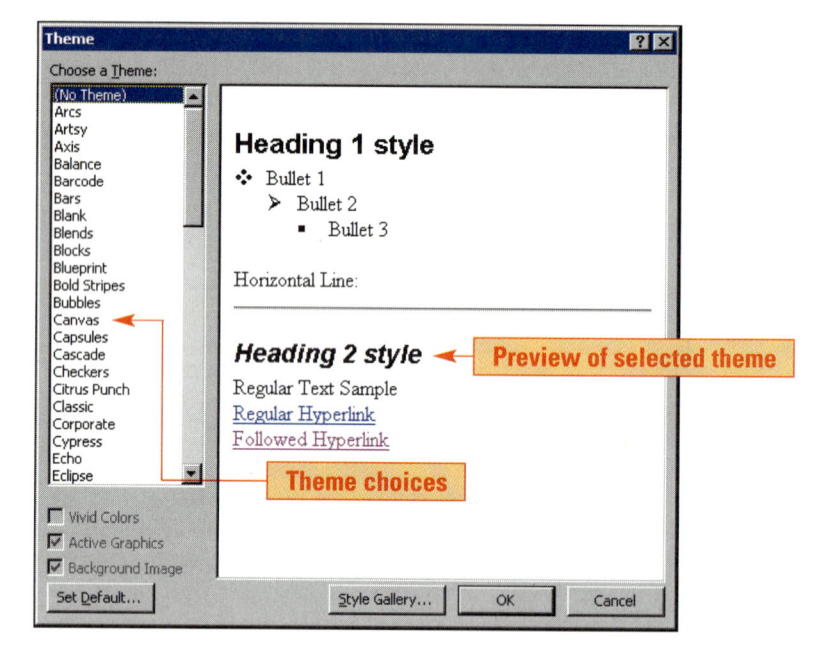

[Screenshot of Theme dialog box showing Choose a Theme list with options including (No Theme), Arcs, Artsy, Axis, Balance, Barcode, Bars, Blank, Blends, Blocks, Blueprint, Bold Stripes, Bubbles, Canvas, Capsules, Cascade, Checkers, Citrus Punch, Classic, Corporate, Cypress, Echo, Eclipse. Preview pane shows Heading 1 style, Bullet 1, Bullet 2, Bullet 3, Horizontal Line, Heading 2 style, Regular Text Sample, Regular Hyperlink, Followed Hyperlink. Check boxes: Vivid Colors, Active Graphics, Background Image. Buttons: Set Default, Style Gallery, OK, Cancel. Annotations point to "Preview of selected theme" and "Theme choices".]

CAUTION TIP

Animated graphics turned on with the Active Graphics option in the Theme dialog box can be viewed only in a Web browser.

Most themes have two color sets: a bright, or vivid color set and a more subdued color set. You can turn on or off the brighter color set with the Vivid Colors check box. Some themes have active graphics, which are graphics that include animation. You turn on or off the use of active graphics with the Active Graphics check box. Each theme has a background image you can add. If you choose not to use a background image, a solid color background is substituted. You turn on or off the use of a background image with the Background Image check box.

Step 3	Click	Blends in the Choose a Theme: list
Step 4	Observe	the theme preview
Step 5	Click	the Vivid Colors, Active Graphics, and Background Image check boxes to insert check marks, if necessary
Step 6	Observe	the theme preview changes
Step 7	Continue	to review the different themes with and without vivid colors, active graphics, and a background image

To apply the Geared Up Factory theme:

Step 1	Click	Geared Up Factory in the Choose a Theme: list
Step 2	Click	the Vivid Colors, Active Graphics, and Background Image check boxes to insert check marks, if necessary
Step 3	Click	OK

Integrating Word Documents with the Internet WA 245

The background image is applied to the page, the Bullets button option is modified, the horizontal divider line style is added to the Borders grid, and the Style button and Styles and Formatting task pane contain styles based on the applied theme.

To add the company name as a centered heading at the top of the page:

Step 1	Click	Heading 1 in the Style button list `Normal` on the Formatting toolbar
Step 2	Turn on	the view of nonprinting formatting marks, if necessary
Step 3	Move	the I-beam mouse pointer to the center of the page on the first line

Because Word has switched to Web Layout view, the I-beam mouse pointer becomes the Click and Type pointer. Your screen should look similar to Figure 24-2.

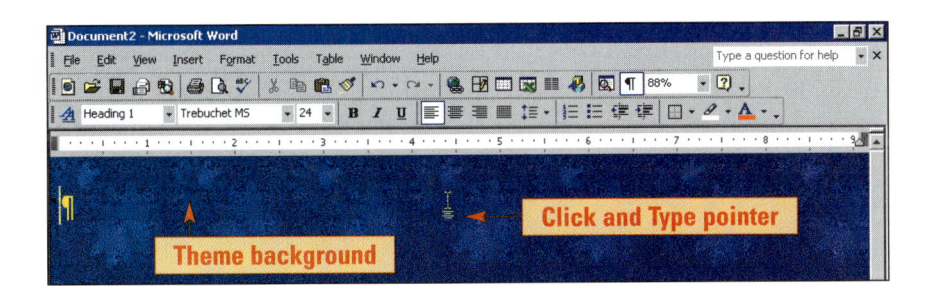

MOUSE TIP

The **Click and Type** pointer allows you to double-click a blank area of the document in Print Layout or Web Layout view to position the insertion point. Click and Type automatically applies the formatting needed to center, left align, or right align the text or insert left, center, or right tab stops as needed to position the insertion point.

FIGURE 24-2
Click and Type Pointer

Step 4	Double-click	the page at the center position with the Click and Type pointer
Step 5	Observe	that the insertion point is center aligned on the page
Step 6	Key	Worldwide Exotic Foods, Inc.
Step 7	Press	the ENTER key to return the insertion point to the left margin
Step 8	Observe	that the Normal style is turned on at the insertion point

Because HTML does not support tabs and newspaper-style columns, you use tables to organize text and graphic images attractively on Web pages. You key the company's business purpose, called a mission statement, into a table with one row and one column centered below the heading. Below the mission statement, you key the branch office names as a bulleted list inside another table. To insert the mission statement:

| Step 1 | Create | a 1 × 1 Table on the line below the heading |
| Step 2 | Remove | the table border and center it using options in the Table Properties dialog box |

QUICK TIP

You can use AutoCorrect, the Spelling and Grammar checker, and other Word features when you create a Web page.

chapter twenty-four

Step 3	*Show*	the table gridlines, if necessary
Step 4	*Move*	the insertion point into the table, if necessary
Step 5	*Key*	Worldwide Exotic Foods, Inc. is the world's fastest growing distributor of specialty food items. Our mission is to provide our customers with an extensive and unusual selection of meats, cheeses, pastries, fruits, vegetables, and beverages from around the world.
Step 6	*Center*	the text inside the table cell
Step 7	*Click*	at the left margin below the table

Before you add more text to the page, you should save it and then preview the Web page to make sure the text looks like you expect.

Step 8	*Click*	File
Step 9	*Click*	Save as Web Page
Step 10	*Save*	the Web page as *Worldwide Home Page* in the location specified by your instructor
Step 11	*Preview*	the Web page
Step 12	*Maximize*	the Internet Explorer Web browser window, if necessary

Your screen should look similar to Figure 24-3.

FIGURE 24-3
Worldwide Exotic Foods Home Page

| Step 13 | *Close* | the Internet Explorer Web browser |

The mission statement looks good. To create a bulleted list of the branch office locations in a table below the mission statement:

| Step 1 | *Click* | at the left margin on the line below the mission statement table to position the insertion point, if necessary |

Integrating Word Documents with the Internet **WA 247**

Step 2	Press	the ENTER key twice to add blank lines
Step 3	Create	a 1 × 1 Table, remove the border, and center it
Step 4	Drag	the right table boundary to the left until the table is approximately two inches wide
Step 5	Move	the insertion point into the table, if necessary
Step 6	Apply	the Heading 4 style
Step 7	Key	Visit Our Branch Offices and center the text in the cell, if necessary
Step 8	Press	the TAB key to create a new row
Step 9	Apply	the Normal style at the position of the insertion point

> **CAUTION TIP**
>
> When you save a Web page, Word automatically creates a folder for the page at the same location. This folder contains the graphic images, such as bullets or horizontal divider lines, used in the Web page. If you move the saved Web page, remember to also move the associated folder.

Your screen should look similar to Figure 24-4.

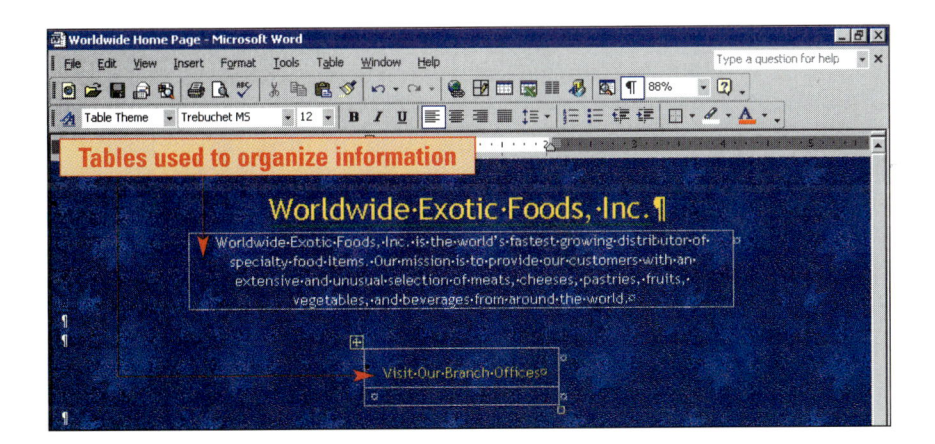

FIGURE 24-4
Tables in a Web Page

Step 10	Click	the Bullets button on the Formatting toolbar
Step 11	Observe	the graphic bullet added by the theme
Step 12	Key	Chicago
Step 13	Press	the TAB key to add a new row
Step 14	Continue	by adding London, Melbourne, and Vancouver to the bulleted list, each in a new row
Step 15	Save	the Web page
Step 16	Preview	the Web page
Step 17	Close	the Web browser

Horizontal lines are used frequently in Web pages to break the text into logical segments. You want to insert a horizontal line to separate the branch office names from the end-of-page contact information.

chapter twenty-four

To add a centered horizontal line below the branch office names:

Step 1	Double-click	at the center position below the bulleted list with the Click and Type pointer
Step 2	Click	the Borders button list arrow on the Formatting toolbar
Step 3	Click	the Horizontal Line button on the Borders grid
Step 4	Observe	the horizontal line graphic inserted at the center position in the document
Step 5	Save	the Web page
Step 6	Preview	the Web page
Step 7	Close	the Web browser

It is important that viewers of your Web page have a way to contact you about the Web page. Because most viewers are looking for current information, it is also important to show the date when the Web page was last updated. Finally, to protect the contents of your Web page, you should add a copyright notice. To key the contact, update date, and copyright information below the horizontal divider line:

Step 1	Move	the insertion point to the left margin below the horizontal divider line
Step 2	Key	Worldwide Exotic Foods, Inc. Gage Building, Suite 2100, Riverside Plaza Chicago, IL 60606-2000 Contact us with questions or comments about this Web site. Updated (insert today's date in the mm/dd/yy format) © (current year), Worldwide Exotic Foods, Inc.
Step 3	Select	all the text below the horizontal divider line
Step 4	Apply	the Heading 5 style
Step 5	Center	the text and then deselect it
Step 6	Observe	the Smart Tag indicator below the Suite 2100 text
Step 7	Display	the Smart Tag Actions button and menu and then close the menu by pressing the ESC key
Step 8	Save	the Web page
Step 9	Preview	the Web page
Step 10	Observe	that the Suite number is marked as a Smart Tag when viewed in the browser

> **QUICK TIP**
>
> You can insert the © symbol with AutoCorrect by keying (c).

Integrating Word Documents with the Internet   WA 249

| Step 11 | *Review* | the Smart Tag Actions button and menu |
| Step 12 | *Close* | the Web browser |

Because the Web page is longer than one screen, Nat suggests you add hyperlinks

Creating Hyperlinks on the Same Page

A **hyperlink**, commonly called a **link**, is text or a picture that provides a shortcut to another document or to another location in the same document. When you position the mouse pointer on a hyperlink, it becomes a hand pointer. When you click a hyperlink, the associated document opens.

When viewers browse the Web looking for information, they often decide whether or not to explore a Web site based on the information they can see as a Web page loads. Because of this, you should position all important information and hyperlinks as close to the top of the page as possible. To help viewers navigate easily through a Web site, each page should include hyperlinks, called **navigational links**, to important areas of the same page and to all other significant pages at the site. For example, you should include a navigational link to the home page on every other page of a Web site.

A well-designed Web page contains a navigational link at the bottom of each page to allow viewers to move quickly back to the top of the page without scrolling. You add a navigational link below the contact information at the bottom of the page. Links can be made to text formatted with the Word built-in heading styles or to a reference point at the destination position called a **bookmark**. Because the Web page formatting may change later, Nat asks you to use a bookmark. To insert a bookmark at the top of the page:

Step 1	*Move*	the insertion point to the top of the page
Step 2	*Click*	Insert
Step 3	*Click*	Bookmark

> **QUICK TIP**
>
> You can create hyperlinks between two Word documents or between a Word document and a Web page. Additionally, you can create hyperlinks between different Office XP applications.
>
> Hyperlinks can be text, pictures, or drawing objects. You can insert pictures and drawing objects in a Web page with the Picture or Object commands on the Insert menu and you can use the AutoShapes feature to add drawing objects to a Web page.

You create a bookmark by assigning it a name and adding it to a list of available bookmarks. Bookmark names must begin with an alphabetic character. You can use numbers following the first character but you cannot use spaces. Use an underscore character to separate words in a bookmark name instead of a space. You should use a descriptive name so that you can easily remember what the bookmark references later.

| Step 4 | *Key* | Top in the Bookmark name: text box |

chapter
twenty-four

| Step 5 | Click | Add |

Next you create a hyperlink between text at the bottom of the page and the bookmark. To insert the hyperlink text:

Step 1	Move	the insertion point to the bottom of the document
Step 2	Press	the ENTER key
Step 3	Center	the insertion point
Step 4	Key	Top of Page
Step 5	Select	the Top of Page text
Step 6	Click	the Insert Hyperlink button on the Standard toolbar

The Insert Hyperlink dialog box opens. You can create hyperlinks to existing external files or Web pages, locations in the current document, new external documents, and e-mail addresses in this dialog box. The selected text "Top of Page" appears in the Text to display: text box and appears on the Web page. You can create a custom ScreenTip for the hyperlink that appears whenever a viewer points to it. You create a hyperlink to the Top bookmark and include a customized hyperlink ScreenTip.

| Step 7 | Click | the Place in This Document icon in the Link to: Places Bar |

Your Insert Hyperlink dialog box should look similar to Figure 24-5.

FIGURE 24-5
Insert Hyperlink Dialog Box

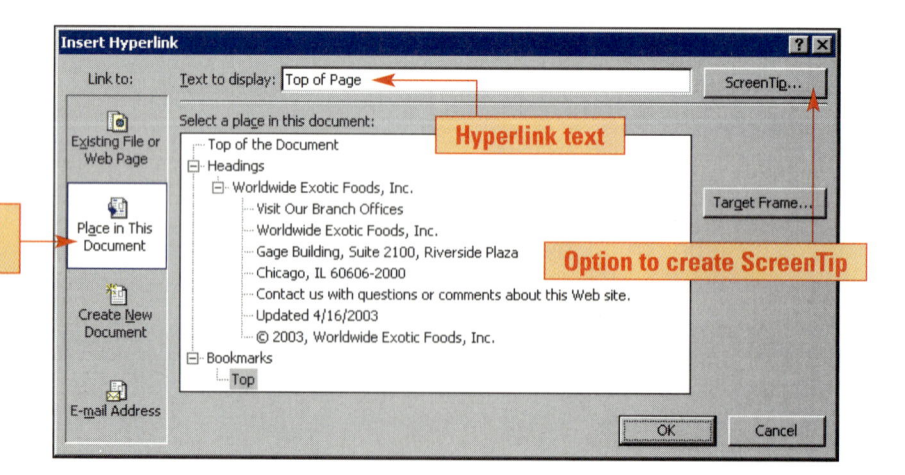

Integrating Word Documents with the Internet   **WA 251**

Step 8	Observe	the list of headings and bookmarks
Step 9	Click	Top in the Select a pla<u>c</u>e in this document: list box
Step 10	Click	Screen<u>T</u>ip to open the Set Hyperlink ScreenTip dialog box
Step 11	Key	Return to the Top of the Page in the Screen<u>T</u>ip text: text box
Step 12	Click	OK to close the Set Hyperlink ScreenTip dialog box
Step 13	Click	OK to close the Insert Hyperlink dialog box

After you create hyperlinks, you should test them to ensure they work correctly. To test the Top navigational link:

Step 1	Save	the Web page
Step 2	Preview	the Web page
Step 3	Scroll	to the bottom of the page, if necessary
Step 4	Move	the mouse pointer to the <u>Top of Page</u> link
Step 5	Observe	the pointing hand mouse pointer and custom ScreenTip

Your screen should look similar to Figure 24-6.

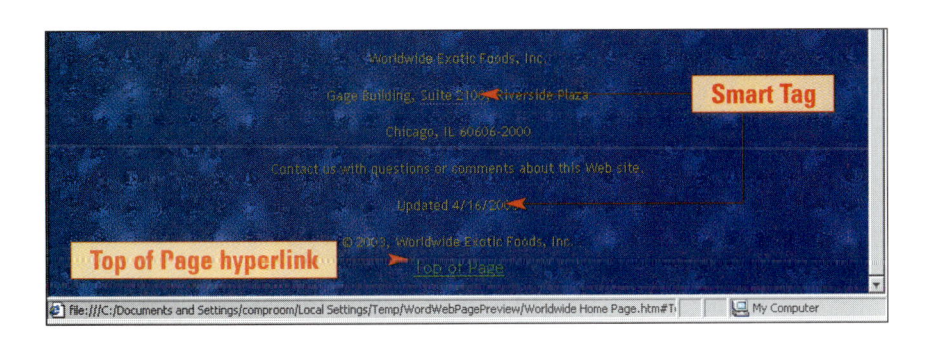

FIGURE 24-6
Hand Pointer and Custom ScreenTip

Step 6	Click	the <u>Top of Page</u> link
Step 7	Observe	that you are now viewing the top of the Web page
Step 8	Close	the Web browser

Often viewers who visit your Web page want to contact you. To make it easy for them to provide feedback or request information, you can add your e-mail address as a hyperlink on every Web page at your Web site. When clicked, the link opens the viewer's e-mail message composition window and automatically inserts your e-mail address in the To: address line. This type of hyperlink is called a **mailto: link**.

chapter
twenty-four

> **QUICK TIP**
>
> A **link bar** is a set of navigational links that allow viewers to move back and forth between pages at a Web site. To use link bars on your Web pages, you must store your Web pages on specifically designated Web servers.

To create a mailto: link in the contact information at the bottom of the home page:

Step 1	Move	the insertion point immediately before the word "with" in the sentence beginning "Contact us" at the bottom of the Web page
Step 2	Key	at staff@wwide.xeon.net
Step 3	Press	the SPACEBAR to have Word automatically create the mailto: link using AutoCorrect
Step 4	Move	the mouse pointer to the new link
Step 5	Observe	the mailto: ScreenTip and the AutoCorrect Options button
Step 6	Click	the AutoCorrect Options button and view the menu options
Step 7	Press	the ESC key to close the AutoCorrect Options menu
Step 8	Save	the Web page
Step 9	Preview	the Web page
Step 10	Close	the browser

Creating Hyperlinks to Other Pages

You can create hyperlinks to other pages at your Web site and to pages at other Web sites. As with hyperlinks on the same page, hyperlinks to other pages can be both pictures and text. You need to create hyperlinks to each of the branch office pages that Nat created. To create a hyperlink to the Chicago branch office home page:

Step 1	Select	the text Chicago in the bulleted list
Step 2	Right-click	the selected text
Step 3	Click	Hyperlink to open the Insert Hyperlink dialog box
Step 4	Click	the Existing File or Web Page icon in the Link to: Places Bar

> **MOUSE TIP**
>
> You can quickly edit, open, copy, or remove a hyperlink by right-clicking the hyperlink and clicking the appropriate menu command on the shortcut menu.

You can key the path and filename of the file to which you are linking, select the path and filename from lists of recently viewed local files or Web pages, or switch to the files stored on a diskette, hard drive, or network server to locate the appropriate file. You locate the Chicago branch office page on the Data Disk.

Step 5	Click	the Look in: list arrow

Step 6	Switch to	the disk drive and folder where the Data Files are stored
Step 7	Click	Chicago
Step 8	Change	the hyperlink ScreenTip to Chicago Branch Office
Step 9	Click	OK in each dialog box
Step 10	Observe	the Chicago hyperlink in the branch office bulleted list
Step 11	Continue	to create hyperlinks with custom ScreenTips to the London, Melbourne, and Vancouver branch office home pages
Step 12	Save	the Web page
Step 13	Preview	the Web page
Step 14	Close	the browser
Step 15	Close	the Web page

Modifying and Reposting Web Pages

If you decide you don't want to use a particular theme you can remove it or replace it with another theme. Before you test the links, Nat reviews the Web page and decides that the theme colors are too dark. He suggests you replace it with the theme he used for the branch office pages. To replace the theme:

Step 1	Open	the Worldwide Home Page Web page
Step 2	Open	the Theme dialog box
Step 3	Double-click	Citrus Punch in the Choose a Theme: list box
Step 4	Observe	the changes to the background, text, bullets, horizontal line, and hyperlinks
Step 5	Save	the Web page
Step 6	Preview	the Web page
Step 7	Test	the Chicago, London, Melbourne, and Vancouver hyperlinks
Step 8	Close	the Web browser

Saving Word Documents to the Web

When you are satisfied with the look and content of your Web pages, you can make them available on the Web by saving or publishing them to a Web server. **Publishing** is the process of transferring your Web pages to a Web server. You can save your Web pages directly to a Web server with options in the Save As dialog box or you can publish your

QUICK TIP

The final test of your Web pages is to have several people (both inside and outside of your organization) review the pages for their look, clarity, ease of use, interest, and so forth. Weigh their suggestions carefully, and revise your Web pages as necessary. It is a good idea to also carefully proofread the Web page text.

CAUTION TIP

The Home hyperlinks on the branch office Web pages are not active.

chapter
twenty-four

CAUTION TIP

The exact steps for publishing Web pages vary from Web server to Web server and from one ISP to another, so contact your system administrator or ISP's technical support personnel for instructions before attempting to publish any Web pages.

QUICK TIP

You can save a Web page as a Web archive file, which saves all the elements of a Web site including text and graphics into a single file. Then you can easily attach this single file to an e-mail message. For more information on saving a Web page as a Web archive file, see online Help.

You can also publish a Web page to a Web server by keying the http://URL of the Web site directly in the File name: text box.

Web pages using an FTP (File Transfer Protocol) program to transfer your Web page files over the Internet to a Web server. Once your Web pages are stored on the Web server, other users can access them.

> **notes**
> The following activity assumes you have access to a Web server. If you do not have access to a Web server, you can read but not perform the activity. Your instructor may also provide additional instructions, as necessary, to access a specific Web server and folder. If you are using Windows 98, your instructor may modify these instructions.

To publish the Worldwide Home Page to a Web server from inside Word:

Step 1	Open	the, *Worldwide Home Page* Web page in Web Layout view if necessary
Step 2	Click	File
Step 3	Click	Save as Web Page
Step 4	Click	My Network Places icon on the Save in: Places Bar to switch to a list of all available Web servers and other network options
Step 5	Open	the appropriate folder on the desired Web server
Step 6	Click	Save

When you need to send an e-mail message while working in Word, you can quickly do so without opening your e-mail software.

24.b Sending E-mail Messages from Word

If you have Outlook 2002 or Outlook Express designated as your e-mail client, you can send e-mail messages directly from Word. If you are using a different e-mail client, the Word e-mail features and options may vary. When you send an e-mail message directly from Word, it is automatically sent in HTML format, which means the message can contain animated graphics, multimedia objects, and other Web page features. Recipients can read the e-mail message in HTML format with a Web browser or with an e-mail client like Outlook 2002 that supports the HTML format.

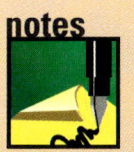

notes The following activities assume you are using Outlook or Outlook Express as your e-mail client. Your instructor may provide additional instructions if you are using a different e-mail client. Your instructor may supplement the following activity to include actually sending and replying to e-mail messages. If you do not have an appropriate e-mail client installed, the E-mail button is not available on the Standard toolbar, and you can read but not perform the following activities.

You want to send the *Worldwide Home Page* to Nat Wong for his review. To create and send an e-mail message from Word:

Step 1	Verify	that the *Worldwide Home Page* is open in Web Layout view
Step 2	Click	the E-mail button on the Standard toolbar
Step 3	Observe	that the e-mail header opens and the *Worldwide Home Page* document is in the message content area

You can key the recipient's e-mail address in the To text box, send a copy to someone else by keying their e-mail address in the Cc text box, and key a brief message in the Introduction: text box.

Step 4	Key	Nat_Wong@wwide.com in the To text box
Step 5	Key	the following text in the Introduction: text box *Nat, please review the Worldwide Home Page document and send me your comments.* *your name*
Step 6	Save	the document as *Wong E-mail* and close it

24.c Distributing Documents for Revision

TASK PANE TIP

You can open the e-mail composition window and create an e-mail message from scratch with the Blank E-mail Message link in the New section in the New Document task pane.

You can distribute documents for revision by sending them to other employees via e-mail. When the recipient receives the document, he or she marks the changes and then returns the document to you. When you receive the document, you can review the changes, accept or reject them, or compare and merge the revised document with the original document.

chapter twenty-four

> **notes**
>
> The following activities assume you are using Outlook for e-mail and that you are working with three classmates. If you do not have e-mail installed on your computer or if you cannot work with three classmates, you can read but not perform the following activities.

Sending Documents for Review

You want to send the *Policy #152* document to three coworkers for their suggestions. You attach a copy of the document to an e-mail message for their review. They each review the document, mark their changes, and return the marked-up document to you. You then merge the three revised documents with your original document. To send a document for revision:

> **MENU TIP**
>
> You can send the current document to someone via e-mail or attach the current document to an e-mail message directly from Word by clicking the File menu, pointing to Send To, and clicking the appropriate e-mail command.

Step 1	Open	the *Policy #152* document located on the Data Disk
Step 2	Click	File
Step 3	Point to	Send To
Step 4	Click	Mail Recipient (for Review)
Step 5	Click	the Please Review Outlook message button on the taskbar, if necessary, to restore the Outlook message window

The Outlook message composition window contains a link to the *Policy #152* document as well as the document attachment. The message composition window on your screen should look similar to Figure 24-7.

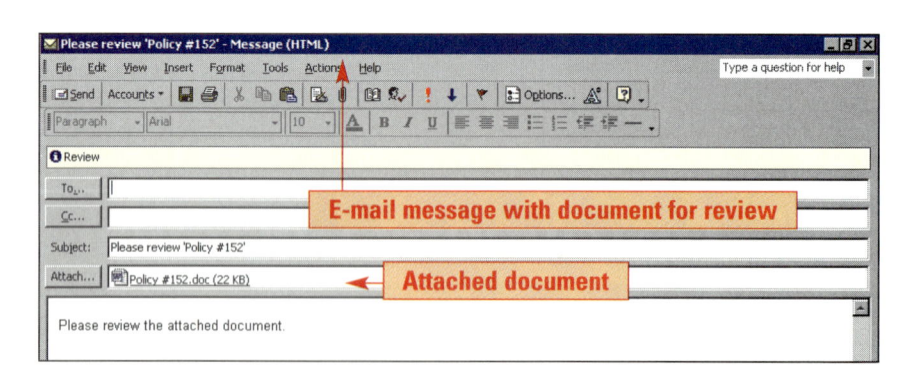

FIGURE 24-7
Outlook Message Composition Window

You key the appropriate e-mail addresses in the message window and send the message.

Integrating Word Documents with the Internet   WA 257

Step 6	Key	three e-mail addresses for other classmates separated by commas in the To text box
Step 7	Click	the Send button [Send] on the Outlook message window Standard toolbar
Step 8	Close	the document without saving and the Reviewing toolbar

Reviewing and Replying With Changes

When a recipient receives the e-mail message, he or she can open the attached document and make revisions to it. When the document opens, the Track Changes feature is turned on and the Reviewing toolbar is displayed. The first message recipient opens Outlook and opens the message:

Step 1	Open	Outlook, if necessary
Step 2	View	the contents of the Inbox
Step 3	Open	the message with the attached document
Step 4	Open	the attachment document in Word

The first message recipient's screen should look similar to Figure 24-8.

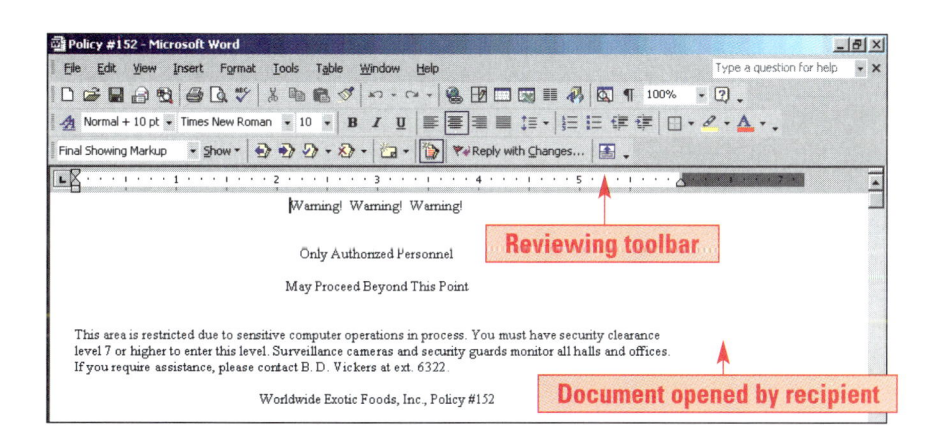

MOUSE TIP

You can attach a document to an e-mail message created directly in Word by first viewing the e-mail header and then clicking the Insert File button on the e-mail header toolbar.

QUICK TIP

Web discussions are threaded discussion items related to individual Office documents that are stored on a server. Individuals with permission to access the server can read and post their own messages about a specific Office document.

FIGURE 24-8
Document Sent for Revision

| Step 5 | Format | the first heading with the centered Heading 1 style and the second two headings with the centered Heading 3 style |
| Step 6 | Delete | the blank paragraph between the second and third heading paragraphs |

After making the changes, the recipient then returns the document to the originator with the Reply with Changes button on the Reviewing

chapter
twenty-four

toolbar or with the Original Sender subcommand under the Send To command on the File menu.

Step 7	Click	File
Step 8	Point to	Send To
Step 9	Click	Original Sender
Step 10	Send	the message and close the document without saving

As the originator, you open Outlook and the message with the revised document. To open the revised document:

Step 1	Open	Outlook, if necessary
Step 2	View	the contents of the Inbox
Step 3	Open	the message with the revised attached document
Step 4	Open	the revised attached document in Word

At this point you are ready to compare and merge the revised document and the original document.

Tracking Changes and Merging Multiple Documents

When you receive the revised document and open it from the e-mail message attachment, you are first asked if you want to merge the changes with the original document. Except for the location of the original document, your dialog box should look similar to Figure 24-9.

FIGURE 24-9
Confirmation Window to Merge Documents

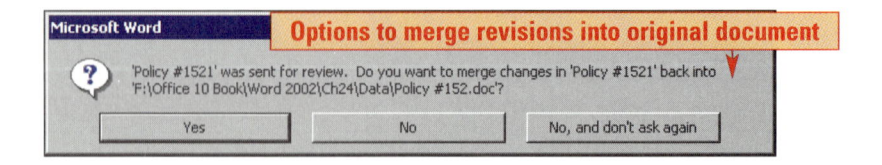

If you click No, the document opens with the Track Changes feature turned on. You have the option of accepting or rejecting the changes and saving the document. If you click Yes, the changes in the revised document are merged with the original document which also opens for your review. To merge the revisions with the original document:

| Step 1 | Click | Yes |

Before the document revisions are merged, you must indicate which document controls the formatting changes: the original (current) document or the revised (target) document. Except for the location of the two documents, your dialog box should look similar to Figure 24-10.

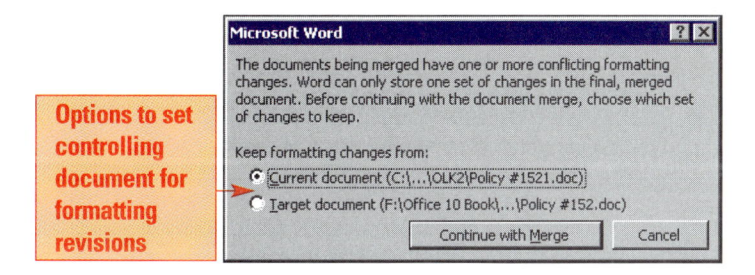

FIGURE 24-10
Dialog Box to Select Controlling Document

If you select the target document as the controlling document for formatting, the original document is opened and the formatting changes from the target document are merged into the original document. You select the target document as the controlling document.

Step 2	Click	the Target document option button
Step 3	Click	Continue with Merge

After comparing and merging the first revised document, the *Policy #152* document on your screen should look similar to Figure 24-11.

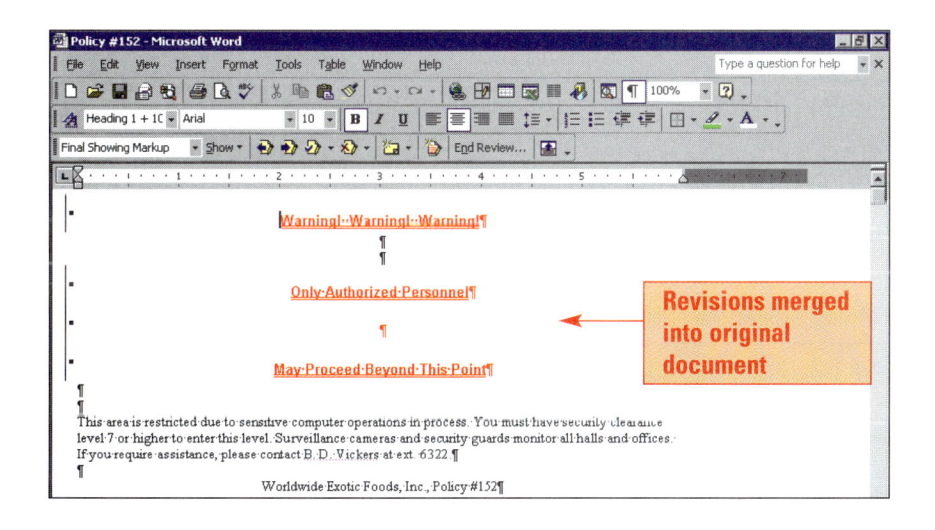

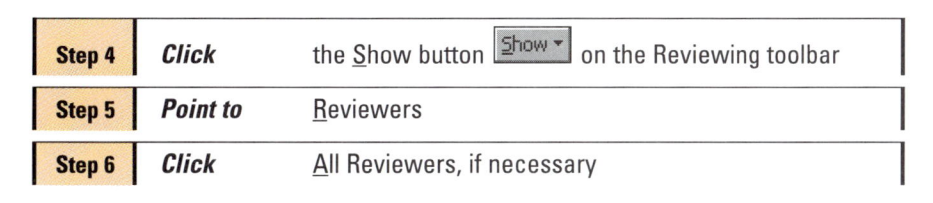

FIGURE 24-11
Revisions Merged into Original Document

Step 4	Click	the Show button [Show] on the Reviewing toolbar
Step 5	Point to	Reviewers
Step 6	Click	All Reviewers, if necessary

chapter twenty-four

| Step 7 | **Accept** | the changes |
| Step 8 | **Save** | the original document with the accepted, merged changes |

To complete the project, the second and third recipients should:

Step 1	**Open**	the Outlook Inbox, if necessary
Step 2	**Open**	the message from the originator
Step 3	**Revise**	the document as necessary
Step 4	**Return**	the revised document to the originator

To complete the project, you, as the originator, should:

Step 1	**Open**	the Outlook Inbox, if necessary
Step 2	**Open**	the message from the second recipient
Step 3	**Merge**	the revised document with the original document, selecting the target document as the controlling document for formatting
Step 4	**Review**	the merged changes, accepting or declining changes as needed
Step 5	**Save**	the original document
Step 6	**Follow**	Steps 1 through 4 to merge the third revised document with the original document and accept or decline the changes
Step 7	**Save**	the original document with a new name

During the review process, the *Policy #152* document was marked as being reviewed. Now that the review is over, you want to update the document to indicate the review process is finished.

Step 1	**Open**	the *Policy #152* document
Step 2	**Click**	the End Review button [End Review...] on the Reviewing toolbar
Step 3	**Click**	Yes to end the review for all reviewers
Step 4	**Close**	the document

MENU TIP

Word provides two other ways to collaborate with coworkers. You can use the Meet Now subcommand under the Online Collaboration command on the Tools menu to host an online meeting now using Microsoft NetMeeting software. To schedule an online meeting for a later date and time using NetMeeting and the Outlook meeting scheduling features, click the Schedule Meeting subcommand under the Online Collaboration command on the Tools menu.

notes The activities in the following section assume a self-created digital certificate or a digital certificate issued by a certification authority is installed on your computer. See online Help, if necessary, for information on creating your own digital certificate or tips on securing one from a certification authority.

24.d Using Digital Signatures

Because collaborating electronically with coworkers is now an important part of each workday, it is critical that coworkers have confidence in the source of an electronically transmitted document.

A **digital signature** is an electronic, encoded, secure mark of authentication added to a file or macro project to assure that the file or macro project originated from a trusted source and has not been altered. To use a digital signature to authenticate a file or macro project, you must first have a digital certificate installed on your computer that can be attached to the file or macro project. A **digital certificate** is an attachment to a file, macro project, or e-mail that vouches for its authenticity. You can create your own digital certificate or secure one from a commercial certification authority such as VeriSign, Inc.

You want to digitally sign the *Policy #113* document before sending it to employees via e-mail. To digitally sign the document:

Step 1	Open	the *Policy #113* document located on the Data Disk
Step 2	Save	the *Policy #113* document as *Signed Policy #113*
Step 3	Open	the Options dialog box
Step 4	Click	the Security tab, if necessary
Step 5	Click	Digital Signatures

The Digital Signature dialog box on your screen should look similar to Figure 24-12. You add and remove digital signatures from this dialog box.

CAUTION TIP

Because a self-created digital certificate can be forged, it is not considered "authenticated." Self-created digital certificates should be used for personal use only. Self-signed macro projects generate a warning if the security level in the Security Warning dialog box is set to High or Medium. A certification authority should issue digital certificates for commercial use.

chapter twenty-four

FIGURE 24-12
Digital Signature Dialog Box

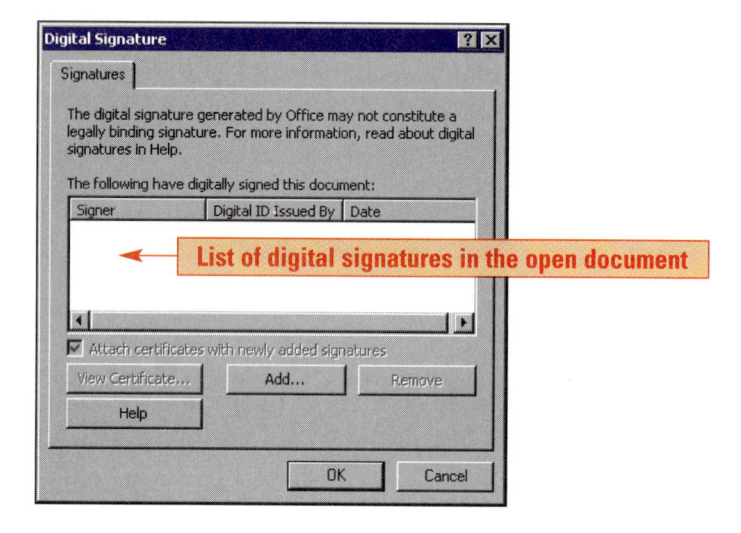

List of digital signatures in the open document

| Step 6 | **Click** | Add |
| Step 7 | **Click** | Yes, if necessary |

The Select Certificate dialog box on your screen should look similar to Figure 24-13.

FIGURE 24-13
Select Certificate Dialog Box

List of available digital signatures

QUICK TIP

You can easily create your own digital certificate for personal use by switching to Windows Explorer and locating the *SelfCert.exe* file generally located in the C:\Program Files\Microsoft Office\Office folder. Simply double-click the *SelfCert.exe* filename and follow the instructions to create the certificate.

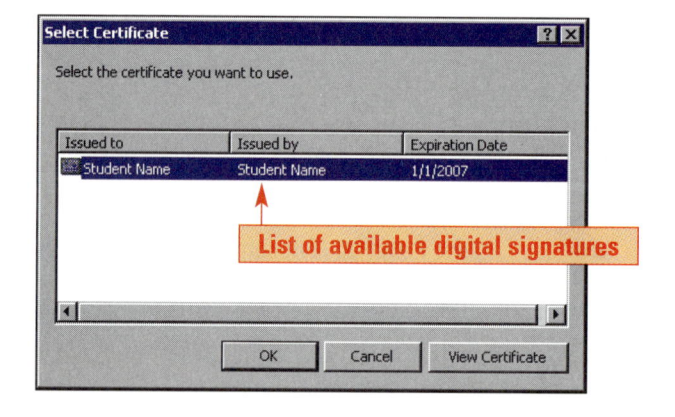

Step 8	**Click**	the desired certificate in the list
Step 9	**Click**	OK three times to close all three dialog boxes
Step 10	**Observe**	the text (Signed) at the end of the filename on the title bar
Step 11	**Save**	and close the document

Integrating the Internet with daily Word activities can help you work more efficiently with others.

Summary

- You can use various templates to create a Web page in Word.
- You can add a Web page title to the document's properties or in the Save As dialog box.
- Word provides Web page themes with coordinated background color and graphics, bullets, horizontal lines, and text.
- A table is an effective way to organize Web page content.
- Horizontal lines break a Web page into logical segments and you can use bulleted lists to itemize text on a Web page.
- You can create hyperlinks within a Web page or between Web pages.
- You should include navigational links to the home page, the top of the current page, and all other Web pages on each Web page at your site.
- After you complete all the pages at your Web site you should review them by testing all the links; checking the spelling and proofreading the contents; and having others review the pages for their look, clarity, and ease of use.
- When you are satisfied with the look and content of your Web pages, you can make them available on the Web by publishing them to a Web server.
- You can send e-mail messages using Outlook or Outlook Express directly from Word.
- You can distribute documents for revision via e-mail and then compare and merge the revised documents with the original document.
- You can digitally sign documents to assure others that the documents, when transmitted electronically, are from a trusted source.

chapter twenty-four

Commands Review

Action	Menu Bar	Shortcut Menu	Toolbar	Task Pane	Keyboard
Create a Web page	File, New.		in Web Layout view	Click the Blank Web Page link in the New Document task pane Click the General Templates link in the New Document task pane and click the Web pages tab in the Templates dialog box	ALT + F, N
Switch to Web Layout view	View, Web Layout				ALT + V, B
Save a Web page	File, Save as Web Page				ALT + F, G
Preview a Web page	File, Web Page Preview				ALT + F, W
Add a title to a Web page	File, Properties				ALT + F, I
Create a bulleted list on a Web page	Format, Bullets and Numbering				ALT + O, N
Insert a horizontal line on a Web page					
Apply a design theme	Format, Theme				ALT + O, H
Create a bookmark	Insert, Bookmark				ALT + I, K
Create a hyperlink	Insert, Hyperlink	Right-click selected link text, click Hyperlink			ALT + I, I CTRL + K
Sending e-mail messages from Word	File, New			Click the Blank E-mail Message link in the New Document task pane	ALT + F, N
Send documents for review with the Track Changes feature	File, Send To, Mail Recipient (for Review)				ALT + F, D, C
Digitally sign a document	Tools, Options				ALT + T, O

Concepts Review

Circle the correct answer.

1. To add a title to a Web page, you click the:
   - [a] Options command on the Edit menu.
   - [b] Properties command on the Edit menu.
   - [c] Internet Options command on the View menu.
   - [d] Properties command on the File menu.

2. To apply a preset design to a Web page, you click the:
   - [a] Color command on the Format menu.
   - [b] Scheme command on the Insert menu.
   - [c] Theme command on the Format menu.
   - [d] Background command on the View menu.

3. When you save a Web page, Word automatically:
   - [a] opens the Insert Hyperlink dialog box.
   - [b] creates a subfolder at the same location as the Web page.
   - [c] applies a theme.
   - [d] browses for files.

4. Publishing is the process of:
   - [a] setting a document's properties.
   - [b] adding a Web page title.
   - [c] creating a bookmark.
   - [d] transferring a Web page to a Web server.

5. A hyperlink is:
   [a] text or a picture that provides a clickable shortcut to another page.
   [b] a text box in which you can key an introduction to an e-mail message.
   [c] the title of a Web page.
   [d] a Smart Tag.

6. Which of the following is not a step in distributing documents for revising and then merging the revisions with the original document?
   [a] Opening Outlook and opening a message attachment.
   [b] Attaching a copy of the document to the recipient's e-mail.
   [c] Publishing the document to a Web server.
   [d] Specifying the controlling document for formatting revisions.

7. A digital certificate is a(n):
   [a] attachment to a file authenticating it.
   [b] hyperlink.
   [c] HTML code.
   [d] security level.

Circle **T** if the statement is true or **F** if the statement is false.

T F 1. A self-generated digital certificate is appropriate for commercial use.

T F 2. You can use text, but not pictures, as hyperlinks.

T F 3. Web pages are created with the Hypertext Markup Language.

T F 4. The Click and Type pointer allows you to position the insertion point in Normal view.

T F 5. You create a hyperlink to a different position on the same page by first creating a bookmark and then linking to that bookmark.

T F 6. It is not important to preview your Web page in a Web browser as you create it.

T F 7. After you create and test your Web pages, you must publish them to a Web server so others can access them.

T F 8. A link bar is a set of navigational links that allows viewers to move between pages at a Web site.

Skills Review

Exercise 1

1. Create a new Web page using the Personal Web Page template located on the Web Pages tab in the Templates dialog box.
2. Add your name as the title in the document properties.
3. Replace the main heading sample text with your name in all-uppercase characters.
4. Complete the Work Information, Favorite Links, Contact Information, Current Projects, Personal Interests, and revised date using your own information.
5. Preview the Web page and make any necessary corrections.
6. Change the theme to a theme of your choice.
7. Save the Web page with your name as the filename.
8. Preview, print, and close the Web page.

chapter twenty-four

Exercise 2

1. Create a new Web page using the Frequently Asked Questions template located on the Web Pages tab in the Templates dialog box.

2. Complete the Web page by including and answering the following questions:

    How do I create a Web page from a template?
    Where can I find the Web page templates?
    What is a template?

3. Select and delete the table of contents text, buttons, and related text for the questions:

    Why doesn't…?
    Who is…?
    When is…?

4. Insert the current date as the last revised date.

5. Apply the theme of your choice.

6. Save the Web page with the title "Frequently Asked Questions" and the filename *Frequently Asked Questions*.

7. Preview, print, and close the Web page.

Exercise 3

1. Open the *Office Information Automation* document located on the Data Disk.

2. Apply the Nature theme with vivid colors, animated graphics, and background image.

3. Format the main heading with the Heading 2 style and center it.

4. Add a centered horizontal line below the main heading.

5. Format the paragraph headings with the Heading 3 style.

6. Add bullets to the items below each paragraph heading.

7. Insert a top-of-page bookmark at the top of the page.

8. Use the AutoShapes feature to draw a blue-filled, up-arrow object centered approximately 1½ lines below the last line of text. Insert a hyperlink from the arrow object to the top-of-page bookmark. Use the text "Top of the Page" as a customized ScreenTip. (*Hint:* Right-click the selected up-arrow drawing object to open the Insert Hyperlink dialog box.)

9. Save the Web page as *OIAS Web Page*.

10. Preview, print, and close the Web page.

Exercise 4

1. Open the *Commonly Misused Words* document located on the Data Disk.

2. Apply the theme of your choice with vivid colors, animated graphics, and background image.

3. Center the major heading COMMONLY MISUSED WORDS formatted with the Heading 1 style one line above the first paragraph.

4. Format the first paragraph with the Heading 3 style.

5. Insert a centered horizontal line between the first paragraph and the list of descriptions.

6. Format the list of descriptions with the Heading 4 style.

7. Add bullets to the list of descriptions.
8. Insert a bookmark at the top of the page.
9. Insert a hyperlink to the top-of-page bookmark centered below the text.
10. Save the Web page with the title "Commonly Misused Words" and the filename *Misused Words Web Page*.
11. Preview, print, and close the Web page.
12. Open the *Misused Words Web Page* document in Word.
13. Apply a different theme of your choice.
14. Save the Web page, and then preview, print, and close it.

Exercise 5

1. Create a new Web page with the Blank Web Page link in the New section in the New Document task pane.
2. Add the title "Worldwide Sales Department" to the file properties.
3. Apply the Blueprint theme with vivid colors, active graphics, and background image.
4. Center the major heading "SALES INFORMATION" formatted with the Heading 1 style.
5. Insert a centered horizontal line below the major heading.
6. Create a 1 × 1 Table approximately 4 inches wide, remove the border, and center the table.
7. Apply the Heading 2 style.
8. Key and center the text "Sales Report Links" in the table.
9. Create a new row and apply the Heading 4 style.
10. Turn on the Bullets feature and key the following filenames in the second row:

    Sales Representatives Web Page
    Annual Beverage Sales Web Page
    Regional Deli Sales Web Page

11. Browse to create a hyperlink from each bulleted item to the file on the Data Disk. Modify the ScreenTip for each hyperlink to contain the filename.
12. Save the Web page as *Sales Information Web Page*.
13. Print and close the Web page.
14. Open the Web browser, load the *Sales Information Web Page*, and test the links.
15. Close the Web browser when finished.

Exercise 6

1. Open the *Winter Schedule* document located on the Data Disk.
2. Apply the Classic theme with vivid colors, active graphics, and a background graphic.
3. Select each date paragraph and convert the text to a table without a border.
4. Apply bold style to the date table contents.
5. AutoFit the table to the contents and then center the table horizontally. (*Hint:* Select all the columns and double-click any column boundary.)

chapter twenty-four

6. Apply the Expedition theme with vivid colors and active graphics. Turn off the background image.

7. AutoFit the tables to the contents again.

8. Apply the Heading 1 style to the major heading and center it.

9. Apply the Heading 2 style to the "Training Sessions" subheading and center it.

10. Apply the Heading 3 style to each of the paragraph headings.

11. Insert a centered horizontal divider line following the "Training Sessions" subheading, each date table, and the last paragraph on the page.

12. Create a bulleted list from the text following each paragraph heading. (*Hint:* Each sentence in the paragraph should be a new paragraph with a bullet.)

13. Add a top-of-page bookmark and an AutoShape hyperlink with the modified ScreenTip "Top of Page" below the last horizontal divider line.

14. Save the document as a Web page with the title "Training Schedule" and the filename *Winter Schedule Web Page*.

15. Preview, print, and close the Web page.

Exercise 7

1. Open the *Policy #113* document located on the Data Disk.

2. Apply the theme of your choice and format the document attractively using the theme options.

3. Save the document as a Web page with the title "Policy #113" and filename *Policy #113 Web Page*. Preview, print and close it.

4. Open the *Policy #152* document located on the Data Disk.

5. Apply the theme of your choice and format the document attractively using the theme options.

6. Save the document as a Web page with the title "Policy #152" and filename *Policy #152 Web Page*. Preview, print and close it.

7. Create a new, blank Web page and apply the theme of your choice. Use the theme formatting options to format the page as desired.

8. Insert the major heading "PERSONNEL POLICIES" centered at the top of the page and text hyperlinks to the *Policy #113 Web Page* and *Policy #152 Web Page* files. Modify the ScreenTip for each hyperlink appropriately.

9. Save the new Web page with the title "Personnel Policies" and the filename *Personnel Policies Web Page*.

10. Open the Web browser, load the *Personnel Policies Web page*, and test the links.

11. Close the Web browser when you finish.

Exercise 8

1. Open the *Preparing For A Speech* document located on the Data Disk.

2. Save the document as a Web page formatted with a theme of your choice. Use the title "How to Prepare for a Speech" and the filename *Preparing For A Speech Web Page*.

3. Preview, print, and close the Web page.

Case Projects

Project 1

The sales manager, Dick Montez, asks you to create a Web page describing Worldwide Exotic Foods new holiday products. Create a blank Web page and apply the theme of your choice. Use fictitious information about five holiday products for the headings, text, and bulleted lists. Format the page attractively. Save, preview, and print the Web page.

Project 2

Nat Wong thinks it would be helpful for you to learn more about creating a Web page with the Hypertext Markup Language (HTML) and suggests you locate online guides for working with HTML. Connect to the Internet and search for Web sites that provide information on how to create Web pages using HTML. Print at least four Web pages. Write Nat an interoffice memorandum describing the results of your research. Save, preview, and print the memo.

Project 3

Jody Haversham calls to ask for help in reviewing a digital certificate. She wants to know what the critical things are to look for when reviewing a digital certificate. Using online Help, look up the topic "Review digital certificates for a file or macro project" topic. Then write Jody a memo listing the three important things she should look for when reviewing the digital certificate details. Save, preview, and print the memo.

Project 4

Mary Boyer, the Marketing Department representative to the Web site development committee, asks you to research online options for getting the company Web site noticed. Connect to the Internet and search for Web sites that provide information on marketing Web sites. Print at least five Web pages. Write an interoffice memorandum to Mary with a Cc: to the Web site development committee listing the Web sites you find. Save, preview, and print the memo.

Project 5

Nat Wong recently read an article about Office XP that mentioned team sites. He asks you to find out what team sites are and how they are used. Using online Help research the "team sites" topics. Then write a memo to Nat describing team sites and listing ways a team site can be used. Save, preview, and print the memo.

Project 6

Viktor Winkler, the public affairs officer, wants to add a Web page to the company intranet that provides hyperlinks to important government Web sites. He asks you to create the Web page. Using the template and theme of your choice, create a Web page that contains hyperlinks to ten local, state, and federal Web sites. Save, preview, and print the Web page.

If you have access to a Web server complete the following additional steps. Your instructor will provide any additional instructions you need to access the Web server. (1) Save the Web page to the Web server. (2) Open the Web page from the Web server and change the theme. (3) Save the modified Web page to the Web server.

Project 7

During lunch with Jody Haversham and Bob Markham, from the Sales Department, you mention how helpful it is to send documents for review. Bob asks you to give him more information on the topic. Using online Help review topics related to sending files for review. Then write Bob an interoffice memo discussing sending documents for review. Save, preview, and print the memo.

Project 8

Kelly Armstead is having trouble creating Web pages and asks for your help. When she saves existing Word documents as Web pages, some of the formatting is different when she views the Web page in a browser. Use the Ask A Question Box to search for information on how to troubleshoot viewing Web pages. Write Kelly a memo describing the likely cause of her problem. Save, preview, and print the memo.

chapter twenty-four

Word 2002

Using Macros

Chapter Overview

Organizations often create macros—programs that automate tasks—to save their employees time. Rather than performing a series of common tasks, you can automate them into a single macro and then select only one command to perform the entire series. In this chapter, you learn to record, run, edit, copy, rename, and delete macros.

LEARNING OBJECTIVES

- Record and run macros
- Edit macros
- Copy, rename, and delete macros

Case profile

Several departments at Worldwide Exotic Foods want to automate routine word processing tasks by using macros. Chris Lofton, the word processing manager, asks you to tackle the project. You agree to learn how to record, edit, and run macros and then create the macros requested by each department. You create and modify a macro that prints two copies of any active document and create a macro that performs a multilevel sort on five columns of text and then formats the text as a table.

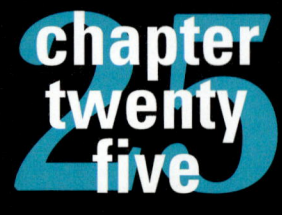

chapter twenty five

25.a Recording and Running Macros

A **macro** is a set of commands saved together in one step to automate a multiple step task. Macros are especially useful for performing detailed, repetitive tasks that existing Word features—such as toolbar buttons, AutoCorrect, AutoText, styles, and document templates—do not perform efficiently. You can use a macro to speed up editing and formatting, to combine multiple commands, and to automate a series of tasks. For example, you could use a macro to create and format a header or footer or to convert text to a table and apply a table style, or AutoFormat, to the table.

You can create a macro by writing the Word commands in the Visual Basic for Applications programming language. Another method of creating a macro is to turn on the macro recorder and actually perform all the steps of a task, such as clicking menu commands, keying text, or moving the insertion point. As you complete each step, Word translates the actions into Visual Basic for Applications programming statements. For most macros that automate routine tasks, you simply record the steps to create the macro.

Executing a macro is called "running" it. You can run a macro by assigning it to a menu, toolbar, or keyboard shortcut and then clicking the menu command or toolbar button, or pressing the shortcut keys. By default, macros are stored in the Normal template so that they are available for all documents you open each time you start Word, but they may be stored in any template or document. For example, you may want to restrict a macro's use to a single document or template rather than use it with all documents. Individual macros are stored in a **macro project**, which is a group of macros saved in a document or template that you can copy, delete, or rename using the Organizer feature. The default name for a macro project is NewMacros.

Before you begin to record a macro, it is helpful to first write down all the steps in the task that you want to automate. Then you practice the steps to be certain you haven't accidentally omitted any steps. After you are certain that the written steps are correct, you record the macro. This technique helps you record the macro correctly the first time so that you do not have to rerecord or edit it.

Worldwide Exotic Foods employees often print two copies of documents—one for their files and one to distribute. Chris asks you to automate this task by creating a macro that prints two copies of any active document, which users can run by clicking a command on the menu bar. To begin:

| Step 1 | **Write down** the commands you click, in the exact order, to print two copies of any active document |

QUICK TIP

You can create flexible, powerful macros using the Visual Basic for Applications programming that includes instructions that you cannot record. For more information on using the Visual Basic for Applications programming language, see online Help.

MENU TIP

You can create, record, run, edit, and delete macros with the Macro command on the Tools menu.

| Step 2 | *Practice* | the steps until you are certain no steps have been omitted |

Once you know the steps are correct and complete, you can record the macro. To record the macro:

| Step 1 | *Create* | a new, blank document, if necessary |
| Step 2 | *Double-click* | the REC mode indicator on the status bar |

The Record Macro dialog box that opens on your screen should look similar to Figure 25-1.

FIGURE 25-1
Record Macro Dialog Box

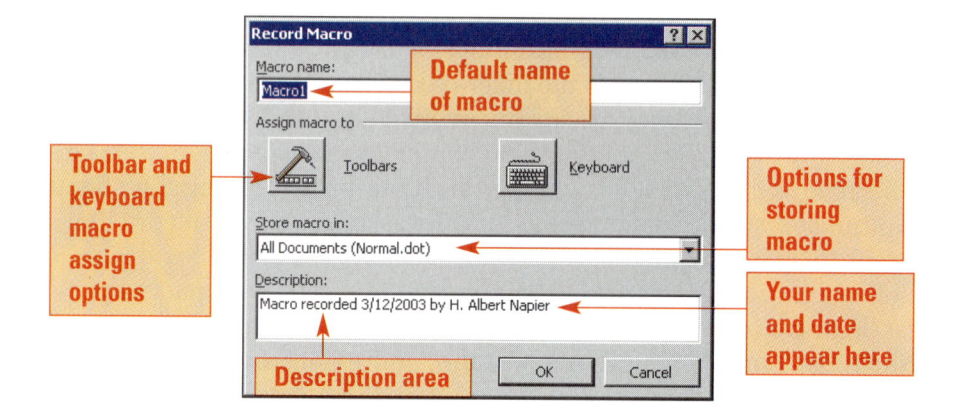

[Screenshot of Record Macro dialog box with callouts: "Default name of macro" pointing to Macro name field (Macro1); "Toolbar and keyboard macro assign options" pointing to Toolbars and Keyboard buttons; "Options for storing macro" pointing to Store macro in dropdown (All Documents (Normal.dot)); "Your name and date appear here" and "Description area" pointing to Description field (Macro recorded 3/12/2003 by H. Albert Napier)]

This dialog box allows you to assign a macro to a toolbar button or keyboard shortcut. The Store macro in: list allows you to store the macro in the attached template or in the document. If a macro is going to be used widely, it is a good idea to store it in the Normal template. If a macro is used only with a specific template or document, you can store it in that template or document. To help you remember what a macro does, you enter a short description of your macro in the Description: text box.

Because this macro is used on many documents, you store it in the Normal template. You name the macro and add a short description.

Step 3	*Key*	PRINTMACRO in the Macro name: text box
Step 4	*Key*	Prints two copies of the active document. in the Description: text box
Step 5	*Click*	Toolbars
Step 6	*Click*	the Commands tab, if necessary

QUICK TIP

The menu bar is a toolbar just like the Standard and Formatting toolbars. To add a macro to a specific menu, click the Toolbars button in the Record Macro dialog box and drag the macro to the appropriate menu.

The Commands tab in the Customize dialog box on your screen should look similar to Figure 25-2.

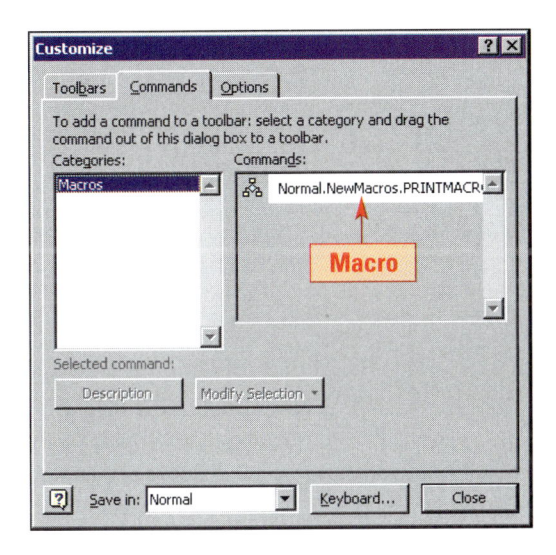

FIGURE 25-2
Commands Tab in the Customize Dialog Box

To assign the PRINTMACRO command to the menu bar, you simply drag the macro command to the desired position.

| Step 7 | Drag | the Normal.NewMacros.PRINTMACRO command from the Commands: list to the menu bar |

To make the command easier to read, you can edit the macro command text.

Step 8	Right-click	the Normal.NewMacros.PRINTMACRO command on the menu bar
Step 9	Edit	the Name: text box to contain only the text PRINTMACRO
Step 10	Press	the ENTER key to close the menu
Step 11	Close	the dialog box

The Stop Recording toolbar appears and the mouse pointer has a cassette icon, indicating the macro recorder is turned on. Every keyboard and mouse action you perform is recorded when the macro recorder is turned on. The two buttons on the Stop Recording toolbar allow you to stop recording your actions or to pause recording your actions while you do something that is not part of the macro. Your screen should look similar to Figure 25-3.

chapter twenty-five

FIGURE 25-3
Document with Macro Recorder Turned On

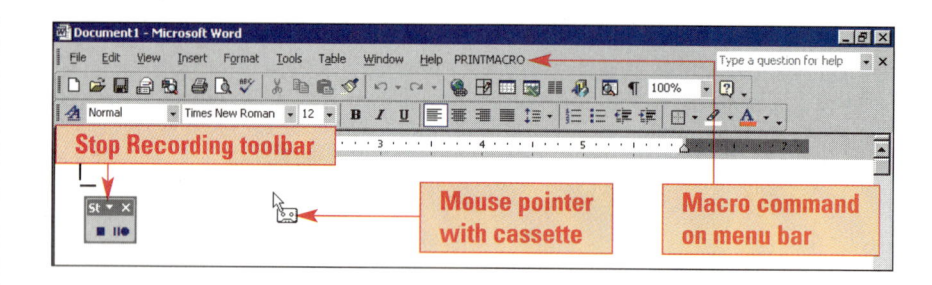

To record the steps in the print macro:

Step 1	Click	File
Step 2	Click	Print
Step 3	Key	2 in the Number of copies: text box
Step 4	Click	OK
Step 5	Click	the Stop Recording button ■ on the Stop Recording toolbar

The Stop Recording toolbar no longer appears and the REC mode indicator on the status bar is not bold, indicating that Word is no longer recording your keystrokes.

After you record a macro, you should test it to ensure it works properly. You run a macro to test it. To test the PRINTMACRO:

Step 1	Open	the *Chicago Warehouses Audit* document located on the Data Disk
Step 2	Click	the PRINTMACRO command on the menu bar
Step 3	Observe	that two copies of the active document print
Step 4	Close	the document

The Sales Department wants to print two copies of a sales representatives list formatted as a table. Because the list is used in a variety of ways, they do not want to permanently change the formatting. Chris asks you to create the macro that sorts five columns of text alphabetically by the first and then second columns, converts the sorted text to a table, sizes and centers the table, and prints two copies. This macro applies only to this specific document, so you store it in the document

CAUTION TIP

When recording a macro, you can use the mouse to click commands and dialog box options, but you cannot use the mouse to move the insertion point or select, copy, or move text in the document window. Use the keyboard for these tasks.

and run it from the Macros dialog box. This is a complex macro; therefore, it is important that you write down and practice the steps before you begin recording. To begin:

| Step 1 | *Write down* | the steps for the macro |
| Step 2 | *Practice* | the steps for the macro |

After writing down and practicing the steps you can begin recording the macro. To turn on the macro recorder:

Step 1	*Open*	the *Sales Representatives* document located on the Data Disk
Step 2	*Double-click*	the REC mode indicator on the status bar
Step 3	*Key*	TABLE in the Macro name: text box
Step 4	*Select*	Sales Representatives (document) in the Store macro in: list box
Step 5	*Key*	Sorts text; creates table; prints document. in the Description: text box
Step 6	*Click*	OK

The Stop Recording toolbar appears and the mouse pointer has a cassette icon attached, indicating that the macro recorder is on and you can begin to record your actions. To select the five columns of text using the keyboard:

| Step 1 | *Move* | the insertion point to the beginning of the first Jones line using the keyboard |
| Step 2 | *Press* | the CTRL + SHIFT + END keys to select from the insertion point to the end of the document |

Next you sort the selected text in ascending order. To sort the text:

Step 1	*Click*	Table
Step 2	*Click*	Sort
Step 3	*Select*	Field 1 in the Sort by list box, if necessary
Step 4	*Click*	the Ascending option button, if necessary

chapter
twenty-five

Step 5	*Select*	Field 2 in the Then by list box
Step 6	*Click*	the As**c**ending option button, if necessary
Step 7	*Click*	OK

Now that the text is sorted correctly, you convert it to a centered table. To convert the text to a table and size and center it:

Step 1	*Click*	T**a**ble
Step 2	*Point to*	Con**v**ert
Step 3	*Click*	Te**x**t to Table
Step 4	*Click*	OK
Step 5	*AutoFit*	the table to its contents using the **A**utoFit command on T**a**ble menu
Step 6	*Center*	the table using the Table Properties dialog box
Step 7	*Print*	two copies of the document
Step 8	*Click*	the Stop Recording button on the Stop Recording toolbar
Step 9	*Observe*	the formatted table and two printed copies

Now that you've recorded the macro you want to remove all the formatting changes you made while recording it, and then run it to verify that it works. Because you didn't assign the macro to a keyboard, toolbar, or menu, you use the Macros dialog box to run it. To test the macro:

Step 1	*Undo*	all the previous formatting actions with the Undo button list arrow on the Standard toolbar
Step 2	*Move*	the insertion point to the top of the document
Step 3	*Click*	**T**ools
Step 4	*Point to*	**M**acro
Step 5	*Click*	**M**acros

The Macros dialog box on your screen should look similar to Figure 25-4.

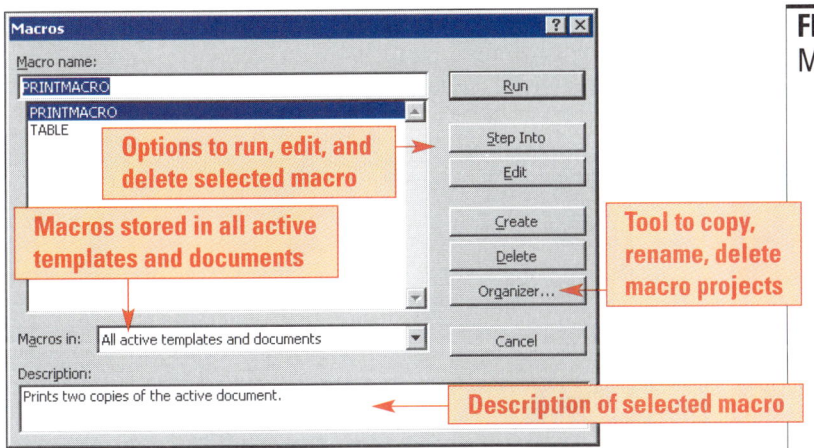

FIGURE 25-4
Macros Dialog Box

[Macros dialog box screenshot with annotations:
- Options to run, edit, and delete selected macro
- Macros stored in all active templates and documents
- Tool to copy, rename, delete macro projects
- Description of selected macro]

You can run, edit, create, and delete macros in this dialog box. You run the TABLE macro.

Step 6	Double-click	TABLE in the Macro name: list box
Step 7	Observe	that the five columns of text are sorted, converted to an automatically sized table, and printed

You need to save the document with the macro, but you do not want to save the new formatting. To remove the formatting and save the document with the macro:

Step 1	Undo	all the previous formatting actions
Step 2	Save	the document as *Sales Representatives Automated* and close it

Sometimes you need to modify macros. You do this by editing them with the Visual Basic Editor.

25.b Editing Macros

You use the Visual Basic Editor to create new macros or to edit existing macros. The **Visual Basic Editor** is a feature that contains its own windows, menus, and tools you use to write or revise the Visual Basic programming statements for a macro. Chris tells you that the PRINTMACRO must be modified to print three copies of the active document instead of two. Rather than record the entire macro again, you decide to edit it in the Visual Basic Editor by selecting it in the Macros dialog box and clicking the Edit button. You also decide to add the modification date as an

> **QUICK TIP**
>
> To correct a macro that is not running correctly, rerecord the steps and save it with the same name.
>
> Word has several supplied macros you can use for manipulating data and troubleshooting and fixing problems in a document. These macros are stored in the Macros subfolder in the folder where the Word program is stored. For more information on Word supplied macros, see online Help.

additional comment to the macro and change the number of printed copies in the comments from "two" to "three."

To open the PRINTMACRO in the Visual Basic Editor:

Step 1	Click	Tools
Step 2	Point to	Macro
Step 3	Click	Macros
Step 4	Click	PRINTMACRO in the Macro name: list box, if necessary
Step 5	Click	Edit

The Visual Basic Editor window on your screen should look similar to Figure 25-5.

FIGURE 25-5
Microsoft Visual Basic Editor

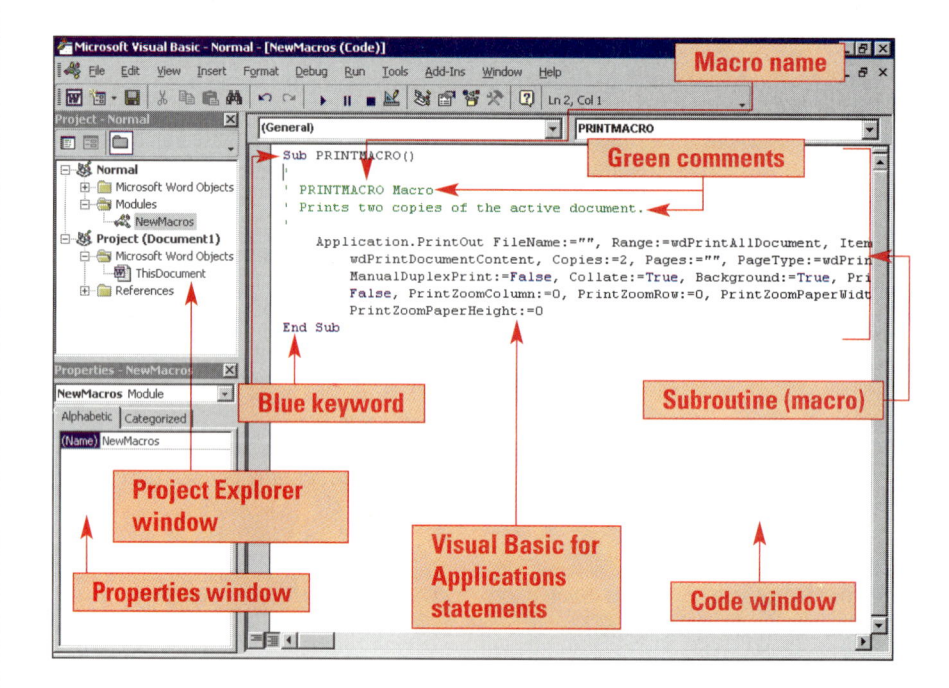

The Visual Basic Editor contains three windows: the Code window, the Project Explorer window, and the Properties window. The Code window displays the contents of a macro written in the Visual Basic for Applications programming language. When you record the PRINTMACRO macro, Word translates your recorded steps into this code. The Project Explorer window displays a list of macro projects currently open; programmers use this window to add or delete macro project components and reorganize macro projects. If the Project Explorer window is not visible, you can open it by clicking the Project Explorer button on the Standard toolbar. The Properties window allows programmers to change the settings or characteristics of a macro. If the Properties window is not visible, you can open it by clicking the Properties Window button on the toolbar. Because you are going to modify the code, you close the Project Explorer and Properties windows. To close the windows:

Step 1	Click	the Close button ⊠ in the Project Explorer window title bar
Step 2	Click	the Close button ⊠ in the Properties window title bar
Step 3	Maximize	the Code window, if necessary

> **MENU TIP**
>
> You can print a selected macro subroutine, a macro module, or macro project by opening the Visual Basic Editor and clicking the Print command on the File menu.

The Visual Basic for Applications code is created in a special format called a **subroutine**. Macros are sometimes called subroutines. Each subroutine (macro) is part of a larger component, called a **module**. The subroutine (macro) begins with the reserved word, or **keyword**, "Sub" in blue font; it ends with the keyword "End Sub" in blue font. Between these two keywords is the name of the subroutine (macro), any comments in green font, and the Visual Basic for Applications program statements that perform the macro tasks in black font. You want to add the modification date as a comment and change the comment text "two" to "three." To add and modify the comment text:

Step 1	Move	the insertion point to the end of the green comment line beginning with "Prints"
Step 2	Key	Modified on (today's date).
Step 3	Select	the text "two" and replace it with "three" in the first comment sentence

Now you want to edit the Visual Basic for Applications statement to print three copies instead of one. To edit the Visual Basic for Applications statement:

Step 1	Select	the number 2 in the code Copies:=2 in the Visual Basic for Applications statement
Step 2	Key	3
Step 3	Click	the Project Explorer button on the Standard toolbar to open the Project Explorer window
Step 4	Click	the Properties Window button on the Standard toolbar to open the Properties window
Step 5	Click	File
Step 6	Click	Close and Return to Microsoft Word

chapter
twenty-five

Caution Tip

It is a good practice to install the most current version of antivirus software on your computer system so that you can check routinely for computer viruses. Opening files you receive as e-mail attachments and downloading files from the Web may place your computer system at a higher risk for a virus infection. You should consider saving e-mail attachments and downloaded files to a disk and then checking them with your antivirus software before opening them to avoid infection. To learn more about computer viruses and antivirus software see your instructor, visit a local computer store, or search the Web for computer virus topics.

As before, you run the macro to verify that it works. To test the PRINTMACRO modifications:

Step 1	*Open*	the *Chicago Warehouses Audit* document located on the Data Disk
Step 2	*Run*	the PRINTMACRO macro
Step 3	*Close*	the document without saving changes

Because macro viruses can be a serious problem, Word provides a macro security feature to protect your computer files.

Changing the Security Level

A **virus** is a computer program that "infects" your computer by inserting copies of itself into other files. When this happens, the virus can infect still other files when the infected file is loaded into your computer's memory. Some viruses are harmful and may damage your hard disk, use computer memory that could otherwise be used by other programs, or destroy files. A **macro virus** is a virus included in a macro that is activated when the macro runs.

By default, Word sets a high security level that automatically disables any macros in a document when you open the document. Unless you switch to a lower security level, Word automatically disables macros, without a warning message, when you open any document that contains a macro—such as the *Sales Representatives Automated* document you created earlier. You can modify this security level so you can choose whether to open a document with macros enabled or disabled.

To modify the security level:

Step 1	*Click*	Tools
Step 2	*Point to*	Macro
Step 3	*Click*	Security
Step 4	*Click*	the Security Level tab, if necessary

The Security dialog box on your screen should look similar to Figure 25-6. Because macro viruses can only damage your files when the macro runs, you might want to modify the security level so that you can choose to open a document with the macros enabled or disabled. The medium security level allows you to do this. If you are comfortable with the source of the document and trust that you are not exposing your system to a macro virus, you can elect to open the document with the macros enabled. If you are not comfortable with the source of the document, you can choose to cancel the open process or open the document as read-only with the macros disabled.

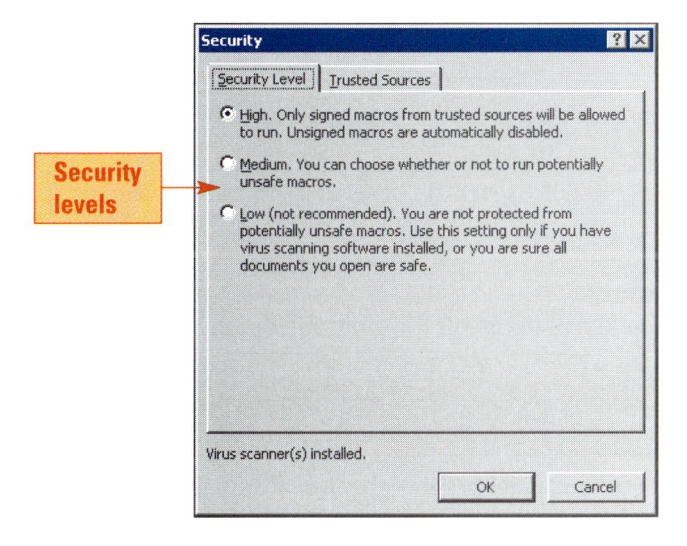

FIGURE 25-6
Security Level tab in the Security Dialog Box

Security levels

You want to open the *Sales Representatives Automated* document you created earlier with the macro enabled. To do this, you can change the security level to medium.

Step 5	Click	the Medium option button, if necessary
Step 6	Click	OK

You can see how the security level works by opening the *Sales Representatives Automated* document you created earlier. To open the document with macros enabled:

Step 1	Open	the *Sales Representatives Automated* document
Step 2	Click	the Enable Macros button in the confirmation dialog box

Despite the care you take to write down, practice, and then record a macro, you might find errors when you test it. If a macro is not working properly, you can work through it step-by-step to find the errors.

Debugging Macros

If you record a macro that doesn't run properly, you can look for errors in each Visual Basic for Applications statement by working through the macro one step at a time. A macro "bug" is an error in a Visual Basic for Applications statement. The process of stepping through the statements to find errors is called **debugging** the macro.

> **QUICK TIP**
>
> You can digitally sign macros to authenticate them as originating from a trusted source. For more information on digitally signing macros, see Visual Basic Editor online Help.

chapter twenty-five

CAUTION TIP

Extensive editing of complex macros requires some knowledge of the Visual Basic for Applications programming language and experience using the Visual Basic Editor. In many cases it is easier and faster to simply rerecord the macro. If a macro is not working properly, first review your written steps, then practice the steps again, and finally rerecord the macro.

Although the macro in the *Sales Representatives Automated* document should be working properly, you can use it to view the debugging process. To open the TABLE macro:

Step 1	Open	the Macros dialog box
Step 2	Select	the TABLE macro
Step 3	Click	Edit to open the Visual Basic Editor window

As you process the macro step by step, you can switch to the Word document to view the results of that step. To begin the debugging process:

Step 1	Click	Debug on the menu bar
Step 2	Click	Step Into
Step 3	Observe	the first line of the subroutine is highlighted and the left side of the Code window contains a yellow arrow pointing to the highlighted text
Step 4	Press	the F8 key to proceed to the first statement in the subroutine
Step 5	Observe	the statement that moves the insertion point down three lines is highlighted
Step 6	Press	the F8 key to run the highlighted statement and move to the next statement
Step 7	Press	the F8 key to finish running the statements that move the insertion point and select the five columns of text (Selection. Sort step)
Step 8	Switch to	the Word document using the taskbar button and observe the selected text
Step 9	Switch to	the Visual Basic Editor using the taskbar button
Step 10	Continue	to process each step of the macro by pressing the F8 key
Step 11	Close	the Visual Basic Editor and return to Word when finished
Step 12	Close	the document without saving any changes

When you have several macros, it is important to be able to organize them.

25.c Copying, Renaming, and Deleting Macros

Over time you may need to edit your macros to meet new processing requirements or delete those macros that are no longer useful. Also, as you develop your macros others in your work group may want to use them. You can manage your macros using the Organizer, options in the Macros dialog box, or with the Visual Basic Editor.

Using the Organizer

You can access the Organizer from the Macros dialog box or from the Templates and Add-ins dialog box, both of which are opened from the Tools menu. From the Organizer dialog box, you can copy macros to other documents or templates, rename macros when necessary, and delete macros when they are no longer needed.

Chris asks you to copy the NewMacros macro project (which contains the PRINTMACRO macro) from the Normal template to another document, rename the PRINTMACRO in the new document, and then delete the PRINTMACRO from the Normal template. To open the new document and the Organizer dialog box:

Step 1	**Open**	the *Chicago Warehouses Audit* document located on the Data Disk
Step 2	**Open**	the Macros dialog box
Step 3	**Click**	Organizer

The Macro Project Items tab in the Organizer dialog box on your screen should look similar to Figure 25-7.

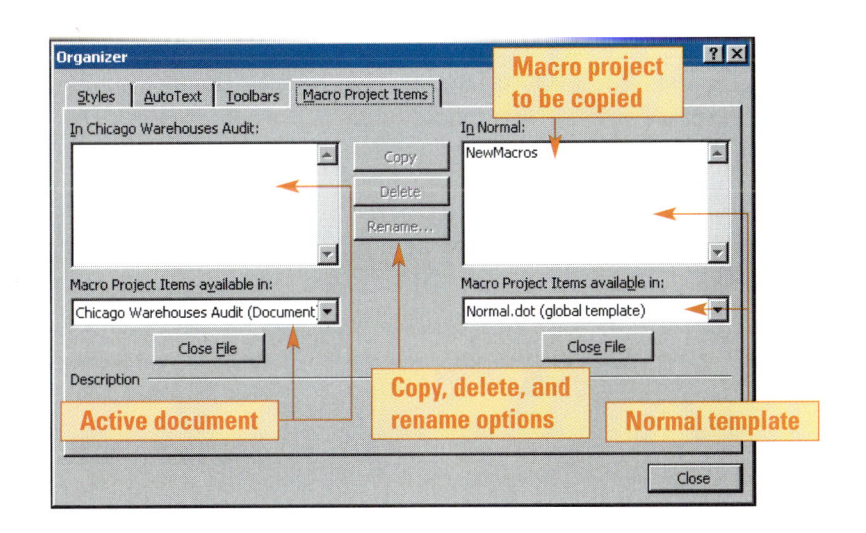

FIGURE 25-7
Macro Project Items Tab in the Organizer Dialog Box

> **QUICK TIP**
>
> You can also copy AutoText, styles, and custom toolbars from one template or document to another in the Organizer.
>
> If the only open macro projects are in the Normal template, you might see a list of macro names without a macro project reference in the Macros dialog box.

You copy, rename, and delete entire macro projects in this dialog box. Because you opened the *Chicago Warehouses Audit* document before you opened the Organizer dialog box, both the Normal template and the destination document are open and ready for the copy process. You copy the selected NewMacros project to the destination document.

Step 4	Click	the NewMacros project in the In Normal: list to select it, if necessary
Step 5	Click	the << Copy button in the Organizer dialog box
Step 6	Observe	that the NewMacros project is copied to the *Chicago Warehouses Audit* document
Step 7	Close	the Organizer dialog box
Step 8	Save	the document as *Chicago Warehouses With Print Macro* and leave it open

Using the Visual Basic Editor

You also can manage individual macros using the Visual Basic Editor. To rename the PRINTMACRO in the *Chicago Warehouses With Print Macro* document, you edit the name in the Visual Basic Editor. To edit the macro name:

Step 1	Open	the Macros dialog box
Step 2	Select	the Project.NewMacros.PRINTMACRO item in the Macro name: list box
Step 3	Click	Edit
Step 4	Select	the macro name PRINTMACRO following the blue keyword Sub in the Chicago Warehouses With Print Macro Code window
Step 5	Key	PrintsThree
Step 6	Click	File
Step 7	Click	Close and Return to Microsoft Word
Step 8	Open	the Macros dialog box and observe the new macro name "PrintsThree"

Using the Macros Dialog Box

You want to delete the PRINTMACRO macro from the NewMacros project in the Normal template. You can do this in the Macros dialog box. To delete the PRINTMACRO in the Normal template:

Step 1	Select	PRINTMACRO, if necessary

Step 2	**Click**	<u>D</u>elete
Step 3	**Click**	<u>Y</u>es to confirm the deletion
Step 4	**Close**	the dialog box

Because the PRINTMACRO in the Normal template is no longer available, you also must remove the PRINTMACRO command from the menu bar. To remove the macro command:

Step 1	**Press & hold**	the ALT key
Step 2	**Drag**	the PRINTMACRO command downward off the menu bar until you see an X on the mouse pointer
Step 3	**Release**	the mouse button and the ALT key
Step 4	**Save**	the *Chicago Warehouses With Print Macro* document and close it

You can use macros to automate many of your routine word processing tasks.

MOUSE TIP

You can remove a macro command or button by opening the Customize dialog box and dragging the command or button off the menu or toolbar.

---

chapter
twenty-five

Summary

- A macro is a set of Word commands and instructions you combine into a single step to automate tasks.

- Macros are especially useful when you perform detailed, repetitive tasks that you cannot do as efficiently with other Word features, such as toolbar buttons, AutoCorrect, AutoText, Styles, and document templates.

- You can assign a macro to a toolbar button, menu, or keyboard shortcut.

- When you record a macro, Word writes the instructions you record in a macro programming language called Visual Basic for Applications.

- By default, Word stores macros in the Normal template, but you can store macros in any template or document.

- When recording a macro, you cannot use the mouse to move the insertion point or to select, copy, or move text in the document window.

- The process of stepping through a macro to find errors is called debugging the macro.

- You can copy, rename, or delete macro projects in the Organizer dialog box.

- You can copy, rename, or delete individual macros in the Macros dialog box or from the Visual Basic Editor.

- When you delete a macro, you should remember to remove the custom toolbar button or custom menu command that executes the macro.

- A macro virus is a potentially harmful program included in a macro that may damage your files or hard disk.

- By default, Word sets a high security level that automatically disables any macros in a document when you open the document.

- You can modify the security level to allow you the choice of opening a document with macros enabled or disabled.

Using Macros   WA 287

Commands Review

Action	Menu Bar	Shortcut Menu	Toolbar	Task Pane	Keyboard
Record a macro	Tools, Macro, Record New Macro		Double-click the REC mode indicator		ALT + T, M, R
Run or edit a macro	Tools, Macro, Macros Click a custom menu command assigned to the macro		Click a custom toolbar button assigned to the macro		ALT + T, M, M Press custom keyboard shortcut keys assigned to the macro ALT + F8
Change the security level	Tools, Macro, Security, Security Level tab				ALT + T, M, S, S

Concepts Review

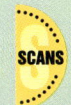

SCANS

Circle the correct answer.

1. **A macro:**
   [a] cannot be recorded as you perform actions.
   [b] can be created using the Word Basic programming language.
   [c] is useful for performing tasks not covered by the toolbar buttons, AutoText, Styles, AutoCorrect, and templates.
   [d] must be edited in the Word Basic Editor window.

2. **You cannot run a macro by:**
   [a] double-clicking the REC mode indicator on the status bar.
   [b] clicking a custom button on a toolbar.
   [c] clicking a custom command on a menu.
   [d] pressing keyboard shortcut keys.

3. **By default, macros are stored in the:**
   [a] active document.
   [b] Normal template.
   [c] Macro template.
   [d] Macros dialog box.

4. **When you need to automate a task, you should first:**
   [a] open the Macros dialog box.
   [b] turn on the recorder and record the steps to automate it.
   [c] write down all the commands and instructions required in exact order.
   [d] practice performing the task you want to automate.

5. **The best candidate for automation with a macro is the routine task of:**
   [a] inserting standard wording in a document.
   [b] adding a standard header and footer to multiple-page letters.
   [c] applying boldface or italic formatting to text.
   [d] creating a basic 4 × 3 Table.

6. **A group of macros in a document or template are stored in:**
   [a] the Visual Basic Editor.
   [b] macro projects.
   [c] the Organizer.
   [d] the Macros dialog box.

7. **To select text or position the insertion point when recording a macro, you must use the:**
   [a] mouse.
   [b] keyboard.
   [c] ALT + M keys.
   [d] Visual Basic Editor.

8. **The process of looking for errors in a macro line by line is called:**
   [a] step-by-step processing.
   [b] debugging.
   [c] managing.
   [d] editing.

chapter twenty-five

9. The cassette icon on the mouse pointer means:
  [a] a macro is running.
  [b] every mouse and keyboard actions is being recorded.
  [c] you are deleting a macro.
  [d] you are renaming a macro.

10. Macros are also called:
  [a] keywords.
  [b] viruses.
  [c] debuggers.
  [d] subroutines.

Circle **T** if the statement is true or **F** if the statement is false.

T   F   1. Macros can be created or edited in the Macro Editor window.
T   F   2. You double-click the TRK mode indicator on the status bar to begin editing a macro.
T   F   3. You can copy, rename, or delete individual macros in the Organizer dialog box.
T   F   4. If a macro contains errors, you can edit it or simply rerecord it.
T   F   5. The Stop Recording toolbar has buttons for Stop Recording and Pause Recording actions.
T   F   6. A macro is an appropriate alternative when you cannot automate a task with existing Word toolbar buttons, AutoCorrect, AutoText, styles, and document templates.
T   F   7. Macros can be created only by keying the Visual Basic for Applications code in the Visual Basic Editor Code window.
T   F   8. Macros can be assigned to a command on the menu bar and to keyboard shortcuts, but not to any other toolbar.
T   F   9. A keyword is a reserved word in the Visual Basic for Applications language.
T   F   10. A macro virus can infect your computer system even if you do not run the macro.

Skills Review

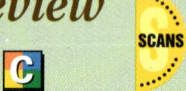

Exercise 1

1. Write down the steps to open a document, save it with a new name, print two copies, and close it.
2. Practice the steps to assure their accuracy.
3. Record a macro named "OPENDOCUMENT" to open the *Internet Training* document located on the Data Disk, save it as *Internet Macro*, print two copies, and close it.
4. Store the macro in the Normal template.
5. Assign the macro to the ALT + M keys.
6. Close all open documents and run the macro.
7. Select the OPENDOCUMENT macro in the Macros dialog box, open the Visual Basic Editor, and select and print the OPENDOCUMENT subroutine.

Exercise 2

1. Create a new, blank document.
2. Copy the NewMacros project created in Exercise 1 from the Normal template to the new document.

3. Save the document as *NewMacros Document*.

4. Edit the OPENDOCUMENT macro in the *NewMacros Document* to print one copy using the Visual Basic Editor.

5. Enter the text "Testing the modified macro." in the document.

6. Save the document to update the copy on the disk.

7. Run the macro from the Macros dialog box.

8. Close the document.

Exercise 3

1. Write down the steps needed to create a custom header and footer that right-aligns the date in the header and centers the page number in the footer.

2. Practice the steps to assure their accuracy.

3. Record a macro named "HEADER" to insert the custom header and footer.

4. Store the macro in the Normal template.

5. Assign the macro to a command on the menu bar.

6. Customize the macro command to read "Custom Header."

7. Open the *Understanding The Internet* document located on the Data Disk.

8. Run the macro.

9. Print and close the document without saving any changes.

10. Select the HEADER macro in the Macros dialog box, open the Visual Basic Editor window, select the HEADER subroutine (macro) in the Code window, and print the selection.

Exercise 4

1. Write down the steps to open, print, and close three single-page documents of your choice from the Data Disk. (*Hint:* Use the SHIFT + Click method of opening multiple documents.)

2. Practice the steps to assure their accuracy.

3. Record a macro named "THREE" to open, print, and close the documents.

4. Store the macro in the Normal template.

5. Run the macro from the Macros dialog box.

6. Select the THREE macro in the Macros dialog box, open the Visual Basic Editor, and select and print the THREE subroutine.

Exercise 5

1. Use the Visual Basic Editor to edit the THREE macro created in Exercise 4 and rename it "THREEPAGES."

2. Select and print the THREEPAGES subroutine.

chapter twenty-five

Exercise 6

1. Write down the steps to create a new interoffice memorandum template, including setting the appropriate margins and tab stops, text, formatting, and line spacing. Center the text "MEMORANDUM" at the top of the document. Insert the current date as a field and insert the name "B. Michaels" as the From: name. Position the insertion point at the left margin of the first body paragraph line.
2. Practice the steps to assure their accuracy.
3. Record a macro named "MEMO" to create the template.
4. Store the macro in the Normal template.
5. Assign the macro to a command on the menu bar.
6. Run the macro.
7. Save the document as *Michaels Memo Template*.
8. Print and close the document.
9. Open the MEMO macro in the Visual Basic Editor and select and print the MEMO subroutine.

Exercise 7

1. Write down the steps to sort (in descending order) the product list in the *List Of Products* document located on the Data Disk, and then print the document.
2. Practice the steps to assure their accuracy.
3. Open the *List Of Products* document and record a macro named "SORTPRINT" to sort the list and print the document.
4. Store the macro in the document.
5. Undo all the previous actions with the Undo button on the Standard toolbar.
6. Save the document as *List Of Products Automated*.
7. Run the macro from the Macros dialog box.
8. Open the document in the Visual Basic Editor and select and print the SORTPRINT subroutine.
9. Close the document without saving any changes.

Exercise 8

1. Using the Macros dialog box delete the OPENDOCUMENT, HEADER, THREEPAGES, and MEMO macros from the Normal template. (If you did not create all the macros, delete the ones you created.)
2. Remove any macro commands from the menu bar using the ALT + Drag method.

Case Projects

Project 1

While demonstrating to Chris Lofton how to record a macro, a question arises about the purpose of the Microsoft Script Editor command on the Macro submenu. Chris asks you to research the command. Using the Ask A Question Box, search for the "macro" topic. Open the "About macros" subtopic and click the "Automating tasks in Web pages" link. Review the topic and any other related subtopics. Write Chris an interoffice memorandum describing, in general, how the command is used. Include steps for creating a Web script on the company home page. Save, preview, and print the memorandum.

Project 2

Jody Haversham is eager to create a macro that applies a standard footer on her purchasing reports including the text "Purchasing Department" at the left margin, a centered page number, and the current date at the right margin. She also wants to be able to run the macro on any document using a keyboard shortcut. She asks for your help in recording the macro. Create an outline containing the steps required to record, test, and delete the macro. Create the macro and test it by running it on the outline document. Save, preview, and print the outline. Delete the macro. With your instructor's permission, use the outline to guide a classmate through the process of recording, testing, and deleting the macro.

Project 3

This week's edition of the *Secretarial Guide* e-mail newsletter contains a brief reference to the macros supplied by Word. You want to know more about them. Using the Ask A Question Box, review the macros supplied with Word topic and the macros for troubleshooting topics. Write an interoffice memorandum to Chris Lofton describing two of the supplied macro templates. Save, preview, and print the memorandum.

Project 4

Because of your experience using Word, Chris asks you to update the macros portion of the Word Processing Department procedure manuals. Some of the junior operators are experiencing problems recording and running macros. Using the Ask A Question Box, research how to troubleshoot problems encountered when recording or running macros. Create an unbound report document describing four common problems and their suggested solutions. Save, preview, and print the document.

Project 5

During lunch with Marisa DaFranco, the executive assistant to the CEO, she tells you that her boss must be able to connect to the Internet when traveling both in the United States and internationally. She asks for your help in locating an Internet service provider that has local phone numbers in major U.S. cities plus a toll-free service for international calls. Connect to the Internet and search the Web for pages that list Internet service providers. Review several Web pages to compare service and price. Print at least three Web pages. Write Marisa an interoffice memorandum describing the results of your research and recommending a service provider that meets the CEO's needs. Save, preview, and print the memorandum.

Project 6

Kelly Armstead asks you to create a macro that centers the title text "PURCHASING DEPARTMENT" and formats it with 12-point, Arial font, with the words only underlined. After thinking about how to create the macro, you decide that existing Word features offer ways to create, store, and insert preformatted text without creating a macro. Write Kelly an interoffice memorandum explaining why a macro is not necessary to accomplish the task and noting two Word features that she can use instead of a macro. Save, preview, and print the memorandum.

Project 7

Chris Lofton wants to publish a Web page to the company intranet that offers weekly tips on using Word 2002 and asks you to create the Web page. The first set of tips covers recording a macro. Using online Help and what you learned in this chapter, create a Web page with a bulleted list of five to ten tips for recording a macro. Apply the theme of your choice. Save, preview, and print the Web page.

Project 8

Nat Wong has recently upgraded to Word 2002 from the previous version of Word (Word 2000) and he calls with concerns about whether or not his Word 2000 macros will run properly in Word 2002. You agree to research the problem and get back to him. Using online Help, find the answer to Nat's question and then draft an e-mail message (using a new Word document) providing the answer. Save, preview, and print the e-mail message.

chapter twenty-five

Word 2002

Managing Files

Chapter Overview

Managing your Word document files is a very important task. During the course of a business day, you may need to locate Word document files to modify them or quickly print them. You also may need to protect important documents from unauthorized changes or add identifying text to documents to help locate them later. In this chapter, you learn how to search for specific files, how to add and use document properties, and how to protect files from unauthorized changes. Additionally, you learn how to make these tasks easier by modifying toolbars and menus.

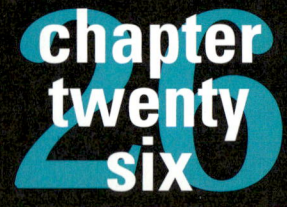

Learning Objectives

- Search for specific files
- View and modify file properties
- Protect documents
- Define the default location for workgroup templates
- Customize toolbars and menus

Case profile

You are promoted to the position of executive assistant to Randall Holmes, the president of Worldwide Exotic Foods, Inc. The president thinks that publishing standardized company-wide procedures for locating, identifying, and protecting important Word document files saves time and reduces errors. He asks you to set up the procedures for managing Word document files.

chapter twenty six

26.a Searching for Specific Files

Often you are called on to locate document files and then modify or print them. When files are stored in different locations, it may be necessary to search these different locations to find the files you need. You can quickly perform a simple search using the Basic Search task pane. You receive a request to print the *Confidential Legislative Report* Word document created several weeks ago by someone who is no longer with the company. Because you did not create the document, you are not certain where it is stored; therefore, you must search for it.

To display the Basic Search task pane:

Step 1	**Create**	a new, blank document, if necessary
Step 2	**Click**	the Search button on the Standard toolbar to view the Basic Search task pane

To locate a file you can key search keywords in the Search text: text box in the Basic Search task pane. Word then uses these keywords to search in the body text of a document, the filename, or other file properties. Word also searches using different word forms. For example, if you key the word "swim" in the Search text: text box, Word finds any documents containing the word "swim," "swam," or "swimming." Keying more search keywords in the Search text: text box makes your search more specific and limits the number of documents Word finds.

> **notes**
> To make the search processes more efficient, it is recommended that the Data and Solution Files for this chapter be stored in their own, separate folders.

After you specify the search keywords, you can then specify both the locations in which to look and the type of file to look for using the Search in: and Results should be: lists in the task pane. To search for the *Confidential Legislative Report* Word document located in the folder where the Data Files for this chapter are stored:

Step 1	**Key**	Confidential Legislative Report in the Search text: text box in the Basic Search task pane
Step 2	**Click**	the Search in: list arrow in the Basic Search task pane

TASK PANE TIP

For additional help on using the options in the Basic Search task pane, click the Search Tips link.

chapter twenty-six

The Search in: list on your screen should look similar to Figure 26-1.

FIGURE 26-1
Search in: List in the Basic Search Task Pane

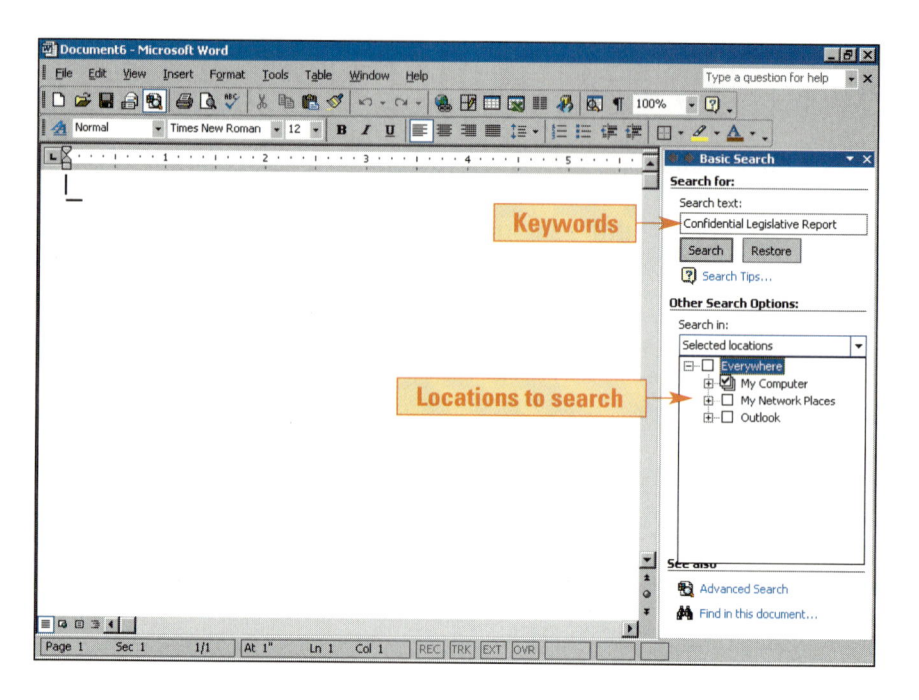

You can search one or more locations by inserting or removing the check mark from the location's check box. You can expand or collapse the view of available locations just as you would in Windows Explorer. For this activity, you search only the location where the Data Files are stored.

Step 3	Locate	the folder in which the Data Files for this chapter are stored (see your instructor for the location, if necessary)
Step 4	Click	the folder check box to insert a check mark, if necessary
Step 5	Remove	the check marks from all other check boxes
Step 6	Close	the Search in: list
Step 7	Click	the Results should be: list arrow in the Basic Search task pane

You can specify one or more file types in this list. You are searching for a Word document.

Step 8	Click	the Word Files check box to insert a check mark, if necessary
Step 9	Remove	the check marks from the other check boxes

The Results should be: list on your screen should look similar to Figure 26-2.

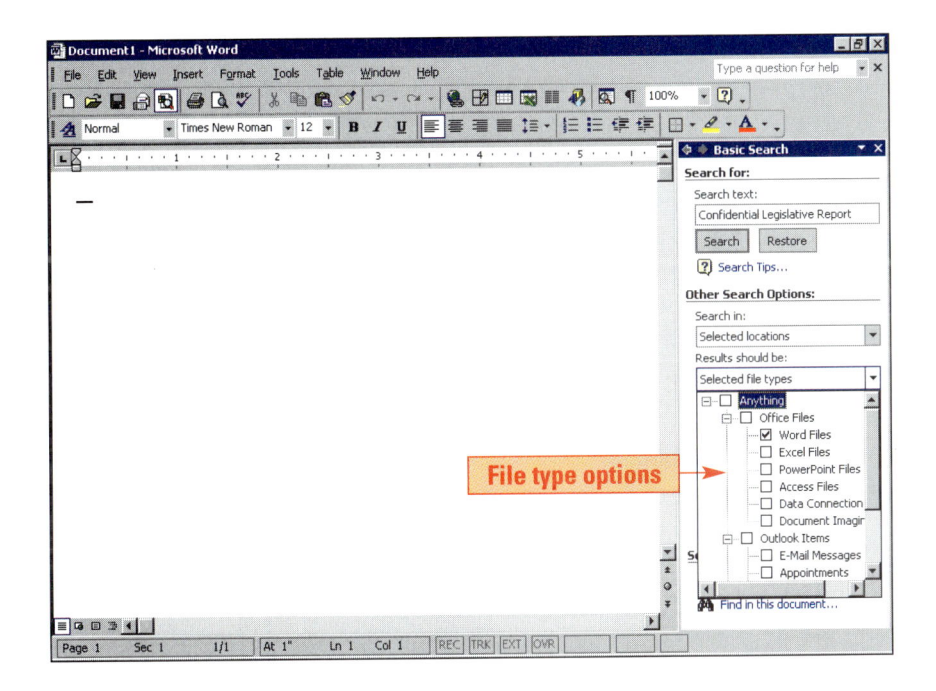

FIGURE 26-2
Results should be: List in the Basic Search Task Pane

| Step 10 | *Close* | the Results should be: list |
| Step 11 | *Click* | the Search button in the Basic Search task pane |

It may take a few seconds to locate Word documents containing the text "Confidential Legislative Report," depending on the number of locations, folders, and files being searched. The Search Results task pane automatically opens. As the search process runs, the text "Searching" appears at the top of the task pane; a Stop button, which allows you to halt the search process, appears at the bottom of the task pane. When the search process is complete, the document or documents containing the keywords are listed in the Search Results task pane. The Stop button becomes the Modify button, which allows you to revise the search criteria for another search. One Word document matches the search criteria.

The Search Results task pane on your screen should look similar to Figure 26-3.

chapter twenty-six

FIGURE 26-3
Search Results Task Pane

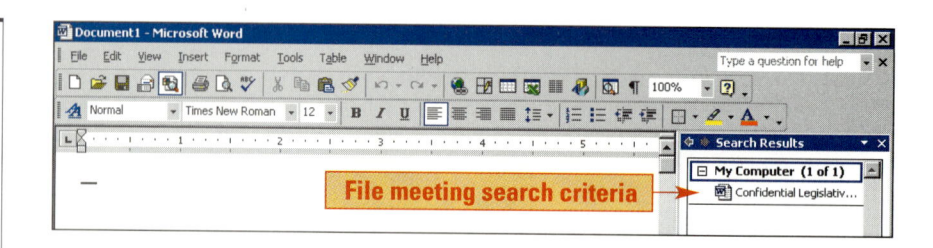

File meeting search criteria

When you move the mouse pointer to the *Confidential Legislative Report* document in the Search Results task pane, a ScreenTip appears indicating the complete path to the document and a list arrow appears to the right of the document name. You can click this list arrow to see a menu with commands to open the document for editing, to create a new document based on the *Confidential Legislative Report* document, copy a shortcut link to the document, or view the document's characteristics or properties. You can also open the document by clicking the document name in the task pane. To open the document:

Step 1	Click	the *Confidential Legislative Report* document in the Search Results task pane
Step 2	Print	the document
Step 3	Close	the document without saving changes
Step 4	Click	the Modify button in the Search Results task pane to return to the Basic Search task pane

When the search criteria are more complicated, you can search by specific file properties.

Advanced Searching Using File Properties

File **properties** are details about a file that help identify it, including a descriptive filename, the author's name, date last modified, printed, or saved, and a number of other properties. You can use the Advanced Search task pane to set search criteria for specific file properties such as the File name property.

If you know that the filename of the file you want to find starts with a certain letter, you can search any location for files of any type or a specific type that begin with that letter. Suppose you want to find Word documents beginning with "c" located in the folder where the data files for this chapter are stored. You can use the File name property and the asterisk (*) wildcard character to do this.

QUICK TIP

You can use wildcard characters to search for files. The asterisk (*) wildcard character represents any group of one or more characters. For example, the keyword "s*t" finds files containing "sit," "sent," or "sentiment." The question mark (?) wildcard character represents a single character. The keyword "s?t" finds documents containing "sit," "sat," or "set."

Managing Files   WA 297

To display the Advanced Search task pane:

Step 1	Verify	that the Basic Search task pane is visible
Step 2	Delete	the text in the Search text: text box
Step 3	Click	the Advanced Search link in the Basic Search task pane

The Advanced Search task pane on your screen should look similar to Figure 26-4.

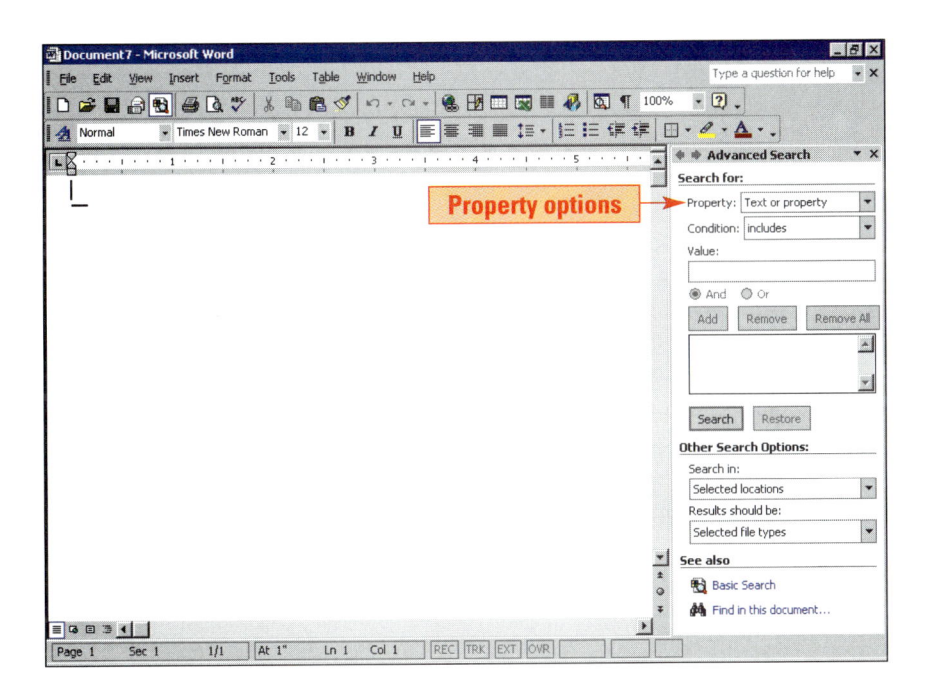

FIGURE 26-4
Advanced Search Task Pane

You can select one or more file properties, set conditions for each property, look for files in specific locations, and specify a file type in this task pane. The find process is not case sensitive so you can use "c" or "C" in your search criteria to find a list of files beginning with "c." To find all the filenames beginning with the character "c" in the folder containing the Data Files for this chapter:

Step 1	Click	the Property: list arrow in the Advanced Search task pane
Step 2	Scroll	the Property: list to view the different property options
Step 3	Click	File name in the Property: list
Step 4	Verify	that the Condition: text box contains "includes"
Step 5	Key	c* in the Value: text box

chapter
twenty-six

Step 6	Click	the Add button in the Advanced Search task pane to add the search criteria to the search criteria list
Step 7	Verify	that the Search in: list is set to look only in the folder containing this chapter's Data Files
Step 8	Verify	that the Results should be: list is set to look only for Word documents
Step 9	Click	the Search button in the Advanced Search task pane

In a few seconds the Search Results task pane appears. Your screen should look similar to Figure 26-5.

FIGURE 26-5
List of Word Documents That Begin with "c"

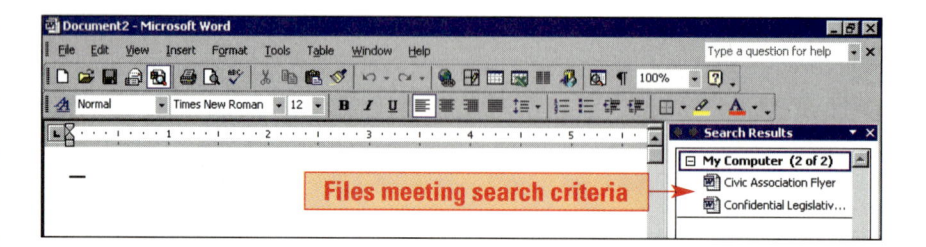

Step 10	Click	the Modify button in the Search Results task pane to return to the Advanced Search task pane

One of the details or properties that can be added to a document is subject text. Adding subject text to a document's properties allows you to later search for all documents that have the same subject property text. To find all the Word documents with the "Art Show" subject property in the folder that contains the Data Files for this chapter:

Step 1	Verify	that the Advanced Search task pane is visible
Step 2	Click	the File name includes c* item in the criteria list in the Advanced Search task pane to select it
Step 3	Click	the Remove button in the Advanced Search task pane to remove the previous criteria
Step 4	Click	Subject in the Property: list
Step 5	Click	in the Value: text box
Step 6	Verify	that "is (exactly)" appears in the Condition: text box
Step 7	Key	Art Show in the Value: text box
Step 8	Click	the Add button in the Advanced Search task pane

Managing Files   WA 299

Step 9	Verify	that the Search in: list is set for the folder that contains the Data Files for this chapter
Step 10	Verify	that the Results should be: list is set only for Word documents
Step 11	Click	the Search button in the Advanced Search task pane
Step 12	Observe	that the new search results indicate the *Civic Association Flyer* document is the only document with the specified subject property

After locating the desired file, you can quickly view its properties and modify them, if necessary.

26.b Viewing and Modifying File Properties

In addition to the filename, file type, location, size, and dates, file properties include statistics, such as the number of words in a Word document. You can also add user information, such as the subject or special comments, to the file properties.

You want to add special comment text to a copy of the *Civic Association Flyer* document. You can add or modify file properties in the document's Properties dialog box. To view the document's advanced properties in its Properties dialog box:

Step 1	Click	the *Civic Association Flyer* filename list arrow in the Search Results task pane to view the menu
Step 2	Click	Properties
Step 3	Click	the Summary tab, if necessary
Step 4	Click	the Advanced >> button, if visible, to see the advanced property options

The advanced property options on the Summary tab in the Civic Association Flyer Properties dialog box on your screen should look similar to Figure 26-6.

MENU TIP

You can right-click a filename in Windows Explorer, the Open dialog box, or the Save As dialog box and click Properties to display the properties for the file. You can click the Properties command on the Tools button list in the Open or Save As dialog box to view a selected file's properties. Finally, you can open a file and click the Properties command on the File menu to view its properties.

chapter twenty-six

FIGURE 26-6
Civic Association Flyer Properties Dialog Box

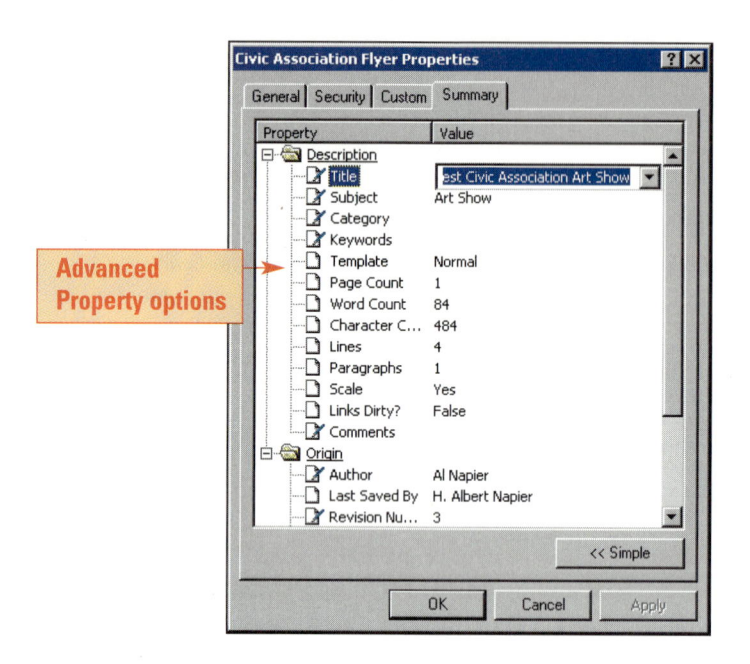

[Screenshot of Civic Association Flyer Properties dialog box, Summary tab, showing Description properties (Title: est Civic Association Art Show, Subject: Art Show, Category, Keywords, Template: Normal, Page Count: 1, Word Count: 84, Character C...: 484, Lines: 4, Paragraphs: 1, Scale: Yes, Links Dirty?: False, Comments) and Origin properties (Author: Al Napier, Last Saved By: H. Albert Napier, Revision Nu...: 3), with a "<< Simple" button and OK, Cancel, Apply buttons. A callout labeled "Advanced Property options" points to the property list.]

You can change the properties in this dialog box and the change is immediately made in the document. For this example, you want to make a change in a copy of this document.

To open the document, save it with a new name, and add the comment text:

Step 1	*Cancel*	the dialog box without making changes
Step 2	*Open*	the *Civic Association Flyer* document from the Search Results task pane
Step 3	*Save*	the document as *Civic Association Flyer With Revised Properties*
Step 4	*Click*	File
Step 5	*Click*	Properties
Step 6	*Click*	the Summary tab in the Properties dialog box, if necessary
Step 7	*Key*	Annual Sponsorship in the Comments: text box
Step 8	*Click*	OK
Step 9	*Save*	the document and close it

You verify that you can locate the file from the comment you just added. To search for the document using the Comments property:

| Step 1 | *Click* | the Modify button in the Search Results task pane to switch to the Advanced Search task pane |

Step 2	Change	the search criteria to look for Word documents that include the text "annual sponsorship" in the Comments property and that are stored in the folder where the completed files for this chapter are stored (don't forget to first remove any previous search criteria)
Step 3	Verify	that only the *Civic Association Flyer With Revised Properties* document is returned as the search results
Step 4	Open	the document from the Search Results task pane
Step 5	Close	the Search Results task pane

You also might want to make sure others don't access or change certain documents.

26.c Protecting Documents

There are several ways to protect a document from unauthorized changes. In Chapter 23 you learned how to protect an online form so that users can only key the variable data in the document. You also can protect other types of documents. You can assign a password to prevent others from opening a document or you can assign a password that allows others to open the document but prevents them from modifying it. You can have Word recommend that others open specific documents as "read-only." If they open the file as "read-only" and modify it, they must save the file with a different name. Finally, you can specify that individuals reviewing documents online can add only comments to the document but not tracked changes.

You want to protect the *Civic Association Flyer With Revised Properties* document by assigning a password that must be used to open the document. To save the document with a new name and password protect it:

Step 1	Open	the Save As dialog box
Step 2	Switch to	the location where you store your completed Data Files, if necessary
Step 3	Click	the Tools button Tools on the dialog box toolbar
Step 4	Click	Security Options

The Security tab from the Options dialog box opens in its own dialog box. The dialog box on your screen should look similar to Figure 26-7.

> **QUICK TIP**
>
> You can print document properties by opening the document, and then selecting the Document properties option in the Print what: list in the Print dialog box.

> **MENU TIP**
>
> Instead of using Windows Explorer to manage your files, you can use a shortcut menu to open, print, move, copy, delete, rename, or otherwise manage a file from inside the Open or Save As dialog boxes. This saves time when you are already working in Word. For example, if you are working on a Word document and a coworker asks for a hard copy of another Word document, you can quickly print it from the Open dialog box without first opening the document in Word (or opening Windows Explorer).

FIGURE 26-7
Security Options

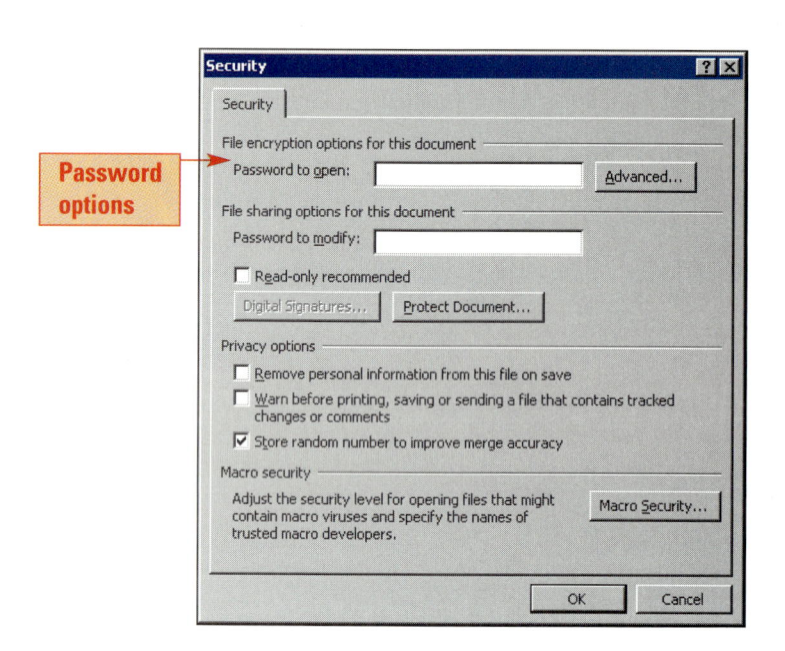

[Figure: Security dialog box with Password options indicated — showing Password to open, Password to modify fields, Read-only recommended checkbox, Digital Signatures, Protect Document buttons, Privacy options, and Macro security section.]

QUICK TIP

For more information on each of the different ways to protect a document, use the Ask A Question Box to search online Help using the keywords "protect document."

A password can have a maximum of 15 characters in any combination of letters, numbers, spaces, and symbols. Passwords are case sensitive so if you use upper- and lowercase letters when you assign a password, users who try to open the document must also use the same upper- and lowercase letters. If you need a longer password, up to 255 characters, you can use the advanced encryption options to create it.

When you key password characters in the password text boxes, you see only asterisks (*). This prevents others from learning the password. After you key the password, you confirm it by keying it again in a confirmation dialog box. To set the password to open the document:

Step 1	Key	Password in the Password to open: text box
Step 2	Click	OK
Step 3	Key	Password in the Reenter password to open: text box in the Confirm Password dialog box
Step 4	Click	OK
Step 5	Save	the document as *Password Protected Document* and close it

As verification of the password protection, you open the document and enter the password. To test the password protection:

Step 1	Open	the *Password Protected Document* you just saved
Step 2	Key	Password in the Password dialog box
Step 3	Click	OK
Step 4	Close	the document

CAUTION TIP

When you create a password you must be careful to write it down and keep it in a safe place for future reference. If you lose or forget the password you cannot open the password-protected document!

26.d Defining the Default File Location for Workgroup Templates

When templates are used by many members of the same workgroup, it is a good idea to have the network system administrator store the templates as read-only or on a server with limited access permissions. This helps to prevent users from inadvertently altering the templates. So that Word can locate your workgroup templates, you can set the default file location for them on the File Locations tab in the Options dialog box. To review the File Locations tab:

Step 1	Create	a new, blank document, if necessary
Step 2	Open	the Options dialog box
Step 3	Click	the File Locations tab
Step 4	Observe	the Workgroup templates option in the File types: list

You change the location by selecting the Workgroup templates option, clicking the Modify button to open the Modify Location dialog box, and then selecting the disk drive and folder that contains the templates. You cancel the Options dialog box without changing the Workgroup templates location.

Step 5	Cancel	the dialog box

Often it is easier to work with and manage files when using customized menus or toolbars.

26.e Customizing Toolbars and Menus

You can customize the menu bar or other toolbars by adding or removing commands and buttons with the Add or Remove Buttons command also on the Toolbar Options list. You can also add and remove buttons and commands on the menu bar or other toolbars with options in the Customize dialog box.

QUICK TIP

To remove the password protection from a document, open the document using the password, and open the Security tab in the Options dialog box. Select and delete the password and click the OK button. Then save the document to update the copy on the disk.

You also set the read-only recommendation and modification password for a document on the Security tab in the Options dialog box.

chapter
twenty-six

MENU TIP

You can display the Customize dialog box with the Customize command on the Tools menu or the Customize subcommand under the Toolbars command on the View menu.

To view the Customize dialog box:

Step 1	*Right-click*	any toolbar (the menu bar, the Standard toolbar, or the Formatting toolbar)
Step 2	*Click*	Customize
Step 3	*Click*	the Commands tab, if necessary

The Customize dialog box on your screen should look similar to Figure 26-8.

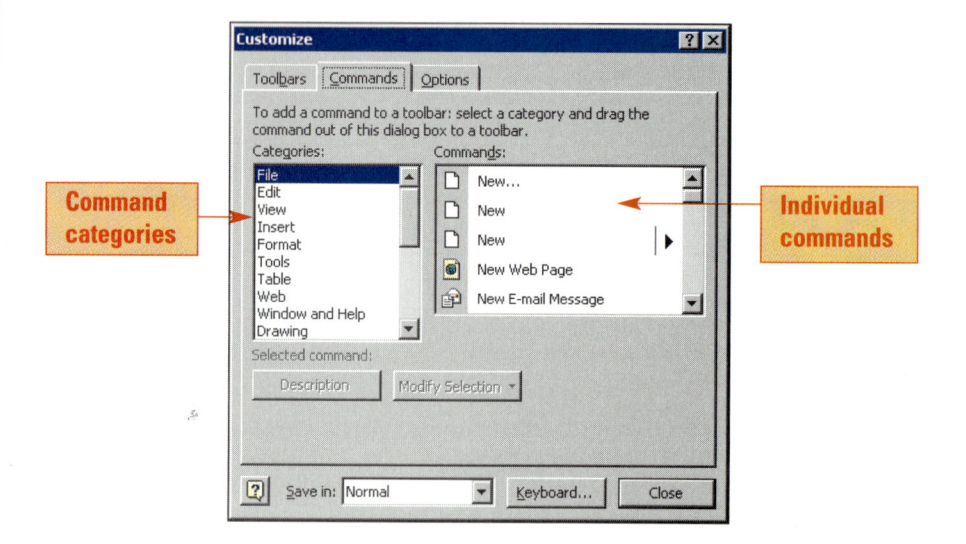

FIGURE 26-8
Commands Tab in the Customize Dialog Box

MOUSE TIP

You can display the Customize dialog box with the Customize command on the Add or Remove Buttons menu displayed from the Toolbar Options list.

The Commands tab in the Customize dialog box contains a list of category names and a list of commands available for a selected category. You can view a description of a command by selecting it and clicking the Description button. When you find the command you want to add, drag it from the dialog box to the menu bar or another visible toolbar.

You can more easily view and modify an open document's properties by clicking a command or toolbar button. To customize the menu bar by adding the Properties command:

Step 1	*Verify*	that File is selected in the Categories: list
Step 2	*Click*	Properties in the Commands: list (scroll the list to view this command)
Step 3	*Click*	Description to view the Properties (File menu) ScreenTip
Step 4	*Press*	the ESC key to close the ScreenTip
Step 5	*Drag*	the Properties command to the right of Help on the menu bar

Managing Files **WA 305**

| Step 6 | *Click* | Close to close the dialog box |
| Step 7 | *Observe* | the Prope<u>r</u>ties command on the menu bar |

To test the new menu bar command:

Step 1	*Create*	a new, blank document, if necessary
Step 2	*Click*	the Prope<u>r</u>ties command on the menu bar to view the document's Properties dialog box
Step 3	*Cancel*	the Properties dialog box

You can remove a command or button from a toolbar just as quickly. You can open the Customize dialog box and then drag the command or button off the toolbar. You can remove a command or button without opening the Customize dialog box by pressing the ALT key while dragging a command or button off a toolbar. To remove the Prope<u>r</u>ties command from the menu bar:

Step 1	*Press & hold*	the ALT key
Step 2	*Drag*	the Properties command down from the menu bar until you see an "X" at the end of the mouse pointer
Step 3	*Release*	the mouse button and then ALT key
Step 4	*Observe*	that the command is removed from the menu bar

Creating a Custom Menu

Just as you can customize existing toolbars and create new toolbars, you can also customize existing menus or create new menus. Suppose you want to add a custom menu that contains commands you can use to quickly apply character formatting to text without opening the Font dialog box. To add a custom menu to the menu bar:

Step 1	*Open*	the <u>C</u>ommands tab in the Customize dialog box using a shortcut menu
Step 2	*Click*	the New Menu item in the Cate<u>g</u>ories: list (scroll to view the item) to select it
Step 3	*Drag*	the New Menu item in the Comman<u>d</u>s: list to the right of the Font Color button on the Formatting toolbar (do not drag to the right of the Toolbar Options button)
Step 4	*Right-click*	New Menu on the menu bar to view a shortcut menu

QUICK TIP

Remember, the menu bar is also a toolbar. You customize the menu bar and other toolbars the same way.

chapter twenty-six

Step 5	Drag	to select New Menu in the Name: text box on the shortcut menu
Step 6	Key	Font Effects in the Name: text box
Step 7	Press	the ENTER key to close the shortcut menu and accept the new menu command

Next, you add the individual font effects commands to the custom menu. To add several font effects commands to the Font Effects menu:

Step 1	Click	Format in the Categories: list to view the list of commands in the Format category
Step 2	Drag	the Double Underline command from the Commands: list to the Font Effects menu (scroll to view this command)
Step 3	Pause	until a blank box drops down below the Font Effects menu
Step 4	Drop	the Double Underline command in the blank box
Step 5	Drag	the Double Strikethrough, Small Caps, All Caps, Superscript, and Subscript commands to the Font Effects menu, dropping each one below the other on the new Font Effects menu
Step 6	Close	the Customize dialog box
Step 7	Click	the Font Effects menu [Font Effects] on the Formatting toolbar

Your screen should look similar to Figure 26-9.

QUICK TIP

You can press the ESC key to close a menu without making a selection from the menu. You can point to a menu command and then press the ENTER key to select that command.

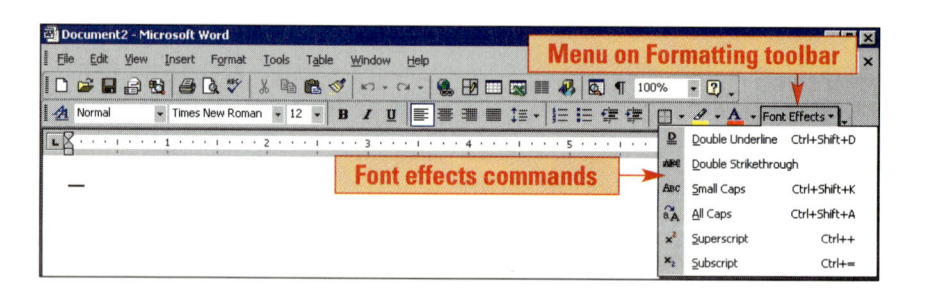

FIGURE 26-9
Font Effects Menu with Commands

When you no longer need a custom menu, you can easily remove it from the toolbar. To remove the Font Effects custom menu:

Step 1	Drag	the Font Effects menu from the Formatting toolbar using the ALT key

Using efficient techniques to manage your Word documents enhances your job productivity.

Managing Files   WA 307

Summary

- You can use the Basic Search and Advanced Search task panes to search for specific files by keywords or file properties.
- File properties include the filename, file type, location, file size, date created, date modified, last date accessed, user summary information, and document statistics.
- File properties can be viewed by opening the document's Properties dialog box from the File menu, the Open dialog box shortcut menu, the Properties command on the Tools button list in the Open or Save As dialog box, or by clicking a file in the Search Results task pane.
- You can add information such as comments to a document property and then search for files based on the comment text.
- You can add or remove buttons and commands on toolbars and menus.

Commands Review

Action	Menu Bar	Shortcut Menu	Toolbar	Task Pane	Keyboard
Display the Basic or Advanced Search task pane	File, Search				ALT + F, H
View file properties	File, Properties	Right-click a filename, click Properties	Tools button, Properties	Click the document list arrow in the Search Results task pane, Properties	ALT + F, I
Protect a document	Tools, Protect Document Tools, Options, Security tab		Tools button, Security Options		ALT + T, P ALT + T, O
Change the default file locations	Tools, Options, File Locations tab				ALT + T, O
Customize a menu or toolbar	View, Toolbars, Customize	Right-click any menu or toolbar, then click Customize			ALT + V, T, C ALT + Drag (when Customize dialog box is closed)

chapter twenty-six

Concepts Review

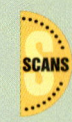

Circle the correct answer.

1. You cannot set options in the Basic Search task pane to:
   - [a] specify location.
   - [b] specify a file type.
   - [c] find a document containing specific keywords.
   - [d] protect a document.

2. Which of the following items is not a file property?
   - [a] Last modified
   - [b] Files of type
   - [c] Contents
   - [d] Application size

3. When entering a search keyword, use the "*" wildcard character to represent:
   - [a] only the first character.
   - [b] an unlimited number of unknown characters.
   - [c] the letter "c."
   - [d] one unknown character.

4. Which search criteria will find only Word documents only in the My Documents folder whose filename begins with "b"?
   - [a] ?b and file type is Word and location is My Documents
   - [b] b* and file type is Word and location is Everywhere
   - [c] b?t and file type is Anything and location is My Documents
   - [d] b* and file type is Word and location is My Documents

5. To search by the contents of a specific file property, you use options in the:
   - [a] Reveal Formats task pane.
   - [b] Basic Search task pane.
   - [c] Advanced Search task pane.
   - [d] Property Search task pane.

6. To prevent unauthorized access to a document you should:
   - [a] mark it "read-only" recommended.
   - [b] password-protect it to open.
   - [c] password-protect it for comments.
   - [d] password-protect it for tracked changes.

7. Which property can be searched to find all files related to the same topic?
   - [a] Size
   - [b] Author
   - [c] Subject
   - [d] Creation Date

8. If you password-protect a document, you should be careful to:
   - [a] mark the document "read-only."
   - [b] write down the password and save it in a safe place.
   - [c] turn on the track changes feature.
   - [d] insert a comment.

Circle **T** if the statement is true or **F** if the statement is false.

T F 1. You can search for different types of files based on the file properties.

T F 2. You cannot delete search criteria once you specify it.

T F 3. The Properties dialog box can be opened from the Basic Search task pane.

T F 4. Word keeps track of document statistics, such as the number of words, in the Properties dialog box.

T F 5. If you can't remember the name of a file, you can search for it using different keywords and file properties.

T F 6. A password can have any combination of letters, numbers, spaces, and symbols up to a maximum of 25 characters.

T F 7. To make it easier to manage your documents, you can add frequently used commands and buttons or a custom menu to the menu bar or a toolbar.

> **notes**
> In order to expedite the search processes in the following Skills Review exercises, it is recommended that you temporarily place *this chapter's Data Files and completed files* in separate folders that can be accessed from the Basic and Advanced Search task panes.

Skills Review

Exercise 1

1. Display the Basic Search task pane and find all the Word documents in the folder containing the Data Files for this chapter that contain the keyword "web."

2. Verify that the following five documents are listed in the Search Results task pane:
   About Master Documents
   About the New Economy
   Unformatted E-Commerce Report
   Unformatted Report
   Using the World Wide Web

3. Open the *Unformatted E-Commerce Report* from the Search Results task pane.

4. Open the Save As dialog box and protect the document with the password "unformatted" and then save it as *Protected E-Commerce Report* and close it.

5. Close the Search Results task pane.

> **notes**
> You must complete Exercise 1 before you begin Exercise 2.

chapter twenty-six

Exercise 2

1. Display the Basic Search task pane, delete any previous search keywords, and search the folder containing your completed files for all Word documents whose filenames include the word "Protected."

2. Verify that the following two files appear in the Search Results list:
   Password Protected Document
   Protected E-Commerce Report

3. View the advanced properties on the Summary tab in the Protected E-Commerce Report Properties dialog box.

4. Change the Title property to "Protected E-Commerce Report."

5. Open the *Protected E-Commerce Report* document using the appropriate password.

6. Close the document and the Search Results task pane.

Exercise 3

1. Open the *Australia* document located on the Data Disk.

2. Create a new custom menu named "Quick Formats" and place it on the menu bar.

3. Add the Change Case command from the Format group to the Quick Formats custom menu.

4. Select all the uppercase paragraph headings and the uppercase title using the CTRL key.

5. Click the Change Case command on the Quick Formats custom menu to change the case to lowercase; click the Change Case command on the Quick Formats custom menu a second time to change the case to title case.

6. Save the document as *Australia With Reformatted Headings*, and then preview, print, and close it.

7. Open the Customize dialog box and remove the Quick Formats custom menu from the menu bar; then close the Customize dialog box.

Exercise 4

1. Display the Basic Search task pane and using the advanced search options search for all documents in the folder where the Data Files for this chapter are stored and whose author property contains "Jody Haversham." (*Hint:* Don't forget to remove any previous search criteria.)

2. Verify that the following three documents are listed in the Search Results:
   About Master Documents
   Answering the Telephone
   Using the World Wide Web

3. Verify the contents of the author property for each document by displaying the Summary tab in its Property dialog box using the Search Results task pane.

4. Close the Search Results task pane when finished.

Exercise 5

1. Open the Customize dialog box and drag the Page Break button from the Insert group to the right of the Microsoft Word Help button on the Standard toolbar. (Don't drag the button to the right of the Toolbar Options button.)

2. Right-click the new Page Break button and click the Image and Text command to view both the button image and the text "Page Break."

3. Close the Customize dialog box and observe the new button and text.

4. Open the *Confidential Legislative Report* document located on the Data Disk.

5. Using the new Page Break button on the Standard toolbar, insert a page break at each paragraph heading.

6. Save the document as *New Page Breaks*, and then preview, print, and close it.

7. Remove the Page Break button from the Standard toolbar by dragging it off the toolbar while pressing the ALT key.

Exercise 6

1. Display the Basic Search task pane and search for all Word documents that are stored in the folder that contains your completed files for this chapter and whose Number of pages property is more than 1. (*Hint:* Switch to the Advanced Search task pane and set the Number of pages property to more than 1. Don't forget to remove all previous search criteria.)

2. View the advanced property options for the *New Page Breaks* document and change the Title property to "New Page Breaks" and the Author property to your name.

3. Close the Search Results task pane.

Exercise 7

1. Display the Basic Search task pane and search for all Word documents containing the keyword "exotic" that are stored in the folder containing the Data Files for this chapter.

2. Verify that the *Confidential Legislative Report* document is the only file listed in the Search Results.

3. Create a new document based on the *Confidential Legislative Report* document using New from this file command on the document menu in the Search Results task pane.

4. Select all the text in the new document and clear all the formats.

5. Save the document as *Legislative Draft*, and then preview, print, and close it.

Exercise 8

1. Open the *Legislative Draft* document created in Exercise 7. If you have not created the document, do so now.

2. Use the AutoFormat command and let Word automatically format the document.

3. Review the document and apply the appropriate Heading style to any paragraph headings not automatically formatted by Word.

4. Save the document as a password protected document using the password "draft." Name the document *Protected Draft*, and then close it.

5. Open the *Protected Draft* document using the appropriate password, print it, and then close it.

Case Projects

Project 1

As the recently promoted administrative assistant to the president, you are replacing an employee who resigned after several years of employment. You must frequently find documents created before you were hired and the president cannot provide filenames for the documents. Although you have successfully searched for files by various criteria, you often experience the following problems: (a) it takes a long time to search for files, and (b) you can't search for a specific file type. Use Ask A Question Box to troubleshoot searching for files. Create an unbound report document describing each problem and its suggested solution. Save, preview, and print the document.

chapter twenty-six

Project 2

After receiving several questions from other employees about file properties, you decide to create a Web page for the company intranet that contains an explanation and examples of file properties. Use the Ask A Question Box to review the "About file properties" topic in online Help, and then create a Web page that describes file properties and gives examples of different types of file properties. Use a theme of your choice. Save, preview, and print the Web page.

Project 3

The president asks you how to change the setup on his personal computer so that the new company intranet Web search page appears when he clicks the Search the Web button in the Open dialog box or on the Web toolbar instead of the default search page. Use the Ask A Question Box to research how to set the default search page. Then create an interoffice memorandum to the president describing the process. Save, preview, and print the document.

Project 4

Jody Haversham meets you for lunch and asks how she can use passwords to protect her confidential documents from being opened by others and how to protect her nonconfidential documents from being modified by others. Use online Help to research how to use passwords, if necessary. Write Jody an interoffice memorandum suggesting how to protect confidential documents and how to protect documents from unauthorized changes. Save, preview, and print the memo.

Project 5

Bill Martin, from Human Resources, calls to ask for your help in locating a Word document. He cannot remember the name but knows he created the document last week. Write Bill an e-mail message suggesting how he can search for the document. Save and print the e-mail message.

Project 6

Jody Haversham calls you and she is very upset and asks for your help. She used a password to protect a confidential document and now she cannot open the document when she keys the password. Search online Help for suggestions on troubleshooting passwords. Create an e-mail message to Jody suggesting ways to prevent this problem. Save and print the e-mail message.

Project 7

Kelly Armstead is preparing a document she plans to route to several reviewers and she wants to know how she can protect the document for comments and tracked changes. Use the Ask A Question Box to search for topics on tracking changes and how to prepare copies of a document to be reviewed. Write Kelly a memo describing what she should do to protect her document. Save, preview, and print the memo.

Project 8

Bill Martin uses the same search criteria several times a week to create a list of Word documents; he asks you if there is an easy way to repeat the same search without recreating the search criteria each time. Use the Ask A Question Box, if necessary, to review the "search for files" topic. Write Bill an e-mail message telling him whether or not he can save search criteria. Save and print the e-mail message.

Microsoft
Excel 2002
Advanced

Excel 2002

Linking Worksheets and Workbooks

Chapter Overview

Grouping worksheets can reduce repetitious formatting and worksheet preparation chores. Consolidating data from multiple worksheets is an important task. You do this by using 3-D references in formulas or by using the Data Consolidation command. You can use named ranges to select and identify important cell references. Providing a summary worksheet can help other users understand a complex workbook more quickly. To effectively work with multiple workbooks, you can create hyperlinks between workbooks. You can even save workspaces, which automatically open and arrange workbooks the way you like them.

Learning Objectives

- Group worksheets to share data, formatting, and formulas
- Insert and format a documentation worksheet
- Use named ranges
- Consolidate data from multiple worksheets
- Create 3-D references and links between workbooks
- Work with multiple workbooks

Case profile

With four regional offices and a central office all collecting and combining data, Super Power Computers relies on numerous workbooks to keep track of the stream of information. One of your responsibilities is to combine the information from those various sources and ensure that your data stays up to date, even though the information may be revised daily. You use linked formulas to gather data from other worksheets and other workbooks, and you use hyperlinks to quickly open related documents.

chapter seven

7.a Grouping Worksheets to Share Data, Formatting, and Formulas

A worksheet **group** consists of several worksheets you have selected for editing. When you group worksheets, you can enter data and formulas on one worksheet and have that information appear simultaneously on all of the other grouped worksheets. You also can format cells and perform operations, such as spell checking and printing, across grouped worksheets.

The *Super Power Computers - Central Region* workbook contains most of the data you need to create a company sales summary. None of the formulas or titles that you need for your report has been added to the workbook. You decide to group the worksheets so that you can enter information simultaneously on multiple pages. To group worksheets:

Step 1	Open	the *Super Power Computers - Central Region* workbook located on the Data Disk
Step 2	Save	the workbook as *Super Power Computers - Central Region Revised*
Step 3	Click	the Store #1 sheet tab
Step 4	Press & hold	the SHIFT key
Step 5	Click	the Store #11 sheet tab

> **QUICK TIP**
>
> Select nonadjacent worksheets by holding the CTRL key down while clicking sheet tabs. You also can use this method to remove worksheets from a group.

Your screen should look similar to Figure 7-1. The store tabs are selected, or grouped, as indicated by the white sheet tabs. The title bar also indicates that a group has been formed. When you group worksheets, any information that you enter and all formatting that you apply, appear on all sheets in the group.

FIGURE 7-1
Grouped Worksheets

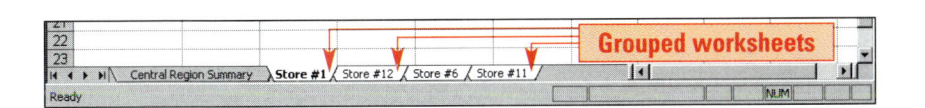

Table 7-1 lists the data you need to add to the worksheet group. As you enter the data on the Store #1 sheet tab, the same information is added to the other worksheets in the group. To enter data and format cells on the worksheet group:

Step 1	Enter	the data shown in Table 7-1

TABLE 7-1
Data for the Worksheet Group

Cell Reference	Enter
A4	Employee Name
B4	Q1
C4	Q2
D4	Q3
E4	Q4
F4	Total
A9	Total

You can use AutoSum to automatically sum the cells to the left and above a selected range.

| Step 2 | Select | the ranges F5:F8 and B9:F9 using the CTRL key |
| Step 3 | Click | the AutoSum button Σ on the Standard toolbar |

Now you can apply an AutoFormat to the table.

Step 4	AutoFit	columns B, C, D, E, and F to fit the entries in row 9
Step 5	Format	the range F6:F8 with no dollar sign symbol
Step 6	Click	cell A4
Step 7	Click	Format
Step 8	Click	AutoFormat
Step 9	Verify	that Simple is selected
Step 10	Click	OK

> **QUICK TIP**
> You can also group worksheets for printing.

Your screen should look similar to Figure 7-2. You can examine the changes to the other worksheets by clicking any tab in the group. The group remains selected as long as you select a tab in the group.

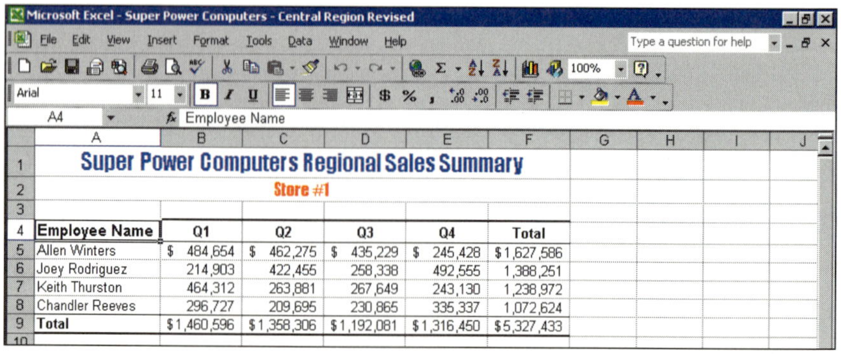

FIGURE 7-2
Data and Formatting Added to Grouped Worksheets

| Step 11 | Click | the Store #11 sheet tab to view the formatting applied to the worksheet data |

As you can see, the formatting and data have been applied to this worksheet as well as to the original worksheet. You're finished setting up the table, so you need to ungroup the worksheets to avoid overwriting important data. To ungroup the worksheets:

Step 1	Right-click	the Store #11 sheet tab
Step 2	Click	Ungroup Sheets
Step 3	Save	the workbook

> **MOUSE TIP**
>
> You can click a sheet tab outside the group to ungroup worksheets.

7.b Inserting and Formatting a Documentation Worksheet

Documenting a workbook is very important, especially when you share your workbooks with other people. One way to document a workbook is to provide a documentation worksheet. This page explains the content of the other worksheets in the workbook, and might include the following sections: Identification; Map of the Workbook; and Description, Assumptions, and Parameters.

The **Identification** section includes information about the workbook owner (usually a company name), the developer's name (the person who created the workbook), and the user's name (the person who is using the workbook). In addition, it may indicate the date the workbook was created and the date of the workbook's last revision. The **Map of the Workbook** provides a table of contents, describing the order and contents of the worksheets in the workbook. The **Description, Assumptions, and Parameters** section provides a place to describe the workbook's purpose and details any assumptions or parameters necessary for using it. To create a documentation worksheet:

Step 1	Insert	a new worksheet in front of the Central Region Summary worksheet
Step 2	Name	the worksheet Documentation
Step 3	Enter	the data and format as shown in Figure 7-3

chapter seven

FIGURE 7-3
Data and Format for Documentation Worksheet

QUICK TIP

Before you distribute the workbook to anyone, use the spell check command to check for errors.

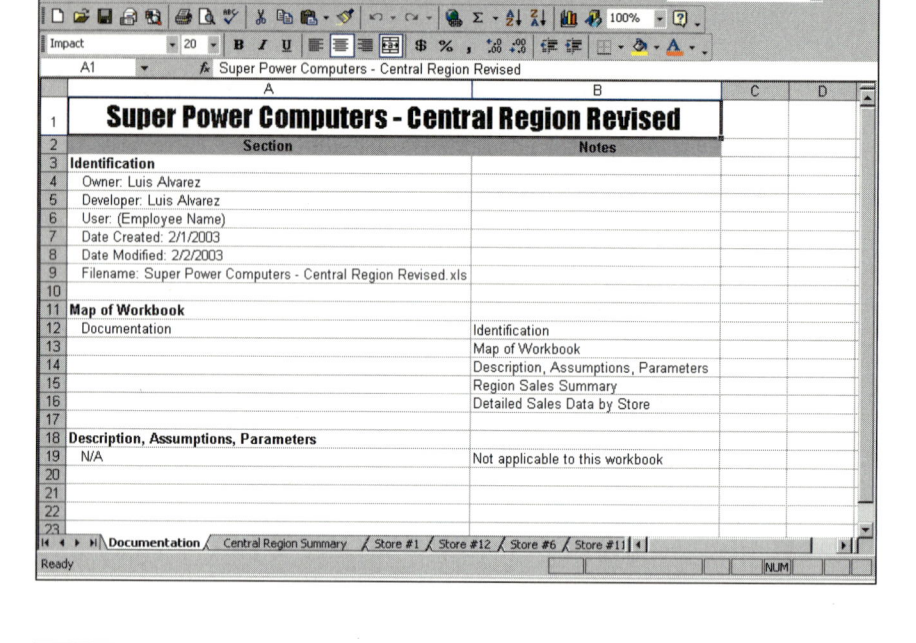

| Step 4 | **Save** | your workbook |

7.c Using Named Ranges

A **named range** is a meaningful name given to a cell or a range. You can use the name in place of cell references to help you easily find and reference the cells. For example, the named range Store11Totals is easier to remember than Store #11!B9:E9. Named ranges can be used simply to locate and select cells, or they can be used in formulas to replace cell addresses.

When naming ranges, you can use letters, numbers, and the underscore (_) character, but you cannot use spaces. Named ranges are not case sensitive. SouthTotal, SOUTHTOTAL, and southtotal would all refer to the same range of cells.

Add and Delete a Named Range

The Super Power Computers summary report is a consolidation of data located on many worksheets. To make referencing this data easier, you use named ranges in place of cell references. You can create a named range in the Name Box to the left of the Formula Bar. To create a named range:

| Step 1 | **Select** | the range B9:E9 on the Store #11 worksheet |

Step 2	Click	in the Name Box to the left of the Formula Bar
Step 3	Key	Store11Totals
Step 4	Press	the ENTER key

The named range is added to the Name Box list. You can then use this list to select the named range. To select a named range:

Step 1	Click	the Central Region Summary sheet tab
Step 2	Click	the Name Box list arrow
Step 3	Click	Store11Totals

Excel activates the Store #11 worksheet and selects the cells referenced by the named range. To manage your named ranges, you use the Define Name dialog box. To use the Define Name dialog box to name ranges:

Step 1	Click	Insert
Step 2	Point to	Name
Step 3	Click	Define

The Define Name dialog box on your screen should look similar to Figure 7-4.

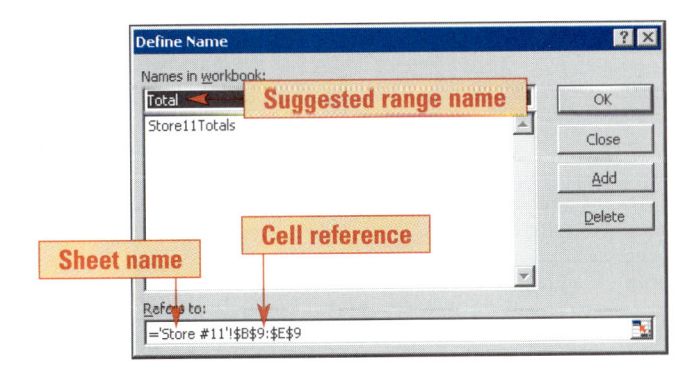

FIGURE 7-4
Define Name Dialog Box

The cell reference in the Refers to: text box begins with an equal sign (=), because the reference is essentially a formula that references the range name you chose. The sheet name appears next, enclosed between single quotation marks. As in 3-D references, an exclamation point separates the sheet name from the cell references. Finally, notice that the cell references are absolute references. You can modify the cell references in the Refers to: text box, select new ones from the worksheet by clicking the Collapse Dialog button, add new named ranges, or delete existing ones. Excel suggests a name for the named range in the Names in workbook: text box. To create a named range using the Define Names dialog box:

| Step 1 | Key | Store1Totals in the Names in workbook: text box |
| Step 2 | Click | the Collapse Dialog button in the Refers to: text box |

The dialog box collapses and the title bar changes to Define Range - Refers to: text box, and the status bar prompts you to point to the cells that should be added to your named range.

Step 3	Select	the range B9:E9 on the Store #1 worksheet
Step 4	Click	the Expand Dialog button in the dialog box
Step 5	Click	Add to add the new named range to the Names in workbook: list
Step 6	Follow	Steps 1 through 5 to add named ranges for Stores #12 and #6 (the range B9:E9)
Step 7	Click	OK to close the Define Name dialog box

Using a Named Range in a Formula

You can use range names instead of cell references in formulas. You need to sum the totals from all the stores on the Central Region Summary worksheet. To create a formula using a named range:

Step 1	Click	the Central Region Summary sheet tab
Step 2	Key	=sum(in cell B12
Step 3	Click	Insert
Step 4	Point to	Name
Step 5	Click	Paste to open the Paste Name dialog box
Step 6	Click	Store11Totals in the Paste name list
Step 7	Click	OK
Step 8	Click	the Enter button on the Formula Bar

> **QUICK TIP**
>
> To delete a named range, open the Define Name dialog box, select the range name in the list, then click the Delete button.

Excel automatically adds the closing parenthesis for the SUM argument and calculates the value as 4778585. Your formula should match the one shown in Figure 7-5.

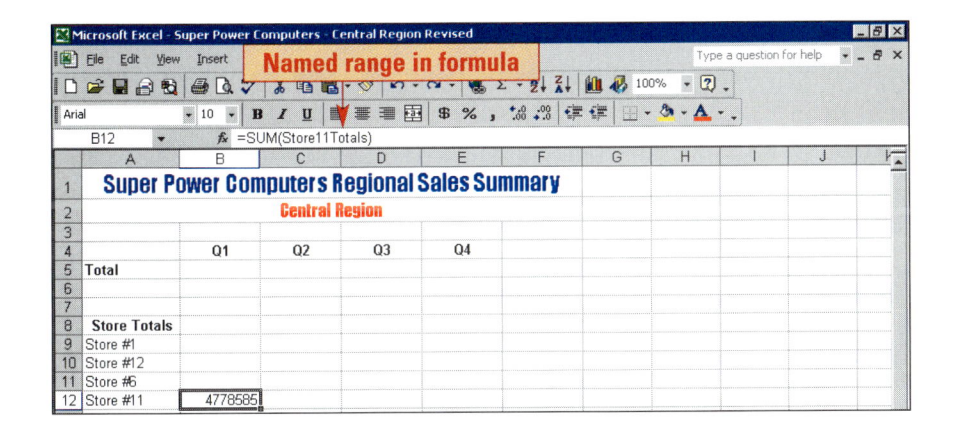

FIGURE 7-5
Named Ranges in a Formula

Step 9	Follow	Steps 2 through 8 to add formulas to calculate the remaining stores' totals in cells B9, B10, and B11
Step 10	Enter	a formula in cell B13 to sum cells B9:B12
Step 11	Select	the range B9:B13
Step 12	Click	the Currency Style button on the Formatting toolbar
Step 13	Click	the Decrease Decimal button on the Formatting toolbar twice
Step 14	AutoFit	column B to show the formatted values
Step 15	Save	the workbook

7.d Consolidating Data from Multiple Worksheets

Consolidating data for use in reports is a common business task. One way of consolidating data is to use 3-D references between worksheets. Another way to do this is with the Consolidate Data feature, which helps automate the process. When combined with named ranges, consolidating data can be a fast and effective way to build a summary report.

chapter seven

As part of your summary report, you want to consolidate the data for each quarter. You have already created named ranges for each store's quarter totals. To consolidate data:

Step 1	*Activate*	cell B5 on the Central Region Summary worksheet
Step 2	*Click*	Data
Step 3	*Click*	Consolidate

The Consolidate dialog box on your screen should look similar to Figure 7-6. In this dialog box, you can select the consolidation formula and the ranges to be used in the consolidation.

FIGURE 7-6
Consolidate Dialog Box

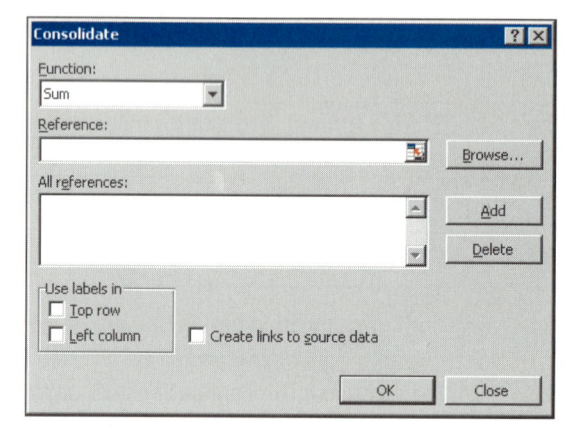

| Step 4 | *Verify* | that Sum is selected in the Function: list box |

Next, you add the named range to the All references: list. As you add the reference, the named range is selected in the worksheet.

Step 5	*Key*	Store1Totals in the Reference: text box
Step 6	*Click*	Add
Step 7	*Follow*	Steps 5 and 6 to add Store12Totals, Store6Totals, and Store11Totals to the All references: list
Step 8	*Click*	OK

The data is consolidated and added in cells B5:E5.

| Step 9 | *AutoFit* | columns C, D, and E |
| Step 10 | *Activate* | cell B5 |

Notice in the Formula Bar that a linking formula is not added to the cell by default, just the calculated value. To add linking formulas, formulas that update the calculated values when the cell references used in the formulas are updated, you need to change a setting in the Consolidate dialog box.

Step 11	*Open*	the Consolidate dialog box
Step 12	*Click*	the Create links to source data check box
Step 13	*Click*	OK

When you create links to source data, Excel automatically links to all source data, creates an outline by inserting new rows into the worksheet, adds the SUM function in each column, then hides the data. An **outline** allows you to view data in hierarchies, or levels. To view this data:

| Step 14 | *Click* | the Expand Outline button [+] to the left of row 9 |

Your screen should look similar to Figure 7-7. The outline expands to show the sublevel, and the plus outline button changes to a minus sign. All of the data from the Store worksheets is now linked to the Central Region Summary worksheet. Rows 5 through 8 contain the quarterly totals for Stores 11, 12, 1, and 6, respectively.

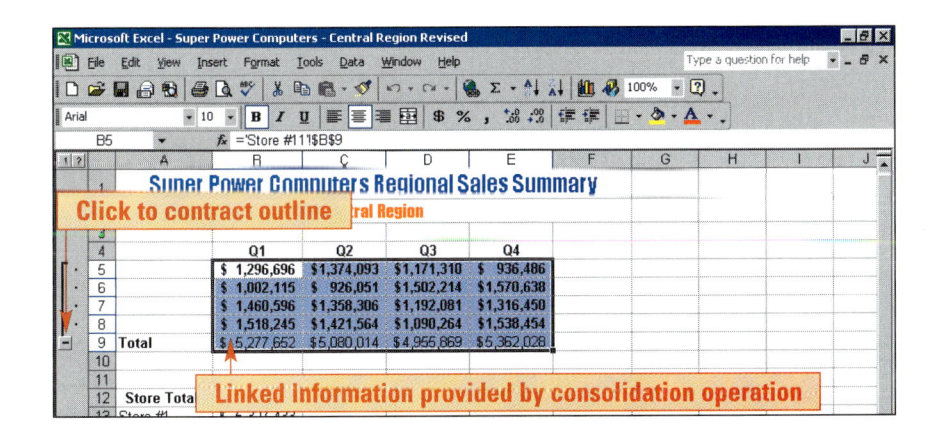

FIGURE 7-7
Summary Created Using Consolidate Data

| Step 15 | *Save* | the workbook and leave it open |

chapter seven

7.e Creating 3-D References and Links Between Workbooks

You know how to create 3-D references between worksheets in the same workbook. A 3-D reference is a link between a cell on one worksheet and a cell on another worksheet. You can also create 3-D references between workbooks. You do this by creating a linking formula or a hyperlink.

Creating Linking Formulas Between Workbooks

You need to combine the summary data in the *Central Region Revised* workbook with the summary data in the *Super Power Computers - East Coast Region* workbook to create a new summary workbook. To create linking formulas between workbooks:

Step 1	Open	the *Super Power Computers - Region Summary* workbook located on the Data Disk
Step 2	Save	the workbook as *Super Power Computers - Region Summary Revised*
Step 3	Open	the *Super Power Computers - East Coast Region* located on the Data Disk

You want to activate the *Super Power Computers - Region Summary Revised* workbook and move it in front of the other workbooks.

Step 4	Click	Window
Step 5	Click	Super Power Computers - Region Summary Revised
Step 6	Key	= in cell B5
Step 7	Click	Window
Step 8	Click	Super Power Computers - Central Region Revised
Step 9	Click	cell B17 on the Central Region Summary worksheet
Step 10	Click	the Enter button ✓ on the Formula Bar

The formula ='[**Super Power Computers - Central Region Revised.xls]Central Region Summary'!$B$17** is displayed in the Formula Bar. In this case, the formula is just a cell reference to cell B17 on the Central Region Summary worksheet in the *Super Power Computers - Central Region Revised* workbook. The worksheet name is separated from the cell reference by an exclamation point, and the workbook name is in brackets. You want to add a linking formula in cell B6 to cell B12 in the *Super Power Computers - East Coast Region* workbook.

Step 11	**Key**	= in cell B6
Step 12	**Switch to**	the *Super Power Computers - East Coast Region* workbook
Step 13	**Click**	cell B12 on the East Coast Region Summary worksheet
Step 14	**Click**	the Enter button ✓ on the Formula Bar

When you link between workbooks, the links are updated as changes are made.

Step 15	**Activate**	the *Super Power Computers - East Coast Region* workbook
Step 16	**Activate**	cell B5 on the Store #2 worksheet
Step 17	**Enter**	425000
Step 18	**Activate**	the *Super Power Computers - Region Summary Revised* workbook

The value in cell B6 has been updated from 17,890,348 to 18,115,348.

Step 19	**Activate**	the *Super Power Computers - East Coast Region* workbook
Step 20	**Close**	the *Super Power Computers - East Coast Region* workbook without saving your changes

Because you closed the *Super Power Computers - East Coast Region* workbook without saving changes, the value you changed was not saved. The *Super Power Computers - Region Summary Revised* workbook was not updated immediately, but will be updated the next time you open the workbook.

MENU TIP

You can create links to cells on other worksheets or workbooks by using the Copy and Paste Special commands. Copy the cell(s) to which you want to link, then switch to the workbook, worksheet, and cell where the new link should appear. Click Paste Special on the Edit menu, then click the Paste Link option to create an absolute reference to the cells you copied.

chapter seven

Creating Hyperlinks Between Workbooks

By adding a hyperlink to the workbooks you just linked, you can quickly reopen the workbooks. You should still have the *Super Power Computers - Region Summary Revised* workbook open. To create a hyperlink:

Step 1	Right-click	cell A5 in the *Super Power Computers - Region Summary Revised* workbook
Step 2	Click	Hyperlink

The Insert Hyperlink dialog box opens.

Step 3	Click	Existing File or Web Page in the Link to: bar, if necessary

The Insert Hyperlink dialog box changes, allowing you to insert a file or Web page name. The list in the middle of the dialog box displays filenames, network drives, and Internet addresses that you've visited recently, depending on which button is selected to the left of the list.

Step 4	Click	the *Super Power Computers - Central Region Revised* workbook in the list
Step 5	Verify	that Central appears in the Text to display: text box

This text will appear in the cell. Your dialog box should look similar to Figure 7-8.

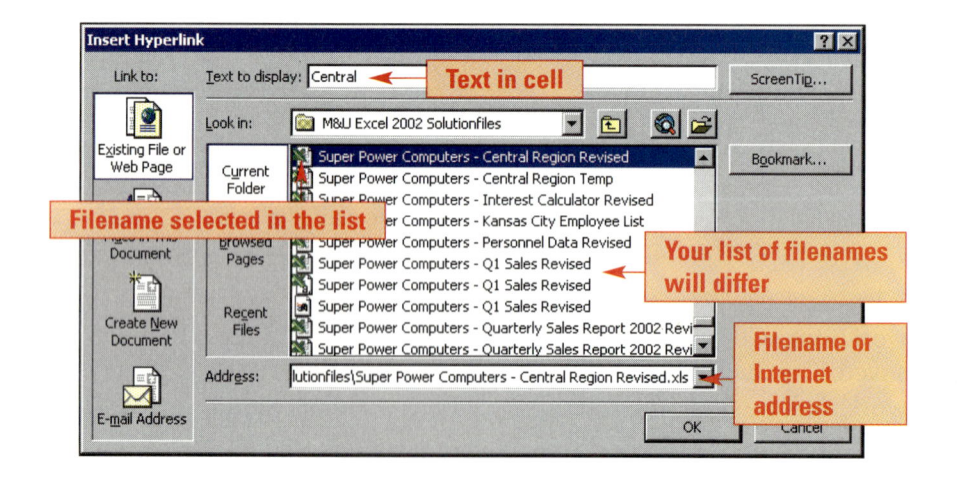

FIGURE 7-8
Insert Hyperlink Dialog Box

Step 6	Click	ScreenTip
Step 7	Key	Central in the ScreenTip text: text box in the Set Hyperlink ScreenTip dialog box

MENU TIP
Click Hyperlink on the Insert menu to open the Insert Hyperlink dialog box.

QUICK TIP
When creating hyperlinks to a Web page, you don't have to key the URL. Instead, open the Insert Hyperlink dialog box, then click Web Page on the right to open your browser. Use your browser to find the Web page, click in the address box in the browser, then switch to Excel. The address currently in your browser appears in the Address: text box.

MOUSE TIP
Click the Insert Hyperlink button on the Standard toolbar to insert a hyperlink.

Step 8	Click	OK
Step 9	Click	OK to change the value in cell A5 to a hyperlink
Step 10	Follow	Steps 1 through 9 to add a hyperlink in cell A6 to the Super Power Computers - East Coast Region workbook with the ScreenTip East Coast

Now check your new hyperlinks.

Step 11	Position	the mouse pointer over cell A6 to view the ScreenTip with the text "East Coast"
Step 12	Click	the East Coast hyperlink

The *Super Power Computers - East Coast Region* workbook opens. The Web toolbar also opens.

Step 13	Right-click	the Web toolbar
Step 14	Click	Web to close the Web toolbar

Hyperlinks make it easy to connect to a variety of information sources. By creating links to Web pages on the Internet or to other Office documents, you can quickly open documents associated with the workbook(s) with which you are working.

7.f Working with Multiple Workbooks

When working with multiple workbooks, you can arrange them so as to view several workbooks at once. If you must repeatedly manipulate the same workbooks simultaneously, you can save a workspace, which speeds the editing process when you need to work with the same set of workbooks again. **Workspaces** remember which files are open and how the workbooks are arranged.

Arranging Workbooks

When working with multiple workbooks, you may want to display more than one workbook window at a time. Using the Arrange

---

QUICK TIP

You can modify the formatting of a cell containing a hyperlink by using the normal formatting commands. Altering the formatting does not affect the hyperlink.

CAUTION TIP

If you move a file to which you have created hyperlinks, you must edit the hyperlink to point to the new location. Right-click the hyperlink or object and select Hyperlink, then Edit Hyperlink.

MOUSE TIP

When you add a hyperlink to an object, you cannot click the object to select it, because clicking the object activates the hyperlink. Instead, to select an object with a hyperlink attached, right-click the object. You can then use the shortcut menu to modify the object, or press ESC to close the shortcut menu and move or resize the object.

chapter seven

Windows dialog box, you can create several different arrangements. To arrange the workbook windows:

Step 1	Click	Window
Step 2	Click	Arrange
Step 3	Click	the Tiled option button, if necessary
Step 4	Click	OK

Your screen should look similar to Figure 7-9.

FIGURE 7-9
Tiled Windows

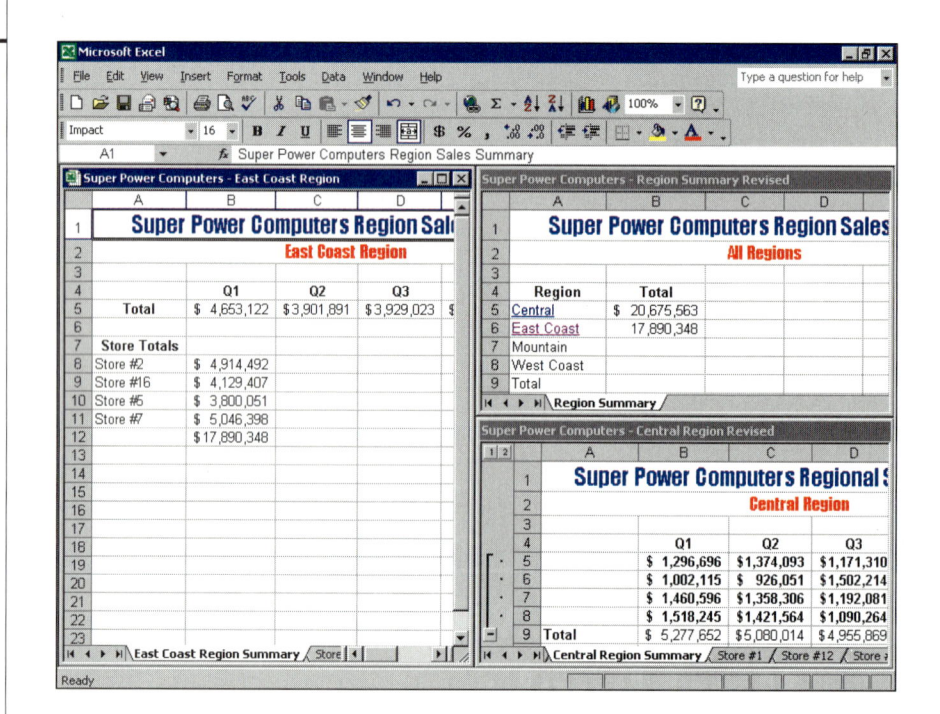

Using a Workspace

Workspaces are great time savers when you frequently use the same files simultaneously. Instead of opening several files and then using the Arrange Windows dialog box every time you need to work with that particular set of files, you can open a workspace, which will automatically open and arrange the desired files. Because you will be using this set of Super Power Computers workbooks frequently, you decide to create a workspace. To create a workspace:

| Step 1 | Click | File |
| Step 2 | Click | Save Workspace |

The Save Workspace dialog box opens with Workspaces in the Save as type: list box. This is the only option available when you save a workspace. If your computer is set to display file extensions, the Excel workspace file extension, .xlw, also appears.

Step 3	Save	the workspace as *Region Summary* to the same location as your Data Files
Step 4	Click	Yes To All to save any changes in the workbooks
Step 5	Press & hold	the SHIFT key
Step 6	Click	File
Step 7	Click	Close All

> **MENU TIP**
>
> When you press the SHIFT key before clicking the Close command on the File menu, the command changes to Close All.

Next you open your workspace. Opening a workspace is very similar to opening a workbook. To open a workspace:

Step 1	Click	the Open button on the Standard toolbar
Step 2	Click	the Files of type: list arrow
Step 3	Click	Workspaces (you may need to scroll)
Step 4	Click	Region Summary
Step 5	Click	Open

Because the *Super Power Computers - Region Summary Revised* workbook contains links to another workbook, Excel prompts you to update the links.

Step 6	Click	Update

> **TASK PANE TIP**
>
> You can click the More Workbooks link under Open a workbook in the New Workbook task pane.

All of the workbooks are open exactly the way you had them arranged previously.

Step 7	Close	all open workbooks, saving changes as needed

With the links between the workbooks added and the workspace saved, it will be very easy to update this information.

> **QUICK TIP**
>
> If you change the arrangement of the workbooks, remember to resave the workspace.

chapter seven

Summary

- To group worksheets, use SHIFT + Click or CTRL + Click. Grouping worksheets makes it easy to add the same data, titles, headings, and formatting to several worksheets at a time. You can also group worksheets for printing.
- Documentation worksheets contain documentation that explains the content of the workbook.
- You can add and delete named ranges to refer to ranges by name instead of by cell reference.
- You can use named ranges in formulas as you would use cell references.
- The Data Consolidation command enables you to automatically include data from the worksheets in a workbook in a formula.
- Use 3-D references when ranges must span multiple worksheets or workbooks. In a 3-D reference, workbook names are enclosed within brackets.
- You can add hyperlinks to cell values or drawing objects in other workbooks or on Web pages. Click the hyperlink to open other files or access an Internet Web site.
- The Arrange Windows command enables you to arrange several windows simultaneously.
- Workspaces enable you to open and arrange several workbooks in the same way each time.

Commands Review

Action	Menu Bar	Shortcut Menu	Toolbar	Task Pane	Keyboard
Ungroup worksheets		Right-click, Ungroup Sheets			
Add named range	Insert, Name, Define				CTRL + F3 ALT + I, N, D
Paste a named range	Insert, Name, Paste				ALT + I, N, P
Consolidate data	Data, Consolidate				ALT + D, N
Add a hyperlink to an object or cell	Insert, Hyperlink	Right-click, Hyperlink			CTRL + K ALT + I, I
Arrange workbooks	Window, Arrange				ALT + W, A
Create workspace	File, Save Workspace				ALT + F, W
Close all open workbooks	SHIFT + File, Close All				SHIFT + ALT + F, C

Concepts Review

Circle the correct answer.

1. **Hyperlinks can link to:**
   - [a] other cells.
   - [b] other workbooks.
   - [c] Web pages.
   - [d] other cells, other workbooks, and Web pages.

2. **Which of the following formulas contains a valid reference to a range on another worksheet?**
   - [a] =sum(Totals!A1:B5)
   - [b] =sum('Totals'!A1:B5)
   - [c] =sum("Totals"!A1:B5)
   - [d] =sum(Totals:A1:B5)

3. **Which of the following formulas contains a valid reference to a range in another workbook?**
   - [a] =sum(RegionSales['Sheet1'!A1:B5])
   - [b] =sum('[RegionSales]Sheet1'!A1:B5)
   - [c] =sum('[RegionSales]Sheet1!A1:B5')
   - [d] =sum("[RegionSales]Sheet1"!A1:B5)

4. **To simultaneously add data and formatting to multiple worksheets, you must first:**
   - [a] group the worksheets.
   - [b] link the worksheets.
   - [c] add the data and formatting, then copy and paste from one worksheet to another.
   - [d] join worksheets together.

5. **A summary page might include which of the following sections?**
   - [a] Map of the Workbook
   - [b] Identification
   - [c] Descriptions, Assumptions, and Parameters
   - [d] all of the above

6. **3-D references in formulas:**
   - [a] cannot be modified.
   - [b] allow formatting to be applied across multiple worksheets.
   - [c] span worksheets.
   - [d] none of the above.

7. **An workspace is used to store:**
   - [a] which workbooks were open but not their arrangement.
   - [b] which workbooks were open and their arrangement.
   - [c] the arrangement only so you can apply it to currently open workbooks.
   - [d] the toolbar arrangement.

8. **A referenced workbook name is surrounded by:**
   - [a] [ ].
   - [b] { }.
   - [c] ( ).
   - [d] < >.

9. **You create named ranges by:**
   - [a] using the name box next to the formula bar or the Define Name dialog box.
   - [b] using the Formula Bar.
   - [c] right-clicking a selected range and choosing Name.
   - [d] double clicking a range.

10. **Hyperlinks can be attached to:**
    - [a] lines.
    - [b] clip art.
    - [c] cells.
    - [d] lines, clip art, and cells.

chapter seven

Circle **T** if the statement is true or **F** if the statement is false.

T F 1. You can select groups of worksheets only if they are in one continuous group.

T F 2. You can use the SHIFT or CTRL key to create a worksheet group.

T F 3. You can group worksheets for printing, but not for formatting.

T F 4. Hyperlinks between workbooks and linking formulas between workbooks are the same thing.

T F 5. Hyperlinks cannot be made to other types of documents, such as a Word document.

T F 6. You cannot link worksheet text to charts.

T F 7. If linked workbooks are open simultaneously, changes are immediately reflected in both workbooks.

T F 8. Once a workbook is open, you cannot update its links to other workbooks without closing the original workbook and reopening it.

T F 9. Use Paste Link from the Paste Special dialog box to create a quick reference to another cell or cells.

T F 10. Named ranges can be used in formulas in place of cell references.

Skills Review

Exercise 1

1. Open the *Sweet Tooth Summary* workbook located on the Data Disk.

2. In cells B5:B10 on the Summary worksheet, use a linking formula to link to the total items sold, which is calculated in cell D24 of each item's worksheet.

3. In cells C5:C10 on the Summary worksheet, use a linking formula to link to the total gross sales, which is calculated in cell F24 of each item's worksheet.

4. Activate cell B12 and open the Consolidate dialog box from the Data menu.

5. Enter qty123 in the Reference: text box and click Add. Repeat to add references to qty124, qty125, qty126, qty127, and qty128. Click OK when you are finished.

6. Enter =SUM(in cell C12, then click the Item 123 sheet tab, click cell F24, press and hold the SHIFT key and click the Item 128 tab, then press the ENTER key.

7. Print the Summary worksheet.

8. Save the workbook as *Sweet Tooth Summary Revised*, and then print and close it.

Exercise 2

1. Create a new workbook.

2. Add the name of five Internet search engines in cells A1–A5 (such as Google, Yahoo!, and Northern Light).

3. Add a hyperlink to each of the search engines. Click the Browse the Web button in the Insert Hyperlink dialog box to open your Web browser and locate a Web address. Switch back to Excel, and the address should be inserted into the Address: text box. If it's not, key in the address.

4. Add a ScreenTip and text to the objects to identify the hyperlinks.

5. Save the workbook as *Search Links*, and then print and close it.

Exercise 3

1. Open the *Central Region*, *Mountain Region*, *West Coast Region*, and *East Coast Region* workbooks located on the Data Disk.
2. Save the workbooks as *Mountain 1*, *West Coast 1*, *East Coast 1*, and *Central 1*.
3. In cell D4 of the *Central 1* workbook, enter "Go to Mountain." Add a hyperlink to jump to the *Mountain 1* workbook with a ScreenTip that says, "Mountain 1 workbook."
4. In cell D4 of the *Mountain 1* workbook, enter "Go to West Coast." Add a hyperlink to jump to the *West Coast 1* workbook with a ScreenTip that says, "West Coast 1 workbook." (*Hint*: Use the Recent Files button in the Insert Hyperlinks dialog box.)
5. In cell D4 of the *West Coast 1* workbook, enter "Go to East Coast." Add a hyperlink to jump to the *East Coast 1* workbook with a ScreenTip that says, "East Coast 1 workbook."
6. In cell D4 of the *East Coast 1* workbook, enter "Go to Central." Add a hyperlink to jump to the *Central 1* workbook with a ScreenTip that says, "Central 1 workbook."
7. Arrange all the open workbooks.
8. Save the workspace as *Region Workbooks*.
9. Save and close all of the workbooks, leaving only the *Central 1* workbook open.
10. Test the hyperlinks, printing the Summary tab of each workbook as it opens.
11. Close all open workbooks.

Exercise 4

1. Create a new workbook.
2. In cell A1, enter "Jump to Cell."
3. In cell A2, enter "Jump to Worksheet."
4. In cell A3, enter "Jump to Workbook."
5. In cell A4, enter "Jump to Web."
6. Create a hyperlink in cell A1 to another cell on the same worksheet.
7. Create a hyperlink in cell A2 to another worksheet in the same workbook.
8. Create a hyperlink in cell A3 to any of the workbooks you created in the Skills Review Exercises.
9. Create a hyperlink in cell A4 to one of your favorite Web site's address.
10. Include ScreenTips to indicate where the hyperlinks point.
11. Save the workbook as *Jump Around*, and then print and close it.

Exercise 5

1. ZXY Accounting is a large accounting firm with offices in Orlando, San Diego, Phoenix, and Washington, D.C. Open the *ZXY Accounting* workbook located on the Data Disk.
2. Group all the worksheets.
3. Insert a column in front of column A.
4. Insert a row above row 1.

chapter seven

5. Add the information indicated in the table below:

Cell	Enter
A2	Auditing
A3	Tax Preparation
A4	Consulting
A5	Total
B1	January
C1	February
D1	March
E1	Total

6. Bold and center the titles in the range B1: E1.

7. Bold cell A5.

8. Use the SUM formula in row 5 and column E to sum the data.

9. Ungroup the worksheets and enter and bold the city name (shown on each tab) in cell A1 of each worksheet.

10. AutoFit columns A, B, C, D, and E.

11. Save the workbook as *ZXY Accounting Revised,* and then print and close it.

Exercise 6

1. Open the *ZXY Accounting Revised* workbook that you created in Exercise 5.

2. Insert a new worksheet named "Summary" to the left of the Washington, D.C. worksheet.

3. Create a summary table to add the totals for each month across all cities.

4. Create a named range for each city's monthly total cell.

5. On the Summary worksheet, insert a linking formula using the named ranges.

6. Sum each column on the Summary worksheet.

7. Format the data in rows 2 and 6 using the Currency format, no decimal places, and format the data in rows 3, 4, and 5 as Comma with no decimal places.

8. Find the average income for each month by adding a formula in row 8 in each column. Format the data in this row as Currency with no decimal places.

9. Create a chart showing the income by month for each category, on a new worksheet called "Summary Chart."

10. Title the chart "1st Quarter Income."

11. Print the chart.

12. Save the workbook as *ZXY Accounting Summary,* and then print and close it.

Exercise 7

1. Open the *ZXY Accounting Summary* workbook that you created in Exercise 6.
2. Group all the worksheets except the Summary Chart worksheet.
3. Use Page Setup command on the File menu to set print options to center the data vertically and horizontally.
4. Add a centered header "ZXY Accounting" and format it as 20 point and boldface.
5. Preview and print all five worksheets.
6. Ungroup the worksheets.
7. Save the workbook as *ZXY Accounting Summary Print,* and close it.

Exercise 8

1. Open the *ZXY Accounting Summary Print* workbook that you created in Exercise 7.
2. Group all the worksheets except the Summary Chart and Summary worksheets.
3. Apply AutoFormat style List 2 to the range A1:E5.
4. Use the Page Setup command on the File menu to set print options to landscape orientation and 150% scale.
5. Print the worksheets.
6. Ungroup the worksheets.
7. Save the workbook as *ZXY Accounting Summary Print 2,* and then close it.

Case Projects

Project 1

You work for the local newspaper. You are currently researching historical weather trends in the United States. Connect to the Internet and use the Web toolbar to search for average monthly temperatures for New York City and Los Angeles in the last year. Create a workbook that includes the temperatures for each city on two separate worksheets. Create a 3-D reference formula on a second workbook to display the average temperature of the two cities for each month of the previous year. Create a chart comparing the average temperatures for each city. Use axis and chart titles to clarify the purpose of the chart. Save the workbook as *Temperature Averages,* and then print and close it.

Project 2

You teach English at a high school. In preparation for the upcoming term, you need to set up a workbook with five worksheets, one for each of five classes. Each worksheet will be used to record five test scores and ten assignment scores. The test scores and the assignment scores must be summed separately. Group worksheets to make your job easier as you input column and row headings, sum formulas, and formatting. Save your workbook as *Fall Semester Scores,* and then print and close it.

chapter seven

Project 3

You work for a small architectural firm that tracks income in one of two categories: contract and consulting work. The firm lumps expenses into four categories: advertising, office, auto, and rent. Create a workbook named *Business Income* showing receipts in both categories for four quarters. Name the worksheet "2002 Income" and remove any unused worksheets. Sum the totals and save the workbook. Create a workbook named *Business Expenses* showing expenses in each category for four quarters. Name the worksheet "2002 Expenses" and remove any unused worksheets. Sum the totals and save the workbook.

Create a workbook named *Business Projection*. Set up separate tables to show both income categories and the four expense categories. Use columns for each quarter. Using a 5% projected growth rate for consulting work, create a formula to link the *Business Income* cells to the *Business Projection* cells, and then add 5% to last year's totals to project this year's consulting income totals. Do the same for contract work, using a projected growth percentage of 7.5%. For expense categories, link the *Business Expenses* figures to the *Business Projection* workbook, and then calculate an inflation adjustment of 4% over last year's totals. Name the worksheet "2003 Projection" and remove any unused worksheets. Print the worksheets in each of the workbooks. Save and close each workbook when you are finished.

Project 4

As a worker in the financial sector, you need to understand the concept of inflation. Connect to the Internet and search the Web for information about inflation. Write a two-paragraph summary explaining what inflation is and how it affects the economy. Save the document as *Inflation.doc*, and then print and close it.

Project 5

As a small business owner who uses Excel for a variety of functions, you need to use your time effectively. When you need help with Excel, you immediately look for information on the Internet. It takes time to locate useful sites, however. Create a new workbook called *Excel Internet Resources*. Connect to the Internet and search the Web for five useful sites containing tips and other information about Excel. Add hyperlinks to each site in the workbook. When you finish adding the hyperlinks, print the worksheet, and save and close the workbook.

Project 6

You have sent several linked workbooks to a colleague. When she opened those workbooks, the links were broken because the source files were stored in a folder system that's different from the one you use on your computer. Using the Ask A Question Box, find out how to reconnect linked objects if the source file is moved. Write a Word document explaining in your own words how to reconnect the links. Save the file as *Reconnect Links.doc*, and then print and close it.

Project 7

You work for a distribution company called Sweet Tooth Candy. Create a sample documentation worksheet for use in other workbooks. Be sure to add Identification, Map of the Workbook, and Description, Assumptions, and Parameters sections to the documentation worksheet. Save the workbook as *Sweet Tooth Candy - Documentation Sheet*, and then print and close it.

Project 8

You would like to set up an Internet e-mail account. Many companies offer free e-mail services. Connect to the Internet and search the Web for at least three companies offering free e-mail. Create a new workbook and insert the company name, the URL, and a brief summary of the terms. Save the workbook as *Free E-mail*, and then print and close it.

Excel 2002

Creating, Sorting, and Filtering Lists

Chapter Overview

Some workbooks in Excel are used to store lists of data, much as a database does. In this chapter, you learn about the components of a list. Validation criteria help ensure proper data entry in a list. Using data forms, you can enter, edit, find, and delete records from a list. You can use advanced filters to view subsets of a list. You can sort lists in ascending or descending order. Creating outlines using the subtotal command offers an easy way to summarize data by easily displaying or hiding levels of detail as needed.

Learning Objectives

- Identify basic terms and guidelines for creating lists
- Enter data in a list using data validation
- Use the data form
- Create custom filters
- Perform single and multilevel sorts
- Use grouping and outlines to create subtotals

Case profile

You need to create a personnel data list for Super Power Computers. You have been asked to make it easy for anyone to enter and find data in this list. By using data validation, you can ensure that other users enter the appropriate data. You can use data forms and filters to locate specific data. You also need to create a sales report, sorted by region and containing subtotals for each region.

chapter eight

8.a Identifying Basic Terms and Guidelines for Creating Lists

So far you have seen the capacity for dealing with numerical data in Excel. However, Excel is also adept at handling **lists** of data, in a manner similar to a database. A **database** stores data in a structure called a **table**. Each row in a data table contains a unique record, and each column contains entries belonging to a particular field. A **field** contains a collection of characters or numbers, such as a person's name or a phone number. The **field name** identifies the contents of that particular field. A group of field entries is known as a **record**. At the top of the list, or data table, is a **header row**, which identifies the field names used in the table.

The *Super Power Computers - Personnel Data* workbook contains several records. This list contains fields for each employee's last name, initial of first name, division, salary, and "Rec. No.," a field that stores a unique record number for each record in the list. To open the workbook:

> **QUICK TIP**
>
> Record numbers are often used in large database tables to speed up indexing and data retrieval. They also provide an easy way to sort the list by the order in which the records were entered into the list.

| Step 1 | Open | the *Super Power Computers - Personnel Data* workbook located on the Data Disk |
| Step 2 | Save | the workbook as *Super Power Computers - Personnel Data Revised* |

The Super Power Computers Personnel list on your screen should look similar to Figure 8-1.

FIGURE 8-1
Typical List in Excel

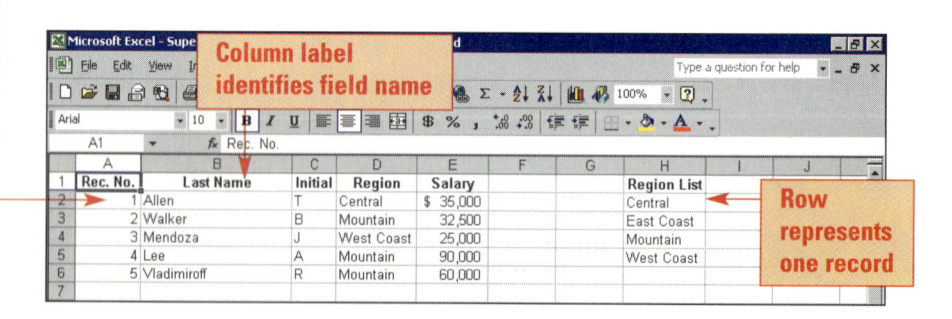

You must remember some important guidelines when creating lists. First, you should format the header row differently from the rest of the data, using bold, italics, or a different font, so that Excel recognizes that it is the header row and not just another record. Second, the header row should appear as the first row of your list. Don't separate the header row from the first row of data by inserting a blank row. If necessary, use borders or the cell fill to distinguish the header row from the data in the list. Third, each field entry in a field must contain the same type of data. For example, don't place a phone number in the Last Name field of a phone directory list. Take note of the following guidelines as well:

- Create only one list per worksheet. If you need more than one list, use a separate worksheet for each new list. This strategy helps you avoid the potential problem of mixing lists when you perform a sort.
- Always leave one column and one row blank on both sides and above and below a list. Excel then can automatically detect the list boundaries, saving you the hassle of selecting the list for sorting, outlining, and AutoFormat operations.
- Avoid using spaces at the beginning of a field entry. Spaces affect the sort order of a list, because the space character comes before alphabetic characters. Entries that have spaces as their first character are placed at the top of a sorted list.
- Format data in a column in a consistent manner. Don't make some names bold and others italic.
- Never place critical data to the left or right of a list. When filters are later applied to the list, you may not be able to see important data.
- Always include a record number field so as to give each record a unique record number. This strategy enables you to return the list to its original entry order after you've performed other sort operations.

> **CAUTION TIP**
>
> The data in the Region field in the Personnel Data file is not considered critical for filtering the personnel list.

8.b Entering Data in a List Using Data Validation

You want to ensure that anyone who uses the *Super Power Computers - Personnel Data Revised* workbook enters the correct data in each field. For example, the Salary field should contain only numerical data. To help the user meet these expectations, you set up data validation for each column. **Data validation** restricts the entry in a field to parameters that you set. You want to limit the entry in the record number field to whole numbers between 1 and 999. To use data validation:

Step 1	*Select*	the range A7:A10
Step 2	*Click*	Data
Step 3	*Click*	Validation

chapter eight

| Step 4 | *Click* | the <u>A</u>llow: list arrow on the Settings tab |

Your Data Validation dialog box should look similar to Figure 8-2. Each choice in the <u>A</u>llow: list restricts the data in the selected cells to a specific type. The options on the Settings tab change for each validation option selected in the <u>A</u>llow: list.

FIGURE 8-2
<u>A</u>llow: List on the Settings Tab of the Data Validation Dialog Box

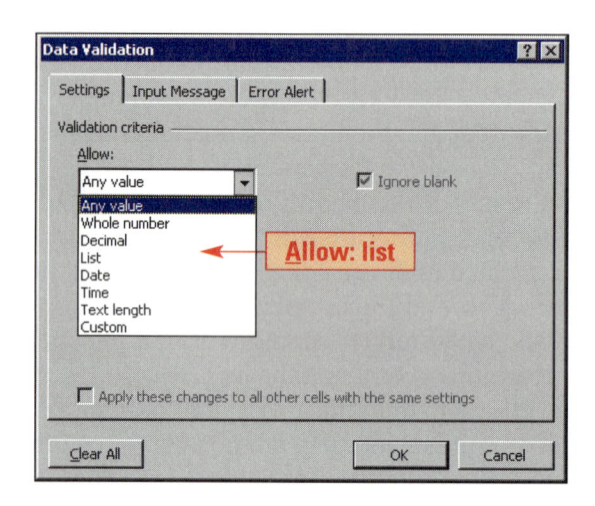

| Step 5 | *Click* | Whole number in the <u>A</u>llow: list |

For whole numbers, you specify an operator (less than, greater than, between, and so on) along with minimum and maximum values to restrict the range of acceptable values.

Step 6	*Verify*	that between is selected in the <u>D</u>ata: list
Step 7	*Key*	1 in the <u>M</u>inimum: text box
Step 8	*Key*	999 in the Ma<u>x</u>imum: text box

You want to ensure that every new record receives a record number. By default, Excel does not count blank entries as invalid.

| Step 9 | *Click* | the Ignore <u>b</u>lank check box to remove the check mark |

Input messages display entry instructions, which make it easier for the user to understand what type of information should be entered into a field. To add an input message to the selected cells:

Step 1	*Click*	the Input Message tab
Step 2	*Key*	Record Number in the Title: text box
Step 3	*Press*	the TAB key to move to the Input message: text box
Step 4	*Key*	A whole number between 1 and 999

Your dialog box should look similar to Figure 8-3.

FIGURE 8-3
Input Message Tab in the Data Validation Dialog Box

When a user enters invalid data, you can have the worksheet display one of three types of error messages. Each option produces a different type of error message alert dialog box. The Stop style generates an alert dialog box that contains Retry and Cancel buttons. The Warning style alert dialog box contains Yes and No buttons. The Information style alert dialog box contains OK and Cancel buttons. Because you do not want to allow the entry of invalid data into the worksheet, you will prompt the user to enter the correct entry or cancel the operation. To set the error messages:

Step 1	*Click*	the Error Alert tab
Step 2	*Verify*	that the Show error alert after invalid data is entered check box contains a check mark
Step 3	*Click*	Stop in the Style: list, if necessary
Step 4	*Key*	Record Number in the Title: text box

| Step 5 | *Press* | the TAB key to move to the Error message: text box |
| Step 6 | *Key* | You must enter a whole number between 1 and 999. |

The dialog box on your screen should look similar to Figure 8-4.

FIGURE 8-4
Error Alert Tab in the Data Validation Dialog Box

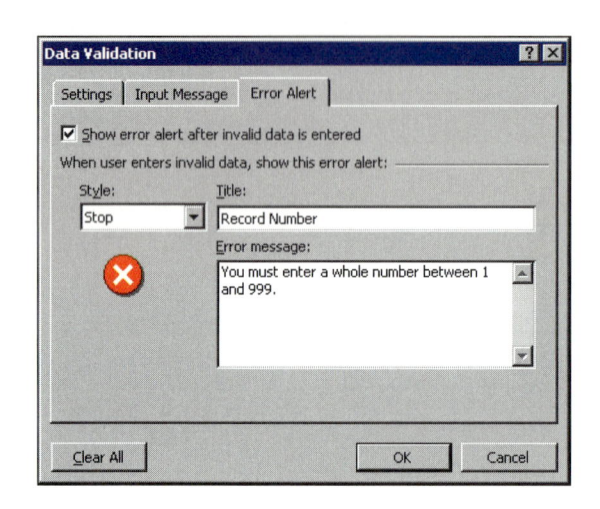

| Step 7 | *Click* | OK |

The dialog box closes, and the input message that you just created appears near the selected cells. Next, you test the new data validation rules. To test data validation:

| Step 1 | *Activate* | cell A7 to display the information message |

Your screen should look similar to Figure 8-5.

FIGURE 8-5
Entering Data with Data Validation

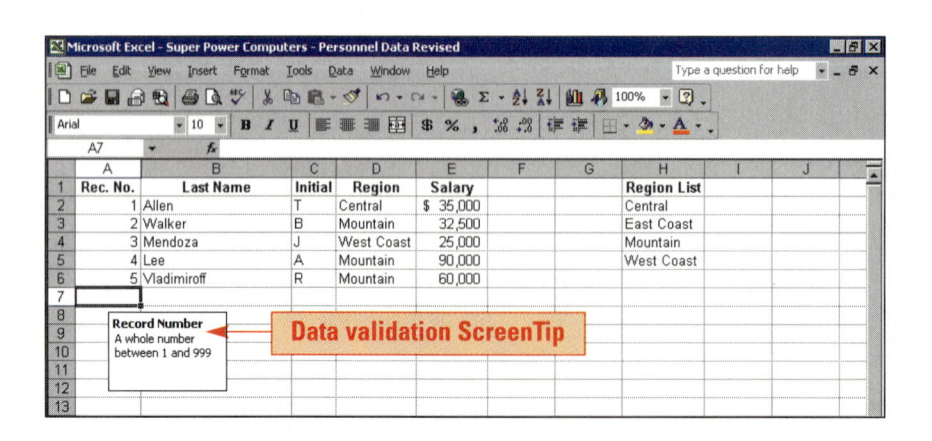

Creating, Sorting, and Filtering Lists — EA 31

Step 2	Key	1000
Step 3	Press	the ENTER key
Step 4	Click	Retry in the error message dialog box that opens
Step 5	Key	6
Step 6	Press	the TAB key

This entry is valid and accepted. For the Last Name and Initial fields, you want users to enter only text, and you want to limit the number of characters permitted in each field. To set data validation for the Last Name column:

Step 1	Select	the range B7:B10
Step 2	Open	the Settings tab in the Data Validation dialog box
Step 3	Click	Text length in the Allow: list
Step 4	Key	1 in the Minimum: text box
Step 5	Key	20 in the Maximum: text box
Step 6	Click	the Ignore blank check box to remove the check mark
Step 7	Key	Last Name in the Title: text box on the Input Message tab
Step 8	Key	Limit last name to 20 characters. Abbreviate if necessary. in the Input message: text box
Step 9	Verify	that Stop is selected in the Style: list on the Error Alert tab
Step 10	Key	Last Name in the Title: text box
Step 11	Key	Please limit last name to 20 characters. Abbreviate if necessary. in the Error message: text box
Step 12	Click	OK
Step 13	Enter	Rawlins in cell B7

Next, you add the validation criteria for the Initial column. To add the validation criteria for the Initial column:

Step 1	Select	the range C7:C10
Step 2	Open	the Data Validation dialog box
Step 3	Set	the validation criteria to Text length and a minimum and maximum of 1, on the Settings tab
Step 4	Click	the Ignore blank check box to remove the check mark

QUICK TIP

If you set data validation for a range of cells but later need to update the validation settings, you can have the update apply to all cells with similar data validation settings. Select any cell that contains the data validation setting you wish to change, then open the Data Validation dialog box to modify the setting. On the Settings tab, click Apply these changes to all other cells with the same settings check box.

chapter eight

QUICK TIP

To prevent changes to data validation, click Protection on the Tools menu, then click Protect Sheet. Verify that the Contents box contains a check mark before you click OK.

Step 5	Key	Initial in the Title: text box on the Input Message tab
Step 6	Key	Enter initial of employee's first name. in the Input message: text box
Step 7	Key	Initial in the Title: text box on the Error Alert tab
Step 8	Key	You must enter a one-character initial. in the Error message: text box
Step 9	Click	OK
Step 10	Enter	J in cell C7

The next field, Region, contains only four valid entries. You can create a list of these valid entries from which the user can select. To set list validation criteria:

Step 1	Select	the range D7:D10
Step 2	Open	the Data Validation dialog box
Step 3	Click	List in the Allow: list on the Settings tab
Step 4	Click	the Collapse button in the Source: text box

The dialog box shrinks to just the title bar and input box.

Step 5	Select	the range H2:H5
Step 6	Click	the Expand button in the Data Validation dialog box
Step 7	Verify	that the In-cell dropdown check box contains a check mark
Step 8	Click	the Ignore blank check box to remove the check mark
Step 9	Key	Region in the Title: text box on the Input Message tab
Step 10	Key	Select a region from the list. in the Input message: text box
Step 11	Key	Region in the Title: text box on the Error Alert tab
Step 12	Key	You must select an entry from the list. in the Error message: text box
Step 13	Click	OK
Step 14	Click	cell D7
Step 15	Click	the list arrow next to cell D7

Your screen should look similar to Figure 8-6.

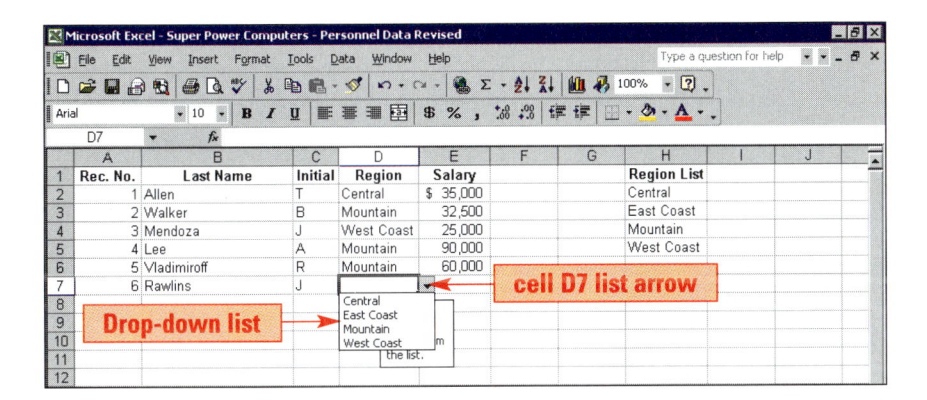

FIGURE 8-6
Using a List to Enter Valid Data in a Field

Step 16	Click	East Coast

Salaries over $75,000 at Super Power Computers must be authorized by Luis Alvarez, the company president, so the error alert message for the salary column must be an Information error alert. To set validation with an Information error alert message:

Step 1	Select	the range E7:E10
Step 2	Open	the Data Validation dialog box
Step 3	Set	the validation criteria to Whole number, less than or equal to 75000
Step 4	Click	the Ignore blank check box to remove the check mark
Step 5	Key	Salary in the Title: text box on the Input Message tab
Step 6	Key	Enter salary amount. in the Input message: text box
Step 7	Click	the Error Alert tab
Step 8	Click	the Style: list arrow
Step 9	Click	Information
Step 10	Key	Salary in the Title: text box on the Error Alert tab
Step 11	Key	Salary must be under $75,000 unless authorized by L. Alvarez. in the Error message: text box
Step 12	Click	OK
Step 13	Enter	80000 in cell E7

chapter eight

MENU TIP

You can use the Paste Special command to copy data validation criteria to other cells. Once you've set the data validation criteria, copy the cell, click Paste Special on the Edit menu, and select the Validation option button to paste only the validation criteria into the selected cells.

The Information dialog box displays the error alert message. In this case, you have been authorized to add this salary to the list. Clicking the OK button accepts the entry; clicking the Cancel button clears the entry so you can key another value.

| Step 14 | Click | OK |
| Step 15 | Save | the workbook |

Data validation is not required to enter data in a list. Nevertheless, data validation is important to ensure that the user enters the appropriate type of data in each field. Next, you enter the rest of the data in the list. To enter the data in the list:

| Step 1 | Enter | the records as shown in Table 8-1 |

TABLE 8-1 Additional Records

Rec. No.	Last Name	Initial	Region	Salary
7	Munns	R	East Coast	45000
8	Greenwood	J	West Coast	30000

Your screen should look similar to Figure 8-7.

FIGURE 8-7 Completed Data List

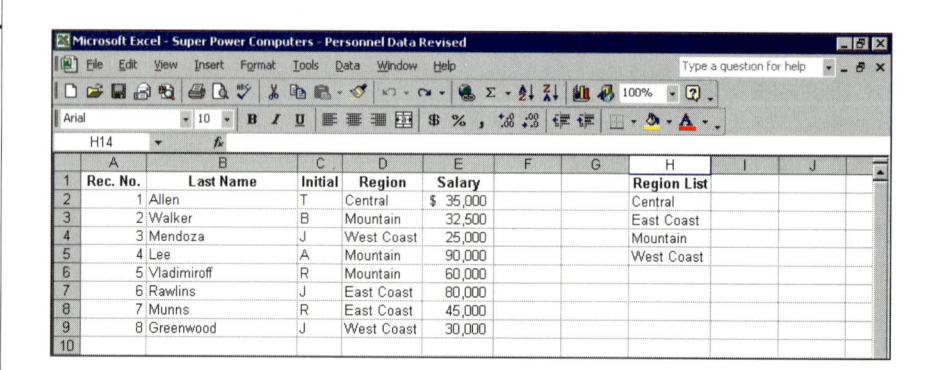

| Step 2 | Save | the workbook |

8.c Using the Data Form

An alternate method of entering data in a list is to use a data form. A data form simplifies data entry by allowing the user to enter each field of a record using a simple dialog box, rather than the worksheet itself. You also can use the data form to edit and locate specific records in a list.

Entering Data in a List Using the Data Form

You need to add another record to the list. This time, you try the data form. To use a data form to enter a new record:

Step 1	Activate	any cell that is part of the list, including the header row
Step 2	Click	Data
Step 3	Click	Form

> **QUICK TIP**
>
> To find out more about data validation options, key "data validation" in the Ask A Question Box.

The Form dialog box opens, with the worksheet tab name as the title of the dialog box. Your dialog box should look similar to Figure 8-8. You use the scroll bar or the Find Prev and Find Next buttons to scroll through records.

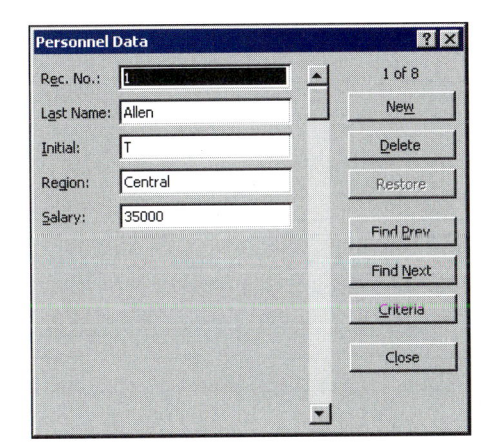

FIGURE 8-8
Form Dialog Box

Step 4	Click	New
Step 5	Key	9 in the Rec. No.: text box
Step 6	Press	the TAB key
Step 7	Key	Tate in the Last Name: text box

Step 8	Press	the TAB key
Step 9	Key	J in the Initial: text box
Step 10	Press	the TAB key
Step 11	Key	Central in the Region: text box
Step 12	Press	the TAB key
Step 13	Enter	65000 in the Salary: text box
Step 14	Press	the ENTER key

The record is added to the bottom of your list, and a new record is started in the Form dialog box. You can enter a new record at this point or close the Form dialog box.

| Step 15 | Click | Close |

Finding Specific Records Using the Data Form

The data form allows you to readily locate specific records in a list. Many lists grow to include hundreds, or even thousands, of records. Scrolling through a list of this length to find a certain record would be very time-consuming. You want to review records of employees whose annual salaries are $40,000 or more. Using the data form, you can set criteria for the records you want to see. To search for specific records:

Step 1	Open	the Form dialog box
Step 2	Click	Criteria
Step 3	Click	in the Salary: text box
Step 4	Key	>40000
Step 5	Click	Find Next

The first record meeting the criteria appears in the Form dialog box.

| Step 6 | Click | Find Next five more times |

The computer indicates that no more records meet your criteria by making a sound. When you have finished searching for records that

---

CAUTION TIP

One drawback to using the Form dialog box is that data validation criteria are not active with this method of data entry. In other words, you do not see input messages or error alert messages, and the list option is not available.

QUICK TIP

You can use the Find Prev button to step back through the records meeting the specified criteria.

meet your criteria, you can clear the criteria. To clear the criteria and view all records again:

Step 1	Click	Criteria
Step 2	Click	Clear
Step 3	Click	Form to return to the Form dialog box

Deleting a Record from a List Using the Data Form

Occasionally, you will need to remove records from a list. To delete a record by using the data form:

Step 1	Scroll	to locate the record for J. Rawlins (record number 6)
Step 2	Click	Delete

A confirmation dialog box opens, indicating that the record will be permanently deleted.

Step 3	Click	OK to remove the record from the list
Step 4	Click	Close
Step 5	Save	the workbook

8.d Creating Custom Filters

When you used the Find command in the data form, you filtered the records displayed in the Form dialog box. Alternately, you can filter records in the worksheet. You already know how to filter for one criterion in a field by using the AutoFilter command. You also can create custom filters (also known as advanced filters) to apply conditional operators (AND and OR) and logical operators (greater than, equal to, and less than).

Using AutoFilter to Create a Custom Filter

When you apply AutoFilter to a list, one of the selections on the filter list is (Custom…). When you select this option, the Custom dialog box opens, allowing you to specify criteria for a custom filter. You need to

> **MOUSE TIP**
>
> You can delete a record by deleting the row in the worksheet or the cells containing the data. Right-click the row number, then click Delete; alternately, select all cells in the record, right-click the selection, click Delete, then choose the appropriate option.

compile a list of the employees in Super Power Computers' Mountain region who make $50,000 or less per year. To apply an AutoFilter:

Step 1	*Activate*	any cell in the list
Step 2	*Click*	Data
Step 3	*Point to*	Filter
Step 4	*Click*	AutoFilter
Step 5	*Click*	the Filter list arrow in the Region field
Step 6	*Click*	Mountain
Step 7	*Click*	the Filter list arrow in the Salary field
Step 8	*Click*	(Custom…)

The Custom AutoFilter dialog box on your screen should look similar to Figure 8-9.

FIGURE 8-9
Custom AutoFilter Dialog Box

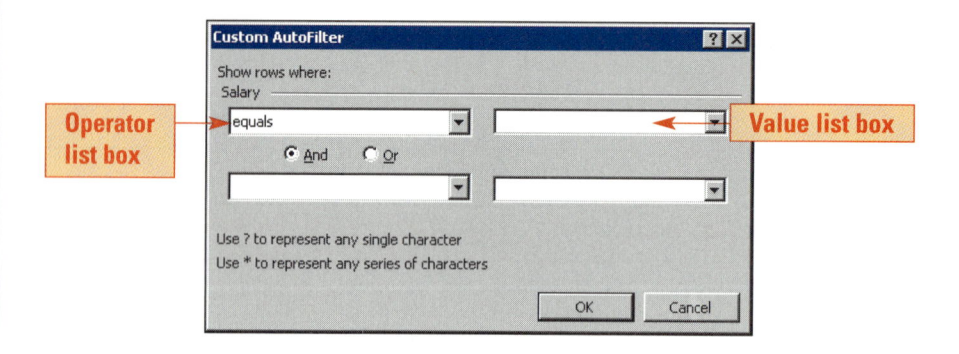

Step 9	*Click*	the operator list arrow on the left side of the dialog box
Step 10	*Click*	is less than or equal to
Step 11	*Key*	50000 in the box on the right side of the dialog box
Step 12	*Click*	OK

The list is filtered. Your screen should look similar to Figure 8-10.

FIGURE 8-10
Filtered List

Creating, Sorting, and Filtering Lists **EA 39**

You can use wildcards in your custom filters. A **wildcard** is used in place of other characters. Suppose you want to filter a list for all last names starting with R. You could enter R* in the Custom AutoFilter dialog box, where the asterisk (*) represents any characters after the R. The question mark (?) can be used in place of a single character. If you used the filter r?n on a list of words, for example, you would see *ran*, *ron*, and *run*. You need to clear the previous filter first unless you want to filter only the records showing from the previous filter. To apply a wildcard filter:

Step 1	Click	Data
Step 2	Point to	Filter
Step 3	Click	Show all
Step 4	Click	the Last Name filter arrow
Step 5	Click	(Custom…)
Step 6	Verify	that equals is selected in the operator list on the left
Step 7	Enter	m* in the value box on the right
Step 8	Click	OK

The list is filtered to show all last names beginning with M.

| Step 9 | Turn off | AutoFilter |
| Step 10 | Save | the workbook |

Creating Custom Filters with Multiple Operators

Another way to filter records is to use advanced filters. Advanced filters allow you to work with multiple AND and OR operators in each field to filter a list. These types of filters are more difficult to set up than AutoFilters, however. To take advantage of advanced filters, you must establish a criteria range in the worksheet. The column labels in the criteria range must match the column labels of your list. Rows beneath the column labels in the criteria range indicate the filter criteria. You should follow these guidelines when using advanced filtering:

- Place the criteria range above or below the rows containing your list data. Do not set up the range in the same rows as the list, because filtered rows remain hidden from view.

chapter eight

- The first row of the criteria range identifies the columns to be filtered. Although its formatting does not have to match that of the column labels in the list you are filtering, the spelling must match exactly.
- Adding multiple criteria in the same row creates an AND condition. For example, to list employees who have an annual salary greater than $40,000 AND who work in the Central division, you would enter ">40000" under the column heading Salary and "Central" under the column label Division; both entries would appear in the same row.
- Entering criteria in subsequent rows specifies an OR condition. For example, if you wanted to find all employees who made more than $40,000 OR less than $30,000 per year, you would enter ">40000" in one row under the Salary column label and "<30000" in the next row under the column label. Each time you add another row to the criteria, you specify another OR condition.

To create a criteria range:

Step 1	Insert	six blank rows above row 1
Step 2	Enter	Last Name in cell D1
Step 3	Enter	Salary in cell E1

The criteria range appears above your list. Next, enter the criteria you want to use in the filter. To add criteria to a criteria range:

| Step 1 | Enter | a* in cell D2 |

This sets up a filter that displays records starting with the letter "A" in the Last Name field.

| Step 2 | Enter | m* in cell D3 |
| Step 3 | Enter | >40000 in cell E3 |

This multiple-column condition displays records that start with the letter "M" in the Last Name field AND have a salary greater than $40,000.

| Step 4 | Enter | g* in cell D4 |

Creating, Sorting, and Filtering Lists — EA 41

This complex filter displays records for all employees whose last name starts with A or G, as well as records for any employee whose last name starts with M and whose salary is more than $40,000. To apply the advanced filter:

Step 1	Click	cell A8

You must select a cell within the list that you want to filter. Excel automatically searches for the header row.

Step 2	Click	Data
Step 3	Point to	Filter
Step 4	Click	Advanced Filter

The Advanced Filter dialog box on your screen should look similar to Figure 8-11. You can select the list range and criteria range and specify whether you want to create a copy of the filtered records or filter the list in place. The default is to filter the list in place. The list range is selected automatically.

QUICK TIP

You can use named ranges as references in the Advanced Filter dialog box.

FIGURE 8-11
Advanced Filter Dialog Box

Step 5	Click	in the Criteria range: text box
Step 6	Key	D1:E4
Step 7	Click	OK

The filtered list displays only records that meet the criteria specified in the criteria range D1:E4. Your screen should look similar to Figure 8-12.

chapter eight

FIGURE 8-12
Filtered List

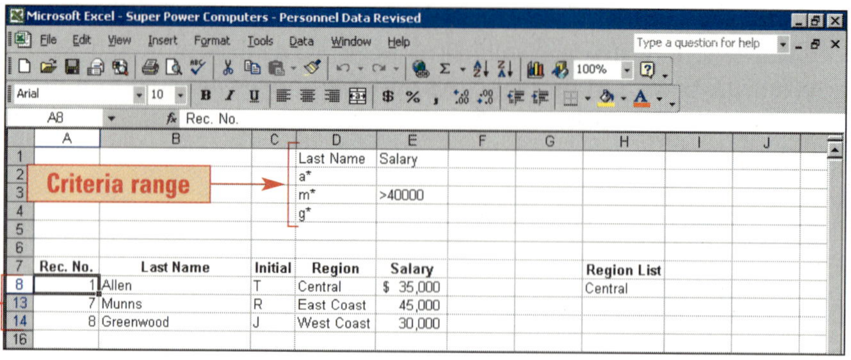

[Screenshot of Excel worksheet showing Criteria range with Last Name (a*, m*, g*) and Salary (>40000), and Filtered records showing Allen/Central/$35,000, Munns/East Coast/45,000, Greenwood/West Coast/30,000, with Region List showing Central]

| Step 8 | *Clear* | the filter |

Extracting Data

When you use the advanced filter copy option, you leave the original list of data unfiltered and **extract** the records meeting your filter criteria, which are copied to a new location. You want to extract a list of all employees who make more than $35,000 per year. To extract data:

Step 1	*Delete*	the contents of cells D2:E4
Step 2	*Enter*	>35000 in cell E2
Step 3	*Click*	any cell in the list
Step 4	*Open*	the Advanced Filter dialog box
Step 5	*Select*	all the text in the Criteria range: text box
Step 6	*Key*	D1:E2
Step 7	*Click*	the Copy to another location option button
Step 8	*Click*	in the Copy to: text box
Step 9	*Click*	cell I1 in the worksheet

Note that you can copy filtered data only to the active worksheet. Once you have extracted the records, you can move or copy them to wherever you like.

Step 10	*Click*	OK
Step 11	*Scroll*	the worksheet to view the extracted data
Step 12	*Increase*	the width of columns J and L to show the data

QUICK TIP

To learn about other advanced filtering techniques, use online Help to search for information about advanced filters and examples of advanced filter criteria.

The filtered records, including the column headings, are copied to the new location, starting in cell I1. Your screen should look similar to Figure 8-13.

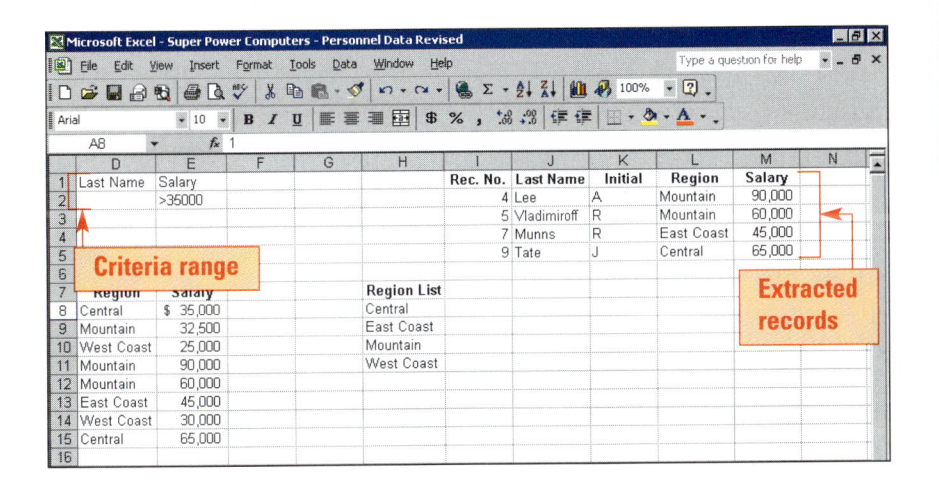

FIGURE 8-13
Extracted Records

> **QUICK TIP**
>
> It may take you some time to become comfortable with working with data lists and filters, but these features represent powerful tools for storing and retrieving data.

Step 13	Save	and close the workbook

8.e Performing Single and Multilevel Sorts

The *Super Power Computers - Sales Rep Data* workbook contains gross sales data for each salesperson. Before you can create a meaningful report, the data needs to be sorted. First open the workbook containing the data. To open the workbook:

Step 1	Open	the *Super Power Computers - Sales Rep Data* workbook on the Data Disk
Step 2	Save	the workbook as *Super Power Computers - Sales Rep Data Revised*

Column A contains the column label Region. This column label acts as your sort **criteria**, indicating the type of data you want to sort by. If you place the active cell in this column, Excel will know which column to sort. To sort the sales representative data:

Step 1	Activate	cell A4
Step 2	Click	the Sort Ascending button on the Standard toolbar

QUICK TIP

To sort on four to six columns, first sort on the columns of least importance. Then, using the sorted data, sort on the other three columns.

The column is sorted in ascending order (alphabetically) by region. When Excel works with lists, it assumes that the top row of the list contains the column labels and does not sort that row. Using the Sort dialog box, you can sort by as many as three criteria. To sort on multiple columns:

Step 1	*Click*	Data
Step 2	*Click*	Sort

Your Sort dialog box should look similar to Figure 8-14. When you open the Sort dialog box, Excel scans for the header row of the active list and adds the column headings to the criteria list boxes. It also assumes that the first sort criterion is the column containing the active cell.

FIGURE 8-14
Sort Dialog Box

Step 3	*Verify*	that Region is selected in the Sort by list box
Step 4	*Click*	the Then by list arrow in the middle of the dialog box
Step 5	*Click*	Gross Sales in the list
Step 6	*Click*	the Descending option button next to Gross Sales
Step 7	*Click*	OK

The list is sorted alphabetically by region, then from highest to lowest by gross sales within each region.

8.f Using Grouping and Outlines to Create Subtotals

Outlines offer a powerful option for viewing data in a worksheet. An **outline** shows data in hierarchies, or levels, up to eight levels.

An easy way to create outlines is to use the Subtotals command. When you create subtotals, you specify at what points subtotals should be calculated. Excel automatically inserts the SUBTOTAL function at the specified points, then creates a grand total at the end. The information appearing above each subtotal is called **detail data**. Applying the Subtotals command automatically creates an outline, and a set of outline symbols appears on the left of the worksheet, providing the controls to display or hide detail data.

You can calculate the subtotals for each region as well as obtain totals for the company as a whole. To create a subtotal outline:

Step 1	Verify	that cell A4 is selected
Step 2	Click	Data
Step 3	Click	Su<u>b</u>totals

The Subtotal dialog box on your screen should look similar to Figure 8-15. Region—the first column in the data set—is automatically selected in the At each change in: list. The Region column is sorted alphabetically. Whenever a new value appears in the Region column, a subtotal will be calculated. In the Add subtotal to: list, Gross Sales—the last column in the data set—is selected.

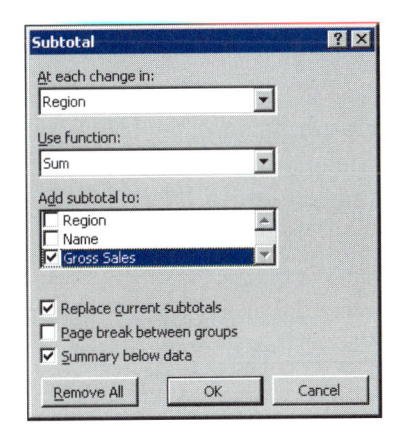

QUICK TIP

You can create an outline by clicking the Data menu, pointing to Group and Outline, then clicking Auto Outline. Use Group and Ungroup to create single levels of data. Your worksheet must be set up properly for this function to work. See online Help for more information about creating an outline manually.

CAUTION TIP

Leaving the Replace current subtotals check box *checked* will replace your current outline with a new one. If you want to add another level of detail to an existing outline, you must remove the check mark.

FIGURE 8-15
Subtotal Dialog Box

chapter eight

Step 4	Click	OK
Step 5	Scroll	the worksheet to view row 71

New rows are inserted at each change in the Region column, and Excel calculates a subtotal for each region. Outline symbols showing a two-level outline appear on the left. At the bottom of the list, a grand total is calculated. Your screen should look similar to Figure 8-16.

FIGURE 8-16
Outline Created Using the Subtotals Command

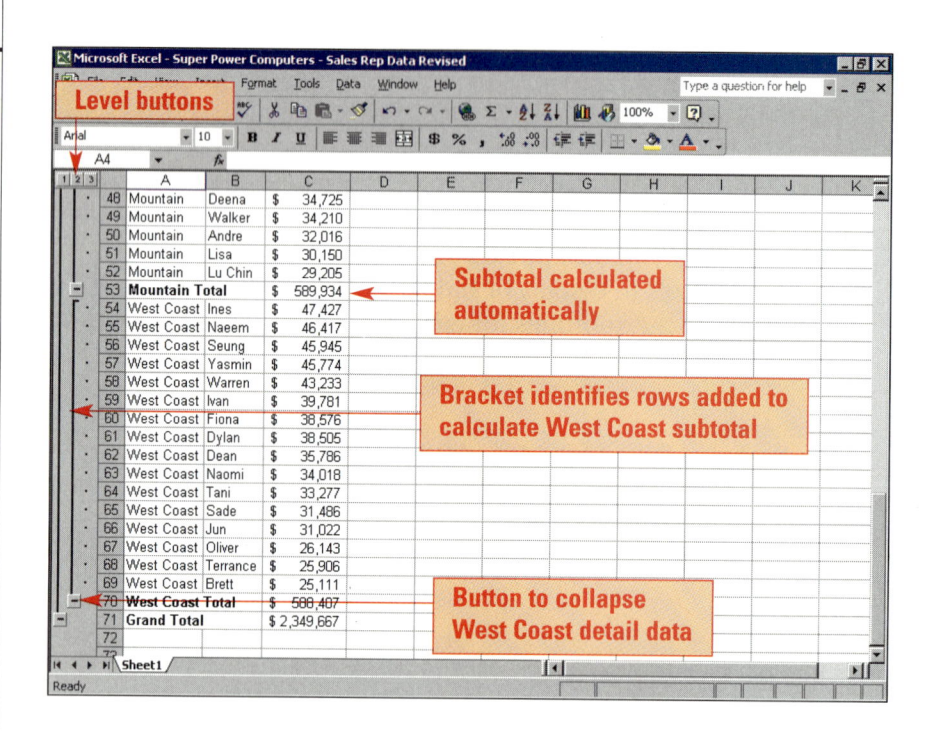

You can hide detail data by collapsing the outline. To collapse outline levels:

Step 1	Click	the Collapse Level button ▬ to the left of row 70

The detail data for the West Coast Region becomes hidden, and only the subtotal for that category appears. The Collapse Level button changes to an Expand Level button.

> **QUICK TIP**
>
> To remove the subtotals and the outline, open the Subtotal dialog box, then click the Remove All button.

Step 2	Click	the 2 Level button ② at the top of the outline to display only subtotals for each region
Step 3	Scroll	to the top of the worksheet to view all of the subtotals
Step 4	Save	the workbook and close it

Summary

▶ You can identify the main components of a list, including field, field name, header row, and record.

▶ Data validation criteria ensure that users enter the proper data in each field of a record.

▶ You can use the data form to add, modify, locate, and delete records.

▶ Custom filters allow you to build complex filters using AND and OR operators.

▶ You can extract records from a list to move or copy them to another location.

▶ You can sort data by using as many as three levels of sort criteria.

▶ You can use subtotals to create outlines automatically. You can add as many as eight levels of subtotals. Select outline symbols to hide or reveal detail.

Commands Review

Action	Menu Bar	Shortcut Menu	Toolbar	Task Pane	Keyboard
Set data validation	Data, Validation				ALT + D, L
Use a data form to enter records	Data, Form				ALT + D, O
Apply an AutoFilter	Data, Filter, AutoFilter				ALT + D, F, F
Apply an advanced filter	Data, Filter, Advanced Filter				ALT + D, F, A
Show all records	Data, Filter, Show All				ALT + D, F, S
Sort data	Data, Sort		A↓Z Z↓A		ALT + D, S
Use subtotals	Data, Subtotals				ALT + D, B
Expand an outline level	Data, Group, Show detail		1 2 3 +		ALT + D, G, S
Collapse an outline level	Data, Group, Hide detail		1 2 3 −		ALT + D, G, H

chapter eight

Concepts Review

Circle the correct answer.

1. **A field name:**
   - [a] is a collection of characters or numbers that make up one part of a record.
   - [b] is the collection of fields that make a complete entry.
   - [c] identifies the contents of each column.
   - [d] can appear anywhere on the worksheet.

2. **A record:**
   - [a] is a collection of characters or numbers that make up one part of a record.
   - [b] is the collection of fields that make a complete entry.
   - [c] identifies the contents of each column.
   - [d] can appear anywhere on the worksheet.

3. **Why should you leave one column and one row blank on all sides of a list?**
   - [a] This approach makes it easier to return the list to its original sort order.
   - [b] Excel can detect list boundaries more easily.
   - [c] You should not leave blank rows or columns, because spaces affect the sort order of a list.
   - [d] It does not matter, as long as you format each field in the same way.

4. **Data validation is used to:**
   - [a] sort fields using criteria you define.
   - [b] restrict the data that can be entered in each field.
   - [c] search for records containing certain characters.
   - [d] make a copy of filtered records in another location.

5. **A data form can be used to:**
   - [a] add records to a list.
   - [b] locate records meeting specific criteria in a list.
   - [c] delete records from a list.
   - [d] all of the above

6. **Multiple criteria in the same row in an advanced filter criteria range indicate:**
   - [a] an AND condition.
   - [b] an OR condition.
   - [c] a wildcard character.
   - [d] the inclusion of additional fields in the result.

7. **Criteria in additional rows beneath a criteria column heading indicate:**
   - [a] an AND condition.
   - [b] an OR condition.
   - [c] a wildcard character.
   - [d] the inclusion of additional records in the result.

8. **Extracted data refers to records:**
   - [a] meeting filter criteria that are moved from the list.
   - [b] meeting filter criteria that are copied from the list.
   - [c] not meeting filter criteria.
   - [d] that are randomly removed from the database.

9. **You can create outlines with as many as:**
   - [a] five levels of detail.
   - [b] six levels of detail.
   - [c] seven levels of detail.
   - [d] eight levels of detail.

10. **One drawback of a data form is that:**
    - [a] you cannot delete records from a list.
    - [b] the data validation criteria are not active.
    - [c] you cannot move from record to record.
    - [d] you cannot edit records once they are entered.

Circle **T** if the statement is true or **F** if the statement is false.

T F 1. Column headings for advanced filter criteria must be spelled exactly like the column headings in the list you are filtering.

T F 2. "Part No." would be a likely field name in a warehouse database.

T F 3. The terms "record" and "field" refer to the same thing.

T F 4. Clicking one of the Sort buttons performs a sort based on the column of the active cell.

T F 5. Spaces at the beginning of a field entry affect the sort order of a list.

T F 6. You cannot specify AND or OR conditions using AutoFilters.

T F 7. The header row can be placed anywhere in a list, as long as it is formatted differently from the rest of the list.

T F 8. Filters allow you to work with a subset of records in a list.

T F 9. When you apply a filter to a list, you hide all other records that don't meet the criteria.

T F 10. A wildcard is used in place of other characters.

Skills Review

Exercise 1

1. Create a new workbook.

2. Use the following field names to create a product list for use in the warehouse: "Part No."; "Description"; "Manufacturer"; "Cost"; "Quantity"; and "Value."

3. Select 15 rows per column. Use data validation to set the rules in the table below, using the following instructions:

   a. Do not allow blank entries for any fields.

   b. The valid manufacturer names are: Price Mfg., Sunrise Products Inc., Watershed Mfg., and Irontown Mfg.

   c. Use a formula in the Value column to calculate the value of stock on hand by multiplying the quantity of each item times the cost.

Field Name	Validation Characteristic	Input Message	Error Alert Type
Part No.	Whole number between 1,000 and 4,999	Yes	Stop
Description	Text limited to 20 characters	Yes	Information
Manufacturer	Use list of four manufacturer names (see Step b)	Yes	Stop
Cost	Decimal number limited to less than $100.00	Yes	Information
Quantity	Whole number limited to less than 1,000	Yes	Stop

4. Review your list setup to make sure that it fits the list guidelines discussed in this chapter.

5. Save the workbook as *Warehouse Parts*, and then print and close it.

chapter eight

Exercise 2

1. Open the *Warehouse Parts* workbook that you created in Exercise 1, change the data validation for the Description column to a maximum of 30 characters.
2. Enter the data shown in the table below. Calculate the Value column by using a formula.

Part No.	Description	Manufacturer	Cost	Quantity	Value
1010	Sugar, 50 lb	Price Mfg.	19.95	333	(use a formula)
1020	Sugar, 125 lb	Price Mfg.	39.95	693	(use a formula)
1030	Molasses	Watershed Mfg.	45.95	282	(use a formula)
2100	Sprinkles, 1,000 gross	Sunrise Products Inc.	70.95	314	(use a formula)
2200	Rainbow Sprinkles, 10 gross	Watershed Mfg.	6.95	838	(use a formula)
3001	Flour, 25 lb	Irontown Mfg.	12.95	940	(use a formula)
3002	Flour, 5 lb	Irontown Mfg.	5.95	412	(use a formula)
3003	Wheat flour, 150 lb	Price Mfg.	99.95	758	(use a formula)
4020	Honey, 30 gallons	Sunrise Products Inc.	89.95	687	(use a formula)
4030	Honey, 2 gallons	Sunrise Products Inc.	6.95	769	(use a formula)
4040	Honey, 1 quart	Watershed Mfg.	1.95	930	(use a formula)

3. Resize columns to fit, as necessary.
4. Format columns D and F using the Accounting format, two decimal places.
5. Save the workbook as *Warehouse Parts Inventory*, and then print and close it.

Exercise 3

1. Open the *Warehouse Parts Inventory* workbook that you created in Exercise 2.
2. Use a data form to edit part number 3002. Change the description to Wheat Flour, 7 lb.
3. Use a data form to delete part number 4040.
4. Use a data form to add a new record using the information in the following table.

Part No.	Description	Manufacturer	Cost	Quantity
4041	Honey, 25 gallons	Price Mfg.	35.95	750

5. Apply AutoFilters to the list.
6. Using the AutoFilter list arrows, filter the list to find all items manufactured by Price Mfg.
7. Print the filtered list, save the workbook as *Warehouse Parts Inventory Filter 1*, and then close it.

Exercise 4

1. Open the *Warehouse Parts Inventory Filter 1* workbook that you created in Exercise 3.
2. Clear any active filters. Create an advanced filter criteria that will find any records with a quantity of more than 500 items, or any item that costs less than $30.00 (be sure you don't create an "AND" condition).
3. Filter the list with the criteria you set in Step 2.

4. Sort the list in ascending order by Quantity.

5. Print the list, save the workbook as *Warehouse Parts Inventory Filter 2*, and then close it.

Exercise 5

1. Open the *Sweet Tooth Sales to Stores* workbook located on the Data Disk.

2. Apply AutoFilters to the list.

3. Filter the list to show only items sold in quantities greater than 200.

4. Save the workbook as *Sweet Tooth Sales to Stores Filter1*, and then print and close it.

Exercise 6

1. Open the *Sweet Tooth Sales to Stores Filter1* workbook that you created in Exercise 5.

2. Remove the filter you created in Exercise 5, then create a new advanced filter to find records of employees whose Total Sales were less than $500 or more than $2000.

3. Filter the list using the filter you created in the previous step.

4. Print the filtered list, save the workbook as *Sweet Tooth Sales to Stores Filter 2*, and then close it.

Exercise 7

1. Open the *Sweet Tooth Sales to Stores Filter 2* workbook that you created in Exercise 6.

2. Display all records.

3. Click any cell in the data list, then use a data form to add the following record to the list:

| East Coast | New York | Jungle Planet | 124 | 240 | 6.95 | Kaili Muafala |

4. Save the workbook as *Sweet Tooth Sales Data 2*, and then print and close it.

Exercise 8

1. Open the *Employee Time* workbook located on the Data Disk.

2. Sort the data by Project (ascending order), and then by Hours (descending order).

3. Create an outline of the data by creating subtotals for each Project.

4. Collapse the outline to level 2.

5. Change the title in cell A1 to Time by Project.

6. Save the workbook as *Project Time Subtotals*, and then print and close it.

Case Projects

Project 1

You have just been promoted to programming director at the radio station where you work. The station manager wants to completely reorganize the way in which the station keeps track of which songs are played. Prepare a workbook that can sort songs by the number of times played in a week, duration, artist, and musical classification. Be sure to format the cells so that they display the correct units. Add the titles of at least 10 songs, and create fictitious data for the number of times played and duration. Save the workbook as *Record Tracker*, and then print and close it.

chapter eight

Project 2

As the personnel director for a small retail sales company, you are in charge of tracking personnel information. Create a list of 15 employees. Include a unique record number for each employee, starting at 1. Each record should include a record number, last name, first initial, hire date (within the last five years), date of last pay increase, current salary, and department (use at least three departments). Use appropriate data validation for each field. Prepare and print a series of sorted reports showing employees sorted by record number, alphabetically by last name, by hire date, by department (alphabetically by last name within each department), and by current salary. Use subtotals to prepare a pie chart showing salary percentages by department. Print the chart. Save the workbook as *Personnel Information*, and then close it.

Project 3

Use the Ask A Question Box to find out how to locate cells that have data validation rules applied. Write a step-by-step summary of this process. Save the document as *Find Data Validation Cells.doc*, and then print and close it.

Project 4

You are a serious baseball card collector. Create a worksheet to organize your card collection by player, card manufacturer, or value. Connect to the Internet and search for Web sites devoted to baseball card collectors. Create a workbook containing the names, card manufacturers, card years, and values for 20 cards. Include at least three different cards for three of the players. Organize the data so that it can be sorted by player name, card manufacturer, year, or value. Filter the data to display only those cards with a worth greater than or equal to $100 and manufactured by Topps or Upper Deck. Save the workbook as *Baseball Card Collection*, and then print and close it.

Project 5

Programmers sometimes add "Easter Eggs" to a program: If a user follows a certain sequence of commands, they might see a special message containing the names of the programmers or something else fun. Connect to the Internet and search the Web for Excel Easter Eggs. See if any of them work with Excel 2002. You also could try searching for Easter Eggs in other programs you use. Print at least one page explaining how to display an Easter Egg.

Project 6

You are the data manager at a shipping company. Create a workbook to track shipping dates, company names, addresses, and four-digit item numbers. Use a data form to add five records to the list. Print the list, save the workbook as *Shipping*, and then close it.

Project 7

Your marketing firm is preparing a commercial that it would like to release in the 10 largest cities in the United States. Connect to the Internet and search the Web for a list of populations of cities in the United States. Create a new workbook, and set up field names for each city, its state, and its population. Apply data validation to each column. Limit the data in the city field to a text length of 15 characters and the state field to a text length of 2 characters. Limit the population field to a whole number greater than 1,000,000 with a Warning message if a number less than this is entered. Enter the data for the 10 largest cities you can find. Save the workbook as *Population*, and then print and close it.

Project 8

You work at a telemarketing company. Create a list to log the date, time, and duration of each call. Use data validation to restrict the data entry for each cell to the appropriate type of data (limit call length to less than 60 minutes). Enter fictitious data for five calls. Save the workbook as *Phone Log*, and then print and close it.

Excel 2002

Increasing Productivity with Macros, Templates, and Custom Toolbars and Menus

Chapter Overview

Many tasks you perform in Excel, such as common formatting tasks, are very repetitive. Macros can record these steps then replay them much more rapidly than you can perform them, and as often as you like. In this chapter, you learn to record, edit, and run macros. Another time-saving strategy is to create and use templates, special workbooks with formatting and formulas already in place. You learn to create, edit, and use templates to become more productive.

Case profile

Every time you create a new worksheet for Super Power Computers, you spend precious time keying worksheet and column titles, adding formulas, and formatting the worksheet titles same way you do all the other worksheet titles. By using macros to automate repetitive tasks, you can save a lot of time. Saving a formatted workbook as a template also increases your productivity. To work even more efficiently, you can customize the menus and the toolbars.

Learning Objectives

- Use macros to automate repetitive tasks
- Edit a macro
- Use workbooks containing macros
- Create and edit templates
- Customize toolbars and menus

chapter nine

9.a Using Macros to Automate Repetitive Tasks

A **macro** is a group of instructions that automatically executes a set of commands. By using macros, you can automate repetitive tasks. For example, you usually format Super Power Computers' worksheet titles with the Impact font, 16-point size, blue color, and centered across several cells. The task described is a perfect candidate for a simple macro: repetitive, specific commands that you use over and over again. Other good candidates for macros include tasks such as adding headers and footers to a print report, creating charts, sorting lists, and setting up worksheets.

Macros are written or recorded in a programming language called Visual Basic, which is used in all of the Office applications. Visual Basic is fairly easy to learn. If you learn its basics, you can create macros that work in Word, Access, PowerPoint, or Excel.

Now, take a deep breath. Yes, we said "programming." And yes, you're going to do it. Keep a few things in mind: (1) programming is not just for geeks anymore, and (2) by learning how to do a little bit of programming (deep breath), you can actually lighten your workload and free yourself to do other things.

Recording a Macro

The simplest way to create a macro is to record it. When you record a macro, Excel takes note of every command you use and every keystroke you press. To start recording a macro:

Step 1	Create	a new, blank workbook
Step 2	Save	the workbook as *Super Power Computers - Title Macro*
Step 3	Click	Tools
Step 4	Point to	Macro
Step 5	Click	Record New Macro

The Record Macro dialog box opens. Macro names cannot contain spaces, so use the underscore (_) character instead. You can choose to store a macro in the workbook in which you created it or in a global workbook called the Personal Macro Workbook. Macros stored in a workbook are only available when that workbook is open. Macros stored in the Personal Macro Workbook are available whenever you are working in Excel. You store the SPC_Title macro in the open workbook.

QUICK TIP

The Personal Macro Workbook is a hidden workbook that opens automatically each time Excel opens. This makes the macros contained in the Personal Macro Workbook, called "global macros," available for use with any open workbook. An example of a global macro is a print macro.

If you work on a shared computer or network, consider storing macros in the workbook in which you created them to ensure that others don't accidentally modify or delete your macros. You can copy macros from one workbook to another.

Step 6	*Key*	SPC_Title in the Macro name: text box
Step 7	*Verify*	that This Workbook is selected in the Store macro in: list box
Step 8	*Drag*	to select all of the text in the Description: text box
Step 9	*Key*	Create and format a worksheet title

Your dialog box should look similar to Figure 9-1.

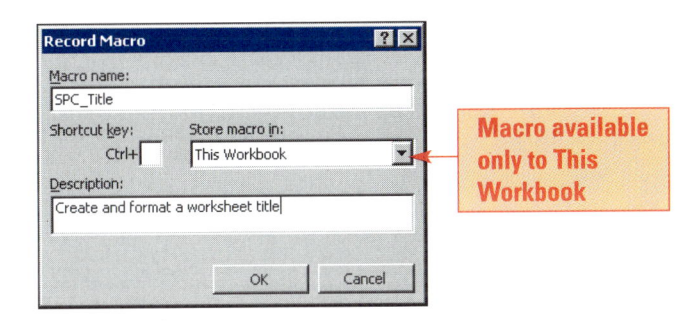

QUICK TIP

When creating macros, a very helpful technique is to write down or practice each step in the task you want to automate. When you are sure that you have written down all of the steps involved, begin recording your macro.

FIGURE 9-1
Record Macro Dialog Box

Step 10	*Click*	OK

The Stop Recording toolbar appears, and Recording appears in the status bar. Your screen should look similar to Figure 9-2.

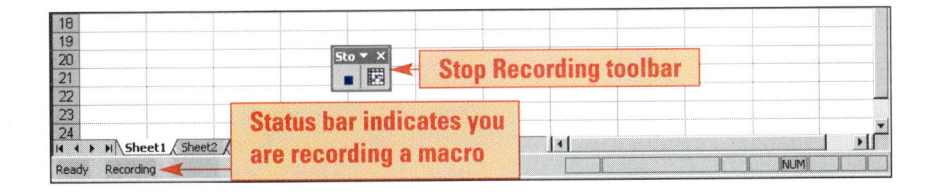

FIGURE 9-2
Stop Recording Toolbar

Next, you enter and format the titles you want on your worksheet. To enter the titles:

Step 1	*Enter*	Super Power Computers in cell A1
Step 2	*Enter*	<Add a subtitle in cell A2> in cell A2 (include the brackets)
Step 3	*Select*	the range A1:F1
Step 4	*Click*	the Merge and Center button on the Formatting toolbar
Step 5	*Repeat*	Steps 3 and 4 with the range A2:F2
Step 6	*Select*	the range A1:A2

chapter nine

Step 7	Open	the Font tab in the Format Cells dialog box
Step 8	Click	Impact in the Font: list
Step 9	Click	16 in the Size: list
Step 10	Click	the Blue box in the Color: palette
Step 11	Click	OK
Step 12	Activate	cell A1
Step 13	Click	the Stop Recording button ■ on the Stop Recording toolbar

The macro is saved as part of the workbook, and the Stop Recording toolbar closes.

Running a Macro

You must run the macro to test it. You can use the Macro dialog box to run macros stored in any currently open workbook or macros stored in your Personal Macro Workbook. To run the macro:

Step 1	Click	the Sheet2 sheet tab
Step 2	Click	Tools
Step 3	Point to	Macro
Step 4	Click	Macros to open the Macro dialog box
Step 5	Click	SPC_Title in the available macros list

The description you keyed when you recorded the macro appears at the bottom of the dialog box. Your Macro dialog box should look similar to Figure 9-3.

FIGURE 9-3
Macro Dialog Box

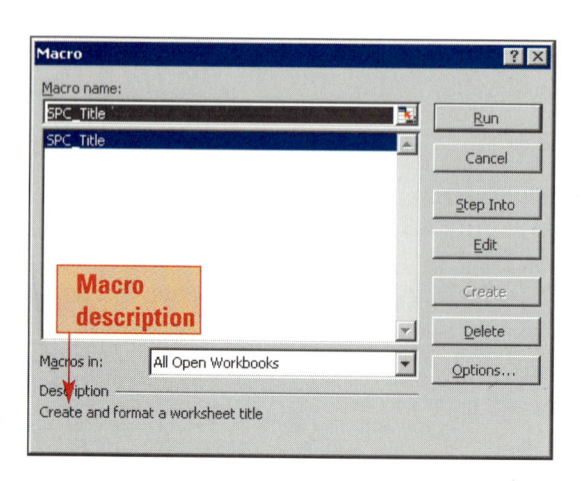

Increasing Productivity with Macros, Templates, and Custom Toolbars and Menus **EA 57**

Step 6	Click	Run

The macro performs the steps that you recorded earlier. Your screen should look similar to Figure 9-4.

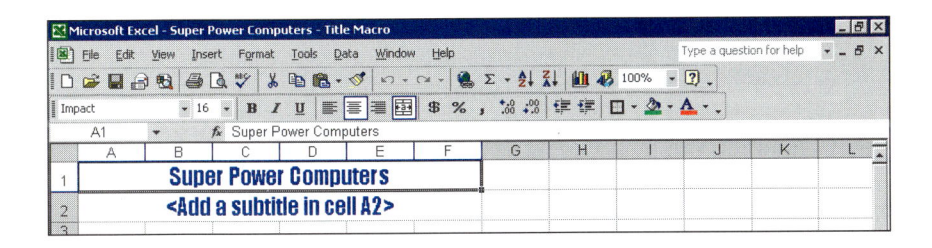

FIGURE 9-4
SPC_Title Macro Results

9.b Editing a Macro

Using the Visual Basic Editor, you can edit macros that you've previously recorded or written. The Visual Basic Editor is a separate program that runs in its own window, outside of Excel, and provides toolbars and menus specifically intended for working with Visual Basic programming code. To edit the SPC_Title macro:

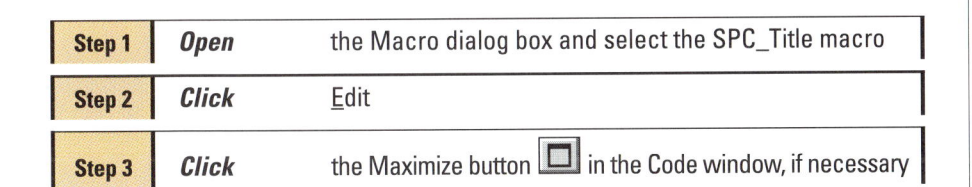

Step 1	Open	the Macro dialog box and select the SPC_Title macro
Step 2	Click	Edit
Step 3	Click	the Maximize button in the Code window, if necessary

Your screen should look similar to Figure 9-5. The selected macro is open in the right side of the Visual Basic Editor. The Visual Basic Editor program button appears in the taskbar.

On the left side of the Visual Basic Editor window, the Project Explorer window displays a hierarchical list of all open projects and each of the items associated with each particular project. A **project** includes objects in the workbook, such as the worksheets, **modules** (where macro code is stored), and **forms** (custom dialog boxes). Projects also can contain other items, such as ActiveX controls, class modules, and references to other projects.

The Properties window, located beneath the Project Explorer window, is used to modify the properties for selected objects. For example, the code module has a (Name) property that you can change. Other types of objects, such as buttons or controls used on forms (dialog boxes), have many additional properties. The Code window to the right contains the macro code for the SPC_Title macro.

QUICK TIP

You can write new macros, test, debug, and delete macros from the Visual Basic Editor.

If you want additional information about recording macros and items that can be included in projects, use Microsoft Visual Basic Help in the Visual Basic Editor.

chapter nine

FIGURE 9-5
Visual Basic Editor

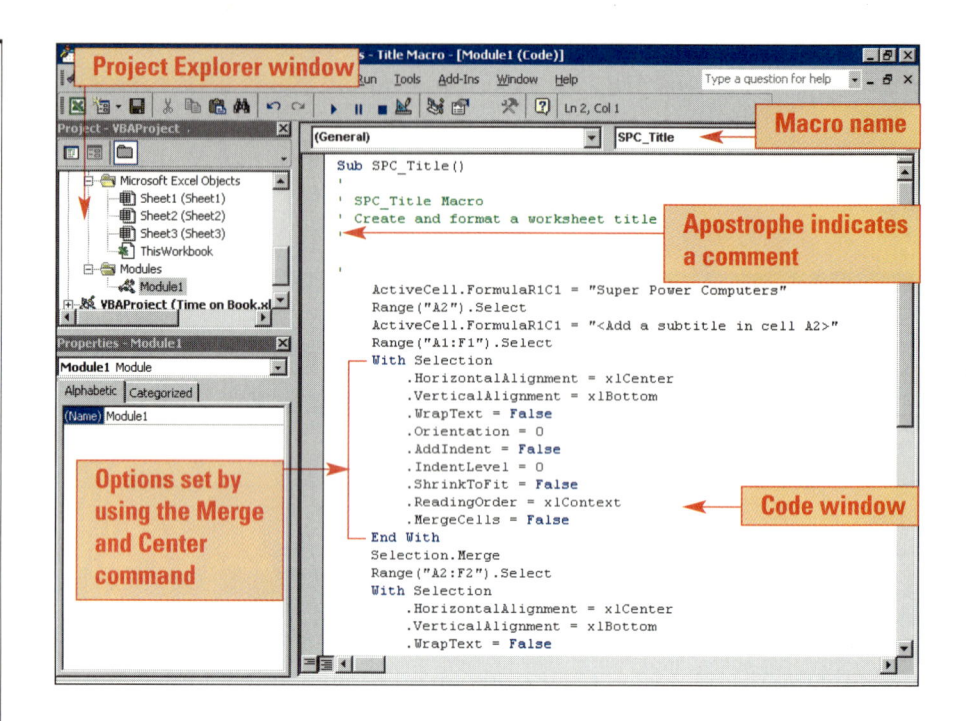

Callouts on figure: Project Explorer window; Macro name; Apostrophe indicates a comment; Code window; Options set by using the Merge and Center command

| Step 4 | **Scroll** | the Code window to review the code |

Table 9-1 describes different sections of the code.

TABLE 9-1
Macro Code Description

Macro Line	Description
Sub SPC_Title()	Sub appears in blue text and defines the beginning of a macro (sometimes called a subroutine). The title of the macro appears on the Sub line and appears in black text.
Green text lines	Green text that appears after an apostrophe is a comment line. Comments are used to explain the steps in your macro. Notice that the description you entered in the Record Macro dialog box appears at the top of your code.
ActiveCell.FormulaR1C1 = "Super Power Computers"	Enters the text "Super Power Computers" in the current cell (using R1C1 style cell references—use online Help to learn more about this topic)
Range("A2").Select	Selects cell A2
All lines starting with Range("A1:F1").Select to Selection.Merge	Merges and centers cells A1:F1
All lines beginning with Range("A1:F2").Select to End With	Selects cells A1:F2 and sets the font options
End Sub	Indicates the end of the macro

Whenever a Super Power Computers employee uses this macro, the current date should be added, in a blue font, to cell A3. To modify the code:

Step 1	Locate	the line that reads Range ("A1:F1").Select near the end of the macro
Step 2	Drag	to select the range reference A1:F1
Step 3	Key	A3
Step 4	Press	the END key to move to the end of the line
Step 5	Press	the ENTER key
Step 6	Key	ActiveCell.FormulaR1C1 = "=TODAY()"

After you key "ActiveCell." a list appears with options belonging to the ActiveCell object. As you continue keying "FormulaR1C1," that option is selected in the list. When the correct option is highlighted, you can press the SPACEBAR or the TAB key, and Visual Basic will finish the typing for you. This feature not only saves time, but also helps reduce errors when you are creating and modifying macro code.

The completed line will enter the TODAY date formula in the current cell, A3, when you run the macro.

Step 7	Press	the ENTER key
Step 8	Key	Selection.Font.ColorIndex = 5

This line sets the font color to 5, which is the color index code for the color blue.

Step 9	Press	the ENTER key
Step 10	Key	Range("A1").
Step 11	Scroll	down the list until you see Select
Step 12	Double-click	Select

Your screen should look similar to Figure 9-6.

FIGURE 9-6
Edited Macro

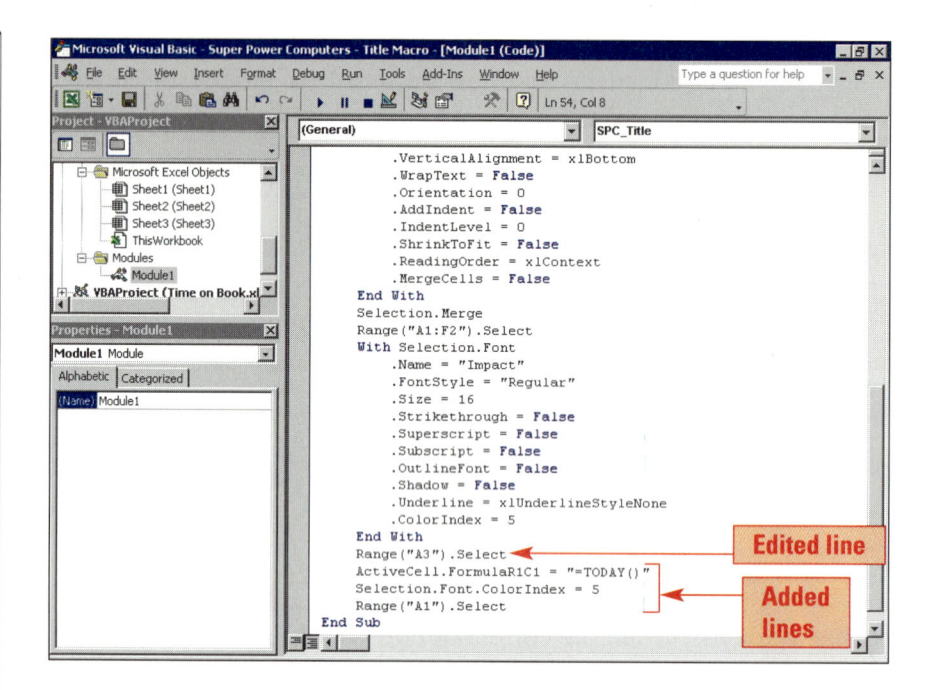

Before you run your macro, it is a good idea to save the workbook. You can save the workbook in the Visual Basic Editor, or in Excel. Then you run your revised macro. To save the workbook and run the revised macro:

Step 1	Click	the Save button in the Visual Basic Editor window
Step 2	Switch to	the Excel program window using the taskbar
Step 3	Click	the Sheet3 sheet tab
Step 4	Open	the Macro dialog box
Step 5	Verify	that SPC_Title is selected in the macros list
Step 6	Click	Run to run the SPC_Title macro

Your screen should look similar to Figure 9-7.

FIGURE 9-7
Results of the Revised Macro

To print the macro code and close the Visual Basic Editor:

Step 1	**Switch to**	the Visual Basic Editor program using the taskbar
Step 2	**Click**	File
Step 3	**Click**	Print
Step 4	**Click**	OK to print the current module
Step 5	**Click**	File
Step 6	**Click**	Close and Return to Microsoft Excel

The Visual Basic Editor closes, and the Excel window becomes the active window.

Step 7	**Save**	the workbook and leave it open

> **CAUTION TIP**
>
> If cell A3 displays TODAY(), click the Visual Basic taskbar button, click before the T in TODAY, and key an equal sign (=). Switch back to Excel and run the macro again.

9.c Using Workbooks Containing Macros

Whenever you share workbooks with other users or download files from the Internet, your file(s)—or the downloaded files—could be infected with viruses. Viruses are malicious programs that can destroy files and data. **Macro viruses** are a special class of viruses that embed themselves in macros. Whenever you open a workbook containing a macro virus, the virus can replicate itself to other workbooks, destroy files on your hard drive, and do other types of damage. Because of this threat, Excel prompts you before opening any file containing macros.

Opening a Workbook with Macros

The *Super Power Computers - Header Macro* workbook contains a previously recorded macro that sets up a header, and you want to edit it. Macros will only run if the Excel security setting is set to Medium or lower. To set the Excel security setting to Medium:

Step 1	**Click**	Tools
Step 2	**Click**	Options
Step 3	**Click**	the Security tab

chapter nine

Step 4	Click	Macro Security
Step 5	Click	the Medium option button, if necessary
Step 6	Click	OK
Step 7	Click	OK

To open a workbook containing a macro:

Step 1	Open	the *Super Power Computers - Header Macro* workbook on your Data Disk

The warning dialog box on your screen should look similar to Figure 9-8.

FIGURE 9-8
Macro Virus Warning Dialog Box

> **QUICK TIP**
>
> To scan your files for viruses, you must purchase special antivirus software capable of scanning your files, hard drive(s), and floppy drive(s). Most newer antivirus programs can scan files containing macros for macro viruses. For more information about macro viruses, refer to online Help.

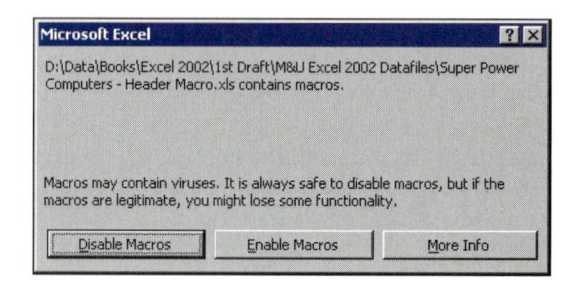

Excel cannot determine whether a macro is actually a macro virus. If you are not sure about the origins of the workbook, you should select Disable Macros. The contents of the workbook can still be edited, but any special macros stored in the workbook cannot be executed. If possible, contact the person who created the workbook to find out which macros should appear in the workbook. Once you've determined that the source of this workbook is safe, you can open the file with macros enabled.

Step 2	Click	Enable Macros

Copying Macro Code to Another Workbook

You want to copy the macro in this workbook to the *Super Power Computers - Title Macro* workbook you created earlier. To copy macro code:

Step 1	Click	Tools
Step 2	Point to	Macro
Step 3	Click	Visual Basic Editor

Increasing Productivity with Macros, Templates, and Custom Toolbars and Menus   **EA 63**

The Project Explorer window contains a new VBAProject (Super Power Computers - Header Macro.xls).

| Step 4 | Click | the + sign next to VBAProject (Super Power Computers - Header Macro.xls) in the Project Explorer window, if necessary |

If a – (minus sign) appears next to VBAProject (Super Power Computers - Header Macro.xls), do not click it.

Step 5	Click	the + sign next to Modules, if necessary
Step 6	Double-click	Module1
Step 7	Press	the CTRL + A keys to select all the code
Step 8	Click	the Copy button on the Visual Basic Editor Standard toolbar

In the Project Explorer window, you can expand the view for the Super Power Computers Title project.

Step 9	Scroll	the Project Explorer window, if necessary
Step 10	Click	the + sign next to VBAProject (Super Power Computers - Title Macro.xls), if necessary
Step 11	Right-click	the Modules folder indented under VBAProject (Super Power Computers - Title Macro.xls)
Step 12	Point to	Insert
Step 13	Click	Module

A blank macro module opens with the name of the Title Macro worksheet in the title bar.

Step 14	Click	Paste button on the Visual Basic Editor standard toolbar
Step 15	Close	the Visual Basic Editor
Step 16	Click	Window
Step 17	Click	Super Power Computers - Title Macro
Step 18	Save	the *Super Power Computers - Title Macro* workbook

chapter nine

| Step 19 | Switch to | the *Super Power Computers - Header Macro* workbook |
| Step 20 | Close | the *Super Power Computers - Header Macro* workbook |

The macro from *Super Power Computers - Header Macro* is pasted into the *Super Power Computers - Title Macro* workbook. To reset the security setting to its default value of High:

Step 1	Open	the Options dialog box
Step 2	Click	Macro Security on the Security tab
Step 3	Click	the High option button
Step 4	Click	OK
Step 5	Click	OK

9.d Creating and Editing Templates

Templates are designed to save you time and effort. You know how to open a new workbook based on one of the Excel predesigned templates. You can also create templates from scratch, save existing workbooks as templates, and modify existing templates.

Creating a Workbook Template

At Super Power Computers, you generate a lot of sales reports. To save time formatting the worksheets, you create a template from an existing workbook. To create a workbook template:

Step 1	Verify	that the *Super Power Computers - Title Macro* workbook is open
Step 2	Open	the *Super Power Computers - Store 2 Sales* workbook located on the Data Disk
Step 3	Select	the range A5:E8
Step 4	Press	the DELETE key to clear the data cells
Step 5	Clear	cell A2

The template should contain as much information as you are likely to reuse, but not data that is likely to change.

CAUTION TIP

Be sure *not* to click the Save button on the Standard toolbar when you intend to save the workbook as a template. Remember, the Undo list starts over after each save!

Increasing Productivity with Macros, Templates, and Custom Toolbars and Menus   **EA 65**

Step 6	Click	File
Step 7	Click	Save As
Step 8	Click	the Save as type: list arrow
Step 9	Click	Template

Notice that the Save in: folder changes to the default Templates folder. Generally, you should save your templates to the default template folder to make them available when you click the General Templates link in the New Workbook task pane. If you save them to another location, as you do here, you click the New from existing workbook link on the task pane, which makes all workbooks *and* templates act as templates.

Step 10	Change	the Save in: location to the folder where you store your completed files
Step 11	Key	*Super Power Computers - Store Sales Template* in the File name: text box
Step 12	Click	Save
Step 13	Close	the template

Once you save a template, you can create new workbooks from this template by clicking the General Templates link in the task pane, then selecting the template you want to use.

Editing a Template

You can modify both templates that you created and the Excel built-in templates. To edit a template, you must open it as a template (instead of as a new workbook). To modify the template you just created:

Step 1	Open	the Open dialog box
Step 2	Change	the Look in: list box to the folder where you store your completed files, if necessary
Step 3	Click	*Super Power Computers - Store Sales Template*
Step 4	Click	Open

Any changes you make and save to the template will be added to new workbooks you create in the future.

Step 5	Enter	Store # in cell A2
Step 6	Save	and close the template

> **INTERNET TIP**
>
> To find more template examples, open the New Workbook task pane, then click the Templates on Microsoft.com link.

> **QUICK TIP**
>
> Creating a new workbook from a template is different from opening the template file itself.

chapter
nine

9.e Customizing Toolbars and Menus

Another way to boost your productivity is to create your own custom toolbars and menus. Excel features many commands that can be added to toolbars or menus, and you can add macros you have recorded as well. You can even add menus to toolbars.

Creating a Custom Toolbar

If there is a set of commands that you use often, it can be more efficient to create your own toolbar. To create a custom toolbar:

Step 1	Verify	that the *Super Power Computers - Title Macro* workbook is the active workbook
Step 2	Right-click	any toolbar
Step 3	Click	Customize
Step 4	Click	the Toolbars tab

Your Customize dialog box should look similar to Figure 9-9. The Toolbars tab helps you create, rename, and delete toolbars.

FIGURE 9-9
Toolbars Tab in the Customize Dialog Box

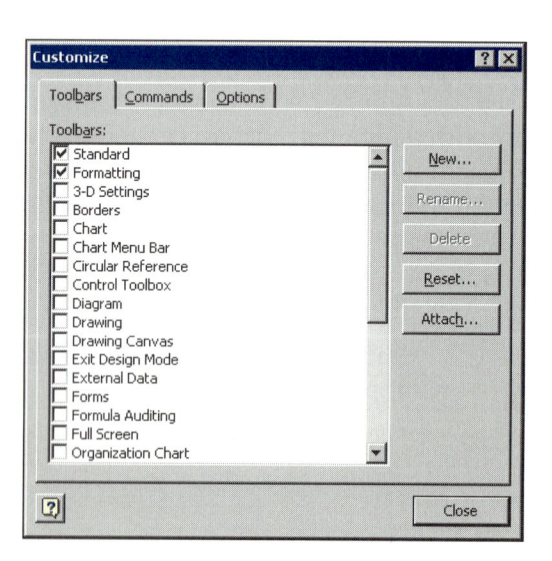

Step 5	Click	New
Step 6	Key	My Custom Toolbar in the Toolbar name: text box in the New Toolbar dialog box

---

MOUSE TIP

You can move a menu from a toolbar to the menu bar, or vice versa, as long as the Customize dialog box remains open. Just drag the menu item from the toolbar to the menu bar or from the menu bar to the toolbar.

You can remove items from a toolbar or menu while the Customize dialog box remains open. Drag the item from the toolbar or menu and drop it anywhere on the worksheet.

| Step 7 | Click | OK |
| Step 8 | Observe | the small empty toolbar, named My Custom Toolbar, that appears on your screen |

You can see only the M of the toolbar name in the title bar. Next, you add buttons or menus to your toolbar. To add a button to a toolbar:

Step 1	Click	the Commands tab in the Customize dialog box
Step 2	Click	Edit in the Categories: list
Step 3	Scroll	down the Commands: list until you see Paste Formatting
Step 4	Drag	Paste Formatting from the Commands: list to your new toolbar

This button is a shortcut for clicking the Paste Special command on the Edit menu, and clicking Formatting.

Creating a Custom Menu

You can modify menus by adding or removing existing commands, or you can create your own menus. You want to create a menu with commands to run your macros. To create a new menu:

Step 1	Verify	that the Commands tab in the Customize dialog box is open
Step 2	Scroll	the Categories: list to locate New Menu
Step 3	Click	New Menu
Step 4	Drag	New Menu from the Commands: list to the new toolbar
Step 5	Right-click	the New Menu menu on the toolbar
Step 6	Drag	in the Name: text box to select all of the text
Step 7	Key	My Macros
Step 8	Press	the ENTER key
Step 9	Click	Macros in the Categories: list in the Customize dialog box
Step 10	Drag	Custom Menu Item to the My Macros menu you added to your custom toolbar, but do not release the mouse button

QUICK TIP

You can assign a macro to a toolbar button. Open the Customize dialog box, and click the Commands tab. Right-click a custom button that you've added to a toolbar, then click Assign Macro. Select the desired macro, then click the OK button.

CAUTION TIP

Toolbars and custom menus are usually saved on your computer. If you want a toolbar to "travel" with a workbook or template, you need to attach it. Open the Customize dialog box, then click Attach on the Toolbars tab. Select an available toolbar in the Custom toolbars: list, then click Copy>>. Click the OK button, then click the Close button, and save the workbook or template.

When you open a workbook with an attached custom toolbar, that toolbar is automatically added to the Toolbars: list in the Customize dialog box. You must delete the toolbar if you don't want it stored on your computer.

chapter nine

MENU TIP

You can key & in front of a menu item character in the Name: text box to create an ALT + key shortcut. For example, key "&My Menu" to create the ALT + M shortcut to access the My Menu menu.

CAUTION TIP

The SPC_Title and SPC_Header macro shortcuts on the custom menu will not run the associated macros unless one of the workbooks that contains the macro is open.

A small menu pop-out appears below the My Macros menu name. Dropping a button or macro on this area adds it as a menu item. A black line appears to indicate where the menu item will be placed.

Step 11	Drop	the menu item on the menu pop-out
Step 12	Right-click	Custom Menu Item
Step 13	Click	Assign Macro
Step 14	Click	SPC_Title
Step 15	Click	OK
Step 16	Rename	the menu item as Title
Step 17	Follow	Steps 10 through 15 to add the SPC_Header macro to the My Macros menu
Step 18	Rename	the menu item as Header
Step 19	Click	Close
Step 20	Save	the workbook and close it

Occasionally, you need to delete a toolbar. To delete a toolbar:

Step 1	Open	the Customize dialog box
Step 2	Click	the Toolbars tab
Step 3	Click	My Custom Toolbar in the Toolbars: list
Step 4	Click	Delete
Step 5	Click	OK
Step 6	Close	the Customize dialog box

The toolbar is removed from Excel. There are many ways to customize Excel to increase your productivity. Macros, templates, and custom toolbars and menus can help you make short work of many common tasks.

Increasing Productivity with Macros, Templates, and Custom Toolbars and Menus EA 69

Summary

- A macro is a set of instructions that executes several commands automatically. Macros can be simple recorded steps, or they can be complex programs capable of making decisions based on user input.
- Recording a macro is the simplest way to create a macro. During the recording process, Excel records exactly what you do.
- Once a macro is recorded, it must be run to perform the desired task.
- You can edit macros using the Visual Basic Editor. Visual Basic is the programming language used by Excel and other Office programs. The Visual Basic Editor is a separate application used to create, edit, delete, and test Visual Basic modules or macros.
- Some macros can contain viruses, or programs that can damage files on your computer system. If you are unsure of a workbook's origin, disable macros when you open the workbook. You can still view and edit data in the workbook.
- You can copy macro code between Visual Basic projects (other workbooks) by using the Cut and Paste commands.
- You can create templates from scratch or by saving existing workbooks as templates. To save a workbook as a template, click Template in the Save as type: list in the Save As dialog box.
- To edit a custom template you created or a built-in template, open it as a template instead of as a new workbook.
- You can create custom toolbars and menus by dragging command buttons onto the toolbar or menu.
- You can drag items from a toolbar or menu to remove them.

Commands Review

Action	Menu Bar	Shortcut Menu	Toolbar	Task Pane	Keyboard
Record a macro	Tools, Macro, Record New Macro				ALT + T, M, R
Run or edit a macro	Tools, Macro, Macros, then Run or Edit button				ALT + T, M, M ALT + F8
Open the Visual Basic Editor	Tools, Macro, Visual Basic Editor				ALT + T, M V ALT + F11
Save a template	File, Save As, then change file type to Template				ALT + F, A
Open a template for editing	File, Open, then change file type to Template				ALT + F, O
Customize a toolbar or menu	Tools, Customize	Right-click toolbar, then Customize			ALT + T, C

chapter nine

Concepts Review

Circle the correct answer.

1. **Macros:**
   - [a] are much too difficult for the average user to program.
   - [b] can waste time because they run every time you open a workbook.
   - [c] consist of a set of instructions that automatically executes a set of commands.
   - [d] can never be modified.

2. **Which of the following tasks can be performed by macros?**
   - [a] printing worksheets
   - [b] creating and modifying charts
   - [c] sorting lists
   - [d] all of the above

3. **To make a macro available in all workbooks, you should save it:**
   - [a] in every workbook you use.
   - [b] in the Personal Macro Workbook.
   - [c] on a floppy disk.
   - [d] to the All Macros folder on your hard drive.

4. **You edit macros in the:**
   - [a] Excel application window.
   - [b] Macro dialog box.
   - [c] Visual Basic Editor program window.
   - [d] Record Macro dialog box.

5. **Visual Basic is the programming language used by:**
   - [a] only Microsoft Excel.
   - [b] only Microsoft Word.
   - [c] only Microsoft Access.
   - [d] all Office applications.

6. **An apostrophe (') in Visual Basic, signifies a:**
   - [a] shortened version of the REMOVE command.
   - [b] blank line follows.
   - [c] comment section.
   - [d] shortened version of REMEMBER, preceding a programmer's reminder section.

7. **When you record a macro, you:**
   - [a] must write all the actions you want to perform, then key them in the Visual Basic Editor program window.
   - [b] start recording, then Excel automatically records every keystroke.
   - [c] must open the Visual Basic Editor first, before Excel will record your keystrokes.
   - [d] click the Record button after each keystroke so that mistakes are not recorded.

8. **If you see a message telling you that a workbook contains macros, you should:**
   - [a] always click Disable Macros because the workbook contains a virus.
   - [b] always click Enable Macros because the workbook will not display all the data unless you do.
   - [c] cancel the operation quickly because the macro may contain a virus.
   - [d] decide whether the workbook comes from a reliable source, then click either Disable or Enable Macros.

9. **Templates:**
   - [a] save time by eliminating repetitious formatting and setup tasks.
   - [b] are difficult to create.
   - [c] cannot be modified.
   - [d] can be used by clicking the New button on the Standard toolbar.

10. **To create a custom toolbar:**
    - [a] drag buttons off the Standard toolbar.
    - [b] drag the name of the toolbar from the Toolbars list in the Customize dialog box.
    - [c] right-click an open toolbar, then click New Toolbar.
    - [d] click the New button on the Toolbars tab of the Customize dialog box.

Increasing Productivity with Macros, Templates, and Custom Toolbars and Menus **EA 71**

Circle **T** if the statement is true or **F** if the statement is false.

T F 1. Macros save a lot of time.

T F 2. You can save any workbook as a template by using the File menu, then clicking Save As and setting the Save As type: list to Template.

T F 3. Custom menus can be added to the menu bar, but not to custom toolbars.

T F 4. You can write macros that work across several Office applications.

T F 5. Learning the basics of Visual Basic can help you write macros in all of the Office applications.

T F 6. The easiest way to create a macro is to open the Visual Basic Editor and key the code by hand.

T F 7. If you make a mistake when recording a macro, you have to record a new macro.

T F 8. Whenever you see the macro virus warning when opening an Excel workbook, the workbook must contain a macro virus and should not be opened.

T F 9. Macro viruses are usually harmful programs embedded in a macro, capable of copying themselves to other files and destroying data.

T F 10. A module is the basic storage unit for macro code.

Skills Review

Exercise 1

1. Create a new workbook.

2. Create a new toolbar named "Special Edit."

3. Add the following Edit category commands: Paste Formatting, Paste Values, Clear Contents, Clear Formatting, and Select Current Region.

4. On the Toolbars tab, select the Special Edit toolbar, click Attach, select Special Edit in the Custom toolbars: list, click Copy >>, then click OK to attach the toolbar to the workbook.

5. Save the workbook as *Special Edit* and close it.

6. Delete the Special Edit toolbar (the toolbar will still be available when you open the *Special Edit* workbook because you attached it).

Exercise 2

1. Open the *Sort List* workbook located on the Data Disk.

2. Click any cell within the list of data on Sheet1.

3. Record a new macro called "Sort1" and save it in the current workbook.

4. Sort the list by name in ascending order.

5. Stop recording the macro.

6. Record a second macro called "Sort2" and save it in the current workbook.

7. Sort the list by region and then by name in ascending order.

8. Stop recording the macro.

9. Save the workbook as *Sort List with Macros*, and then print and close it.

chapter nine

Exercise 3

1. Create a new expense statement workbook, using the Expense Statement template on the Spreadsheet Solutions tab.
2. Enter the following data. Name: "Luis Alvarez," Position: "Owner."
3. Save the workbook as a template named *Sweet Tooth Owner Expenses* and then print and close it.

Exercise 4

1. Open the *Video Rental* workbook located on the Data Disk.
2. Bold and center the column headings in row 2.
3. Use a red cell fill with white text in row 2.
4. Select the range B3:G7 and add All Borders to the selection.
5. Select the range G3:G10 and add a Thick Box Border to the selection.
6. Select the range B1:G10 and add a Thick Box Border to the selection.
7. Set the print area to this selection and print it.
8. Activate cell B3.
9. Save the workbook as a template named *Video Rental*, and then close it.

Exercise 5

1. Create a new workbook using the *Video Rental* template that you created in Exercise 4.
2. Enter fictitious data on the form for two video rentals. Enter today's date in the Check Out Date column for each video. Enter a video title for each video.
3. Print the Video Rental form, save the workbook as *Video Rental1*, and then close it.

Exercise 6

1. Open the *Central Region Sales 2* workbook located on the Data Disk.
2. Record a macro called "Chart." Store the macro in This Workbook.
3. Select the range A4:E8 on the Central Region Summary worksheet, and click the Chart Wizard button on the Standard toolbar.
4. Create a Clustered Column chart with a 3-D visual effect chart subtype. Enter "Central Region Summary" as the Chart title. Create the chart as a new sheet named "Central Region Summary Chart."
5. When the chart appears, click the Stop Recording button to stop recording the macro.
6. Delete the new chart sheet tab.
7. Run the macro to verify that it works correctly.
8. Save the workbook as *Central Region Sales 2 Chart Macro*, and then print and close it.

Increasing Productivity with Macros, Templates, and Custom Toolbars and Menus   EA 73

Exercise 7

1. Open the *Central Region Sales 2 Chart Macro* workbook that you created in Exercise 6.
2. Open the Macro dialog box, and select the Chart macro for editing.
3. In the Visual Basic Editor, edit the macro code as follows (insert the text in bold):
   a. Insert **NM = ActiveSheet.Name** before the line Range("A4:E8").Select
   b. Use Replace (press the CTRL + H keys) to replace "Central Region Summary" (including the quotation marks) with **NM**
   c. Use Replace to replace all occurrences of "Central Region Summary Chart" (including the quotation marks) with **NM & " Summary Chart"** (include a space between the first quotation mark and the letter S).
   d. In the line .ChartTitle.Characters.Text = "Central Region Summary Chart" replace "Central Region Summary Chart" with **NM & " Summary Chart"**

   These changes find the current sheet tab name and assign it to the variable NM. The macro then uses this variable to create and automatically give a title to a new chart on a new chart sheet that it also names automatically.

4. Switch to Excel using the taskbar.
5. Click the South Division tab.
6. Run the Chart macro.
7. Create charts for each of the Division pages of your workbook, using the Chart macro.
8. Print the charts, save the workbook as *Central Region Sales 2 Chart Revised*, and then close it.

Exercise 8

1. Open the *Central Region Sales 2 Chart Revised* workbook that you created in Exercise 7.
2. Create a new toolbar called "Macros."
3. Add the Chart macro to the toolbar.
4. Attach the toolbar to the workbook.
5. Save the workbook as *Central Region Sales 2 Chart Revised 2*.
6. Delete the Macros toolbar from the Toolbars: list in the Customize dialog box.

Case Projects

Project 1

As a busy student who uses Excel for many homework assignments, you find it tedious to constantly add your name, class, and date to your workbooks before you turn them in. In a new workbook, record a macro to insert three rows at the top of your workbook, and insert your name in cell A1, the class name in cell A2, and today's date in cell A3. Name the macro "NameStamp." Test your macro on Sheet2 of the workbook. Save the workbook as *Name Stamp Macro* and then print and close it.

Project 2

Connect to the Internet and search the Web for information about Visual Basic and Visual Basic for Applications. Focus your search on tutorials, especially those intended for beginners. Print at least two beginner tutorials, and save five links in your browser's Favorites or Bookmarks.

chapter nine

Project 3

As the manager of a retail music store, you create a chart every week listing the bestselling CDs. Use the Internet to search for the Top 15 Bestselling CDs for the current week. Create a new workbook containing each album's title, artist's name, and the number of CDs sold. Create records for at least 15 CDs by your favorite bands, or other popular titles. Generate fictitious sales data (for your store) for each CD. Record a macro to do the following: (1) sort the list by number of CDs sold, then by album title, (2) create a chart selecting the top 10 bestselling albums, (3) create a centered header with your store's name, (4) create a footer with the date on the left and the time on the right, (5) change the page layout to landscape orientation, and (6) print the chart. Then, randomly change the number of albums sold, and run the macro again. Save the workbook as *Record Sales*, and then print and close it.

Project 4

As an accountant who deals with a high volume of clients every day, you want to see the current date and time when you switch between clients. Create a new, blank workbook, and save it as *Time Clock*. Open the Visual Basic Editor and double-click Module 1 of the Time Clock.xls project in the Project Explorer window. Use Visual Basic Help to create a message dialog box that displays the current date and time. (*Hint:* Search for the MsgBox, Date, and Time functions.) Assign the macro to your clock object. Print the module code, then save the workbook as *Time Clock*.

Project 5

As an office manager, you receive a large volume of phone calls each day. Create a custom phone message template. Include cells to record the time and date of the call, the name of the person whom the message is for, the message text, the caller's phone number, and the requested response. Be creative in your use of borders, shading, drawing objects, font styles, and so on. Apply number formats as appropriate. Set print settings to print messages correctly. Save the template as *Phone Message*, and then print and close it.

Project 6

As the owner of a small bookstore, you want to create a receipt template to record sales. The template should include the current date and time of the transaction, a place to enter the title of the book(s) purchased, and the price of each book. It also should include formulas to calculate the subtotal of items sold, sales tax, and the total sale amount. Save the template as *Book Sales Receipt*, and then print and close it.

Project 7

You are worried about the security of workbooks that you share with other people over the Internet. Connect to the Internet and search the Web for information about Excel macro viruses. Print at least one page identifying one existing Excel macro virus, explaining what it does, and describing how you can eliminate it.

Project 8

You own a retail computer store. In addition to selling custom computers, you service computers that aren't working. You need a template to enter service order information. In the client information section, you need to enter the client's name, address, city, state, ZIP code, phone number, and e-mail address. In the computer information section, you need to enter the CPU speed, amount of RAM, hard drive space, and operating system. In the problem description section, you need to enter a description of the problem as explained by the client. In the estimate section, you need to enter an estimate of the number of hours it will take a technician to repair the problem, plus the estimated cost of any parts that may need to be replaced. Create formulas to: (1) multiply the number of estimated hours by the current rate of $45/hour, (2) add the estimated technician cost to the estimated parts cost, (3) calculate the sales tax on the estimate, and (4) add the subtotal and the calculated sales tax to provide a total. Create a new template named *Service Order* that includes all these sections, and then print and close it.

Using Problem-Solving Tools

Excel 2002

Chapter Overview

Finding solutions to complex business problems is one of the things that Excel does best. You can create data tables to replace the values used in formulas with variables. Data tables allow you to quickly see the results that occur from changing one or two variables. Goal Seek modifies one variable in a formula to create a desired outcome. Solver allows you to arrive at a desired outcome by changing the values of multiple cells and placing constraints as to what changes can take place. Scenarios let you store multiple sets of values for selected cells, allowing you to quickly view the results of several different situations. Finally, you can add trendlines to a chart to show projected values based on existing data.

Learning Objectives

- Create data tables
- Use Goal Seek and Solver
- Create scenarios
- Create a trendline

Case profile

To be successful in business, you must know how to analyze information and how to make decisions based on the analysis of that information. This month, Super Power Computers is looking to expand its fleet of cars and needs to know how much the company can afford to borrow. The warehouse division is also seeking a solution to some scheduling problems. You use a variety of what-if analysis tools to resolve each of these problems.

chapter ten

> **notes** Several of the tools presented in this chapter require certain Excel Add-In components to be activated. To activate the necessary add-ins, click the Add-Ins command on the Tools menu. Click the Solver Add-In check box and the Analysis ToolPak check box to insert check marks, if necessary. Click the OK button to activate the add-ins.

10.a Creating Data Tables

One of the key strengths of Excel is its ability to help you perform what-if analyses. In a **what-if analysis**, you change data values and then observe the effect on calculations—for example, what if I change the value in cell A2? To make this kind of trial-and-error process easier, you can use **data tables** to show the results of a formula by replacing one or two of the variables with several different values. **One-variable data tables** can be created to show the results of changing one variable in several formulas at once. **Two-variable data tables** can show the results of changing two variables in a single formula.

Creating a One-Variable Data Table

A **variable** is like a container, or placeholder, for a value. When you create formulas in Excel using cell references, the cell reference acts as a variable. As you change the value of the referenced cell, the formula automatically displays the new result. A **one-variable data table** uses a variable to replace one of the arguments in a given formula and then calculates results using several different values for that argument.

Super Power Computers is considering purchasing a fleet of automobiles for its sales representatives. The purchase amount of each car is $25,000, with a loan interest rate of 9.5%. The company wants to determine the monthly payment per car, and the amount of interest to be paid depending on the term of the loan. In this case, the term argument is the variable. To open the workbook and set up a one-variable data table:

Step 1	**Open**	the *Super Power Computers - Interest Calculator* workbook located on the Data Disk
Step 2	**Save**	the workbook as *Super Power Computers - Interest Calculator Revised*

One of the financial functions, CUMIPMT, calculates the cumulative interest paid over the course of a loan. Another related function, PMT, calculates the monthly payment on a loan. Both of these financial functions share common arguments, including the *rate* (percentage), *nper* (number of periods in the life of the loan), and *pv* (present value of the loan). The syntax of the CUMIPMT function is:

=CUMIPMT(rate,nper,pv,start_period,end_period,type)

In this workbook, the loan information has already been entered. Cell B5 holds the value representing the *nper* argument used in both the CUMIPMT and the PMT functions. This value will be replaced by the values in the range C5:C8, which are shaded in green. (In this case, the period of time for the *nper* argument is months.) The payment (PMT) calculation takes place in column D. The cumulative interest (CUMIPMT) is calculated in column E.

| Step 3 | Enter | =PMT(B4/12,B5,B6) in cell D4 on the One Variable worksheet |
| Step 4 | Enter | =CUMIPMT(B4/12,B5,B6,1,B5,1) in cell E4 |

Your screen should look similar to Figure 10-1.

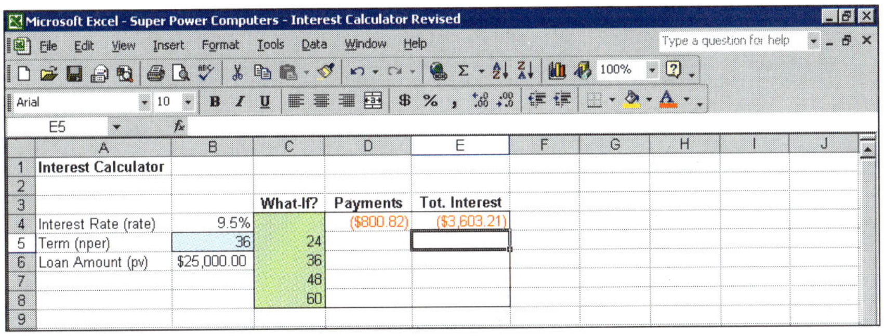

> **QUICK TIP**
>
> For more information about financial functions, use online Help.
> To automatically open a Help window with information about a function you entered, click the function in the Formula Bar to display its ScreenTip, then click the function name link in the ScreenTip.

FIGURE 10-1
One-Variable Data Table

Next you calculate what happens when you change the term of the loan. To perform a what-if analysis using a one-variable data table:

Step 1	Select	the range C4:E8
Step 2	Click	Data
Step 3	Click	Table

The Table dialog box opens. The value that you want to change in the formula is stored in the input cell. Because the replacement values you will use are arranged in a column, you use a Column input cell.

| Step 4 | Click | in the Column input cell: text box |
| Step 5 | Click | cell B5 |

The data table replaces the value in cell B5 with each of the values in the leftmost column of the selected data table. First, Excel calculates the PMT function using the value 24 (the first value in column C) instead of the current value of cell B5. Then, Excel calculates the PMT function again, using the next value in column C, 36, in place of the current value of cell B5. Excel continues this process until it reaches the end of the table you selected. Your screen should look similar to Figure 10-2.

FIGURE 10-2
Choosing the Variable in a One-Variable Data Table

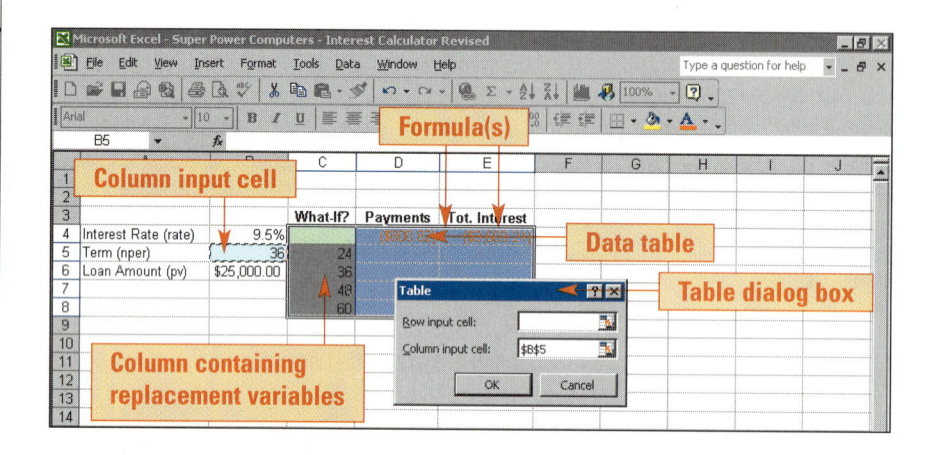

Step 6	Click	OK
Step 7	Click	cell A1

The monthly payment and cumulative interest for each term length are calculated. Your screen should look similar to Figure 10-3.

FIGURE 10-3
One-Variable Data Table Calculated

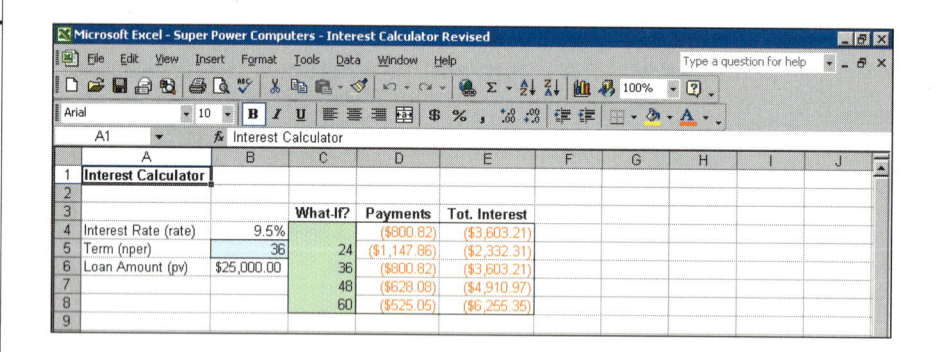

Step 8	Save	the workbook

Using Problem-Solving Tools   EA 79

Creating a Two-Variable Data Table

Two-variable data tables allow you to see the results of a formula that uses two different variables. You want to calculate the monthly payments on the auto loan for various terms at different interest rates. To set up a two-variable data table:

Step 1	**Activate**	the Two Variable worksheet
Step 2	**Enter**	=PMT(B4/12,B5,B6) in cell C4

Two-variable data tables can use only one formula at a time, and this formula must be located in the cell directly above the column of the first replacement values and to the right of the second replacement values. The result of the formula, ($800.82), appears in cell C4.

Now you can perform the what-if calculations. To create a two-way data table:

Step 1	**Select**	the range C4:G8
Step 2	**Click**	Data
Step 3	**Click**	Table
Step 4	**Click**	cell B4 so that it appears as an absolute reference in the Row input cell: text box
Step 5	**Click**	in the Column input cell: text box
Step 6	**Click**	cell B5
Step 7	**Click**	OK
Step 8	**Click**	cell A1

Your final data table should look similar to Figure 10-4.

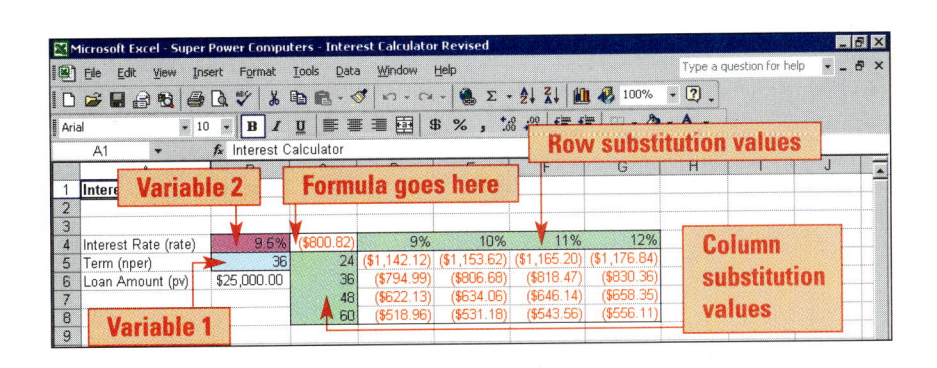

FIGURE 10-4
Two-Variable Data Table

Step 9	**Save**	the workbook

10.b Using Goal Seek and Solver

Excel includes several tools to help you solve complex problems. When you know the desired result of a formula but the values currently used in the formula don't produce the correct result, you can use the Goal Seek tool to change a variable in the formula and obtain the correct result. Goal Seek can modify only one variable. Solver works in much the same way, but it allows you to change the values of several variables; at the same time, it sets constraints on how much you can alter those variables.

Using Goal Seek

Super Power Computers has decided to purchase 40 new cars for the company, at a total cost of $1,000,000. The company wants to pay off the loan in 36 months, but it has a budget of only $30,000 per month available to make payments. The board of directors needs to know how much money Super Power Computers can borrow at 10% to meet this budget limitation. To set up the workbook:

Step 1	Activate	the Car Purchase worksheet
Step 2	Enter	=PMT(B8/12,B9,B10) in cell B13

The monthly payment is calculated at $32,032.95. You need to adjust the loan amount so that the monthly payment fits the budget of $30,000. To use Goal Seek:

Step 1	Activate	cell B13
Step 2	Click	Tools
Step 3	Click	Goal Seek
Step 4	Click	in the To value: text box

The company will pay this amount, so you use a negative number to indicate an expense.

Step 5	Key	-30000
Step 6	Press	the TAB key to move to the By changing cell: text box

| **Step 7** | ***Click*** | cell B10 |

Your Goal Seek dialog box should look similar to Figure 10-5. Goal Seek finds the solution and displays the Goal Seek Status dialog box. When you click OK, Excel changes the value of the variable cell—B10 in this case—so that the formula in cell B13 meets your goal.

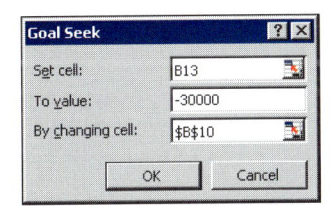

FIGURE 10-5
Goal Seek Dialog Box

| **Step 8** | ***Click*** | OK |

Figure 10-6 shows the results of the Goal Seek operation. To meet the budgeted payment amount of $30,000 per month, Super Power Computers can borrow a maximum of $936,536.

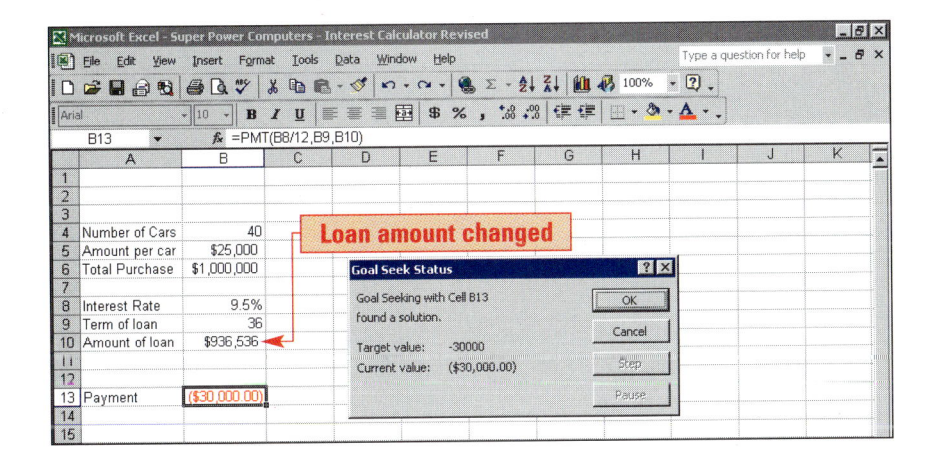

FIGURE 10-6
Goal Seek Status Dialog Box

| **Step 9** | ***Click*** | OK |
| **Step 10** | ***Save*** | the workbook and leave it open |

Using Solver

Luis Alvarez, president of Super Power Computers, has requested that all divisions of the company study ways to save the company money. Many departments are overstaffed, but some departments are understaffed or are not scheduling employees efficiently. The warehouse has especially serious scheduling problems.

The warehouse division currently employs 64 employees and runs seven days a week. Each employee works a schedule of five days on, two days off. Under the current schedule, approximately 45 employees are scheduled each day, but this system creates problems. More employees are needed during the week, when the warehouse is at its busiest. The goal is to minimize the amount of payroll paid out each week, by reducing the staff required to meet the demand for each day. Sound like a complicated problem? It is, and that's why Solver is so useful. To open the workbook and save it with a new name:

| Step 1 | Open | the *Super Power Computers - Warehouse Personnel Scheduling* workbook located on the Data Disk |
| Step 2 | Save | the workbook as *Super Power Computers - Warehouse Personnel Scheduling Solution* |

This worksheet shows the scheduling for employees in the warehouse. The number of employees currently assigned to each shift appears in the range C5:C11, with the total number of employees being displayed in cell C13. The range D13:J13 calculates the number of employees working each day by multiplying the number of employees on each shift by the on value of 1 or the off value of 0 for each day on the schedule. The range D15:J15 indicates the actual numbers of employees that the warehouse needs on staff each day. Cells C18 and C19 calculate the payroll total for each week. Each warehouse employee is paid $100 per day. To use Solver to create the most efficient schedule:

| Step 1 | Click | Tools |
| Step 2 | Click | Solver |

The Solver Parameters dialog box on your screen should look similar to Figure 10-7.

FIGURE 10-7
Solver Parameters Dialog Box

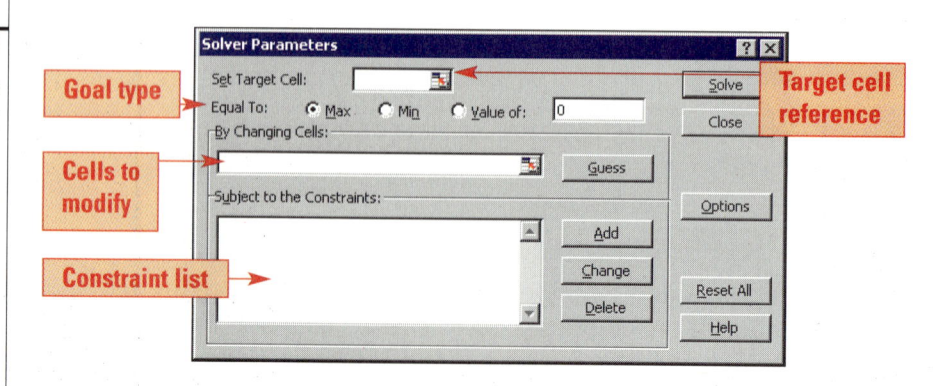

The goal of this exercise is to reduce the total payroll, so cell C19 is the target. To set the Solver target:

Step 1	Click	cell C19
Step 2	Click	the Mi<u>n</u> option button next to Equal To:

Solver will look for the solution that results in the lowest possible value for the target cell C19. Next, you need to specify which cells can be changed to reach the goal. To identify which cells can be changed:

Step 1	Click	the Collapse dialog button in the <u>B</u>y Changing Cells: text box
Step 2	Select	the range C5:C11
Step 3	Click	the Expand dialog button

Solver changes the number of employees on each shift so as to best reduce the amount of payroll paid each week. To ensure that Solver does not eliminate the entire warehouse staff, you must apply some constraints. The first constraint is that the number of employees on each shift must be greater than or equal to the total demand for each day. The second constraint is to force Excel to use whole numbers—after all, it's difficult to get 0.58 of a worker to appear at work on any given day. To add constraints:

Step 1	Click	<u>A</u>dd

The Add Constraint dialog box opens with the insertion point in the Cell <u>R</u>eference: text box.

Step 2	Select	the range D13:J13
Step 3	Click	>= in the constraint type list (in the middle of the dialog box)
Step 4	Select	the range D15:J15 in the <u>C</u>onstraint: list box

This constraint requires the values in the range D13:J13 to be greater than or equal to the values in the range D15:J15. You need the number of employees on each schedule to be a whole number, so you also apply an integer constraint. Your Add Constraint dialog box should look similar to Figure 10-8.

FIGURE 10-8
Add Constraint Dialog Box

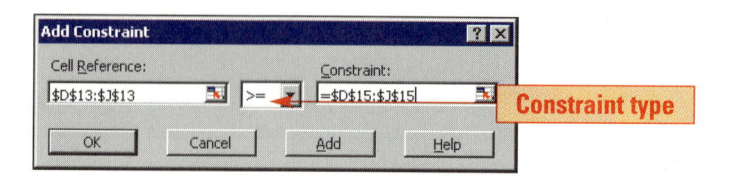

You need to add the constraint you just defined. You also want the result—the number of employees on each schedule—to be a whole number, so you need to define and add an integer constraint.

Step 5	Click	Add
Step 6	Select	the range C5:C11
Step 7	Click	int in the type of constraint list
Step 8	Click	OK
Step 9	Click	Solve

Depending on the worksheet and the speed of your computer, Solver may take a few seconds to perform its calculations. Solver figures out the solution, displays the results on your worksheet, and opens the Solver Results dialog box. Your screen should look similar to Figure 10-9.

> **QUICK TIP**
>
> The Options button provides settings to optimize the calculation methods in Solver; it also allows you to save and load Solver models for use in other worksheets. If you want to change the way that Solver calculates solutions, open the Solver dialog box, then click Options. Use the online Help to learn more about the Solver Options dialog box.

FIGURE 10-9
Solver Results Dialog Box

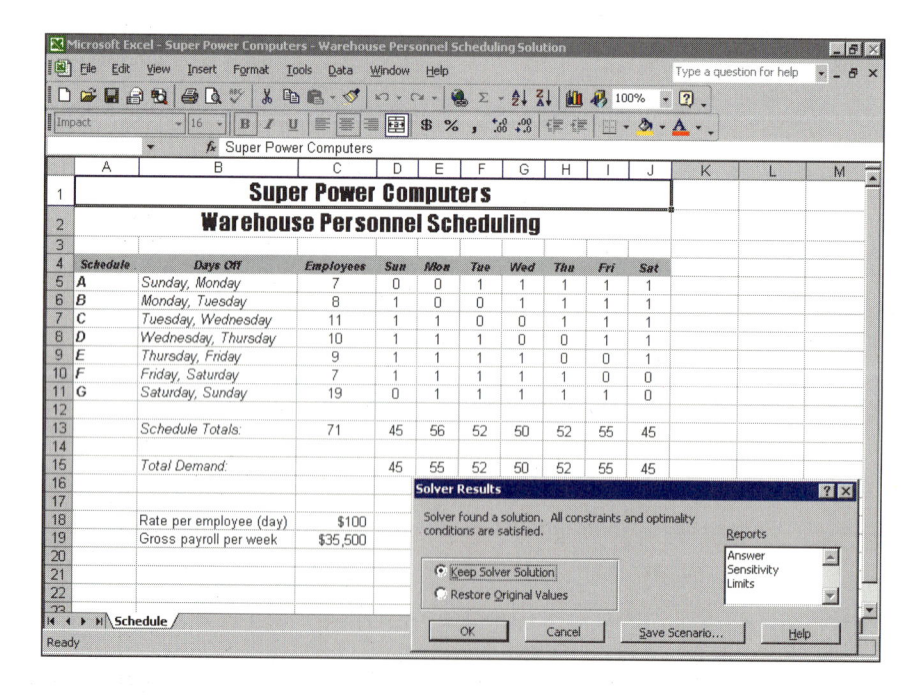

Interestingly, the best solution for the warehouse is to add more employees. By doing so, Solver came up with a scheduling solution that provides the correct number of employees for each day of the week. Only once does the number of employees exceed the required number of employees.

Step 10	Click	Answer in the Reports list box
Step 11	Click	OK
Step 12	Click	the Answer Report 1 sheet tab

Excel generates The Answer Report shown in Figure 10-10. The Answer Report provides information about the calculations and constraints used by Solver to generate the solution. It displays information about the date on which this solution was created, and provides all data used in the solution, including the target cell, adjustable cells, and constraints. Original cell values are shown adjacent to the final cell values after Solver is run.

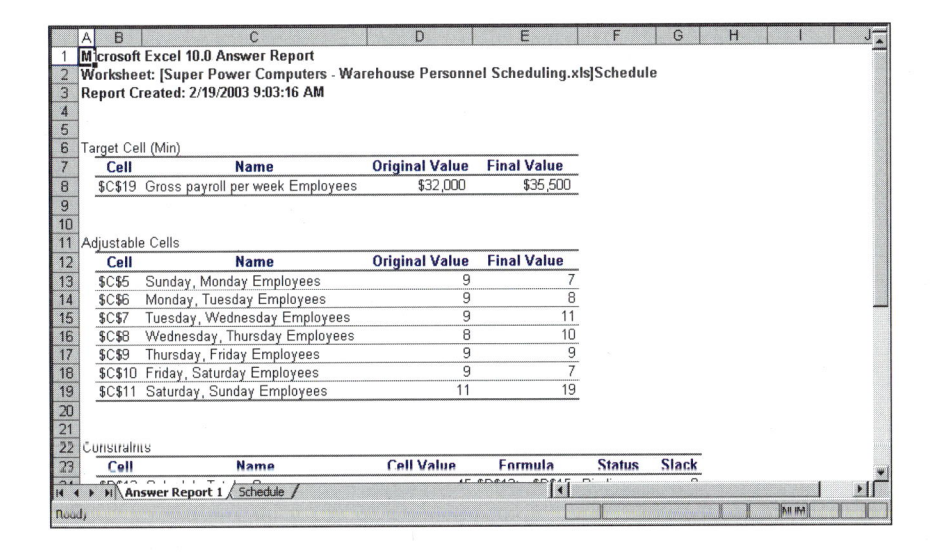

CAUTION TIP

Once you complete the Solver operation, you cannot undo it. Before closing the Solver Results dialog box, you have the option of restoring the original values. To do that, click the Restore Original Values option button, then click OK.

FIGURE 10-10
Solver Answer Report

QUICK TIP

To find out more information about the Limits and Sensitivity reports, use online Help.

Step 13	Save	the workbook

10.c Creating Scenarios

The tools introduced in this chapter—data tables, Goal Seek, and Solver—are designed to allow you maximum flexibility in asking the question, "What if?" Many times, you will need to quickly see the results of several "What if?" situations. For example, what if the current level of

chapter ten

activity in the warehouse drops off? What if the current level of activity in the warehouse increases, as it always does during the holiday season?

The demand values in cells D15:J15 indicate how many employees are needed on a given day. By using scenarios, you can change the values contained in these cells and run Solver using the new set of values to find a solution that satisfies the constraints of the given scenario.

Creating Scenarios

Scenarios allow you to quickly replace the values in several cells with another set of values, which you can then use in formulas throughout the worksheet. To create scenarios:

Step 1	**Click**	the Schedule sheet tab
Step 2	**Select**	the range D15:J15
Step 3	**Click**	Tools
Step 4	**Click**	Scenarios

Your Scenario Manager dialog box should look similar to Figure 10-11.

FIGURE 10-11
Scenario Manager Dialog Box

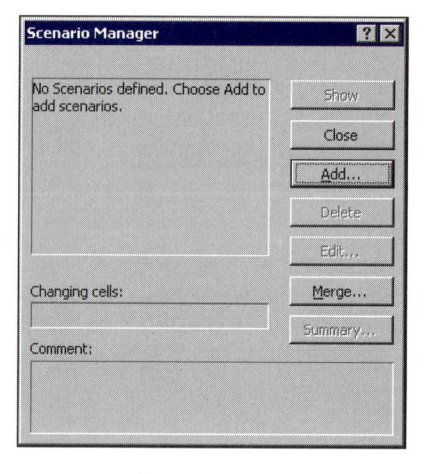

| Step 5 | **Click** | Add |

The Add Scenario dialog box opens. In this dialog box, you can name your scenario, select the cells to be changed under the new scenario, and add descriptive comments about your scenario.

| Step 6 | **Key** | Normal Demand in the Scenario name: text box |
| Step 7 | **Verify** | that the Changing cells: box references D15:J15 |

Step 8	Click	at the end of the Created by…on MM/DD/YY comment in the Comment: text box
Step 9	Press	the ENTER key
Step 10	Key	Normal demand covers April-September.
Step 11	Click	OK

MOUSE TIP

You can drag the scroll box down to see the rest of the cells you selected.

The Scenario Values dialog box on your screen should look similar to Figure 10-12. You can enter different values for each of the changing cells in this dialog box. Because the values currently in those cells are the Normal Demand values, you can leave them alone.

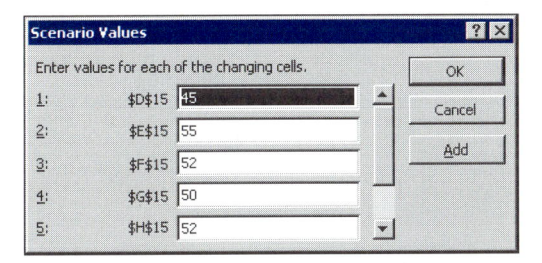

FIGURE 10-12
Scenario Values Dialog Box

Step 12	Click	OK to return to the Scenario Manager dialog box
Step 13	Click	Add and create another scenario named Low Demand that covers January-March
Step 14	Click	OK in the Add Scenario dialog box
Step 15	Key	20 in the 1: text box next to $D$15
Step 16	Press	the TAB key
Step 17	Continue	replacing the values with those listed in Table 10-1

QUICK TIP

Press the TAB key to move from box to box in the Scenarios Values dialog box.

$D$15	$E$15	$F$15	$G$15	$H$15	$I$15	$J$15
20	45	45	40	45	50	20

TABLE 10-1
Low Demand Values

Step 18	Add	a scenario named High Demand that covers October-December and uses the values listed in Table 10-2

$D$15	$E$15	$F$15	$G$15	$H$15	$I$15	$J$15
40	60	60	60	60	65	40

TABLE 10-2
High Demand Values

chapter ten

Displaying Scenarios

Once you've created different scenarios, you can display each one so as to replace the values in row 15, then run Solver to calculate the number of employees needed for each scenario. To display different scenarios:

Step 1	Click	Low Demand in the Scenarios: list box in the Scenario Manager dialog box
Step 2	Click	Show

The values in the range D15:J15 change to display the scenario values you created.

Step 3	Show	the High Demand scenario

A scenario report displays the values contained in each scenario.

Step 4	Click	Summary
Step 5	Verify	that the Scenario summary option button is selected
Step 6	Click	OK

A scenario summary is created and inserted on a new worksheet named Scenario Summary, which automatically becomes the active worksheet. Your summary should look similar to Figure 10-13. This scenario summary lists the current values of the changing cells as well as the values for each of the defined scenarios.

> **QUICK TIP**
>
> To show your scenario as a PivotTable, click the Scenario PivotTable option button. You also must select Result cells that perform calculations on the cells saved in your scenario(s).

> **MOUSE TIP**
>
> Click the Outline symbols to expand the outline and view the comments for each scenario.

FIGURE 10-13
Scenario Summary

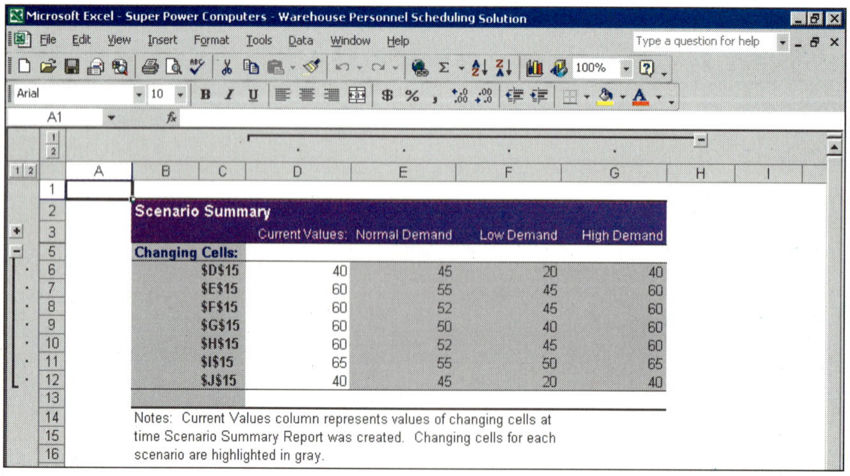

	Current Values	Normal Demand	Low Demand	High Demand
Changing Cells:				
$D$15	40	45	20	40
$E$15	60	55	45	60
$F$15	60	52	45	60
$G$15	60	50	40	60
$H$15	60	52	45	60
$I$15	65	55	50	65
$J$15	40	45	20	40

Notes: Current Values column represents values of changing cells at time Scenario Summary Report was created. Changing cells for each scenario are highlighted in gray.

| Step 7 | **Save** | the workbook and close it |

Using these different scenarios, you can run Solver to find the best solution for each period of the year.

10.d Creating a Trendline

Another type of what-if analysis involves forecasting trends. For example, by analyzing previous sales figures, Super Power Computers can project future growth potential. In a way, forecasting trends is like predicting the weather. Based on existing (past) data, a prediction, or forecast can be made for future events. **Trendlines** are often added to charts to provide a graphical illustration of the direction in which a set of data is headed. Excel can add a trendline to a chart based on the existing data. When you also need to see the actual values associated with a trendline, you use a special group of statistical functions. To add a trendline to a chart:

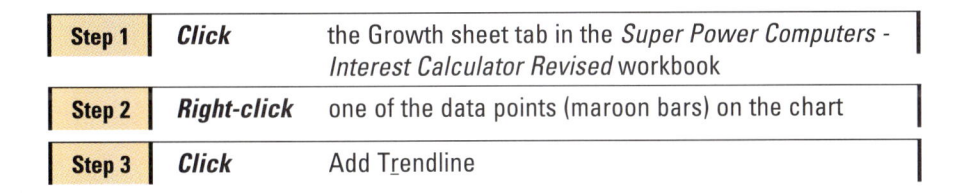

Step 1	**Click**	the Growth sheet tab in the *Super Power Computers - Interest Calculator Revised* workbook
Step 2	**Right-click**	one of the data points (maroon bars) on the chart
Step 3	**Click**	Add T_rendline

The Add Trendline dialog box that opens should look similar to Figure 10-14. Each option in the Trend/Regression type uses a different formula to predict the trend in the data provided. The linear trend averages the differences over the data you supply, then calculates the trend as a straight line continuation of the trend over the number of periods you specify. You want to project a linear trend four months into the future.

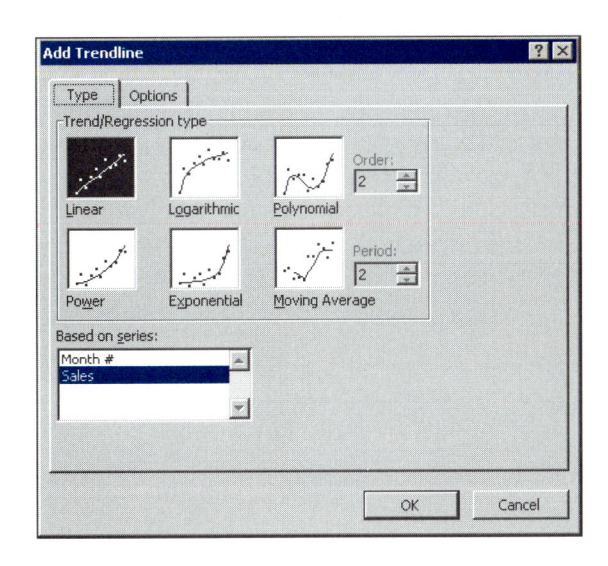

FIGURE 10-14
Add Trendline Dialog Box

Step 4	**Verify**	that Linear is selected
Step 5	**Click**	the Options tab
Step 6	**Double-click**	the Forward: text box
Step 7	**Key**	4
Step 8	**Click**	OK
Step 9	**Resize**	the chart to match the one shown in Figure 10-15

> **QUICK TIP**
>
> For more information about the different types of trends, refer to online Help.

The chart is updated to show a trendline and four additional months. No extra data points are added to the chart. Your chart should look similar to Figure 10-15. To add the projected data points, you need to use a statistical function to calculate the values.

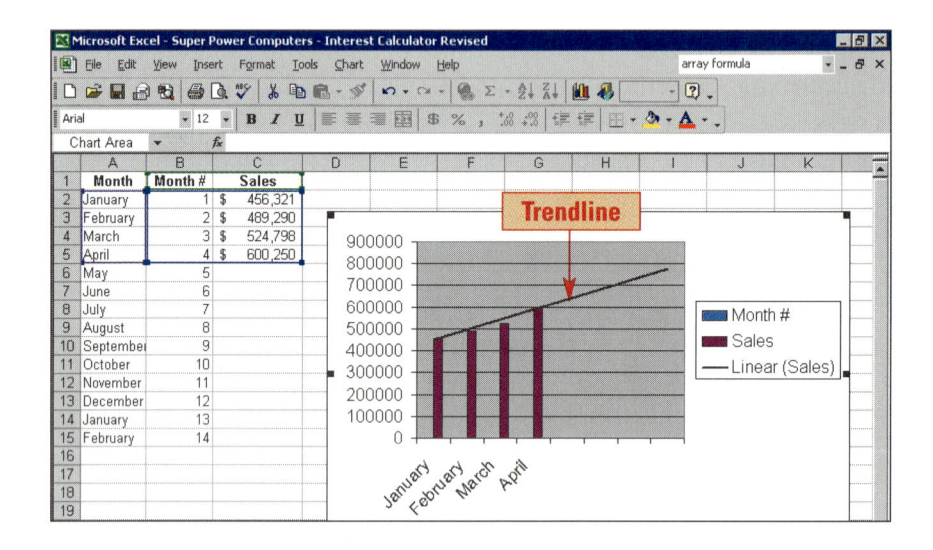

FIGURE 10-15
Chart with Trendline

The TREND function returns values reflecting a linear trend, and uses the following syntax:

=**TREND**(**known_y's**, known_x's, new_x's, const)

The **known_y's** are the actual data that indicate some sort of trend or pattern. In this workbook, the known_y's are the sales amounts. To create the trend, the y values change over time, so the **known_x's** represent an increment in establishing a time frame for the trend. In this workbook, the known_x's are the months corresponding to the known sales figures. The months are represented by their numeric value because the formula calculates a numerical increment. Your task is to project the future sales values (y), for the months ahead.

To have this formula calculate values for several months at a time, you must change it to an **array formula**. An array formula can use a single formula to perform multiple calculations and return multiple results. In this case, you want the TREND function to return values in the range C6:C15, based on the data in the range B2:C5, and projecting across the periods indicated by the range B6:B15. To calculate the sales trend using an array formula:

Step 1	Select	the range C6:C15 to automatically enter the array formula in each of these cells
Step 2	Key	=TREND(C2:C5,B2:B5,B6:B15)
Step 3	Press	the CTRL + SHIFT + ENTER keys simultaneously

This special key combination enters the formula as an array formula. In the Formula Bar, an array formula is surrounded by curly braces, {=**TREND(C2:C5,B2:B5,B6:B15)**}. The array formula calculates a new value in each row of column C based on the value of the adjacent cell in column B. In other words, the TREND function "predicts" the sales for months 5–14 based on the existing data in cells B2:C5. Now, you update your chart.

Step 4	Click	in a blank area of the chart object
Step 5	Drag	the blue Range Finder handle in the worksheet so that it includes the range A2:C15
Step 6	Double-click	the trendline on the chart

The Format Trendline dialog box opens. Because your chart now includes the projected data (as calculated by the TREND function), you want to eliminate the extra four months of projection.

Step 7	Click	the Options tab
Step 8	Key	0 in the Forward: text box
Step 9	Click	OK
Step 10	Resize	the chart as necessary to display the first four months

Your chart displays the additional data points.

| Step 11 | Save | the workbook and close it |

The "What-if" tools presented in this chapter offer powerful ways for businesses to analyze trends and make important financial decisions that often have long-term implications.

Summary

- Use a one-variable data table to replace one variable of a formula(s) with multiple values.
- Use a two-variable data table to replace two variables of a single formula with multiple values.
- Use Goal Seek to change the values of variables used in a formula to obtain a certain result.
- Use Solver to change the values of multiple cells and apply constraints to limit the changes of those cells so as to obtain a certain result.
- Use scenarios to store cell values for different situations.
- Add a trendline to charts to project future data.
- Create data points on a trendline using a variety of statistical functions, including the TREND function.

Commands Review

Action	Menu Bar	Shortcut Menu	Toolbar	Task Pane	Keyboard
Create a data table	Data, Table				ALT + D, T
Use Goal Seek	Tools, Goal Seek				ALT + T, G
Activate an add-in	Tools, Add-Ins				ALT + T, I
Use Solver	Tools, Solver				ALT + T, V
Create scenarios	Tools, Scenarios				ALT + T, E
Add a trendline to a graph	Click data point, then Chart, Add Trendline	Right-click data point, Add Trendline			ALT + C, R
Create an array formula					Key formula, then CTRL + SHIFT + ENTER to accept entry

Concepts Review

Circle the correct answer.

1. **If you want to see how different interest rates and different terms affect the payment of a loan, which of the following tools would you use?**
   - [a] one-variable data table
   - [b] two-variable data table
   - [c] Solver
   - [d] Goal Seek

2. **Solving complex business problems often requires you to:**
   - [a] look at a problem several ways.
   - [b] know the expected outcome of a formula.
   - [c] perform a what-if analysis.
   - [d] all of the above

3. **When you need to calculate values for predicting future sales, you should:**
   - [a] add a trendline to a graph.
   - [b] use the Draw toolbar to draw lines based on your best guess.
   - [c] average the difference between each of the known sales amounts, then add that to the last known sales amount.
   - [d] use a statistical function such as TREND.

4. **Which of the following is not a setting used by Solver?**
   - [a] Target
   - [b] Changing cells
   - [c] Constraints
   - [d] Summary

5. **Goal Seek is useful when you:**
   - [a] know the outcome and have to change only one variable.
   - [b] know the outcome and have to change multiple variables.
   - [c] don't know the outcome, but know one of the variables.
   - [d] don't know the outcome, but know two of the variables.

6. **Constraints:**
   - [a] cannot be modified.
   - [b] set limits regarding how much a cell's value can be changed.
   - [c] help Solver run faster.
   - [d] set limits regarding the speed at which Solver runs.

7. **A what-if analysis can show you:**
   - [a] how changing data affects various calculations.
   - [b] how to set up one-variable data tables if you don't know the value of any of the variables.
   - [c] which feature is the better choice to solve your problem—Goal Seek or Solver.
   - [d] which calculations will change if you change a variable.

8. **In a two-variable data table, you can replace:**
   - [a] two variables in more than one formula.
   - [b] two variables in a single formula.
   - [c] one variable in two formulas.
   - [d] one variable in one formula.

9. **The Scenario Manager allows you to:**
   - [a] add a new scenario.
   - [b] delete a scenario.
   - [c] merge scenarios from other workbooks.
   - [d] all of the above

10. **If you know the outcome you want for a given formula and can change multiple values, which tool should you use?**
    - [a] scenarios
    - [b] Solver
    - [c] one-variable data table
    - [d] Goal Seek

chapter ten

Circle **T** if the statement is true or **F** if the statement is false.

T   F   1. You can use more than one formula in a one-variable data table.

T   F   2. You can use more than one formula in a two-variable data table.

T   F   3. You can create a what-if analysis by manually changing the values of cells referenced in a formula.

T   F   4. Goal Seek can create a report when it finds a solution.

T   F   5. Solver is the best tool to use whenever you're trying to do a what-if analysis.

T   F   6. Solver can create three different reports when it has found a solution.

T   F   7. You can save a scenario from Solver.

T   F   8. The formula for a two-variable data table must appear immediately above the column variables and immediately to the right of row variables.

T   F   9. Once you run Solver, you cannot retrieve your original data.

T   F   10. When you add a trendline to a chart, the type of formula used makes no difference; all the trendlines come out the same.

Skills Review

Exercise 1

1. Open the *Warehouse Personnel Scheduling 2* workbook located on the Data Disk.
2. Set up constraints in the Solver Parameters dialog box to accomplish the following:

    a. The goal is to reduce the value of cell C19 to a minimum.

    b. The values in the range C5:C11 can change, but must be integers and must be greater than or equal to 1.

    c. The values in the range D13:J13 must meet or exceed the total demand in the range D15:J15.

3. Run Solver on the workbook and create an Answer Report.
4. Print the schedule and the Answer Report.
5. Save the workbook as *Warehouse Personnel Scheduling Solution 1*, and close it.

Exercise 2

1. Open the *Warehouse Personnel Scheduling Solution 1* workbook that you created in Exercise 1.
2. Create four scenarios called "1st Quarter," "2nd Quarter," "3rd Quarter," and "4th Quarter" by changing the range D15:J15 on the Schedule tab. Values for each scenario are listed below:

    1st Quarter—use the values currently set

    2nd Quarter—D15 = 37, E15 = 54, F15 = 56, G15 = 56, H15 = 60, I15 = 52, J15 = 40

    3rd Quarter—D15 = 35, E15 = 52, F15 = 52, G15 = 50, H15 = 55, I15 = 48, J15 = 37

    4th Quarter—D15 = 45, E15 = 55, F15 = 55, G15 = 55, H15 = 60, I15 = 55, J15 = 45

3. Save the workbook as *Warehouse Personnel Scheduling Scenarios*, and close it.

Exercise 3

1. Open the *Warehouse Personnel Scheduling Scenarios* workbook that you created in Exercise 2.
2. Rename the Answer Report 1 sheet tab to "1st Quarter Answer."
3. Show the 2nd Quarter scenario.
4. Run Solver and create an Answer Report.
5. Rename the sheet tab "2nd Quarter Answer."
6. Follow Steps 3 through 5 to show the 3rd and 4th Quarter scenarios, run Solver and generate an Answer Report, and rename each Answer Report sheet tab.
7. Print the Answer Reports.
8. Save the workbook as *Warehouse Personnel Scheduling Scenarios 2*, and then print and close it.

Exercise 4

1. Open the *Projected Portfolio* workbook located on the Data Disk.
2. In cell E4, enter the formula =FV(B4/12,B5,B6).
3. Select the range D4:E7.
4. Create a one-variable data table using cell B6 as the Column input cell.
5. Save the workbook as *Projected Portfolio Final*, and then print and close it.

Exercise 5

1. Open the *Home Purchase* workbook located on the Data Disk.
2. Use Goal Seek to find the maximum amount of a loan according to the following parameters:
   a. Use cell B8 as the goal, with a value of 650.
   b. Change the value in cell B5.
3. Save the workbook as *Home Purchase Loan*, and then print and close it.

Exercise 6

1. Open the *System Purchase* workbook located on the Data Disk.
2. Use Solver to find the optimum purchasing solution, given the following parameters:
   a. Seek the minimum total purchase price in cell D7.
   b. Change the range C4:C6.
   c. Use the following constraints:
   - C4:C6 must be integers.
   - You need to buy at least 65 new computers.
   - At least 15 computers need to be P-4 1.4s.
   - At least 20 computers need to be P-III 850s.
   - The total number of Duron 700s cannot exceed 20.

chapter ten

3. Generate an Answer Report.

4. Print your solution and the Answer Report.

5. Save the workbook as *System Purchase Solution* and close it.

Exercise 7

1. Open the *Manufacturing Production* workbook located on the Data Disk.

2. Use Solver to find a solution to maximize total profit (cell H8). Use the following constraints:

   a. The number of cases must be an integer.

   b. The number of cases for each product must be at least 1.

   c. The minimum number of cases of product A-123 to produce is 100.

   d. The maximum number of cases of product A-128 to produce is 25.

   e. The minimum number of cases of product A-128 to produce is 10.

   f. The total storage space must not exceed 25,000.

   g. The maximum production hours is 80.

3. Create an Answer Report.

4. Print the Answer Report and the solution.

5. Create a scenario using the constraint values in the range B11:B17. Name it "Normal Production Schedule."

6. Save the workbook as *Manufacturing Production Solution,* and then print and close it.

Exercise 8

1. Open the *North Region 2003 Sales* workbook located on the Data Disk.

2. Select the range B9:E9.

3. Create a Column chart according to the following parameters:

   a. In Step 2 of the Chart Wizard, click the Series tab, then select the range B4:E4 as the Category (X) axis labels.

   b. In Step 4 of the Chart Wizard, create the chart as an embedded chart.

4. Add a trendline to the chart projecting forward four quarters.

5. Insert two columns between columns E and F.

6. Change the column labels in the range B4:G4 to 1, 2, 3, 4, 5, 6.

7. In cell F9, enter the TREND formula using cells B9:E9 as known_y, B4:E4 as known_x, and F4:G4 as new_x.

8. Select the range F9:G9.

9. Press the F2 key to edit cell F9, then press the CTRL + SHIFT + ENTER keys to enter the formula as an array formula.

10. Click the chart.

11. Use the Range Finder to include the range F9:G9 in the chart.

12. Save the workbook as *North Region 2004 Projected Sales,* and then print and close it.

Case Projects

Project 1

You want to buy a new house. To buy the house you want, you need a loan of $140,000. You've been shopping for loans and have found one offering an interest rate of 9.5% with a 15-year term, 8.5% with a 20-year term, 7.5% with a 25-year term, and 7% with a 20-year term. Use a data table(s) to calculate your monthly payments for each interest rate, and what your total interest would be for each loan. Save the workbook as *Home Loan Calculator*, and print and close it.

Project 2

Connect to the Internet and search the Web for Excel Solver tutorials. Locate at least one tutorial and print the Web page(s) containing the tutorial.

Project 3

You want to buy a car for $28,500. The car dealer has offered to finance your purchase at 8.5% for 48 months. You can afford to make payments of $400.00 per month. Use Goal Seek to find the maximum amount you can borrow at this interest rate. Save the workbook as *Car Loan*, print the solution, and close the workbook.

Project 4

Connect to the Internet and search for stock prices for a company that interests you. Find a closing price on the same day for the last six months. (*Hint:* Search for historical data.) Record these six closing prices in a new workbook. Create a column chart of this data, then add a trendline covering the next six months. Save the workbook as *Stock Trend*, and print and close it.

Project 5

Set up a budget for a sales company with an estimated gross sales income of $25,000 per month. Figure an amount for rent of $5,000, utilities and overhead of $5,000, payroll of $8,500, and advertising costs of $2,500. Set up a workbook to calculate the net profit or loss using these figures. Save the gross sales income, payroll, and advertising costs as a scenario called "Best Case." Create a second scenario called "Worst Case," with the following amounts: income = $17,500, rent = $5,000, utilities/overhead = $5,000, payroll = $5,000, advertising = $1,000. Show the worst-case scenario values, then save the workbook as *Best and Worst Case Sales*, and print and close it.

Project 6

You are deciding between two jobs located in different cities. Job offer #1 provides a salary of $35,000 per year. Job offer #2 includes a salary of $40,000 per year. Create a workbook to calculate a budget based on each scenario. In your budget, you estimate that 30% of your salary can be spent on house payments, 10% can be spent on car payments, 30% on living expenses, and 10% for savings. Also include a formula to sum the total budgeted expenses, then subtract this amount from the salary. Create a scenario summary worksheet and print it. Save the workbook as *Job Offers*, then print and close it.

Project 7

You would like to reduce the length of time needed to pay off your car loan. Instead of paying off the $10,000 loan (at 9%) in 48 months, you want to see what your monthly payments would be if you paid off the loan in 42, 36, and 30 months. Create a one-variable table to calculate these payments. Save the workbook as *Quick Payoff*, and print and close it.

Project 8

You are a broker for an investment firm. Your job is to analyze companies to see whether you should invest in them. Create a fictitious company with sales data for the last seven months. Create a graph with a trendline with data points showing the projected growth for the next seven months. Indicate projected months by shading the cells. Save the workbook as *Growth Analysis*, and print and close it.

chapter ten

Excel 2002

Using Auditing Tools

Chapter Overview

Auditing tools help you identify relationships between cells. The Formula Auditing toolbar provides tools to identify precedents and dependents, trace errors to their source, and locate invalid data. In this chapter, you use Range Finder to check and review data, identify data between precedent and dependent cells, use error checking, and identify invalid data.

Learning Objectives

- Use Range Finder to check and review data
- Identify relationships between precedent and dependent cells
- Use error checking
- Identify invalid data

Case profile

Many Super Power Computers employees use the Excel workbooks you create as well as create their own. As you share workbooks with coworkers, you occasionally notice their errors (and find your own *rare* errors) or need to review the sources of values referenced by a certain formula. The Excel auditing tools help you quickly track down the source of errors or identify locations where values are used throughout even the most complex worksheets.

chapter eleven

Using Auditing Tools   EA 99

11.a Using Range Finder to Check and Review Data

Whenever you open a workbook created by someone else, it is a good idea to review the worksheet's assumptions and calculations before you begin editing data. Previously, you used Range Finder to adjust which cells were used for chart data. Here, Range Finder helps you track down references used in formulas.

The *Super Power Computers - Projected Profit with Errors* workbook contains several errors that should be corrected. To open the workbook and save it with a new name:

| Step 1 | Open | the *Super Power Computers - Projected Profit with Errors* workbook located on the Data Disk |
| Step 2 | Save | the workbook as *Super Power Computers - Projected Profit Revised* |

The Projected Profit worksheet contains projections for income and expenses for the coming year. Rows 17–22 contain multipliers used in some of the formulas on the worksheet to calculate expense amounts. Because the information for the third and fourth quarters consists of projected data, it is italicized.

Excel tools can help you pinpoint errors in formulas and correct them. Several of the cells contain small green triangles in the upper-left corner. Excel automatically checks for errors, and these triangles indicate possible errors in those cells. When you click a cell containing a detected error, the Trace Errors button appears. Clicking that button opens a menu of commands that can help you in fixing the error.

To use Range Finder to revise a formula:

| Step 1 | Click | cell E13 on the Projected Profit worksheet |

The Trace Errors button appears to the left of cell E13. The formula in cell E13 is supposed to calculate the projected profit for the third quarter, but it currently shows a value of zero (shown as a dash in the Accounting format).

| Step 2 | Click | the Trace Errors button |
| Step 3 | Click | Edit in Formula Bar |

> **QUICK TIP**
>
> You can disable automatic error checking by clicking the Options command on the Tools menu. Click the Error Checking tab, then click Enable background error checking check box. Several other error-checking options are available on this tab.

chapter eleven

Your screen should look similar to Figure 11-1. The formula highlights each cell or range reference, using a different color for each reference to make it easier to identify the reference.

FIGURE 11-1
Using Range Finder to Locate References

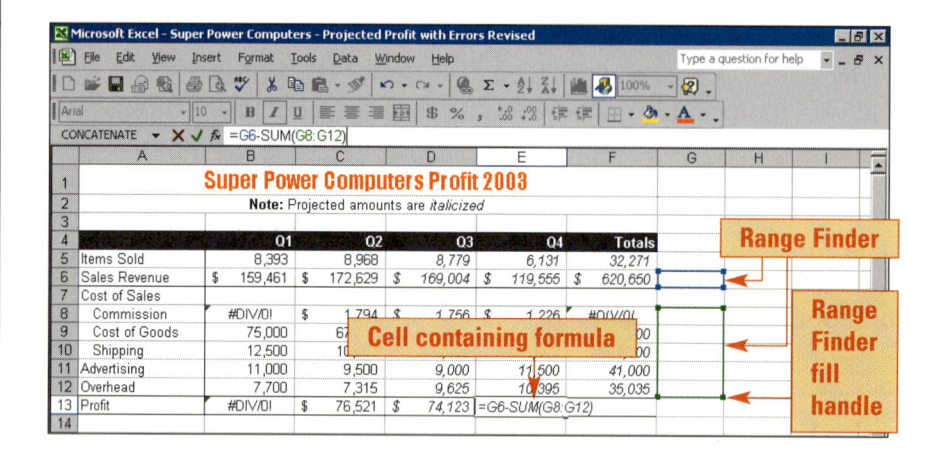

As shown by the Range Finder, the formula refers to empty cells G6 and G8:G12. To adjust a reference, you drag the border of the Range Finder to the correct location in column E. If necessary, you can drag the Range Finder fill handle to increase or decrease the size of the range.

Step 4	*Drag*	the blue Range Finder border to cell E6
Step 5	*Observe*	that as you drag the border, the formula in the Formula Bar adjusts automatically
Step 6	*Drag*	the green Range Finder border to cells E8:E12
Step 7	*Click*	the Enter button on the Formula Bar
Step 8	*Observe*	that the total $11,434 appears in cell E13
Step 9	*Save*	the workbook

11.b Identifying Relationships Between Precedent and Dependent Cells

As workbooks grow larger and more complex, it becomes increasingly difficult to locate and review relationships between cells. Excel provides auditing features to simplify this job.

Using Auditing Tools   EA 101

Tracing Precedents

Precedents are the cells referred to by a formula. You can locate precedents by using the Formula Auditing commands on the Tools menu and on the Formula Auditing toolbar. To show the Formula Auditing toolbar:

Step 1	Click	Tools
Step 2	Point to	Formula Auditing
Step 3	Click	Show Formula Auditing Toolbar

The formula in cell F6 adds the total Sales Revenue figures for each quarter. To trace the precedents for this formula:

Step 1	Click	cell F6
Step 2	Click	the Trace Precedents button on the Formula Auditing toolbar

A heavy blue tracer arrow identifies the precedent(s) for this formula. When the precedent consists of a range of cells, the tracer arrow is indicated with a heavy line, and the range is highlighted with a blue border. When the precedent consists of a single cell, the tracer arrow is indicated with a thin line. Your screen should look similar to Figure 11-2.

> **MENU TIP**
>
> To trace precedents, point to Formula Auditing on the Tools menu, then click Trace Precedents.

> **MOUSE TIP**
>
> You can jump to a referenced cell by using the tracer arrow lines. Double-click an arrow line, and the active cell moves back and forth between the referenced cells and the formula.

FIGURE 11-2
Tracing Precedents

Many times, the results of a formula are not based on a single level of precedents. For example, the formula in cell F6 refers to the range B6:E6, but the values in this range are derived from still other formulas.

chapter eleven

To view a second level of precedents:

| Step 1 | Click | the Trace Precedents button on the Formula Auditing toolbar a second time |

Your screen should look similar to Figure 11-3.

FIGURE 11-3
Tracing Multiple Levels of Precedents

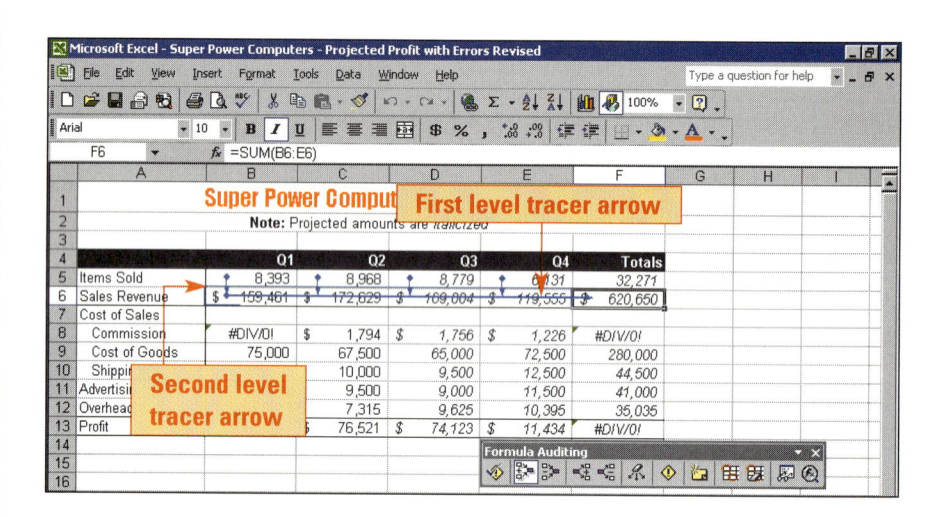

| Step 2 | Click | the Trace Precedents button on the Formula Auditing toolbar |

An alert sound indicates that Excel has reached the last level of precedents. Once you have finished viewing the precedents for a cell, you may want to clear the precedent arrows to view your worksheet more easily. To clear all precedent arrows:

| Step 1 | Click | the Remove All Arrows button on the Formula Auditing toolbar to remove the arrows |

Tracing Dependents

Dependents are cells containing formulas that rely on the value of another cell. A cell may be referenced by one or several formulas throughout a workbook. You can locate dependents in the same manner that you located precedents. To trace dependents:

| Step 1 | Click | cell B5 |
| Step 2 | Click | the Trace Dependents button on the Formula Auditing toolbar |

> **QUICK TIP**
>
> You can preview and print tracer arrows.

Thin blue tracer arrows point to cells B6, B8, and F5. Each of these cells contains a formula that references cell B5. Your screen should look similar to Figure 11-4.

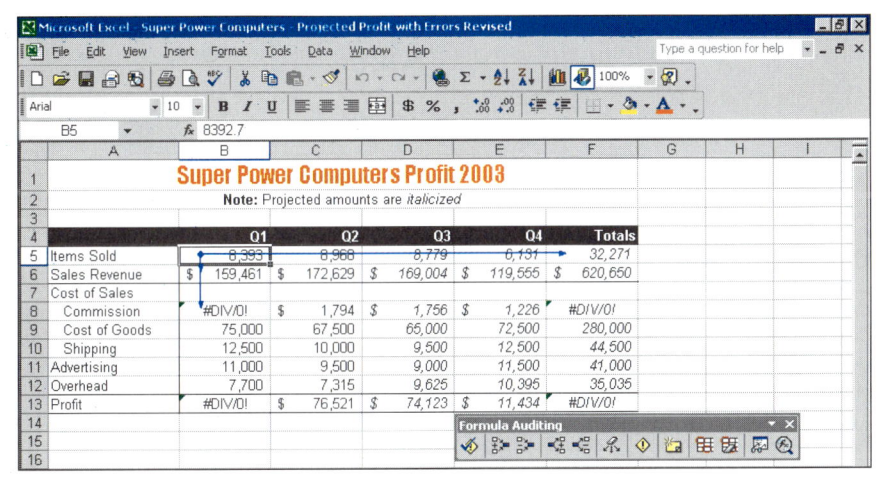

FIGURE 11-4
Tracing Dependents

You can identify multiple levels of dependents by continuing to click the Trace Dependents button on the Formula Auditing toolbar. The number of items sold, which appears in cell B5, is referenced by the formula in cell B8, which calculates the commission expense. This amount is then referenced by still other formulas. Cell B5 is also referenced by the formula in cell B6, which is then referenced by cell F6.

| Step 3 | Click | the Trace Dependents button on the Formula Auditing toolbar a second time |

A second level of tracer arrows is added to the display. A blue tracer arrow now points to cell F6. Because the formula in cell B8 contains an error, red tracer arrows point to the two cells that use cell B8 in their formulas. You fix this error in the next section.

You can remove a single level of arrows rather than removing all arrows at once. To remove a single level of arrows:

Step 1	Click	the Remove Dependent Arrows button on the Formula Auditing toolbar
Step 2	Observe	that the second level of tracer arrows disappears
Step 3	Click	the Remove Dependent Arrows button on the Formula Auditing toolbar
Step 4	Observe	that the first level of tracer arrows disappears

MENU TIP

To remove all precedent and dependent tracer arrows, click Tools, point to Formula Auditing, then click Remove All Arrows.

Tracing Cell Relationships Between Worksheets

As you learned in previous chapters, you can reference cells located on other worksheets as well as those on the current worksheet. The Excel auditing tools help you trace references to these cells. To trace precedents between worksheets:

Step 1	Click	cell B12
Step 2	Click	the Trace Precedents button on the Formula Auditing toolbar

A worksheet icon and a black tracer arrow appear, indicating that a reference in cell B12 is located on another worksheet. Check the formula in the Formula Bar to verify this relationship. Your screen should look similar to Figure 11-5. You can quickly jump to the referenced cell.

FIGURE 11-5
Tracing Relationships Between Worksheets

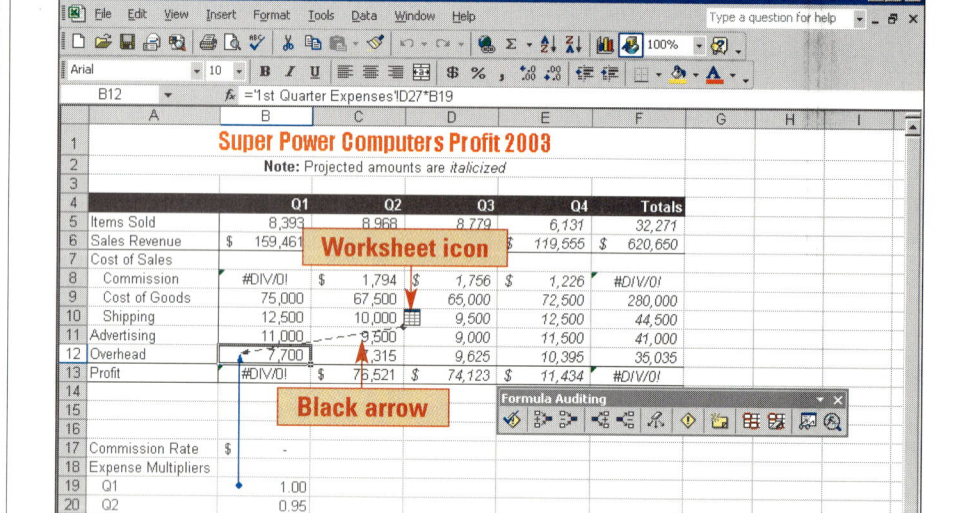

CAUTION TIP

Make sure the mouse pointer is in the shape of an arrow and not the cross when you double-click the black tracer arrow.

Step 3	Double-click	the black tracer arrow

The Go To dialog box opens.

Step 4	Click	the reference listed at the top of the Go to: list
Step 5	Click	OK

The 1st Quarter Expenses worksheet is activated, and the active cell moves to cell D27. The total in cell D27 is used in cell B12 on the Projected Profit worksheet.

Step 6	Click	the Projected Profit sheet tab
Step 7	Click	the Remove All Arrows button on the Formula Auditing toolbar
Step 8	Save	the workbook

11.c Using Error Checking

Excel features several tools to help you pinpoint errors in formulas and correct them. As you've seen, Excel tags cells with detected errors with a small green triangle in the upper-left corner, and when you click a cell containing a detected error, the Trace Errors button appears. Another tool, Error Checking, helps you locate and resolve common errors by scanning the worksheet for errors. When it finds one, the error is flagged, and Error Checking suggests ways to fix it. You can display tracer arrows from a cell containing a formula with errors to identify all cells referenced in the formula.

The formulas in cells B8, F8, B13, and F13 display the #DIV/0! error. This error indicates that at least one of these cells contains a formula that attempts to divide a value by zero. To trace and correct the source of this error:

Step 1	Activate	cell F8
Step 2	Click	the Error Checking button on the Formula Auditing toolbar
Step 3	Click	Trace Error in the Error Checking dialog box

The formula in cell F8 refers to the range B8:E8. Because an error occurs in cell F8, you see a red error arrow, as shown in Figure 11-6. Cell B8, however, is also displaying the #DIV/0! error. Clicking Edit in Formula Bar in the Error Checking dialog box won't do any good, because the source of the error isn't in cell F8, so you keep going to let the Error Checker find the source of the problem.

> **QUICK TIP**
>
> Select a cell, then click the Show Watch Window button on the Formula Auditing toolbar to open the Watch Window toolbar to watch the value in the cell.

> **MENU TIP**
>
> You can trace errors by clicking, pointing to the Formula Auditing command on the Tools menu, and then clicking Trace Error.

FIGURE 11-6
Tracing Errors

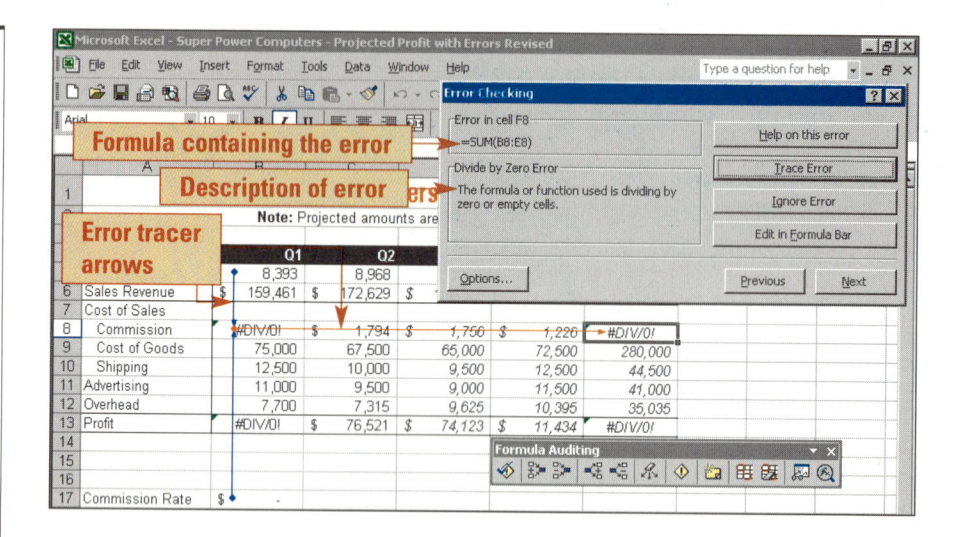

MOUSE TIP

Use the Trace Error button on the Formula Auditing toolbar to display trace arrows from a cell containing an error. This is equivalent to clicking Trace Error in the Error Checking dialog box.

QUICK TIP

Clicking Options in the Error Checking dialog box opens a dialog box in which you can select or deselect the rules that the Error Checker uses to check your workbooks.

Step 4	Click	Next to move to the next error
Step 5	Click	Trace Error
Step 6	Observe	that this error in cell B13 again points to cell B8
Step 7	Click	Next
Step 8	Click	Trace Error
Step 9	Observe	that this error in cell F13 also points to cell B8
Step 10	Click	Next

This time, the command in the Error Checking dialog box changes to Show Calculation Steps. This is because the error originates in this cell, cell B8. Your dialog box should look similar to Figure 11-7.

FIGURE 11-7
Error Checking Dialog Box

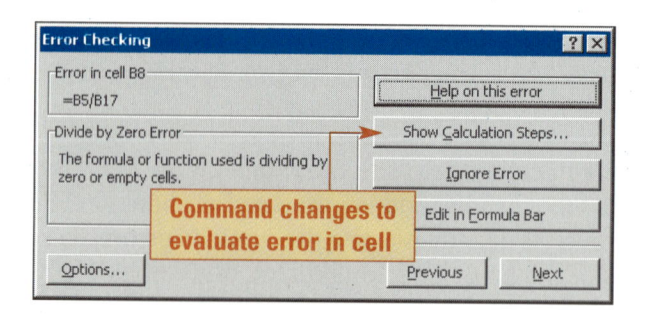

| Step 11 | Click | Show Calculation Steps |

Using Auditing Tools   EA 107

The Evaluate Formula dialog box opens, displaying the actual calculation that takes place. In this case, you are trying to divide the value in cell B5, 8392.7, by the value in cell B17, which is currently 0.

| Step 12 | Click | Evaluate |

This results in an error. Cell B17 is the source of all four errors; it contains a value of 0.

Step 13	Click	Close
Step 14	Click	Next
Step 15	Click	OK in the dialog box that opens, telling you that error checking is complete
Step 16	Enter	5 in cell B17

This correction solves the "divide by 0" error in cell B8, and consequently eliminates the problems in cells B13, F8, and F13. The red error arrows are replaced by blue tracer arrows.

| Step 17 | Click | the Remove All Arrows button on the Formula Auditing toolbar |
| Step 18 | Save | the workbook |

> **MENU TIP**
>
> Another way to track down errors is to display the formulas in the cells instead of the values. To do this, point to the Formula Auditing command on the Tools menu, then click Formula Auditing Mode.

11.d Identifying Invalid Data

In Chapter 8, you learned how to use data validation when creating lists of data. You also learned about the three different types of error alert messages. Two of the error alert messages—Information and Warning—allow a user to input invalid data, even though the user is informed that the information is invalid. To help you identify cells in a list that contain data violating data validation rules, you can use an auditing command.

The 1st Quarter Expenses worksheet has been prepared using data validation. However, several errors were made. To find invalid data:

| Step 1 | Click | the 1st Quarter Expenses sheet tab |
| Step 2 | Click | the Circle Invalid Data button on the Formula Auditing toolbar |

chapter eleven

| Step 3 | Scroll | the worksheet up until you can see row 1 |

All cells containing invalid data are circled in red. Your screen should look similar to Figure 11-8.

FIGURE 11-8
Identifying Invalid Data

> **MOUSE TIP**
>
> You can turn off the circles by clicking the Clear Validation Circles button on the Formula Auditing toolbar.

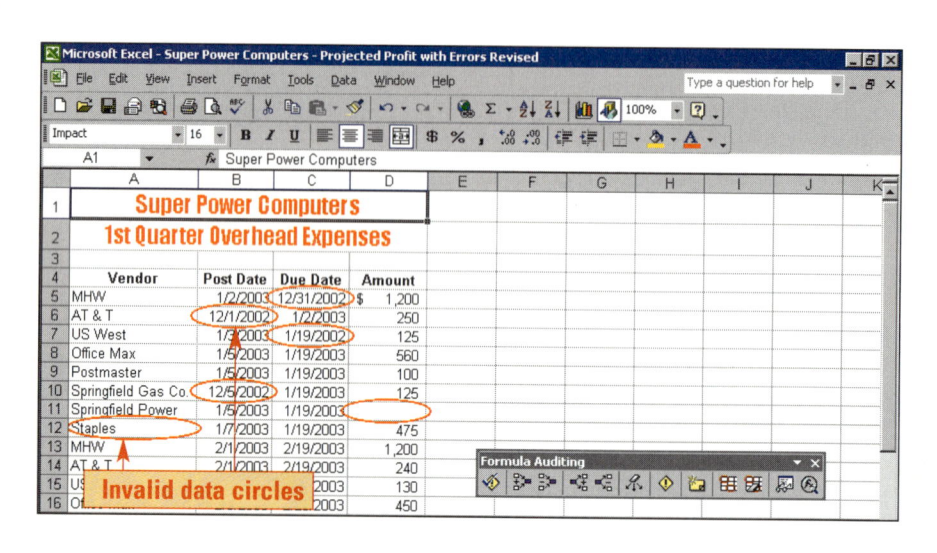

Step 4	Click	cell B6
Step 5	Enter	1/2/03 in cell B6
Step 6	Enter	1/5/03 in cell B10
Step 7	Enter	1/31/03 in cell C5
Step 8	Enter	1/19/03 in cell C7
Step 9	Enter	185 in cell D11
Step 10	Click	the list arrow in cell A12
Step 11	Click	Office Max
Step 12	Click	the Circle Invalid Data button on the Formula auditing toolbar to double-check for additional errors
Step 13	Close	the Formula Auditing toolbar
Step 14	Save	the workbook and close it

The Formula Auditing toolbar can be helpful when your worksheets include complicated formulas that use many precedents.

Summary

- You can use Range Finder to quickly edit cell references in a formula. Click and drag Range Finder borders to move a reference. The Range Finder fill handle enables you to "resize" a range reference.

- Precedents are cells or ranges referenced by a specific formula. You can select a cell containing a formula, then use the Trace Precedents tool to identify cells and ranges referenced in that particular formula.

- Dependents are cells containing formulas that depend on the value of a certain cell. You can select a cell containing a value or formula, then use the Trace Dependents tool to identify other cells containing formulas that reference that particular cell.

- You can use the Error Checker tool to quickly locate and resolve the source of a formula error.

- You can locate data that violates data validation rules by using the Circle Invalid Data auditing tool.

Commands Review

Action	Menu Bar	Shortcut Menu	Toolbar	Task Pane	Keyboard
Trace precedents	Tools, Formula Auditing, Trace Precedents				ALT + T, U, T
Trace dependents	Tools, Formula Auditing, Trace Dependents				ALT + T, U, D
Error checking					
Trace errors	Tools, Formula Auditing, Trace Error				ALT + T, U, E
Remove all arrows	Tools, Formula Auditing, Remove All Arrows				ALT + T, U, A
Circle invalid data					
Clear validation circles					

chapter eleven

Concepts Review

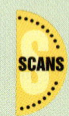

Circle the correct answer.

1. **Precedents are cells that:**
   - [a] are referred to by a formula.
   - [b] depend on the value of another cell.
   - [c] have blue arrow lines showing the relationship between two cells.
   - [d] have red arrow lines showing the source of an error.

2. **Dependents are cells that:**
   - [a] are referred to by a formula.
   - [b] depend on the value of another cell.
   - [c] have blue arrow lines showing the relationship between two cells.
   - [d] have red arrow lines showing the source of an error.

3. **Traced errors are indicated by a:**
   - [a] blue arrow.
   - [b] black arrow.
   - [c] red arrow.
   - [d] blinking cell border.

4. **A black tracer arrow indicates a:**
   - [a] serious error.
   - [b] multiple-cell reference.
   - [c] single-cell reference.
   - [d] reference on another worksheet.

5. **A green triangle in a cell indicates a:**
   - [a] comment placed by you.
   - [b] possible error detected by Excel.
   - [c] comment placed by another user.
   - [d] precedent.

6. **To locate data that violates data validation, use the:**
   - [a] Trace Precedents tool.
   - [b] Trace Error tool.
   - [c] Trace Dependents tool.
   - [d] Circle Invalid Data tool.

7. **To quickly jump to a precedent or dependent in another worksheet that has been traced:**
   - [a] click the worksheet icon that appears in the worksheet.
   - [b] double-click the black tracer arrow.
   - [c] drag the black tracer arrow to the sheet tab.
   - [d] double-click the cell to which the black tracer arrow points.

8. **You can trace errors in worksheet formulas by:**
   - [a] clicking the Trace Error button on the Formula Auditing toolbar.
   - [b] double-clicking the tracer arrows until they point to the errors.
   - [c] clicking the Find Errors button on the Formula Auditing toolbar.
   - [d] dragging the red tracer arrows to the precedent cell.

9. **If data in a worksheet has a red circle around it, you should:**
   - [a] fix the precedent cells.
   - [b] reenter the value currently in the cell.
   - [c] enter a valid entry in the cell.
   - [d] erase the red circles using the Eraser button on the Drawing toolbar.

10. **Range Finder can help you:**
    - [a] adjust the data used in a chart.
    - [b] change cell references in a formula.
    - [c] locate which cell references are used in a formula.
    - [d] all of the above

Circle **T** if the statement is true or **F** if the statement is false.

T F 1. You can view multiple levels of precedents and dependents.

T F 2. It is a good idea to review the relationships between cells when using a workbook prepared by someone else or when using a workbook with which you haven't worked on for a long time.

T F 3. You can jump between ends of a tracer arrow by double-clicking the arrow line.

T F 4. You can open the Formula Auditing toolbar by right-clicking the toolbar and clicking Auditing.

T F 5. The #DIV/0! error indicates a number that Excel cannot display.

T F 6. Red arrows indicate precedents and dependents.

T F 7. If a cell containing a formula that results in an error is a precedent of a formula in another cell, both cells display the error.

T F 8. To move a range with Range Finder, click and drag the Range Finder fill handle.

T F 9. You can use the Trace Error tool to find invalid data entered in a list.

T F 10. As you correct invalid entries in a list, the validation circles disappear.

Skills Review

Exercise 1

1. Open the *Warehouse Inventory Errors* workbook located on the Data Disk.
2. Use the Formula Auditing toolbar to locate cells containing invalid data.
3. Select rows 17–24.
4. Use the Clear All command (open the Data Validation dialog box) to clear data validation settings from rows 17–24.
5. Click the Circle Invalid Data button on the Formula Auditing toolbar again.
6. Print the worksheet with the circles displayed.
7. Correct the errors using data that is compatible with the validation rules.
8. Save the workbook as *Warehouse Inventory Errors Fixed* and print and close it.

Exercise 2

1. Open the *Fee Calculator Errors* workbook located on the Data Disk.
2. Start the Error Checker.
3. Evaluate the first suggestion. Because this formula is not in error, click Next to move to the next error.
4. Trace the #NAME? error to its source.
5. The formula in cell C3 refers to a named range, percentage, that does not exist in the worksheet. Edit the formula to properly refer to cell C2. If necessary, check the formula in the cell to the right.
6. Close Error Checking.
7. Save the workbook as *Fee Calculator Errors Fixed 1* and print and close it.

chapter eleven

Exercise 3

1. Open the *Fee Calculator Errors Fixed 1* workbook that you created in Exercise 2.
2. Click cell H7.
3. Use the Trace Precedents button, and then use the Range Finder to correct the formula so that it adds the range H3:H6.
4. Save the workbook as *Fee Calculator Errors Fixed 2* and print and close it.

Exercise 4

1. Open the *Fee Calculator Errors Fixed 2* workbook that you created in Exercise 3.
2. Trace the source of the #DIV/0! error in cell B10.
3. Remove the arrows.
4. Change the value of the erroneous cell to 5.
5. Print the worksheet.
6. Save the workbook as *Fee Calculator Errors Fixed 3*, and close it.

Exercise 5

1. Open the *XYZ Accounting* workbook located on the Data Disk.
2. Click cell B2 and trace its precedents.
3. Print the worksheet with the arrows displayed.
4. Double-click the black arrow line.
5. Select the reference to the San Diego tab and click OK.
6. Print the worksheet.
7. Save the workbook as *XYZ Accounting 1* and close it.

Exercise 6

1. Open the *XYZ Accounting 1* workbook that you created in Exercise 5.
2. Click cell E5.
3. Display the first-level precedents for cell E5.
4. Display the second-level precedents for cell E5.
5. Print the worksheet.
6. Save the workbook as *XYZ Accounting 2* and close it.

Exercise 7

1. Open the *XYZ Accounting 2* workbook that you created in Exercise 6.
2. Activate cell B2 on the Summary tab.
3. Trace all dependents of cell B2.
4. Print the worksheet.
5. Save the workbook as *XYZ Accounting 3* and close it.

Exercise 8

1. Open the *Day Off* workbook located on the Data Disk.
2. Use Error Checking to help you determine the cause of the error in cell B4.
3. Change the IF function to see if cell B2="Monday."
4. Change the width of column A.
5. Save the workbook as *No Day Off* and print and close it.

Case Projects

Project 1

Use the Ask A Question Box to look up the topic "Find and correct errors in formulas." Using the information you find, create a new workbook and try to create one of each type of error. In another column enter a description of how you "caused" each error (there are several ways to create almost all errors; just describe the one you used). Save the workbook as *Errors* and print and close it.

Project 2

Some of your clients work with other spreadsheet applications that use the R1C1 cell reference style. Use the Ask A Question Box to research the R1C1 reference style. Write a description of the differences between the R1C1 and the A1 reference styles, and how to use absolute and relative cell references in the R1C1 style. Include instructions on how to change Excel to use the R1C1 reference style. Save the document as *R1C1 Instructions.doc* and print and close it.

Project 3

Use the Ask A Question Box to research "circular references." In Word, write a two-paragraph memo explaining what a circular reference is, how to turn on the Circular Reference toolbar, and how to resolve the problem. Save the document as *Circular References.doc* and print and close it.

Project 4

You are in charge of hiring new employees for the Accounting Division. Part of your hiring procedure is to test applicants using a workbook containing several errors, to see how they resolve the problems. Create a workbook similar to the one used in this chapter, using your own row and column headings, and data. Create erroneous formulas using incorrect references, named ranges that don't exist, circular references, and a divide by 0 error. Save your workbook as *Error Test* and print and close it.

Project 5

History hunt! Connect to the Internet and search the Web to find out who invented the first spreadsheet application. Print a Web page explaining who invented it, why (s)he invented it, and what (s)he named it.

Project 6

You are the manager of a retail goods store. Create a template that can be used for calculating a typical sales transaction. Use a formula to add the sum of several items (minimum of five cells), then calculate a sales tax of 7% and add that to the previously calculated sum and display the total for the sale. Save the template as *Sales Transaction Template*. Create a new workbook from this template, enter fictitious sales data, then turn on Trace Precedents to trace the source of the total formula. Print the worksheet, save the workbook as *Sample Sales Transaction*, and then close it.

chapter eleven

Excel 2002

Summarizing Data with Data Analysis, PivotTables, and PivotCharts

Chapter Overview

Excel provides many ways to analyze and summarize data. Data analysis tools help you to prepare reports based on selected data, using a variety of statistical calculations. Using PivotTables and PivotCharts, you can prepare data reports by dragging and dropping report fields. PivotTables are very powerful, allowing you to quickly reorganize data as necessary.

Learning Objectives

- Use data analysis
- Create PivotTable reports
- Modify a PivotTable report
- Format a PivotTable report
- Create PivotChart reports

Case profile

Lately, you have been inundated with requests for information from every department in Super Power Computers. The warehouse needs to know which items are the best-sellers so that it knows how much to keep in stock. Shipping needs to know which stores are selling the most so that it can prepare orders accordingly. Personnel wants to know which sales representatives are ready to be promoted based on their sales performance. You can use data analysis tools, PivotTables, and PivotCharts to make short work of all these requests.

chapter twelve

12.a Using Data Analysis

Data analysis tools comprise a set of statistical analysis tools used to quickly generate reports based on a given set of data. Excel offers nearly 20 such analysis tools. In this section, you learn about the descriptive statistics and the rank and percentile tools. These tools generate statistics using several of the statistical functions with which you are already familiar.

The **descriptive statistics** tool creates a table of statistical data based on a range of numerical data. Statistics generated include Sum, Count, Minimum, Maximum, Range, Median, Mean, and Standard Deviation. By analyzing these types of statistics generated over a certain period of time, Super Power Computers can spot trends in the growth of the company. This information can be very helpful when the company president must make decisions about Super Power Computers' future. To generate a descriptive statistics report:

Step 1	Open	the *Super Power Computers - Store Sales Ranking* workbook located on the Data Disk
Step 2	Save	the workbook as *Super Power Computers - Store Sales Ranking Revised*
Step 3	Click	Tools
Step 4	Click	Data Analysis to open the Data Analysis dialog box
Step 5	Double-click	Descriptive Statistics in the Analysis Tools list (you may need to scroll up the list)

The Descriptive Statistics dialog box on your screen should look similar to Figure 12-1. You use this dialog box to select the input range and set output options for the statistical report.

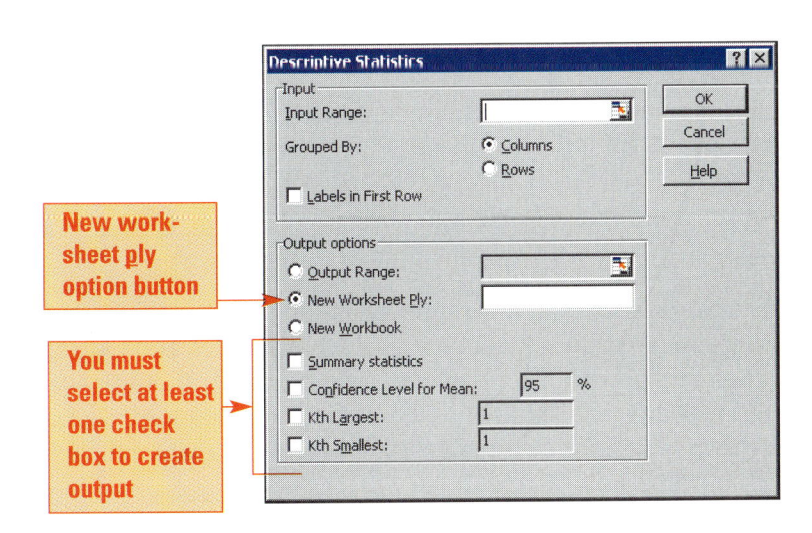

FIGURE 12-1
Descriptive Statistics Dialog Box

New worksheet ply option button

You must select at least one check box to create output

CAUTION TIP

When you use data analysis tools, you do not actually insert formulas in the reports. Instead, creating these reports is analogous to taking a snapshot of the data at a given point in time. Having such a fixed reference point is important when you must evaluate statistical trends over a period of time. If the source data changes, you must create a new statistical report.

Step 6	Click	in the Input Range: text box, if necessary
Step 7	Drag	to select the range B1:B17
Step 8	Click	the Labels in First Row check box

You want to generate the statistical report on a new worksheet named Statistics.

Step 9	Click	in the New Worksheet Ply: text box
Step 10	Key	Statistics
Step 11	Click	the Summary statistics check box to insert a check mark
Step 12	Click	OK

A new worksheet named Statistics is inserted in your workbook.

| Step 13 | AutoFit | columns A and B |
| Step 14 | Click | cell A1 to deselect the cells |

Your worksheet should look similar to Figure 12-2.

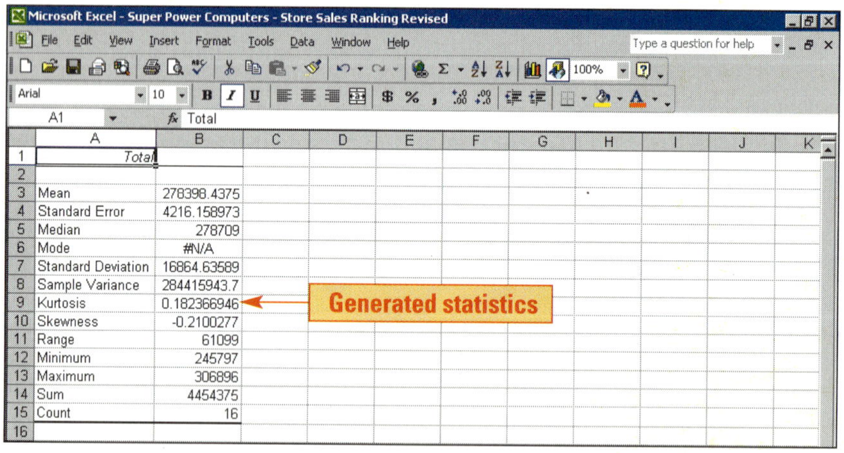

FIGURE 12-2
Report Generated Using the Descriptive Statistics Analysis Tool

Many of the statistics in this report could be derived from statistical functions you already know, such as SUM, MIN, MAX, and COUNT.

The **rank and percentile** tool creates a ranking table that sorts values in order from largest to smallest and provides a percentage based on each item's ranking. You can use this type of table to analyze the relative standing of values in a data set.

To generate a rank and percentile report:

Step 1	Click	the Summary sheet tab
Step 2	Click	Tools
Step 3	Click	Data Analysis
Step 4	Double-click	Rank and Percentile (scroll down the list) to open the Rank and Percentile dialog box
Step 5	Select	the range B1:B17 as the Input range:
Step 6	Click	the Labels in First Row check box to insert a check mark
Step 7	Enter	Rank & Percentile in the New Worksheet Ply: text box
Step 8	Click	OK to insert a new worksheet named Rank & Percentile in your workbook
Step 9	Click	cell A1 to deselect the selected cells

Your worksheet should look similar to Figure 12-3. The rank and percentile report includes four columns of information. The Point column identifies the original position, or order, of the data "point" in the source data (the Summary worksheet). The Total column displays the actual values, or points, from the raw data. The totals for the points are sorted in descending order, from highest to lowest, and placed in the Rank in Ascending order from first to last. The final column, Percent, gives the percentage of each item in terms of its rank.

QUICK TIP

To find out more about any of the other descriptive statistics generated or other data analysis tools, use the Ask A Question Box.

FIGURE 12-3
Report Generated Using Rank & Percentile Analysis Tool

Step 10	Save	the workbook and close it

chapter twelve

12.b Creating PivotTable Reports

Excel is often used to maintain lists of data. You've already learned how to sort lists and create outlines using lists. **PivotTables** are a special kind of table that you create to summarize unsorted data stored in lists. Using PivotTables, you can quickly rearrange how data is displayed and select different data sets to use.

You receive requests for data from Super Power Computers' many departments every day. Rather than maintaining separate lists of data for each department, which increases the chance of introducing errors in your data lists, you can maintain a single list of data. Then, using PivotTable reports, you can quickly display the exact data requested. The *Super Power Computers - Sales* workbook contains a portion of the sales data for the company's Central and East Coast Regions. To respond to the many requests for these data, you construct PivotTables. To create PivotTables:

| Step 1 | Open | the *Super Power Computers - Sales* workbook located on the Data Disk |
| Step 2 | Save | the workbook as *Super Power Computers - Sales Revised* |

This workbook includes several columns of unsorted data. Sorting allows you to readily retrieve certain information for lists. For example, you can easily sort the list by Region and Store, and then add subtotals to generate a summary of sales by store. However, suppose that you were asked to generate a report identifying how many units of Item 123 were sold at Store #7. Or maybe you want to find the quantity of each item sold by a certain sales rep. Gathering this type of information is not easily accomplished through simple sorting. These complex sorting and filtering tasks are easily accomplished using a PivotTable report.

Step 3	Click	in the Name Box
Step 4	Enter	A1:H97 to quickly select that range, which includes all of the data
Step 5	Click	Data
Step 6	Click	PivotTable and PivotChart Report

The PivotTable and PivotChart Wizard guides you through three steps to create your PivotTable or PivotChart report. In Step 1 of the PivotTable and PivotChart Wizard, you can select the source of your

Summarizing Data with Data Analysis, PivotTables, and PivotCharts   EA 119

data and the type of report you wish to create. Because you're using data in the current workbook and creating a PivotTable, you leave the settings in this step at their defaults. Your dialog box should look similar to Figure 12-4.

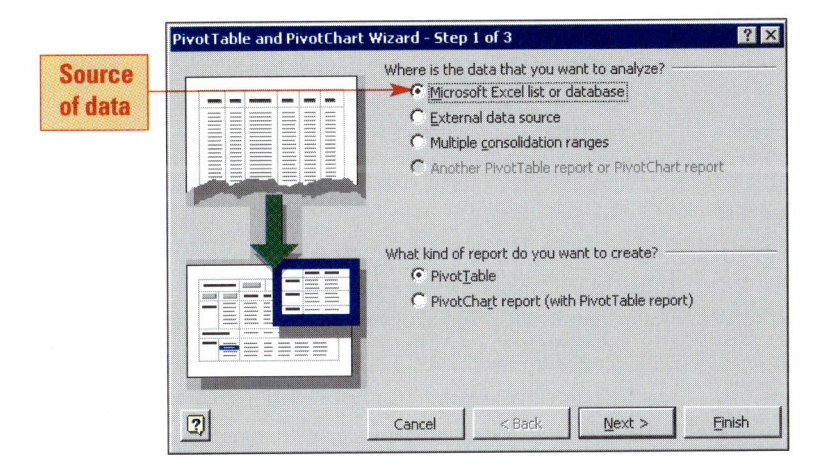

FIGURE 12-4
Step 1 of PivotTable and PivotChart Wizard

Source of data [arrow pointing to "Microsoft Excel list or database" option]

QUICK TIP

If you are using data from another workbook or a database, click the Browse button in Step 2 of the PivotTable and PivotChart Wizard to locate the file.

| Step 7 | Click | Next > |

Step 2 of the wizard should look similar to Figure 12-5. In this dialog box, you specify the data to use in your report. You've already selected the range, so accept the range indicated in this step.

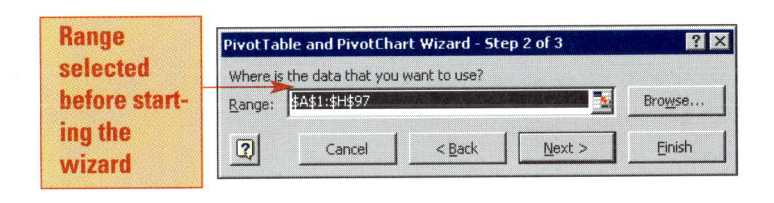

Range selected before starting the wizard [arrow pointing to Range: $A$1:$H$97]

FIGURE 12-5
Step 2 of PivotTable and PivotChart Wizard

| Step 8 | Click | Next > |

Step 3 of the wizard should look similar to Figure 12-6.

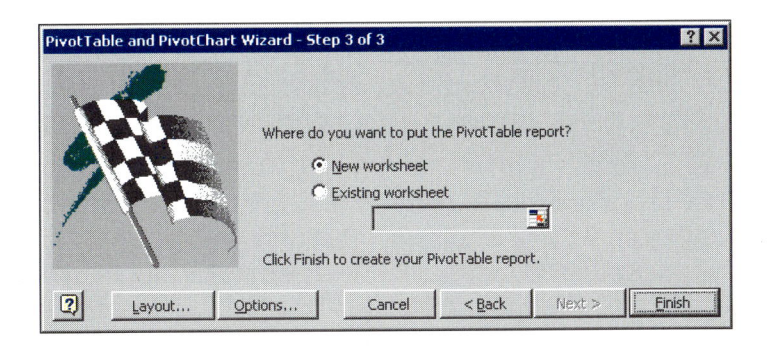

FIGURE 12-6
Step 3 of PivotTable and PivotChart Wizard

chapter twelve

EA 120 Excel 2002

> **MOUSE TIP**
>
> Clicking Layout in Step 3 of the wizard lets you preselect a layout for your data, but you can also make this selection directly on the worksheet when the wizard is finished. Clicking Options lets you set format and data options for your report. You can also change these settings later.

In this dialog box, you specify the report destination as either a new worksheet or an existing worksheet. You want the default settings—to insert the report on a new worksheet.

Step 9	Click	Finish
Step 10	Drag	the PivotTable toolbar by its title bar to the bottom of the screen so it "docks" into place below the sheet tabs, if necessary

Your screen should look similar to Figure 12-7. A new worksheet containing an empty PivotTable is inserted in your workbook and the PivotTable Field List appears with buttons matching the column labels of your worksheet. You create the PivotTable report by dragging field buttons from the field list to different areas of the PivotTable.

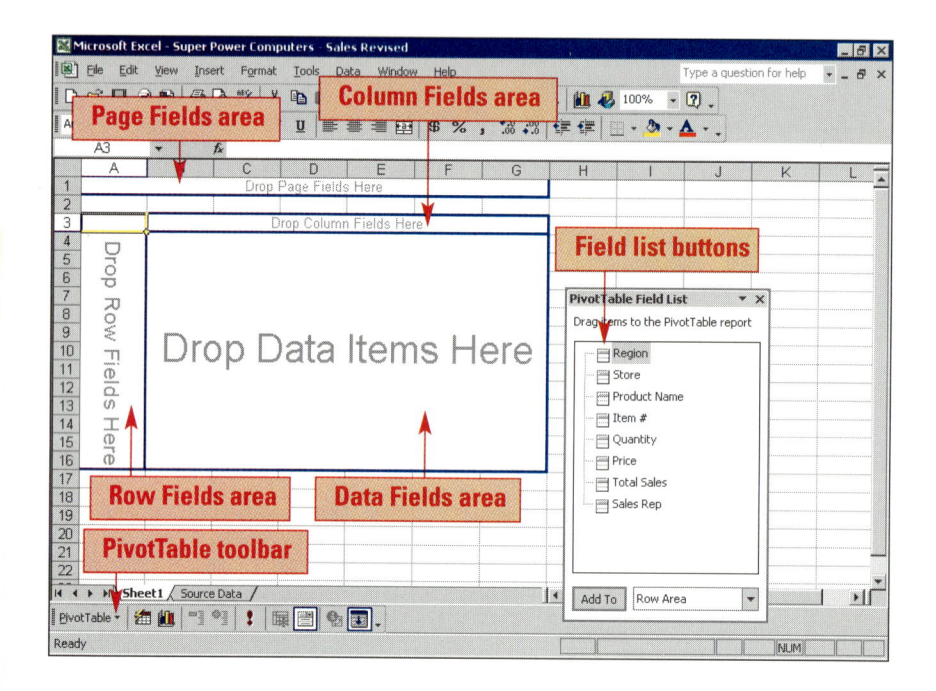

FIGURE 12-7
Empty PivotTable

You want to find out the quantity of items sold by each sales rep. working at Store #2. To create this report:

Step 1	Drag	the Store button in the PivotTable Field List to the Drop Page Fields Here area at the top of the worksheet

The Page Fields area is used when you need to limit the data displayed in the report. Cell A1 displays the Store button. Cell B1 contains a filter list arrow that allows you to filter the data displayed in the

> **CAUTION TIP**
>
> If you click anything outside the PivotTable area, the Field list and the PivotTable toolbar close.

report. This list includes each unique name found in the Store column (column B) of the Source Data tab. For this report, you limit the display of data to only Store #2, one of the company stores, after you've added the other fields to the report.

Your report should include the names of the items that were sold. You add this field to the row area of the PivotTable report.

| Step 2 | Drag | the Product Name button in the PivotTable Field List to the Drop Row Fields Here area at the left of the worksheet |

The Product Name button appears in cell A4 with a filter list arrow. This list includes each unique product name found in the Product Name column (column C) of the Source Data tab. When the report is complete, you can use this filter to display data for all products or only a selected group of products.

Next you add the Sales Rep field to the column field area of the report.

| Step 3 | Drag | the Sales Rep button in the PivotTable Field List to the Drop Column Fields Here area in rows 3 and 4 of the worksheet |

The Sales Rep button appears in cell B3 with a filter list arrow. This list includes each unique name found in the Sales Rep column (column H) of the Source Data tab. As with the other buttons in your report, you can filter the values displayed in the Item # field in your report by using the filter list arrow.

The last item needed in your report is the quantity of items sold to each store. This data is found in the Quantity column (column E) of the Source Data tab. Add the Quantity field to the data area of the report.

| Step 4 | Drag | the Quantity button in the PivotTable Field List to the Drop Data Items Here area on the worksheet |

The final step in creating your report is to filter the list of stores so that only data for Store #2 is displayed.

Step 5	Click	the Store filter list arrow in cell B1 (the Page fields area)
Step 6	Click	Store #2
Step 7	Click	OK

The filtered data on your screen should look similar to Figure 12-8.

FIGURE 12-8
Filtered PivotTable Report

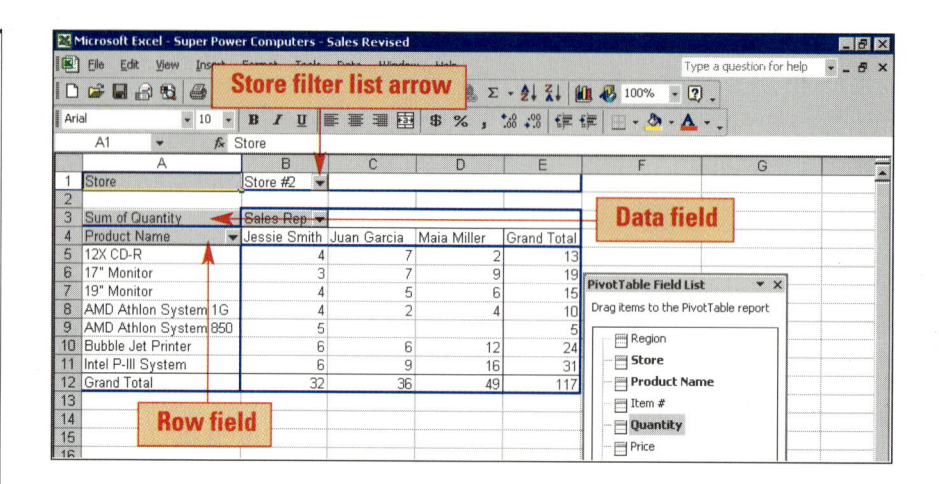

[Screenshot of Excel PivotTable with callouts: "Store filter list arrow", "Data field", "Row field"]

| Step 8 | **Rename** | the sheet tab PivotTable |
| Step 9 | **Save** | the workbook |

An employee from Super Power Computers' Sales Department has just called and asked for the total sales by store. You can quickly gather this information by modifying your PivotTable report.

12.c Modifying a PivotTable Report

The real power of a PivotTable report lies in the variety of ways in which you can quickly display data by rearranging fields included in the report. You also can format PivotTable results easily. Now you want to view the total sales by each employee. To modify the PivotTable report:

| Step 1 | **Drag** | the Sum of Quantity button off the PivotTable to a blank area of the worksheet |

This field is not necessary for the new report you want to create. As you drag button off the PivotTable, a Remove Field pointer appears to indicate that you are removing the field from your report.

| Step 2 | **Drag** | the Total Sales button to the Drop Data Items Here area |

The PivotTable displays the total sales by each sales rep. You want to display this information in the Accounting format.

MOUSE TIP

Access the PivotTable Field dialog box by right-clicking any cell in the PivotTable or a field name button and selecting Field Settings.

Summarizing Data with Data Analysis, PivotTables, and PivotCharts   EA 123

| Step 3 | **Verify** | that cell A3 is selected |
| Step 4 | **Click** | the Field Settings button on the PivotTable toolbar |

The PivotTable Field dialog box opens and should look similar to Figure 12-9.

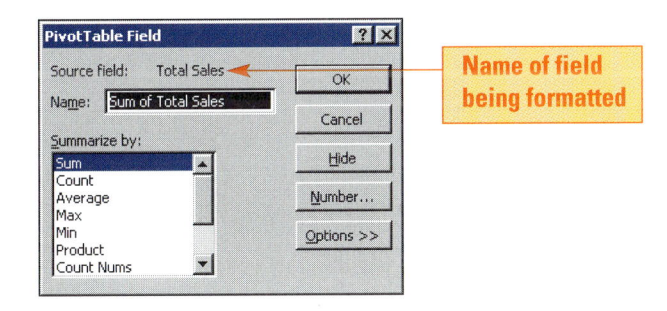

FIGURE 12-9
PivotTable Field Dialog Box

| Step 5 | **Click** | Number to open the Number tab of the Format Cells dialog box |
| Step 6 | **Click** | Accounting in the Category: list |

Applying this number format affects only the data in the Total Sales field. If you change the data in the report, the numerical format changes back to the default setting.

| Step 7 | **Click** | OK |
| Step 8 | **Click** | OK |

Rather than displaying the sales by sales rep, you want to show the total sales of each product by store.

| Step 9 | **Drag** | the Sales Rep field button off the PivotTable |

When you remove the Sales Rep field, the Total column displays only the sum of all sales made at Store #2.

| Step 10 | **Drag** | the Store field from cell A1 (the Page Fields area) to cell B3 (the Column Fields area) |

Using this report, it's easy to spot the leader in sales for a given product. Your screen should look similar to Figure 12-10.

> **QUICK TIP**
>
> You can change the type of summary from Sum to Count, Min, Max, or Average or alter a number of other statistical summaries by selecting an item in the Summarize by list. The Options button allows you to change the way that data is displayed. For example, you might want to show the difference between sales amounts through a store-to-store comparison.

chapter twelve

FIGURE 12-10
Column Fields Organized by Store

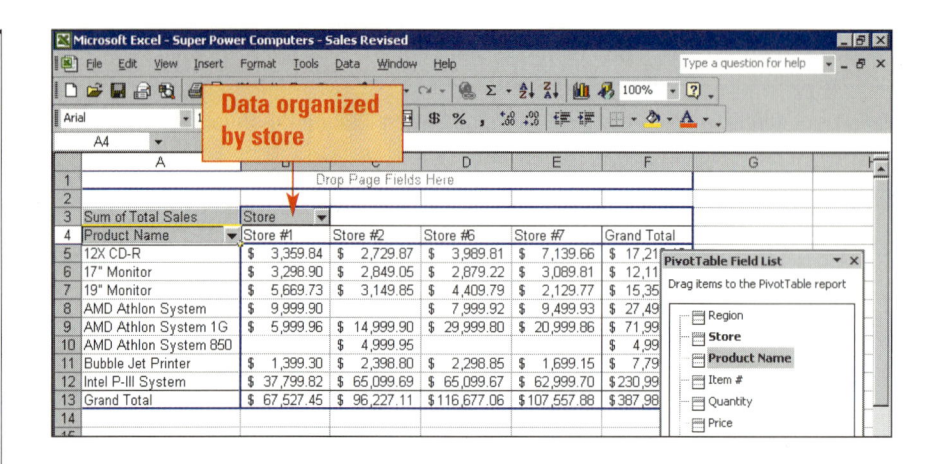

| Step 11 | Drag | the Store field to the left of the Product Name field (cell A4) |

You have successfully reorganized the report, providing a different view of the same data. This view is organized more like an outline, with the Store names appearing in column A and the products sold at each store listed in column B. Your screen should look similar to Figure 12-11.

FIGURE 12-11
Row Fields Organized by Store with Subtotals

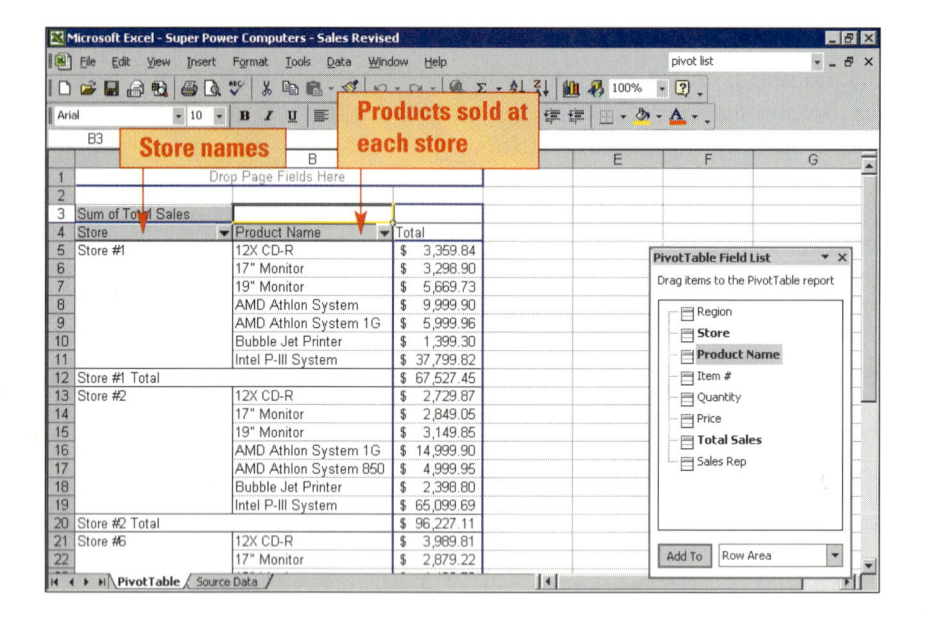

Displaying and Hiding Detail in a Field

Excel provides many ways to display selected data in a PivotTable report. One feature allows you to extract selected data into a new table on a new worksheet. The manager of Store #2 would like to see a detailed report of 12X CD-R sales for her store. Using your PivotTable report, you can quickly extract the desired data to a new worksheet.

To show detailed data:

Step 1	Click	cell C13
Step 2	Click	the Show Detail button on the PivotTable toolbar
Step 3	Click	cell A1 in the new worksheet
Step 4	Rename	the sheet tab Store #2 CD-R

The new worksheet contains a detailed summary of 12X CD-R sales at Store #2. Your worksheet should look similar to Figure 12-12.

FIGURE 12-12
Detail Data Extracted from PivotTable

You also can alter the display of data so as to hide selected records. For example, suppose you want to see only a summary of Store #1 and Store #2, but detailed reports for Store #6 and Store #12. The process used to modify the PivotTable is similar to collapsing levels in an outline. To hide data:

> **MENU TIP**
>
> You can hide data from the Data menu. Point to Group and Outline on the Data menu, then click Hide Detail.

Step 1	Click	the PivotTable sheet tab
Step 2	Click	cell A11

You can actually click any cell in the range A5:B11. The PivotTable has a format similar to that of an outline. Each of the cells in the range belongs to Store #1. Selecting Hide Detail while any of these cells is active hides the details for the entire level.

Step 3	Click	the Hide Detail button on the PivotTable toolbar
Step 4	Click	cell A6
Step 5	Click	the Hide Detail button on the PivotTable toolbar

> **MOUSE TIP**
>
> You can hide data using a shortcut menu. Right-click any of the cells whose data you want to hide to access the PivotTable shortcut menu. Point to Group and Show Detail, then click Hide Detail.

chapter twelve

Unlike outlines, hiding data in a PivotTable does not simply hide rows. The data is actually removed from the PivotTable until you choose to display the data again. To show the details for Store #2:

Step 6	Verify	that cell A6 is still the active cell
Step 7	Click	the Show Detail button on the PivotTable toolbar
Step 8	Click	cell A5
Step 9	Click	the Show Detail button on the PivotTable toolbar

Show Detail acts differently when used to show the detail of a row or column field. Rather than extracting the data to a new worksheet, it includes additional data within the PivotTable report. As you can see, Excel offers a variety of ways in which to organize data with PivotTables. Fortunately, rearranging reports is a simple drag-and-drop matter that has no effect on your source data. As a result, you can experiment, worry-free, with as many different combinations as you can dream up.

Step 10	Save	the workbook

Your PivotTable report will be used in a presentation to the Sales Department. Next, you apply AutoFormats to a PivotTable report.

12.d Formatting a PivotTable Report

Recall that AutoFormats enable you to quickly format tables. PivotTables can also be formatted similarly to other tables. For PivotTables, AutoFormat provides 10 report styles and 10 table styles. Applying AutoFormats rearranges the field layouts to a preset scheme. To format the PivotTable with an AutoFormat:

Step 1	Click	the Format Report button on the PivotTable toolbar to open the AutoFormat dialog box
Step 2	Scroll	down the list of AutoFormats
Step 3	Click	Table 8

| Step 4 | Click | OK |

The report is reorganized and formatted using different font, border, and text orientation settings to emphasize the store names and grand totals in row 13. Table AutoFormat styles arrange the data horizontally in the worksheet.

| Step 5 | Click | cell A1 |

The PivotTable is deselected, and the Page Fields area disappears because the current report does not require its presence. The field buttons on the PivotTable toolbar are not active while the active cell remains outside the PivotTable report. Your screen should look similar to Figure 12-13.

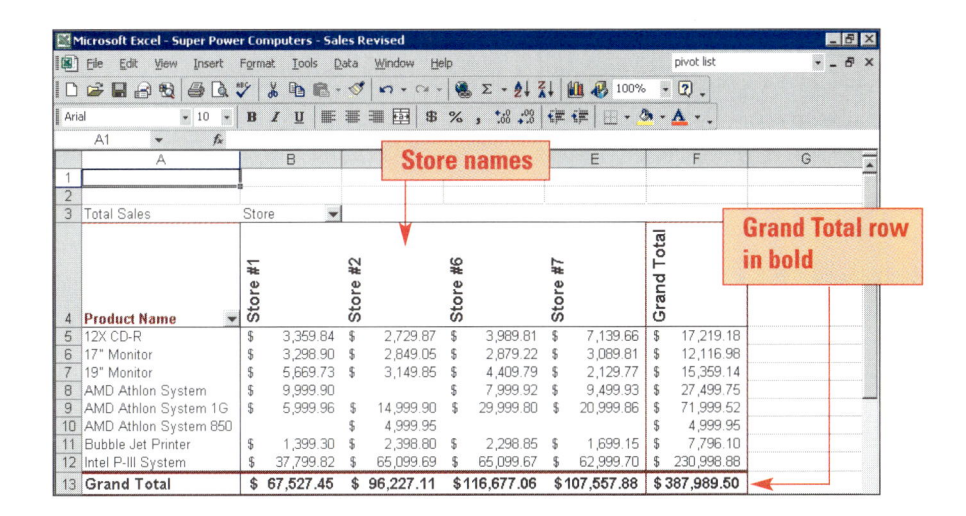

> **MOUSE TIP**
>
> You can turn the Fields display (the blue borders around the PivotTable field areas) on and off by clicking the Hide/Show Field List button on the PivotTable toolbar.

FIGURE 12-13
AutoFormat Table Style Arranges Data Horizontally

Rather than view your data in a simple table layout, you would rather examine the data in a report format.

Step 6	Activate	cell A4 in the PivotTable report
Step 7	Click	the Format Report button on the PivotTable toolbar
Step 8	Click	Report 4
Step 9	Click	OK
Step 10	Click	cell A1 to deselect the PivotTable report

chapter twelve

The PivotTable is rearranged in a report style with a new color format. Report AutoFormat styles arrange the data vertically in the worksheet. Your screen should look similar to Figure 12-14.

FIGURE 12-14
AutoFormat Report Style Arranges Data Vertically

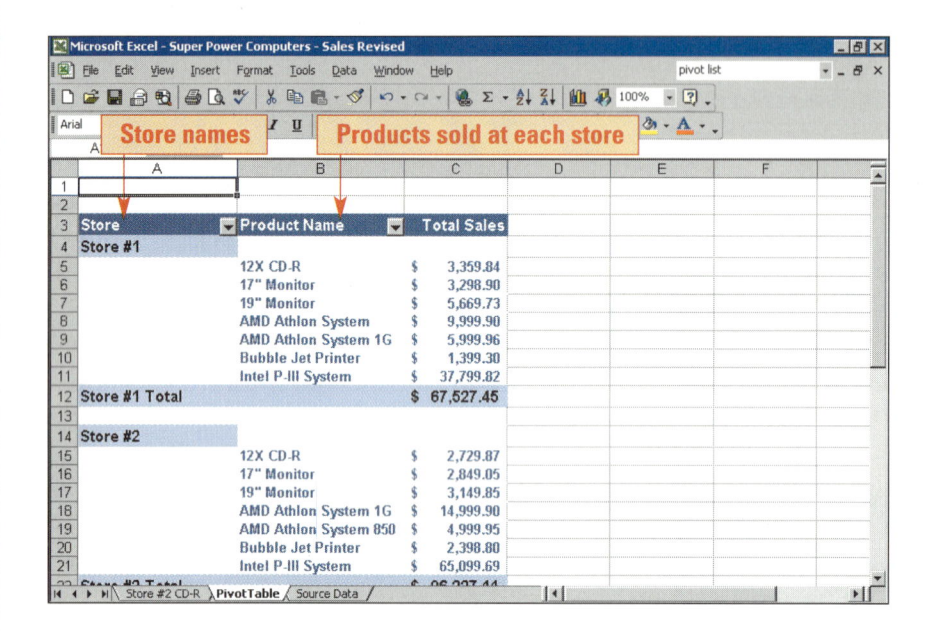

Step 11	*Preview*	the worksheet
Step 12	*Print*	the worksheet
Step 13	*Save*	the workbook

This report will be very useful to the Sales Department. You also can organize the data in a PivotChart, based on the PivotTable report.

12.e Creating PivotChart Reports

PivotCharts present another option for summarizing data. **PivotCharts** combine the features of both charts and PivotTable reports. Field buttons, which you can rearrange to modify how data is grouped and displayed, appear on the PivotChart. When you reorganize PivotChart fields, you also alter the underlying PivotTable structure. In constructing a PivotChart, you can either use an existing PivotTable report or create a new PivotTable report when you create a PivotChart.

Summarizing Data with Data Analysis, PivotTables, and PivotCharts   EA 129

To create a PivotChart from an existing PivotTable:

Step 1	Activate	any cell within the PivotTable
Step 2	Click	the Chart Wizard button on the Standard or PivotTable toolbar

A PivotChart is created on a new worksheet named Chart1. When you use the Chart Wizard to create a chart from a PivotTable, the Chart Wizard makes all decisions for you.

Step 3	Rename	the chart tab PivotChart
Step 4	Close	the PivotTable Field List by clicking the Close button in the title bar, if necessary
Step 5	Drag	the Chart toolbar by its title bar so it docks next to the PivotChart toolbar

The Chart Wizard creates the new chart, which should look similar to Figure 12-15. The field buttons employed in the PivotTable are automatically placed on the chart. You can rearrange the field buttons on the chart to modify the data display.

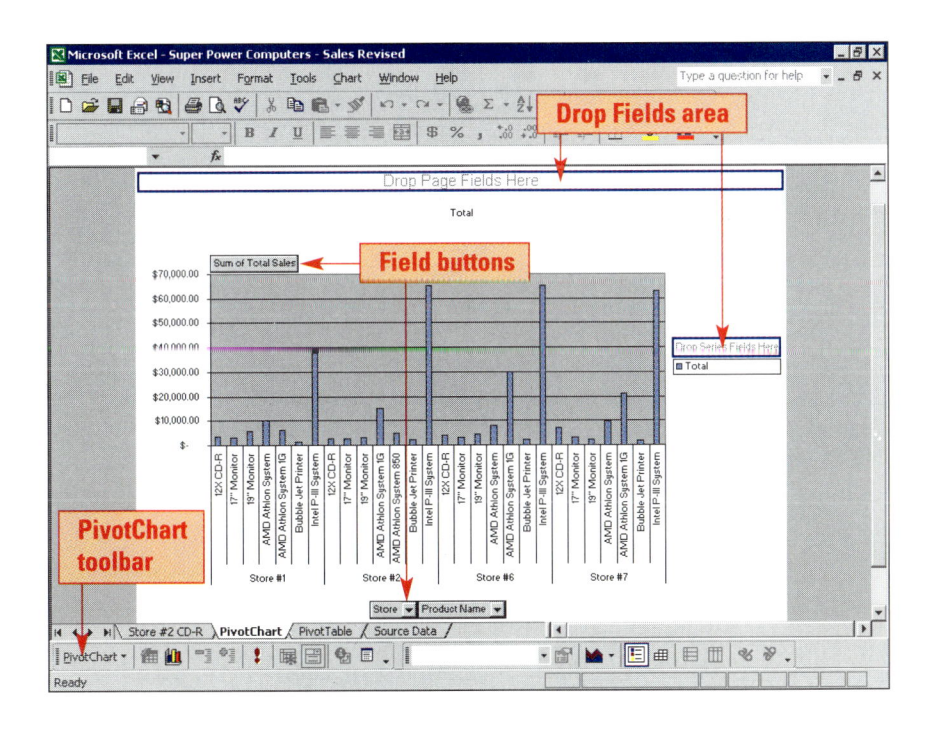

FIGURE 12-15
PivotChart

MOUSE TIP

You can change the chart typo by clicking the Chart Type button on the Chart toolbar.

You decide to change the chart to show total sales for stores located in New York.

chapter
twelve

Step 6	Drag	the Store field button to the Page Fields area at the top of the chart (you may need to scroll)
Step 7	Click	the Store field button list arrow
Step 8	Click	Store #6
Step 9	Click	OK
Step 10	Click	in the gray area outside the chart to deselect the chart

The updated chart on your screen should look similar to Figure 12-16.

FIGURE 12-16
Modified PivotChart

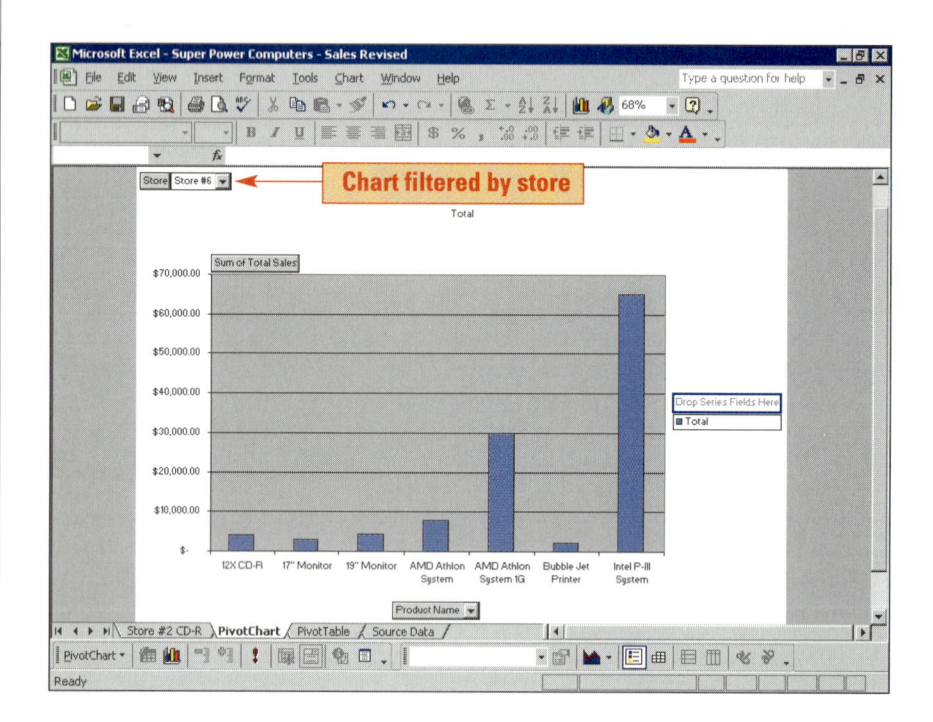

Step 11	Print	the PivotChart
Step 12	Click	the PivotTable sheet tab

When you modify a PivotChart, you also change the PivotTable on which the chart is based. Thus the PivotTable now shows the total sales for stores in New York.

Step 13	Save	the workbook and close it

PivotTables and PivotCharts are very powerful tools for quickly summarizing data.

Summary

▶ Data analysis tools enable you to examine data from a variety of angles using statistical calculations.

▶ You can create PivotTable reports with the PivotTable and PivotChart Wizard to quickly display data in a variety of report layouts.

▶ You can modify PivotTables by dragging and dropping fields at different locations on the PivotTable report.

▶ You can extract data from a PivotTable by using Show Detail on a Data Field item.

▶ You can hide and display data in row and column field items organized into an outline.

▶ You can use AutoFormats to format a PivotTable report with preset report and table styles.

▶ You can create a PivotChart based on a PivotTable report. Drag and drop fields on the PivotChart to modify the chart's data display.

Commands Review

Action	Menu Bar	Shortcut Menu	Toolbar	Task Pane	Keyboard
Use data analysis tools	Tools, Data Analysis				ALT + T, D
Create a PivotTable or PivotChart report	Data, PivotTable and PivotChart Report	Right-click a PivotTable, then PivotChart	Select a PivotTable, then PivotTable		ALT + D, P
Show detail	Data, Group and Outline, Show Detail	Group and Outline, Show Detail			ALT + D, G, S
Hide detail	Data, Group and Outline, Hide Detail	Group and Outline, Hide Detail			ALT + D, G, H
Format a PivotTable		Format Report			
Change field settings of a PivotTable		Field Settings			
Refresh data in a PivotTable or PivotChart	Data, Refresh Data	Refresh Data			ALT + D, R

chapter twelve

Concepts Review

Circle the correct answer.

1. **Clicking the Show Detail button on the PivotTable toolbar while the selected cell is in detail data:**
   - [a] extracts the supporting data to a new worksheet.
   - [b] shows the supporting data in the PivotTable.
   - [c] hides the supporting data in the PivotTable.
   - [d] extracts the supporting data to the same worksheet as the PivotTable.

2. **Which of the following is *not* calculated using the Descriptive Statistics analysis tool?**
   - [a] mean
   - [b] median
   - [c] sum
   - [d] average

3. **Fields that you specify in a PivotTable or PivotChart report are represented by:**
   - [a] field buttons.
   - [b] field icons.
   - [c] data labels.
   - [d] field menus.

4. **PivotTables can be created from:**
   - [a] only the current workbook.
   - [b] only an external file, such as a workbook or database.
   - [c] only another PivotTable or PivotChart report.
   - [d] the current workbook, an external file, or another PivotTable or PivotChart report.

5. **When you modify a PivotChart, the underlying PivotTable:**
   - [a] is not affected.
   - [b] disappears.
   - [c] is reorganized to match the PivotChart changes.
   - [d] is copied to prevent unwanted changes.

6. **Field buttons can be removed from a PivotTable or PivotChart by:**
   - [a] double-clicking the field button.
   - [b] right-clicking the field button and selecting Delete.
   - [c] dragging the field button off the report or chart.
   - [d] clicking Delete Field Button on the Edit menu.

7. **To summarize data for one item at a time, drag the field button to the:**
   - [a] Column Fields area.
   - [b] Row Fields area.
   - [c] Data Items area.
   - [d] Page Fields area.

8. **When you want to show a field as a column header of a PivotTable, drag the field button to the:**
   - [a] Column area.
   - [b] Row area.
   - [c] Data area.
   - [d] Page area.

9. **To see any data in a PivotTable, you need to drag a minimum of:**
   - [a] one item.
   - [b] two items.
   - [c] three items.
   - [d] four items.

10. **To change the number format in a PivotTable report, use the:**
    - [a] Format Report button.
    - [b] PivotTable Wizard button.
    - [c] Field Settings button.
    - [d] Format Cells dialog box.

Summarizing Data with Data Analysis, PivotTables, and PivotCharts   EA 133

Circle **T** if the statement is true or **F** if the statement is false.

T F 1. Rearranging PivotTable fields has no effect on the data used to create the PivotTable report.

T F 2. Rearranging PivotChart fields has no effect on the PivotTable used to create the PivotChart.

T F 3. Using an AutoFormat Report style has no effect on the PivotTable layout, other than changing attributes like colors, borders, and number formatting.

T F 4. Using an AutoFormat Table style has no effect on the PivotTable layout, other than changing attributes like colors, borders, and number formatting.

T F 5. Data analysis reports contain formulas that are automatically updated when the data is changed.

T F 6. The PivotTable and PivotChart Wizard has a total of four steps.

T F 7. PivotTables and PivotCharts are created on new sheets by default.

T F 8. When you are placing multiple field buttons in a row or column, the arrangement of the field buttons does not affect the display of the data.

T F 9. You can change the name of a field button.

T F 10. To remove a field button from a PivotTable or PivotChart, drag it off the report or chart.

Skills Review

Exercise 1

1. Open the *Sweet Tooth Sales to Stores Q2* workbook located on the Data Disk.
2. Sweet Tooth's warehouse Store needs to know the quantity of each item being sold, so that it can keep adequate supplies in the warehouse. Create a new PivotTable report based on the data in cells A1:H97 using the PivotTable Wizard.

    a. Use default settings for all three steps of the wizard.

    b. Rename the tab PivotTable Report.

    c. Drag the Item # field button to the Row fields area.

    d. Drag the Quantity field button to the Data Items area.

3. Format the report using the Table 5 AutoFormat style.
4. Print the PivotTable report.
5. Save the workbook as *Sweet Tooth Sales to Stores Warehouse*, and then close it.

Exercise 2

1. Open the *Sweet Tooth Sales to Stores Warehouse* workbook that you created in Exercise 1.
2. Shipping needs to know the quantity of each item being shipped to stores in Minnesota. Using the PivotTable Report tab, do the following:

    a. Remove all field buttons from the PivotTable report.

    b. Drag the Division field button to the Page Fields area.

    c. Select Minnesota from the filter list.

    d. Drag the Item # field button to the Row area.

chapter twelve

e. Drag the Store field button to the Row area and drop it to the left of the Item # field button.

f. Drag the Quantity field button to the Data area.

3. Format your report using Report 4 style.

4. Print the report.

5. Save the workbook as *Sweet Tooth Sales to Stores Shipping*, and then close it.

Exercise 3

1. Open the *Sweet Tooth Sales to Stores Shipping* workbook that you created in Exercise 2.

2. Marketing has asked you to figure out which stores are buying the most in each region.

    a. Remove all field buttons from the PivotTable.

    b. Drag the Store field button to the Columns area.

    c. Drag the Total Sales field button to the Data area.

    d. Drag the Region field button to the Rows area.

3. Print your report.

4. Save the workbook as *Sweet Tooth Sales to Stores Marketing* and then close it.

Exercise 4

1. Open the *Sweet Tooth Sales to Stores Marketing* workbook that you created in Exercise 3.

2. Create a PivotChart based on the PivotTable report.

3. Change the chart type to Clustered Column with a 3-D visual effect.

4. Drag the Store field button to the Drop Page Fields Here area at the top of the chart.

5. Drag the Region button off the PivotTable.

6. Drag the Sales Rep field button from the PivotTable Field List to the Drop Category Fields Here area at the bottom of the chart.

7. Change the chart title to "Sales by Rep."

8. Change the chart title's font size to 20 and the style to Bold.

9. Rename the chart sheet tab to "Sales Rep Chart," then print the chart.

10. Save the workbook as *Sweet Tooth Sales to Stores Marketing 2* and then close it.

Exercise 5

1. Open the *Sweet Tooth Sales to Stores Marketing 2* workbook that you created in Exercise 4. Management would like to see a breakdown of sales by sales representative within each store.

2. Click the PivotTable Report sheet tab.

3. Format the PivotTable using the Accounting number format.

4. Drag the Division Field button to the left of the Sales Rep field in the Row Fields area.

5. Print the report.

6. Save the workbook as *Sweet Tooth Sales to Stores Management* and then close it.

Exercise 6

1. Open the *Sweet Tooth Sales to Stores Management* workbook that you created in Exercise 5.
2. Drag the Sales Rep field button off the PivotTable.
3. Drag the Store field button to the right of the Division button in the Row Fields area. (*Hint:* Position the mouse pointer below the Division button to the right.)
4. Format the report using the Table 2 style.
5. Print the report.
6. Save the workbook as *Sweet Tooth Sales to Stores Management 2* and then close it.

Exercise 7

1. Open the *Sweet Tooth Sales to Stores Management 2* workbook that you created in Exercise 6.
2. Click the Source Data tab.
3. Generate a Descriptive Statistics report using cells G1:G97 as your source.
4. Place the report on a new worksheet called Stats, using Summary Statistics.
5. AutoFit columns A and B.
6. Print the report.
7. Save the workbook as *Sweet Tooth Sales to Stores Accounting* and then close it.

Exercise 8

1. Open the *Sweet Tooth Sales to Stores Accounting* workbook that you created in Exercise 7.
2. Click the PivotTable Report sheet tab.
3. Display the PivotTable toolbar, if necessary.
4. Drag the Sales Rep field button to the Page Fields area.
5. Filter the Sales Rep to show data for Portia Greene only.
6. Print the worksheet.
7. Save the workbook as *Sweet Tooth Sales to Stores Personnel* and then close it.

chapter twelve

Case Problems

Problem 1

You own a computer retail store. Connect to the Internet and search the Web for computer component prices. Find at least three items in the following categories: hard drive, RAM, monitors, printers. Using the prices and product descriptions that your search turns up, create a table of information using the following column headings: Category, Item Description, Price, Q1 Quantity, Q2 Quantity, Q3 Quantity, Q4 Quantity, and Total Sales (use a formula to multiply Price by the sum of the quantity columns). Use fictitious sales data for the each quarter's quantities. Create a PivotTable that shows total sales for each item by category. Save the workbook as *Computer Sales*, and then print and close it.

Problem 2

You own a successful catering business. Create a table to keep track of your clients. Include column headings for party name, menu item, quantity, price, and total sale. Create a menu of four items with prices for each item. Create fictitious data for three separate parties and indicate how many of each menu item were ordered for each of the parties. Enter a price for each item, then use a formula to calculate the total sales for each item. Create a PivotChart showing which items are bestsellers. Save the workbook as *Catering*, and then print and close it.

Problem 3

You are in charge of recordkeeping at a local veterinarian's office. You must keep track of owner names, pet names, pet visit dates, treatment, and treatment cost. Create five pet/owner combinations. Use fictitious data to show each pet visiting the veterinarian's office at least twice for different treatments. Create a PivotTable showing each pet, the treatments the animal received, and the amount due for treatments provided. Save the workbook as *Veterinarian*, and then print and close it.

Problem 4

Connect to the Internet and search the Web for PivotTable tutorials. Print at least one tutorial you find on the Web.

Problem 5

You work at a busy convenience store. Create a workbook to keep track of sales for 20 items grouped in four different categories. Use fictitious sales data for seven days. Create a PivotTable showing the total items sold each day by category. Save the workbook as *Convenience Store*, and then print and close it.

Problem 6

Connect to the Internet and search the Web for information about the latest trends in spreadsheet applications and/or office suites. Print Web pages containing reviews of at least two competing products.

Problem 7

You are a teacher analyzing the latest test scores. Create a workbook with 30 scores between 40 and 100. Use data analysis to generate a Rank and Percentile report. Save the workbook as *Test Scores*, and then print and close it.

Problem 8

You are analyzing sales made by sales representatives in your company. Create a workbook with fictitious sales figures for 10 sales reps. Use data analysis to generate a Descriptive Statistics report. Save the workbook as *Sales Statistics*, and then print and close it.

Excel 2002

Working with Charts and the Drawing Tools

Chapter Overview

You've already learned to create and print charts. In this chapter, you explore advanced chart types, such as the XY scatter and area charts, and features such as combining two chart types on one chart. Charts are not the only way to dress up a workbook. Using the drawing tools, you can create conceptual and organizational diagrams. You can use the drawing tools to insert company logos and even create newsletters and design colorful visual worksheets.

Learning Objectives

- Create special charts
- Modify charts
- Use the drawing tools
- Create and edit a conceptual diagram

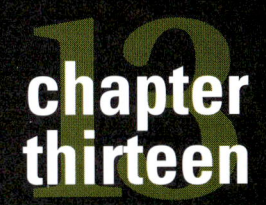

Case profile

At Super Power Computers, company sales are analyzed each quarter to see which stores are selling the highest quantity of goods and which stores are bringing in the most revenue. You are to analyze this data using special types of charts to determine which stores are generating the most income on the fewest sales. You also need to create an organizational chart to show the various leadership positions at Super Power Computers.

chapter thirteen

13.a Creating Special Charts

Charts are a way to visually represent numerical data. For most people, charts make data easier to understand. In this section, you learn about two special types of charts, area and XY scatter charts.

Creating an Area Chart

Area charts are used to show the magnitude of change over time. In the workbook *Super Power Computers - Sales Comparison*, data for all 16 stores is listed. Among this data is the percentage of each store's sales for the last three quarters. An area chart illustrates this data more clearly than looking at the numerical data. You have a worksheet that lists the total number of sales transactions and the total income from those transactions. You need to create an area chart to illustrate these percentages for the last two quarters. To create an area chart:

| Step 1 | Open | the *Super Power Computers - Sales Comparison* workbook located on the Data Disk |
| Step 2 | Save | the workbook as *Super Power Computers - Sales Comparison Revised* |

The percentages calculated in columns D:F indicate the percentage of each store's contribution to the company's total sales.

Step 3	Select	the range D5:E21
Step 4	Click	the Chart Wizard button on the Standard toolbar
Step 5	Click	Area in the Chart type: list
Step 6	Verify	that Stacked Area is selected in the Chart sub-type: area (first row, second column)
Step 7	Click	Next >

You want to show the store numbers as the Category (X) labels. You can do this in Step 2 of the Chart Wizard using the Series tab.

Step 8	Click	the Series tab
Step 9	Click	in the Category (X) axis labels: text box
Step 10	Select	A6:A21
Step 11	Click	Next >

Step 12	Click	Next >
Step 13	Click	the As new sheet: option button
Step 14	Key	Percentage Chart in the As new sheet: box
Step 15	Click	Finish

Your workbook should look similar to Figure 13-1.

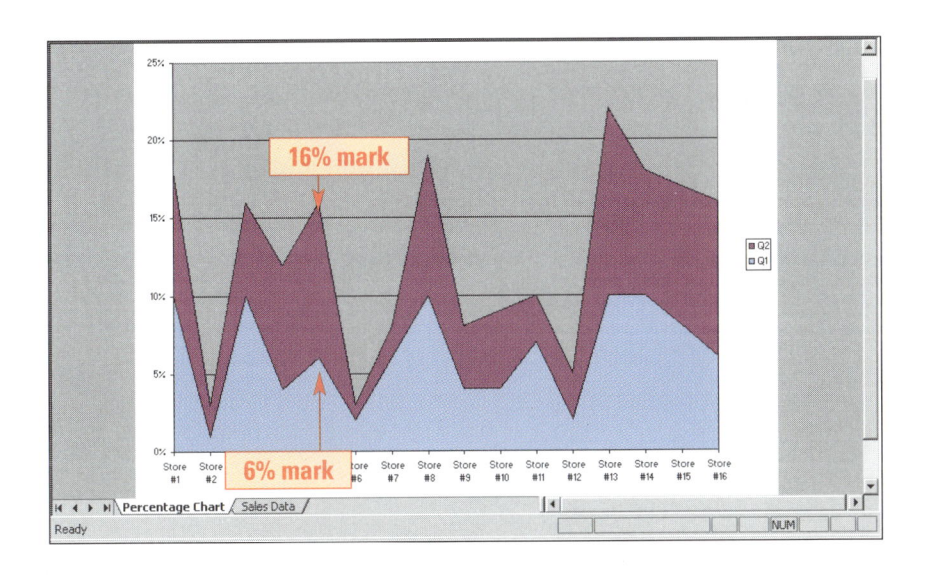

FIGURE 13-1
Area Chart

This chart makes it easy to see each store's contribution to the company's overall sales for the past two quarters. By examining the area chart, you can see that store #5, which accounted for approximately 6% of the company's sales in the first quarter, had a good second quarter, accounting for 10% of the company's sales.

Creating an XY Scatter Chart

Another special type of chart is the XY scatter chart. XY scatter charts are useful for graphing clusters of data. A common example of this use in the computer industry is determining the overall value of a computer system by charting the system cost against the overall system speed. This type of evaluation enables customers to determine whether they are getting a good deal. You use the scatter chart to evaluate which stores are generating the most revenue on the fewest sales. To create an XY scatter chart:

Step 1	Select	the range B5:C21 on the Sales Data worksheet
Step 2	Open	the Chart Wizard
Step 3	Click	XY (Scatter) in the Chart type: list

Step 4	**Verify**	that Scatter is selected in the Chart sub-type: area (first row)
Step 5	**Click**	Next >
Step 6	**Click**	Next >
Step 7	**Click**	the Titles tab, if necessary
Step 8	**Key**	Total Revenue by Number of Sales in the Chart title: text box
Step 9	**Key**	Number of Sales in the Value (X) axis: text box
Step 10	**Key**	Revenue in the Value (Y) axis: text box

Next, you want to place the data from column B next to each point in the chart to make identification easier.

Step 11	**Click**	the Data Labels tab
Step 12	**Click**	the X Value check box to insert a check mark
Step 13	**Click**	Next >
Step 14	**Add**	the chart as a new sheet named Revenue by Sales
Step 15	**Click**	Finish

The XY scatter chart is added to the worksheet, as shown in Figure 13-2. This chart makes it relatively easy to find a few standouts.

FIGURE 13-2
XY Scatter Chart

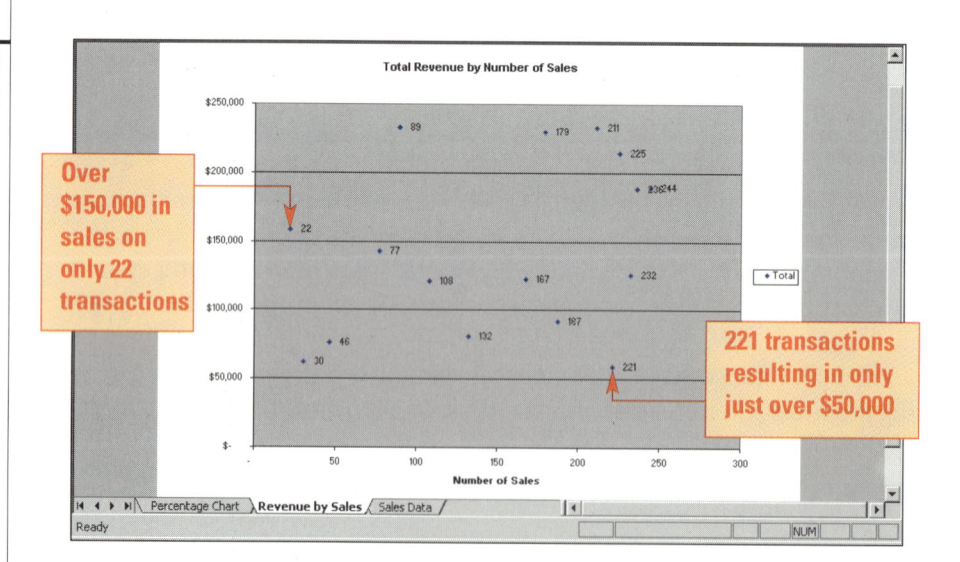

Working with Charts and the Drawing Tools   EA 141

13.b Modifying Charts

There are many ways to modify charts in Excel. You can add a data series to or remove it from a chart after it has been created. You also can combine chart types to show different kinds of data on the same chart.

Adding, Deleting, and Moving a Data Series

Once a chart is created, you may want to add, remove, or change the data series used in the chart. In the area chart, you are currently displaying two data series. You want to add a third. To add a data series:

Step 1	*Right-click*	the area chart on the Percentage Chart sheet tab
Step 2	*Click*	Source Data
Step 3	*Click*	the Series tab

Your Source Data dialog box should look similar to Figure 13-3. You use the Series tab to add, remove, or change the location of data series used in a chart. Q1 and Q2 are already listed. You need to add another series for the Q3 data in column F.

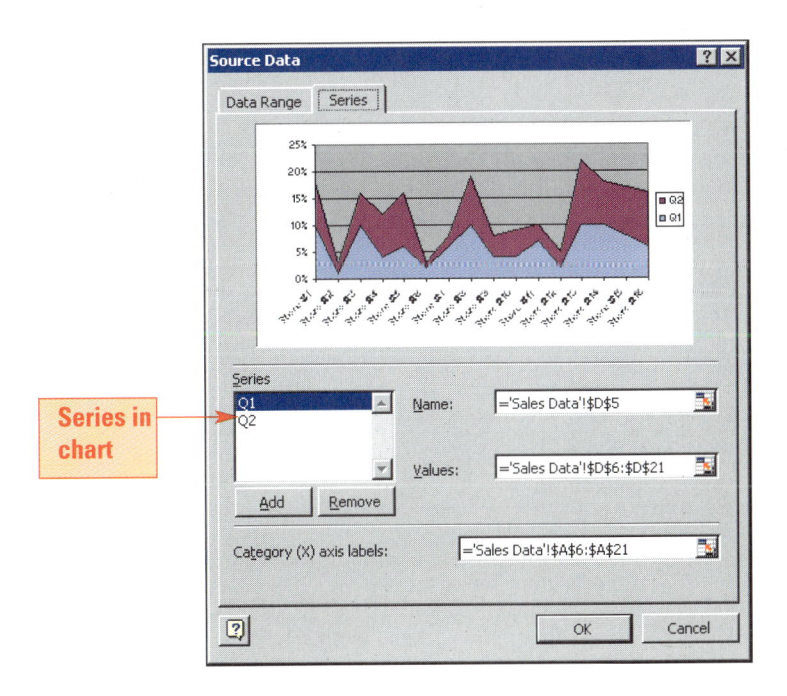

FIGURE 13-3
Series Tab of the Source Data Dialog Box

chapter thirteen

QUICK TIP

To remove a series, select the series name on the Series tab in the Source Data dialog box, then click Remove. To move a series, highlight the series name, collapse the dialog box in the Values text box, select a new range in your worksheet, expand the dialog box again, and click OK.

Step 4	Click	Add
Step 5	Click	the Collapse dialog button in the Name: text box
Step 6	Click	cell F5 on the Sales Data worksheet
Step 7	Click	the Expand dialog button in the Source Data - Name: text box
Step 8	Click	the Collapse dialog button in the Values: text box:
Step 9	Select	the range F6:F21 on the Sales Data worksheet
Step 10	Click	the Expand dialog button in the Source Data - Values: text box
Step 11	Click	OK

The chart is updated to include the new series. To make the data clearer, you decide to add value data labels to the chart.

Step 12	Right-click	in a gray area in the chart
Step 13	Click	Chart Options
Step 14	Click	the Data Labels tab, if necessary
Step 15	Click	the Value check box to insert a check mark
Step 16	Click	OK

The percentage values are added beneath each data point in the chart.

Combining Chart Types on One Chart

Combining chart types can be a good way to compare data. The Store Sales sheet tab includes some other data that can be effectively shown using a combination chart. To combine chart types:

Step 1	Verify	that the range B5:C21 on the Sales Data worksheet is selected
Step 2	Open	the Chart Wizard
Step 3	Click	the Custom Types tab
Step 4	Click	Line - Column on 2 Axes in the Chart type: list (you may need to scroll)
Step 5	Click	Next >

Step 6	Click	the Series tab
Step 7	Click	in the Category (X) labels: text box
Step 8	Select	the range A6:A21
Step 9	Click	Next >
Step 10	Click	Next >
Step 11	Add	the chart as a new sheet called Revenue by Sales 2
Step 12	Click	Finish

The chart, shown in Figure 13-4, makes it easy to see that Stores #12 and #16 had great total sales on relatively few sales transactions.

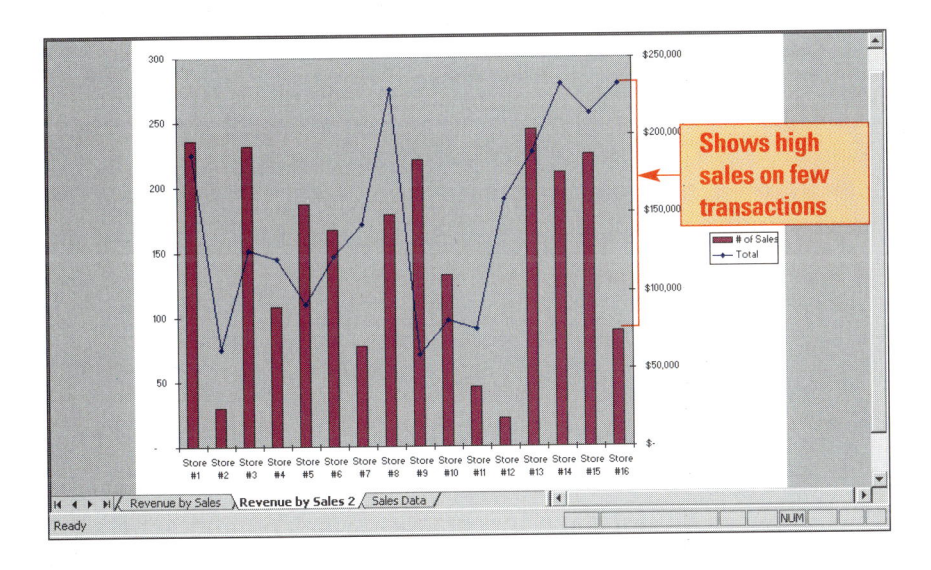

FIGURE 13-4
Combination Chart

Step 13	Save	the workbook and close it

13.c Using the Drawing Tools

The Excel drawing tools help you create a variety of useful diagrams and enhance worksheets and charts. **Clip art** is ready-made graphics you can insert in a worksheet. Office XP includes the **Clip Organizer**, a feature that indexes clip art on your computer and on the Web, making it easier to find the graphic you want to use. **AutoShapes** are simple outlined shapes, such as squares, circles, arrows, and banners, that you can insert in your worksheet. The AutoShape called a connector line helps you create diagrams.

chapter thirteen

Inserting Clip Art Objects

Using clip art, you create a network diagram for Super Power Computers' central office. A network diagram is useful as a map showing how computers on the network communicate with one another. You want to add a network diagram to a workbook that contains information about the computer equipment used in Super Power Computers' central office. To open the workbook:

> **MOUSE TIP**
>
> You can use the Zoom button list box on the Standard toolbar to zoom a worksheet from 10% to 400%.

Step 1	Open	the *Super Power Computers - Computer Equipment Inventory* workbook located on the Data Disk
Step 2	Edit	cell A1 to read "Central Office Computer Equipment Diagram"
Step 3	Save	the file as *Super Power Computers - Computer Equipment Diagram*

This file has been zoomed to 75% to allow you to view more of the worksheet area. Several objects are already inserted in this worksheet, but you need to add a printer and a laptop to the diagram. You insert a printer by using the Clip Organizer. To open the Clip Organizer and search for appropriate clips art:

| Step 1 | Click | the Drawing button on the Standard toolbar to display the Drawing toolbar if necessary |
| Step 2 | Click | the Insert Clip Art button on the Drawing toolbar |

The Insert Clip Art task pane appears with search options to help you search through the Clip Organizer.

| Step 3 | Key | printer in the Search text: text box in the Insert Clip Art task pane |

> **CAUTION TIP**
>
> You might see a message asking if you want to catalog the media on your computer. This process takes a while, as your computer is searched for media that can be added to the Clip Organizer. If this message appears, click the Later button.

The Search in: list under Search Options allows you to specify which collections you search. These collections include Office Collections (clip art that comes with Office), My Collections (media on your computer that you have catalogued), and Web Collections (clip art available online). The Results should be: list allows you to limit the type of media searched, such as clip art, photographs, movies, or sounds.

| Step 4 | Click | the Search in: list arrow |

Working with Charts and the Drawing Tools EA 145

Step 5	Click	the Web collections check box to remove the check mark, if necessary
Step 6	Click	anywhere in the task pane to close the list
Step 7	Click	the Results should be: list arrow
Step 8	Click	the Clip Art and Photographs check boxes to insert check marks, if necessary
Step 9	Click	the Movies and Sounds check boxes to remove the check marks, if necessary
Step 10	Click	anywhere in the task pane to close the list
Step 11	Click	Search in the task pane

> **MENU TIP**
>
> You can insert clip art from the Insert menu. Point to Picture, then click Clip Art to open the Insert ClipArt dialog box.

Any clips found that match the keyword are displayed in the task pane, and similar to the ones shown in Figure 13-5. (The clips on your screen may not match the one in the figure exactly.)

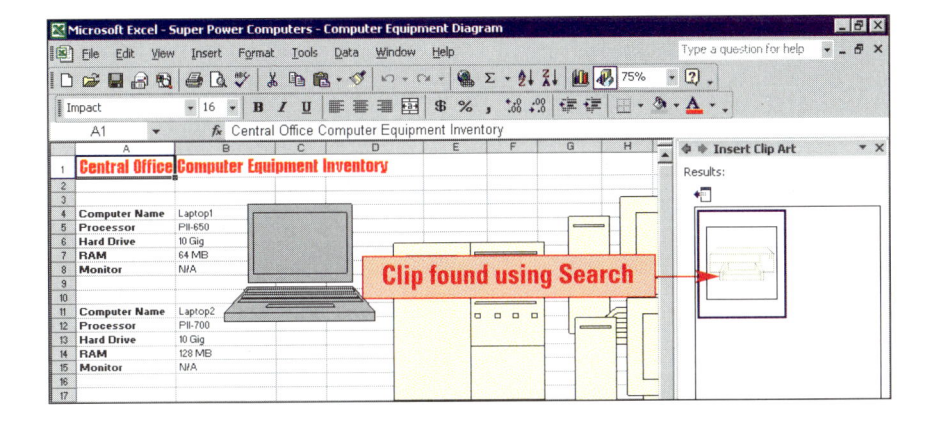

FIGURE 13-5
Insert Clip Art Task Pane

You can drag clips from the task pane right into your worksheet. When you point to a clip, a ScreenTip appears displaying information about the clip art, such as the file size and file type. To drag clip art from the task pane to the worksheet:

Step 1	Point to	the clip resembling a drawing of a printer in the task pane (if you don't have the printer clip art, drag a similar clip instead)
Step 2	Drag	the line art drawing of a printer clip art onto the worksheet near cell H26

As you drag the clip, a large dotted outline appears in your worksheet. Your clip will probably be much smaller than the outline seems to indicate. It may be difficult to accurately position the clip art with the task pane in the way. You can reposition a clip later.

chapter thirteen

You may want to browse for clip art rather than searching by keywords. The Clip Organizer indexes clip art by allowing you to add categories and keyword information to a media file. Its categories display related clips. For example, the Networking category displays clip art of several computers and computer peripherals, such as printers, scanners, and a CD-ROM drive.

Step 3	*Click*	the Clip Organizer link in the task pane
Step 4	*Click*	the + sign next to the Office Collections folder in the Collection List
Step 5	*Click*	the + sign next to the AutoShapes folder in the Collection List
Step 6	*Click*	the Networking folder

Clip Organizer categorizes clip art into categories and subcategories, and displays them as folders, even though the clip art might be stored in different locations on your computer. Your Clip Organizer should look similar to Figure 13-6.

FIGURE 13-6
Clip Organizer

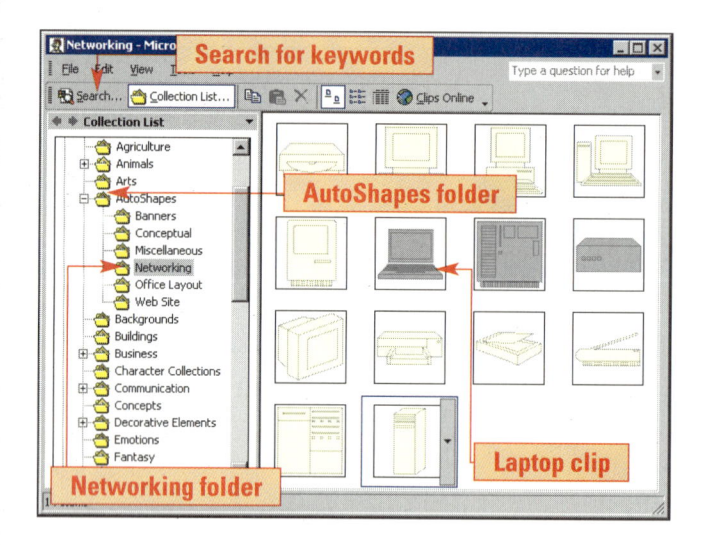

| Step 7 | *Point to* | the clip resembling a laptop computer |
| Step 8 | *Drag* | the clip art image onto your worksheet near cell C13 |

The laptop images may overlap because they are too large, but you scale and reposition them later. After you drop the clip art, Clip Organizer minimizes itself on the taskbar.

Step 9	Right-click	the Clip Organizer button on the taskbar
Step 10	Click	Close
Step 11	Close	the Insert Clip Art task pane

Scaling and Moving Objects

You can reposition and resize drawing objects. At present, the clips are too large for the area on your worksheet. You can select multiple objects for editing, by holding down the SHIFT key as you click each object. To select and resize the objects:

Step 1	Press & hold	the SHIFT key
Step 2	Click	each of the clips on the worksheet (a total of six) to select them (observe the sizing handles)
Step 3	Right-click	one of the objects
Step 4	Click	Format Object to open the Format Object dialog box
Step 5	Click	the Size tab

The dialog box on your screen should look similar to Figure 13-7. When you modify the height or width of an object with lock aspect ratio turned on, the object scales equally in the other dimension.

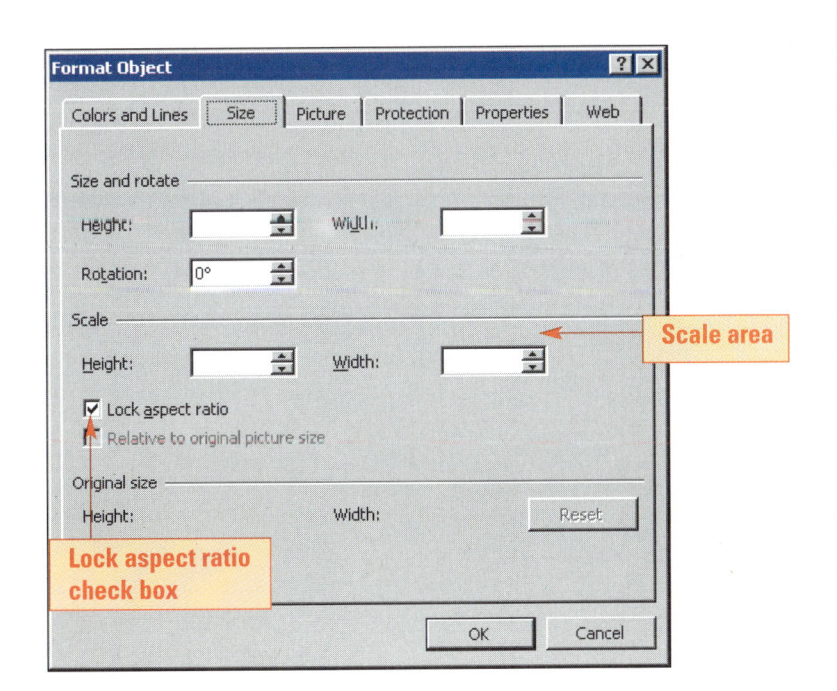

> **QUICK TIP**
>
> You can switch between Clip Organizer and Excel or other open applications by pressing the ALT + TAB keys.
>
> The Picture toolbar appears when you select a clip.

> **MOUSE TIP**
>
> If you need to remove an object from a multiple object selection, press and hold the SHIFT key as you click the object again.

FIGURE 13-7
Size Tab in the Format Object Dialog Box

Step 6	Click	the Lock aspect ratio check box to insert a check mark, if necessary
Step 7	Key	65 in the Height: text box in the Scale group
Step 8	Press	the TAB key to move to the Width: text box and automatically adjust the width to 65%

The width automatically adjusts to the same percentage as the height because the Lock aspect ratio check box is checked.

Step 9	Click	OK
Step 10	Observe	that all of the objects are scaled to 65% of their original size
Step 11	Press	the ESC key to deselect the drawing objects

To move the printer object above its description in cells G26:H26:

| Step 1 | Move | the mouse pointer over the printer clip until it changes to a four-headed arrow move pointer |
| Step 2 | Drag | the clip above row 26 in columns G and H |

As you drag the clip, a dashed box matching the width and length of the actual clip appears, helping you to position the clip more precisely.

| Step 3 | Follow | Steps 1 and 2 to reposition the other objects as necessary to match Figure 13-8 |

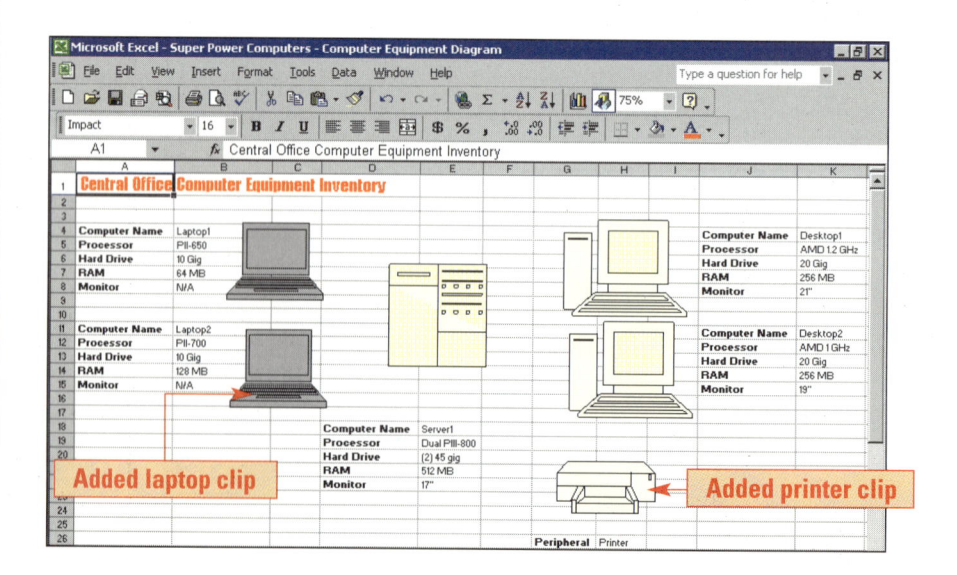

FIGURE 13-8
Scaling and Moving Objects

Working with Charts and the Drawing Tools   EA 149

Using an AutoShape

AutoShapes come in a variety of styles and shapes, making it easy to add interest to your diagrams. Shapes are grouped into categories such as arrows, callouts, and banners and include everything from ovals, rectangles, and triangles to stars, lightning bolts, and smiley faces.

To diagram Super Power Computers' network properly, you must connect the clips using connector lines. A **connector line** is a special type of AutoShape that automatically snaps to connection points on an object. When you move objects connected with connector lines, the line stays attached. To add connector lines:

| Step 1 | Click | the AutoShapes button [AutoShapes] on the Drawing toolbar |

There are several AutoShapes categories, which you may want to spend a few minutes exploring. As you move your pointer across the displayed AutoShape styles, a ScreenTip description appears.

Step 2	Point to	Connectors
Step 3	Point to	a button on the Connectors submenu
Step 4	Observe	the ScreenTip description
Step 5	Click	Elbow Double-Arrow Connector
Step 6	Move	the mouse pointer close to the top laptop clip (Laptop #1)

Near a clip, the mouse pointer changes to a connection pointer, and blue connection points surround the edges of the clip. Your screen should look similar to Figure 13-9.

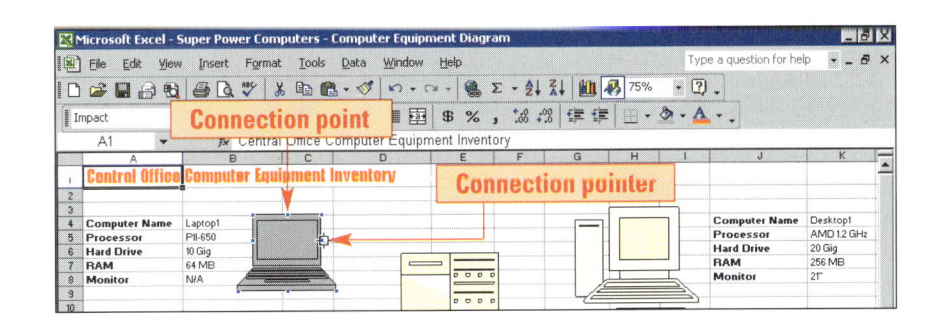

> **MENU TIP**
>
> You can use the AutoShapes toolbar to insert AutoShapes. To display the AutoShapes toolbar, click the Insert menu, point to Picture, then click AutoShapes.

FIGURE 13-9
Using Attachment Points

| Step 7 | Click | the middle-right connection point on the first laptop clip |

chapter thirteen

MOUSE TIP

You may find it difficult to draw on top of cells while the gridlines remain on. You can turn gridlines on or off by using the Options dialog box. Click Options on the Tools menu, click the View tab, click the Gridlines check box in the Window options group, then click the OK button.

Step 8	**Move**	the mouse pointer to the server clip
Step 9	**Observe**	that as you drag across the worksheet, a dotted line extends from the point you clicked to the mouse pointer position
Step 10	**Click**	the middle-left connection point on the server clip

Your screen should look similar to Figure 13-10. When a connector line is attached, a red circle appears at the end of the line. When a connector line is unattached, a green circle is displayed. You can drag the yellow adjustment handle to change the position of the line.

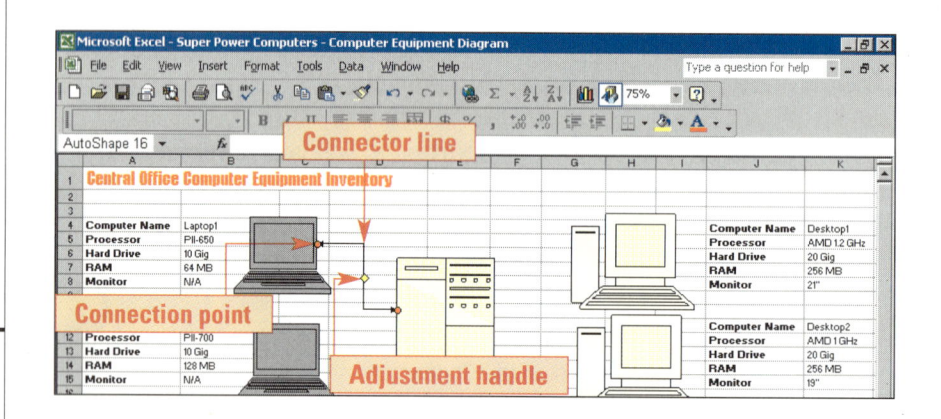

FIGURE 13-10
Completed Connector Line

Step 11	**Follow**	Steps 1 through 10 to attach each of the clips to the server clip
Step 12	**Drag**	the yellow adjustment handle to reposition any lines if necessary

Your screen should look similar to Figure 13-11.

FIGURE 13-11
Final Diagram

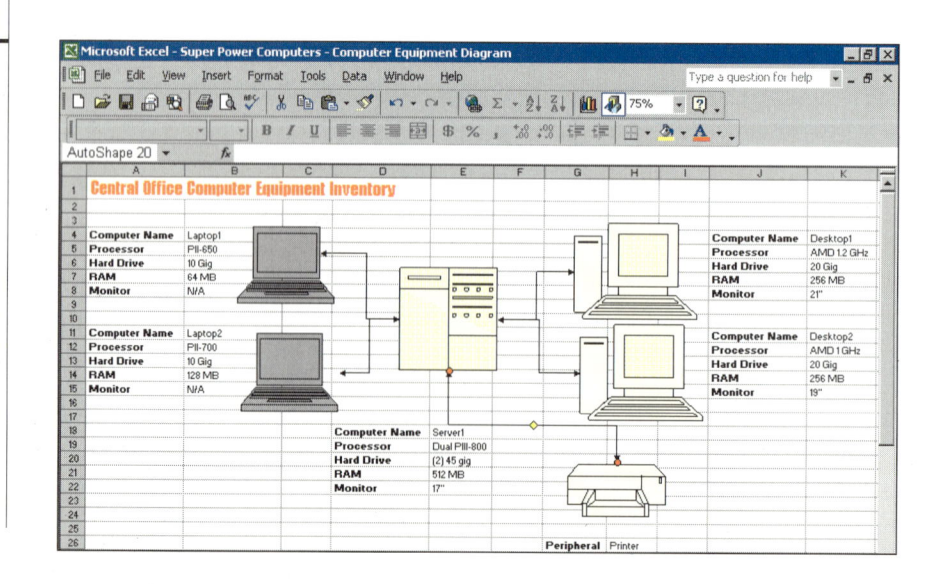

| Step 13 | Press | the ESC key to deselect the connector line |
| Step 14 | Save | the workbook and close it |

13.d Creating and Editing a Conceptual Diagram

Conceptual diagrams are used for showing different types of relationships. One example of this is an organization chart, which is a hierarchical diagram of a company's management structure.

Creating an Organization Chart

Organizational charts show the reporting structure of employees in a company. To create a diagram:

Step 1	Create	a new, blank workbook
Step 2	Save	the workbook as *Super Power Computers - Management Diagram*
Step 3	Click	the Insert Diagram or Organization Chart button on the Drawing toolbar

The Diagram Gallery dialog box on your screen should look similar to Figure 13-12. This dialog box allows you to select the type of chart you wish to create.

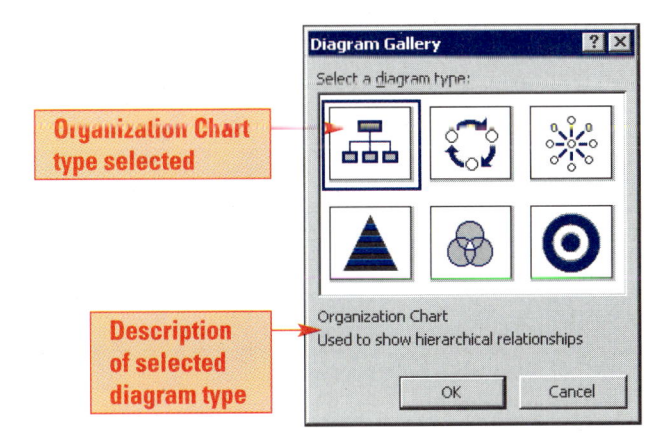

FIGURE 13-12
Diagram Gallery Dialog Box

| Step 4 | Verify | that Organization Chart is selected |
| Step 5 | Click | OK |

The Organization Chart is added to your worksheet. Your worksheet should look similar to Figure 13-13. The area inside the border is the drawing space.

FIGURE 13-13
Organization Chart

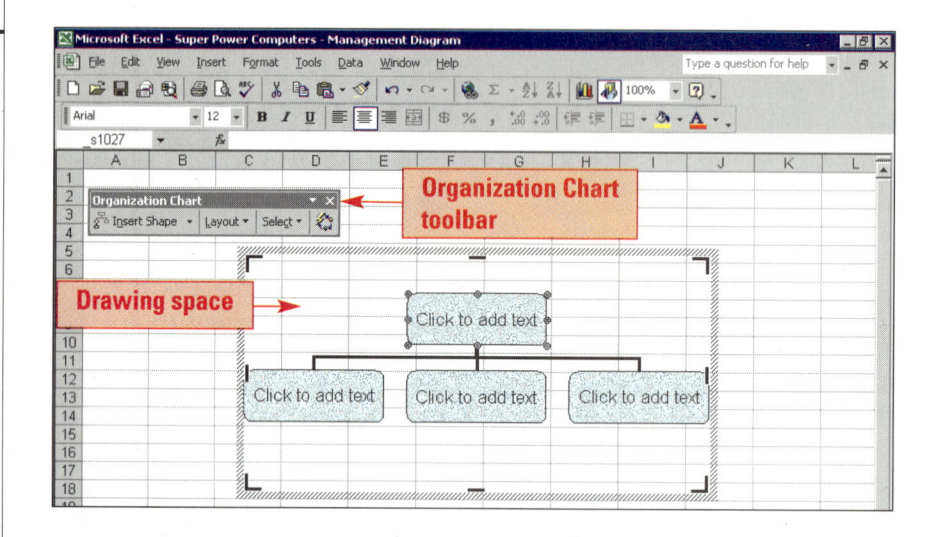

Editing an Organization Chart

Editing a conceptual diagram involves entering text in different boxes, and adding and deleting coworkers, assistants, or subordinates. To edit the organization chart:

Step 1	Click	the box at the top of the organization chart
Step 2	Key	President
Step 3	Press	the ESC key
Step 4	Right-click	the President box border
Step 5	Click	Assistant

A new assistant box is inserted.

Step 6	Click	the new box
Step 7	Key	Assistant
Step 8	Click	the left box on the bottom row
Step 9	Key	Regional Manager
Step 10	Right-click	the Regional Manager box border
Step 11	Click	Subordinate

QUICK TIP

You can click the Insert Shape button on the Organization Chart toolbar, then click an option on the list that appears to add boxes to an organization chart.

A new subordinate box is placed beneath the Regional Manager box.

Step 12	Click	the new box
Step 13	Key	Store Manager
Step 14	Right-click	the Store Manager box border
Step 15	Click	Coworker
Step 16	Click	the new box
Step 17	Key	Store Manager
Step 18	Change	the other two boxes on the third level to Regional Manager
Step 19	Add	two Subordinate Store Manager boxes to each Regional Manager box

As you add the new items, the font sizes will adjust to odd sizes. To readjust font sizes in an organization chart:

Step 20	Click	in the organization chart drawing space
Step 21	Click	8 in the Font size list

Selecting the entire organization chart and changing font settings sets all boxes to use the same settings. Your chart should look similar to Figure 13-14.

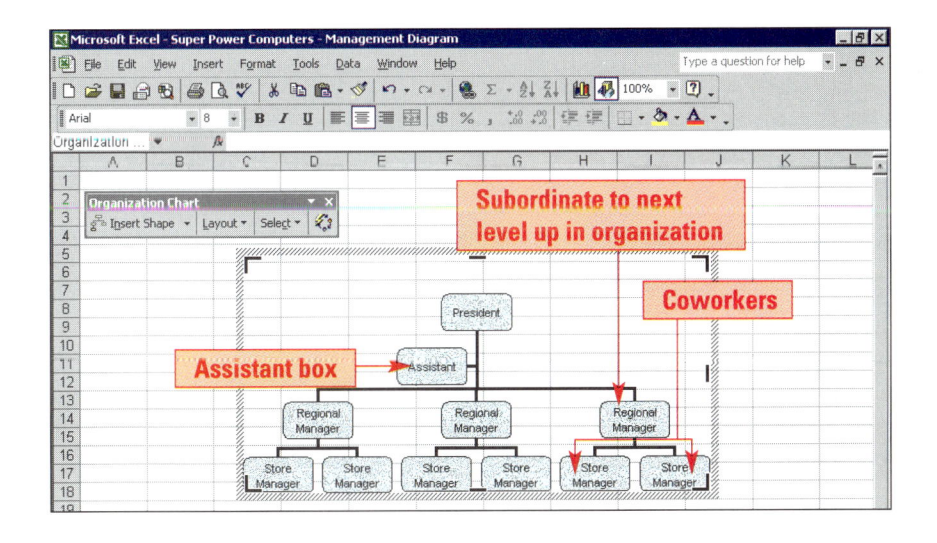

FIGURE 13-14
Completed Organization Chart

chapter
thirteen

Mouse tip

You can add text to most AutoShapes, not just to text boxes. To add text to an AutoShape, right-click the AutoShape, then click Add Te_x_t.

Quick tip

You can use the Format Object dialog box to change Font settings for text added to AutoShapes, or you can click buttons on the Formatting toolbar to accomplish the same task. For example, if you want the text in an AutoShape object to be bold, select the object, then click the Bold button on the Formatting toolbar.

Inserting a Text Box Object

Text boxes are useful in diagrams because you can freely reposition the box so it doesn't interfere with other objects in your diagram. To add a text box:

Step 1	Click	the Text Box button on the Drawing toolbar
Step 2	Drag	from cell A2 to cell C10
Step 3	Key	Super Power Computers Organizational Diagram
Step 4	Drag	one of the text box corner handles to resize the text box so it is not so tall
Step 5	Click	the Center button on the Formatting toolbar
Step 6	Click	the Bold button on the Formatting toolbar
Step 7	Press	the ESC key to deselect the Text Box object

Printing a Worksheet with Drawing Objects

Drawing objects are printed along with anything else on the worksheet. You can preview and change the page setup of the worksheet with a drawing object. To preview and print the worksheet:

Step 1	Click	the Print Preview button on the Standard toolbar
Step 2	Click	the Setup button on the Print Preview toolbar
Step 3	Click	the Landscape option button on the Page tab
Step 4	Click	the Horizontally and Vertically check boxes on the Margins tab to insert check marks
Step 5	Click	OK
Step 6	Print	the worksheet
Step 7	Save	the workbook and close it

The drawing objects enhance your printed workbook.

Summary

- Area and XY scatter charts show complex relationships between data.
- You can add, delete, or modify data series to change the information shown in a chart.
- Custom chart types enable you to combine chart types on one chart.
- The Clip Organizer allows you to insert clip art symbols. You can locate clip art by browsing categories or by searching for keywords either in Clip Organizer or on the Insert Clip Art task pane.
- You can scale objects by dragging their resize handles or by using the Size tab of the Format AutoShape dialog box.
- Connector lines connect objects. Connector lines automatically route around objects and stay attached when you move either connected object. You can choose from a variety of connector styles, including straight, elbow, and curved.
- The Insert Diagram or Organizational Chart tool enables you to create conceptual and organizational diagrams. These types of diagrams simplify the illustration of complex hierarchical relationships.
- You can insert drawing objects, such as text boxes, to further enhance diagrams and worksheets.
- You print a worksheet with drawing objects as you would any other worksheet.

Commands Review

Action	Menu Bar	Shortcut Menu	Toolbar	Task Pane	Keyboard
Use the Chart Wizard	Insert, Chart				ALT + I, H
Change chart type	Chart, Chart Type	Chart Type			ALT C + Y
Change chart options	Chart, Chart Options	Chart Options			ALT C + O
Add a data series	Chart, Add data				ALT + C, A
View Drawing toolbar	View, Toolbars, Drawing				ALT + V, T
Open Insert ClipArt dialog box	Insert, Picture, Clip Art			Insert Clip Art	ALT + I, P, C
Switch between applications					ALT + TAB

chapter thirteen

Action	Menu Bar	Shortcut Menu	Toolbar	Task Pane	Keyboard
Open Format AutoShape dialog box	Format, AutoShape	Format AutoShape			ALT + O, O CTRL + 1
View AutoShapes toolbar	Insert, Picture, AutoShape				ALT + I, P, A
Insert AutoShapes			AutoShapes		
Insert Text box					
Change AutoShape			Draw, then Change AutoShape		
Insert line object					
Insert arrow object					
Change line color					
Change line style					
Change dash style					
Change arrow style					
Deselect objects					ESC
Rotate objects			Draw, then Rotate or Flip		
Flip objects			Draw, then Rotate or Flip		
Insert WordArt	Insert, Picture, WordArt				ALT + I, P, W
Add or modify color fill					
Add shadow to an object					
Create 3-D objects					
View 3-D Drawing toolbar			, then 3-D Settings		
Change stack order		Order	Draw, then Order		
Group objects		Grouping, Group	Draw, then Group		
Ungroup objects		Grouping, Ungroup	Draw, then Ungroup		
Zoom	View, Zoom		100%		ALT + V, Z

Concepts Review

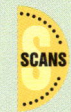

Circle the correct answer.

1. **To select multiple objects for editing, press and hold the:**
   - [a] SHIFT key while selecting objects.
   - [b] END key while selecting objects.
   - [c] CTRL key while selecting objects.
   - [d] ALT key while selecting objects.

2. **Area charts are used to:**
   - [a] show the magnitude of change over time.
   - [b] compare pairs of values.
   - [c] compare values across categories.
   - [d] show trends in values across two dimensions.

3. **To deselect an object, press the:**
   - [a] SHIFT key.
   - [b] ESC key.
   - [c] CTRL key.
   - [d] ALT key.

4. **Connection lines are more useful than line objects when diagramming because:**
   - [a] you can't change the arrow style of a line object.
   - [b] connection lines stay attached even when objects are moved.
   - [c] connection lines reroute around the objects to which they are attached.
   - [d] connection lines stay attached when objects move, and also reroute around the objects to which they are attached.

5. **XY scatter charts are used to:**
   - [a] show the magnitude of change over time.
   - [b] compare values across categories.
   - [c] compare pairs of values.
   - [d] show trends in values across two dimensions.

6. **A data table is used:**
   - [a] in place of a chart.
   - [b] to override chart data.
   - [c] as a different type of chart.
   - [d] to show numerical data along with the chart.

7. **Which of the following media types can be catalogued in Clip Organizer?**
   - [a] images
   - [b] sounds
   - [c] movies
   - [d] images, sounds, and movies

8. **Connector lines are a type of:**
   - [a] AutoShape.
   - [b] line.
   - [c] rectangle.
   - [d] WordArt.

9. **An organizational diagram shows:**
   - [a] a foundation-based relationship.
   - [b] a continuous cycle process.
   - [c] relationships of a core element.
   - [d] a hierarchical organization.

10. **Adding a coworker to an organization chart places a new element:**
    - [a] above the currently selected element.
    - [b] below the currently selected element.
    - [c] adjacent to the currently selected element.
    - [d] between the selected element and the next lower level element.

chapter thirteen

Circle **T** if the statement is true or **F** if the statement is false.

T F   1. You must turn off gridlines before using drawing tools.

T F   2. Once you create a chart you cannot add or remove data series from the chart.

T F   3. When you are adding connector lines, tiny blue connection points appear when the pointer is moved close to an object.

T F   4. A green handle on a connector indicates that the connector is attached to a connection point.

T F   5. A red handle on a connector indicates that the connector is attached to a connection point.

T F   6. To change the font settings for an entire diagram, select the diagram object and change the font settings using the Formatting toolbar.

T F   7. AutoShapes can be resized.

T F   8. You can add media collected on your computer to the Clip Organizer.

T F   9. You cannot print diagrams or drawings created using drawing tools.

T F   10. Clip Organizer can look for clip art on the Web.

> **notes**
> In the following Skills Review Exercises, several drawing tools are used that were not explicitly covered in the chapter. Use the Drawing toolbar and watch the status bar for instructions on using the tools.

Skills Review

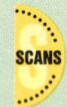

Exercise 1

1. Create a new, blank workbook.

2. Use AutoShapes to do the following:

  a. Click the Rectangle AutoShape on the Drawing toolbar, then drag to create a rectangle about 2½ inches by 3 inches.

  b. Click the Oval AutoShape on the Drawing toolbar, then drag to create an oval about 4 inches wide.

  c. Click AutoShapes on the Drawing toolbar, point to Basic Shapes, click the Isosceles Triangle shape (fourth column, second row), then drag to create a triangle about 3 inches tall.

  d. Click AutoShapes on the Drawing toolbar, point to Basic Shapes, click the Cross shape (third column, third row), then drag to create a cross about 4 inches tall.

3. Double-click the triangle.

4. On the Colors and Lines tab, change the fill color to Bright Green.

5. Double-click the rectangle.
6. Change the fill color to Blue.
7. Change the transparency to 50%.
8. Click the Cross shape.
9. Click the Dash Style button on the Drawing toolbar to change the dash style to Square Dot.
10. Save the workbook as *Drawing Objects*, and then print and close it.

Exercise 2

1. Create a new, blank workbook.
2. Open the Clip Organizer.
3. Search for clips related to sports.
4. Insert three clips representing sports you enjoy (playing or watching).
5. Add a drop shadow to the clips by selecting all three clips, then clicking the Shadow Style button on the Drawing toolbar.
6. Save the workbook as *Sports*, and then print and close it.

Exercise 3

1. Open the *Computer Price Chart* workbook located on the Data Disk.
2. Add cells A3:A9 on Sheet1 to the Category (X) axis labels using the Source Data dialog box.
3. Display the Drawing toolbar, if necessary.
4. Click AutoShapes on the Drawing toolbar, point to Callouts, click the Rectangular Callout shape (first row, first column), then drag the callout shape over the AMD 900 MHz system.
5. With the callout object selected, key "Biggest Price Drop!" and then click the Center button on the Formatting toolbar to center the text.
6. With the callout object selected, click the Fill Color list arrow on the Drawing toolbar and change the fill color to Red.
7. Drag the yellow object handle to point the callout to the "Now" price of the AMD 900 MHz system.
8. Save the workbook as *Computer Price Chart Revised*, and then print and close it.

Exercise 4

1. Open the *Business Transactions* workbook located on the Data Disk.
2. Zoom in on the worksheet, if necessary.
3. Click the Line button on the Drawing toolbar, then drag to draw a line between the Total Income in cells C22 and F16.
4. Draw a line between the Total Distributions in cells K15 and F17.
5. Draw a line between the Total Expenses in cells D42 and F18.
6. Select all three lines, then change the line style of the lines to 3 pt by clicking the Line Style button on the Drawing toolbar.

chapter thirteen

7. With all three lines selected, change the line color to lavender by clicking the Line Color button list arrow on the Drawing toolbar.

8. Change the arrow style of all three lines to Arrow Style 7 by clicking the Arrow Style button on the Drawing toolbar, then clicking the seventh style in the list.

9. Zoom the worksheet to 50% if you changed it earlier.

10. Save the workbook as *Business Transactions Revised*, and then print and close it.

Exercise 5

1. Open the *Temperature Data* file located on the Data Disk.
2. Create an XY Scatter chart using all the data shown on Sheet1.
3. Use Chart Options to:
    a. Add the title "Recorded Temperatures."
    b. Add the Value (X) axis title "Date."
    c. Add the Value (Y) axis title "Temperature."
4. Save the workbook as *Temperature Data Chart*, and then print and close it.

Exercise 6

1. Open the *Half Marathon Mile Splits 2* workbook located on the Data Disk.
2. Select the range B3:B15.
3. Open the Chart Wizard.
4. Create an area type chart as an embedded chart in Sheet1.
5. Right-click the Y-axis on the left side of the chart, then click Format Axis.
6. On the Scale tab, set the Minimum to 0.004 and click OK.
7. Save the workbook as *Half Marathon Mile Splits Chart*, and then print and close it.

Exercise 7

1. Open a new, blank workbook.
2. Using the Rectangle button on the Drawing toolbar, draw a box representing a house.
3. Click the Fill Color button list arrow on the Drawing toolbar, click Fill Effects, click the Pattern tab, then select a brick pattern to add to the house.
4. Using more rectangles, add windows to the house with a light blue fill color.
5. Add another rectangle and a circle for a door.
6. Using a triangle AutoShape, add a roof with a brown fill color.
7. Add a rectangle for a tree trunk with dark red fill color.
8. Click AutoShapes on the Drawing toolbar, point to Stars and Banners, then click the Explosion 2 AutoShape (first row, second column) and create the top of the tree with a green fill color.
9. Print the drawing, save the workbook as *House Drawing*, and then close it.

Working with Charts and the Drawing Tools   EA 161

Exercise 8

1. Open the *Product Quantities* workbook located on the Data Disk.

2. Select the range A1:B4, then use the Chart Wizard to create a Line - Column on 2 Axes chart.

3. Insert the chart on the worksheet.

4. Save the workbook as *Product Quantities Chart*, and then print and close it.

Case Projects

Project 1

You work for a mortgage company that is seeking ways to promote its low interest rates on home loans. Open the *Interest* workbook located on the Data Disk. Using AutoShapes with text and clip art, create a newsletter-type document in Excel advertising a 6.9% interest rate. To add an eye-catching title, draw an AutoShape, then add text. Select the text and format it, then add a fill color to the shape. Target your newsletter toward first-time homebuyers. Try searching for clip art associated with homes, saving money, and families. Save the workbook as *Interest Advertisement*, and then print and close it.

Project 2

You own a successful restaurant. You train your employees to always follow a four-step system to serve clients. The steps are as follows: (1) Greet Customers, (2) Take the Order, (3) Prepare the Order, and (4) Collect the Amount Due. Using AutoShapes with text, add each of the steps to a new workbook. Then use curved connector lines to create a flow chart that you can use in training meetings to emphasize this system. You may need to resize the objects to fit on-screen. Save the worksheet as *Serve System*, and then print and close it.

Project 3

Connect to the Internet and search the Web for a food pyramid. Using the Excel organizational charts, recreate the food pyramid. Save the workbook as *Food Pyramid*, and then print and close it.

Project 4

This one's just for fun but might prove useful in Algebra class. Open a new, blank workbook. Select cells A1:B21 and create an XY scatter chart using smoothed lines (one of the chart subtypes). In column A, enter the following values (leave cells empty when you see EMPTY): X, 0.5, 0.75, 0.5, 0.25, 0.5, EMPTY, -0.5, -0.75, -0.5, -0.25, -0.5, EMPTY, 0, -0.25, 0.25, 0, EMPTY, -1, 0, 1. In column B, place the following values: Y, 0.5, 0.25, 0, 0.25, 0.5, EMPTY, 0.5, 0.25, 0, 0.25, 0.5, EMPTY, 0, -0.5, -0.5, 0, EMPTY, -0.2, -0.8, -0.2. Save the completed workbook as *XY Fun*, and then print and close it.

Project 5

Prediction time! Randomly select five classmates. In a new workbook, predict what score you think they earned on a recent assignment (do this before you find out their actual score). Next, record the actual score they earned. Create a Line-Column on 2 Axes chart to show how well you were able to predict their scores. To maintain anonymity, be sure to assign each student a number instead of using his or her name in the workbook. Save the workbook as *Score Prediction*, and then print and close it.

chapter thirteen

Project 6

Your cookie company has been tremendously successful. You want to find out which cookies have been contributing most to your success. Create fictional sales data for five types of cookies. Include quantities for each of the last four quarters. Create an area chart with a data table to illustrate the data. Save your workbook as *Cookie Sales Chart*, and then print and close it.

Project 7

You work for an interior design company creating layouts of office furniture. Use Clip Organizer to insert clip art of office furniture (*Hint:* Use the Office Layout category or search for furniture). Save your workbook as *Office Layout*, and then print and close it.

Project 8

You work as a technical support engineer. Each day you receive calls from customers who are having problems opening Excel workbooks. To make it easier for you to do your job, create a troubleshooting flow chart of questions you can ask to determine the source of the problem. Each question should have a Yes or No answer. If the answer is Yes, you ask the next question on your list; if the answer is No, include steps to solve the problem. Place each question and each solution set in its own text box, then connect the boxes using connectors. Save the workbook as *Troubleshooting*, and then print and close it.

Excel 2002

Importing and Exporting Data from Other Applications

Chapter Overview

Excel worksheets and charts can be used in a variety of ways outside of Excel. For example, you can create reports in Word using Excel data, and you can enhance PowerPoint presentations with Excel data and charts. In addition, you can create Access tables from existing Excel lists or query Access databases from Excel to analyze data. You can paste or link workbook data to documents created in other programs. You can also embed workbooks within other documents to share the functionality of Excel with other programs.

Learning Objectives

- Integrate Excel data with Word and PowerPoint
- Integrate Excel with Access
- Import data from text files

Case profile

You are responsible not only for gathering data from each store at Super Power Computers, but also for distributing the data to regional and store managers. For example, you periodically write memos to regional managers, distribute reports to management, and prepare presentations for potential investors. By integrating Excel-based data into other Office documents, and by querying existing Access databases for information, you can save time and ensure accurate data.

chapter fourteen

> **notes** It is assumed that you have a basic knowledge of the Word, Access, and PowerPoint applications. Your instructor may provide additional instructions as you complete the activities in this chapter.

14.a Integrating Excel Data with Word and PowerPoint

Excel data can be integrated with other applications, such as Word, PowerPoint, and Access. In Word and PowerPoint documents, worksheets and charts can be linked or embedded. Alternately, you can create a "table" from within Word or PowerPoint, using Excel features.

There are several ways to integrate Excel data with Word documents and PowerPoint presentations. First, you can insert an Excel file (the **source file**) in a Word document or PowerPoint presentation (the **target file**). Second, you can embed an Excel object in a Word document or PowerPoint presentation. Third, you can create a link between an Excel workbook and a Word document or PowerPoint presentation.

When you **insert** Excel data into a Word document, you place the data in a Word table that can be edited using the Word table editing commands. When you insert Excel data into a PowerPoint presentation, the data is inserted as a graphic object, similar to a picture of the data, which cannot be edited. All links to the original data are lost. Thus, if you modify the data in the target file, the original Excel workbook is not updated. Likewise, if you update the Excel workbook, the target file is not updated. Because you can use the Copy and Paste commands to insert Excel data into the target file, this method is very fast.

Embedding an Excel object in a target file creates a connection between the target application and Excel. When you double-click an embedded worksheet object to edit it, the target application's menu bar and toolbars are replaced with the Excel menu bar and toolbars. Using an embedded worksheet is like opening a window in the target application to the Excel application. Although you use the familiar Excel menu bar and toolbars to edit the data, you are not actually altering the original data. That is, your changes are not reflected in the original Excel workbook. When you do not need to maintain a link to the original data, but do want access to Excel features to format and edit data, use this method.

When you **link** an Excel worksheet to a target file, you create a reference to the original Excel worksheet. Double-clicking a linked object opens the original file. Because the workbook is linked to the target file, any changes you make in Excel are reflected in your target file. Linking files saves hard drive space, because you do not create a second copy of the data in the target file. If having up-to-date data in the target file is essential, linking is your best option.

Integrating Excel with Access involves sharing data normally used in a database. Data stored in lists in Excel can be used to create new data tables in Access, and data stored in an Access database can be queried and extracted into an Excel workbook.

Embedding Excel Data in a Word Document

You need to send a memo to the management personnel at Super Power Computers showing the sales totals for 2003. You wrote the memo in Word, and you collected the data in Excel. You want to embed the Excel data, so the managers can correct the data if necessary. To embed Excel data in a Word document:

Step 1	Start	Word
Step 2	Open	the *Memo to Store 3 Manager* document located on the Data Disk
Step 3	Save	the Word document as *Memo to Store 3 Manager with Embedded Data*
Step 4	Click	the Show/Hide button ¶ on the Standard toolbar to display the nonprinting formatting marks in Word, if necessary
Step 5	Key	your name on the From: line, replacing Your Name
Step 6	Press	the CTRL + END keys to move the insertion point to the end of the document
Step 7	Press	the ENTER key to create a new line
Step 8	Start	Excel
Step 9	Open	the *Super Power Computers - Mountain Region Sales* workbook located on the Data Disk
Step 10	Click	the Store #3 sheet tab
Step 11	Select	the range A1:F9
Step 12	Click	the Copy button on the Standard toolbar
Step 13	Click	the Word button on the taskbar
Step 14	Click	<u>E</u>dit
Step 15	Click	Paste <u>S</u>pecial

The Paste Special dialog box opens in Word.

QUICK TIP

You can click the Paste link: option button to link the worksheet to the document. Then you can change the data from either file.

Step 16	**Click**	Microsoft Excel Worksheet Object in the A̲s: list box
Step 17	**Verify**	that the P̲aste: option button is selected
Step 18	**Click**	OK

The worksheet is embedded in the document as an object. When a worksheet is embedded in the target file, you must change it from within the Word target file. To edit the embedded Excel object in the Word document:

| Step 1 | **Double-click** | the embedded worksheet object to edit it with Excel tools |

Your screen should look similar to Figure 14-1.

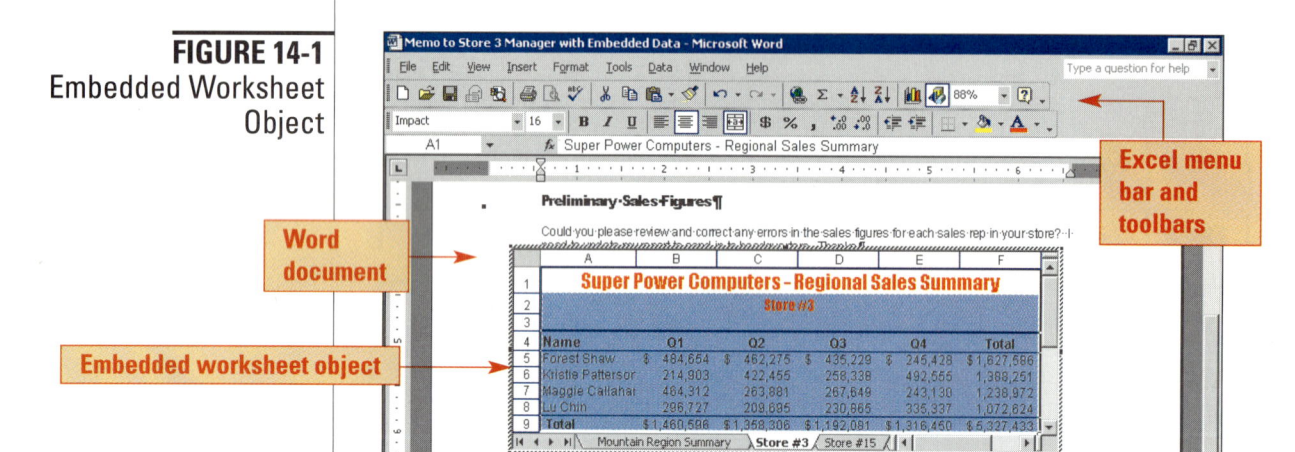

FIGURE 14-1
Embedded Worksheet Object

Step 2	**Select**	the range A4:F4
Step 3	**Click**	the Fill Color button list arrow on the Formatting toolbar
Step 4	**Click**	the Gray-25% square
Step 5	**Activate**	cell A1
Step 6	**Click**	anywhere in the Word document to deactivate the Excel object

You can drag the object in Word to reposition it or align it on the page using the Formatting toolbar. To center the embedded object:

| Step 1 | **Click** | the embedded worksheet object to select it |

| Step 2 | Click | the Center button on the Formatting toolbar |
| Step 3 | Click | in a blank area of the document to deselect the object |

Your document should look similar to Figure 14-2.

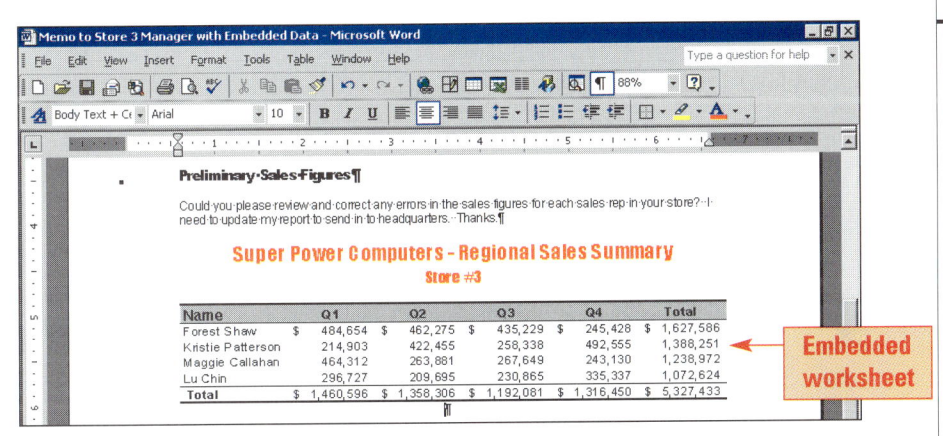

FIGURE 14-2
Embedded Worksheet Object after Formatting

| Step 4 | Save | the Word document |

Creating a Chart in Word Using Excel Data

An alternate method of creating charts in Word is to use Excel data along with the Microsoft Chart Object. To create a chart in Word using Excel data:

Step 1	Click	the Excel button on the taskbar
Step 2	Copy	the range A4:F8 on the Store #3 sheet tab
Step 3	Click	the Word button on the taskbar
Step 4	Press	the ENTER key to move the insertion point below the embedded worksheet object
Step 5	Click	Insert
Step 6	Click	Object
Step 7	Click	Microsoft Graph Chart in the Object type: list
Step 8	Click	OK

The Microsoft Graph Chart object appears in your document, along with the Datasheet window. Your screen should look similar to Figure 14-3.

The datasheet contains sample data, on which the chart is. In the datasheet, you can paste and modify data used in the chart.

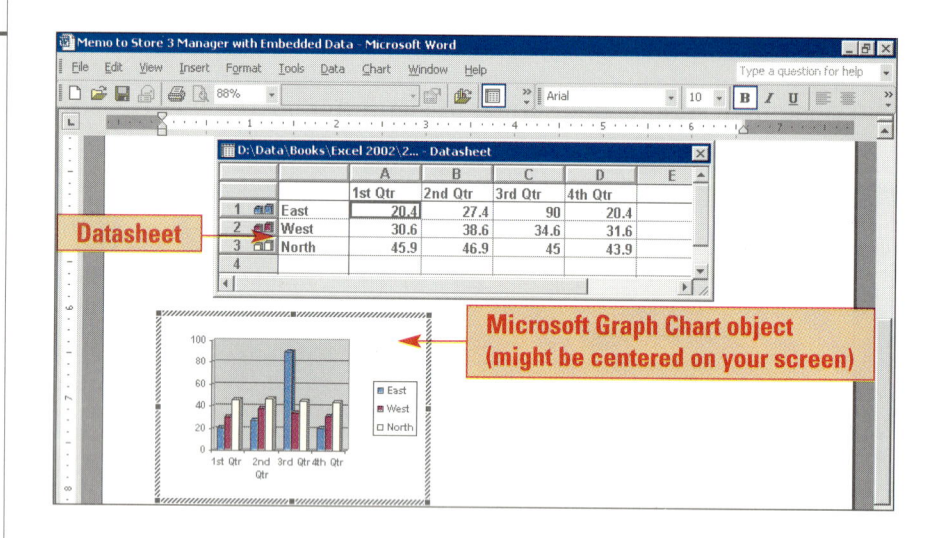

FIGURE 14-3
Microsoft Graph Chart Object

> **CAUTION TIP**
>
> If you double-click a column head rather than a column divider in the Datasheet window, you may deactivate the column. If the data in a column is gray, double-click the column header again to reactivate it.

Step 9	Right-click	the upper-left cell in the datasheet, the blank cell to the left of 1st Qtr
Step 10	Click	Paste
Step 11	Double-click	the boundaries between each column to AutoFit each column, if necessary

You added the Total column to the chart, which you want to deactivate. To modify the chart:

Step 1	Double-click	the column E header to deactivate the column

The Total data disappears from the chart and appears grayed out in the Datasheet window.

Step 2	Click	outside the chart object to deselect it and close the Datasheet window
Step 3	Click	the chart object once to select it
Step 4	Drag	the sizing handle at the lower-right corner to make the chart as large as possible without jumping to the next page
Step 5	Save	the Word document and close it
Step 6	Exit	Word
Step 7	Close	the *Super Power Computers - Mountain Region Sales* workbook

> **CAUTION TIP**
>
> If you make the chart too large, it may slip onto the next page. If this happens, resize the chart, making it a little smaller until it returns to the first page of the document.

Linking an Excel Worksheet to a PowerPoint Presentation

You are working on a PowerPoint presentation showing sales data for the South Region. You want to include a chart showing this year's data in the presentation. You know that the worksheet will be updated later, so you decide to link it to the presentation. You then can update the chart right before your presentation. To add a link to the data:

Step 1	Open	the *Super Power Computers - Store #10 Summary* workbook located on the Data Disk
Step 2	Start	PowerPoint
Step 3	Open	the *Super Power Computers - Store #10 Presentation* file located on the Data Disk
Step 4	Save	the presentation as *Super Power Computers - Store #10 Presentation Final*
Step 5	Click	the Excel button on the taskbar
Step 6	Verify	that the Summary Chart sheet is active
Step 7	Click	the Copy button on the Standard toolbar

Excel automatically selects and copies the chart on the Summary Chart worksheet.

Step 8	Click	the PowerPoint button on the taskbar
Step 9	Click	the Slide 2 slide icon in the Outline tab to move to the second slide
Step 10	Click	Edit
Step 11	Click	Paste Special
Step 12	Click	the Paste link option button
Step 13	Click	OK

The chart is linked to the PowerPoint presentation, but you need to resize it so it fits on the slide. When you press and hold the CTRL key while you resize an object, the object resizes proportionally toward or from the center of the object. To resize the chart object:

Step 1	Press & hold	the CTRL key

Step 2	*Drag*	a corner sizing handle until the object fits nicely on the slide
Step 3	*Move*	the object so it is visually centered on the slide
Step 4	*Press*	the ESC key to deselect the object
Step 5	*Save*	the presentation

Your screen should look similar to Figure 14-4.

FIGURE 14-4
Excel Data Linked to PowerPoint Slide

> **CAUTION TIP**
>
> If you move or rename a workbook that has been linked to other files, the link must be corrected for the data to be updated. However, the most recently updated data (before the link was broken) is displayed until you update the link. For more information about breaking and reestablishing links in a PowerPoint presentation, refer to PowerPoint online Help.

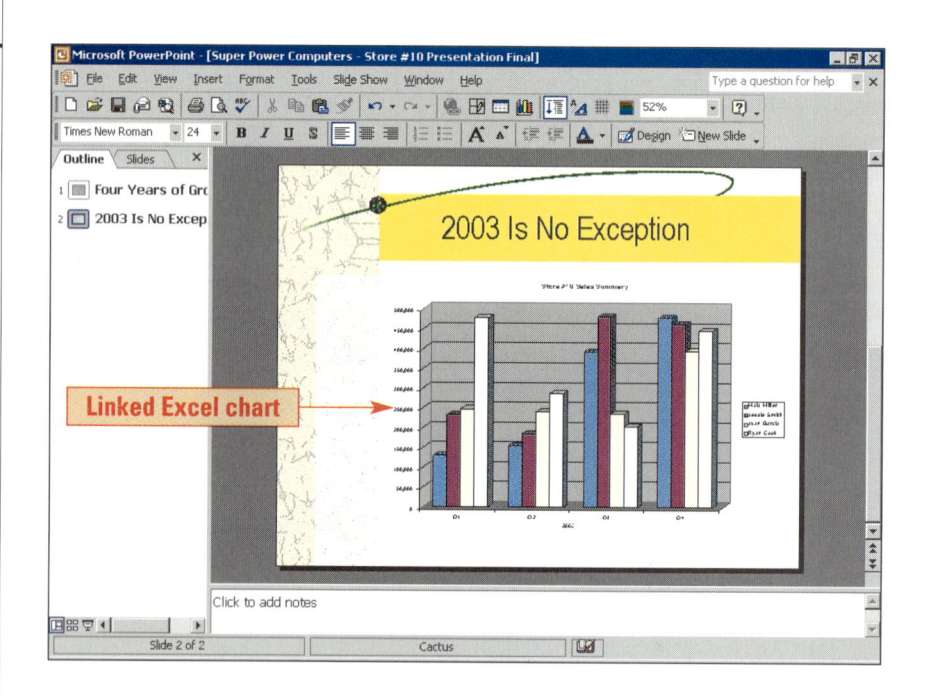

| Step 6 | *Close* | the *Super Power Computers - Store #10 Summary* workbook in Excel |

The chart is linked to the PowerPoint presentation. When an Excel worksheet is linked to a target file, double-clicking the Excel object takes you directly to Excel and opens the linked file, if necessary. As you edit the linked data, the target file is updated automatically. To modify the worksheet object:

| Step 1 | *Click* | the PowerPoint button on the taskbar, if necessary |
| Step 2 | *Double-click* | the linked chart object |

Excel becomes the active program, and the workbook containing the chart object appears in the active window.

Step 3	Maximize	the Excel workbook window, if necessary
Step 4	Save	the workbook as *Super Power Computers - Store #10 Summary Revised*
Step 5	Right-click	the taskbar
Step 6	Click	Tile Windows Vertically to display both program windows
Step 7	Click	in the Excel window to make it active

Your screen should look similar to Figure 14-5.

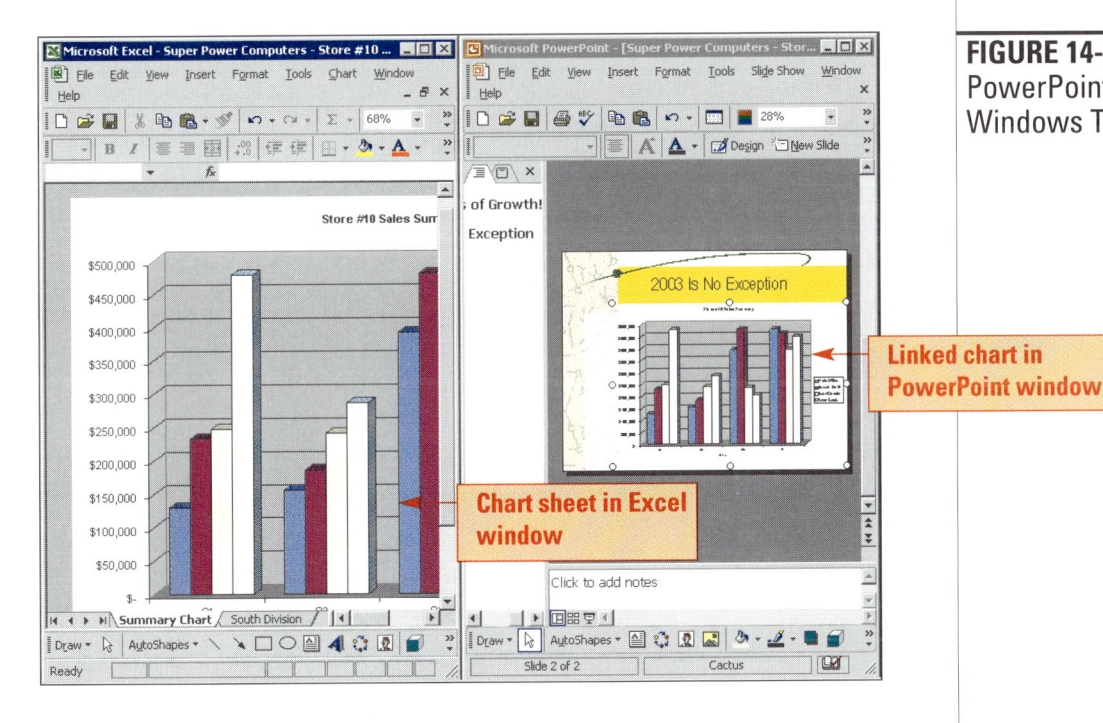

FIGURE 14-5
PowerPoint and Excel Windows Tiled Vertically

Step 8	Select	the Chart Title object in Excel
Step 9	Press	the DELETE key to delete the Chart Title object in the Excel window
Step 10	Click	in the PowerPoint window to make it active
Step 11	Right-click	the Chart object in PowerPoint
Step 12	Click	Update Link

The chart title no longer appears on the PowerPoint slide.

Step 13	Maximize	the PowerPoint program window
Step 14	Save	the PowerPoint presentation and close it

Step 15	Exit	PowerPoint
Step 16	Maximize	the Excel program window
Step 17	Save	the workbook and close it

14.b Integrating Excel with Access

> **QUICK TIP**
>
> Even though databases store large amounts of data efficiently, Excel still offers advantages when it comes to performing calculations on that information. As a result, you may prefer to import data from Access databases to Excel to perform more complex calculations and create charts.

Although Excel can store a large volume of data in list form, a database application—such as Access—is better suited to holding large amounts of this type of data. As your Excel lists grow in size, you can export them to create Access tables.

Exporting Excel Data to an Access Database

You can use existing lists of Excel data to build data tables in Access. The *Sales Rep Data* workbook contains a variety of information about the sales for each of Sweet Tooth's divisions. You think it would be a good idea to store the data in a database rather than in Excel. Before you import Excel-based data into Access, however, you need to prepare the information. To prepare the Excel data:

| Step 1 | Open | the *Super Power Computers - Sales Rep Data 2* workbook located on the Data Disk |
| Step 2 | Save | the workbook as *Super Power Computers - Sales Rep Data to Import* |

You should delete any worksheet titles and blank rows that appear above the data to be imported into Access. The labels in the first row become the field names in the database, so you want the column headings in the first row.

Step 3	Delete	rows 1 through 4
Step 4	Verify	that the column headings appear in the first row of the worksheet you want to import
Step 5	Activate	cell A1
Step 6	Delete	the PivotTable and PivotChart worksheets
Step 7	Save	the workbook and close it

To start Access and create a new database:

Step 1	Start	Access
Step 2	Click	the Blank Database link in the New File task pane
Step 3	Switch to	the drive and folder containing your completed files
Step 4	Key	Super Power Computers - Sales Rep Data in the File name: text box
Step 5	Click	Create

To import data from Excel:

Step 1	Click	File
Step 2	Point to	Get External Data
Step 3	Click	Import
Step 4	Click	the Files of type: list arrow in the Import dialog box
Step 5	Click	Microsoft Excel
Step 6	Click	Super Power Computers - Sales Rep Data to Import
Step 7	Click	Import

The Import Spreadsheet Wizard opens. The first row of data in the workbook contains the column headings.

Step 8	Click	the First Row Contains Column Headings check box to insert a check mark

Notice that in the bottom half of the dialog box the column headings from the worksheet become the field headings for the new Access table. Below those headings, you see how the data divides into records (horizontally) and fields (vertically).

Step 9	Click	Next >
Step 10	Click	Next > to accept the default option of creating the database in new table
Step 11	Click	Next > to accept the default information about each of the fields you are importing

In a database, a primary key is used to uniquely identify each record in a table and to speed up data retrieval in large databases. Access adds a primary key by default in Step 4 of the Wizard.

Step 12	Click	Next >

The next step names the new Access database table.

Step 13	Verify	Sales Report Data is entered in the Import to Table: text box
Step 14	Click	Finish
Step 15	Click	OK to close the message dialog box

The new table name appears in the Database window.

Step 16	Double-click	the Sales Report Data table icon

Your screen should look similar to Figure 14-6.

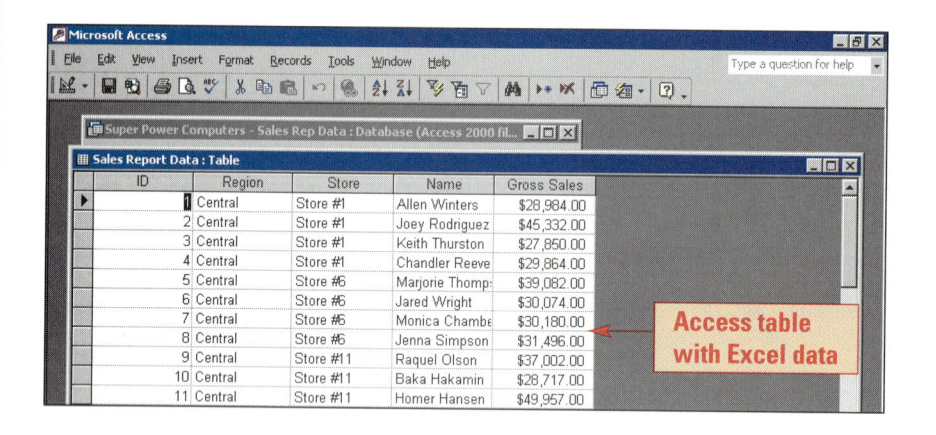

FIGURE 14-6
Access Table Created Using an Excel List

Step 17	Exit	Access

Querying Data from an Access Database

A **query** is a method of extracting information from a database. You can use Excel to query data stored in Access and search for records meeting certain criteria. Then, you can import only those records that meet your criteria into Excel so as to create charts, develop PivotTable reports, or perform statistical analysis. To query a database, you use Microsoft Query in Excel.

Importing and Exporting Data from Other Applications   **EA 175**

To query the database:

Step 1	Create	a new workbook in Excel
Step 2	Click	Data
Step 3	Point to	Import External Data
Step 4	Click	New Database Query
Step 5	Click	MS Access Database* in the Choose Data Source dialog box
Step 6	Verify	that the Use the Query Wizard to create/edit queries check box contains a check mark
Step 7	Click	OK
Step 8	Switch to	the drive and folder containing your completed files
Step 9	Click	*Super Power Computers - Sales Rep Data.mdb* in the Database Name list box in the Select Database dialog box
Step 10	Click	OK

Once you have selected a database source, the Query Wizard starts. In Step 1 of the wizard, you select which columns you want to include from your table in your query. If you omit a column, the data in that column is not extracted from the database. To add columns to your query:

Step 1	Click	the + next to Sales Report Data in the Available tables and columns: list box
Step 2	Verify	that Sales Report Data is selected
Step 3	Click	the > button to add the entire table to the Columns in your query: list box
Step 4	Click	Next >

Step 2 of the Query Wizard enables you to set query filters. **Filters** allow you to view only records meeting criteria you define. For this query, you want to extract only the records of sales representatives who work in the West Coast Region and whose gross sales exceed $35,000. To set query filters:

Step 1	Click	Gross Sales in the Column to filter: list box
Step 2	Click	the Operator list arrow in the active box on the right
Step 3	Click	is greater than in the list of operators
Step 4	Key	35000 in the Value list box on the right

chapter fourteen

Your query extracts all records in which the value of the Gross Sales column exceeds $35,000, as shown in Figure 14-7.

FIGURE 14-7
Step 2 of the Query Wizard

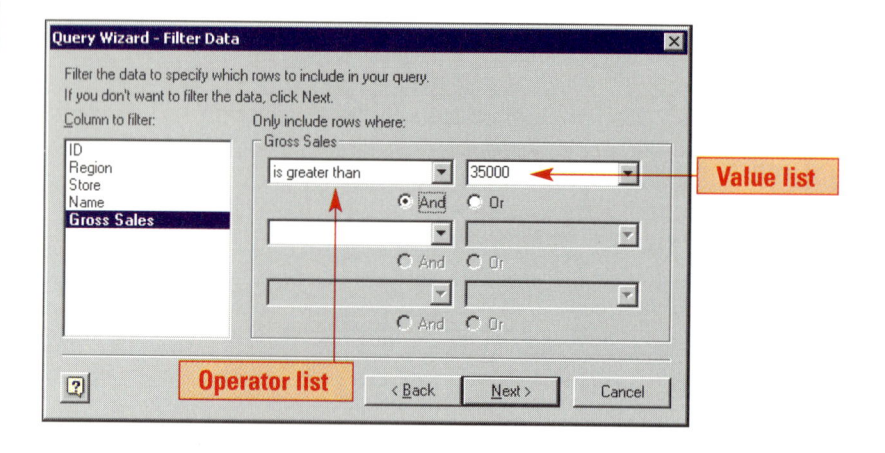

Step 5	*Click*	Region in the Column to filter: list box
Step 6	*Click*	equals in the operator list
Step 7	*Click*	West Coast in the value list

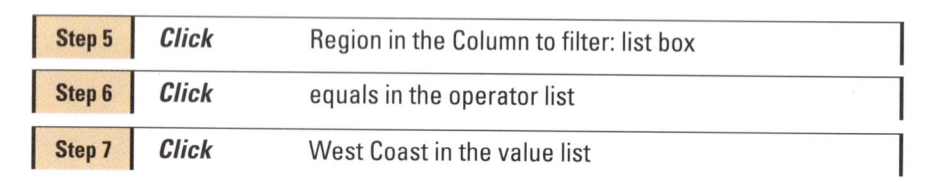

Notice that both Region and Gross Sales are highlighted in the Column to filter: list box. This indicates that both columns have a filter applied. The query extracts all records where the value in the Gross Sales column is greater than $35,000 *and* where the region equals West Coast.

| Step 8 | *Click* | Next > |

The third step of the Query Wizard allows you to define a sort order for the records. To set the sort order:

Step 1	*Click*	the Sort by list arrow
Step 2	*Click*	Gross Sales
Step 3	*Click*	the Descending option button
Step 4	*Click*	Next >

The final step of the Query Wizard allows you to specify where the data should appear. You want to create a new list in Excel.

> **QUICK TIP**
>
> If you plan to reuse this query to update data at a later time, you can save it by clicking the Save Query button in the last step of the Query Wizard.

To specify the output option of your query results:

Step 1	Verify	that the Return Data to Microsoft Excel option button is selected
Step 2	Click	Finish

The Import Data dialog box opens. You need to select a location where the data will be placed. Cell A1 (the default) is just fine.

Step 3	Click	OK
Step 4	Save	the workbook as *Super Power Computers - Database Query*

Your query results should look similar to Figure 14-8.

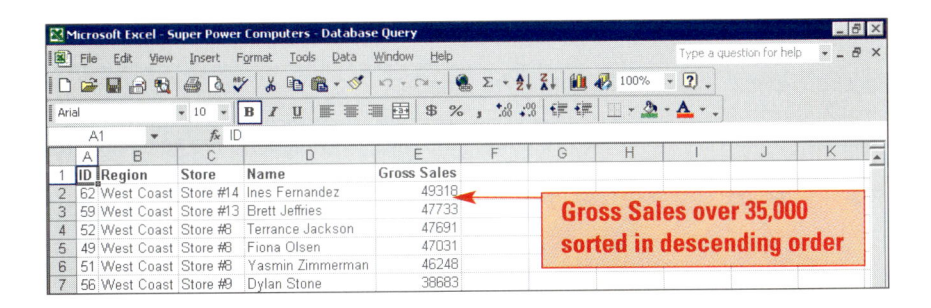

FIGURE 14-8
Results of Database Query

Step 5	Close	the workbook

14.c Importing Data from Text Files

A common method of exchanging data between applications involves **comma-separated** or **tab-delimited** text files. These files can be created in any text editor and use commas, tabs, or other characters to separate columns of data. You can import these files into an open workbook, or you can create a new workbook using the text file. You have located an old document containing financial data that was exported from an accounting program. This file uses tabs to separate information into columns. To import data from a text file into Excel:

Step 1	Create	a new workbook
Step 2	Click	Data

MOUSE TIP

The External Data toolbar appears after you run a query. Using this toolbar, you can refresh the data source, modify the query to extract other records, or modify the data range properties.

QUICK TIP

You could use other characters as well, including commas, semicolons, or even spaces, to separate columns of data.

Step 3	Point to	Import External Data
Step 4	Click	Import Data

The Select Data Source dialog box opens.

Step 5	Click	the Files of type: list arrow
Step 6	Click	Text Files
Step 7	Select	Monthly Cash Flow located on the Data Disk
Step 8	Click	Open

Step 1 of the Text Import Wizard appears. This wizard walks you through three steps to help you import and properly separate the text file into columns of data. Because the data is delimited, you can leave the settings at their defaults.

Step 9	Click	Next > to go to Step 2
Step 10	Click	Next > to accept the default choice of tabs as delimiters
Step 11	Click	Finish to accept the default settings for specifying how columns of data are formatted
Step 12	Click	OK in the Import Data dialog box

You can format and rearrange the imported data as necessary. Because Super Power Computer's file is a plain text file, it cannot carry formulas with it; thus all totals and subtotals are included only as values. Upon reviewing the information, you notice that the totals in the workbook are not correct. You decide to correct the totals by replacing them with functions. To replace values with functions:

Step 1	Activate	cell B10
Step 2	Click	the AutoSum button Σ on the Standard toolbar
Step 3	Press	the ENTER key
Step 4	Follow	Steps 1 through 3 to sum the total outflows in cells B14:B28 in cell B30
Step 5	Enter	=B10-B30 in cell B33
Step 6	Save	the workbook as Old Monthly Cash Flow and close it

Importing and exporting data enables you to accurately and quickly use Excel data in other Office applications.

> ### QUICK TIP
>
> Virtually any character can be used as a delimiter, so Excel permits you to specify a character in the Other box. If the data is not divided into columns automatically, you need to specify a character other than a tab.

Importing and Exporting Data from Other Applications   EA 179

Summary

▶ You can paste Excel data into a Word document to use the Word table tools.

▶ You can embed Excel data to use the functionality of Excel without providing for data to be updated from the source.

▶ You can create charts in Word using Excel data and the Microsoft Graph Chart object.

▶ You can link Excel documents when data must be kept up to date.

▶ You can embed or link charts and data to PowerPoint slides to enhance presentations.

▶ You can use Excel lists to create tables in Access. You also can query Access databases from Excel to create charts, reports, and statistical analysis.

▶ You can import data from different types of files using the Import Text Wizard.

Commands Review

Action	Menu Bar	Shortcut Menu	Toolbar	Task Pane	Keyboard
Insert a copy of Excel data in a Word document	Insert, File				ALT + I, L
Place Excel data in a Word document as a Word table	Edit, Copy Edit, Paste	Right-click selected data, Copy Right-click, Paste			ALT + E, C ALT + E, P CTRL + C CTRL + V
Embed Excel data in a Word document	Insert, Object Edit, Copy Edit, Paste Special, Paste				ALT + I, O ALT + E, C ALT + E, S ALT + P
Link Excel data in a Word document	Edit, Copy Edit, Paste Special, Paste link	Right-click Excel range, Copy			ALT + E, C ALT + E, S ALT + L CTRL + C
Link Excel worksheet data or chart to PowerPoint slide	Edit, Copy Edit, Paste Special, Paste link	Right-click Excel range, Copy			ALT + E, C ALT + E, S ALT + L CTRL + C
Embed Excel worksheet data or chart in PowerPoint slide	Edit, Copy Edit, Paste Special, Paste	Right-click Excel range or chart, Copy Right-click PowerPoint slide, Paste			ALT + E, C ALT + E, S ALT + P CTRL + C CTRL + V

chapter fourteen

Concepts Review

Circle the correct answer.

1. To embed worksheet data in a Word document:
   - [a] use Copy and Paste.
   - [b] use Copy and Paste Special.
   - [c] press the CTRL key and drag a selection from Excel to Word.
   - [d] use Copy and Paste Special or drag a selection from Excel to Word.

2. Integrating Excel with other applications:
   - [a] is difficult and creates outdated copies of data.
   - [b] is unnecessary because Excel can format a worksheet any way you want.
   - [c] increases your productivity and enhances your options for presenting data.
   - [d] cannot be done.

3. Embedding an Excel file in Word or PowerPoint:
   - [a] creates a link to the Excel application and the source data.
   - [b] creates a link to the Excel application but not to the source data.
   - [c] makes a copy of the Excel data using a Word table structure.
   - [d] makes a picture object of the data that can be only resized or moved.

4. When creating a Word document with integrated Excel data that might change later, you should use:
   - [a] embedded data.
   - [b] linked data.
   - [c] inserted data.
   - [d] copied data.

5. If you need to keep a "snapshot" of Excel data in another document at a given time, you should:
   - [a] use embedded data.
   - [b] use linked data.
   - [c] use a screen shot.
   - [d] save the workbook using a different filename.

6. Text files can use which of the following characters as delimiters?
   - [a] comma
   - [b] tab
   - [c] semicolon
   - [d] comma, tab, or semicolon

7. When Excel lists become very large, a better option may be to:
   - [a] remove infrequently used records.
   - [b] create a second workbook and move half the records there.
   - [c] convert the worksheet to an Access database.
   - [d] condense the data by abbreviating names and other information.

8. You can output the results of a query to:
   - [a] the Microsoft Query window.
   - [b] an Excel worksheet.
   - [c] the Excel Query dialog box.
   - [d] all of the above

9. A comma-delimited file uses what character as a delimiter?
   - [a] ,
   - [b] ;
   - [c] TAB
   - [d] `

10. Which application is best suited to storing large lists of data?
    - [a] Excel
    - [b] Word
    - [c] PowerPoint
    - [d] Access

Circle **T** if the statement is true or **F** if the statement is false.

T F 1. Inserting and embedding data create copies of the data that are not linked to the source data.

T F 2. Linking Excel data to a Word document requires more disk space than embedding, because it creates an additional copy of the Excel workbook.

T F 3. You cannot create a simultaneous link to the same data in both a Word document and a PowerPoint presentation.

T F 4. The Paste Special dialog box can be used to embed or link data.

T F 5. Right-click and drag an object from Excel to a Word document to create a linked object.

T F 6. When editing embedded or linked Excel data in a Word document, you stay "in" the Word document, but the Excel menu and toolbars appear.

T F 7. Double-clicking the column head in the Datasheet window of a Microsoft Graph Chart object toggles the column on and off.

T F 8. Double-clicking a linked worksheet opens the linked worksheet document in Excel.

T F 9. Double-clicking an embedded worksheet opens the linked worksheet document in Excel.

T F 10. Learning to use the right software tool for the job can save time and effort.

Skills Review

Exercise 1

1. Create a new, blank workbook.

2. Use Microsoft Query (Data, Import External Data, New Database Query) to query the *Excel List.mdb* database located on the Data Disk.

3. Create a query to extract records from the Mountain or Central regions where the gross sales exceed $40,000.

4. Sort the results by gross sales in descending order.

5. Output the results to Excel.

6. Create a chart on a new sheet listing the top 10 sales representatives and their gross sales totals.

7. Add a title to your chart that describes its contents.

8. Print the chart.

9. Save the workbook as *Top 10*, and close it.

Exercise 2

1. Open the *Top 10* workbook that you created in Exercise 1.

2. Open the *Top 10 Sales Representatives.ppt* presentation located on the Data Disk using PowerPoint.

3. Save the presentation as *Top 15.ppt*.

4. Link the Top 10 Chart to the first slide in the presentation by using Copy and Paste Special, then selecting the Paste link option.

5. Resize and reposition the chart as necessary.

6. Click the Excel button on the taskbar.
7. Modify the Chart Source Data to include the top 15 sales representatives.
8. Remove the chart title.
9. Click the PowerPoint button on the taskbar and update the link.
10. Rename the Slide title as "Top 15 Sales Representatives."
11. Print the PowerPoint slide, then save the PowerPoint presentation and exit PowerPoint.
12. Save the workbook as *Top 15* and close it.

Exercise 3

1. Open the *Warehouse Inventory* workbook located on the Data Disk.
2. Sort the list by Part No., then save the workbook as *Warehouse Inventory Modified*.
3. Select the range A4:F16 and click the Copy button on the Standard toolbar, then close the workbook.
4. Open the Word application.
5. Open the *Letter to Warehouse Division Manager.doc* document located on the Data Disk.
6. Save the Word document as *Letter with Data.doc*.
7. Insert a blank line between the first and second paragraphs of the letter.
8. Use the Paste Special command on the Edit menu to embed the data as a Microsoft Excel worksheet object.
9. Resize and reposition the embedded object as necessary.
10. Double-click the embedded object to make the following modifications:
    a. Change the cost of item 1020 to $29.95.
    b. Change the quantity of item 3001 to 500.
    c. Center the data in the range E5:E16. (*Hint:* If you scroll the worksheet so that the visible range changes, scroll it back so that the visible range is again A4:F16.)
    d. Turn off the display of gridlines by using the Options dialog box.
11. Print, save, and close the letter.

Exercise 4

1. Open the *Letter with Data.doc* document that you created in Exercise 3, and delete the embedded object.
2. Open the file *Warehouse Inventory Modified* workbook that you created in Exercise 3, then save it as *Warehouse Inventory Modified 2*.
3. Copy the range A4:F16.
4. Use the Paste Special command in Word to create a linked worksheet object in the document, then resize it and reposition the object as necessary.
5. Double-click the linked object to edit the data as follows:
    a. Center the range E5:E16.
    b. Change the cost of item 1020 to $35.95.
    c. Change the quantity of item 3001 to 750.
    d. Select the range A5:A16 and left-justify the range.

6. Save the workbook.

7. In Word, right-click the linked object and click Update Link.

8. Save the Word document as *Letter with Linked Data.doc*.

9. Print and close the workbook and the Word document.

Exercise 5

1. Create a new, blank workbook.

2. Create a database query using the *Excel List.mdb* database located on the Data Disk to extract all records where the gross sales exceed $45,000.

3. Sort the results by gross sales in descending order.

4. Output the results to Excel.

5. Copy the data.

6. Start a new Word document.

7. Embed the data as a Microsoft Excel worksheet object in a new Word document.

8. Save the Word document as *Sales Above 45000.doc* and close it.

9. Save the workbook as *Sales Above 45000* and close it.

Exercise 6

1. Create a new, blank workbook.

2. Use Import Data (Data, Import External Data, Import Data) to import the tab-delimited text file *Movie Times.txt*.

3. Save the workbook as *Movie Times Imported*, then print and close it.

Exercise 7

1. Create a new, blank workbook.

2. Create a database query using the *Sales Data.mdb* database located on the Data Disk.

3. Extract records from the West Coast Region whose Q1 sales and Q2 sales each exceeded $2,000.

4. Sort the records by Name in ascending order.

5. Format columns E and F with Currency format.

6. Hide column A.

7. Rename the sheet tab as "West Coast."

8. Save the workbook as *Sales Data Extracted*, then print and close it.

Exercise 8

1. Open the *Sales Data Extracted* workbook that you created in Exercise 7.

2. On Sheet2 create another database query using the *Sales Data.mdb* database located on the Data Disk.

3. Extract records from the North subregions whose Q1 sales are not more than $1,500.

4. Sort the records by Region in ascending order.

5. Format columns E and F with Currency format.

chapter fourteen

6. Hide column A.

7. Rename the sheet tab to "North Subregions."

8. Save the workbook as *Sales Data Extracted 2*, then print and close it.

Case Projects

Project 1

You work for a framing company that builds houses. You are preparing a bid on a new job. In a new workbook, create categories for materials, labor, and markup. Include fictitious data for the materials and labor costs. Calculate the markup as 10% of the sum total of materials and labor costs. Calculate the grand total of your bid. Save the workbook as *Framing Bid*. In a new Word document, write a letter explaining your proposal. Embed the workbook data in the Word document. Save the document as *Final Bid.doc*, then print and close it. Close the workbook.

Project 2

You are a busy stockbroker. In an effort to drum up investment business, you decide to send a letter to your clients showing the recent results of several stocks that have been performing well lately. Use the Internet to research two or three companies that might pique your clients' interest. Create a workbook to record high/low/close prices for each stock over the last week. Save the workbook as *Recent Stock Prices*. Create a chart for each stock and link the charts to your letter. If you are having problems positioning the linked charts, turn on the Drawing toolbar in Word, then use the Text Wrapping button to change the wrapping (Top and Bottom or Square work pretty well). Print the letter and save the document as *Stock Letter.doc*. Close the document and the workbook.

Project 3

You are the assistant to the president of a large advertising company. One of your responsibilities is to prepare a monthly report showing the amounts collected from your five largest clients. Create a workbook with fictitious data for 10 clients over the last three months. Sort the data by totals for the quarter to find your five largest clients. Create a pie chart of the data for these clients. Save the workbook as *Client Data*. Working in PowerPoint, create a new presentation. Link the chart from your workbook to the first slide. Link the data, including all 10 clients, to the second slide. Save the presentation as *Clients.ppt*, then print and close it. Close the workbook.

Project 4

You are the personnel director for a large firm. You have been keeping a list of employee data, including first and last names, ages, phone extensions, and departments in an Excel workbook. Because the list keeps growing larger, you decide to maintain this information in an Access database. Create a workbook containing data for 20 fictitious employees. Save the workbook as *Personnel Data*. In Access, create a new blank database called *Personnel Data.mdb* and import the data from this newly created workbook. Print the database table, then close the table and the database. Close the workbook.

Project 5

Your sales company has been forced to release some of its sales staff. Using the *Excel List* database located on the Data Disk, create a new workbook using a database query. Query the database for records in the Central Region whose gross sales are less than $30,000. Sort the results by gross sales in descending order. Save the workbook as *Cutback*, then print and close it.

Project 6

You are in charge of application licensing for your firm. Create a new workbook in which you can record the application name, version number, and upgrade cost for each application installed on your computer. Using your own computer, add information for as many applications installed on your computer as you can. Try and find upgrade prices for each of the applications by looking at the vendor's Web site. Save the workbook as *Application Licensing*. Create a Word document addressed to management explaining which applications you think need to be upgraded in the near future and why. Link the data from your workbook to this document and save it as *Application Licensing.doc*. Print the letter, then close the document. Close the workbook.

Project 7

As a travel broker, you use "open house" presentations to encourage your existing clients to travel more often. This month, you are featuring a special on travel to Europe. Use the Internet to look up the current exchange rate between U.S. dollars and the euro. Record this information in a workbook and save the workbook as *Travel to Europe*. Embed this data in a PowerPoint slide. Save the PowerPoint presentation as *Travel to Europe.ppt*, then print and close it. Close the workbook.

Project 8

You are a columnist for the local newspaper covering the NBA (or another sport that interests you or is in season). Prepare a workbook covering the score of a recent game, including a column for each team, column labels for four quarters (periods, or innings, depending on the sport you chose), plus a total column. Add a formula in the total column that sums the total number of points scored by each team. Save the workbook as *Sports Scores.ppt*. Create a chart, then embed the chart in a Word document. Save the document as *Embedded Sports Scores.doc*, then print and close it. Close the workbook.

chapter fourteen

Excel 2002

Sharing Workbooks with Others

Chapter Overview

Changes in today's software reflect the way the business world works. Documents are shared between departments and among coworkers and can be edited simultaneously by many people connected to a network. During the editing process, Excel tracks all changes made to a workbook. Workbooks can be distributed electronically, then merged into a single workbook after several people make modifications. You can add comments to cells to clarify results or add an informative note. You can customize by creating custom number formats, then using lookup functions to create highly specialized workbooks.

Learning Objectives

- Create and apply custom number and conditional formats
- Use lookup and reference functions
- Use workgroup features

Case profile

Super Power Computers uses Excel to look up and track inventory. Using custom number formats and special reference functions in this workbook saves a lot of time during data entry and retrieval. Working efficiently often requires several people to collaborate, or work together in a workbook. The Excel collaboration features make this a simple task.

chapter fifteen

15.a Creating and Applying Custom Number and Conditional Formats

Number formats speed data entry by inserting symbols, text, or extra zeroes in entries to maintain a consistent look to data entered on a worksheet. These number format styles don't change the value entered in the cell; they just add special formatting and symbols, such as monetary symbols, comma separators, and so on. You have seen these formats at work when applying the Currency, Percent, and Accounting styles to cells. Excel also provides other specialized number formats such as ZIP codes, telephone numbers, and Social Security numbers. In addition to the number formats provided, you can create and apply your own specialized number formats. You also can apply number formats to a cell or cells based on the value or condition of another cell's content.

Creating Custom Number Formats

At the Super Power Computers warehouse, each item receives a special sorting code made up of a mixture of letters and numbers, to make it easier to locate specific items. The *Super Power Computers - Warehouse Receiving Log* keeps track of all merchandise received at the warehouse. To start:

| Step 1 | Open | the *Super Power Computers - Warehouse Receiving Log* workbook located on the Data Disk |
| Step 2 | Save | the workbook as *Super Power Computers - Warehouse Receiving Log Revised* |

The January 2003 worksheet contains a list of items received at the warehouse in January. You see an example of the number format that the warehouse department would like to apply in the Item # column. These entries are text values and therefore are not recognized as numbers. Each character must be entered by hand. Correct entries use the ##-SPC-#### format, where # represents a significant digit. Your worksheet, which includes several incorrect entries, should look similar to Figure 15-1.

chapter fifteen

FIGURE 15-1
Incorrect Data Entry

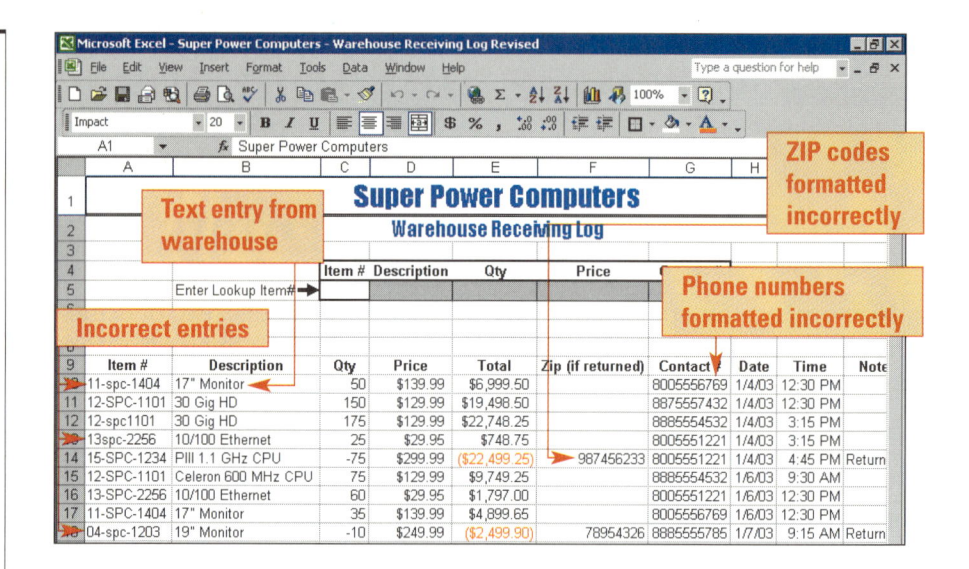

As part of an effort to reduce data entry errors, you create a custom numeric format that corresponds to the company's existing system. To create a custom number format:

| Step 1 | Key | 111404 in cell A10, replacing the previous entry |

This value is the numerical portion of the item number.

Step 2	Click	the Enter button on the Formula Bar
Step 3	Click	F_ormat
Step 4	Click	C_ells
Step 5	Click	the Number tab, if necessary
Step 6	Click	Custom in the C_ategory: list

You can set the color of the entry, and you can determine how and where the numerical data will be placed. The formats listed in the Type: list can serve as starting points for your own custom format. The formats use special codes to specify various types of formatting. Table 15-1 describes these codes.

TABLE 15-1
Custom Number Format Codes

Format Code	Use
#	Displays significant digits, but not insignificant zeroes
0	Displays insignificant zeroes if a number has fewer digits than the number of zeroes specified in the format
?	Adds spaces for insignificant zeroes to line up decimals; also used for fraction formats with varying numbers of digits
,	Thousands separator
*	Repeats the next character in the format code to fill any blank spaces in a cell
"text"	Inserts any text within the quotes as part of the number format
\	Displays a single character as part of the number format
_	Inserts a space character in the number format
;	Separates sections of a custom number format; each format can have four sections to format positive, negative, zero, and text values
<=, <, >=, >, <>, =	Conditional operators that apply the custom format only if a numerical value meets the specified condition
[Color]	Use one of eight colors (Black, Blue, Cyan, Green, Magenta, Red, White, and Yellow) to display values; colors must be listed first in a section
@	Used as the last entry in a custom number format to display text; if this symbol is omitted from the custom format, any text entered is not displayed

> **QUICK TIP**
>
> Significant digits on the left of a decimal point start with the number farthest to the left that is not a zero. Significant digits to the right of the decimal point do not include ending zeroes.

For each custom number format you define, you can specify four formats in the following order: positive numbers, negative numbers, zero values, and text. Each section is separated by a semicolon. If you omit the negative and zero value formats from the style definition, those values are displayed in the same way as the positive number format. If you omit the text style from the style definition, text entered in the cell is stored but not displayed.

Step 7	**Double-click**	the Type: text box to select the previous entry
Step 8	**Key**	[Blue]00-"SPC"-0000

The Custom category of the Number tab should look similar to Figure 15-2. As you enter the code, the preview displays the formatted number the way it will appear in your worksheet. The first part of this number format, **[Blue]**, sets the text color of the entry to blue. The rest of the code determines how and where numerical data is placed. The first two digits are separated by **-SPC-** followed by the last four digits.

chapter fifteen

FIGURE 15-2
Creating a Custom Number Format

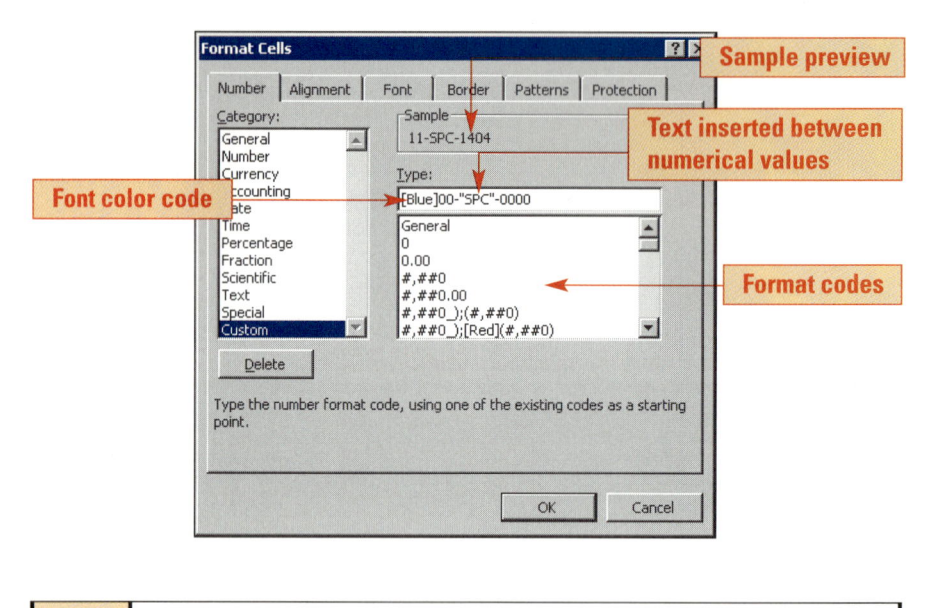

| Step 9 | *Click* | OK |

The formatting applied to cell A10 of your worksheet should look similar to Figure 15-3.

FIGURE 15-3
Custom Format Applied to Cell A10

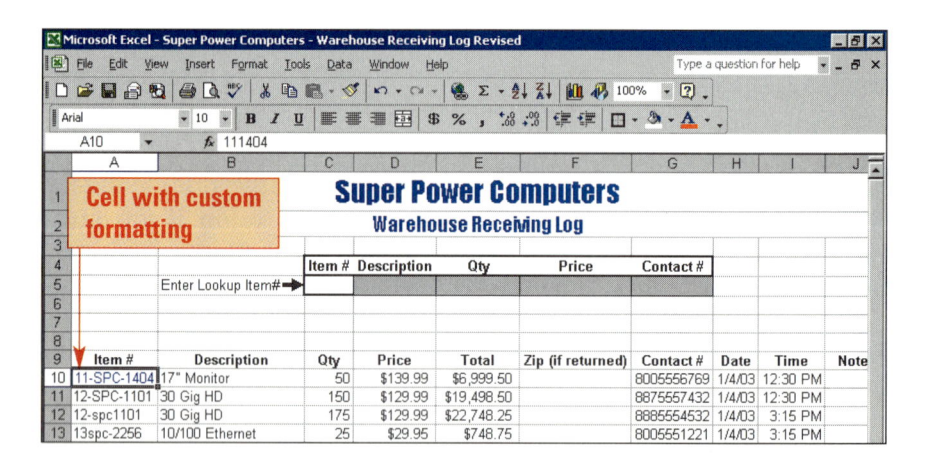

Applying Custom Number Formats

Once you've created a custom number format, it is added to the Type: list. You apply that format by selecting the cell and then selecting the format in the list. To apply custom number formats:

Step 1	*Select*	the range A11:A21
Step 2	*Open*	the Number tab in the Format Cells dialog box
Step 3	*Click*	Custom in the Category: list

Step 4	Scroll	down the Type: list
Step 5	Click	[Blue]00-"SPC"-0000
Step 6	Click	OK

Even though the number format has been applied, the data in the cell doesn't match the "picture" Excel expects to find. You need to reenter the numerical portion of each entry.

Step 7	Enter	121101 in cell A11

Notice that the font changes to blue, and the extra information is inserted into the middle of the numerical data.

Step 8	Repeat	Step 7 to reenter the numerical values only in cells A12:A21

Next you finish formatting the workbook.

Step 9	Select	the range F10:F21
Step 10	Open	the Number tab in the Format Cells dialog box
Step 11	Click	Special in the Category: list box
Step 12	Click	Zip Code + 4 in the Type: list box
Step 13	Click	OK
Step 14	Apply	the Special format "Phone Number" to column G
Step 15	Save	the workbook

CAUTION TIP

When applying the Zip Code + 4 format, double check to make sure the Locale is set to English (United States).

Applying Conditional Formatting

Conditional formatting evaluates the value of a cell for a true or false condition and applies different formatting to the cell based on the results of that evaluation. For example, you can apply a conditional format to the cell containing the quantity of an item in the warehouse so that the format changes when inventory levels in the warehouse fall below a certain level.

When you apply conditional formatting to a cell, you can test for as many as three conditions by using cell-to-cell comparisons or a logical function; you can then apply shading and borders to the cell itself, in addition to changing the font style and color. You can use conditional formatting to apply as many as three different formatting styles, based on either a comparison of the cell value to another value or the results of a logical function.

In the worksheet, you want to flag the quantity when the inventory falls to certain levels. To apply conditional formatting:

Step 1	*Activate*	cell C10
Step 2	*Click*	F<u>o</u>rmat
Step 3	*Click*	Con<u>d</u>itional Formatting

The Conditional Formatting dialog box on your screen should look similar to Figure 15-4.

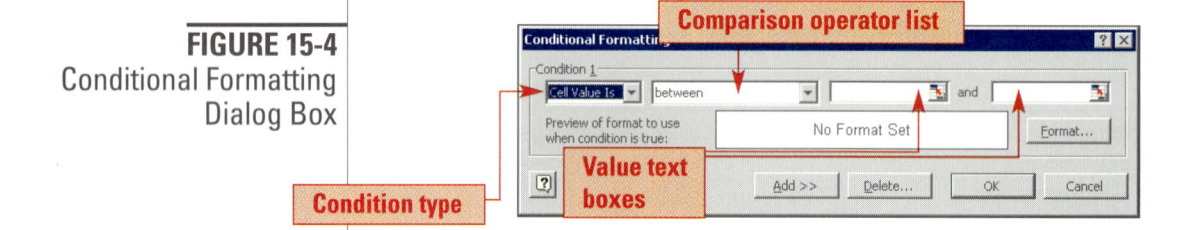

FIGURE 15-4
Conditional Formatting Dialog Box

When the quantity of any item falls below 50, you want the cell to show a red background.

Step 4	*Press*	the TAB key
Step 5	*Select*	less than from the list
Step 6	*Press*	the TAB key
Step 7	*Key*	50 in the value text box
Step 8	*Click*	F<u>o</u>rmat
Step 9	*Change*	the font color to White (you must select the White box instead of the default Automatic)
Step 10	*Click*	the Border tab
Step 11	*Click*	<u>O</u>utline
Step 12	*Click*	the Patterns tab
Step 13	*Click*	the red box
Step 14	*Click*	OK

You want to add another condition in case the inventory of an item falls between 50 and 75.

Step 15	Click	Add >>
Step 16	Press	the TAB key twice
Step 17	Key	50
Step 18	Press	the TAB key
Step 19	Key	75
Step 20	Change	the font color to blue and the cell shading color to yellow
Step 21	Click	OK twice
Step 22	Observe	the formatting in cell C10

To copy the conditional formatting to the range C11:C21:

Step 1	Click	the Format Painter button on the Standard toolbar
Step 2	Select	the range C11:C21 to apply the conditional formatting to all the quantity cells
Step 3	Select	A1

Your worksheet should look similar to Figure 15-5.

FIGURE 15-5
Conditional Formatting Applied to Worksheet

Step 4	Save	the workbook

15.b Using Lookup and Reference Functions

Lookup functions are a special class of functions that can be used to locate information in a workbook. Certain lookup functions can be used to lookup and retrieve associated data. For example, when you search for an ISBN number at an online bookseller, information about the book's title, author, number of pages, and the price are returned.

The **VLOOKUP** function searches for a value in the leftmost column of an array, an arrangement or list of items, usually in columns and rows.

The VLOOKUP function has the following syntax:

=VLOOKUP(lookup_value,table_array,col_index_num,range_lookup)

The lookup_value is the Item # you will input in cell A2. The table_array is the list set up in cells A5:E11. When VLOOKUP finds a match to the Item #, it retrieves the value located in the same row as the matching Item # and in the column number in the array specified as the col_index_num argument.

VLOOKUP searches for an exact match. The default value of the optional range_lookup argument is TRUE, which means that if VLOOKUP cannot find an exact match, it returns the next largest value that is less than the lookup value. Using the default range_lookup setting requires your data to be sorted in ascending order. If you set the range_lookup argument to FALSE, VLOOKUP returns only an exact match.

The Inventory worksheet contains a list of items available in the warehouse. As this list grows, it will become more difficult to quickly look up information. By adding the VLOOKUP formula to cells B2:E2, an item number can be entered in cell A2, and data from the list matching the item # will be returned. To use the VLOOKUP function:

Step 1	*Activate*	cell D5
Step 2	*Click*	the Insert Function button to the left of the Formula Bar
Step 3	*Double-click*	the VLOOKUP function in the Lookup & Reference function category
Step 4	*Key*	C5 in the Lookup_value argument text box
Step 5	*Key*	A10:J21 in the Table_array argument text box

Next, you want to retrieve the value located in the second column of the array, the Description.

Step 6	*Key*	2 in the Col_index_num text box
Step 7	*Key*	FALSE in the Range_lookup text box
Step 8	*Click*	OK

Cell D5 displays the #N/A error because cell C5 does not yet contain a value to look up.

MOUSE TIP

If you drag to select a range as an argument, the Function Arguments dialog box automatically collapses when you start your selection and expands when you release the mouse button.

QUICK TIP

In practice, you would probably key a row number well beyond row 21 so that additional items could be entered into the lookup array without adjusting the formulas.

Sharing Workbooks with Others   EA 195

| Step 9 | Enter | 111404 in cell C5 |

Cell D5 displays the correct product description, 17" Monitor. Now finish adding VLOOKUP formulas to the remaining cells.

Step 10	Enter	=VLOOKUP(C5,A10:J21,3,false) in cell E5
Step 11	Enter	=VLOOKUP(C5,A10:J21,4,false) in cell F5
Step 12	Enter	=VLOOKUP(C5,A10:J21,7,false) in cell G5

Now look up another Item #.

| Step 13 | Enter | 151234 in cell C5 |

The information is retrieved from the list and displayed in cells D5:G5. Your worksheet should look similar to Figure 15-6.

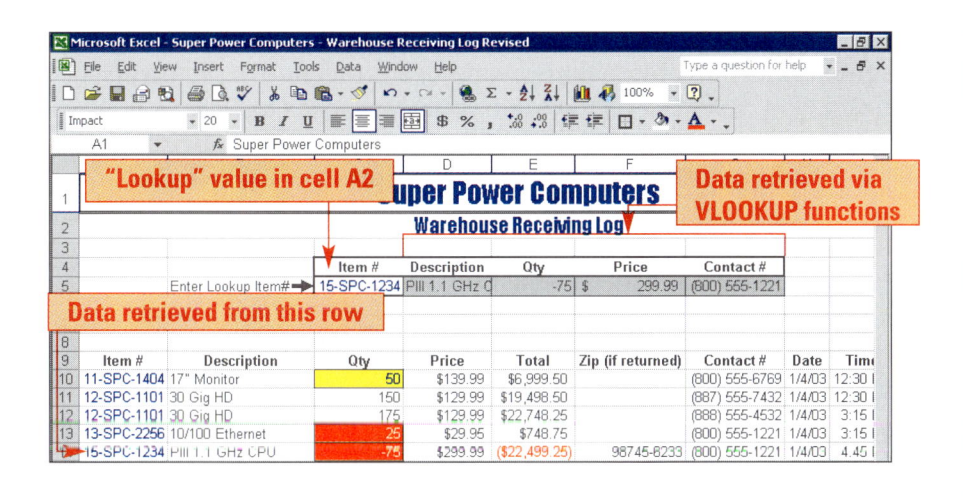

CAUTION TIP

The #VALUE! error occurs when you use the wrong type of argument or operand. For example, entering "hello" as the range_lookup argument in the VLOOKUP function would produce this error. Supply the correct type of argument required by the function to fix this error.
  The #N/A! error occurs when a value is not available to a function or formula.

FIGURE 15-6
Using the VLOOKUP Reference Function

QUICK TIP

Excel provides more than 15 lookup and reference functions. To find out more about functions not covered in this section, use online Help.

| Step 14 | Save | the workbook |

The HLOOKUP function works similarly to the VLOOKUP function, but searches for values in a row rather than a column. When it finds a match, the HLOOKUP function retrieves data located in a specified row of the column where the match was found. This allows for flexibility in the way you set up your worksheets. The syntax of the HLOOKUP function is the same as that of the VLOOKUP function except that you supply a row index number to return instead of a column index number.

chapter fifteen

15.c Using Workgroup Features

Often, you need to create a workbook that many people will have access to. The Warehouse Receiving Log will be used by many people. You are still developing the format of the workbook, and you want to collect input from several other people at Super Power Computers. You also want to allow warehouse workers to use the lookup function you added to find the current inventory of any product, but you don't want someone to inadvertently change a formula. You can protect the formulas in the workbook from changes, then put the workbook on the company network and allow many people to access it and make any changes they want to the unprotected cells. You can collect their revisions and then merge the results.

Protecting Cells, Worksheets, and Workbooks

When a workbook is used by many people, you may want to prevent other users from changing the data or formatting in that workbook. You accomplish this task by enabling workbook protection. If security is a concern, you can add a password to your workbooks as well.

Excel provides two ways to protect individual cells from being altered. **Hiding** cells prevents the formula from appearing in the Formula Bar when a user clicks the cell, but still calculates the result as usual. **Locking** cells prevents other users from changing them. To set these options, you use the Format Cells dialog box, then enable worksheet protection.

You want to protect the cells containing the VLOOKUP functions you just entered. To set cell protection options:

Step 1	Select	the range D5:G5
Step 2	Open	the Format Cells dialog box
Step 3	Click	the Protection tab
Step 4	Click	the Hidden check box to insert a check mark

The Locked check box is selected by default. When checked, the Hidden option prevents other users from seeing formulas in the Formula Bar. Neither option affects the selected cells until you protect the worksheet.

Step 5	Click	OK

You want warehouse personnel to be able to add new entries, as well as use cell D5 for data entry. You need to unlock these cells specifically, then apply worksheet protection.

Step 6	Click	cell C5
Step 7	Press & hold	the CTRL key
Step 8	Select	the range A10:J35
Step 9	Open	the Format Cells dialog box
Step 10	Click	the Locked check box on the Protection tab to remove the check mark
Step 11	Click	OK

To apply worksheet protection:

Step 1	Click	Tools
Step 2	Point to	Protection
Step 3	Click	Protect Sheet

The Protect Sheet dialog box on your screen should look similar to Figure 15-7. It allows you to protect cell contents, formatting, drawing objects, scenarios, and more. If security is an issue, you can apply a password to prevent anyone who does not have that password from changing the settings.

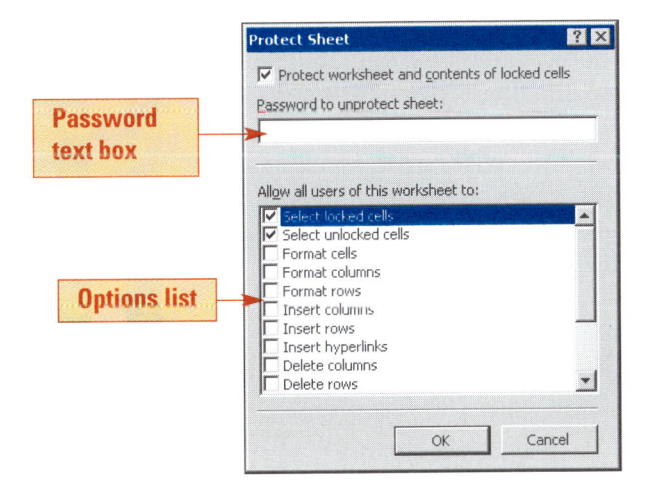

FIGURE 15-7
Protect Sheet Dialog Box

> **CAUTION TIP**
>
> Be sure to remember your password. If you forget it, you may not be able to access your workbook.

To apply a password:

| Step 1 | Enter | your first name in the Password to unprotect sheet: text box (use lowercase letters) |

As you enter your password, an asterisk (*) replaces each letter you type, as a security measure.

| Step 2 | Click | OK |

Excel prompts you to reenter your password to ensure that you entered it correctly. Passwords are case-sensitive, so *Your Name* is not the same password as *your name*.

Step 3	Enter	your first name again, exactly as you entered it before
Step 4	Click	OK
Step 5	Click	cell D5
Step 6	Observe	that you can no longer see the formula in the Formula Bar
Step 7	Press	any letter key to change the contents of the cell

Excel notifies you that the cell is protected.

| Step 8 | Click | OK |

In the Protect Workbook dialog box, you are given two options. Checking the Structure check box prevents users from deleting, moving, renaming, or inserting worksheets into a workbook. Checking the Windows check box prevents users from resizing, minimizing or restoring the document window. This option is useful for a specially formatted workbook designed to work as a form for entering data, such as a sales receipt. To turn on workbook protection:

Step 1	Click	Tools
Step 2	Point to	Protection
Step 3	Click	Protect Workbook
Step 4	Key	your first name in lowercase letters in the Password (optional): text box

Step 5	Click	OK
Step 6	Key	your first name in lowercase letters again
Step 7	Click	OK
Step 8	Right-click	the January 2003 sheet tab

Most of the options normally available, such as Rename, Insert, and Delete, are disabled now that workbook protection is enabled. When you no longer need the workbook or worksheet protection, you can disable them. To remove worksheet and workbook protection:

Step 1	Click	Tools
Step 2	Point to	Protection
Step 3	Click	Unprotect Sheet
Step 4	Key	your password (your first name) exactly as you entered it previously
Step 5	Click	OK
Step 6	Observe	that the formula contained in cell D5 reappears in the Formula Bar
Step 7	Click	Tools
Step 8	Point to	Protection
Step 9	Click	Unprotect Workbook
Step 10	Key	your password
Step 11	Click	OK
Step 12	Save	the workbook

Sharing a Workbook

You can share a workbook by routing it to other users via e-mail or by working simultaneously with other users on a network. When you collaborate with others via a network, each user is notified when another user has saved changes.

The warehouse personnel need to begin using the workbook, even though you are still finalizing the workbook features. Sharing the workbook allows multiple users to work on the same workbook at the same time. To share a workbook:

Step 1	Click	Tools

MENU TIP

You can change your user name in the Options dialog box. Click the Options command on the Tools menu. On the General tab, key your name in the User name box, then click OK.

QUICK TIP

The Advanced tab of the Share Workbook dialog box includes advanced tracking options. For more information about these settings, click the Help button, then click the setting about which you want to learn.

chapter fifteen

| Step 2 | Click | S<u>h</u>are Workbook to open the Share Workbook dialog box |
| Step 3 | Click | the <u>A</u>llow changes by more than one user at the same time check box to insert a check mark |

The Share Workbook dialog box on your screen should look similar to Figure 15-8.

FIGURE 15-8
Share Workbook Dialog Box

Registered user's name appears here

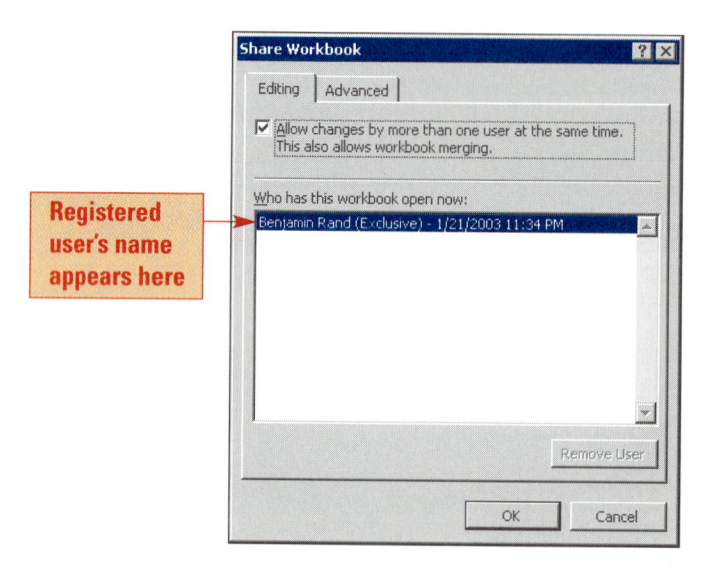

| Step 4 | Click | OK |
| Step 5 | Click | OK to save changes to the workbook |

The workbook is saved automatically, and the title bar reflects the fact that the workbook is [Shared].

Tracking Changes

When you share a workbook, you can track modifications to it. When you track changes, highlighted borders quickly identify cells whose contents have been edited. When several people work together on the same workbook, each user's changes are assigned a different color, making it easy to see who made changes to various cells. Note that the color assigned to each user's changes may differ each time you open the workbook. To highlight changes:

Step 1	Click	<u>T</u>ools
Step 2	Point to	<u>T</u>rack Changes
Step 3	Click	<u>H</u>ighlight Changes

CAUTION TIP

When you share a workbook, certain limitations exist regarding what changes can and cannot be made to it. For example, all elements in place before the workbook is shared, such as charts, conditional formatting, and drawing objects, can be viewed by others, but not edited. Once you turn off workbook sharing, you can edit the workbook as usual. To obtain a complete list of these limitations, use online Help.

QUICK TIP

A quick way to enable workbook sharing and to track changes simultaneously is to open the Track Changes dialog box, then click the <u>T</u>rack changes while editing check box.

The Highlight Changes dialog box should look similar to Figure 15-9. In this dialog box, you select which changes to show.

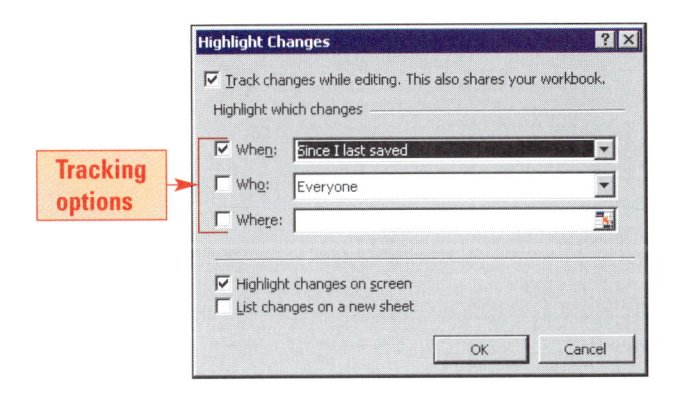

FIGURE 15-9
Highlight Changes Dialog Box

MOUSE TIP

Excel keeps track of changes on a separate worksheet. Normally, this worksheet remains hidden from view, but you can display it by clicking the List changes on a new sheet check box in the Highlight Changes dialog box. This history list displays detailed information about all changes made to the workbook since the "track changes" feature was enabled.

Step 4	Click	the When: list arrow
Step 5	Click	All
Step 6	Click	OK

Excel notifies you that it did not find any changes since the last time the workbook was saved.

Step 7	Click	OK
Step 8	Enter	10250 in cell A14
Step 9	Move	the mouse pointer over cell A14

Your worksheet should look similar to Figure 15-10.

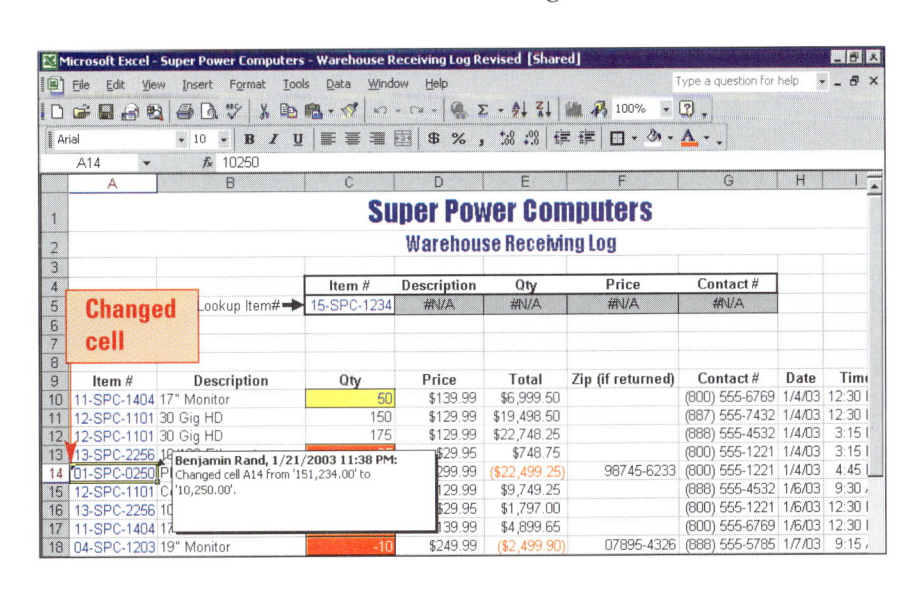

FIGURE 15-10
Changes to a Shared Workbook

chapter fifteen

QUICK TIP

When working simultaneously with multiple users, conflicting changes may occur. Excel can either save the latest changes—known as the "whoever saves last, wins" rule—or it can open the Resolve Conflicts dialog box to allow you to select which change to accept. This option appears on the Advanced tab of the Share Workbook dialog box.

A ScreenTip indicates the user name of the person who made the change, the date and time when the change was made, and the modification that was made to the cell. The border of the cell changes to a colored border and a small triangle is added in the upper-left corner, indicating that the cell's contents have changed.

| Step 10 | *Enter* | 19.95 in cells D13, D16, and D19 |

You can accept or reject any change to the workbook. To accept or reject changes:

Step 1	*Click*	Tools
Step 2	*Point to*	Track Changes
Step 3	*Click*	Accept or Reject Changes
Step 4	*Click*	OK to save the changes to the workbook

The Select Changes to Accept or Reject dialog box opens. This dialog box allows you to filter the changes made since a certain date, changes made by a certain user, or changes affecting certain cells. The default is to select changes that you haven't reviewed yet.

| Step 5 | *Click* | OK |

When you click the OK button, the Accept or Reject Changes dialog box opens, allowing you to accept or reject individual or group changes. Your dialog box should look similar to Figure 15-11.

MOUSE TIP

Click Accept All or Reject All to quickly accept or reject all cells currently being reviewed.

FIGURE 15-11
Accept or Reject Changes Dialog Box

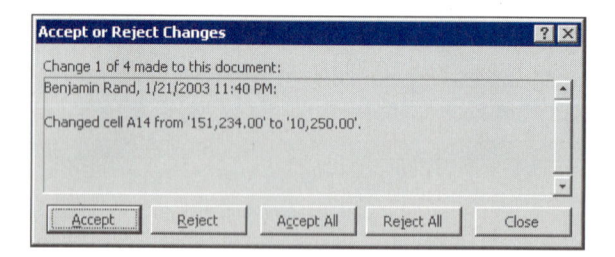

| Step 6 | *Click* | Accept to accept the first change |
| Step 7 | *Click* | Reject three times to reject the second, third, and fourth changes |

The values in cells D13, D16, and D19 return to their original values, and the colored triangle and border that indicated a change disappears from each cell.

| Step 8 | Save | the workbook |

Merging Workbooks

When you merge workbooks, you must follow several rules. First, you must create copies of a workbook for which the sharing and track changes features are enabled. Second, each copy must have a unique filename. Third, all workbooks must have a common password or no password. Fourth, when you enable workbook sharing, you can specify the length of time for which you want to track changes on the Advanced tab of the Share Workbook dialog box (the default is 30 days). You must merge the copies within this period. For example, if you set the "keep change" history to 30 days, and the workbook copies were made 45 days ago, you can no longer merge the workbooks. If necessary, you can set the "keep change" history to 32,767 days (about 90 years), which should give you plenty of time to merge workbooks.

When you perform the merge, only the destination (workbook receiving the changes) can be open. Your workbook should still be open, with track changes and sharing enabled. To create a copy and merge changes:

Step 1	Save	the workbook as *Super Power Computers - Warehouse Receiving Log Warehouse Copy*
Step 2	Save	the workbook again as *Super Power Computers - Warehouse Receiving Log Office Copy*
Step 3	Enter	89.95 in cell D11
Step 4	Enter	20 in cell C10
Step 5	Save	the *Office Copy* workbook and close it
Step 6	Open	the *Super Power Computers - Warehouse Receiving Log Warehouse Copy* workbook
Step 7	Open	the Highlight Changes dialog box
Step 8	Select	All in the Whe<u>n</u>: list
Step 9	Click	OK
Step 10	Enter	80 in cell C10
Step 11	Save	the *Warehouse Copy* workbook and close it
Step 12	Open	the *Super Power Computers - Warehouse Receiving Log Revised* workbook
Step 13	Click	<u>T</u>ools

QUICK TIP

Occasionally, you may need to distribute copies of a shared workbook to users who do not have access to your network. Although you can route the workbook via e-mail, if you must continue editing the workbook simultaneously, this option may not work. In this case, you can save copies of the workbook and distribute them. When other users return these copies to you with their changes, you can incorporate the additional changes into the original workbook by using the Merge workbooks command.

Step 14	*Click*	Compare and Merge <u>W</u>orkbooks
Step 15	*Press & hold*	the CTRL key
Step 16	*Click*	the *Office Copy* and the *Warehouse Copy* workbooks you saved earlier
Step 17	*Click*	OK

The changes in the revised (source) workbook are merged into the target workbook.

Step 18	*Open*	the Highlight Changes dialog box
Step 19	*Select*	All in the Whe<u>n</u>: list
Step 20	*Click*	OK

The colored border indicates the changed cells. Your screen should look similar to Figure 15-12.

FIGURE 15-12
Merging Workbooks

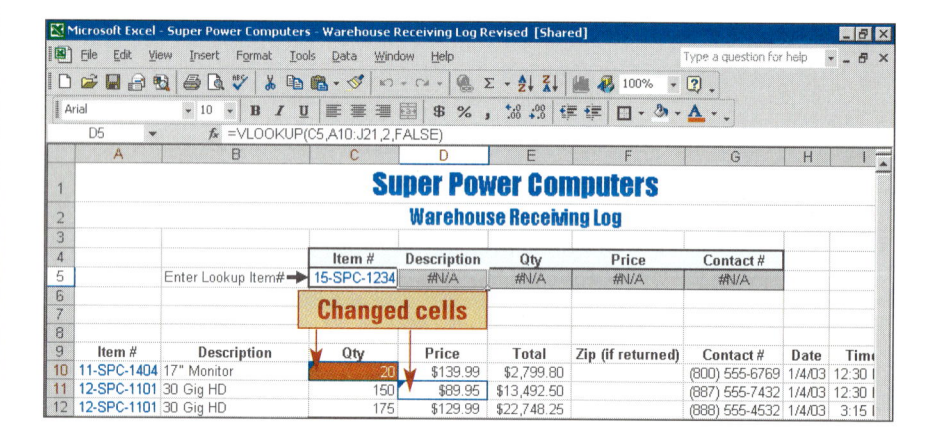

| Step 21 | *Save* | the workbook |

Changing Workbook Properties

Workbook **properties** comprise information about the workbook that can be stored with the workbook. This information includes file size, creation date, company and author name, and date that the workbook was last modified or accessed. You can change some of this information in the workbook Properties dialog box. Before you can change properties, you need to turn off workbook sharing. To disable workbook sharing:

| Step 1 | *Open* | the Share Workbook dialog box |

Sharing Workbooks with Others EA 205

Step 2	Click	the Allow changes check box to remove the check mark
Step 3	Click	OK
Step 4	Click	Yes after reading the warning about turning off the sharing feature

CAUTION TIP

When you disable workbook sharing, you also turn off the track changes feature and erase the History list.

Now you can change the workbook's properties. To change a workbook's properties:

Step 1	Click	File
Step 2	Click	Properties
Step 3	Key	your name in the Author: text box
Step 4	Key	Super Power Computers in the Company: text box

Your dialog box should look similar to Figure 15-13.

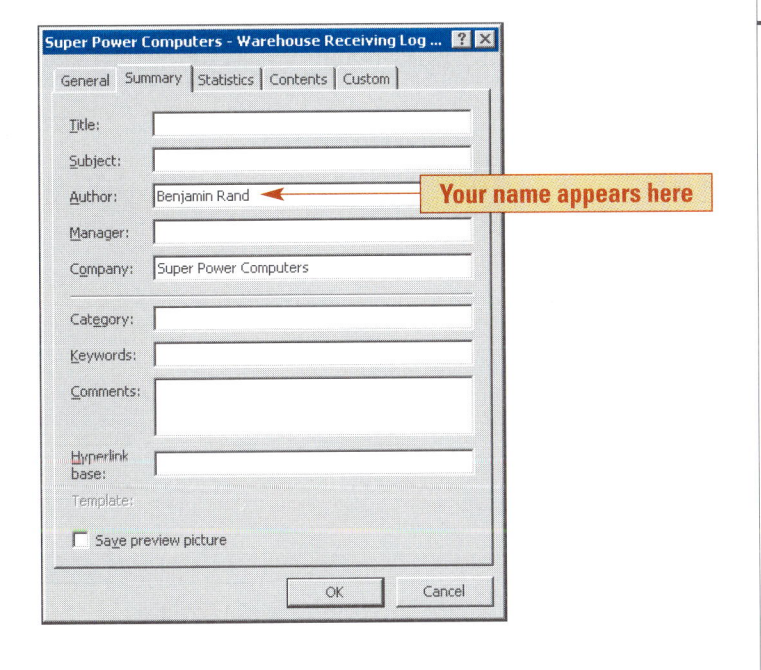

FIGURE 15-13
Workbook Properties Dialog Box

MOUSE TIP

You can view a workbook's properties without opening the workbook. In Windows Explorer or in the Open dialog box, right-click any workbook, then click Properties on the shortcut menu.

Step 5	Click	OK
Step 6	Save	the workbook and close it

Sharing workbooks and tracking changes can be a good way to boost productivity by allowing multiple users to work on and modify the same workbook simultaneously. Protecting cells, worksheets, or entire workbooks ensures that critical data and formulas are not changed.

chapter fifteen

Summary

- Number formats change the manner in which numerical values are displayed; they do not change the underlying values.

- You can create custom number formats to display additional characters, text, comma styles, and decimal options.

- You can apply conditional formatting to cells. You use cell value comparisons or logical formula evaluations to determine which formatting should be applied to a cell. You can assign as many as three conditions with which to test a cell.

- Lookup functions, including VLOOKUP and HLOOKUP, search for a value in a row or column, then return another value in the table or array, depending on the arguments supplied.

- You can protect a workbook from changes by enabling protection. You also can add a level of security by providing password protection to a worksheet or workbook.

- Multiple users can edit a workbook simultaneously on a network. While a workbook is shared, certain features remain unavailable, such as chart and drawing tools.

- You can track changes to see which modifications have been made and who made them.

- You can merge workbooks to combine information from multiple copies of a shared workbook.

- You can add comments to clarify information or to act as a reminder.

Commands Review

Action	Menu Bar	Shortcut Menu	Toolbar	Task Pane	Keyboard
Format cells	Format, Cells	Right-click cell, Format Cells			CTRL + 1 ALT + O, E
Apply conditional formatting	Format, Conditional Formatting				ALT + O, D
Protect a worksheet	Tools, Protection, Protection Sheet				ALT + T, P, P
Unprotect a worksheet	Tools, Protection, Unprotect Sheet				ALT + T, P, P
Protect a workbook	Tools, Protection, Protect Workbook				ALT + T, P, W
Unprotect a workbook	Tools, Protection, Unprotect Workbook				ALT + T, P, W
Share a workbook	Tools, Share workbook				ALT + T, H
Highlight changes	Tools, Track changes, Highlight changes				ALT + T, T, H
Accept or reject changes	Tools, Track changes, Accept or Reject changes				ALT + T, A
Merge workbooks	Tools, Merge Workbooks				ALT + T, W
Modify Workbook	File, Properties				ALT + F, I

Concepts Review

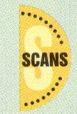

Circle the correct answer.

1. **When you hide formulas using worksheet protection:**
   - [a] formulas are not calculated.
   - [b] the formula is displayed but not the calculated value.
   - [c] formulas are calculated but are not displayed in the Formula Bar.
   - [d] formulas appear and are calculated as usual.

2. **You can identify modified cells when using Track Changes by a colored:**
   - [a] border and triangle in the upper-right corner.
   - [b] border and triangle in the upper-left corner.
   - [c] triangle in the upper-right corner.
   - [d] triangle in the upper-left corner.

3. **The 0 symbol in a custom number format code:**
   - [a] displays an @ symbol in the cell.
   - [b] acts as a repeat code; the character following it will be repeated to fill a cell.
   - [c] allows the displaying of text in a cell formatted with a number format.
   - [d] displays nonsignificant zeroes.

4. **To select view options for changes, click Tools, then:**
   - [a] Merge Workbook.
   - [b] Share Workbook.
   - [c] Track Changes, Highlight changes.
   - [d] Track Changes, Accept or Reject changes.

5. **Conditional formatting (*not* conditional number format) can check a maximum of:**
   - [a] one condition.
   - [b] two conditions.
   - [c] three conditions.
   - [d] four conditions.

chapter fifteen

6. When merging workbooks:
   [a] both workbooks can be open.
   [b] only the target workbook can be open.
   [c] only the source workbook can be open.
   [d] neither of the workbooks has to be open.

7. Given a value of 9995551234, what is displayed when the cell is formatted using the following custom number format code: (###) ###-####?
   [a] 9995551234
   [b] 999 555 1234
   [c] (999) 555-1234
   [d] (###) ###-####

8. Workbook properties:
   [a] cannot be modified.
   [b] contain fields of additional data that are stored with the workbook.
   [c] cannot be displayed unless the workbook is open.
   [d] can be displayed only outside of Excel.

9. The VLOOKUP function:
   [a] searches for a specific value in the leftmost column of a table or an array.
   [b] searches for a specific value in the topmost row of a table or an array.
   [c] returns the relative position of an item in a table or an array that matches a specific value.
   [d] returns a value or the reference to a value from within a table or an array.

10. In Excel, you can protect:
    [a] worksheets, but not workbooks.
    [b] only selected cells.
    [c] selected cells, entire worksheets, or entire workbooks.
    [d] only worksheets in which changes are highlighted.

Circle **T** if the statement is true or **F** if the statement is false.

T F 1. Changing a cell's number format alters the actual value of the cell.

T F 2. You must enable sharing before multiple users can access a workbook simultaneously.

T F 3. You can track changes without enabling workbook sharing.

T F 4. You can view a workbook's properties in Windows Explorer.

T F 5. ###-####[Yellow] is a valid custom number format.

T F 6. Excel automatically saves a workbook before enabling the sharing feature.

T F 7. The logical test of a conditional format can only test the cell to which the formatting is applied.

T F 8. The VLOOKUP function looks in any column of a data array to find a match.

T F 9. You can protect a worksheet or workbook without applying a password.

T F 10. You can set all font options, including font size, when setting conditional formatting options.

Skills Review

Exercise 1

1. Create a new, blank workbook.

2. Enter "Division" in cell A1, "Sales Rep" in cell B1, and "Total Sales" in cell C1. Enter "East" in cells A2:A5, enter "West" in cells A6:A9, enter "North" in cells A10:A13, and enter "South" in cells A14:A17.

3. Save the workbook as *Divisional Sales*.

4. Share the workbook.

5. Save the workbook, then print and close it.

Exercise 2

1. Open the *Divisional Sales* workbook that you created in Exercise 1.

2. Save the workbook as *Divisional Sales 1*.

3. Enable Track Changes and set the When option to All.

4. In column B, add fictitious sales representative names for each division. Resize the column as necessary.

5. Replace the text in cell A14 with "North."

6. Reject the change in cell A14; accept the rest of your changes.

7. In column C, create fictitious sales data between $1,000 and $5,000. Resize the column as necessary.

8. Save the workbook, then print and close it.

Exercise 3

1. Open the *Divisional Sales 1* workbook that you created in Exercise 2.

2. Open the Highlight Changes dialog box, check the box next to List changes on a new sheet, and set the When option to All.

3. Print the History worksheet.

4. Save the workbook. Note that when you save the workbook, the History list becomes hidden again.

5. Close the workbook.

Exercise 4

1. Open the *Divisional Sales 1* workbook that you created in Exercise 2.

2. Save the workbook as *Divisional Sales 2*.

3. Change the column heading "Sales Rep" to "Rep Name."

4. Save and close the workbook, then open the *Divisional Sales* workbook you created in Exercise 1.

5. Compare and merge the *Divisional Sales 1* and *Divisional Sales 2* workbooks with the open workbook. Click OK in the alert dialog box that appears.

6. Disable workbook sharing.

chapter fifteen

7. Add a title to the workbook properties, change the Author name to your name, and change the company name to Sweet Tooth.

8. Save the workbook as *Divisional Sales Merged*, then print and close it.

Exercise 5

1. Create a new, blank workbook.

2. Create a table containing tax rates for the following income levels: 0–12,000 = 12%; $12,001–$18,000 = 15%; $18,001–$30,000 = 21%; $30,001–$42,000 = 28%; >$42,000 = 39%.

3. Create a formula using the VLOOKUP function to multiply a given income by the proper tax percentage.

4. Save the workbook as *Choose Tax*, then print and close it.

Exercise 6

1. Open the *Warehouse* workbook located on the Data Disk.

2. Create a custom number format to display the Part No. as shown, using only numerical entries. All part numbers start with the letter *A* and end with the letter *B*.

3. Create a custom number format to display the Storage location as shown, using only numerical entries.

4. Reenter the data in cells A2 and B2 as the numerical values 1240 and 1125, respectively, to test your number format.

5. Enter four other four-digit numbers in each column, and apply the correct number format to each column.

6. Print the worksheet.

7. Save the workbook as *Warehouse Numbers*, and close it.

Exercise 7

1. Create a new, blank workbook.

2. Enter five different times in column A.

3. Enter five different dates in column B.

4. Select the values in column A.

5. Create a new time format that inserts the text string "Time: " in front of the time format. (*Hint:* Look at the custom number formats for illustrations of custom date and time formats.)

6. Select the values in column B.

7. Create a new time format that inserts the text string "Date: " in front of the time format. (*Hint:* Look at the custom number formats for illustrations of custom date and time formats.)

8. Protect the range A1:B5 to hide the formulas, protect the sheet, then protect the workbook.

9. Save the workbook as *Custom Date and Time*, then print and close it.

Exercise 8

1. Open the *Semi-Annual Results* workbook located on the Data Disk.
2. Apply a conditional format to cell B2 that does the following:
    a. If the value in the cell is less than 100, format the cell with red and italics.
    b. If the value in the cell is equal to or greater than 100, format the cell with a yellow fill.
3. Use Format Painter to format cells B3:B6 with the same format as cell B2.
4. Deselect the cells.
5. Print the worksheet.
6. Save the workbook as *Semi-Annual Results Formatted*, and close it.

Case Projects

Project 1

You are the personnel manager for a small company. You maintain information about the company's employees using a worksheet. Create a workbook with fictitious names, home phone numbers, and Social Security numbers for 10 employees. You want to prevent unauthorized users from viewing the contents of this workbook. In addition to protecting worksheets and workbooks, you can add a password to keep users from opening a workbook, when you save the file. Use the Save As command on the File menu to save your workbook as *Employee Info*. Before clicking Save, click the Tools menu button, then click General Options. Add a password consisting of your first name in uppercase letters in the Password to open text box. Print and close the workbook.

Project 2

Your boss is concerned about securing information contained in some workbooks that you are sharing with other staff members. Use the Ask A Question Box to research how to limit what others can see and change in a shared workbook. Write a half-page summary of your findings, including any steps necessary to hide or protect portions of a workbook from other users. Name your document *Securing Workbook Information*, then print and close it.

Project 3

As a small business owner just learning Excel, you want to take a class to help you become familiar with this program more rapidly. Connect to the Internet and search the Web for organizations offering Excel training in your area. Print a Web page containing contact information for an organization near you.

Project 4

You are looking for a new job where you can apply your Excel skills. Connect to the Internet and search the Web for jobs where Excel is a required skill. (*Hint:* Search for Job Sites first.) Print at least two job descriptions that sound intriguing.

Project 5

Play a game of Othello using a shared Excel workbook. Open the *Othello* workbook located on the Data Disk. Share the workbook, then start a game of Othello. View comments for instructions or ask someone who knows how to play Othello for help. Make sure that both players save their workbooks after each player's turn ends.

chapter fifteen

Project 6

You are in charge of keeping track of donations to a local charity. Create a workbook with five fictitious donors and amounts between $50 and $1,000. Use column headings and widen columns to fit the data as necessary. Create and apply a number format that inserts the text "Gift:" in front of the gift amount, displays a $ symbol in front of the amount, and uses a decimal and two zeros after the decimal. Apply a conditional format that highlights donations exceeding $500 with red text and a border around the cell. Save the workbook as *Donations*, then print and close it.

Project 7

You are a sales manager who is evaluating cell phone calling plans for the sales representatives who you manage. You want to see if your usage in the last year warrants changing your cellular calling plan. Create a worksheet with columns for local and long-distance minutes. Randomly generate numbers between 0 and 400 for each month for local airtime, and numbers between 0 and 150 for long-distance airtime. Use conditional formatting to identify total airtimes exceeding 500 minutes for any given month. Copy the cells containing the airtime data, then use the Paste Special command to paste only the values (not the formulas) in the same cells from which you copied. Save the workbook as *Cell Phone*, then print and close it.

Project 8

You work for a retail company that uses a special inventory numbering system. If the inventory number is less than 1000, the inventory number is entered in the form: "A-0999-B"; if the inventory number is greater than or equal to 1000, the inventory number is entered in the form: "C-1001-D." Create a new workbook with a custom number format that allows you to enter just the numerical portion of the entry. Add 20 inventory numbers between 0 and 2000. Save the workbook as *Part Numbers*, then print and close it.

Excel 2002

Integrating Excel with the Internet or an Intranet

Chapter Overview

Integrating Excel with the Internet enables a whole new level of communication. Worksheets and workbooks can be published as interactive Web pages, allowing users to check data and perform calculations via the Internet. Data can be exchanged easily between Web pages and Excel workbooks through importing, Web queries, and XML. You can look up important up-to-the-minute financial data, such as stock quotes. You can distribute workbooks via e-mail to other users.

Learning Objectives

- Import data from the Internet
- Work with XML
- Publish worksheets and workbooks to the Web
- Send a workbook via e-mail

Case profile

You need to monitor local competitors of Super Power Computers by checking their Web pages for current pricing. You can do this by copying the data to an Excel worksheet. You also can use Web queries to monitor the major stock market indices, and keep tabs on individual stock prices. In addition, you need to set up a process that allows customers to "create" a custom computer from a list of available options, and to compute the price. You can do this by using interactive Web pages.

chapter sixteen

16.a Importing Data from the Internet

The Internet is a gold mine of data that can be imported directly into Excel. Tables in Web pages can be copied and pasted into worksheets. Using Web queries, dynamic data can be updated continually. In this section, you learn to make the most of the Internet and Excel.

Copying Data from a Web Page

Many Web pages use tables to display information in columns and rows, much like a worksheet. You can select this data in your Web browser, then use the Copy and Paste features or the drag-and-drop process to import the information directly into Excel.

Once a month, you visit the Web sites of competitors to check their current prices. You prepare a report of your findings for Luis Alvarez, the president of Super Power Computers. For this activity, you use a Web page located on the Data Disk. To copy data from a Web page:

Step 1	*Create*	a new, blank workbook
Step 2	*Save*	the workbook as *Competitor Pricing*
Step 3	*Close*	the New Workbook task pane, if necessary

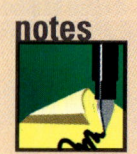

notes: This activity requires Internet Explorer 5.0 and higher. If you are using another browser, your instructor may modify the steps or provide additional information.

Step 4	*Start*	Internet Explorer
Step 5	*Click*	File
Step 6	*Click*	Open
Step 7	*Click*	Browse
Step 8	*Click*	the Look in: list arrow
Step 9	*Switch to*	the disk drive and folder where your Data Files are stored
Step 10	*Double-click*	*MegaComputers*
Step 11	*Click*	OK

Step 12	Press	the CTRL + A keys to select the entire Web page
Step 13	Right-click	anywhere on the selected data in the browser window
Step 14	Click	Copy
Step 15	Click	the Excel button on the taskbar
Step 16	Right-click	cell A1
Step 17	Click	Paste

The data is copied into the worksheet, but is difficult to read. You reformat the data for better legibility.

Step 18	Click	Format
Step 19	Point to	Column
Step 20	Click	AutoFit Selection
Step 21	Activate	cell A1
Step 22	Rename	the Sheet1 tab as Mega Computers' Prices

Your workbook should look similar to Figure 16-1. The Excel worksheet isn't formatted exactly the same as the data on the Web page, but the data is identical.

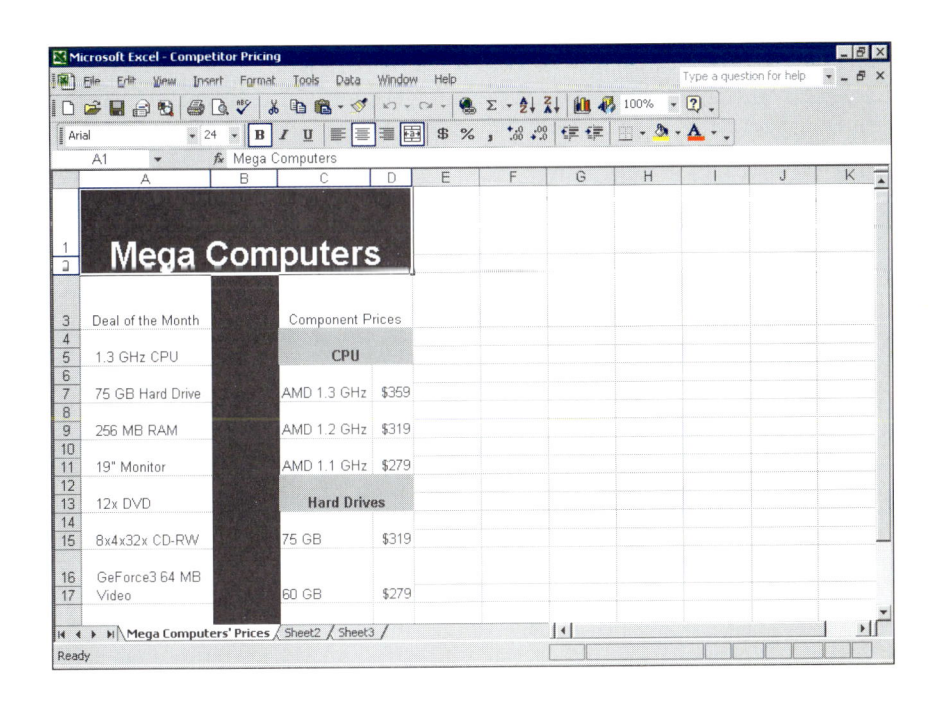

MOUSE TIP

Once you've selected data in your Internet browser, you can drag-and-drop it into Excel. If Excel is open but you can't see it, drag the information to the Excel button on the Windows taskbar, but do not release the mouse button. After a few seconds, the Excel window moves to the front, and you can drag the information into place on the worksheet.

FIGURE 16-1
Data Copied from a Web Page

| Step 23 | Save | the workbook |

Importing Data from External Sources

In Chapter 14, you learned to import data from database and text file sources. In the fast-paced business climate, these sources may not be updated quickly enough. Excel can import real-time information from the Internet, helping you to stay up to date on important events.

Super Power Computers invests a portion of its income in the stock market. Tracking the stock market indices and major companies within the computer industry helps you evaluate the investments currently held by the company. In your monthly report to Luis, you also need to report on the major stock indices and your competitors' stock prices. You can set up a Web query that keeps track of major market indices or individual stock quotes.

notes You must be connected to the Internet to complete these steps. If you are not, you can read the steps, but you won't be able to complete them.

To set up a Web query:

Step 1	Click	the Sheet2 sheet tab
Step 2	Rename	the sheet tab as Market Indices
Step 3	Click	Data
Step 4	Point to	Import External Data
Step 5	Click	Import Data

The Select Data Source dialog box opens, allowing you to choose from a variety of data sources.

Step 6	Click	MSN MoneyCentral Investor Major Indices
Step 7	Click	Open
Step 8	Click	OK in the Import Data dialog box to accept cell A1 in the existing worksheet as the destination

QUICK TIP

You can add data sources to this list by clicking New Source in the Select Data Source dialog box. The Data Connection Wizard starts and takes you through the steps necessary to set up a connection to a database server.

Integrating Excel with the Internet or an Intranet   EA 217

After a few moments, data from the major stock indices appears, as shown in Figure 16-2. The External Data toolbar is also displayed. The imported data on your screen will differ from that shown in the figure because stock prices fluctuate constantly.

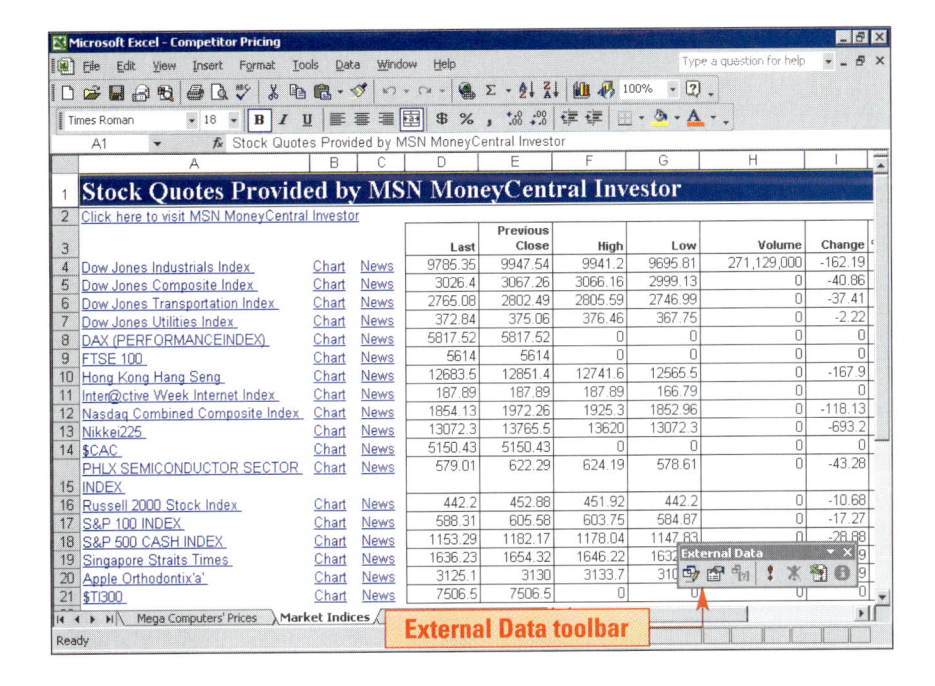

FIGURE 16-2
Results of Web Query

As you can see, the data displayed includes indices for stock markets around the world. You want to narrow the report by selecting indices that better reflect conditions in the U.S. stock market as a whole. The Dow Jones Industrials, the Nasdaq and the S&P 500 are considered leading indicators of the stock market conditions in the United States. To edit the Web query:

Step 1	**Verify**	that cell A1 is the active cell
Step 2	**Click**	the Edit Query button on the External Data toolbar

The Edit Web Query window opens, as shown in Figure 16-3. The query is listed in the Address text box at the top of the dialog box.

The Edit Web Query window is a special, enhanced browser that displays the portions of a Web page that show the result of your query. The small yellow squares that contain a black arrow are the areas on the Web page that you can query.

chapter sixteen

FIGURE 16-3
Edit Web Query Window

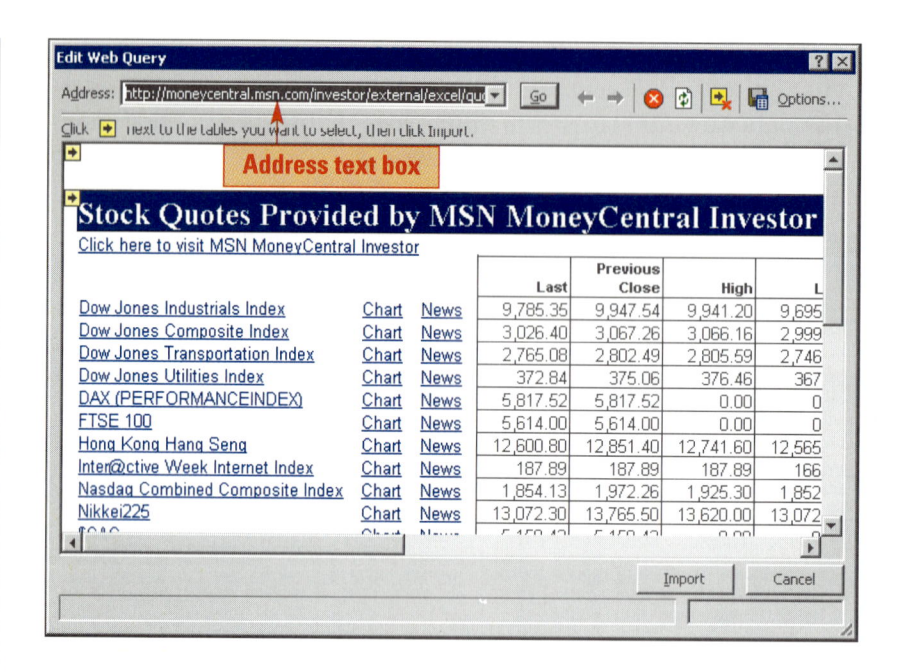

[Screenshot of Edit Web Query window showing the Address text box highlighted near the top, displaying a MoneyCentral MSN URL. Below is a table titled "Stock Quotes Provided by MSN MoneyCentral Investor" listing indices such as Dow Jones Industrials Index, Dow Jones Composite Index, Dow Jones Transportation Index, Dow Jones Utilities Index, DAX (PERFORMANCE INDEX), FTSE 100, Hong Kong Hang Seng, Inter@ctive Week Internet Index, Nasdaq Combined Composite Index, and Nikkei225, with columns for Last, Previous Close, High, and L. Import and Cancel buttons appear at the bottom.]

Step 3	**Click**	in the A<u>d</u>dress: text box

Near the end of the Web address, you should see "symbol=" followed by several index symbols such as "$INDU,$COMP…" Each variable listed after the = sign is a symbol of a market index that is listed in the table in the window; for example, $INDU is the symbol for the Dow Jones Industrial index, and $COMP is the symbol for the Dow Jones Composite index. You need to edit the Web query to show only the Dow Jones Industrial, Nasdaq, and S&P 500 indices. First, you need to position the insertion point immediately following the equal sign.

Step 4	**Press**	the RIGHT ARROW key until the insertion point is to the right of the = sign

The first symbol after the equal sign should be "$INDU," the symbol for the Dow Jones Industrial index. You still want to display that index.

Step 5	**Press**	the RIGHT ARROW key six times to position the insertion point after the comma
Step 6	**Press**	the SHIFT + END keys to select the remaining text
Step 7	**Press**	the DELETE key

$COMPX is the symbol for the Nasdaq, and $INX is the symbol for the S&P 500 index.

Step 8	Key	$COMPX,$INX
Step 9	Click	Go to update the table
Step 10	Click	Import

After a few moments, the worksheet displays the results of the revised query. Over the course of a day, this data can be refreshed to keep you informed up to the minute. The data can be refreshed periodically throughout the day while the major markets are open. After a few minutes, you want to update the data. To update a Web query:

| Step 1 | Click | the Refresh Data button on the External Data toolbar |

The data is refreshed after a few seconds.

| Step 2 | Save | the workbook |

16.b Working with XML

XML, short for eXtensible Markup Language, is fast emerging as a standard language for exchanging data on the Internet and between applications. In this section, you learn what XML is, how to create XML documents using Excel, and how to create Web Queries that take advantage of XML.

Understanding XML

Years ago, a special computer language was invented called Hypertext Markup Language, or HTML. HTML uses a system of format codes, or tags, to describe the visual appearance of content in a document. As the Internet expanded, people began to recognize some serious limitations of HTML. HTML tags describe how information should *look*, they don't describe what that information *means*, so although HTML is great for creating pages that are "pretty" to look at, it is not very good at exchanging data with other applications, such as databases.

Databases are often used to collect data in a table. A good example of this is a phone directory. Each entry in the phone book is a record, and within each record are the fields: name, address, and phone number. These fields define the meaning of the data in the record. The number 8005551234 could mean many things, but when identified as a member of the phone number field, the meaning becomes clear: (800) 555-1234. Data stored this way is called **structured data**.

XML uses a system of tags, similar to the formatting tags in HTML, to describe the meaning and structure, or organization, of data. Applications can easily process and analyze structured data, because it has meaning.

XML provides a way for different applications, including Web browsers, to exchange structured data. For example, data stored in a database can be extracted and analyzed, then formatted and displayed on the Internet. Information obtained from a Web site can be formatted as an XML document and fed directly into a database. Figure 16-4 shows an XML file displayed in a Web browser. This file contains data about a computer system at Super Power Computers.

FIGURE 16-4
Sample XML File

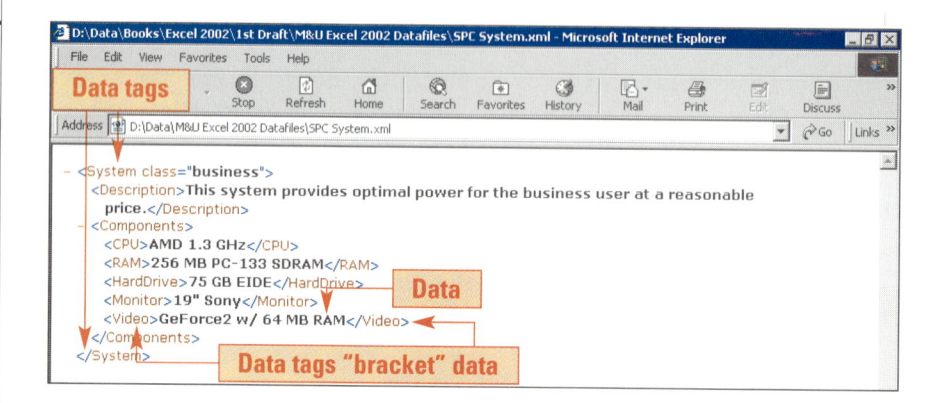

For an XML file to be displayed on the Web in a meaningful way, a style sheet is used to describe how the data should be formatted.

It is important to realize that XML does not do anything by itself. It is a storage container for data that shows the relationship, or organization, of the data. The way it stores data makes it easy for other applications to use the data.

Using XML to Share Excel Data on the Web

How does XML apply to Excel? Worksheets store data in columns and rows, very similarly to the way databases store data in tables. You know how to store data in lists in Excel, which also could be described as structured data. You can save Excel files as XML documents. An XML version of an Excel workbook describes the data in the workbook in such a way that other applications can be written to make use of this data.

You can save the data in the *Competitor Pricing* workbook as an XML file. To save a workbook as an XML file:

Step 1	**Open**	the Save As dialog box
Step 2	**Click**	the Save as type: list arrow
Step 3	**Click**	XML Spreadsheet

Integrating Excel with the Internet or an Intranet EA 221

Step 4	Key	Competitor Pricing XML File in the File name: text box
Step 5	Click	Save

Now you can view the file in your Web browser.

Step 6	Switch to	the Internet Explorer window
Step 7	Click	File
Step 8	Click	Open
Step 9	Click	Browse
Step 10	Click	the Look in: list arrow
Step 11	Switch to	the disk drive and folder where you store your completed files
Step 12	Click	the Files of type: list arrow
Step 13	Click	All Files
Step 14	Click	Competitor Pricing XML File
Step 15	Click	Open
Step 16	Click	OK

Your screen should look similar to Figure 16-5.

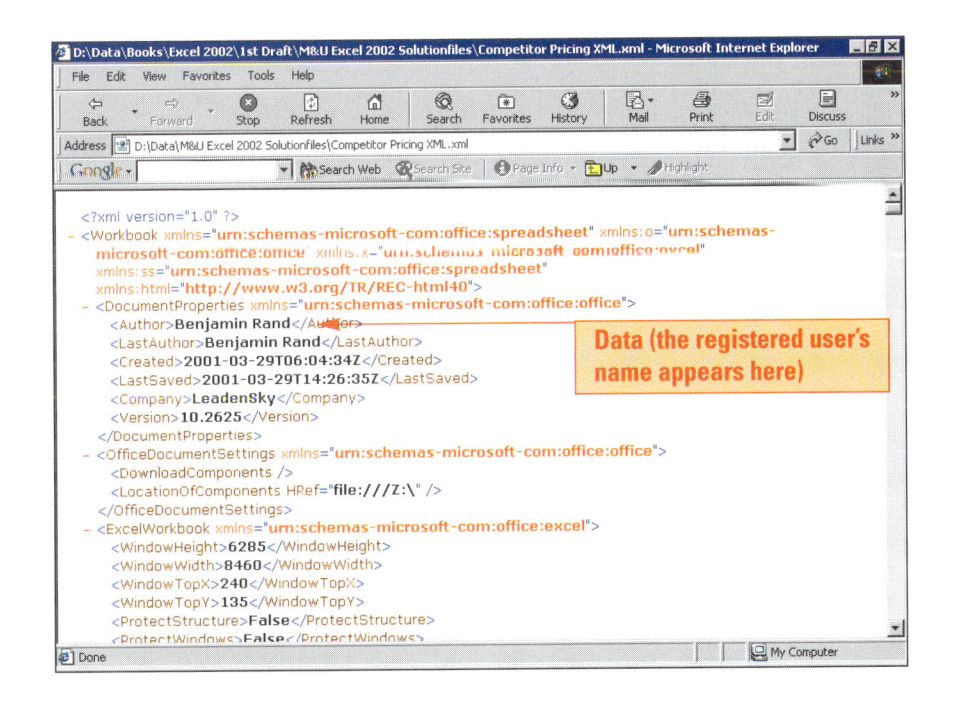

FIGURE 16-5
XML Spreadsheet Data

Remember that the XML file does not look like a reproduction of the workbook. Instead, it provides a description of the structure of the workbook, including the data it holds. Although XML files are stored as text files and are meant to be simple in nature, they are really intended to be read and processed by computers.

Before continuing, you need to close the XML workbook in Excel and reopen the Excel workbook.

Step 17	*Click*	the Close button ⊠ in the browser application window
Step 18	*Close*	the *Competitor Pricing XML File* workbook in Excel
Step 19	*Open*	the *Competitor Pricing* workbook

Creating XML Queries

An XML query is a special type of Web query you can use to keep track of important, dynamic data, such as stock prices. Fortunately, this sounds a lot more difficult than it really is. Creating an XML query is as simple as starting the New Web Query command and selecting a specific area of a Web page to query (or link to) using a specially modified browser.

As part of your efforts to track information to use to help Super Power Computers set computer prices, you watch the stock prices of some of the leading technology companies. You decide to use an XML query to make Excel do the work for you, allowing you to update the current stock prices with the click of a button. You add this query to your workbook. To create an XML query:

Step 1	*Activate*	cell A20 on the Market Indices worksheet
Step 2	*Click*	Data
Step 3	*Point to*	Import External Data
Step 4	*Click*	New Web Query

The New Web Query dialog box opens. You want to set up a query to update stock prices, so you need to locate a site that displays up-to-date stock quotes.

| Step 5 | *Key* | moneycentral.msn.com in the Address: text box |

Integrating Excel with the Internet or an Intranet   EA 223

Step 6	Click	Go

The New Web Query window opens. This window is similar to the Edit Query window you saw earlier in this chapter.

Before linking to this site, you want to locate the exact information you are looking for, in this case, the current stock quotes for Microsoft and Intel Corporation. Companies are listed on the stock market by unique three or four letter names, such as MSFT for Microsoft and INTC for Intel Corporation.

Step 7	Key	intc,msft in the Enter Symbol(s): text box on the Web page
Step 8	Click	Go next to the Enter Symbols(s): text box on the Web page (not at the top of the New Web Query window)

The returned data should look similar to Figure 16-6.

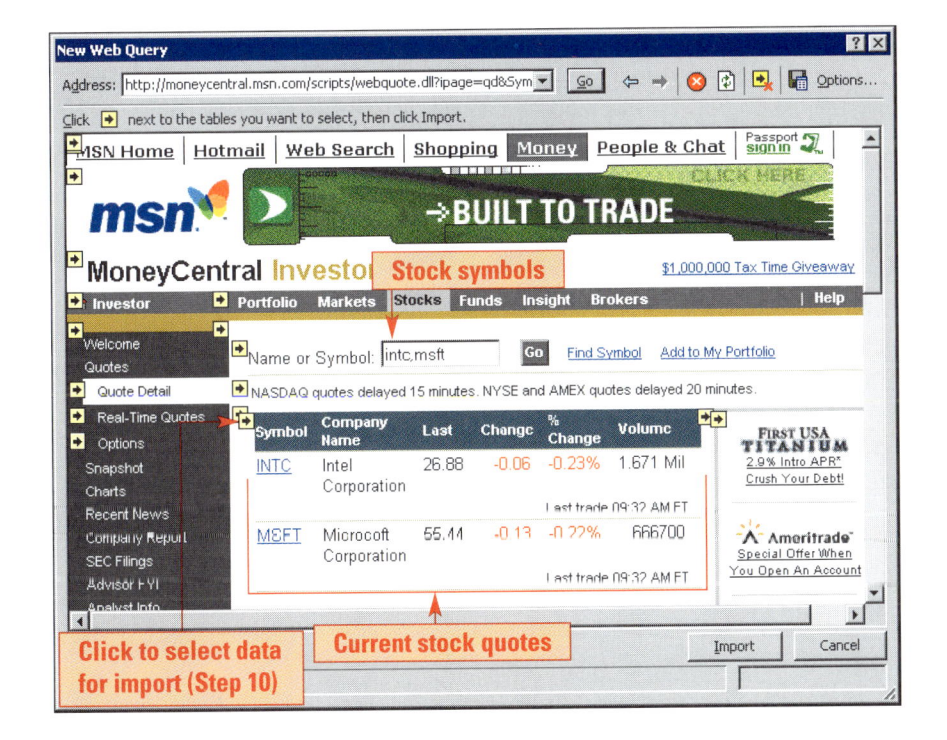

CAUTION TIP

If a dialog box opens, telling you that it might be possible for others to see the information you are sending over the Internet and asking if you want to continue, click Yes.

FIGURE 16-6
Located Stock Prices

Step 9	Move	the mouse pointer over the yellow square with the arrow symbol in the top left corner of the stock quotes as shown in Figure 16-6 (the yellow square becomes a green square when the mouse point is positioned over it)

A border appears around the data.

chapter sixteen

| Step 10 | Click | the green square with the arrow symbol to select the stock quotes |

The green square contains a check mark, and the selected area is shaded. Your screen should look similar to Figure 16-7.

FIGURE 16-7
Web Data Selected for Import

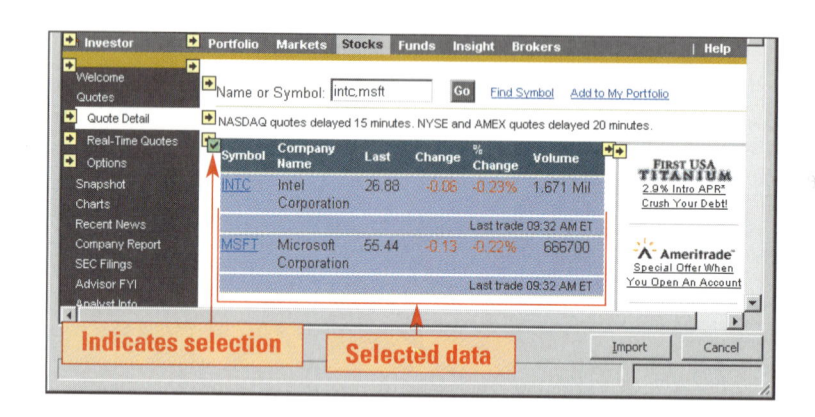

Step 11	Click	Import
Step 12	Verify	that =$A$20 is entered in the Existing worksheet: text box
Step 13	Click	OK
Step 14	Scroll	the worksheet to view rows 20 through 24

After a moment, the data is downloaded to your worksheet. Your screen should look similar to Figure 16-8. This query can be updated when needed by using the Refresh button on the External Data toolbar.

FIGURE 16-8
Data Imported into Excel

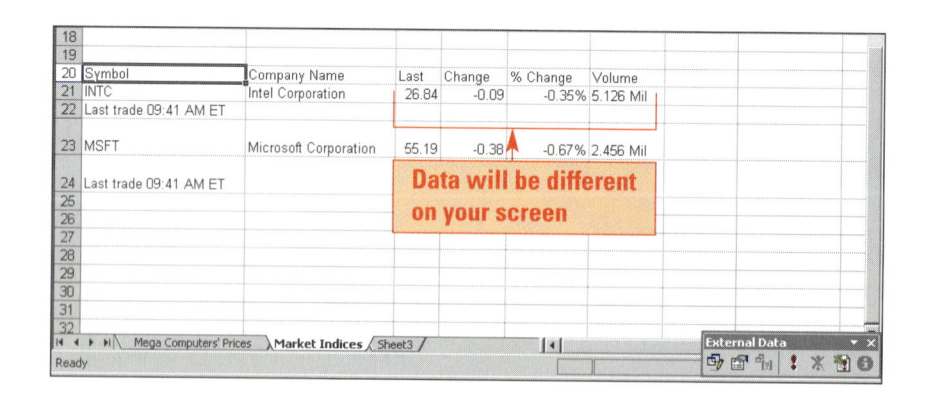

| Step 15 | Save | the workbook and close it |

16.c Publishing Worksheets and Workbooks to the Web

In just a few short years, businesses around the world have embraced the Internet as an essential part of doing business. The ability of a Web site to attract potential customers from around the world is just one of the many benefits. Information can also be communicated more readily to employees, customers, and other business partners in a fraction of the time it once took.

Preparing a Workbook to Be Used as an Interactive Web Page

Super Power Computers sells several different computer system packages. Each package requires the same components: a CPU, RAM, a hard drive, a monitor, a video card, and so forth. For each component, there are many options. For example, the monitor selection includes several manufacturers, sizes, and types. You have created a worksheet to help sales reps when they fill out orders for new computers. You realize that by providing this worksheet as an interactive Web page, customers could create and price their own custom systems on the Web, providing a valuable service to customers and speeding up the sales process. To prepare a workbook to be used as an interactive Web page:

Step 1	**Open**	the *Super Power Computers - Build System* workbook located on the Data Disk
Step 2	**Save**	the workbook as *Super Power Computers - Build System Complete*

This workbook allows customers to "build" a custom computer by entering item numbers of their choice of available components. Item numbers are entered in the white cells in column B. The Invoice area at the bottom of the page uses the VLOOKUP formula to automatically create an invoice using the items selected by the customer.

Step 3	**Scroll**	to row 33
Step 4	**Activate**	cell B25

chapter sixteen

In the Formula Bar, you see the formula =VLOOKUP(B5,$C$5:$E$7,2). The #N/A error appears because a value has not been entered in cell B5. If a value is entered and located in the first column of the range C5:E7, the matching description in the second column of the array (D5:D20) will be returned.

| Step 5 | Activate | cell B17 |

The formula =IF(OR(B11=200,B11=201),400,401) appears in the Formula Bar. This special logical formula uses the IF function to evaluate the condition of cell B11 and select the correct motherboard for the selected CPU. The nested OR function is used to test cell B11 for either of two conditions, item 200 OR item 201. If the item number in cell B11 is 200 or 201, then the value of cell B17 will be set to item 400, otherwise the value of cell B17 will be set to item 401. Notice that the value of B17 is already 401, even though cell B11 is currently blank. A blank cell fails either of the criteria in the OR statement, so the IF statement evaluates to the FALSE condition.

Before saving your workbook as a Web page, you should verify that everything works correctly.

Step 6	Enter	122 in cell B5
Step 7	Enter	131 in cell B8
Step 8	Enter	201 in cell B11
Step 9	Enter	301 in cell B14
Step 10	Enter	500 in cell B19
Step 11	Scroll	the worksheet to row 33 again

The Invoice total should be $1,064.35, as shown in Figure 16-9.

FIGURE 16-9
Tested Worksheet

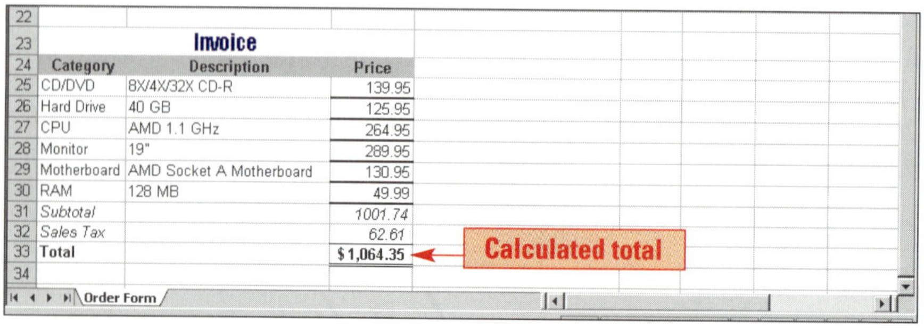

| Step 12 | **Delete** | the contents of cells B5, B8, B11, B14, and B19 |
| Step 13 | **Save** | the workbook |

Using Web Page Preview

Previewing a workbook as a Web page is a simple task. To preview your workbook:

| Step 1 | **Click** | File |
| Step 2 | **Click** | We**b** Page Preview |

Your browser opens with the workbook in HTML format.

| Step 3 | **Maximize** | the browser window, if necessary |

Your screen should look similar to Figure 16-10. Although you prepared the worksheet to be used as an interactive Web page, the preview is not interactive.

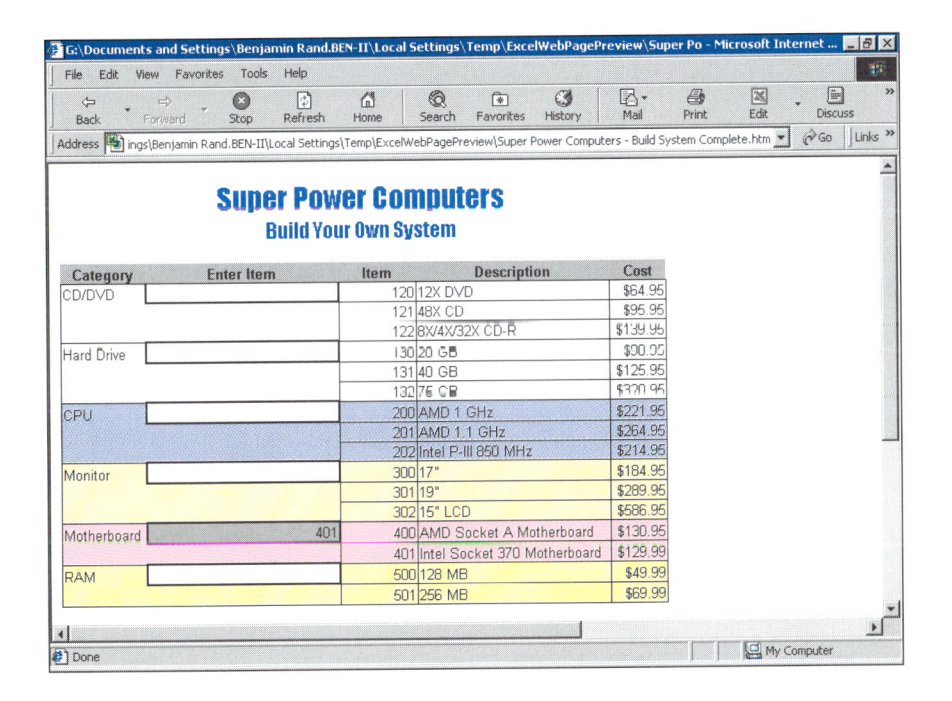

FIGURE 16-10
Web Page Preview of a Workbook

| Step 4 | **Close** | the browser window |

Publishing a Worksheet or Workbook to the Web

Publishing a worksheet or a workbook is also easy. When a worksheet or workbook is published, new options are available in the Save As dialog box. These options allow you to choose which portions of the workbook are published, where the finished documents are saved, and whether to add interactivity.

> **notes**
> The interactivity feature only works with Internet Explorer version 4.01 or higher.

To publish your worksheet:

Step 1	Click	File
Step 2	Click	Save as Web Page

The Save As dialog box on your screen should look similar to Figure 16-11.

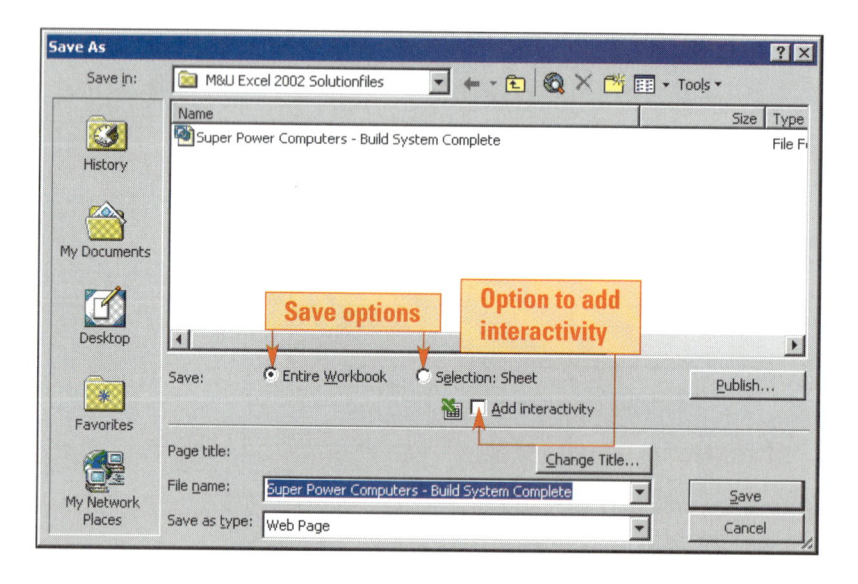

FIGURE 16-11
Save As Dialog Box with Web Page Options

The Save As dialog box shows Save options (Entire Workbook / Selection: Sheet) and an Option to add interactivity (Add interactivity checkbox).

Publishing the workbook differs from saving it by providing additional options. Using this feature, you can choose to automatically republish the workbook every time you save it, select specific areas of the workbook to publish, and select the interactive functionality (spreadsheet or PivotTable).

Integrating Excel with the Internet or an Intranet   EA 229

Step 3	Click	Publish

The Publish as Web Page dialog box on your screen should look similar to Figure 16-12.

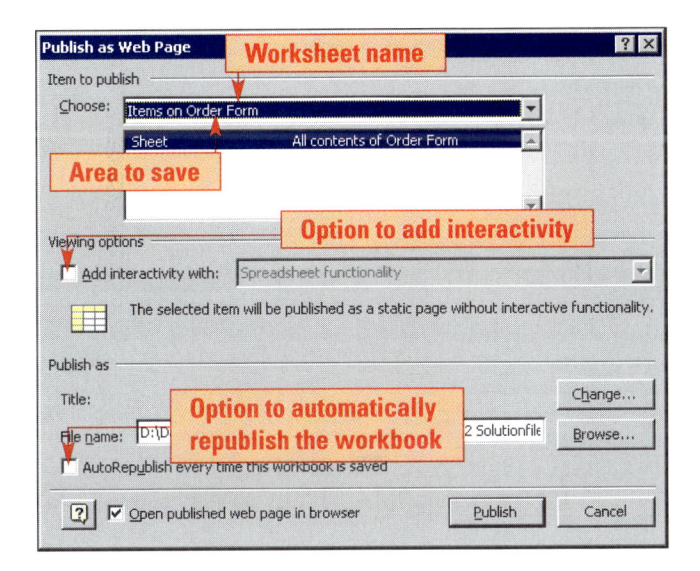

FIGURE 16-12
Publish as Web Page Dialog Box

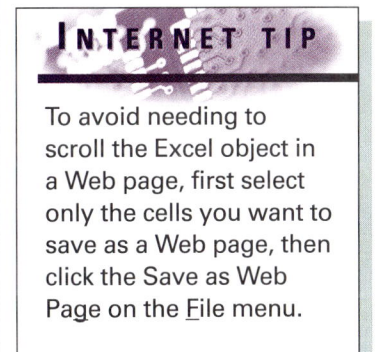

INTERNET TIP

To avoid needing to scroll the Excel object in a Web page, first select only the cells you want to save as a Web page, then click the Save as Web Page on the File menu.

Step 4	Verify	that Items on Order Form is selected in the Choose: list
Step 5	Click	the Add interactivity with: check box to insert a check mark
Step 6	Verify	that Spreadsheet functionality is selected in the Add interactivity with: list
Step 7	Click	the Open published web page in browser check box to insert a check mark, if necessary
Step 8	Click	Browse
Step 9	Key	Super Power Computers - Build System Complete in the File name: text box
Step 10	Verify	that the Save in: list box lists the folder in which you store your completed files
Step 11	Click	OK
Step 12	Click	Publish

QUICK TIP

To publish an entire workbook, you would click Entire Workbook in the Choose: list.

The workbook is published and your browser opens. Because this workbook was saved with interactivity, you can use the workbook as though you were working in Excel.

chapter sixteen

Step 13	**Enter**	121 in cell B5
Step 14	**Enter**	130 in cell B8
Step 15	**Enter**	202 in cell B11
Step 16	**Enter**	300 in cell B14
Step 17	**Enter**	500 in cell B19
Step 18	**Scroll**	the Excel object window to view the Invoice section

Your screen should be similar to Figure 16-13.

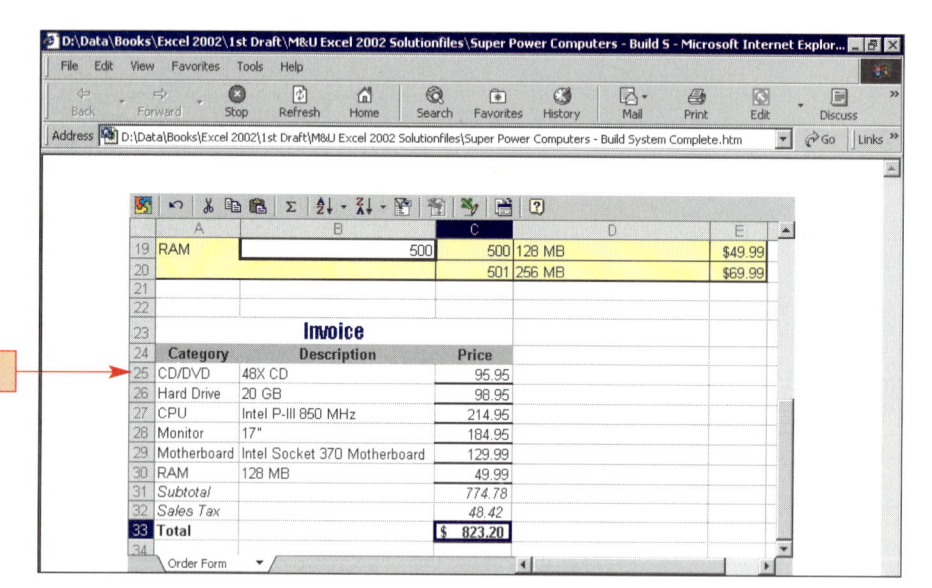

FIGURE 16-13
Interactive Workbook

| Step 19 | **Close** | the browser window |

16.d Sending a Workbook via E-mail

Using e-mail capabilities built in to Excel, you can quickly send a worksheet or an entire workbook to a colleague. You can transmit a single worksheet as an HTML-formatted mail message—an option that allows the recipient to see all the formatting of the original message. The recipient can select the data in his or her message and drag it into Excel. When you need to send an entire workbook, you can transmit it as an attachment. **Attachments** accompany a regular e-mail message and allow you to send any type of document or program.

notes This section describes how to send workbooks via e-mail using Microsoft Outlook as the e-mail application. If you are using a different e-mail application, your instructor may modify the steps.

Sending a Worksheet as HTML Mail

HTML mail is a newer form of e-mail that allows you to send a Web page as the body of an e-mail message. All the formatting, alignment, and drawing objects can be sent and viewed in HTML mail-enabled mail readers. Microsoft Outlook, which is part of the Office suite, can receive and display HTML mail. To test this method, you send the *Super Power Computers - Build System Complete* workbook to yourself.

notes You must have Internet access and an e-mail account to complete these steps. Otherwise you can read the steps but you cannot complete them.

To send a worksheet as part of a message:

Step 1	**Activate**	cell A1
Step 2	**Click**	the E-mail button on the Standard toolbar

Your screen should look similar to Figure 16-14.

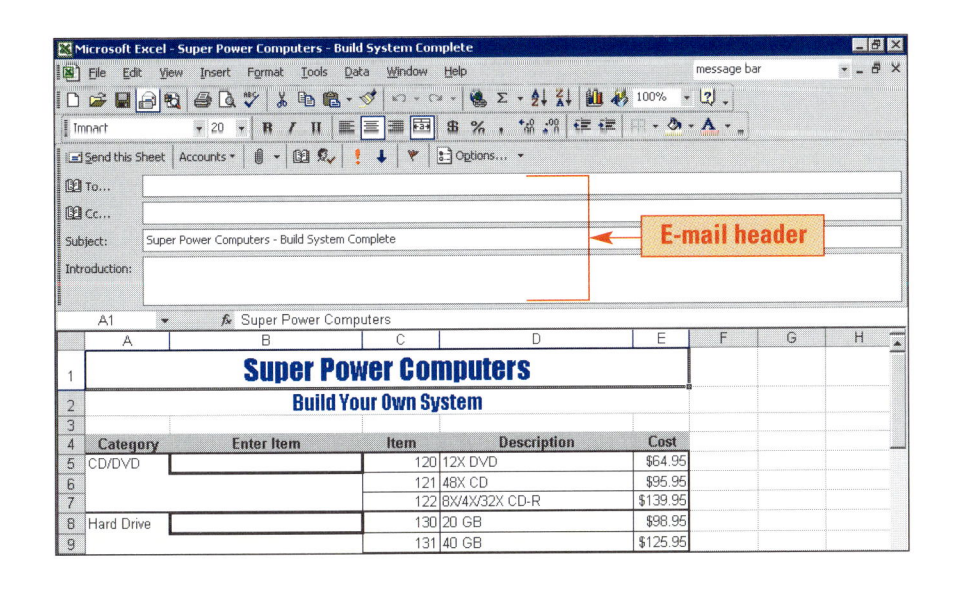

MENU TIP

You can send a worksheet by pointing to Send to on the File menu, and then clicking Mail recipient.

To send the entire workbook as an attachment, point to Send to on the File menu, then click Mail Recipient (as Attachment). When you send a workbook as an attachment, the recipient can then open the file in Excel.

FIGURE 16-14
E-mailing a Workbook

> **MOUSE TIP**
>
> If you want to use the Address Book to fill in e-mail addresses, click the To button or the Address Book button on the toolbar.

| Step 3 | **Enter** | your e-mail address in the To text box |
| Step 4 | **Click** | the Send this Sheet button [Send this Sheet] |

The message is sent to the Outbox. You need to start Outlook, connect to your ISP, and send the message.

Step 5	**Start**	Outlook
Step 6	**Click**	the Send/Receive button [Send/Receive] to send the message
Step 7	**Open**	the message you sent yourself

If your e-mail program can display HTML mail, your message should look similar to Figure 16-15.

FIGURE 16-15
Viewing HTML Mail

> **QUICK TIP**
>
> Change your mind about sending a worksheet? To turn off the messaging toolbar without sending the message, click the E-mail button on the Standard toolbar again.

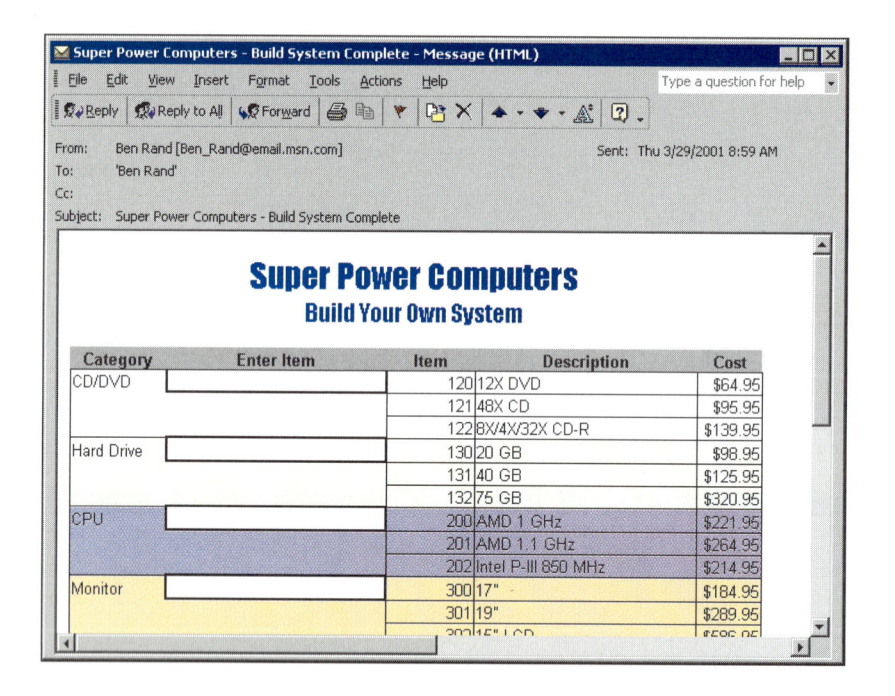

| Step 8 | **Close** | the e-mail message |
| Step 9 | **Switch to** | the Excel application window |

Sending a Workbook as an Attachment

Often, you need to send a copy of an entire workbook so that it can be opened and edited directly in Excel. To do this, you need to send the workbook as an attachment. To send a workbook as an e-mail attachment:

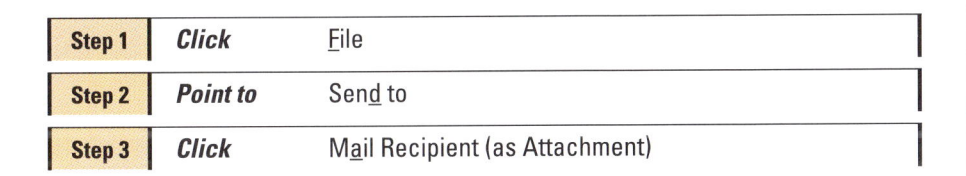

Step 1	Click	File
Step 2	Point to	Send to
Step 3	Click	Mail Recipient (as Attachment)

A new message is created with the workbook attached, and should look similar to Figure 16-16.

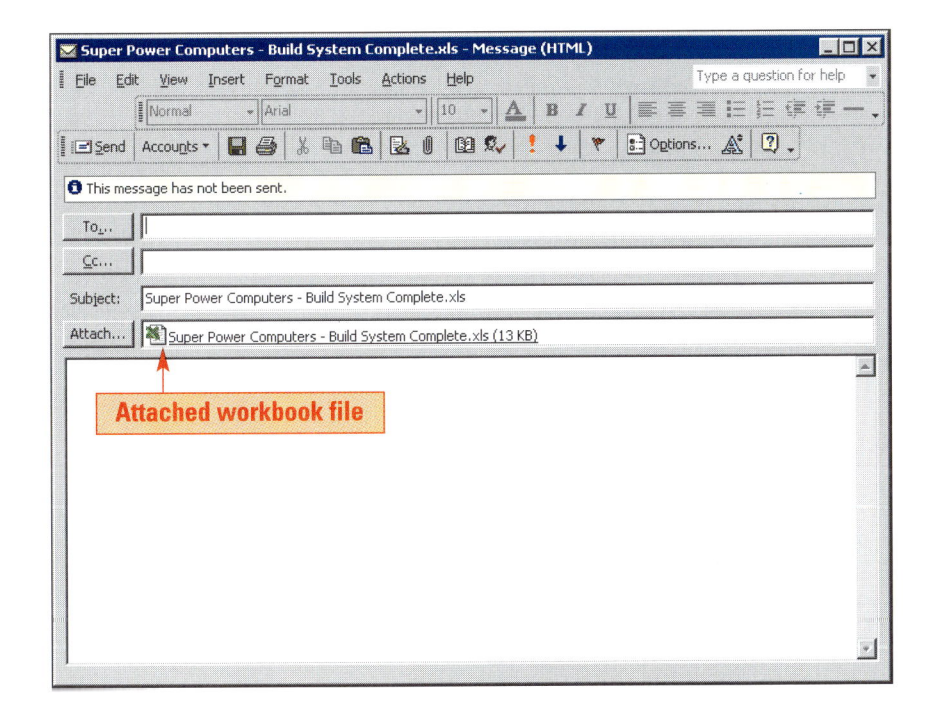

FIGURE 16-16
Workbook Attached to E-mail Message

CAUTION TIP

While most newer e-mail applications can properly display HTML mail, many older applications cannot. If this is the case with your system, you should be able to send the message but may not be able to view it properly when you receive it.

At this point, you fill in the recipient address and send the message as you would normally. For this activity, you don't send the message.

Step 4	Close	the e-mail message
Step 5	Close	the Outlook window, if necessary
Step 6	Save	the workbook and close it

Excel makes it easy to share workbook information with others via e-mail.

Summary

▶ You can copy data from Web pages and paste it into Excel. You also can select information on a Web page, then drag and drop it directly onto a worksheet.

▶ You can import data from a variety of sources, including the Internet. Use Web queries to extract data and update dynamic data, such as stock quotes and market indices.

▶ XML makes it easier for applications to share data, such as that found in databases, with the Web.

▶ Excel can save XML-formatted workbooks.

▶ You create custom XML queries by selecting areas of a Web page using the New Web Query dialog box.

▶ You can use Web Page Preview to preview a workbook or worksheet you want to publish to the Web. Previews are not interactive.

▶ You can publish a worksheet or workbook to the Web to share data. AutoPublish automatically updates the published Web page each time the workbook is modified and saved. Published workbooks can be interactive, allowing users to input data while the Web page correctly calculates the results.

▶ You can send worksheets or workbooks to others without leaving Excel by e-mailing worksheets as HTML mail, or sending workbooks as e-mail attachments.

Commands Review

Action	Menu Bar	Shortcut Menu	Toolbar	Task Pane	Keyboard
Import external data	Data, Import External Data, Import Data				ALT + D, D, D
Create a Web query	Data, Import External Data, New Web Query				ALT + D, D, W
Edit a Web Query	Data, Import External Data, Edit Query		☐		ALT + D, D, E
Refresh data in a Web query	Data, Refresh Data	Refresh Data	❗		ALT + D, R
Preview a workbook as a Web page	File, Web Page Preview				ALT + F, B
Publish a workbook as a Web page	File, Save as Web Page				ALT + F, G
Send a workbook as HTML mail	File, Send to, Mail Recipient		☐		ALT + F, D, M
Send a workbook as an attachment	File, Send to, Mail Recipient (as Attachment)		☐		ALT + F, D, A

Concepts Review

Circle the correct answer.

1. **You can import data into Excel from:**
   - [a] databases.
   - [b] text files.
   - [c] the Internet.
   - [d] databases, text files, and the Internet.

2. **A Web query:**
   - [a] must be recreated every time you want to update the data.
   - [b] requires in-depth programming knowledge.
   - [c] can be refreshed easily whenever you want.
   - [d] cannot be edited.

3. **XML is short for:**
   - [a] hyper teXt Markup Language.
   - [b] eXtended Markup Language.
   - [c] Standardized General Markup Language.
   - [d] structured data.

4. **XML is not used to:**
   - [a] display data.
   - [b] store data.
   - [c] exchange data between applications.
   - [d] describe structured data.

5. **When you refresh the data in a Web query:**
   - [a] the new data overwrites the old data.
   - [b] the new data is appended after the old data.
   - [c] the new data is inserted before the old data.
   - [d] You can't refresh Web queries.

6. **XML files are intended to be:**
   - [a] displayed in Web browsers without any additional files.
   - [b] read by human beings.
   - [c] extremely complex.
   - [d] processed and analyzed by computer applications.

7. **A worksheet sent as HTML mail:**
   - [a] can be edited directly in the e-mail message.
   - [b] is a good way to transfer a workbook file.
   - [c] can be copied and pasted into Excel for editing.
   - [d] can have interactivity enabled.

chapter sixteen

8. To send a workbook as an e-mail attachment:
  [a] you must first save and close the document.
  [b] you must first open your e-mail program.
  [c] click the Attachment button in Excel.
  [d] click the E-mail button, then choose to send the workbook as an attachment.

9. The OR function is used to evaluate:
  [a] whether a single condition is true.
  [b] whether any of several conditions are true.
  [c] whether all of several conditions are true.
  [d] a set of conditions, then return one value if the conditions are true, and another value if the conditions are false.

10. HTML is used on the Internet to:
  [a] describe how data should appear.
  [b] define what data means.
  [c] exchange data between applications.
  [d] store structured data.

Circle **T** if the statement is true or **F** if the statement is false.

T F 1. Enabling AutoPublish in the Publish dialog box means that the Web page will be updated every time the workbook is saved.

T F 2. Once you turn on the messaging (e-mail) toolbar, you cannot turn it off until you send the file.

T F 3. You can send most types of documents or computer files as attachments.

T F 4. Interactive worksheets allow users to enter data, but formulas are disabled and do not calculate results.

T F 5. An XML spreadsheet in a Web browser looks just like an Excel worksheet.

T F 6. XML uses tags to describe the way data should appear when it is viewed.

T F 7. Sending a workbook as an e-mail attachment and sending a workbook as HTML mail are identical operations.

T F 8. You can enable interactivity in a Web page preview.

T F 9. Interactive Web pages enable users to interact with the Web page's data.

T F 10. Although you can copy and paste data from a Web page into Excel, you cannot drag and drop selected data from a Web page into Excel.

Skills Review

Exercise 1

1. Create a new, blank worksheet.

2. Create a new Web Query.

3. In the Address box, go to *www.msnbc.com*.

4. Click the headlines link and wait for the headlines to appear.

5. Move the pointer over the box next to News (all the headlines should be highlighted). Click the box to select the headlines area.

6. Click Import and place the results in cell A1.

7. Save the workbook as *Today's News*. Print the workbook and close it.

Exercise 2

1. Open the *Annual Sales by Country* workbook located on the Data Disk.
2. Create an Area Blocks chart (*Hint:* look on the Custom Types tab) with the following settings:
   a. Chart title should be "Annual Sales by Country."
   b. Turn on the legend.
   c. Turn on the data table.
   d. Create the chart as a new chart sheet.
3. Save the workbook as *Annual Sales by Country with Chart.*
4. E-mail the workbook as an attachment to a classmate.
5. You should also receive a workbook from your classmate via e-mail. Open the workbook in the e-mail message.
6. Change the value of cell B4 to 2,500,000, then print the chart.
7. Save the workbook as *Annual Sales by Country with Chart Revised*. Print the workbook and close it.

Exercise 3

1. Open the *Annual Sales by Country with Chart Revised* workbook you created in Exercise 2.
2. You cannot save a workbook as an XML spreadsheet if it contains a chart, so delete the chart sheet.
3. Save the workbook as an XML spreadsheet named *Annual Sales by Country XML*, and then close the workbook.
4. Open the *Annual Sales by Country XML* file in your browser.
5. Print the XML document, then close your browser.

Exercise 4

1. Create a new, blank workbook.
2. In cell A1, enter the text "Enter Stock Symbol". Shade the cell with Gray-25%.
3. From the Data menu, point to Import External Data, then click Import Data.
4. Select MSN MoneyCentral Investor Stock Quotes, then click Open.
5. Click the Parameters button.
6. Click the Get the value from the following cell option button, click the box underneath the option button, then click cell B1 in the worksheet.
7. Click the Refresh automatically when cell value changes check box to insert a check mark.
8. Click OK.
9. Click cell A4 as the output cell.
10. Click OK.
11. Enter the stock symbol for Dell computers, dell, in cell B1.
12. Save the workbook as *Stock Lookup*.
13. Print the worksheet and close the workbook.

chapter sixteen

Exercise 5

1. Open the *Car Loan Payments* workbook located on the Data Disk.
2. Select cells E1:E2.
3. Open the Format Cells dialog box, click the Protection tab, and click the Locked check box to remove the check mark.
4. Click Tools, point to Protection, and click Protect Sheet.
5. Turn off Select locked cells and make sure Select unlocked cells is on.
6. Select the range A1:I20, click Save as Web Page on the File menu, then save the selection as an interactive Web page named *Car Loan Payment Calculator*.
7. Open the *Car Loan Payment Calculator* in your Web browser.
8. Enter 12,500 as the loan amount in cell E1.
9. Enter 2.5% as the interest rate in cell E2.
10. Print the Web page from your browser, then close the browser.
11. Save the workbook as *Car Loan Payment Calculator* and close it.

Exercise 6

1. Use the *Month Calendar* template located on the Data Disk to create a new calendar workbook. (*Hint:* In the Open dialog box, click All Microsoft Excel files in the Files of type: list box.)
2. Enter the correct dates for the current month.
3. Modify the calendar title in cell A1 to display the current month.
4. Modify the cell shading to correspond to the current month.
5. Select the calendar area.
6. Save the calendar as a Web page with interactivity. Name the Web page *Calendar Web Page.htm*.
7. Print the Web page and close your browser.
8. Close the workbook without saving it and close the custom Calendar toolbar, if necessary.

Exercise 7

1. Open the *Calendar Web Page.htm* file in your browser.
2. Add at least five appointments to the calendar.
3. Click the Export to Excel button in the browser to create a copy of the appointments.
4. Save the workbook as an Excel workbook named *Calendar Export*, and print it.
5. Close the browser and the workbook.

Exercise 8

1. Open the *Calendar Export* workbook that you created in Exercise 7.
2. Send the workbook as an HTML message to a classmate.
3. You should receive a similar message from a classmate. View the e-mail message in Outlook, and then print the HTML mail message.
4. Close the workbook without saving changes.

Case Projects

Project 1

As a mortgage officer, you want to provide the best possible service to your clients. One tool that you find helpful is a mortgage loan calculator, which calculates the monthly payment for a loan at a given percentage. (*Hint:* Use online Help to find out how to use the PMT functions.) Use Excel to create an interactive Web page where visitors to your site can input a loan amount, a term in months, and an interest rate, and then calculate a monthly payment and total interest. Save the workbook as *MLC* and the Web page as *MLC.htm*. Print the Web page. Close your browser and the workbook.

Project 2

Connect to the Internet and search the Web for a table of data displaying current stock prices for Microsoft (stock symbol: MSFT). Select the table in your browser and drag it into a new Excel workbook. Save the workbook as *Imported Stock Price*, and then print and close it.

Project 3

As an investment advisor for a small mutual fund that caters to first-time investors, you want to help your clients see how ups and downs in the stock market have affected their investments. Create a worksheet with an initial investment of 250 shares purchased at a price of $40 per share. Create a formula to calculate the value of the investment. Save the workbook as *Investment*. Next, save only the cells you use as an Interactive Web page called *Investment Interactive*. Change the title to "Enter Share Price" in the Publish Web Page dialog box. Test your Web page in a browser by changing the price of the shares (the calculated value of the investment should change). Print the Web page and close your browser. Close the workbook.

Project 4

You are a busy stockbroker with clients who are very interested in technology stocks. Create a worksheet with a Web query that looks up stocks for the following companies: Microsoft, Intel Corporation, IBM, Dell, Gateway, AMD, and Apple. (*Hint:* Most financial sites help you locate company stock symbols by entering the company name in a lookup box.) After you import the data, use the Data Range Properties button on the External Data toolbar to refresh the data every 30 minutes. Save the workbook as *Technology Stock Updates*. Print the workbook and close it.

Project 5

You and some friends are planning an outdoor activity, but your plans depend on the weather. Connect to the Internet and search for a Web site that forecasts the local weather four or five days in advance. Select the forecast and drag and drop (or copy and paste) it into a new, blank workbook. Add a hyperlink in your workbook to the site from which you copied the forecast. Save the workbook as *Weather Forecast*, then print and close it.

Project 6

COMDEX is one of the computer industries biggest trade shows. You decide you want to attend, but first, you need to find out when and where the event takes place this year. Connect to the Internet and search for the COMDEX Web site. Search the Web site to find out when and where the show is being held this year, then copy the information into a new workbook. Next search the Web for plane fares to and from your city to the site of the event, and copy the results into your workbook. Save the workbook as *Plane Fares* to *COMDEX*, then e-mail the workbook as HTML mail to a colleague who is interested in attending. Print the workbook and close it.

chapter sixteen

Project 7

Your company is trying to integrate its customer data from a variety of sources. After looking into different alternatives, you've decided that using XML to store and exchange the data is the way to go. Create a workbook containing column headings for customer data, including names, addresses, city, state, zip, and phone number. Include fictitious information for at least five customers. Save the workbook as an XML spreadsheet named *Customer Data XML.xml*, then print and close it.

Project 8

You work in the Marketing Department for Widgit, Inc. To help increase sales, you need to create a Web page that allows clients to input the number of Widgits they want to order and then the worksheet calculates the total price of the transaction. To encourage customers to buy more Widgits, the company is offering special pricing based on the quantity purchased. If the customer buys between 1 and 50 Widgits, they cost $19.95 each; if a customer buys between 51 and 100 Widgits, they cost $17.95 each; and if a customer buys more than 100 Widgits, they cost $14.95 each. In the price cell, use a formula to display the correct price based on the number entered in the quantity cell. Unlock the quantity cell then protect the worksheet to prevent data being entered in any cell except the quantity cell. Save the workbook as *Widgits*, then print it. Select the cells that make up your "form" and save them as an interactive web page named *Widgits.htm*. Close the workbook and the Web page files.

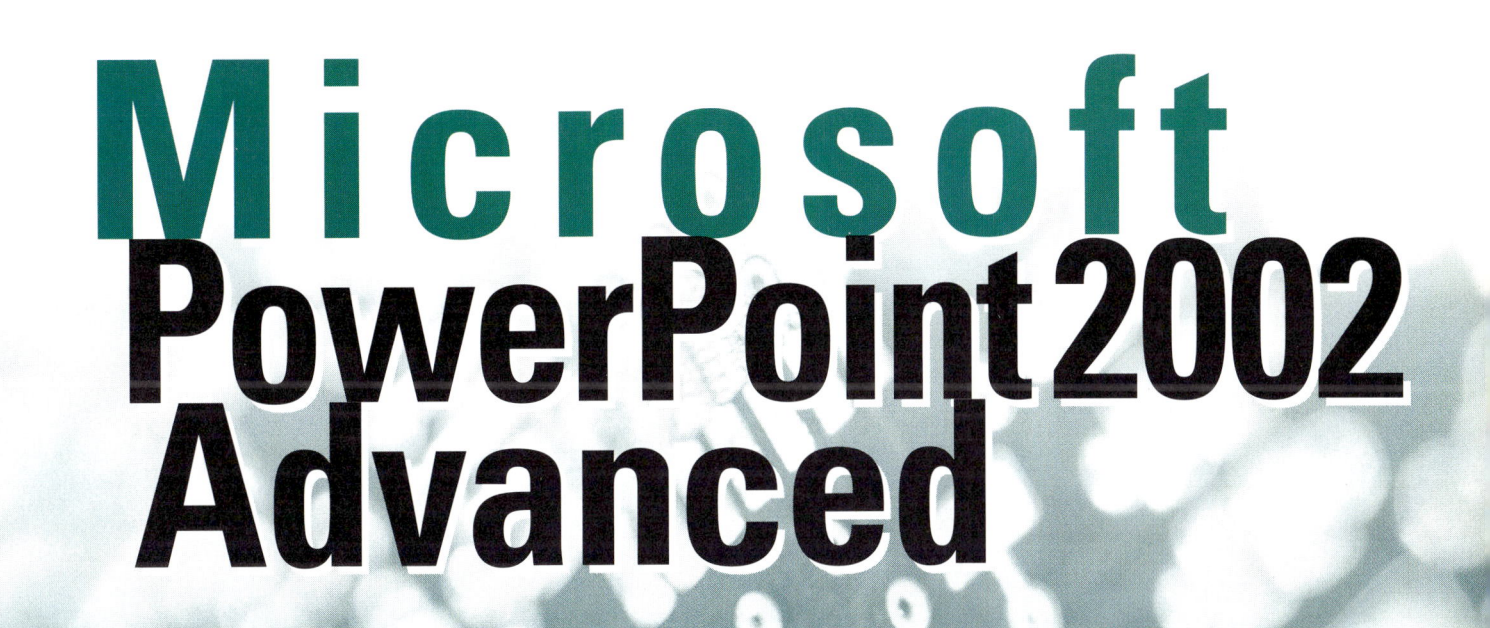

Microsoft PowerPoint 2002 Advanced

PowerPoint 2002

Working with Organization Charts and Diagrams

Chapter Overview

You can use organization charts and other diagrams in PowerPoint slides to present information in a graph-based format. Organization charts are diagrams that show the hierarchical structure of an organization, such as a company, division, or department, and how its parts relate to one another. Other diagrams illustrate different types of conceptual information, such as the relationships of elements to a core element, areas of overlap among related elements, the phases of a process involving a continuous cycle, or steps toward a goal. This chapter introduces you to the process of creating, editing, and formatting organization charts and other diagrams.

Learning Objectives

- Add an organization chart slide
- Format an organization chart
- Add a diagram slide
- Format a diagram

Case profile

Mr. Theodore Rimes, president of Teddy Toys, just increased the annual budget for the New Products Division. Ms. Hill now can produce more new products for Teddy Toys and hire more employees. Ms. Hill asks you to add slides to an existing presentation that introduce the current new products, the organizational structure of the New Products Division, and the role of new departmental employees. She plans to run the presentation during the interviews with prospective employees.

chapter nine

Working with Organization Charts and Diagrams PA 3

9.a Adding an Organization Chart Slide

An **organization chart** is a graphical representation of the hierarchical reporting relationships within an organization. It usually consists of individual shapes, which are objects that are positioned at different levels and connected by lines. Levels show the chain of command within a company, division, and/or department. PowerPoint allows you to create organization charts easily by using a predesigned placeholder that you can customize for almost any type of organizational structure. To add a new slide and create an organization chart on the slide:

Step 1	Open	the *Teddy Toys New Products* presentation located on the Data Disk
Step 2	Save	the presentation as *Teddy Toys Organization*
Step 3	Add	a new Title slide to the end of the presentation using the Slide Layout task pane
Step 4	Key	New Products Division as the title and Working Toward the Future as the subtitle
Step 5	Click	the New Slide button on the Formatting toolbar
Step 6	Click	the Title and Diagram or Organization Chart layout in the Other Layouts area in the Slide Layout task pane

The new slide with a title placeholder and a diagram or organization chart layout placeholder should look similar to Figure 9-1.

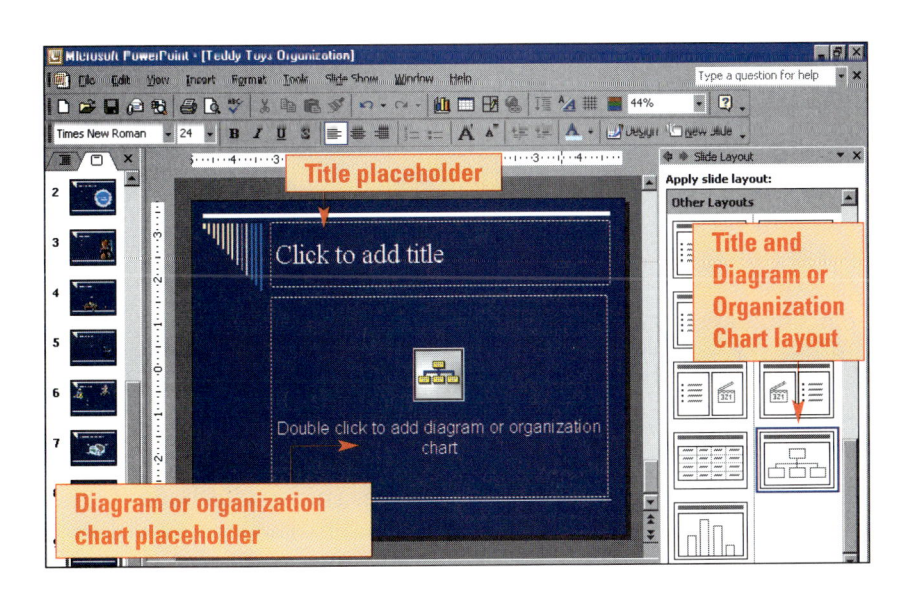

TASK PANE TIP

You can create an organization chart by clicking the New Slide command on the Insert menu and then clicking the Title and Diagram or Organization Chart layout in the Slide Layout task pane.

You also can create an organization chart by clicking the New Slide button on the Formatting toolbar, clicking any of the Content Layouts in the Slide Layout task pane, and then clicking the Insert Diagram or Organization Chart icon.

FIGURE 9-1
Slide with Diagram or Organization Chart Placeholder

chapter nine

Entering Information in an Organization Chart

The process of entering information in an organization chart is similar to entering information in other objects on a slide; you just click the shape and key the text. To enter a slide title and create an organization chart:

Step 1	Key	New Products Division as the title
Step 2	Double-click	the diagram or organization chart placeholder

The Diagram Gallery dialog box opens, with six diagram types from which to choose. PowerPoint offers one type of organization chart, and it is selected by default. The dialog box on your screen should look similar to Figure 9-2.

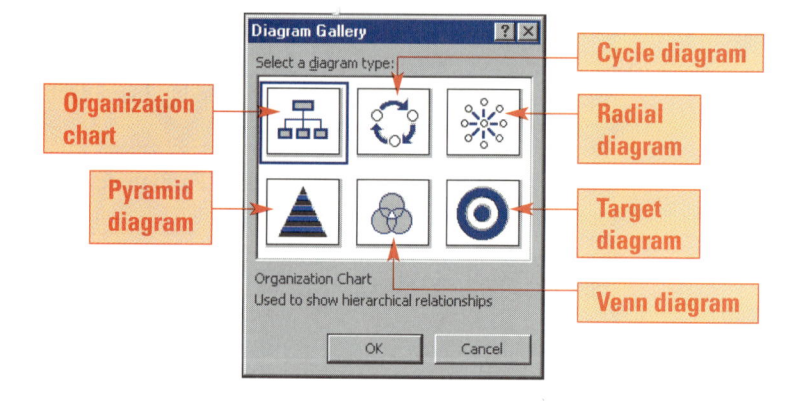

> **MENU TIP**
>
> You can create an organization chart by clicking the Organization Chart subcommand under the Picture command on the Insert menu.

FIGURE 9-2
Diagram Gallery Dialog Box

Step 3	Double-click	the Organization Chart diagram type

A default organization chart appears on the slide surrounded by a drawing border with sizing handles, and the Organization Chart toolbar displays for working with the chart. The **drawing border** is a nonprinting border that defines the drawing area of the chart. It can be resized by dragging the sizing handles. The default organization chart consists of a superior shape and three subordinate shapes. Each shape has placeholders for data. The **superior shape** represents the highest position in the company, division, or department you are charting. **Subordinate shapes** represent individuals reporting to the superior position or to higher-level subordinate positions. The Organization Chart toolbar contains four buttons: Insert Shape, Layout, Select, and AutoFormat. The Insert Shape button enables you to add shapes to the chart for subordinates, coworkers, and assistants. The Layout button

> **MOUSE TIP**
>
> You can create an organization chart by clicking the New Slide button on the Formatting toolbar and then clicking the Insert Diagram or Organization button on the Drawing toolbar.
>
> You can add an organization chart to any slide by right-clicking a blank area of the slide (not a placeholder or object), clicking Slide Layout, and then clicking the Title and Diagram or Organization Chart layout in the Slide Layout task pane.

enables you to change the layout style and resize the organization chart. The Select button enables you to select an entire level, branch, all assistants, or all connecting lines so that you can make multiple formatting changes at once. The AutoFormat button enables you to select a different overall diagram style for the shapes and connecting lines in your chart.

Each shape can hold multiple lines of text—usually a name followed by a title. By default, the superior shape is already selected. To enter names and titles into the organization chart shapes:

Step 1	Key	Sandra Hill in the superior shape
Step 2	Press	the ENTER key
Step 3	Key	Manager

> **DESIGN TIP**
>
> Although you can create multiple levels and multiple positions in an organization chart, common sense should prevail. Consider using only one type of organization structure and at least three, but no more than twenty, shapes in the chart. The more shapes and levels you have, the smaller the shapes and text become. If necessary, use a separate organization chart to show a close-up view or a section of another chart.

The size of the shape will change to accommodate the text. Before entering text in another shape, you must first select the shape. To enter text for the rest of the organization chart:

Step 1	Click	the first shape at the left of the second level to select the shape
Step 2	Key	Gordon Pedersen (press the ENTER key) Team Coordinator
Step 3	Click	the second shape on the second level
Step 4	Key	Ruth Pedersen (press the ENTER key) Product Coordinator
Step 5	Click	the third shape on the second level
Step 6	Key	Karen Peer (press the ENTER key) Design Coordinator

Adding an Additional Level of Subordinates

You can add additional subordinate shapes to an organization chart by first clicking the shape to which the subordinates report and then clicking the Insert Shape button on the Organization Chart toolbar. Multiple subordinate shapes can be created by clicking the Insert Shape button as many times as the shapes you need. For example, if you want to show three subordinate positions for one shape, click the Insert Shape button three times after clicking the shape to which the subordinates report. To add a new level of subordinate shapes to existing subordinate shapes:

Step 1	Click	the first subordinate shape (Gordon Pedersen) to select it

> **QUICK TIP**
>
> You can create four different positions in a PowerPoint organization chart: a superior position (for a president or manager) in level 1, subordinate positions in levels 2–50, coworker shapes in any level, and assistant positions in any level.

chapter nine

Mouse Tip

You can add text to a shape in an organization chart by right-clicking the shape and then clicking Edit Text.

| Step 2 | Click | the Insert Shape button on the Organization Chart toolbar four times |

Four subordinate shapes now appear horizontally beneath the Gordon Pedersen shape.

Step 3	Click	the Gordon Pedersen shape, if necessary
Step 4	Click	the Layout button on the Organization Chart toolbar
Step 5	Click	Left Hanging

The four shapes are now hanging below and to the left of the Gordon Pedersen shape. Your slide should look similar to Figure 9-3.

FIGURE 9-3
Left-Hanging Subordinate Shapes

(Screenshot showing Microsoft PowerPoint - [Teddy Toys Organization] with labels: Organization Chart toolbar, Superior shape, Subordinate shape, Left-hanging subordinates)

Quick Tip

You can move from shape to shape by pressing the CTRL + UP, DOWN, RIGHT, or LEFT arrow keys if the shape is selected. If you click in one box to edit, the arrow keys move you within the shape.

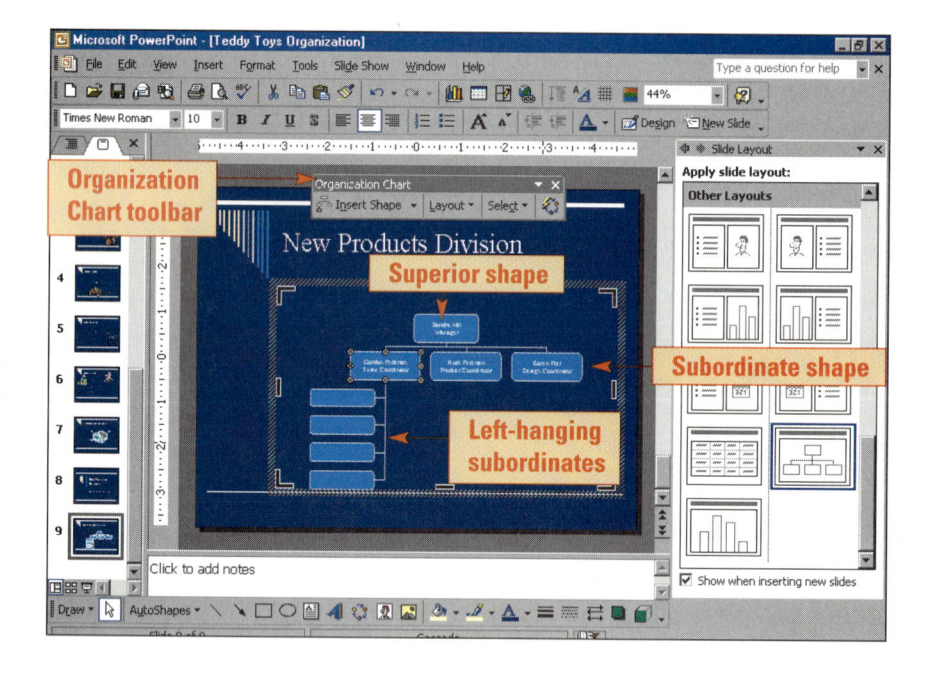

Step 6	Zoom	to 75% to key text more easily
Step 7	Click	the first newly added subordinate shape
Step 8	Key	Leslie Skylar
Step 9	Key	Juan Ortiz in the shape under Leslie Skylar
Step 10	Key	Ran Un in the shape under Juan Ortiz
Step 11	Key	Sara Jackson in the shape under Ran Un
Step 12	Select	the Ruth Pedersen subordinate shape

| Step 13 | Click | the Insert Shape button `Insert Shape` on the Organization Chart toolbar two times |

The two subordinate shapes appear below, both hanging side by side.

Step 14	Key	Roxie Rickens in the first new shape
Step 15	Key	Peter Surs in the second new shape
Step 16	Select	the Roxie Rickens subordinate shape
Step 17	Click	the Insert Shape button `Insert Shape` on the Organization Chart toolbar
Step 18	Key	New Position in the new shape
Step 19	Select	the Karen Peer subordinate shape
Step 20	Click	the Insert Shape button `Insert Shape` on the Organization Chart toolbar two times
Step 21	Click	the Layout button `Layout` on the Organization Chart toolbar
Step 22	Click	Right Hanging
Step 23	Key	Kari Harris in the first new shape
Step 24	Key	New Position in the second new shape
Step 25	Change	the zoom to 44%
Step 26	Run	the slide show from the current slide

The organization chart shows a top level, three subordinates, and third and fourth levels of subordinates displayed using various hanging effects. Your slide should look similar to Figure 9-4.

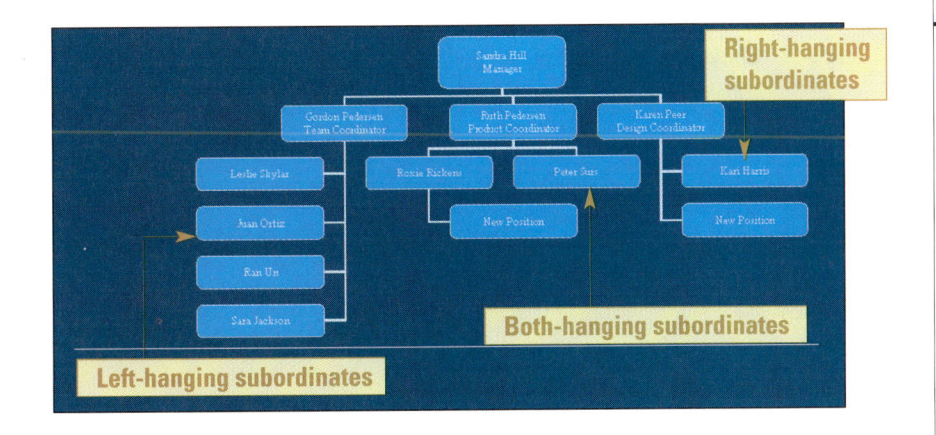

MOUSE TIP

You can add a subordinate, coworker or assistant by right-clicking the shape and then clicking Subordinate, Coworker, or Assistant.

QUICK TIP

You can end a slide show at any time by pressing the ESCAPE key.

FIGURE 9-4
New Products Division Organization Chart

Adding an Assistant Shape

An **assistant** reports directly to a given position and gives administrative assistance and advice to the person in that position. By default, assistant shapes do not automatically appear; they must be added. To add an assistant shape to an existing organization chart:

Step 1	Select	the superior shape (Sandra Hill)
Step 2	Click	the Insert Shape button list arrow [Insert Shape] on the Organization Chart toolbar
Step 3	Click	Assistant
Step 4	Key	Your Name in the Assistant shape
Step 5	Click	anywhere in the chart object to deselect the shape
Step 6	Save	the *Teddy Toys Organization* presentation

> **QUICK TIP**
>
> You can delete a shape in an organization chart by selecting the shape and pressing the DELETE key or by right-clicking the shape and then clicking Delete.

9.b Formatting an Organization Chart

You can format an organization chart by changing the look of one or more shapes in the chart (or all shapes at a particular level), lines that connect the shapes, the style of the organization chart layout, the alignment of text, the size of the organization chart, the color of the chart background, and the chart's position on the slide. If you want to format the shapes, shape styles, shape borders, text, color of text, alignment of text, style of chart, or any other element of the organization chart, you need to first select the chart, shape, shapes, or lines and then use the commands you use to format any object. To select the organization chart and format the font, font size, and connecting lines:

Step 1	Click	the drawing border of the organization chart to select the entire chart
Step 2	Click	the Font button list arrow [Comic Sans MS] on the Formatting toolbar
Step 3	Click	Comic Sans MS
Step 4	Click	the Font Size button list arrow [24] on the Formatting toolbar
Step 5	Click	16

> **MENU TIP**
>
> You can edit the text in a single shape of the organization chart by clicking the Text Object command on the Edit menu.

Working with Organization Charts and Diagrams **PA 9**

The text is too large for the shapes in the chart. You correct this later in the chapter.

Step 6	Click	the Sele**c**t button [Select ▾] on the Organization Chart toolbar
Step 7	Click	All **C**onnecting Lines
Step 8	Click	the Line Color button list arrow on the Drawing toolbar
Step 9	Click	the light yellow color (ScreenTip displays: Follow Shadows Scheme Color)

> **MOUSE TIP**
>
> You can edit the text in a single shape by right-clicking the shape and then clicking Edit Te**x**t.

Applying a Chart AutoFormat

AutoFormats are predesigned formatting combinations for shapes, fill colors, lines, and/or shadows within an organization chart. Using an AutoFormat can speed the formatting process because it saves you from having to format many individual elements separately. The Organization Chart Style Gallery provides 16 different AutoFormats including a Default style. To change the style of the organization chart using the AutoFormat button:

| Step 1 | Click | the AutoFormat button on the Organization Chart toolbar |

The Organization Chart Style Gallery dialog box on your screen should look similar to Figure 9-5.

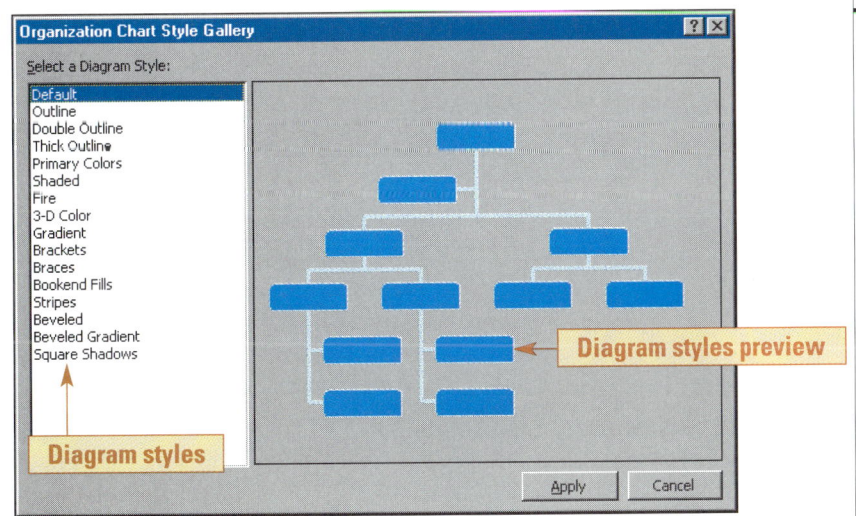

FIGURE 9-5
Organization Chart Style Gallery Dialog Box

> **DESIGN TIP**
>
> Break long lines of text into two lines of text to prevent text from being too small to read by pressing the ENTER key after desired words.

| Step 2 | Click | Gradient |

chapter nine

QUICK TIP

You can select multiple shapes within an organization chart by pressing and holding the CTRL key or the SHIFT key as you click the desired shapes or by using the Sele_c_t button on the Organization Chart toolbar.

Step 3	Click	Apply
Step 4	Observe	the changes to the color of the shapes and lines of the chart
Step 5	Repeat	Steps 1 through 4 for each available AutoFormat
Step 6	Apply	Default style to the chart

Changing Shape and Text Colors

You can change the fill color of one or more shapes in a chart. Because an organization chart is typically used to show hierarchical structure within an organization, you need to consider levels and branches when selecting multiple shapes for formatting. Formatting shapes within an organization chart can help distinguish a **level**, shapes of equal position within an organization, or a **branch**, shapes representing a functional group within the hierarchy (finance, manufacturing, marketing, or administration). In addition, shape colors can be changed to enhance the appearance of the slide, aid in readability, or just to satisfy personal preferences. To select multiple shapes and format them:

Step 1	Click	the Gordon Pedersen shape in the second level
Step 2	Click	the Sele_c_t button [Select ▼] on the Organization Chart toolbar
Step 3	Click	_L_evel to select all three shapes at this level
Step 4	Click	the Fill Color button list arrow [icon] on the Drawing toolbar
Step 5	Click	the light yellow (ScreenTip displays: Follow Shadows Scheme Color)

MOUSE TIP

You can change the color of shapes by right-clicking any shape, clicking Format Aut_o_Shape, clicking the Fill _C_olor list arrow, and then clicking the desired color.

You can change the border color and style of a shape by right-clicking the shape, clicking Format Aut_o_Shape, clicking the Line C_o_lor or Line _S_tyle list arrows, and then clicking a specific color or style.

If you make changes to the look of the shapes that were originally determined by the presentation design, you may need to make changes to the text within the shapes. In the level of the chart you just changed, for example, the shape text is somewhat difficult to read against the lighter color. Formatting shape text is similar to formatting other slide text. To change shape text color for the selected shapes:

Step 1	Click	the Font Color button list arrow [icon] on the Drawing toolbar
Step 2	Click	the dark blue color (ScreenTip displays: Follow Background Scheme Color)
Step 3	Run	the slide show from the current slide
Step 4	Observe	the changes in the connecting lines and the level-three shapes

Changing Shadow Style

Adding a shadow style to a shape creates a 3-D effect that helps the shape stand out. To add a different shadow effect to the top of shapes:

Step 1	Select	the Sandra Hill shape
Step 2	Click	the Sele<u>c</u>t button [Select ▼] on the Organization Chart toolbar
Step 3	Click	<u>B</u>ranch
Step 4	Click	the Shadow Style button [■] on the Drawing toolbar
Step 5	Click	Shadow Style 1 (first row, first column)

Resizing and Moving an Organization Chart

Depending on the size of the organization chart, it may be necessary to resize it to fit attractively on a slide. Before resizing, the chart object must be selected. Once selected, you can use the <u>L</u>ayout button on the Organization Chart toolbar to <u>F</u>it Organization Chart to its Contents (decrease the size of the chart object to fit the shapes), <u>E</u>xpand Organization Chart (increase the size of the chart object), or S<u>c</u>ale Organization Chart (increase or decrease the chart object and the shapes) using any one of the sizing handles. To resize an organization chart object using the <u>L</u>ayout button on the Organization Chart toolbar:

Step 1	Select	the organization chart object, if necessary
Step 2	Click	the <u>L</u>ayout button [Layout ▼] on the Organization Chart toolbar
Step 3	Click	<u>F</u>it Organization Chart to Contents
Step 4	Click	the <u>L</u>ayout button [Layout ▼] on the Organization Chart toolbar
Step 5	Click	S<u>c</u>ale Organization Chart
Step 6	Drag	the top middle circle on the selection border up approximately 1 inch
Step 7	Point to	the chart's selection border
Step 8	Drag	the chart to the center of the slide
Step 9	Observe	that the font size changes as the chart is resized
Step 10	Run	the slide show from the current slide

CAUTION TIP

Once you have applied the <u>F</u>it Organization Chart to Contents option, you can then resize an organization chart and its shapes using the S<u>c</u>ale Organization Chart option. However, if after resizing the organization chart you click outside the chart, you must click the S<u>c</u>ale Organization Chart option again to make additional changes.

QUICK TIP

Holding down the CTRL key while dragging sizes the object vertically, horizontally, or diagonally from the center of the slide. If you want to maintain the proportion of the chart object and its shapes, drag a corner sizing handle when you scale the chart.

chapter nine

Your slide should look similar to Figure 9-6.

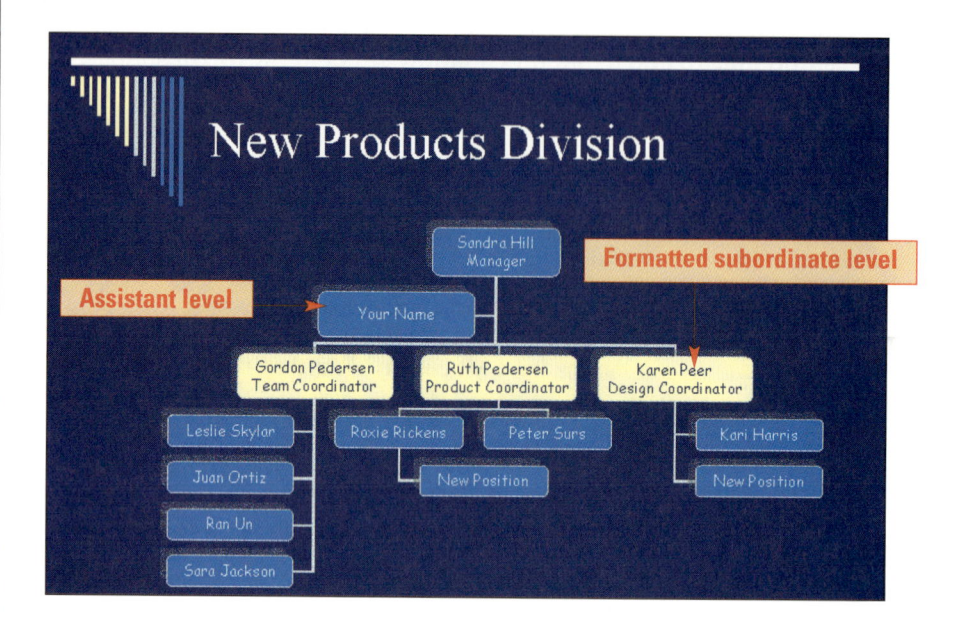

FIGURE 9-6
Resized and Repositioned Organization Chart

[Figure 9-6: Organization chart slide titled "New Products Division" showing Sandra Hill (Manager) at top, with "Your Name" as Assistant level, and three coordinators below: Gordon Pedersen (Team Coordinator), Ruth Pedersen (Product Coordinator), and Karen Peer (Design Coordinator) as Formatted subordinate level. Under Gordon: Leslie Skylar, Juan Ortiz, Ran Un, Sara Jackson. Under Ruth: Roxie Rickens, Peter Surs, New Position. Under Karen: Kari Harris, New Position.]

CAUTION TIP

Whenever you make editing or formatting changes that affect the size or number of shapes in the chart, the size of the chart automatically adjusts. You may need to resize a chart again after making additional formatting changes.

| Step 11 | Save | the *Teddy Toys Organization* presentation |

9.c Adding a Diagram Slide

Diagrams are used to add visual variety to your slides while illustrating conceptual ideas. The intent is to provide information in a manner that is interesting and can be comprehended and retained easily by those viewing the chart. PowerPoint enables you to create Cycle, Target, Radial, Venn, and Pyramid diagrams. You use a **Cycle diagram** to show a process that has a continuous cycle, such as managerial tasks that involve planning, organizing, leading, and control. You use a **Target diagram** to show the required steps that lead toward fulfilling a goal, such as obtaining information via a process of input, processing, output, and storage. You use a **Radial diagram** to show relationships of elements to a central element, such as a product and what is involved in the making of that product. You use a **Venn diagram** to show how areas or elements overlap, such as various degree programs at a college that overlap in the area of technology. You use a **Pyramid diagram** to show foundation-based relationships, such as how the hierarchy of an organization relates down to the nonmanagement, clerical, and production workers (one down to many).

To create a Radial diagram on a new slide:

TASK PANE TIP

You can create a diagram by clicking the New Slide command on the Insert menu and then clicking the any Content Layout or the Title and Diagram or Organization Chart layout in the Slide Layout task pane.

| Step 1 | Display | Slide 9, if necessary |

Working with Organization Charts and Diagrams PA 13

Step 2	Click	the <u>N</u>ew Slide button [New Slide] on the Formatting toolbar
Step 3	Click	the Title and Content layout in the Slide Layout task pane

A new slide appears with title and content placeholders. Your screen should look similar to Figure 9-7. The content placeholder contains icons for inserting a table, chart, clip art, picture, diagram or organization chart, or media clip to the slide.

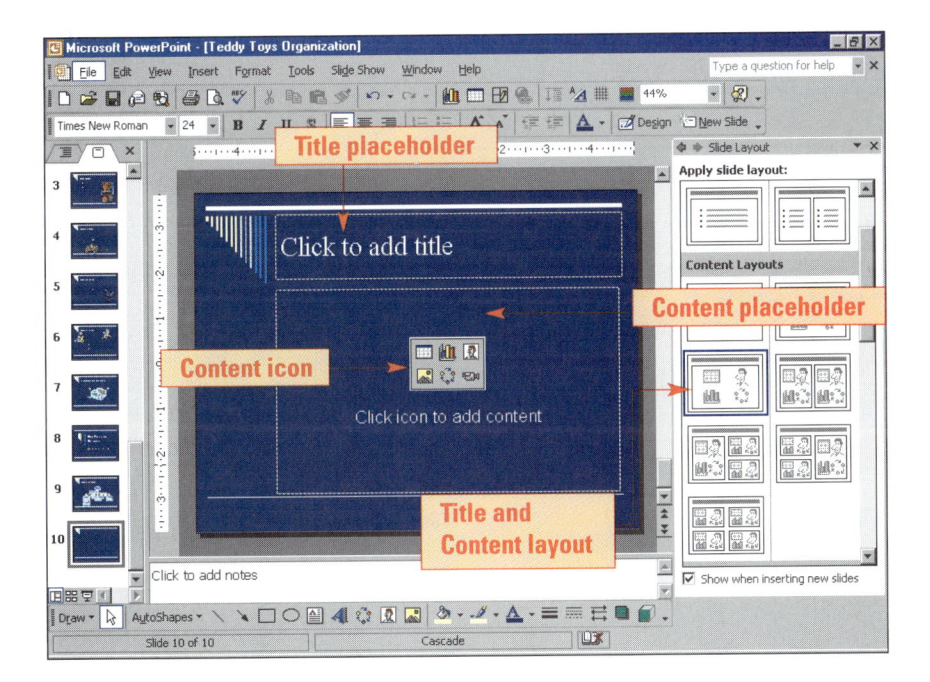

FIGURE 9-7
Slide with Content Placeholder

> **MOUSE TIP**
>
> You can create a diagram or an organization chart by clicking the <u>N</u>ew Slide button on the Formatting toolbar and then clicking the Insert Diagram or Organi<u>z</u>ation tool on the Drawing toolbar.

Creating a Diagram and Entering Information

The process of entering information in a diagram is similar to entering information in other slide elements: you key data in the placeholders. A default diagram consists of a core shape and three relationship shapes. Each shape has placeholders. The **core shape** is for the central position in a company, division, department, product, or concept. The **relationship shapes** are the shapes for divisions, departments, products, or concepts that relate to the core shape. To enter a title and diagram information:

Step 1	Key	Teddy Toys' Success Factors as the title
Step 2	Click	the Insert Diagram or Organization Chart button on the Content icon
Step 3	Double-click	the Radial Diagram example (first row, third column)

chapter nine

> **MOUSE TIP**
>
> You can add a shape to a diagram by right-clicking any shape and then clicking Insert Shape.
>
> You can add text to a shape in a diagram by right-clicking the shape and then clicking Edit Text.

A default Radial diagram displays within a drawing border with sizing handles, and the Diagram toolbar opens. The drawing border is a nonprinting border that lets you resize the diagram by dragging the sizing handles. The Diagram toolbar contains seven buttons: Insert Shape, Move Shape Backward, Move Shape Forward, Reverse Diagram, Layout, AutoFormat, and Change to. The Insert Shape button enables you to add relationship shapes. The Move Shape Backward and Move Shape Forward buttons enable you to move shapes forward and backward within the diagram. The Reverse Diagram button enables you to reverse shapes (move from one side to another). The Layout button enables you to change the size of the diagram. The AutoFormat button enables you to change the style of any given diagram. The Change to button enables you to change the type of diagram.

Step 4	Click	the core shape in the middle of the diagram, if necessary, to select it
Step 5	Key	Teddy (press the ENTER key) Toys
Step 6	Click	the relationship shape at the top of the core shape
Step 7	Key	Mfg.
Step 8	Click	the relationship shape at the lower right of the core shape
Step 9	Key	Marketing
Step 10	Click	the relationship shape at the lower left of the core shape
Step 11	Key	Sales

Adding Additional Relationships to a Diagram

The process of adding additional shapes to a Radial diagram, or any diagram, is similar to adding a subordinate shape to the superior in an organization chart, except that you do not have to select a shape first. All relationship shapes are added to the core shape. To add three relationship shapes to the core shape:

> **QUICK TIP**
>
> You can delete a shape in a diagram by selecting the shape and pressing the DELETE key, or by right-clicking the shape and then clicking Delete Shape.

Step 1	Click	the Insert Shape button [Insert Shape] on the Diagram toolbar four times
Step 2	Key	New (press the ENTER key) Products in the relationship shape to the left of the Mfg. shape
Step 3	Key	Distrib. in the shape under New Products
Step 4	Key	Admin. in the shape under Distribution

| Step 5 | **Key** | Finance in the shape to the right of Admin. |
| Step 6 | **Run** | the slide show from the current slide |

Your slide should look similar to Figure 9-8.

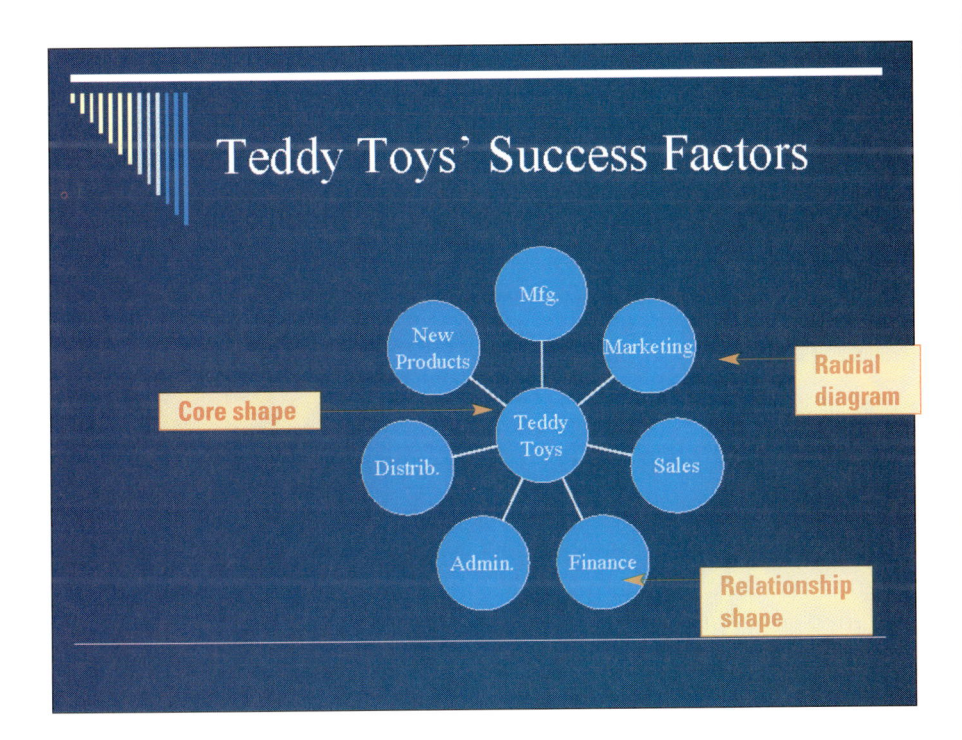

FIGURE 9-8
Radial Diagram

[Diagram: "Teddy Toys' Success Factors" radial diagram with Teddy Toys as the core shape and surrounding shapes: Mfg., Marketing, Sales, Finance, Admin., Distrib., New Products. Labels point to "Core shape," "Radial diagram," and "Relationship shape."]

9.d Formatting a Diagram

You can format a diagram using preset styles or by formatting individual elements. You can change the arrangement and/or look of one or more shapes in the diagram; the color, size, and style of the lines that connect the shapes; the alignment of text; the size of the diagram; the color of the background; and the diagram's position on the slide.

The Diagram toolbar displays three buttons for rearranging selected shapes in a diagram: Move Shape Backward (counterclockwise), Move Shape Forward (clockwise), and Reverse Diagram (flip shapes horizontally). To change the position of the shapes:

Step 1	**Click**	the New Products shape
Step 2	**Click**	the Move Shape Backward button twice
Step 3	**Observe**	that the New Products shape moves two places counterclockwise in the diagram

QUICK TIP

If you want to format the shapes, shape styles, shape borders, text, color of text, alignment of text, style of diagram, or any other element of the diagram, you need to first select the diagram, shape, shapes, or lines and then use the commands you use to format any object.

chapter nine

| Step 4 | *Click* | the Move Shape Forward button until the New Products shape is at the top |

Applying a Diagram AutoFormat

AutoFormats are predesigned formatting combinations for shapes, fill colors, lines, and/or shadows within a diagram. Using an AutoFormat can speed the formatting process because it saves you from having to format many individual elements separately. The Diagram Style Gallery provides 10 different AutoFormats including a Default style. To change the style of the diagram using the AutoFormat button:

| Step 1 | *Click* | the AutoFormat button on the Diagram toolbar |
| Step 2 | *Double-click* | Gradient |

Changing the Diagram Type

In addition to an organization chart, you can select from five other diagrams to illustrate different conceptual ideas. Once created, any diagram type can be changed to a diagram that may better reflect the intended concept being projected. The Change to button on the Diagram toolbar enables you to quickly change from one diagram type to another. To change the type of diagram:

Step 1	*Click*	the Change to button on the Diagram toolbar
Step 2	*Click*	Cycle to view the Cycle diagram
Step 3	*Click*	the Change to button on the Diagram toolbar
Step 4	*Click*	Pyramid to view the Pyramid diagram
Step 5	*Change*	the diagram to Venn
Step 6	*Change*	the diagram to Target
Step 7	*Change*	the diagram to Radial
Step 8	*Click*	the drawing border of the diagram, if necessary
Step 9	*Click*	the Font Color button list arrow on the Drawing toolbar
Step 10	*Click*	the dark blue color (ScreenTip displays: Follow Background Scheme Color)

Formatting Individual Elements of a Diagram

Formatting of individual elements within a diagram is accomplished by selecting the element and formatting as you would any shape or object. However, if you applied an AutoFormat to a diagram at a prior point (as you did when you applied the Gradient AutoFormat), you must first turn off the AutoFormat feature before attempting to manually format any individual element. To remove AutoFormat and format the core shape:

Step 1	*Right-click*	the drawing border of the diagram
Step 2	*Click*	to remove the check mark in front of Use AutoFormat
Step 3	*Select*	the Teddy Toys core shape
Step 4	*Click*	the Fill Color button list arrow on the Drawing toolbar
Step 5	*Click*	Fill Effects
Step 6	*Click*	the Color 2: list arrow
Step 7	*Click*	the pale yellow color (ScreenTip displays: Follow Shadows Scheme Color)
Step 8	*Click*	the From center Shading style
Step 9	*Click*	the variant on the right
Step 10	*Click*	OK
Step 11	*Select*	the Diagram
Step 12	*Change*	the font to Comic Sans MS and the font size to 16

> **DESIGN TIP**
>
> You can make the core shape of a Radial diagram stand out from the relationship shapes by changing its text and fill formatting.

Resizing and Moving a Diagram

Depending on the size of the diagram, it may be necessary to resize it to fit attractively on the PowerPoint slide. You can use the Layout button on the Diagram toolbar to Fit Diagram to Contents (decrease the size of the chart object to fit the shapes), Expand Diagram (increase the size of the chart object), or Scale Diagram (increase or decrease the chart object and the shapes) using any one of the sizing handles. If you want to maintain the proportion of the chart object and its shapes, drag a corner sizing handle when you scale the diagram. To resize a diagram object using the Layout button on the Diagram toolbar:

Step 1	*Select*	the Diagram, if necessary
Step 2	*Click*	the Layout button on the Diagram toolbar

Step 3	Click	Fit Diagram to Contents
Step 4	Click	the Layout button [Layout ▼] on the Diagram toolbar
Step 5	Click	Scale Diagram
Step 6	Drag	a corner sizing handle on the drawing border approximately 1 inch larger
Step 7	Point to	the chart's drawing border
Step 8	Drag	the diagram object to the center of the slide
Step 9	Change	the font size as needed so all the text fits inside the shapes
Step 10	Run	the slide show from the current slide

Your slide should look similar to Figure 9-9.

FIGURE 9-9
Completed Radial Slide

Repositioned diagram

Formatted relationship shape

CAUTION TIP

Once you have applied the Fit Diagram to Contents option, you can then resize a diagram and its shapes using the Scale Diagram option. However, if after resizing the diagram you click outside the object, you must click the Scale Diagram option again to make additional changes.

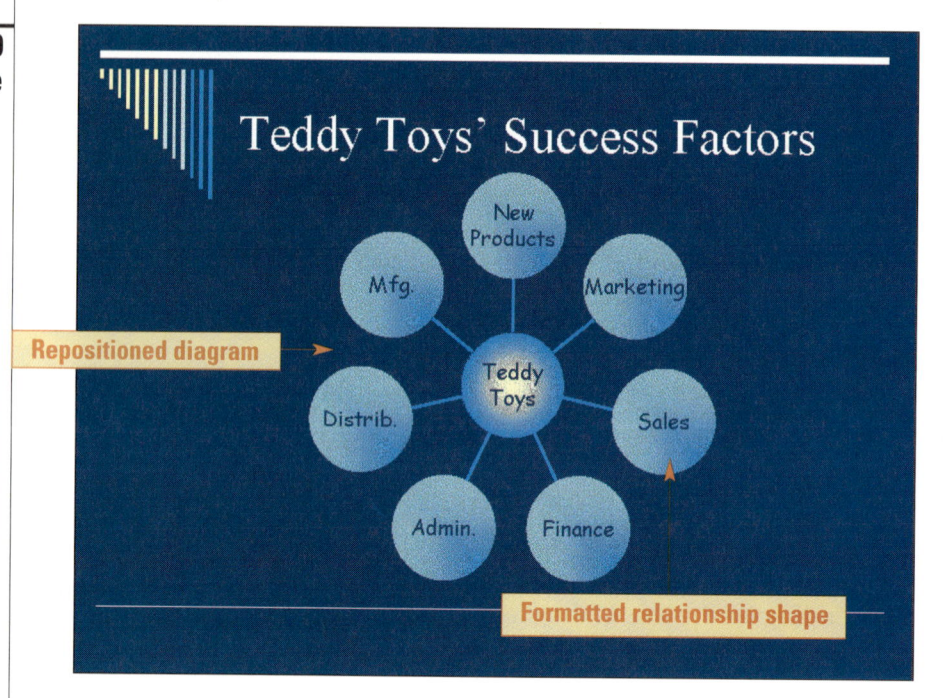

| Step 11 | Save | the *Teddy Toys Organization* presentation and close it |

The diagram is attractively formatted, sized, and positioned on the slide.

Summary

- Organization charts are graphical representations of the hierarchical reporting relationships within an organization.
- Before making editing or formatting changes to any elements in an organization chart or diagram, such as text or shapes, you must first select that element.
- Each shape in an organization chart can contain multiple lines of data.
- The process of entering information in a shape within an organization chart is the same as entering text in any text placeholder.
- Organization charts in PowerPoint display within a drawing border that contains sizing handles.
- In an organization chart or other diagram, you can change shape colors, text, borders, and font style to enhance readability.
- Additional subordinate shapes can be added to the superior shape and subordinate shapes within an organization chart.
- Formatting changes involving shape styles, shape borders, color of text, alignment of text, and style of chart can be made to any shape of the organization chart.
- You can resize, change the fill color, and add lines around the shapes.
- Diagrams are used to add visual variety to slides while illustrating conceptual ideas.
- A Cycle diagram shows a process that has a continuous cycle, such as managerial tasks that involve planning, organizing, leading, and control.
- A Target diagram shows the required steps that lead toward fulfilling a goal, such as obtaining information via a process of input, processing, output, and storage.
- A Radial diagram shows relationships of elements to a central element, such as a product and what is involved in the making of that product.
- A Venn diagram shows how areas or elements overlap, such as various degree programs at a college that overlap in the area of technology.
- A Pyramid diagram is used to show foundation-based relationships, such as how the hierarchy of an organization relates down to the non-management, clerical, and production workers (one down to many).

chapter nine

Commands Review

Action	Menu Bar	Shortcut Menu	Toolbar	Task Pane	Keyboard
Add an organization chart	Insert, Picture, Organization Chart			Click Title and Diagram or Organization Chart in the SlideLayout task pane under Other Layouts; click Insert Diagram or Organization Chart icon on placeholder on any content layout	ALT + I, P, O
Edit a selected chart shape	Edit, Text Object	Right-click shape, Edit Text			ALT + E, O
Add a subordinate for the selected shape		Right-click shape, Subordinate	Insert Shape		
Add a coworker for the selected shape		Right-click shape, Coworker	Insert Shape		
Add an assistant for the selected shape		Right-click shape, Assistant	Insert Shape		
Delete a selected shape		Right-click shape, Delete or Delete Shape			DELETE
Select specific levels		Right-click the selected shape, Select	Select		SHIFT + Click each box; or CTRL + Click
Change selected shape(s) fill color	Format, AutoShape, Color	Right-click selected shape(s), Format AutoShape, Color or double-click selected shape			ALT + O, O, C
Change organization chart style			Layout		
Change organization shape style					
Change border of shapes	Format, AutoShape, Style	Right-click selected shape(s), Format AutoShape, Style or double-click selected shape			ALT + O, O, S
Change shape text color	Format, Font, Color				ALT + O, F, C
Change shape text font	Format, Font		Comic Sans MS		ALT + O, F
Add a diagram	Insert, Diagram			Click Title and Diagram or Organization Chart in the Slide Layout task pane under Other Layouts; click Insert Diagram or Organization Chart icon on placeholder on any content layout	ALT + I, G
Add shapes to a diagram		Right-click shape, Insert Shape	Insert Shape		
Arrange shapes in a diagram					
Change diagram style			Change to		
Change diagram shapes					

Concepts Review

Circle the correct answer.

1. **The vice president of a corporation would be on what level of an organization chart that included all employees in positions of authority?**
   - [a] superior
   - [b] subordinate
   - [c] coworker
   - [d] assistant

2. **To add an organization chart to a slide, click the:**
   - [a] Organization Chart button on the Standard toolbar.
   - [b] Organization Chart button on the Formatting toolbar.
   - [c] Insert Diagram or Organization Chart button on the Drawing toolbar.
   - [d] Object command on the Edit menu.

3. **When creating an organization chart, consider all of the following *except*:**
   - [a] using at least three but no more than twenty shapes in the chart.
   - [b] breaking long lines of text into two lines of text to prevent text from being too small to read.
   - [c] choosing a different color for each individual shape of the organization chart.
   - [d] choosing a shape color that complements your presentation design colors.

4. **To format any shape in an organization chart:**
   - [a] select the organization chart object.
   - [b] select the shape you want to format.
   - [c] click the Layout button, then click Insert Shape.
   - [d] click the Change to button on the Organization Chart toolbar.

5. **To add a subordinate shape to the organization chart:**
   - [a] right-click the chart object and then click Insert, Object.
   - [b] double-click the organization chart object and click Insert Shape.
   - [c] select the shape to receive the subordinate and click Insert Shape.
   - [d] select the shape to receive the subordinate and click the Subordinate button on the Organization Chart toolbar.

6. **To show the required steps that lead toward fulfilling a goal, you would use a:**
   - [a] Cycle diagram.
   - [b] Target diagram.
   - [c] Radial diagram.
   - [d] Venn diagram.

7. **Which of the following statements is not true?**
   - [a] Organization charts are graphic illustrations of the hierarchy within an organization.
   - [b] Organization charts usually use lines to connect shapes.
   - [c] Organization charts always display rectangular shapes.
   - [d] You may create multiple levels and multiple positions in an organization chart.

8. **To format text within shapes of a diagram:**
   - [a] double-click the shape(s), then click Font.
   - [b] select the shape(s), click Format, then click Font.
   - [c] select the shape(s), click the Fill Color tool on the Drawing toolbar.
   - [d] right-click the shape(s), then click Format Text.

9. **To maintain the proportions (height and width ratio) of an object when resizing, you need to:**
   - [a] drag any sizing handle.
   - [b] press and hold the ALT + CTRL keys while dragging a middle sizing handle.
   - [c] press and hold the SHIFT key while dragging a middle sizing handle.
   - [d] drag the chart object to the right.

10. **To move shapes within a diagram:**
    - [a] select the shape and drag it to a new location.
    - [b] right-click the shape, click Move Forward.
    - [c] select the shape and click Change to, and then change the position.
    - [d] select the shape and click the Move Shape Backward or Move Shape Forward button.

chapter nine

Circle **T** if the statement is true or **F** if the statement is false.

T F 1. An organization chart is a graphical arrangement of shapes showing the personnel structure of a company or other hierarchical relationships within a given entity.

T F 2. The shapes in an organization chart are usually connected by lines.

T F 3. Assistant shapes can only report to superior shapes.

T F 4. There can be multiple superior shapes in any organization chart.

T F 5. The more shapes you can add to your organization chart the better.

T F 6. You can make changes to an entire organization chart, to individual shapes of the chart, or to each level of the chart.

T F 7. Diagrams are used to add visual variety to slides while illustrating conceptual ideas.

T F 8. Venn diagrams are used to show how the hierarchy of an organization relates down to the nonmanagement, clerical, and production workers.

T F 9. In a diagram or an organization chart, the border refers to a line around the selected object or objects.

T F 10. You can change the appearance of text in the shapes of a diagram or an organization chart by using a command on the F*o*rmat menu.

Skills Review

Exercise 1

1. Open the *PowerPoint Advanced* presentation located on the Data Disk, and save it as *PowerPoint Organization*.
2. Add a new slide for an organization chart at the end of the presentation with the title "PowerPoint Augments Presentations."
3. Complete the organization chart using the information as shown in the following table:

SHAPE TEXT	LEVEL
PowerPoint	First Level
Handouts	Second Level
Notes Pages	Second Level
Slides	Second Level
Outlines	Second Level

4. Change the color of the shapes to the orange color (ScreenTip displays: Follow Title Text Scheme Color).
5. Add the Shadow Style 5 shadow effect in the second row, first column to all the shapes.
6. Change the color of the text in the shapes to the blue color in the first row, first column.
7. Change the text in the shapes to Bold.
8. Change the color of the connecting lines to the orange color in the first row, fourth column and change the line weight to 1 point. (*Hint:* Be sure the AutoFormat feature is turned off by right-clicking the chart area and removing the Use A*u*toFormat check mark.)
9. Spell check and proofread the presentation.

Working with Organization Charts and Diagrams   PA 23

10. Scale and reposition the organization chart.

11. Save the presentation, print the organization chart slide, and then close the presentation.

Exercise 2

1. Open the *Office Advanced* presentation located on the Data Disk, and save it as *Office Organization*.

2. Add a new slide for an organization chart at the end of the presentation with the title "Office XP."

3. Complete the organization chart using the information in the following table:

SHAPE TEXT	LEVEL
Minimum System (press the ENTER key) *Requirements*	First Level
Chip	Second Level
RAM	Second Level
Hard Drive	Second Level
Operating (press the ENTER key) *System*	Second Level

4. Edit the organization chart by adding an additional level and shapes and using the information in the following table: (*Hint:* Be sure the AutoFormat feature is turned on by right-clicking the chart area and clicking Use AutoFormat.)

SHAPE TEXT	LEVEL	REPORTS TO
x86	Third Level	Chip
32 MB	Third Level	RAM
350 MB	Third Level	Hard Drive
Windows 98	Third Level	Operating System

5. Using the AutoFormat button on the Organization Chart toolbar, select the 3-D Color style.

6. Change the text for all the shapes to Times New Roman and 20 point.

7. Spell check and proofread the presentation.

8. Save the presentation, print the organization chart slide, and then close the presentation.

Exercise 3

1. Open the *Design Advanced* presentation located on the Data Disk, and save it as *Design Organization*.

2. Add a new slide for a Radial diagram at the end of the presentation with the title "Presentation Design."

3. Complete the Radial diagram using the information in the following table:

SHAPE TEXT	LEVEL
Good Design	Core Shape
Objective	Relationship Shape
Audience	Relationship Shape
Medium	Relationship Shape

chapter nine

4. Add the following relationship shapes for the Good Design core shape:

SHAPE TEXT	LEVEL
Tone	Relationship Shape
Color	Relationship Shape
Typeface	Relationship Shape
Size	Relationship Shape

5. Reverse the relationship shapes. (*Hint:* Use the Reverse Diagram button on the Diagram toolbar.)
6. Access the Diagram Style Gallery dialog box, and change the style to Gradient.
7. Change the text color within the shapes to dark green.
8. Bold the text in the core shape.
9. Spell check and proofread the presentation.
10. Save the presentation, print the Radial diagram slide, and then close the presentation.

Exercise 4

1. Open the *Precision Builders Advanced* presentation located on the Data Disk, and save it as *Precision Builders Organization*.
2. Add a new slide for a Cycle diagram at the end of the presentation with the title "Construction Process."
3. Complete the Cycle diagram using the information in the table below, keying data in the text boxes following the shapes in a clockwise direction:

SHAPE TEXT
Create (press the ENTER key) *Architectural* (press the ENTER key) *Blueprints*
Organize (press the ENTER key) *Material* (press the ENTER key) *& Labor*
Create (press the ENTER key) *Construction* (press the ENTER key) *Schedule*

4. Edit the Cycle diagram to add the information after the Create Construction Schedule shape and in a clockwise direction:

SHAPE TEXT
Supervise (press the ENTER key) *Construction*
Final (press the ENTER key) *Customer* (press the ENTER key) *Approval*

5. Access the Diagram Style Gallery, and change the style of the Cycle diagram to Fire.
6. Make any adjustments necessary to improve the appearance of the chart.

Working with Organization Charts and Diagrams PA 25

7. Select all text shapes, and use the Bring to Front subcommand of the Order command on the Draw menu to bring the text in front of the shapes.

8. Bold all the text shapes and change the font to 16-point Arial Narrow.

9. Spell check and proofread the presentation.

10. Save the presentation, print the Cycle diagram slide, and then close the presentation.

Exercise 5

1. Open the *Nature Tours Advanced* presentation located on the Data Disk, and save it as *Nature Tours Organization*.

2. Add an organization chart slide at the end of the presentation with the title "The Bottom Line."

3. Complete the organization chart using the information in the following table:

SHAPE TEXT	LEVEL
Proper (press the ENTER key) *Footwear*	Superior
Hiking Boots	Subordinate
Biking Shoes	Subordinate

4. Delete the remaining subordinate shape.

5. Edit the organization chart by adding the following subordinate positions to the subordinates Hiking Boots and Biking Shoes:

SHAPE TEXT	LEVEL	REPORTS TO
Full Grain (press the ENTER key) *Leather*	Subordinate Third Level	Hiking
Minimal (Press the ENTER key) *Seams*	Subordinate Third Level	Hiking
Good (press the ENTER key) *Soles*	Subordinate Third Level	Hiking
Lightweight	Subordinate Third Level	Biking
Stiff Soles	Subordinate Third Level	Biking

6. Access the Organization Chart Style Gallery, and select the Beveled Gradient style.

7. Change the text of all shapes to the yellow color in the Fill Color dialog box (Follow Title Text Scheme Color) and 16 point.

8. Change the text of the Superior shape to 18 point.

9. Make any other adjustments necessary to improve the appearance of the chart.

10. Spell check and proofread the presentation.

11. Scale and reposition the organization chart.

12. Save the presentation, print the organization chart slide, and then close the presentation.

chapter nine

Exercise 6

1. Open the *A Healthier You Advanced* presentation located on the Data Disk, and save it as *A Healthier You Organization*.
2. Add a Venn diagram slide at the end of the presentation with the title "Sources of Daily Water Intake."
3. Complete the Venn diagram using the information in the following table (you may have to look outside the shapes—left, right, above, below—for the text boxes that accompany the shapes):

SHAPE TEXT
Drinking Water (press the ENTER key)   100%
Milk (press the ENTER key)   8%
Meat (press the ENTER key)   40% – 75%
Vegetables (press the ENTER key)   93%

4. Make any style changes you desire.
5. Make any text changes you desire, such as font size, color, and style.
6. Using the Move Shape Forward or Move Shape Backward button, rearrange the shapes in order of the percentage of water composition (100%, 93%, 40%–75%, 8% respectively).
7. Resize the chart for readability, if necessary.
8. Make any adjustments necessary to improve the appearance of the chart.
9. Spell check and proofread the presentation.
10. Save the presentation, print the Venn diagram slide, and then close the presentation.

Exercise 7

1. Open the *Buying A Computer Advanced* presentation located on the Data Disk, and save it as *Buying A Computer Organization*.
2. Add a Radial diagram slide at the end of the presentation with the title "Computer Information."
3. Complete the Radial diagram using the information in the following table:

SHAPE TEXT	LEVEL
Sources	Core Shape
Friends	Relationship Shape
Magazines	Relationship Shape
Internet	Relationship Shape
Stores	Relationship Shape

4. Choose a different Radial diagram style.
5. Turn off the AutoFormatting feature, and make changes to the individual shapes.
6. Make changes to the thickness and color of the connecting lines.
7. Change the look of the shapes (gradients, shadows, etc.), if desired.
8. Change the typeface of the text, and resize the text in the shapes.

9. Change the color of the text, if necessary.
10. Rearrange the shapes by moving the shapes or reversing the shapes.
11. Make any additional adjustments necessary to improve the appearance of the chart.
12. Spell check and proofread the presentation.
13. Save the presentation, print the Radial diagram slide, and then close the presentation.

Exercise 8

1. Open the *Leisure Travel Advanced* presentation located on the Data Disk, and save it as *Leisure Travel Organization*.
2. Add an organization chart slide at the end of it with the title "Canada's Splendor."
3. Complete the organization chart using the information in the following table:

SHAPE TEXT	LEVEL
Canada's(press the ENTER key) *Rivers*	Superior
Tatshensine	Subordinate
Alsek	Subordinate
Yukon	Subordinate

4. Edit the organization chart by adding an additional level and shapes and using the information in the following table: (*Hint:* Be sure the AutoFormat feature is turned on by right-clicking the chart area and clicking Use AutoFormat.)

SUBORDINATE LEVEL 2	SUBORDINATE LEVEL 3	SUBORDINATE LEVEL 3	SUBORDINATE LEVEL 3	SUBORDINATE LEVEL 3
Tatshensine	*Canoeing*	*Kayaking*		
Alsek	*Fishing*	*Hiking*		
Yukon	*Canoeing*	*Kayaking*	*Fishing*	*Hiking*

5. Access the Organization Chart Style Gallery, and determine a new style or keep the default style.
6. Change the Organization Chart layout for the third level to left hanging or right hanging.
7. Change the color of the shapes to complement the presentation design colors.
8. Change the text font, color, and size, if necessary for readability.
9. Change the connecting lines to a color that complements the shape color.
10. Make any adjustments necessary to improve the appearance of the chart.
11. Spell check and proofread the presentation.
12. Save the presentation, print the organization chart slide, and then close the presentation.

Case Projects

Project 1

You pride yourself on being able to create the various slide types in PowerPoint. Having recently created organization charts and diagrams, you decide to learn as much as you can about the various chart types that can be created in PowerPoint. Using online Help, display and print information on the various chart types.

chapter nine

Project 2

The director of the Human Resources Department likes the variety of slide types you used in the *Communicate Advanced* presentation. She asks, however, that you add an organization chart to the end of the presentation that displays the same information presently on the table slide of the presentation. She believes an organization chart would better display the correct and incorrect actions to use when dealing with irate customers. Consider adding a coworker to the superior position to set up the correct and incorrect actions. Then add two to four subordinates to each defining the actions. After completing the organization chart slide, make any adjustments to shapes, text, or size that are necessary to aid readability. Save the presentation as *Communicate Organization*, and print the organization chart slide.

Project 3

Several people who have seen your *Souner Advanced* presentation suggest that you create a organization chart slide that provides information about the hierarchy of the training corporation.

Include the president, sales manager, training manager, and several trainer positions in the organization chart. After completing the organization chart slide, make any adjustments necessary to aid readability. Be sure to spell check the presentation. Save the presentation as *Souner Organization*, and print the organization chart slide.

Project 4

To reinforce what you have been learning, you decide to create an organization chart slide for *My Presentation Advanced* that provides information on the structure of your organization. After completing the organization chart slide, make any adjustments necessary to aid readability. Be sure to spell check the presentation. Save the presentation as *My Presentation Organization*, and print the organization chart slide.

Project 5

The zoo is very proud of their new ape house. You want to add a diagram to the *Zoo Advanced* presentation to display what people will see in the ape house. The core shape can identify the ape house, and the relationship shapes can display the residents. Make any formatting decisions with regard to shape colors, line styles, and shadows, as well as text typeface, size, and color. If possible, make some changes to the style of the diagram that aid layout, size, and readability. Be sure to spell check the presentation. Save the presentation as *Zoo Organization*, and print the diagram slide.

Project 6

You want to be creative in how you use the chart types in your presentations. Connect to the Internet and search the Web for examples of organization charts and diagrams. Create an organization chart or diagram slide that displays the various ways in which organization chart or diagrams were used in your search. Print the organization chart or diagram slide and a sample of a unique organization chart or diagram you found on the Internet.

Project 7

You think that by adding a diagram slide to your *Cars Advanced* presentation you can best display at least four of the models available by the specific car manufacturer of the car you select. Make the shape containing your car model a different color than the rest of the shapes or lines. Be sure to use colors that complement one another. Make any formatting decisions with regard to shape border style, shape colors, shadows, and text enhancements. Connect to the Internet and search the Web to find out the various models offered. Save the presentation as *Cars Organization* and print the diagram slide.

Project 8

Your partner suggests adding an organization chart or diagram slide at the end of the *Internet Advanced* presentation to convey information about Web addresses on the Internet. You determine what type of information to include in the organization chart or diagram. Connect to the Internet and search the Web for your research. Make any formatting decisions with regard to shape border style, shape colors, lines, shadows, and text enhancements. Resize the chart, if necessary, to aid in readability. Save the presentation as *Internet Organization*, and print the organization chart or diagram slide.

PowerPoint 2002

Customizing a Slide Show

Chapter Overview

Previously you learned to set timings, slide transitions, and animation schemes for a slide show presentation. In this chapter, you learn additional techniques for customizing a slide show. You learn how to apply animation effects to text, clip images, and charts. You also learn how to add sounds and music to slides. This chapter also teaches you how to set up a slide show to run continuously for situations such as kiosk viewing, and how to customize the ending of a slide show to accommodate different viewing situations.

Learning Objectives

- Add custom animation effects to slide objects
- Add sound effects to slides
- Set up presentations to run continuously
- Customize the end of a slide show presentation

Case profile

Teddy Toys is sending one of its sales representatives to a toy exposition to promote the company's new products. Teddy Toys will have a booth at the exposition. The representative has flyers about products, reports about the company's timely production schedules, samples of the toys currently being manufactured, and a computer to display a self-running PowerPoint presentation in a booth or kiosk. Ms. Hill wants you to add animation, sounds, and music, and set up the slide show presentation to run continuously.

chapter ten

10.a Adding Custom Animation Effects to Slide Objects

For situations where a preset animation scheme doesn't meet your needs, you can apply custom animation effects. **Custom animation effects** are visuals and sounds you apply to the objects, images, charts, and/or text of your choice on a slide. For example, you can set text and bullet items to fly in from the top, one letter at a time, with sound effects, onto the slide during the slide show. You also can apply more than one animation effect to an object. The Custom Animation task pane provides options for adding, modifying, and removing effects; starting effects manually or automatically; and changing the direction and speed of the effects. You can play the effects directly on your slide to view the effects as you choose them, using the Preview option in the Custom Animation task pane, or you can display the slide show from the current slide. To add custom animation to a title slide:

Step 1	Open	the *Teddy Toys New Products* presentation located on the Data Disk
Step 2	Save	the presentation as *Teddy Toys Animation*
Step 3	Display	Slide 1, if necessary
Step 4	Click	Sli<u>d</u>e Show
Step 5	Click	Custo<u>m</u> Animation

Your screen should look similar to Figure 10-1.

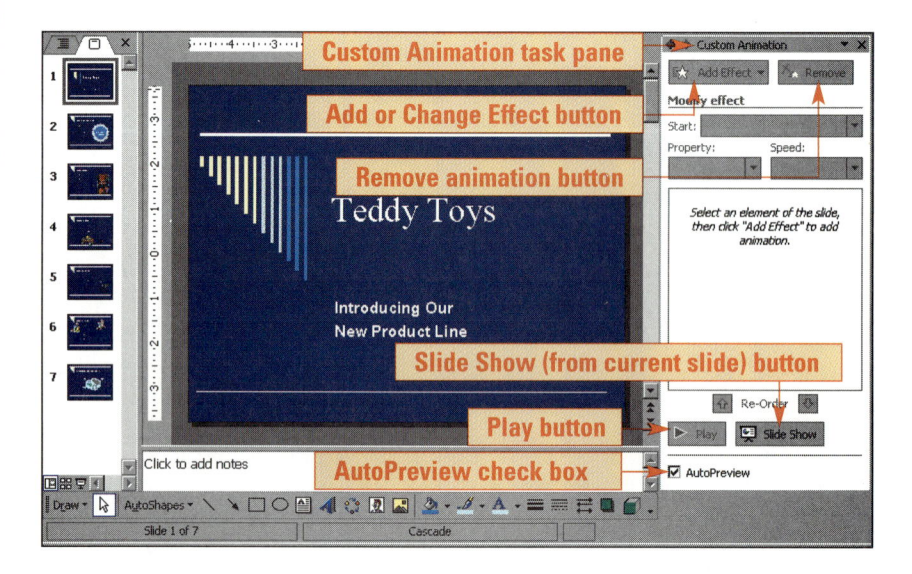

FIGURE 10-1 Custom Animation Task Pane

Task Pane Tip

If the task pane is open, you can display the Custom Animation task pane by clicking the Other Task Panes list arrow and then clicking Custom Animation.

Menu Tip

You can access the Custom Animation task pane by clicking the Custo<u>m</u> Animation command on the Sli<u>d</u>e Show menu.

Mouse Tip

You can add custom animation to an object by right-clicking the object and then clicking Custo<u>m</u> Animation.

Step 6	Verify	that the AutoPreview check box in the Custom Animation task pane contains a check mark
Step 7	Select	the Teddy Toys title object
Step 8	Click	the Add Effect button [Add Effect ▼] in the Custom Animation task pane

The Add Effect submenu opens, listing four variations of custom animation that can be added to objects: Entrance, Emphasis, Exit, and Motion Paths. Each of these variations opens a submenu of effects. **Entrance** effects determine the way objects enter or come onto a slide during a slide show; **Emphasis** effects animate objects that are already on the slide; **Exit** effects animate objects as they leave the slide; and **Motion Paths** create a path that the object follows as part of the animation. You can apply more than one type of effect to the same object. When you add multiple effects to one object, or effects to different objects, they are listed in the Custom Animation list in the order the animation was added.

| Step 9 | Point to | Entrance |
| Step 10 | Click | Blinds |

The AutoPreview shows the effect of this custom animation on the slide, and the animation tag at the left of the animated object displays the number 1, indicating that this is the first animated object for the slide. Each animated object appears with a number or icon to the left of the object animated to visually indicate the way the animation starts. Numbers indicate the order of the effect. Icons indicate whether the animation starts with a mouse click, with the previous effect, or after the previous effect. If you want to change the order of any animation, you can click the Re-Order up or down arrows in the Custom Animation task pane to change the order to accomplish a more logical or visual flow of objects on the slide.

Step 11	Deselect	the title object
Step 12	Select	the subtitle object (Introducing Our New Product Line)
Step 13	Click	the Add Effect button [Add Effect ▼] in the Custom Animation task pane
Step 14	Point to	Entrance
Step 15	Click	Diamond

DESIGN TIP

The goal of multimedia (animation, sounds, music) is to enhance the presentation, not overtake it.

If you want all the objects on all slides in a presentation (except title slides) to animate with the same effect, you can animate that placeholder or object on the slide master. This saves time and ensures consistency throughout a presentation.

QUICK TIP

You can see all the Entrance effects by clicking More Effects at the bottom of the Entrance effects list.

You can remove an animation effect by selecting the animated item in the Custom Animation list in the Custom Animation task pane and then clicking the Remove button.

chapter ten

Each line of the subtitle enters with the diamond effect, displaying animation tags 2 and 3 to the left of the text box. The first line of the subtitle is the second animated object on the slide, and the second line of the subtitle is the third animated object. Your slide should look similar to Figure 10-2.

FIGURE 10-2
Title Slide Displaying Animation Tags

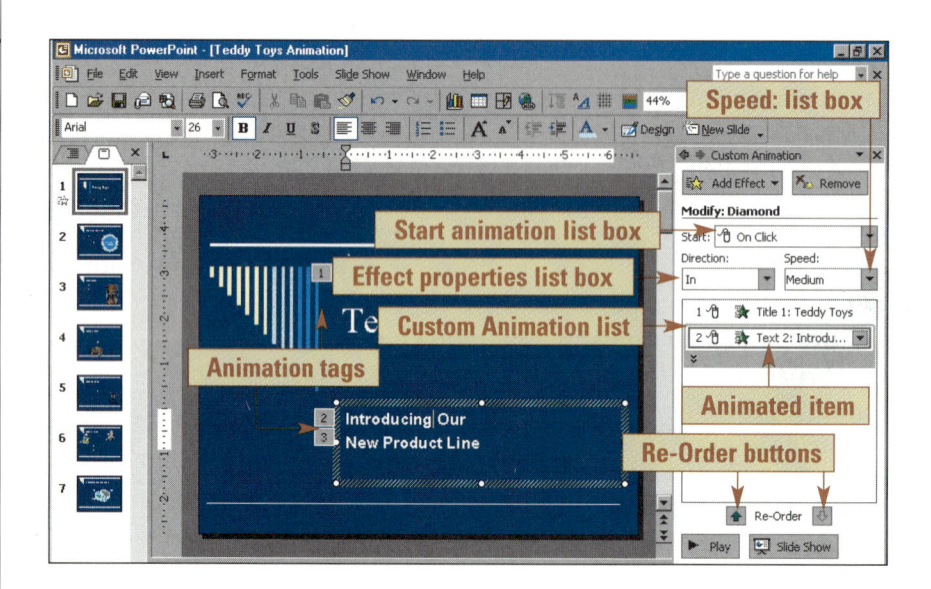

After you apply animation effects to the objects, the Custom Animation list in the Custom Animation task pane displays the list of animated items for the slide, as shown in Figure 10-2. Each item has an **animation tag** displayed on the slide indicating the order or sequence of the animated item(s), an icon indicating the timing of the animation event in relation to the other events on the slide (such as on mouse click, with previous, after previous), an icon representing the type of animation (Blinds, Diamond, etc.), and a portion of the text used in the animation (such as Title 1: "Teddy Toys" or "Text 2: Introducing…"). If only a portion of the text is visible, you can see a ScreenTip by pointing to the animated item.

Step 16 *Click* the Play button in the Custom Animation task pane

The Teddy Toys title object comes on to the slide with the blinds animation effect while the subtitle object uses the diamond animation effect. Each line of the subtitle object is animated separately. In the Custom Animation task pane, there are only two items listed in the Custom Animation list. The gray bar with the double-down arrow directly below the subtitle item indicates that there are additional sequences for a particular list item. You can click the double-down arrow to display the third animated object. When you click the Play

---

MOUSE TIP

You can display the Advanced Timeline in the Custom Animation list by clicking the arrow on any animated list item and then clicking Show Advanced Timeline.

button and view the custom animations, **time blocks** and a **moving timeline** display on each animated item in the Custom Animation list, indicating seconds and including zooming options. In addition, an advanced timeline displays at the bottom of the Custom Animation list that allows you to edit the timings for animations by selecting the item and dragging the timeline marker.

You can also change the speed of the animation effects. To change the animation speed using the Custom Animation task pane:

Step 1	*Select*	the title and subtitle objects on the slide
Step 2	*Click*	Medium in the Speed: list in the Custom Animation task pane
Step 3	*Click*	the Slide Show (from current slide) button ![Slide Show] in the Custom Animation task pane
Step 4	*Click*	to view each of the animation effects on the first slide
Step 5	*End*	the slide show after the subtitle displays

Both the title and subtitle objects on the slide are animated when you click during the slide show to view their animation effects. You can set the animation to begin automatically during a slide show by clicking Start With Previous or Start After Previous in the list for each animated item. The Start With Previous feature starts the animation event at the same time as a previous item in the list or, if first, as soon as the slide appears in the Slide Show. The Start After Previous feature starts the animation immediately after a previous event has finished playing, without using a mouse click. You also can customize the effects for each animated object. To set the animation to automatically start:

Step 1	*Click*	the list arrow on the first animated item in the Custom Animation list
Step 2	*Click*	Start With Previous
Step 3	*Click*	the list arrow on the second animated item in the Custom Animation list
Step 4	*Click*	Start After Previous
Step 5	*Run*	the slide show from the current slide
Step 6	*Observe*	that the objects are animated and appear on the slide automatically
Step 7	*End*	the slide show
Step 8	*Observe*	that the animation tags now display 0

> **QUICK TIP**
>
> When animated items are set to start with or after another item, the animation effect becomes one event for those items. Even though each item comes in a set order, the entire animation is treated as a combined event.

chapter ten

Adding a Motion Path

Motion paths can be drawn or applied to objects to create a path that the object follows as part of the animation. PowerPoint provides preset motion paths, or you can create your own motion paths using the Freeform (contains curved and straight segments), Scribble (contains smooth curves similar to being drawn with a pen), Line (straight path), and/or Curve (creates a curved line between two mouse clicks) tools. To add a motion path:

Step 1	Select	the title object
Step 2	Click	the Add Effect button in the Custom Animation task pane
Step 3	Point to	Motion Paths
Step 4	Click	More Motion Paths
Step 5	Double-click	the 4 Point Star in the Basic category

The Teddy Toys title object moves in the shape of a 4-point star and then returns to its original position on the slide. When you select the motion path object, it displays a green triangle indicating the starting and ending point of the motion path. A second animation event for the title item displays in the Custom Animation list, directly below the original title and subtitle items, with an icon indicating a star shape motion effect. Your slide should look similar to Figure 10-3.

FIGURE 10-3
Motion Path Displayed

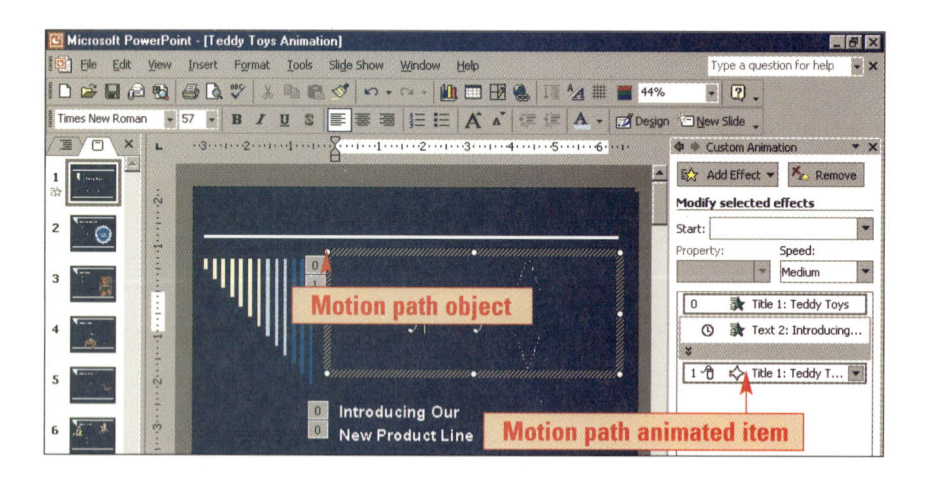

Step 6	Click	the Title 1: Teddy Toys motion path item list arrow
Step 7	Click	Start After Previous

Design Tip

PowerPoint provides a variety of motion paths to enhance your presentation, separated into the following categories: Basic, Lines and Curves, and Special. When adding a motion path to an object, choose an appropriate path for the tone of the presentation. For example, a path that uses a bouncing or jumping motion in a presentation would be inappropriate when discussing the financial stability of an organization.

| Step 8 | **Save** | the *Teddy Toys Animation* presentation |

Adding a Sound to an Animation

If you have a sound card in your computer, you also can add sound to accompany animation. Text, visual animations, and sound work together to attract attention, aid comprehension, and increase retention. Sound effects can enhance the animated object by drawing attention to the object by sound as it animates on the slide. An object must first be animated before you can apply a sound effect to it. You can further customize the animation by changing the direction of the animation, changing the timing per animated object, repeating the animation, and adding sounds as each animated object displays on the slide. In addition, you have the option of animating text all at once, by word, or letter by letter. To add sounds to animations:

| Step 1 | **Double-click** | the first animated item in the Custom Animation list |

The Blinds dialog box opens, allowing you to further customize the selected animation. The dialog box name corresponds to the type of animation applied to the object or to the type of animation object itself. The Effect tab of the Blinds dialog box displays settings for direction, sound, after animation effect, and custom text animation. Your dialog box should look similar to Figure 10-4.

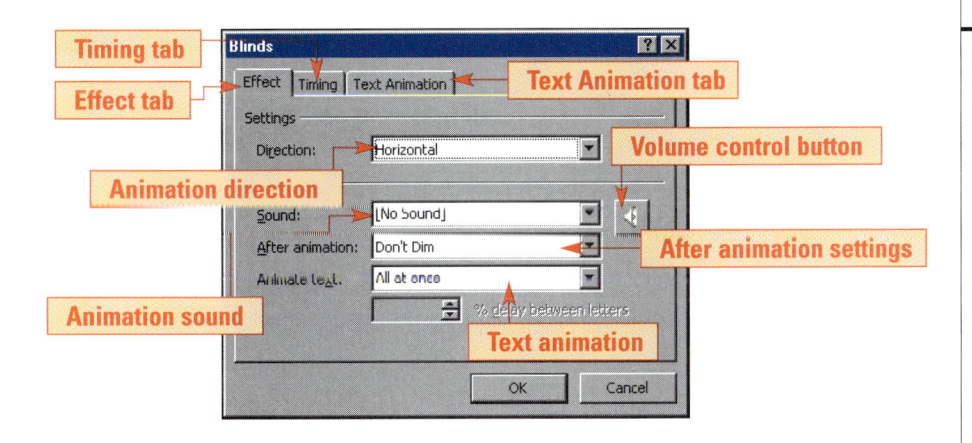

> **QUICK TIP**
>
> The volume control button next to the Sound: list box enables you to adjust the volume for the sound effect that plays with the animation. The indicator can be dragged to increase or decrease the volume of the sound. You can mute the sound by clicking the Mute check box.

FIGURE 10-4
Blinds Dialog Box

| Step 2 | **Click** | Applause in the Sound: list |
| Step 3 | **Click** | OK |

chapter ten

PowerPoint 2002

DESIGN TIP

Adding sound to individual slides takes time, and it may become distracting to the audience to keep switching music and sounds as new slides appear.

QUICK TIP

If a trigger is used as an animation event, the trigger displays as a gray bar directly above the animated item in the Custom Animation list. Triggers are additional animation events that act as links to trigger or activate other animation events when clicked during the slide show. When you use a trigger, any previous start animation event on that item automatically reverts back to an On Click start.

FIGURE 10-5
Timing Options in Blinds Dialog Box

If your computer is equipped with a sound card, you hear the sounds of applause accompany the title object animation.

In addition to adding sound to an animation in the dialog box for an animated object, you can customize an object with other effects. For example, you can animate the text of an object so that it enters the slide by word or by letter. To add sound and additional enhancements to an animation:

Step 1	*Double-click*	the second item in the Custom Animation list
Step 2	*Click*	Chime in the Sound: list of the Diamond dialog box
Step 3	*Click*	By word in the Animate text: list
Step 4	*Click*	OK
Step 5	*Observe*	the effects

Another enhancement you can add to an animation is setting individual timings for objects, so that they enter and exit the slide automatically at different time intervals. To change animation timings:

| Step 1 | *Double-click* | the first item in the Custom Animation list |
| Step 2 | *Click* | the Timing tab in the Blinds dialog box |

The timing options include starting animation, delaying animation, setting the animation speed, and repeating the animation. You can rewind an animation effect to return the object to its original position after the animation has played. In addition, you can set triggers that animate an object upon the animation of another object. Your dialog box should look similar to Figure 10-5.

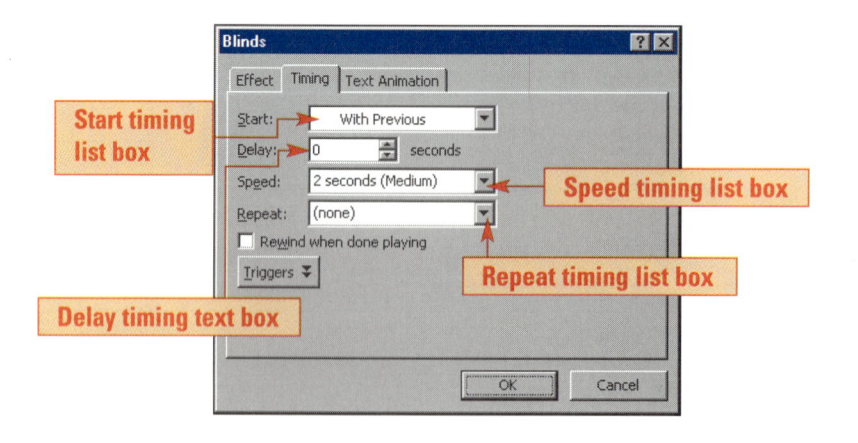

Step 3	Change	the Start: list box to After Previous
Step 4	Key	2 in the Delay: text box
Step 5	Click	OK
Step 6	Double-click	the second animated item in the Custom Animation list
Step 7	Click	the Timing tab
Step 8	Verify	that After Previous appears in the Start: list box
Step 9	Key	2 in the Delay: text box
Step 10	Click	OK
Step 11	Run	the slide show from the current slide
Step 12	End	the slide show after observing the effects
Step 13	Save	the *Teddy Toys Animation* presentation

When you select an object containing more than one line of text, the animation is applied to all lines of text. If you click the animation order number to the left of a line, the animation effects are applied to only that line of text. When the entire text object is selected, you use the list arrow that appears at the bottom of the selected lines of text in the animation order section in the Custom Animation task pane. To add animation to a text slide:

Step 1	Display	Slide 2
Step 2	Select	the bullet text object
Step 3	Click	the Add Effect button in the Custom Animation task pane
Step 4	Point to	Entrance
Step 5	Click	More Effects
Step 6	Drag	the Add Entrance Effect dialog box to the right (see Figure 10-6 for placement)

Your screen should look similar to Figure 10-6. The Add Entrance Effect dialog box contains choices for adding entrance animation effects, beyond those available on the submenu. All available entrance animation effects are organized into Basic, Subtle, Moderate, and Exciting categories. When the Preview Effect check box contains a check mark, you can preview the animation effect you select on the slide without applying it to your object.

DESIGN TIP

When adding animation and sound to a slide or a presentation, do so sparingly. Too many animations and sounds begin to annoy an audience instead of capturing their attention.

When using sound effects, be sure they add impact or reinforcement to your slides. The audience is quickly attuned to the needless use of sounds when they do not help to add impact, bring attention to the slide, or reinforce an idea or concept.

CAUTION TIP

The preview of the animation effect is not visible if the dialog box obscures the area of the slide where the effect will occur.

chapter ten

FIGURE 10-6
Add Entrance Effect Dialog Box

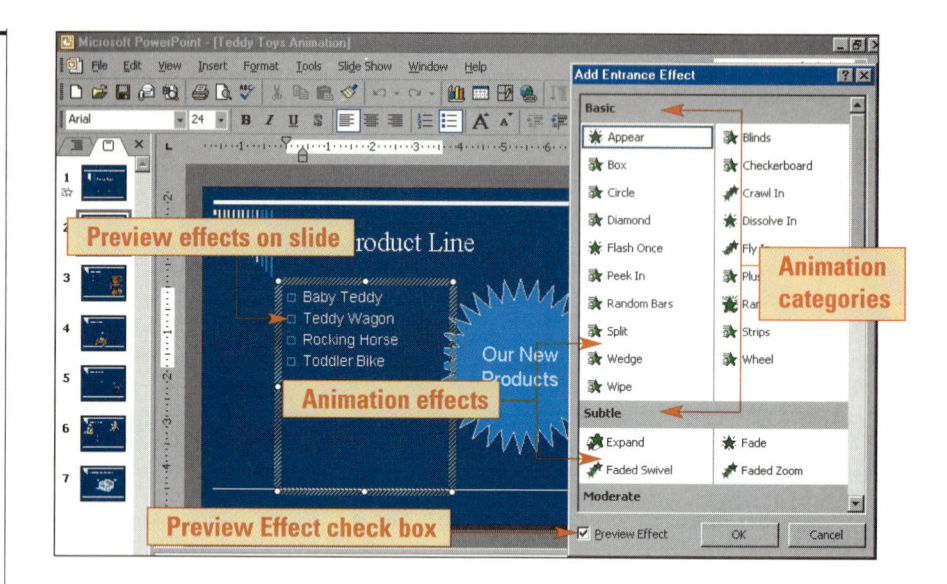

[Screenshot of PowerPoint Add Entrance Effect dialog box with callouts: "Preview effects on slide", "Animation effects", "Animation categories", "Preview Effect check box"]

Step 7	Scroll	to the Exciting category
Step 8	Click	Bounce and view the animation
Step 9	Click	OK
Step 10	Click	After Previous in the Start: list in the Custom Animation task pane
Step 11	Double-click	the first item in the Custom Animation list
Step 12	Click	the Drum Roll sound in the Sound: list
Step 13	Click	the light blue color (second from left) in the After animation: list
Step 14	Click	the Timing tab
Step 15	Key	1 in the Delay: text box
Step 16	Click	OK
Step 17	Run	the slide show from the current slide

Each bullet item bounces as it enters the slide with the drum roll sound on each bullet. The title should be the first object to enter the slide during the slide show because it introduces the bullet text. To animate the title and AutoShape and change the animation order:

Step 1	Select	the title object on Slide 2
Step 2	Click	the Add Effect button [Add Effect] in the Custom Animation task pane
Step 3	Point to	Entrance
Step 4	Click	More Effects

Step 5	Click	Stretch in the Moderate category
Step 6	Click	OK
Step 7	Double-click	the Title 1: New Pro item in the Custom Animation list
Step 8	Add	the Whoosh sound in the Stretch dialog box
Step 9	Click	the Timing tab
Step 10	Click	With Previous in the Start: list
Step 11	Key	1 in the Delay: text box
Step 12	Click	2 seconds (Medium) in the Speed: list
Step 13	Click	OK
Step 14	Click	the Title 1: New Pro item in the Custom Animation list, if necessary
Step 15	Click	the Re-Order up button until the Title 1: New Pro item is the first in the list

The title item is the first animated item in the list; however the star AutoShape displays on the slide first because it is not yet animated with an entrance effect. To add custom animation to an AutoShape:

Step 1	Select	the star AutoShape with the Our New Products text
Step 2	Click	the Add Effect button in the Custom Animation task pane
Step 3	Point to	Emphasis
Step 4	Click	Spin
Step 5	Change	the AutoShape item to start After Previous
Step 6	Click	the Play button in the Custom Animation task pane
Step 7	Save	the *Teddy Toys Animation* presentation

Animating Images and Charts

In addition to animating text, you can add custom animation to clip art images and charts, such as organization, diagram, column, bar, and pie charts. To add animation effects to images:

Step 1	Display	Slide 3
Step 2	Select	the title and bullet text objects

QUICK TIP

The Animate grid and legend check box allows you to animate the grid and legend with the chart elements. If you remove the check mark, the grid and legend display before any animation.

Options for animating a diagram include animating as one object, all at once, clockwise-inward, clockwise-outward, counterclockwise-inward, counterclockwise-outward, inward by ring, and outward by ring.

Step 3	Open	the Add Entrance Effect dialog box
Step 4	Add	the Wedge effect from the Basic category
Step 5	Change	the title item to start With Previous
Step 6	Change	the bullet text item to start After Previous
Step 7	Select	the teddy bear image
Step 8	Add	the Wedge effect as the Entrance effect
Step 9	Double-click	the teddy bear item (Object 3) in the Custom Animation list
Step 10	Add	the Camera sound
Step 11	Change	the timing to start After Previous
Step 12	Change	the delay to 2 seconds
Step 13	Run	the slide show from the current slide
Step 14	Follow	Steps 2 through 8 for the Teddy Wagon, Rocking Horse, and Toddler Bike slides, replacing applicable images for the "teddy bear" image
Step 15	Save	the *Teddy Toys Animation* presentation

Just as with text and objects, you can animate charts containing statistical data (pie, bar, and line charts), tables, organization charts, and diagrams. To add custom animation to chart slides:

Step 1	Display	Slide 7
Step 2	Select	the title and pie chart objects

You want to add the Wedge animation effect to these selected objects to provide a consistent animation look to your presentations. Because you have applied this effect to other objects in this presentation, the effect is now available in the Entrance Effect submenu.

Step 3	Add	the Wedge effect as the Entrance effect
Step 4	Change	the title item to start With Previous

You can animate a table by animating the entire table object. You can animate a chart, diagram, or statistical chart by animating the entire object as a whole or individual chart elements. When you animate the chart as a whole, the animation effects determine how the chart enters or animates as one entire object. When you animate elements of the chart, you can animate by series, categories, branches, shapes, levels, clockwise, counterclockwise, inward, and outward. To add effects and animate a pie chart by category:

Step 1	Double-click	the Chart 2 item in the Custom Animation list
Step 2	Add	the Cash Register sound
Step 3	Change	the timing to start After Previous, the delay to 2 seconds, and the speed to 3 seconds (Slow)
Step 4	Click	the Chart Animation tab
Step 5	Click	By category in the Group chart: list
Step 6	Click	OK
Step 7	Run	the slide show from the current slide
Step 8	Observe	that the title displays first on the slide, followed by the pie chart building slice by slice
Step 9	End	the slide show

10.b Adding Sound Effects to Slides

You can also apply sound effects and music to individual slides that play during a slide show presentation. Sound clips help to create a polished, professional slide show that appeals to the auditory senses of the viewer. Unlike a sound effect that accompanies the animation of an object on a slide, a slide sound effect plays when the slide displays during slide show. It is not associated with any one object on the slide. Sound files or clips can be inserted from the Clip Organizer or from a folder containing the clips. PowerPoint supports various types of sound files, such as AIFF Audio (.aif, .aiff, .aifc), CD Audio Track (.cda), MIDI Sequence (.mid, .rmi, .midi), MP3 (.mp3), Sound Clip (Basic) (.au, .snd), Wave Sound (.wav), and Windows Media Audio file (.wma). You can add sound clips to play automatically or when you click the sound clip icon. Sounds can be repeated to continue playing more than one time per slide. As sound files vary in length, you can loop sound or music files to play until the slide show finishes.

Adding Sound Clips from Clip Organizer

Sound and music clips can be added to a PowerPoint presentation using the Clip Organizer. When you browse the Clip Organizer by categories, the sound clips are usually found at the bottom of the clip previews. Sound clips display a sound icon in the Clip Organizer, whereas music clips display a musical note icon. When you add a sound or music clip to a slide, the sound icon is the same. You can organize

---

MOUSE TIP

Although the position of the sound clip on the slide does not affect the playing of the sound, it can become a distraction if left in the center of the slide. You can drag it to a position anywhere on the slide, even off the slide, to avoid any possible interference when editing or formatting objects on the slide.

CAUTION TIP

Sounds added to slides are automatically linked (connection between sound and PowerPoint) to the PowerPoint presentation rather than embedded (part of the presentation) in it, if the sound file is greater than 100 KB in size. When the sounds are linked, the sound files must be copied to the same location as the PowerPoint presentation if the presentation will be given on a different computer.

chapter ten

MENU TIP

You can find additional sounds available on your computer system by clicking Insert, Movies and Sounds, Sound from File, and then clicking the Microsoft Windows Media folder (in the Windows folder) and selecting the desired sound.

QUICK TIP

You can delete a sound clip just as you delete any other object, by selecting it and pressing the DELETE key.

INTERNET TIP

If you cannot find an appropriate sound clip from the Clip Organizer and you have access to the Internet, you can access the Microsoft Design Gallery Live Web site by clicking the Clips Online button in the Insert ClipArt task pane.

sound clips by adding them to folders in the collection list in the Clip Organizer. You can search for sound and music clips by text using the Insert Clip Art search task pane. To add a sound clip to a slide:

Step 1	Display	Slide 1
Step 2	Click	the Insert Clip Art button on the Drawing toolbar
Step 3	Key	music in the Search text: text box
Step 4	Change	the Results should be: list box to Sounds
Step 5	Click	Search
Step 6	Scroll down	to the *Action News Theme* sound file (Screen Tip displays: Action News Theme)
Step 7	Click	the sound clip

The sound clip is inserted at the center of the slide, and a dialog box opens asking whether you want the sound to play automatically in the slide show or only when you click the clip.

Step 8	Click	Yes
Step 9	Drag	the sound clip to the lower-right corner of the slide
Step 10	Double-click	the sound clip to play the sound
Step 11	Run	the slide show from the current slide

The text objects are animated before the sound clip plays. Once added to a slide, a sound clip is simply an item in the Custom Animation list and can be moved or customized. To change animation order:

Step 1	Display	the Custom Animation task pane
Step 2	Select	the Media item in the Custom Animation list
Step 3	Click	the Re-Order up button three times to move the Media clip item to the top of the Custom Animation item list
Step 4	Double-click	the Media item in the Custom Animation list

The Play Sound dialog box opens with options for starting and stopping playing, adjusting the volume, and hiding the sound clip object.

| Step 5 | Click | the From beginning option button in the Start playing section, if necessary |

Customizing a Slide Show   PA 43

Step 6	Click	the After: option button in the Stop playing section
Step 7	Verify	that 1 appears in the After: slides text box
Step 8	Click	the Hide while not playing check box to insert a check mark
Step 9	Click	the Timing tab
Step 10	Click	With Previous in the Start: list
Step 11	Click	OK
Step 12	Change	the timing of the title object to start 7 seconds After Previous
Step 13	Run	the slide show from the current slide and observe that the sound clip begins playing before any animation begins
Step 14	Save	the *Teddy Toys Animation* presentation

Adding Sound Clips from Another Source

You can add music to the slide show presentation that will play the duration of the slide show. You can find music clips on the Internet, a folder on disk, a network, or a CD-ROM. To add a music clip from another source to the slide show:

Step 1	Display	Slide 2
Step 2	Click	Insert
Step 3	Point to	Movies and Sounds
Step 4	Click	Sound from File
Step 5	Switch to	the drive or folder where your Data Files are stored
Step 6	Double-click	the *FLMOON01.mid* clip file
Step 7	Click	Yes
Step 8	Drag	the sound clip to the lower right corner of the slide
Step 9	Move	the sound clip to be the first item in the Custom Animation list

The music sound clip is the first animated object on the slide. You want the music to play for the remaining slides to keep a consistent sound playing throughout. To change sound settings:

Step 1	Double-click	the *FLMOON01.mid* item in the Custom Animation list
Step 2	Verify	that the From beginning option button is selected in the Start playing section
Step 3	Click	the After: option button in the Stop playing section

MENU TIP

You can add sound clips to slides by clicking the Sound from Clip Organizer command on the Movies and Sounds submenu on the Insert menu.

You can also play sound from a CD track by clicking the Play CD Audio Track command on the Movies and Sounds submenu on the Insert menu.

TASK PANE TIP

You can use the back or forward buttons on any task pane to display the task panes previously used during your PowerPoint session.

INTERNET TIP

When you download sound or music files from the Internet, right-click the file, click Save Target As, and save it to a desired location. You then insert the sound or music files into your presentation. Do not copy the shortcut to your PowerPoint slide because that copies only the link or path to the Internet.

chapter ten

CAUTION TIP

It is important to verify if sound or music files on the Internet are free for your downloading. Many files are copyrighted, and it is illegal to use them in your PowerPoint presentations.

QUICK TIP

Wave sound (.wav) files stop playing when other objects start their animation. MIDI sequence (.mid) files continue playing when other objects start their animation.

MENU TIP

You can record narration for an entire slide show in Slide Show by clicking the Record Narration command on the Slide Show menu. The recorded narrations are created much the same as rehearsing timings in slide show and can be saved with the slide timings.

Step 4	Key	6 in the After: slides text box
Step 5	Click	the Hide while not playing check box to insert a check mark
Step 6	Click	the Timing tab
Step 7	Change	the timing to start With Previous
Step 8	Click	OK
Step 9	Right-click	the sound clip object
Step 10	Click	Edit Sound Object
Step 11	Click	the Loop until stopped check box to insert a check mark
Step 12	Click	OK
Step 13	Change	the timing delay of the title object to 5 seconds
Step 14	Run	the slide show from the beginning

The music begins playing before the animated objects enter the screen and continues throughout the presentation. The music begins playing again if the slide show takes longer than the length of the music clip.

| Step 15 | Click | to view the remaining slides in the presentation |
| Step 16 | Save | the *Teddy Toys Animation* presentation |

10.c Setting Up Presentations to Run Continuously

You can set up a presentation to run without a presenter. A full-screen presentation displayed in a kiosk, on a computer connected to a projection device, or on a computer screen can be set up either as a continuous, self-running presentation or as a self-paced presentation that involves the user clicking the mouse button to advance the slides.

When you set up a slide show using the Set Up Show dialog box, the Presented by a speaker (full screen) option enables you to manually advance the slides and animations or use automatic timings. The Browsed by an individual (window) option enables you to run a slide show with custom menus and commands that make it easy for an individual to browse your presentation. The Browsed at kiosk (full screen) option runs the slide show automatically and restarts it after five minutes of inactivity. The audience can advance the slide and navigate the presentation, but they cannot make changes to the presentation. With the kiosk option, PowerPoint selects the Loop continuously until 'Esc' option. A **kiosk** is a small structure with one or more open sides

Customizing a Slide Show **PA 45**

that is used to vend merchandise (such as newspapers) or services (such as film developing or wedding registry), similar to a booth.

To set up a show to run continuously, you first set timings for each slide. Timings determine the length of time the slide displays on the screen before the next slide automatically replaces it. You can set slide timings individually or use the rehearse timings feature. To set up automatic times and a continuous, self-running presentation:

Step 1	Display	the Slide Transition task pane
Step 2	Key	6 in the Automatically after list box
Step 3	Click	Apply to All Slides
Step 4	Run	the slide show from the beginning
Step 5	End	the slide show when the End of slide show, click to exit, message appears
Step 6	Click	Sli_d_e Show
Step 7	Click	Set Up Show

> **DESIGN TIP**
>
> Slide times should be set that are appropriate for the content and discussion necessary to fully convey the intent of the slides. You will preview and make changes many times before the slide timings are perfect for each presentation.

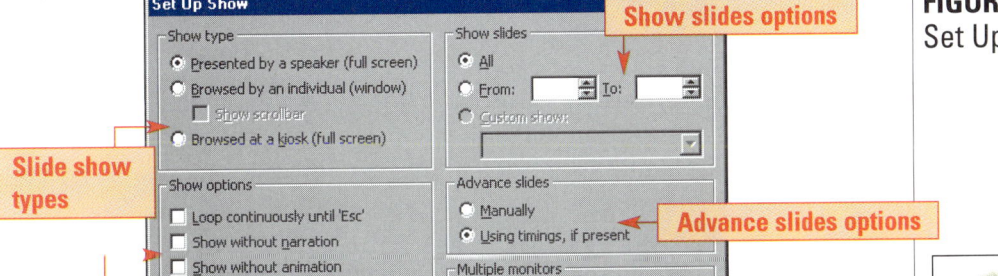

The Set Up Show dialog box opens with options for setting up a slide show. Your dialog box should look similar to Figure 10-7.

FIGURE 10-7
Set Up Show Dialog Box

> **MOUSE TIP**
>
> You can access the Set Up Show dialog box by holding down the SHIFT key and clicking the Slide Show button when the ScreenTip displays Set Up Show.

Step 8	Click	the Presented by a speaker (full screen) option button, if necessary
Step 9	Click	the Loop continuously until 'Esc' check box in the Show options section to insert a check mark
Step 10	Click	the All option button in the Show slides section, if necessary

chapter ten

QUICK TIP

Instead of creating a black slide at the end of the presentation, you could create a blank slide that uses the same color background as the existing slides. Because a blank slide has no visual attraction, the audience is no longer interested in looking at the overhead or the screen.

CAUTION TIP

A slide show set up to loop continuously until the ESC key is pressed will not loop automatically if the timing on the last, blank slide has been removed.

DESIGN TIP

A blank or black slide a the end of the presentation adds a polished look to the presentation and is a clear indication to the audience that the slide show is over, without returning to the PowerPoint window. This slide remains on the screen until the question and answer period is over, if there is one, or until the audience leaves. If, however, the slide show is set to loop and repeat, a black slide is not necessary.

Step 11	Click	the Using timings, if present option button in the Advance slides section, if necessary
Step 12	Click	OK
Step 13	Run	the slide show from the beginning
Step 14	End	the slide show after you view the presentation twice
Step 15	Save	the *Teddy Toys Animation* presentation

10.d Customizing the End of a Slide Show Presentation

By default, PowerPoint ends a presentation with a black slide with the text "End of slide show, click to exit" at the top of the slide. It is a good idea to end your presentation with a black or blank slide.

To remove the black slide option from the end of a presentation:

Step 1	Click	Options on the Tools menu, then click the View tab
Step 2	Click	the End with black slide check box to remove the check mark, if necessary
Step 3	Click	OK

When a blank slide is added to the end of the presentation, be sure to remove the timing from the slide. If the last slide includes a slide timing, the presentation will either start again (if the slide show is looped to start again), or return to the last PowerPoint view. To add a blank slide that matches the presentation design:

Step 1	Display	Slide 7
Step 2	Add	a new slide based on the Blank content layout
Step 3	Right-click	the slide
Step 4	Click	Background
Step 5	Click	the Omit background graphics from master check box to insert a check mark
Step 6	Click	Apply
Step 7	Display	the Slide Transition task pane
Step 8	Remove	the check mark in the Automatically after check box
Step 9	Run	the slide show from the beginning
Step 10	Save	the *Teddy Toys Animation* presentation and close it

Summary

- Custom animation effects are special visual effects and sounds applied to objects, clip images, charts, and text.
- Custom animation effects can be applied to objects in the slide master to save time and provide consistency.
- You can change the path an object follows by applying a preset motion path or by creating your own custom path.
- Custom animation of objects involves determining the order of animation, effects, times for effect, and sounds.
- When customizing charts containing statistical data, you can add timings and chart effects affecting each category or series on the chart.
- You can add sound or music clips to a slide or slides from the Microsoft Clip Organizer, a disk or drive, network, or from the Internet.
- Music clips can be set to play during one or any number of slides in the presentation.
- If you have the necessary equipment, PowerPoint enables you to record narration to add to an individual slide or the entire presentation.
- You can add a sound clip to a presentation that continuously plays through the slide show.
- A presentation can be displayed as a full-screen presentation in a kiosk, either running continuously or viewer paced.
- You can customize a presentation to end with a blank slide that matches the background of the presentation, instead of the standard black slide containing a message that the slide show is over.
- If you add a blank slide to a slide show you have set up to run continuously, you can ensure that the presentation will end in a blank slide and viewers will be able to start the slide show again when they click or press a key at the kiosk.

chapter ten

Commands Review

Action	Menu Bar	Shortcut Menu	Toolbar	Task Pane	Keyboard
Display the Custom Animation task pane	Sli<u>d</u>e Show, Cust<u>o</u>m Animation	Right-click object, Custom Animation		Custom Animation	ALT + D, M
Add custom animation effect to a selected object				Add Effect	
Remove animation effect from a selected object				Remove	
Change animation effect on a selected object		Double-click selected object in Custom Animation list		Change	
Add a motion path effect to a selected object				Add Effect	
Change or edit a motion path		Right-click selected motion path object on slide, <u>E</u>dit Points Drag start and/or end points			
Add sound to an animated object		Double-click selected object in Custom Animation list, Effect tab, <u>S</u>ound			
Add sound clips to slide	<u>I</u>nsert, Mo<u>v</u>ies and Sounds, <u>S</u>ound from Clip Organizer or Sou<u>n</u>d from File				ALT + I, V, S ALT + I, V, N
Save sound clip from Internet		Right-click sound object, Save Target <u>A</u>s			
Edit sound object	<u>E</u>dit, Sound <u>O</u>bject	Right-click sound object, Edit Sound <u>O</u>bject			ALT + E, O
Add narration to a slide	<u>I</u>nsert, Mo<u>v</u>ies and Sounds, <u>R</u>ecord Sound				ALT + I, V, R
Add narration to a presentation	Sli<u>d</u>e Show, Record Narration				ALT + D, N
Set up a self-running show	Sli<u>d</u>e Show, <u>S</u>et Up Show		SHIFT+		ALT + D, S
Add or remove black slide at end of presentation	<u>T</u>ools, <u>O</u>ptions, View tab, <u>E</u>nd with black slide				ALT + T, O, E

Concepts Review

Circle the correct answer.

1. Custom animation effects that can be added to slides include all of the following *except*:
   [a] entrance animation.
   [b] emphasis animation.
   [c] picture animation.
   [d] exit animation.

2. Text is introduced during entry animation by all of the following effects *except*:
   [a] phrase by phrase.
   [b] word by word.
   [c] letter by letter.
   [d] all at once.

3. The path that an object or text follows as part of an animation during slide show is called the:
   [a] entrance path.
   [b] exit path.
   [c] motion path.
   [d] emphasis path.

4. Which of the following enables you to change the order of the animated items on a slide?
   [a] change order
   [b] modify order
   [c] re-order
   [d] remove order

5. Sound clips are inserted in slides at the:
   [a] lower-left corner of the slide.
   [b] lower-right corner of the slide.
   [c] center of the slide.
   [d] lower-right corner of the slide master.

6. Which of the following effects requires special computer equipment to use?
   [a] custom animation
   [b] voice narration
   [c] transitions
   [d] preset animations

7. You can add sounds to slides in a presentation using all of the following *except*:
   [a] the Internet.
   [b] the Clip Organizer.
   [c] a disk, drive, or CD-ROM.
   [d] the Custom Animation task pane.

8. Which of the following statements is *not* true?
   [a] A kiosk is another term for booth.
   [b] A self-running presentation can be shown in a booth or kiosk.
   [c] A self-paced presentation involves the user clicking the mouse button to advance slides.
   [d] A self-paced presentation always uses slide timings.

9. To run a presentation continuously without stopping requires:
   [a] expensive slide show equipment.
   [b] establishing a loop.
   [c] adding a blank slide to the end of the presentation to signal the presentation is over.
   [d] pressing a Rerun button.

10. To add a polished look to any presentation, you would:
    [a] add a blank or black slide to the end of the presentation.
    [b] use a different color for each character of a bullet line to display important points.
    [c] use a different background for each slide of the presentation.
    [d] use different typefaces and font sizes for the titles of each slide in the presentation.

Circle **T** if the statement is true or **F** if the statement is false.

T F 1. To remove animation from an object, select the object and then press the DELETE key.

T F 2. You cannot add sounds to animated objects.

T F 3. You can change the animation order of various objects on a slide.

T F 4. You can apply custom animation effects to only charts.

T F 5. To add an animated object to all slides except the title slides, use the slide master.

T F 6. To record narration, you need a sound card and microphone.

T F 7. When using sound or music clips, it is best to use a different sound and music clip throughout the presentation because each slide covers a different topic.

T F 8. To loop continuously means the same slide displays over and over.

T F 9. Kiosk is a term describing a booth where a self-running presentation may be displayed.

T F 10. Creating a blank slide for the end of a presentation adds a polished look to the presentation.

Skills Review

Exercise 1

1. Open the *PowerPoint Advanced* presentation located on the Data Disk, and save it as *PowerPoint Animation*.
2. Using the Slide Transition task pane, set a 4-second timing to advance all the slides automatically.
3. Animate all the title objects with the same Entrance effect on all the slides using With Previous for the start option. (*Hint:* Use the slide and title masters.)
4. Animate all text objects with the same Entrance effect on all the slides using After Previous for the start option. (*Hint:* Use the slide and title masters.) The Entrance should be different than the title objects Entrance effect.
5. Add sound to some of the animated objects.
6. Animate the image and table objects using Entrance effects.
7. Set up a continuously, self-running presentation for a kiosk.
8. Save the *PowerPoint Animation* presentation.
9. Run the slide show.
10. Print the presentation as a six-slides-per-page handout, and then close it.

Exercise 2

1. Open the *Office Advanced* presentation located on the Data Disk, and save it as *Office Animation*.
2. Add a blank slide at the end of the presentation, then remove the slide's graphic elements, if any.
3. Add slide timings to all slides.
4. Add custom animation for Emphasis to both text objects on the title slide.
5. Add custom animation for Entrance effects with sound to the slide with the AutoShapes or a slide of your choice.
6. Add custom animation with the Whoosh sound to the pie chart slide.
7. Add the *FLWERS01.mid* sound clip from the Data Disk to the first slide in the presentation and play the sound automatically. Change the animation order so that sound clip is first in the animation list.

8. Hide the sound clip, and have the music play throughout the presentation and loop continuously.
9. Run the slide show.
10. Save the *Office Animation* presentation.
11. Print the presentation as a six-slides-per-page handout, and then close it.

Exercise 3

1. Open the *Design Advanced* presentation located on the Data Disk, and save it as *Design Animation*.
2. Select the title and subtitle objects on the title master, add an Entrance effect to start With Previous, and add the *PHANTM01.mid* sound clip from the Data Disk to run continuously for the entire presentation. Hide the sound clip, and change the animation order so that sound clip is first in the animation list.
3. Add the same custom animation effect to the title of each slide, except the title slide, start the animation with the previous effect, and change the speed to medium (do not use the slide master).
4. Add custom animation with an Entrance effect to the bullet objects on the Presentation Fonts slide, change the speed to medium, and start the animation after the previous effect.
5. Add custom animation with an Entrance effect to the table object on the AutoShapes slide and start the animation after the previous effect with a 2-second delay.
6. Add custom animation with Entrance effects to the shapes on the AutoShapes slide and start the animation after the previous effect, with a medium speed for each of the shapes.
7. Add custom animation with the click sound to the chart slide.
8. Set up the slide show to be presented by a speaker and loop continuously.
9. Add slide timings to all the slides.
10. Run the slide show.
11. Save the *Design Animation* presentation.
12. Print the presentation as a six-slides-per-page handout, and then close it.

Exercise 4

1. Open the *Precision Builders Advanced* presentation located on the Data Disk, and save it as *Precision Builders Animation*.
2. Set up the presentation so it can be browsed at a kiosk.
3. Add custom animation Entrance effects to the title and subtitle objects on the title master.
4. Add custom animation effects to the title and bullet objects on the slide master.
5. Add custom animation with sound to the WordArt object on the Distinctive Designs slide.
6. Add a motion path to the shapes on the Distinctive Designs slide.
7. Add custom animation effects with delay times for Entrance, Emphasis, and/or Exit effects to the text objects on the Customer Comments slide.
8. Add slide timings to the entire presentation.
9. View the slide show.
10. Save the *Precision Builders Animation* presentation.
11. Print the presentation as a six-slides-per-page handout, and then close it.

chapter ten

Exercise 5

1. Open the *Nature Tours Advanced* presentation located on the Data Disk, and save it as *Nature Tours Animation*.
2. Add custom animation to the title, subtitle, and bullet objects on the slide and title masters.
3. Add the *TOBAGO05.mid* sound clip from the Data Disk to the title slide, and play it through the first five slides. The sound clip should play before any other animation appears on the slide.
4. Add custom animation with sound to the shapes and text boxes on the Special Tours slide.
5. Add custom animation to the table slide.
6. Add a blank slide at the end of the presentation that matches the presentation design.
7. Run the slide show.
8. Save the *Nature Tours Animation* presentation.
9. Print the presentation as a six-slides-per-page handout, and then close it.

Exercise 6

1. Open the *A Healthier You Advanced* presentation located on the Data Disk, and save it as *A Healthier You Animation*.
2. Set up the presentation to be presented by a speaker and loop continuously.
3. Add custom animation for Entrance effects for the title and subtitle on the title masters.
4. Add custom animation and sound to each of the slides in the presentation, and add the slide timings.
5. Change the start options, delay times, and order of the animated objects on the last slide.
6. Run the slide show.
7. Save the *A Healthier You Animation* presentation.
8. Print the presentation as a six-slides-per page-handout, and then close it.

Exercise 7

1. Open the *Buying A Computer Advanced* presentation located on the Data Disk, and save it as *Buying A Computer Animation*.
2. Animate the text boxes and the image on the Reasons to Buy a Computer slide, delaying the animation on the second text box and image.
3. Add custom animation for Entrance effects to the table and chart slides.
4. Add custom animation for Entrance and Emphasis effects for each AutoShape and image on the Places to Buy a Computer slide.
5. Add a black slide at the end of the presentation.
6. Run the slide show.
7. Save the *Buying A Computer Animation* presentation.
8. Print the presentation as a six-slides-per-page handout, and then close it.

Exercise 8

1. Open the *Leisure Travel Advanced* presentation located on the Data Disk, and save it as *Leisure Travel Animation*.
2. Add custom animation for the title and subtitle on the title master.
3. Add custom animation to the title and graphic on the slide master.
4. Add slide timings to all the slides.
5. Add the *CUBADA01.mid* sound clip from the Data Disk to the title slide that plays throughout the entire presentation.
6. Remove the black slide at the end of the presentation, if necessary, and set up the presentation to run on a kiosk.
7. Animate the AutoShape slide with both Entrance and Emphasis effects. Add an Exit effect to the four season shapes.
8. Add delay times to the four season shapes.
9. Add custom animation effects to the column chart, and build the chart by series.
10. Run the slide show.
11. Save the *Leisure Travel Animation* presentation.
12. Print the presentation as a six-slides-per-page handout, and then close it.

Case Projects

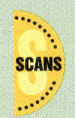

Project 1
You want to learn more about using a CD Audio track that plays throughout the presentation. Using online Help, review and print information on adding a CD Audio track to a presentation. Find and print the steps involved for accessing an audio track from a CD and inserting it into a presentation.

Project 2
After experimenting with the custom animation features of PowerPoint, you are anxious to add custom animation to the *Communicate Advanced* presentation to show your boss. You hope she finds such features viable for her use. Add custom animation effects to the slides of *Communicate Advanced*. Set the presentation to loop continuously at a kiosk. Set the same transition and timing on all slides of the presentation to show the presentation quickly for your boss. Save the presentation as *Communicate Animation*. Print the presentation as a six-slides-per-page handout.

Project 3
Your employer asks you to add custom animation to the slides of your presentation. He asks you to be consistent in the animation effects you use. He also wants a sound clip to play throughout the entire presentation—something calming. Open the *Souner Advanced* presentation. Add custom animation to the slides and a sound clip that plays throughout the viewing of the slide show. Connect to the Internet and search the Web for an appropriate sound clip. In addition, add a blank slide at the end of the presentation that matches the presentation. Save the presentation as *Souner Animation*. Print the presentation as a six-slides-per-page handout.

Project 4
While viewing a slide show of your presentation, you decide to add custom animation to the slides of a presentation. You also decide to manually progress through the slide show, and you like the idea of

chapter ten

adding a blank slide at the end of the presentation that can stay on the screen until the audience leaves. Add motion paths to several text boxes on the slides, and add a sound clip from the Clip Organizer. Open *My Presentation Advanced,* and make the changes you decided on. Save the presentation as *My Presentation Animation*. Print the presentation as a six-slides-per-page handout.

Project 5

Your employer wants to set up the *Zoo Advanced* presentation to run as a continuous, self-running presentation viewed at any time, by anyone passing by. To catch the attention of passersby, especially the children, you decide to add custom animation and sounds to the objects on the slides. You want to keep the existing *Zoo Advanced* presentation as is, so you decide to save the new presentation as *Zoo Animation*. Print the presentation as a six-slides-per-page handout.

Project 6

You are interested in accessing Design Gallery Live on the Web. Access the Design Gallery Live site on the Internet. Download at least two sound clips. Search the Web and find at least two music files and save them for future use. Create a presentation consisting of a title and a bullet slide regarding the use of sound and music files. Add sound clips to either text or clip images on these slides. Add one of the music files to play through both slides. Save and print the presentation as a two-slides-per-page handout.

Project 7

You think it would be a good idea to add some custom animation to some or all of the slides in the *Cars Advanced* presentation. You also want to add a sound clip from the Internet to the clip images on the slides. To surprise your students, you want the presentation running continuously as they enter the classroom until you are ready to start class. As your students are really into current music groups, you decide to add music from one of their CD-ROMs or MP3 files from the Internet to keep their interest in the *Cars Advanced* presentation. Open the *Cars Advanced* presentation, add custom effects, add a sound clips to clip images, add music, and set up the presentation to run continuously. Save the presentation as *Cars Animation*. Print the presentation as a six-slides-per-page handout.

Project 8

Your professor wants you to get the presentation ready to upload to the Internet in the next couple of weeks. He wants you to add custom animation to the slides, as well as add a high-tech type of sound that runs continuously throughout the entire *Internet Advanced* presentation. He asks you and your partner to be creative, but consistent. If you can't find a high-tech sound in PowerPoint, he advises you to connect to the Internet and search the Web for an appropriate sound or music clip. When you finish, save the presentation as *Internet Animation*. Print the presentation as a six-slides-per-page handout.

Customizing a Presentation

Chapter Overview

PowerPoint provides many choices for applying a presentation template to a new or existing presentation. In this chapter, you learn how to apply a template from other sources, including other presentations, and to apply more than one presentation design to a presentation. You also learn how to modify an existing template by formatting and editing the title and slide masters of the template. In addition, you learn how to customize slide format and backgrounds by changing the presentation fonts, headers and footers, and slide color scheme. To maintain good file management, you learn to create folders for storing presentations. Finally, you learn how to create a custom slide show.

Case profile
Ms. Hill is pleased with the new *Teddy Toys New Products* presentation you created for the Sales Department to introduce the upcoming new product line to prospective clients. She asks you to save this presentation with a different name, and apply a different template to it. She wants to give the sales people a choice of presentation looks, so they can choose the one that best suits each client. You explore several options to find a different look and tone.

PowerPoint 2002

LEARNING OBJECTIVES

- Apply a presentation design template from a different source
- Modify a presentation template
- Customize slide formats and backgrounds
- Customize a template
- Create folders for storing presentations
- Create a custom show

chapter eleven

11.a Applying a Presentation Design Template from a Different Source

> **QUICK TIP**
>
> Web sites might include a site created by a company where members of the company or team at the company can go to share template or presentation files or commercial Web sites where you can download for free or buy unique, professionally designed templates. If a company Web site has a folder that stores existing presentations that use a design template created especially for the company, any company employee that has rights to the folder may access the design template from any presentation.

As you have learned, each presentation is based on a template. A design template contains its own unique title and slide masters. Masters contain placeholders for text, font size, style and color, background colors, and any special effects applied to objects or text (such as shadowing or bullets). For example, the *Teddy Toys New Products* presentation is based on the design template named Cascade. The background is dark blue with a design element that uses bars of pale yellow, light blue, and blue. You can apply a template when you start a new presentation or at any time after creating the presentation. If you apply a different template to an existing presentation, PowerPoint automatically updates the text style, placement, graphics, background, and color scheme.

In addition to applying the standard design templates to a presentation, you can apply a content template, templates from Microsoft Office Template Gallery at *www.Microsoft.com*, templates from other Web sites, or templates attached to other presentations. The Microsoft Office Template Gallery, located at the Microsoft Web site, provides PowerPoint users with additional templates that can be downloaded for free and that are periodically updated to provide new "looks" to presentations.

Applying a Content Template to an Existing Presentation

Like design templates, **content templates** contain predesigned placement for objects, formatting for fonts, color schemes, and text suggestions for creating common business presentations. Content templates provided by PowerPoint include categories such as projects, sales and marketing, corporate, and general, with suggestions for the types of slides and the information that should appear on the slides. Content templates can be applied to new or existing presentations without using the content suggestions. In addition, content design templates, without the content, can be accessed and applied to existing presentations. Because your presentation is already complete, you want to use one of the content design templates, without the content. To apply a content template:

Step 1	*Open*	the *Teddy Toys New Products* presentation located on the Data Disk
Step 2	*Save*	the presentation as *Teddy Toys Customized*
Step 3	*Double-click*	Cascade on the status bar

Customizing a Presentation PA 57

| Step 4 | Click | the Browse link at the bottom of the Slide Design task pane |

The Apply Design Template dialog box opens. Two of the folders listed contain templates. The Presentation Designs folder contains design templates, the same templates you access through the Design Templates link in the New Presentation task pane. The 1033 folder contains presentation templates, templates that contain both formatting and suggested content.

| Step 5 | Double-click | the 1033 folder |

The folder opens, listing additional folders and displays the content design presentation templates. Your dialog box should look similar to Figure 11-1.

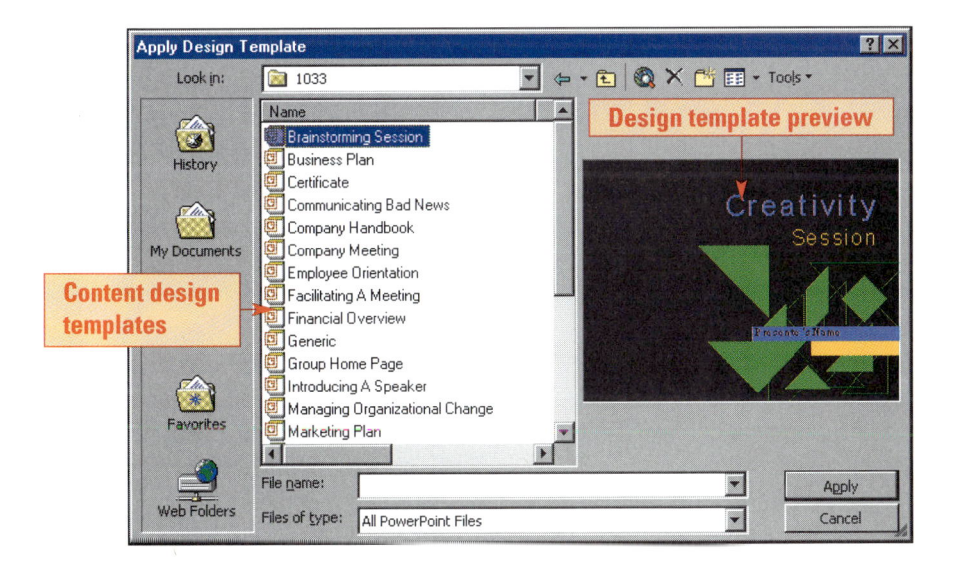

(Screenshot of Apply Design Template dialog box with callouts "Content design templates" and "Design template preview")

> **notes**
> The template files may display a .pot extension if your file extensions are displayed through Windows 98/2000 options. A PowerPoint template file has a .pot extension, whereas a PowerPoint presentation file has a .ppt extension.

| Step 6 | Click | each design in the list and observe the preview |
| Step 7 | Double-click | the Business Plan design template |

QUICK TIP

You also can apply content templates that have been developed by Dale Carnegie Training & Associates that provide coaching for the following topics: Selling Your Ideas, Motivating A Team, Facilitating A Meeting, Presenting A Technical Report, Managing Organization Change, and Introducing A Speaker.

FIGURE 11-1
Apply Design Template Dialog Box with Content Design Templates

INTERNET TIP

Presentation tips and courses developed by Dale Carnegie Training & Associates can be accessed via the Internet through the Web link on the Design Templates task pane or by connecting directly to the Dale Carnegie Training and Associates site by keying the following URL: www.dalecarnegie.com.

chapter eleven

The *Teddy Toys Customized* presentation has now been updated with the formatting, color scheme, and typeface of the content design template. The status bar now displays the Business Plan design template. Your screen should look similar to Figure 11-2.

FIGURE 11-2
Business Plan Design Template Applied to *Teddy Toys Customized* Presentation

[Screenshot showing Business Plan design template applied to the Teddy Toys presentation, with callouts pointing to: "Business Plan design template", "Business Plan design template name in status bar", and "Design templates"]

TASK PANE TIP

You can access content templates when creating a new presentation by clicking the General Templates link in the New Presentation task pane and then clicking the Presentations tab in the Templates dialog box.

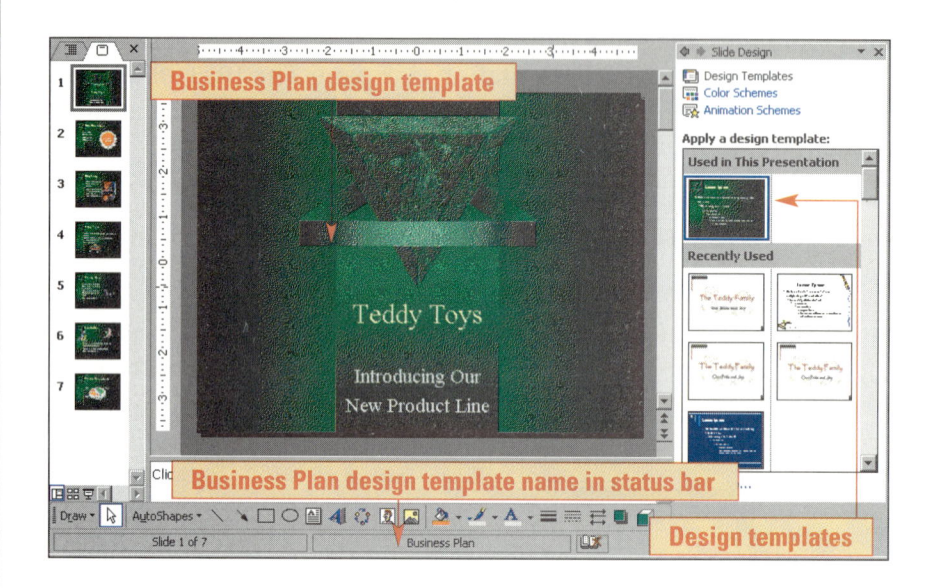

Step 8	Run	the slide show and observe the changes to various portions of each slide
Step 9	Save	the *Teddy Toys Customized* presentation

The colors of the new design template changed the colors of the original design template. The layouts used on each slide remain the same, but the clip art images were resized to fit the layout placeholders of the applied presentation design template. Default effects of the new presentation design won't override any changes made by the user, such as those in a peripheral program used in PowerPoint (Microsoft Graph, for instance).

Applying a Design Template from an Existing Presentation

As mentioned earlier, the design template of any existing presentation can be applied to another presentation. So, if you viewed a presentation on the company intranet or the Internet and liked the design template, or a friend sent you a presentation that uses a design template he/she created and you like it, you can use that design template on your presentation. To apply a design template from an existing presentation:

| Step 1 | Click | the Browse link at the bottom of the Slide Design task pane |

Customizing a Presentation   PA 59

| Step 2 | **Switch to** | the drive or folder where your Data Files are stored |
| Step 3 | **Double-click** | *Teddy Family* |

The *Teddy Toys Customized* presentation has now been updated with a new color scheme and a new customized look. Your screen should look similar to Figure 11-3.

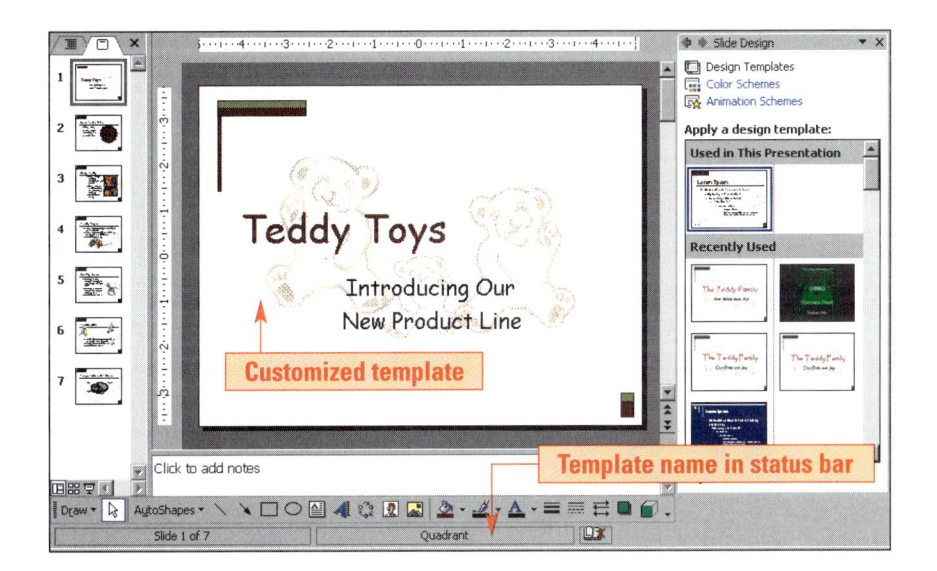

FIGURE 11-3
Slide with Customized Presentation Design Template

The presentation design on the status bar displays Quadrant. When you apply a design template that has been modified from an existing presentation, the modified version of the presentation template appears, but the name of the template refers to the original design. The original design template called Quadrant appears in the task pane as a template (.pot). The edited Quadrant design template applied to the Teddy Family presentation appears in the task pane as Teddy Family (.ppt).

| Step 4 | **Run** | the slide show |

Because of formatting differences between your original template and the Teddy Family presentation, the text in the star AutoShape does not display clearly on the New Product Line slide. To format text within an AutoShape:

MENU TIP

You can edit a title master template by clicking the <u>M</u>aster command on the <u>V</u>iew menu and then clicking the <u>S</u>lide Master command on the submenu.

| Step 1 | **Display** | the New Product Line slide |
| Step 2 | **Select** | the AutoShape object |

chapter eleven

Step 3	Click	the Font Color button list arrow [A] on the Drawing toolbar
Step 4	Click	the white color (first color)
Step 5	Run	the slide show and observe the changes
Step 6	Save	the *Teddy Toys Customized* presentation

Applying More than One Design Template to a Presentation

When creating a presentation that has several parts that are related but separate, such as the chapters in a book, you can apply different design templates to one or more of the slides. When a different design template is applied to a slide or slides within a presentation, another master template is created for those slides. The second master template controls the placement and formatting of title and text placeholders for the slides using the second design template. To apply more than one design template to slides in a presentation:

Step 1	Display	the Slides tab in the outline/slides pane
Step 2	Select	Slides 3 through 6
Step 3	Double-click	the Quadrant in the status bar if necessary to display the Slide Design task pane
Step 4	Scroll	to the Quadrant design template under the Available for use section of the Slide Design task pane (do not use the Quadrant design under the Used in this Presentation section)
Step 5	Click	the Quadrant list arrow
Step 6	Click	Apply to Selected Slides
Step 7	Resize	and/or reposition any image or text box in the presentation to improve the slide's appearance
Step 8	Run	the slide show

The four new product slides now have the Quadrant design. The design element uses the same two colors but is displayed across the top of the screen, the teddy bears no longer display in the background, and the text is Times New Roman.

DESIGN TIP

Although multiple design templates may be applied to a presentation, you should limit the use of multiple templates. Remember that a key to good presentation design is consistency. Having all slides use the same design template creates the impression that all the slides displayed are intended to accomplish a goal. In addition, the audience gets comfortable with a given look and expects to see it each time a slide is displayed.

11.b Modifying a Presentation Template

The master templates, color schemes, and design templates provide a consistent look to any presentation. You access the title and slide masters when you want to add a picture or text to all the slides in the presentation, resize the placeholders, or change font, font size font color, and alignment. Because each design template has its own master, it is possible to have several master templates in each presentation, each of which is edited or formatted apart from the other master templates. When multiple masters are applied to a presentation, each master is listed in the title and slide master views. You can personalize any presentation design by changing the font, size, style, or background color in the master templates, as well as adding footers, date and time, and page numbers.

Formatting Title and Slide Masters

The title master contains formatting for slides that follow the title slide layout. When you make changes to the title master, those changes affect only title slides. The slide master contains formatting for slides that follow all other layouts other than a title slide. When you make changes to either master, those changes take effect on all slides using that master, unless you made individual formatting changes to the slides. The *Teddy Toys Customized* presentation now has one title master and two slide masters. To format the font on the master template:

Step 1	Verify	that one of the new product slides (Baby Teddy, Teddy Wagon, etc.) is the current slide
Step 2	Point to	the Normal View button located to the left of the horizontal scroll bar
Step 3	Press & hold	the SHIFT key until the ScreenTip displays Slide Master View
Step 4	Click	the Slide Master View button

The Slide Master displays placeholders for the title, bullet, date, footer, and slide number areas. It displays existing formats in terms of font, point size, alignment, color scheme, graphic elements, and bullet symbols dependent on the design template used. A Slide Master View toolbar opens in the Slide Master, with options for inserting a new slide master, inserting a new title master, deleting a master, preserving a master, renaming a master, accessing the Master Layout dialog box, and closing the master view. Your screen should look similar to Figure 11-4.

DESIGN TIP

Changes made to the slide master affect all slides using that master unless changes were made individually to a slide. For example, if you change the bullet on one slide, then change the bullet on the master, the individual change remains in effect. To override changes made to individual slides, you reapply the master.

FIGURE 11-4
Slide Master with Slide Master View Toolbar

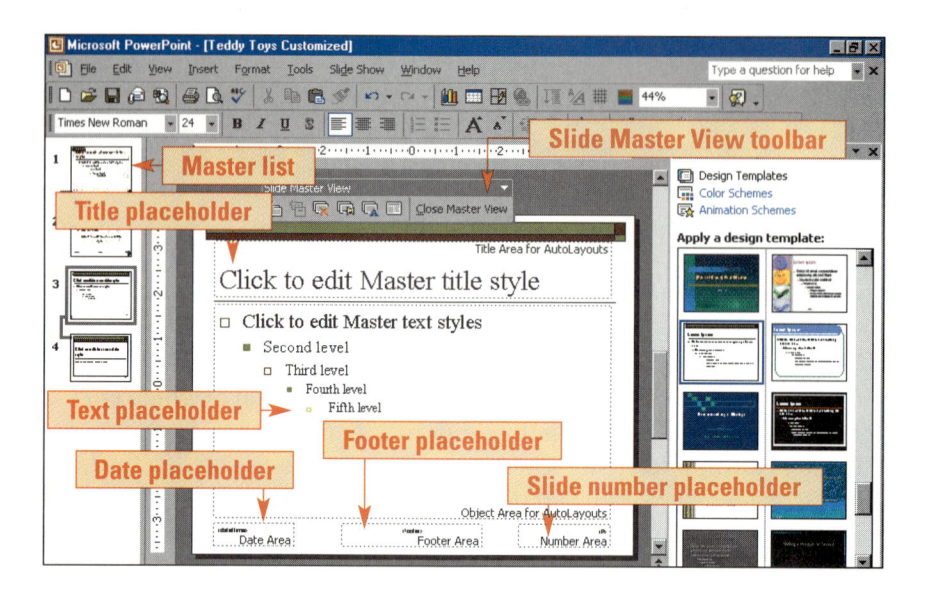

(Screenshot of PowerPoint Slide Master view with labeled callouts: Master list, Title placeholder, Slide Master View toolbar, Text placeholder, Footer placeholder, Date placeholder, Slide number placeholder)

Step 5	*Select*	all five placeholders on the master using CTRL + A
Step 6	*Change*	the font to Comic Sans MS
Step 7	*Deselect*	the selected placeholders
Step 8	*Run*	the slide show from the beginning of the presentation

Adding a Footer to the Slide Master

Headers and footers are slide elements that appear on each slide in a presentation to display repetitive information. **Headers** display information that you want to appear at the top of all printed handouts, outlines, notes pages, and slides; **footers** display information that you want to appear at the bottom. This information might include document titles, filenames, author names, a company logo, dates, or even clip art. Adding the company name to the footer of the master results in all slides based on that slide master to display the company name.

To delete a placeholder, add text to the footer, and change the location of the footer:

Step 1	*Click*	the Date Area placeholder
Step 2	*Press*	the DELETE key
Step 3	*Click*	<footer> in the Footer Area placeholder
Step 4	*Key*	Teddy Toys
Step 5	*Click*	the Align Left button on the Formatting toolbar
Step 6	*Press*	the SHIFT key

Step 7	Drag	the footer placeholder to the left (see Figure 11-5 for placement)
Step 8	Release	the SHIFT key and then the mouse

When you drag to move a placeholder, the SHIFT key maintains the alignment. Your screen should look similar to Figure 11-5.

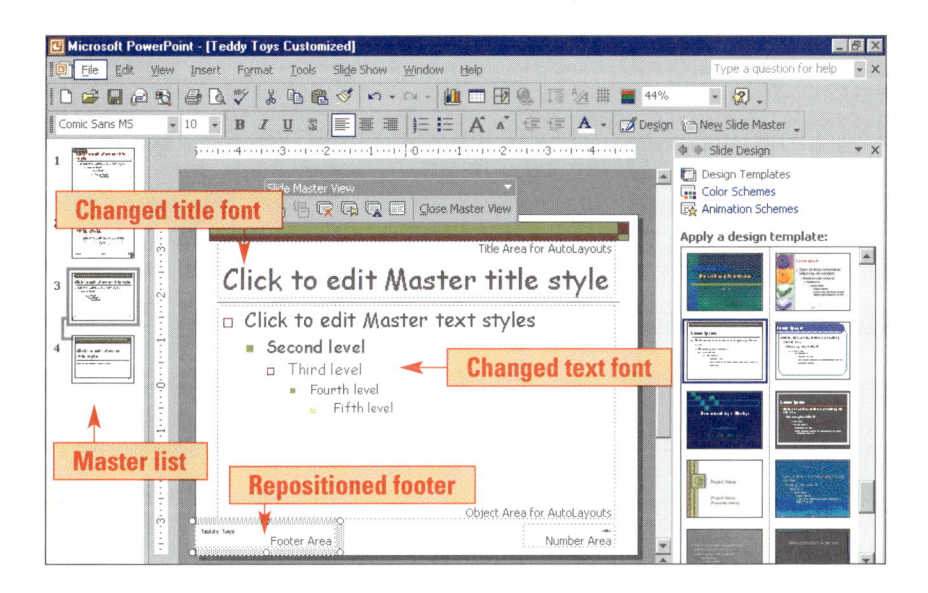

FIGURE 11-5
New Fonts and Footer Location on Slide Master

> **QUICK TIP**
>
> You can create a new slide or title master by clicking the Insert New Slide Master or Insert New Title Master button on the Slide Master View toolbar.

Step 9	Run	the slide show from the beginning

The slides using the slide master of the Quadrant design template now display the company name in the footer.

Creating and Managing Multiple Slide Masters

Whenever you use more than one presentation template in a presentation, PowerPoint creates a master list. The **master list** is displayed in the slide thumbnails pane located at the left of the master views and displays the title and slide masters used in each presentation template. When you use multiple masters in a presentation, they are grouped in slide-title master pairs, each containing a slide master and a title master. To aid the managing of masters in your presentation, you use the buttons on the Slide Master View toolbar. To explore the master list and rename a slide-title master:

Step 1	Point to	the first master in the thumbnails pane

The ScreenTip displays Quadrant Slide Master: used by slide(s) 2, 7.

| Step 2 | Point to | the second master of the first master pair |

The ScreenTip displays Quadrant Title Master: used by slide(s) 1.

| Step 3 | Point to | each slide master of the second master pair |

The ScreenTips display 1_Quadrant Slide Master: used by slide(s) 3-6 and 1_Quadrant Title Master: used by no slides. Because both templates use the Quadrant name, you decide to rename the Quadrant design template containing the teddy bears in the background.

Step 4	Click	the first slide master (ScreenTip displays: Quadrant Slide Master: used by slide(s) 2, 7)
Step 5	Click	the Rename Master button on the Slide Master View toolbar
Step 6	Key	Teddy Bears
Step 7	Click	Rename
Step 8	Point to	the title and slide masters with the teddy bears

The ScreenTips now display Teddy Bears: Slide Master: used by slide(s) 2, 7 and Teddy Bears Title Master: used by slide(s) 1. To make additional changes on the slide masters:

Step 1	Delete	the Date placeholder on the Teddy Bear slide master
Step 2	Key	Teddy Toys in the footer placeholder on the Teddy Bear slide master
Step 3	Change	the footer alignment to the left
Step 4	Drag	the footer placeholder to the extreme left of the slide
Step 5	Change	the font color of the title placeholder on the 1_Quadrant slide master to medium brown (ScreenTip displays: Follow Shadows Scheme color)
Step 6	Run	the slide show
Step 7	Close	Master View
Step 8	Save	the *Teddy Toys Customized* presentation

> **MENU TIP**
>
> You can add slide numbers to each slide individually by creating a text box and then clicking the Slide Number command on the Insert menu.

Adding Slide Numbers Using the Header and Footer Command

Slide numbers can be added to the slides of a presentation so that the slide number appears on each slide when displayed during the slide show presentation. You can add slide numbers to any slide by using the slide master, where the default for the slide numbers is the lower-right corner of the slide.

You can use the Header and Footer dialog box to add a header and/or footer to your presentation which will be displayed throughout the entire presentation, regardless of the number of masters. Using this method eliminates the necessity of separately editing the two masters you applied to your presentation. Any slides added at a later time will also have slide numbers assigned to them because of the automatic slide number code in the footer. To add a slide number to the footer area of all the slides, except the title:

Step 1	Click	View
Step 2	Click	Header and Footer

The Header and Footer dialog box opens, with options for adding the date and time, slide numbers, and a footer to the slide, notes pages, or handouts. Your dialog box should look similar to Figure 11-6.

> **QUICK TIP**
> Any placeholder on the slide master can be moved anywhere on the slide master or deleted.

FIGURE 11-6
Header and Footer Dialog Box

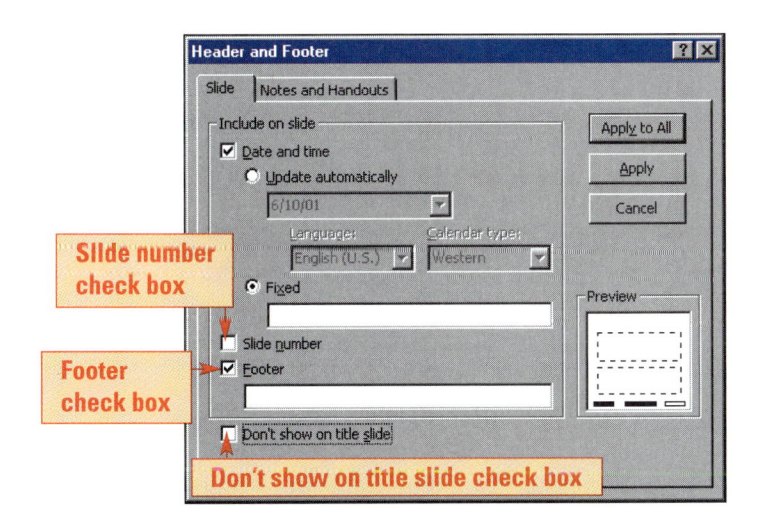

Step 3	Click	the Slide number check box to insert a check mark

The slide number placeholder in the lower-right corner of the Preview box is now bolded. Check marks appear before the Date and time and Footer options, but they do not appear on the slide unless data is

chapter eleven

inserted in the appropriate text boxes. It is not necessary to number the title slide of a presentation because title slides are either the first slide of a presentation or the start of a new section within a presentation.

| Step 4 | **Click** | the Don't show on title <u>s</u>lide check box to insert a check mark |
| Step 5 | **Click** | Appl<u>y</u> to All |

By clicking the Appl<u>y</u> to All button, you assign a page number to the slides of the two presentation design templates, without accessing each master separately.

| Step 6 | **Run** | the slide show and observe the slide numbers |

A slide number appears on every slide in the presentation, except the title slide. On the slides with the teddy bear background, the slide numbers display in the graphic image.

| Step 7 | **Save** | the *Teddy Toys Customized* presentation and close it |

11.c Customizing Slide Formats and Backgrounds

Any presentation design template can be customized by changing the fonts, background and text colors, as well as adding additional elements to the slide master to create the desired look, feel, and tone you are seeking. In addition to modifying presentation design templates using the slide masters, you can change the fonts, backgrounds, and color schemes to customize the slides of a presentation without accessing the slide master. Accessing the <u>R</u>eplace Fonts or Bac<u>k</u>ground commands on the <u>F</u>ormat menu or the Color Schemes command on the Slide Design task pane allows you to customize slide formats without accessing the slide master. Either method of customizing slide formats is effective, but if you are not adding additional elements to the background of the slides, using the menu and task pane commands to format slides is more efficient.

Changing presentation fonts changes all the text within the presentation that uses the existing fonts to a different font. Changing the background of slides involves removing any objects or changing the color of the background, if any. Changing text, graphic, and element colors involves changing the existing color scheme that is part of any presentation design template. A slide color scheme is the set of eight balanced colors used on various elements of the slides in a presentation. If you select a presentation design but want to change various color elements, you can use the presentation design color schemes. You also have the option of creating and saving your own color scheme.

Replacing Presentation Fonts

You can change text font by selecting a text box or multiple text boxes on a slide or slide master and making formatting changes. As another faster alternative, you can change all the fonts in the presentation by using the Replace Fonts command on the Format menu. Replacing fonts affects all text placeholders, text within tables, diagrams, organization charts, and shapes that use the font being replaced. The replace fonts feature does not replace text that was created in the peripheral program Microsoft Graph. The Cascade presentation design template used on the *Teddy Toys New Products* presentation uses Times New Roman for all the titles on all the slides and it uses Arial for all the slide text (bullets, labels, shapes, etc.). You want to change all instances of the Times New Roman and Arial fonts to Comic Sans MS, a friendlier-looking font, in a new presentation based on the *Teddy Toys New Products* presentation. To save the presentation under a new name and replace the presentation fonts:

Step 1	*Open*	the *Teddy Toys New Products* presentation
Step 2	*Save*	the presentation as *Teddy Toys New Look*
Step 3	*Verify*	that no placeholder is selected on the current slide
Step 4	*Click*	Format
Step 5	*Click*	Replace Fonts

The Replace Font dialog box opens. Here, you first specify the font you want to replace, and then you specify the font you want to replace it with. Your dialog box should look similar to Figure 11-7.

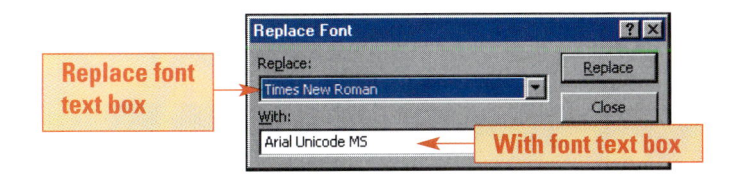

| Step 6 | *Click* | Comic Sans MS in the With: list |
| Step 7 | *Click* | Replace |

> **QUICK TIP**
>
> When you change and edit a color scheme, you have the option of saving that color scheme for use in future presentations.

> **CAUTION TIP**
>
> When you change the slide color scheme, PowerPoint displays an information box indicating that charts are now updated with the color scheme. Depending on the speed of your machine, you have to wait until all slides are updated with the new color scheme.

FIGURE 11-7
Replace Font Dialog Box

TASK PANE TIP

You can display the Slide Design - Color Schemes task pane by clicking Color Schemes on the Slide Design task pane.

You can display the Slide Design task pane by clicking Slide Design on the Format menu or by right-clicking the slide background and then clicking Slide Design.

CAUTION TIP

If you want to control the slides changed by a color scheme, be sure to click the color scheme list arrow to display the options for either applying the color scheme to all slides or selected slides. If you click the color scheme instead of the color scheme list arrow, the color scheme is applied to all the slides of the presentation.

If you change your mind after applying a color scheme to the selected slides or all the slides of a presentation, click the Undo button on the Standard toolbar.

FIGURE 11-8
Slide Design Task Pane with Color Schemes

Step 8	Click	Arial in the Replace: list
Step 9	Verify	that Comic Sans MS is displayed in the With: list
Step 10	Click	Replace
Step 11	Click	Close
Step 12	Run	the slide show

Changing the Slide Color Scheme

The color scheme of a design template includes eight balanced colors for various parts of a slide such as background, text and lines, shadows, title text, fills, accent, accent and hyperlink, and accent and followed hyperlink. You see the eight colors appear when you change the colors of text, fills, and lines of drawing objects. Design templates have varying color schemes available; however, you can choose to further customize each of the available color schemes per design template. To change the slide color scheme:

| Step 1 | Click | the Color Schemes link on the Slide Design task pane |

The Slide Design task pane displays the various color schemes that can be applied to your presentation. The Slide Design task pane enables you to change the entire color scheme automatically. You screen should look similar to Figure 11-8. Notice that on each new color scheme each element of the slide is assigned a color that is complementary to all the other colors in the presentation. You can, however, customize various parts of the color scheme you select by editing that color scheme.

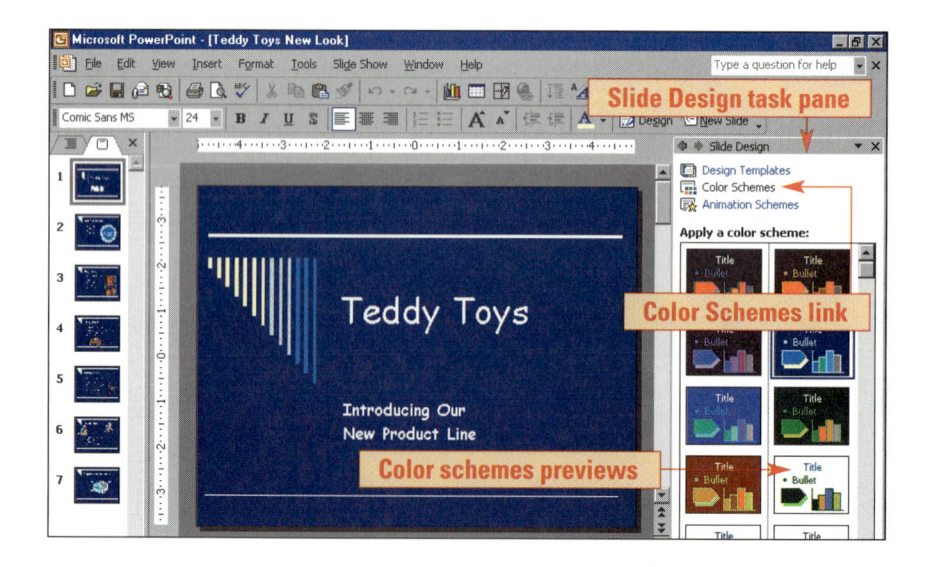

Step 2	Click	the color scheme list arrow in the first row, first column (black background with red fill)
Step 3	Click	Apply to Selected Slides
Step 4	Observe	that the new color scheme is applied only to Slide 1
Step 5	Click	the color scheme that displays the white background with dark blue text and orange bullet colors to apply this color scheme to all the slides

An information bar appears across the slides, indicating that the charts are being updated with the new color scheme.

All the slides in the presentation now have the same color scheme. The background is very important because it sets the tone of the presentation. The background of a slide consists of the colors and objects, if any, that appear behind the text.

The output format of your presentation is a major consideration in determining the appropriate background. If the presentation is printed only, you should use a light background. If you display an electronic slide show with an overhead projection system, you should use a darker background. Depending on your slides, you can choose a solid, gradient, texture, pattern, or picture for your slide backgrounds.

To edit the background and bullets color scheme:

| Step 1 | Click | Edit Color Schemes at the bottom of the Slide Design task pane |

The Edit Color Scheme dialog box opens with options for changing the slide color scheme. You can choose another color scheme in the Standard tab dialog box, or you can change individual scheme colors in the Custom tab dialog box.

| Step 2 | Click | the Custom tab, if necessary |

Your dialog box should look similar to Figure 11-9.

TASK PANE TIP

You can apply a color scheme to all slides in the presentation by clicking the color scheme in the Slide Design - Color Schemes task pane.

CAUTION TIP

Individual changes override default changes in a master template. Any changes made individually to the master templates do not change when the color scheme is changed.

QUICK TIP

You can use the Preview button to preview the changes in the preview window and directly on your slide. You need to drag the title bar of the Color Scheme dialog box so that you can read the text boxes on the slide.

FIGURE 11-9
Edit Color Scheme Dialog Box

Edit Color Scheme dialog box showing Standard colors tab, Custom colors tab, Scheme colors, Change Color button, and Color scheme preview.

MOUSE TIP

You can change the background fill of a presentation by right-clicking a blank area of the slide and then clicking Bac<u>k</u>ground.

DESIGN TIP

For transparencies or printouts, use white or pastel backgrounds and dark colors for text to create a sharp contrast. For slides or slide shows, in which a stronger light is projected behind each slide, use dark colors for backgrounds and light colors for text to create a sharp contrast.

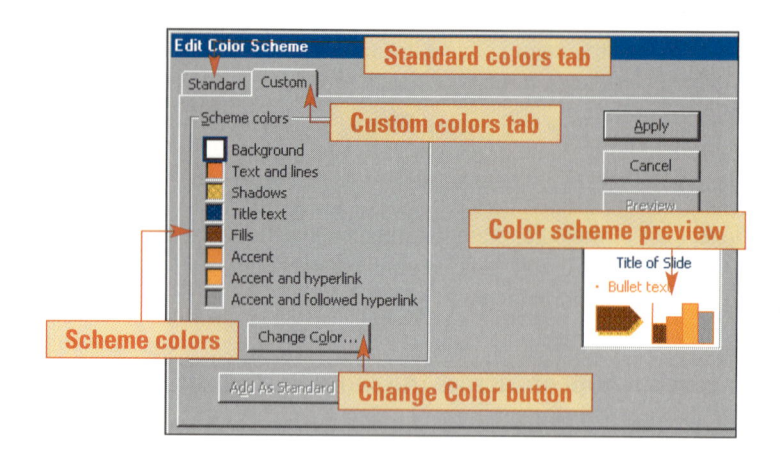

Step 3	Click	the Background color box (white), if necessary
Step 4	Click	Change C<u>o</u>lor
Step 5	Click	the dull yellow color (eighth row, sixth column)
Step 6	Click	OK
Step 7	Click	the Accent and hyperlink color box
Step 8	Click	Change C<u>o</u>lor
Step 9	Click	the dark brown (last row, first column)
Step 10	Click	OK
Step 11	Change	the Fills color to a light gold color (fourth row from bottom, fifth column)
Step 12	Click	<u>A</u>pply
Step 13	Run	the slide show and observe the background and bullet color changes
Step 14	Save	the *Teddy Toys New Look* presentation and close it

11.d Customizing a Template

Customizing a template enables you to create the perfect look that fits the exact image you want to project. That look could be the result of adding design elements to the background of the slide masters, changing colors of backgrounds and text, changing fonts and font sizes, changing alignment within placeholders, and repositioning placeholders.

You can easily create a customized template by first creating a presentation based on any existing design or presentation template. If you don't want the presentation to contain any special formatting, you can base it on the blank design template. You then make all necessary modifications to the presentation, including formatting choices, adding graphic

Customizing a Presentation   PA 71

elements, and adding any text you want to appear in the template. Then you save the presentation as a template.

To customize an existing design template:

Step 1	Open	the New Presentation task pane
Step 2	Click	From Design Template in the New Presentation task pane
Step 3	Click	the Balloons design template
Step 4	Access	the title master
Step 5	Right-click	an empty area of the title master
Step 6	Click	Background
Step 7	Click	the Background fill list arrow
Step 8	Click	Fill Effects
Step 9	Click	the Texture tab
Step 10	Double-click	Pink tissue paper (third row, second column)
Step 11	Click	Apply to All
Step 12	Delete	the Date Area object
Step 13	Align	the Footer Area object at the left
Step 14	Left Align	the <footer> placeholder
Step 15	Increase	the font size for the title to 72 point and the font size for the subtitle to 40 point

The title master on your screen should look similar to Figure 11-10.

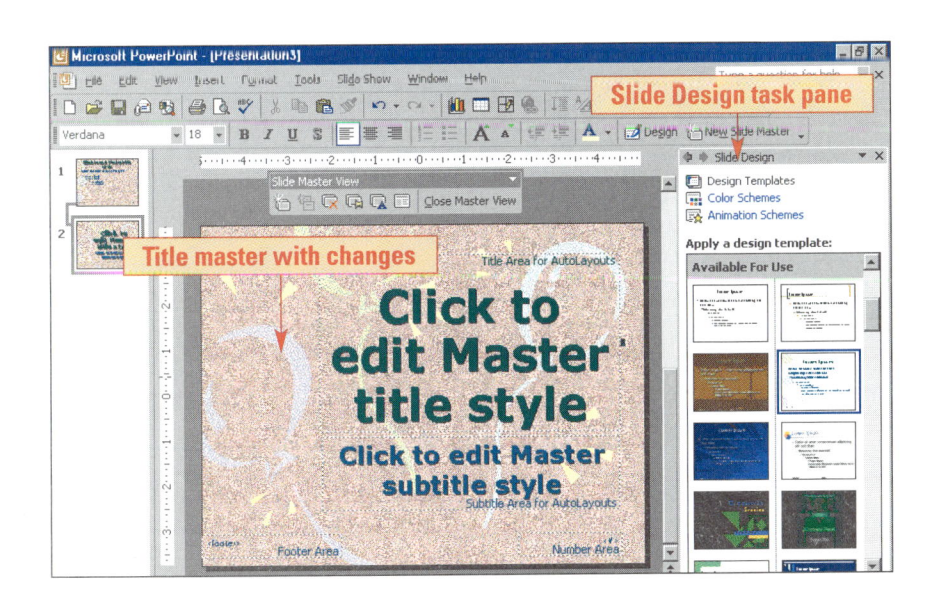

> **MENU TIP**
>
> You can change the slide background by clicking the Background command on the Format menu.

FIGURE 11-10
Title Master with Edited Changes

chapter eleven

Step 16	**Drag**	the scroll bar up on the title master until the ScreenTip displays Slide Master Balloons to display the slide master
Step 17	**Increase**	the font size for the title to 54 point
Step 18	**Increase**	the font size of the first-level bullet to 36 point and the font size of the second-level bullet to 32 point

To personalize a presentation, you can add information at the bottom of every slide that identifies the name of the company, the date, and/or slide numbers. Although the date area placeholder displays at the lower-left corner of a slide and the footer area placeholder displays at the bottom-center of a slide and the slide number placeholder displays at the lower-right of a slide, these locations can be moved or deleted. To edit the footer placeholders:

Step 1	**Delete**	the Date Area placeholder
Step 2	**Align**	the Footer Area object at the left
Step 3	**Left Align**	the <footer> placeholder

> **QUICK TIP**
>
> You can move between the title master and the slide master by clicking either master in the slides tab.

In addition to formatting text, moving placeholders, and changing backgrounds, you can add or delete design elements on the slide masters. **Design elements** are images or objects that complement the background, attract the eye of the viewer, and add consistency to the look of the slides in a presentation. The Balloons design template currently has a set of three balloons, aligned vertically, at the left of the slide master. To copy and add images on the slide master:

Step 1	**Copy**	the balloons clip art image at the left of the slide
Step 2	**Paste**	and reposition the second balloons clip art image to the right of the slide
Step 3	**Flip**	the balloons clip art image on the right horizontally
Step 4	**Draw**	a horizontal line below the title placeholder and above the text placeholder that reaches from one balloon stem to the other
Step 5	**Change**	the style of the line to 4½ pt
Step 6	**Open**	the Insert Clip Art task pane
Step 7	**Search**	for a single teddy bear image with a party theme
Step 8	**Insert**	the teddy bear image and move it inside the first balloon at the upper left
Step 9	**Resize**	the image to fit inside the balloon

Step 10	Copy	the teddy bear image to the last balloon at the lower right
Step 11	Flip	the second teddy bear image horizontally
Step 12	Resize	the second teddy bear image to fit inside the last balloon

The slide on your screen should look similar to Figure 11-11.

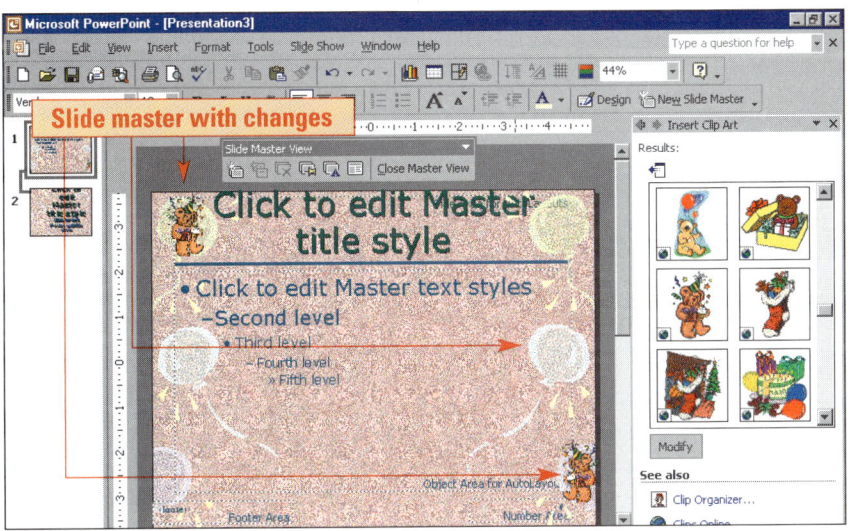

FIGURE 11-11
Slide Master with Changes

Step 13	Close	the slide master

Once you have made substantial changes to the look of a presentation, you can save your design efforts as a new presentation template. It becomes a template that you can apply to other new or existing presentations and even share with others.

When you save a template in PowerPoint, you identify it as a template file (.pot) and not a presentation file (.ppt). PowerPoint then saves it to the location where other templates are saved, so it is available when you create a new presentation. Templates created in Microsoft Office are saved to the Templates folder located in the Microsoft folder, which is in the Application Data folder of Windows. All templates that are created in Word, Excel, Access, and PowerPoint are saved to the Templates folder. Such file management enables the various software packages to operate efficiently. To save a presentation as a design template:

Step 1	Click	File
Step 2	Click	Save As

chapter eleven

Task Pane Tip

You can create a presentation from a new template by clicking General Templates under New from template in the New Presentation task pane. The Templates dialog box enables you to choose design templates, content templates, and user-defined templates.

Step 3	Click	Design Template in the Save as type: list
Step 4	Observe	that the folder automatically changes to Templates
Step 5	Key	Teddy Toys Birthday Template in the File name: text box
Step 6	Click	Save

The template you created has been saved in the Templates folder for easy retrieval at a future date. It will appear in the Slide Design task pane under Available for Use the next time you open PowerPoint.

| Step 7 | Close | the *Teddy Toys Birthday Template* and PowerPoint |

Applying a Newly Created Presentation Template

You apply a newly created template in the same manner as any other template in PowerPoint. You can create a new presentation or you can apply the new template to an existing presentation. If you want your templates to appear under Available for Use in the Slide Design task pane, you must close PowerPoint after creating the template. When you reopen PowerPoint, your newly created presentation displays in the Slide Design task pane.

To create a presentation based on a template you have created:

Step 1	Start	PowerPoint
Step 2	Display	the Slide Design task pane
Step 3	Click	the *Teddy Toys Birthday Template* design template under Available for Use
Step 4	Key	the title Teddy Toys
Step 5	Key	the subtitle We're Having a Birthday
Step 6	Add	a new slide

A text slide appears with the balloon clip art images at the left and right with the two teddy bear clip art images.

| Step 7 | Key | the title Join the Celebration |
| Step 8 | Key | Honoring as the first-level bullet |

Step 9	Key	the following second-level bullets under Honoring: Papa Teddy (press the ENTER key) Mama Teddy (press the ENTER key) Baby Teddy
Step 10	Run	the slide show from the beginning
Step 11	Save	the presentation as *Teddy Toys Celebration* and close it

11.e Creating Folders for Storing Presentations

Design templates are saved to a Templates folder in Windows, unlike regular presentations that are saved to a default folder on the C:\ or network drive. The reason for using folders to store files is efficient file management. The goal of file management is fast, easy access and retrieval. File management enables you to organize your files much like an office file cabinet. If you were asked to retrieve a letter from a file cabinet, you would not want to have to look through all the letters in the file cabinet to find the one you are looking for. You would want to go directly to the appropriate folder, within the appropriate drawer and find the letter. Folders can be created in Windows Explorer or the Save As or Open dialog boxes from within PowerPoint, Word, Excel, or Access.

To create a folder within PowerPoint:

Step 1	Click	the Open button on the Standard toolbar
Step 2	Switch to	the folder that contains your Data Files
Step 3	Click	the Create New Folder button in the Open dialog box

The New Folder dialog box opens. It displays a text box for keying the name of your new folder.

Step 4	Key	Teddy Toys Presentations in the Name: text box
Step 5	Click	OK

The Teddy Toys Presentations folder opens in the Open dialog box displaying no presentations because you have just created the folder.

Step 6	Click	the Up One Level button in the Open dialog box

> **QUICK TIP**
>
> Pressing the CTRL key when selecting multiple files in the contents window enables you to select nonadjacent files. Pressing the SHIFT key when selecting multiple files enables you to select adjacent files.
>
> You can add any folder to the My Places Bar in the Open or Save As dialog box. You select the folder, click the Tools button, and then click Add to "My Places." This enables you to quickly access your presentations by simply clicking the folder on the My Places Bar. In addition, you can change the order of the folders, remove folders, or change from large to small icons.

chapter eleven

Step 7	*Click*	the *Teddy Toys Celebration* presentation
Step 8	*Press & hold*	the CTRL key
Step 9	*Click*	the following presentations: *Teddy Toys Customized* and *Teddy Toys New Look*
Step 10	*Release*	the CTRL key
Step 11	*Right-click*	any selected file
Step 12	*Click*	Cu*t*
Step 13	*Double-click*	the *Teddy Toys Presentations* folder
Step 14	*Right-click*	in the folder list
Step 15	*Click*	*P*aste
Step 16	*Close*	the Open dialog box

11.f Creating a Custom Show

A **custom show** is a presentation within a presentation saved under a separate name. Instead of creating multiple, nearly identical presentations for different audiences, you can group together and name the slides that differ and then use these slides at the appropriate time for the appropriate audience.

For example, you might want to give a presentation to two groups in your company that work at two different sites or in two different departments. To do so, you create a presentation that includes slides that are identical and pertinent to both groups. Next, you create slides within the same presentation that contain information specific to each group. Finally, you create two custom shows, each containing slides specific to each group. The result is one presentation that can be given to two groups, but displays only the slides relevant to each group.

To create a custom show from existing slides:

Step 1	*Open*	the *Teddy Toys Customized* presentation
Step 2	*Save*	the presentation as *Teddy Toys Custom Show*
Step 3	*Click*	Sli*d*e Show
Step 4	*Click*	Custom Sho*w*s
Step 5	*Click*	*N*ew in the Custom Shows dialog box

The Define Custom Show dialog box opens enabling you to select the slides you want to appear in the custom show. Your dialog box should look similar to Figure 11-12.

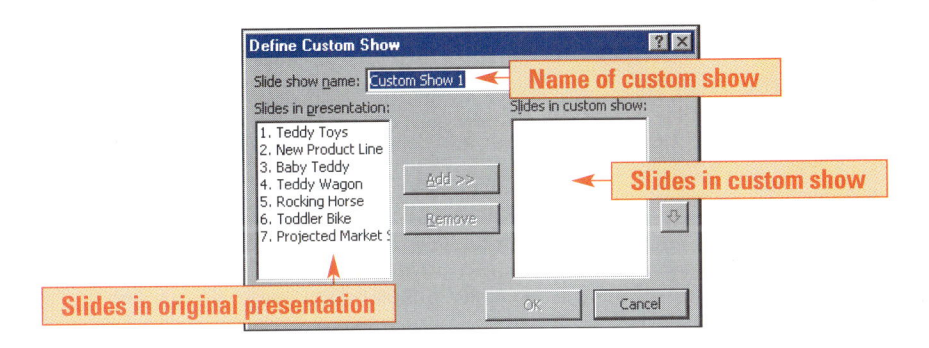

FIGURE 11-12
Define Custom Show Dialog Box

| Step 6 | *Key* | New Products Custom in the Slide show name: text box |
| Step 7 | *Double-click* | the following slides: Teddy Toys; Baby Teddy; Teddy Wagon; Rocking Horse; and Toddler Bike |

The title and four new product slides appear in the Slides in custom show: list box. If you need to rearrange the order in which the slides appear in the custom show, click the slide or slides you wish to move and then click the up or down arrow at the right of the list box.

| Step 8 | *Click* | OK |

New Products Custom appears in the Custom shows: list box. If you wanted to create another show, edit, remove, or copy the existing show, you would click one of the command buttons displayed at the right. To create a second custom show from existing slides:

Step 1	*Click*	New
Step 2	*Key*	Introducing New Products in the Slide show name: text box
Step 3	*Double-click*	the following slides: Teddy Toys; New Product Line; and Projected Market Share
Step 4	*Click*	OK
Step 5	*Click*	Close

QUICK TIP

You can add multiple slides in the Define Custom Show dialog box by pressing CTRL as you click the slides you want to include in the custom show and then clicking Add.

MOUSE TIP

You can run a custom show during a slide show presentation by accessing the shortcut menu, pointing to Go, pointing to Custom Show, and then clicking the desired custom show.

chapter eleven

When it is time to display the slides of a custom show, you can set up the custom show prior to running the slide show. You set up the custom show using the Set Up Show dialog box and selecting the desired custom show you want to display. You can also run a custom show during a slide show presentation using the shortcut menu to access the desired custom show. To set up the custom show and run it in slide show:

Step 1	*Click*	Sli<u>d</u>e Show
Step 2	*Click*	<u>S</u>et Up Show to open the Set Up Show dialog box
Step 3	*Click*	the <u>C</u>ustom show: option button under Show slides

New Products Custom displays in the <u>C</u>ustom show: list box. If you want to run a different show, you can click the list arrow and select the show. You want to run the New Products Custom slide show.

Step 4	*Click*	OK
Step 5	*Run*	the slide show to view the title and four new product slides
Step 6	*Save*	the *Teddy Toys Custom Show* presentation and close it

A custom show enables you to use one presentation for a variety of audiences.

MENU TIP

You can run a custom show by clicking Sli<u>d</u>e Show, clicking Custom Sho<u>w</u>s, selecting the custom show, and then clicking <u>S</u>how.

MOUSE TIP

You can run a custom show from your desktop by opening Microsoft Windows Explorer, locating the folder where the presentation is located, right-clicking the file, and then clicking S<u>h</u>ow.

Summary

- Presentation and design templates contain their own unique title and slide masters that include formats for font styles, sizes, colors, backgrounds, graphic elements, and color schemes.
- You can change the design template of a presentation using one of the following methods: applying a presentation design from the Slide Design task pane, applying a content template, or applying a design template from an existing presentation.
- AutoContent presentations include a design template as well as actual text that focus on common business needs.
- The current master styles can be reapplied to any slide after a new design template has been applied to override any previous manual changes to individual slides.
- The master templates, color schemes, and design templates provide a consistent look to a presentation.
- The slide master template holds the graphics and text that you want to appear on every slide in the presentation.
- The title master affects all title slides in the presentation; the slide master affects all slides other than the title slides.
- Title master templates contain title, subtitle, date, footer, and slide number placeholders.
- Multiple presentation design templates can be added to a presentation.
- A master list displays the title and slide masters from each presentation template used in a presentation that uses multiple templates.
- Slides are numbered in a presentation using the Header and Footer options.
- Bullet symbols are determined by the presentation design template, but can be changed.
- Any presentation design template can be edited to better suit individual preferences or needs.
- All the fonts in the presentation can be changed by using the replace fonts feature in PowerPoint, regardless of the number of presentation design templates that have been applied.
- A slide color scheme is a set of eight balanced colors that are used on various components of the slides in a presentation so that all components complement each other.
- Customized design templates can be saved as new templates to use again at a later date.

chapter eleven

- Folders for saving files can be created in the Save As dialog box or the Open dialog box.
- When saving a design template, it must be saved with a .pot extension.
- To save a design template, select the Design Template presentation type in the Save as type: list box.
- The goal of file management is fast, easy access and retrieval of files and/or presentations.
- Good file management uses folders to organize your files much like an office file cabinet.
- A custom show is a presentation within a presentation, consisting of different slides and a separate name for the custom show.
- You can use custom shows to show different slides of the same presentation to different groups of people.

Commands Review

Action	Menu Bar	Shortcut Menu	Toolbar	Task Pane	Keyboard
Apply one or multiple design templates	Format, Slide Design	Right-click slide background, Slide Design	Design Templates	Design templates in the Slide Design task pane	ALT + O, D
Reapply current master styles	Format, Slide Layout	Right-click slide background, Slide Layout		List arrow on layout in the Slide Layout task pane, Reapply Layout	ALT + O, L
Access the title master	View, Master, Slide Master on title slide		SHIFT + on title slide		ALT + V, M, S
Access the slide master	View, Master, Slide Master		SHIFT + on any slide other than a title slide		ALT + V, M, S
Replace presentation fonts	Format, Replace Fonts				ALT + O, R
Adding a footer	View, Header and Footer, Footer				ALT + V, H, F
Add slide numbers	View, Header and Footer, Slide number			Slide Design	ALT + V, H, N
Change color scheme	Format, Slide Design, Color Schemes		Design, Color Schemes	Slide Design - Color Schemes	ALT + O + D
Change background	Format, Background	Right-click slide background, Background		Slide Design – Color Schemes, Edit Color Schemes	ALT + O, K
Save a design template	File, Save As, Save as type: Design Template				ALT + F, A, T
Create a folder			in Open or Save As dialog box		
Create a custom show	Slide Show, Custom Shows, New				ALT + D, W, N
Run a custom show	Slide Show, Set Up Show, Custom show	Right-click in slide show, Go, Custom Show, click desired show, click through custom show			ALT + D, S, then ALT + C

Concepts Review

Circle the correct answer.

1. To change the design of a presentation, you can apply all of the following *except*:
   - [a] a content design template.
   - [b] PowerPoint design templates from the Slide Design task pane.
   - [c] templates from another presentation.
   - [d] a background template.

2. Which of the following does not provide a consistent look to any presentation?
   - [a] master templates
   - [b] color scheme
   - [c] presentation design
   - [d] clip art on an individual slide

3. The goal of presentation designs is to:
   - [a] provide consistency within the presentation.
   - [b] add variety to the presentation.
   - [c] create extra work.
   - [d] make every presentation look the same.

4. The slide master holds all of the following *except*:
   - [a] clip art images.
   - [b] text.
   - [c] clip art and text for the title slides.
   - [d] text, clip art images, colors, backgrounds, and formatting for all placeholders.

5. You can access the Background command by:
   - [a] right-clicking the slide background, then clicking Format, Background.
   - [b] pressing the CTRL + B keys.
   - [c] pressing ALT + B keys.
   - [d] right-clicking the slide background, then clicking Background.

6. The types of placeholders on the title master template are best described as:
   - [a] title, subtitle, and footer area.
   - [b] title, subtitle, date area, footer area, and number area.
   - [c] title, subtitle, date area, footer area, and time area.
   - [d] title, subtitle, date area, and footer area.

7. The formatting and placement for the title and body of text on the slides of a presentation is determined by the:
   - [a] title or slide master.
   - [b] outline master.
   - [c] handouts master.
   - [d] notes master.

8. All the same fonts within a presentation, regardless of the number of design templates, can be changed at the same time using the:
   - [a] Format, Font command.
   - [b] Format, Slide Design command.
   - [c] Format, Replace Fonts command.
   - [d] Format, Change Case command.

9. Creating your own presentation design may involve all of the following *except*:
   - [a] formatting the fonts and bullets on the masters.
   - [b] adding clip art images or text to the masters.
   - [c] changing the color scheme and background of the design.
   - [d] using the AutoContent Wizard.

10. To save a presentation design as a new template you use:
    - [a] File, Save As, Save as type: Presentation Template (*.pot).
    - [b] File, Save As, Save as type: Design Template (*.pot).
    - [c] File, Save As, Save as type: Presentation (*.ppt).
    - [d] File, Save As HTML, Design Template (*.htm).

chapter eleven

Circle **T** if the statement is true or **F** if the statement is false.

T F 1. You can apply a content design template to an existing PowerPoint presentation.
T F 2. Editing the title master affects all the slides in a presentation.
T F 3. Bullet symbols are originally determined by the presentation design.
T F 4. You must reapply the current master styles if you want the slides to follow the new presentation design if you manually made changes to individual slides.
T F 5. The term "title master" is an alternate name for the term "slide master."
T F 6. Slide numbers can only be added by editing the master template.
T F 7. Color schemes consist of ten complementary colors that work together to present a professional, polished look to a presentation.
T F 8. You can customize a color scheme by changing the colors of various slide components.
T F 9. Backgrounds for slide show presentations look best if they are light or transparent.
T F 10. When you save your own custom presentation design template, PowerPoint automatically adds a .pto extension.

Skills Review

Exercise 1

1. Open the *PowerPoint Advanced* presentation located on the Data Disk, and save it as *PowerPoint Customized*.
2. Access the title master. Format the title in 60 point Tahoma. Format the subtitle in 40 point Times New Roman.
3. Access the slide master and make the following changes:

   Title: 48 point Tahoma.
   First-level bullet text: 36 point Times New Roman.
   Second-level bullet text: 32 point Times New Roman.

4. Change the color scheme of the presentation to the brown color scheme.
5. View the slide show.
6. Save and print the presentation as a four-slides-per-page handout, and then close it.

Exercise 2

1. Open the *Office Advanced* presentation located on the Data Disk, and save it as *Office Customized*.
2. Apply the Selling a Product or Service content template to the presentation. (*Hint:* Look in folder 1033 or look in the Available for use in the Slide Design task pane.)
3. Access the title master, and change the title font to 60 point Garamond with shadow and the subtitle font to 36 point Garamond.
4. Access the slide master, and change the title font to 44 point Garamond with shadow; the bullet text to Arial Narrow; and the Date Area, Footer Area, and Number Area placeholders to Arial Narrow.
5. Add slide numbers to all the slides in the presentation, except the title slide.
6. Delete the Date Area placeholder on the slide master.
7. Add a footer that reads "Office."
8. Move the footer to the left and left-align the text.

9. View the slide show.
10. Save and print the presentation as a six-slides-per-page handout, and then close it.

Exercise 3

1. Open the *Design Advanced* presentation located on the Data Disk, and save it as *Design Customized*.
2. Apply the Studio design template.
3. Change all the placeholder text on the title master to Book Antiqua.
4. Change the size of the title on the title master to 54 point and center it
5. Change the size of the subtitle to 36 point.
6. Change all the text placeholders on the slide master to Book Antiqua.
7. Change the title text placeholder on the slide master to 40 point.
8. Change the first-level bullet symbol on the slide master to a symbol of your choice.
9. Change all bullet text on the slide master to italic.
10. Change the color scheme to the last green background with the colors that complement the background.
11. View the slide show.
12. Save and print the presentation as a six-slides-per-page handout, and then close it.

Exercise 4

1. Open the *Precision Builders Advanced* presentation located on the Data Disk, and save it as *Precision Builders Customized*.
2. Change the slide color scheme to the black background and complementary colors.
3. Edit the new Color Scheme by changing the title text color to the gray-blue color (second row, third column) and the text and line color to the pale yellow color (eighth row, sixth column).
4. Add slide numbers to all the slides except the title slide.
5. View the slide show.
6. Save the *Precision Builders Customized* presentation.
7. Print the presentation as a six-slides-per-page handout.
8. Delete all the slides except the title slide.
9. Save the presentation design template as *Precision Builders*.
10. Create a new presentation using the *Precision Builders* template.
11. Create a text slide with the following information:

    Title: *Great New Subdivisions*
    Bullets: *Mountain Meadows*
               TreeTop Terrace
               Brookside Estates
               Paradise Cliffs

12. Save the presentation as *Precision Builders Subdivisions*.
13. Print the presentation as a two-slides-per-page handout, and then close it.

chapter eleven

Exercise 5

1. Open the *Nature Tours Advanced* presentation located on the Data Disk, and save it as *Nature Tours Customized*.
2. Apply the Mountain Top presentation design.
3. Change the color scheme to reflect a more earthy look.
4. Add the text "Nature Tours" in the footer, and position it attractively.
5. Make changes to the title font and subtitle font on the title master and slide master to complement the presentation design.
6. Change the fill color on the AutoShapes to complement the design.
7. View the slide show.
8. Make changes as necessary to see all text and images on all the slides.
9. If necessary, resize, reposition, or delete any clip art image that does not go well with the new presentation design.
10. Save and print the presentation as a six-slides-per-page handout, and then close it.

Exercise 6

1. Open the *A Healthier You Advanced* presentation located on the Data Disk, and save it as *A Healthier You Customized*.
2. Change the slide color scheme to a lighter background.
3. Change the title font on the title master to 60 point Bookman Old Style.
4. Change the subtitle on the title master to Arial Narrow.
5. Change the title font on the slide master to Bookman Old Style.
6. Change the remaining text placeholders on the slide master to Arial Narrow (do not include the title placeholder).
7. Add your name to the footer, and arrange the footer attractively on the page.
8. Change the bullet symbols for the first- and second-level bullets to enhance the look of the slides.
9. Add slide numbers to all the slides in the presentation, except the title slide.
10. Make any additional changes to coordinate the look of the slides in the presentation.
11. View the slide show.
12. Save and print the presentation as a three-slides-per-page handout, and then close it.

Exercise 7

1. Open the *Buying A Computer Advanced* presentation located on the Data Disk, and save it as *Buying A Computer Customized*.
2. Apply the Marketing Plan content design template.
3. Make any changes that will complement the *Buying A Computer Customized* presentation
4. Print the *Buying A Computer Customized* presentation as a six-slides-per-page handout.
5. Add the Pixel design template to Slides 3, 4, and 5.
6. Using the slide master, add "Buying A Computer" to the footer on the Pixel slide master.
7. Create a custom show, called *Computers*, consisting of the following slides: Computer Essentials, Places to Buy a Computer, and Home Computer Prices.
8. Run the *Computers* custom show using the shortcut menu during the *Buying A Computer Customized* slide show.
9. Save the presentation.
10. Delete all the slides except the title slide.

Customizing a Presentation   PA 85

11. Delete the text on the title slide.
12. Save the presentation design template as *Buying A Computer*, and then close the presentation template.
13. Create a new presentation using the *Buying A Computer* design template.
14. Create a title and bullet slide relating to banking.
15. Save the presentation as *Banking Customized*, print it as a two-slides-per-page handout, and then close it.

Exercise 8

1. Open the *Leisure Travel Advanced* presentation located on the Data Disk, and save it as *Leisure Travel Customized*.
2. Change the presentation design using a content design, presentation designs, or another presentation to create a feeling of luxury that will appeal to travelers.
3. Change the color scheme of the presentation design, and customize colors as desired.
4. Access the slide master, and change the font, font size, and font color, if necessary, to create the feeling you want.
5. Change the graphic on the slide master, and move it to a new location on the slide master.
6. Add the text *Leisure Travel* to the footer, and position it attractively on the slide.
7. Change the fill colors of the AutoShapes slide to match the slide color scheme.
8. Change the chart to the default chart colors, and make any other adjustments on the chart slide.
9. Make any other necessary changes to each slide to aid readability and enhance the slide's appearance.
10. View the slide show.
11. Save and print the presentation as a six-slide-per-page handout, and then close it.

Case Projects

Project 1

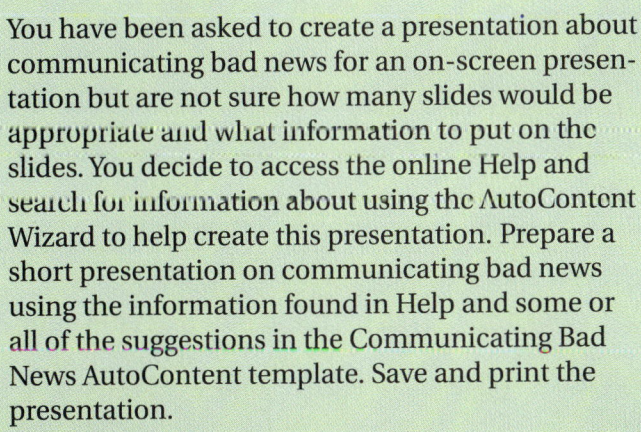

You have been asked to create a presentation about communicating bad news for an on-screen presentation but are not sure how many slides would be appropriate and what information to put on the slides. You decide to access the online Help and search for information about using the AutoContent Wizard to help create this presentation. Prepare a short presentation on communicating bad news using the information found in Help and some or all of the suggestions in the Communicating Bad News AutoContent template. Save and print the presentation.

Project 2

You decide to change the look of your *Communicate Advanced* presentation. Change the color scheme to a scheme that best displays the presentation as overhead transparencies. Change the fills and accent colors in your new color scheme, if necessary, to clearly display all text. Make any changes regarding the slide master font, font color and size, or bullets. Make any changes regarding AutoShapes or AutoShape text. Add slide numbers to all the slides in the presentation except the title slide. Add the word "Communicate" in the footer, and move the footer to the left. Save the presentation as *Communicate Customized*, and print it as a six-slides-per-page handout.

Project 3

Your employer wants you to create a presentation design template based on the *Souner Advanced* presentation. He would like you to edit the color scheme to add color to the background, but he does not want you to use a black or white background. He likes the text, bullets, shapes, and chart and only wants you to change their appearance by

chapter eleven

changing the presentation fonts and text colors to complement the background you choose. He wants you to increase the size of the text in the title and text placeholders on the slide master and add the name of the company, Souner & Associates, to the lower-left corner and a page number at the lower-right corner of all slides, except the title slide. Save the presentation as *Souner Customized,* and save the presentation design template as *Souner Master* so it can be accessed at a later date. View the presentation, and make any necessary changes to coordinate all the slides in the presentation. Print the presentation as a four-slides-per-page handout.

Project 4

You are asked to create a new presentation design from scratch. Begin with a new presentation, and select either an AutoContent design or a presentation design. Change the color scheme, background, and fonts to your liking. Add either a clip art image or a company logo to the slide master. Save the design template as *My New Presentation.* Close the newly created design template. Open the *My Presentation Advanced* presentation, and apply the *My New Presentation* template to this presentation. Save the presentation as *My Presentation Customized.* Print your new presentation as a nine-slides-per-page handout.

Project 5

As the zoo director views the slide show for the *Zoo Advanced* presentation, she indicates that she wants a lion, tiger, polar bear, or elephant to appear on the title and a smaller version of any of those animals to appear on all the slides. In addition, she also wants more color on the slides and a more playful font to be used. Apply a presentation design either from the content design templates, presentation designs, or from an existing presentation. Make sure to change the color scheme and background if needed. Check to see that all text, bullets, shapes, and clip art images are seen and easily read on all slides. Reapply the slide layout of the new presentation design template, if necessary, to resize the table or chart placeholders so they fit the new template. Add the clip art images the zoo director requested on the slide masters, making sure they do not interfere with the new presentation design. Save the new presentation as *Zoo Customized.* Print your new presentation as a four-slides-per-page handout.

Project 6

You have worked with PowerPoint for quite some time, and now you want to find additional template designs for your presentations. Access online Help, and search for information about creating a presentation using Web templates or using templates from the Office Update Web site. Create a short presentation listing the steps you need to follow to apply a template from the Web or an Internet site. Apply a design presentation from the Web, and indicate the Web address in the footer. Save and print the presentation.

Project 7

Before giving your *Cars Advanced* presentation to your class, you want to view the presentation in a classroom with an overhead projection system. You find that the color scheme, background, and font colors and sizes do not display well with the lights out. You decide to make changes so that the color scheme and background are easily seen and the font colors easily read by the entire class. Make any changes in regard to clip art images, shapes, and other text boxes. Create two custom shows from the slides in the presentation that you can use for customized presentations. Save the new presentation as *Cars Customized,* and print the presentation as a six-slides-per-page handout.

Project 8

Your professor is pleased with your *Internet Advanced* presentation thus far. In fact, he wants you and your partner to create two new presentation designs that he could use for any presentation he plans to present in his classes. One presentation should use a light background, whereas the other presentation should use a dark background. This gives your professor some flexibility depending on how he displays the presentations. Include the professor's name on the slide master. Change fonts, bullets, and color schemes so his presentations stand out among his colleagues. Save each presentation as a design template including his name in the template name. Create a sample presentation consisting of a title and bullet slide using each new template. Print the presentations as a two-slides-per-page handout.

PowerPoint Presentations and the Internet

PowerPoint 2002

Chapter Overview

One of the most dramatic trends in organizations today is increased connectivity across networks. PowerPoint enables you to take advantage of this by sharing information through presentations published to an Internet or intranet site and by using hyperlinks to presentations. In this chapter, you learn how to add hyperlinks to slides so that when you run a slide show you can quickly jump to another slide in the presentation or to another presentation. You also learn how to preview a presentation in Web page format, save a presentation as a Web file, and publish a presentation to the Internet or an intranet.

Case profile

Ms. Hill plans to show the *Teddy Toys New Products* presentation to a group of staff members. She wants you to create hyperlinks on selected slides in the presentation so that she can link to different slides, a different presentation, and the Internet during her talk. In addition, Ms. Hill wants you to publish the *Teddy Toys New Products* presentation to the Internet, so that staff members who do not attend the meeting have access to viewing the presentation.

LEARNING OBJECTIVES

- Understand hyperlinks
- Add hyperlinks to slides
- Preview a presentation as a Web page
- Save a PowerPoint presentation as a Web page
- Edit a Web page presentation
- Publish a presentation to the Web

chapter twelve 12

QUICK TIP

You also can create a hyperlink that starts a program, runs a macro, or opens an embedded object. In addition, hyperlinks can be added to any text or object on a slide to jump to a presentation that is yet to be created. When the presentation is eventually created, the hyperlink will link to it.

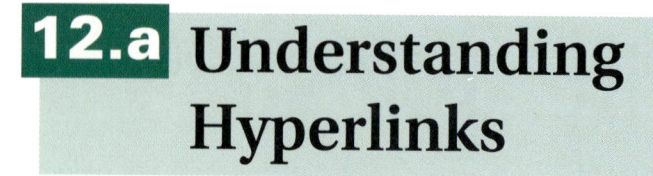

12.a Understanding Hyperlinks

A **hyperlink** is specially formatted text or a graphic in a presentation that you click to move or "jump" to another slide in the presentation, to another presentation, or to another location, such as a Web page or file. A hyperlink is a reference in a presentation that points to or represents a linked location. Although created in Normal or Outline views, hyperlinks can be activated only during a slide show presentation. When you click the linked text or graphic, the link activates and the linked location opens. You can add sounds to hyperlinks that activate as you click the hyperlink in a slide show. Hyperlinks make it easy to access a variety of information sources quickly to get just the information you need during a slide show. You can create a hyperlink in a PowerPoint presentation that points to a specific slide or custom show in the current presentation, a different presentation, a Word document, an Excel workbook file, an Access database, a Web page on the Internet or an intranet, a new file, or an e-mail address.

12.b Adding Hyperlinks to Slides

You can add a hyperlink to text, images, charts, or any element on a slide. When you create a hyperlink, it's important to name it appropriately because the name of the hyperlink displays when the user points to it in a slide show presentation. You can use the slide title or create a name identifying the content of the slide for the hyperlink.

Adding Hyperlinks to Text

To add a hyperlink to text, you first select the text and then create the hyperlink. To add hyperlinks to text:

Step 1	Open	the *Teddy Toys New Products* presentation located on the Data Disk
Step 2	Save	the presentation as *Teddy Toys Hyperlinks*
Step 3	Display	Slide 2
Step 4	Select	the first bullet item (Baby Teddy)
Step 5	Click	the Insert Hyperlink button on the Standard toolbar

PowerPoint Presentations and the Internet   PA 89

The Insert Hyperlink dialog box opens with options for linking to an Existing File or Web page, a Place in This Document, Create New Document, or to an E-mail address. Your dialog box should look similar to Figure 12-1.

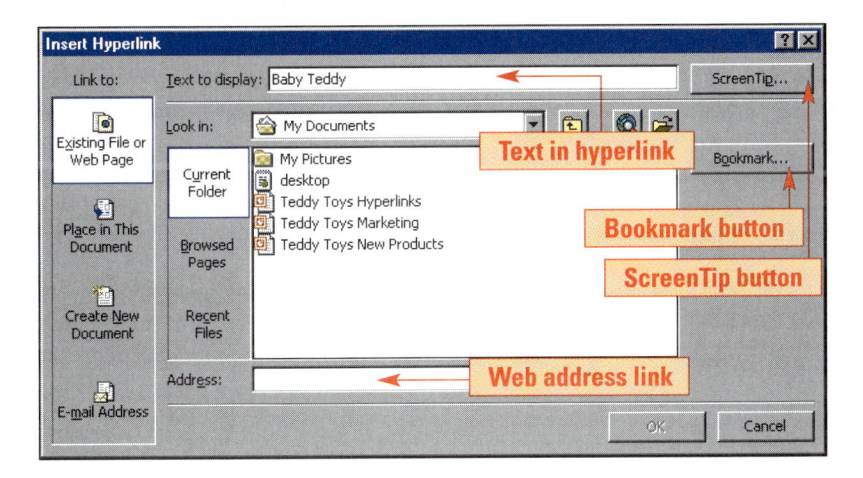

FIGURE 12-1
Insert Hyperlink Dialog Box

(Screenshot of Insert Hyperlink dialog box with callouts: Text in hyperlink, Bookmark button, ScreenTip button, Web address link)

MOUSE TIP

You can add a hyperlink by right-clicking a text box or object and then clicking Hyperlink or Action Settings.

When you link to a Place in This Document, you can link to the First Slide, the Last Slide, the Next Slide, the Previous Slide, a specific Slide Title, or a Custom Show. When the Place in This Document button is active, the dialog box provides a Slide preview so you can see which slide you're linking to. When you link to an Existing File or Web Page, you select Current Folder, Browsed Pages, Recent Files, or key an Internet Address. When you link to Create New Document, you enter the full path and name of new document you edit later or now. When you link to an E-mail Address, you key the E-mail address and the Subject. A Recently used e-mail addresses: list box is provided for future reference.

MENU TIP

You can add a hyperlink to a text box or object by clicking the Hyperlink command on the Insert menu.

| Step 6 | Click | Place in This Document under Link to: on the left, if necessary |
| Step 7 | Click | 3. Baby Teddy in the Select a place in this document: list box |

The Baby Teddy slide becomes the linked location or destination for the hyperlink and appears when the user clicks the Baby Teddy text on the New Product Line slide during a slide show. The text in the Text to display: text box is the text you selected to be the hyperlink. This text does not appear in the ScreenTip. If you don't specify any custom text, then the ScreenTip displays the link path of the hyperlink only if it points to a location outside the current presentation.

| Step 8 | Click | ScreenTip |
| Step 9 | Key | Baby Teddy in the ScreenTip text: text box in the Set Hyperlink ScreenTip dialog box |

chapter twelve

QUICK TIP

Custom ScreenTips are supported in Microsoft Internet Explorer version 4.0 or later.

Step 10	Click	OK twice
Step 11	Click	outside the bullet object
Step 12	Observe	that the Baby Teddy bullet item displays in a different color and with an underline to indicate that it is hyperlinked
Step 13	Select	the second bullet item (Teddy Wagon)
Step 14	Click	the Insert Hyperlink button on the Standard toolbar
Step 15	Click	4. Teddy Wagon in the Select a place in this document: list box
Step 16	Click	ScreenTip
Step 17	Key	Teddy Wagon in the ScreenTip text: text box in the Set Hyperlink ScreenTip dialog box
Step 18	Click	OK twice
Step 19	Follow	Steps 13 through 18 to add hyperlinks on the Rocking Horse and Toddler Bike bullet items to the appropriate slides
Step 20	Click	outside the bullet object

Your slide should look similar to Figure 12-2. Text that represents a hyperlink appears underlined and in a color that coordinates with the color scheme of the presentation design.

FIGURE 12-2
Slide with Hyperlinked Bullet Items

CAUTION TIP

It's a good idea to test all the hyperlinks in a presentation before showing it to an audience to make sure all the links point to the correct locations.

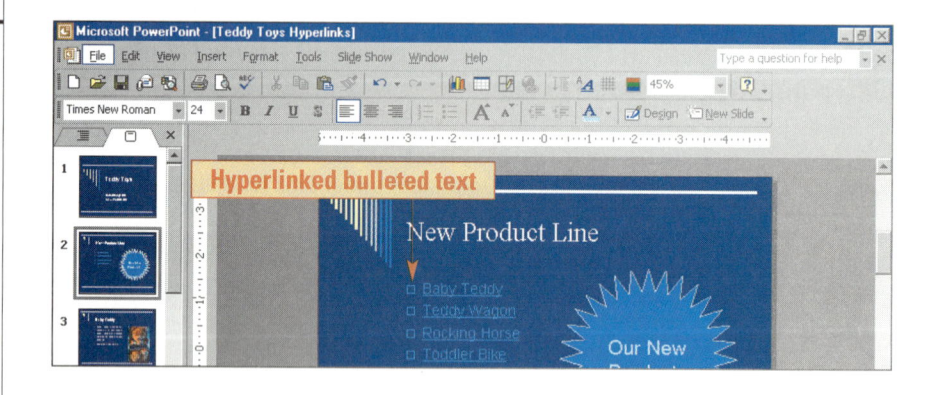

Using Hyperlinks in a Presentation

Once you have added hyperlinks to a presentation, the presenter or viewer can use them during a slide show. To use hyperlinks during a slide show:

Step 1	Run	the slide show from the current slide
Step 2	Point to	the Baby Teddy hyperlink

Step 3	*Observe*	that the mouse changes to the pointing hand, indicating a hyperlink, and the ScreenTip displays Baby Teddy
Step 4	*Click*	the Baby Teddy hyperlink to display the Baby Teddy slide
Step 5	*Right-click*	in the slide show
Step 6	*Point to*	G̲o
Step 7	*Point to*	By T̲itle
Step 8	*Click*	New Product Line
Step 9	*Observe*	that the color of the Baby Teddy hyperlink on the New Product Line slide has changed, indicating that you already visited that hyperlink
Step 10	*Click*	the Teddy Wagon hyperlink to display the Teddy Wagon slide
Step 11	*Display*	the New Product Line slide in the slide show

Your slide should look similar to Figure 12-3.

FIGURE 12-3
Slide with Visited Hyperlinks

Step 12	*Continue*	testing each of the remaining hyperlinks
Step 13	*End*	the slide show
Step 14	*Save*	the *Teddy Toys Hyperlinks* presentation

Adding Action Buttons

Instead of manually navigating through a slide show, you have the option of adding action buttons to slides to return you to the first, last, next, or previous slides, as well as individual slides. **Action buttons** are predesigned onscreen buttons that contain hyperlinks. They function just like other hyperlinks and can be placed anywhere on an individual slide or on the slide master. They are useful when you do not want to use slide text

MENU TIP

You can add an action button by clicking the desired action button on the Action Buttons submenu on the Slid̲e Show menu.

QUICK TIP

If you plan to create several buttons for hyperlinking, you can drag the Action Buttons menu away from the Slide Show menu so it becomes a floating toolbar.

MOUSE TIP

You can draw an action button anywhere on the screen and then move it to the desired location.

or a graphic as the hyperlink. Once you select a particular button, you then draw the shape anywhere on the slide where you want the hyperlink button to appear. Action buttons are commonly understood symbols for navigating to next, previous, first, and last slides in a slide show.

You can add an action button to the slide master if you want that button to appear on every slide in the same place. Because action buttons are graphic elements, they appear on each slide in the slide show presentation except those slides where you omitted the graphic elements from the background. To add an action button with a sound to the slide master:

Step 1	Access	the slide master
Step 2	Click	Sli_d_e Show
Step 3	Point to	Act_i_on Buttons
Step 4	Click	the Action Button: Back or Previous button (second row, first column)
Step 5	Observe	that the mouse pointer changes to a crosshair, the pointer shape you use to draw shapes
Step 6	Drag	using the SHIFT key to draw a button approximately 1 inch wide by 1 inch high on the slide master

After you release the mouse button, the Action Settings dialog box opens with options for hyperlinking the button to another slide, another presentation, a different program, a different file type, or a location on the Internet. Your dialog box should look similar to Figure 12-4.

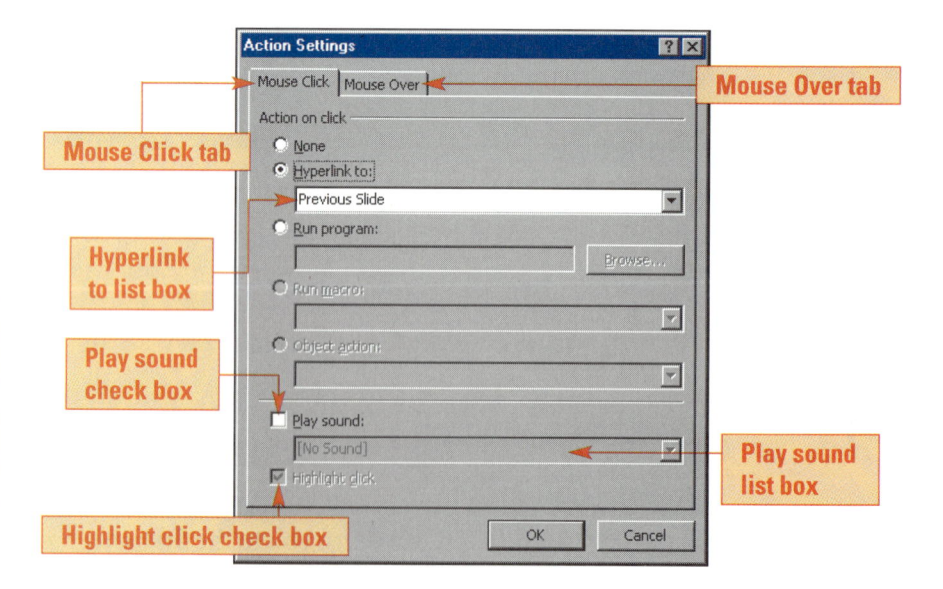

FIGURE 12-4
Action Settings Dialog Box

The tabs for Mouse Click and Mouse Over are used to specify how you want users to activate a hyperlink. You can use either method for text hyperlinks, image hyperlinks, AutoShape hyperlinks, or action button hyperlinks. **Mouse Click** (the default method) means the user clicks the hyperlink to jump to the linked location and points to it to see a ScreenTip that displays the path of the hyperlink. **Mouse Over** means the user simply points to the hyperlink to activate it. Another feature in the Action Settings dialog box lets you add sound to a hyperlink. You can add a sound that plays when the user clicks the action button during a slide show presentation. To utilize the sound option, the computer you plan to run the presentation on must have a sound card and speakers. For some hyperlinked objects, such as action buttons, you have an option of highlighting when you click the object for a visual effect. You cannot, however, use the highlight click option on hyperlinked text.

> **QUICK TIP**
>
> It is best to use the mouse-click method when setting the way hyperlinks start because using the mouse-over method may cause the link to activate when you don't intend it.

Step 7	*Click*	the list arrow in the Hyperlink to: list box
Step 8	*Click*	Slide…
Step 9	*Double-click*	New Product Line in the Slide title: list box
Step 10	*Click*	the Play sound: check box to add a check mark
Step 11	*Click*	the list arrow in the Play sound: list box
Step 12	*Click*	Chime
Step 13	*Click*	OK

Your screen should look similar to Figure 12-5.

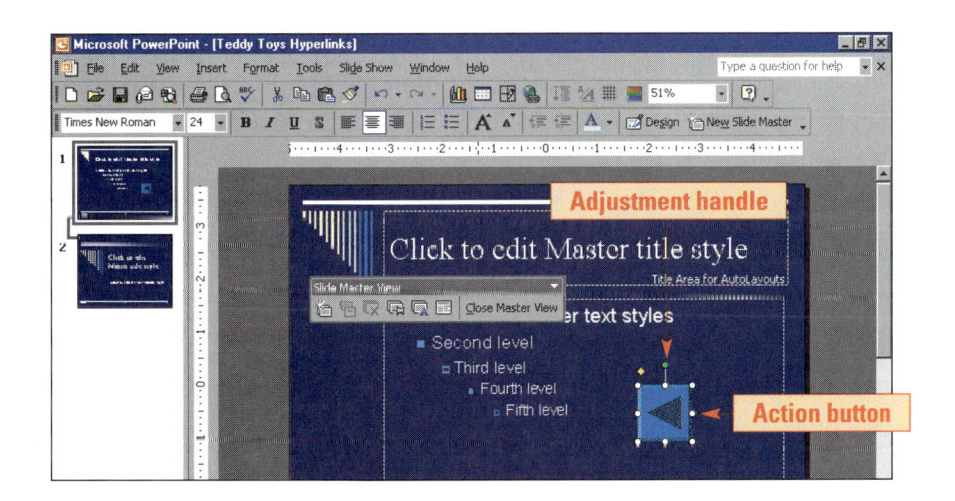

FIGURE 12-5
Action Button on Slide Master

The action button appears on the slide master. The selection handles indicate it is currently selected. The yellow diamond-shaped adjustment handle above and to the left of the button lets you quickly apply a 3-D look to the button by dragging the handle. To format the action button:

Step 1	*Click*	the Fill Color button list arrow on the Drawing toolbar

chapter twelve

QUICK TIP

When working in the slide master, you can zoom in and zoom out to resize and position the action button. An action button placed on the slide master appears on each slide that uses the slide master and its background and graphics.

MOUSE TIP

You can resize a shape or an action button by right-clicking the shape, clicking Format AutoShape, clicking the Size tab, and then changing the Height and Width.

You can resize a shape or an action button by double-clicking the shape, clicking the Size tab, and then changing the Height and Width.

Step 2	Click	the medium blue color (ScreenTip displays: Follow Accent and Hyperlink Scheme Color)
Step 3	Drag	the yellow diamond shaping handle as far to the right as possible
Step 4	Resize	the button to approximately 0.3 inches wide by 0.3 inches high
Step 5	Drag	the action button to the lower-right corner of the slide master
Step 6	Run	the slide show to Slide 2
Step 7	Click	the Baby Teddy hyperlink
Step 8	Click	the action button on the Baby Teddy slide to return to the New Product Line slide
Step 9	Continue	clicking each hyperlink on the New Product Line slide, using the action button to return to the New Product Line slide
Step 10	End	the slide show
Step 11	Close	the Slide Master view
Step 12	Save	the *Teddy Toys Hyperlinks* presentation

Adding a Hyperlink to a Slide in Another Presentation

You can use hyperlinks to jump from a slide in one presentation to a slide in a different presentation. This process requires that you know the exact location (including any subfolders) of the presentation to which you want the hyperlink to link. After you select the desired destination presentation, you use the Bookmark feature to select the exact slide in the destination presentation.

notes The *Teddy Toys Marketing* presentation contains hyperlinks to link you to the various slides in the *Teddy Toys Hyperlinks* presentation. You can hyperlink presentations saved in different folders if you specify the folder location of the presentation when you create the hyperlink. For the following activities, however, the preset hyperlinks assume both presentations are in the My Documents folder on the hard drive. Move or copy the *Teddy Toys Marketing* presentation from the Data Disk to the My Documents folder on the C: drive before continuing.

To format a shape as a hyperlink and link it to another presentation:

Step 1	Display	the New Product Line slide

Step 2	**Select**	the star AutoShape (do not click in the text)
Step 3	**Open**	the Insert Hyperlink dialog box
Step 4	**Click**	E_xisting File or Web Page in the Places bar
Step 5	**Click**	*Teddy Toys Marketing*
Step 6	**Click**	B_ookmark

The Select Places in Document dialog box opens with a list of the slides in the current presentation.

Step 7	**Double-click**	Slide 5
Step 8	**Click**	ScreenTi_p
Step 9	**Key**	The Future in the ScreenTip: text box
Step 10	**Click**	OK twice
Step 11	**Run**	the slide show from the current slide
Step 12	**Point to**	the star AutoShape

The mouse displays the pointing finger and the ScreenTip displays The Future.

| Step 13 | **Click** | the star AutoShape |

The Future slide in the *Teddy Toys Marketing* presentation appears.

| Step 14 | **Point to** | the action button in the lower-right corner of the slide |

The ScreenTip displays that the action button is hyperlinked to C:\My Documents\Teddy Toys Hyperlinks.ppt#2. Slide 2.

| Step 15 | **Click** | the action button |

The slide show returns to the New Product Line slide in the *Teddy Toys Hyperlinks* presentation. The column chart slide in the *Teddy Toys Marketing* presentation contains a hyperlink back to the pie chart slide in the *Teddy Toys Hyperlinks* presentation.

> **MENU TIP**
>
> You can change the Action Settings of a shape by clicking the Action Settings command on the Sli_de Show menu.

Mouse Tip

You can edit a hyperlink by right-clicking the hyperlink and then clicking Edit Hyperlink.

Step 16	Click	the star AutoShape hyperlink
Step 17	Right-click	in The Future slide
Step 18	Click	Previous
Step 19	Point to	the action button in the lower-right corner

The ScreenTip displays C:\My Documents\Teddy Toys Hyperlinks.ppt #7. Projected Market Share.

| Step 20 | Click | the action button |

The Projected Market Share slide from the *Teddy Toys Hyperlinks* presentation appears.

| Step 21 | End | each slide show |
| Step 22 | Save | the *Teddy Toys Hyperlinks* presentation |

Adding a Hyperlink to an Internet Location

In addition to inserting hyperlinks to slides and presentations, you can insert a hyperlink to a Web page on the Internet, as well as to Gopher, Telnet, newsgroups, and FTP sites. A **Web page** is a document on the World Wide Web that can be accessed using Web browser software, such as Internet Explorer or Netscape Navigator. **Gopher** is a resource that helps you find files and resources on the Internet through a series of linked menus. **Telnet** is a resource that allows you to log onto another computer through a Telnet host such as a library catalog. **Newsgroups** are online discussion groups in which participants exchange ideas and opinions by posting messages to a public area. **FTP** (**File Transfer Protocol**) is a method you use to transfer files between computers over the Internet.

Hyperlinking to a Web site during a presentation is a means of providing the audience with additional information about a specific product or company, already provided on the Web site, with additional hyperlinks to other locations within the site or different sites that provide more information. To hyperlink to a Web site during a presentation, the computer that you plan to run the slide on must be equipped with an Internet connection and have an Internet browser program installed, such as Microsoft Internet Explorer. **Browsers** are programs that interpret and display HTML files, allowing Internet users to visit sites on the Internet. Internet Explorer is the browser that is included with Office XP; when you preview a presentation as a Web page, Internet Explorer opens so that you can see exactly how the presentation looks when viewed in a typical browser.

Quick Tip

When you hyperlink to the Internet during a slide show, you can click the Back button on the Internet Explorer toolbar or your browser toolbar to return to the PowerPoint presentation.

notes To hyperlink to the Internet sites during the slide show, you must have access to the Internet. You can set the hyperlinks on the slides, but they will not work during slide show without an Internet connection. If the Internet sites indicated here are unavailable, use different, appropriate sites to complete the steps.

To hyperlink an image to a Web page:

Step 1	Display	Slide 3
Step 2	Select	the teddy bear image
Step 3	Open	the Insert Hyperlink dialog box
Step 4	Click	E*x*isting File or Web Page in the Places bar, if necessary
Step 5	Key	www.Toysrus.com in the Addr*e*ss: text box
Step 6	Click	ScreenTi*p*
Step 7	Key	Toys on the Web in the Screen*T*ip text: text box
Step 8	Click	OK twice
Step 9	Run	the slide show from the current slide
Step 10	Point to	the teddy bear image (ScreenTip displays: Toys on the Web)
Step 11	Click	the teddy bear hyperlink
Step 12	View	the toysrus Web site at Amazon.com
Step 13	Close	the Web browser
Step 14	End	the slide show
Step 15	Save	the *Teddy Toys Hyperlinks* presentation

Changing Hyperlinks

You can modify a hyperlink by changing its color, its destination, or the hyperlink text. The Accent and hyperlink or the Accent and followed hyperlink color can be changed in the Slide Design Color Schemes dialog box. The destination of a hyperlink can be changed in the Edit Hyperlink dialog box. The hyperlink text can be changed by simply selecting the hyperlinked text and keying the next text. The action button destination can be changed in the Action Settings dialog box. When making changes to the destination, you select the hyperlinked text or object, click the Insert Hyperlink button on the Standard

QUICK TIP

It is always a good idea to test your hyperlinks before a presentation. In the case of a Web address, take the time to connect to the Internet and visit the site to make sure it still exists and that the URL is accurate.

MENU TIP

You can edit or remove a hyperlink by clicking the Hyperl*i*nk command on the *I*nsert menu to open the Edit Hyperlink dialog box.

chapter twelve

Mouse Tip

When you no longer need a hyperlink, you can remove it from any text or object. Simply select the hyperlink text or object, click the Insert Hyperlink button on the Standard toolbar and click the Remove Link button in the Edit Hyperlink dialog box. You can also remove a hyperlink by right-clicking the object and then clicking Remove Hyperlink.

Design Tip

Hyperlinks help make your presentations more flexible, effective, and up to date.

toolbar, or right-click and then click Edit Hyperlink. The Edit Hyperlink dialog box allows you to edit changes to text and object hyperlinks. The Action Settings dialog box allows you to edit hyperlinks that were created with an action button. To edit the path of a hyperlink:

Step 1	Display	Slide 3, if necessary
Step 2	Right-click	the teddy bear image
Step 3	Click	Edit Hyperlink
Step 4	Change	the text in the Address: text box to www.drtoy.com
Step 5	Click	OK
Step 6	Run	the slide show
Step 7	Click	the teddy bear image
Step 8	Browse	through the www.drtoy.com Web site
Step 9	Close	the Internet browser
Step 10	End	the slide show
Step 11	Save	the *Teddy Toys Hyperlinks* presentation

12.c Previewing a Presentation as a Web Page

The opening or primary page of a Web site is called the **home page** or **start page**. Home pages are created and saved as HTML documents on the Internet or on an intranet. **HTML** is an acronym for Hypertext Markup Language, the file format for documents that are published on the Internet that can be read and displayed by browsers.

An **intranet** is an intraorganizational (internal use) network. The **Internet** consists of sets of networks located worldwide that are interconnected. The Internet is the physical connection of existing computer networks that carry the information from site to site, computer to computer.

When you save a PowerPoint presentation as a Web page, PowerPoint makes changes to the presentation to make it suitable for viewing in a Web browser. In addition, PowerPoint creates a separate .htm file for the presentation, each slide, an *outline.htm* file, two *master.htm* files, a *fullscreen.htm* file and a *frame.htm* file, as well as other files needed for Internet viewing. PowerPoint converts the slides and their contents into HTML language, which enables Internet browsers to interpret the files so that they display properly over the Internet.

To preview a presentation as a Web page:

Step 1	**Display**	Slide 1
Step 2	**Click**	F̲ile
Step 3	**Click**	We̲b Page Preview
Step 4	**Maximize**	the Teddy Toys - Microsoft Internet Explorer window

The Internet Explorer browser application opens with the *Teddy Toys Hyperlinks* presentation displayed. Your screen should look similar to Figure 12-6.

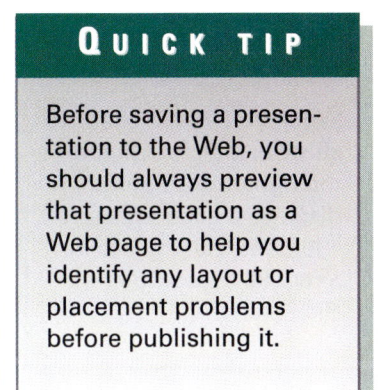

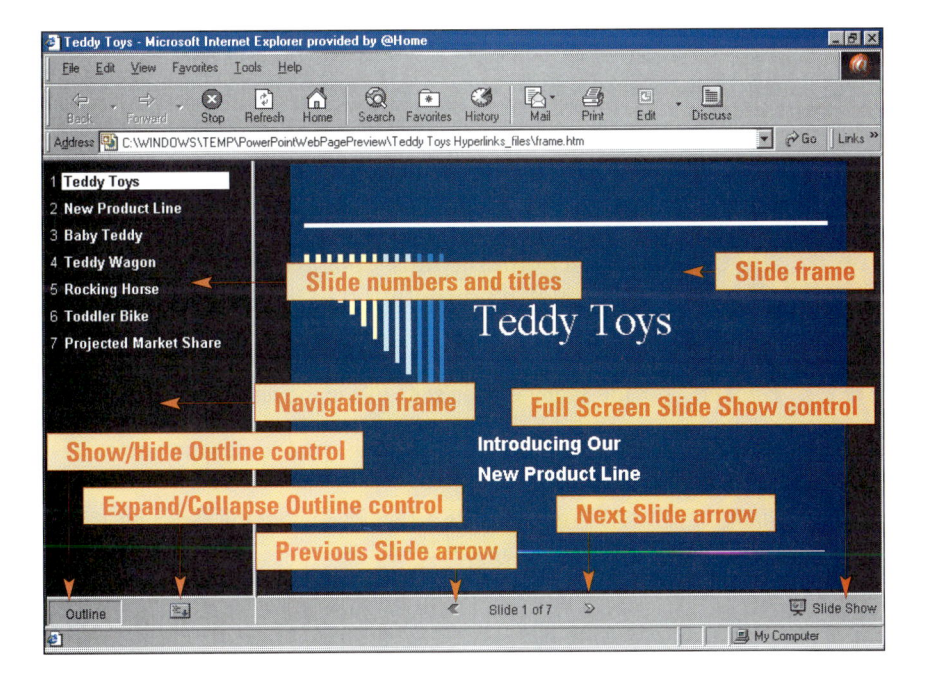

> **QUICK TIP**
>
> Before saving a presentation to the Web, you should always preview that presentation as a Web page to help you identify any layout or placement problems before publishing it.

FIGURE 12-6
Teddy Toys Hyperlinks Presentation in Internet Browser

The Internet Explorer window contains the title bar, the menu bar, the Standard Buttons toolbar, the Address bar, and the Links bar. The left side of the window is the **navigation frame**, a frame similar to the Web site frames on the Internet. The navigation frame contains the titles of the presentation in outline format. You can scroll through the navigation frame to see the titles of the slides in the *Teddy Toys Hyperlinks* presentation. If no scroll bar appears, then you can see all the slide titles in the presentation. The right frame is the **slide frame**, which displays the current slide in the presentation. When you click a title in the navigation frame, the appropriate slide displays in the slide frame.

Below the navigation frame are the Show/Hide Outline and the Expand/Collapse Outline controls. Controls are elements that enable you to navigate in the Web page preview. The **Show/Hide Outline** control displays the presentation in outline format without graphics. The

chapter twelve

> **MOUSE TIP**
>
> When you view a slide show in Internet Explorer, the right mouse button displays a different shortcut menu than it does in a regular PowerPoint slide show.

Expand/Collapse Outline control expands to display the title and bullet text of the slides or collapses to display only the title of each slide. A **Show/Hide Notes** control displays to the right of the Expand/Collapse Outline control if your presentation contains notes pages. This control displays the text "Notes" and a red circle with a white check mark to the left of the text. Directly above the Show/Hide Notes control is a line or two of the notes page text.

The number of the current slide you see is listed below the slide with Previous Slide and Next Slide arrows to navigate through the slides. A Full Screen Slide Show control appears on the far right that allows you to view the presentation as a slide show through the Web page.

Navigating Through a Presentation in a Web browser

Web Page Preview allows you to preview and practice navigating through the presentation as you would on the Internet or intranet. In Web Page Preview, you can progress from slide to slide, show or hide the slide titles in the navigation frame so you can advance quickly to various slides in the presentation, and show or hide any notes pages that may accompany a slide. When you point to a slide title in the navigation frame, it changes color and a pointing hand appears, indicating that it is a hyperlink. To navigate through a presentation in Internet Explorer:

Step 1	Point to	the Teddy Wagon slide title in the navigation frame
Step 2	Click	the Teddy Wagon hyperlink in the navigation frame
Step 3	Click	the Previous Slide arrow under the slide until it displays Slide 2 of 7
Step 4	Click	the Next Slide arrow until you display the Toddler Bike slide
Step 5	Click	the Full Screen Slide Show control on the far right

The slide show starts from the current slide, displaying your PowerPoint presentation as it will look when published to the Internet. The Full Screen view is identical in appearance to Slide Show in the PowerPoint application. Only the slides appear on the screen; no toolbars, menus, or panes appear. You must click to advance each slide individually as no times are set on this presentation. You can right-click in the Web Page Preview slide show and choose to go to the Next or Previous slide or end the show.

Step 6	Click	the left mouse button to advance to each slide until you view the entire presentation

The Show/Hide Outline control displays or hides the outline in the navigation frame directly above it. Displaying the outline allows you to quickly navigate through the presentation. The Expand/Collapse Outline control, to the right of the Show/Hide Outline control, displays either the title when the outline is collapsed or the title and bullet items when the outline is expanded in the navigation frame. Collapsing the outline in the navigation frame allows you to easily navigate to various slides in the presentation. Expanding the outline allows you to view the bullet items on each slide in the navigation frame without navigating to the individual slides. The Expand/Collapse Outline control displays only when you show the outline. To use the Show/Hide Outline and Expand/Collapse Outline controls:

Step 1	Click	the Show/Hide Outline control Outline to hide the navigation frame
Step 2	Click	the Show/Hide Outline control Outline to display the navigation frame with the numbered slide titles
Step 3	Click	the Expand/Collapse Outline control to display the bulleted text under each slide title
Step 4	Scroll	through the outline until you view all the bullet items
Step 5	Click	the Expand/Collapse Outline control to hide the bulleted text
Step 6	Click	the Close button on the Internet Explorer window

12.d Saving a PowerPoint Presentation as a Web Page

When you save a presentation as a Web page, you save it in HTML format, the required format of all Web documents. You can save a presentation to a specific server by saving it to Web Folders in the Save As dialog box. Use Web Folders to store saved presentations for easy access of a presentation from a Web server. You can add a Web folder by clicking the Create New Folder button in the Save As or Open dialog boxes and providing a Web server URL. As you have learned, when PowerPoint saves a presentation as a Web page, it actually creates multiple files and sometimes multiple folders for storing the Web presentation. These files and folders are necessary for publishing the presentation to the Internet. If you publish a presentation without saving it first, the files are automatically saved to

> **MENU TIP**
>
> You can also save your presentation as a Web page by clicking the Save As command on the File menu and then changing the Save as type: to Web Page.

chapter twelve

TASK PANE TIP

You can create or add a Web folder by clicking the Add Web Folder link in the New Presentation task pane.

the current drive and folder location. It is a good idea to save the presentation first as a Web page, specifying the correct save location, before you publish it.

To save a presentation as a Web page:

| Step 1 | *Click* | File |
| Step 2 | *Click* | Save as Web Page |

The Save As dialog box opens with options for changing the title of the Web page in the browser and for publishing a Web page to the Internet. The default title is the text in the title placeholder on the title slide. The page title provides a professional look to others visiting your Web site on the Internet. The page title displays in the Internet browser title bar when you access this page on the Internet and appears in the History list and Favorites list of the people that view this presentation online. The folders and files in the dialog box on your screen may vary from Figure 12-7.

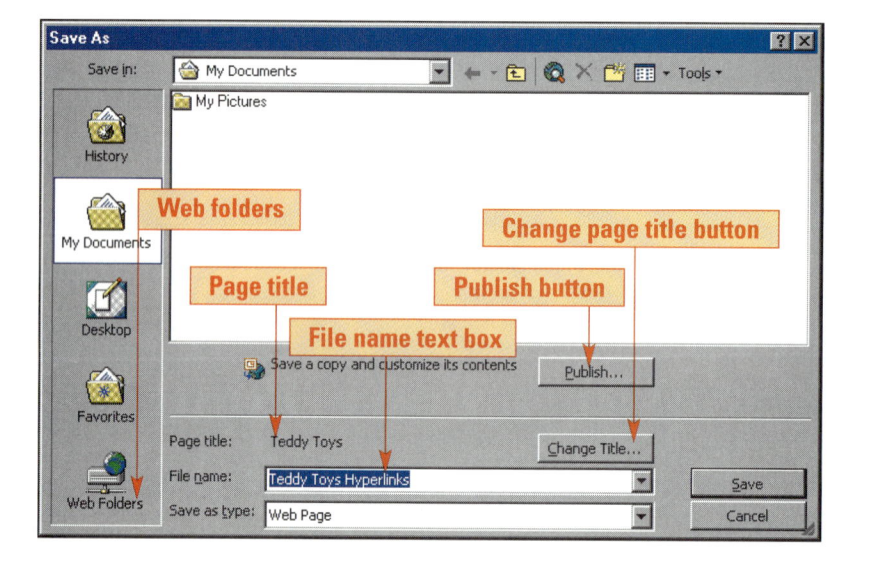

FIGURE 12-7
Save As Dialog Box

[Screenshot of Save As dialog box with callouts labeling: Web folders, Page title, File name text box, Change page title button, Publish button. File name shows "Teddy Toys Hyperlinks", Page title shows "Teddy Toys", Save as type: Web Page.]

Step 3	*Key*	Teddy Toys Web in the File name: text box
Step 4	*Click*	Change Title
Step 5	*Key*	Teddy Toys New Products in the Page title: text box
Step 6	*Click*	OK
Step 7	*Click*	Save

The *Teddy Toys Web* presentation is saved with an .htm extension, the file extension for HTML files. If your system is set to display file extensions, the title bar displays *Teddy Toys Web.htm*.

| Step 8 | Close | the *Teddy Toys Web.htm* file |

12.e Editing a Web Page Presentation

When you need to make changes to a presentation you have saved as a Web page, you should edit only the .htm file for the presentation. You do not need to open the folder created during the save as a Web page process for editing purposes, and you should not manually edit any of the other files. Editing the .htm file automatically changes any necessary individual files.

To edit and update a particular page on the Web site, you need to edit and open the appropriate .htm file. To open the *Teddy Toys Web.htm* file:

| Step 1 | Click | the Open button on the Standard toolbar |
| Step 2 | Switch to | the folder where you saved the *Teddy Toys Web.htm* file |

You also see the *Teddy Toys Web_files* folder that was automatically created when you saved the *Teddy Toys Hyperlinks* presentation as a Web page.

| Step 3 | Double-click | the *Teddy Toys Web_files* folder |
| Step 4 | Observe | that the files displayed are .htm files |

If the Files of type: list box contains only Web Pages and Web Archives or All PowerPoint Presentations, you see only .htm files displayed. If you select All Files in the Files of type: list box, you can see other files that are automatically created when saving a PowerPoint presentation as a Web page. Your presentation consists of seven slides, but some slide files consist of coding for the Internet.

| Step 5 | Click | the Up One Level button on the Open dialog box toolbar |

The *Teddy Toys Web.htm* file is listed in the same folder as the *Teddy Toys Web_files* folder. The *Teddy Toys Web.htm* file icon is different than a regular PowerPoint presentation icon. The .htm extension indicates that this file is a Web page and the .htm extension displays if your computer settings are set to display the extensions.

QUICK TIP

When you save a presentation as an .htm file, the presentation becomes an .htm file, and a new folder is created at the same level as the .htm file. Each individual slide of the presentation is set up as a separate file along with other files for the slides, and all are stored in the newly created folder.

chapter twelve

MENU TIP

Find and Replace are listed as separate commands on the Edit menu; however, both commands use the Find feature.

QUICK TIP

You can open the Find dialog box by pressing the CTRL + F keys; you can open the Replace dialog box pressing the CTRL + H keys.

FIGURE 12-8
Replace Dialog Box

| Step 6 | Double-click | the *Teddy Toys Web.htm* file |
| Step 7 | Observe | that the title bar displays *Teddy Toys Web.htm* if your system is set to display file extensions |

Using Find and Replace

The Find and Replace features in PowerPoint allow you to automatically find text and replace it quickly within a presentation, thereby eliminating the necessity of finding each and every occurrence yourself and manually making changes. The **Find** feature finds a certain string of text, and the **Replace** feature replaces it with whatever text you type in the Replace with: text box. To find and replace text in a presentation:

Step 1	Display	Slide 1, if necessary
Step 2	Click	Edit
Step 3	Click	Replace

The Replace dialog box opens with the Find what: and Replace with: text boxes, along with options for matching the case, finding whole words separately, and matching half/full width forms (characters). Your dialog box should look similar to Figure 12-8.

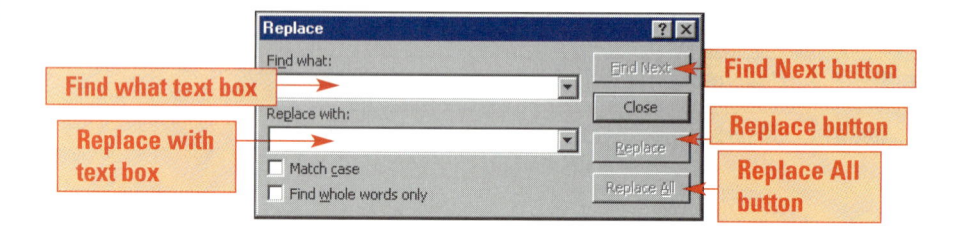

[Replace dialog box figure with callouts: Find what text box, Replace with text box, Find Next button, Replace button, Replace All button]

Step 4	Key	Baby in the Find what: text box
Step 5	Key	Cuddly in the Replace with: text box
Step 6	Click	Find Next to locate the first occurrence of Baby

Clicking the Find Next button allows you to control when an occurrence of the word you are finding is replaced with a new word. There may be instances when you do not want an occurrence of the word you are finding replaced with a new word or term. If that is the case, you just click the Find Next button again.

| Step 7 | Click | Replace All |

After all replacements are made, a PowerPoint dialog box displays a message that it has finished searching the presentation and indicates how many replacements were made.

Step 8	Click	OK
Step 9	Close	the Replace dialog box
Step 10	Run	the slide show from the beginning

Notice that Baby Teddy still appears in the label on the Project Market Share slide. This text did not change because the labels are part of the Microsoft Graph program that is not affected by the find and replace feature. You need to manually edit the pie chart and change the label on the datasheet to reflect the change. To edit the pie chart label:

Step 1	Display	the Projected Market Share slide in Normal view
Step 2	Double-click	the pie chart object
Step 3	Display	the datasheet
Step 4	Change	Baby Teddy to Cuddly Teddy
Step 5	Close	the datasheet
Step 6	Click	outside the chart object
Step 7	Run	the slide show
Step 8	Observe	the ScreenTips on the New Product Line slide and end the slide show
Step 9	Edit	the Cuddly Teddy hyperlink on the New Product Line slide
Step 10	Change	the ScreenTip to display Cuddly Teddy
Step 11	Save	the *Teddy Toys Web.htm* file with the changes

12.f Publishing a Presentation to the Web

Publishing a presentation to the Web saves a copy of the presentation in HTML format (a Web page) to a server on the Web or on an intranet server. When you save a presentation as a Web page, you are preparing the folder and files necessary for Web publication. When you publish a presentation, you have the opportunity to publish the complete presentation or individual slides, display speaker notes, select a browser, and change the page title and filename and location. In addition, you can

---

CAUTION TIP

Be sure to proofread any text you key into the Replace dialog box before clicking Replace or Replace All. An error in the Find what: text box results in 0 occurrences found, and an error in the Replace with: text box results in an error or errors in the presentation.

QUICK TIP

The Find and Replace features in PowerPoint do not affect any text created in a peripheral program used by PowerPoint; instead, you have to manually make changes to text created in Microsoft Graph and WordArt.

chapter twelve

CAUTION TIP

You must have access to a Web server before you can publish, copy, or manage folders and files on a Web server. Check with your instructor as to whether you should publish to a hard drive, a local network drive, or an Internet server.

make changes to the Web options, such as adding slide navigation controls, selecting presentation colors, showing slide animation while browsing, and resizing graphics to fit browser window.

If your company uses an intranet based on Internet protocols, you can use Web folders to save copies of your presentations to a Web server. A **Web server** hosts Web pages and responds to requests from browsers. To make your presentations available on the Internet, you need to use an Internet service provider that allocates space for Web presentations or you need to install Web server software on your computer.

To begin publishing a presentation to the World Wide Web:

Step 1	Verify	that the *Teddy Toys Web.htm* file is open
Step 2	Click	File
Step 3	Click	Save as Web Page
Step 4	Click	Publish

The Publish as Web Page dialog box opens with options for publishing the entire presentation, publishing various slides, publishing a custom show, speaker notes, changing browsers, and changing the page title and filename of the Web page. Your dialog box should look similar to Figure 12-9.

FIGURE 12-9
Publish as Web Page Dialog Box

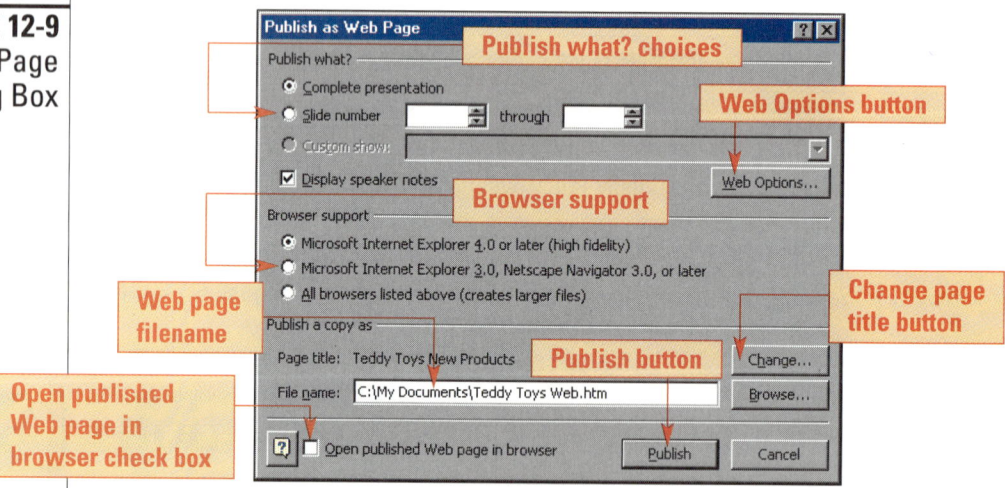

Changing Web Page Options

You can add slide navigation controls, change the appearance of colors in a presentation, display slide show animation effects while browsing, and resize the graphics to fit the browser window in the General tab. On the Browsers tab, you can choose the browser for the target audience, allow PNG as a graphics format, rely on VML for displaying graphics in browsers, save an additional version of the presentation for older browsers, or save new Web pages as Web archives. On the Files tab, you can organize supporting files in a folder, use long filenames whenever possible, update links on save, and choose Office as the default editor for Web pages created in Office. You can change the screen size for target monitors in the Pictures tab. The Encoding tab allows you to save the Web page in a different language format. The Fonts tab allows you to choose a different character set for the default font and change the proportional and fixed-width font default sizes.

The Vector Markup Language format (VML) is recommended if others view your Web page in a Web browser that supports graphics in VML format—for example, Microsoft Internet Explorer 5.0 or later. Your Web page saves faster in HTML, takes up less disk space, and takes less time to download. Portable Network Graphics (PNG) is a graphic file format supported by many Web browsers. It is a good format for compressing and storing graphic images, and there is no loss of graphic image data when an image is uncompressed.

You want to change the presentation colors for the Web page. When you change the presentation colors, you select the text and background color scheme that you want for the notes and outline panes. To change Web page options and complete publishing the presentation:

> **QUICK TIP**
>
> PNG supports variable transparency of images (alpha channels) and control of image brightness on different computers (gamma correction). It is used for a wide range of graphics from small images (such as bullets and banners) to complex images (such as photographs).

Step 1	Verify	that Complete presentation is selected under Publish what?
Step 2	Click	the Display speaker notes check box to remove the check mark
Step 3	Click	Web Options

The Web Options dialog box opens with options for changing the appearance of the Web page on the Internet. Your dialog box should look similar to Figure 12-10.

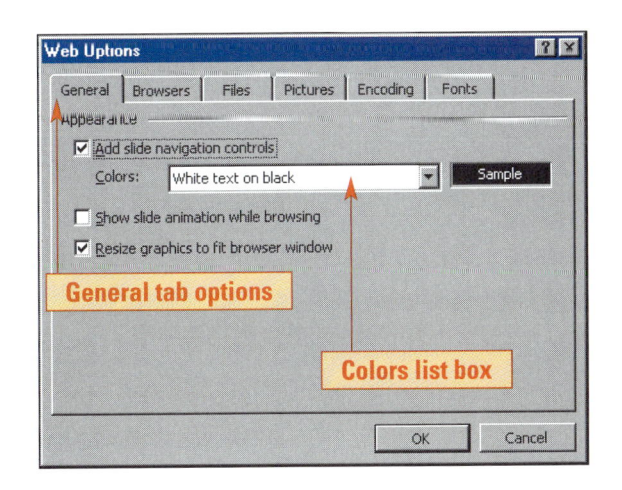

FIGURE 12-10
Web Options Dialog Box

Step 4	Click	the Colors: list arrow

chapter twelve

Step 5	*Click*	Presentation colors (accent color)
Step 6	*Click*	OK
Step 7	*Verify*	that Microsoft Internet Explorer 4.0 or later (high fidelity) is selected under Browser support
Step 8	*Verify*	that *C:\My Documents\Teddy Toys Web.htm* appears in the File name: text box
Step 9	*Click*	the Open published Web page in browser check box to add a check mark
Step 10	*Click*	Publish
Step 11	*Click*	Yes to replace the existing Web page
Step 12	*Click*	OK if you receive a message indicating the presentation is currently in use
Step 13	*Click*	File
Step 14	*Click*	Web Page Preview
Step 15	*Maximize*	the Internet Explorer window
Step 16	*Observe*	that the Web page title is Teddy Toys New Products, the outline frame has a background that coordinates with the presentation design colors, the text displays with accent colors, and there are no speaker notes
Step 17	*Close*	the Internet Explorer window
Step 18	*Save*	the *Teddy Toys Web.htm* file and close it

The presentation is ready to be viewed as a Web page on the Internet.

Summary

- A hyperlink is a reference on a slide that represents another location you want to access during a slide show.
- During a slide show, you can click a hyperlink to activate or jump to the location the hyperlink represents.
- You can add a hyperlink from a slide in one presentation to a different slide in the same presentation, a different presentation, a Web page, or a new document.
- Action buttons are predesigned hyperlink buttons that provide a means of jumping from slide to slide or presentations.
- Hyperlinks can be added to or removed from text and images.
- Sounds can be added to hyperlinked images.
- A hyperlinked image can be set to change color when you click it.
- Web pages are in the HTML (Hypertext Markup Language) text formatting language.
- The Web Page Preview provides a realistic view of how your presentation appears in an Internet browser.
- You can navigate through Web Page Preview with the Previous and Next Slide buttons and the Full Screen Slide Show button.
- The file extension for HTML documents is .htm.
- PowerPoint automatically adds an .htm extension to a presentation that is saved as a Web page.
- The page title on a Web page appears in the title bar in the Internet browser.
- A folder of files with codes is created when you save a presentation as a Web page.
- You can publish a presentation to the Web.
- You can set specific Web options in your PowerPoint presentation to change its appearance on the Internet.

chapter twelve

Commands Review

Action	Menu Bar	Shortcut Menu	Toolbar	Task Pane	Keyboard
Insert a hyperlink	Insert, Hyperlink	Right-click, Hyperlink	[icon]		ALT + I, I CTRL + K
Add an action button	Slide Show, Action Button		AutoShapes, Action Buttons		ALT + D, I ALT + U, I
Change action settings	Slide Show, Action Settings	Right-click, Action Settings			ALT + D, A CTRL + K on action button
Edit a hyperlink	Insert, Hyperlink	Right-click, Edit Hyperlink	[icon]		ALT + I, I
Add sound to hyperlink	Slide Show, Action Settings, Play sound	Right-click, Action Settings, Play sound			ALT + D, A, P
Add highlight click	Slide Show, Action Settings, Highlight click	Right-click, Action Settings, Highlight click			ALT + D, A, C
Add hyperlink to Web page	Insert, Hyperlink, Existing File or Web Page	Right-click, Hyperlink, Existing File or Web Page	[icon], Existing File or Web Page		ALT + I, I, X
Remove a hyperlink	Insert, Hyperlink, Remove Link; Slide Show, Action Settings, None	Right-click, Remove Hyperlink; Right-click, Action Settings, None	[icon], Remove Link		ALT + I, I, R ALT + D, A, N
Preview a presentation as a Web page	File, Web Page Preview				ALT + F, B
Save a presentation as a Web page	File, Save as Web Page				ALT + F, G
Publish a presentation to the Web	File, Save as Web Page, Publish				ALT + F, G, P

Concepts Review

Circle the correct answer.

1. To jump from one slide to another in a slide show presentation, you use a(n):
   - [a] action.
   - [b] hyperlink.
   - [c] image.
   - [d] slide show.

2. Which of the following enables you to place an action button on all slides in a presentation except the title slides?
   - [a] the title master
   - [b] the handout master
   - [c] the slide master
   - [d] the notes master

3. After clicking hyperlinked text, the text:
   - [a] changes to a different color indicating you have already visited that hyperlink.
   - [b] changes to a different color and you cannot click that hyperlink again.
   - [c] changes to a different color each time you click that hyperlink.
   - [d] color does not change at all.

4. When clicking a hyperlink to jump to one PowerPoint presentation from a different one:
   - [a] both presentations must be open.
   - [b] both presentations must use the same presentation template design.
   - [c] both presentations must be located in the same folder.
   - [d] only the presentation with the hyperlink needs to be open.

5. Objects that are hyperlinked to a different presentation should display a ScreenTip with:
[a] Yes or No as to whether the presentation is linked.
[b] the location and filename of linked presentation.
[c] hyperlinked object.
[d] the original presentation.

6. When creating hyperlinks to Web pages, you:
[a] must be connected to the Internet.
[b] must know the exact Web site address to hyperlink.
[c] cannot hyperlink using images.
[d] must link all the objects on the slide to only one Web page.

7. To remove a hyperlink from existing text while keeping the text, you cannot:
[a] select the Remove Link option in the Edit Hyperlink dialog box.
[b] select the None option in the Action Settings dialog box.
[c] right-click hyperlink, Hyperlink, Remove Hyperlink.
[d] highlight the existing text and press the DELETE key.

8. What term correctly describes Internet Explorer?
[a] Web site
[b] Web page
[c] Web browser
[d] Web address

9. HTML stands for:
[a] Hypertext Mailable Layout.
[b] Hypertext Machine Language.
[c] Hypertext Markup Language.
[d] Hypertext Transfer Language.

10. When you save a presentation as a Web page, PowerPoint automatically adds the:
[a] .ppt extension.
[b] .pot extension.
[c] .web extension.
[d] .htm extension.

Circle **T** if the statement is true or **F** if the statement is false.

T F 1. A hyperlink is a link that allows you to jump from one location to another in PowerPoint slide shows.

T F 2. You can hyperlink objects only from one slide to another slide in the same presentation.

T F 3. Hyperlinks automatically return to the same slide without you designating the location.

T F 4. Hyperlinked text, images, or objects work only in slide show.

T F 5. Sound can be heard when you jump from one presentation to a hyperlinked location in another presentation even if you do not have a sound card or speakers on your computer.

T F 6. The highlight click feature is not available with text hyperlinks.

T F 7. Once you create an action button, you cannot delete it.

T F 8. HTML is a presentation software language.

T F 9. You can save and publish PowerPoint presentations to display them over the Internet or an intranet.

T F 10. You can use an Internet browser to view and navigate through a presentation on the Web.

chapter twelve

Skills Review

Exercise 1

1. Open the *PowerPoint Advanced* presentation located on the Data Disk, and save it as *PowerPoint Hyperlinks*.
2. Display the What is PowerPoint? slide.
3. Add a hyperlink to the title text to link to the Internet at the following Web address: *www.microsoft.com/office/powerpoint*.
4. Add the ScreenTip "Microsoft PowerPoint" to the hyperlink.
5. Add an image to the upper-right corner of the "Slide Types" table slide and hyperlink the image to the What is PowerPoint? slide in the presentation.
6. Add the ScreenTip "PowerPoint" to the hyperlinked image.
7. Run the slide show from the beginning using the hyperlinks.
8. Save the presentation. Print any slide containing a hyperlink, and then close the presentation.

Exercise 2

1. Open the *Office Advanced* presentation located on the Data Disk.
2. Save the *Office Advanced* presentation as a Web page with the filename *Office Web*.
3. Change the page title to "Office Professional."
4. Preview the *Office Web* presentation as a Web page in the Internet browser.
5. Navigate through the Web page using the navigation frame and the previous and next slide controls.
6. Expand the outline in the navigation frame to see the bullet items, and then collapse the outline.
7. Run the slide show in the Web page preview.
8. Change the Web options (under the Publish feature) to display Presentation colors (accent color).
9. Save the *Office Web* presentation. Preview the *Office Web* presentation as a Web page.
10. Print the slide as a four-slides-per-page handout, and then close the presentation.

Exercise 3

1. Open the *Design Advanced* presentation located on the Data Disk, and save it as *Design Hyperlinks*.
2. Change the presentation design template to Fireworks.
3. Add a drawing shape or action button to the slide master to return to the previous slide.
4. Make the shape 3-D and change the color.
5. Using the Action Settings dialog box, add the Explosion sound to the shape.
6. Select the individual colors in the table, and add hyperlinks to Internet sites containing more information about the psychology of using color, what colors mean, or the color wheel.
7. Add appropriate ScreenTips that describe the Web sites.
8. Save the *Design Hyperlinks* presentation.
9. Save the *Design Hyperlinks* presentation as a Web page with the filename *Design Web*.
10. Change the page title to "Designing a Presentation."

11. Run the slide show in the Web page preview and use the hyperlinks to view Web sites.

12. Save the presentation, print the slide with the hyperlink, and then close the presentation.

Exercise 4

1. Open the *Precision Builders Advanced* presentation located on the Data Disk.

2. Save the *Precision Builders Advanced* presentation as a Web page with the filename *Precision Builders Web*.

3. Add an image to the Why Precision Builders slide, and hyperlink it with a sound and a ScreenTip and link it to an Internet site displaying pictures of new homes, new construction, or floor plans.

4. Preview the *Precision Builders Web* presentation as a Web page in the Internet browser.

5. Change the presentation design or color scheme to an appropriate design or color scheme for an Internet site showing builders of distinction.

6. Save the *Precision Builders Web* presentation.

7. Run the slide show in the Internet browser using the hyperlink to the Internet site.

8. Print the slide with the hyperlink, and then close the presentation.

Exercise 5

1. Open the *Nature Tours Advanced* presentation located on the Data Disk, and save it as *Nature Tours Hyperlinks*.

2. Open the *National Parks* presentation, and save it as *National Parks Hyperlinks*.

3. Add an action button hyperlink on the last slide ("Leg Tours") in the *Nature Tours Hyperlinks* presentation that hyperlinks to the second slide ("National Park Tours") in the presentation.

4. Make the action button 3-D and change the color.

5. Add a hyperlink with the Wind sound to the climber image on the third slide ("Available Tours") to hyperlink to the table slide ("Leg Tours").

6. Add hyperlinks to the bullet items on the second slide ("National Park Tours") that link to the appropriate slides in the *National Parks Hyperlinks* presentation, and add a ScreenTip to each park's link that identifies the destination.

7. Add an action button on the slides of the *National Parks Hyperlinks* presentation that links back to the National Park Tours slide in the *Nature Tours Hyperlinks* presentation.

8. Save the *National Parks Hyperlinks* presentation. Save the *Nature Tours Hyperlinks* presentation.

9. Run the slide show using the hyperlinks to navigate through the presentations.

10. Print the slides with the hyperlinks, and then close the presentation.

Exercise 6

1. Open the *A Healthier You Advanced* presentation located on the Data Disk, and save it as *A Healthier You Hyperlinks*.

2. Add the following hyperlinks and ScreenTips to the bullet items that link to the Internet on the Good Health Helps Everyone slide (*Hint:* If these addresses change, use the Search feature to locate appropriate sites per link.):

Exercise regularly	hyperlink to an Internet site about exercising
Eat a balanced diet	hyperlink to the Food Pyramid Guide (*www.nal.usda.gov/fnic*)
Drink plenty of water	hyperlink to an Internet health site discussing water intake
Visit your doctor periodically	hyperlink to a page on the WebMD Internet site (*www.webmd.com*)

chapter twelve

3. Add a hyperlink with sound to the Reduce Your Stress AutoShape that links to an Internet site showing calming pictures.

4. Save the presentation.

5. Print the slides with the hyperlinks, and then close the presentation.

Exercise 7

1. Open the *Buying A Computer Advanced* presentation located on the Data Disk, and save it as *Buying A Computer Hyperlinks*.

2. Using the Action Settings dialog box, add hyperlinks to the AutoShapes on the Where to Buy My Computer? slide to link to the appropriate slides in the *Computer Resources* presentation.

3. Add sounds to each hyperlink.

4. Run the slide show using the hyperlinks and the return action button provided on the *Computer Resources* presentation.

5. Add a hyperlink with sound and a ScreenTip to the chart object that links to a computer Internet site that lists current prices of computers.

6. Save the *Buying A Computer Hyperlinks* presentation. Print the slides with the hyperlinks, and then close the presentation.

Exercise 8

1. Open the *Leisure Travel Advanced* presentation located on the Data Disk.

2. Save the presentation as a Web page with the filename *Leisure Travel Web*.

3. Add hyperlinks to the bullet items on the Vacation Packages for Everyone slide to hyperlink to Internet sites relating to each bullet.

4. Run the slide show in the Web page preview using the previous and next slide controls and the hyperlinks.

5. Save the presentation, print the slide with the hyperlinks, and then close the presentation.

Case Problems

Project 1

You want to be prepared for any problems that may come up when working with hyperlinks. To find out how to resolve any difficulties, you decide to use the online Help to research how to troubleshoot hyperlinks. Find and print the information on troubleshooting hyperlinks and include all the links.

Project 2

Your employer wants you to add hyperlinks for the *Communicate Advanced* presentation. Create hyperlinks for various text, clip art images, or drawing shapes. Add sound where desired. Use the slide master if necessary to add return action buttons. Save the presentation as *Communicate Hyperlinks*. View the slide show and display it for your instructor. Print the slides with the hyperlinks in a two-slides-per-page handout.

Project 3

Souner & Associates uses PowerPoint to present many slide show presentations. You want to add hyperlinks to the *Souner Advanced* presentation to jump from the bullet items to different locations on the Internet dealing with Microsoft Office, Microsoft MOUS, and Web page design. Save the presentation as *Souner Hyperlinks*. View the slide show and display it for your instructor. Print the slides with the hyperlinks in a four-slides-per-page handout.

Project 4

As you prepare your own presentation, you decide to add hyperlinks that connect you to Web pages on the Internet. Create hyperlinks to jump you from slide to slide. Use text, clip art, WordArt, or drawing objects as hyperlinks. Add a text or image hyperlink to jump to a Web page that relates to your topic in your presentation. Save the *My Presentation Advanced* presentation as *My Presentation Hyperlinks*. Save the *My Presentation Hyperlinks* presentation as a Web page with the filename *My Presentation Web*. Run the slide show in the Web page preview, and navigate using the hyperlinks. Print the slides with the hyperlinks as a two-slides-per-page handout.

Project 5

Some grammar schools in your area have Internet access in the classroom. Your employer wants you to create a Web page for the Internet that the children can access regarding the Zoo's scheduled events. Save the *Zoo Advanced* presentation as *Zoo Web*, and make changes to enhance the appearance on the Internet. Add transitions, animation effects, and sound as children notice movement and sound quickly. Add a new slide to the presentation indicating the Zoo recently joined the Internet as a means of advertising upcoming events. Print the new slide.

Project 6

You want to get your PowerPoint presentations published on the Internet. Connect to the Internet and search the Web for information on Web pages. You might start with the Microsoft Office home page at *http://www.microsoft.com/office* and search for recent articles on intranet and Internet Web pages. Create a presentation detailing the specific information you found, and list the Web site addresses as a resource on one of the slides. Print the presentation as a six-slides-per-page handout.

Project 7

Your district superintendent asks if you can publish your *Cars Advanced* presentation on the school district's intranet so that all the consumer education instructors in the four high schools in the district can benefit from your information on cars. Save the *Cars Advanced* presentation as *Cars Web*, and preview it as a Web page before publishing it. Make any necessary changes to color, clip art images, and fonts before publishing it to the intranet. Add hyperlinks to link to your Secretary of State's Web site to locate information regarding state licenses for vehicles. Add a slide at the end of the presentation that lists you as the creator of the *Cars Web* Web page with your school name and telephone number for inquiries. Print the new slide.

Project 8

You and your partner work on the *Internet Advanced* presentation for your professor. He asks you to hyperlink various slides to other slides in the presentation. You use both text hyperlinks and image hyperlinks. In addition, as this is a PowerPoint presentation dealing with the Internet, your professor provides you with some Web site addresses to which you can hyperlink. Add sound and highlight click options where desired. Add action buttons to the slide master if you plan to return to certain slides. Save the presentation as *Internet Hyperlinks*. Create a second PowerPoint presentation called *Internet Search Engines* consisting of at least three slides. Hyperlink from slides in the *Internet Hyperlinks* presentation to various slides in the *Internet Search Engines* presentation. Run the slide show with all the hyperlinks, and print the slides with the hyperlinks as a two-slides-per-page handout.

chapter twelve

PowerPoint 2002

Using Additional Features in PowerPoint

Chapter Overview

In this chapter, you learn to use PowerPoint features that help you further polish presentations and share them in variety of situations. First, you learn to check styles to ensure your presentation adheres to basic style principles. Then, you learn how to prepare and send a presentation for review to others and then accept or reject the changes they suggest. You also learn to prepare a presentation for use on computers that do not have PowerPoint installed. Finally, you learn how to set up and schedule online broadcasts via the Internet or an intranet.

Learning Objectives

- Check styles in a presentation
- Set up a review cycle
- Review presentation comments and changes
- Use Pack and Go
- Set up and schedule online broadcasts

Case profile

Ms. Hill ask you perform a final check for clarity and consistency within the *Teddy Toys New Products* presentation before you e-mail a copy of it to Kathleen Lerek, vice president of sales, for her review. When the presentation is returned with Ms. Lerek's comments, Ms. Hill wants you to review the comments and make any suggested adjustments to the presentation. In addition, she wants you to prepare the presentation for an online broadcast that she plans to give next week.

chapter thirteen

13.a Checking Styles in a Presentation

By default, PowerPoint automatically checks your presentation for consistency and style. Based on a default set of rules stored in the program, PowerPoint checks for consistent use of capitalization and end punctuation, a maximum number of fonts and minimum number of font sizes, and the number of bullets used on a slide and the number of lines of text per bullet item. If PowerPoint encounters any style inconsistencies on a slide, such as too many bullets on a slide, a light bulb appears next to the placeholder indicating the inconsistency and suggesting a correction if available.

To make sure PowerPoint is set to alert you of style inconsistencies and to view the style options for the style check feature, you need to open the Spelling and Style dialog box. To view and turn on style checks:

| Step 1 | Open | the *Teddy Toys New Products* presentation located on the Data Disk |
| Step 2 | Save | the presentation as *Teddy Toys Styles* |

To use the Office Assistant to alert you to inconsistencies, it must be turned on. If you do not see the Office Assistant on your screen, complete Steps 3 and 4. Otherwise, skip to Step 5 to view the style options available when checking for style inconsistencies.

Step 3	Click	Help
Step 4	Click	Show the Office Assistant
Step 5	Click	Tools
Step 6	Click	Options
Step 7	Click	the Spelling and Style tab
Step 8	Click	the Check style check box to insert a check mark, if necessary
Step 9	Click	Style Options

The Style Options dialog box on your screen should look similar to Figure 13-1. The Case and End Punctuation tab enables you to determine whether you want the titles and body text to use title case, sentence case, lowercase, uppercase, or consistent case, and what type of end punctuation to use.

> **QUICK TIP**
>
> If you want to review or modify the rules PowerPoint is using to check styles, you open the Style Options dialog box by clicking Style Options on the Spelling and Style tab of the Options dialog box. Style rules in the Style Options dialog box are organized in two tabs: Case and End Punctuation and Visual Clarity.

> **CAUTION TIP**
>
> The light bulb is not available if the Office Assistant is turned off. If the Office Assistant is only hidden, the light bulb displays and the Office Assistant pops up when you click the light bulb.

chapter thirteen

FIGURE 13-1
Style Options Dialog Box

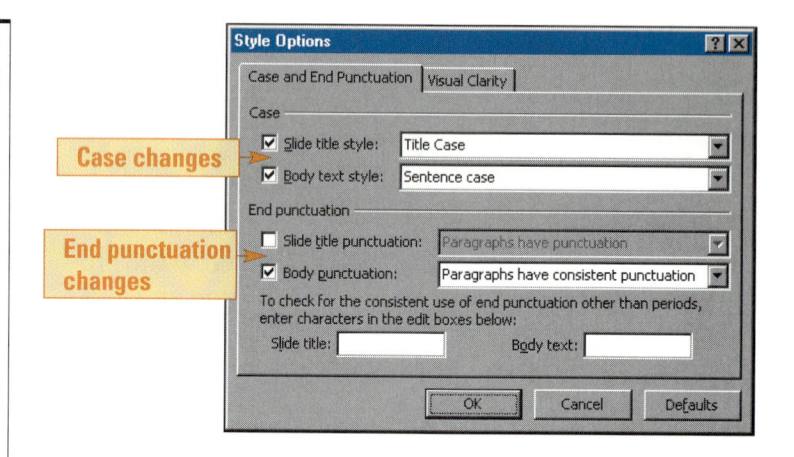

Case changes →

End punctuation changes →

| Step 10 | **Click** | the Visual Clarity tab |

The Visual Clarity tab of the Style Options dialog box enables you to determine the maximum number of different fonts to be used in your presentation, the minimum size of the title text, the minimum size of the body text on the text slides, the maximum number of bullets per slide, the maximum number of lines per title, and the number of lines per bullet.

Step 11	**Verify**	that the Number of fonts should not exceed: check box contains a check mark and the text box displays 3
Step 12	**Verify**	that the Title text size should be at least: check box contains a check mark and the text box displays 36
Step 13	**Verify**	that the Body text size should be at least: check box contains a check mark and the text box displays 20

The legibility options may or may not be activated. To view and turn on legibility style checks:

Step 1	**Click**	to insert check marks in the Number of bullets should not exceed:, Number of lines per title should not exceed:, and Number of lines per bullet should not exceed check boxes
Step 2	**Verify**	that the Number of bullets should not exceed: text box displays 6
Step 3	**Verify**	that the Number of lines per title should not exceed: text box displays 2
Step 4	**Verify**	that the Number of lines per bullet should not exceed: text box displays 2
Step 5	**Click**	OK twice

To check styles in the presentation:

| Step 1 | *Display* | Slide 1, if necessary |

A light bulb does not appear on Slide 1, because the slide does not contain any style inconsistencies as established in the Style Options dialog box.

| Step 2 | *Display* | Slide 2 and look for the light bulb |
| Step 3 | *Click* | the light bulb next to the bullet placeholder |

The Office Assistant pops up and displays the Capitalization style and four suggestions: Change the text to sentence case, Ignore this style rule for this presentation only, Change style checker options for all presentations, and Don't show me this tip again. If you select Change the text to sentence case, the bullets start with a capital letter and the remaining characters are lowercase. If you select Change style checker options for all presentations, the Style Options dialog box opens enabling you to change the style options.

Step 4	*Click*	Ignore this style rule for this presentation only
Step 5	*Display*	Slide 3
Step 6	*Click*	the light bulb next to the bullet placeholder

The Office Assistant pops up and displays the Punctuation style and five suggestions: Add end punctuation, Remove end punctuation, Ignore this style rule for this presentation only, Change style checker options for all presentations, and Don't show me this tip again.

| Step 7 | *Click* | Remove end punctuation |

The periods at the end of the bullets are removed, but the Presentation Assistant light bulb is still active.

| Step 8 | *Click* | the light bulb next to the bullet placeholder |

The Office Assistant pops up and displays the Long paragraphs message and three suggestions: Ignore this style rule for this presentation only, Change style checker options for all presentations, and Don't show

chapter
thirteen

me this tip again. You decide to follow the advice of the Office Assistant by editing the bulleted text on the slide to shorten the bullet items.

Step 9	Click	OK
Step 10	Edit	the first and second bullets to read as follows: Designed especially for your toddler Travels in his own car seat next to your children
Step 11	Display	Slide 4
Step 12	Click	the light bulb next to the bullet placeholder
Step 13	Click	Remove end punctuation
Step 14	Edit	the first and second bullets to read as follows: Designed especially for your preschooler Pulls your child's toys and friends up to 100 pounds
Step 15	Display	Slide 5 and click the light bulb next to the bullet placeholder
Step 16	Click	Remove end punctuation
Step 17	Click	the light bulb next to the bullet placeholder

The Office Assistant pops up and displays the Long paragraphs message and three suggestions for remedying the problem.

Step 18	Click	OK, and then edit the first and second bullets to read as follows: Designed especially for children 4 to 10 years of age Entertains children for hours
Step 19	Display	Slide 6 and click the light bulb next to the bullet placeholder
Step 20	Click	Remove end punctuation
Step 21	Edit	the first and second bullets to read as follows: Designed especially for toddlers and preschoolers Available in two styles
Step 22	Right-click	the Office Assistant
Step 23	Click	Hide
Step 24	Save	the Teddy Toys Styles presentation

Embedding Fonts in a Presentation

If TrueType fonts are used in a presentation, you can embed the fonts within the presentation. This ensures that the TrueType fonts used in the presentation display if the presentation is shown on a computer on which the font is not installed.

DESIGN TIP

When embedding fonts in a presentation, you can embed just the characters in use or you can embed all the characters in the font set, used or not used. When sending a presentation out for review, it is best to embed the full font set in case the reviewers decide to use a character that was not originally included in the presentation, even though embedding all characters in the font set will increase the size of the file.

To learn whether a font is a TrueType font, check the font list box; TrueType fonts are displayed with a ^T_T notation displayed before the font name.

Using Additional Features in PowerPoint — PA 121

To embed fonts in a presentation:

Step 1	Click	Tools
Step 2	Click	Options
Step 3	Click	the Save tab

The Save tab in the Options dialog box on your screen should look similar to Figure 13-2.

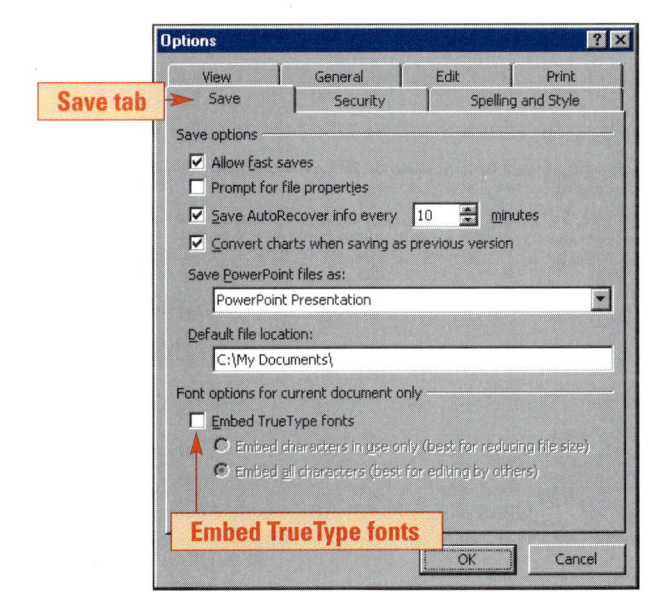

FIGURE 13-2
Options Dialog Box with Save Tab

QUICK TIP

You can also embed fonts when you save a presentation by clicking the Tools button in the Save As dialog box, clicking Save Options, and then clicking Embed TrueType fonts.

Step 4	Click	the Embed TrueType fonts check box to add a check mark
Step 5	Verify	that the Embed all characters (best for editing by others) option button is selected
Step 6	Click	OK
Step 7	Save	the *Teddy Toys Styles* presentation

13.b Setting Up a Review Cycle

Today, electronic mail, commonly known as e-mail, has become a fast, economical form of communication. **E-mail** is the electronic transmission of data over the Internet or intranet via communication

chapter thirteen

> **QUICK TIP**
>
> If you want more than one person to review and comment on a presentation, you can route it in e-mail or you can send it to people on a distribution list. To route a presentation for review, indicate the individuals to review the presentation and send the presentation to the first reviewer. The first reviewer sends it to the next reviewer and so forth; each recipient sees the previous reviewer's comments. You can set deadlines for each reviewer and for the final return of the presentation.
>
> You can send a presentation to people on a distribution list by sending an attachment of the presentation to each recipient at the same time. This method does not enable all reviewers to see comments and changes from other reviewers.

lines. Business employees, researchers, writers, teachers, and students have found that e-mail is an efficient means of exchanging ideas and documents, as well as editing and critiquing each others work. Rather than sending hard copies of a document to review, you send the document electronically. In that way, editing can be done electronically as well.

If your goal is to have another person preview and comment on a presentation, you can send that presentation as an attachment that accompanies an e-mail message.

You can send a presentation for review by using Outlook or by saving the presentation for review and attaching it to an e-mail message. If you use Outlook as your e-mail application, Outlook sends the presentation to designated individuals, creates an e-mail message that they are receiving a presentation for review, enabling you to create follow-up flags for returning the document, and automatically tracks changes made by the reviewers. If you send the entire presentation as an attachment, you must first save a copy of the presentation in Presentation for Review format before attaching the presentation to an e-mail message. When the presentation returns, you are responsible for tracking the changes of the reviewer or reviewers. With either method, recipients can use any version of PowerPoint to review the presentation and make comments. Sending a presentation as an attachment or for review can be accomplished via Outlook or any other 32-bit e-mail program compatible with the Messaging Application Programming Interface (MAPI), a Microsoft Exchange server, or a disk.

The Reviewing toolbar contains tools for reviewing changes and adding comments. To display the Reviewing toolbar and add comments to slides:

| Step 1 | *Display* | Slide 1 |
| Step 2 | *Display* | the Reviewing toolbar, if necessary |

The Reviewing toolbar has buttons for displaying comments and changes; viewing names of reviewers; moving from previous to next items; applying and unapplying changes; inserting, editing, and deleting comments; and opening the Revisions Pane. When you open a presentation that was previously saved for review, an End Review button appears on the Reviewing toolbar, allowing you to end the review process.

| Step 3 | *Click* | the Insert Comment button on the Reviewing toolbar |

A comment marker displays at the upper-left corner of the slide with a comment box displaying the reviewer's name, review date, and a flashing insertion point where you key your comments.

| Step 4 | Key | Please review the presentation and make any comments and edits you feel would improve the slides. Thanks! |

The text for the comment appears in the comment box. Your screen should look similar to Figure 13-3, except that the name in the comment box reflects the user information for a particular computer, so the name Sandra Hill does not appear in your comment box.

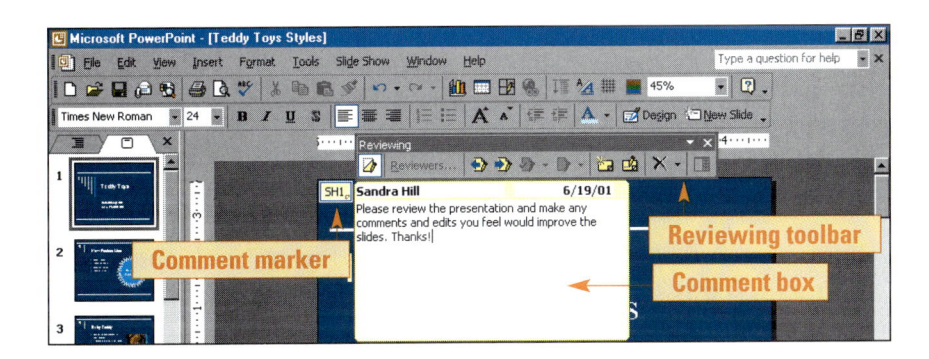

FIGURE 13-3
Comment Box

Step 5	Click	outside the comment box
Step 6	Display	Slide 7
Step 7	Click	the Insert Comment button on the Reviewing toolbar
Step 8	Key	In preparation for the online broadcast, I think we should delete this slide. Do you agree?
Step 9	Click	outside the comment box

Next you save the presentation for review so you can send the file as an attachment to an e-mail message. To save a presentation for review:

Step 1	Click	File
Step 2	Click	Save As
Step 3	Click	the Save as type: list arrow in the Save As dialog box
Step 4	Click	Presentation for Review
Step 5	Key	Teddy Toys Styles-Lerek in the File name: text box
Step 6	Click	Save

Although you just saved the presentation as a presentation for review with a different name, the title bar still displays the original presentation filename (*Teddy Toys Styles*). The *Teddy Toys Styles-Lerek* presentation is a

MENU TIP

When you send a copy of a presentation for reviewing using Microsoft Outlook, you save the file as a regular PowerPoint presentation and then click the Mail Recipient (for Review) subcommand on the Send To submenu on File menu.

When you send a copy of a presentation as an attachment for reviewing using other e-mail programs, you save the presentation in Presentation for Review format in the Save as type: text box in the Save As dialog box. Otherwise, the review copy cannot be compared to the original copy when it is returned, and it replaces the original copy unless renamed.

chapter
thirteen

CAUTION TIP

Outlook may be configured differently on your computer. You may be asked to select a different profile to use the Outlook application. If this happens, key your name, click OK, and then in the E-mail accounts dialog box that opens, specify the e-mail account and directory that Outlook should use. If you need assistance, see your instructor.

QUICK TIP

When you use the File, Send To Mail Recipient (for Review) option, a review request e-mail message is automatically created in Microsoft Outlook using Word as the E-mail editor displaying To, Cc, Subject, and Attach text boxes. A body text area displays below them.

copy of the *Teddy Toys Styles* presentation that will contain reviewer's changes, and you can compare and merge this copy of the presentation with the original presentation. To send a presentation for review via e-mail:

Step 7	Close	the *Teddy Toys Styles* presentation
Step 8	Click	No if prompted to save changes to the *Teddy Toys Styles* presentation
Step 9	Open	the *Teddy Toys Styles-Lerek* presentation
Step 10	Click	No to merge changes
Step 11	Click	the E-mail (as Attachment) button on the Standard toolbar

Outlook opens with the Subject: Teddy Toys Styles-Lerek.ppt and the attachment, Teddy Toys Styles-Lerek.ppt (410 KB), in the Attach box. You then key in the reviewer's e-mail address, any message text, and then click Send. You do not send the attachment at this time.

| Step 12 | Close | the Outlook window |
| Step 13 | Close | the *Teddy Toys Styles-Lerek* presentation |

13.c Reviewing Presentation Comments and Changes

The advantage of sending a presentation electronically to others for review is that when it returns, you can combine the reviewed presentation with the original and view all the comments and changes at the same time. If multiple people reviewed the presentation, each reviewer's comments or changes are displayed with a color-coded icon indicating each change or comment made by a reviewer and a short description of the change or the comment. PowerPoint also indicates if one reviewer's change conflicts with another's, letting the originator determine which change to accept and which to reject.

The *Teddy Toys Styles-Lerek Compare* presentation on the Data Disk has comments and changes so you can complete the compare and merge process. To review comments and changes to the *Teddy Toys Styles* presentation and manually merge the *Teddy Toys Styles* presentation with the *Teddy Toys Styles-Lerek Compare* presentation:

| Step 1 | Open | the *Teddy Toys Styles* presentation |

Using Additional Features in PowerPoint   PA 125

Step 2	Click	the Close button [X] in the open task pane, if necessary
Step 3	Click	Tools
Step 4	Click	Compare and Merge Presentations
Step 5	Switch to	the drive or folder that contains your Data Files
Step 6	Double-click	the *Teddy Toys Styles-Lerek Compare* presentation

The *Teddy Toys Styles* original presentation is displayed and the Revisions Pane opens displaying tabs for Gallery and List. Your screen should look similar to Figure 13-4. The Gallery tab of the Revisions Pane lists the reviewers and displays thumbnails with suggested changes to the current slide for each reviewer. The Reviewers: list box allows you to select which reviewer's comments you want to review at this time. By default, the All Reviewers check box contains a check mark, as does the name of every reviewer who reviewed the document. To hide comments from any reviewer, remove the check mark next to the reviewer's name. The List tab shows all comments and objects that contain revisions for the current slide, as well as presentation changes.

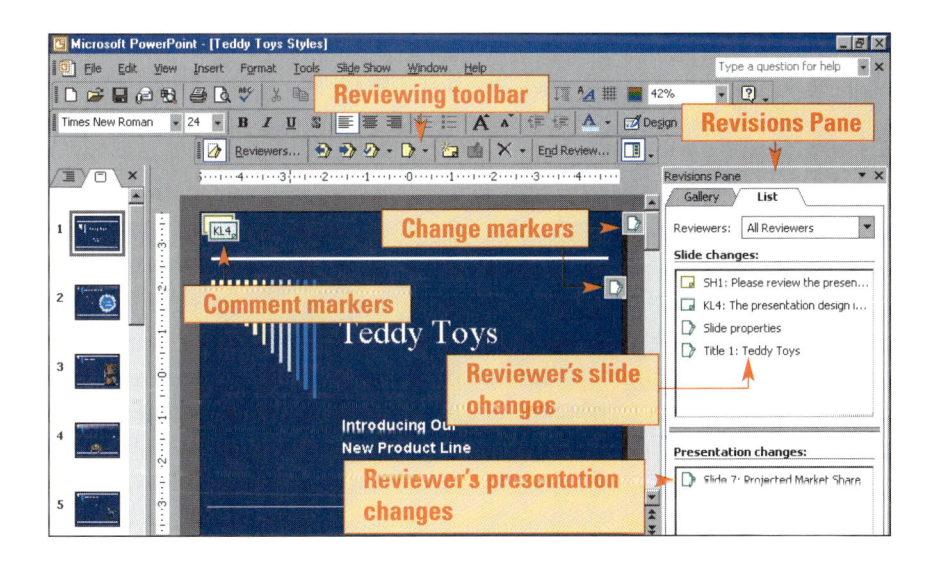

CAUTION TIP

When sending a presentation for review that has links to other presentations or documents, you need to include all linked files in your e-mail message.

TASK PANE TIP

You can display a comment by clicking the appropriate comment in the Slide changes: list in the List tab in the Revisions Pane.

FIGURE 13-4
Revisions Pane

To view the reviewer's comments in the merged presentation:

Step 1	Display	Slide 1, if necessary
Step 2	Click	the List tab in the Revisions Pane, if necessary
Step 3	Click	the All Reviewers list arrow

MOUSE TIP

You can send a presentation as an e-mail attachment from within your e-mail program by clicking the Attachment or Insert file button, keying the filename, clicking OK or Insert, and then clicking Send.

chapter
thirteen

Menu Tip

You can display the Revisions Pane by clicking View, pointing to Toolbars, and then clicking Revisions Pane.

Task Pane Tip

You can apply or unapply changes by each individual reviewer by clicking the list arrow on the thumbnail and then clicking Apply Changes By This Reviewer or Unapply Changes By This Reviewer. You can also Show Only This Reviewer's Changes, Preview Animation, or choose Done With This Reviewer. In the List tab, the Reviewers: list box allows you to select All Reviewers or Multiple Reviewers the same as in the Gallery tab.

Quick Tip

When comparing and merging presentations, the Revisions Pane provides a quick method for viewing and applying reviewer's changes. If another task pane is already open, the Revisions Pane appears directly to the left of the open task pane. You can close any open task pane to increase the size of the slide in Normal view.

The All Reviewers list shows Kathleen Lerek as the reviewer. If Ms. Hill sent the presentation to other reviewers as well, their names would appear in the list. A Reviewers button is available on the Reviewing toolbar as well.

Step 4	Click	away from the Reviewers: list
Step 5	Display	the Reviewing toolbar, if necessary

All comments and changes are displayed on the individual slides as well as in the Revisions Pane. If comments and changes do not display on the slides, you can click the Markup button on the Reviewing toolbar to display them.

Step 6	Click	the Markup button on the Reviewing toolbar, if necessary, to display comment markers
Step 7	Point to	the KL4 comment marker on the first slide

The comment marker displays the reviewer's initials and the number of the reviewer's comment. Because you opened this presentation from the Data Disk, you are looking at comments made by Kathleen Lerek. The comment displays with the reviewer's name, review date, and reviewer comments regarding changes on this slide.

Step 8	Read	the reviewer's comment

Kathleen Lerek suggests a different template design in her comment. In addition to comments, reviewers make changes to the slides such as changes to text, objects, placement, sizing, color schemes, and design templates. A change marker displays at the right corner of the Teddy Toys title slide. The change marker provides a summary of the change. To view, accept, and reject changes:

Step 1	Point to	the change marker at the upper-right corner of the slide
Step 2	Read	the reviewer's change

The change marker displays Slide property changes: Design template, but does not indicate which design template.

Step 3	Click	the Gallery tab in the Revisions Pane

Using Additional Features in PowerPoint   PA 127

The Gallery tab displays the thumbnail of the Teddy Toys title slide with a different template. You have five choices for applying the suggested change: you can click the thumbnail; point to the list arrow that displays at the right of the thumbnail and click to Apply Changes By This Reviewer; click to add a check mark in the reviewer check box above the thumbnail; click the change marker and add a check mark in the check box; click the Slide properties item in the Slides changes: list in the List tab and add a check mark in the check box; or click the Apply button on the Reviewing toolbar. Your screen should look similar to Figure 13-5.

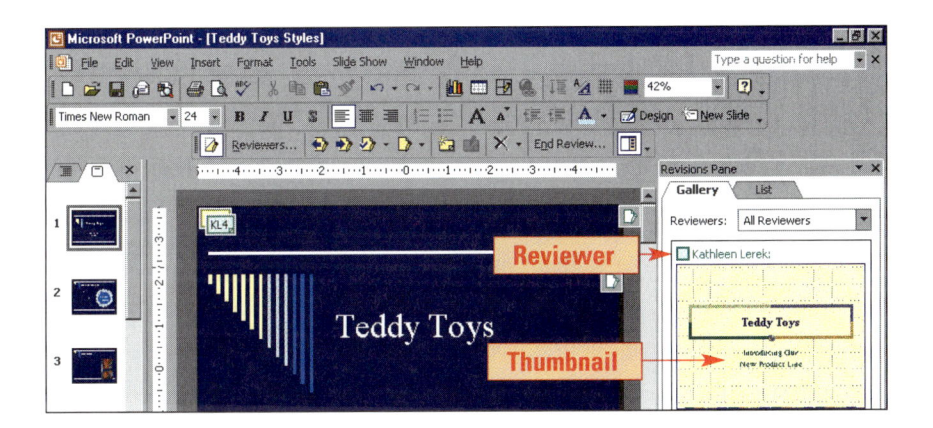

> **MOUSE TIP**
>
> You can display the Revisions Pane by right-clicking any toolbar button and then clicking Revisions Pane.

FIGURE 13-5
Gallery Tab in the Revisions Pane

Step 4	Point to	the change marker near the Teddy Toys title object
Step 5	Read	the reviewer's change
Step 6	Click	the thumbnail in the Gallery tab in the Revisions Pane

By clicking the thumbnail in the Gallery, you are accepting all changes made by this reviewer on this slide, the new presentation design template as well as the formatting changes.

Step 7	Display	Slide 2
Step 8	Read	the comment and change markers
Step 9	Accept	all changes on Slide 2

After viewing the new AutoShape, you decide to reject this change.

| Step 10 | Click | the change marker near the AutoShape |
| Step 11 | Click | the AutoShape (Kathleen Lerek) check box to remove the check mark |

> **QUICK TIP**
>
> When you use Outlook to track changes, Outlook automatically combines the presentations to be merged. If you do not use Outlook for tracking the changes, you can open the reviewed presentation and then manually compare revisions between the original and the reviewed presentation by using Compare and Merge Presentations on the Tools menu.

chapter
thirteen

The AutoShape is returned to the original shape. To finish reviewing the presentation and accept the remaining changes:

Step 1	Display	Slide 3 and read the change markers
Step 2	Accept	the design template and the Size/Position changes on the bullet text and image on Slide 3
Step 3	Display	Slide 4 and accept all changes
Step 4	Remove	the check mark in the Inserted "pre-school age child" (Kathleen Lerek) check box

After you accept the changes on the fourth slide, you notice that text was deleted and additional text inserted in the bullet item.

Step 5	Accept	all changes on Slide 5 and Slide 6
Step 6	Remove	the check mark in the Inserted "pre-school age child" (Kathleen Lerek) check box on Slide 6
Step 7	Display	Slide 7

The original comment from Sandra Hill to Kathleen Lerek displays at the upper-left corner of the slide. It appears that Kathleen did not return a comment nor make any changes to this slide as shown in the Gallery tab, but you notice a change marker in the Slides tab on Slide 7. A change marker with text displays in the Presentation changes: list in the List tab in the Revisions Pane.

Step 8	Click	the List tab and observe the Presentation changes: list
Step 9	Click	the change marker on Slide 7 in the Slides tab
Step 10	Click	the Deleted "Projected Market Share" (Kathleen Lerek) check box to add a check mark

When you end the review, you end the review for all reviewers and any unapplied changes are lost. To end a review:

Step 1	Click	the End Review button [End Review...] on the Reviewing toolbar

A warning dialog box displays, asking whether you are sure you want to end the review for your presentation and informing you that if you do end the review, this would end the review for all reviewers and any unapplied changes would be lost.

MOUSE TIP

When you point to the comment marker, the comment displays when the mouse rests on the comment marker, similar to a ScreenTip on a toolbar button. If you want the comment to remain displayed, you click either the comment marker on the slide or the comment in the Slide changes: list in the List tab in the Revisions Pane.

You can accept a change by clicking the Apply button on the Reviewing toolbar; you can reject a change by click the Unapply button on the Reviewing toolbar.

QUICK TIP

Clicking the thumbnail slide in the Gallery tab accepts all changes on the slide. After the originator of the presentation for review has accepted a change, a check mark displays in the change marker, indicating acceptance of that change. The changes on the slide are made automatically as you click the check boxes. When you check the check boxes, you are accepting the change. When you leave the check box empty, you are rejecting the change.

| Step 2 | Click | Yes to end the review |
| Step 3 | Save | the *Teddy Toys Styles* presentation |

Printing Comments Pages

When printing a presentation that has been compared and merged with reviewed presentations, you also can print the comments pages. Comments are printed on a separate slide if you print slides or on a separate page if you print a handout or notes page. Comment markers print on each slide of the printout and the comments page includes the slide number, reviewers' initials, comments, reviewer's name, and review date. To print comments with handouts:

Step 1	Click	File
Step 2	Click	Print
Step 3	Click	the Print what: list arrow
Step 4	Click	Handouts
Step 5	Verify	that 6 appears in the Slides per page: list box
Step 6	Click	the Include comment pages check box to add a check mark
Step 7	Click	OK

After ending a review comparing presentations, the change markers disappear but the comment markers are still displayed. You can turn off the comments using the Reviewing toolbar. To turn off comments after ending a review:

Step 1	Display	the Reviewing toolbar, if necessary
Step 2	Click	the Markup button on the Reviewing toolbar to hide comment markers
Step 3	Close	the Reviewing toolbar
Step 4	Save	the *Teddy Toys Styles* presentation

13.d Using Pack and Go

There may be times when you need to make a PowerPoint presentation on a computer that does not have PowerPoint installed. The **Pack and Go Wizard** allows you to pack your presentation with all its files,

> **QUICK TIP**
>
> You can apply all changes to a slide by clicking the Apply button list arrow on the Reviewing toolbar and then clicking Apply All Changes to the Current Slide. You can unapply all changes to a slide by clicking the Unapply button list arrow on the Reviewing toolbar and then clicking Unapply All Changes to the Current Slide.
>
> You can apply all changes to a presentation by clicking the Apply button list arrow on the Reviewing toolbar and then clicking Apply All Changes to the Presentation. You can unapply all changes to a slide by clicking the Unapply button list arrow on the Reviewing toolbar and then clicking Unapply All Changes to the Presentation.

chapter thirteen

Task Pane Tip

You can apply or unapply all changes made by a reviewer on one slide by clicking the Gallery tab in the Revisions Pane and then clicking the slide thumbnail. You can also apply or unapply all changes made by a reviewer on one slide by clicking the Gallery tab in the Revisions Pane and then clicking Apply (or Unapply) Changes By This Reviewer.

fonts, and images, and save it in a format that you can unpack and run on a computer that does not have PowerPoint. Presentations can be packed to a floppy disk, a Zip disk, your hard drive, or a location on your network. If your presentation contains links to other files, you must include those files with the presentation being packed. If linked files are not packed with the presentation, you cannot open the files containing the most recent changes on the destination computer. In addition, you want to consider embedding fonts during the packing process so those fonts will display correctly if the font is not installed on the destination computer.

To pack a presentation:

Step 1	Save	the *Teddy Toys Styles* presentation as *Teddy Toys Pack and Go*
Step 2	Click	File
Step 3	Click	Pack and Go

The Pack and Go Wizard dialog box opens with the Office Assistant offering help and with a diagram of the steps for packing the presentation. Your dialog box should look similar to Figure 13-6.

FIGURE 13-6
Pack and Go Wizard Dialog Box

Caution Tip

When you pack a presentation to a floppy disk, it may require many floppy disks, depending on the size of the presentation file.

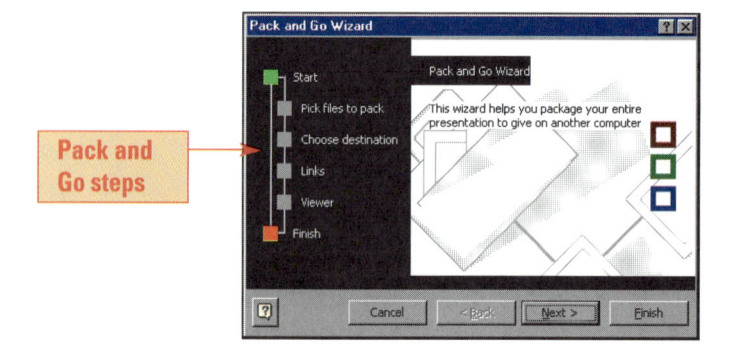

Step 4	Click	Next>
Step 5	Verify	that Active presentation is checked
Step 6	Click	Next>
Step 7	Click	the A: drive (or the drive designated by your instructor)
Step 8	Click	Next>
Step 9	Verify	that Include linked files is checked
Step 10	Click	the Embed TrueType fonts check box to add a check mark
Step 11	Click	Next>
Step 12	Click	Viewer for Microsoft Windows

If the Viewer for Microsoft Windows option is ghosted, you must first download the viewer to your computer and then you can include it in the Pack and Go process.

Step 13	Click	N̲ext>
Step 14	Click	F̲inish

A Pack And Go Status window displays, indicating what Pack and Go is doing: packaging the presentation, files, viewer, and other essential files. If you are saving to disks, the Pack and Go Wizard prompts you if you need to insert additional disks for storing the Viewer and the presentation.

Step 15	Close	the *Teddy Toys Pack and Go* presentation
Step 16	Exit	the PowerPoint application

You can now take the floppy disk(s) or Zip disk to a computer that does not have PowerPoint and run the *Teddy Toys Pack and Go* presentation. When you run your slide show on a different computer, you need to unpack the presentation and the Viewer. To unpack and run the slide show presentation:

Step 1	Insert	the disk containing the packed presentation into the new computer
Step 2	Access	Windows Explorer
Step 3	Click	the 3½ Floppy [A:] drive icon or Zip drive
Step 4	Double-click	the *pngsetup.exe* file
Step 5	Create	a new destination folder to which you want to copy the packed presentation
Step 6	Click	OK until all disks have been unpacked
Step 7	Click	N̲o to Would you like to run slide show now?

If you are unpacking to show the presentation as a slide show only one time, you would then answer Yes to the Would you like to run slide show now? question. If you want to access the presentation more than once, you would then proceed to the drive when you unpacked.

Step 8	Click	the drive and folder where you copied the presentation
Step 9	Double-click	the *Teddy Toys Pack and Go* presentation

QUICK TIP

The PowerPoint Viewer is an application used to run a slide show on a computer without PowerPoint. You can add the Viewer to the same disk as the presentation by using the Pack and Go Wizard. You then unpack the viewer and the presentation and run the slide show on any computer. You can download the PowerPoint Viewer (free of charge) from the Microsoft Office Download Center Web site at *http://office.microsoft.com/downloads*. The Viewer supports all PowerPoint 2002, 2000, and 97 features, as well as files created in PowerPoint for Windows and PowerPoint for the Macintosh. The Pack and Go Wizard does not, however, run on Microsoft Windows 3.1.

Step 10	*Run*	the slide show
Step 11	*Close*	the *Teddy Toys Pack and Go* presentation
Step 12	*Close*	Windows Explorer

13.e Setting Up and Scheduling Online Broadcasts

PowerPoint enables you to increase your productivity by broadcasting a presentation over the Web, including any video and/or audio with the presentation. **Broadcasting** a presentation enables you to show your presentation to several different groups, at several remote locations, thereby reaching a greater audience.

You schedule a broadcast of the presentation via Microsoft Outlook or any e-mail program you use just as you schedule any meeting. While scheduling, the person setting up the broadcast can also review a list of things to do before, during, and/or after the broadcast by viewing the tips for broadcast that are available. The presentation must be saved in HTML format (Hypertext Markup Language) so that the audience at the remote locations can view the presentation on their browser.

> **notes**
> Due to variations in intranet and Internet setup and access, you cannot complete the entire process of setting up and scheduling online broadcasts and online collaborations in this chapter. Instead, you look at the various dialog boxes and stop at a point prior to actual scheduling.

If you are using Microsoft Outlook as your e-mail application, an online broadcast can be scheduled the same as any other meeting you schedule using Outlook. To set up and schedule an online broadcast:

Step 1	*Open*	the *Teddy Toys Styles* presentation you saved earlier in this chapter
Step 2	*Save*	the presentation as *Teddy Toys Broadcast*
Step 3	*Click*	Sli<u>d</u>e Show
Step 4	*Point to*	<u>O</u>nline Broadcast
Step 5	*Click*	<u>S</u>chedule a Live Broadcast

> **QUICK TIP**
>
> To broadcast a presentation, the sender and audience need PowerPoint 2002 and Microsoft Internet Explorer 5.1 or later. If you are broadcasting with audio, a microphone must be attached to the computer of the person broadcasting, and each audience member needs sound cards and speakers attached to their computers to hear the audio. If you are broadcasting with video, a video camera must be attached to the computer broadcasting the presentation and to the audience computers.

Using Additional Features in PowerPoint   PA 133

The Schedule Presentation Broadcast dialog box opens, enabling you to set up a lobby page for the broadcast that the audience reads before the broadcast. The dialog box lets you key the Title of the presentation, a brief Description of what the broadcast will cover, the Speaker, a Copyright if applicable, Keywords used in the presentation, and an Email address of the speaker. In addition, you can access tips for broadcasting that help you prepare for the broadcast. Your dialog box should look similar to Figure 13-7.

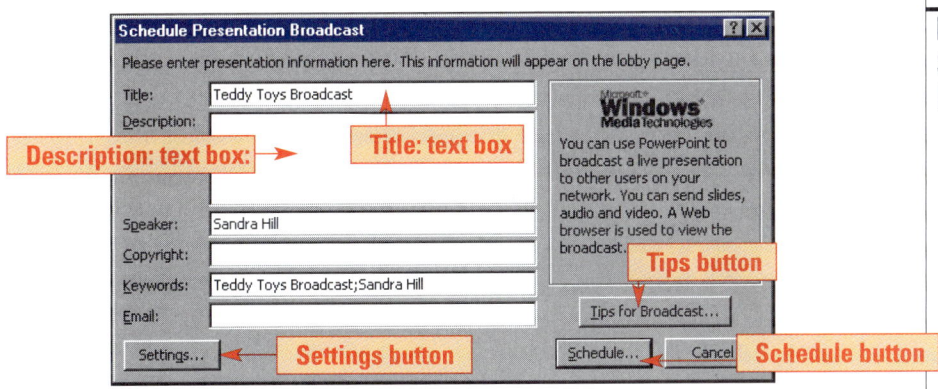

FIGURE 13-7
Schedule Presentation Broadcast Dialog Box

Step 6	Click	Tips for Broadcast
Step 7	Read	the Help topic tips

The Tips for Broadcast include information about setting up a broadcast, working with audio and video, and things to do before, during, and after a broadcast.

Step 8	Close	the Tips for broadcasting Help screen
Step 9	Verify	that *Teddy Toys Broadcast* is in the Title: text box
Step 10	Key	the following information in the Description: text box: The purpose of this broadcast is to make the Teddy Toys Broadcast presentation available to sales managers across the nation. Feedback on the Teddy Toys Broadcast presentation is requested.
Step 11	Key	Sandra Hill in the Speaker: text box
Step 12	Click	Settings and observe the settings

The Broadcast Settings dialog box opens with Presenter and Advanced tabs to define settings. You do not make any changes to this dialog box.

DESIGN TIP

If you do not embed fonts and the destination computer does not have those fonts, the destination computer substitutes a font for the one it does not have. If you have not embedded the fonts in a presentation before using the Pack and Go Wizard, you can do so while completing the wizard. Embedding the TrueType fonts ensures that the presentation displays with the correct fonts.

chapter thirteen

CAUTION TIP

You need to set the options you need for broadcasting only the first time you set one up; after that, these options are used for all future broadcasts unless you make changes.

Your system administrator may have already set up the options so you do not need to.

QUICK TIP

The Presenter tab in the Broadcast Settings dialog box enables you to select audio/video options, set the display from a resizable screen to a full screen, select whether to display speaker notes, and determine the location to save the broadcast files. The location to save the broadcast files is a folder to which all participants have access and where PowerPoint will put the presentation. The Advanced tab enables you to set the URL for a chat room and set the media server that will be used for the broadcast.

| Step 13 | *Click* | Cancel |
| Step 14 | *Click* | S<u>c</u>hedule |

If your system administrator has not set up a shared folder, a prompt displays indicating that you must specify a shared file location in the Broadcast Settings dialog box before proceeding with your broadcast. At this point, you cannot progress further unless your system administrator sets up a shared folder. If your service provider sets up the options for a broadcast, you then click the Start <u>L</u>ive Broadcast Now button and your e-mail program starts. If you have Microsoft Outlook, use it to arrange a broadcast as you would any other meeting. For more information, see Outlook online Help. If you do not use Outlook, you would enter the broadcast date, time, and the URL of the broadcast side in the e-mail message sent to the participants.

| Step 15 | *Click* | OK to close the prompt |
| Step 16 | *Click* | Cancel |

Once you set up and schedule a broadcast, you are ready to start the broadcast. To start a broadcast:

Step 1	*Click*	Sli<u>d</u>e Show
Step 2	*Point to*	<u>O</u>nline Broadcast
Step 3	*Click*	Start <u>L</u>ive Broadcast Now

If you have not saved the presentation in HTML format prior to this point, the presentation is automatically saved in HTML format at the designated server location. A Microsoft Outlook information dialog box displays telling you that a program is trying to access e-mail addresses you have stored in Outlook and asking if you want to allow this. These Outlook addresses are usually the addresses Outlook needs to invite people to the online broadcast. Audience members are invited through an e-mail message sent through Outlook using the Address Book and Contacts list.

| Step 4 | *Click* | <u>Y</u>es |
| Step 5 | *Click* | <u>B</u>roadcast in the Live Presentation Broadcast dialog box |

The Live Presentation Broadcast dialog box expands with a button enabling you to invite the audience.

| Step 6 | Click | Invite Audience |

You are prompted if you do not have a shared file location (on a server) specified in the Settings dialog box. Otherwise, the Outlook Meeting window opens indicating, "This is an online meeting. Invitations have not been sent for this meeting." You then address the meeting invitation to those you want to view the broadcast. After addressing the invitation, you click the Send button and the sales managers are invited via e-mail. If your computer is set up for Outlook, your screen should look similar to Figure 13-8.

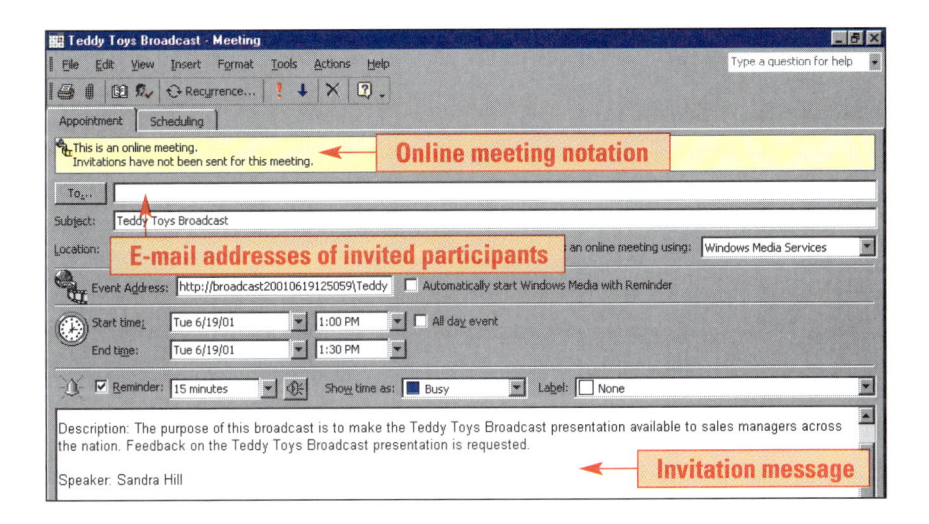

FIGURE 13-8
Teddy Toys Broadcast Meeting Window

| Step 7 | Click | OK |

If you have specified a shared file location on a server, then you are ready to start the broadcast. If you do not have a specified shared file location on a server, you cancel the broadcast.

| Step 8 | Click | Cancel |

If participants in the broadcast use Microsoft Outlook, they are notified of the approaching broadcast via e-mail before the broadcast. Participants then click View this NetShow that appears on the message to see the lobby page. At the designated time for broadcast, the broadcast begins. If participants do not use Outlook, they open the e-mail message containing the broadcast information and click the URL for the broadcast. The lobby page displays on the screen, informing you of how much time remains before the broadcast.

| Step 9 | Close | the *Teddy Toys Broadcast* presentation |

chapter thirteen

Summary

▶ As you work, PowerPoint checks a presentation for spelling, visual clarity, and punctuation.

▶ You set style-checking rules PowerPoint should adhere to when checking a presentation by changing options on the Case and End Punctuation and Visual Clarity tabs in the Style Options dialog box.

▶ If style inconsistencies are found during a style check and the Office Assistant is turned on, the Office Assistant pops up with a message indicating the inconsistency and suggesting ways to correct the problem.

▶ You can embed the TrueType fonts in a presentation to ensure that these fonts are used in the presentation display even if the presenting computer does not have the embedded font.

▶ Presentations can be sent electronically to individuals via e-mail for reviewing and editing.

▶ PowerPoint enables you to send a copy of a presentation for review two ways: as a presentation for review using Outlook or by saving the presentation for review and attaching it to an e-mail message.

▶ The advantage of sending a presentation for review electronically is that when it returns, you can combine the reviewed presentation with the original and view all comments and changes at once.

▶ You can use the Reviewing toolbar to apply or unapply changes from a reviewer, add, edit, or delete comments, move through comments and changes, and names of reviewers.

▶ You can use Compare and Merge Presentations to combine reviewed presentations sent by an e-mail program other than Outlook.

▶ The Pack and Go feature allows you to pack your presentation for use on another computer that does not have PowerPoint installed.

▶ The PowerPoint Viewer is needed to view a PowerPoint presentation on a computer that does not have PowerPoint installed.

▶ Broadcasting enables you to send a presentation to remote locations over the Internet or a network (intranet).

▶ To use a presentation for broadcast, the presentation must be saved in HTML format (Hypertext Markup Language) so that the audience at the remote locations can view the presentation on their browser.

▶ You can schedule a broadcast of the presentation via Microsoft Outlook or any e-mail program you use just as you would schedule any meeting.

Commands Review

Action	Menu Bar	Shortcut Menu	Toolbar	Task Pane	Keyboard
Editing spelling and style (Presentation Assistant)	Tools, Options, Spelling and Style tab, Style Options button				ALT + T, O, T
Embed TrueType fonts	File, Save As, Tools, Save Options, Embed TrueType fonts; Tools, Options, Save tab, Embed TrueType fonts				ALT + F, A, then ALT + L, S, E ALT + T, O, E
Send a presentation as an e-mail attachment	File, Send To, Mail Recipient (as Attachment)		📧		ALT + F, D, A
Send a presentation for review	File, Send To, Mail Recipient (for Review)				ALT + F, D, C
Save a presentation for review	File, Save As, Presentation for Review in the Save as type: list box				ALT + F, A
Add comments	Insert, Comment		📝 on Reviewing toolbar		ALT + I, M
Print comments	File, Print, click Include comment pages				ALT + F, P, U
Display Revisions Pane	View, Toolbars, Revisions Pane	Right-click any toolbar button, then click Revisions Pane			ALT + V, T
Compare and merge presentations for review	Tools, Compare and Merge Presentations				ALT + T, P
Accept or reject changes during a review		Click change marker, then click to add or remove check mark in check box	🔲 🔲	In Gallery tab: Click thumbnail to apply or unapply all changes; Click list arrow on thumbnail, click Apply Changes By This Reviewer or Unapply Changes By This Reviewer; In List tab: click change marker under Slide changes: then click to add or remove a check mark In check box	
End review			End Review…		
Pack a presentation for use on another computer	File, Pack and Go				ALT + F, K
Schedule a live broadcast	Slide Show, Online Broadcast, Schedule a Live Broadcast				ALT + D, O, S
Start live broadcast now	Slide Show, Online Broadcast, Start Live Broadcast Now				ALT + D, O, L

chapter thirteen

Concepts Review

Circle the correct answer.

1. **A light bulb displays on the slides in Normal view to indicate when:**
   - [a] AutoShapes could be used.
   - [b] a typographical error occurs.
   - [c] a grammar error occurs.
   - [d] inconsistencies occur in case or end punctuation, as well as visual clarity guidelines.

2. **When sending a presentation out for review, it is best to embed the:**
   - [a] full font set.
   - [b] characters in use.
   - [c] characters and symbols in use.
   - [d] characters, symbols, and numbers in use.

3. **Which of the following statements is not true?**
   - [a] E-mail can be sent and received 24 hours a day, seven days a week.
   - [b] E-mail is a fast, economical form of communication over the Internet or intranet via communication lines.
   - [c] E-mail is an inefficient means of exchanging ideas and documents for editing and critiquing.
   - [d] E-mail can be accessed from locations all over the world.

4. **If you do not save a presentation as a Presentation for Review, the review copy cannot be:**
   - [a] compared to the original copy when it is returned.
   - [b] resaved.
   - [c] opened by the reviewer as a file for review.
   - [d] reviewed.

5. **Which of the following is not an advantage of sending a presentation electronically to others for review?**
   - [a] When multiple reviewers are used, PowerPoint will indicate if one reviewer's change conflicts with another, letting the originator determine which change to accept and which to reject.
   - [b] A hard copy is always used.
   - [c] When multiple reviewers are used, each reviewer's comments or changes are displayed with a color-coded icon.
   - [d] You can combine a reviewed presentation with the original presentation and view all the comments and changes at the same time.

6. **Which of the following allows you to print reviewers' comments?**
   - [a] File, Print Comments
   - [b] File, Print, Include comment pages
   - [c] Insert, Comments
   - [d] View, Comments

7. **You can use the Pack and Go feature to save your presentation for use on a:**
   - [a] computer on another network that contains the PowerPoint application.
   - [b] computer on your own network that contains the PowerPoint application.
   - [c] computer that does not contain the PowerPoint application.
   - [d] laptop computer that contains the PowerPoint application.

8. Which of the following terms best describes the PowerPoint Viewer?
   [a] monitor
   [b] wizard
   [c] application
   [d] slide

9. Broadcasting a presentation enables you to broadcast your presentation to all of the following *except*:
   [a] several different groups.
   [b] several different locations.
   [c] individuals in realtime.
   [d] individuals with televisions.

10. When broadcasting with audio, you do not need:
    [a] a video camera.
    [b] a microphone.
    [c] sound cards.
    [d] speakers.

Circle **T** if the statement is true or **F** if the statement is false.

T F 1. PowerPoint automatically checks each slide in the presentation and displays a light bulb where there is a style error.

T F 2. If a case inconsistency is found, you must manually rekey the text in the correct case.

T F 3. It is possible to send your presentation to another person via an e-mail application.

T F 4. The change marker in a merge and compared presentation provides a summary of the changes made to an element on a slide.

T F 5. When you use Outlook to track changes in reviewer presentations, Outlook automatically tracks the presentations and combines them together.

T F 6. You can download the PowerPoint Viewer (free of charge) from the PowerPoint Web site at *http://officeupdate.microsoft.com*.

T F 7. The Pack and Go feature allows you to pack your presentation with all its files, fonts, and images and save it in a format that you can unpack on any computer that does not have PowerPoint installed.

T F 8. Pack and Go is just another term for saving a presentation.

T F 9. PowerPoint 2002 enables you to increase productivity by broadcasting a presentation over the Web, including any video and/or audio with the presentation.

T F 10. The benefit of broadcasts is that you can broadcast a real-time presentation or record and save the broadcast on your Internet service provider for playback at a later time.

Skills Review

Exercise 1

1. Open the *PowerPoint Advanced* presentation located on the Data Disk, and save it as *PowerPoint Styles*.
2. Set the following style options for fonts in visual clarity: title text size should be at least 48 point, body text size should be at least 28 point.

chapter thirteen

3. Remove the following checks in the Legibility section: Number of bullets should not exceed: and Number of lines per bullet should not exceed.

4. Starting from the first slide, view each slide

5. If PowerPoint notifies you of style inconsistencies, click the change option for all inconsistencies except capitalization or long paragraphs. If a capitalization or long paragraphs inconsistency is reported, click the Ignore the style rule for this presentation only.

6. Save the presentation as *PowerPoint Styles,* print it as a six-slides-per-page handout, and the close the presentation.

Exercise 2

1. Open the *Office Advanced* presentation located on the Data Disk, and save it as *Office Review*.

2. Set the following visual clarity style options: Title text size should be at least 36 point, Body text size should be at least 22 point, Number of bullets should not exceed 6, and Number of lines per bullet should not exceed 3.

3. View the slides, and accept or reject suggestions for fixing style inconsistencies.

4. Compare and merge the *Office Review* with *Office Review - Kim* presentation located on the Data Disk.

5. Read comments and changes, accepting all changes.

6. Do not end the review.

7. Print the presentation as a six-slides-per-page handout.

8. Save and close the *Office Review* presentation.

Exercise 3

1. Open the *Design Advanced* presentation located on the Data Disk, and save it as *Design Packed*.

2. Change the style options back to the defaults. (*Hint:* Click the Defaults button.)

3. Use the Pack and Go Wizard to embed the fonts, and pack the presentation and Viewer to a floppy disk(s) or a Zip disk.

4. Add a bullet slide to the end of the *Design Packed* presentation.

5. Use Windows Explorer to view the data displayed in the folder where the presentation was packed. On the Title and Text slide key the title " Pack and Go Files" and for the bullets key the names of the packed files displayed in Windows Explorer.

6. Save the *Design Packed* presentation, print the new slide, and the close the presentation.

Exercise 4

1. Open the *Precision Builders Advanced* presentation located on the Data Disk, and save it as *Precision Builders Review*.

2. View each slide and check for style inconsistencies. Change any inconsistencies that are appropriate.

3. Create the following comment on Slide 1: "Please let me know if the presentation design I selected for this presentation fits the presentation. I chose the design for the circular elements. Feel free to change the design or color scheme to better fit the contents of the presentation."

4. Create the following comment on Slide 2: "I welcome any changes or additions to the bullets."

5. Create the following comment on Slide 4: "What do you think? Should I keep this slide or delete it?"

6. Create the following comment on Slide 5: "Suggestions?"

7. Save the presentation for review as *Precision Builders Review - Hernandez*.
8. Save the presentation for review again as *Precision Builders Review - Nichols*.
9. Print the comments.
10. Save and close the *Precision Builders Review* presentation.

Exercise 5

1. Open the *Nature Tours Advanced* presentation located on the Data Disk, and save it as *Nature Tours Review*.
2. View each slide for style inconsistencies. Change the capitalization inconsistency on the title slide. Ignore the capitalization inconsistency on the second slide.
3. Compare and merge *Nature Tours Review* with *Nature Tours Review - Heston* presentation located on the Data Disk.
4. Read all comments and accept all changes, except to delete the slide with the AutoShapes.
5. End the review.
6. Delete all comments.
7. Print the presentation as a six-slides-per-page handout.
8. Save and close the *Nature Tours Review* presentation.

Exercise 6

1. Open the *A Healthier You Advanced* presentation located on the Data Disk, and save it as *A Healthier You Comments*.
2. View each slide and check for style inconsistencies. Change any inconsistencies that are appropriate.
3. Create the following comment on Slide 1: "I'm looking for a presentation design that is more athletic in tone. Can you help?"
4. Create the following comment on Slide 2: "I'd like to change the animated gif on this slide but can't seem to find one I like. Do you have an animated gif that reflects the WordArt text? Or can you create a more interesting WordArt design or phrase?"
5. Create the following comment on Slide 3: "Any additional bullet suggestions?"
6. Create the following comment on Slide 5: "What do you think? Suggestions?"
7. Save the presentation for review as *A Healthier You Comments - Franz*.
8. Print the presentation as a six-slides-per-page handout along with the comments.
9. Save and close the *A Healthier You Comments* presentation.

Exercise 7

1. Open the *Buying A Computer Advanced* presentation located on the Data Disk, and save it as *Buying A Computer Packed*.
2. View each slide and check for style inconsistencies. Change any inconsistencies that are appropriate.
3. Use the Pack and Go Wizard to embed the fonts and pack the presentation (do not include the Viewer) to a floppy disk(s) or a Zip disk.

chapter thirteen

4. Add a bullet slide to the end of the *Buying A Computer Packed* presentation, and list the Pack and Go filenames that appear on the floppy disk.

5. Save the *Buying A Computer Packed* presentation, print the new slide, and the close the presentation.

Exercise 8

1. Open the *Leisure Travel Advanced* presentation located on the Data Disk, and save it as *Leisure Travel Review-Your Last Name*.

2. View each slide and check for style inconsistencies. Change any inconsistencies that are appropriate.

3. With the *Leisure Travel Review-Your Last Name* presentation open, compare and merge with the *Leisure Travel - Jennings* presentation.

4. Read and accept all of the reviewer's changes on Slide 1.

5. Read all of the reviewer's changes on Slide 2. Accept only the design change.

6. Read and accept all of the reviewer's changes on Slides 3 and 4.

7. Display Slide 5 and delete it.

8. Display Slide 2 and delete all the AutoShapes. Add four clipart images that reflect a summer, fall, winter, and spring activity, no text.

9. Turn off the comments.

10. End the review.

11. Print the presentation as a four-slides-per-page handout.

12. Save and close *Leisure Travel Review-Your Last Name*.

Case Projects

Project 1

You are unsure about the procedures for sending a presentation for review via e-mail. Using online Help, find and print information on sending a presentation for review.

Project 2

You are asked to send the *Communicate Advanced* presentation for review to five other managers at Communicate Corporation. Before sending the presentation for review, view all the slides of the presentation for style. Make any style changes deemed appropriate. Using the comment feature of PowerPoint, indicate which slides in the presentations for which you want their comments, edits, and suggestions for changes. Print the comments.

Save and close the presentation as *Communicate Comments*.

Project 3

Your employer wants to present the *Souner Advanced* presentation at the Trainers Convention in Miami. He is not sure if the available computer has the newest version of PowerPoint. Just to be safe, he asks you to pack a copy of the *Souner Advanced* presentation along with the PowerPoint Viewer. Save the *Souner Advanced* presentation *as Souner Packed* and use the Pack and Go Wizard to pack the *Souner Packed* presentation to a floppy disk(s) or a Zip disk. Add a bullet slide to the end of the presentation that contains the files included in the packed presentation. Print the last bullet slide.

Project 4

You finally finish your *My Presentation Advanced* presentation. A friend in another state asks to see what you did with the presentation when you visit there next week. Your friend does not have PowerPoint on his computer. Pack the presentation and Viewer so that you may show the presentation on your friend's computer. Print a listing of the filenames that appear on the floppy disk(s) or a Zip disk you used for packing. Close the presentation.

Project 5

The head caretaker of the Ape House at the zoo is going to Chicago's Brookfield Zoo to check out the exhibits and houses. She asks you for a copy of the *Zoo Advanced* presentation to show the caretakers at Brookfield Zoo what your zoo has to offer the public. When you ask her if she knows whether they have a computer with PowerPoint, she responds that she does not know. To be safe, you decide to use the Pack and Go Wizard to pack the files and Viewer onto some disks. This way, she can show the presentation even if they do not have PowerPoint. Before packing the presentation, you decide to run a style check to make sure that no slide in the presentation has more than six bullets on a bullet slide and that all the titles of the presentation are 48 point or larger. Save the presentation as *Zoo Styles*. Print the presentation as a six-slides-per-page handout. Close the presentation when you fulfill your responsibilities.

Project 6

You somehow damage the PowerPoint Viewer file on your hard drive. You are not upset because you know you can download it free from the Internet. Connect to the Internet and download the PowerPoint Viewer from the PowerPoint Web site to the My Documents folder on your computer.

Project 7

The semester is over and even though you feel the *Cars Advanced* presentation was successful, you want several of your more outspoken students to critique it. Open the *Cars Advanced* presentation and save it as *Cars Review*. Add a comment to the first slide asking your students to critique the presentation. Save the *Cars Review* presentation as a presentation for review with the name *Cars Review-Students*. Before sending the presentation to your students, you decide to test the comments and compare and merge features by sending the presentation to several friends as an e-mail attachment indicating that they are to route the presentation to the next person on the route list when they are done. Print the comments.

Project 8

The semester is over and you and your partner are off for three glorious weeks touring the southwestern states. Your professor asks you and your partner to visit a few southwestern colleges in your vacation area where his fellow colleagues are employed. He is very proud of your *Internet Advanced* presentation, and he wants to share this presentation with his colleagues. You are not sure if they have access to PowerPoint, so you decide to use the Pack and Go Wizard to pack the presentation and load the Viewer. In addition, you want to incorporate the fonts you have chosen to ensure that they are always available as part of this presentation. Save the *Internet Advanced* presentation as *Internet Packed* and embed the TrueType fonts.

chapter thirteen

PowerPoint 2002

Integrating Word and Excel with PowerPoint

Chapter Overview

One of the benefits of using Microsoft Office is the ability to exchange information among software packages that make up the Office suite. For example, PowerPoint presentations can be used in Word documents, and Word documents can be used in PowerPoint presentations. PowerPoint charts can be used in Excel, and Excel worksheets and charts can be used in PowerPoint. This chapter teaches you how to integrate, or share data, and embed and link objects between PowerPoint and Word, and PowerPoint and Excel. You also learn how to open files from other applications to create slides for a PowerPoint presentation.

Learning Objectives

- Save a slide presentation as a Word outline
- Open a Word outline as a presentation
- Embed and link in PowerPoint and Word
- Embed and link in PowerPoint and Excel

Case profile

Ms. Hill asks you to send the presentation you created for an upcoming regional sales meeting directly to an outline in Word so that she can include some of the information in a quarterly report. She also wants you to create an entertaining presentation about Disney movies that she can present during an afternoon break at the sales meeting. Her daughter, Tracy, a Disney movie buff, has prepared a Word outline and a Word table for the presentation. Tracy also created an Excel workbook and an Excel chart that you import into the presentation.

chapter fourteen 14

14.a Saving a Slide Presentation as a Word Outline

> **QUICK TIP**
> When you save a presentation in .rtf format, you can open the outline in any program that supports .rtf files.

You have two choices for creating a Word outline using a PowerPoint presentation. You can save the presentation in Outline/RTF format, or you can directly send the presentation to Word as an outline. The first method saves the document as an .rtf file; the second method saves the document in the Word native .doc format. By sending a presentation to Word, anyone can view the outline if they have Word on their computer.

Saving a Slide Presentation as an RTF Outline

When you save a presentation as an RTF outline, the file is saved in .rtf format. An .rtf (Rich Text Format) file contains no graphical information (such as slide design or art elements in a PowerPoint presentation), but does contain text formatting. Once saved as an .rtf file, you can open the file in Word and can then work with the document as an .rtf file or save it as a Word document (.doc), which allows you to use all of the design features available in Word. In the .rtf file, each slide title becomes a first-level heading in the outline and the bullets become second-level topics. To save a PowerPoint presentation as an .rtf file:

Step 1	Open	the *Teddy Toys New Products* presentation located on the Data Disk
Step 2	Click	File
Step 3	Click	Save As
Step 4	Click	the Save as type: list arrow
Step 5	Click	Outline/RTF
Step 6	Key	Teddy Toys RTF Outline in the File name: text box
Step 7	Click	Save

> **INTERNET TIP**
> An outline in Word takes up less storage space when sending the outline as an attachment in an e-mail message. Sending the entire PowerPoint presentation as an attachment includes the designs, graphics, drawing shapes, and backgrounds and is a much larger document.

The *Teddy Toys RTF Outline* file is saved to your disk, and the *Teddy Toys New Products* PowerPoint presentation remains open on the screen. To switch to Microsoft Word and open the .rtf file:

| Step 1 | Click | Start |

chapter fourteen

Step 2	**Point to**	Programs
Step 3	**Click**	Microsoft Word
Step 4	**Click**	the Open button on the Standard toolbar
Step 5	**Switch to**	the drive or folder that contains your saved files

The Microsoft Word Open dialog box opens with the Word icon immediately to the left of the *Teddy Toys RTF Outline* file, indicating that it is an .rtf file that can be opened with the Word application.

Step 6	**Double-click**	the *Teddy Toys RTF Outline* file

The *Teddy Toys RTF Outline* file opens on the screen. Notice that the hierarchical format of the slide text is converted into heading styles in this document. Your screen should look similar to Figure 14-1.

FIGURE 14-1
Teddy Toys RTF Outline Document in Microsoft Word

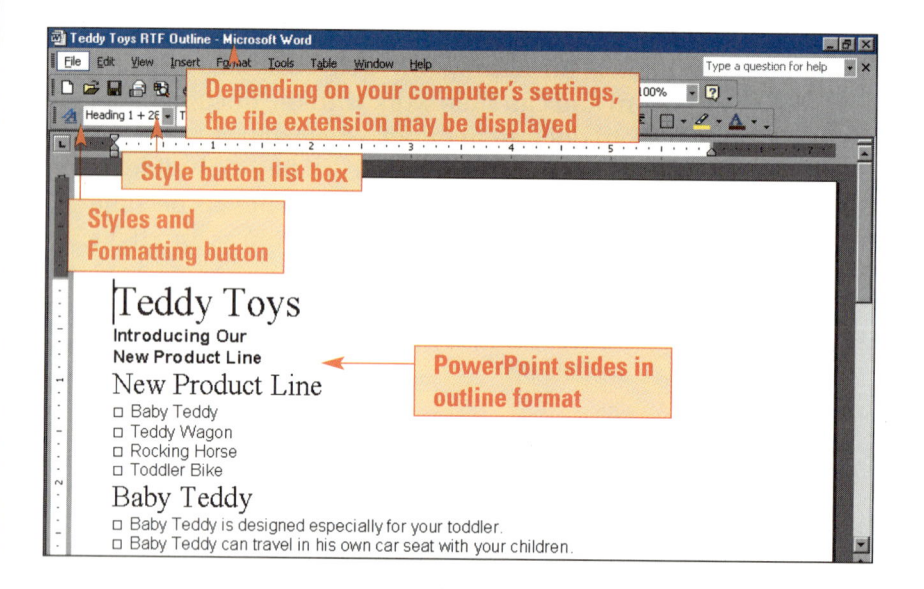

A **style** is a set of formatting characteristics that can be applied to text in a document to quickly change the formatting of the selected text to match the formatting assigned to the style. For example, the Heading 1 style in Word assigns the following formatting to a paragraph: Arial, 16 pt, Bold, Kern at 16 pt; space before 12 pt, space after 3 pt, keep with text, Level 1. Because the PowerPoint presentation you opened contained different formatting, the styles in this document differ slightly from the default Word styles. The Heading 1 + 28.5 style includes the following differences: Times New Roman, 28.5 pt, left alignment.

Styles can be classified as paragraph, character, table, or list styles. Paragraph styles assign formatting to a paragraph, and character styles assign formatting to selected text. Table styles assign consistent formatting to tables that you want to have the same "look" within a document. List styles assign formatting to a particular outline level including numbering, bullets, and indentations. The Teddy Toys title from the title slide is tagged with the Heading 1 + 28.5 style. The subtitle from the title slide, Introducing Our New Product Line, is tagged with the Heading 2 + 13 style. Each slide title is tagged with the Heading 1 style. All bullets are tagged with the Heading 2 + 12 style. To view the styles in the RTF outline:

| Step 1 | Click | the Styles and Formatting button on the Formatting toolbar |

The Styles and Formatting task pane opens, displaying the formatting of any selected text as well as styles available to use in this document. Your screen should look similar to Figure 14-2.

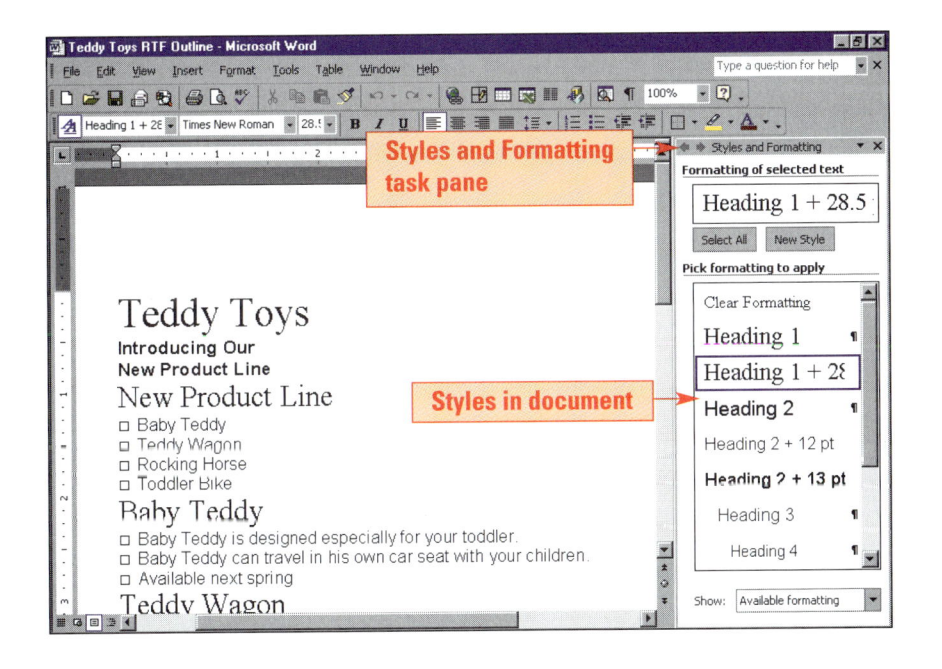

FIGURE 14-2
Styles and Formatting Task Pane

Step 2	Click	in each line of the outline
Step 3	Observe	the styles shown in the Pick formatting to apply list in the Styles and Formatting task pane
Step 4	Close	Word without saving changes
Step 5	Verify	that the *Teddy Toys New Products* presentation is still open in PowerPoint

chapter fourteen

> **QUICK TIP**
>
> When you save a PowerPoint presentation as an RTF outline, the file is saved and you need to open the saved file in Word or another word processing program to view it. When you send a PowerPoint presentation to Word as an outline only, the file is not saved until you save it in Word, at which point the default .doc file extension is applied.

Sending a PowerPoint Presentation to Word as an Outline

Another way to create a Word outline using a PowerPoint presentation is to send the presentation to Word as an outline. When you use this method, the outline is automatically sent to Word. When it is saved, it is saved as a Word document with the .doc file extension by default. The results are visually the same—text in an outline format with no graphics, design templates, backgrounds, or AutoShapes. Each slide title becomes the first-level topic in an outline, with the bullets as second-level topics under each first-level topic. In addition to saving a presentation as an .rtf outline format, you can send a presentation to Word as an outline. When the presentation is sent to Word as an outline, it is created as a Word document with the .doc file extension. To send a presentation to Word as an outline:

Step 1	Click	File
Step 2	Point to	Send To
Step 3	Click	Microsoft Word

The Send To Microsoft Word dialog box opens, with options for placing Notes next to slides, Notes below slides, Blank lines next to slides, Blank lines below slides, or an Outline only. You can Paste the presentation to embed it into Word, or you can Paste link to link the presentation to the Word document. When you send a presentation as an outline only, you do not have the option of pasting or pasting the links.

| Step 4 | Click | Outline only |
| Step 5 | Click | OK |

Microsoft Word opens with the *Teddy Toys New Products* presentation displayed in outline format.

Step 6	Observe	that the styles are the same as those in the RTF outline file
Step 7	Save	the outline as *Teddy Toys Word Outline*
Step 8	Observe	the filename in the Word title bar (depending on your Windows settings, you may see the .doc file extension)
Step 9	Close	Word

14.b Opening a Word Outline as a Presentation

A Word outline saved as an RTF outline or a Word document (.doc) can be opened in PowerPoint and viewed as a presentation. The styles assigned to the text in the Word outline are converted to titles, subtitles, and bullet items, depending on the style of the text in the RTF outline. To open a Word outline in PowerPoint:

Step 1	**Verify**	that PowerPoint is open
Step 2	**Close**	any open presentations
Step 3	**Click**	the Open button on the Standard toolbar
Step 4	**Switch to**	the disk drive and folder that contains your Data Files
Step 5	**Click**	the Files of type: list arrow
Step 6	**Click**	All Outlines
Step 7	**Double-click**	the *Movies I.rtf* file

When an outline opens as a PowerPoint presentation, text slides are created based on the text from the outline document. This new PowerPoint presentation consists of a text slide for each Heading 1 style in the Word outline, and the Heading 2 styles display as first-level bullets. Any Heading 3 styles under each Heading 2 style in the Word outline become second-level bullets. You have a title on Slide 1 and a title and seven bullet items on Slides 2 and 3. The Default Design is black text on a white background. To format the new presentation:

Step 1	**Double-click**	Default Design on the status bar
Step 2	**Apply**	the Curtain Call design template in the Slide Design task pane
Step 3	**Display**	Slide 1, if necessary
Step 4	**Change**	the slide layout to a title slide
Step 5	**Key**	your name in the subtitle placeholder
Step 6	**Save**	the presentation as *Teddy Movies I* and close it

Sending a Word Outline to PowerPoint

You can send a Word outline saved either as a Word document or an .rtf file to PowerPoint. The results are the same as opening an outline file in PowerPoint. Instead of opening a Word outline in PowerPoint, you can send a Word document to PowerPoint from within Word. The text in the Word document must be formatted with the styles Heading 1, Heading 2, and/or Heading 3. This is done by applying the styles or by clicking the Numbering button on the Formatting toolbar and formatting the numbers with the outline format. Once formatted with styles, the outline can be sent to PowerPoint using the Sen_d To command on the _File menu. This results in a presentation consisting of slides determined by the style levels assigned in Word. All text formatted with the Heading 1 style become titles of slides; all text formatted with the Heading 2 style become bullets; and all text formatted with Heading 3 become second-level bullets. To send a Word outline to PowerPoint:

Step 1	*Start*	Word
Step 2	*Open*	the *Movies II* Word outline located on the Data Disk
Step 3	*View*	the styles displayed in the outline
Step 4	*Click*	_File
Step 5	*Point to*	Sen_d To
Step 6	*Click*	Microsoft _PowerPoint

Microsoft PowerPoint opens and displays a new presentation that contains text slides created from the Word outline. You decide to apply a design template, change the color scheme, and change the first slide from a text slide to a title slide.

Step 7	*Apply*	the Curtain Call design template
Step 8	*Change*	the color scheme to the darker royal blue background
Step 9	*Display*	Slide 1, if necessary
Step 10	*Change*	the slide layout to a title slide
Step 11	*Key*	your name in the subtitle placeholder
Step 12	*Save*	the PowerPoint presentation as *Teddy Movies II* and close it
Step 13	*Switch to*	Word
Step 14	*Close*	the *Movies II* Word document and Word

Inserting Slides from a Word RTF Outline

You can insert slides from a Word RTF outline into an existing PowerPoint presentation. To do so, the Word document must be closed, the PowerPoint application must be open, and the existing presentation (or a new presentation, if you plan to add a Word outline to a new presentation) must be open. To insert slides from a Word RTF outline:

Step 1	Verify	that you are in the PowerPoint application
Step 2	Open	the *Teddy Movies I* presentation saved previously
Step 3	Display	the last slide in the presentation
Step 4	Click	Insert
Step 5	Click	Slides from Outline
Step 6	Double-click	the *Movies III* Word .rtf document in the Insert Outline dialog box
Step 7	Run	the slide show from the beginning

The *Teddy Movies I* presentation consists of six slides, with the last three slides inserted from the Word outline to the end of the presentation.

Step 8	Save	the *Teddy Movies I* presentation

Inserting Slides from One PowerPoint Presentation to Another

Inserting slides from one presentation to another is helpful even if you use only part of the slide that you insert. Although the slide, text, and clip art images are added to the existing presentation, the slide design template is not brought into the existing presentation. You insert slides using the Slide Finder dialog box to find individual slides in a presentation or the entire presentation. Using the Slide Finder dialog box, you can choose to keep the formatting of the source presentation by clicking the Keep source formatting check box to add a check mark in the box. If you do not elect to keep the source formatting, the presentation design template of the destination presentation automatically applies formatting to the newly inserted slides. To insert slides from one presentation to another:

Step 1	Display	the last slide in the *Teddy Movies I* presentation
Step 2	Click	Insert

> **MENU TIP**
>
> You also can copy and paste slides from one open presentation to another using Slide Sorter view and the Arrange All command on the Window menu.

chapter fourteen

QUICK TIP

You can create a new presentation using existing slides by starting a new presentation and then using the Slide Finder dialog box to add slides from an existing presentation. When you insert slides or outlines into a PowerPoint presentation, they are inserted after the currently viewed slide. If you want to add slides to the end of the presentation, you must be on the last slide of the presentation before you start inserting slides.

FIGURE 14-3
Slide Finder Dialog Box with *Teddy Movies II* Slides

MOUSE TIP

You can select an individual slide or slides by clicking each desired slide.

| Step 3 | Click | Slides from Files |

The Slide Finder dialog box opens with Find Presentation and List of Favorites tabs. You can browse to find a PowerPoint presentation from which to insert slides, or you can use the presentations that have been saved to your favorites.

Step 4	Click	Browse
Step 5	Switch to	the disk drive or folder that contains the *Teddy Movies II* presentation
Step 6	Double-click	the *Teddy Movies II* presentation
Step 7	Click	Display, if necessary

Your Slide Finder dialog box should look similar to Figure 14-3. You can find a presentation from which to insert slides into the current presentation. A slide miniature of each slide in the presentation appears in the Select slides: area. You can view all the slides by scrolling through the presentation. The dialog box displays the slides with numbers and text below or the slide number and text only.

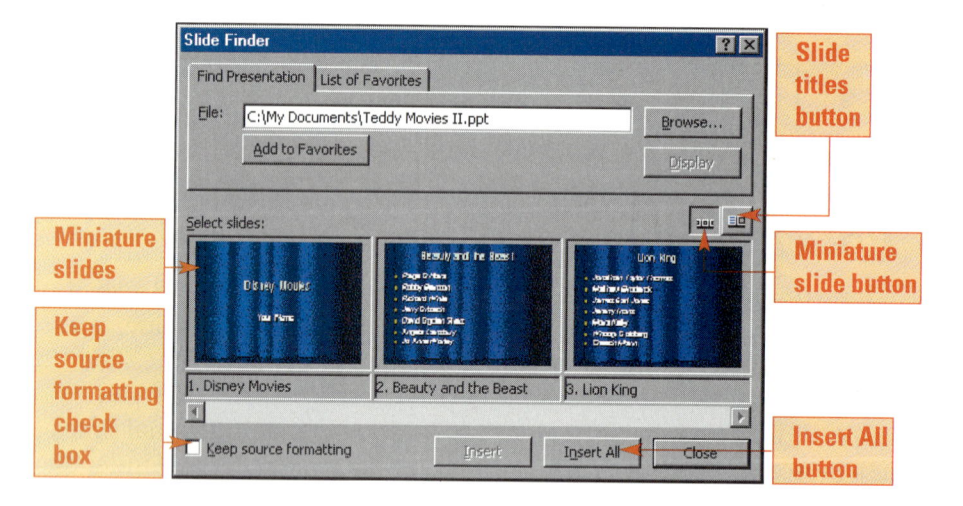

[Figure 14-3: Slide Finder dialog box showing File: C:\My Documents\Teddy Movies II.ppt, with three slide miniatures labeled 1. Disney Movies, 2. Beauty and the Beast, 3. Lion King. Callouts identify: Miniature slides, Keep source formatting check box, Slide titles button, Miniature slide button, Insert All button.]

Step 8	Verify	that the Keep source formatting check box does not contain a check mark
Step 9	Click	Insert All to insert all the slides
Step 10	Click	Close
Step 11	Run	the slide show from the beginning, observing the two slides with titles only between the text slides
Step 12	Select	and delete Slides 4 and 7 from the Slides tab
Step 13	Save	the *Teddy Movies I* presentation and close it

14.c Embedding and Linking in PowerPoint and Word

Integrating is the process of sharing information within various software applications. Included in this process of sharing is embedding and linking objects from one application to another. You can send slides, notes, or outlines from a PowerPoint presentation directly to Word and then use the presentation as a Word document. When you send notes and slides from PowerPoint to Word, you actually copy the notes and embed the slides into a Word document. An object created in one application (**source file**) can be inserted or copied into another application (**destination file**).

In addition to copying, you can embed or link objects between applications. When you **embed** an object, the object becomes a part of the destination file, but retains the editing capabilities of the source application. You edit and format the object using the source application features, but your changes do not affect the source file. There is no connection between the source file and the embedded object, so any changes that are made to the embedded object do not affect the source file, and any modifications that are made to the source file do not affect the embedded object.

When you **link** an object, you are actually creating a dynamic connection between the source file and the destination file. Linking inserts a reference or pointer to the object (rather than the object itself) in the destination file. When you edit a linked object, you work with the source file. You can open a linked object either by opening it from the destination file or by opening the source file from within the source application; when you change the source file, the linked information is updated automatically.

Embedding a PowerPoint Presentation in a Word Document

When you embed or link a PowerPoint presentation in a Word document, the slides are placed in a Word table. This gives you greater versatility in the arrangement of the slides, the placement of the notes lines, and the creation of a Word outline from a PowerPoint presentation. To send a presentation to Word without linking files:

Step 1	Open	the *Teddy Toys New Products* presentation located on the Data Disk
Step 2	Save	the presentation as *Teddy Toys Embed and Link*
Step 3	Click	File
Step 4	Point to	Send To

QUICK TIP

When you create slides in PowerPoint from a Word outline and create a Word outline from a PowerPoint presentation, the source document remains the same and a copy is sent to another application, where it is converted to the format of the destination application. The Word outline (source) still exists, and a PowerPoint presentation (destination) is created. The same is true for the PowerPoint presentation (source) sent to Word; it remains a PowerPoint presentation, and a copy of it becomes a different Word document (destination).

Quick Tip

You do not have to close the PowerPoint presentation to view the changes in the Word document; however, you must save the PowerPoint presentation to view the changes in the Word document. You can use the taskbar to switch between different documents in different applications quickly. Each open Office file has its own button on the taskbar.

Step 5	*Click*	Microsoft Word
Step 6	*Click*	Blank lines next to slides
Step 7	*Click*	Paste, if necessary
Step 8	*Click*	OK

Word opens and displays a new document containing your PowerPoint slides in a three-column tabular format. The first column displays the slide number, the second displays a miniature slide, and the third displays blank lines.

| Step 9 | *Save* | the Word document as *Teddy Toys Embedded* |

The slides in the Word document are embedded objects; as such, edits made to them do not affect the source document. To edit an embedded object, you double-click it. To edit the embedded slide object in Word:

| Step 1 | *Scroll* | to the first slide object, if necessary |
| Step 2 | *Double-click* | the Slide 1 object |

A border appears around the slide object; you can edit the object using the PowerPoint application features.

Step 3	*Click*	directly to the right of Teddy Toys in the title area
Step 4	*Press*	the SPACEBAR
Step 5	*Key*	Embedded
Step 6	*Click*	outside the slide object border
Step 7	*Save*	the *Teddy Toys Embedded* Word document and close it
Step 8	*Click*	the Teddy Toys Embed and Link PowerPoint presentation button on the taskbar to switch to the PowerPoint application
Step 9	*Display*	the first slide, if necessary

Notice that the title still reads Teddy Toys. This document is not affected by any changes you made to the Word document.

Linking a PowerPoint Presentation to a Word Document

You can link a PowerPoint presentation to a Word document when you want the information in the destination file to be updated every time the information in the source file changes. Each time you open a PowerPoint presentation containing links, the application asks if you want to update the links. If you click OK, all links to the presentation automatically reestablish upon opening the file. You must, however, be sure that the location of the linked file (source) does not change. If the location of the files changes, the presentation cannot reestablish the links. To link the *Teddy Toys Embed and Link* PowerPoint presentation to a Word document, edit text, and update the link to reflect editing changes in the source document:

Step 1	*Click*	File
Step 2	*Point to*	Send To
Step 3	*Click*	Microsoft Word
Step 4	*Click*	Blank lines next to slides
Step 5	*Click*	Paste link under Add slides to Microsoft Word document
Step 6	*Click*	OK

The PowerPoint slides have been sent to Word in a three-column tabular format again. This time, however, the slide objects directly link to your PowerPoint presentation.

| Step 7 | *Save* | the Word document as *Teddy Toys Linked* |
| Step 8 | *Double-click* | the Slide 1 object |

The linked slide opens in PowerPoint. Observe that you are viewing the source file (*Teddy Toys Embed and Link* presentation) in the PowerPoint application window; you are not merely accessing PowerPoint editing features, but actually working in the application.

Step 9	*Edit*	the title slide in the *Teddy Toys Embed and Link* PowerPoint presentation to read Teddy Toys Linked
Step 10	*Save*	the *Teddy Toys Embed and Link* PowerPoint presentation
Step 11	*Click*	the *Teddy Toys Linked* Word document button in the taskbar

---

QUICK TIP

You should link any time there is limited disk space; a link takes less disk space than an embedded object.

CAUTION TIP

Any changes you make to a linked object while you are working in the destination file are automatically updated as you make the changes. However, if you make the changes in the source file, save the source file before any changes are updated in the destination file. Every time you open a file with links, the links are updated.

Teddy Toys Linked displays in the slide title of the first slide. Your screen should look similar to Figure 14-4.

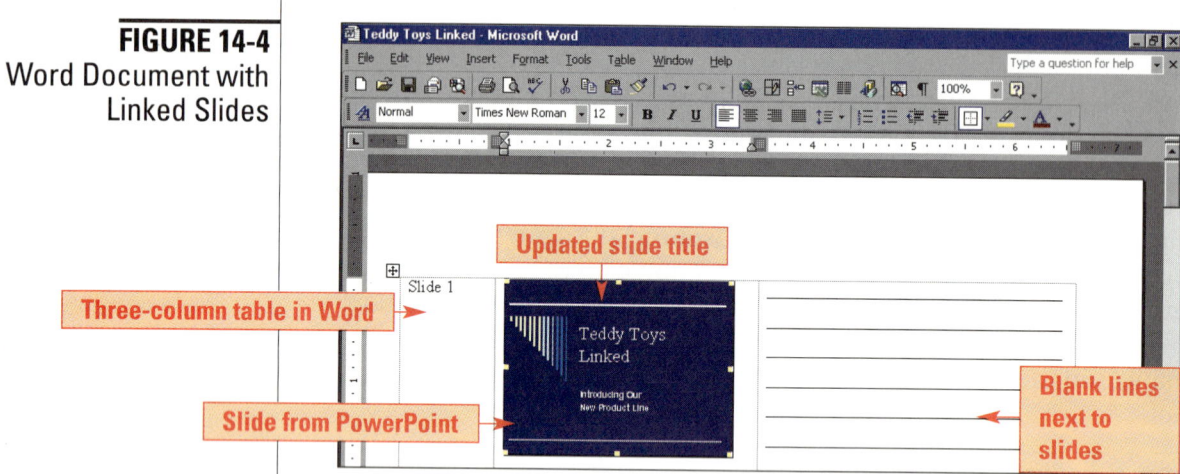

FIGURE 14-4
Word Document with Linked Slides

- Updated slide title
- Three-column table in Word
- Slide from PowerPoint
- Blank lines next to slides

| Step 12 | **Save** | the *Teddy Toys Linked* Word document and close Word |
| Step 13 | **Save** | the *Teddy Toys Embed and Link* presentation and close it |

When you make any changes to the *Teddy Toys Embed and Link* PowerPoint presentation, those changes are automatically updated when you open the *Teddy Toys Linked* Word document because the slide objects are linked.

Inserting a Word Table in a PowerPoint Slide

You can insert a Word table on a PowerPoint slide either by embedding or linking it. To insert a Word table on a PowerPoint slide without linking:

Step 1	**Open**	the *Teddy Movies I* presentation that you modified earlier in this chapter
Step 2	**Add**	a Title Only slide at the end of the presentation
Step 3	**Key**	Early Disney Movies as the title
Step 4	**Click**	Insert
Step 5	**Click**	Object
Step 6	**Click**	the Create from file option button in the Insert Object dialog box
Step 7	**Browse**	to select the *Early Disney Movies* Word document located on the Data Disk
Step 8	**Click**	OK

The Word table appears on the PowerPoint slide. To edit an embedded object, you access the source application by double-clicking the object and make the changes using the source application's features. To format and resize the embedded table:

Step 1	Double-click	the Word table
Step 2	Drag	to select all the text in the table
Step 3	Click	the Font Color button list arrow on the Formatting toolbar
Step 4	Click	Dark Red
Step 5	Click	the Shading Color button list arrow on the Tables and Borders toolbar (display this toolbar if necessary)
Step 6	Click	Gray-10%
Step 7	Click	the Font Size button list arrow on the Formatting toolbar
Step 8	Click	22
Step 9	Click	outside the Word table
Step 10	Resize	the table to 4 inches high and 7.5 inches wide using the Format Object dialog box
Step 11	Drag	the table to center it under the title
Step 12	Deselect	the table object
Step 13	Save	the *Teddy Movies I* presentation

Your slide should look similar to Figure 14-5.

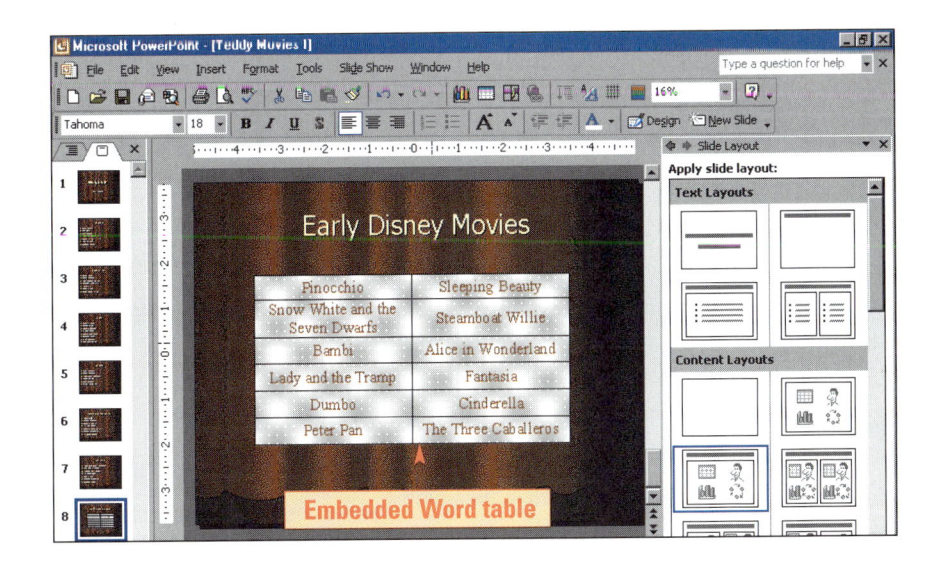

QUICK TIP

You can add or embed a table from Word by copying and pasting it into a PowerPoint slide. If you want to link the Word table to a PowerPoint slide, you must use the Paste link option in the Paste Special dialog box.

FIGURE 14-5
Slide with Embedded Word Table

chapter fourteen

14.d Embedding and Linking in PowerPoint and Excel

One of the advantages of integrating applications is that you can create an object in the most efficient application and then copy, embed, or link it to any of the other applications. For example, when it comes to creating tables and charts, Excel is more feature-rich and versatile than PowerPoint, so you may prefer creating these objects in Excel and then integrating them with PowerPoint. Or, you may want to use an existing Excel chart, table, or worksheet from a coworker or your own files in a presentation. You can easily copy, embed, or link the chart or worksheet instead of re-creating it yourself.

Embedding an Excel Worksheet in a PowerPoint Slide

When you insert an Excel worksheet or chart into a presentation, you have the option of embedding it or linking it to the PowerPoint presentation. If the Excel object is linked, the PowerPoint presentation automatically updates each time you make changes to the Excel worksheet or chart. To link an Excel worksheet to a PowerPoint slide:

Step 1	Add	a Title Only slide at the end of the presentation
Step 2	Key	Disney Movies Gross Sales as the title
Step 3	Click	Insert
Step 4	Click	Object
Step 5	Click	the Create from file option button
Step 6	Click	Browse
Step 7	Switch to	the disk drive and folder that contains your Data Files
Step 8	Double-click	the *Disney Movies* Excel workbook file located on the Data Disk
Step 9	Click	OK

A small object appears on the slide. To resize and edit the embedded object:

| Step 1 | Resize | the Excel object from the center using the CTRL key and a corner handle to resize the object until it is approximately 2.5 inches high |
| Step 2 | Double-click | the Excel object |

QUICK TIP

If you are experienced in different software applications, that experience translates into greater productivity on the job because of the ability to recognize the best application and method to use to complete tasks.

Integrating Word and Excel with PowerPoint   PA 159

You now edit in Excel, the source application. To view the worksheet data, you use the sheet tab (Movie Data) in the Excel file so that you can see the text and numbers.

Step 3	Click	the Movie Data sheet tab, if necessary
Step 4	Drag	to select cells A1 through B5
Step 5	Click	the Font Color button list arrow on the Formatting toolbar
Step 6	Click	White
Step 7	Drag	to select cells B1 through B5
Step 8	Right-click	the selected cells
Step 9	Click	Format Cells
Step 10	Click	the Number tab, if necessary
Step 11	Click	Currency
Step 12	Click	the Symbol: list arrow and select the $ symbol
Step 13	Key	0 in the Decimal places: text box
Step 14	Click	OK
Step 15	Click	outside the Excel object twice to deselect it

> **QUICK TIP**
>
> If an Excel workbook file contains more than one worksheet, the most recently active worksheet is inserted in the slide.

Your slide should look similar to Figure 14-6. The changes you make affect only the PowerPoint presentation because you did not link the Excel file to the PowerPoint slide.

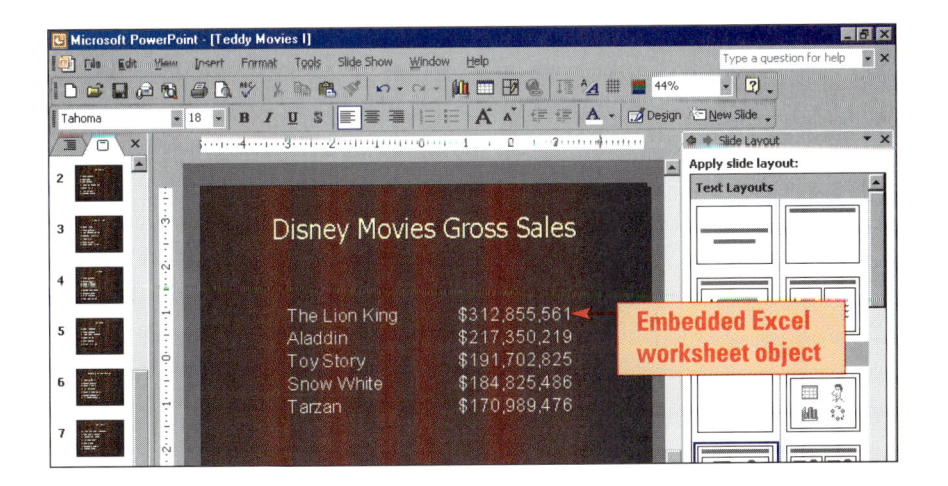

FIGURE 14-6
Slide with Embedded Excel Worksheet Object

| Step 16 | Save | the *Teddy Movies I* presentation |

chapter fourteen

Linking an Excel Chart to a PowerPoint Slide

You can link an object by copying it in the source program and then pasting it in a PowerPoint slide using the copy and paste special features in PowerPoint. To copy a chart from Excel, you select it before you start the copy process. You can copy an object from Word or Excel, then use the Paste Special command on the Edit menu to paste the link between the two applications. To link an Excel Chart to a PowerPoint slide:

Step 1	Add	a Title Only slide at the end of the presentation
Step 2	Key	Disney Movies Percentages in the title placeholder
Step 3	Start	Excel
Step 4	Click	the Open button on the Standard toolbar
Step 5	Switch to	the disk drive and folder that contains your Data Files
Step 6	Double-click	the *Disney Movies* Excel workbook file located on the Data Disk
Step 7	Save	the *Disney Movies* Excel file as *Teddy Disney Movies*
Step 8	Click	the Movie Chart sheet tab at the bottom
Step 9	Click	the Chart Area (wait until ScreenTip displays Chart Area) to select the pie chart
Step 10	Click	the Copy button on the Standard toolbar
Step 11	Click	the Teddy Movies I PowerPoint button on the taskbar
Step 12	Click	Edit
Step 13	Click	Paste Special

The Paste Special dialog box opens with options to paste the Excel Chart Object with or without a link.

Step 14	Click	Paste link
Step 15	Click	OK

The chart is inserted as a linked object on the slide. Observe the sizing handles on the object. The Smart Tag, the Automatic Layout Options button, appears at the lower-right sizing handle.

QUICK TIP

In the same way that you link a Word document to a presentation, you can link an Excel object (or any object) by opening the Insert Object dialog box, selecting the file you want to insert, and then adding a check mark in the Link check box.

MOUSE TIP

You can copy a chart in Excel by right-clicking the chart and then clicking Copy.

MENU TIP

You can copy the selected chart by clicking the Copy command on the Edit menu.

| Step 16 | **Deselect** | the pie chart object |

Your slide should look similar to Figure 14-7.

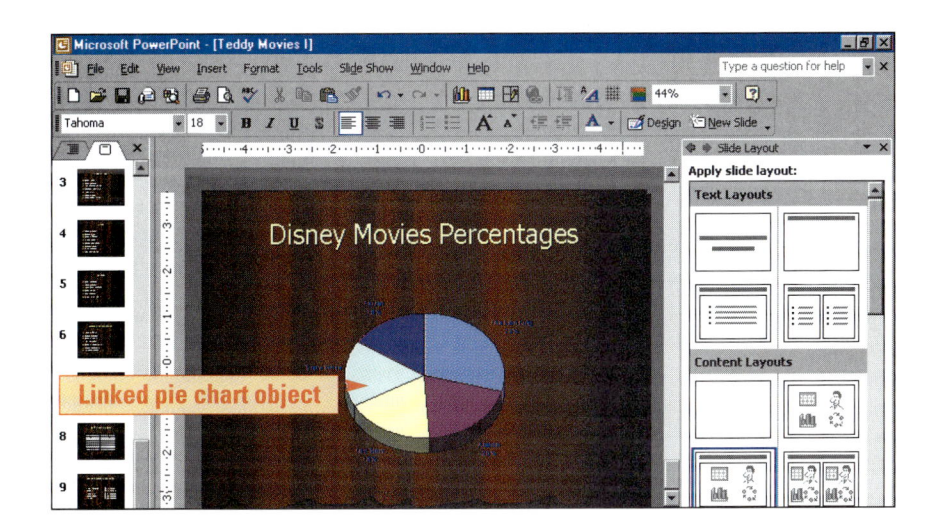

FIGURE 14-7
Slide with Linked Pie Chart Object

| Step 17 | **Close** | any open task pane in PowerPoint |
| Step 18 | **Close** | Excel |

If you want to make any formatting changes to the 3-D view, rotation of the pie, slice colors, font colors, and size, you make those changes using the Excel features. You find it hard to read the dark text labels on the slide background. To format the linked object:

| Step 1 | **Double-click** | the chart object |

When you double-click the linked chart object, the Excel application opens and you edit the original *Teddy Disney Movies* file. You can switch between Excel and PowerPoint using the taskbar; however, you can also tile the two application windows so you can see changes take place.

Step 2	**Right-click**	an empty area on the taskbar
Step 3	**Click**	Tile Windows Vertically to see the Excel and the PowerPoint application windows side by side
Step 4	**Scroll**	in PowerPoint and Excel to view the pie chart in each window

CAUTION TIP

When tiling application windows, be sure to minimize any windows you do not want tiled.

chapter fourteen

Your screen should look similar to Figure 14-8.

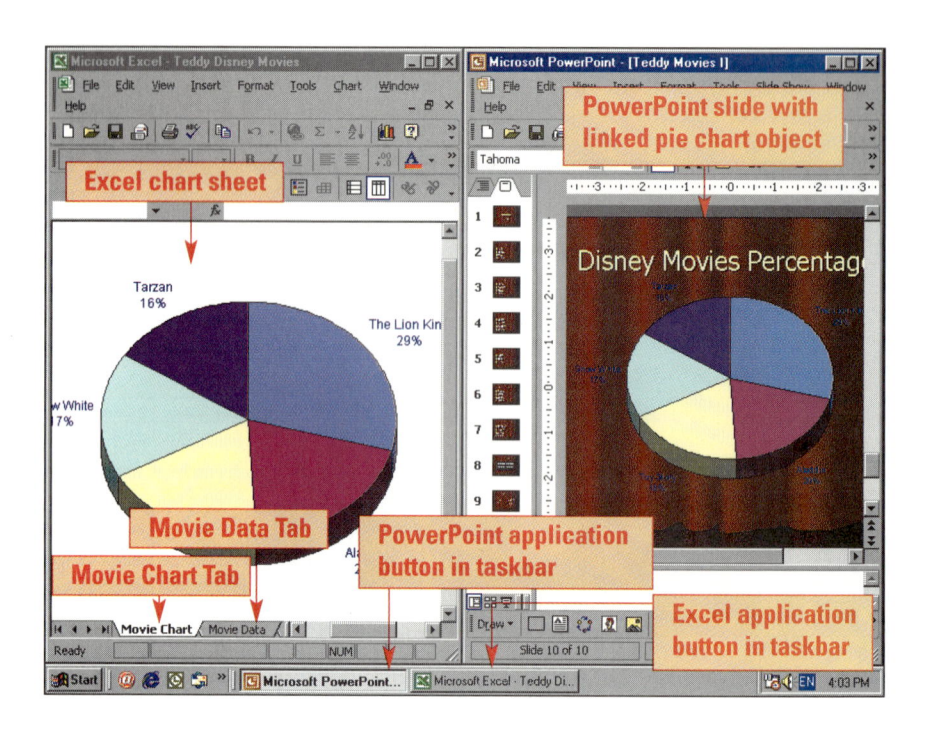

FIGURE 14-8
PowerPoint and Excel Windows Tiled Vertically

Quick Tip

When you next open a PowerPoint presentation containing links (destination file), an information message displays indicating that the PowerPoint presentation contains links that can be updated. You have a choice to update the links or cancel, which allows you to open the presentation without updating the links. When you update the links, any changes made to the source file are reflected in the PowerPoint slides.

Step 5	Click	the The Lion King slice in the Excel file until only that slice is selected
Step 6	Drag	the The Lion King slice away from the rest of the pie
Step 7	Click	a data label to select all data labels in the Excel chart
Step 8	Change	the font color to Ivory
Step 9	Change	the font size to 20 point
Step 10	Click	the *Teddy Movies I* PowerPoint presentation button on the taskbar
Step 11	Right-click	the pie chart object in the PowerPoint application
Step 12	Click	Update Link
Step 13	Observe	that the names and percentages have changed and the The Lion King slice has been pulled out from the rest of the pie chart on the PowerPoint slide
Step 14	Save	and close the *Teddy Disney Movies* Excel file and Excel
Step 15	Maximize	the *Teddy Movies I* presentation
Step 16	Run	the slide show from the beginning
Step 17	Save	the *Teddy Movies I* presentation and close it

Linking ensures that changes made in one file also appear in the other file.

Summary

- You can send a PowerPoint presentation as an outline to Word by saving it as an RTF (Rich Text Format) file and then opening the file in Word or by sending it directly to Word.

- The styles applied to text in a Word outline determine the format of the title and bullets on slides sent to PowerPoint.

- You can send slides, notes, or an outline from a PowerPoint presentation (source file) to a Word document (destination file).

- You can open a Word outline in PowerPoint and view it as a presentation.

- You can link or embed an object from another application (source file) into a PowerPoint presentation (destination file).

- Slides can be inserted into PowerPoint from either an outline format or slides from a different PowerPoint presentation.

- An embedded object becomes part of the destination file with no links to the source file.

- A linked object does not become part of the destination file; it remains linked to the source file.

- When you modify an embedded object, the source file does not change.

- When you modify a linked object, you actually modify the source file, so the change is reflected in both the source file and the destination file.

- You can embed and link a Word table into PowerPoint slides.

- You can embed and link Excel worksheet data and charts into PowerPoint slides.

- You can view two or more applications at the same time by using the Tile commands on the taskbar.

chapter fourteen

Commands Review

Action	Menu Bar	Shortcut Menu	Toolbar	Task Pane	Keyboard
Save a presentation as an RTF outline	File, Save As, Save as type: Outline/RTF				ALT + F, A; ALT + T, Outline/RTF
Send a PowerPoint presentation to Word	File, Send To, Microsoft Word				ALT + F, D, W
Send a Word outline to PowerPoint	File, Send To, Microsoft PowerPoint				ALT + F, D, P
Insert a Word outline into PowerPoint	Insert, Slides from Outline				ALT + I, L
Insert slides from one PowerPoint presentation to another	Insert, Slides from Files				ALT + I, F
Embed an object	Insert, Object				ALT + I, O
Copy an object (in source application)	Edit, Copy	Right-click object, Copy			ALT + E, C CTRL + C
Paste a link (in destination application)	Edit, Paste Special				ALT + E, S
Tile windows		Right-click taskbar, Tile Windows Horizontally or Tile Windows Vertically			

Concepts Review

Circle the correct answer.

1. When you save a file as an Outline/RTF, the RTF stands for:
   - [a] Rich Text Font.
   - [b] Rich Text Format.
   - [c] Real Text Format.
   - [d] Rich Type Format.

2. When creating a PowerPoint presentation from a Word outline, the title in a PowerPoint slide is created from which heading level in the Word outline?
   - [a] Heading 1
   - [b] Heading 2
   - [c] Subheading 1
   - [d] Subheading 2

3. All of the following can be sent from PowerPoint into the Word application *except*:
   - [a] slides.
   - [b] outlines.
   - [c] notes.
   - [d] masters.

4. When you insert a Word outline into a PowerPoint slide, you create:
   - [a] text slides.
   - [b] chart slides.
   - [c] title slides.
   - [d] table slides.

5. Linking or embedding objects from one application to another is called:
   - [a] copying.
   - [b] pasting.
   - [c] integrating.
   - [d] multiple pasting.

6. An object placed in a document in another application that retains no ties to the original source file is called a(n):
   - [a] linked object.
   - [b] template design.
   - [c] graphic image.
   - [d] embedded object.

7. When linking or embedding, the original file is called the:
   - [a] destination file.
   - [b] source file.
   - [c] input file.
   - [d] output file.

8. Which of the following is true with regard to linking an Excel chart to a PowerPoint slide?
   [a] If you change the color of the pie slices in Excel, only the Excel chart changes.
   [b] If you change the color of the pie slices, only the PowerPoint slide changes.
   [c] If you change the chart type, the chart changes in both Excel and PowerPoint.
   [d] If you change the chart data (values), only the Excel chart changes.

9. When copying an object from one application to another, you do which of the following to link the object?
   [a] Edit, Link
   [b] Edit, Embed
   [c] Edit, Paste
   [d] Edit, Paste Special

10. Which of the following taskbar commands can you use to view two or more applications side by side?
    [a] Tile All Windows
    [b] Tile Windows Vertically
    [c] Cascade Windows
    [d] Minimize All Windows

Circle **T** if the statement is true or **F** if the statement is false.

T F 1. You can save a PowerPoint presentation as an outline in Rich Text Format.
T F 2. If you create five top-level headings in a Word outline, you get one title slide with four separate bullets.
T F 3. To insert an existing object into a PowerPoint slide, you must first start the application that contains the object you want to insert.
T F 4. The Slide Finder dialog box enables you to copy one or more slides from one PowerPoint presentation to another.
T F 5. The source file is the original file from which an object is embedded and linked.
T F 6. Linking allows you to make simultaneous changes to separate files in separate software applications.
T F 7. Embedding and linking achieve exactly the same result when inserting an object from another application into a PowerPoint slide.
T F 8. You cannot insert a Word table into a PowerPoint slide.
T F 9. You can edit an embedded chart by double-clicking it.
T F 10. When you change the font and alignment of a linked object in the source file, you also make those changes to the destination file.

Skills Review

Exercise 1

1. Open the *PowerPoint Advanced* presentation located on the Data Disk, and then send it to Word as an embedded object, choosing the Blank lines next to the slides layout option.
2. Save the Word document as *PowerPoint Integrated*. (Remember to change the type of document to a Word Document in the Save as type: list box.)
3. Print and close the Word document.
4. Save the *PowerPoint Advanced* presentation as *PowerPoint Outline.rtf* in Outline/RTF format. (Remember to change the type of document to Outline/RTF in the Save as type: list box.)
5. Open the *PowerPoint Outline.rtf* file in Word and print it. Close all Word documents and PowerPoint presentations.

Exercise 2

1. Open the *Office Advanced* presentation located on the Data Disk, and save it as *Office Integrated*.

chapter fourteen

2. Add a Title Only slide at the end of the presentation, and then add the following title: "Office Users By Department."
3. Embed an Excel chart using the Paste option in the Paste Special dialog box, from the *Office Workbook* file located on the Data Disk on the Office Users By Department slide.
4. Resize and reposition the chart, if necessary, and change the font size, color, style, etc., so the chart is easy to read in PowerPoint.
5. Using Chart Options on the Chart menu, add titles to the axes to further aid readability of the chart.
6. Reposition and format the legend as desired.
7. Print the new slide, and then save and close the *Office Integrated* presentation.

Exercise 3

1. Open the *Design Advanced* presentation located on the Data Disk, and save it as *Design Integrated*.
2. Display the last slide in the presentation.
3. Use the Slide Finder to insert all the slides from the *Planning a Presentation* presentation located on the Data Disk, matching destination formatting.
4. Make any necessary changes to the newly added slides to aid readability.
5. Print the presentation as a four-slides-per-page handout, and then save and close the *Design Integrated* presentation.

Exercise 4

1. Open the *Precision Builders Outline* Word document located on the Data Disk in the Word application.
2. Send the *Precision Builders Outline* document to PowerPoint.
3. Save the new PowerPoint presentation as *Precision Builders PowerPoint Outline*, and close it.
4. Close the Word application.
5. Open the *Precision Builders Advanced* presentation located on the Data Disk in PowerPoint, and save it as *Precision Builders Integrated*.
6. Insert all the slides from the *Precision Builders PowerPoint Outline* presentation, matching the destination formatting, after the third slide (Our Motto) of the *Precision Builders Integrated* presentation.
7. Make any necessary adjustments to the newly inserted slides, print them, and then save and close the *Precision Builders Integrated* presentation.
8. From within PowerPoint, open the *Precision Builders Outline* Word document located on the Data Disk.
9. Add a title slide at the beginning of the presentation with the title "Precision Builders" and the subtitle "Goals for the Future."
10. Apply any design template to the newly created PowerPoint presentation, save it as *Precision Builders Future*, print it as a three-slides-per-page handout, and then close the presentation.

Exercise 5

1. Open the *Nature Tours Advanced* presentation located on the Data Disk, and save it as *Nature Tours Integrated*.
2. Send the *Nature Tours Integrated* presentation to Word as an Outline only.
3. Save the Word document as *Nature Tours Outline* and print it. (Remember to save it as a Word Document.)
4. Close *Nature Tours Outline* and the Word application.
5. Send the *Nature Tours Integrated* presentation as a linked object to Word, choosing the Notes next to the slides option.
6. Add a clip art image to one of the slides in the PowerPoint application, readjusting the slide layout if necessary.
7. Save and close the *Nature Tours Integrated* presentation.
8. Save the Word document as *Nature Tours Linked*.
9. Print the linked Word document, and then close the document and Word.
10. Open the *Nature Tours Advanced* presentation located on the Data Disk, and save it as *Nature Tours Table*.
11. Add a Title Only slide at the end of the presentation with the following title: "Bike Tours."

12. Insert and embed the Word table object from the *Bike Tours Table* document.
13. Change the color of the text and borders in the newly inserted Word table to white and bold the column heading, and use the Font dialog box to change the font to Verdana, shadow.
14. Resize and reposition the table for readability, if necessary.
15. Save the presentation as *Nature Tours Table*, print it as a six-slides-per-page handout, and then save and close the presentation.

Exercise 6
1. Open the *A Healthier You Advanced* presentation located on the Data Disk, and save it as *A Healthier You Integrated*.
2. Add a Title Only slide at the end of the presentation with the following title: "Daily Water Sources."
3. Open the *A Healthier You Workbook* file located on the Data Disk in Excel.
4. Copy the data cells in the Excel worksheet, and use the Paste Special feature to link to the new PowerPoint slide.
5. Resize and reposition the Excel linked object, if necessary.
6. Change the font size, color, style, etc., to enhance the look of the chart.
7. Add borders to the Excel worksheet.
8. Remove the gridlines under Tools, Options, and View in Excel, if necessary.
9. Resize the chart in PowerPoint, if necessary.
10. Update and print the slide with the linked Excel chart.
11. Save and close the *A Healthier You Workbook* file and the *A Healthier You Integrated* presentation.

Exercise 7
1. Create a new presentation in PowerPoint with a design template of your choice.
2. Insert the slides from the *Computer Reference Manuals Outline.rtf* (Rich Text Format) located on the Data Disk.
3. Delete the first blank title slide.
4. Change the first slide to a Title slide and key "By" (press the ENTER key) "Your Name" in the subtitle placeholder.
5. Make adjustments to font size, color, style, and placement on slides.
6. Save the new presentation as *Computer Reference Manuals*, print it as a four-slides-per-page handout and then close it.
7. Open the *Buying A Computer Advanced* presentation located on the Data Disk, and save it as *Buying A Computer Integrated*.
8. Insert The Internet and Your Kids slide from the *Computer Reference Manuals* presentation after Slide 2 in the *Buying A Computer Integrated* presentation (have the new slide match the formatting of the presentation.)
9. Print the presentation as a six-slides-per-page handout, and then save and close it.

Exercise 8
1. Open the *Leisure Travel Advanced* presentation located on the Data Disk, and save it as *Leisure Travel Integrated*.
2. Add a Title Only slide at the end of the presentation with the following title: "Current Bookings."
3. Insert an Excel chart with a link from the *Leisure Travel Workbook* file located on the Data Disk.
4. Tile the windows so that you can see both applications open at the same time, and then change the color of the slices to match the *Leisure Travel Integrated* presentation design.
5. Change the font size, color, style, etc., to enhance the readability of the chart, and then resize and reposition it so it is placed attractively on the slide.
6. Print the new slide, and then save and close the *Leisure Travel Integrated* presentation and the *Leisure Travel Workbook* file.

chapter fourteen

Case Projects

Project 1
You want to explain how to link and embed objects to your classmates. Use online Help to research information on linking and embedding objects. Print all the Help topics on using linked objects and embedded objects to share information between Office products. Include all the links.

Project 2
An administrative assistant at Communicate Corporation created an Excel workbook that contains a column chart comparing last year's typical calls with this year's typical calls. Open the *Communicate Advanced* presentation located on the Data Disk and save it as *Communicate Integrated*. Copy and paste a link between the Excel chart from the *Communicate Workbook* file and a slide in your *Communicate Integrated* presentation. Add a Title Only slide at the end of the presentation with a title suggesting this comparison. Use the *Communicate Workbook* file located on the Data Disk, and link the chart when you paste it from Excel into PowerPoint. Make any formatting changes to the chart to fit your presentation design. Remember that all changes made in the *Communicate Workbook* file automatically update the chart slide in the *Communicate Integrated* presentation. Print the new slide. Save and close both files.

Project 3
At Souner & Associates, your employer finds an RTF outline from a previous employee with helpful information. Open the *Souner Advanced* presentation located on the Data Disk, and save it as *Souner Integrated*. Insert the *Souner Outline.rtf* located on the Data Disk into the *Souner Integrated* presentation. Decide where the slides belong in the presentation. Make any changes to the slides as desired. Print the new slides. Save and close the *Souner Integrated* presentation.

Project 4
You plan to travel, and you want to review *My Presentation Advanced*, modifying the content, but not the background, colors, or clip art images. Open the *My Presentation Advanced* presentation located on the Data Disk, and save it as *My Presentation Integrated*. Send the presentation to Word as a Word document with blank lines next to the slides. Link the slides to the original PowerPoint presentation. Save the RTF outline as *My Presentation Integrated Outline*, and save the linked Word document as *My Presentation Integrated Slides* and print it. Close the Word documents and the presentation.

Project 5
Another summer zoo employee created slides for you to incorporate into your presentation. Open the *Zoo Advanced* presentation located on the Disk, and save it as *Zoo Integrated*. Insert the slides from the *Zoo PowerPoint Presentation* located on the Data Disk. Decide on the order of the new slides in the presentation. Make any changes to the presentation to maintain a consistent look. Print the presentation as a nine-slides-per-page handout. Save and close the *Zoo Integrated* presentation.

Project 6
Connect to the Internet and search the Microsoft Web site for recent articles on OLE (Object Linking and Embedding). Print at least three current articles, and include a summary indicating how you could use linking or embedding in your next PowerPoint presentation.

Project 7
One of your consumer education students created a worksheet and a chart in Excel that shows the current market share of popular vehicles. You want to add this information to your presentation. Open the *Cars Advanced* presentation located on the Data Disk, and save it as *Cars Integrated*. Copy the Excel chart from the *Cars Workbook* file located on the Data Disk and paste it without links on a new slide in the *Cars Integrated* presentation. Make any changes to the chart in the *Cars Integrated* presentation with regard to data labels, rotating slices, tilting the pie, etc. Save the *Cars Workbook* file. Save the *Cars Integrated* presentation and print the new slide. Close both documents.

Project 8
Your professor decides to manually enter notes for his lecture on the Internet. He asks you and a fellow teaching assistant to work together to send the *Internet Advanced* presentation to Word as a document with blank lines below the slides so he can handwrite his notes. Open the *Internet Advanced* presentation located on the Data Disk. Link the slides to the Word document and save it for future semesters. Save the Word document as *Internet Integrated Outline* and print it. Save and close both documents.

Microsoft
Access 2002
Advanced

Access 2002

Building and Modifying Tables

Chapter Overview

As your use of databases becomes more sophisticated, you need a way to ensure the integrity of data and relationships within a database. Data validation rules, masks, and other Access features ensure that the data and the relationships reflect the tasks you want to accomplish using your database. In this chapter, you define data validation rules, learn how to establish data validation for a field, modify lookup field properties, modify an input mask, and modify relationships between tables.

Learning Objectives

- Define data validation rules
- Modify lookup field properties
- Modify an input mask
- Define table relationships

Case profile

The administrators of Online University want you to improve the accuracy of data entered in the OLU database. You want to set up data validation rules as well as learn more about input masks and lookup fields. You also need to look at join properties and ensure that the foreign keys found in related tables reflect changes to primary keys.

chapter nine

9.a Defining Data Validation Rules

Data validation is a set of procedures that ensure that data fields contain consistent and valid values. Access provides several layers of data validation that do not require you to establish an explicit validation rule. This saves time. To validate data after you enter it, Access looks at field properties and makes sure that you entered data values consistent with those properties. You establish field properties in Design view. The fields that you later add to forms and reports inherit most of these properties. Through inheritance, Access enforces data validation on objects.

Access provides data validation at the field level through two field properties. The **Validation Rule** property is an expression in a field that must be true for any value entered or modified in that field. The **Validation Text** property is a text message that indicates violation of a data validation rule. You must provide values for these properties; Access does not supply them by default.

Because it is important to prohibit invalid data *at the time it is entered*, a validation rule is the best way to detect and correct invalid data. Table 9-1 shows some sample validation rule expressions for single fields.

Desired Data Condition	Validation Rule Expression	Validation Text Message
Numeric value must be non-negative	>=0	Value cannot be negative
Text value must be within this set of choices	In("Cash","Credit")	Sale type must be Cash or Credit
Numeric value must be in this range	Between 12 and 24	Value must be greater than 11 and less than 25
Text value must start with a pattern	Like "MIS*"	Course prefix must begin with MIS

If you establish a validation rule for a field, you cannot suspend the rule temporarily. Access forces you to enter a data value that meets the validation rule expression before you leave the field.

You know that classes at OLU can have 0, 1, 2, 3, or 4 credits, so you decide to create a validation rule that restricts entries to these values in the Credits field of the tblCourses table. To create a field validation rule:

| Step 1 | **Create** | a copy of the *mdbOnlineU9-* database located on the Data Disk |
| Step 2 | **Open** | the tblCourses table in Design view |

QUICK TIP

You can establish record validation rules that apply to the entire record before it is saved in the table. Unlike the field validation rule, the table validation rule property can refer to more than one field. For example, you can specify that one date field's value must be after another date field's value. You can access the table's data validation rule properties in Design view.

TABLE 9-1
Sample Validation Rules

MENU TIP

To display table properties, use the Properties command on the View menu.

> **MOUSE TIP**
>
> Click the Properties button on the Table Design toolbar to display table properties.

Step 3	Click	the Credits field
Step 4	Click	the Validation Rule text box
Step 5	Key	Between 0 and 4 to force the value entered to less than 5
Step 6	Click	the Validation Text text box
Step 7	Key	Credits must be a number less than 5

You must save your changes to the table before you can activate the validation rule. Access checks the records in the table to make sure the existing data meets your new rule. If it does not meet the rule, you have an opportunity to eliminate the rule.

> **QUICK TIP**
>
> For information about validation rules, click the Validation Rule text box in the Field Properties pane, and then press the F1 key.

Step 8	Click	the Save button on the Table Design toolbar
Step 9	Click	Yes to allow Access to check existing data against the data validation rule
Step 10	Close	the table

9.b Modifying Lookup Field Properties

A **lookup field** is a control in a form that displays a list of choices for a field. Access can generate the list from the data in another table or query or from a static set of values that you key into the table properties. One use of the lookup field occurs when two tables are related. In such a situation, you can provide a list of primary key values for the foreign key in the related table. This is useful because you then can click a valid choice for the foreign key instead of keying a matching value. You create the lookup field in the Lookup tab of the table properties in Design view.

OLU wants to create a combo box lookup field for the course code in tblRegistrations. The lookup field would find the class information in the tblClasses table. Linking these fields is helpful: Although the tblRegistration table contains the ClassCode field, the persons who enter the schedule prefer to see both the department prefix and the course number, which makes entering the correct data easier. To create a combo box lookup field:

Step 1	Open	the tblRegistration table in Design view
Step 2	Click	the ClassCode field

Step 3	Click	the Lookup tab in the Field Properties pane
Step 4	Click	the Display Control text box
Step 5	Click	the list arrow
Step 6	Click	Combo Box

The combo box lookup properties appear. Your screen should look similar to Figure 9-1.

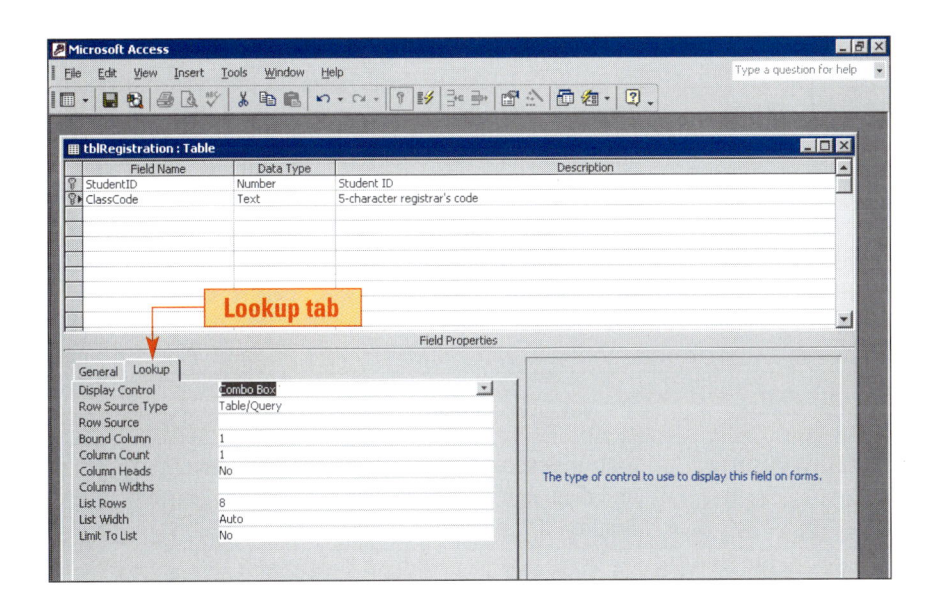

FIGURE 9-1
Combo Box Lookup Properties

| Step 7 | Click | the Row Source text box |
| Step 8 | Key | tblClasses in the Row Source text box |

The Column Count property indicates how many columns from the Row Source appear in the combo box. In this case, the data in the first three columns of the tblClasses table appear: ClassID, DeptPrefix, and CourseNumber. The Bound Column property of 1 indicates that the value in the first column of the tblClasses table (ClassID) will be stored in this field in the tblRegistration table.

Step 9	Select	the text in the Column Count text box
Step 10	Key	3 in the Column Count text box to establish the number of columns
Step 11	Click	the Column Widths text box
Step 12	Key	0.5,0.5,0.5 in the Column Widths text box to establish the width for each of the three columns as .5 inches

QUICK TIP

By default, users can enter values other than those a lookup field provides. However, you can use the Limit To List property to restrict users' entries.

chapter nine

| Step 13 | *Save* | the changes to the table |

By widening the Class Code column, you can see the three columns from the tblClasses table (ClassID, DeptPrefix, and CourseNumber) for each row in the combo box. To view the class code information:

Step 1	*Switch to*	Datasheet view
Step 2	*Drag*	the right border of the Class Code column to make the column approximately 2.5 inches wide
Step 3	*Click*	the first row of the Class Code column
Step 4	*Click*	the list arrow to display choices for that field and then close the list

If you add a record to the tblClasses table, that record appears in the combo box the next time you open the tblRegistration table. To add a record to the tblRegistration table using the new combo box list:

Step 1	*Click*	the New Record button
Step 2	*Observe*	that Access adds a new row at the bottom of the table and displays the lookup field that already exists for the Student ID column
Step 3	*Key*	51
Step 4	*Press*	the TAB key to move to the next column
Step 5	*Click*	the list arrow in the Class Code column
Step 6	*Click*	00154 BUS 1011 to insert the class code
Step 7	*Close*	the tblRegistration table, saving your changes

Access saves the value 00154 in the new row along with the student ID 51. The advantage of the Class Code lookup field combo box is that the user sees valid choices for the Class Code field, including the class name, which makes recognizing the proper value easier.

9.c Modifying an Input Mask

An **input mask** is a template or pattern for each character in a field that controls what users can key. Access provides the Input Mask Wizard to create common input masks. After you create the mask, you might need to modify it. In addition, you might need to create an input mask for a field that the Input Mask Wizard does not include. This situation occurs, for example, when a user needs to enter a coded part number. To do either task, you need to know how Access interprets the input mask property.

An input mask can mask a variety of data, such as a telephone number or Social Security number. A standard telephone number input mask from the wizard is !\(999") "000\-0000;0;_ (without an ending period). The input mask for this field has three parts:
- The character pattern for the field: !\(999") "000\-0000.
- A status value that determines if the data field in the table contains the literal display characters: 0 means the field contains the literal characters; 1 or blank means the field does not contain the literal characters.
- The placeholder character that represents a character position within the field. To save storage space in the database, you usually do not store the literal display characters in the field. However, if you plan to export data to Word, Excel, or another database, storing the literal characters in the field is important.

Access uses different characters in the mask for different purposes. Each character in the mask indicates what users can key in that position in the field. These characters reserve spots in the input field for a particular digit, decimal point, or character, and indicate whether that character is required or optional. Table 9-2 shows the use of the most common input mask characters.

TABLE 9-2 Common Input Mask Characters

Character	Requires
0	a digit (0 through 9, entry required, plus and minus prohibited)
9	a digit or space (entry not required, plus and minus prohibited)
L	a letter (A through Z, entry required)
?	a letter (A through Z, entry not required)
A	a letter or digit (entry required)
a	a letter or digit (entry not required)
&	any character or space (entry required)
C	any character or space (entry not required)
<	conversion of all characters that follow to lowercase
>	conversion of all characters that follow to uppercase
!	displays input mask from right to left, rather than from left to right
\	displays the character that follows as a literal character; used when the literal character (such as \A) is another input mask special character, such as those that appear in this table
others	displays other characters in the field as a literal characters, such as parentheses around an area code or hyphens in Social Security numbers
Password	displays characters in the field as asterisks, and stores them as text characters (in this case, Password is the complete input mask)

The Input Mask Wizard is available from the field properties in Design view. You can select a sample mask from the wizard and then modify it, or you can build an input mask from scratch. You want to create an input mask to help the user enter the supervisor's identification number correctly. You need an input mask to handle entering a Social Security number. The mask requires the entry of a digit in each of nine character positions. To create an input mask:

> **QUICK TIP**
>
> The \- combination indicates that the hyphen following the back slash is a literal character to appear as is. The ;; indicate that mask literal characters are not to be stored in the field value in the table. Finally, the # character is the placeholder for entering digits in a field.

Step 1	Open	the tblInstructors table in Design view
Step 2	Click	the SupervisorID field (you might need to scroll down)
Step 3	Click	the Input Mask text box in the Field Properties pane
Step 4	Key	000\-00\-0000;;# in the Input Mask text box
Step 5	Save	the changes to the table design
Step 6	Switch to	Datasheet view
Step 7	Click	the left side of the SupervisorID field in the last record (scroll to view the Supervisor column)
Step 8	Key	999114999

Notice that the input mask displays the hyphens and placeholders. Your screen should look similar to Figure 9-2.

FIGURE 9-2
SupervisorID Field Input Mask

> **CAUTION TIP**
>
> Depending on whether your computer's operating system is Windows 98 or Windows 2000, Access displays dates with a two-digit or four-digit year format by default.

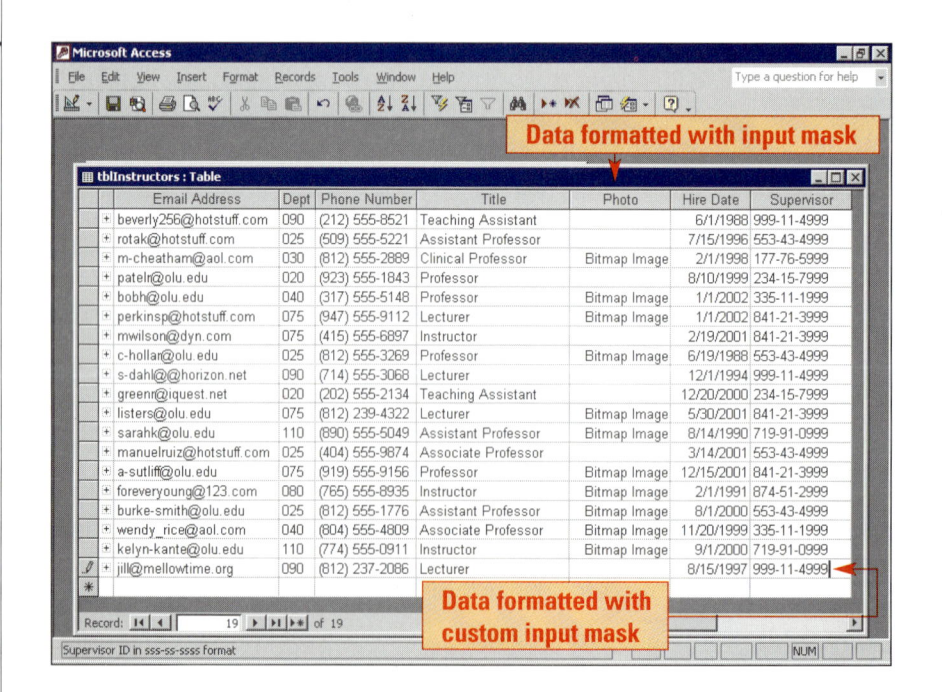

| Step 9 | Close | the table |

9.d Defining Table Relationships

You establish a relationship between two tables in the Relationships window by linking a value from one field in one table to a common value in another field in another table. For instance, the tblStudents and tblInstructors tables share a relationship based on common values in the AdvisorID and the InstID fields.

Setting One-to-Many and Many-to-Many Relationships

Many students enrolled in one class is an example of a one-to-many relationship. You can establish this relationship for the tblStudents and tblRegistration tables based on the StudentID field. To set a one-to-many relationship between two tables:

Step 1	Click	the Relationships button on the Database toolbar
Step 2	Click	the Show Table button on the Relationships toolbar
Step 3	Double-click	tblRegistration to add it to the Relationships window
Step 4	Click	Close
Step 5	Drag	the StudentID field in the tblStudents table to the StudentID field in the tblRegistration table
Step 6	Click	Create to create the relationship
Step 7	Drag	the ClassID field in the tblClasses table to the ClassCode field in the tblRegistration table
Step 8	Click	Create to create the relationship

Your screen should look similar to Figure 9-3.

> **QUICK TIP**
>
> Consider these tips when choosing the data type for fields in Access tables: When you do not plan to do arithmetic with a field, leave it as a Text type rather than as a number. Make the field size as small as possible to avoid wasted space. For Number fields, choose the smallest field size that matches the data. For joining tables, the data types of the two fields must match. Use a Yes/No field rather than a one-character text field when you have data with two values. Because Access does not round numbers internally, use Currency type for money fields to maintain accuracy to the penny. Avoid changing the data type *after* you add data to the table.

FIGURE 9-3
Relationships Window

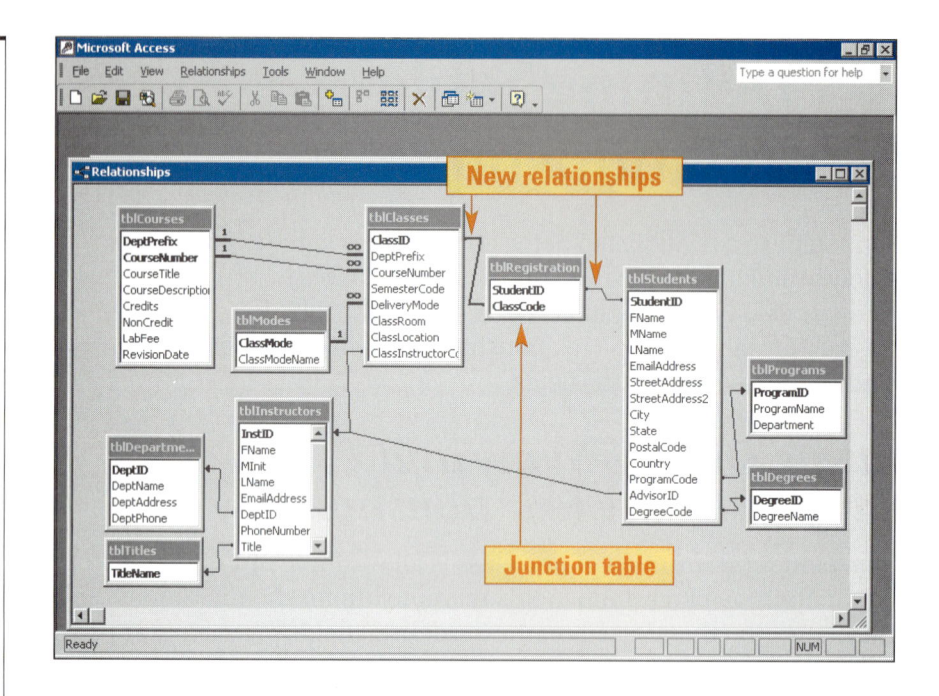

Access creates a **junction table** to support a many-to-many relationship. A junction table may have fields other than the primary keys from the related tables. For example, consider the many-to-many relationship between students and classes. The junction table in the OLU database is the tblRegistration table, which contains the StudentID field from the tblStudents table and the ClassID field from the tblClasses table. Each row of the tblRegistration table represents one student enrolled in one class; if the student takes three classes, the student has three rows in the tblRegistration table. The tblRegistration table also contains nonprimary key fields that describe the registration.

You just created a one-to-many relationship between the tblStudents and tblRegistration tables and another one-to-many relationship between the tblClasses and tblRegistration tables. Together, the three tables implement the many-to-many relationship. To implement this relationship in the Relationships window, you join each table with the junction table.

Setting Join Properties for Relationships

A **join** is a relationship between a field in one table and a field with the same value in another table. A join is the actual link that defines the relationship between two tables. Access lets you set up three types of joins: inner join, outer join, and self-join. The type of join that you use in your table relationships depends on the information that you want from your data.

Inner Join

An **inner join**, the most common type, includes only the rows of records where the join fields match exactly. If the related table contains no matching field, Access does not select the row from the primary table. For example, because the ClassID field in the tblClasses table exactly matches the ClassCode field in the tblRegistration table, you use an inner join. Because this is the default join type, you do not need to make any changes in the Join Properties dialog box to establish the inner join.

Outer Join

An **outer join** includes every record from one table and only those records from the other table that match exactly. For example, you've joined the tblStudents and tblRegistration tables. Suppose you add a new student who has yet to schedule a class. This student's ID would therefore not appear in the tblRegistration table. If you set up an outer join, you can show all records in the tblStudents table, even those of students who have not scheduled classes. This also lets you to find students who have no classes.

You decide to change the join type for the tblStudents/tblRegistration relationship to an outer join. To set join properties:

Step 1	Double-click	the join line between the tblStudents and tblRegistration tables to open the Edit Relationships dialog box
Step 2	Click	Join Type in the Edit Relationships dialog box

The Join Properties dialog box opens, offering you the three join type options shown in Figure 9-4. The first option button represents an inner join. The other two option buttons represent left-outer and right-outer joins, respectively. **Left-outer join** uses all records from the primary table and only those from the related table with matching foreign key values. **Right-outer join** uses all records from the related table and only those from the primary table with matching primary key values.

> **CAUTION TIP**
>
> If you select the default inner join type and the related table contains no matching records some records in the primary table appear to be lost when you open a query that joins both tables.

FIGURE 9-4
Join Properties Dialog Box

Step 3	Click	the second option button to choose the left-outer join type to include all student records and only those registration records with matching StudentID fields

Caution Tip

You could create an outer join that lists all registration records and only those student rows that match. However, if any registration/student combination matched the criteria, it violates referential integrity, because every record in the tblRegistration table must have a matching StudentID in the tblStudents table. In essence, you use the outer join to discover flaws in your database design.

Step 4	Click	OK
Step 5	Click	OK to close the Edit Relationships dialog box

Self-Join

A **self-join** joins a table to a second copy of the same table. You use a self-join to link tables that have different fields but that contain the same type of information. For example, the tblInstructors table includes the InstID and SupervisorID fields. Each instructor reports to a supervisor. However, because supervisors are also considered instructors, they are listed in the same table. If you copy the tblInstructors table to join the InstID and SupervisorID fields, you can create a query that shows the name of each instructor's supervisor. To create a self-join for the tblInstructors table:

Step 1	Click	the Show Table button on the Relationship toolbar
Step 2	Double-click	tblInstructors in the Show Table dialog box
Step 3	Click	Close
Step 4	Drag	the left border of the second copy of the tblInstructors table to see its entire title bar

You added a copy of the tblInstructors table, called tblInstructors_1. Your screen should look similar to Figure 9-5.

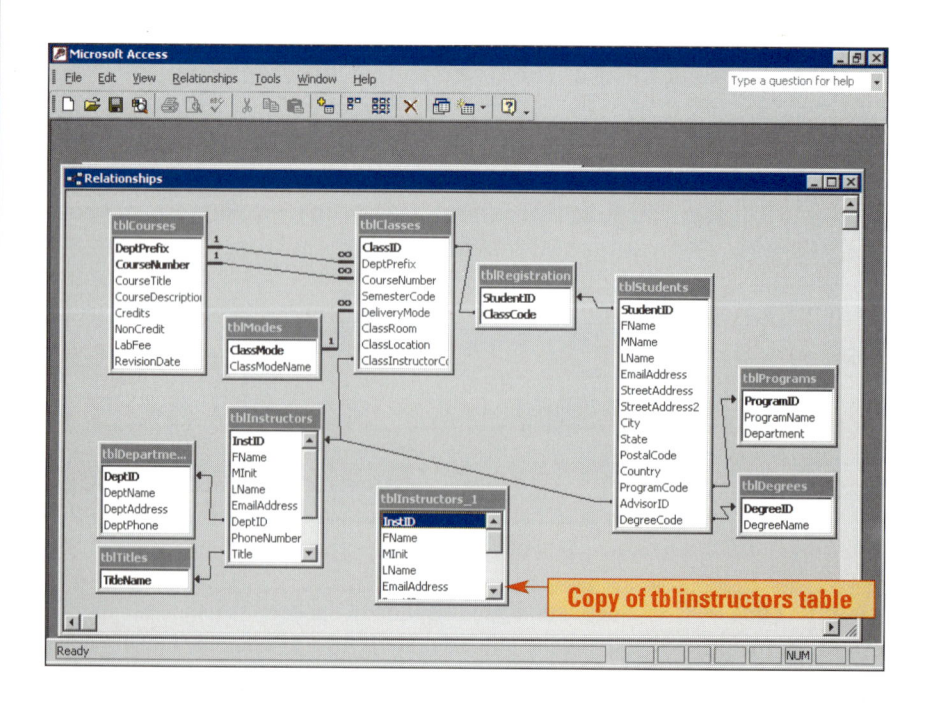

FIGURE 9-5
Relationships Window with Copy of tblInstructors Table

| Step 5 | Drag | the InstID field in the tblInstructors table to the SupervisorID field in the tblInstructors_1 table |
| Step 6 | Click | Create to create the relationship |

This method creates a one-to-many relationship between the tblInstructors and tblInstructors_1 tables. Next you learn how to use cascade options to ensure that changes in the primary field are automatically made to the related field.

Setting Cascade Options and Enforcing Referential Integrity

Access helps you manage changes to a primary table that affect related records in the related tables. You can change the key value in both tables or even delete records from a child table when you delete the matching record in the parent table. Doing so ensures that a primary record always matches each related record. You ensure that related records match by using the cascade update and cascade delete options. To use these options, you must enforce referential integrity.

Cascade Update

Suppose you want to change the value of the primary key field in the primary table. If you change the primary key value with referential integrity enforced, many students can be enrolled in one class. The **cascade update** feature automatically changes the foreign key value in all related records in the related table. With referential integrity enforced, unchecking the Cascade Update Related Fields check box prevents you from changing the value of the primary key if the related table contains related records; that is, you cannot select the cascade update feature if referential integrity is not enforced.

Cascade Delete

If you delete the matching record in the primary table and referential integrity is enforced, the **cascade delete** feature in Access automatically deletes related records in related tables. This feature ensures that the related table contains no orphaned records. With referential integrity enforced, unchecking the Cascade Delete Related Records check box prevents you from deleting a record from the primary table when the related table contains related records. You cannot check the cascade delete feature if the Enforce Referential Integrity check box is not checked. You can select cascade delete without selecting cascade update.

> **CAUTION TIP**
>
> Because StudentID in the tblStudents table is an AutoNumber field, you cannot change its value for an existing record. Thus, you cannot test cascade update with this table.

chapter nine

Quick Tip

For documentation and discussion purposes, you can create a report that includes the Relationships window. First, display the Relationships window with the Relationships command on the Tools menu. Then click the Print Relationships command on the File menu. Access creates a report that includes the Relationships window and displays the report in Print Preview view. You can edit a relationships report in Design view to add comments or notes to the report. Of course, subsequent changes to the relationships in the database are not incorporated in the initial report. If you change the relationships, you must recreate the report.

To use the cascade update and cascade delete features:

Step 1	Double-click	the join line between the tblRegistration and tblStudents tables to open the Edit Relationships window
Step 2	Click	the Enforce Referential Integrity check box to insert a check mark
Step 3	Click	the Cascade Update Related Fields check box to insert a check mark
Step 4	Click	the Cascade Delete Related Records check box to insert a check mark
Step 5	Click	OK
Step 6	Save	the Relationships window and close it

Access establishes internal rules that enable the cascade options. Next you verify that cascade delete indeed works for this relationship. To verify that cascade delete works:

Step 1	Open	the tblStudents table in Datasheet view
Step 2	Select	record 19, Javier Orozco
Step 3	Click	the Delete Record button on the Table Datasheet toolbar

Javier has a record in the tblRegistration table and cascade delete is enforced in the relationship between the tblStudents and tblRegistration tables. As a result, Access displays a warning message that indicates you are about to delete related records. *You do not want to delete the records.*

| Step 4 | Click | No to cancel the deletion |
| Step 5 | Close | the tblStudents table without saving the changes and close the database |

If you had not activated cascade delete and enforced referential integrity, Access would make the deletion and the related record would be orphaned, with no matching primary record.

Building and Modifying Tables   AA 15

Summary

- A data validation rule presents a condition that each value of a field must meet. The rule ensures accurate data entry. Data validation text is the message that appears when data in the field violates the validation rule.
- A lookup field provides a list of values from another table or query for a field. It helps the user select a valid entry when two tables are related.
- An input mask provides a template for entering data in a field. Special characters in the input mask indicate what type of character can be keyed in that position and whether an entry is mandatory.
- In a one-to-one relationship, each table has only one related field. In a one-to-many relationship, the primary table can have more than one related record in the secondary table. In a many-to-many relationship, each table can have many related records.
- A join is the actual link that defines the relationship between related tables.
- You can set up three types of joins. An inner join matches the same field in two different tables. An outer join matches only records that both tables include. A self-join links copies of the same table.
- You can enforce referential integrity to ensure that related tables stay related even if you change the data in one table.

Commands Review

Action	Menu Bar	Shortcut Menu	Toolbar	Task Pane	Keyboard
Set table properties		Right-click table, click Design View			
View a relationship	Tools, Relationships	Right-click, click Edit Relationship			ALT + T, R
Create a relationship			Drag between tables		
View a join	Relationships, Edit Relationship	Right-click, click Show All	Double-click the join line		ALT + R, R
Create a join			Click join type		
Show a table	Relationships, Show table	Right-click, click Show Table			ALT + R, S
Enforce referential integrity	Relationships, Edit Relationship	Double-click the join line, click Enforce Referential Integrity			ALT + R, R, E
Add a table to a relationship	View, Show Table				ALT + V, H
Cascade Update	Relationships, Edit Relationships	Double-click the join line, click Cascade Update Related Field			ALT + R, R, U
Cascade Delete	Relationships, Edit Relationships	Double-click the join line, click Cascade Delete Related Records			ALT + R, R, D

chapter nine

Concepts Review

Circle the correct answer.

1. The validation rule that excludes numeric values less than 10 is:
   - [a] like 10.
   - [b] between 10 and 20.
   - [c] in ("10","20","30").
   - [d] <=10.

2. If no validation rule is set for a field:
   - [a] Access checks that the value entered is the proper data type.
   - [b] that field accepts any value.
   - [c] you cannot make an entry in that field.
   - [d] Access prompts you to create a validation rule.

3. Which of the following is not a possible row source for a combo box lookup field?
   - [a] a table
   - [b] a query
   - [c] a list of values
   - [d] a form

4. The data obtained through a combo box lookup field is:
   - [a] found in the bound column of the row source.
   - [b] in a text box.
   - [c] stored in the bound row of the table.
   - [d] found only in the list.

5. Which character in an input mask converts the characters that follow it to uppercase?
   - [a] >
   - [b] !
   - [c] U
   - [d] \

6. To edit a join, you must:
   - [a] open the Edit Relationships dialog box.
   - [b] double-click the table that you want.
   - [c] click the referential integrity button.
   - [d] draw a line between two fields.

7. The most common type of relationship is a:
   - [a] one-to-one relationship.
   - [b] one-to-many relationship.
   - [c] many-to-many relationship.
   - [d] self-relationship.

8. Creating an outer join:
   - [a] automatically creates referential integrity.
   - [b] includes every record from one table and only matching records from another table.
   - [c] includes only fields that match exactly.
   - [d] links tables in two different databases.

9. An inner join:
   - [a] is the most common type of join.
   - [b] eliminates referential integrity.
   - [c] is indicated by a dotted line.
   - [d] links two orphans.

10. The Relationships window shows related tables and the fields linked in each:
    - [a] join.
    - [b] data type.
    - [c] record.
    - [d] relationship.

Circle **T** if the statement is true or **F** if the statement is false.

T F 1. A validation rule is the text that appears if a field violates a rule.

T F 2. Two one-to-many relationships supported by a junction table create a many-to-many relationship.

T F 3. You cannot save the literal characters from the input mask in the field value stored in the table.

T F 4. The ? character displays the input mask from right to left, rather than from left to right.

T F 5. A join is a relationship between a field in one table and a field with the same value in another table.

T F 6. An inner join displays all records in one table and matching records in another table.

T F 7. A self-join matches a record to another record in the same table.

T F 8. A junction table supports a one-to-many relationship.

T F 9. You cannot establish cascade update without enforcing referential integrity.

T F 10. In a one-to-many relationship, one student record could be related to many class records.

Skills Review

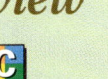

Exercise 1

1. Create a copy of the *mdbFanTours9-* database located on the Data Disk.
2. Open the tblEmployees table in Design view.
3. Create a validation rule that requires the employee hire date to be on or after July 1, 1999. (*Hint:* Use the greater than or equal to symbols (>=) and the number sign (#) to structure the validation rule as >=#7/1/1999#.)
4. Create validation text that states that the hire date must be on or after July 1, 1999.
5. Save the table and let Access validate the existing data.
6. Close the table, and then close the database.

Exercise 2

1. Open *the mdbFanTours9-1* database you created in Exercise 1.
2. Open the tblEmployees table in Datasheet view.
3. Change the HireDate for the first employee to June 1, 1999. Key it in this format: 06/01/1999. The validation rule you created in Exercise 1 prevents you from entering the date. The validation text you created in Exercise 1 tells you that.
4. Press the ESC key to abort the change to the hire date or rekey 3/14/2001 as the original hire date.
5. Close the table, and then close the database.

Exercise 3

1. Open the *mdbFanTours9-1* database you modified in Exercise 2.
2. Open the tblBookings table in Design view.
3. Create an input mask for the EmplID field that lets users enter a Social Security type number (123-45-6789). Store the literal characters in the field.
4. Save and close the table, and then close the database.

chapter nine

Exercise 4

1. Open the *mdbFanTours9-1* database you modified in Exercise 3.
2. Open the tblCustomers table in Design view.
3. Create an input mask for the PostalCode field. Require that users enter the first five digits and provide an optional set of four more digits for the Zip+4 portion. Display the literal dash or hyphen character between the required and optional digits.
4. Save and close the table, and then close the database.

Exercise 5

1. Open the *mdbFanTours9-1* database you modified in Exercise 4.
2. Click the Relationships button on the Database toolbar to open the Relationships window.
3. Print the Relationships window in a report using the Print Relationships command on the File menu.
4. Switch to Landscape orientation in Print Preview view using the Setup button, and print another copy of the report.
5. Save the report, and then close it.
6. Close the Relationships window, and then close the database.

Exercise 6

1. Open the *mdbFanTours9-1* database you modified in Exercise 5.
2. Click the Relationships button on the Database toolbar to open the Relationships window.
3. Identify the junction table in this database. Which tables have a many-to-many relationship, as expressed through this junction table? Save your answers in a Word document.
4. Close the Relationships window, and then close the database.

Exercise 7

1. Open the *mdbFanTours9-1* database you modified in Exercise 6.
2. Click the Relationships button on the Database toolbar to open the Relationships window. Double-click the center of the join line between the tblEvents table and the tblBookings table.
3. In the Edit Relationships dialog box, enforce referential integrity on the join between the tblEvents table and the tblBookings table. Select both cascade options in the Edit Relationships dialog box. Select Join type 2 for this join.
4. Save and close the Relationships window, and then close the database.

Exercise 8

1. Open the *mdbFanTours9-1* database you modified in Exercise 7.
2. Click the Relationships button on the Database toolbar to open the Relationships window. Double-click the center of the join line between the tblCustomers table and the tblBookings table.
3. In the Join Properties dialog box, set the join type as type 2 to include all records from the tblCustomers table and all records from the tblBookings table where the join fields match.
4. Save and close the Relationships window, and then close the database.

Case Projects

Project 1

During a power outage, you lost part of the work you did to set up relationships in the FanTours database. In addition, you need to set up new relationships. Open the *mdbFanTours9-2* database located on the Data Disk. Create a one-to-many relationship for the following tables: tblPayments and tblCustomers, and tblVendors and tblVCategories. Save the relationships and close the database.

Project 2

Open the *mdbFanTours9-2* database from Project 1. Create a many-to-many relationship for the tblEvents and tblCustomers tables by using the tblBookings table as a junction table. Enforce referential integrity in both relationships, and make both relationships type 2 joins. Save the relationships and close the database.

Project 3

Open the *mdbFanTours9-2* database from Project 2. Open the Relationships window and print a relationships report in Landscape orientation. Save the report and close the Relationships window. Close the database.

Project 4

Open the *mdbFanTours9-2* database from Project 3. Open the tblEvents table in Design view. Establish a data validation rule for the EventDate field. The EventDate should be no earlier than 10/1/2002 and no later than 1/1/2004. Create an appropriate validation text message that appears when users enter invalid dates. Save the table, allow Access to validate the existing data, and then close the table and close the database.

Project 5

Open the *mdbFanTours9-2* database from Project 4. Open the Relationships window. Set referential integrity for the relationship between the tblBookings and tblEmployees tables. The company wants to protect this relationship so that any time you change an EmployeeID, Access automatically updates the EmployeeID in all related records in the tblBookings table. Do this by setting the cascade update option for the relationship between the two tables. In the Relationships window, double-click the relationship line for the relationship between the tblBookings and tblEmployees tables. Click the Cascade Update Related Fields check box to add a check mark. Save the relationships, and then close the database.

Project 6

Open the *mdbFanTours9-2* database from Project 5. Open the tblCustomers table in Design view. Establish a data validation rule for ContactType field in this table. The contact type must be M, E, W, or P. However, some records have no contact type value, so you also must allow a blank. Create an appropriate data validation text message that appears when users enter invalid contact types. Save the table and then close the database.

Project 7

Connect to the Internet and load the home page for a search engine, such as *www.google.com*. Search for an online computer dictionary or encyclopedia, and find definitions for terms covered in this chapter, such as *referential integrity, relationships, one-to-many relationship*, and *joins*. Save at least two definitions in a Word document, print and close the document.

Project 8

Open the *mdbFanTours9-2* database from Project 6. Open the tblEventDetails table in Design view. Add a new 12-character text field named "VendorCategory." Create a combo box lookup control for the new field using the tblVCategories table as the row source. Modify the Column Count property to display two columns from the row source. Modify the Column Widths property so that the two columns are sized .25 and .75, respectively. Save the tblEventDetails table with your changes and switch to Datasheet view. Use the new VendorCategory combo box lookup field to update the records, then close the table and the database.

chapter nine

Access 2002

Working with Advanced Filters and Queries

Chapter Overview

With advanced filtering techniques, you can use complex criteria to narrow the number of records in a table or query. Special query types enable you to calculate total values, enter search criteria from a dialog box as you run the query, permanently change data in a table, and summarize large amounts of complex data. In this chapter, you create an advanced filter. Then you create and run total, parameter, action, and crosstab queries.

Learning Objectives

- Create and apply advanced filters
- Specify multiple query criteria
- Modify query properties
- Use aggregate functions in a query
- Create a parameter query
- Create an action query
- Create a crosstab query

Case profile

Michael Golden, who works in the registrar's office, wants to view a list of classes by delivery mode. Giang Hu, the accounting manager, wants to permanently modify the OLU database by removing all accepted students from the prospect list and changing the salary for all OLU teaching assistants. You use advanced filtering techniques and queries to make these changes.

chapter ten

10.a Creating and Applying Advanced Filters

You can use the advanced filter/sort techniques when specifying complex criteria that involve one or more fields. The advanced filter/sort grid is very similar to the query design grid. Each column represents a field for which you enter criteria expressions and set sort fields. You need to include only fields in the advanced filter that contain criteria expressions or sort instructions; the underlying table or query determines which fields appear in Datasheet view. The criteria expressions in an advanced filter are identical to those used in a query.

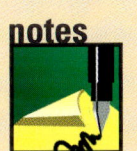

> **notes**
> In this chapter and the remaining chapters in this book, it is assumed that you know the correct button on the Objects bar to use when instructed to view an object. These chapters provide no detailed instructions to click a button on the Objects bar in the Database window.

Classes at OLU are delivered in one of four modes: classroom, correspondence, the Web, and television. The master list of delivery modes is maintained in the tblModes table. Michael needs a list of business (BUS), accounting (ACCT), and information technology (IT) classes that OLU does not deliver in a conventional classroom mode. To review the OLU class delivery modes:

Step 1	Create	a copy of the *mdbOnlineU10-* database located on the Data Disk
Step 2	Open	the tblModes table in Datasheet view
Step 3	Observe	the four delivery modes and their Mode IDs: 1=Classroom, 2=Correspondence, 3=Web, and 4=Television
Step 4	Close	the table

Now you are ready to create an advanced filter to show the business, accounting, and information technology classes that OLU does not deliver in a classroom mode (those that do not have Mode ID=1). To create the advanced filter:

Step 1	Open	the tblClasses table in Datasheet view
Step 2	Click	Records
Step 3	Point to	Filter

Step 4	Click	A̲dvanced Filter/Sort
Step 5	Double-click	DeptPrefix in the tblClasses table to add it to the filter design grid
Step 6	Double-click	DeliveryMode in the tblClasses table (you may need to scroll to view this field)
Step 7	Click	the Criteria: row beneath the DeptPrefix field
Step 8	Key	In (BUS, ACCT, IT)
Step 9	Press	the ENTER key
Step 10	Click	the Criteria: row beneath the DeliveryMode field, if necessary
Step 11	Key	Not 1
Step 12	Press	the ENTER key
Step 13	Click	the Apply Filter button on the Filter/Sort toolbar to apply the filter

Access filters the tblClasses table and displays the 13 records that meet the filter conditions. Your screen should look similar to Figure 10-1.

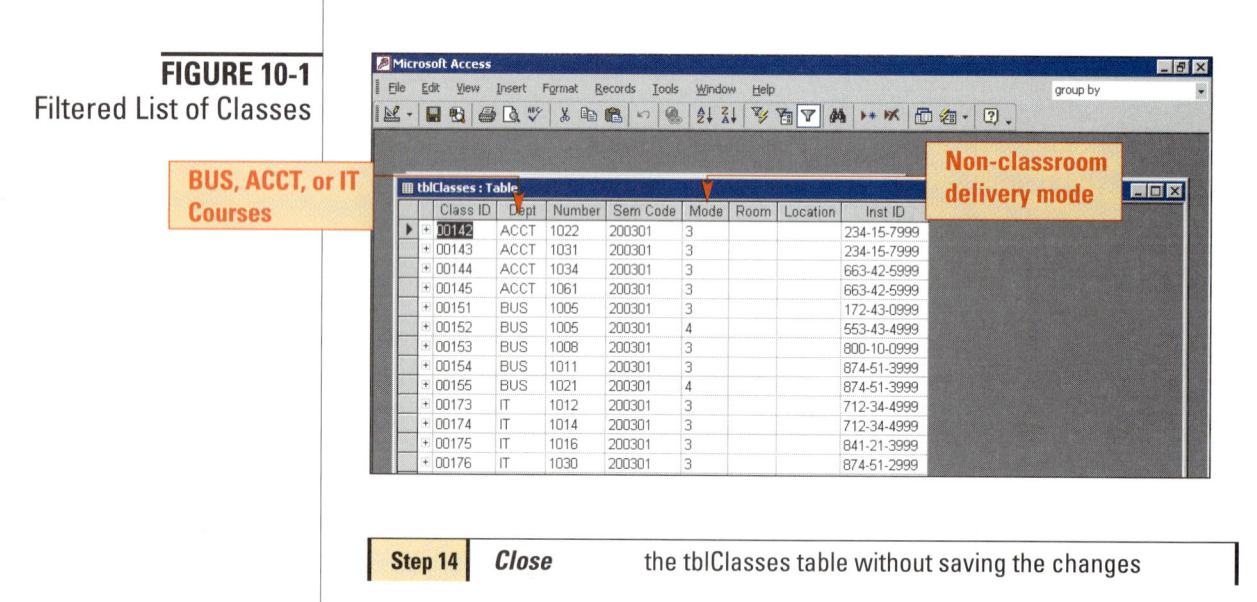

FIGURE 10-1
Filtered List of Classes

BUS, ACCT, or IT Courses

Non-classroom delivery mode

Class ID	Dept	Number	Sem Code	Mode	Room	Location	Inst ID
00142	ACCT	1022	200301	3			234-15-7999
00143	ACCT	1031	200301	3			234-15-7999
00144	ACCT	1034	200301	3			663-42-5999
00145	ACCT	1061	200301	3			663-42-5999
00151	BUS	1005	200301	3			172-43-0999
00152	BUS	1005	200301	4			553-43-4999
00153	BUS	1008	200301	3			800-10-0999
00154	BUS	1011	200301	3			874-51-3999
00155	BUS	1021	200301	4			874-51-3999
00173	IT	1012	200301	3			712-34-4999
00174	IT	1014	200301	3			712-34-4999
00175	IT	1016	200301	3			841-21-3999
00176	IT	1030	200301	3			874-51-2999

| Step 14 | Close | the tblClasses table without saving the changes |

You also can use compound criteria in a query to view a list of specific records.

10.b Specifying Multiple Query Criteria

You can use the query design grid to specify the fields included in a query as well as the criteria and sort instructions for a query. Multiple query criteria, also called **compound criteria**, occur when you specify more than one criteria expression for one or more fields. One way to specify multiple criteria for a single field is to place one criterion on the Criteria row and the other criteria on successive "or:" rows in the same column of the design grid. You can also create a compound criteria expression that involves multiple values for a single field by using a single expression with AND or OR. To create a query with multiple query criteria for a single field:

Step 1	Open	the qryInstructors query in Design view
Step 2	Click	the Criteria: row beneath the Title field (you may need to scroll right to view this field)
Step 3	Key	Lecturer
Step 4	Press	the DOWN ARROW key to move to the or: row beneath the Title field
Step 5	Key	Instructor
Step 6	Press	the ENTER key
Step 7	Run	the query to view the seven records where the Title field contains either Lecturer or Instructor

Next, you convert this query to a single criteria expression using the OR operator. To convert the query to a single criteria expression:

Step 1	Switch to	Design view
Step 2	Clear	the criteria expression in the or: row beneath the Title field
Step 3	Clear	the criteria expression in the Criteria: row beneath the Title field
Step 4	Key	Lecturer Or Instructor in the Criteria: row beneath the Title field
Step 5	Press	the ENTER key
Step 6	Observe	that Access converts your expression to "Lecturer" Or "Instructor"
Step 7	Run	the query

> **CAUTION TIP**
>
> You can specify criteria for more than one field in a query by placing the criteria expression in the Criteria: row for each field. Multiple criteria that appear on the *same row* in the query must all be true for a record to appear when you run the query; this is known as an AND query. If you specify criteria in a column on *different rows*, at least one of the criteria expressions must be true for a record to appear when you run the query; this is known as an OR query.

QUICK TIP

When you have criteria from more than one field in a query, it is better to use the OR operator for multiple values from one field so that the expressions can be placed on a single row in the query grid.

Access does not require that the case match your criteria expression. Thus, "BUS" and "Bus" and "buS" all match the BUS criteria.

| Step 8 | *Observe* | that the converted query returns the same seven records |
| Step 9 | *Close* | the query without saving the changes |

Michael wants to know which business or accounting classes OLU offers on the Web. Because each class record includes the delivery mode code, you can use a query to provide this information. To create a query that returns records for business or accounting classes delivered on the Web:

Step 1	*Open*	the qryClassOfferings query in Design view
Step 2	*Click*	the Criteria row beneath the DeptPrefix field
Step 3	*Key*	BUS Or ACCT
Step 4	*Click*	the Criteria: row beneath the DeliveryMode field (scroll to view this field)
Step 5	*Key*	3
Step 6	*Run*	the query
Step 7	*Observe*	that seven records match the multiple criteria you specified: delivery mode 3 (Web) with either BUS or ACCT department prefix

Your screen should look similar to Figure 10-2.

FIGURE 10-2
Web-based Business or Accounting Courses

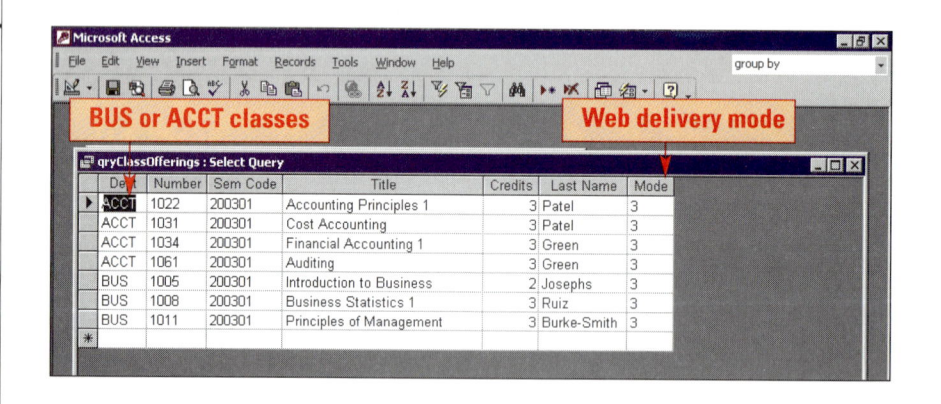

| Step 8 | *Close* | the query without saving the changes |

You can modify a query's field properties to further control how the results appear and which records are retrieved.

10.c Modifying Query Properties

Like other Access objects, queries have properties that affect fields' appearance and the records retrieved. Query **field properties** include Format, Input Mask, and Caption. Query field properties affect how records are displayed and include the following (default value are shown in bold):

- Default View for the query (**Datasheet**, PivotTable, or PivotChart)
- Top Values (**All**, 5, 25, 100, 5%, or 25% of the records appear)
- Unique Records (**No**, or Yes; if yes, this property causes the query to display only the first instance of duplicate records)
- Order By (specify a list of sort fields that is not in the query design itself; if a field appears in the list, it is assumed to be an ascending sort unless DESC follows the field name; by default, this is blank)
- Max Records (a long integer field that gives the maximum number of records returned by the query; by default, this is blank and all records are returned)

Michael wants to view a list of the first 25% of the new semester's class offerings. You already have a select query, qryClassOfferings, which returns a list of classes offered. You first run that query to view all classes offered, and then you modify it to return only the first 25% of classes offered. To run the query:

Step 1	Run	the qryClassOfferings query
Step 2	Observe	the list of records and the total number of records returned, which is 26

To modify the query to return the first 25% of the records:

Step 1	Switch to	Design view
Step 2	Click	the Properties button on the Query Design toolbar to display the Field Properties sheet
Step 3	Click	the top pane in the Query Design window to change the Field Properties sheet to the Query Properties sheet
Step 4	Click	the Top Values text box in the Query Properties sheet to view its list arrow
Step 5	Click	the list arrow
Step 6	Click	25%
Step 7	Run	the query

> **QUICK TIP**
>
> As with forms and reports, fields added to a query inherit field properties from the underlying table. If you set a caption for the field in Table Design view and add that field to a query, the query uses the same caption when the query appears in Datasheet view.
>
> You do not have to close the Query Properties sheet to run the query, but you may need to move it out of the way.

The query returns the first 7 records instead of 26 records. To modify the query to show all 26 records:

Step 1	**Switch to**	Design view
Step 2	**Click**	the top pane in the Query Design window to display the Query Properties sheet
Step 3	**Click**	the Top Values text box to view its list arrow
Step 4	**Click**	the list arrow in the Top Values text box
Step 5	**Click**	All
Step 6	**Run**	the query to view all 26 records
Step 7	**Switch to**	Design view
Step 8	**Close**	the Field Properties sheet
Step 9	**Close**	the query without saving the changes

Sometimes you need to perform calculations for groups of records returned by a query. You can do that by creating a totals query.

10.d Using Aggregate Functions in a Query

A **totals query** uses the Access aggregate functions (Sum, Avg, Count, Min, Max, StDev, and Var) to perform a calculation for groups of records retrieved by the query. You can do the calculation for all records in the query or perform the calculation for groups of records that share a common characteristic. Giang Hu, the accounting manager, wants to know how many instructors are in each department. You can query the tblInstructors and tblDepartments tables to find that information. You use the Count aggregate function in the query to calculate the number of instructors by department. To create a totals query to calculate the number of instructors in each department:

Step 1	**Create**	a new query in Design view
Step 2	**Double-click**	tblDepartments in the Show Table dialog box
Step 3	**Double-click**	tblInstructors in the Show Table dialog box
Step 4	**Close**	the Show Table dialog box
Step 5	**Double-click**	DeptName in the tblDepartments table

Working with Advanced Filters and Queries　　AA 27

Step 6	**Double-click**	Salary in the tblInstructors table
Step 7	**Click**	<u>V</u>iew
Step 8	**Click**	Tota<u>l</u>s to add the Total: row to the query grid

To calculate the number of instructors in each department, you group the records by department name. Access then counts the number of instructors for each distinct value in the DepartName field.

Step 9	**Verify**	that Group By is in the Total: row beneath the DeptName field
Step 10	**Click**	the Total: row beneath the Salary field to view its list arrow
Step 11	**Click**	the list arrow
Step 12	**Click**	Count (you may need to scroll to view this function)
Step 13	**Run**	the query

Your screen should look similar to Figure 10-3.

QUICK TIP

The Group By option defines the groups for which you want to perform the calculations. The Expression option creates a calculated field. The Where option specifies criteria for a field you are not using to define groups. For more information about these options and about creating calculations in a query, see online Help.

FIGURE 10-3
Number of Instructors by Department

Next, you calculate the average salary of instructors in each department and the sum of salaries in each department. You can do this easily using the Avg and Sum functions in a totals query. To modify the current totals query to calculate the average instructor's salary and to total all instructors' salaries in each department:

Step 1	**Switch to**	Design view
Step 2	**Double-click**	Salary in the tblInstructors table to add this field again to the query design grid (there will be two Salary fields)
Step 3	**Click**	the Total: row beneath the first Salary field
Step 4	**Click**	the list arrow

chapter
ten

Step 5	*Click*	Avg
Step 6	*Click*	the Total: row beneath the second Salary field
Step 7	*Click*	the list arrow
Step 8	*Click*	Sum
Step 9	*Run*	the query

Your screen should look similar to Figure 10-4. The first Salary column displays the average salary for each department, and the second Salary column displays the sum of salaries in each department.

FIGURE 10-4
Average and Total Salaries by Department

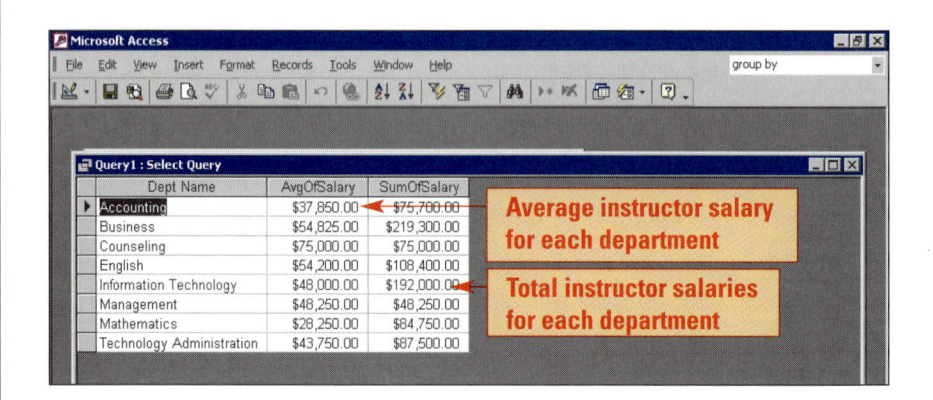

To save the modified query with a new name:

Step 1	*Click*	the Save button on the Query Datasheet toolbar
Step 2	*Key*	qryInstructorTotals in the Query Name text box of the Save As dialog box
Step 3	*Click*	OK
Step 4	*Close*	the query

When you need to enter different search criteria each time you run a query and do not want to modify the query design, you can use a parameter query.

10.e Creating a Parameter Query

A **parameter query** is an advanced select query that enables you to enter search criteria in a dialog box rather than specify the search criteria in the query's design grid. When you run a parameter query, you first see the Enter Parameter Value dialog box asking you to enter the specific search criteria. Access then returns the records that match the search criteria you enter.

Michael asks for an easy way to update prospective student status. Each prospective student has a record in the tblProspects table, and each record contains a status code: 1=prospect, 2=applicant, 3=admitted, and 4=no longer interested. You can use a parameter query to quickly find all prospective students by status. To create a parameter query to locate prospective students by status:

| Step 1 | Open | the qryProspects query in Design view |

You are ready to enter brief instructions for the prompt in the Enter Parameter Value dialog box. Because Michael is looking for prospect status, you can use "Enter status request (1-4)" as the prompt.

Step 2	Click	the Criteria: row for the Status field
Step 3	Key	[Enter status request (1-4)] (remember to include the brackets)
Step 4	Press	the ENTER key
Step 5	Widen	the Status column to display the entire expression
Step 6	Run	the query

The Enter Parameter Value dialog box on your screen should look similar to Figure 10-5.

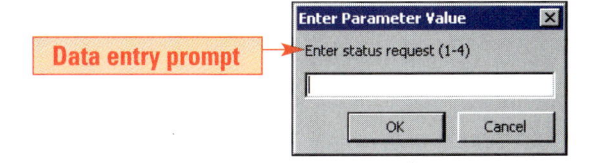

QUICK TIP

Parameter queries are handy when used with forms, reports, and data access pages. For example, you can create a monthly orders report based on a parameter query. When you print the report, Access displays a dialog box that asks for the month you want the report to include. You enter a month and Access prints the appropriate report.

CAUTION TIP

The square brackets in a query expression indicate that the query is a parameter query. Make sure to include them. If you omit the brackets, you receive an error message when you run the query.

FIGURE 10-5
Enter Parameter Value Dialog Box

Step 7	Key	1 in the Enter Parameter Value dialog box to select those records of prospective students with Status=1
Step 8	Click	OK

The parameter query returns the four records for prospective students with Status=1. Your screen should look similar to Figure 10-6.

FIGURE 10-6
Prospective Students with Status=1

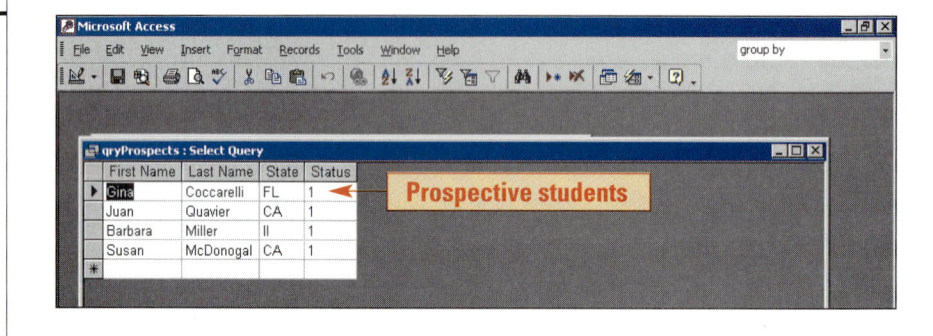

Quick Tip

By default, Access uses Text as the data type for parameters, but you can define the data type for each query parameter. To define the data type, open the Query Parameters dialog box from the Query menu. You must use this approach when you include a Yes/No data type as a parameter or when you use fields that come from a table in an external SQL database.

Creating Multiple Parameters

You can create queries that prompt for several parameters to find exactly the data you want. You can specify parameters in a number of different fields, or you can enter multiple parameters in one field. When you run a query with multiple parameters, Access prompts you to enter criteria for each parameter you set in successive dialog boxes. Michael wants to find prospective student records with a certain status in a certain state, such as all prospects from California. To create and run a query to find all prospective students from California:

Step 1	Switch to	Design view
Step 2	Click	the Criteria: row for the State field
Step 3	Key	[Enter state abbrev]
Step 4	Run	the query
Step 5	Key	CA in the first Enter Parameter Value dialog box
Step 6	Click	OK
Step 7	Key	1 in the second Enter Parameter Value dialog box
Step 8	Click	OK

The query returns all records for prospective students (Status=1) in California (State=CA).

Changing a Parameter Order

The leftmost parameter appearing in the query design grid is the first parameter the user is asked to enter. You change the parameter order in the query design grid by dragging the fields into the proper sequence.

Because entering the status code before entering the state is more efficient, you modify the query to move the Status column to the left of the State column. To reposition the Status column in the query grid:

Step 1	Switch to	Design view
Step 2	Click	the column selector box at the top of the Status column
Step 3	Drag	the Status column to the left of the State column

When you run the query, Access first prompts you to enter the status code and then prompts you for the state code.

Step 4	Run	the query
Step 5	Key	1 in the first Enter Parameter Value box
Step 6	Click	OK
Step 7	Key	CA in the next Enter Parameter Value box
Step 8	Click	OK to return the same two records
Step 9	Close	the qryProspects query and save the changes

When you need to modify a number of records very quickly, you can use an action query.

10.f Creating an Action Query

Unlike a select query, which retrieves records based on criteria you specify, an **action query** can change many records in one operation. For example, you can create new tables or permanently change data in existing tables. There are four types of action queries: (1) A **delete query** removes a group of records from one or more tables. You can use a delete query to remove discontinued courses. (2) An **update query** makes global changes to a group of records in one or more tables. For example, you can automatically raise lab fees by 10% for all classes, or

> **CAUTION TIP**
>
> Because you cannot use the Undo command to reverse changes made by an action query, making a backup copy of the table you are changing is a good idea. If you have sufficient hard drive space, make a backup copy of the entire database.

you can raise salaries by 5% for people within a certain job category. (3) A **make-table query** creates a new table from all or part of the data in one or more tables. (4) An **append query** inserts a group of records from one or more tables to the end of one or more different tables. For example, suppose that OLU acquires new students from the prospect list. You could simply append the list of new students to the current students table.

Creating a Delete Query

Michael asks you to remove all records of students who are no longer interested in enrolling at OLU (Status=4) from the tblProspects table. You use a delete query to do that. Before you create and run the delete query, you need to review the tblProspects table. To review the table:

Step 1	Open	the tblProspects table in Datasheet view
Step 2	Observe	the two student records with Status=4
Step 3	Close	the table

Because you cannot retrieve records after a delete query removes them, you decide to make a backup copy of the tblProspects table. After you test the query and are satisfied with its results, you can delete the backup table. To create a backup copy of the tblProspects table:

Step 1	Right-click	tblProspects in the Database window
Step 2	Click	Copy
Step 3	Right-click	the Database window
Step 4	Click	Paste
Step 5	Key	tblProspectsBackup in the Table Name: text box in the Paste Table As dialog box
Step 6	Verify	that the Structure and Data option button is selected
Step 7	Click	OK
Step 8	Observe	the new backup table, tblProspectsBackup, in the Database window

With a backup copy of the tblProspects table available in case a problem occurs, you can modify the qryProspects query to make it a delete query. Before you run a delete query, you should test the query as a select query to make sure that the query retrieves the proper records. Remember that Status 4 indicates students are no longer interested in enrolling at OLU. First, you create and run a select query to verify that it returns only the records with Status=4. Then you change the query type to a delete query and run it to remove the records with Status=4. To create and run the select query:

Step 1	Open	the qryProspects query in Design view
Step 2	Key	4 in the Criteria text box in the Status column
Step 3	Clear	the criteria from the State column
Step 4	Run	the query to view the two records that meet the criteria

To create and run the delete query:

Step 1	Switch to	Design view
Step 2	Click	the Query Type button list arrow on the Query Design toolbar
Step 3	Click	Delete Query
Step 4	Close	the qryProspects query and save the design changes
Step 5	Observe	the X indicating a delete query and the ! indicating an action query in front of qryProspects

When you run the qryProspects query, you delete the records with a Status=4.

Step 6	Run	the query
Step 7	Observe	the warning message
Step 8	Click	Yes
Step 9	Observe	the second message warning that you are about to delete two rows
Step 10	Click	Yes to run the query

To verify that you removed the two records with Status=4 from the tblProspect table:

Step 1	Open	the tblProspects table in Datasheet view
Step 2	Observe	that the two records with Status=4 are no longer in the table
Step 3	Close	the table

Because you have verified that the delete query executed properly, you can safely delete the tblProspectsBackup table. To delete the tblProspectsBackup table:

Step 1	*Right-click*	the tblProspectsBackup table in the Database window
Step 2	*Click*	Delete
Step 3	*Click*	Yes

Creating an Update Query

The university wants to increase teaching assistants' salaries by 4%. To change the current teaching assistants' salaries easily, you create an update query. You can simply modify an existing select query for instructors that includes title and salary. Because an update query permanently changes data in the tblInstructors table, you create a backup copy of the table in case the query changes records incorrectly. To create a backup copy of tblInstructors:

| Step 1 | *Create* | a backup copy of the tblInstructors table, and name it tblInstructorsBackup using the copy and paste method |
| Step 2 | *Observe* | the new backup table, tblInstructorsBackup, in the Database window |

Before creating the update query, you also want to review current teaching assistants' salaries. You can do this by running the existing select query. To run the qryUpdateInstructors query:

Step 1	*Run*	the qryUpdateInstructors query
Step 2	*Observe*	that the salary for each of the two teaching assistants is $8,500
Step 3	*Close*	the query

To create an update query that increases the teaching assistants' salaries by 4%:

Step 1	*Open*	the qryUpdateInstructors query in Design view
Step 2	*Click*	the Query Type button list arrow on the Query Design toolbar
Step 3	*Click*	Update Query

Working with Advanced Filters and Queries   AA 35

The Query window adds an Update To: row in the design grid. Enter the text in this row that you want the query to use to update those records that meet the query criteria.

Step 4	Key	[Salary]*1.04 in the Update To: row beneath the Salary field
Step 5	Click	the Criteria: row beneath the Title field
Step 6	Key	Teaching Assistant
Step 7	Press	Enter
Step 8	Run	the query
Step 9	Observe	the message warning that you are about to update two rows and cannot undo the query
Step 10	Click	Yes to update the salaries
Step 11	Close	the qryUpdateInstructors query and *do not save the changes*

To verify that the query updated the teaching assistants' salaries in the tblInstructors table:

Step 1	Open	the tblInstructors table in Datasheet view
Step 2	Observe	that the update query changed the two teaching assistants' salaries from $8,500 to $8,840
Step 3	Close	the tblInstructors table

You verified the actions of the update query, so you can now safely delete the backup table.

| Step 4 | Delete | the tblInstructorsBackup table |

Creating a Make-table Query

Michael wants you to create a new table containing records for prospective students who applied to OLU. You can do this by creating a make-table query based on the qryNewStudents query. The new table should contain records for prospective students with Status=2. To create and run a make-table query that creates a new table containing records for prospective students who have applied to OLU:

| Step 1 | Open | the qryNewStudents query in Design view |

QUICK TIP

You can update many fields at the same time by using an update query. Just fill in as many of the Update To: fields as necessary, and the query updates them all at once.

CAUTION TIP

Each time you run an update query, the data changes. For example, if you run the update query to change the teaching assistants' salaries twice, the query increases the salary field by 4% *twice*. Because of the danger of accidentally duplicating the update action, it is best not to save an update query.

If you inadvertently change a table that you do *not* want to keep, you cannot undo that operation. For example, to undo the salary update, you must modify the update query with an Update To expression of Salary/1.04 and use the same criteria. Running this update query changes the teaching assistants' salaries back to $8,500.

chapter ten

Step 2	Click	the Query Type button list arrow on the Query Design toolbar
Step 3	Click	Make-Table Query
Step 4	Key	tblNewStudents in the Table Name: list box in the Make Table dialog box
Step 5	Click	OK
Step 6	Run	the query
Step 7	Key	2 in the Enter Parameter Value dialog box to select only prospective students who are applicants
Step 8	Click	OK
Step 9	Observe	the message indicating that you are about to paste four rows into a new table and that you cannot undo the changes
Step 10	Click	Yes
Step 11	Close	the qryNewStudents query without saving the changes

To view the new tblNewStudents table:

Step 1	Open	the tblNewStudents table in Datasheet view
Step 2	Observe	that the query added four records from the tblProspects table with Status=2 to the tblNewStudents table
Step 3	Close	the table

Creating an Append Query

Michael asks you to also add any admitted students (Status=3) to the tblStudents table. You can add those records by creating an append query based on the qryNewStudents query, which already contains much of the information you need. Before you create the append query, you want to review the total number of students in the tblStudents table and create a backup copy of the table. To review the total number of students in the tblStudents table and create a backup of the tblStudents table:

Step 1	Open	the tblStudents table in Datasheet view
Step 2	Observe	that the last record is for Jeffrey Webb and that the table includes 54 records
Step 3	Close	the table
Step 4	Create	a backup copy of the tblStudents table named tblStudentsBackup using the copy and paste method

Working with Advanced Filters and Queries **AA 37**

To create and run an append query to add the new students to the tblStudents table:

Step 1	Open	the qryNewStudents query in Design view
Step 2	Click	the Query Type button list arrow on the Query Design toolbar
Step 3	Click	Append Query
Step 4	Click	tblStudents on the Table Name drop-down list in the Append dialog box
Step 5	Click	OK
Step 6	Run	the query
Step 7	Key	3 to select all admitted students' records
Step 8	Click	OK
Step 9	Observe	the message warning that you are about to append three rows and that you cannot undo the change
Step 10	Click	Yes
Step 11	Close	the qryNewStudents query without saving the changes

To review the results of the append query:

Step 1	Open	the tblStudents table in Datasheet view
Step 2	Scroll	to the bottom of the table
Step 3	Observe	that the three appended records follow Jeffrey Webb's record and that the number of records now totals 57
Step 4	Close	the table
Step 5	Delete	the tblStudentsBackup table

If you need to summarize data, you can use a crosstab query.

chapter ten

10.g Creating a Crosstab Query

Crosstab queries take a large amount of complex data and summarize some or all of that data in row-and-column format. This format helps you make comparisons and see trends in your data. You also can use a crosstab query as the basis for a report. Because a select query produces a long list of information, comparisons are difficult due to the amount of scrolling needed. A crosstab query, on the other hand, produces a more compact summary of the same information.

Michael wants you to summarize information from the tblStudents table. He wants to know the total number of students in each major by state. You can use the Crosstab Query Wizard to step through the creation of a crosstab query to summarize that information. To create a crosstab query to summarize information from the tblStudents table:

Step 1	*Create*	a new query using the New button [New] in the Database window
Step 2	*Double-click*	Crosstab Query Wizard
Step 3	*Click*	the Queries option button to view the queries in the database
Step 4	*Click*	qryStudents as the data source for this query (you may have to scroll to view this selection)
Step 5	*Click*	Next >

Because you are summarizing information in a row-and-column format, your first step is to choose the field values you want to use as row headings. Because there are so many states, listing the states on each row is practical. The crosstab report fits better on a sheet of paper.

| Step 6 | *Double-click* | State in the Available Fields: list |
| Step 7 | *Click* | Next > |

The next step is to choose the field values to use as column headings. The ProgramName field contains the name of each student's major, so you choose it for your column headings. Because Michael also wants to know the number of students in each major from each state, you then calculate the total number of students for each column and row intersection.

Working with Advanced Filters and Queries　　AA 39

Step 8	Click	ProgramName
Step 9	Click	Next >
Step 10	Click	FName in the Fields: list to specify the field to count, if necessary
Step 11	Click	Count in the Functions: list, if necessary
Step 12	Click	Next >
Step 13	Click	the Modify the design. option button, if necessary
Step 14	Click	Finish to accept the name of the query (qryStudents_Crosstab) and view the design
Step 15	Run	the query

MOUSE TIP

You can modify the column headings after you finish using the wizard by modifying the crosstab query's ColumnHeadings property. After you complete the query, open it in Design view, and then right-click the background to see the property list for the query.

Your screen should look similar to Figure 10-7.

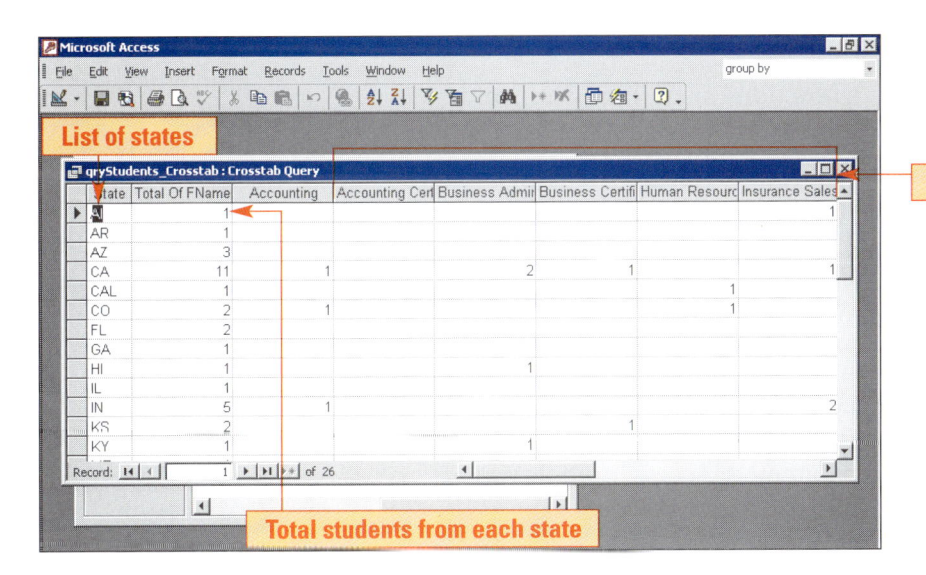

FIGURE 10-7
Crosstab Query Results

Step 16	Close	the qryStudent_Crosstab query and the database

Queries enable you answer specific questions about the data in a database.

chapter ten

Summary

▶ Advanced filter/sort lets you establish multiple filter criteria and/or sorting conditions for a table or a query without creating a query.

▶ You can specify multiple query criteria, called compound criteria, in the query design grid. Criteria that appear on the same row in the query design grid are AND conditions—all must be true for a record to appear. Criteria expressions on different lines are OR conditions—only one of the expressions must be true for a record to appear in the query datasheet. You can use AND and OR in the same criteria expression to set multiple conditions.

▶ You can modify the field properties in a query to change the caption, format, and input mask for a field. Queries inherit those field properties from the underlying data source if they exist when you create the query. You can also change query properties to change the way the records appear when the query runs.

▶ A totals query lets you use aggregate functions like Count, Sum, and Avg to perform calculations on grouped records.

▶ A parameter query is an advanced select query that asks you to enter search criteria in a dialog box. When you run a parameter query, the Enter Parameter Value dialog box lets you enter specific search criteria, which Access then uses to return the data that matches the criteria.

▶ You can create queries that prompt for several parameters to find exactly the data you want. You can specify parameters in a number of different fields, or you can enter multiple parameters in one field. When you run a query with multiple parameters, Access prompts you to enter criteria for each parameter you set in successive dialog boxes.

▶ The parameter listed first in the Query Parameters dialog box is the first parameter the user is asked to enter. You change parameter order in the Query Parameters dialog box by rekeying the information and changing data types, if necessary.

▶ Action queries change many records in just one operation. There are four types of action queries: A delete query removes a group of records from one or more tables. An update query makes global changes to a group of records in one or more tables. A make-table query creates a new table from all or part of the data in one or more tables. An append query inserts a group of records from one or more tables to the end of one or more different tables.

▶ Crosstab queries take a large amount of complex data and summarize some or all of that data in a row-and-column format. That format helps you make comparisons and see trends in your data. You can also use a crosstab query as the basis for a report.

Commands Review

Action	Menu Bar	Shortcut Menu	Task Pane	Toolbar	Keyboard
Create an advanced filter	Records, Filter, Advanced Filter/Sort				ALT + R, F, A
Create a totals query	View, Totals			Σ	ALT + V, L
Create a make-table query	Query, Make Table Query	Query Type, Make-Table Query			ALT + Q, K
Create an update query	Query, Update Query	Query Type, Update Query			ALT + Q, U
Create an append query	Query, Append Query	Query Type, Append Query			ALT + Q, P
Create a delete query	Query, Delete Query	Query Type, Delete Query			ALT + Q, D
Create an action query	Query, *query type*	Query Type			ALT + Q
Create a crosstab query	Query, Crosstab Query				ALT + Q, B

Concepts Review

Circle the correct answer.

1. Which filter is best to use when you have multiple criteria from two or more fields?
   - [a] Advanced Filter/Sort
   - [b] Parameter Filter
   - [c] Filter By Form
   - [d] Filter By Selection

2. The purpose of an update query is to:
   - [a] limit the number of records shown.
   - [b] display records that match the criteria entered.
   - [c] delete records from a table.
   - [d] replace information in a table.

3. You can use a totals query to:
   - [a] retrieve all records in a table.
   - [b] permanently change data in a table.
   - [c] perform calculations on fields in sub-groups of records.
   - [d] substitute criteria when you run the query.

4. If you have multiple parameters in a parameter query:
   - [a] the leftmost parameter field appears first when you run the query.
   - [b] the rightmost parameter field appears first when you run the query.
   - [c] the first parameter you added to the query appears first when you run the query.
   - [d] only the first parameter that you enter affects which records the query retrieves.

5. If you have criteria expressions in two columns of a query in the same row:
   - [a] both criteria must be true for a record to appear when you run the query.
   - [b] either criteria can be true for a record to appear when you run the query.
   - [c] only one criteria can be true for a record to appear when you run the query.
   - [d] combine the criteria into an OR expression in one column.

6. Which type of action query adds records to an existing table?
   - [a] update query
   - [b] append query
   - [c] make-table query
   - [d] delete query

chapter ten

7. To summarize a large amount of data in a compact row-and-column format, you use a(n):
   [a] parameter query.
   [b] update query.
   [c] crosstab query.
   [d] select query.

8. You can use a make-table query to:
   [a] create a new table from all or part of the data in one or more tables.
   [b] make global changes to a group of records in one or more tables.
   [c] add records to a selected table.
   [d] prompt users to enter criteria for each parameter.

9. Action queries differ from select queries because they:
   [a] permanently change data in the database for selected records.
   [b] retrieve records based on multiple criteria.
   [c] use backup copies of tables instead of originals.
   [d] require you to use parameters.

10. You should make a backup copy of a table:
    [a] before running an action query that changes data in the table.
    [b] each time you exit Access.
    [c] after you create a parameter query.
    [d] after you run a delete query.

Circle **T** if the statement is true or **F** if the statement is false.

T F   1. You can limit the output of a query to the first 25 records.
T F   2. You should make copies of a table before you run an action query on the table.
T F   3. Parentheses surround a parameter query's criteria prompt in the query design grid.
T F   4. You can change the criteria in a parameter query when you run the query.
T F   5. A crosstab query is a type of action query.
T F   6. An append query adds groups of records to the end of a table.
T F   7. If an error results from running an action query, simply click the Undo command to reverse the query's actions.
T F   8. You should test your action query as a select query before you convert it to an action query.
T F   9. You can use an update query to delete records.
T F   10. A crosstab query shows calculated results for subgroups of data.

Skills Review

Exercise 1

1. Create a copy of the *mdbFanTours10-* database located on the Data Disk.
2. Open the tblProspects table in Design view, and review the ContactType description. Then switch to Datasheet view, and filter the table to identify the number of records with a "W" contact type. Remove the filter and close the table without saving the changes.
3. Open the qryProspects query in Design view.
4. Create a parameter query to retrieve records from qryProspects based on the ContactType field.
5. Prompt the user to enter the customer contact type (M, E, W, or P).

6. Run the query and test it by keying "W" when prompted. Verify that the number of records returned by the query agrees with the number of W contact types you identified in Step 2.

7. Use the Save As command on the File menu to save the query as "qryProspectsContactType," close the query, and then close the database.

Exercise 2

1. Open the *mdbFanTours10-1* database you modified in Exercise 1.

2. Open the tblProspects table in Datasheet view, and filter the table to identify the records with the contact type W and a contact date after 2/1/2002. Remove the filter and close the table without saving changes.

3. Open the qryProspectsContactType query that you created in Exercise 1 in Design view.

4. Add another parameter to the query to retrieve prospect records that occur *after* the contact starting date. The criteria expression has this form: > [parameter prompt message].

5. Prompt the user to enter the starting contact date.

6. Run and test the query by keying "W" when prompted for the contact type and 2/1/2002 when prompted for the starting contact date. Verify that the query returns the records that you identified in Step 2.

7. Save the query as "qryProspectsContactDate," close the query, and then close the database.

Exercise 3

1. Open the *mdbFanTours10-1* database you modified in Exercise 2.

2. Open the tblCustomers table in Datasheet view, and filter the table to identify the total number of records for each contact type, including the total number of records with no contact type. Remove any filters and close the table without saving any changes.

3. Create a new query in Design view using the ContactType and State fields from the tblCustomers table.

4. Convert the query to a totals query. Group the records by ContactType, and count the State field.

5. Run the query. Verify that the number of query results match your count in Step 2.

6. Save the query as "qryCustomersContactType," close the query, and then close the database.

Exercise 4

1. Open the *mdbFanTours10-1* database you modified in Exercise 3.

2. Make a backup copy of tblBookings named "tblBookingsBackup." Open the tblBookingsBackup table in Datasheet view, and filter the EventID field to identify the number of records with an EventID=4. Remove the filter and close the table without saving changes.

3. Create a new query in Design view using the CustID and EventID fields from the tblBookingsBackup table.

4. Add criteria to select customers with EventID=4. Run the query to make sure it returns the same number of records you identified in Step 2.

5. Switch to Design view, and convert the query to a delete query that removes all records with EventID=4.

6. Run the delete query, and verify that you deleted the same number of records you identified in Steps 2 and 4.

7. Save the query as "qryDeleteBookings" and close it. *Do not delete the tblBookingsBackup table.*

8. Close the database.

chapter ten

Exercise 5

1. Open the *mdbFanTours10-1* database you modified in Exercise 4.

2. Run the qryCustomerBookings query and review the results. Identify the number of records in which the Event is Rose Bowl.

3. Switch to Design view, and add a criterion to select only those records with the EventName Rose Bowl. Run the query to test it, and verify that the number of records returned equals the number of records you identified in Step 2.

4. Switch to Design view, and convert the query to a make-table query that makes a new table called "tblRoseBowl."

5. Run the query to test it, and confirm the number of records you are pasting into the new table equals the number of records you identified in Steps 2 and 3.

6. Save the query as "qryRoseBowl," and close it.

7. Open the tblRoseBowl in Datasheet view, review the records, and then close the table.

8. Close the database.

Exercise 6

1. Open the *mdbFanTours10-1* database you modified in Exercise 5.

2. Open the tblBookings table and use the Advanced Filter/Sort command to filter the table to view all records with EventID=3 or a registration date after 12/31/2002.

3. Print the filtered table.

4. Remove the filter and close the table without saving any changes.

5. Close the database.

Exercise 7

1. Open the *mdbFanTours10-1* database you modified in Exercise 6.

2. Open the tblCustomers table in Datasheet view, and use the Advanced Filter/Sort command to filter the table to show only those records for customers who live in NM or NC.

3. Print the filtered table.

4. Remove the filter and close the table without saving any changes.

5. Close the database.

Exercise 8

1. Open the *mdbFanTours10-1* database you modified in Exercise 7.

2. Create a new query using the Crosstab Query Wizard.

3. Select the tblCustomers table as the data source for crosstab query results.

4. Make State the row headings field and ContactType the column headings field.

5. Calculate the count of the CustID field. (You use this field because it is required for all records.)

6. Save the query as the "qryCustomers_Crosstab," run the query, and print a copy of the crosstab query's datasheet.

7. Close the query and close the database.

Case Projects

Project 1
Using the Office on the Web command on the Help menu, open the Microsoft Office Update home page and then link to pages that provide information about action queries. Print at least one Web page.

Project 2
Connect to the Internet and search for an online computer dictionary or encyclopedia, such as *www.webopedia.com*, and find definitions for terms covered in this chapter, such as *parameter, filter, query, append,* and *action query*. Print at least two definitions or explanations.

Project 3
Open the *mdbFanTours10-2* database located on the Data Disk. Catherine Emmen, the marketing manager, wants to produce a query that shows prospects by state. Create a parameter query that Catherine can use to identify prospects by state. Print one datasheet for a particular state, such as CA. Save the query as "qryProspectsByState." Close the query, and then close the database.

Project 4
Open the *mdbFanTours10-2* database that you modified in Project 3. Catherine also wants to calculate the average down payment received for all bookings. You can do this by creating a totals query and using the Avg function. Open the qryCustomerBookings query in Design view, and then remove all but the EventName and DownPaymentRecd fields. Add the Total: row to the query design grid. Group by EventName and calculate the average of the down payments received. Run the query to view the results. Save the query as "qryAveragePayment," close the query, and then close the database.

Project 5
Open the *mdbFanTours10-2* database that you modified in Project 4. Catherine wants you to create a new table with complete information about each customer who booked the Rose Bowl trip, EventID=1. Call the table "tblRoseBowlers" and call the query "qryRoseBowlers." Print a copy of the new table. Close the table, and then close the database.

Project 6
Open the *mdbFanTours10-2* database that you modified in Project 5. FanTours just learned that an employee who requested emergency family leave needs to be replaced in the tblEventDetails table. Create an update query to replace StaffID 123417999 with 872234781 for EventID=3. Call this query "qryReplaceEmployee." Run the query, open the table, and confirm the changes. Close the table, and then close the database.

Project 7
Open the *mdbFanTours10-2* database that you modified in Project 6. Open the qry2001Prospects query in Design view. Add the Status field to this query. Create criteria to select only those prospective customers from 2001 whose Status field values are not 2. Run the query, print a copy of the results, and save the query. Close the query, and then close the database.

Project 8
Open the *mdbFanTours10-2* database that you modified in Project 7. Create a crosstab query that shows which employees (by name) are working on which events (by name). First create a select query that includes the tblEmployees, tblEvents, and tblEventDetails tables. Create a single field that concatenates the FirstName and LastName fields from the tblEmployees table, named "Employee." Save the query as "qryEventEmployees," and then create a crosstab query using this query as the data source. The row heading field should be Employee. The column heading field should be EventName. Use the Count function for the EventID field in the query. Save the crosstab query as "qryEventEmployees_Crosstab." Close the query, and then close the database.

chapter ten

Access 2002

Advanced Form Features

Chapter Overview

Creating a form in Design view enables you to control the placement and appearance of form controls. A subform is a form within a form. A switchboard form helps users navigate a database. In this chapter, you create a form from scratch in Design view, insert and position the appropriate form controls, and then insert a subform. You also create a switchboard form to display menu choices when a database is opened.

Learning Objectives

- Create a form in Design view
- Create a subform
- Create a switchboard form

Case profile

Jung Me, an assistant registrar at OLU, wants you to create a form that makes it easier to review student information, including the classes for which students are registered. You use a subform to provide the information Jung needs. Finally, you add a switchboard form to help Jung and his staff use the OLU database more easily.

chapter eleven 11

Advanced Form Features   AA 47

11.a Creating a Form in Design View

Form Design view is frequently used to modify a form created by the Form Wizard. You also can create a new form in Design view, which lets you customize the form by placing controls at precise locations, use the types of controls you want, and adjust control properties to best fit the data.

Creating a form in Design view is a four-step process:
1. Create a blank form in Design view.
2. Open the Field List window, and drag fields to the Detail section.
3. Open the Toolbox and add controls.
4. Modify the properties of these controls.

You decide to create a student form that has room for registration information. To create the student registration form in Design view:

Step 1	Create	a copy of the *mdbOnlineU11-* database located on the Data Disk
Step 2	Create	a new form using the New button [New] in the Database window
Step 3	Click	Design View in the New Form dialog box, if necessary
Step 4	Click	qryStudentAdvisors in the Choose table or query where the object's data comes from: list
Step 5	Click	OK

Access opens a new form in Design view and automatically displays the Field List window. The Toolbox may also be visible. If not, you can display it.

| Step 6 | Click | the Toolbox button [tool] on the Form Design toolbar to display the Toolbox, if necessary |

notes The illustrations in this chapter show the Formatting (Form/Report) toolbar docked at the top of the window below the Form View or Form Design toolbars. Your Formatting (Form/Report) toolbar may be positioned differently.

QUICK TIP

A form contains up to five sections: the **Detail section** contains the controls that display data from the underlying data source; the **Form Header section** appears at the top of the form and can be used to display a title or graphic image like a logo; the **Form Footer section** appears at the end of the form and can contain command buttons that cause some action, such as printing a form; the **Page Header section** appears only at the top of a *printed* form; the **Page Footer section** appears only at the end of the *printed* form.

chapter eleven

QUICK TIP

The gridlines in Design view help you place and align controls. You can use the vertical and horizontal rulers to place controls at specific locations.

You can use the ARROW keys to nudge a selected control left, right, up, or down. This is a great way to fine-tune the positioning of controls.

CAUTION TIP

The form's tab order is the sequence in which the insertion point moves as you tab from control to control. By default, the tab order is the same sequence in which the fields are added to the form. If you make changes or add controls out of order, you can modify the tab order with the Tab Order command on the View menu in Design view.

You drag fields from the Field List window to the Detail section of the form to create label and text box controls. To add the label and text box controls for the StudentID, FName, MName, LName, DeptName, and Advisor fields to the form:

Step 1	**Drag**	the StudentID field from the qryStudentAdvisors Field List window to the Detail section and drop it at the 1-inch horizontal and the 0-inch vertical position
Step 2	**Observe**	that a pair of controls, a label, and a text box bound to the StudentID field are inserted

Next, you add the three name fields, but use one label.

Step 3	**Drag**	the FName field from the Field List window to the Detail section and drop it one gridline below the StudentID field text box control
Step 4	**Drag**	the MName field from the Field List window to the Detail section and drop it one gridline to the right of the FName text box control (the MName label control overlaps the FName text box control)
Step 5	**Click**	the MName label control to select it
Step 6	**Press**	the DELETE key to delete the MName label control (do not delete the MName text box control)
Step 7	**Follow**	Steps 4 through 6 to drag the LName field from the Field List window to the Detail section, drop it one gridline to the right of the MName text box control, and then delete the overlapping LName label control
Step 8	**Drag**	the DeptName field from the Field List window to the Detail section and drop it one gridline below the FName text box control
Step 9	**Drag**	the Advisor field from the Field List window to the Detail section and drop it one gridline below the LName text box control
Step 10	**Verify**	that the Advisor label and text box controls are still selected
Step 11	**Press**	the LEFT ARROW key twice to nudge the controls two gridlines to the left until only one gridline remains between the DeptName text box control and the Advisor label control

Modifying Form and Control Properties

Sometimes it is helpful to be able to modify the properties of a form, form sections, or the controls within a form. Some properties are accessible through buttons on the Form Design toolbar or through commands on the menu bar. You can view and modify other properties within the appropriate Properties sheet. In Design view, you can display a form or form control's Properties sheet in a variety of ways:

- Double-click a control in the form's Design window.
- Right-click a control and select Properties.
- Click the Properties button on the Form Design toolbar.
- Click Properties on the View menu.

After the Properties sheet is open, you can click a control in the Design window to display that control's properties. You also can select a control's name from the list box at the top of the Properties sheet. The Properties sheet has multiple tabs to organize individual properties. The All tab contains all properties for the control; the other tabs contain subsets of the properties.

Because the fields for a student's entire name are now on one row, you need to change the FName label control's caption property from "First Name" to "Student Name." You then want to size the label control to fit its contents. To modify the FName label control's caption property and size the label control:

Step 1	Double-click	the FName label control (contains the First Name caption) to open its Properties sheet
Step 2	Click	the Format tab, if necessary
Step 3	Select	the contents of the Caption text box, if necessary
Step 4	Key	Student Name:
Step 5	Close	the Properties sheet
Step 6	Right-click	the FName label control (contains the Student Name: caption)
Step 7	Point to	Size
Step 8	Click	To Fit to expand the size of the control to fit its contents

> **QUICK TIP**
>
> When you need more information about a specific property, click the property's text box in the Properties sheet and press the F1 key to display online Help for that property.

Aligning Controls

If necessary, you can select and align multiple controls. You can align the selected controls at the top, bottom, left, or right. To align the student name controls:

Step 1	Click	the FName (Student Name) label control in the Detail section to select it, if necessary
Step 2	Select	the FName, MName, and LName text box controls using the SHIFT + Click method
Step 3	Verify	that the label and all three student name text box controls are selected
Step 4	Click	Format

Step 5	*Point to*	<u>A</u>lign
Step 6	*Click*	<u>T</u>op to align the group of selected controls
Step 7	*Deselect*	the controls
Step 8	*Select*	and nudge the remaining controls into place, if necessary, using Figure 11-1 as your guide

Your screen should look similar to Figure 11-1.

FIGURE 11-1
Completed Form in Design View

MOUSE TIP

The Select Objects button in the Toolbox enables you to select a group of controls in one form section using the mouse pointer to draw a selection rectangle around the desired controls. Starting at an empty spot in the design grid, press and hold the mouse button and drag over the controls you want to include in the selection group. When you release the mouse button, all controls within the selection rectangle are selected.

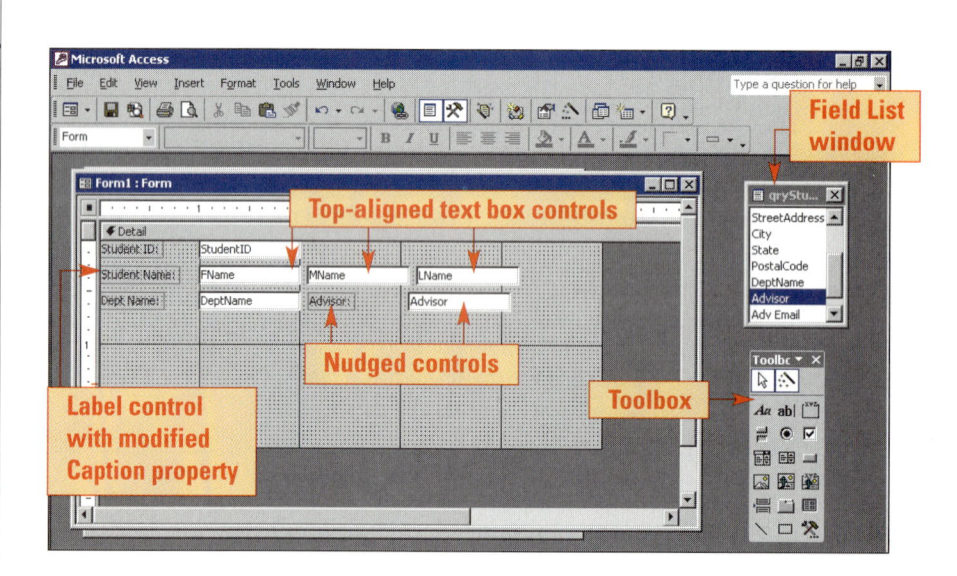

Step 9	*Click*	the Save button on the Form Design toolbar
Step 10	*Key*	frmStudentClasses in the Form Name: text box
Step 11	*Click*	OK

When you want to view related information from two or more tables at the same time, you can use a subform.

11.b Creating a Subform

A **subform** is a smaller form within a form. The outer form is the **primary form** and contains the subform. You can use subforms when you want to show data from tables or queries that have a one-to-many relationship—one field in the subform is related to many fields in the primary form. For example, Jung wants to add a subform to the frmStudentClasses form to show class data from the tblRegistrations table. The data in the tblStudents table is the "one" side of the relationship.

The data in the tblRegistration table is the "many" side of the relationship—each class can have many students. The primary form and the subform in this type of form are linked so that the subform displays only records related to the current record in the primary form. This means that when Jung displays the primary frmStudentClasses form, he sees the classes for which the current student is registered in the subform.

Planning a Subform

Before you create a primary form and subforms, you should plan what to include and how to use the subform. Jung wants his staff to answer questions about class registration as they speak to students on the phone. When a student calls, Jung wants a student service representative to open the student's record, see the classes the student took in the past, and then enter new class information. He also wants the representative to verify billing address information and change it if necessary. To do this, Jung and his staff need to work with the frmStudentClasses form and the frmRegistration form at the same time.

You can create a form with subforms in a number of ways. You can use the Form Wizard to create a form and a subform at the same time, based on existing tables. Even if you already created the forms that serve as the primary form and the subform, you can use the Form Wizard to step through the creation of a form with subforms. The Form Wizard also is the best choice if you already set up a one-to-many relationship between the tables or queries you want to use to create the form and subform.

If you already created the primary form, you can open it in Design view and use the Control Wizard to add the subform. Once you become familiar with forms and subforms, you can add an existing form to another form in Design view to create a subform. You also can modify the design of any form with subforms in Design view. If you created a subform with a datasheet layout, you can modify its layout in Form view.

Adding a Subform Control

You are ready to create a subform that shows the classes taken by each OLU student. To add a subform control to an existing form using the SubForm Wizard:

Step 1	**Verify**	that the frmStudentClasses form is open in Design view
Step 2	**Click**	the Control Wizards button in the Toolbox to select it, if necessary
Step 3	**Click**	the Subform/Subreport button in the Toolbox

> **QUICK TIP**
>
> A primary form can have any number of subforms. You also can nest a subform within a subform. To create a new form with subforms using the Form Wizard, add fields from *more than one* related table or query to the Selected Fields. Access automatically determines that your form should have a subform and asks you questions about how to display your data. You then indicate which table/query should be in the primary form and which table/query should be in the subform. See online Help for more information about creating forms with subforms.

| Step 4 | Click | in the Detail section at the 1-inch vertical and 0-inch horizontal position to place the upper-left corner of the subform at the left margin of the primary form, approximately eight gridlines below the DeptName label |

The first SubForm Wizard dialog box opens. The SubForm Wizard, similar to other wizards, guides you step-by-step through the process of creating a subform. In this case, you use an existing form for the class information. The form already contains fields for Student ID, Class Code, Department, Course Number, and Semester Code.

Step 5	Click	the Use an existing form option button
Step 6	Click	frmRegistration in the list box
Step 7	Click	Next >

The wizard asks whether you want to define the fields to link your primary form to the subform yourself or choose from the list. You want to define your own fields to set up Jung's primary form and subform so that related class information is in the subform for each student in the primary form. The field that links the primary and subform is the StudentID field.

Step 8	Click	the Define my own. option button
Step 9	Click	the list arrow in the first Form/report fields: list box
Step 10	Click	StudentID
Step 11	Click	the list arrow in the first Subform/subreport fields: list box
Step 12	Click	StudentID
Step 13	Click	Next >
Step 14	Key	sbfRegisteredClasses as the name of the subform
Step 15	Click	Finish
Step 16	Deselect	the Subform
Step 17	Size	the frmStudentClasses: form window, if necessary, to view the complete subform

> **QUICK TIP**
>
> If you do not use a wizard to create a form and subform, you still can show related records in the subform. Do so by linking (also called **synchronizing**) the primary form and the subform, using the Link Child Fields and Link Master Fields properties of the subform control. Use online Help to learn more about creating subforms.

Your screen should look similar to Figure 11-2.

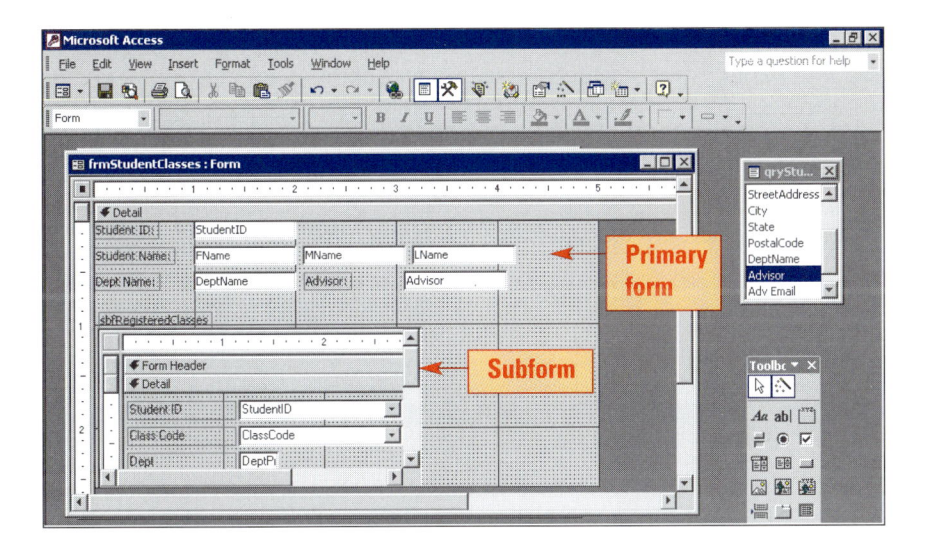

FIGURE 11-2
Primary Form and Subform in Design View

The primary form window now includes another Design view window complete with rulers for viewing and editing the subform.

Modifying Subform Properties

After you create a primary form with a subform, you can change the layout of the subform either in Form view or Design view. Use Form view to modify how the subform presents data. You can change the width of a column, the order of the columns, and the height of the rows. You also can hide, show, or freeze a column. Use Design view to change the size and position of the subform within the primary form. Jung wants to adjust the size of the subform. To size the subform within the primary form in Design view:

Step 1	Verify	that the frmStudentClasses primary form and the sbfRegisteredClasses subform are open in Design view
Step 2	Click	the subform to select it and view its sizing handles
Step 3	Point to	the subform's middle-right sizing handle to view the double-headed arrow sizing pointer
Step 4	Drag	the sizing handle to the right to the 4-inch mark on the horizontal ruler to increase the width of the subform

You also need to modify the primary form by moving the Advisor label control to the right so that it is closer to the Advisor text box control and enlarging the DeptName text box control. To reposition and resize controls in the primary form:

Step 1	Click	the Advisor label control in the primary form to select it

chapter eleven

Step 2	*Drag*	the Advisor label control move handle to the right and drop it one gridline to the left of the Advisor text box control
Step 3	*Click*	the DeptName text box control to select it
Step 4	*Drag*	the middle-right sizing handle on the DeptName text box control to the right until one gridline is between it and the Advisor label control
Step 5	*Deselect*	the DeptName text box control

Your screen should look similar to Figure 11-3.

FIGURE 11-3
Modified Primary Form and Subform Layout

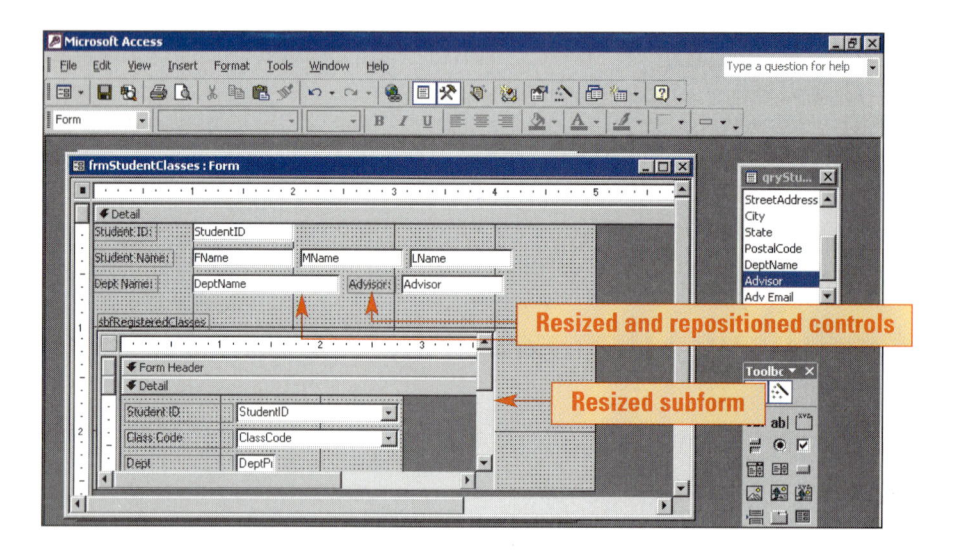

| Step 6 | *Save* | the form |
| Step 7 | *Close* | the Field List window and the Toolbox |

Viewing a Primary Form and Subform

In the frmStudentClasses form, the primary form shows student information and the subform shows the classes for which a student has registered. To view student records using the frmStudentClasses form:

| Step 1 | *Switch to* | Form view |
| Step 2 | *Observe* | that the primary form shows student information, but the subform is blank because this student has not registered for any classes |

Your screen should look similar to Figure 11-4.

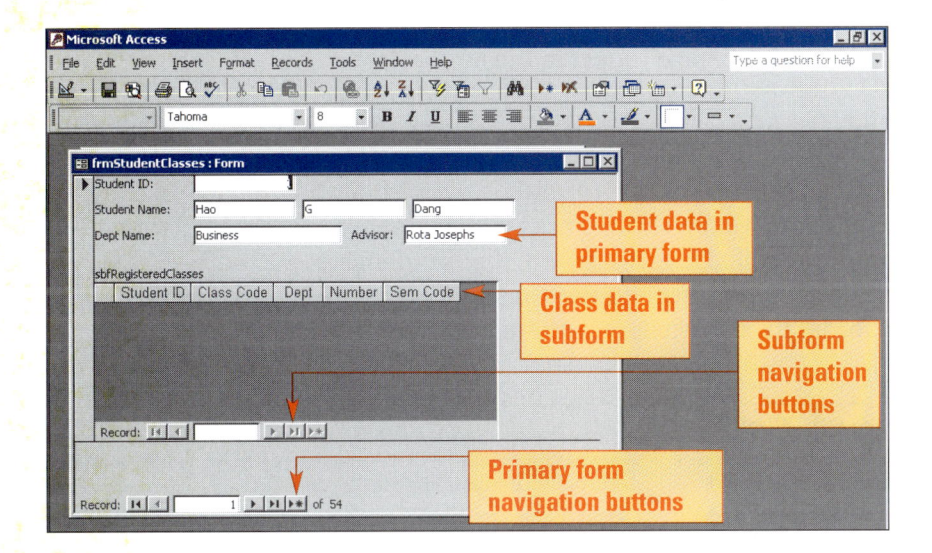

FIGURE 11-4
Form and Subform in Form View

The outside (lower) navigation buttons apply to the primary form and the inside navigation buttons apply to the subform. If you want to view a different student, use the outside navigation buttons. If you want to scroll to see which classes a particular student took, use the inside navigation buttons.

Step 3	Click	the Next Record button in the outside navigation area twice to view Judy Falk's record, record 3
Step 4	Observe	that Judy registered for three classes
Step 5	Click	the Next Record button in the inside navigation buttons to move to Judy's second class in the subform
Step 6	Close	the form

You can help users navigate around a database by adding a switchboard form.

11.c Creating a Switchboard Form

A **switchboard form** is a form that contains command buttons in a menu format. A **command button** is a button on a form or report that starts an action or series of actions. If desired, you can specify that a switchboard form open automatically when a database opens. You also can have a switchboard form command button open another switchboard. For example, you might have a Print Reports command button in the main switchboard that opens another switchboard form with buttons for each report in the application.

Using the Switchboard Manager

You can create, customize, and delete a switchboard using the Switchboard Manager. Jung asks you to create a switchboard form, commonly called a switchboard, that his department can use to quickly access the frmStudentClasses form and other forms in the OLU database. To create a new switchboard for the OLU database:

Step 1	*Click*	<u>T</u>ools
Step 2	*Point to*	<u>D</u>atabase Utilities
Step 3	*Click*	<u>S</u>witchboard Manager
Step 4	*Click*	Yes to create a new switchboard

The Switchboard Manager dialog box on your screen should look similar to Figure 11-5.

FIGURE 11-5
Switchboard Manager Dialog Box

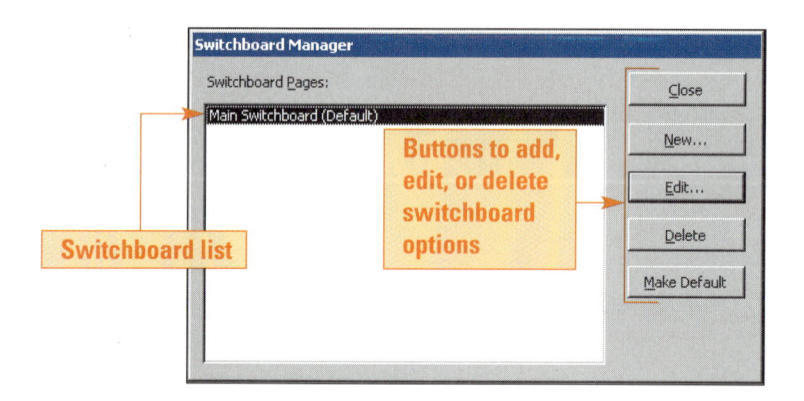

You can edit the default Main Switchboard or create a new switchboard. You need to create a new switchboard for Jung named "frmSwitchboard."

Step 5	*Click*	New
Step 6	*Key*	frmSwitchboard in the Switchboard Page <u>N</u>ame: text box in the Create New dialog box
Step 7	*Click*	OK

| Step 8 | Observe | that the new switchboard page, frmSwitchboard, is added to the list of switchboard pages in the Switchboard Manager dialog box |

You are ready to edit the frmSwitchboard form to add a command button to open the frmStudentClasses form. To edit the switchboard:

Step 1	Click	frmSwitchboard in the Switchboard Pages: list to select it
Step 2	Click	Edit to open the Edit Switchboard Page dialog box
Step 3	Click	New

The Edit Switchboard Item dialog box on your screen should look similar to Figure 11-6.

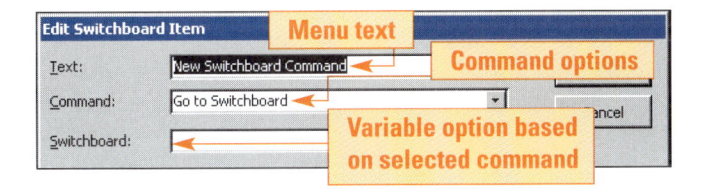

FIGURE 11-6
Edit Switchboard Item Dialog Box

You key the text you want to appear on the switchboard item and select the appropriate command for the item. The command you select determines the remaining dialog box options. Jung wants to be able to open the frmStudentClasses, frmStudents, frmInstructors, frmDepartments, and frmRegistration forms quickly from the new switchboard and add or edit the records.

CAUTION TIP

When you use the Switchboard Manager to create a switchboard, Access creates a Switchboard Items table that describes what buttons on the switchboard form display and do. If you modify the switchboard form in Design view, the switchboard may no longer work properly.

Step 4	Key	Open the StudentClasses Form in the Text: text box
Step 5	Click	the Command: list arrow
Step 6	Click	Open Form in Edit Mode
Step 7	Observe	that the third list in the dialog box now becomes the Form: list, which allows you to specify which form to open
Step 8	Click	the Form: list arrow
Step 9	Click	frmStudentClasses
Step 10	Click	OK

chapter eleven

The Open the StudentClasses Form item is added to the Items on this Switchboard: list in the Edit Switchboard Page dialog box. To add the remaining form items—frmStudents, frmInstructors, frmDepartments, and frmRegistration—to the frmSwitchboard form:

Step 1	*Click*	New in the Edit Switchboard Page dialog box listing the frmSwitchboard items
Step 2	*Key*	Open the Students Form in the Text: text box
Step 3	*Click*	Open Form in Edit Mode in the Command: list
Step 4	*Click*	frmStudents in the Form: list
Step 5	*Click*	OK
Step 6	*Follow*	Steps 1 through 5 to add the frmInstructors, frmDepartments, and frmRegistration items to the switchboard

The Edit Switchboard Page dialog box on your screen should look similar to Figure 11-7.

FIGURE 11-7
Edit Switchboard Page Dialog Box

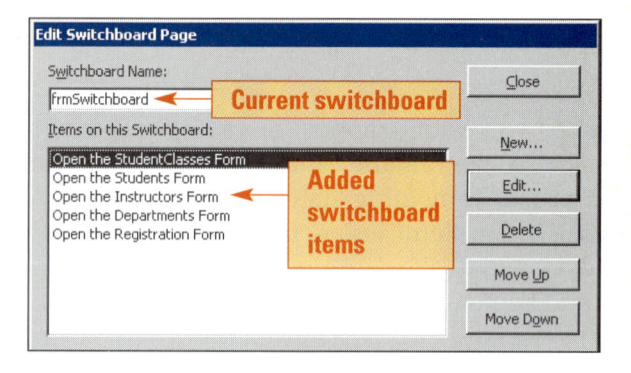

| Step 7 | *Close* | the Edit Switchboard Page and Switchboard Manager dialog boxes |
| Step 8 | *Observe* | that the Switchboard form is added to the database |

Setting Startup Options for a Switchboard Form

Jung wants the new switchboard to be the default switchboard for the database and to open automatically when the database opens. You set the default switchboard in the Switchboard Manager dialog box. To have a switchboard automatically open when the database opens, you must add the switchboard name to the startup information for the database. To make the frmSwitchboard form the default switchboard:

Step 1	*Open*	the Switchboard Manager dialog box
Step 2	*Click*	frmSwitchboard in the Switchboard Pages: list to select it
Step 3	*Click*	Make Default
Step 4	*Observe*	that the frmSwitchboard form is now marked as the default switchboard
Step 5	*Close*	the Switchboard Manager dialog box

To add the frmSwitchboard to the database startup options:

Step 1	*Click*	Tools
Step 2	*Click*	Startup
Step 3	*Click*	the Display Form/Page: list arrow in the Startup dialog box
Step 4	*Click*	Switchboard
Step 5	*Click*	OK

Changes to the database startup options don't take effect until the next time you open the database. To test the new switchboard:

Step 1	*Close*	the *mdbOnlineU11-1* database
Step 2	*Open*	the *mdbOnlineU11-1* database

The new frmSwitchboard form opens. Your screen should look similar to Figure 11-8.

FIGURE 11-8
frmSwitchboard Form

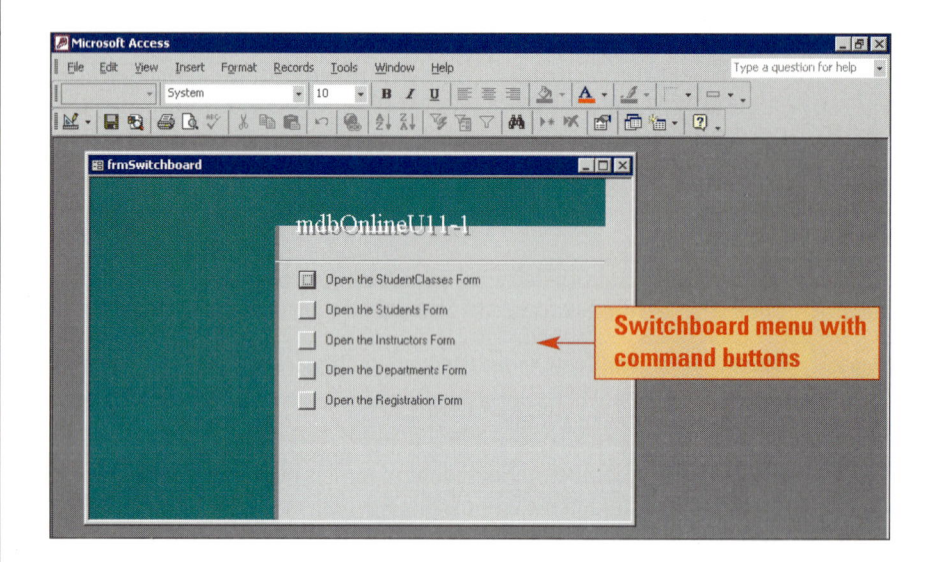

Step 3	Click	the Open the StudentClasses Form command button
Step 4	Observe	that the frmStudentClasses form opens in Form view and provides access to 54 student records
Step 5	Close	the frmStudentClasses form
Step 6	Continue	to test the new switchboard by clicking each command button, verifying that the correct form opens in Form view, and then closing the form
Step 7	Close	the switchboard and the database

The switchboard form makes it simple to open the forms in the database.

> **QUICK TIP**
>
> You can edit or delete an existing switchboard form by opening the Switchboard Manager, selecting the switchboard, and clicking the Edit or Delete buttons.

Summary

- Creating a form from scratch in Design view lets you add and position controls and modify their properties. To create a form in Design view, you first create a blank form and then drag fields from the Field List window to create label and text box controls or add other controls using the Toolbox. You can use the rulers, gridlines, and alignment options to position controls in the Design window.

- A Properties sheet displays the properties for form objects, including the form, its sections, and its controls.

- A subform is a smaller form within a form. The primary form, or outer form, contains the subform.

- You can link the primary form and subform so that the subform displays only those records related to the current record in the primary form.

- You can use the Form Wizard to create a form and subform at the same time based on existing tables. The Form Wizard also is the better choice if you already set up a one-to-many relationship between the tables or queries you want to use to create the form and subform.

- To add a subform to an existing form, open the form in Design view and then use the Subform/Subreport button in the Toolbox to add the subform.

- After you create a form with a subform, you can modify a subform in either Form view or Design view. Use Form view to modify how the subform presents data. Use Design view to modify the size and position of the subform within the primary form.

- A switchboard form is a form that contains command buttons in a menu format. You can create, edit, and delete a switchboard form with the Switchboard Manager.

chapter eleven

Commands Review

Action	Menu Bar	Shortcut Menu	Toolbar	Task Pane	Keyboard
Display Field List window	View, Field List				ALT + V, L F8
Nudge a control to the next gridline position					LEFT ARROW, RIGHT ARROW, UP ARROW, DOWN ARROW
View properties for form objects and controls	View, Properties	Right-click object or control, Properties Double-click the form object or control			ALT + V, P
Add a subform to an existing form					
Move from the last field in the primary form to the first field in the subform		Click the first field in the subform			TAB
Move from the first field in the subform to the last field in the primary form		Click the last field in the primary form			CTRL + SHIFT + TAB
Create, edit, or delete a switchboard	Tools, Database Utilities, Switchboard Manager				ALT + T, D, S
Set startup options for a switchboard	Tools, Startup				ALT + T, U

Concepts Review

Circle the correct answer.

1. In which form section do the fields in the underlying table appear?
   - [a] Form Header
   - [b] Page Header
   - [c] Record
   - [d] Detail

2. To create a form from scratch in Design view:
   - [a] open the Field List window, drag fields to the form, create a blank form, open the Toolbox, add other controls, and modify control properties.
   - [b] create a blank form, open the Field List window, drag fields to the form, open the Toolbox, add other controls, and modify control properties.
   - [c] modify control properties, open the Toolbox, add other controls, open the Field List window, drag fields to the form, and create a new blank form.
   - [d] create a blank form, modify form controls, open the Field List window, drag fields to the form, open the Toolbox, and add other controls.

3. A subform is a:
   - [a] link to a Web site.
   - [b] way to set a one-to-many relationship.
   - [c] smaller form within a form.
   - [d] primary form.

4. You can use a subform to:
   - [a] print a form.
   - [b] give instructions to users within the form.
   - [c] provide a way for Access users to work with an on-screen menu.
   - [d] show related data from other tables or queries.

5. To move a control up, down, left, or right in small increments in Design view, you can press the:
   [a] TAB key.
   [b] ENTER key.
   [c] ARROW keys.
   [d] SHIFT key.

6. To select a group of controls in Design view, you click the first control and then:
   [a] click each remaining control in succession.
   [b] SHIFT + Click each remaining control.
   [c] ALT + Click each remaining control.
   [d] press the TAB key for each remaining control.

7. To create a primary form and a subform at the same time, you use the:
   [a] Primary Wizard.
   [b] Form Wizard.
   [c] Switchboard Wizard.
   [d] Link Wizard.

8. You use the *inner* navigation buttons in a form with a subform to navigate through records in the:
   [a] primary form.
   [b] subform.
   [c] Properties sheet.
   [d] Form Wizard.

9. A switchboard form contains command buttons in a:
   [a] subform.
   [b] PivotTable.
   [c] menu.
   [d] datasheet.

10. To delete a switchboard, you can use the:
    [a] Event Manager.
    [b] Form Manager.
    [c] Command Manager.
    [d] Switchboard Manager.

Circle **T** if the statement is true or **F** if the statement is false.

T F 1. You can use a Properties sheet to adjust the properties of form controls.

T F 2. You can select and align multiple controls at the top, bottom, left, and right edge of the first control.

T F 3. When working with subforms, the inner form is the primary form and the outer form is the subform.

T F 4. A primary form can have only one subform.

T F 5. A command button is a button on a form or report that starts an action or a series of actions.

T F 6. To have a switchboard open automatically when the database opens, you should make the switchboard the default switchboard and then modify the database startup options.

T F 7. You can link a form and a subform by specifying the Link Master Fields and Link Child Fields properties.

T F 8. When you enter information on a subform, Access stores the data in a new table.

T F 9. Once you create a switchboard, you cannot edit its contents.

T F 10. A database can have only one switchboard form.

chapter eleven

Skills Review

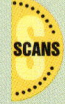

Exercise 1

1. Create a copy of the *mdbFanTours11*- database located on the Data Disk.
2. Create a blank form in Design view based on the tblEmployees table.
3. Open the tblEmployees Field List window, if necessary, drag the following fields from the Field List window to the Detail section of the form, and drop them in the following locations:
   - the EmployeeID and HireDate fields on the first line
   - the FirstName and LastName fields on the second line
4. Reposition the label and text box controls attractively in the form using the alignment options and the ARROW keys.
5. Save the new form as "frmEmployees."
6. Close the new form and close the database.

Exercise 2

1. Open the *mdbFanTours11-1* database you created in Exercise 1.
2. Open the frmEmployees form in Design view.
3. Delete the label control for LastName. Modify the caption property for the FirstName label control (currently First) to "Employee Name:" and size the label control to fits its contents.
4. Switch to Form view and scroll through the records to see if the field widths are appropriate and if the fields are positioned attractively on the form.
5. Switch to Design view and adjust the width of the EmployeeID and HireDate text box controls to make them approximately 25% smaller.
6. Use the ARROW keys to nudge the LastName text box control until it is one gridline to the right of the FirstName field.
7. Drag the HireDate text box control to the left until it is one gridline to the right of the HireDate label control.
8. Drag the ID label control to the right until it is one gridline to the left of the EmployeeID text box control.
9. Use the ARROW keys to nudge the EmployeeID label control (caption is Employee Name) to the right until it is one gridline to the left of the FirstName text box control.
10. Save and close the form, and then close the database.

Exercise 3

1. Open the *mdbFanTours11-1* database you modified in Exercise 2.
2. Open the frmEmployees form in Design view.
3. Display the form header and footer sections with the Form Header/Footer command on the View menu. Close the Form Footer section by dragging up its bottom border.
4. Insert the image file *fst.bmp* located on the Data Disk into the upper-left corner of the Form Header section using the Picture command on the Insert menu. Size the height of the Form Header section as needed to fit the image.

5. Add a label with the company name, Fantastic Sports Tours, to the Form Header section and position it to the right of the logo image. Format the label text with the bold, italic, 16-point font, and then resize the label to view the entire text, if necessary.

6. Save and close the form, and then close the database.

Exercise 4

1. Open the *mdbFanTours11-1* database you modified in Exercise 3.

2. Open the frmProspects form in Design view.

3. Rearrange the controls on the frmProspects form so that they meet the following requirements:

- At least one horizontal gridline should be between each line of controls and at least one vertical gridline should be between controls on the same line.
- The ProspectID controls should be at the top of the Detail section.
- The ContactType and ContactDate controls should be on the same line below the ProspectID controls.
- Add the Status label and text box controls to the Detail section, placing them on the same line and to the right of the ContactType and Contact Date controls.
- The FName, MName, and LName text box controls should appear on the third line, with one label control with the caption "Name."
- The EmailAddress controls should appear on one line below the name controls.
- The City, State, and PostalCode controls should appear on one line, with one label control containing the caption "Address."
- The Country controls should appear on one line below the other address controls.
- All label controls are sized to fit their contents (use the SHIFT + Click method to select the label controls).

4. Switch to Form view and review the text box control sizes in relation to their contents. Then switch to Design view and resize the individual text box controls as necessary.

5. Save and close the form, and then close the database.

Exercise 5

1. Open the *mdbFanTours11-1* database you modified in Exercise 4.

2. Open the frmEmployees form in Design view.

3. Use the SubForm Wizard to create a subform positioned at the 1-inch vertical position and the 0-inch horizontal position in the Detail section below the other controls. Use the qryStaffEvent query for the data source, and include all fields in the subform: EventName, DetailName, DetailLocation, DetailDate, DetailTime, and StaffID. Define your own link using the EmployeeID field in the primary form and the StaffID field in the subform. Name the subform "sbfEventDetails."

4. Save and close the form, and then close the database.

chapter eleven

Exercise 6

1. Open the *mdbFanTours11-1* database you modified in Exercise 5.

2. Open the tblEventDetails table in Datasheet view, and sort the Staff column in ascending order. Count the number of events assigned to each staff member, remove the sort, and then close the table without saving any changes.

3. Open the frmEmployees form in Form view. Size the form so that the entire subform appears, including its navigation area, if necessary.

4. Scroll the records in the primary form using the outer navigation buttons. Verify that the number of records shown in the subform for each employee equals the number of records you counted in Step 2.

5. Close the form and close the database.

Exercise 7

1. Open the *mdbFanTours11-1* database you modified in Exercise 6.

2. Create a new switchboard named "frmSwitchboard."

3. Edit the frmSwitchboard form to add menu and control button items to open the following forms in edit mode: frmBookings, frmCustomers, frmEmployees, and frmProspects.

4. Make the frmSwitchboard form the default switchboard.

5. Open the switchboard form (double-click its icon), and then test the command buttons by opening and closing their respective forms.

6. Close the switchboard form and close the database.

Exercise 8

1. Open the *mdbFanTours11-1* database you modified in Exercise 7.

2. Modify the database startup options to open the default switchboard each time the *mdbFanTours11-1* database opens.

3. Close the database and then reopen it to verify that the default switchboard opens automatically.

4. Close the switchboard and close the database.

Case Projects

Project 1

Using the Office on the Web command on the Help menu, open the Microsoft Web site and then link to pages that provide information about switchboards. Print at least one Web page.

Project 2

You want to create more forms and subforms on your own, but need to know more about how Access synchronizes primary forms and subforms. Search online Help for information about subforms to learn how Access synchronizes primary forms and subforms. Print the Help topics and then summarize the information in a Word document.

Project 3

Open the *mdbFanTours11-2* database located on the Data Disk. Create a blank form in Design view, using the tblEvents table as the data source. Use all fields from the table in the form, and position them attractively in the Detail section of the form. Size the labels as necessary. Save the form as "frmEvents," and then close the form and close the database.

Project 4

Open the *mdbFanTours11-2* database you modified in Project 3. You want to make the frmEvents form more useful and informative by adding a title to the form header and the current date with a control to the form footer. Open the form in Design view, add the header and footer sections, and then click the header section. Add the title label using the text "List of Events." Format the title text as desired, and resize the label and header section as necessary. To add the current date, click the footer section and insert a text box control at the left margin. Enter the expression "=Date()" in the unbound text box control. Save the form, test your changes in Form view, and then close the form and the database.

Project 5

Open the *mdbFanTours11-2* database you modified in Project 4. You want to customize the form sections to make the frmEvents form more visually appealing. Change the color of fields in the form to bright red. Open the form in Design view, and select all the fields with the Select All command on the Edit menu. Right-click a field, point to Font/Fore Color, and then click the Red color (the first color in the third row) on the color palette. Save the form, review it in Form view, and then close the form and the database.

Project 6

Open the *mdbFanTours11-2* database you modified in Project 5. You decide to create a switchboard form from which users can open other forms. Create a blank form and then add menu items and command buttons to open the following forms: frmEmplPhotos, frmProspects, frmVendors, and frmCustomers. Use the name of the form as part of the label for each command button. Save the form as "frmSwitchboard" and make it the default form. Test the switchboard form and then close the form and the database.

Project 7

Open the *mdbFanTours11-2* database you modified in Project 6. Edit the frmSwitchboard form using the Switchboard Manager to add the rptEvents, rptProspectList, and rptVendors reports and to delete the frmVendors form from the switchboard. Save the form as "frmReportSwitchboard," and then close the database. Test the switchboard, and then close the switchboard and the database.

Project 8

Open the *mdbFanTours11-2* database you modified in Project 7. You want the frmSwitchboard form to open automatically when the database opens. Change the database startup settings so that happens. Then close the database and reopen it to test your changes. Close the switchboard and the database.

chapter eleven

Access 2002

Customizing Reports

Chapter Overview

When you create a custom report from scratch in Design view, you can control the content, layout, and formatting of the report. In this chapter, you create a report in Design view, and then sort and group the data in the report. You modify properties of report objects and use the subreport control to create a subreport in Design view. Then you create a grouped report from a parameter query and customize the report in Design view.

Learning Objectives

- Create a custom report in Design view
- Sort and group data on a report
- Add a subreport to an existing report
- Run a grouped report from a parameter query

Case profile

Denise Washington, a supervisor in the registrar's office, often requests a variety of student reports from the OLU database. She recently asked you to create a new report that provides class information by student. She also requested modifications to an existing report to include a subreport. To create and modify these reports, you use advanced report features in Access.

chapter twelve

12.a Creating a Custom Report in Design View

Recall that the Report Wizard can quickly create a report for you. If you want more control over a report's layout and formatting, you can create a custom report from scratch in Design view. When you create a custom report in Design view, each field must be placed in the proper location in the correct section, and that requires planning. Before you begin to create the report, you should first sketch how the report should look. Consider issues such as what fields to include; the amount of space each field requires; the appropriate formatting choices; the page orientation; whether to include calculated fields (such as subtotals) and report footers (such as page numbers or dates); and whether to group report data in a special way. Because making changes in the report's design is easy, you do not need to make all report design decisions before you create the report; however, you should have at least a basic plan in mind.

Denise needs a report that lists each student and the classes in which he or she is enrolled, including the class instructors' names. Because you intend to build this report in Design view, you must be sure the relevant tables are joined. In this case, you need fields from the following tables: tblStudents, tblRegistration, tblClasses, tblCourses, and tblInstructors. To open the database and verify the table relationships:

Step 1	Create	a copy of the *mdbOnlineU12-* database located on the Data Disk
Step 2	Open	the Relationships window
Step 3	Verify	the relationships between the tblStudents, tblRegistration, tblClasses, tblCourses, and tblInstructors tables
Step 4	Close	the Relationships window

The report Denise needs contains student information provided by the qryStudentClasses query. You use this query as the basis for the report. To create a report in Design view based on the qryStudentClasses query:

Step 1	Click	Reports on the Objects bar
Step 2	Click	the New button in the Database window
Step 3	Switch to	Design view, if necessary

chapter twelve

| Step 4 | Click | qryStudentClasses in the Choose the table or query where the object's data comes from: list box |
| Step 5 | Click | OK |

The blank report opens in Design view, and the qryStudentClasses Field List window also opens. The Toolbox may also open. If it does not, you can open it.

| Step 6 | Click | the Toolbox button on the Report Design toolbar to display the Toolbox, if necessary |

notes The illustrations in this chapter show the Formatting (Form/Report) toolbar docked below the Report Design toolbar. Your Formatting (Form/Report) toolbar's position may differ.

Denise wants the report title and column heading label controls on each page of the report, so you place these controls in the Page Header section. To add the title and column header label controls to the Page Header section:

Step 1	Click	the Label button in the Toolbox
Step 2	Click	the upper-left corner of the Page Header section to place the title label control
Step 3	Key	OLU Student Classes Report
Step 4	Press	the ENTER key to complete the label
Step 5	Click	the Font Size button list arrow on the Formatting (Form/Report) toolbar
Step 6	Click	20 in the Font Size list box
Step 7	Right-click	the title label control
Step 8	Point to	Size
Step 9	Click	To Fit to enlarge the label control to fit the resized text

notes When you use the To Fit option, sometimes you still have to adjust the label control manually to make the text totally visible.

| Step 10 | Drag | the bottom edge of the Page Header section down to approximately the .75-inch position to enlarge the Page Header section and make room for the column headings |

When you add fields to the report, Access creates two controls—a label control and a bound text box control that takes its value from a field in the underlying table or query. Because Denise wants column headings (label controls) on each page, you move each text box's label control to the Page Header section after adding the controls to the Detail section. You can drag related label and text box controls from one report section to another, but to reposition just the label control, you must use the Cut and Paste method. To add the StudentID field to the Detail section and then reposition its label control in the Page Header section:

Step 1	Drag	the StudentID field from the Field List window to the 1-inch horizontal position and the 0-inch vertical position in the Detail section
Step 2	Right-click	the StudentID label control
Step 3	Click	Cu<u>t</u>
Step 4	Click	the Page Header section
Step 5	Click	the Paste button on the Report Design toolbar to paste the label in the Report Header section
Step 6	Observe	that the StudentID label pasted in the upper-left corner of the Page Header section overlaps the title label control
Step 7	Verify	that the StudentID label control is selected
Step 8	Press	the DOWN ARROW several times to nudge the StudentID label control down to approximately the .5-inch vertical position below the title label control

To save space in the report, you want to change the StudentID label control caption from "StudentID" to "ID" and then resize the control. To change the StudentID label control caption and resize the control:

Step 1	Right-click	the StudentID label control
Step 2	Click	<u>P</u>roperties to display the control's Properties sheet
Step 3	Click	the Format tab, if necessary
Step 4	Key	ID in the Caption text box
Step 5	Close	the Properties sheet

chapter twelve

Caution Tip

Pasting a control in a section automatically places it in the upper-left corner, sometimes on top of a previous control. To move the top control from that stack, point to the move handle in the upper-left corner of the control until the mouse pointer becomes a hand with one pointing finger. Then drag the top control to the desired location. If it is difficult to see and point to the control's move handle, you can use the ARROW keys to nudge the selected control into the desired position.

Step 6	Size	the StudentID label control (its current caption is ID) to fit using the shortcut menu
Step 7	Click	the Center button on the Formatting (Form/Report) toolbar to center-align the caption

To reposition, resize, and format the StudentID text box control:

Step 1	Select	the StudentID text box control
Step 2	Drag	the StudentID text box control to the left edge of the Detail section (0-inch horizontal position) to position it directly below its label control
Step 3	Resize	the StudentID text box control to the same size as its label control using the mouse pointer
Step 4	Click	the Center button on the Formatting (Form/Report) toolbar to center the contents of the control

To add the FName, tblStudents.LName, and ClassCode fields to the Detail section and then reposition the label controls and text box controls:

Step 1	Drag	the FName field from the Field List window to the Detail section and drop it at the 1-inch horizontal position and 0-inch vertical position
Step 2	Cut	the FName label control
Step 3	Paste	the FName label control in the Page Header section
Step 4	Reposition	the FName label control one gridline to the right of the StudentID label control
Step 5	Reposition	the FName text box control in the Detail section below its label control, approximately one gridline to the right of the StudentID text box control
Step 6	Size	the FName text box control approximately the same size as its label control
Step 7	Follow	Steps 1 through 6 above to drag the tblStudents.LName field from the Field List window to the Detail section, move its label control to the Page Header section and reposition it one gridline to the right of the FName label control, and reposition and resize its text box control
Step 8	Follow	Steps 1 through 6 above to drag the ClassCode field from the Field List window to the Detail section, move its label control to the Page Header section and reposition it one gridline to the right of the tblStudents.LName label control, and reposition and resize its text box control

| Step 9 | Select | the ClassCode label and text box controls and center their contents |
| Step 10 | Drag | the lower border of the Detail section up so it's just high enough to display the controls |

To edit the Caption properties for the FName, tblStudents.LName, and ClassCode label controls:

Step 1	Display	the Format tab in the Properties sheet for the FName label in the Page Header section
Step 2	Remove	the colon (:) from the FName Caption property
Step 3	Click	the tblStudents.LName label control
Step 4	Remove	the colon (:) from the tblStudents.LName label's Caption property
Step 5	Click	the ClassCode label control
Step 6	Remove	the colon (:) from the ClassCode label control
Step 7	Close	the Properties sheet

You want to clearly separate the report column labels (label controls) from the report details (text box controls), so you insert a horizontal line in the Page Header section below the label controls. To insert a horizontal line:

Step 1	Click	the Line button in the Toolbox
Step 2	Move	the mouse pointer to the 0-inch horizontal position at the first gridline below the label controls in the Page Header section
Step 3	Drag	to the right across the horizontal gridline to the 2.5-inch position, taking care to keep the mouse pointer on the horizontal gridline, which keeps the line straight (when the line is straight, you cannot see it as you drag; if you can see the line as you drag, the mouse pointer is either above or below the horizontal gridline)
Step 4	Deselect	the horizontal line
Step 5	Compare	your screen to Figure 12-1, and adjust the positions and sizes of the controls in your report, if necessary

After making any necessary adjustments to the position of the report controls, your screen should look similar to Figure 12-1.

FIGURE 12-1
Custom Report in Design View

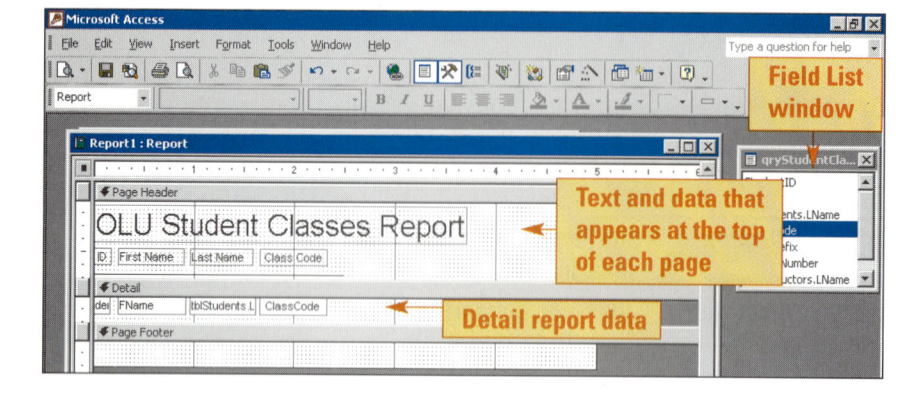

To preview the report:

Step 1	Switch to	Print Preview
Step 2	Observe	the layout of the report, noting that each student registered for multiple classes is listed multiple times
Step 3	Switch to	Design view
Step 4	Save	the report as rptStudentClasses, and leave it open in Design view

After reviewing the report, Denise asks you to modify the report so that each student's ID and name appear only once, followed by his or her class information, including total number of credit hours.

> **MOUSE TIP**
>
> You can drag one corner of a line control up or down to align it horizontally. Click the line to select it, and then drag the left or right move handle as necessary. Dragging the center move handle moves the whole line.

12.b Sorting and Grouping Data on a Report

When you create a report with the Report Wizard, you define the sorting and grouping criteria as part of the wizard process. When you create a report from scratch in Design view, you use the Sorting and Grouping dialog box to define sorting and grouping criteria. In order for the rptStudentClasses report to list each student's name once followed by his or her class information, you should group the report by StudentID. To define the grouping criteria for the rptStudentClasses report:

Step 1	Verify	that the rptStudentClasses report is open in Design view

| Step 2 | Click | the Sorting and Grouping button on the Report Design toolbar to open the Sorting and Grouping dialog box |

The Sorting and Grouping dialog box lets you specify the field(s) used for sorting and grouping. When you select a field to sort or group on, you can choose whether to show group header and footer sections. The **group header section** is typically used to introduce the group. The **group footer section** follows the last entry in the group and is often used to show cumulative values such as the number of records in the group or other subtotals.

| Step 3 | Click | the list arrow in the first row in the Field/Expression column |
| Step 4 | Click | StudentID from the list of fields |

Denise wants students listed in ascending order by StudentID. Also, to enhance the report's readability, she wants the report to include introductory and summary information for each student. You can provide this introductory and summary information by adding StudentID group header and footer sections to the report.

Step 5	Verify	that Ascending appears in the Sort Order column for the StudentID field
Step 6	Click	the Group Header text box to view its list arrow
Step 7	Click	Yes in the Group Header list
Step 8	Press	the TAB key to select the contents of the Group Footer text box and display its list arrow
Step 9	Click	Yes in the Group Footer list

The Sorting and Grouping dialog box on your screen should look similar to Figure 12-2.

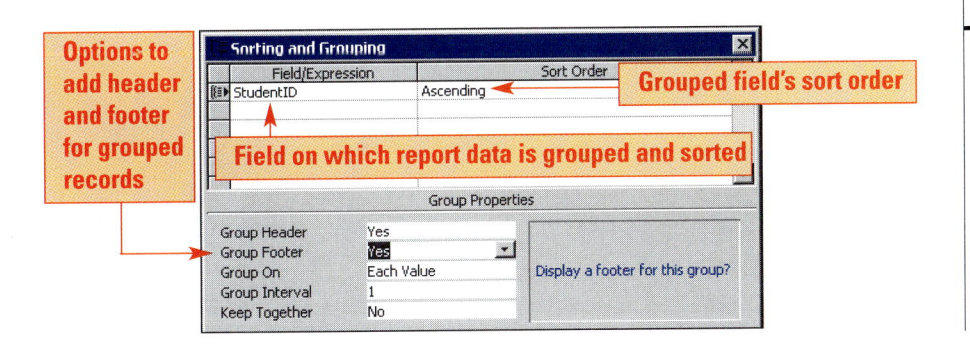

> **MENU TIP**
>
> You can display the Sorting and Grouping dialog box with the Sorting and Grouping command on the shortcut menu or the Sorting and Grouping command on the View menu.

> **QUICK TIP**
>
> You can group up to 10 variables in Access.

FIGURE 12-2
Sorting and Grouping Dialog Box

chapter twelve

| Step 10 | **Close** | the Sorting and Grouping dialog box |
| Step 11 | **Observe** | that the StudentID Header and StudentID Footer sections are added to the report design |

Because the StudentID header section introduces each group of student records, you need to move the StudentID, FName, and tblStudents.LName text box controls from the Detail section to this section. The Detail section then contains only the ClassCode text box control. To move the StudentID, FName, and tblStudents.LName text box controls to the Student ID Header section:

Step 1	**Click**	the StudentID text box control in the Detail section to select it
Step 2	**Select**	the FName and tblStudents.LName text box controls in the Detail section using the SHIFT + Click method (three text box controls are selected)
Step 3	**Drag**	the three selected controls into the StudentID Header section and drop them at the 0-inch vertical position
Step 4	**Switch to**	Print Preview view
Step 5	**Scroll**	the report to view the information for the first three students listed
Step 6	**Observe**	that each student is now listed once followed by the class code for each of his or her classes

Your screen should look similar to Figure 12-3.

> **QUICK TIP**
>
> The report now has just *one* row for each student in the StudentID Header section and as many rows in the Detail section as classes in which that student is enrolled. That's because you set up the join between the tblStudents and tblRegistration tables so only rows from each table that contains a matching key field (in this case, StudentID) appear.

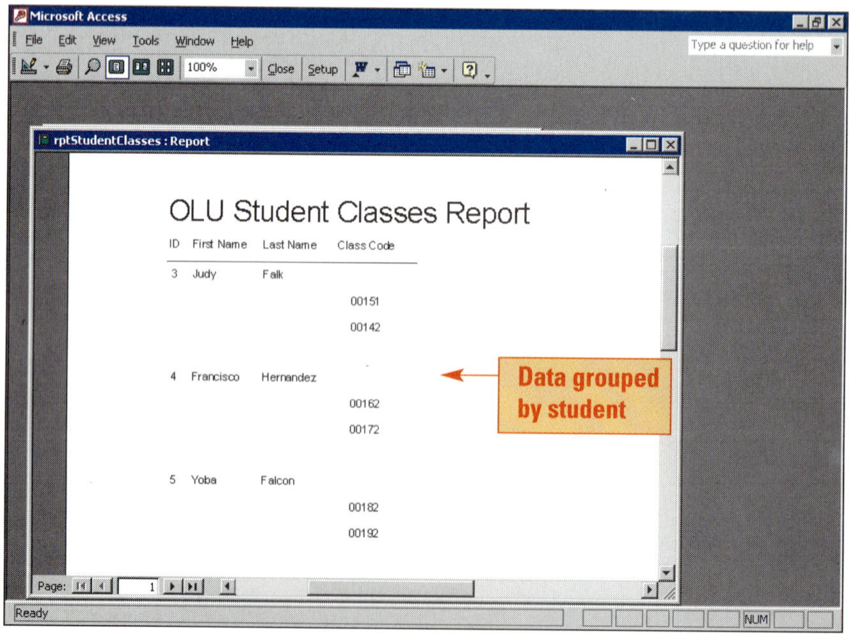

FIGURE 12-3
Report Grouped by StudentID

After consulting with Denise, you decide to add the DeptPrefix, CourseNumber, tblInstructors.LName, and CreditHours fields to the report to provide more detailed information for each class in which a student is enrolled. To add the additional fields:

Step 1	Switch to	Design view
Step 2	Drag	the DeptPrefix field from the Field List window to the Detail section anywhere to the right of the ClassCode text box control
Step 3	Move	the DeptPrefix label control to the Page Header, and reposition it approximately one gridline to the right of the ClassCode label control
Step 4	Edit	the DeptPrefix label control's caption property to remove the colon (:)
Step 5	Reposition	the DeptPrefix text box control in the Detail section to the right of the ClassCode text box control so that it aligns with its label control
Step 6	Resize	the DeptPrefix text box control in the Detail section so that it is approximately one gridline wider than its label control
Step 7	Follow	Steps 2 through 5 to add the CourseNumber field to the Detail section, move the CourseNumber label control to the Page Header section one gridline to the right of the DeptPrefix label control and edit its caption, and reposition the CourseNumber text box control
Step 8	Size	the CourseNumber text box control so that it is approximately the same size as its label
Step 9	Follow	Steps 2 through 5 to add the tblInstructors.LName field to the Detail section, move the tblInstructors.LName label control to the Page Header section one gridline to the right of the CourseNumber label control, and reposition the tblInstructors.LName text box control
Step 10	Edit	the tblInstructors.LName label control's caption property to change it to Instructor
Step 11	Size	the tblInstructors.LName text box control approximately one gridline wider than its label control
Step 12	Follow	Steps 2 through 5 to add the CreditHours field to the Detail section, move the CreditHours label control to the Page Header section one gridline to the right of the tblInstructors.LName label control, and reposition the CreditHours text box control
Step 13	Edit	the CreditHours label control's caption property to Credit Hours
Step 14	Size	the CreditHours text box control so that it is approximately the same size as its label and then center its contents

Now that you added label controls to the Page Header section, you want to extend the horizontal line so that it appears under all the label controls. To edit the horizontal line in the Page Header section:

Step 1	Click	the horizontal line in the Page Header section to select it
Step 2	Drag	the horizontal line's right sizing handle to the right to the 5-inch horizontal position to extend the line below the newly added label controls
Step 3	Deselect	the horizontal line

Denise calls to remind you to include the total credit hours for each student. To do this, you add an unbound text box control to the StudentID Footer section that contains a calculated field, which sums the credit hours for each student. To add a calculated field to the StudentID group footer section:

Step 1	Click	the Text box button ab	in the Toolbox
Step 2	Click	the StudentID Footer section beneath the CreditHours text box control to add a label and unbound text box control
Step 3	Click	the unbound text box control in the StudentID Footer section to position the insertion point in the control
Step 4	Key	=Sum(CreditHours) in the unbound text box control in the StudentID Footer section
Step 5	Press	the ENTER key to complete the expression
Step 6	Size	the unbound text box control the same size as the CreditHours text box control and center its contents
Step 7	Select	the text in the unbound text box's label control in the StudentID Footer section
Step 8	Key	Total Credits
Step 9	Press	the ENTER key
Step 10	Reposition	the unbound text box's label control approximately one gridline to the left of the unbound text box control

Denise's last request for this report is to add and center the page number and the total number of pages at the bottom of each page of the report and to insert the current date at the bottom-right margin of each page of the report. You make these changes by adding controls to the Page Footer section using menu commands. To insert centered page numbers at the bottom of each page:

| Step 1 | Click | Insert |
| Step 2 | Click | Page Numbers |

The Page Numbers dialog box on your screen should look similar to Figure 12-4. You select the page number format and location in this dialog box.

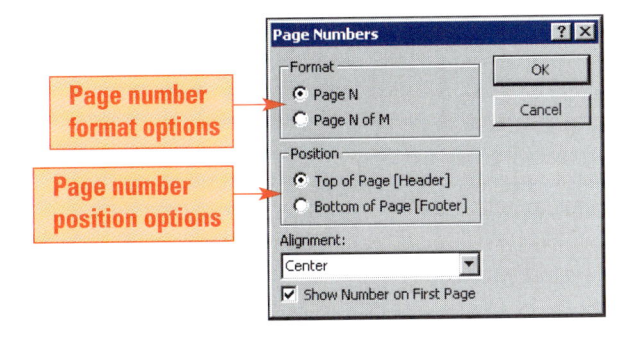

FIGURE 12-4
Page Numbers Dialog Box

QUICK TIP

Another way to insert the current date or current date and time in a report is to insert an unbound text box control and key a calculated expression such as "=Now()" or "=Date()" in the text box control.

Step 3	Click	the Page N of M option button to add the page number and the total number of pages
Step 4	Click	the Bottom of Page [Footer] option button to position the page numbers in the Page Footer section
Step 5	Click	Center in the Alignment: list, if necessary
Step 6	Click	the Show Number on First Page check box to insert a check mark, if necessary
Step 7	Click	OK
Step 8	Observe	the centered page number control added to the Page Footer section

To insert the current date at the right margin of the Page Footer section:

| Step 1 | Click | Insert |
| Step 2 | Click | Date and Time |

chapter
twelve

The Date and Time dialog box on your screen should look similar to Figure 12-5.

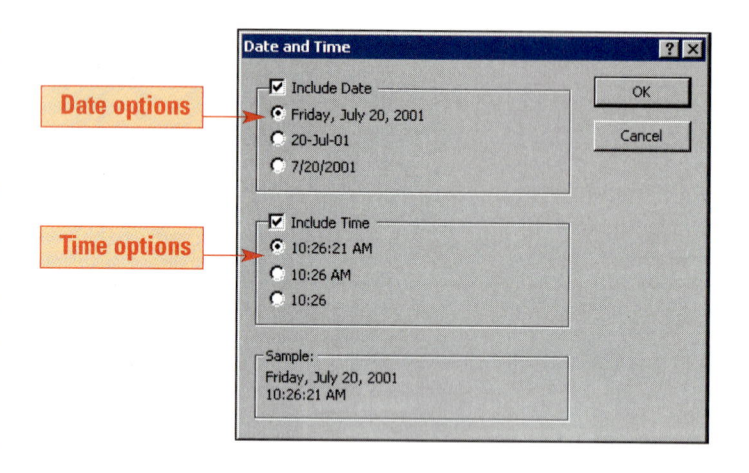

FIGURE 12-5
Date and Time Dialog Box

Caution Tip

Depending on whether your computer's operating system is Windows 98 or Windows 2000, Access displays dates with a two-digit or four-digit year format by default. The date options in Figure 12-5 show the Windows 2000 four-digit default.

Step 3	*Click*	the Include Date check box to insert a check mark, if necessary
Step 4	*Click*	the *mm/dd/yyyy* or *mm/dd/yy* option button (this option displays the current date, for example, 10/19/2003 or 10/19/03)
Step 5	*Click*	the Include Time check box to remove the check mark, if necessary
Step 6	*Click*	OK
Step 7	*Observe*	the unbound control containing the calculated expression "=Date()" inserted at the left margin of the Detail section
Step 8	*Drag*	the unbound control containing the date expression to 0-inch vertical position at the right margin of the Page Footer section and size it to approximately one-half its current width
Step 9	*Compare*	your report to Figure 12-6 and adjust the position of the controls, if necessary

After adjusting the position of the controls, your screen should look similar to Figure 12-6.

FIGURE 12-6
Completed Report in Design View

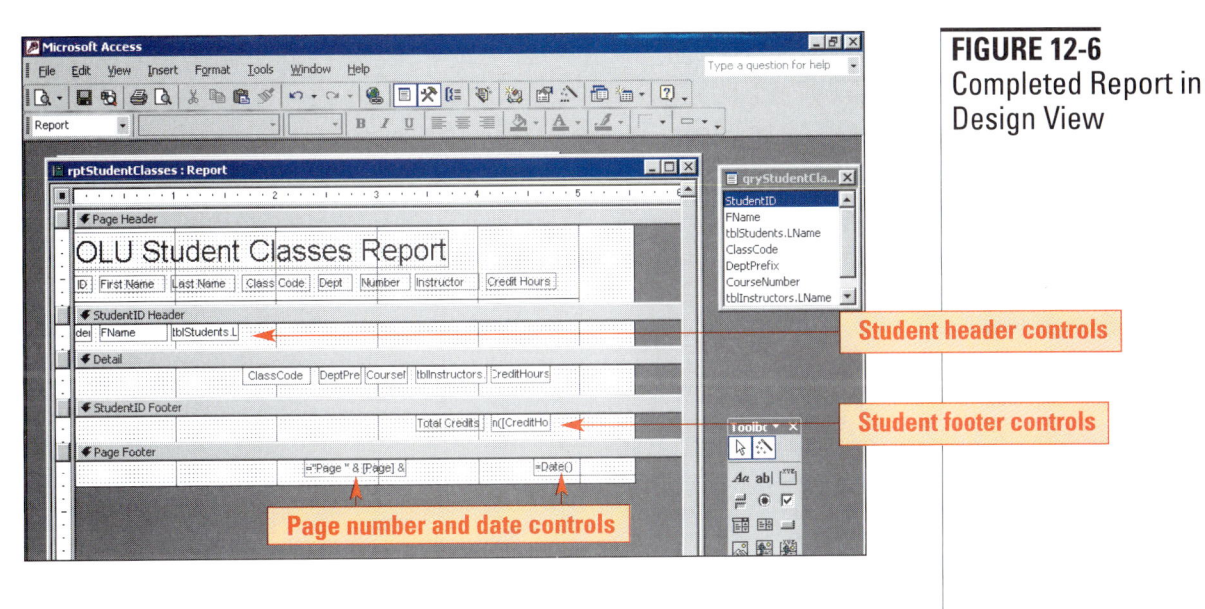

Step 10	Switch to	Print Preview
Step 11	Verify	the report's layout, including its group headers and footers and its page header and footers
Step 12	Switch to	Design view
Step 13	Save	the report and leave it open in Design view

Sometimes you need to modify a report's properties to get just the report layout you need.

Modifying Report Properties

Denise likes the new rptStudentClasses report. However, she tells you that sometimes she needs to print each student's information on a separate page and asks you to create a second report to do that. To print each student's information on a separate page, you can change the report properties. You decide to save time in creating the new report by saving the rptStudentClasses report with a new name and then modifying the new report's properties. To save the rptStudentClasses report with a new name:

Step 1	Verify	that the rptStudentClasses report is open in Design view
Step 2	Click	File
Step 3	Click	Save As
Step 4	Key	rptStudentPage in the Save Report 'rptStudentClasses' To: text box in the Save As dialog box
Step 5	Click	OK

MOUSE TIP

You can click the StudentID Footer bar and then click the Properties button on the Report Design toolbar to open the StudentID Footer's Properties sheet.

chapter twelve

You can force a new page each time the value in the StudentID field changes by modifying the group's footer properties. To view the Properties sheet for the StudentID Footer section and modify its Force New Page property:

Step 1	Right-click	the StudentID Footer section to view the shortcut menu
Step 2	Click	Properties
Step 3	Click	the Format tab, if necessary
Step 4	Click	the Force New Page text box to display its list arrow, if necessary
Step 5	Click	the list arrow
Step 6	Click	After Section in the list to insert a page break after each StudentID Footer section
Step 7	Close	the Properties sheet

Another way to modify report properties is to use the Formatting (Form/Report) toolbar buttons to make changes to the font, font size, and font color. The Properties sheet for the control reflects the changes you make using the Formatting (Form/Report) toolbar. Denise wants to emphasize each student's name in the new report. To apply bold formatting to the FName and tblStudents.LName text box controls:

Step 1	Select	the FName and tblStudents.LName text box controls in the StudentID Header section using the SHIFT + Click method
Step 2	Click	the Bold button **B** on the Formatting (Form/Report) toolbar

Because each student's information is on a separate page, the page number control in this report's Page Footer section is unnecessary. To delete the page number control and preview the report:

Step 1	Click	the page number control in the Page Footer section to select it
Step 2	Press	the DELETE key
Step 3	Switch to	Print Preview
Step 4	Verify	that each student's information is on a separate page and that boldface emphasizes each student's name
Step 5	Switch to	Design view
Step 6	Save	the report and close it

Denise is satisfied with both the student reports. Michael, who works with Denise, asks you to add a subreport to an existing instructors report.

12.c Adding a Subreport to an Existing Report

When you use the Report Wizard to create a report, you can automatically add a nested subreport if you use fields from two or more properly linked tables. You also can add a subreport control to an existing report in Design view with the Subform/Subreport button in the Toolbox. Michael wants to add a list of classes each individual instructor is teaching to the existing rptInstructors report. This information is available in the rptClasses report. To provide the information Michael needs, you can insert the rptClasses report as a nested subreport in the existing rptInstructors report. To insert the nested subreport:

Step 1	Open	rptInstructors in Design view
Step 2	Display	the Toolbox, if necessary
Step 3	Verify	that the Control Wizards button in the Toolbox is selected
Step 4	Click	the Subform/Subreport button in the Toolbox
Step 5	Click	the Detail section at the 1-inch horizontal and .25-inch vertical position to start the SubReport Wizard

notes When you start the SubReport Wizard for the first time, you might see a dialog box asking whether you want to install it. Go ahead and accept the installation.

Step 6	Click	the Use an existing report or form option button
Step 7	Select	rptClasses, if necessary
Step 8	Click	Next >
Step 9	Click	the Define my own. option button to define which fields link the report and subreport
Step 10	Key	InstID in the first Form/report fields: list box
Step 11	Key	InstID in the first Subform/subreport fields: list box

The two reports, rptInstructors and rptClassessubreport, are **synchronized** through the use of the subreport control's LinkChildFields and LinkMasterFields properties. These properties link the field with matching values, the InstID field, that you specified in this SubReport Wizard step. This linking insures that the individual courses taught by each instructor are listed following each instructor's personnel information.

Step 12	Click	Next >
Step 13	Key	rptClassesSubreport for the subreport name
Step 14	Click	Finish
Step 15	Switch to	Print Preview view and zoom the report
Step 16	Scroll	to view the report
Step 17	Observe	that the subreport contains duplicate instructor and department identification information and that the repeating label "rptClassesSubreport" makes the report difficult to read

To modify the subreport by removing the duplicate information and the repeating title label:

Step 1	Switch to	Design view
Step 2	Size	the subreport control, if necessary, by dragging down the bottom sizing handle so you can more easily view the subreport design
Step 3	Select	and delete the rptClassesSubreport label in the primary report Detail section
Step 4	Select	and delete the InstID and Dept label controls in the subreport Report Header section
Step 5	Right-click	the CourseNumber label control in the subreport Report Header section and change its caption property to "Course Number"
Step 6	Size	the CourseNumber label control in the subreport Report Header section to see the entire new caption
Step 7	Scroll	to view the subreport Detail section
Step 8	Select	and delete the InstID and DeptPrefix text box controls in the subreport Detail section
Step 9	Select	the CourseNumber, CreditHours, and DeliveryMode text box controls in the subreport Detail section and center their contents
Step 10	Switch to	Print Preview

Customizing Reports   AA 85

| Step 11 | Observe | that the subreport title label and duplicate instructor and department information are removed and the report is much easier to read |

Your screen should look similar to Figure 12-7.

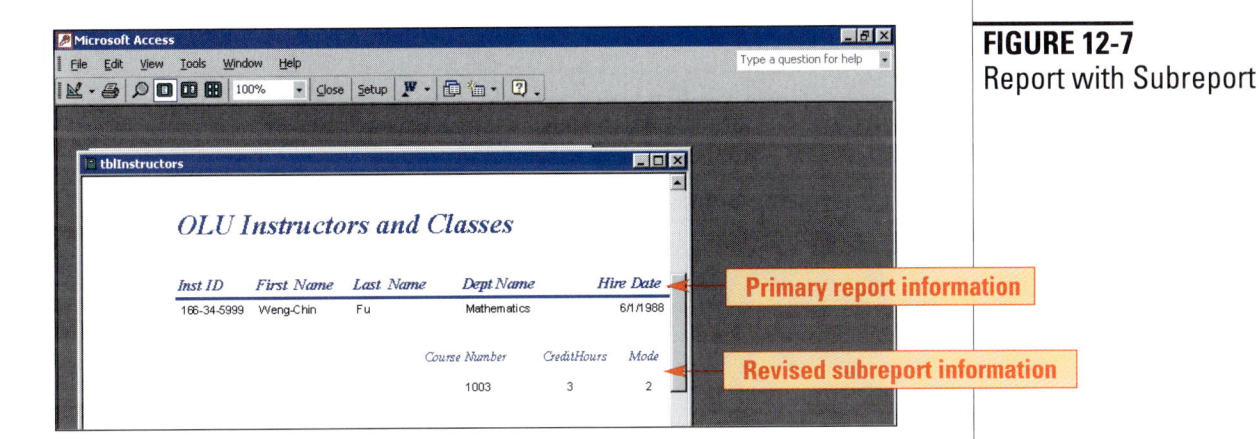

FIGURE 12-7
Report with Subreport

| Step 12 | Switch to | Design view |
| Step 13 | Save | the report and close it |

Sometimes you want to group a report as the report is being run. You can do this with a parameter query.

12.d Running a Grouped Report from a Parameter Query

As you learned earlier in this chapter, a grouped report lets you separate groups of records visually and to display introductory and summary information for each group. If you use a parameter query as the data source for a grouped report, you can specify which group of records to include in the report. During lunch with Denise and Michael, you learn that they are often asked to create a report that lists the courses offered by a particular department. You offer to create such a report based on the existing qryCourses parameter query. To create a report that list courses offered by a specified department:

| Step 1 | Click | Reports   Reports   on the Objects bar, if necessary |

chapter
twelve

Step 2	**Double-click**	Create report by using wizard
Step 3	**Click**	Query: qryCourses in the Table/Queries list
Step 4	**Move**	all the fields to the Selected Fields: list
Step 5	**Click**	Next >
Step 6	**Double-click**	DeptPrefix to group the data by prefix
Step 7	**Click**	Next >

Now you can choose how you want to sort the data. Denise and Michael want the data in the report sorted by course number and then formatted with the Stepped format in Portrait orientation.

Step 8	**Click**	CourseNumber in the first sort list box and verify that Ascending order is selected
Step 9	**Click**	Next > to see the page layout
Step 10	**Click**	Stepped to see a preview of that format, if necessary
Step 11	**Click**	the Portrait option button, if necessary
Step 12	**Click**	the Adjust field widths check box to insert a check mark, if necessary
Step 13	**Click**	Next >
Step 14	**Click**	Corporate, if necessary
Step 15	**Click**	Next >
Step 16	**Key**	rptDepartmentalCourses as the report title
Step 17	**Click**	Finish to preview the report
Step 18	**Key**	ACCT in the parameter box to specify the Accounting department
Step 19	**Click**	OK to preview the report
Step 20	**Observe**	that although the report contains most of the information Denise and Michael want, the information presented is incomplete or poorly presented

Editing a Report Created by the Report Wizard

Although using the Report Wizard is a good way to start a report, most reports created with the Report Wizard benefit from fine-tuning in Design view. The rptDepartmentalCourses report is a good example. You need to modify its design to present the information completely and attractively, and thus increase the report's usability and readability. You can modify this report in Design view to resize and reposition controls, add new controls, delete unneeded controls, resize report sections, and modify properties of report objects. To modify the rptDepartmentalCourses report in Design view:

Step 1	**Switch to**	Design view
Step 2	**Change**	the title in the title label control in the Report Header to Departmental Courses
Step 3	**Change**	the Caption property for the DeptPrefix label control in the Page Header section to Department
Step 4	**Select**	the DeptPrefix label control in the Page Header section and the DeptPrefix text box control in the DeptPrefix Header section using the SHIFT + Click method, and then reduce the size of both controls at once by dragging the middle-right sizing handle on one of the selected controls approximately four gridlines to the left
Step 5	**Select**	the CourseNumber label control in the Page Header section and the CourseNumber text box control in the Detail section using the SHIFT + Click method, and then enlarge both controls at once by dragging the middle-left sizing handle on one of the selected controls approximately four gridlines to the left
Step 6	**Select**	the CourseDescription label control (its caption is Description) in the Page Header section and the CourseDescription text box control in the Detail section using the SHIFT + Click method, and then reduce the size of both controls at once by dragging the middle-left sizing handle on one of the select controls approximately six gridlines to the right
Step 7	**Select**	the CourseDescription text box control in the Detail section, and enlarge the control vertically by dragging down the bottom middle sizing handle until the control is approximately 1½ inches tall
Step 8	**Select**	the CourseTitle text box control in the Detail section, and then enlarge the CourseTitle text box control by dragging the middle-right sizing handle approximately five gridlines to the right
Step 9	**Change**	the caption for the Credits label control (its caption is Cr Hrs) in the Page Header section to Hrs
Step 10	**Select**	the Credits label control (its caption is Hrs) in the Page Header section and the Credits text box control in the Detail section using the SHIFT + Click method, and then center the contents of the selected controls
Step 11	**Select**	the NonCredit label control (its caption is Non) in the Page Header section and the NonCredit text box control (a check box) in the Detail section using the SHIFT + Click method, and then delete the selected controls

Step 12	Select	the LabFee label control (its caption is Lab Fee) in the Page Header section and the LabFee text box control in the Detail section using the SHIFT + Click method, reposition the selected controls approximately one gridline to the right of the CourseDescription controls, and then center the selected controls contents
Step 13	Select	the RevisionDate label control (its caption is Rev.) in the Page Header section and the RevisionDate text box control in the Detail section using the SHIFT + Click method, and then size the selected controls by dragging the middle-left sizing handle approximately four gridlines to the left
Step 14	Save	the report

To review the revised report:

Step 1	Switch to	Print Preview
Step 2	Key	ACCT in the Enter department prefix text box in the Enter Parameter Value dialog box
Step 3	Click	OK
Step 4	Observe	that the layout is more attractive and easier to read and that the revised report shows complete information for the course title and description
Step 5	Switch to	Design view
Step 6	Adjust	the position and size of the report controls so that the report looks similar to Figure 12-8, if necessary, switching between Print Preview and Design view to test the results

Your screen should look similar to Figure 12-8.

FIGURE 12-8
Completed Report

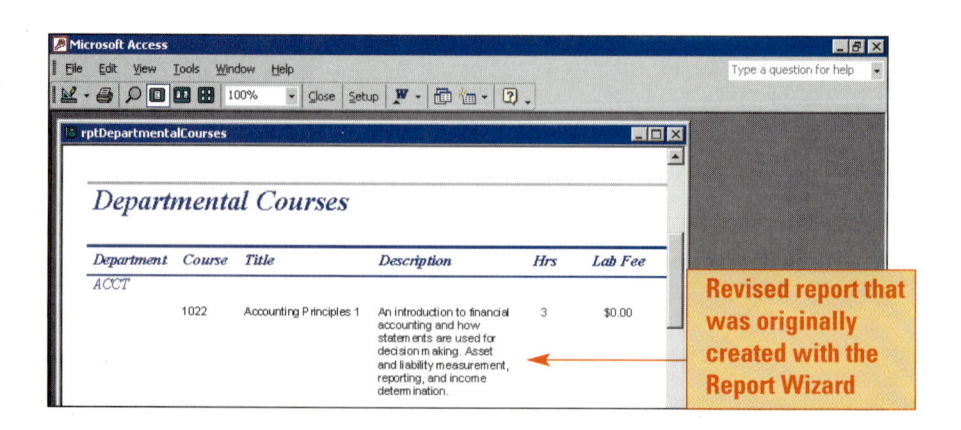

Revised report that was originally created with the Report Wizard

Step 7	Save	the report when you are satisfied with its design and then close the report and the database

Summary

▶ You can create a custom report in Design view by placing label and text box controls exactly where you want them. In a typical three-section (Page Header, Detail, and Page Footer) custom report, the Detail section contains the individual records from the underlying data source; column headings and the report's title usually appear in the Page Header section; and the date and page number information frequently appear in the Page Footer section.

▶ A grouped report lets you separate groups of records visually and display introductory and summary information for each group.

▶ You can specify a sort order for a group in a grouped report.

▶ Report sections and controls have properties you can modify in the section or control's Properties sheet.

▶ To make a calculation in a report, you create and insert an unbound text box, and then key a formula in the text box control.

▶ You can add a subreport control to an existing report in Design view to display information from two or more properly linked tables in the primary report and its subreport.

▶ You can use a parameter query as the basis for a grouped report. When you print the report, the parameter query prompts you to enter the grouping criteria.

▶ A report created with the Report Wizard usually benefits from fine-tuning in Design view.

chapter twelve

Commands Review

Action	Menu Bar	Shortcut Menu	Toolbar	Task Pane	Keyboard
Create a new report in Design view	Insert, Report	New	New		ALT + I, R CTRL + N
Insert a new control into a report	Insert, ActiveX Control		Click a control button in the Toolbox Drag a field from the Field List window		ALT + I, C
Create groups	View, Sorting and Grouping	Sorting and Grouping			ALT + V, S
Select multiple controls	Edit, Select All	Click selection boxes to the left of section headers	SHIFT + Click each control		ALT + E, A CTRL + A
Display the Toolbox	View, Toolbox				ALT + V, X
Display report properties	View, Properties	Properties			ALT + V, P F4
Insert page numbers	Insert, Page Numbers				ALT + I, U
Insert the date	Insert, Date and Time				ALT + I, T

Concepts Review

Circle the correct answer.

1. To select multiple controls in a report design, you can click the first control and then:
   - [a] click each remaining control.
   - [b] CTRL + Click subsequent controls.
   - [c] SHIFT + Click subsequent controls.
   - [d] ALT + Click subsequent controls.

2. In a typical three-section custom report, which section do you use for column headings?
   - [a] Detail
   - [b] Page Header
   - [c] Group Header
   - [d] Report Header

3. Which report section often provides a subtotal for a group of records?
   - [a] Detail
   - [b] Report Footer
   - [c] Group Header
   - [d] Group Footer

4. You can change the grouping of a report in:
   - [a] the Properties sheet.
   - [b] Print Preview.
   - [c] the Sorting and Grouping dialog box.
   - [d] the Summary Options dialog box.

5. Which expression inserts only the current date in a report?
   - [a] =NOW()
   - [b] =DATE
   - [c] =DATE()
   - [d] ="June 1, 2002"

6. To add summary information to a grouped report, you can place unbound text boxes containing calculated expressions in the:
   - [a] Field List.
   - [b] Properties sheet.
   - [c] Group Header section.
   - [d] Group Footer section.

7. When you want each group to appear on a new page in a grouped report, you can change the:
   [a] Force New Page property.
   [b] Start New Page property.
   [c] Begin New Page property.
   [d] Set New Page property.

8. To change the grouping criteria for a grouped report when you run it, you can base the report on a(n):
   [a] Report Wizard.
   [b] parameter query.
   [c] update query.
   [d] calculated field.

9. Access synchronizes a primary report and subreport by linking fields with matching values in the:
   [a] Autosynchronize and Synchronize properties.
   [b] LinkChildFields and LinkMasterFields properties.
   [c] MatchingChildFields and MatchingMasterFields properties.
   [d] PrimaryFields and SubReportFields properties.

10. To insert the date in a custom report, you can use the:
    [a] Date and Time command on the Edit menu.
    [b] Date command on the Format menu.
    [c] Date and Time command on the Insert menu.
    [d] Date and Time button in the Toolbox.

Circle **T** if the statement is true or **F** if the statement is false.

T F 1. Access expands a newly created label control as you key text in it.

T F 2. In a grouped report, you must always include the group header and group footer sections.

T F 3. You cannot drag a single control from one report section to another section.

T F 4. When you add a field from the Field List to the report, Access creates two kinds of controls: a label control and a bound text box control.

T F 5. A bound text box control takes its value from a field in the underlying table or query.

T F 6. You cannot reposition a report control with the keyboard.

T F 7. You can modify report control properties by formatting the control with buttons on the Formatting (Form/Report) toolbar.

T F 8. It is often necessary to fine-tune the design of a report created with the Report Wizard.

T F 9. You can select multiple controls in a section with the CTRL + Click method.

T F 10. You cannot change the sorting order for grouped records when you create a report from scratch in Design view.

chapter twelve

Skills Review

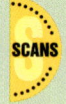

Exercise 1

1. Create a copy of the *mdbFanTours12-* database located on the Data Disk.
2. Create a new report in Design view based on the qry2001Prospects query.
3. Add the FName field to the Detail section. Move the FName label to the Page Header section.
4. Position the FName text box control in the Detail section below the FName label control in the Page Header section.
5. Follow Steps 3 and 4 to add the LName, ContactDate, and Status fields. Move the label controls to the Page Header section, and position them to the right of the FName label control. Position the text box controls in the Detail section below their label controls in the Page Header section.
6. Print Preview the report and observe the layout. Then switch to Design view, reposition the controls, and align the controls' contents as desired to create an attractive report layout.
7. Save the report as "rpt2001Prospects," and then print and close it. Close the database.

Exercise 2

1. Open the *mdbFanTour12-1* database you created in Exercise 1.
2. Open the rpt2001Prospects report in Design view. Increase the height of the Page Header section to make room for a title label.
3. Select the four labels in the Page Header section, and move them to the bottom of the Page Header section.
4. Display the Toolbox, if necessary. Add a label control at the 0-inch vertical and horizontal position in the Page Header section, and key "FST 2001 Prospects" as the text. Format the label with 14-point italic font, and resize the label to fit its contents.
5. Reduce the height of the Detail section to fit the controls.
6. Print Preview the report then return to Design view and make any desired adjustments to the size or position of the controls.
7. Save and print the report, and then close it. Close the database.

Exercise 3

1. Open the *mdbFanTour12-1* database you modified in Exercise 2.
2. Open rpt2001Prospects in Design view. Add a horizontal line control across the Page Header section below the column headings. (Resize the Page Header section to accommodate the line, if necessary.)
3. Use the Date and Time command on the Insert menu to place the date at the far left side of the Page Footer section. Use the first date format but exclude the time.
4. Print Preview the report and verify the date at the bottom of each page.
5. Save and print the report, and then close it. Close the database.

Exercise 4

1. Open the *mdbFanTour12-1* database you modified in Exercise 3.

2. Open the rpt2001Prospects report in Design view. Add a calculated unbound text box to rpt2001Prospects to concatenate the FName and LName fields. (*Hint:* Use =FName&" "&LName as the expression.) This text box should replace the separate FName and LName text boxes in the Detail section.

3. Delete the LName label control and replace the text in the FName label control with "Prospect Name." Size the unbound text box control appropriately.

4. Print Preview the report to review the change and then switch back to Design view and make any necessary adjustments to the calculated expression or the new caption in the label.

5. Save and print the report, and then close it. Close the database.

Exercise 5

1. Open the *mdbFanTour12-1* database you modified in Exercise 4.

2. Open the rpt2001Prospects report in Design view.

3. Add the label "Fantastic Sports Tours" centered at the bottom of the Page Footer section.

4. Select all report controls. Change the font color to Red.

5. Print Preview the report and observe the changes, and then switch to Design view and make any adjustments necessary.

6. Save and print the report, and then close it. Close the database.

Exercise 6

1. Open the *mdbFanTour12-1* database you modified in Exercise 5.

2. Create a new blank report based on the qryProspectsByState query using the Report Wizard. Include all fields in the report. Group the report by State. Sort the grouped records by ContactType in descending order. Use the Stepped layout, Portrait orientation, and Formal style for the report's format. Save the report as "rptProspectsByState."

3. Use the state code "CA" to run the report.

4. Switch to Design view and change the report title to "Prospects by State." Reduce the size of the State label control and text box control, and then resize and reposition the remaining controls to create an attractive and easy-to-read report.

5. Print Preview the report and review your changes, and then switch to Design view and make any necessary adjustments.

6. Save and print the report, and then close it. Close the database.

chapter twelve

Exercise 7

1. Open the *mdbFanTour12-1* database you modified in Exercise 6.
2. Create a new report in Design view based on the tblEmployees table. Group the report by EmployeeID sorted in ascending order. Include a group header.
3. Place the EmployeeID, FirstName, LastName, City, and State fields in the EmployeeID Header section. Move the label controls to the Page Header section, and position the text box controls in the EmployeeID Header section below their respective labels. Change the caption for the EmployeeID label control to "Employee." Change the captions for the FirstName and LastName labels to "First Name" and "Last Name," and size the label controls to fit. Remove the colon (:) from the City and State label controls' captions. Size and position the labels to provide an attractive and useful report.
4. Preview the report, and then switch to Design view and make any necessary adjustments. (You complete the Detail section in Exercise 8.)
5. Save the report as "rptEmployees," and then print and close it. Close the database.

Exercise 8

1. Open the *mdbFanTour12-1* database you modified in Exercise 7.
2. Open the rptEmployees report in Design view.
3. Add a subreport control to the Detail section and base the subreport on the tblBookings table. Use all fields from the tblBookings table in the subreport. Link the tables with the EmployeeID field in the primary report and the EmpID field in the subreport. Name the subreport tblBookingsSubreport.
4. Edit the tblBookingsSubreport to remove the EmpID label control from the subreport Report Header section and the EmpID text box control from the subreport Detail section.
5. Add a report title label containing the text "FST Employees Paid and Unpaid Bookings" to the Page Header section, format the text with 16-point font, and then size the label control to fit. (*Hint:* Resize the Page Header section, and move the label controls down before adding the title label control.)
6. Bold and italicize the label controls in the Page Header section, and bold the text box controls in the EmployeeID Header section.
7. Insert the centered page number in the Page Footer section, and insert the current date at the right edge of the Page Footer section.
8. Print Preview the report, and then switch to Design view and make any desired adjustments to the report design.
9. Save and print the report, and then close it. Close the database.

Case Projects

Project 1

Using the Office on the Web command on the Help menu, open the Microsoft home page and then link to pages that provide information about the topics covered in this chapter, such as grouped reports. Print at least one Web page.

Project 2

Using the Office on the Web command on the Help menu, open the Microsoft home page and then link to pages that provide information about unbound controls. Print at least one Web page.

Project 3

Open the *mdbFanTours12-2* database located on the Data Disk. Create a custom report in Design view based on the tblProspects table. Include the prospect's first and last names, e-mail address, status, and state. Title the report "FST Prospects Report," and print the title on each page. Use the field's label controls as column headings on each page. Edit the first and last name fields' label controls so only one label control contains the caption "Prospect Name." Edit the first and last name text box controls so only one text box control contains the concatenated first name and last name. Insert a centered page number at the bottom of each page. Sort the report on the State field. Arrange the label and text box controls attractively. Save the report as "rptProspectsByState," print and close the report, then close the database.

Project 4

Open the *mdbFanTours12-2* database you modified in Project 3. Modify the rptProspectsByState report in Design view to group the report by state. Show the state information in the first column on each page and as the group header by repositioning the State label control and text box control. Reposition the remaining controls and format their contents as desired. Include a count of the number of prospects in each state in the group footer section using the calculated expression (=Count(State)) in an unbound text box. Use the label text "Total Prospects." Save and print the report, and then close the database.

Project 5

Open the *mdbFanTours12-2* database you modified in Project 4. You want to ensure that information for each group (including the State reference, the detail information, and the prospect count) appears together on the same page. To do that, you must modify the sorting and grouping properties. Open the rptProspectsByState report in Design view, and then open the Sorting and Grouping dialog box. Use online Help to review the Keep Together group properties, and then make the appropriate change. Save and print the report, and then close the database.

Project 6

Open the *mdbFanTours12-2* database you modified in Project 5. Create an employee report using the Report Wizard based on the tblEmployees table that includes the employee's ID, first and last names, hire date, and salary. Group the report by salary, and sort the detail records in ascending order by the employee's last name. Use the Stepped layout and Portrait orientation. Let Access adjust the field widths. Apply the Bold style. Save the report as "rptEmployeeSalary." Review the report in Print Preview, note ways that you can fine-tune the report, and then switch to Design view. Change the Salary field sort order to Descending in the Sorting and Grouping dialog box, and remove the Salary group header. Add the Salary field back to the Detail section of the report, and delete the duplicate Salary label control in the Detail section. Fine-tune the report, making the format changes you identified in your review. Save, print, and close the report, and then close the database.

chapter twelve

Project 7

Open the *mdbFanTours12-2* database you modified in Project 6. You want to display the Average Salary in the rptEmployeeSalary report in the Report Footer section. Open the report in Design view, and drag down the Report Footer boundary to display the footer area. Create a calculated field in an unbound text box using the expression =Avg(Salary) to calculate the average salary. Change the unbound text box's label to "Average Salary." Change the Format property of the unbound text box control to Currency. Position the controls at the left edge of the Report Footer area. Save, print, and close the report, and then close the database.

Project 8

Open the *mdbFanTours12-2* database you modified in Project 7. Create a new report in Design view based on the tblCustomers table. Group the report by state, and sort it in ascending order by state and by city within each state group. Add the title "Customer List" to each page. Add the state, city, customer ID, first and last names, e-mail address, and contact type to the report. Create appropriate column headers for each page. Add a horizontal line to separate the column labels from the detail information. Insert today's date (not the time) and a page number at the bottom of each page. Format the controls, modify their properties, and reposition them as necessary to create an attractive and easy-to-read report. Save the report as "rptCustomersByStateandCity," print and close the report, and then close the database.

Using Access Tools

Chapter Overview

You can secure a database and its objects in a variety of ways, including encryption, password access, and assigning user permissions. You also can compact, repair, split, and replicate a database with Access tools. In this chapter, you learn how to encrypt a database, set database passwords, and employ user-level security to assign user permissions for a database. You also learn how to compact and repair a database, split a database, manage linked tables, create an MDE file to protect the design of forms and reports, and replicate a database. Finally, you learn how to create an Access module containing an event procedure in Visual Basic code.

Case profile

Maria Mendez in the provost's office asks you to explore ways to protect and secure the OLU database and repair it if it becomes damaged. Maria also wants you to automate opening a form in the OLU database. Finally, Maria wants to work with a copy of the OLU database and asks you to ensure that her copy and the original database contain the same information.

Access 2002

LEARNING OBJECTIVES

- Assign database security
- Compact and repair a database
- Use the Database Splitter
- Use the Linked Table Manager
- Create an MDE file
- Replicate a database
- Create an Access module

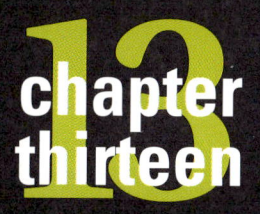

chapter thirteen

13.a Assigning Database Security

Security plays a key role in protecting information within an organization. You can control access to a database and its objects in a number of ways. The three most common ways to secure a database are encryption, password protection, and user-level security. You can **encrypt** a database so that no utility program or word processing application can decipher it. You can require users to enter a **password** before they can open a database. You can establish **user-level security** by giving individual users or groups of users specific permissions to open a database and work with its objects. Before your next meeting with Maria, you want to review these three security strategies.

Encrypting and Decrypting a Database

Encryption is the simplest way to protect a database. When Access encrypts a database, it compacts the database file and protects sensitive data, such as salary information, from anyone who tries to open the database without using the Access application. Encryption is very useful for transmitting a database electronically or when it is stored on a diskette, magnetic tape, or CD-ROM. However, encryption alone does not protect a database from being opened by anyone using the Access application, and it does not protect a database's objects from unauthorized use.

You begin by encrypting a copy of the OLU database. Because you can encrypt a database only when it's closed, you first create and then close a copy of the OLU database. To encrypt a copy of the OLU database:

Step 1	Create	a copy of the *mdbOnlineU13*- database located on the Data Disk
Step 2	Close	the *mdbOnlineU13-1* database
Step 3	Click	Tools
Step 4	Point to	Security
Step 5	Click	Encrypt/Decrypt Database

The Encrypt/Decrypt dialog box, which is similar to the Open and Save As dialog boxes, opens. If you specify the same name, drive, and folder as the original database, Access automatically replaces the original file with the encrypted one. You can create the encrypted file in another location or with a different name to maintain an original, unencrypted copy. You want to replace the *mdbOnlineU13-1* database with the encrypted version.

QUICK TIP

One strategy for securing a database is to set startup options to control what the user sees, such as a switchboard form, when a database is opened. Startup options are set in the Startup dialog box that you open by clicking the Startup command on the Tools menu. Another strategy to protect database objects is to hide them from the casual user. You can hide a database object by selecting it in the Database window, viewing the object's properties, and clicking the Hidden check box to insert a check mark. For more information on setting database startup options or hiding database objects, see online Help.

CAUTION TIP

Operations on an encrypted database are slower than operations on a normal database.

Step 6	**Double-click**	*mdbOnlineU13-1* to select it as the database you want to encrypt and open the Encrypt Database As dialog box
Step 7	**Double-click**	*mdbOnlineU13-1* in the Encrypt Database As dialog box to replace the original *mdbOnlineU13-1* with the encrypted version
Step 8	**Click**	Yes to replace the existing file

The *mdbOnlineU13-1* database now cannot be opened in a word processing application or utility program. Because encryption alone does not secure a database from unauthorized access by anyone using the Access application, adding password protection to an encrypted database is useful.

Setting Password Protection

Another simple way to protect a database is to require users to enter a password before opening the database. When a user enters the password correctly, the database opens; if a user enters the password incorrectly, the database remains closed. That method secures the database from being opened by someone who does not know the password. After the database is opened, the user can work with all its objects.

To review setting password protection, you use the password "go4ward" to protect the encrypted *mdbOnlineU13-1* database. You can open a database for shared use, as **read-only** (users cannot make changes to the database), and in **exclusive mode** (in which you are the only user). Before adding a database password, you must open the database in exclusive mode so that no one else can open it. To open the *mdbOnlineU13-1* database in exclusive mode:

Step 1	**Open**	the Open dialog box
Step 2	**Switch to**	the location where the *mdbOnlineU13-1* database is stored
Step 3	**Click**	*mdbOnlineU13-1* to select it (do not double-click)
Step 4	**Click**	the Open button list arrow
Step 5	**Click**	Open Exclusive

The *mdbOnlineU13-1* database opens in exclusive mode. Now you are ready to set the password. To set the "go4ward" password for the database:

Step 1	**Click**	Tools
Step 2	**Point to**	Security
Step 3	**Click**	Set Database Password

CAUTION TIP

Before you can encrypt a database, you must (1) either own the database or, if user-level security is in force for the database, be a member of the Admins group with full access permissions, and (2) be able to open the database in exclusive mode if the database is shared over a network. For more information on these encryption restrictions, see online Help.

QUICK TIP

If the database is already encrypted, the Encrypt/Decrypt Database command decrypts the database. To decrypt a database, follow the same basic steps as you followed when you encrypted it.

chapter
thirteen

The Set Database Password dialog box on your screen should look similar to Figure 13-1.

FIGURE 13-1
Set Database Password Dialog Box

Options for keying and rekeying password

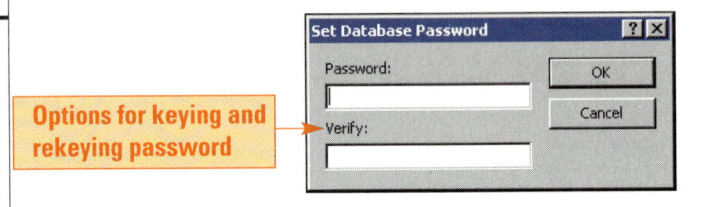

You key the password characters once in the Password: text box and then again in the Verify: text box to confirm your entry. A warning message appears if you key a different set of characters in the Verify: text box, enabling you to try again. As you key the password characters, you see only asterisks (*****) to prevent others from observing the password characters you key.

A database password can be from one to twenty characters and can include letters, accented characters, numbers, spaces, and symbols. Database passwords cannot contain leading spaces, control characters, or the following characters: \ {[ ] : \ < > + = ; , . ? * . For more information on password guidelines, see online Help.

Step 4	Key	go4ward in the Password: text box
Step 5	Press	the TAB key to move the insertion point to the Verify: text box
Step 6	Key	go4ward in the Verify: box
Step 7	Click	OK

To test password protection:

Step 1	Close	the *mdbOnlineU13-1* database
Step 2	Open	the *mdbOnlineU13-1* database
Step 3	Observe	that the Password Required dialog box opens
Step 4	Key	go4ward in the Enter database password: text box
Step 5	Click	OK
Step 6	Observe	that the database opens and you now can work with all its objects
Step 7	Close	the database

Because setting a database password does not protect the individual objects in the database, you must use user-level security to secure those objects from unauthorized access.

CAUTION TIP

Make a backup copy of the database before you set a password. Also write down your password, and store it in a safe place—if you lose or forget your password, you cannot recover it, and you cannot open the database. Passwords are case sensitive, which means users must key the exact uppercase and lowercase letters you keyed when you originally set the password. Do not password-protect a database if you plan to replicate that database. For more information on restrictions to setting a database password, see online Help.

MENU TIP

To change the database password, you must first unset the database password, and then set a new database password. To unset a database password, use the current password to open the database in exclusive mode. Then click Tools, point to Security, click Unset Database Password, key the password, and then click OK.

Setting User-Level Security

The most flexible and secure way to protect a database and its objects is to set **user-level security**, which is similar to security methods used with operating systems such as Windows 2000. The two most important reasons for setting user-level security are: (1) to prevent users from accidentally changing database objects, and (2) to prevent access to sensitive data. User-level security requires a user to log in to an Access database with a valid username and password. Access then reads a workgroup information file that contains the user's unique identification code and authorization status, and it uses that information to validate that the user is an authorized individual user or a member of an authorized user group. By default, Access creates two groups and one user in the workgroup information file: the Admins group (for database administrators), the Users group, and the Admin user (a member of the Admins group).

When you set user-level security for a database, you give each individual user or user group **permission** to work with objects within that database. Individual users or user groups may have different levels of permission. For example, one user group may have permission to view, edit, or change a table's data but not to alter that table's design. Another user group may have permission to both work with a table's data and modify its design.

You activate user-level security by providing a password for the default Admin user and then closing and reopening the Access application. When you reopen Access, you log on as the Admin user and then set permissions for groups or individuals. To activate user-level security:

Step 1	*Click*	Tools
Step 2	*Point to*	Security
Step 3	*Click*	User and Group Accounts

The User and Group Accounts dialog box on your screen should look similar to Figure 13-2.

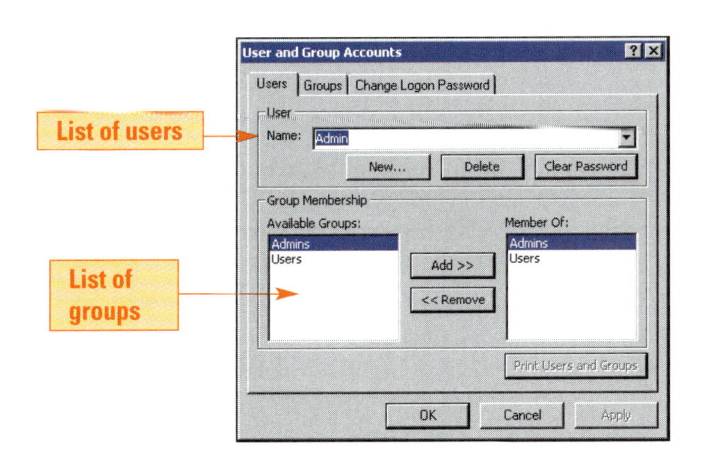

> **QUICK TIP**
>
> There are two types of permissions: explicit and implicit. **Explicit permissions** are granted directly to an individual user and do not affect other users. **Implicit permissions** are granted to a group of users. Adding a new member to the group grants the group's permissions to the new member. Removing a member from the group also removes the group's permissions from that user. For more information on how permissions work and who can assign them, see online Help.

FIGURE 13-2
User and Group Accounts Dialog Box

chapter thirteen

CAUTION TIP

Before setting user-level security, you should back up the databases on your computer. Further, when you create user names and passwords, write them down carefully so that you can remember what you entered. If you inadvertently lose or forget user names and passwords, you may have problems working with Access or opening databases.

Step 4	Observe	the default Admin user in the Name: text box and the default Admins and Users groups in the Available Groups: list
Step 5	Click	the Change Logon Password tab
Step 6	Key	web165 in the New Password: text box to set the Admin user password
Step 7	Press	the TAB key
Step 8	Key	web165 in the Verify: text box to verify the Admin user password
Step 9	Click	OK to save the password
Step 10	Close	the Access application

To log on as the Admin user and create a new user:

Step 1	Open	the Access application
Step 2	Click	Tools
Step 3	Point to	Security
Step 4	Click	User and Group Accounts to display the Logon dialog box
Step 5	Verify	that Admin is in the Name: text box
Step 6	Key	web165 in the Password text box
Step 7	Click	OK to complete the log on

The User and Group Accounts dialog box opens. Now that you have activated user-level security, you can add a user and set database permissions. By default, all new users are added to the Users group. To add a user:

Step 1	Click	the Users tab, if necessary
Step 2	Click	New
Step 3	Key	Mendez in the Name: text box
Step 4	Press	the TAB key
Step 5	Key	1234 in the Personal ID: text box
Step 6	Click	OK to add this user to the Users group
Step 7	Click	OK to close the User and Group Accounts dialog box

Next, you create another copy of the *mdbOnlineU13-* database and then assign Mendez permissions for the database objects. To create a copy of the *mdbOnlineU13-* database and assign Mendez permissions:

Step 1	Create	a copy of the *mdbOnlineU13-* database located on the Data Disk (the copy is named *mdbOnlineU13-2*)
Step 2	Click	Tools
Step 3	Point to	Security
Step 4	Click	User and Group Permissions
Step 5	Click	the Permissions tab, if necessary

The Permissions tab in the User and Group Permissions dialog box on your screen should look similar to Figure 13-3.

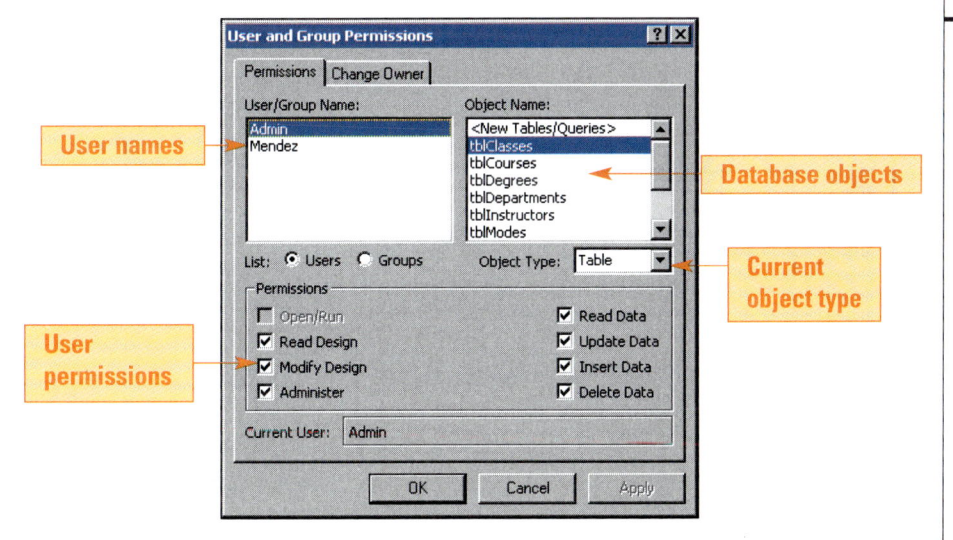

FIGURE 13-3
User and Group Permissions Dialog Box

Step 6	Observe	that the default Admin user has full permissions for each table object
Step 7	Click	Mendez in the User/Group Name: list
Step 8	Observe	that Mendez has no specific permissions assigned for any table objects
Step 9	Click	the Groups option button to view the permissions assigned to the two default groups: Admins and Users
Step 10	Observe	that the Admins group has full permissions for each table object
Step 11	Click	Users in the User/Group Name: list and observe that the Users group also has full permissions for each table object

MOUSE TIP

To see permissions for other objects for a user or group, click the Object Type: list arrow.

chapter thirteen

Although Mendez has no individual permissions for the table objects, the Users group of which Mendez is a member has full permissions for table objects; therefore, Mendez, who inherits the group's permissions, also has full permissions. Assigning permissions to groups rather than to individual users is recommended to assure that every member of the group has the same permissions. With this in mind, you should modify the Users group permissions order to prevent Mendez (and other group members) from modifying the design of a specific table. To restrict the Users group permissions so that no group member can modify the tblClasses table design:

Step 1	Verify	that the Groups option button is selected and that you are viewing group permissions
Step 2	Verify	that Users is selected in the User/Group Name: list
Step 3	Verify	that tblClasses is selected in the Object Name: list
Step 4	Click	the Modify Design check box to remove the check mark
Step 5	Observe	that both the Modify Design and Administer check boxes do not contain check marks, indicating that members of the Users group can no longer modify the design of the tblClasses table
Step 6	Click	OK to close the User and Group Permissions dialog box
Step 7	Close	the Access application

Access adds the new user-level security information to the database. However, the Mendez user has no assigned password, and none is required for the following activity. When you open Access and the *mdbOnlineU13-2* database, you need to log on as Mendez without a password. To open the database, log on as Mendez, and open the tblClasses table in Design view:

Step 1	Open	the Access application and open the *mdbOnlineU13-2* database using the link in the New File task pane
Step 2	Select	the contents of the Name: text box
Step 3	Key	Mendez in the Name: text box
Step 4	Click	OK (no password is set for Mendez)
Step 5	Open	the tblClasses table in Design view
Step 6	Observe	the message warning that Mendez does not have permission to modify the design of the tblClasses table
Step 7	Click	No to close the warning message

> **CAUTION TIP**
>
> For this chapter, it is not necessary to modify permissions for other database objects. However, in a real situation, you would likely modify permissions for more than one database object. You can select more than one object within an object type by using the SHIFT + Click or CTRL + Click methods.
>
> Also, in a real situation you would assign a password for Mendez and other users you add to the Users group.

| Step 8 | Close | the database |
| Step 9 | Close | the Access application so that you can log on as a different user in the next activity |

You also can remove users and deactivate user-level security. To remove Mendez from the Users group and deactivate user-level security:

Step 1	Open	the Access application
Step 2	Open	the User and Group Accounts dialog box
Step 3	Log on	as the Admin user with the web165 password
Step 4	Click	Mendez in the Name: list on the Users tab
Step 5	Click	Delete and then click Yes to delete the Mendez user
Step 6	Verify	that Admin is in the Name: text box
Step 7	Click	Clear Password
Step 8	Click	OK
Step 9	Close	and then reopen the Access application to deactivate user-level security

> **MENU TIP**
>
> The User-Level Security Wizard command on the Security menu provides a comprehensive way to establish workgroups, users, and security restrictions for a particular database. It creates an unsecured copy of the database that you can use in case you encounter a problem assigning permissions. The original database is encrypted and only designated users can open the secured database. Developers of Access applications would use the wizard to create tight security for the database application.

Access features a built-in tool for compacting and repairing databases.

13.b Compacting and Repairing a Database

As you work with a database and change its objects' designs, the database grows larger. Also, deleting data or objects from a database can cause the database to become fragmented and use space inefficiently. Compacting a database can significantly reduce its size and optimize its performance. Occasionally a database that is open when a computer "crashes" or the power fails becomes damaged. That can corrupt database objects or possibly remove information needed to open objects. You can use the Compact and Repair Database command to both compact a database and repair damage. When you compact and repair a database, Access closes the current database and performs compact and repair operations. After a few moments, Access reopens the database.

QUICK TIP

Access usually detects a damaged database when you try to open it and allows repairs. If a damaged database opens, you may see damage indicators, such as #Deleted next to certain records. If a database or its objects behave unpredictably, compact and repair the database.

CAUTION TIP

Compacting and repairing databases regularly is a good idea. One way to do that is to specify that Access compact a database when you close it. It also is a good idea to back up your databases on a regular schedule and to avoid quitting the Access application unexpectedly to prevent damage to the open database. For more information about compacting and repairing databases, see online Help.

To create another copy of the *mdbOnlineU13-* database, and then compact and repair the database copy:

Step 1	*Create*	a copy of the *mdbOnlineU13-* database located on the Data Disk (the copy is named *mdbOnlineU13-3*)
Step 2	*Click*	Tools
Step 3	*Point to*	Database Utilities
Step 4	*Click*	Compact and Repair Database
Step 5	*Close*	the database

Although you do not anticipate damage, take comfort knowing that a tool exists to repair a damaged database and reduce its size.

13.c Using the Database Splitter

Many Access applications use a **front-end/back-end** approach. In this approach, tables reside in a database called the **back-end database**. The **front-end database** consists of all remaining database objects and links to the tables in the back-end database. Users receive a copy of the front-end database while the back-end database resides on a network file server where it is shared. Splitting a database lets users customize their own forms and reports while providing a single data source that can be protected against modification.

To make splitting the database easier, the Database Splitter Wizard automates the process. When the wizard finishes, you have two databases: the front-end database with the linked tables and other objects such as forms and reports, and the back-end database with the original tables. To split a copy of the *mdbOnlineU13-* database:

Step 1	*Create*	a copy of the *mdbOnlineU13-* database located on the Data Disk (the copy is named *mdbOnlineU13-4*)
Step 2	*Click*	Tools
Step 3	*Point to*	Database Utilities
Step 4	*Click*	Database Splitter
Step 5	*Click*	Split Database in the Database Splitter dialog box

Using Access Tools   AA 107

The Create Back-end Database dialog box opens at the location of your Data Files, and Access automatically gives the back-end database the original database filename with _be appended.

Step 6	Verify	that *mdbOnlineU13-4_be* appears in the File name: text box
Step 7	Click	Split
Step 8	Click	OK when Access indicates that the database is successfully split
Step 9	Verify	that the *mdbOnlineU13-4* front-end database is open in Access

Your screen should look similar to Figure 13-4.

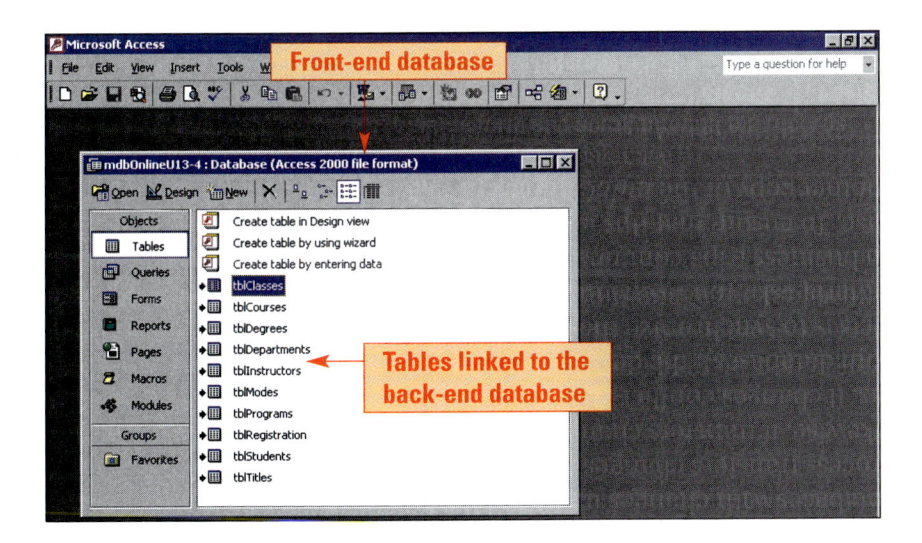

FIGURE 13-4
Linked Tables in the Front-End Database

Step 10	Observe	the link icon in front of each table in the Database window
Step 11	Open	the frmStudents form and scroll through the records provided by the back-end database
Step 12	Close	the frmStudents form

You can use the Linked Table Manager tool to manage the tables in a split database.

QUICK TIP

You can protect the tables in the back-end database in several ways. For example, if the data is to be read-only, you can set user-level security with read-only permissions. One advantage of the front-end/back-end approach is that changes can be made to the front-end database objects without changing the data values in the tables. You can easily distribute to users a revised front-end database, linked to the original back-end database.

chapter thirteen

13.d Using the Linked Table Manager

When you link tables in one database to tables in another database, you can use the Linked Table Manager to refresh those links. If you move the tables to a new location, you can use the Linked Table Manager to change the links and refresh the data stored in the linked tables. To refresh the link to the tblClasses table in the *mdbOnlineU13-4* front-end database:

Step 1	**Verify**	that the *mdbOnlineU13-4* front-end database is open
Step 2	**View**	the table objects, if necessary
Step 3	**Click**	Tools
Step 4	**Point to**	Database Utilities
Step 5	**Click**	Linked Table Manager

The Linked Table Manager dialog box that opens on your screen should look similar to Figure 13-5.

FIGURE 13-5
Linked Table Manager Dialog Box

List of linked tables

Caution Tip

If you move a back-end database to a new location, you must use the Linked Table Manager to refresh the front-end database links before you can open any database object.

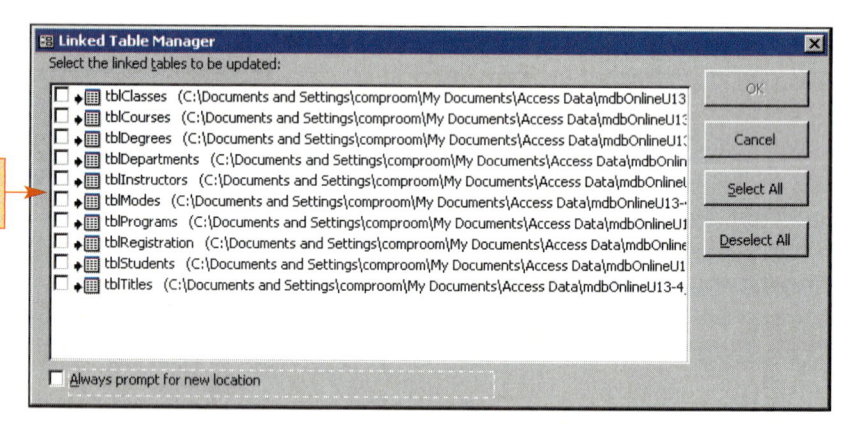

Step 6	**Click**	the tblClasses check box to insert a check mark
Step 7	**Click**	OK to refresh the table links
Step 8	**Click**	OK to close the confirmation dialog box
Step 9	**Close**	the Linked Table Manager dialog box
Step 10	**Close**	the database

You can use an MDE file to prevent users from altering the design of database forms and reports.

13.e Creating an MDE File

An **MDE file** is a special database that prevents users from changing the design of forms and reports without having to set user-level security. To create an MDE file, the database must be in Access 2002 file format. Because the default file format is Access 2000, you first convert it to 2002 format. You want to convert the *mdbOnlineU13-4* front-end database file to an MDE file. To convert the *mdbOnlineU13-4* front-end database file to the Access 2002 format:

Step 1	Verify	that no database is open
Step 2	Click	Tools
Step 3	Point to	Database Utilities
Step 4	Point to	Convert Database
Step 5	Click	To Access 2002 File Format
Step 6	Double-click	mdbOnlineU13-4 in the Database to Convert From dialog box
Step 7	Key	mdbOnlineU13-4 2002 in the File name: text box in the Convert Database Into dialog box
Step 8	Click	Save
Step 9	Click	OK to complete the conversion

To create the MDE file:

Step 1	Open	the mdbOnlineU13-4 2002 database
Step 2	Click	Tools
Step 3	Point to	Database Utilities
Step 4	Click	Make MDE File
Step 5	Click	Save to save the database as a MDE file
Step 6	Close	the database

Now you can distribute the MDE file to users who can work with the database but who cannot change the design of its forms and reports. You can use database replication to ensure that the copy of a database and the original database contain the same information.

> **CAUTION TIP**
>
> You create an MDE file *after* the database has been fully developed. If you need to change the database after you create the MDE file, you simply delete the previous MDE file, modify the original MDB file, and then create another MDE file. Because you need to update the data in the original MDB file to match the MDE data, the MDE approach is more appropriate for the front-end portion (which contains queries, forms, reports, and macros) of a split database than for the back-end portion (which contains the tables). For more information about MDE files, see online Help.

chapter thirteen

13.f Replicating a Database

Replication is the process of creating a copy of a database to be used independently of the original database. Together, the original database, called the **design master**, and the copy, called a **replica**, make a replica set. To ensure that the databases have the same content, the original database and the database copy are **synchronized** to update both databases with changes made to either database. The synchronization process transfers changes made in the replicas to the design master. Likewise, it transfers changes made in the design master to the replicas. If changes conflict (for example, the same record was changed in both databases), the design master has priority. One way to avoid conflicts is to synchronize the replica set frequently.

Maria asks you to ensure that the copy of the OLU database she uses on business trips contains the same information as the original database. To ensure that this is the case, you use replication. To create another copy of the *mdbOnlineU13-* database and then replicate it:

Step 1	Create	a copy of the *mdbOnlineU13-* database located on the Data Disk (the copy is named *mdbOnlineU13-5*)
Step 2	Click	Tools
Step 3	Point to	Replication
Step 4	Click	Create Replica
Step 5	Click	Yes to close the database and convert it to a design master
Step 6	Click	Yes when asked if you want Access to make a backup copy of the database before it converts the database to the design master
Step 7	Click	OK to accept the default name of the replica, *Replica of mdbOnlineU13-5.mdb*
Step 8	Click	OK to complete the process

Access takes a few moments to create the design master and the replica. When the Database window reopens, you see a special replication icon attached to each object in the design master. The replica database has the same replication icon in front of each database object. Your screen should look similar to Figure 13-6.

CAUTION TIP

Replication increases the size of the database and causes database operations to occur more slowly than in a regular database.

QUICK TIP

As you create the replica of a database, make a copy of the original database and set it aside, just in case something goes wrong during the replication process. You cannot synchronize the replica with the backup copy, but at least you have the original database. Access offers to create this copy during the replication process. The replica set can have more than one replica. You also can adjust the priority of replica set members to resolve updating conflicts.

Access also provides several other methods for replicating and synchronizing databases, such as Briefcase replication. For more information on this and other replication methods, see online Help.

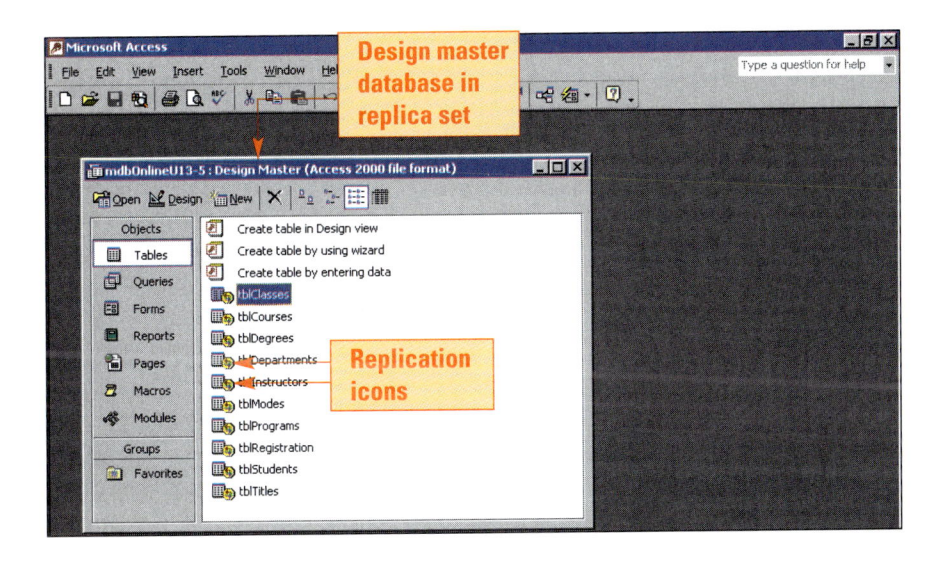

FIGURE 13-6
Design Master Database in Replica Set

[Screenshot of Microsoft Access showing mdbOnlineU13-5 : Design Master (Access 2000 file format) window with tables list. Callouts point to "Design master database in replica set" and "Replication icons"]

| Step 9 | Close | the *mdbOnlineU13-5* design master database |

> **MENU TIP**
>
> You can synchronize members of a replica set by clicking the Tools command, pointing to Replication, and clicking Synchronize Now.
>
> If a design master is damaged, lost, or moved, you can convert a replica into a design master with the Recover Design Master command on the Replication submenu.

You can use event procedures written in Visual Basic code to add automation to forms and reports.

13.g Creating an Access Module

An **event** is a specific action that occurs on or with an object, such as a mouse click or opening and closing a form. A **procedure** is a piece of Visual Basic code that contains a series of instructions that perform some operation or calculation. An **event procedure** is a Visual Basic procedure that runs automatically following a specific event. A **module** is a collection of Visual Basic declarations and procedures stored together as one unit and used to organize the Visual Basic code. The two kinds of modules are class modules and standard modules. Form and report modules, which often contain event procedures, are **class modules**. **Standard modules** contain general procedures not associated with any specific object.

Maria wants you to add a command button that users can click when working with the frmInstructors form to open the frmDepartments form. You can use a Visual Basic event procedure to do this. When you

QUICK TIP

Many Access databases contain Visual Basic code, either as event procedures attached to an object such as a form or report, or as macros written by database developers. A **macro** is set of instructions, often called a subroutine, that performs specific actions. While creating and debugging macros is fairly simple in Access, macros fall short in three areas when compared to event procedures: (1) When a macro fails, errors cannot be trapped and handled under program control; (2) Macros are stored separately from objects such as forms and reports, whereas event procedures are stored within the object itself; and (3) Macros work on an entire set of records at once, whereas you can use a procedure to manipulate an individual record when necessary. For more information on writing macros or creating event procedures, see online Help.

---

create the first event procedure for the frmInstructors form, an associated **form module** also is created. The next time you create an event procedure for the frmInstructors form, the Visual Basic code is added as a new procedure to the existing form module. First, you create another copy of the *mdbOnlineU13-* database, and then you add the command button and event procedure to the frmInstructors form in Design view. To create the database copy and add a command button with a Visual Basic event procedure to the frmInstructors form:

Step 1	Create	a copy of the *mdbOnlineU13-* database located on the Data Disk (the copy is named *mdbOnlineU13-6*)
Step 2	Open	the frmInstructors form in Design view
Step 3	Display	the Toolbox, if necessary
Step 4	Click	the Control Wizards button in the Toolbox, if necessary, to deselect it (it should not have a white background)
Step 5	Click	the Command Button button in the Toolbox
Step 6	Click	in the form Detail section at the 3-inch horizontal position to the right of the Full Name text box control and approximately two gridlines below the image control (scroll to view the Full Name and image controls)
Step 7	Observe	that the selected command button is added to the Detail section of the form
Step 8	Display	the command button's Properties sheet using the shortcut menu
Step 9	Click	the Event tab, if necessary
Step 10	Click	the On Click property text box to view its list arrow and Build button
Step 11	Click	the On Click property Build button
Step 12	Double-click	Code Builder in the Choose Builder dialog box to open the Microsoft Visual Basic window

Your screen should look similar to Figure 13-7. Although this is a very complex window, a small section (sometimes called the **code window**) in the center of the screen contains most of what you need.

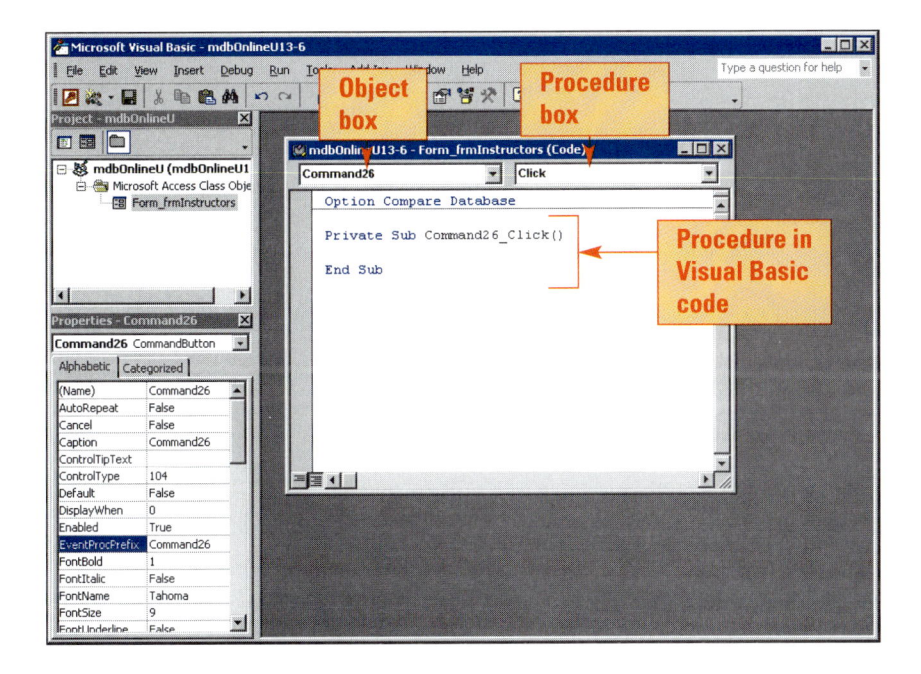

FIGURE 13-7
Microsoft Visual Basic Window

Observe that the phrase Private Sub Command#_Click() appears in the central window. (Command# is the command button's caption—yours may differ.) Table 13-1 describes the function of each part of the phrase.

Phrase	Meaning
Private	beginning of an internal Visual Basic procedure
Sub	beginning of a series of instructions
Command#	name of the command button
_Click()	Click property; the procedure executes when the Click event occurs
End Sub	end of a series of instructions

TABLE 13-1
Visual Basic Explanation

Next you key a single-line instruction to open the frmDepartments form using Visual Basic commands and syntax. As you key the single-line instruction, a drop-down list appears from which you select the appropriate command. To enter the Visual Basic procedure commands in the code window:

Step 1	Verify	that the insertion point is on the line above End Sub in the code window
Step 2	Key	DoCmd. (including the period)
Step 3	Observe	that a drop-down list appears
Step 4	Double-click	OpenForm in the list (scroll to view)
Step 5	Press	the SPACEBAR (ignore the ScreenTip that appears)

chapter thirteen

QUICK TIP

The Command Button Control Wizard provides another way to create a Visual Basic event procedure for a command button. When you answer the questions the wizard poses, the wizard creates the appropriate Visual Basic code and stores it as an event procedure with the button. For more information on using the Command Button Control Wizard, see online Help.

Step 6	Key	"frmDepartments" (including the quotation marks)
Step 7	Close	the Microsoft Visual Basic window
Step 8	Change	the command button caption to Open Departments Form in the Format tab of its Properties sheet
Step 9	Close	the Properties sheet
Step 10	Size	the command button to fit using the shortcut menu
Step 11	Save	the form
Step 12	Switch to	Form view
Step 13	Click	the Open Departments Form button to view the frmDepartments form
Step 14	Close	both forms and the database

Access modules enable you to automate forms and reports.

Summary

- ► You can protect sensitive information by securing a database against being opened by a word processing application or a utility program when you encrypt it.

- ► To prevent unauthorized access, you can require users to enter a password before they can open database.

- ► To prevent unauthorized access to database objects, you set user-level security, which requires that users log on to open a database and have permission to work with individual database objects. You can set permissions for individuals or groups; however, setting group permissions is recommended to control access to database objects for all group members.

- ► By compacting a database, you can reduce its size and optimize its performance. You also can have Access automatically repair a damaged database as it compacts that database.

- ► By splitting a database into front-end and back-end databases, you can let users customize the database's forms and reports but not modify its tables. The back-end database includes the original tables, whereas the front-end database contains links to those tables and other database objects.

- ► You can refresh the links to linked tables with the Linked Table Manager.

- ► Another way to protect the design of database forms and reports from being modified is to convert the database to an MDE file.

- ► When a user needs to work with a copy of a database and then make certain that the contents of the copy agree with the original database, you can create a replica set consisting of the design master (original database) and one or more replicas (database copies). Then the design master and replicas can be synchronized to update both the design master and the replicas with changes made to either one.

- ► You can create an event procedure to perform some action when an event occurs. A module stores the Visual Basic code for this event procedure.

chapter thirteen

Commands Review

Action	Menu Bar	Shortcut Menu	Toolbar	Task Pane	Keyboard
Encrypt/decrypt a database	Tools, Security, Encrypt/Decrypt Database				ALT + T, T, E
Open a database exclusively	File, Open, Open Exclusive				ALT + F, O, V
Set a database password	Tools, Security, Set Database Password				ALT + T, T, D
Unset a database password	Tools, Security, Unset Database Password				ALT + T, T, D
Set user-level security	Tools, Security, User and Group Accounts				ALT + T, T, A
Assign permissions	Tools, Security, User and Group Permissions				ALT + T, T, P
Compact and repair a database	Tools, Database Utilities, Compact and Repair Database				ALT + T, D, C
Split a database using the Database Splitter	Tools, Database Utilities, Database Splitter				ALT + T, D, D
Refresh linked tables with the Linked Table Manager	Tools, Database Utilities, Linked Table Manager				ALT + T, D, L
Convert a database in Access 2000 format to another format	Tools, Database Utilities, Convert Database, To Access (97, 2000, 2002) File Format				ALT + T, D, T, 7 or 0 or 2
Create an MDE file	Tools, Database Utilities, Make MDE File				ALT + T, D, M
Create a replica set	Tools, Replication, Create Replica				ALT + T, P, C
Synchronize a replica set	Tools, Replication, Synchronize Now				ALT + T, P, S

Concepts Review

Circle the correct answer.

1. Which of the following security methods requires an administrator to assign database permissions to group members?
   [a] user-level security
   [b] database password
   [c] startup options
   [d] encryption

2. Which of following security methods protects sensitive information from being opened with an application other than Access?
   [a] database password
   [b] user-level security
   [c] encryption
   [d] startup options

3. Database passwords can have a maximum of:
   [a] 10 characters.
   [b] 40 characters.
   [c] 30 characters.
   [d] 20 characters.

4. To activate user-level security, you first:
   [a] assign a database password.
   [b] make a replica of the database.
   [c] assign a password to the Admin user.
   [d] use the User command on the Tools menu.

Using Access Tools AA 117

5. In a split database, the original tables are stored in the:
   [a] front-end database.
   [b] back-end database.
   [c] replica database.
   [d] MDE file.

6. Implicit permissions are granted to:
   [a] an individual user.
   [b] all members of a user group.
   [c] a database administrator.
   [d] a database manager.

7. It's best to assign permissions to:
   [a] an individual user.
   [b] the Admin user.
   [c] groups.
   [d] no one.

8. To reduce the size of a database and optimize its performance, you should:
   [a] create an MDE file.
   [b] password-protect the database.
   [c] set user-level security.
   [d] compact and repair the database.

9. When you need to refresh the links to linked tables, you can use the:
   [a] Database Splitter.
   [b] Compact and Repair Wizard.
   [c] Linked Table Manager.
   [d] Database Replicator.

10. Which file type prevents the user from changing the design of database objects?
    [a] MKE
    [b] MDE
    [c] MDB
    [d] MDC

Circle **T** if the statement is true or **F** if the statement is false.

T F 1. To set a database password, you must open the database in exclusive mode.

T F 2. The database password cannot contain an asterisk (*) character.

T F 3. Once you set a database password, you cannot remove or change it.

T F 4. Encryption is particularly useful for databases transmitted electronically.

T F 5. As you work with a database, it usually grows larger.

T F 6. An event is a piece of Visual Basic code that performs a series of actions.

T F 7. The two kinds of modules are class modules and standard modules.

T F 8. Each time you associate an event procedure with a form, a new form module is created.

T F 9. The process of updating changes in members of a replica set is called synchronization.

T F 10. Setting a database password prevents users from changing the design of the database's objects.

Skills Review

Exercise 1

1. Create a copy of the *mdbFanTours13-* database located on the Data Disk.
2. Close the *mdbFanTours13-1* database, and then reopen it in exclusive mode so that you can set a database password.
3. Set the database password as oSHKosh.
4. Close and then reopen the database to test the password.
5. Close the database.

chapter thirteen

Exercise 2

1. Create a copy of the *mdbFanTours13-1* database you created in Exercise 1, and then close it. (*Hint:* You must use the database password you set in Exercise 1.)

2. Encrypt the *mdbFanTours13-11* database with the same name, replacing the existing file. (*Hint:* You must use the database password you set in Exercise 1.)

Exercise 3

1. Create a copy of the *mdbFanTours13-11* database you created in Exercise 2, and then close it. (*Hint:* You must use the database password you set in Exercise 1.)

2. Open the *mdbFanTours13-111* database in exclusive mode, unset the database password, and then close the database.

3. Decrypt the *mdbFanTours13-11* database following the same steps you used to encrypt it.

Exercise 4

1. Create a copy of the *mdbFanTours13-* database located on the Data Disk.

2. Open Windows Explorer and determine the size of the *mdbFanTours13-3* database file you just created.

3. Compact and repair the database and then close it.

4. Return to Windows Explorer and determine the size of the compacted database.

Exercise 5

This exercise assumes you do not have user-level security set.

1. Open the User and Group Accounts dialog box, set the 00ABC log on password for the Admin user, and then close the Access application.

2. Open the Access application and the User and Group Accounts dialog box, logging on as the Admin user with the 00ABC password.

3. Add a user named "Roberts" with the personal ID of "1234" to the Users group, click OK, and then click OK.

4. Open the *mdbFanTours13-3* database you created in Exercise 4.

5. Change the Users and Group permissions for the tblCustomers table to prevent any group member from changing the design of the table.

6. Close the database and close Access. Open Access and the database again, logging on as the Roberts user with no password.

7. Attempt to modify the design of the tblCustomers table.

8. Close the database and close Access. Reopen Access and open the User and Group Accounts dialog box, logging on as the Admin user with the appropriate password.

9. Delete Roberts from the Users group, and clear the Admin users password.

10. Close and then reopen Access to remove the user-level security.

Exercise 6

1. Create a copy of the *mdbFanTours13-* database located on the Data Disk.

2. Use the Database Splitter to split the database into a front-end database (*mdbFanTours13-4*) and a back-end database (*mdbFanTours13-4_be*).

3. Open the frmVendors form in Design view in the front-end database, and add a command button associated with an event procedure that prints the rptVendors report when clicked. (*Hint:* Use DoCmd.OpenReport "rptVendors" as your instructions.) Change the button's caption to "Print Vendors Report," and size the button to fit.

4. Save the form, switch to Form view, test the button, and then close the form.

5. Close the front-end database.

Exercise 7

1. Open the *mdbFanTours13-4* front-end database you created in Exercise 6.

2. Convert the database file to the Access 2002 format with the filename *mdbFanTours13-4 2002,* and then close the database.

3. Open the *mdbFanTours13-4 2002* database, create an MDE file named *mdbFanTours13-4 MDE,* and then close the database.

4. Open the *mdbFanTours13-4 MDE* database, and use the Linked Table Manager to refresh the links to all linked tables.

5. Open the frmVendors form and review several records. Attempt to view the frmVendors form in Design view, close the form, and close the MDE database.

Exercise 8

1. Create a copy of the *mdbFanTours13-* database located on the Data Disk.

2. Replicate the *mdbFanTours13-5* database, and let Access create a backup database. Accept the default filename.

3. Close the design master database, and open the replica database. Add the following record to the tblCustomers table in the replica: Mary D Jeffers, mdj@aol.com, 200 West Seneca Blvd., Houston, TX, 77082, E, 2/1/2002. Then close the table and the replica database.

4. Open the *mdbFanTours13-5* design master database, and use the Synchronize Now command on the Replication submenu to synchronize the design master directly with the replica.

5. Open the tblCustomers table in the design master database, and locate the added Mary Jeffers record.

6. Close the table, and then close the design master database.

Case Projects

Project 1

Using online Help, locate and print the topic "About User Level Security." Review the topic and, in a Word document, discuss how permissions work and who can assign them.

Project 2

Betty tells you she cannot remember her Access password, and she asks what she should do. Using online Help, research the "Troubleshooting Passwords" topic and, in a Word document, write what Betty should do.

Project 3

Alan Golden wants a staff member to take the FanTours database on one of the sports tours and update it on the road. Create a copy of the *mdbFanTours13-2* database located on the Data Disk. Create a replica set using the *mdbFanTours13-21* database, and let Access create a backup copy of the database. Open the replica and add a new employee to the tblEmployees table. Then synchronize the replica with the design master, and open the design master to verify that the changes were made. Close the design master database.

chapter thirteen

Project 4

Alan wants you to split the FanTours database. Create a copy of the *mdbFanTours13-2* database located on the Data Disk. Use the Database Splitter to split the *mdbFanTours13-22* database into a front-end database and a back-end database. Use a form to verify that you can view data found in the back-end database. Close the database.

Project 5

Alan calls to tell you that he cannot open the frmVendors form and gets an error message indicating that the linked tables cannot be found. Open the *mdbFanTours13-22* front-end database you created in Project 4. Use the Linked Table Manager to refresh the links to the files in the back-end database. Then open the frmVendors form, and review several records. Close the database.

Project 6

Alan wants to increase security for the FanTours database. Create a copy of the *mdbFanTours13-2* database located on the Data Disk. Open the *mdbFanTours13-23* database in exclusive mode, and set the database password "fSt420" for the database (do not include the quotation marks). Close and then reopen the database to see if the password works. Deliberately key an incorrect password to observe how Access handles this security feature. Key the correct password. Close the database.

Project 7

Alan wants you to set user-level security for the FanTours database. Using the correct password, open the *mdbFanTours13-23* database you created in Project 6 in exclusive mode. Unset the database password and close the database. Set the log on password for the Admin user to "AG9945." Close the Access application.

Project 8

You need to add Alan's new assistant, Mimi Clark, to the Users group so she can work with the FanTours database. Log on as the Admin user with the correct password, and add a user named "Clark" with a personal ID of "1234" to the Users group. Open the *mdbFanTours13-23* database you modified in Project 7, and restrict permissions for the Users group so that group members can only read data in the tblCustomers table but not add to, edit, or delete it. Close the database and close Access. Start Access, open the *mdbFanTours13-23* database, log on as Clark (with no password), and verify that Clark cannot change records in the tblCustomers table. Close the database and close the Access application. Open the Access application, log on as the Admin user with the correct password, delete the Clark user from the Users group, and clear the Admin users password. Close the Access application.

Access 2002

Integrating Access with the Internet

Chapter Overview

You can integrate an Access database with the Internet in a variety of ways: by storing hyperlinks in a table, by importing and exporting data and the data's structure to XML documents, and by creating data access pages (DAPs). In this chapter, you create and follow hyperlinks stored in a table, import from and export to an XML document, create and preview a DAP, create a PivotTable view and a PivotChart view, and save the PivotChart view as a DAP.

Learning Objectives

- View Web sites and send e-mail messages from a database
- Work with XML documents
- Create and preview a data access page
- Use PivotTable and PivotChart views

Case profile

Maria Mendez in the provost's office wants to take advantage of Internet technologies to expand the use of the OLU database. She wants to display Web pages and send e-mail while working in the database, import data collected from the Web into the database, and export data to documents she can then import to Internet applications. She also wants to make some data from the database available to others over the university's intranet.

chapter fourteen

> **notes**
> The activities in this chapter assume that you are using Internet Explorer as your Web browser and Outlook as your e-mail software. Your instructor may provide alternate instructions if you are using a different Web browser or different e-mail software. Your instructor may also provide alternate e-mail addresses and Web site URLs, if necessary.

14.a Viewing Web Sites and Sending E-mail Messages from a Database

The **Internet** is a worldwide public network of private networks over which users view and transfer information between computers. You can use the Internet to communicate with others, for example, by sending and receiving e-mail and finding information on Web pages stored on servers at **World Wide Web** (commonly called the Web) sites. You can integrate an Access database with the Internet to view sites on the Web as well as to send e-mail messages.

Viewing Web Sites

Maria Mendez maintains a list of other schools in the OLU database and wants to be able to access a school's Web site as she works on the database. To help Maria do this, you add a field with the Hyperlink data type to the tblSchools table in the OLU database. Recall that the Hyperlink data type lets you store the path and filename to a Web page (called the *Web address* or *URL*) in a table record.

To add a field with a Hyperlink data type to the tblSchools table:

Step 1	*Create*	a copy of the *mdbOnlineU14-* database located on the Data Disk
Step 2	*Open*	the tblSchools table in Design view
Step 3	*Add*	a new field named WebSite with the Hyperlink data type, School's Web site address as the description, and Web Site as the caption
Step 4	*Save*	the table

You can now enter the Web site addresses (URLs) in the tblSchools table in Datasheet view. To enter the Web addresses:

Step 1	Switch to	Datasheet view
Step 2	Enter	www.asu.edu in the Arizona State University Web Site field
Step 3	Observe	that the *www.asu.edu* text changes to colored, underlined text, indicating that the text is a hyperlink
Step 4	Continue	by entering the following URLs: Florida State University www.fsu.edu Indiana State University www.indstate.edu State University of New York www.suny.edu University of Southern California www.usc.edu University of Tennessee www.utenn.edu University of Texas www.utsystem.edu
Step 5	Widen	the Web Site column to view the complete URL for each school
Step 6	Save	the table
Step 7	Click	the www.indstate.edu hyperlink to open your browser and view the Indiana State University Web site home page
Step 8	Close	the browser
Step 9	Close	the table

You also can send e-mail messages from a database.

Sending E-Mail Messages

Maria wants to be able to send e-mail messages to instructors when she is working on the OLU database. To do that, she needs a field with a Hyperlink data type in the tblInstructors table that contains mailto: hyperlinks. A **mailto: hyperlink** is a hyperlink in the format *mailto:username@domain*. When you click a mailto: hyperlink in a table record, Access opens your e-mail application, creates a new e-mail message, and places the e-mail address from the mailto: hyperlink in the To: address text box.

The tblInstructors table already has a field named EmailAddress. First, you need to modify the table's data to add the mailto: prefix to the e-mail address for each record in the table. Next, you need to modify the table's EmailAddress field in Design view to change its data type to Hyperlink.

MOUSE TIP

When you point to a hyperlink, a ScreenTip appears that shows the full path to or the URL of the Web site.

QUICK TIP

You can insert a specific e-mail address in a form in Design view. Use the Hyperlink command on the Insert menu to open the Insert Hyperlink dialog box. Then click the E-mail Address option in the Link to: bar, and key the e-mail address in the E-mail address: text box. Access inserts a mailto: hyperlink on the form. When you switch to Form view, you can click the link to open the e-mail message window.

You also can insert a specific URL as a hyperlink in a form in the same way—by opening the Insert Hyperlink dialog box and keying the URL in the Address: text box. For more information on creating and formatting hyperlinks, see online Help.

To modify the tblInstructors table data in Datasheet view to add the mailto: prefix to each e-mail address:

Step 1	Open	the tblInstructors table in Datasheet view
Step 2	Click	in the Email Address field for the first record and move the insertion point in front of the e-mail address
Step 3	Key	mailto:
Step 4	Select	the mailto: text and copy it to the Office Clipboard
Step 5	Paste	the mailto: text in front of the e-mail address for the second record
Step 6	Continue	to paste the mailto: text in front of the remaining e-mail addresses
Step 7	Save	the table

To change the EmailAddress field's data type and test a mailto: hyperlink:

Step 1	Switch to	Design view
Step 2	Change	the EmailAddress field to the Hyperlink data type
Step 3	Save	the table
Step 4	Switch to	Datasheet view
Step 5	Observe	that the e-mail addresses in the Email Address field are now hyperlinks

Your screen should look similar to Figure 14-1.

FIGURE 14-1
Mailto: Hyperlinks

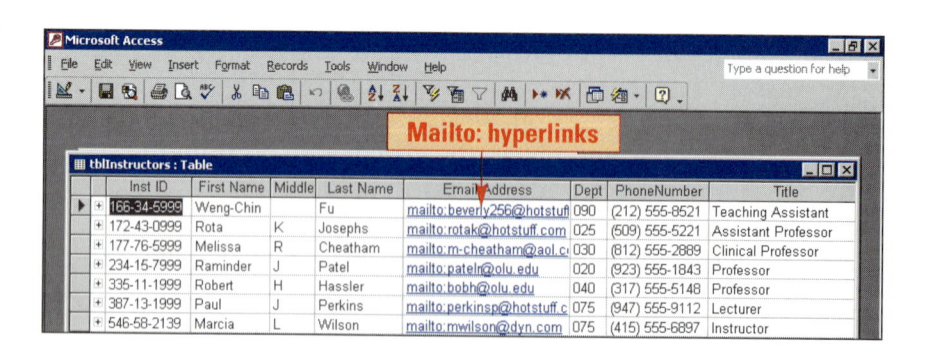

Step 6	Click	the mailto: hyperlink e-mail address for any record to test the mailto: hyperlink
Step 7	Observe	that the Outlook e-mail message window opens (it may open maximized or minimized with just a button on the taskbar)

Step 8	Maximize	the Outlook e-mail message window, if necessary, to observe that the To: address text box contains the e-mail address from the tblInstructors table
Step 9	Close	the Outlook e-mail message window without saving changes
Step 10	Close	the table

Hyperlinks in an Access table make it easy for Maria and other OLU managers to connect to specific Web sites or send e-mail messages.

14.b Working with XML Documents

The **World Wide Web Consortium** (**W3C**) is an international consortium of companies involved with the Internet and the Web founded in 1994 by Tim Berners-Lee, the original architect of the Web. The purpose of the W3C is to develop open standards for the Web such as the **HyperText Transfer Protocol** (**HTTP**), which defines how information on the Web is transmitted, and the **HyperText Markup Language** (**HTML**), which defines the layout and formatting of Web pages. The W3C developed the **Extensible Markup Language** (**XML**) as a way to define, transmit, validate, and interpret data sent between applications. For example, XML enables Internet applications to use data from an Access database or an Excel worksheet.

Importing an XML Document into Access

Typically you import data from an XML document into an existing Access table for which you already have the structure or schema. A **schema** is the structure of a relational database system that defines tables and fields and the relationships between them. XML also supports a format for importing the schema for a set of data, which lets you create a new table with field names, data types, field widths, and field properties already embedded in the data.

Maria wants to import some class data from a local community college into the OLU database. She already created an empty table named xmlCCCclasses, and she asks you to import an XML document named *xmlCCCclasses*, which contains the desired data, into the table. When you import an XML document, Access looks for an existing table with *the same name* as the XML document, and appends the data records to that table. To import data from an XML document into an existing table:

| Step 1 | View | the Tables objects in the Database window, if necessary |

> **QUICK TIP**
>
> Many people believe that XML may become the next industry standard. For example, Microsoft Corporation, a big proponent of XML, touts its Microsoft.NET XML Web services platform as the next generation of software to communicate and share data over the Internet, regardless of operating system or programming language. For more information on Microsoft.NET, go to the Microsoft Web site.

INTERNET TIP

You can search the Web for more information on XML and how to use it. An excellent place to start is the W3C Web page entitled "XML in 10 points," available on the Web at *www.w3.org/XML/1999/XML-in-10-points*.

Step 2	Click	File
Step 3	Point to	Get External Data
Step 4	Click	Import
Step 5	Switch to	the Data Disk, if necessary
Step 6	Click	XML Documents in the Files of type: list
Step 7	Double-click	xmlCCCclasses
Step 8	Click	Options >> in the Import XML dialog box to expand the dialog box

The Import XML dialog box on your screen should look similar to Figure 14-2.

FIGURE 14-2
Expanded Import XML Dialog Box

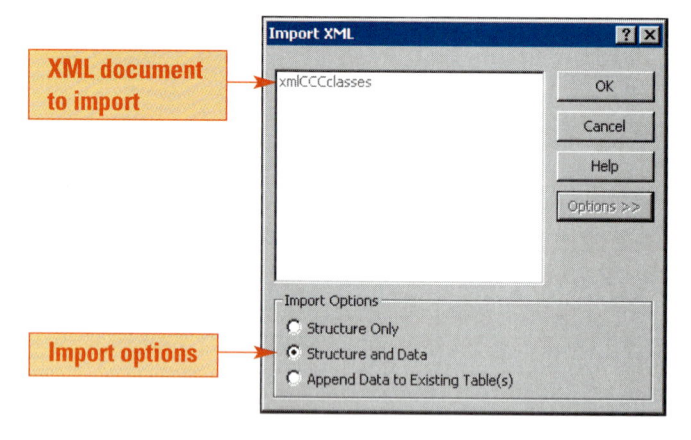

[Dialog box image: Import XML with "xmlCCCclasses" listed, labeled "XML document to import"; Import Options section labeled "Import options" with Structure Only, Structure and Data (selected), Append Data to Existing Table(s); buttons OK, Cancel, Help, Options >>]

You can define the type of import you want in this dialog box: structure only, structure and data, or append the data in the XML document to an existing table. Because an empty table already exists, you want to append the data.

Step 9	Click	the Append Data to Existing Table(s) option button
Step 10	Click	OK
Step 11	Click	OK to acknowledge that Access has finished importing the XML file
Step 12	Double-click	the xmlCCCclasses table to open it in Datasheet view
Step 13	Observe	that 23 records from the XML document were imported into the table
Step 14	Close	the table

Integrating Access with the Internet   AA 127

Exporting Access Data to an XML Document

It is easy to export an Access table or query (the data and the schema) to an XML document for use in Internet applications. Maria asks if you can export the list of programs that the tblPrograms table contains to a document she can use later in Internet applications. You can export the tblPrograms table data to an XML document to do this. To export the tblPrograms table to an XML document:

Step 1	*Right-click*	tblPrograms
Step 2	*Click*	E̲xport
Step 3	*Key*	xmlPrograms in the File n̲ame: text box
Step 4	*Click*	XML Documents in the Save as t̲ype: list
Step 5	*Click*	E̲xport

The Export XML dialog box that opens on your screen should look similar to Figure 14-3.

FIGURE 14-3
Export XML Dialog Box

You specify what to export in this dialog box: the data in XML format and/or the structure in an XML schema document. Specifying both the data and the structure creates a separate XML schema document.

Step 6	*Verify*	that both the D̲ata (XML) and S̲chema of the data check boxes contain check marks
Step 7	*Click*	OK to export the schema and the data

Access creates a file named *xmlPrograms.xml* that contains the data for the fields in the tblPrograms table and a file named *xmlPrograms.xsd* that contains the schema. Both files are stored in the same folder, which also stores the database file. To view the *xmlPrograms* file in Internet Explorer:

Step 1	*Open*	Internet Explorer

MOUSE TIP

You can click the Advanced button in the Export XML dialog box to specify whether to save the schema in a separate file, called an XSD file, or embedded within the XML file. Click the desired option for the Export L̲ocation.

chapter fourteen

Step 2	**Click**	<u>F</u>ile
Step 3	**Click**	<u>O</u>pen
Step 4	**Click**	the Browse button and switch to the location where your completed files are stored
Step 5	**Click**	All Files in the Files of <u>t</u>ype: list
Step 6	**Double-click**	xmlPrograms.xml
Step 7	**Click**	OK to open this file

Your screen should look similar to Figure 14-4.

FIGURE 14-4
xmlPrograms Document

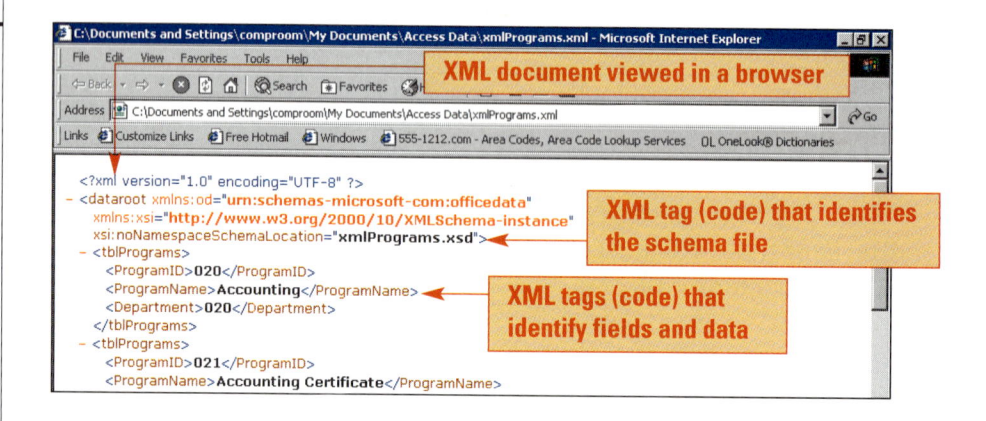

Step 8	**Observe**	that Access added a special tag that identifies the schema file, xmlPrograms.xsd
Step 9	**Close**	the browser

Maria can use the *xmlPrograms* file to import the OLU program data into Internet applications. Data access pages provide a way to view database data via a Web page.

14.c Creating and Previewing a Data Access Page

Recall that a data access page (DAP) is a dynamic HTML file linked to a database object viewed in a browser. In other words, whenever you open the DAP in your browser, the DAP displays current data from the database to which it is connected. You can use the Save <u>A</u>s command to convert a database object (a table, a form, or a report) to an equivalent DAP. You already know how to create a simple DAP using the Page Wizard. You also can create a DAP from scratch in Design view.

QUICK TIP

HTML and XML both use markup code called **tags** (words enclosed in angle brackets, < >). HTML also uses attributes (in the format name="value") for tags. HTML uses the tags and attributes to specify the position and format of items such as text and images and to define how a Web page looks in a browser. XML uses tags only to delimit pieces of data and leaves the interpretation of the data completely to the application into which the data is imported.

Creating a Data Access Page in Design View

Maria wants to add a DAP to the university's intranet that displays the class information contained in the tblClasses table. To do that, you want to create a DAP from scratch. Creating a DAP from scratch in Design view is similar to creating a form in Design view: You drag fields from the Field List window or add controls from the Toolbox to a design grid. To create a DAP from scratch that displays class information:

Step 1	*View*	the Pages objects in the Database window
Step 2	*Double-click*	Create data access page in Design view
Step 3	*Observe*	the message warning that a DAP created in Design view in Access 2002 cannot be opened in Design view in Access 2000
Step 4	*Click*	OK

Access opens a blank data access page with a design grid, the Field List window, and the Alignment and Sizing toolbar. The Toolbox may also open. If the Field List window, Toolbox, and Alignment and Sizing toolbar do not automatically open, you can open them manually.

> **notes**
> The illustrations in this section show the Formatting (Page) toolbar below the Page Design toolbar. The position of your Formatting (Page) toolbar may differ. Also, the Field List window has been resized to show more of the design grid area.

To open the Toolbox, the Alignment and Sizing toolbar, and the Field List window, if necessary:

Step 1	*Click*	the Toolbox button on the Page Design toolbar
Step 2	*Click*	the Field List button on the Page Design toolbar
Step 3	*Right-click*	any toolbar
Step 4	*Click*	Alignment and Sizing

> **QUICK TIP**
>
> You can modify a DAP in Design view much as you would modify a form in Design view, although you cannot select more than one control at a time. You can add fields from the Field List window, move fields, and change fields' sizes. The Toolbox is available to add other controls.

To display the fields in the tblClasses table and drag the desired fields to the design grid:

Step 1	**Click**	the plus sign (+) in front of tblClasses in the Field List window to display the table's fields
Step 2	**Drag**	the ClassID field from the Field List window to the first vertical gridline in the design grid and drop it at the top of the design grid
Step 3	**Drag**	the DeptPrefix field from the Field List window to the first vertical gridline in the design grid and drop it one horizontal gridline below the ClassID field
Step 4	**Drag**	the CourseNumber field from the Field List window to the third vertical gridline in the design grid to the right of the DeptPrefix field and drop it, leaving approximately one gridline between the Course Number label and the DeptPrefix text box
Step 5	**Drag**	the ClassRoom field from the Field List to the first vertical gridline in the design grid and drop it one horizontal gridline below the DeptPrefix field
Step 6	**Drag**	the ClassLocation field from the Field List to the third vertical gridline in the design grid and drop it one horizontal gridline below the CourseNumber field
Step 7	**Rearrange**	the fields to match the spacing and alignment shown in Figure 14-5, if necessary

Your screen should look similar to Figure 14-5.

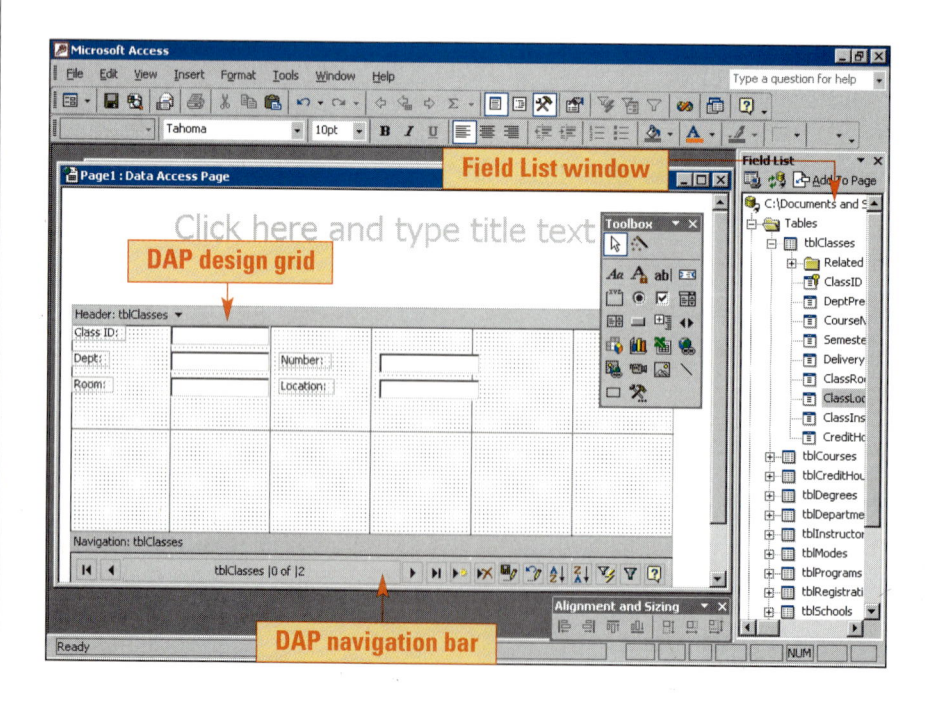

FIGURE 14-5
DAP Design View

Integrating Access with the Internet **AA 131**

Next you add a title to the DAP.

Step 8	Click	in the gray title text area
Step 9	Key	OLU Classes
Step 10	Save	the DAP as dapClasses
Step 11	Click	OK if a message warns you about the absolute path for the DAP and not being able to open the DAP on a network
Step 12	Switch to	Page view to view the DAP as it appears in a Web browser

You can use the navigation area to maneuver through the data in the DAP and work with the filter and sort features. To navigate, sort, and filter records:

Step 1	Click	the Next button in the navigation area to view the second record
Step 2	Click	in the Dept: text box to position the insertion point
Step 3	Click	the Sort Descending button to sort the records in descending order
Step 4	Observe	that Class ID 00196 is now the first record
Step 5	Sort	the Dept: field in Ascending order to return the records to their original order
Step 6	Click	the Dept: field to position the insertion point
Step 7	Click	the Filter by Selection button in the navigation area to filter the list to view the four ACCT records
Step 8	Click	the Filter Toggle button in the navigation area to remove the filter
Step 9	Switch to	Design view

In Design view, you can display the Group Properties window. From this window, you can control whether users are allowed to add or modify records via the DAP, and you can provide additional sorting features within the DAP. To examine the GroupLevel properties in a DAP:

Step 1	Verify	that the dapClasses DAP is open in Design view
Step 2	Click	the Header: tblClasses list arrow in the design grid
Step 3	Click	Group Level Properties to display the GroupLevel Properties sheet for the tblClasses table

> **CAUTION TIP**
>
> Access saves a DAP in a separate file and places it in the same folder as the database file. A DAP connects to the database via its connection string property. A DAP works only if the database is located on the same path and has the same name as those given by the connection string property. If you move the DAP and/or database, you must reestablish the connection before you can view the DAP. To reestablish the connection, open the DAP in Design view and display the Field List window. Click the Page connection properties button in the Field List window to view the Data Link Properties dialog box. On the Connection tab, browse to select the database name and path. Then switch to Page view and close the DAP, saving the changes.

chapter fourteen

> **QUICK TIP**
>
> The ideal environment for a DAP is within an organization's intranet so you can ensure that users have the proper software to view it. The user must be licensed for Microsoft Office 2000 or later and be running Internet Explorer 5.0 or later. DAPs are less appropriate for the Internet because some users may not be able to view the HTML file produced by the DAP.

The first three properties, all True by default, permit additions, deletions, and edits to data stored in the DAP. If you do not want users to add, delete, or edit records, you must change the True values of these properties to False. You do not want users to be able to add, delete, or edit the records, so you set the AllowAdditions, AllowDeletions, and AllowEdits properties to False. Because users cannot add, delete, or edit records, they also cannot sort or filter them.

Step 4	Change	the AllowAdditions, AllowDeletions, and AllowEdits properties to False
Step 5	Close	the GroupLevel Properties sheet
Step 6	Switch to	Page view
Step 7	Observe	that the only active buttons in the navigation area allow users to view records
Step 8	Close	the page, saving the changes

Previewing a Data Access Page

After you finish creating or modifying a DAP, you should preview it in a Web browser. You can preview a DAP in a Web browser from within Access. To preview the dapClasses DAP:

Step 1	Right-click	dapClasses in the Database window
Step 2	Click	We**b** Page Preview to open Internet Explorer and view the *dapClasses* file in the browser
Step 3	Close	the browser

> **INTERNET TIP**
>
> To publish a DAP, you must have permission to write to a Web server attached to the intranet or Internet. FTP, File Transport Protocol, is one way to transfer files from your computer to the Web server. Remember that *both* the HTML file and the database to which it connects must be available on the Web server for users to view data in the DAP.

14.d Using PivotTable and PivotChart Views

Access provides a way for you to analyze data dynamically and perform calculations on subgroups of records in a table or query datasheet or form: PivotTable view and PivotChart view. **PivotTable view** is an interactive view that you can use to summarize table or query datasheets or forms quickly in a variety of ways. You can rotate rows and columns to see different summaries of the underlying source data and filter the data. For example, you can display all students by major and by credit hours earned and then filter by major to list only accounting majors. **PivotChart view** lets you create dynamic interactive charts based on the data underlying a table or query datasheet or form.

Viewing Query Data in PivotTable View

Maria asks if there is some way you can help her analyze class registrations. She wants to see which students are enrolled in each course offered by each department. Then she wants to be able to filter this information by instructor. The basic information is available from the qryStudentClasses query, which gets its data from four underlying source tables: tblStudents, tblRegistration, tblClasses, and tblInstructors. You decide to create a PivotTable view based on the qryStudentClasses data to help Maria get the information she needs. To create a PivotTable view based on the qryStudentClasses query:

Step 1	View	the Queries objects in the Database window
Step 2	Open	the qryStudentClasses query in Datasheet view
Step 3	Click	the View button list arrow on the Datasheet toolbar
Step 4	Click	PivotTable View to view the PivotTable view workspace and PivotTable Field List

Your screen should look similar to Figure 14-6.

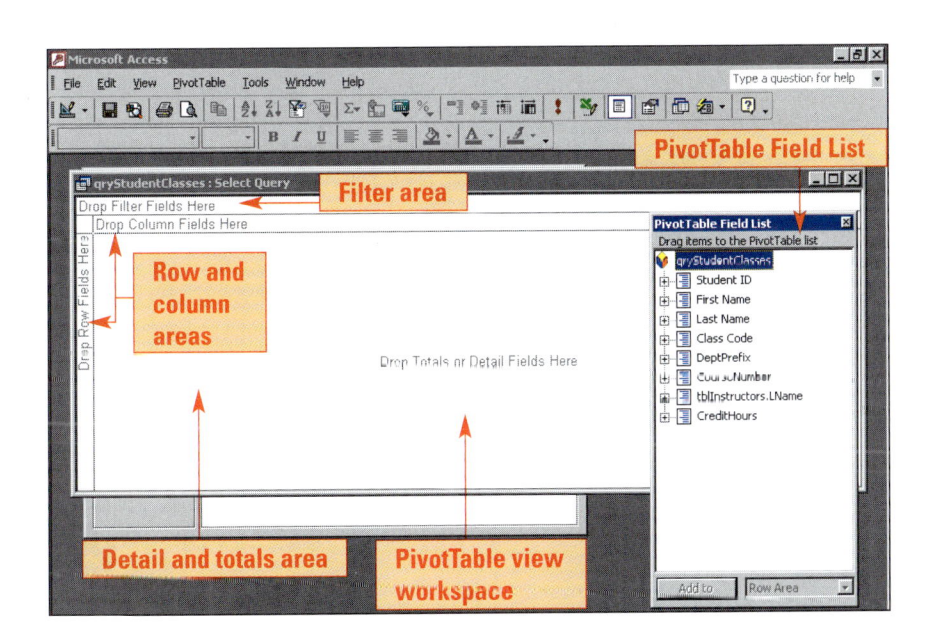

FIGURE 14-6
Blank PivotTable View Workspace and PivotTable Field List

You summarize the underlying data by dragging fields from the PivotTable Field List window to the predefined drop areas in the PivotTable view workspace. You use the **Drop Row Fields Here** and **Drop Column Fields Here** areas to summarize the data and display unique data items down rows or across columns. You use the **Drop Total or Detail Fields Here** area to display all the detail records from

QUICK TIP

You can remove a field from the PivotTable view workspace by dragging the field out of the workspace with the mouse pointer. Removing fields from the PivotTable view workspace does not remove the field from the underlying source data; the field remains in the PivotTable Field List so that you can add it back to the PivotTable view workspace, if desired. Filter settings are retained if you remove a field. If you remove a field and later add it back to the PivotTable view workspace, the same items are again filtered. For more information on adding, moving, and removing fields in PivotTable view, see online Help.

the underlying source data. You use the **Drop Filter Fields Here** area to view a specific part of the data. You can add new fields by adding total fields summarizing the detail data. To eliminate data you do not want to see, you can remove fields from the PivotTable view workspace.

To provide the information Maria needs, you want to summarize each department by row and each class by column. The students' last names should appear in the detail area for each department and class, and the entire view should be filtered by instructor last name. To drag the appropriate fields to the PivotTable view workspace:

Step 1	*Drag*	the tblInstructors.LName field from the PivotTable Field List window and drop it in the Drop Filter Fields Here area of the PivotTable view workspace
Step 2	*Drag*	the DeptPrefix field from the PivotTable Field List window and drop it in the Drop Row Fields Here area of the PivotTable view workspace
Step 3	*Drag*	the Class Code field from the PivotTable Field List window and drop it in the Drop Column Fields Here area of the PivotTable view workspace
Step 4	*Drag*	the Last Name field from the PivotTable Field List window and drop it in the Drop Totals or Detail Fields Here area of the PivotTable view workspace

Your screen should look similar to Figure 14-7.

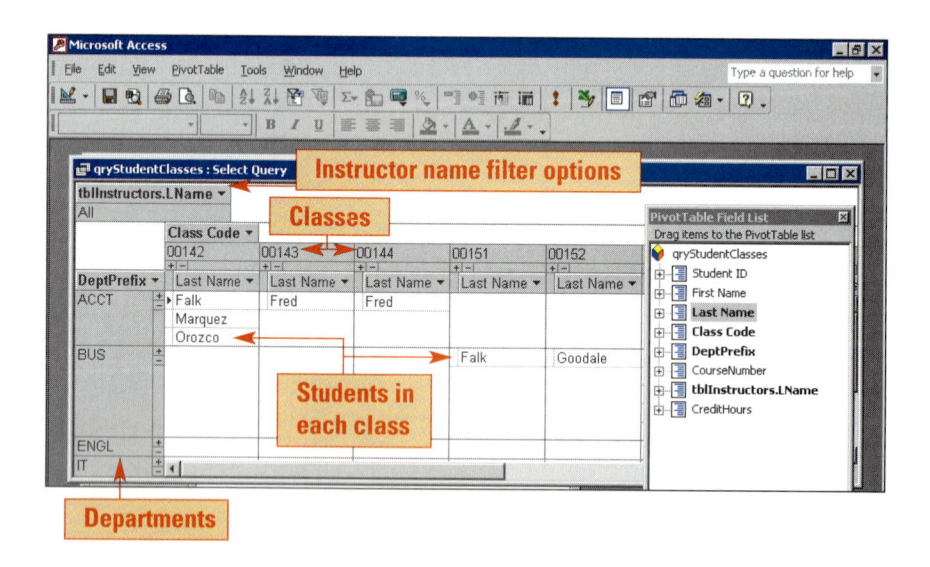

FIGURE 14-7
qryStudentClasses Query in PivotTable View

Currently you are viewing information for all instructors, all classes, and all departments. To view a subset of the records, you can filter the records by clicking the list arrow for the tblInstructors.LName, Class

Code, or DeptPrefix fields. You want to filter the view to see only those students of instructor Patel. To filter the view by instructor last name:

Step 1	Click	the tblInstructors.LName field list arrow to view a list of instructors
Step 2	Observe	that all instructors have check marks in their check boxes, indicating that all are selected for viewing
Step 3	Click	the All check box to remove the check mark and deselect all the instructors
Step 4	Click	the Patel check box to insert a check mark and select Patel for viewing
Step 5	Click	OK
Step 6	Observe	that instructor Patel teaches two classes in the ACCT department—three students are registered for the 00142 class and one student is registered for the 00143 class
Step 7	Click	the tblInstructors.LName field list arrow to view a list of instructors
Step 8	Click	the All check box to insert a check mark and select all the instructors
Step 9	Click	OK to again view information for all instructors

When you close the PivotTable view, Access automatically saves the PivotTable view workspace layout so that the next time you open the object in PivotTable view, you see the same workspace layout you were viewing when you closed the PivotTable view.

Step 10	Close	the PivotTable view and save the changes to the query

Another way to analyze data is in PivotChart view.

Viewing Query Data in PivotChart View

You can create dynamic charts to display data graphically in PivotChart view. Access provides 10 chart types, including standard types such as area, column, bar, line, and pie charts. Access also offers several specialty charts for displaying stock price information (high-low-close), XY (scatter), radar, and polar charts for certain kinds of data series. You create a PivotChart view manually in the same way you create a PivotTable view—by opening a table or query datasheet or form, switching to PivotChart view, and then dragging the desired fields to the PivotChart view workspace.

> **QUICK TIP**
>
> If you first create a PivotTable view for a table or query datasheet or for a form, Access automatically uses the PivotTable view to create a chart that you see when you open the underlying object in PivotChart view. If you first create a PivotChart view, Access automatically creates a PivotTable view for the object.

Maria wants to view a chart that displays the credit hours generated by department over two semesters. The qryCreditHours query, based on the underlying source tables, tblCreditHours and tblDepartments, provides the basic data for this chart. To create a PivotChart view that displays credit hours generated by department for two semesters:

Step 1	*Open*	the qryCreditHours query in Datasheet view
Step 2	*Click*	the View button list arrow [Design] on the Standard toolbar
Step 3	*Click*	PivotChart View

The **Drop Filter Fields Here** area lets you determine which records appear in the chart. The **Drop Data Fields Here** area should contain values to be plotted on the vertical Value (y) axis. The **Drop Category Fields Here** area should contain values to be plotted on the horizontal Category (x) axis. The **Drop Series Fields Here** area should contain values that appear in the chart legend identifying each data series. You drag the fields from the Chart Field List window to the PivotChart view workspace to create the chart. If the Chart Field List window does not automatically open, you can open it.

Step 4	*Click*	the Field List button on the PivotChart toolbar to view the Chart Field List window, if necessary
Step 5	*Drag*	the CreditHoursGenerated field from the Chart Field List window to the Drop Data Fields Here area to summarize the credit hours
Step 6	*Drag*	Dept Name field from the Chart Field List window to the Drop Category Fields Here area to place the department names on the chart's Category (x) axis
Step 7	*Drag*	SemesterCode from the Chart Field List window to the Drop Series Fields Here area to create the legend (you may need to drag the Chart Field List window out of the way to see the drop area)
Step 8	*Close*	the Chart Field List window to view the chart better
Step 9	*Observe*	that each department on the Category (x) axis has two credit hour (data) columns, one for each semester code

Your screen should look similar to Figure 14-8.

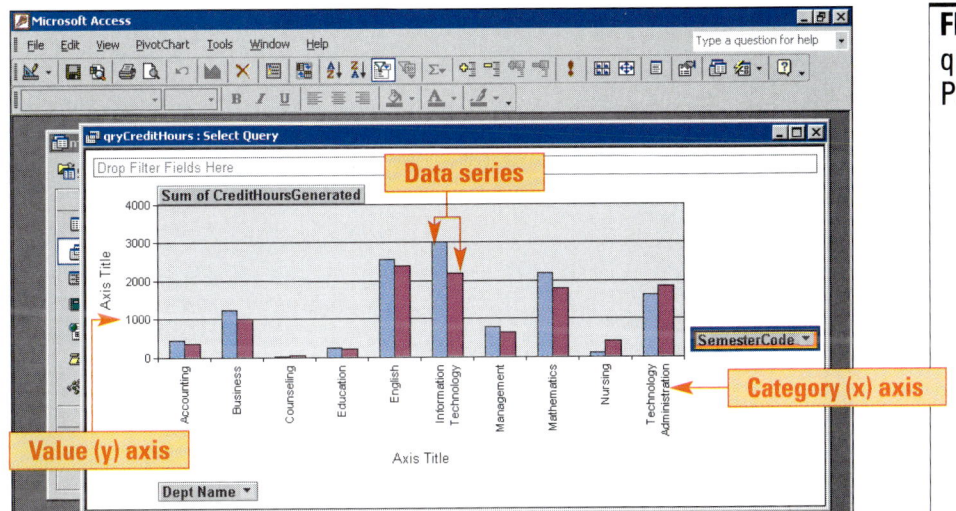

FIGURE 14-8
qryCreditHours Query in PivotChart View

You can customize a PivotChart in a variety of ways by modifying the properties of the chart's objects, such as its axis titles. You want to use "Departments" for the Category (x) axis title and "Cumulative Credit Hours" for the Value (y) axis title. To modify the axis titles:

Step 1	Open	the Category (x) axis title Properties dialog box using a shortcut menu
Step 2	Click	the Format tab
Step 3	Key	Departments in the Caption: text box
Step 4	Press	the ENTER key
Step 5	Click	the Value (y) axis title to select its properties in the Properties dialog box
Step 6	Key	Cumulative Credit Hours in the Caption: text box
Step 7	Press	the ENTER key
Step 8	Close	the Properties dialog box
Step 9	Observe	the new axes titles
Step 10	Close	the PivotChart view, saving changes to the query

To enable others on a company intranet to work with an object's PivotTable or PivotChart view, you can save the views as DAPs.

chapter fourteen

Saving a PivotTable or PivotChart View as a DAP

When you save a PivotTable or PivotChart view as a DAP and then publish the DAP on a company intranet, other users can take advantage of the dynamic nature of the PivotTable or PivotChart view to manipulate and rearrange the data to meet their information needs. You create a PivotTable or PivotChart view DAP by opening the PivotTable or the PivotChart view and then using the Save As command on the File menu to save the view as a DAP. Maria wants to publish the qryCreditHours chart on the university's intranet as a DAP. To save the qryCreditHours PivotChart view as a DAP:

Step 1	Open	the qryCreditHours query in PivotChart view
Step 2	Click	File
Step 3	Click	Save As
Step 4	Click	Data Access Page in the As list
Step 5	Click	OK
Step 6	Key	dapCreditHours in the File name: text box
Step 7	Click	OK

Access saves the PivotChart view as *dapCreditHours.htm* in the same folder as the database file and displays a preview of the DAP. You want to preview the DAP in your Web browser.

Step 8	Close	the DAP and close the PivotChart view
Step 9	View	the Pages objects in the Database window
Step 10	Right-click	dapCreditHours
Step 11	Click	Web Page Preview to open your browser and view the DAP

Users can now open the DAP in their browsers and manipulate the chart by viewing the credit hour summary for an individual semester or individual department.

| Step 12 | Close | the browser and close the database |

You can use Access databases with the Internet in a variety of ways.

Summary

- ▶ You can add fields with a Hyperlink data type to a table and then add Web site URLs or e-mail addresses to the data, which then become live hyperlinks you can click to view Web sites or send e-mail.

- ▶ The World Wide Web Consortium (W3C) sets open standards for the Web, such as HTTP for transmitting information on the Web and HTML for structuring and formatting Web pages.

- ▶ The W3C developed Extensible Markup Language (XML) as a way to define, transmit, validate, and interpret data sent between applications.

- ▶ You can import data from an XML document directly into an existing table that matches the schema of the data in the XML document, or you can import both the data and the schema to create a new table.

- ▶ You can export a table or query to an XML document and export the data or the schema or both.

- ▶ You can create data access pages (DAPs) in Design view much like you create a form or report in Design view by dragging fields and controls to the design grid.

- ▶ PivotTable view and PivotChart view provide two ways to analyze dynamically the data in a table or query datasheet or in a form.

- ▶ You can save a PivotTable view or PivotChart view as a DAP.

chapter fourteen

Commands Review

Action	Menu Bar	Shortcut Menu	Toolbar	Task Pane	Keyboard
Import an XML document	File, Get External Data, Import				ALT + F, G, I
Export an XML document	File, Save As; specify XML Documents	Right-click object, click Save As, specify XML documents			ALT + F, A F12
Display Group Level Properties of a DAP in Design view	View, Properties	Right-click design grid, click Group Level Properties			ALT + V, P
Web Page Preview of a DAP	File, Web Page Preview	Right-click DAP, click Web Page Preview			ALT + F, B
Open table or query datasheet or form in PivotTable view	View, PivotTable View	Right-click object, click PivotTable View			ALT + V, O
Open table or query datasheet or form in PivotChart view	View, PivotChart View	Right-click object, click PivotChart View			ALT + V, V
Add a field to PivotTable or PivotChart view			Drag the field from the Field List window to the drop area in the workspace		
Remove a field from a PivotTable		Right-click the field in the PivotTable grid, click Remove	Drag the field a PivotTable out of the workspace		
Save PivotTable or PivotChart as a DAP	File, Save As				ALT + F, A F12

Concepts Review

Circle the correct answer.

1. You can convert a table field data type from Text to Hyperlink in:
   - [a] Design view.
   - [b] Datasheet view.
   - [c] Form view.
   - [d] Hyperlink view.

2. To convert an e-mail address in a text field to a hyperlink, which of the following must you key before the e-mail address?
   - [a] http://
   - [b] mailto:
   - [c] email://
   - [d] XML

3. XML is an abbreviation for:
   - [a] Exciting Markup Language.
   - [b] Excruciating Markup Language.
   - [c] Extensible Markup Language.
   - [d] Exemplary Markup Language.

4. A schema defines:
   - [a] tables and fields and the relationship between them.
   - [b] a mailto: hyperlink.
   - [c] the design of a DAP.
   - [d] Group Level Properties.

5. PivotTable view is used to:
   - [a] import data and its schema from an XML document.
   - [b] create a Hyperlink data type.
   - [c] analyze data dynamically.
   - [d] display data graphically.

6. The Drop Filter Fields Here area of a PivotChart workspace is used to:
   [a] plot values on the Value (y) axis.
   [b] determine which records appear in the chart.
   [c] plot values on the Category (x) axis.
   [d] create a chart legend.

7. The Internet is:
   [a] the World Wide Web.
   [b] a public network of private networks.
   [c] used to create XML documents.
   [d] too difficult to use, so most people avoid it.

8. The ideal environment for a DAP is:
   [a] the Internet.
   [b] the World Wide Web.
   [c] a company intranet.
   [d] an XML document.

9. To summarize data by row in PivotTable view, you should drag a field to which area of the PivotTable view workspace?
   [a] Drop Column Fields Here
   [b] Drop Filter Fields Here
   [c] Drop Row Fields Here
   [d] Drop Total or Detail Fields Here

10. When you create a PivotChart view for a table or query datasheet or a form, which of the following does Access automatically create if one has not already been created?
    [a] PivotTable view
    [b] XML document
    [c] Mailto: hyperlink
    [d] DAP

Circle **T** if the statement is true or **F** is the statement is false.

T F 1. An XML document can contain the schema and the data values.

T F 2. By modifying a DAP's Group Level Properties, you can control whether viewers can add, delete, or edit records when viewing the DAP.

T F 3. You cannot create a DAP from scratch in Design view.

T F 4. If you move a DAP or its database or store it in a different folder than the one in which it was originally stored, you need to reestablish the connection between the DAP and the database.

T F 5. A PivotTable view is a view of a table or query datasheet or a form.

T F 6. Once you filter a PivotTable or PivotChart view, you must delete the view and start over with a new PivotTable or PivotChart view to remove the filter's effects.

T F 7. Microsoft developed XML to lay out and format Web pages.

T F 8. You can save a PivotTable or PivotChart view as a DAP that can be viewed in a Web browser.

T F 9. A DAP is a dynamic XML document.

T F 10. The mailto: hyperlink has this format: mailto:domain@username.

Skills Review

Exercise 1

1. Create a copy of the *mdbFanTours14-* database located on the Data Disk.
2. Open the tblCustomers table in Datasheet view.
3. Add the mailto: text to each e-mail address in the Email column.

chapter fourteen

4. Switch to Design view and change the data type for the EmailAddress field to Hyperlink.

5. Save the changes and switch to Datasheet view.

6. Click one of the e-mail addresses values to confirm that your e-mail message window opens and contains that address in the To: address text box. Close the e-mail message window without sending the message.

7. Close the table and close the database.

Exercise 2

1. Open the *mdbFanTours14-1* database you created in Exercise 1.

2. Open the tblEvents table in Design view.

3. Add a new field named "EventWebSite," with the Hyperlink data type, the "Event's Web site address" description, and the "Web Site" caption.

4. Save the table.

5. Switch to Datasheet view and add the follow URLs to the appropriate record:

   Rose Bowl   *www.tournamentofroses.com*
   Orange Bowl   *www.orangebowl.org*
   Super Bowl   *www.superbowl.com*
   The Masters   *www.masters.org*
   PGA   *www.pgatour.com*
   Indy 500   *www.indy500.com*

6. Widen the Web Site column to view the complete URLs.

7. Test the URLs by clicking them to open the pages in the browser.

8. Close the browser, close the table saving the changes, and close the database.

Exercise 3

1. Open the *mdbFanTours14-1* database you modified in Exercise 2.

2. Open the tblProspects table in Datasheet view.

3. Export this table to an XML document named "xmlProspects" *without* schema.

4. Close the table and close the database.

5. Open the XML file in your browser to view its contents, and then close the browser.

Exercise 4

1. Open the *mdbFanTours14-1* database you modified in Exercise 3.

2. Open the qryCustomerBookings query in Datasheet view.

3. Export this query to an XML document named "xmlCustomerBookings" and export the schema in an XSD file.

4. Close the query and close the database.

5. Open the *xmlCustomerBookings* file in your browser to view its contents, and then close the browser.

Exercise 5

1. Open the *mdbFanTours14-1* database you modified in Exercise 4.

2. Open the tblVendors table in Datasheet view, verify the number of records in the table, and then close the table.

3. Import the *xmlVendors* XML document into the database, and append the XML document data to the existing tblVendors table.

4. Open the tblVendors table in Datasheet view and confirm that one new record (#19) was appended.

5. Close the table and close the database.

Exercise 6

1. Open the *mdbFanTours14-1* database you modified in Exercise 5.

2. View the Pages objects in the Database window.

3. Create a DAP in Design view. Add all fields from the tblEvents table, and arrange them attractively in the Design grid. Add the title "FanTours Events" to the DAP.

4. Switch to Page view, review the DAP layout, and then view the records. Sort the records by Event: in Descending order and then in Ascending order.

5. Switch to Design view and save the page as "dapEvents."

6. Close the DAP, preview it in your browser, and then close the browser.

7. Open the dapEvents DAP in Design view, and change the Group Level Properties so that viewers cannot add, edit, or delete records.

8. Switch to Page view and verify that records in the DAP cannot be added, edited, or deleted.

9. Save and close the DAP, and then close the database.

Exercise 7

1. Open the *mdbFanTours14-1* database you modified in Exercise 6.

2. Open the tblProspects table in Datasheet view.

3. Switch to PivotTable view.

4. In the PivotTable view workspace, drag the State field to the Drop Column Fields Here area and drag the Last field to the Drop Totals or Detail Fields Here area.

5. How many prospects are from each of these states: AZ, CA, FL, and GA?

6. Close the PivotTable view, saving the changes, and then close the database.

Exercise 8

1. Open the *mdbFanTours14-1* database you modified in Exercise 7.

2. Open the tblProspects table in PivotTable view.

3. Save the PivotTable as a DAP named "dapProspects."

4. Close DAP and close the PivotTable view.

5. Preview the DAP in your browser, close the browser, and then close the database.

chapter fourteen

Case Projects

Project 1

Monica Lewis wants to access vendor Web sites and send e-mail to vendors while working on the FanTours database. Open the *mdbFanTours14-2* database located on the Data Disk. Open the tblVendors table in Design view. Add e-mail and Web site fields, each with a Hyperlink data type. Save the table, switch to Datasheet view, and add a URL and e-mail address to three vendors. Use fictitious URLs and e-mail addresses. Print the table datasheet, close the table, and close the database.

Project 2

Dave Browning asks you to create a document containing event information that he then can use to import the information into other Internet applications. Open the *mdbFanTours14-2* database. Export the tblEvents table as an XML document named "xmlEvents" and the schema as an XSD document. Open the *xmlEvents* document in your Web browser, and then print it. Close the browser, table, and database.

Project 3

Natalie Jabonsky tells you she placed an XML document, *xmlProspectsZipOrder*, on the network and asks you to import the document into the FanTours database. Import the *xmlProspectsZipOrder* document located on the Data Disk into the *mdbFanTours14-2* database, importing both the data and the schema to create a new table. Rename the new table "tblProspectsZipOrder." Open the tblProspectsZipOrder table in Datasheet view to view the records, and then print the Datasheet. Close the table and close the database.

Project 4

Monica Lewis wants to make the qryTours query information available to other employees via the company intranet. Open the *mdbFanTours14-2* database. Create a data access page from scratch in Design view named "dapTours" based on the qryTours query. Preview the DAP in the browser. Close the DAP and close the database.

Project 5

Liz Niarchos needs to quickly analyze the FanTours customer base by contact type and date and then filter the analysis by state. Open the *mdbFanTours14-2* database. View the tblCustomers table in PivotTable view. Create a PivotTable view that meets Liz's needs. (*Hint:* Analyze ContactType by column and ContactDate by row; show customers' last names as the detail, and filter by state.) Print a PivotTable view. Save the PivotTable view and the changes to the table, and then close the database.

Project 6

Liz Niarchos needs a chart identifying the number of customers by Contact Type. Open the *mdbFanTours14-2* database, and view the tblCustomers table in PivotChart view. Remove all current fields from the PivotChart workspace. Then place the ContactType field on the Category (x) axis, use count the Last fields for the chart values, and filter the chart values by State. Open the Properties sheet for the Category (x) axis title using a shortcut menu, change the caption on the Format tab to "Contact Type," and then change the Value (y) axis title caption to "Number of Customers." Print a copy of the PivotChart view. Save the PivotChart view and the changes to the table. Then close the PivotChart view and close the database.

Project 7

You recently read a brief magazine article about the Extensible Markup Language, XML, and want to know more about it. Using Internet search tools or information in this chapter, locate Web pages that contain information explaining what XML is and how it is used. Print several Web pages.

Project 8

Liz Niarchos wants to make the information in the PivotChart view you created in Project 6 available to other employees on the company intranet. She asks you to create a DAP based on the tblCustomers PivotChart view. Open the *mdbFanTours14-2* database. Open the tblCustomers table in PivotChart view, and save the PivotChart view as a DAP named "dapChart." Preview the DAP in your browser. Then close the browser and close the database.

Appendix

Working with Windows 2000

Appendix Overview

The Windows 2000 operating system creates a workspace on your computer screen, called the desktop. The desktop is a graphical environment that contains icons you click with the mouse pointer to access your computer system resources or to perform a task such as opening a software application. This appendix introduces you to the Windows 2000 desktop by describing the default desktop icons and showing how to access your computer resources, use menu commands and toolbar buttons to perform a task, and review and select dialog box options.

LEARNING OBJECTIVES

- Review the Windows 2000 desktop
- Access your computer system resources
- Use menu commands and toolbar buttons
- Use the Start menu
- Review dialog box options
- Use Windows 2000 shortcuts
- Understand the Recycle Bin
- Shut down Windows 2000

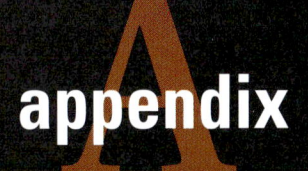

appendix

A.a Reviewing the Windows 2000 Desktop

Whenever you start your computer, the Windows 2000 operating system automatically starts. You are prompted to log on with your user name and password, which identify your account. Then the Windows 2000 desktop appears on your screen. To view the Windows 2000 desktop:

| Step 1 | **Turn on** | your computer and monitor |

The Log On to Windows dialog box opens, as shown in Figure A-1.

FIGURE A-1
Log On to Windows Dialog Box

Text boxes for your account info

Step 2	**Key**	your user name in the User name: text box
Step 3	**Key**	your password in the Password: text box
Step 4	**Click**	OK
Step 5	**Click**	the Exit button in the Getting Started with Windows 2000 dialog box, if necessary
Step 6	**Observe**	the Windows 2000 desktop work area, as shown in Figure A-2

The Windows 2000 desktop contains three elements: icons, background, and taskbar. The icons represent Windows objects and shortcuts to opening software applications or performing tasks. Table A-1 describes some of the default icons. The taskbar, at the bottom of the window, contains the Start button and the Quick Launch toolbar, and tray. The icon types and arrangement, desktop background, or Quick Launch toolbar on your screen might be different.

QUICK TIP

If you don't see the Log On to Windows dialog box, you can open the Windows Security window at any time by pressing the CTRL + ALT + DELETE keys. From this window, you can log off the current user and log back on as another user. You can also change passwords, shut down Windows 2000 and your computer, and use the Task Manager to shut down a program.

Working with Windows 2000 **AP 3**

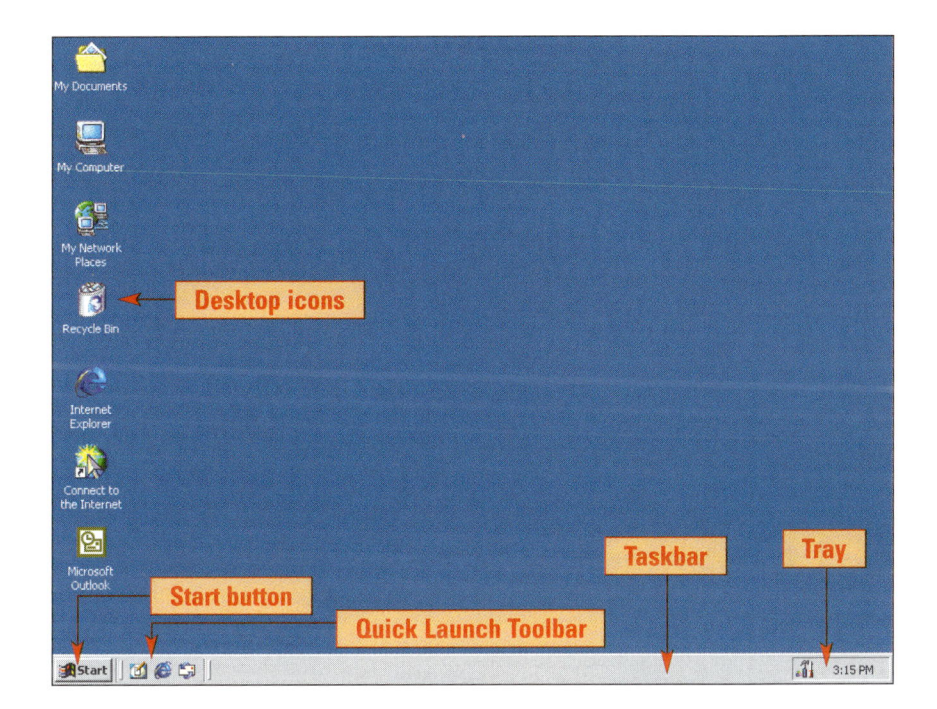

FIGURE A-2
Windows 2000 Desktop

TABLE A-1
Common Desktop Icons

Icon	Name	Description
	My Computer	Provides access to computer system resources
	My Documents	Stores Office documents (by default)
	Internet Explorer	Opens Internet Explorer Web browser
	Microsoft Outlook	Opens Outlook 2002 information manager software
	Recycle Bin	Temporarily stores folders and files deleted from the hard drive
	My Network Places	Provides access to computers and printers networked in your workgroup

The Start button on the taskbar displays the Start menu, which you can use to perform tasks. By default, the taskbar also contains the **Quick Launch toolbar**, which has shortcuts to open the Internet Explorer Web browser and Outlook Express e-mail software, and to switch between the desktop and open application windows. You can customize the Quick Launch toolbar to include other shortcuts.

appendix A

QUICK TIP

An **active desktop** can contain live Web content. You can create an active desktop by adding windows to the desktop that contain automatically updated Web pages. To add Web pages to your desktop, right-click the desktop, point to Active Desktop, click Customize my Desktop, and click the Web tab in the Display Properties dialog box. For more information on Active Desktop features, see online Help.

FIGURE A-3
My Computer window

A.b Accessing Your Computer System Resources

The My Computer window provides access to your computer system resources. Double-click the My Computer desktop icon to open the window. To open the My Computer window:

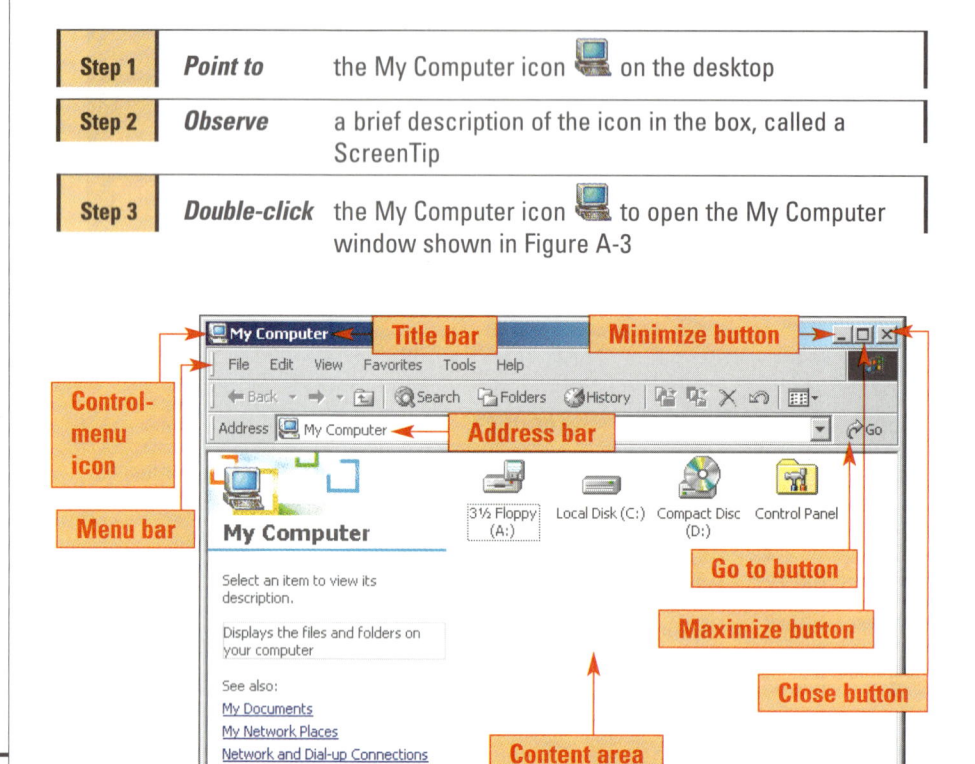

Step 1	**Point to**	the My Computer icon on the desktop
Step 2	**Observe**	a brief description of the icon in the box, called a ScreenTip
Step 3	**Double-click**	the My Computer icon to open the My Computer window shown in Figure A-3

A window is a rectangular area on your screen in which you view operating system options or a software application, such as Internet Explorer. Windows 2000 has some common window elements. The **title bar**, at the top of the window, includes the window's Control-menu icon, the window name, and the Minimize, Restore (or Maximize), and Close buttons. The **Control-menu icon**, in the upper-left corner of the window, accesses the Control menu that contains commands for restoring, moving sizing, minimizing, maximizing, and closing the window. The **Minimize** button, near the upper-right corner of the window, reduces the window to a taskbar button. The **Maximize** button, to the right of the Minimize button, enlarges the window to fill the entire screen viewing area above the taskbar. If the window is already maximized, the Restore button appears in its place. The **Restore** button reduces the window size. The **Close** button, in the upper-right corner, closes the window. To maximize the My Computer window:

Step 1	Click	the Maximize button 🗖 on the My Computer window title bar
Step 2	Observe	that the My Computer window completely covers the desktop

When you want to leave a window open, but do not want to see it on the desktop, you can minimize it. To minimize the My Computer window:

Step 1	Click	the Minimize button ▬ on the My Computer window title bar
Step 2	Observe	that the My Computer button remains on the taskbar

The minimized window is still open but not occupying space on the desktop. To view the My Computer window and then restore it to a smaller size:

Step 1	Click	the My Computer button on the taskbar to view the window
Step 2	Click	the Restore button 🗗 on the My Computer title bar
Step 3	Observe	that the My Computer window is reduced to a smaller window on the desktop

You can move and size a window with the mouse pointer. To move the My Computer window:

Step 1	Position	the mouse pointer on the My Computer title bar
Step 2	Drag	the window down and to the right approximately ½ inch
Step 3	Drag	the window back to the center of the screen

Several Windows 2000 windows—My Computer, My Documents, and Windows Explorer—have the same menu bar and toolbar features. When you size a window too small to view all its icons, a vertical or horizontal scroll bar may appear. A scroll bar includes scroll arrows and a scroll box for viewing different parts of the window contents.

> **QUICK TIP**
>
> This book uses the following notations for mouse instructions. **Point** means to place the mouse pointer on the command or item. **Click** means to press the left mouse button and then release it. **Right-click** means to press the right mouse button and then release it. **Double-click** means to press the left mouse button twice very rapidly. **Drag** means to hold down the left mouse button as you move the mouse pointer on the mouse pad. **Right-drag** means to hold down the right mouse button as you move the mouse pointer on the mouse pad. **Scroll** means to use the application scroll bar features or the IntelliMouse scrolling wheel.

appendix A

Mouse Tip

You can display four taskbar toolbars: Address, Links, Desktop, and Quick Launch. The Quick Launch toolbar appears on the taskbar by default. You can also create additional toolbars from other folders or subfolders and you can add folder or file shortcuts to an existing taskbar toolbar. To view other taskbar toolbars, right-click the taskbar, point to Toolbars, and then click the desired toolbar name.

To size the My Computer window:

Step 1	Position	the mouse pointer on the lower-right corner of the window
Step 2	Observe	that the mouse pointer becomes a black, double-headed sizing pointer
Step 3	Drag	the lower-right corner boundary diagonally up until the horizontal scroll bar appears and release the mouse button
Step 4	Click	the right scroll arrow on the horizontal scroll bar to view hidden icons
Step 5	Size	the window to a larger size to remove the horizontal scroll bar

You can open the window associated with any My Computer icon by double-clicking it. The windows open in the same window, not separate windows. To open the Control Panel Explorer-style window:

Step 1	Double-click	the Control Panel icon
Step 2	Observe	that the Address bar displays the Control Panel icon and name, and the content area displays the Control Panel icons for accessing computer system resources

A.c Using Menu Commands and Toolbar Buttons

You can click a menu command or toolbar button to perform specific tasks in a window. The **menu bar** is a special toolbar located below the window title bar that contains the File, Edit, View, Favorites, Tools, and Help menus. The **Standard Buttons toolbar**, located below the menu bar, contains shortcut "buttons" you click with the mouse pointer to execute a variety of commands. You can use the Back and Forward buttons on the Standard Buttons toolbar to switch between My Computer and the Control Panel. To view My Computer:

Step 1	Click	the Back button on the Standard Buttons toolbar to view My Computer
Step 2	Click	the Forward button on the Standard Buttons toolbar to view the Control Panel
Step 3	Click	View on the menu bar
Step 4	Point to	Go To
Step 5	Click	the My Computer command to view My Computer

| Step 6 | Click | the Close button ☒ on the My Computer window title bar |

A.d Using the Start Menu

The **Start button** on the taskbar opens the Start menu. You use this menu to access several Windows 2000 features and to open software applications, such as Word or Excel. To open the Start menu:

| Step 1 | Click | the Start button **Start** on the taskbar to open the Start menu, as shown in Figure A-4 |

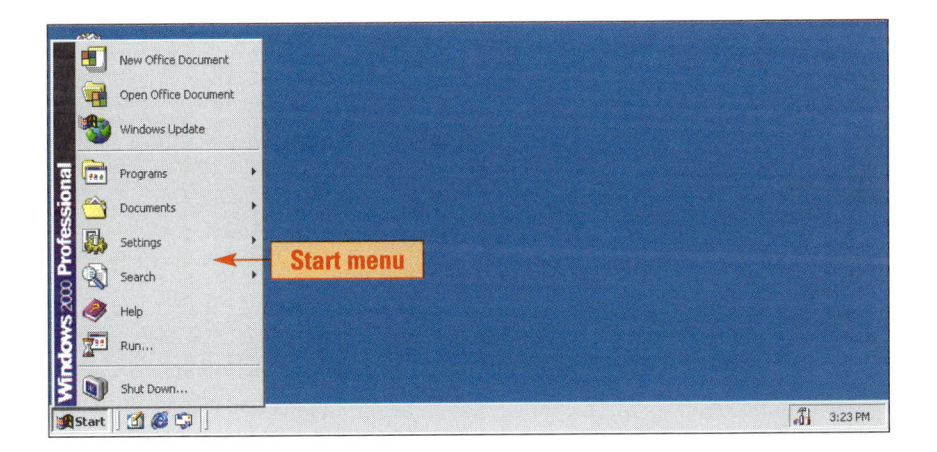

QUICK TIP

You can use Start menu commands to create or open Office XP documents, connect to the Microsoft Web site to download operating system updates, open software applications, open a favorite folder or file, or open one of the last fifteen documents you worked on. You can also change the Windows 2000 settings, search for files, folders, and resources on the Internet, get online Help, run software applications, log off a network, and shut down Windows 2000.

FIGURE A-4
Start Menu

| Step 2 | Point to | Programs to view the software applications installed on your computer |
| Step 3 | Click | the desktop outside the Start menu and Programs menu to close them |

A.e Reviewing Dialog Box Options

A **dialog box** is a window that contains options you can select, turn on, or turn off to perform a task. To view a dialog box:

| Step 1 | Right-click | the desktop |
| Step 2 | Point to | Active Desktop |

appendix A

Appendix

QUICK TIP

Many dialog boxes contain sets of options on different pages organized on **tabs** you click. Options include drop-down lists you view by clicking an arrow, text boxes in which you key information, check boxes and option buttons you click to turn on or off an option, and buttons that access additional options.

| Step 3 | *Click* | Customize My Desktop to open the Display Properties dialog box |
| Step 4 | *Click* | the Effects tab (see Figure A-5) |

FIGURE A-5
Effects Tab in the Display Properties Dialog Box

Labels on figure: Title bar, Tabs, Icon list options, Close button, Help button, Button with additional options, Check box options

MOUSE TIP

One way to speed up tasks is to single-click (rather than double-click) a desktop icon just like you single-click a Web page hyperlink. You can create a Web-style, single-click environment by opening the Folder Options dialog box from the Tools menu in any Windows 2000 window or the Control Panel from the Settings command on the Start menu. The Single-click to open an item (point to select) and Underline icon titles consistent with my browser options add an underline to icon titles, similar to a hyperlink.

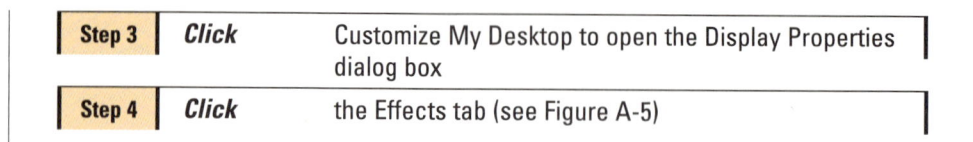

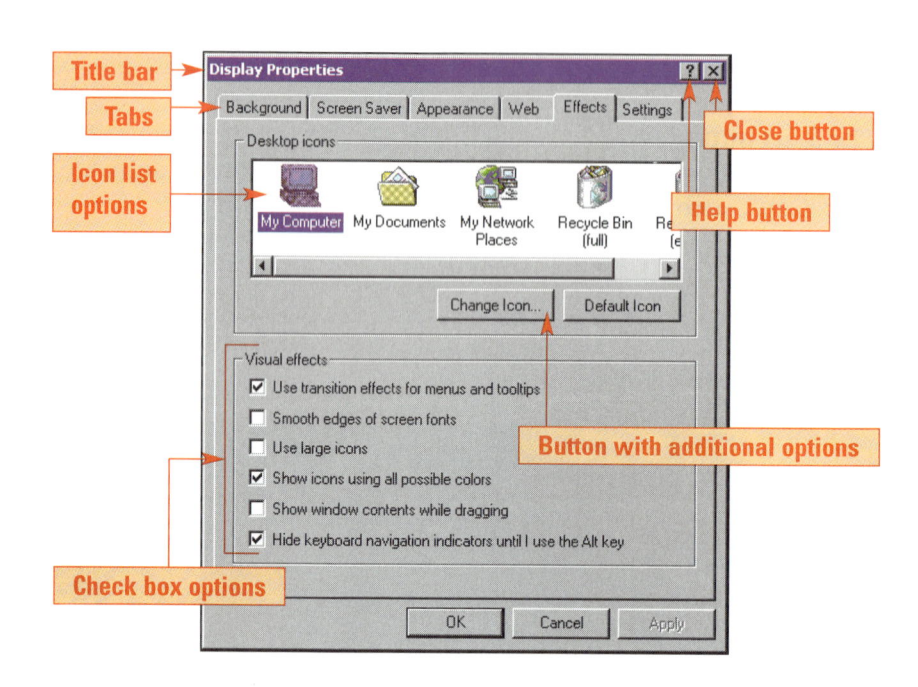

Step 5	*Click*	each tab and observe the different options available (do not change any options unless directed by your instructor)
Step 6	*Right-click*	each option on each tab and then click What's This? to view its ScreenTip
Step 7	*Click*	Cancel to close the dialog box without changing any options

A.f Using Windows 2000 Shortcuts

You can use the drag-and-drop method to reposition or remove Start menu commands. You can also right-drag a Start menu command to the desktop to create a desktop shortcut. To reposition the Windows Update item on the Start menu:

Step 1	*Click*	the Start button [Start] on the taskbar
Step 2	*Point to*	the Windows Update item
Step 3	*Drag*	the Windows Update item to the top of the Start menu

Working with Windows 2000   AP 9

To remove the Windows Update shortcut from the Start menu and create a desktop shortcut:

Step 1	Drag	the Windows Update item to the desktop
Step 2	Observe	that the desktop shortcut appears after a few seconds
Step 3	Verify	that the Windows Update item no longer appears on the Start menu

To add a Windows Update shortcut back to the Start menu and delete the desktop shortcut:

Step 1	Drag	the Windows Update shortcut to the Start button on the taskbar and then back to its original position when the Start menu appears
Step 2	Close	the Start menu
Step 3	Drag	the Windows Update shortcut on the desktop to the Recycle Bin

You can close multiple application windows at one time from the taskbar using the CTRL key and a shortcut menu. To open two applications and then use the taskbar to close them:

Step 1	Open	the Word and Excel applications (in this order) from the Programs menu on the Start menu
Step 2	Observe	the Word and Excel buttons on the taskbar (Excel is the selected, active button)
Step 3	Press & hold	the CTRL key
Step 4	Click	the Word application taskbar button (the Excel application taskbar button is already selected)
Step 5	Release	the CTRL key
Step 6	Right-click	the Word or Excel taskbar button
Step 7	Click	Close to close both applications

You can use the drag-and-drop method to add a shortcut to the Quick Launch toolbar for folders and documents you have created. To create a new subfolder in the My Documents folder:

| Step 1 | Double-click | the My Documents icon on the desktop to open the window |
| Step 2 | Right-click | the contents area (but not a file or folder) |

CAUTION TIP

Selecting items in a single-click environment requires some practice. To **select** (or highlight) one item, simply point to the item. *Be careful not to click the item; clicking the item opens it.*
You can use the SHIFT + Click and CTRL + Click commands in the single-click environment. Simply *point to* the first item. Then press and hold the SHIFT or CTRL key and *point to* the last item or the next item to be selected.

MENU TIP

In the Windows environment, clicking the right mouse button displays a **shortcut menu** of the most commonly used commands for the item you right-clicked. For example, you can use a shortcut menu to open applications from the Programs submenu. You can right-drag to move, copy, or create desktop shortcuts from Start menu commands.

appendix A

Step 3	*Point to*	New
Step 4	*Click*	Folder
Step 5	*Key*	Example
Step 6	*Press*	the ENTER key to name the folder
Step 7	*Drag*	the Example folder to the end of the Quick Launch toolbar (a black vertical line indicates the drop position)
Step 8	*Observe*	the new icon on the toolbar
Step 9	*Close*	the My Documents window
Step 10	*Position*	the mouse pointer on the Example folder shortcut on the Quick Launch toolbar and observe the ScreenTip

You remove a shortcut from the Quick Launch toolbar by dragging it to the desktop and deleting it, or dragging it directly to the Recycle Bin. To remove the Example folder shortcut and then delete the folder:

Step 1	*Drag*	the Example folder icon to the Recycle Bin
Step 2	*Open*	the My Documents window
Step 3	*Delete*	the Example folder icon using the shortcut menu
Step 4	*Click*	Yes
Step 5	*Close*	the My Documents window

A.g Understanding the Recycle Bin

The **Recycle Bin** is an object that temporarily stores folders, files, and shortcuts you delete from your hard drive. If you accidentally delete an item, you can restore it to its original location on your hard drive if it is still in the Recycle Bin. Because the Recycle Bin takes up disk space you should review and empty it regularly. When you empty the Recycle Bin, its contents are removed from your hard drive and can no longer be restored.

MENU TIP

You can open the Recycle Bin by right-clicking the Recycle Bin icon on the desktop and clicking Open. To restore an item to your hard drive after opening the Recycle Bin, click the item to select it and then click the Restore command on the File menu. You can also restore an item by opening the Recycle Bin, right-clicking an item, and clicking Restore.

To empty the Recycle Bin, right-click the Recycle Bin icon and then click Empty Recycle Bin.

A.h Shutting Down Windows 2000

It is very important that you follow the proper procedures for shutting down the Windows 2000 operating system when you are finished, to allow the operating system to complete its internal "housekeeping" properly. To shut down Windows 2000 correctly:

Step 1	Click	the Start button [Start] on the taskbar
Step 2	Click	Shut Down to open the Shut Down Windows dialog box shown in Figure A-6

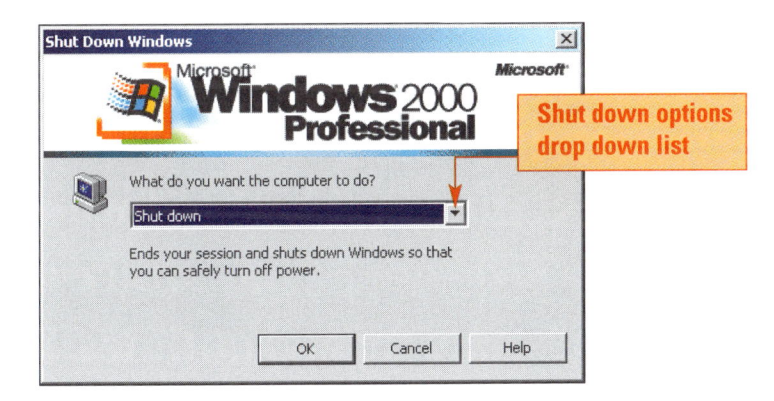

FIGURE A-6
Shut Down Windows Dialog Box

You can log off, shut down, and restart from this dialog box. You want to shut down completely.

Step 3	Click	the Shut down option from the drop-down list, if necessary
Step 4	Click	OK

appendix A

Appendix

Formatting Tips for Business Documents

Appendix Overview

Most organizations follow specific formatting guidelines when preparing letters, envelopes, memorandums, and other documents to ensure the documents present a professional appearance. In this appendix you learn how to format different size letters, interoffice memos, envelopes, and formal outlines. You also review a list of style guides and learn how to use proofreader's marks.

Learning Objectives

- Format letters
- Insert mailing notations
- Format envelopes
- Format interoffice memorandums
- Format formal outlines
- Use style guides
- Use proofreader's marks

appendix B

Formatting Tips for Business Documents   AP 13

B.a Formatting Letters

Most companies use special letter paper with the company name and address (and sometimes a company logo or picture) preprinted on the paper. The preprinted portion is called a **letterhead** and the paper is called **letterhead paper**. When you create a letter, the margins vary depending on the style of your letterhead and the length of your letter. Most letterheads use between 1 inch and 2 inches of the page from the top of the sheet. There are two basic business correspondence formats: block format and modified block format. When you create a letter in **block format**, all the text is placed flush against the left margin. This includes the date, the letter address information, the salutation, the body, the complimentary closing, and the signature information. The body of the letter is single spaced with a blank line between paragraphs.[1] Figure B-1 shows a short letter in the block format with standard punctuation.

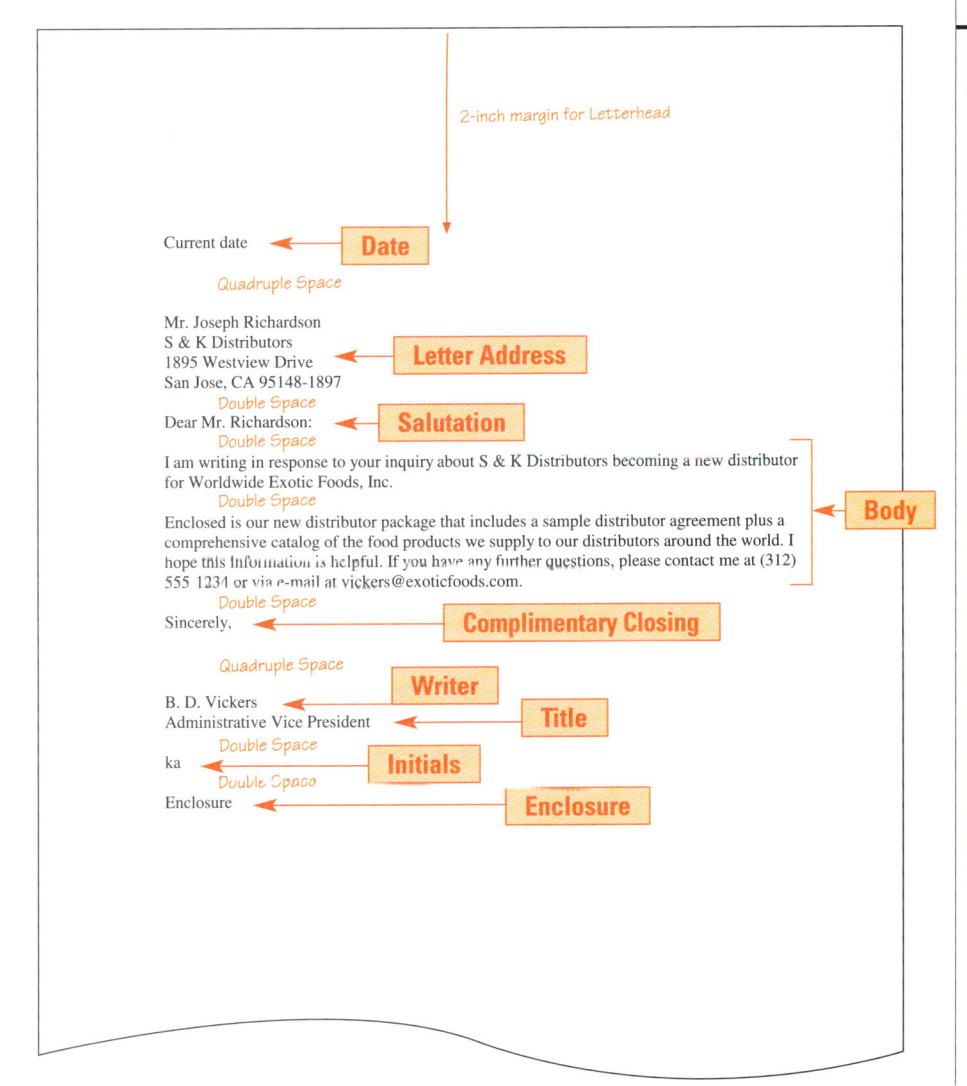

FIGURE B-1
Block Format Letter

Sample Letter

2-inch margin for Letterhead

Current date ← **Date**

Quadruple Space

Mr. Joseph Richardson
S & K Distributors ← **Letter Address**
1895 Westview Drive
San Jose, CA 95148-1897

Double Space

Dear Mr. Richardson: ← **Salutation**

Double Space

I am writing in response to your inquiry about S & K Distributors becoming a new distributor for Worldwide Exotic Foods, Inc.

Double Space

Enclosed is our new distributor package that includes a sample distributor agreement plus a comprehensive catalog of the food products we supply to our distributors around the world. I hope this information is helpful. If you have any further questions, please contact me at (312) 555-1234 or via e-mail at vickers@exoticfoods.com. ← **Body**

Double Space

Sincerely, ← **Complimentary Closing**

Quadruple Space

B. D. Vickers ← **Writer**
Administrative Vice President ← **Title**

Double Space

ka ← **Initials**

Double Space

Enclosure ← **Enclosure**

> **QUICK TIP**
>
> The quality and professionalism of a company's business correspondence can affect how customers, clients, and others view a company. That correspondence represents the company to those outside it. To ensure a positive and appropriate image, many companies set special standards for margins, typeface, and font size for their business correspondence. These special standards are based on the common letter styles illustrated in this section.

appendix B

AP 14 Appendix

In the **modified block format**, the date begins near the center of the page or near the right margin. The closing starts near the center or right margin. Paragraphs can be either flush against the left margin or indented. Figure B-2 shows a short letter in the modified block format with standard punctuation.

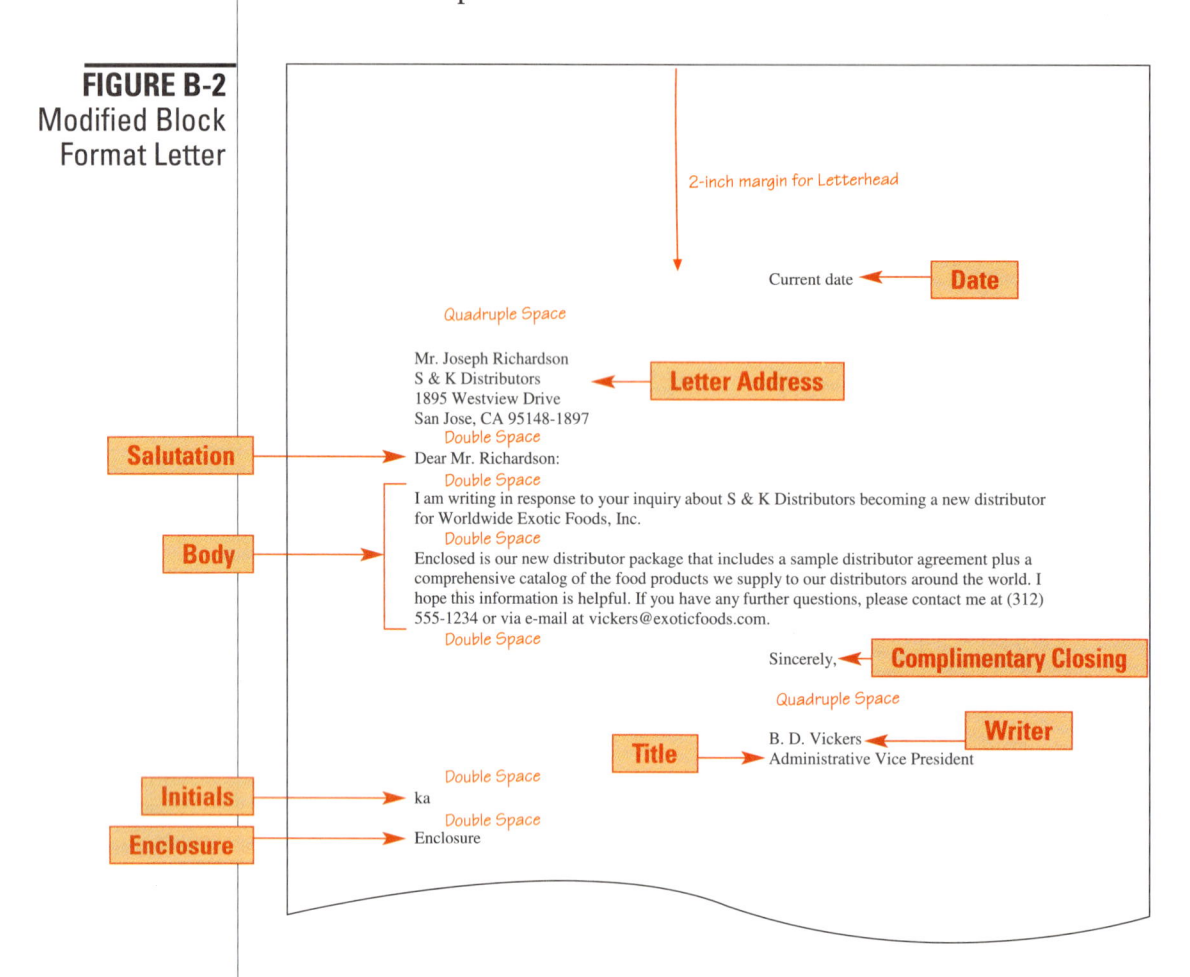

FIGURE B-2
Modified Block Format Letter

```
                                    2-inch margin for Letterhead
                                              ↓

                                                    Current date    ← Date
         Quadruple Space

         Mr. Joseph Richardson
         S & K Distributors           ← Letter Address
         1895 Westview Drive
         San Jose, CA 95148-1897
         Double Space
Salutation →  Dear Mr. Richardson:
         Double Space
         I am writing in response to your inquiry about S & K Distributors becoming a new distributor
         for Worldwide Exotic Foods, Inc.
         Double Space
Body →   Enclosed is our new distributor package that includes a sample distributor agreement plus a
         comprehensive catalog of the food products we supply to our distributors around the world. I
         hope this information is helpful. If you have any further questions, please contact me at (312)
         555-1234 or via e-mail at vickers@exoticfoods.com.
         Double Space
                                              Sincerely,    ← Complimentary Closing
                                              Quadruple Space
                                              B. D. Vickers    ← Writer
                                    Title →   Administrative Vice President
         Double Space
Initials →  ka
         Double Space
Enclosure → Enclosure
```

QUICK TIP

When you key a letter on plain paper in the modified block format, the return address usually appears near the right margin and above the date, with one blank line between the return address and the date.

Both the block and modified block styles use the same spacing for the non-body portions. Three blank lines separate the date from the addressee information, one blank line separates the addressee information from the salutation, one blank line separates the salutation from the body of the letter, and one blank line separates the body of the letter from the complimentary closing. There are three blank lines between the complimentary closing and the writer's name. If a typist's initials appear below the name, a blank line separates the writer's name from the initials. If an enclosure is noted, the word "Enclosure" appears below the typist's initials with a blank line separating them. Finally, when keying the return address or addressee information, one space separates the state and the postal code (ZIP+4).

B.b Inserting Mailing Notations

Mailing notations add information to a business letter. For example, the mailing notations CERTIFIED MAIL or SPECIAL DELIVERY indicate how a business letter was sent. The mailing notations CONFIDENTIAL or PERSONAL indicate how the person receiving the letter should handle the letter contents. Mailing notations should be keyed in uppercase characters at the left margin two lines below the date.[2] Figure B-3 shows a mailing notation added to a block format business letter.

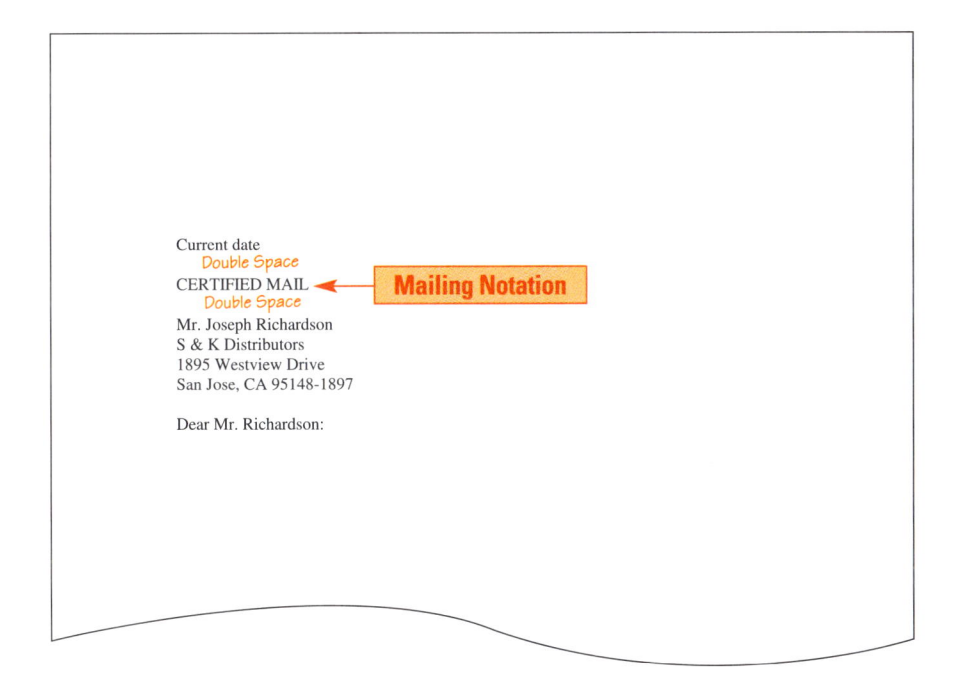

```
Current date
   Double Space
CERTIFIED MAIL  ◄─── Mailing Notation
   Double Space
Mr. Joseph Richardson
S & K Distributors
1895 Westview Drive
San Jose, CA 95148-1897

Dear Mr. Richardson:
```

FIGURE B-3
Mailing Notation on Letter

B.c Formatting Envelopes

Two U.S. Postal Service publications, *The Right Way* (Publication 221), and *Postal Addressing Standards* (Publication 28) available from the U.S. Post Office, provide standards for addressing letter envelopes. The U.S. Postal Service uses optical character readers (OCRs) and barcode sorters (BCSs) to increase the speed, efficiency, and accuracy in processing mail. To get a letter delivered more quickly, envelopes should be addressed to take advantage of this automation process.

Table B-1 lists the minimum and maximum size for letters. The post office cannot process letters smaller than the minimum size. Letters larger than the maximum size cannot take advantage of automated processing and must be processed manually.

TABLE B-1
Minimum and Maximum Letter Dimensions

Dimension	Minimum	Maximum
Height	3½ inches	6⅛ inches
Length	5 inches	11½ inches
Thickness	.007 inch	¼ inch

The delivery address should be placed inside a rectangular area on the envelope that is approximately ⅝ inch from the top and bottom edge of the envelope and ½ inch from the left and right edge of the envelope. This is called the **OCR read area**. All the lines of the delivery address must fit within this area and no lines of the return address should extend into this area. To assure the delivery address is placed in the OCR read area, begin the address approximately ½ inch left of center and on approximately line 14.[3]

The lines of the delivery address should be in this order:

1. any optional nonaddress data, such as advertising or company logos, must be placed above the delivery address
2. any information or attention line
3. the name of the recipient
4. the street address
5. the city, state, and postal code (ZIP+4)

The delivery address should be complete, including apartment or suite numbers and delivery designations, such as RD (road), ST (street), or NW (northwest). Leave the area below and on both sides of the delivery address blank. Use uppercase characters and a sans serif font (such as Arial) for the delivery address. Omit all punctuation except the hyphen in the ZIP+4 code.

Figure B-4 shows a properly formatted business letter envelope.

> **QUICK TIP**
>
> Foreign addresses should include the country name in uppercase characters as the last line of the delivery address. The postal code, if any, should appear on the same line as the city.

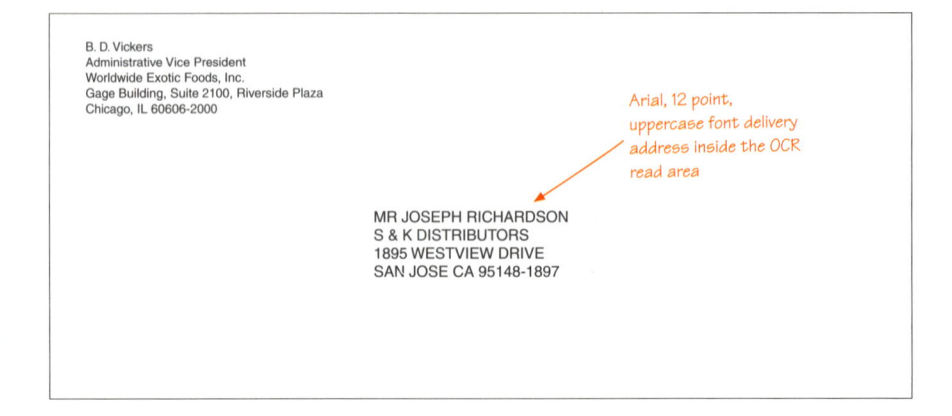

FIGURE B-4
Business Letter Envelope

```
B. D. Vickers
Administrative Vice President
Worldwide Exotic Foods, Inc.
Gage Building, Suite 2100, Riverside Plaza
Chicago, IL 60606-2000




                    MR JOSEPH RICHARDSON
                    S & K DISTRIBUTORS
                    1895 WESTVIEW DRIVE
                    SAN JOSE CA 95148-1897
```

Arial, 12 point, uppercase font delivery address inside the OCR read area

B.d Formatting Interoffice Memorandums

Business correspondence that is sent within a company is usually prepared as an **interoffice memorandum**, also called a **memo**, rather than a letter. There are many different interoffice memo styles used in offices today, and word processing applications usually provide several memo templates based on different memo styles. Also, just as with business letters that are sent outside the company, many companies set special standards for margins, typeface, and font size for their interoffice memos.

A basic interoffice memo should include lines for "TO:", "FROM:", "DATE:", and "SUBJECT:" followed by the body text. Memos can be prepared on blank paper or on paper that includes a company name and even a logo. The word MEMORANDUM is often included. Figure B-5 shows a basic interoffice memorandum.

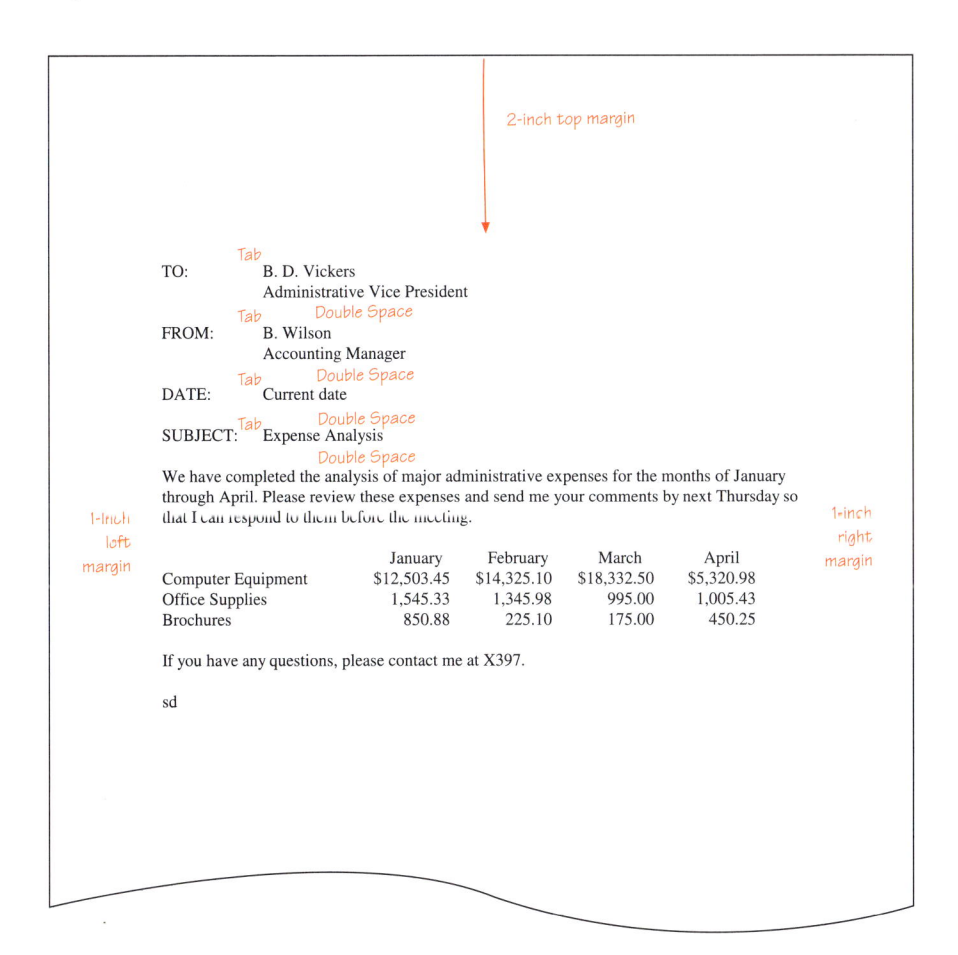

FIGURE B-5
Interoffice Memorandum

2-inch top margin

TO: [Tab] B. D. Vickers
              Administrative Vice President
              Double Space
FROM: [Tab] B. Wilson
              Accounting Manager
              Double Space
DATE: [Tab] Current date
              Double Space
SUBJECT: [Tab] Expense Analysis
              Double Space

We have completed the analysis of major administrative expenses for the months of January through April. Please review these expenses and send me your comments by next Thursday so that I can respond to them before the meeting.

1-inch left margin   *1-inch right margin*

	January	February	March	April
Computer Equipment	$12,503.45	$14,325.10	$18,332.50	$5,320.98
Office Supplies	1,545.33	1,345.98	995.00	1,005.43
Brochures	850.88	225.10	175.00	450.25

If you have any questions, please contact me at X397.

sd

appendix B

B.e Formatting Formal Outlines

Companies use outlines to organize data for a variety of purposes, such as reports, meeting agenda, and presentations. Word processing applications usually offer special features to help you create an outline. If you want to follow a formal outline format, you may need to add formatting to outlines created with these special features.

Margins for a short outline of two or three topics should be set at 1½ inches for the top margin and 2 inches for the left and right margins. For a longer outline, use a 2-inch top margin and 1-inch left and right margins.

The outline level-one text should be in uppercase characters. Second-level text should be treated like a title, with the first letter of the main words capitalized. Capitalize only the first letter of the first word at the third level. Double space before and after level one and single space the remaining levels.

Include at least two parts at each level. For example, you must have two level-one entries in an outline (at least I. and II.). If there is a second level following a level-one entry, it must contain at least two entries (at least A. and B.). All numbers must be aligned at the period and all subsequent levels must begin under the text of the preceding level, not under the number.[4]

Figure B-6 shows a formal outline prepared using the Word Outline Numbered list feature with additional formatting to follow a formal outline.

B.f Using Style Guides

A **style guide** provides a set of rules for punctuating and formatting text. There are a number of style guides used by writers, editors, business document proofreaders, and publishers. You can purchase style guides at a commercial bookstore, an online bookstore, or a college bookstore. Your local library likely has copies of different style guides and your instructor may have copies of several style guides for reference. Some popular style guides are *The Chicago Manual of Style* (The University of Chicago Press), *The Professional Secretary's Handbook* (Barron's), *The Holt Handbook* (Harcourt Brace College Publishers), and the *MLA Style Manual and Guide to Scholarly Publishing* (The Modern Language Association of America).

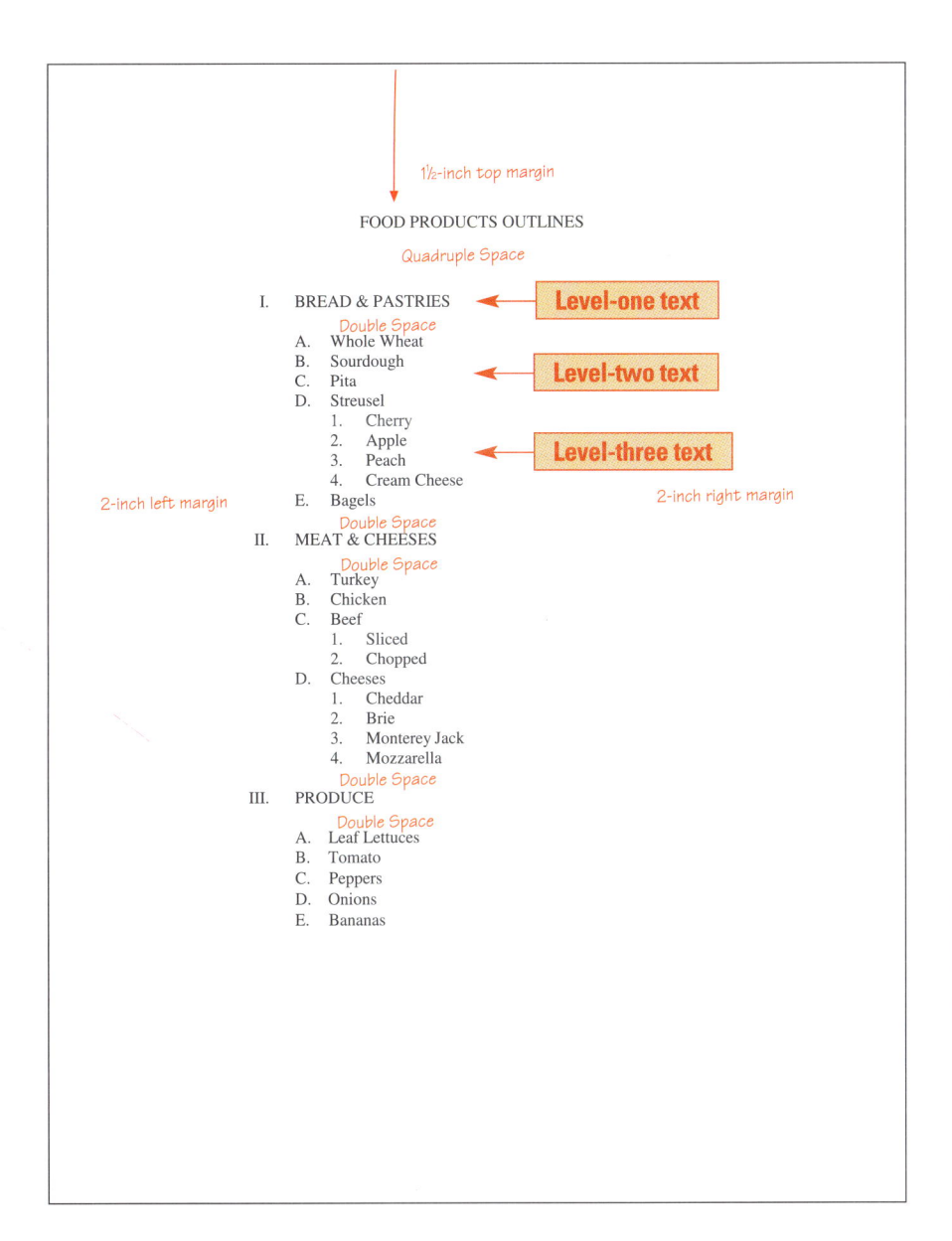

FIGURE B-6
Formal Outline

```
                    1½-inch top margin

                 FOOD PRODUCTS OUTLINES
                      Quadruple Space
           I.   BREAD & PASTRIES        ← Level-one text
                   Double Space
                A.  Whole Wheat
                B.  Sourdough            ← Level-two text
                C.  Pita
                D.  Streusel
                    1.  Cherry
                    2.  Apple            ← Level-three text
                    3.  Peach
                    4.  Cream Cheese
                E.  Bagels
                   Double Space
           II.  MEAT & CHEESES
                   Double Space
                A.  Turkey
                B.  Chicken
                C.  Beef
                    1.  Sliced
                    2.  Chopped
                D.  Cheeses
                    1.  Cheddar
                    2.  Brie
                    3.  Monterey Jack
                    4.  Mozzarella
                   Double Space
           III. PRODUCE
                   Double Space
                A.  Leaf Lettuces
                B.  Tomato
                C.  Peppers
                D.  Onions
                E.  Bananas
```

2-inch left margin   2-inch right margin

B.g Using Proofreader's Marks

Standard proofreader's marks enable an editor or proofreader to make corrections or change notations in a document that can be recognized by anyone familiar with the marks. The following list illustrates standard proofreader's marks.

Defined		Examples
Paragraph	¶	¶ Begin a new paragraph at this
Insert a character	∧	point. Insrt a letter here.
Delete	ℓ	Delete these words. Disregard
Do not change	stet or ...	the previous correction. To
Transpose	tr	transpose is to around turn.
Move to the left	⌐	[Move this copy to the left.
Move to the right	¬	M]ove this copy to the right.
No paragraph	No ¶	No ¶ Do not begin a new paragraph
Delete and close up	℘	here. Delete the hyphen from pre-empt and close up the space.
Set in caps	Caps or ≡	a sentence begins with a capital
Set in lower case	lc or /	letter. This Word should not
Insert a period	⊙	be capitalized. Insert a period⊙
Quotation marks	∨∨	∨Quotation marks and a comma
Comma	∧	should be placed here∧ he said.
Insert space	#	Space between these#words. An
Apostrophe	∨'	apostrophe is what's needed here.
Hyphen	=	Add a hyphen to Kilowatt=hour. Close
Close up	⌢	up the extra spa⌢ce.
Use superior figure	∨	Footnote this sentence.∨ Set
Set in italic	ital. or —	the words, sine qua non, in italics.
Move up	⎡⎤	This word is too ⎡low.⎤ That word is
Move down	⎣⎦	too ⎣high.⎦

Endnotes

[1] Jerry W. Robinson et al., *Keyboarding and Information Processing* (Cincinnati: South-Western Educational Publishing, 1997).

[2] Ibid.

[3] Ibid.

[4] Ibid.

Appendix

Using Office XP Speech Recognition

Appendix Overview

You are familiar with using the keyboard and the mouse to key text and select commands. With Office XP, you also can use your voice to perform these same activities. Speech recognition enables you to use your voice to perform keyboard and mouse actions without ever lifting a hand. In this appendix, you learn how to set up Speech Recognition software and train the software to recognize your voice. You learn how to control menus, navigate dialog boxes, and open, save, and close a document. You then learn how to dictate text, including lines and punctuation, correct errors, and format text. Finally, you learn how to turn off and on Speech Recognition.

LEARNING OBJECTIVES

- ► Train your speech software
- ► Use voice commands
- ► Dictate, edit, and format by voice
- ► Turn Microsoft Speech Recognition on and off

G
appendix

C.a Training Your Speech Software

Speech recognition is an exciting new technology that Microsoft has integrated into its XP generation of products. Microsoft has been working on speech recognition for well over a decade. The state-of-the-art is advancing. If you haven't tried it before, this is a great time for you to experience this futuristic technology.

Voice recognition has important benefits:

- Microsoft's natural speech technologies can make your computer experience more enjoyable.
- Speech technology can increase your writing productivity.
- Voice recognition software can greatly reduce your risk for keyboard- and mouse-related injuries.

In the following activities, you learn to use your voice like a mouse and to write without the aid of the keyboard.

Connecting and Positioning Your Microphone

Start your speech recognition experience by setting up your microphone. There are several microphone styles used for speech recognition. The most common headset microphone connects to your computer's sound card, as shown in Figure C-1. Connect the microphone end to your computer's microphone audio input port. Connect the speaker end into your speech output port.

FIGURE C-1
Standard Sound Card Headset (Courtesy Plantronics Inc.)

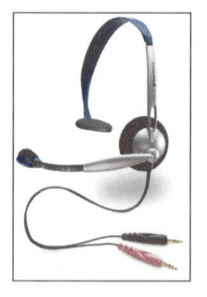

USB speech microphones, such as the one shown in Figure C-2, are becoming very popular because they normally increase performance and accuracy. USB is short for Universal Serial Bus. USB microphones bypass the sound card and input speech with less distortion into your system.

USB microphones are plugged into the USB port found in the back of most computers. Windows automatically installs the necessary USB drivers after you start your computer with the USB microphone plugged into its slot.

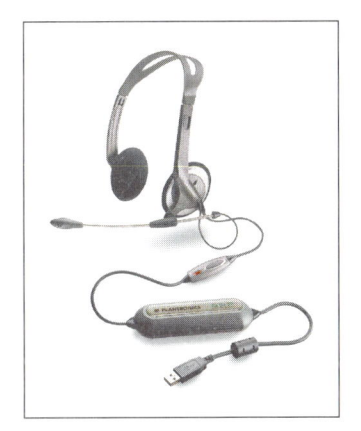

FIGURE C-2
A USB Headset (Courtesy Plantronics Inc.)

After your headset has been installed, put on your headset and position it comfortably. Remember these two important tips:
- Place the speaking side of your microphone about a thumb's width away from the side of your mouth, as shown in Figure C-3.
- Keep your microphone in the same position every time you speak. Changing your microphone's position can decrease your accuracy.

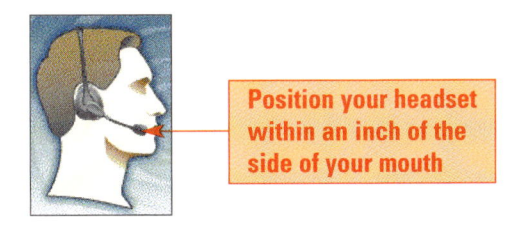

Position your headset within an inch of the side of your mouth

FIGURE C-3
Proper Headset Position

CAUTION TIP

If you see additional buttons on the Language Bar than shown in Figure C-4, click the Microphone button to hide them.

Installing Microsoft Speech Recognition

Open Microsoft Word and see if your speech software has already been installed. As Word opens, you should see either the floating Language Bar, shown in Figure C-4, or the Language Bar icon in the Windows Taskbar tray, as shown in Figure C-5.

FIGURE C-4
Floating Language Bar

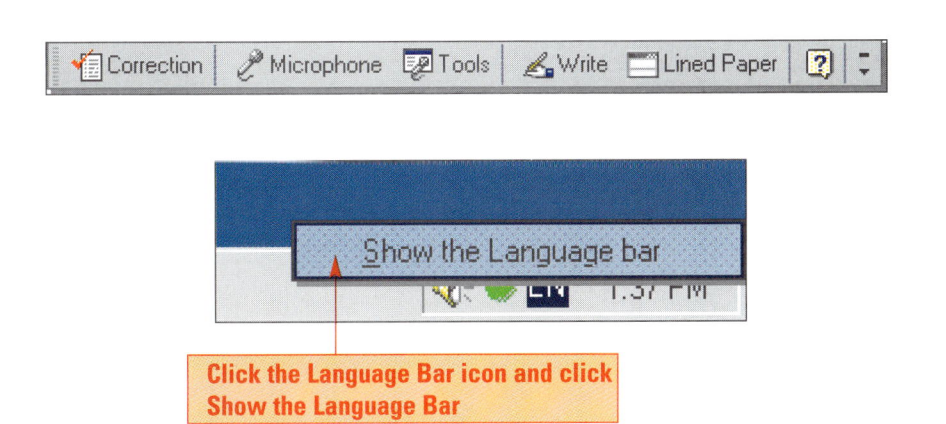

FIGURE C-5
Language Bar Icon

Click the Language Bar icon and click Show the Language Bar

appendix C

If you can open and see the Language Bar, jump to Step-by-Step C.2. However, if this essential tool is missing, proceed with Step-by-Step C.1.

Step-by-Step C.1

| Step 1 | To install Microsoft speech recognition, open Microsoft Word by clicking **Start**, **Programs**, **Microsoft Word**. |
| Step 2 | Click **Tools**, **Speech** from the Word menu bar, as shown in Figure C-6. |

FIGURE C-6
Click Speech from the Tools menu

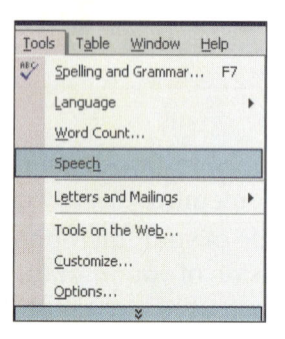

| Step 3 | You are prompted through the installation procedure. The process is a simple one. Follow the onscreen instructions. |

Training Your System

Microsoft speech recognition can accommodate many different voices on the same computer. In order to work properly, your Microsoft Office Speech Recognition software must create a user **profile** for each voice it hears—including your voice.

If you are the first user and have just installed your speech software, chances are the system is already prompting you through the training steps. Skip to Step 3 in Step-by-Step C.2 for hints and help as you continue. However, if you are the second or later user of the system, you need to create a new profile by starting with Step 1.

Step-by-Step C.2

| Step 1 | To create your own personal speech profile, click the **Tools** button on the Language Bar and click **Options**, as shown in Figure C-7. This opens the Speech Properties dialog box. |

Using Office XP Speech Recognition   **AP 25**

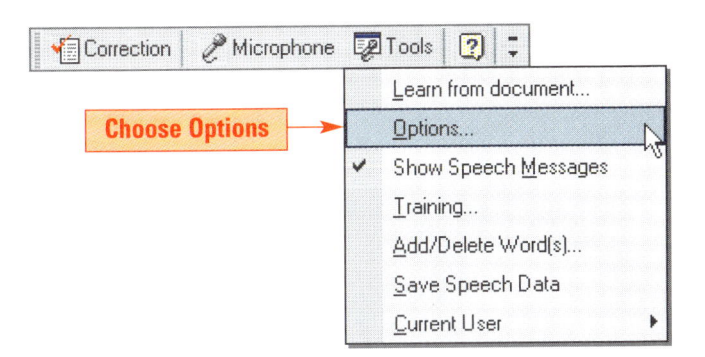

FIGURE C-7
Language Bar's Tools Menu

Step 2 In the Speech Properties dialog box, click **New**, as indicated in Figure C-8.

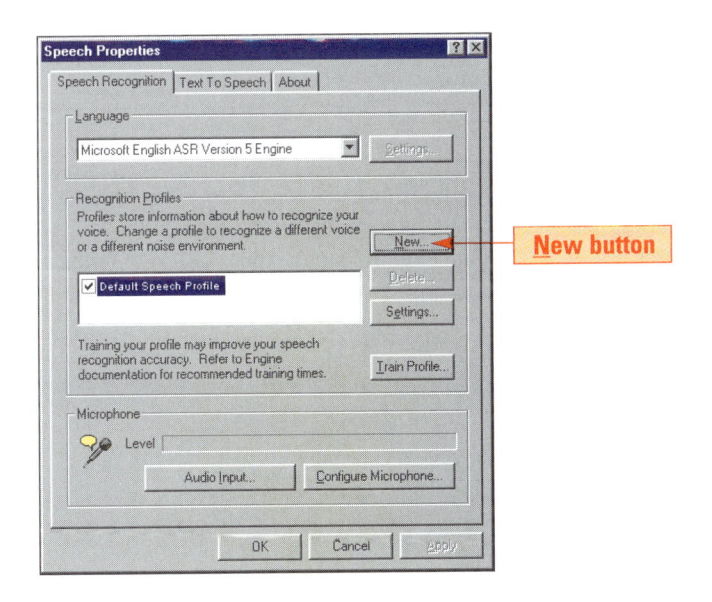

FIGURE C-8
Speech Properties Dialog Box

Step 3 Enter your name in the Profile Wizard, as shown in Figure C-9, and click **Next>** to continue. (*Note:* If you accidently click Finish instead of Next>, you must still train your profile by clicking Train Profile in the Speech Properties dialog box.)

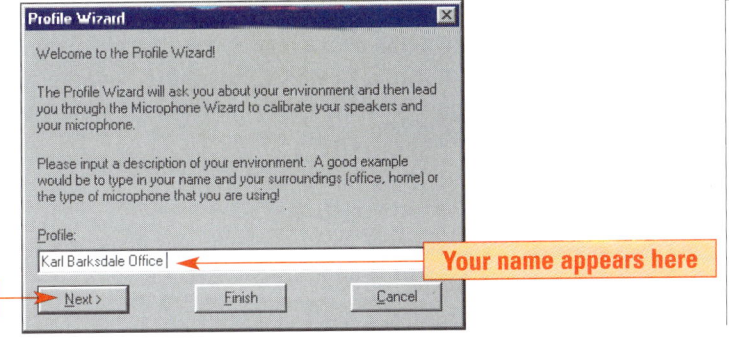

FIGURE C-9
New Profile Dialog Box

appendix C

Step 4 Adjust your microphone, as explained on the Microphone Wizard Welcome dialog box, as shown in Figure C-10. Click **Next>** to begin adjusting your microphone.

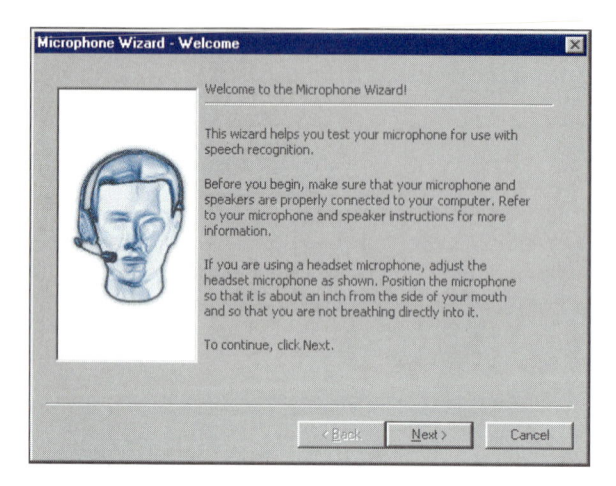

FIGURE C-10
Correctly Position Your Microphone

Step 5 Read the test sentence indicated in Figure C-11 until the volume adjustment settings appear consistently in the green portion of the volume adjustment meter. Your volume settings are adjusted automatically as you speak. Click **Next>** to continue.

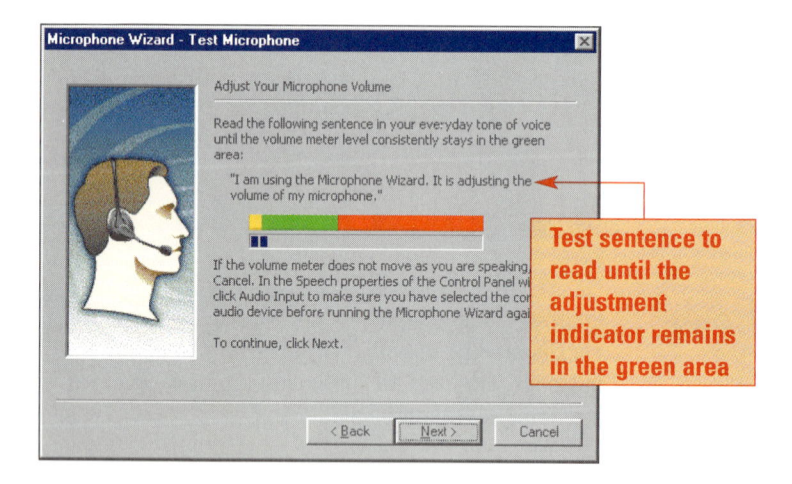

FIGURE C-11
Read Aloud to Adjust Your Microphone Volume

Test sentence to read until the adjustment indicator remains in the green area

QUICK TIP

Microsoft Office Speech Recognition tells you if your microphone is not adequate for good speech recognition. You may need to try a higher quality microphone, install a compatible sound card, or switch to a USB microphone. Check the Microsoft Windows Help files for assistance with microphone problems.

Step 6 The next audio check tests the output of your speakers. Read the test sentence indicated in Figure C-12 and then listen. If you can hear your voice, your speakers are connected properly. Click **Finish** and continue.

FIGURE C-12
Read Aloud to Test Your Sound Output

Test sentence

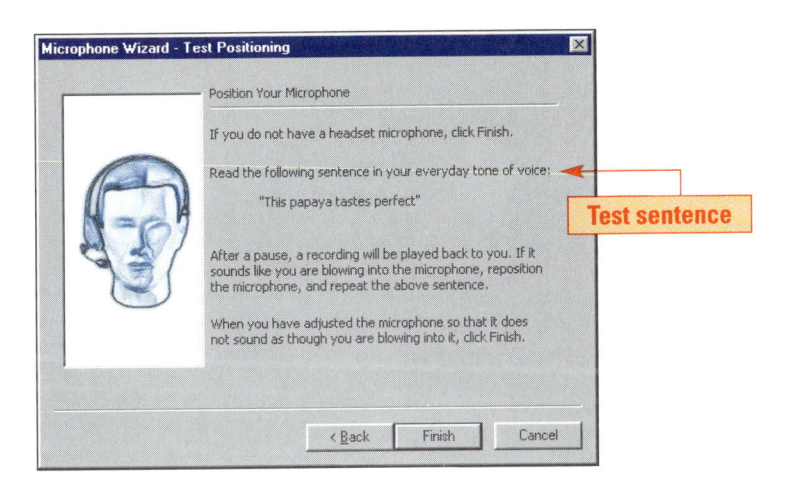

Training Your Software

Next, you are asked to train your software. During the training session, you read a training script or story for about 10 to 15 minutes. As you read, your software gathers samples of your speech. These samples help the speech software customize your speech recognition profile to your way of speaking. As you read, remember to:

- Read clearly.
- Use a normal, relaxed reading voice. Don't shout, but don't whisper softly either.
- Read at your normal reading pace. Do not read slowly and do not rush.

Step-by-Step C.3

Step 1 — Microsoft Office Speech Recognition prepares you to read a story or script. Read the instruction screen shown in Figure C-13 and click **Next>** to continue.

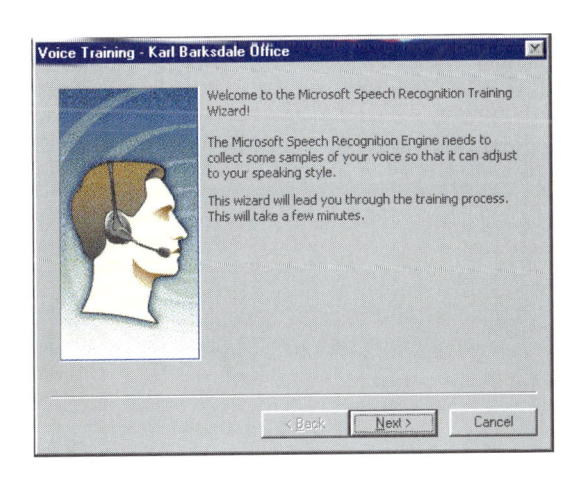

Step 2 — Enter your gender and age information (see Figure C-14) to help the system calibrate its settings to your voice. Click **Next>** to continue.

> **QUICK TIP**
>
> Your user file will remember your microphone settings from session to session. However, if others use the system before you, you may need to readjust the audio settings by clicking **Tools**, **Options**, **Configure Microphone**.

> **CAUTION TIP**
>
> Never touch any part of your headset or microphone while speaking. Holding or touching the microphone creates errors.

FIGURE C-13
Read the Onscreen Instructions Carefully

appendix C

FIGURE C-14
Enter Your Gender and Age Information

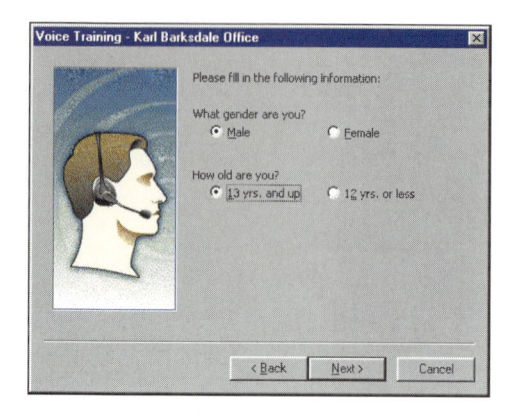

Step 3 Click **Sample** and listen to a short example of how to speak clearly to a computer. See Figure C-15. After the recording, click **Next>** to review the tips for the training session, and then click **Next>** to continue.

FIGURE C-15
Listen to the Speech Sample

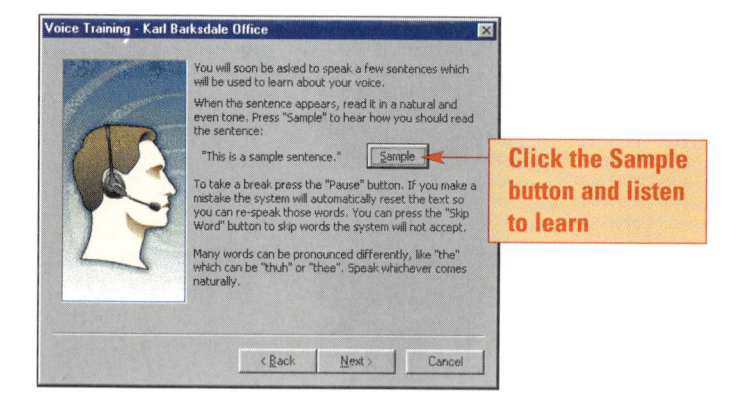

Click the Sample button and listen to learn

Step 4 Begin reading the training session paragraphs, as shown in Figure C-16. Text you have read is highlighted. The Training Progress bar lets you know how much reading is left. If you get stuck on a word, click **Skip Word** to move past the problem spot.

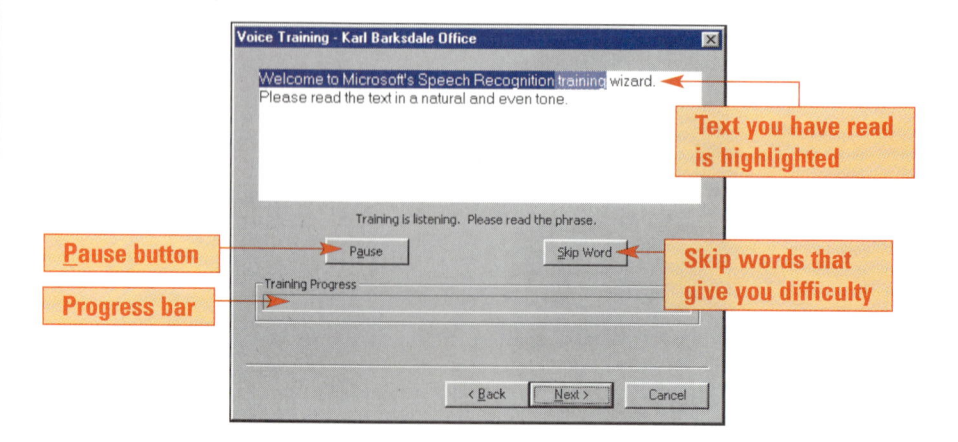

FIGURE C-16
Software Tracks Your Progress

Pause button
Progress bar
Text you have read is highlighted
Skip words that give you difficulty

Using Office XP Speech Recognition   **AP 29**

Step 5 The screen shown in Figure C-17 appears after you have finished reading the entire first story or training session script. You now have a couple of choices. Click **More Training**, click **Next>**, and continue reading additional scripts as explained in Step 6 (or you can click **F**inish and quit for the day).

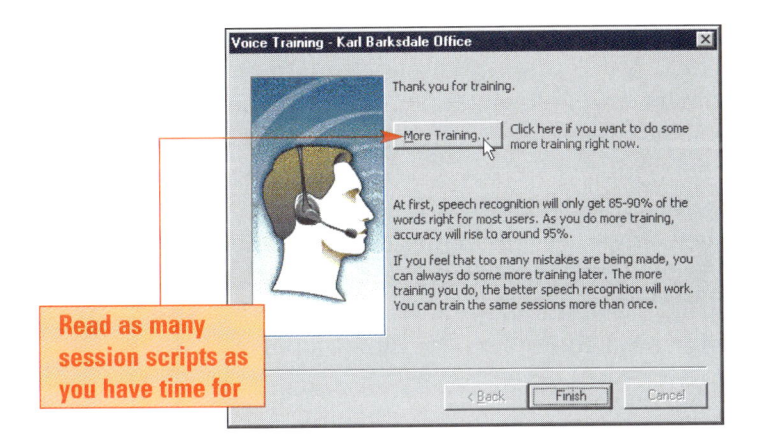

Read as many session scripts as you have time for

QUICK TIP

The more stories you read, the better. Users with thick accents, or accuracy below 90 percent, must read additional stories. You can read additional training session scripts at any time by clicking **Tools**, **Training** on the Language Bar.

FIGURE C-17
First Training Script Completed

Step 6 Choose another training session story or script from the list, as shown in Figure C-18, and then click **Next>**.

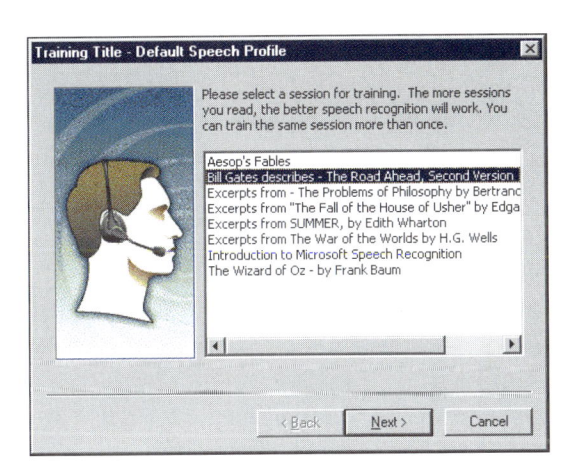

FIGURE C-18
Choose Another Story or Training Script to Read

CAUTION TIP

You must read until Microsoft Office Speech Recognition has a large enough sample of your voice to process and adjust to your unique way of speaking. Click **Pause** to take a break. However, it is best to read the entire session training script in one sitting.

Step 7 At the end of the training process, Microsoft Office Speech Recognition shows you a multimedia training tutorial (you may need to install Macromedia Flash to view the tutorial). Enjoy the tutorial before continuing.

appendix C

C.b Using Voice Commands

Microsoft makes it easy to replace mouse clicks with voice commands. The voice commands are very intuitive. In most cases, you simply say what you see. For example, to open the File menu, you can simply say **File**.

Microsoft Office XP voice commands allow you to control dialog boxes and menu bars, and to format documents by speaking. You can give your hands a rest by speaking commands instead of clicking them. This can help reduce your risk for carpal tunnel syndrome and other serious injuries.

Before you begin using voice commands, remember that if more than one person is using speech recognition on the same computer, you must select your user profile from the Current Users list. The list is found by clicking the Language Bar Tools menu, as shown in Figure C-19.

FIGURE C-19
Current Users List

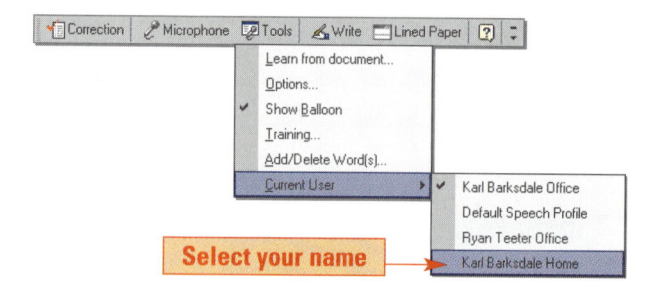

Switching Modes and Moving the Language Bar

Microsoft Office Speech Recognition works in two modes. The first is called **Dictation mode**. The second is called **Voice Command mode**. Voice Command mode allows you to control menus, give commands, and format documents.

When using Voice Command mode, simply *say what you see on the screen or in dialog boxes.* You see how this works in the next few exercises. In Step-by-Step C.4, you learn how to switch between the two modes.

Step-by-Step C.4

Step 1	Open **Microsoft Word** and the **Language Bar**, if necessary.
Step 2	The Language Bar can appear collapsed (see Figure C-20) or expanded (see Figure C-21). You can switch between the two options by clicking the **Microphone** button.

MENU TIP

After you have selected your user profile, you may wish to refresh your audio settings by clicking **Tools**, **Options**, **Configure Microphone**. This will help adjust the audio settings to the noise conditions in your current dictation environment.

FIGURE C-20
Collapsed Language Bar

Microphone button

Clicking the Microphone button with your mouse turns on the microphone and expands the Language Bar.

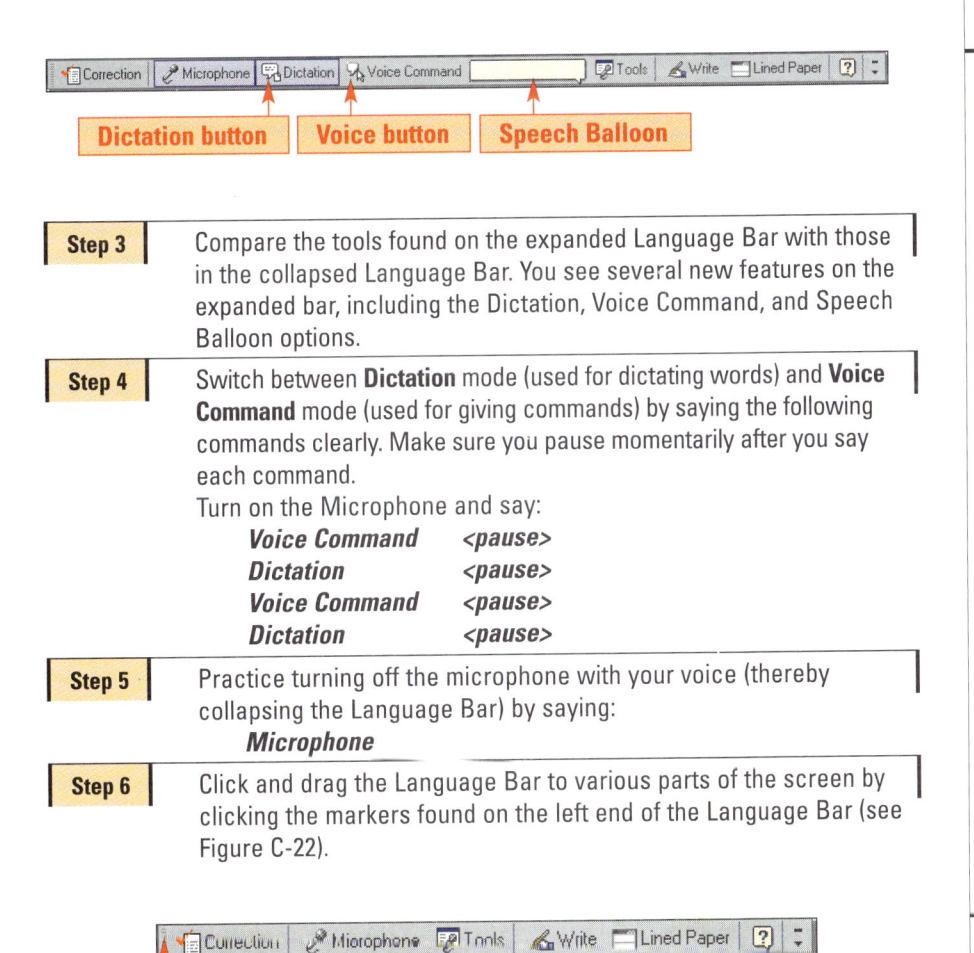

FIGURE C-21
Expanded Language Bar

Dictation button *Voice button* *Speech Balloon*

Step 3	Compare the tools found on the expanded Language Bar with those in the collapsed Language Bar. You see several new features on the expanded bar, including the Dictation, Voice Command, and Speech Balloon options.

Step 4	Switch between **Dictation** mode (used for dictating words) and **Voice Command** mode (used for giving commands) by saying the following commands clearly. Make sure you pause momentarily after you say each command.
	Turn on the Microphone and say:
	   Voice Command <pause>
	   Dictation <pause>
	   Voice Command <pause>
	   Dictation <pause>

Step 5	Practice turning off the microphone with your voice (thereby collapsing the Language Bar) by saying: **Microphone**
Step 6	Click and drag the Language Bar to various parts of the screen by clicking the markers found on the left end of the Language Bar (see Figure C-22).

> **QUICK TIP**
>
> The Language Bar can float anywhere on the screen. Move the Language Bar to a spot that is convenient and out of the way. Most users position the Language Bar in the title bar or status bar when using speech with Microsoft Word.

Click and drag the Language Bar marker

FIGURE C-22
Move the Language Bar to a Convenient Spot

Giving Menu Commands

When you use Microsoft Office Voice Commands, your word will be obeyed. Before you begin issuing commands, take a few seconds and analyze Figure C-23. The toolbars you will be working with in the next few activities are identified in the figure.

appendix C

FIGURE C-23
Customize Microsoft Word with Your Voice

QUICK TIP

In Voice Command mode, you can say almost any command you would click with your mouse, and achieve the same result. For the most part, simply say what you see on the screen. Voice Commands are very easy to learn.

QUICK TIP

The Escape and Cancel commands are like pressing the ESC key on the keyboard. These commands cancel whatever menu you have voice-selected.

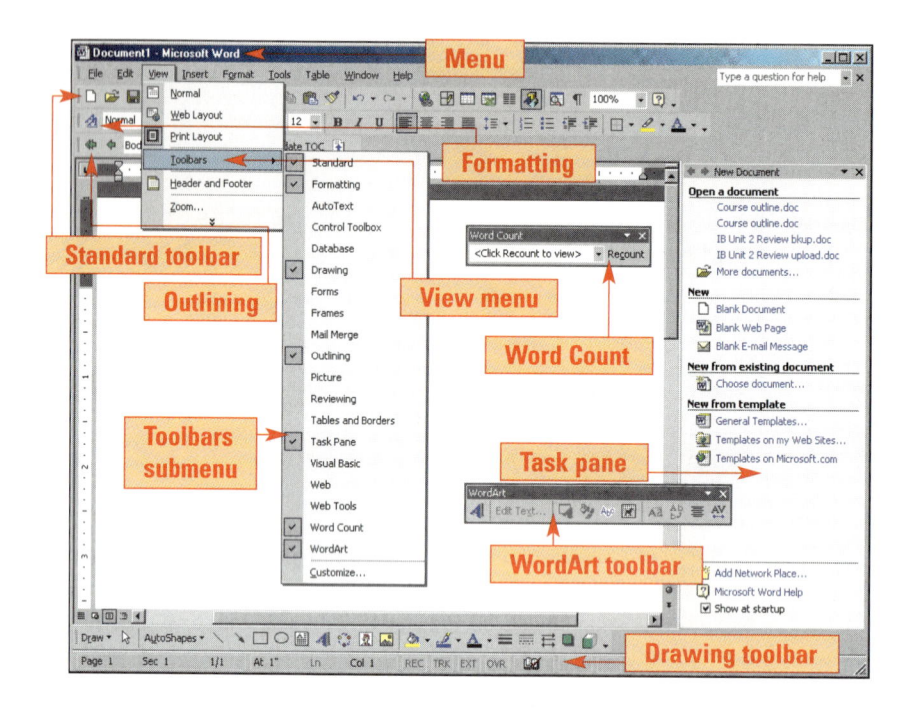

Step-by-Step C.5

Step 1	Switch on the **Microphone** from the Language Bar.
Step 2	Switch to Voice Command mode by saying: *Voice Command*
Step 3	Open and close several menus by saying: *File* (Pause briefly between commands) *Escape* *Edit* *Cancel* *View* *Escape*
Step 4	Close or display a few of the popular toolbars found in Microsoft Word by saying the following commands: *View* *Toolbars* *Standard* *View* *Toolbars* *Formatting* *View* *Toolbars* *Drawing*

Step 5	Close or redisplay the toolbars by saying the following commands: ***View*** ***Toolbars*** ***Drawing*** ***View*** ***Toolbars*** ***Formatting*** ***View*** ***Toolbars*** ***Standard***
Step 6	Practice giving voice commands by adding and removing the Task Pane and WordArt toolbar. Try some other options. When you are through experimenting, turn off the microphone and collapse the Language Bar by saying: ***Microphone***

Navigating Dialog Boxes

Opening files is one thing you do nearly every time you use Microsoft Office. To open files, you need to manipulate the Open dialog box (Figure C-24). A dialog box allows you to make decisions and execute voice commands. For example, in the Open dialog box you can switch folders and open files by voice.

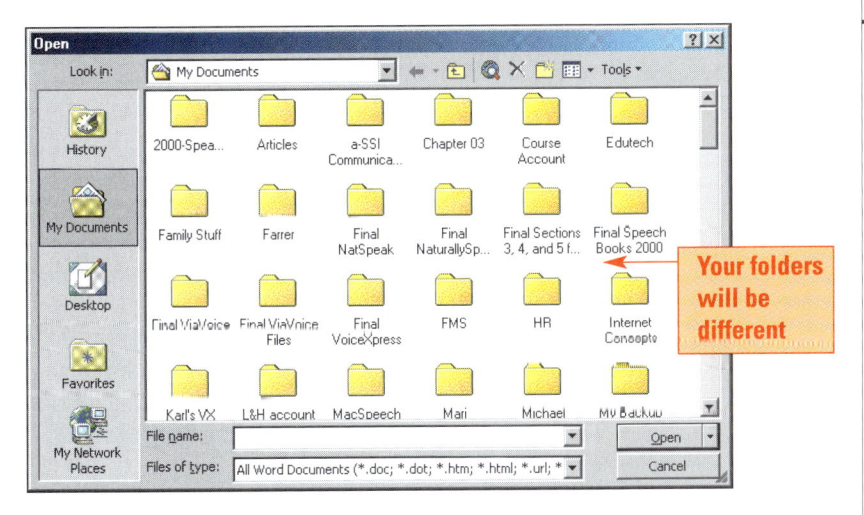

FIGURE C-24
Open Dialog Box

Step-by-Step C.6

Step 1	Turn on the **Microphone**, switch to Voice Command mode, and access the Open dialog box, as shown in Figure C-25, using the following commands: ***Voice Command*** ***File*** ***Open***

FIGURE C-25
Say File, Open

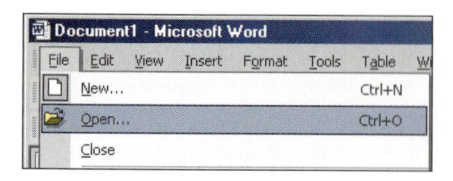

Step 2 Switch between various folder locations with your voice. In this case, you're going to switch between the Desktop, My Documents, and other folders located on the side of the Open dialog box, as shown in Figure C-26. Say the following voice commands to switch between folder locations. Pause slightly after saying each command:
Desktop
My Documents
History
Desktop
Favorites
My Documents

FIGURE C-26
Switch Between Various Folder Locations

> **QUICK TIP**
>
> Any time a button in a dialog box appears dark around the edges, the button is active. You can access active buttons at any time by saying the name of the button or by saying **Enter**. You can also move around dialog boxes using the **Tab** or **Shift Tab** voice commands, or move between folders and files by saying **Up Arrow**, **Down Arrow**, **Left Arrow**, and **Right Arrow**. When selecting files, you'll probably find it much easier to use your mouse instead of your voice.

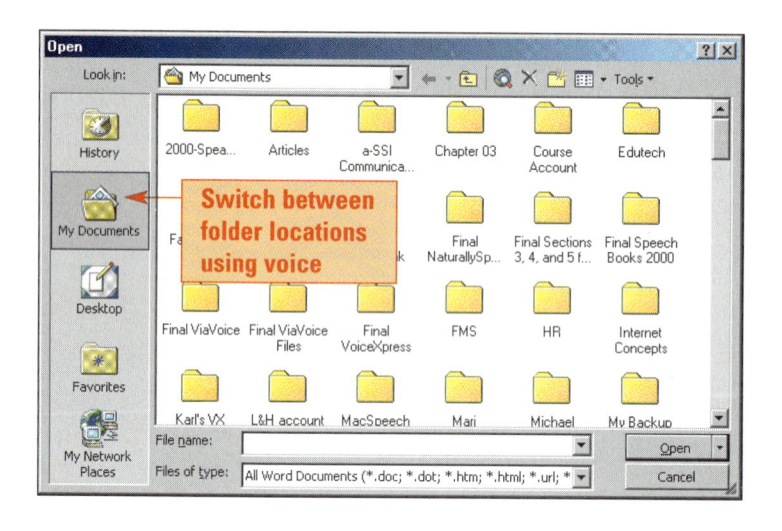

Step 3 You can change how your folders and files look in the Open dialog box by manipulating the Views menu, as shown in Figure C-27. Say the following voice commands to change the look of your folders and files:
Views
Small Icons
Views
List
Views
Details
Views
Thumbnails
Views
Large icons
Views
List

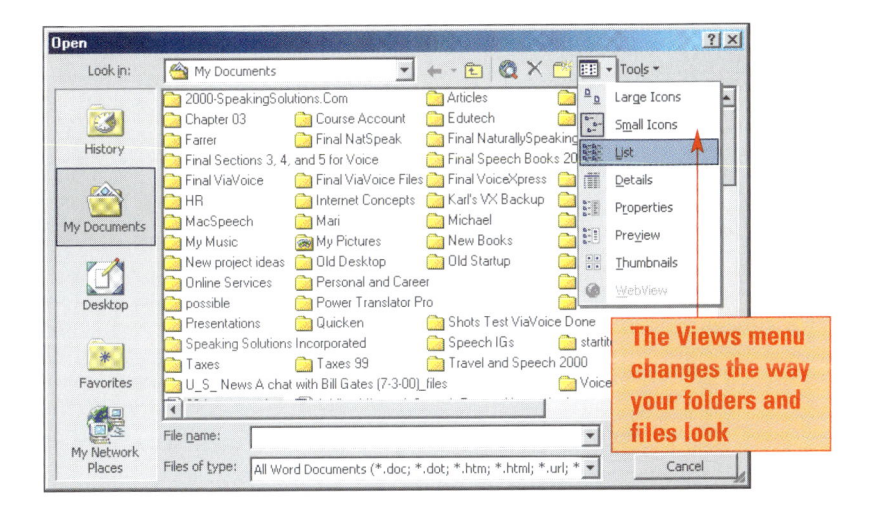

FIGURE C-27
Change the Look of Folders with the Views Menu

The Views menu changes the way your folders and files look

| Step 4 | Close the Open dialog box by using the Cancel command. Say: ***Cancel*** |

Open and Count a Document

In Step-by-Step C.7, you combine your traditional mouse skills with voice skills to accomplish tasks more conveniently. Use your skills to open a file. Then, use your menu selecting technique to open the Word Count toolbar and count the number of words in a document.

Step-by-Step C.7

Step 1	Using your voice, say **File**, **Open** and select the **My Documents** folder (or the location of your Data Disk). View the folders and files in **List** view. (Review Step-by-Step C.6 if you have forgotten how to make these changes in the Open dialog box.)
Step 2	Scroll through the list of files with your mouse until you see the file called ***Prevent Injury***. To open the file, select it with your mouse and say: ***Open*** (or you also may say ***Enter***)
Step 3	As the file opens, notice that the document title is PREVENT INJURY WITH SPEECH. Speech recognition can help you avoid serious keyboarding and mouse injuries. Count the words in the article. Open the Word Count toolbar by saying the following: ***View*** ***Toolbars*** ***Word Count***
Step 4	With the Word Count toolbar open, say the following command to count the words: ***Recount***

QUICK TIP

To complete Step-by-Step C.7, the *Prevent Injury* document should be moved from the Data Disk to the My Documents folder on your computer.

| Step 5 | How many words are contained in the article? |
| Step 6 | Leave the *Prevent Injury* document open for the next activity. |

Save a Document and Exit Word

Saving a file will give you a chance to practice manipulating dialog boxes. Switching from the keyboard and mouse to your voice has several benefits. For example, have you heard of carpal tunnel syndrome and other computer keyboard-related injuries caused by repetitive typing and clicking? By using your speech software even part of the time, you can reduce your risk for these long-term and debilitating nerve injuries.

In Step-by-Step C.8, you change the filename *Prevent Injury* to *My prevent injury file* using the Save As dialog box.

Step-by-Step C.8

Step 1	Make sure the **Prevent Injury** document appears on your screen. If you closed the document, repeat Step-by-Step C.7.
Step 2	Open the **Save As** dialog box. Notice that it is a lot like the Open dialog box. Try the following commands: **Voice Command** *(if necessary)* **File** **Save as**
Step 3	Switch to the **My Documents** folder and display the folder in **List** view as you learned to do in Step-by-Step C.7.
Step 4	Click your mouse in the **File name:** text box and type the filename or switch to Dictation mode and name the file with your voice by saying: **Dictation** **My prevent injury file**
Step 5	Save your document and close the Save As the box by saying: **Voice Command** **Save**
Step 6	Close the **Word Count** toolbar using the steps you learned earlier.
Step 7	Close Microsoft Word and collapse the Language Bar with the following commands: (When asked whether to save other open documents, say **No**.) **File** **Close** **Microphone**

C.c Dictating, Editing, and Formatting by Voice

If you have always dreamed of the day when you could sit back, relax, and write the next great American novel by speaking into a microphone, well, that day has arrived. It is possible to write that novel, a report, or even a simple e-mail message at speeds of 130–160 words per minute. However, it takes practice to achieve an acceptable level of accuracy. This section is designed to help you build accuracy.

Microsoft Office Speech Recognition is not made for complete handsfree use. You still need to use your keyboard and mouse much of the time. But, if you're willing to put in some effort, you can improve your speaking accuracy to the point that you can dramatically improve your output.

Dictating

Microsoft Speech Recognition allows you to work in **Dictation** mode when voice writing words into your documents. Switching from Voice Command mode to Dictation mode is as easy as saying ***Dictation***.

In Dictation mode, don't stop speaking in the middle of a sentence—even if your words don't appear immediately. The software needs a few seconds to process what you're saying. Microsoft Office Speech Recognition lets you know it is working by placing a highlighted bar with dots in your document, as shown in Figure C-28. A few seconds later, your words appear.

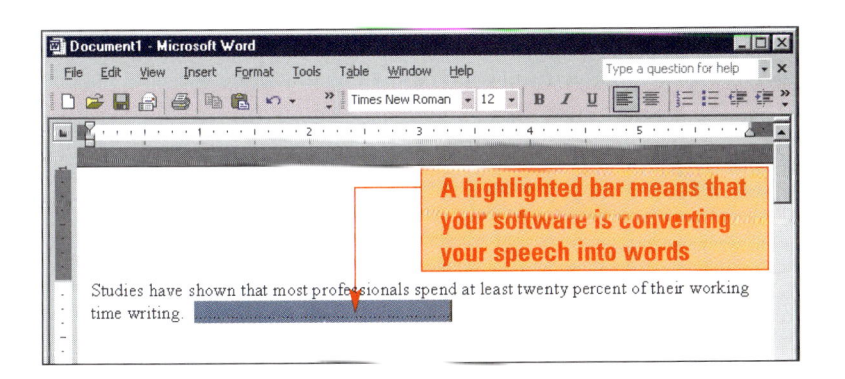

> **QUICK TIP**
>
> The best way to improve dictation accuracy is to read additional training session stories to your computer. You should read at least three to five stories. Do this by clicking **Tools**, **Current User**, and double-checking to see if your user profile name has a check mark by it. Then, click **Tools**, **Training** from the Language Bar and follow the onscreen instructions.

FIGURE C-28
Continue Talking Even If Your Words Don't Appear Instantly

QUICK TIP

Think about the following as you begin voice writing:
- Speak naturally, without stopping in the middle of your sentences.
- Don't speak abnormally fast or slow.
- Say each word clearly. Don't slur your words or leave out sounds.

QUICK TIP

You'll need to dictate punctuation marks. Say the word **Period** to create a (.), say **Comma** to create a (,), say **Question Mark** for a (?), and **Exclamation Mark/Point** for (!).

During the next steps, don't be overly concerned about making mistakes. You learn some powerful ways to correct mistakes in the next few exercises. For now, experiment and see what happens.

Step-by-Step C.9

Step 1	Open **Microsoft Word** and the **Language Bar**, if necessary. Don't forget to select your user profile.
Step 2	Turn on the **Microphone**, switch to **Dictation mode**, and read this short selection into Microsoft Word. **Dictation** *Studies have shown that most professionals spend at least twenty percent of their working time writing <period> You can use speech recognition software to help you in any career you choose <period> Microsoft speech can be used in the medical <comma> legal <comma> financial <comma> and educational professions <period>* **Microphone**
Step 3	Examine your paragraph. How well did you do? Count the mistakes or word errors. How many errors did you make?
Step 4	Now delete all the text on your screen. Start by turning on the **Microphone** and then switching to **Voice Command** mode by saying (remember to pause briefly after each command): **Voice Command** **Edit** **Select All** **Backspace**
Step 5	Repeat the selection from Step 2. This time, say any word that gave you difficulty a little more clearly. See if your computer understands more of what you say this time around.
Step 6	Did you improve? Yes/No
Step 7	Delete all the text on your screen again before you continue, using the **Voice Command**, **Edit**, **Select All**, **Backspace** commands.

Using the New Line and New Paragraph Commands

In this next set of exercises, you have a chance to use the New Line and New Paragraph commands to organize text. These essential commands allow you to control the look and feel of your documents. (See Figure C-29.) It helps to pause briefly before and after you say each command.

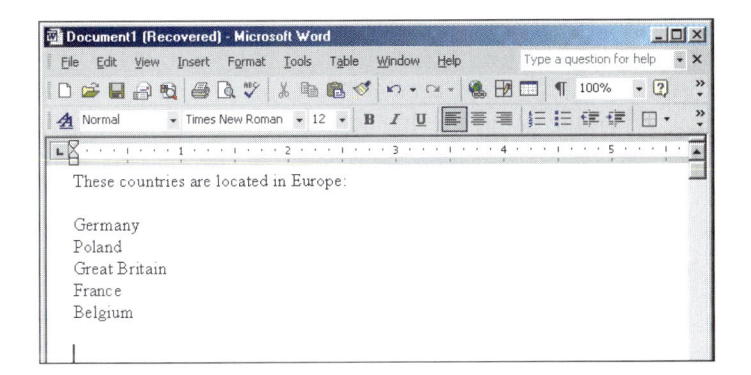

FIGURE C-29
New Line and New Paragraph Commands Organize Text

Step-by-Step C.10

Step 1	The New Line and New Paragraph commands help organize lists of information. Dictate the following list of European countries. Turn on the **Microphone**, if necessary, and say: **Dictation** *These countries are located in Europe <colon> <New Paragraph>* *Germany <New Line>* *Poland <New Line>* *Great Britain <New Line>* *France <New Line>* *Belgium <New Paragraph>*
Step 2	Save the file in the Save As dialog box with the **Voice Command**, **File**, **Save As** commands.
Step 3	Click your mouse in the **File name:** text box and enter **Countries of Europe** as the filename. (*Note:* If you speak the filename, remember to switch to Dictation mode.)
Step 4	Close the Save As dialog box with the **Voice Command**, **Save** commands, and then clear your screen by saying **Edit**, **Select All**, **Backspace**.

QUICK TIP

Say the word **Colon** to create a (:).

QUICK TIP

When dictating words in a list, it helps to pause slightly before and after saying the commands, as in *<pause> New Line <pause>* and *<pause> New Paragraph <pause>*.

Using Undo

Microsoft Office Speech Recognition offers powerful ways to make corrections and train the software to recognize difficult words, so they appear correctly when you say them again. For example, erasing mistakes is easy with the Undo command. That's the first trick you learn in this section.

The Undo command works like pressing the Undo button or clicking Edit, Undo with your mouse. You can quickly erase the problem when you misspeak. All you need to do is switch to Voice Command mode and say **Undo**.

appendix C

> **CAUTION TIP**
>
> A common speech mistake occurs when speakers break words into syllables. For example, they may say **speak keen clear lee** instead of **speaking clearly.**

> **QUICK TIP**
>
> A key to great accuracy in speech recognition is to speak in complete phrases and sentences. Complete sentences and phrases make it easier for the software to understand what you're trying to say. The software makes adjustments based on the context of the words that commonly appear together. The more words you say as a group or phrase, the more information your software has to work with.

Step-by-Step C.11

Step 1	In this step, say the name of the academic subject, then erase it immediately with the Undo command and replace it with the next subject in the list. Erase the subject regardless of whether it is correct. Switch to Voice Command mode before saying Undo.

Dictation
Biology	Voice Command	Undo	Dictation
French	Voice Command	Undo	Dictation
American history	Voice Command	Undo	Dictation

Step 2	The Undo command deletes the last continuous phrase you have spoken. Say each of the following phrases, then use Undo to erase them.

To infinity and beyond	Voice Command	Undo	Dictation
The check is in the mail	Voice Command	Undo	Dictation
Money isn't everything	Voice Command	Undo	
Microphone			

Correcting Errors

Correcting mistakes is obviously important. There are several ways to make corrections effectively.

Because speech recognition software recognizes phrases better than individual words, one of the best ways to correct a mistake is to use your mouse to select the phrase where the mistake occurs and then repeat the phrase. For example, in the sentence below the software has keyed the word *share* instead of the word *sure*. Select the phrase (like the boldface example) with your mouse, then say the phrase again:

What you should select: You sound **very share of yourself**.
What you would repeat: **very sure of yourself**

If you still make a mistake, select the misspoken word with your mouse and take advantage of the power of the **Correction** button on the Language Bar. Carefully read through these steps and then practice what you learned in Step 5.

Step-by-Step C.12

Step 1	If you make an error, select the mistake, as shown in Figure C-30.
Step 2	With your microphone on, say **Correction** or click the Correction button with your mouse.
Step 3	If the correct alternative appears in the correction list, click the correct alternative with your mouse.

Using Office XP Speech Recognition   AP 41

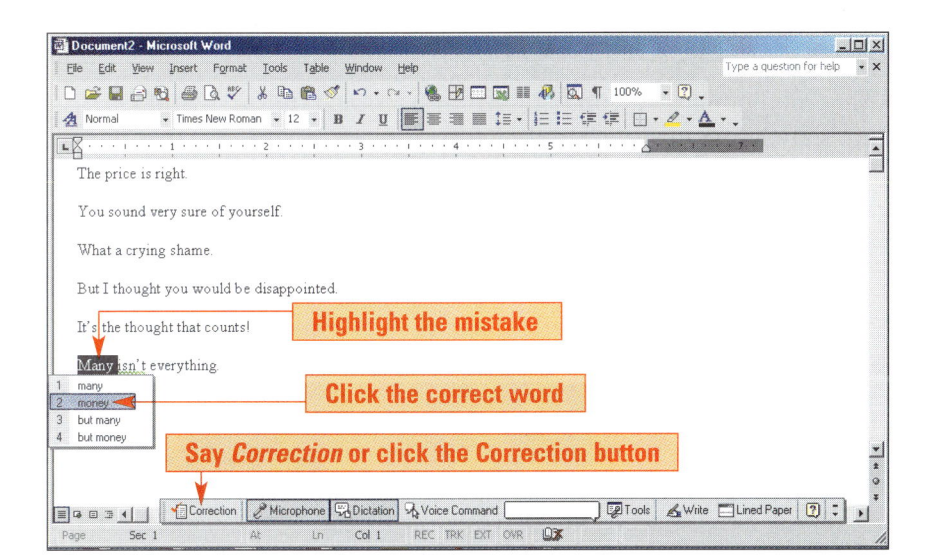

FIGURE C-30
Select the Mistake and Say *Correction*

- Highlight the mistake
- Click the correct word
- Say *Correction* or click the Correction button

Step 4 If the correct word does not appear, as in Figure C-31, key the correct response with your keyboard.

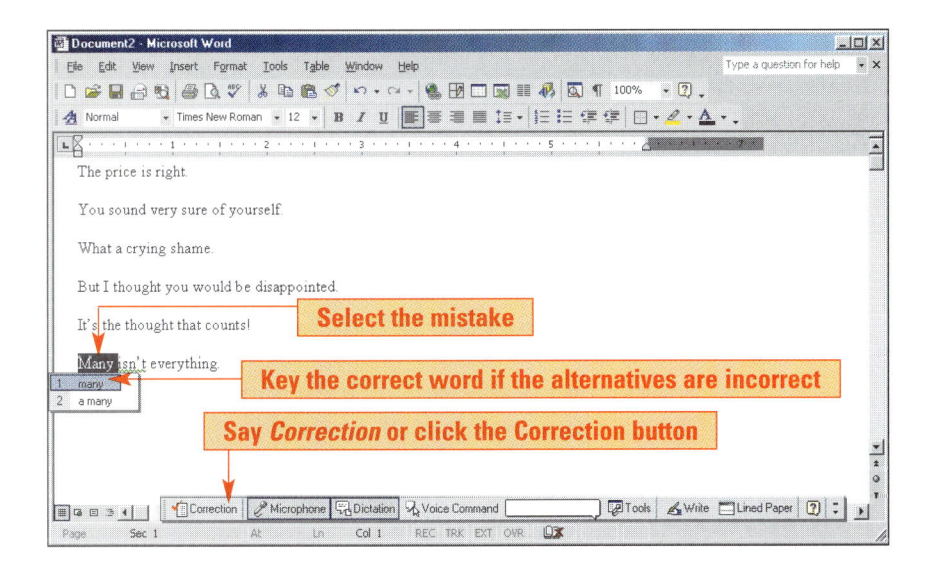

FIGURE C-31
If the Correct Word Doesn't Appear, Key the Word

- Select the mistake
- Key the correct word if the alternatives are incorrect
- Say *Correction* or click the Correction button

Step 5 Now give it a try. Speak the following sentences. (*Hint:* Say the complete sentence before you make any corrections.) Try to correct the error first by repeating the phrase. Then, select individual word errors and use the Correction button to help you fix any remaining mistakes:
The price is right.
You sound very sure of yourself.
What a crying shame.
But, I thought you would be disappointed.
It's the thought that counts!
Money isn't everything.

appendix C

Formatting Sentences

After you dictate text, you can format it, copy it, paste it, and manipulate it just like you would with a mouse. In this exercise, you dictate a few sentences, and then you change the font styles and make a copy of the sentences. That is a lot to remember, so take a look at what you are about to accomplish. Review Figure C-32 to get a sneak preview of this activity.

FIGURE C-32
Dictate, Format, and Copy and Paste These Lines

> **MOUSE TIP**
>
> When you correct a mistake using the Correction button, Microsoft Office Speech Recognition plays back what you said and remembers any corrections that you make. This helps to ensure that the software won't make the same mistake the next time you say the same word or phrase. Use the Correction button as often as you can. This helps to improve your speech recognition accuracy.

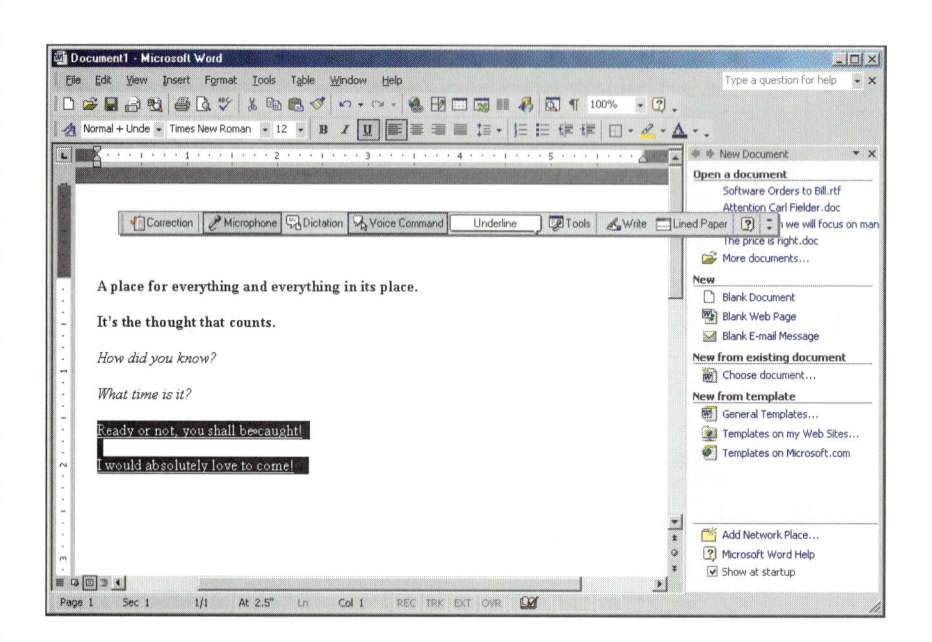

A few quick reminders before you begin:
- Use your mouse and voice together to bold, italicize, and underline text.
- Say the basic punctuation marks, exclamation point/mark (!), period (.), comma (,), question mark (?), semicolon (;), colon (:).
- Start a new line with the New Paragraph command.

Step-by-Step C.13

Step 1 — Speak the following sentences, using the New Paragraph command to space between each. Do not pause in the middle of any sentence. If you make mistakes, correct them using the Correction button, as explained in Step-by-Step C.12.
Dictation
A place for everything and everything in its place.
It's the thought that counts.
How did you know?
What time is it?
Ready or not, you shall be caught!
I would absolutely love to come!

Using Office XP Speech Recognition   AP 43

Step 2	With your mouse, select the first two sentences and make them bold with the following commands: ***Voice Command*** ***Bold***
Step 3	Select the two questions and italicize them by saying: ***Italic***
Step 4	Select the final two exclamatory sentences and underline them by saying: ***Underline***
Step 5	Copy all the text on your screen and paste a copy at the bottom of your document by saying: ***Edit*** ***Select All*** ***Copy*** ***Down Arrow*** ***Paste***
Step 6	Print your document with the following commands: ***File*** ***Print*** ***OK***
Step 7	Close your document without saving using the **File**, **Close** command and then say **No** when you are asked to save.
Step 8	Open a new document with your voice with the **File**, **New**, **Blank Document** commands and turn off your **Microphone** before you continue.

Adding and Training Names

Your speech software can remember what you teach it as long as you follow these simple steps. When you click Add/Delete Word(s) from the Tools menu, the Add/Delete Word(s) dialog box opens. This is a very powerful tool. It allows you to enter a name or any other word or phrase, click the **Record pronunciation** button, and record your pronunciation of the word or phrase.

Step-by-Step C.14

Step 1	Click **Tools**, **Add/Delete Word(s)** from the Language Bar, as shown in Figure C-33.

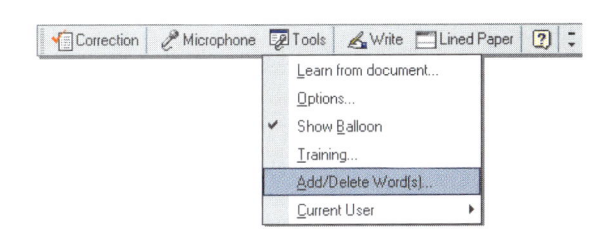

FIGURE C-33
Click the Add/Delete Word(s) Option

appendix C

Step 2 Enter your name into the **Word** text box as shown in Figure C-34.

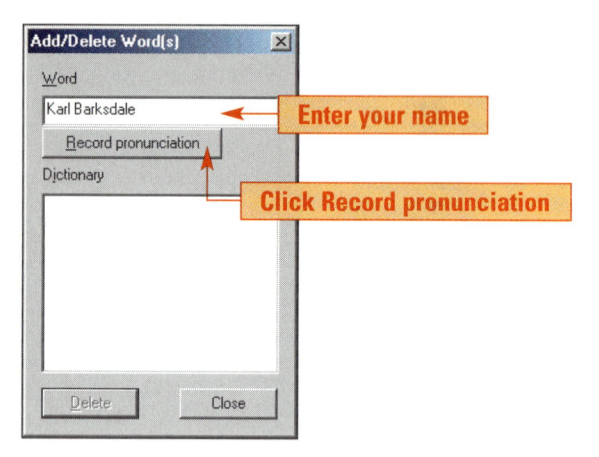

FIGURE C-34
Enter Your Name in the Word Text Box

QUICK TIP

If your speech recognition software doesn't hear you properly, your name does not appear in the Dictionary. If this happens, try again. When the system has accepted your pronunciation of the word, the name appears in the Dictionary.

Step 3 Click the **Record pronunciation** button and say your name aloud.

Step 4 Your name appears in the Dictionary list. Double-click your name to hear a digitized voice repeat your name. (See Figure C-35.)

FIGURE C-35
Add/Delete Word(s) Dialog Box

CAUTION TIP

If your name doesn't appear properly when you say it, return to the Add/Delete Word(s) dialog box, select your name, then click the **Record pronunciation** button and re-record the correct pronunciation of your name.

Step 5 Close the Add/Delete Word(s) dialog box by clicking the **Close** button.

Step 6 Return to Microsoft Word, turn on your **Microphone**, switch to **Dictation** mode. Say your name several times and see if it appears correctly.

Step 7 To improve your accuracy, it's important to add troublesome words to your dictionary. Pick five words that have given you difficulty in the past. Train the software to recognize these words as explained in Steps 1 through 6. As you add and train for the pronunciation of those words, your accuracy improves bit by bit.

C.d Turning Microsoft Speech Recognition On and Off

Microsoft Office Speech Recognition isn't for everybody—at least not in its present form. It requires a powerful CPU and a lot of RAM. It also takes a quality headset. If you don't have the necessary hardware, chances are speech recognition isn't working very well for you.

Perhaps you are simply uncomfortable using speech software. You may be an expert typist with no sign of carpal tunnel syndrome or any other repetitive stress injury. Whatever your reason for choosing not to use Microsoft speech software, it is important to know how to disable the feature.

There are two ways to turn off your speech software. You can minimize the toolbar and place it aside temporarily, or you can turn it off entirely. If you decide you want to use speech recognition at a later time, you can always turn it back on again.

Turning Off Speech Recognition

Microsoft Speech Recognition allows you to minimize the Language Bar, putting it aside temporarily. Minimizing places the Language Bar in the taskbar tray in the form of the Language Bar icon. After the Language Bar has been minimized, it is then possible to turn the system off altogether. To see how this is accomplished, follow Step-by-Step C.15.

Step-by-Step C.15

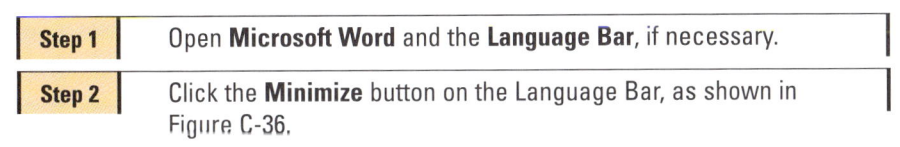

Step 1	Open **Microsoft Word** and the **Language Bar**, if necessary.
Step 2	Click the **Minimize** button on the Language Bar, as shown in Figure C-36.

FIGURE C-36
Click the Minimize Button on the Language Bar

Step 3 When you minimize for the first time, a dialog box explains what is going to happen to your Language Bar, as shown in Figure C-37. Read this dialog box carefully, then click **OK**.

FIGURE C-37
Read This Information Carefully

Step 4 Right-click the **Language Bar** icon in the taskbar. Several options appear, as shown in Figure C-38. Click C**lose the Language Bar**.

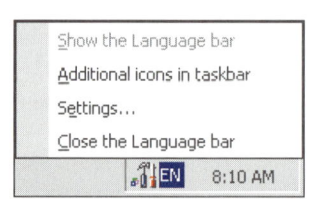

FIGURE C-38
Right-Click the Language Bar Icon

Step 5 Another dialog box opens to explain a process you can follow for restoring your speech operating system after you have turned it off. Click **OK**. The system is turned off and your language tools disappear, as shown in Figure C-39. Close Word. (*Note:* If you click **Cancel**, you return to normal and can continue using the speech recognition system by opening the Language Bar.)

FIGURE C-39
Click OK to Turn Off Speech Recognition

Turning On Speech Recognition

There are several ways to turn your speech recognition system back on. Follow Step-by-Step C.16.

Step-by-Step C.16

Step 1 — Open **Microsoft Word** and click **Speech** on the **Tools** menu, as shown in Figure C-40. Your speech recognition software is restored and you can begin using it again.

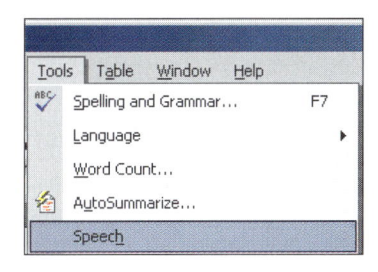

FIGURE C-40
Click Speech on the Tools Menu

If your speech software did not restore itself after Step 1, continue with Steps 2 through 5.

Step 2 — Click the **Start** button, **Settings**, **Control Panel**. Then double-click the **Text Services** icon to open the Text Services dialog box, as shown in Figure C-41.

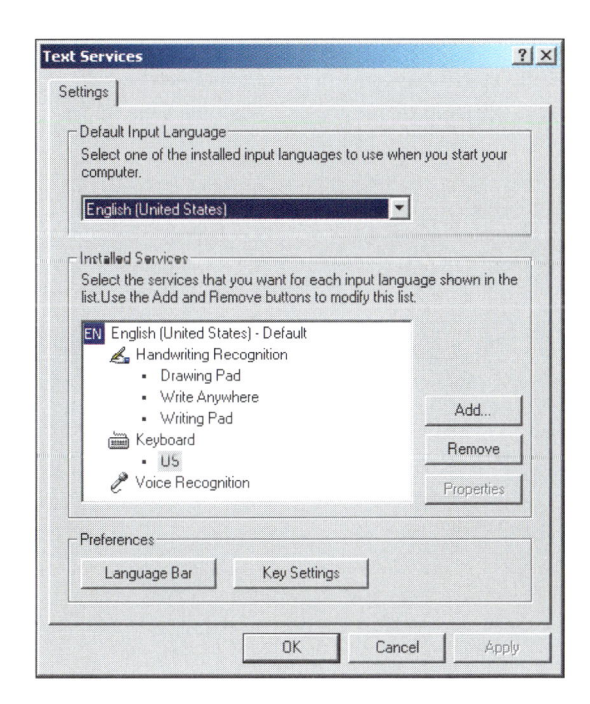

FIGURE C-41
Click Language Bar in the Text Input Settings Dialog Box

appendix C

FIGURE C-42
Language Bar Settings Dialog Box

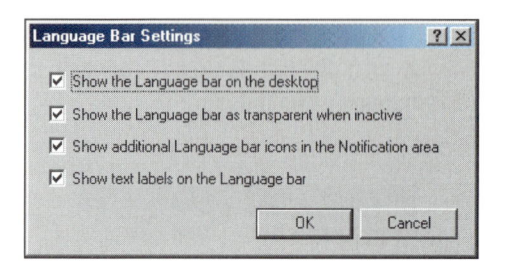

Step 3 Click **Language Bar** in the Text Services dialog box.

Step 4 In the Language Bar Settings dialog box, click the **Show the Language bar on the desktop** check box to insert a check mark, as shown in Figure C-42.

Step 5 Click **OK**, then exit and restart your computer. The speech software should be restored and you can begin speaking again. (*Note:* If the Language Bar is still missing after you launch Word, try selecting Tools, Speech one more time.)

Office XP **MOUS 1**

Mastering and Using Office XP

APPROVED COURSEWARE

Expert MOUS Objectives

Microsoft Word 2002

Standardized Coding Number	Skill Sets and Skills Being Measured	Chapter Number	Chapter Pages	Exercise Pages	Exercises
W2002e-1	**Customizing Paragraphs**				
W2002e-1-1	Control Pagination	16 and throughout text	WA 66	WA 71, 73	Skills Review 6 Case Project 7
W2002e-1-2	Sort paragraphs in lists and tables	19	WA 117, 119, 122, 123	WA 129–132	Skills Review 1–9 Case Projects 1–8
W2002e-2	**Formatting documents**				
W2002e-2-1	Create and format document sections	15	WA 38, 40, 41, 43	WA 52–55	Skills Review 2, 3, 4, 6, 7 Case Projects 1, 2, 4, 6, 8
W2002e-2-2	Create and apply character and paragraph styles	16	WA 57	WA 70–73	Skills Review 1–5, 7, 8 Case Projects 1–6
W2002e-2-3	Create and update document indexes and tables of contents, figures, and authorities	20	WA 142, 146	WA 157, 160	Skills Review 5 Case Projects 7, 8
W2002e-2-4	Create cross-references	20	WA 140	WA 157, 160	Skills Review 4 Case Project 8
W2002e-2-5	Add and revise endnotes and footnotes	20	WA 135	WA 157, 159	Skills Review 2, 3 Case Projects 1, 2, 3
W2002e-2-6	Create and manage master documents and subdocuments	22	WA 196	WA 210–213	Skills Review 3, 4, 5, 7 Case Projects 1, 3, 4
W2002e-2-7	Move within documents	20	WA 134, 152	WA 156–157, 159–160	Skills Review 1, 2 Case Projects 4, 5, 6, 8
W2002e-2-8	Create and modify forms using various form controls	23	WA 215, 227	WA 231–240	Skills Review 1–8 Case Projects 1–8
W2002e-2-9	Create forms and prepare forms for distribution	23	WA 227	WA 231–240	Skills Review 1–8 Case Projects 1–8

MOUS 2 — Office XP

Standardized Coding Number	Skill Sets and Skills Being Measured	Chapter Number	Chapter Pages	Exercise Pages	Exercises
W2002e-3	**Customizing Tables**				
W2002e-3-1	Use Excel data in tables	Excel 14	EA 319	EA 337–339	Skills Review 3, 4, 5 Case Projects 1, 6
W2002e-3-2	Perform calculations in Word tables	14	WA 14, 25	WA 30–35	Skills Review 1–5, 8 Case Projects 2, 6, 8
W2002e-4	**Creating and Modifying Graphics**				
W2002e-4-1	Create, modify, and position graphics	21	WA 162, 174, 176, 179	WA 191–194	Skills Review 2, 4–6, 9, 10 Case Projects 1–6
W2002e-4-2	Create and modify charts using data from other applications	Excel 14	EA 321	EA 339	Case Project 2
W2002e-4-3	Align text and graphics	21	WA 177	WA 193	Skills Review 10
W2002e-5	**Customizing Word**				
W2002e-5-1	Create, edit, and run macros	25	WA 271, 277, 283	WA 288–291	Skills Review 1–8 Case Projects 1–4, 6–8
W2002e-5-2	Customize menus and toolbars	26	WA 303, 305	WA 310–311	Skills Review 3, 5
W2002e-6	**Workgroup Collaboration**				
W2002e-6-1	Track, accept, and reject changes to documents	24	WA 255, 258	WA 269	Case Project 7
W2002e-6-2	Merge input from several reviewers	24	WA 255	WA 269	Case Project 7
W2002e-6-3	Insert and modify hyperlinks to other documents and Web pages	24	WA 249, 252	WA 266–269	Skills Review 3–8 Case Projects 1, 2, 6
W2002e-6-4	Create and edit Web documents in Word	24	WA 242, 253	WA 265–269	Skills Review 1–8 Case Projects 1, 6
W2002e-6-5	Create document versions	22	WA 202	WA 211, 213	Skills Review 5 Case Project 7
W2002e-6-6	Protect documents	23 26	WA 227 WA 301	WA 231–240 WA 309–312	Skills Review 1–8 Case Projects 2, 4, 8 Skills Review 1, 2, 8 Case Projects 4, 6, 7
W2002e-6-7	Define and modify default file locations for workgroup templates	24 26	WA 253 WA 303	WA 265–269	Skills Review 1, 4, 7 Case Project 6
W2002e-6-8	Attach digital signatures to documents	24	WA 261	WA 269	Case Project 3

Standardized Coding Number	Skill Sets and Skills Being Measured	Chapter Number	Chapter Pages	Exercise Pages	Exercises
W2002e-7	**Using Mail Merge**				
W2002e-7-1	Merge letters with a Word, Excel, or Access data source	17	WA 76, 78, 80	WA 86–90	Skills Review 1–8 Case Projects 1–8
W2002e-7-2	Merge labels with a Word, Excel, or Access data source	18	WA 96	WA 110	Skills Review 2
W2002e-7-3	Use Outlook data as mail merge data source	17 18	WA 78	WA 111, 115	Skills Review 3 Case Project 3

Microsoft Excel 2002

Standardized Coding Number	Skill Sets and Skills Being Measured	Chapter Number	Chapter Pages	Exercise Pages	Exercises
Ex2002a-1	**Importing and Exporting Data**				
Ex2002e-1-1	Import data to Excel	16	EA 214–219	EA 237–239	Skills Review 4, 7 Case Projects 2, 4, 5, 6
Ex2002e-1-2	Export data from Excel	16	EA 220, 224	EA 238, 240	Skills Review 5, 6, 7 Case Project 7
Ex2002e-1-3	Publish worksheets and workbooks to the Web	16	EA 228–230	EA 238–240	Skills Review 5, 6, 8 Case Projects 1, 3, 6, 8
Ex2002e-2	**Managing Workbooks**				
Ex2002e-2-1	Create, edit, and apply templates	9	EA 64, 65	EA 72, 74	Skills Review 3, 4, 5 Case Projects 5, 6, 8
Ex2002e-2-2	Create workspaces	7	EA 16–17	EA 21	Skills Review 3
Ex2002e-2-3	Use Data Consolidation	7	EA 9–11	EA 20, 22–24	Skills Review 1, 6 Case Projects 1, 3
Ex2002e-3	**Formatting Numbers**				
Ex2002e-3-1	Create and apply custom number formats	15	EA 187–191	EA 210, 212	Skills Review 6, 7 Case Projects 6, 8
Ex2002e-3-2	Use conditional formats	15	EA 191–193	EA 210, 212	Skills Review 8 Case Projects 6, 7
Ex2002e-4	**Working with Ranges**				
Ex2002e-4-1	Use named ranges in formulas	7	EA 6-9	EA 22	Skills Review 6
Ex2002e-4-2	Use Lookup and Reference functions	15	EA 193–195	EA 210	Skills Review 5
Ex2002e-5	**Customizing Excel**				
Ex2002e-5-1	Customize toolbars and menus	9	EA 66–68	EA 71, 73	Skills Review 1, 8
Ex2002e-5-2	Create, edit, and run macros	9	EA 54–61	EA 71–74	Skills Review 2, 6, 7 Case Projects 1, 3, 4
Ex2002e-6	**Auditing Worksheets**				
Ex2002e-6-1	Audit formulas	11	EA 100–103	EA 112–113	Skills Review 3, 5, 6, 7 Case Projects 4, 6
Ex2002e-6-2	Locate and resolve errors	11	EA 99–100, 105–107	EA 111–113	Skills Review 2, 4, 8 Case Project 4
Ex2002e-6-3	Identify dependencies in formulas	11	EA 100–107	EA 111–113	Skills Review 2, 4, 7, 8 Case Project 4

Standardized Coding Number	Skill Sets and Skills Being Measured	Chapter Number	Chapter Pages	Exercise Pages	Exercises
Ex2002e-7	**Summarizing Data**				
Ex2002e-7-1	Use subtotals with lists and ranges	8	EA 45–46	EA 51–52	Skills Review 8 Case Project 2
Ex2002e-7-2	Define and apply filters	8	EA 37–43	EA 50–52	Skills Review 4, 5, 6 Case Project 4
Ex2002e-7-3	Add group and outline criteria to ranges	8	EA 45–46	EA 51	Skills Review 8
Ex2002e-7-4	Use data validation	8	EA 27–34	EA 49–50, 52	Skills Review 1, 2 Case Projects 2, 7, 8
Ex2002e-7-5	Retrieve external data and create queries	16	EA 220–222	EA 237, 240	Skills Review 3 Case Project 7
Ex2002e-7-6	Create Extensible Markup Language (XML) Web queries	16	EA 222–224	EA 236, 239	Skills Review 1 Case Project 4
Ex2002e-8	**Analyzing Data**				
Ex2002e-8-1	Create PivotTables, PivotCharts, and PivotTable/PivotChart Reports	12	EA 118–122, 128–130	EA 133–136	Skills Review 1–6, 8 Case Projects 1, 2, 3, 5
Ex2002e-8-2	Forecast values with *what-if* analysis	10	EA 76–79, 80–85, 89–91	EA 94–97	Skills Review 1, 4–8 Case Projects 1, 3, 4, 7, 8
Ex2002e-8-3	Create and display scenarios	10	EA 85–89	EA 94–97	Skills Review 2, 3, 7 Case Projects 5, 6
Ex2002e-9	**Workgroup Collaboration**				
Ex2002e-9-1	Modify passwords, protections, and properties	15	EA 196–199	EA 210–211	Skills Review 7 Case Project 1
Ex2002e-9-2	Create a shared workbook	15	EA 199–200	EA 209–211	Skills Review 1, 4 Case Project 5
Ex2002e-9-3	Track, accept, and reject changes to workbooks	15	EA 200–202	EA 209–210	Skills Review 2, 3, 4
Ex2002e-9-4	Merge workbooks	15	EA 203–204	EA 209–210	Skills Review 4

Microsoft Access 2002

Standardized Coding Number	Skill Sets and Skills Being Measured	Chapter Number	Chapter Pages	Exercise Pages	Exercises
Ac2002e-1 Creating and Modifying Tables					
Ac2002e-1-1	Use data validation	9	AA 3–4	AA 17, 19	Skills Review 1, 2 Case Projects 4, 6
Ac2002e-1-2	Link tables	13	AA 107–108	AA 119–120	Skills Review 7 Case Project 5
Ac2002e-1-3	Create Lookup fields and modify Lookup field properties	9	AA 4–6	AA 19	Case Project 8
Ac2002e-1-4	Create and modify input masks	9	AA 6–8	AA 17–18	Skills Review 3, 4
Ac2002e-2 Creating and Modifying Forms					
Ac2002e-2-1	Create a form in Design View	11	AA 47–50	AA 64–67	Skills Review 1–4 Case Projects 3, 4, 5
Ac2002e-2-2	Create a Switchboard and set startup options	11	AA 55–60	AA 66, 67	Skills Review 7, 8 Case Projects 6, 7, 8
Ac2002e-2-3	Add Subform controls to Access forms	11	AA 50–55	AA 65–66	Skills Review 5, 6
Ac2002e-3 Refining Queries					
Ac2002e-3-1	Specify multiple query criteria	10	AA 23–24	AA 43–45	Skills Review 2, 5–7 Case Project 7
Ac2002e-3-2	Create and apply advanced filters	10	AA 21–22	AA 44	Skills Review 6, 7
Ac2002e-3-3	Create and run parameter queries	10	AA 29–31	AA 42–43, 45	Skills Review 1, 2 Case Projects 3, 7
Ac2002e-3-4	Create and run action queries	10	AA 31–39	AA 43–45	Skills Review 4, 5, 8 Case Projects 5, 6, 8
Ac2002e-3-5	Use aggregate functions in queries	10	AA 26–28	AA 43, 45	Skills Review 3 Case Project 4
Ac2002e-4 Producing Reports					
Ac2002e-4-1	Create and modify reports	12	AA 69–74	AA 92–96	Skills Review 1–8 Case Projects 3, 6–8
Ac2002e-4-2	Add Subreport controls to Access reports	12	AA 83–85	AA 94	Skills Review 8
Ac2002e-4-3	Sort and group data in reports	12	AA 74–83	AA 93–96	Skills Review 6, 7 Case Projects 3–6, 8

Office XP **MOUS 7**

Standardized Coding Number	Skill Sets and Skills Being Measured	Chapter Number	Chapter Pages	Exercise Pages	Exercises
Ac2002e-5 Defining Relationships					
Ac2002e-5-1	Establish one-to-many relationships	9	AA 9–13	AA 18, 19	Skills Review 5, 6 Case Projects 1, 2, 3
Ac2002e-5-2	Establish many-to-many relationships	9	AA 13–14	AA 18, 19	Skills Review 7, 8 Case Projects 2, 5
Ac2002e-6 Operating Access on the Web					
Ac2002e-6-1	Create and modify a Data Access Page	14	AA 129–132	AA 143, 144	Skills Review 6 Case Project 4
Ac2002e-6-2	Save PivotTables and PivotCharts views to Data Access Pages	14	AA 138	AA 143, 144	Skills Review 7, 8 Case Projects 5, 6, 8
Ac2002e-7 Using Access Tools					
Ac2002e-7-1	Import XML documents into Access	14	AA 125–126	AA 143, 144	Skills Review 5 Case Project 3
Ac2002e-7-2	Export Access data to XML documents	14	AA 127–128	AA 142, 144	Skills Review 3, 4 Case Project 2
Ac2002e-7-3	Encrypt and decrypt databases	13	AA 98–99	AA 118	Skills Review 2, 3
Ac2002e-7-4	Compact and repair databases	13	AA 105–106	AA 118	Skills Review 4
Ac2002e-7-5	Assign database security	13	AA 99–105	AA 117–120	Skills Review 1–3, 5 Case Projects 1, 2, 6–8
Ac2002e-7-6	Replicate a database	13	AA 110–111	AA 119	Skills Review 8 Case Project 3
Ac2002e-8 Creating Database Applications					
Ac2002e-8-1	Create Access Modules	13	AA 111–114	AA 118–119	Skills Review 6
Ac2002e-8-2	Use the Database Splitter	13	AA 106–107	AA 118–120	Skills Review 6 Case Project 4
Ac2002e-8-3	Create an MDE file	13	AA 109	AA 119	Skills Review 7

Index

.doc (Microsoft Word) extension, PA 149
.pot (PowerPoint template) extension, PA 57, PA 59, PA 73
.ppt (PowerPoint file) extension, PA 57, PA 59, PA 73
.rtf (Rich Text Format) extension, PA 145, PA 148, PA 150
© symbol, inserting, WA 248
3-D effect, PA 11
    assigning to action buttons, PA 93
3-D reference between networks, EA 12–15
3-D style
    adding and modifying, WA 168–169
    button, WA 166

A

Accept Changes dialog box, EA 202
Access 2002, integrating with Excel, EA 172–177
action button
    adding, PA 91
    adding 3-D effects to, PA 93
    resizing, PA 94
    using as hyperlink, PA 91–92
Action Buttons menu, setting as toolbar, PA 92
action query, AA 31–32, AA 41
action settings
    changing, PA 95
    dialog box, PA 92
active desktop, AP 4
Add Constraint dialog box, EA 84
Add Trendline dialog box, EA 89
adding
    data series, EA 141–142
    effect, PA 30, PA 31, PA 34, PA 37, PA 38, PA 39
    named range, EA 6–8
Address toolbar, AP 6
addresses, foreign, AP 16
Admins group, AA 101

Advanced Filter dialog box, EA 41
advanced filter/sort grid, AA 21
Advanced Timeline, displaying, PA 32
aggregate functions, AA 26–28, AA 41
AIFF audio formats, PA 41
Align grid, WA 21
All Reviewers list, PA 125, PA 126
alpha channels, PA 107
AND criteria, AA 23, AA 41
animated item list, PA 32
animation. *See also* custom animation.
    direction, PA 35
    event, combined, PA 33
    options, PA 40
    tags, PA 32
animation effect
    adding sound to, PA 35
    applying to all objects, PA 31
    applying to text, PA 29–41
    order of, PA 31
    previewing, PA 31, PA 37, PA 38
    removing, PA 31
    settings for, PA 35
    timing, PA 35, PA 47
    triggers for, PA 36
animations, changing order of, PA 31
antivirus software, WA 280
append query, AA 32, AA 36–37, AA 41
applications
    sending data between, AA 125
    viewing two or more simultaneously, PA 162, PA 163
Apply button, PA 128, PA 129
Apply Design Template dialog box, PA 57
Apply Filter button, AA 32
Apply/Unapply Changes, PA 126, PA 130, PA 136
area chart, EA 138–139
Arrange Windows dialog box, EA 15–16

array formula, EA 90–91
Arrow button, WA 163
Arrow Style button, WA 166
ascending order, WA 117
assistant
    defined, PA 8
    shape, PA 8
asterisk (*), AA 7, AA 100
attachment, EA 230
auditing tools, EA 98
    error checking, EA 105–107
    invalid data, EA 107–108
    precedent and dependent cells, EA 100–105
    Range Finder, EA 99–100
AutoContent presentations, PA 79
AutoCorrect Options
    button, WA 252
    dialog box, WA 185
AutoFilter
    create custom, EA 37–39
    Custom, dialog box, EA 38
    multiple operators in, EA 39–42
AutoFormat, WA 195, WA 203–206, WA 208
    button, PA 14, WA 185
AutoFormat As You Type feature, WA 185
AutoFormats, PA 9, PA 16
Automatic Layout Options button, PA 160
AutoPreview, PA 30
AutoShapes, EA 143, EA 149–151, WA 162, WA 189
    button, WA 171
    drawing, editing, and deleting, WA 170–173
    tool, WA 170
AutoSum, WA 14
AutoSummarize, WA 195, WA 206–207, WA 208
    Find All Forms Tool used with, WA 207

B

back-end database
　creating, AA 107, AA 115
　protecting tables in, AA 107,
　　AA 108, AA 115
background fill, changing, PA 70
backup copy, AA 100
barcode sorters (BCSs), AP 15
black slide, PA 46
blank slide, PA 46, PA 47
　removing timing from, PA 46,
　　PA 47
Blinds dialog box, PA 35
block format
　letter, AP 13
　modified, AP 14
boilerplate (fixed) text, WA 215
bookmark, WA 249
　button, PA 89
　deleting, WA 135
　feature, using to select slide, PA 94
　hidden, WA 142
　inserting, WA 134–135, WA 154
　turning brackets on and off in,
　　WA 135
Border Color button, WA 5
borders and shading, applying to
　paragraph, WA 61
Borders button, WA 248
Bound Column property, AA 5
branch, indicating in organization
　chart, PA 10
Briefcase replication, AA 110
Broadcast, Tips for, PA 133
Broadcast Settings dialog box, PA 134
broadcasting, PA 132
broadcasts
　setting up and scheduling,
　　PA 132–135, PA 136
　use of audio and video with,
　　PA 132
browsers, PA 96
　adding hyperlinks to, PA 90–91
button, active, AP 35
　changing symbols in, PA 61, PA 79

C

calculations, creating in query, AA 27
Capitalization style guidelines,
　PA 119
captions, adding to tables, equations,
　and figures, WA 177, WA 179
Cascade Delete feature, AA 13
Cascade Update feature, AA 13
Case and End Punctuation rules,
　PA 117
case matching, AA 24
CD Audio Track format, PA 41
cell
　dependent, EA 100, EA 102–104
　hiding, EA 196
　inserting tab formatting mark in,
　　WA 23
　locking, EA 196–199
　merging, WA 2, WA 25–27, WA 28
　precedent, EA 100, EA 101–102
　protection, EA 196
　relationships between worksheets,
　　EA 104–105
　splitting, WA 2, WA 25–27, WA 28
certification authority, WA 261
chain of command, displaying, PA 3
change marker, PA 125, PA 126,
　PA 127, PA 128, PA 129
Change Page button, PA 102
changes, tracking, EA 200–203
characters, AA 7, AA 8, AA 100
　display, AA 7
　literal, AA 7, AA 8, AA 100
　pattern, AA 7
　placeholder, AA 7
　text, AA 7
charts. See also organization chart.
　area, EA 138–139
　AutoFormats in, PA 9
　combination, EA 142–143
　creating in Word, EA 167–168
　inserting, PA 13
　organization, EA 151–153
　specialty, AA 135
　trendline, EA 90
　XY scatter, EA 139–140
check box options, AP 8
check styles, modifying rules for,
　PA 117

Chicago Manual of Style, AP 18
child table, AA 13
class module, AA 111
Click and Type pointer, WA 10,
　WA 245
client list, creating, WA 108
clip art
　inserting, EA 144–147, PA 13
　scaling and moving, EA 147–148
Clip Organizer, EA 143, EA 144–146,
　PA 41
　adding sound clips from, PA 41–43
Clips Online button, PA 42
Close button, AP 8
color scheme
　applying to slides, PA 68–70, PA 79
　changing, PA 67, PA 68–70, PA 79
column and row headers, formatting,
　WA 15
Column Count property, AA 5
Column Heads property, AA 5
Column Widths property, AA 5
column/row boundaries
　drawing, WA 6
　removing, WA 7
columns
　naming conventions for, WA 16
　sorting data in, WA 124–126,
　　WA 127
combination chart, EA 142–143
comma-separated text file,
　EA 177–178
command
　button, AA 55
　choosing, WA 306
Command Button Control Wizard,
　AA 114
comment
　box, PA 123
　marker, PA 122, PA 125, PA 126,
　　PA 128, PA 129
comments. See also review
　comments.
　adding to document properties,
　　WA 300, WA 307
　pages, printing, PA 129
Compare and Merge Presentations
　command, PA 125, PA 136

comparison
  operator, WA 104
  value, WA 104
compound criteria, AA 23. *See also* query criteria, compound.
conceptual diagram, EA 151–154
conditional formatting, EA 191–193
connector line, EA 149–150
consolidating data, EA 9–11
content templates, PA 56–58
Continuous section break, WA 41
control
  aligning, AA 49–50
  nudging, AA 72
Control-menu icon, AP 4
copying
  data from Web page, EA 214–216
  macro code, EA 62–64
copyright, verifying, PA 44
core shape, PA 13, PA 15, PA 17
Correction button, AP 42
correspondence, business, AP 12–19
criteria, specifying in multiple fields, AA 23
Criteria: row, AA 23, AA 24
cross-reference
  creating, WA 140–142
  dialog box, WA 141
  updating field, WA 142
crosstab query, creating, AA 38–39, AA 41
Current date/time form field, WA 220
custom animation
  adding to object, PA 30–33
  command, PA 30
  effects, PA 30, PA 47
  list, PA 32
  task pane, PA 30
custom design templates, PA 70–75, PA 79
custom show
  creating, PA 55, PA 76–78, PA 79
  running, PA 77, PA 78
custom style
  creating, WA 20–22
  deleting, WA 22

Customize
  dialog box, EA 66, WA 304
  menu, EA 67–68
  toolbar, EA 66–67
Cycle diagram, PA 4, PA 12, PA 19

D

Dale Carnegie Training, content templates from, PA 57
DAP. *See* data access page.
data
  adding, deleting, and moving, EA 141–142
  analysis, EA 115–117
  changing, AA 20
  consolidating, EA 9–11
  copying, EA 214–216
  deleting, AA 105
  detail, EA 45
  displaying in data access page, AA 129–132
  displaying in PivotChart view, AA 135–137
  displaying in PivotTable view, AA 132–134
  ensuring conditions of, AA 3
  entering in list, EA 27–34, EA 35–36
  extracting, EA 42–43
  importing and exporting, EA 164–185, EA 216–219
  importing/exporting to XML document, AA 121, AA 127, AA 139
  integrity of, AA 2
  invalid, EA 107–108
  query, EA 174–177
  sharing between applications, AA 125, EA 3–5, PA 144–163
  sorting, EA 43–44
  summarizing, AA 20, EA 114
  validation of, AA 2, AA 3–4, AA 15, EA 27–34
data access page (DAP), AA 121
  connecting to database with, AA 131
  creating, AA 128–132, AA 139
  design grid, AA 130
  in intranet environment, AA 132
  modifying, AA 129

  navigating, sorting, and filtering records in, AA 31
  previewing, AA 132
  publishing, AA 132, AA 138, AA 139
data analysis, EA 115–117
  PivotTable chart for, EA 128–130
  PivotTable report for, EA 118–128
data fields, adding to records, WA 102–103
Data form, EA 35
  deleting record from, EA 37
  entering data in, EA 35–36
  finding records in, EA 36–37
data records
  adding and deleting, WA 101–102, WA 108
  querying, WA 103–105, WA 108
data source, WA 77–80, WA 85, WA 94, WA 97
  modify existing table, WA 101, WA 102
data table
  creating, EA 96
  one variable, EA 76–78
  two variable, EA 79
database, EA 26
  Admins group, AA 101
  back-end, AA 107
  backing up, AA 100, AA 102, AA 106, AA 110
  compacting, AA 105–106, AA 115
  deleting objects, AA 105
  design master for, AA 110, AA 111, AA 115
  encrypting, AA 98–99, AA 115
  exclusive mode, AA 99
  fragmentation, AA 105
  front-end/back-end approach in, AA 107, AA 115
  indications of damage to, AA 106
  linking front-end and back-end tables in, AA 107, AA 115
  management tools for, AA 97–115
  object type, AA 103
  objects, AA 103
  permission, AA 101, AA 115
  read-only access, AA 99
  relationships in, AA 2, AA 9–15
  repairing, AA 105–106, AA 115

replication, AA 110
splitting, AA 106–107, AA 115
user names, AA 102
user permissions, AA 103, AA 115
Users group, AA 101
database design, protecting, AA 107
date and time
    inserting, WA 77
    separator, WA 117
    sorting, WA 117–118, WA 127
deadlines, setting for review, PA 122
debugging, WA 281
Define Custom Show dialog box, PA 77
Define Name dialog box, EA 7
deleting
    data series, EA 141–142
    named range, EA 6–8
    record, EA 37
delivery address, order of, AP 16
dependent cells, EA 100, EA 102–104
descending order, WA 117
descriptive statistics tool, EA 115–116
design
    applying from existing presentation, PA 58–60
    applying multiple, PA 60
    elements, PA 72
    templates, PA 56, PA 58–60, PA 79
design master database, AA 110, AA 111, AA 115
    recovering, AA 111
design tips
    for printouts, PA 70
    for sounds, PA 36, PA 37
    for transparencies, PA 70
Design view, AA 3, AA 4, AA 53, AA 61, AA 81
    creating data access page in, AA 129–132
    rulers, gridlines, alignment options in, AA 48, AA 61
desktop
    customizing, AP 4, AP 6
    icons, AP 3
    toolbar, AP 6
destination file, PA 151, PA 153, PA 155, PA 162, PA 163
detail data, EA 45

detail records, displaying, AA 133
diagram
    changing type, PA 16
    creating, PA 12
    formatting, PA 15–17
    formatting individual elements of, PA 17
    inserting, PA 13
    resizing and moving, PA 17, PA 19
    sizing to fit contents, PA 18
    styles, PA 9
    toolbar, PA 14
    types of, PA 12, PA 20
Diagram Gallery dialog box, EA 151, PA 4, PA 16
dialog box
    defined, AP 7
    navigating with voice commands, AP 33, AP 35
Dictation mode, AP 30, AP 31, AP 37–38
Dictionary, AP 44
digital certificate, WA 261
digital signature, WA 261–263
digits, AA 7
directories, WA 98–99
discussion, threaded, WA 257
Display Control property, AA 5
Document Map, WA 133, WA 152–153, WA 154
document properties, adding comments to, WA 300, WA 307
document references, WA 127–154
documents
    business, AP 12–20
    creating from template, WA 227–229
    creating multiple versions of, WA 202–203
    displaying and modifying properties of, WA 299–301
    distributing for revision, WA 255–258, WA 263
    integrating with the Internet, WA 241–263
    large, WA 195–208
    merging, WA 258–260
    multipage, WA 36–50
    navigating with voice commands, AP 35–36

navigating/browsing, WA 37–38, WA 50
    protecting, WA 301–302
    reviewing changes to, WA 257–258
    tracking changes in, WA 258
drag-and-drop, WA 12–13
dragging with SHIFT key, WA 165
Draw Table
    button, WA 5, WA 7
    command, WA 4
drawing border, PA 4, PA 20
Drawing button, WA 162
drawing canvas, WA 162, WA 164, WA 184
    moving, WA 166
    resizing, WA 166
drawing objects, WA 161–189
    creating, WA 162–165
    deleting, WA 169–170
    editing, WA 165–169
drawing tools, EA 143–154
drop cap effect, WA 178–179, WA 189
Drop Data Fields Here area, AA 136
Drop Filter Fields Here area, AA 134, AA 136
Drop Row Columns Here area, AA 133
Drop Row Fields Here area, AA 133
Drop Total or Detail Fields Here area, AA 133
Drop-Down form field, WA 220

E

Edit Color Scheme dialog box, PA 70
Edit Switchboard Item dialog box, AA 58
Edit Switchboard Page dialog box, AA 59
Edit Web Query window, EA 218
effect
    adding, PA 30, PA 31, PA 34, PA 37, PA 38, PA 39
    properties list box, PA 32
element. *See* shape(s).
e-mail. *See also* e-mail messages (as Attachment) button, PA 124

adding workbook as attachment, EA 233
defined, PA 121
sending workbook in, EA 230–231
sending worksheet as HTML mail, EA 231–232
E-mail button, WA 255
e-mail messages, WA 241, WA 254–255, WA 263
attachment to, PA 122, PA 123, PA 124, PA 136, WA 257
checking attachments for viruses, WA 280
distribution list for, PA 122
editing, PA 157
embedding, PA 153, PA 157, PA 158–159, PA 163
inserting address into form, AA 123
mass mailings. See mail merge.
replying to, WA 257
sending and receiving, AA 123–125
em dash, WA 47
inserting, WA 139–140, WA 154
embedding
data in Word, EA 165–167
object, EA 164
Emphasis, PA 31
Encrypt/Decrypt command, AA 99
encryption, AA 98–99, AA 115
End Review button, PA 122, PA 128
endnotes, AP 20
Entrance effects, PA 31, PA 38
envelopes
Address Block merge field for, WA 95
formatting, AP 15
mail merge for, WA 92–96, WA 108
repositioning delivery address on, WA 95
equation, creating, WA 186–188
Equation Editor (Microsoft Equation 3.0), WA 186, WA 189
equation object, WA 187
Eraser button, WA 8
error
checking, EA 105–107
correcting in speech recognition, AP 40–41, AP 42

trapping, macros and, AA 112
Evaluate Formula dialog box, EA 107
Even Page section break, WA 41
event procedure, AA 111, AA 115
Excel 2002
importing text files to, EA 177–178
integrating with Access, EA 172–177
integrating with Internet and intranet, EA 213–240
integrating with PowerPoint, EA 164–165, EA 169–172
integrating with Word, EA 164–168
Excel chart. See Excel object.
Excel object
embedding in PowerPoint slide, PA 158–159, PA 163
linking to PowerPoint slide, PA 160–162, PA 163
Excel worksheet. See Excel object.
exclusive mode, AA 99
Exit effects, PA 31
Expand/Collapse Outline, PA 100
Export XML dialog box, AA 127
Expression option, AA 27
eXtensible Markup Language (XML), AA 125. See also XML document.

F

fax software, WA 96
field(s), EA 26, WA 118
adding and removing from Word table data source, WA 100
adding to form, AA 48
code, WA 14
displaying and hiding detail, EA 124–126
managing, WA 292–307
primary, WA 120
properties, AA 25
searching for, WA 293, WA 299
secondary, WA 120
sorting by, WA 119–120
sorting by multiple, WA 120–121
tertiary, WA 120
updating multiple, AA 35
validation rule, AA 3

Field Properties pane, AA 4
file management, PA 75–76
file properties
displaying, WA 299, WA 307
viewing and modifying, WA 299–301
File Transfer Protocol (FTP), AA 132, PA 96
files
created when saving as Web page, PA 98, PA 109
manipulating with voice commands, AP 33
opening from other applications, PA 144
fill color, WA 166
Fill Color button, WA 166
Fill Effects dialog box, WA 167
Filter by Selection button, AA 131
Filter Toggle button, AA 131
filtering techniques, AA 20–41
filters
applying advanced, AA 21–22, AA 41
AutoFilter, EA 37–39
extracting data via, EA 42–43
fields, AA 132–134
multiple operators in, EA 39–42
query using, EA 175
Find All Word Forms tool, WA 207
Find and Replace
precautions for, PA 105
using, PA 104–105
Find feature, PA 104
Fit Diagram to Contents option, PA 18
Fit Organization Chart to Contents option, PA 11
folders
managing with voice commands, AP 33, AP 35
using to manage presentations, PA 75–76
fonts. See also presentation fonts.
embedding in a presentation, PA 120–121, PA 133, PA 136
TrueType, PA 120, PA 136

footer, PA 62, WA 43–46
footnote. *See also* endnote.
   converting to endnote, WA 139
   creating and modifying,
     WA 135–136
   indenting, WA 139
   inserting, WA 136–138
   using symbol instead of numbers
     in, WA 138
Footnote and Endnote dialog box,
  WA 137
footnote separator line, WA 137
   removing, WA 140
footnote text
   location of, WA 136
   revising, WA 138–139
form, EA 57
   adding subform to, AA 51–53
   creating in Design view, AA 46,
     AA 47–50
   designing, WA 215, WA 229
   tab order of, AA 48
form control. *See also* form field.
   nudging, AA 48
   positioning, AA 48
   Properties sheet, AA 49
Form Design toolbar, AA 47
Form dialog box, EA 35–36
form field
   creating, WA 219–226
   help messages in, WA 226, WA 229
   Options button, WA 221
   shading button, WA 220
   text, WA 220
   types of, WA 220
Form Footer section, AA 47
Form Header section, AA 47
form module, AA 112, AA 115
form template
   creating, WA 215–227, WA 229
   protecting, WA 227, WA 229
Form view, AA 53, AA 55
Form Wizard, AA 47, AA 51
formal outlines, formatting, AP 17
format
   conditional, EA 191–193
   custom, EA 187–191

documentation worksheet, EA 5–6
PivotTable report, EA 126–128
worksheets, EA 3–6
Format AutoShape command, PA 94
Format Object dialog box, EA 147
Format Trendline dialog box, EA 91
formatting, AA 70, AA 82
   business documents, AP 12–20
   clearing, WA 40
   comparing, WA 39, WA 50
   creating sections with different,
     WA 41
   for formal outlines, AP 18
   inconsistencies in, WA 40
   letters, AP 13–14
   task pane, WA 59
forms, online. *See* online forms.
formula, WA 14
   array, EA 90–91
   Auditing toolbar, EA 108
   creating in table, WA 14–16, WA 28
   creating in worksheet, EA 3–5
   editing, WA 16–18
   link, EA 12–13
   named range, EA 8–9
Formula dialog box, WA 15, WA 16
Fraction and Radical templates button, WA 187
frame.htm file, PA 98
front-end database, AA 107, AA 115
front-end/back-end approach,
  AA 107, AA 115
FTP sites, PA 96. *See also* File Transfer
  Protocol.
fullscreen.htm file, PA 98
function, reference, EA 193–195

G

gamma correction, PA 107
General Templates link, PA 58
Goal Seek, EA 80–85
Gopher, PA 96
Greek characters button, WA 187
group
   footer/header section, AA 75
   sort order of, AA 89

subtotals, EA 45–46
worksheet, EA 3–5
Group by option, AA 27

H

handle
   rotation, WA 164
   sizing, WA 163
header, PA 62
Header and Footer toolbar, WA 45
header row, EA 26
headers and footers
   creating, WA 43–46
   different first page options in,
     WA 43, WA 50
   setting alternate, WA 44
headset, connecting, AP 22–23
Help
   button, AP 8
   messages in form field, WA 226,
     WA 229
hidden bookmark, WA 142
hide cell, EA 196
Hide White Space pointer, WA 5
Highlight changes dialog box, EA 201
Holt Handbook, AP 18
Horizontal Line button, WA 248
HTML. *See also* HyperText Markup
  Language.
   mail, EA 231–232
   tags, AA 128, WA 242
hyperlink, WA 199
   activating with mouse click, PA 92,
     PA 93
   activating with mouse over, PA 92,
     PA 93
   adding sound to, PA 92, PA 93
   adding to slides, PA 87, PA 88–90,
     PA 109
   adding to text box or object, PA 87,
     PA 88–90, PA 109
   appearance of, PA 90, PA 91
   between workbooks, EA 14–15
   changing, PA 96, PA 97–98
   creating for formatting, AA 123
   creating, inserting, and testing,
     WA 248–253, WA 263
   defined, PA 88

editing, copying, and removing, WA 252
original, PA 91
removing, PA 97, PA 98, WA 217
storing in table, AA 121
testing, PA 90–91
to Internet, PA 96–97
using in presentation, PA 90–91, PA 97
using to jump to another slide, PA 94–95
viewing path of, AA 123
visited, PA 91
Hyperlink data type, AA 122, AA 139
Hypertext Markup Language (HTML), AA 125, AA 139, PA 96, PA 98, PA 103, PA 109, PA 132, PA 134, PA 136, WA 242. See also HTML.
hyphen
character, AA 7, AA 8
nonbreaking, WA 48, WA 50
optional, WA 49, WA 50
soft. See hyphen, optional.
hyphenation, WA 46–49, WA 50
automatic, WA 47
zone, WA 47

I

icon list options, AP 8
images, rotating, WA 177
Import data dialog box, EA 177
Import Spreadsheet Wizard, EA 173–174
Import XML dialog box, AA 126
index
compiling, WA 149
concordance file for, WA 150
creating, WA 145–149
modifying, WA 150–151
range of pages in, WA 148
Index and Tables dialog box, WA 143
information
entering in diagram, PA 13, PA 19
entering in organization chart, PA 4, PA 19
sharing over networks, PA 89–110
sharing with other applications, PA 153
inner join, AA 10, AA 11, AA 15

input fields, AA 7
input mask, AA 6, AA 7, AA 15
common characters for, AA 7
hyphens and placeholders in, AA 7, AA 8
modifying, AA 2, AA 6–8
Input Mask Wizard, AA 6, AA 7, AA 8
Insert Clip Art task pane, EA 145, WA 170
Insert Comment button, PA 122
Insert Diagram or Organization Chart button, WA 184
Insert Hyperlink
button, WA 250
dialog box, EA 14, PA 89
Insert Shape button, PA 14, WA 185
inserting
clip art, EA 144–147
dialog box, EA 14
documentation worksheet, EA 5–6
Internet
adding hyperlink to, PA 96
defined, AA 122, PA 98
files, saving, PA 43
importing data via, EA 214–219
integrating database with, AA 121–139
integrating with Excel, EA 213
publishing to, EA 225–230
security, WA 261–262
sending e-mail via, EA 230–233
working with XML, EA 219–224
interoffice memos, formatting, AP 17
intranet, PA 98, WA 241
invitations, sending, PA 135

J

join, AA 10, AA 15
properties, setting, AA 10–13
types, AA 11
Join Properties dialog box, AA 11
junction table, AA 10

K

key value, AA 13
keyword, WA 279
kiosk, PA 44
viewing, PA 29

L

Label
button, AA 70
control, AA 50, AA 71, AA 89
labels, mail merge for, WA 96–99
Language Bar, AP 23–25
icon, AP 23, AP 46
minimizing, AP 45
moving, AP 31
switching modes, AP 3–30
last slide, removing timing from, PA 46
Layout button, PA 14
check box for, PA 40
left-outer join, AA 11
legibility options, PA 118
letterhead, AP 13
letters, minimum and maximum dimensions, AP 16
level 1 position, PA 5
levels
creating multiple, PA 5
distinguishing, PA 10
library catalog, PA 96
light bulb icon, indicating style inconsistencies, PA 117
Lightening button, WA 167
Limit to List property, AA 5
line
control, AA 73, AA 74
linking, PA 153, PA 157, PA 160–162, PA 163
Line button, WA 162
Line Color button, WA 166
Line Style button list, WA 5, WA 166
Line Weight button list, WA 5, WA 21
link. See hyperlink.
Link Child Fields property, AA 52
Link Master Fields property, AA 52
Linked Table Manager tool, AA 107, AA 115
linking vs. embedding
disk space requirements for, PA 155
updating information with, PA 154, PA 155
linking worksheets, EA 2–11, EA 164

Links bar, AP 6, WA 252
List Rows property, AA 5
List Width property, AA 5
lists, EA 25
    basic terms, EA 26–29
    create subtotals, EA 45–46
    custom filter, EA 37–43
    data form, EA 35–37
    data validation, EA 27–34
    single and multiple sort, EA 43–44
    sorting, WA 119–121, WA 127
lock cell, EA 196
Lock Document button, WA 199
Log On to Windows dialog box, AP 2
Long paragraph guidelines, PA 119
lookup
    field, AA 2, AA 4–6, AA 15
    function, EA 193–195
    tab, AA 5

M

macro, AA 112, WA 221, WA 270, WA 271, WA 286
    assigning to button, menu, or keyboard, WA 272, WA 286
    code description, EA 57–58
    copying, renaming, and deleting, WA 283–286
    copying code, EA 62–64
    correction, WA 277
    creating with Visual Basic for Applications program, WA 271
    debugging, WA 281–283, WA 286
    dialog box, EA 56
    editing code, EA 57–61, WA 277–280, WA 282
    project, WA 271
    recording and running, EA 54–57, WA 270–286
    records and, AA 112
    Stop Recording toolbar for, WA 274
    storage and, AA 112
    using keyboard to record, WA 274, WA 286
    virus, EA 61, WA 280, WA 286
    Virus Warning dialog box, EA 62
    workbooks, EA 61–64

Macros dialog box, using to delete macros, WA 284–285, WA 286
mail merge, WA 74–85
    defining data source in, WA 77–80
    defining main document in, WA 76–77
    merging main document and data source in, WA 80–84, WA 85
    selecting data source in, WA 78–79
    templates with, WA 77
    types of, WA 75, WA 76
Mail Merge
    Recipients dialog box, WA 94
    toolbar, WA 76
    Wizard, WA 76–84
mailing notations, AP 15
mailings. *See* mail merge.
mailto: hyperlink, AA 123, AA 124, WA 251
main document, WA 76–77, WA 85
make-table query, creating, AA 32, AA 35–36, AA 41
many-to-many relationship, AA 9–10
Mark formatting inconsistencies, WA 40
Mark Index Entry dialog box, WA 147
Markup button, PA 126, PA 129
mask. *See* input mask.
master. *See also* title master, slide master.
    document, WA 195, WA 196–198, WA 208
    list, PA 63, PA 79
    style, PA 61, PA 79
    template, PA 55, PA 61–66, PA 79
master.htm file, PA 98
matching key field, AA 76
Maximize button, AP 4–6
MDE file, creating, AA 109, AA 115
media clip, inserting, PA 13
Meet Now command, WA 260
meetings, online, WA 260
memorandums, formatting, AP 17
menu
    bar, AP 6
    closing, WA 306

    commands, AP 6
    custom, EA 67–68
    customizing, WA 305–306, WA 307
merge field, WA 75, WA 97–98
merge workbooks, EA 203–204
Messaging Application Programming Interface (MAPI), PA 122
Microphone
    button, AP 30
    connecting and positioning, AP 22–23
    turning on, AP 30
Microsoft Graph, EA 167–168, PA 58, PA 105
Microsoft NetMeeting, WA 260
Microsoft Office Template Gallery, PA 56
Microsoft Outlook 2002
    sending e-mail via, PA 122, PA 123, PA 124
    using to schedule broadcasts, PA 132, PA 134, PA 135, PA 136
    using to track changes, PA 127
Microsoft Windows Media folder, PA 42
Microsoft Word, customizing with voice controls, AP 32–33
Microsoft.net, AA 125
MIDI (.mid), interaction with animation, PA 44
MIDI Sequence formats, PA 41
Minimize button, AP 4
MLA Style Manual, AP 18
Modify Style dialog box, WA 19
module, WA 279
    class, AA 111
    creating, AA 111, AA 115
    form, AA 112
    standard, AA 111
motion path, PA 31, PA 47
    applying to objects, PA 34
    options for, PA 34, PA 47
mouse pointer, WA 166. *See also* pointer.
move handle, WA 8, WA 12
Move Shape Backward button, PA 14

Move Shape Forward button, PA 14
moving
    data series, EA 141–142
    object, EA 147–148
    timeline, PA 33
MP3 format, PA 41
multimedia, goal of, PA 31
music clips, adding, PA 42, PA 47
My Computer window, AP 4

N

named range, EA 6
    adding and deleting, EA 6–8
    in formula, EA 8–9
names, adding and training in speech recognition, AP 43–44
narration, recording for slide show, PA 44, PA 47
navigation frame, PA 99
navigational link. *See* hyperlink.
nesting, WA 10
NetMeeting, WA 260
NetShow, PA 135
New Line
    break, WA 177
    command, AP 38–39
New Paragraph command, AP 38–39
New Presentation task pane, PA 58
New Slide command, PA 12
New Style
    button, WA 60
    dialog box, WA 20, WA 62
New Web Query window, EA 223
newsgroup, PA 96
Next Heading button, WA 38
Next Page section break, WA 41
No Border option, WA 10
Normal template, WA 59, WA 60, WA 64
    adding new style to, WA 64–65
    deleting style from, WA 22, WA 65
    macros stored in, WA 272, WA 286
note pane, WA 136, WA 138
note reference mark, WA 136, WA 137
notes
    inserting from one PowerPoint presentation to another, PA 151–152

    inserting into PowerPoint from Word RTF outline, PA 151, PA 163
Nudged controls, AA 50
nudging, WA 165
Number form field, WA 220
numbers
    adding to slides, PA 64, PA 79
    custom format, EA 187–191
numeric picture switch, WA 15

O

objects
    bar, AA 70
    deleting, AA 105
    embedding, EA 164, PA 144
    linking, PA 144
    nudging, WA 165
    resizing, PA 158
    scaling and moving, EA 147–148
    selected, WA 163, WA 164
    selecting multiple, WA 169
OCR read area, AP 16. *See also* optical character readers.
Odd Page section break, WA 41
Office Assistant
    using to identify style inconsistencies, PA 117
    using to help pack presentations, PA 130
one-to-many relationship, AA 9–10, AA 13, AA 15, AA 50
one-to-one relationship, AA 15
online
    broadcasts. *See* broadcasts.
    forms, WA 214–229
    Help, accessing, AA 49
    meetings, PA 135, WA 260
Online Collaboration command, WA 260
open workbook with macro, EA 61–62
operating system, AA 8
operator, multiple, EA 39–42
optical character readers (OCRs), AP 15
option buttons, AP 8
OR criteria, AA 23, AA 24, AA 41

organization chart, EA 151–153, PA 2, PA 3–12, PA 19
    adding assistants to, PA 7, PA 8
    adding coworkers to, PA 7
    adding subordinates to, PA 5–6, PA 19
    adding to presentation, PA 3, PA 4
    creating, WA 183–185, WA 189
    editing, WA 185
    entering information in, PA 4, PA 19
    formatting, PA 8–12
    inserting, PA 13
    maintaining proportions while resizing, PA 11
    positions on, PA 5
    resizing and moving, PA 11, PA 19
    sizing to fit contents, PA 11, PA 19
    toolbar, WA 184
    using separate for close-up views, PA 5
Organization Chart Style Gallery, PA 9, PA 13
Organizer
    dialog box, WA 66
    using to delete macros, WA 283–284
    using to delete styles, WA 22, WA 65–66
orphan, WA 56, WA 66, WA 68
outer join, AA 10, AA 11, AA 15
Outline view, WA 199, WA 208
outline.htm file, PA 98
Outlining toolbar, WA 143
outlines
    formatting, AP 18, EA 11, EA 45
    subtotals, EA 45–46
Outlook 2002, WA 96
Oval button, WA 165

P

Pack and Go
    Status window of, PA 131
    steps in process, PA 130
    wizard, PA 129, PA 130–132, PA 136
page borders, decorative, WA 173–174
page break, WA 56
Page Footer section, AA 47, AA 89
Page Header section, AA 47, AA 89

page number
 creating alternate, WA 44
 inserting, AA 79, WA 44
 starting, WA 46
pagination, controlling, WA 66–67, WA 68
paragraph
 formats, verifying, WA 38–39, WA 50
 sorting, WA 122, WA 127
parameters
 changing order in, AA 31
 creating in query, AA 30
 data types of, AA 30
parent table, AA 13
parentheses, AA 7
password
 characters, AA 7
 characters prohibited in, AA 100
 guidelines, AA 100
 keying, AA 100
 removing protection, WA 303
 rules for creating and protecting, WA 302
 storing, AA 100
password protection
 setting, AA 98, AA 99–100, AA 115
 testing, AA 100
permission, AA 101, AA 115
 assigning, AA 101, AA 115
 explicit, AA 101, AA 115
 implicit, AA 101
 viewing, AA 103
Personal Macro Workbook, EA 54
picture
 deleting, WA 177
 Enhanced MetaFile (EMF) data type, inserting and positioning, PA 13, WA 176–177, WA 189
Picture toolbar, WA 177
PivotChart, EA 128–130
 customizing, AA 137
 saving as DAP, AA 138, AA 139
 using, AA 121, AA 132, AA 139
 Wizard, EA 119, EA 129
PivotTable, EA 118–122
 Field dialog box in, EA 123
 field list, AA 133

format, EA 126–128
 modify, EA 122–124
 saving as DAP, AA 138, AA 139
 using, AA 121, AA 132, AA 139
 workspace, AA 133, AA 134
placeholders, AA 7, AA 8, PA 3, PA 61, PA 62, PA 63, PA 65
pointer
 Click and Type, WA 10
 converting to eraser, WA 7, WA 8
 I-beam, WA 7
 move, WA 8
 pencil, WA 6, WA 8
 pointing hand, PA 91
pointer-movement key, WA 165
positions, creating multiple, PA 5
PowerPoint 2002
 integrating with Excel, EA 164–165, EA 169–172
 Viewer, PA 131, PA 136
precedent cells, EA 100–102
presentation
 accessing, PA 75
 checking styles in, PA 116, PA 117–120, PA 136
 comparing and merging, PA 126, PA 127, PA 136
 creating from new template, PA 74
 creating from template, PA 55, PA 56–60
 displaying outline of, PA 99
 displaying slide titles in, PA 99
 embedding fonts in, PA 120–121, PA 136
 embedding in a Word document, PA 153–154
 files created for Web display, PA 98
 formatting in Word, PA 149
 linking to a Word document, PA 155–156
 moving between, PA 87, PA 94–97, PA 109
 navigating in Web browser, PA 100
 opening Word outline as, PA 149
 packing, PA 129–132
 previewing in Web page format, PA 87, PA 98–103
 publishing to Internet or intranet, PA 87, PA 105–108, PA 109

reviewing and editing, PA 124–129, PA 136
 reviewing comments and changes, PA 124–129, PA 136
 routing for review, PA 122, PA 123, PA 136
 saving as RTF outline, PA 145–147, PA 163
 saving as Web page file, PA 87, PA 101–102, PA 103, PA 105–108
 sending to Word as outline, PA 145, PA 148, PA 163
 setting to run continuously, PA 44–46
 storing, PA 55, PA 67–68, PA 75–76, PA 79
presentation fonts, replacing, PA 67–68, PA 79
Presentation for Review format, saving document as, PA 122, PA 123
Preview button, PA 69
preview Web page, EA 227
primary form, AA 50, AA 51, AA 52, AA 53, AA 54–55, AA 61
 synchronizing with subform, AA 52, AA 115
primary key, AA 10
 values, AA 4
primary record, AA 13
primary table, AA 11, AA 15
printouts, design tips for, PA 70
problem-solving tools, EA 75–76
 data tables, EA 76–79
 Goal Seek and Solver, EA 80–85
 scenarios, EA 85–89
 trendline, EA 89–91
procedure, AA 111
Professional Secretary's Handbook, AP 18
project, EA 57
Properties
 button, AA 4, AA 25
 changing workbook, EA 204–205
 sheet, AA 49, AA 61
Protect Sheet dialog box, EA 197
Protect Workbook dialog box, EA 198
Publish as Web Page dialog box, EA 229, PA 106

Publish button, PA 102, PA 106
publishing, WA 253
Punctuation
    dictating, AP 38–39, AP 42
    style guidelines, PA 119
Pyramid diagram, PA 4, PA 12, PA 19

Q

query, WA 103
    action, AA 31–32, AA 41
    aggregate properties in, AA 26–28, AA 41
    appending, AA 32, AA 36–37, AA 41
    changing parameter order in, AA 31
    compound criteria in, AA 23–24
    creating multiple parameters for, AA 30
    crosstab, AA 38–39, AA 41
    data, EA 174–177
    deleting, AA 31, AA 32–34, AA 41
    filters, EA 175
    make-table, AA 32, AA 35–36, AA 41
    modifying properties of, AA 25–26, AA 41
    types, AA 20, AA 23–41
    updating, AA 31, AA 34–35, AA 41
    viewing data in PivotTable view, AA 133–135
    Web, EA 216–217
    XML, EA 222–224
query design grid
    adding Update to: row in, AA 35
    changing parameter order in, AA 31
Query Parameters dialog box, AA 30
Query Type button, AA 33, AA 34, AA 36, AA 37
Query Wizard, EA 175–176
Quick Launch toolbar, AP 2–3, AP 6–7

R

Radial diagram, PA 4, PA 12, PA 14, PA 19
range
    Finder, EA 99–100
    named. *See* named range.

rank and percentile, EA 116–117
read-only access, AA 99
record, AA 3. *See also* primary record, related record.
Record Macro dialog box, WA 272
Record pronunciation button, AP 43–44
recording a macro, EA 54–56
records
    deleting, EA 37
    finding, EA 36–37
    setting criteria for selection, WA 103–105
    sorting, WA 127
Recover Design Master command, AA 111
Rectangle button, WA 163
Recycle Bin, AP 10
reference. *See also* document reference.
    function, EA 193–195
    locating, EA 100
referential integrity, AA 12, AA 13–14, AA 15
Reject Changes dialog box, EA 202
related record, AA 13
related table, AA 11, AA 15
Relationship
    shape, PA 13, PA 14
    toolbar, AA 12
    window, AA 12, AA 14
relationships, adding to diagram, PA 14
Rename Master button, PA 64
Re-Order buttons, PA 32, PA 39
Replace feature, PA 104
Replace Font dialog box, PA 67, PA 79
replica set, AA 110, AA 111, AA 115
    converting to design master, AA 111, AA 115
    synchronizing, AA 111, AA 115
replication, AA 110
    Property sheet controls, AA 89
Report Design toolbar, AA 70
Report Wizard, AA 69, AA 74, AA 86, AA 89
reports
    as objects, AA 68

    creating custom, AA 68, AA 69–74, AA 89
    Detail section of, AA 89
    editing, AA 86–88
    grouped, AA 68, AA 85–86, AA 89
    modifying properties of, AA 81–82
    sorting and grouping data in, AA 68, AA 74–81
Reports button, AA 69
Reveal Formatting task pane, WA 38, WA 50
Reverse Diagram button, PA 14
review
    ending, PA 128–129
    routing for, PA 122, PA 123, PA 136
    sending as e-mail attachment, PA 122, PA 123, PA 125, PA 136
review change
    applying (accepting), PA 127, PA 128, PA 129
    unapplying (rejecting), PA 128
review comments, PA 124–129, PA 136
review cycle, setting up, PA 116, PA 121–124
reviewer, PA 125, PA 126, PA 127, PA 136
Reviewers button, PA 126
Reviewing toolbar, PA 122, PA 124, PA 125, PA 126, PA 127, PA 128, PA 129, PA 136, WA 257
Revisions Pane, PA 125, PA 126, PA 127, PA 128
    displaying, PA 126, PA 127
    Gallery tab of, PA 125, PA 126, PA 127, PA 128, PA 130
    List tab of, PA 125
right mouse button, WA 225
right-outer join, AA 11
rotation handle, WA 164
row, naming conventions for, WA 16
Row Source property, AA 5
Row Source Type property, AA 5
run macro, EA 56–57

S

Save As dialog box, EA 228, PA 102
Scale Diagram option, PA 18

scaling, EA 147–148
Schedule Meeting command, WA 260
Schedule Presentation Broadcast dialog box, PA 133
scenario, EA 85–89
   creating, EA 85–86
   displaying, EA 88
   Manager dialog box, EA 86
   summary, EA 88
   Values dialog box, EA 87
schema, definition of, AA 125
schema (XSD) file, AA 127
ScreenTip, AA 123
   adding to hyperlink, PA 89–90
   button, PA 89
   custom, PA 90
search
   Advanced Search task pane, WA 297, WA 307
   Basic Search task pane, WA 295, WA 307
   criteria, AA 20
   file properties, WA 296
   file types, WA 295
   keywords, WA 293, WA 295
   locations, WA 294
   wildcard, WA 296
Search Results task pane, WA 296, WA 298
Search Tips link, WA 293
section, formatting, WA 42
section break
   creating, WA 41–43, WA 50
   types of, WA 41
section header panes, viewing, WA 45
security level
   changing, WA 280–281, WA 286
   user level, AA 98, AA 99, AA 101–105, AA 115
Select Browse Object
   button, WA 37, WA 50
   grid, WA 37, WA 50
Select Data Source dialog box, EA 216
Select Objects button, AA 50
selecting, AP 8
   objects, WA 169
self-join, AA 10, AA 11, AA 12, AA 15

self-paced presentation, PA 44
Send To Microsoft Word dialog box, PA 148
sentences, formatting with speech recognition, AP 42
Set Up Show dialog box, accessing, PA 45
Shadow effects, adding and modifying, WA 167–168
shadow style, PA 11
Shadow Style button, WA 167
shape(s)
   adding shadow style to, PA 11
   adding to core, PA 14
   adding to diagram, PA 14
   changing, PA 10
   changing border color and style of, PA 10
   changing color of, PA 10, PA 11, PA 19
   deleting, PA 14
   editing text in, PA 8
   resizing, PA 94
   selecting multiple, PA 10
share
   data, EA 3–5
   workbook, EA 186–212
shortcut menu, AP 8
show, custom. *See* custom show.
Show Table button, AA 12
Show/Hide button, WA 40
Show/Hide Notes control, PA 100
Show/Hide Outline control, PA 99
signature, digital, WA 241
single-click environment, AP 8
sizing handle, WA 8, WA 163
slide
   adding hyperlinks to, PA 87, PA 88–90, PA 109
   changing background of, PA 70, PA 71
   copy and paste, PA 151
   customizing format of, PA 55, PA 66–70, PA 79
   frame, PA 99
   inserting from one PowerPoint presentation to another, PA 151–152

   inserting into PowerPoint from Word RTF outline, PA 151, PA 163
   timings, PA 45, PA 47
Slide Design task pane, PA 68
Slide Finder dialog box, PA 151, PA 152
Slide Layout task pane, PA 12
slide master, PA 61, PA 63, PA 73, PA 79
   adding action buttons to, PA 93, PA 94
   adding footer to, PA 62
   creating new, PA 63
   making changes to, PA 61
   switching to/from title master, PA 72
   view button, PA 61
   view toolbar, PA 62
   zooming in and out on, PA 94
slide numbers, adding, PA 64, PA 65–66, PA 79
slide show
   automatic looping of, PA 46
   customizing, PA 29–48
   customizing end of presentation in, PA 46
   ending, PA 7
   running on computer without PowerPoint, PA 129–132
   viewing in browser, PA 100–101
Slide Show button, PA 33
slides, miniature, PA 152, PA 154
Smart Tags, PA 160, WA 248
Solver, EA 81–85
   Answer Report, EA 85
   Parameters dialog box, EA 82
   Results dialog box, EA 84
sort data, EA 43–44
Sort dialog box, EA 44, WA 118
sort order, WA 117
Sort Text dialog box, WA 117
sorting, WA 116–127
Sorting and Grouping dialog box, AA 75
sound
   adding to hyperlinks, PA 109
   changing settings of, PA 43–44
   design tips for, PA 36, PA 37

from Clip Organizer, PA 43
linking to presentation, PA 41
locating additional, PA 42
repeating, PA 41
Sound Clip formats, PA 41
sound clips
adding from another source, PA 43–44
adding from Clip Organizer, PA 41–43
adding to slides, PA 42, PA 47
deleting, PA 42
positioning on slide, PA 41
sound effect, adjusting volume of, PA 35
sound files
copying to presentation folder, PA 41
looping, PA 41
Source Data dialog box, EA 141
source file, EA 164, PA 151, PA 153, PA 154, PA 155, PA 157, PA 159, PA 160, PA 163
space, AA 7
speech recognition, AP 21–48
adding and training names in, AP 43–44
adjust audio settings for, AP 30
context in, AP 40
correcting errors in, AP 40–42
Dictionary, AP 44
formatting sentences in, AP 42
highlighted bar in, AP 37
installing, AP 23–29
microphone quality check, AP 26
New Line command in, AP 38–39
New Paragraph command in, AP 38–39
restoring software in, AP 47
training software for, AP 22–29
training system for, AP 24–26
turning on and off, AP 45–48
Undo in, AP 39
user profile for, AP 24
standard module, AA 111
Standard toolbar, AP 6
Start animation list box, PA 32
Start button/menu, AP 2–3, AP 7

Start Live Broadcast Now button, PA 134
status value, AA 7
Stop Recording toolbar, EA 55–56
structured data, EA 219
style, PA 146, PA 147, PA 149, PA 150, PA 163
classes of, PA 157
indicating inconsistencies in, PA 117
Style area, WA 57, WA 68
button, WA 40
button list, WA 59
style-checking rules, reviewing and modifying, PA 117
Style Gallery
button, WA 65
templates in, WA 65
style guides, using, AP 18
style names, custom, WA 62
Style Options dialog box, PA 117, PA 118
styles
character, WA 56, WA 68
custom, WA 56–66
custom character, WA 64–65, WA 68
custom paragraph, WA 59–64, WA 68
list, WA 57, WA 58, WA 59, WA 68
paragraph, WA 56, WA 60, WA 68
Pick format to apply list, WA 59
table, WA 57, WA 68
types of, WA 57, WA 68
Styles and Formatting
button, PA 157, WA 18
task pane, PA 157, WA 20, WA 28, WA 59, WA 60
subdocument, WA 195, WA 196, WA 198–201
button, WA 197
combining, removing, deleting, WA 200
locking, WA 199
splitting, WA 201, WA 208
subform, AA 46, AA 50–55, AA 61
adding to form, AA 51–53
modifying properties of, AA 53–54

nesting within subform, AA 51
planning, AA 51
synchronizing with primary form, AA 52
SubForm Wizard, AA 51, AA 52
Subform/Subreport button, AA 83
control, AA 89
subordinate shape, defined, PA 4
subordinates, adding to organization chart, PA 5, PA 19
subreport, AA 68, AA 85
adding to existing report, AA 83–85
SubReport Wizard, AA 83
subroutine, WA 279
Subscript and Superscript templates button, WA 187
subtotal, EA 45–46
Sum function, WA 14, WA 17
Summation templates button, WA 187
superior shape, defined, PA 4
switch, WA 223
setting startup options for, AA 59–60, AA 61
switchboard list, AA 56, AA 84
Switchboard Manager, AA 56, AA 57
synchronizing, AA 52
system resources, accessing, AP 4–6

T

tab delimited text file, EA 177
tab formatting mark, WA 23
tab order, modifying, AA 48
tab stops in table, WA 22–23, WA 28
table(s), EA 26, EA 76–79
complex, WA 3, WA 28
converting to text, WA 28
copying, PA 157, WA 12–13, WA 28
creating custom style for, WA 20–22, WA 28
customizing, WA 2–28
distributing columns or rows in, WA 7
drawing, WA 2, WA 4–9, WA 28
formatting options for, WA 19
joining, AA 76

many-to-many relationships in, AA 9–10
nesting, WA 9–10, WA 28
one variable, EA 76–78
one-to-many relationships in, AA 9–10
option to view properties, WA 19
pasting, PA 157
performing calculations in, WA 14–18
positioning options, WA 11
related, AA 4
relationships between, AA 2, AA 9–15
repeat heading row in, WA 24
rotating text in, WA 10, WA 28
side-by-side, WA 10
special features of, WA 3
style applied to, WA 20, WA 28
style preview for, WA 19
two variable, EA 79
using as framework for forms, WA 217–219, WA 229
using tab stops in, WA 22–23
Validation Rule property of, AA 3
Validation Text property of, AA 3
Table AutoFormat dialog box, WA 20
table borders, setting options for, WA 5, WA 10
table cell. *See* cell.
table move handle, WA 8
table of authorities, WA 145
table of contents
    applying heading styles to entries, WA 142
    applying outline levels to, WA 143
    creating and modifying, WA 142–146
    formatting, WA 144
    modifying, WA 145–146
    moving, WA 145
    using to view specific text, WA 144
table of figures, WA 145
Table Positioning dialog box, WA 11
tables
    side-by-side, WA 218
    sorting, WA 123–126
Tables and Borders
    button, WA 4
    toolbar, WA 4, WA 5, WA 21

tabs, AP 8
tag delimiters (< >), AA 128. *See also* HTML, XML.
tags, AA 128
Target diagram, PA 4, PA 12, PA 19
target file, EA 164
task panes
    Advanced Search, WA 297, WA 307
    Basic Search, WA 295, WA 307
    Formatting, WA 59
    Insert Clip Art, WA 170
    Reveal Formatting, WA 38, WA 50
    Search Results, WA 296, WA 298
taskbar, using to switch between files, PA 154
Telnet, PA 96
templates, AA 6, AA 15
    applying new, PA 74–75
    applying to presentation, PA 55, PA 56–60
    content, PA 56. *See also* content templates.
    creating document, WA 219
    creating workbook, EA 64–65
    customizing, PA 55, PA 70–75, PA 79
    default location for workgroup, WA 303
    design, PA 56, PA 79. *See also* custom design templates.
    editing, EA 65
    master list of, PA 63
    modifying, PA 55, PA 61–66, PA 79, WA 227
    sharing over company Web site, PA 56
Templates and Add-Ins command, WA 65
text
    aligning graphics with, WA 177
    box, EA 154
    breaking lines in, PA 9
    changing color of, PA 10
    converting to table, WA 2, WA 20, WA 23–25, WA 28
    copying and pasting with speech recognition, AP 42–44
    files, integrating with Excel, EA 177–178

formatting with speech recognition, AP 42–44
    rotating, WA 10–12
    sorting, WA 117–122, WA 127
text box
    button, WA 162
    controls, AA 50, AA 71, AA 89
    formatting, WA 181–183
text effects, special, WA 174–176
text flow, controlling, WA 56, WA 68
Text form field, WA 220
Text wrapping break option, WA 177
Text Wrapping button, WA 176
theme, WA 243–244. *See also* Web page theme.
Theme dialog box, WA 65
thumbnail, slide, PA 125, PA 127, PA 128, PA 130
time blocks, PA 33
timing options, PA 36, PA 47
Tips for Broadcast button, PA 133
title bar, AP 4, AP 8
title master, PA 61, PA 71, PA 79
    creating new, PA 63
    switching to slide master and back, PA 72
To Fit option, AA 70
toolbar buttons, adding, AP 6
toolbars, *See also* individual toolbars.
    customizing, EA 66–67, WA 303–305, WA 307
Toolbox, AA 50
    button, AA 47, AA 70
totals query, AA 26, AA 41
trace errors, Range Finder, EA 99–100
track changes, EA 200–203
transition, design tips for, PA 70
trendline, EA 89–91
TrueType fonts, PA 120, PA 136

U

U.S. Postal Service standards, AP 15
Unapply button, PA 128
Undo command/button, AP 39
Uniform Resource Locator (URL), AA 122, AA 123

as hyperlink, AA 123, AA 139
   setting for broadcast, PA 134, PA 135
Universal Serial Bus (USB), AP 22
update query
   creating, AA 31, AA 34–35, AA 41
   multiple fields in, AA 35
   running, AA 35
updating information
   in embedded file, PA 154, PA 163
   in linked file, PA 155, PA 163
URL. *See* Uniform Resource Locator.
user, creating, AA 102
User and Group Accounts dialog box, AA 101, AA 102
user-level security, AA 98, AA 99, AA 101–105, AA 115
   activating, AA 101, AA 115
User-level Security Wizard, AA 105
Users group, AA 101

V

variable data, saving, WA 225
Vector Markup language (VML), PA 107
Venn diagram, PA 4, PA 12, PA 19
VeriSign, Inc., WA 261
Visual Basic Editor, EA 57–58, WA 277–280, WA 282, WA 286
   using to delete macros, WA 284, WA 286
Visual Clarity
   rules, PA 117
   settings, PA 118
VLOOKUP function, EA 194–195
Voice Command mode, AP 30–32
voice commands, navigating dialog boxes with, AP 35

W

watermarks, creating, WA 179–181, WA 189
wave (.wav) sound format, PA 41
   and animation, PA 44
Web
   address, AA 122
   sites, AA 122, AA 139

Web archive file, WA 254
   attaching to e-mail, WA 254
Web discussions, WA 257
Web folder
   creating new, PA 101, PA 102
   icon, PA 102
   saving presentation to, PA 101
Web Layout view, WA 242–255
Web Options
   button, PA 106, PA 107
   dialog box, PA 107
Web page, PA 96
   advanced features of, WA 242
   AutoCorrect and Spelling and Grammar check with, WA 245
   bulleted list on, WA 245–247, WA 263
   changing options for, PA 106–108, PA 109
   contact and update information on, WA 248
   copying data from, EA 214–216
   creating, WA 241–248, WA 263
   folder associated with, WA 247
   horizontal lines on, WA 247–248, WA 263
   inserting picture or drawing object, WA 249
   modifying and reposting, WA 253
   Preview, PA 100
   previewing, EA 227
   publishing to, EA 225–230, WA 253–254, WA 263
   tables and graphic images with, WA 245
   testing, WA 253
   theme, WA 243–244, WA 263
   title of, PA 102, PA 109
   using tables to organize information on, WA 245, WA 263
Web page presentation
   changing, PA 103–105
   editing, PA 103–104
   saving, PA 87, PA 101–103, PA 109
Web page title, adding and changing, WA 243, WA 263
Web query, EA 216–217
Web server, PA 106
Web toolbar, WA 199
what-if analysis, EA 76

What's This? pointer, WA 39
Where options, AA 27
widow, WA 56, WA 66, WA 68
windows, tiling, PA 161–162
Windows 2000
   desktop, AP 2–3
   operating system, AP 1–11
   shortcuts, AP 8–10
   shutting down, AP 11
Windows Media Audio file, PA 41
Word
   field, inserting, WA 105–107
   integrating with Excel, EA 164–168
   outline, opening and sending to PowerPoint, PA 149–150
   special fields, WA 108
   table, inserting (embedding) in PowerPoint slide, PA 156–157
   table, using to display PowerPoint presentation, PA 154, PA 156
WordArt, PA 105, WA 174–176, WA 189
   Shape button, WA 176
   toolbar, WA 175
workbook(s)
   3-D reference, EA 12–15
   arranging multiple, EA 15–16
   as interactive Web page, EA 225–227
   changing properties of, EA 204–205
   copying macro code, EA 62–64
   features, EA 196–205
   hyperlinks in, EA 14–15
   linking, EA 2, EA 12–17
   macros, EA 61–62
   merging, EA 203–204
   multiple, EA 15
   opening, EA 61–62
   Personal Macro, EA 54
   properties, EA 204–205
   protection, EA 196–199
   publishing to Web, EA 228–230
   sending as attachment, EA 233
   sharing, EA 186, EA 199–200
   sharing custom numbers and conditional formats, EA 187–193
   sharing lookup and reference functions, EA 193–195
   template for, EA 65

using multiple workspaces in, EA 16–17
workbook protection feature, EA 196–198
workgroup templates, default location, WA 303
worksheet(s)
  cell relationships between, EA 104–105
  consolidating data in, EA 9–11
  Description, Assumptions and Parameters, EA 5
  documentation, EA 5–6
  drawing objects, EA 154
  embedding data in Word, EA 165–167
  format, EA 3–6
  group, EA 3–5
  Identification, EA 5
  linking, EA 2–11, EA 164
  Map of the Workbook, EA 5
  protection, EA 196–199
  publish to Web, EA 228–230
  sending as HTML mail, EA 231–232
workspace, EA 15, EA 16–17
World Wide Web (the Web), defined, AA 122
World Wide Web Consortium (W3C), AA 125, AA 139

X

XML (eXtensible Markup Language) document, AA 125, EA 219–220
  exporting, AA 127
  importing into Access, AA 125–126
  learning about, AA 126
  query, EA 222–224
  sharing data via, EA 220–222
  tag delimiters (< >), AA 128
  tags, AA 128
  viewing in browser, AA 128
XML standard, AA 125, AA 139
XY scatter chart, EA 139–140

Z

ZIP code, sorting by, WA 103